154/14124

D1823465

SYRIA

IRAQ

non

Jordan

Kuwait

Bahrain

Qatar

U.A.E.

SAUDI ARABIA

OMAN

R E D   S E A

North
Yemen

South Yemen

Djibuti

SOMALIA

THE INTERNATIONAL

WHO'S

WHO

of the

ARAB

WORLD

The International Who's Who of the Arab World Limited
London

The International Who's Who of the Arab World
Second Edition 1984
Published by the International Who's Who of the Arab World Ltd
37 Park Street, London W1Y 3HG, UK
Telephone: 01-409 1525   Telex: 268663 IWWAW G
ISSN 0261-0310
ISBN 0 9506122 1 9

Publisher
Sabih M Shukri

Printed in England by Unwin Brothers Limited, The Gresham Press
Old Woking, Surrey

CONTENTS

PREFACE TO THE SECOND EDITION

In the past two decades, the world has witnessed an unprecedented development in the field of communication. During this same period, the Arab countries began to play an increasingly important role in world affairs, and in particular at the economic, political and social levels. However, the contemporary Arab world, its people, its culture and its vast geographical area remain relatively unknown, or at best badly represented. In more recent years, most Arab countries have embarked upon large scale economic and social plans for development. Development plans by their nature require sound channels for communication between partners in development, and better understanding and appreciation of the human resources and potentials that exist. Thus the need for an international volume of Who's Who of the area, which is an established tradition in itself in most regions of the world, has led to the publication of the First edition (1978/79) of *The International Who's Who of the Arab World*. The biographical entries are listed in alphabetical order, which transcend national boundaries, clearly indicating the common heritage and identity of the people of the area.

The objectives of this publication are: firstly, to put the Arab world into a better perspective; secondly, to promote better understanding between the people of the area and the rest of the world; finally, this directory seeks to recognise the contributions of the Arab People. Our criteria for selection are broad, and recognise achievements or prominence, foremost through ability and merit, the formal office or position.

The publisher has been greatly encouraged by the success of the First edition and the response of the biographees, hence the expanded and updated Second edition (1984). It must be pointed out that this publication is not a systematic survey of all those who merit inclusion. However, it is hoped that more people will indicate their wishes to be included in future editions, as such inclusion usually follows upon the expressed wishes of the people concerned.

THE PUBLISHER
Sabih M Shukri
London, December 1983

EDITORIAL INTRODUCTION TO THE SECOND EDITION

This book represents the Second edition, of what is now an established reference work, THE INTERNATIONAL WHO'S WHO OF THE ARAB WORLD.

As in the First edition, the biographies have been listed in alphabetical order. The subjects included, are citizens of member states of the Arab League, naturalised citizens of other countries, who have maintained links with the Arab world, and those of Arab descent. We have endeavoured to include Mauritania, Somalia and Djibuti, but the response has been inadequate, and did not justify inclusion. However, it is our hope that we will be able to include these countries in future editions.

A proof of every entry which appeared in the First edition was sent to its subject for updating. Approximately seventy five per cent of the biographees responded with amendments. Those who did not respond were contacted again, either by us or by our representatives, who are based in various parts of the Arab world. A number of entries have been deleted either due to death or to the lack of any current data, and new entries of those who completed our questionnaire have been added.

The Second edition (1984), is an updated and more broadly based volume. It includes the biographical data of those who through their chosen profession or vocation have contributed to the economic, political, scientific and artistic life of their country. Professional people such as judges, lawyers, businessmen, bankers, scientists, doctors, journalists, artists and writers have been included. In addition, prominent people who occupy formal positions and play a role in the political and economic life of their country, such as Heads of State, Cabinet Ministers, Heads of Development Funds, Research Institutions and quasi official bodies. International and regional officials of the United Nations and the League of Arab States, have been included. Finally, we have also included the biographies of prominent people, who have contributed in the past to the life and culture of their country.

Each entry has been presented within our standard format, which consists of the following headings: full name and nationality, followed by profession/position, date of birth and other personal details, education, career, publications, decorations, interests and recreations, languages and address. The biographical data are computer-compiled and will be up-dated regularly.

As a book of reference, one of the main objectives in the presentation of the biographical entries, is to enable the reader to readily locate the name of an individual biographee. There are however, specific cultural differences in the listing of names of individuals, in a directory of Arabic proper nouns, which the non Arabic speaking reader may not be aware of. For instance, the inheritance of a formally recognised surname, is on the whole not an established tradition, although is becoming more widespread. The use of father's first name is still widespread, thus a biographee may not necessarily be listed under the same name as his father. In addition, there are other differences, particularly in relation to some of the ruling families. In the case of the ruling families of Saudi Arabia, Jordan and Morocco, individual members are traditionally listed under their first name (eg KHALID AL-FAISAL BIN ABDUL AZIZ, HRH Prince, Saudi Arabian Prince/administrator, or HASSAN BIN TALAL, HRH Prince, Jordanian Crown Prince). Finally, we have been particularly aware of the variations in the transliteration of Arabic proper nouns and place-names, and the possible confusion that can ensue. In the absence of definitive rules for the transliteration of names, we have devised our in-house general guide-lines, which we have adhered to as much as possible (see A NOTE ON TRANSLITERATION). But, our first rule has been to use the form of transliteration which the biographees themselves prefer. The main part of the directory consists of the alphabetical listing of biographies, preceded by a list of ABBREVIATIONS and A NOTE ON TRANSLITERATION.

At the end of the book, there is an index of all the names listed by country (see LIST OF COUNTRIES) and cross-referenced with a professional category (see LIST OF PROFESSIONAL CATEGORIES), with page number on which the entry can be found. The main purpose of this index, is to provide the reader with another way of locating a biographical entry.

The 1984 edition of *The International Who's Who of the Arab World*, IS A UNIQUE REFERENCE SOURCE, which is a must for all those who wish to establish sound channels of communication with the ARAB WORLD, be it in the field of economics, politics, science or the arts.

Whilst the publisher has made every effort to ensure that the information included is correct, no responsibility or liability can be accepted for any errors or omissions, or for the consequences thereof.

London,
December, 1983

A NOTE ON TRANSLITERATION

As in any directory containing Arabic proper nouns and place-names, the main aim is to avoid variations and confusion. Our general guide-lines are more practical than scientific. We have avoided the use of diacritical marks other than the inverted comma, as in Sana'a. Above all, the form of transliteration which the biographees themselves prefer, have been used. We have tried to be consistent in the case of familiar proper nouns and place-names such as Abdullah or Abdallah, Ali, Muhammad, Ahmad, Hussain, Hassan, Khartoum, Cairo. There are regional variations in the transliteration of names such as Abdul Salam (not Abdel), Bin Salim, which are usually written as two separate words, except in the case of subjects from the Maghreb countries, they are transliterated as Abdelslam and Benslim.

All names which contain the word al-Din, have been transliterated as one word, and not separated from the first part of the name. The most common examples are Takiyddin, Gamaluddin, Muhiyddin, Izziddin, and not Takiy al-Din, Gamal al-Din etc. Finally, names which begin with the word Abu (and not Abou) is usually separated from the second part of the name with a space, for example: Abu Ghazala, and not Abughazala. All surnames with the definite article will be listed as follows, for example: Abdul Aziz Ahmad al-Bahar, will appear under the letter B as BAHAR, Abdul Aziz Ahmad al-.

The alphabetical ordering used is a strict one and arranged as though the surname including the first name and initials is one word.

ABBREVIATIONS

AA — Associate in Arts
AUB — American University of Beirut
ARAMCO — Arabian American Oil Company
AFCAC — African Civil Aviation Commission
ACAC — Arab Civil Aviation Council
AP-AP TV — Arab People to American People Television
ALA — Associate of Library Association
AUC — American University of Cairo
ALIA — Royal Jordanian Airlines
APU — Arab Pharmacists Union; Arab Postal Union
AIDA — Arab Institute for the Development of Arts
ALESCO — Arab League Educational, Cultural & Scientific Organisation
AACO — Arab Air Transport Association Conference
AGFUND — Arab Gulf Fund for UN Development Organisation
ASFEC — Arab States Training Center for Community Development
ARLO — Arab Literacy & Adult Education Organisation
AID — United States Agency for International Development

BA — Bachelor of Arts
BSc — Bachelor of Science
BS — Bachelor of Science; Bachelor of Surgery
BEd — Bachelor of Education
BLitt — Bachelor of Letters
BBA — Bachelor of Business Administration
BCh — Bachelor of Surgery
BCom — Bachelor of Commerce
BLL — Bachelor of Law
BVMS — Bachelor of Veterinary Medicine and Surgery
BSSS — British Society of Soil Science
BBC — British Broadcasting Corporation
BRSMES — British Society for Middle East Studies
BDSc — Bachelor or Dental Scienceet

CPA — Certified Public Accountant; Chartered Patent Agent
ChB — Bachelor of Surgery
CAEU — Council of Arab Economic Unity
CChem — Chartered Chemist
CNAA — Council of National Academic Awards
CMA — Certificate in Management Accountancy
CAFRAD — Centre Africaine de Formation de Recherches Administratives pour le Developpement
CPM — Crucial Passage Method
CIEC — Conference on International Economic Co-operation
CDR — Council for Development & Reconstruction
Co — Company
Corp — Corporation

DDS — Doctor of Dental Surgery
DSc — Doctor of Science
DPhil — Doctor of Philosophy

DIC — Diploma of Membership of the Imperial College of Science and Technology (University of London)
DPH — Diploma of Public Health
D Litt — Doctor of Letters; Doctor of Literature
DCO — Dominion Colonial Overseas
DLC — Diploma of the Loughborough College of Technology
DTMH — Diploma of Tropical Medicine & Hygiene
DPA — Diploma of Public Administration

ESDUCK — Egyptian Society for the Dissemination of Universal Culture and Knowledge
ECWA — UN Economic Commission for Western Asia
EdD — Doctor of Education
EEC — European Economic Community
ECAFE — UN Economic Commission for Asia and the Far East
ECLA — UN Economic Commission for Latin America
ECOSOC — UN Economic & Social Council
ECA — UN Economic Commission for Africa

FACS — Fellow of the American College of Surgeons
FAO — Food & Agriculture Organisation (UN)
FIFA — International Federation of Association Football
FRCP — Fellow of the Royal College of Physicians
FACC — Fellow of the American College of Cardiology
FRSC — Fellow of the Royal Society of Canada; Fellow of the Royal Society of Chemistry
FICE — Fellow of the Institution of Civil Engineers
FICA — Fellow of the International College of Angiology
FCCP — Fellow of the American College of Chest Physicians
FICS — Fellow of the International College of Surgeons
FRCOG — Fellow of the Royal College of Obstetricians & Gynaecologists
FLA — Fellow of the Library Association
FRCSI — Fellow of the Royal College of Surgeons for Ireland

GBE — Knight (or Dame) Grand Cross of the Order of the British Empire
GEC — General Electric Company
GATT — General Agreement for Trade & Tariffs
hc — honoris causa
HH — His (or Her) Highness
HRH — His (or Her) Royal Highness
HM — His (or Her) Majesty
HEC — Higher Education Certificate
ILO — International Labour Organisation (UN)
IBRD — International Bank for Reconstruction & Development (World Bank)
IMF — International Monetary Fund
ISA — International Sociological Association
IFC — International Finance Corporation

INSTRAW	Institute for Training & Research for the Advancement of Women	NIH	National Institute of Health (USA)
IDCAS	Industrial Development Centre for Arab States	NASA	National Aeronautics & Space Administration (USA)
IDF	International Dental Federation	NAMRU	US Naval Medical Research Unit
INOC	Iraq National Oil Company	NIHM	National Institute for Mental Health (USA)
IAEA	International Atomic Energy Agency (UN)	NPT	Non Proliferation Treaty
IUCW	International Union for Child Welfare		
IPC	Iraq Petroleum Company	OPEC	Organisation for Petroleum Exporting Countries
ISSS	International Society of Social Science		
INMARSAT	International Maritime Satellite Organisation	OAPEC	Organisation for Arab Petroleum Exporting Countries
INTELSAT	International Satellite Organisation	OAU	Organisation for African Unity
ITU	International Telecommunication Union	OND	Ordinary National Diploma
ICAO	International Civil Aviation Organisation		
ITA	Industrial Transport Association	PhD	Doctor of Philosophy
INSEAD	Institute of Social & Economic Development (University of Paris)	PMD	Programme of Management Development
ITT	International Telephones & Telegraphs	RIBA	Royal Institute of British Architects
IATA	International Air Transport Association	RCP	Royal College of Physicians
ISDC	International Studies & Development Center	RCS	Royal College of Surgeons
		RCPS	Royal College of Physicians & Surgeons of Glasgow
IBM	International Business Machines		
ICARDA	International Centre for Agriculture Research in Dry Areas	RAS	Royal Asiatic Society
		RSS	Royal Statistical Society
Inc	Incorporated	RAF	Royal Air Force
		SM	Master of Science
KCMG	Knight Commander for the Memorable Order of the Garter	SC	South Caroline; Senior Counsel (Republic of Ireland)
KISR	Kuwait Institute for Scientific Research	SAK	Societe Anonyme Kuwaitien
KOC	Kuwait Oil Company	SAL	Societe Anonyme Libanese
KFAED	Kuwait Fund for Arab Economic Development	SJD	Doctor of Juristic Science
KCVO	Knight Commander of the Royal Victorian Order	SPA	Society for Personnel Administration (USA)
		SAUDIA	Saudi Arabian Airlines
LLB	Bachelor of Law	SRTH	Society for Religion and Theology
LLM	Master of Law		
LLD	Doctor of Law	TH	Technical University
		TMP	Trade Marks and Patents
MD	Doctor of Medicine	TIT	Technical Institute for Telecommunications
MAS	Master of Applied Science		
MA	Master of Arts	UNESCO	United Nations Educational, Scientific & Cultural Organisation
MSc	Master of Science		
MBA	Master of Business Administration	UCLA	University of California, Los Angeles
MEd	Master of Education	USC	University of Southern California
MS	Master of Science; Master of Surgery	UNIDO	UN Industrial Development Organisation
MBBCh	Bachelor of Medicine and Surgery	USAF	United States Air Force
MB	Bachelor of Medicine	USPHS	United States Public Health Service
MPH	Master of Public Helath	UN	United Nations
MLitt	Master of Letters	UAR	United Arab Republic
MCh	Master of Surgery	UNCTAD	UN Conference on Trade & Development
MED	Master of Education	UNCHS	UN Centre for Human Settlements
MCST	Manchester College of Science & Technology	UAE	United Arab Emirates
		UNCHBP	UN Committee for Housing, Building & Planning (Economic Commission for Europe)
MIT	Massachusetts Institute of Technology		
MICE	Member of the Institution of Civil Engineers	UNICEF	UN International Children's Emergency Fund
MRCPath	Member of the Royal College of Pathologists		
		UNECWA	UN Economic Commission for Western Asia
MRCP	Member of the Royal College of Physicians		
MACI	Member of the American Concrete Institute	UNRWA	UN Relief & Works Agency
MPhil	Master of Philosophy	UNEP	UN Environment Programme
MEA	Middle East Airlines	UNFPA	United National Family Planning Association
MDS	Master of Dental Surgery		
MRCOG	Member of the Royal College of Obstetricians & Gynaecologists	UFO	Unidentified Flying Object
		UNRISD	UN Research Institute for Social Development
MSBCh	Master of Surgery and Bachelor of Surgery		
MSE	Master of Science in Engineering		
MESAA	Middle Eastern Society of Associated Accountants	WMO	World Meteorological Organisation
		WHO	World Health Organisation
MPA	Master of Public Administration	WLL	With Limited Liability

BIOGRAPHIES

A

ABA HUSSAIN, Mansur Muhammad, Saudi Arabian academic/official; born 23 December 1942, Saudi Arabia; married; two sons; *Religion:* Muslim; *Education:* BSc, American University of Beirut, 1965; MSc, University of Arizona, 1969; PhD, University of California, 1972; *Career:* Professor of Agriculture, University of Riyadh, 1972; successively in the Ministry of Agriculture and Water, Saudi Arabia, Director General of Development, 1975; Assistant Deputy Minister, 1976; Deputy Minister, 1976; President, Harad Agricultural and Aminal Production Company; represented Ministry of Agriculture and Water in the Saudi-US Joint Economic Commission, 1975, and in the Arab-European Dialogue, 1976; Chairman, Saudi-Dutch Potato Development Programme, of Al-Faisal Settlement Project, of al-Hasa Irrigation and Drainage Authority, of the Saudi Agricultural Bank; *Publications: Mineralogy of Al-Hasa Desert Soils,* 1977, in *Clays and Clay Minerals Journal,* vol 25 No 2, page 138–47; and several other research articles; *Interests and Recreations:* reading, table tennis, fishing; *Languages:* Arabic, English; *Address:* Harad Agricultural and Animal Production Company, P O Box 2557, Riyadh, Saudi Arabia; telephone: 4642552.

ABAAKIL, Najim, Moroccan banker; born 1934, Morocco; *Religion:* Muslim; *Career:* President and Director General, Banque Marocaine pour l'Afrique et l'Orient; Vice President, Allgemeine Bank Maroc; President and Director General, Chamber of Commerce and Industry of Casablanca; Vice President of the Federation of the Chambers of Commerce and Industry of Morocco; Vice President of the Union of the Arab Chambers of Commerce and of Agriculture; *Languages:* Arabic, English, Spanish; *Address:* Banque Marocaine pour l'Afrique et l'Orient, 80 Avenue Lalla Yacout, BP 880 Casablanca, Morocco.

ABALKHAIL, Abdul Rahman, Saudi Arabian diplomat; *Religion:* Muslim; *Education:* BA, Arabic and Eastern Languages, Cairo University, Egypt, 1952; *Career:* Diplomatic Attaché, later 3rd Secretary, Embassy to Egypt; 2nd Secretary, Embassy to Lebanon; Director General, Ministry of Finance, 1959–60; 1st Counsellor, Ministry of Foreign Affairs; Minister of Labour and Social Affairs, 1962; Ambassador to Egypt; member of the Board, Arab Cement Company Ltd; member of the Board, Medina Press Organization; President of the Advisory Social Security Board; Chairman of the Board of General Social Insurance Organization; member of Social Affairs Conferences, through UN agencies; attended Arab Ministers of Social Affairs Conferences; *Address:* c/o Ministry of Foreign Affairs, P O Box 495, Baghdadiah, Jeddah, Saudi Arabia; telephone: Residence — Riyadh 22632.

ABALKHAIL, Shaikh Muhammad Ali, Saudi Arabian politician; born 1935, Bureida, Saudi Arabia; married; two sons, two daughters; *Religion:* Muslim; *Education:* BSc in Public Administration, Faculty of Commerce, Cairo University, Egypt,1956; *Career:* Assistant Director, Minister of Communication's Office; Director of the Office of the Minister of Communication; established the Institute of Public Administration, Saudi Arabia; Director General of the Institute of Public Administration; Deputy Minister of Finance and National Economy, 1964; Vice Minister, 1970; Minister of State and member of the Council of Ministers, 1971; Minister of Finance and National Economy, 1975–; Chairman of the Board of Directors of Public Investment Fund, of the Board of Directors of Retirement and Pensions Fund, of Institute of Public Administration, of Saudi International Bank, London, of the Saudi Fund for Development; member of the Supreme Consultative Council of Petroleum and Mineral, of the Royal Commission for Industrial Estates in Jubail and Yanbou, of the Board of Directors of Saudi Airlines, of the Civil Service Council, of the Manpower Council, of the Board of Directors of Equestrian Club; *Decorations:* Medal of King Abdul Aziz, Saudi Arabia; Medal of the Republic, Egypt; Pakistan Crescent Medal, Pakistan; Leopald II Saah, Belgium; Ordre de Mérite du Grand Duche, Luxembourg; Médaille du Mérite, France; and several others; *Languages:* Arabic, English; *Address:* Ministry of Finance and National Economy, Airport Road, Riyadh, Saudi Arabia; telephone: 4034734; telex: 201021 FINANS SJ.

ABASSI, Izzeddine, Tunisian official/ engineer; born 1920, Tunis, Tunisia; married; five children; *Religion:* Muslim; *Education:* Diploma, National Higher School of Mines, St. Etienne; *Career:* Engineer, Government Department of Public Works; member of the Administrative Commission of the Union Générale des Travailleurs Tunisiens; Minister of Public Works in the first Bourguiba Government, 1956; Minister of Industry and Transport, 1957–61; Manager of the Compagnie des Phosphates et des Chemins de Fer de Gafsa, 1961–65; President and Director General of the government controlled commercial and industrial group, AL-Bouniane, 1966; Director General of the Mining and Iron Ore Group, SOMTEMI, and of the Société Djebel Djerissa, 1968–69; Director General of the Office Nationale des Mines, 1969–74; *Languages:* Arabic, French; *Address:* Office Nationale des Mines, 26 Rue d'Angleterre, Tunis, Tunisia; telephone: 253122, 258263.

ABAZA, Muhammad Tharwat, Egyptian writer; born 28 June 1927, Cairo, Egypt; married;one daughter, one son; *Religion:* Muslim; *Education:* Licence in Law, Cairo University, Egypt, 1950; *Career:* Lawyer, 1950–54; Editor, *Al-Masri,* 1952–54; Editor, *Al-Qahira,* 1954–55; Publishing Consultant, 1956–57, and 1961–; member of Committee on Fiction, Supreme Council of Arts, Literature and Social Services; Chairman of Radio and Television Magazine; Head of Literature and Cultural Department, *Al-Ahram* newspaper; member of Board of Literary Association; *Publications:* numerous novels and short story collections; *Decorations:* Order of Arts and Sciences, 1st Class; *Address:* 17 Aziz Abaza Street, Zamalek, Cairo, Egypt; telephone: 809429.

ABAZA, Sami Abdullah, Egyptian politician; born 10 June 1934, Minia al-Kamh, Sharqiyah Governorate, Egypt; married; one son, two daughters; *Religion:* Muslim; *Education:* Diploma of the Higher Institute for Commercial Co-operation; studies in Arabic and Egyptian literature; studies in history; *Career:* Chairman, Minia al-Kamh town, 1964–67; Public Relations Manager, Madhareb al-Sharqiyah Company, 1963; Secretary of the Arab Socialist Union for Minia al-Kamh; member of the People's Assembly, 1968–; Chairman of the People's Assembly Youth Committee, 1971–76; Chairman of the Cultural, Information and Tourism Committee of the People's Assembly, 1976–; represented Egypt in delegations to Ireland, USA, France, Italy, UK, Czechoslovakia, East Germany, West Germany; Secretary General of Egypt Party in Minia al-Kamh; Director General, Madhareb al-Sharqiyah Company; re-elected to the People's Assembly, 1979–; Secretary General for the National Democratic Party, Minia al-Kamh; Assistant Secretary General for the National Democratic Party, Sharqiyah Governorate; *Decorations:* Order of the 6th of October; *Interests and Recreations:* archaeology, theatre, literature, cinema; member of the Board of Directors of Zamalek Sporting Club; Chairman of the Board of *Sawt Baladna* magazine, published in Sharqiyah Governorate; *Languages:* Arabic, English; *Address:* 427 Ramsis Street, Cairo, Egypt; telephone: Office — 31718; Residence — 833133; Minia al-Kamh, Sharqiyah Governorate, Egypt.

ABBAD, Abdul Muhsin Bin Hamad al-, Saudi Arabian academic; born 1933; *Religion:* Muslim; *Education:* MA, Al-Azhar University, Cairo, Egypt; *Career:* Sidirah Religious Institute; Riyadh Religious Institute; Teacher, Faculty of Islamic Law (Shari'a), the Islamic University, Medina; Vice Rector of the Islamic University of Medina, 1973–; *Publications:* several verified and annotated editions of groups of the Prophet's Traditions, mainly *Ishrun Hadithan min Sahilal Bokhary* (20 annotated verified traditions of the Prophet); *Address:* The Islamic University, Medina, Saudi Arabia; telephone: Office — Medina 24045; Residence — Medina 21368.

ABBADAN, Abdul Aziz Abdullah al-, Saudi Arabian diplomat/educationalist; born 1928; *Religion:* Muslim; *Education:* BA, Arabic Language and Islamic Law; *Career:* Director of Education, Abha Province; Director of Education, City of Taif; Director General of Secondary School Education, Ministry of Education; Cultural Attaché, Embassy to Iraq; member of Board of *Al-Jazira* daily newspaper; delegate to several conferences on education in Saudi Arabia and abroad; *Address:* Office of the Saudi Cultural Attache, Al-Mansour, Baghdad, Iraq; telephone: Office— Baghdad 512941; Residence— Baghdad 515220.

ABBADI, Abdul Muhsin al-, Egyptian academic; born 19 August 1924, Alexandria, Egypt; married; one son, two daughters; *Religion:* Muslim; *Education:* BSc in Chemistry, Alexandria University, Egypt, 1947; PhD, Synthetic Pharmaceutical Organic Chemistry, London University, UK, 1952; Fellowship at University of Michigan, Faculty of Chemistry, University of Detroit, Ann Arbor, USA, 1956–57; *Career:* Demonstrator, Chemistry Department, Faculty of Science, Alexandria University, Egypt, 1947; Lecturer, Chemistry Department, University College for Girls, Ain Shams University, Egypt, 1953; Lecturer, Chemistry Department, Faculty of Education, Baghdad University, Iraq, 1958–59; Assistant Professor, Chemistry Department, University College for Girls, Ain Shams University, 1961; Assistant Professor, Chemistry Department, Faculty of Science and Faculty of Agriculture, Baghdad Universtiy, Iraq, 1964–66; Professor, Chemistry Department, University College for Girls, Ain Shams University, 1969; Professor of Organic Chemistry, Faculty of Science, Tanta University, Egypt, 1969; Deputy Dean of Faculty of Science, Tanta University, 1972; Acting Dean, Faculty of Education, Tanta University, 1972; Dean of Faculty of Science, Sana'a University, Yemen Arab Republic, 1974–79; Acting President, Sana'a University, Yemen Arab Republic, 1975; Consultant, Faculty of Science, Sana'a University, 1979–80; Assistant Secretary General of the Scientific, Synthetic, Organic Chemistry Unit, National Research Centre, Cairo, Egypt, 1960–64; *Publications:* numerous research papers on various aspects of analytical chemistry; translated two books; *Interests and Recreations:* reading, tennis, travelling; *Languages:*

Arabic, English, French, German; *Address:* Faculty of Science, University of Sana'a, P O Box 1247, Sana'a, Yemen Arab Republic.

ABBADI, Bashir Ahmad, Sudanese politician/engineer; born 1936, Omdurman, Sudan; married; three children; *Religion:* Muslim; *Education:* Degree in Engineering, Faculty of Engineering, University of Khartoum, Sudan, 1961; MA, Northwestern University, Evanston, Illinois, USA, 1963; PhD, Mechanical Engineering and Space Science, Northwestern University, USA; *Career:* Lecturer in Engineering, University of Khartoum, 1966; member of the Board of Directors of Sudan Railways, 1968–69; Chairman of the Board of Directors of Sudan Airways, 1969–70; Head of the Department of Mechanical Engineering, University of Khartoum, 1970; Minister of Communications , 1971; Transportation Affairs added to the portfolio, May 1973; member of the Political Bureau, Sudanese Socialist Union, 1976–; Minister of Transport and Communications, 1976–77; Minister of Industry, 1977; Chairman, Kenama Sugar Co, 1977–; *Languages:* Arabic, English; *Address:* Kenama Sugar Co, P O Box 2632, Khartoum, Sudan.

ABBAS, Abbas Khudhair, Iraqi lawyer; born 1922, Diyala, Iraq; *Religion:* Muslim; *Education:* LLB, Baghdad University, Iraq; Social Leadership Diploma, Saint Francis Xavier University, Canada; Social Policy Course, Swansea University College, Wales, UK; Certificate in Community Recreation, The National Recreation School, New York, USA; Certificate in Farm Management, American University of Beirut; Post Graduate Diploma in Comprehensive Development Planning, Kuwait Institute of Economic and Social Planning in the Middle East; attended and contributed to many other short courses and conferences held by UN and ILO; *Career:* Civil Servant, Iraqi Government, 1941; Director of Planning and Researches, Ministry of Labour and Social Affairs, 1973; Editor of *Social Sciences Bulletin,* issued by the Iraqi Association of Social Sciences; member of the Bar Association, the Journalists Union, the Deaf and Dumb Society, the Association of Social Sciences and Human Rights Association, the Union of Authors and Writers; *Publications:* several articles on manpower planning and community works and other subjects in professional journals; *Interests and Recreations:* travel, swimming;

3

Languages: Arabic, English, French; *Address:* P O Box 3289, Al Sadoon, Baghdad, Iraq; telephone: 8882540.

ABBAS, Al-Obeid Khalifa, Sudanese diplomat; born 1915; *Religion:* Muslim; *Education:* Gordon Memorial College, Khartoum, Sudan; *Career:* Sudan Railway Service, 1933–44, 1948–54; Deputy Under Secretary for Special Functions, 1955; Deputy Permanent Under Secretary, Ministry of Foreign Affairs, 1956–57; Ambassador to Ethiopia, 1957–59; Ambassador to Iraq, Lebanon, Jordan, Turkey, 1959–61; Ambassador to USA, 1965–66; Permanent Under Secretary for Foreign Affairs, 1966–69; Chairman of Board of Directors for Foreign Affairs, 1966–69; Chairman of Board of Directors, Omdurman National Bank, 1969–70; Diplomatic Adviser, Embassy of Qatar, London, UK, 1972–76; now retired; *Address:* Ministry of Foreign Affairs, Khartoum, Sudan.

ABBAS, Ferhat, Algerian politician; born 1899; *Religion:* Muslim; *Education:* Algiers University; *Career:* pharmacist in Setif; leader of General Union of Algerian Muslim Students, 1926–31; took part in organizing Algerian People's Union, 1938; published Manifesto of the Algerian People, 1943; founded Amis du Manifeste et de la Liberté (AML), 1944; imprisoned, 1945–1946; took part in establishment of Union Démocratique du Manifeste Algérien (UDMA), 1946; elected representative to French Constitutional Assembly, 1946; later member of French Union Assembly; elected to Algerian Assembly, 1948 and 1954; leader of UDMA, 1946–56; founded National Liberation Front (FLN), 1955; member of FLN delegation to 11th General Assembly of the United Nations, 1957; Prime Minister of Algerian Provisional Government in Tunisia, 1958–61; President of the Chamber of Algeria, 1962–63; detained, 1964–65; now retired; *Publications: Le Jeune Algérien,* 1931; *La Nuit Coloniale,* 1962; *Languages:* Arabic, French; *Address:* c/o Front de Libération Nationale (FLN), Place Amir Abdel Kader, Algiers, Algeria.

ABBAS, Makki, Sudanese UN official; born 1 January 1911, Gezira Province, Sudan; married; *Education:* Diploma in Education, University College of the Southwest, Exeter, UK, 1938–40; BA in Literature, Oxford University, UK, 1948–50; LLD, University of Exeter, UK, 1959; *Career:* Director and Managing Director, Sudan Gezira Board, Government of Sudan, 1955–58; Executive Secretary, Economic Commission for Africa (ECA), UN, 1958–62; Assistant Director General, Economic and Social Policy Department (ESPD), FAO, Rome, Italy, 1963–68; member, Society for International Development; *Publications: The Sudan Question – Dispute Over the Anglo-Egyptian Condominium, 1884–1951; Interests and Recreations:* chess, walking, economic development; *Languages:* Arabic, English: *Address:* Economic and Social Policy Department, FAO, P O Box 30234, Nairobi, Kenya; telephone: 61272.

ABBAS, Muhammad Hamza, Jordanian UN official/economist; born 21 March 1928, Jerusalem, Palestine; married; *Religion:* Muslim; *Education:* BA, Business Administration and Economics, Colorado State College, USA, 1950; MA and PhD in Economics, University of Wisconsin, USA, 1950–53; *Career:* Economist, Government of Jordan, Amman, 1954–56; Chief, Economic Division, UN Relief and Works Agency for Palestine Refugees in the Near East, (UNRWA), Beirut, 1956–58; Project Officer, UNDP, New York, 1959–62; Chief Programme Coordinator, Food and Agriculture Organisation, 1962–65; Deputy Chief, Operations Service, FAO, Rome, 1965–68; Senior Officer, Policy and Planning Unit, Land and Water Development Division, FAO, Rome, 1969–78; Assistant Director General, Economic and Social Policy Department, 1978–; member of the Society for International Development; *Interests and Recreations:* sports, music; *Languages:* Arabic, English, French, Italian; *Address:* Economic and Social Policy Department, Food and Agriculture Organisation, Via delle Terme di Caracalla, 00100 Rome, Italy; telephone: 5797; telex: 61181 FOODAGRI.

ABBAS, Salih Muhammad, Yemen Arab Republic politician/educationalist born 1934; married; two sons, three daughters; *Religion:* Muslim; *Education:* general; *Career:* Assistant Director General of the Arab Affairs Office, UN, New York, USA, 1954; 1st Secretary, Yemeni Legation to Saudi Arabia, 1955; Director, Minister's Office; member and Secretary of the Technical Committee, Ministry of Education, 1960; Director, Hodeida Schools, 1962; Administrative Inspector, Department of Education, Hodeida Province, 1962; Assistant Secretary General, Council of Ministers, 1962–65; Secretary General, Council of Ministers with rank of Minister, 1965–; *Interests and Recreations:* Arabic literature, history, tennis, table tennis, swimming; member of the Yemeni Cultural Association; *Languages:* Arabic, some English; *Address:* Prime Minister's Office, Sana'a, Yemen Arab Republic; telephone: Office — 533105; Residence — 3135.

ABBO, Bakri Hassan, Sudanase official; born 1933, El-Obaid, Sudan; married; two daughters, two sons; *Religion:* Muslim; *Education:* MA in Business Administration, Syracuse University, Syracuse, USA; *Career:* Industrial Relations Officer, Ministry of Labour, Sudan, 1957; technical and administrative positions in Industrial Bank of Sudan, 1961; Deputy Managing Director, Industrial Bank of Sudan, 1970; Labour Expert on secondment from Sudan Government to United Arab Emirates, Ministry of Labour, 1972; professional posts in ADMA-OPCO (oil company), Abu Dhabi, 1977; Head of Government and Employee Relations, ADMA-OPCO, 1981–82; *Interests and Recreations:* tennis, travel, photography; *Languages:* Arabic, English; *Address:* ADMA-OPCO, P O Box 303, Abu Dhabi, United Arab Emirates; telephone: Office — 320778.

ABBOUD, General Ibrahim, Sudanese army commander/politician; born 1900; *Religion:* Muslim; *Education:* Gordon Memorial College, Khartoum, Sudan; Military College, Khartoum; *Career:* joined Sudan Defence Force; served in World War II with Sudanese contingent, British Army in Eritrea, Ethiopia, Libya; Deputy Commander in Chief, Sudanese Army, 1954; Commander in Chief, 1956–64; President, Supreme Military Council; Prime Minister, Minister of Defence, 1958–64; *Address:* Suakin, Sudan.

ABBOUSHI, Nassib, Jordanian journalist/economist; born 3 August 1939, Hammana, Lebanon; *Religion:* Muslim; *Education:* Diploma in Economics, Munich University, West Germany; Philosophy and Modern History Studies, Munich University; *Career:* Senior Economic Researcher in the Libyan General Press Association, Tripoli, Libya, 1974–75; Chief Editor of *Deutsche Wirtschaft,* weekly magazine published in Munich on Arab economic affairs, 1975; *Publications:* econo-

mic and political articles in Libyan press; *Development of International Demand for Oil until 2000 A.D.; Interests and Recreations:* classical music, reading philosophy and history, mountain-climbing, ice-skating; *Languages:* Arabic, German, English; *Address:* c/o Arabisch-Deutsche Vereinigung Für Handel und Industrie. E.V., Godesberger Allee 125/1, 5300 Bonn 2, West Germany; telephone: (02221) 373637; telex: c/o 886672.

ABSY, Salim R., Bahraini diplomat/official; born 1925, Bahrain; married; two sons; *Religion:* Muslim; *Education:* special courses in Legal Translation, School of Oriental and African Studies, London, UK; *Career:* school master, 1943; journalist, 1956; translator, 1954–71; Director of the Prime Minister's Office in Bahrain, 1976; Ambassador of Bahrain to Jordan, 1977–81; *Interests and Recreations:* history, politics and social affairs, swimming; *Languages:* Arabic, English; *Address:* P O Box 1040, Manama, Bahrain.

ABD, Hamid Abdul Aziz al-, Egyptian academic; born 26 November 1928, Egypt; married; one son, one daughter; *Religion:* Muslim; *Education:* BSc Ain Shams University, 1952; Diploma in Higher Studies for Teachers, Cairo, 1955, MA in Education, University of London, 1961; PhD in Educational Psychology, University of London, 1964; *Career:* Professor and Chairman, Educational Psychology Department, University of Makarere, Kampala, Uganda, 1965–71; Professor and Chairman, Educational Psychology Departments, Assuit and Minia Universities, Egypt, 1971–76; Professor and Chairman; Child Studies Department, Ain Shams University, Cairo, 1976–78; Professor and Chairman, Psychology Department, University College of Arts, Science and Education, Bahrain, 1978–; UNESCO Specialist/Adviser in Educational Pyschology, University College of Bahrain, 1978–; Associate member of the British Pyschological Society; member of American Educational Research Association, of American Psychological Association; *Publications: Educational Psychology Research and the African Teacher,* Cairo, 1973, in English; *Psychology of Thinking and Ability,* Cairo, 1976; *Interests and Recreations:* reading, writing; *Address:* University College of Bahrain, P O Box 1082, Bahrain; telephone: 682 748, 251 113.

ABD RABBO, Yassir, Palestinian politician; born 1944, Palestine; *Religion:* Muslim; *Education:* in Cairo, Egypt; *Career:* member of the Palestine Liberation Organization (PLO) Executive Committee; representative of the Popular Democratic Front for the Liberation of Palestine (PDFLP) in PLO; former member of the Arab Nationalist Movement; left Popular Front for the Liberation of Palestine (PFLP) in 1968–69 to form PDFLP; went on PDFLP delegation to Moscow, 1975; Head of PLO Information and Culture Department, 1977.

ABDALLAH, HRH Prince Moulay, Moroccan Royal Prince; born 1934; younger son of late HM King Mohammed V whom he accompanied into exile; married; one son, one daughter; *Religion:* Muslim; *Education:* on return from exile continued studies in Paris, 1955; *Career:* led Moroccan delegation to the Algeria-Morocco talks, at Maghreb Foreign Ministers Conference, Rabat, 1963; accompanied HM King Hassan II on state visits to USA and France; led Moroccan delegation to Arab Summit Meeting, September 1964, and to anniversary celebrations of the Chinese People's Republic, October 1964; Personal Representative of HM King Hassan, 1972–74; *Interests and Recreations:* aviation, golf; *Languages:* Arabic, French; *Address:* Palais Royale, Rabat, Morocco.

ABDALLAH, Ibrahim A., Jordanian UN official; born 5 June 1923, Palestine; married; two sons, four daughters; *Religion:* Muslim; *Education:* BA in Commerce and Business Administration, Arab University of Beirut, Lebanon, 1965; Diploma in Credit, Cooperatives and Management; *Career:* Teacher in Palestine, 1941–46; Cooperative Officer, Palestine, 1946–48; Teacher, Jordan Government, 1949–58; Cooperative Officer, Jordan, 1958–60; Deputy General Manager, Jordan Central Cooperative Union, 1960–66; Cooperative and Credit Expert FAO, Iraq, 1966–71; Cooperative and Credit Expert, and Project Manager, Afghanistan, 1971–77; Regional Credit, Cooperatives and Marketing Officer, Jordan, 1977–; Secretary General, Near East-North Africa Regional Agricultural Credit Association, NENARACA, 1977–; *Publications: Management of Agricultural Loans,* Amman 1982; numerous studies and lectures on Agricultural Credit and Cooperative Theories; *Languages:* Arabic, English, Persian; *Address:* P O Box 35286 Amman, Jordan; telephone: Office — 668632; Residence — 668372; telex: ALOUN 21835 JO.

ABDALLAH, Salahiddin, Tunisian diplomat; born 25 March, Kairouan, Tunisia; married; two daughters, one son; *Religion:* Muslim; *Education:* BA in History; Diploma in Political Studies, University of Lyon, France; *Career:* Secretary, Tunisian Embassy in Cairo, Egypt, 1957; Chargé d'Affaires, Tripoli, Libya, 1958; Counsellor, Rabat, Morocco, 1959–60; Director of the Department of Asia and Africa, Ministry of Foreign Afairs, Tunis, 1960–68; Minister Plenipotentiary, Tunisian Embassy in Cairo, 1964; Minister Plenipotentiary, Tunisian Embassy in Washington D.C., USA, 1965–68; Ambassador to Addis Ababa, Nairobi, Dar es Salaam, Kampala, and Permanent Representative of Tunisia at the OAU, 1968–70; Ambassador to Beirut, Amman, Damascus, Baghdad, 1970–73; Secretary of State for Information, 1974; Ambassador to Cairo, and Permanent Representative of Tunisia at the Arab League, 1975–78; Ambassador to Rabat, 1978–; *Decorations:* Grand Officier de l'Ordre d'Indépendence, Tunisia, 1974; Grand Officier de l'Ordre de la République Tunisienne, 1974; Grand Cordon de l'Ordre de la République, Egypt, 1978; Grand Cordon de l'Ordre du Cèdre, Lebanon, 1973; *Interests and Recreations:* swimming, golf; Arabic poetry and literature, history; *Languages:* Arabic, French, English; *Address:* Embassy of Tunisia, 6 rue de Fes, Rabat, Morocco; telephone: 31309, 30636.

ABDEL GHANI, Colonel Muhammad Ben Ahmad, Algerian politician/army commander; *Religion:* Muslim; *Career:* served in French Armed Forces; served in Oran Wilaya during Revolution; Commander, First Military Region, Algiers, 1962–65; Commander, Fourth Military Region, 1965–67; President, Revolutionary Court at Oran, 1969; promoted Colonel, 1969; Commander of the Fifth Military Region, Constantine; member of the Revolutionary Council; Minister of the Interior, 1976; Prime Minister 1980–; *Languages:* Arabic, French; *Address:* Prime Minister's Office, Palais du Government, Algiers, Algeria; telephone: 606360; telex: 52045/47.

ABDEL-MEGUID, Abdel Razak, Egyptian economist/politician; born 1931; *Religion:* Muslim; *Education:* PhD in Economics, Oxford University, UK, 1957, and Texas University, USA, 1962; *Career:* Adviser to Prime Minister Abdel Aziz Hegazi, 1975; shared in drafting Five-Year Plan and Law on Foreign Investments; Deputy Minister of Planning; Economic Adviser to Prime Minister Mamdouh Salem; Director of General Authority for Foreign Investments and Free Zones (GAFIFZ), 1977–; Minister of Economy, 1978; *Address:* Ministry of Economy, Cairo, Egypt.

ABDERRAZAK, Muhammad Larbi, Tunisian journalist; born 13 January 1936, Tunis, Tunisia; married; four sons; *Religion:* Muslim; *Education:* Doctorate, University of Paris, France; *Career:* Teacher, 1959; Assistant Director, Tunisian Radio and Television, 1966; Director of National Guidance, Ministry of Information, 1970; Assistant Director of Political Affairs in the Prime Minister's Office, 1971; Assistant Professor, Faculty of Literature, Tunis, 1972; Director of *Al-Amal,* newspaper of the Socialist Destour Party, 1972; Deputy in the National Assembly, 1974–; Vice President of Tunis Municipality; Administrator, Counsellor of the Tunisian Government; *Decorations:* Officer of the Order of Tunisian Independence; Grand Officer of the Order of Tunisian Republic; Grand Officer of Cultural Merit; *Interests and Recreations:* literature, music, painting, tennis, gymnastics; Director of a youth cultural centre; *Languages:* Arabic, French, English; *Address: Al-Amal* newspaper, La Kasbah, Tunis, Tunisia; telephone: 264899, 263600.

ABDESSALAM, Belaid, Algerian politician; born 6 July 1928, Algeria; *Religion:* Muslim; *Education:* Medicine, Universities of Algiers and Grenoble, France; *Career:* founding member and Honorary President of the Union Générale des Etudiants Musulmans d'Algérie during the Revolution; instructor at National Liberation Front (FLN) School at Oujda, Morocco; Political Adviser to Ben Khedda in Tunis and later appointed Delegate for Economic Affairs to the Provisional Executive; technical posts in various ministries; founder and first President of national oil company SONATRACH, 1964; Head of the Algerian team for negotiations with France which led to Franco-Algerian Agreement of 1965; Minister of Industry and Energy in Boumedienne Government, 1965, retaining SONATRACH post, 1965–1966;

Minister of Light Industry, 1977–; *Languages:* Arabic, French; *Address:* Ministry of Industry and Energy, La Colisée, rue Ahmed Bey de Constantine, Algiers, Algeria; telephone: 6002 804.

ABDUH, Ghanim Muhammad, Yemen Arab Republic academic; born 15 January 1912, Aden; married; four sons, two daughters; *Religion:* Muslim; *Education:* BA, Education, Beirut, 1936; BA, PhD; Diploma in Education, London, 1969; *Career:* teacher, Government Secondary School, Aden, 1937–56; Education Officer, Department of Education, Aden, 1947–56; Deputy Director of Education, 1956–60; Director of Education, Aden, 1960–63; Professor, Department of Arabic, Faculty of Arts, University of Khartoum, Sudan, 1974–77; Professor, Department of Arabic, Faculty of Arts, University of Sana'a, 1977–; Dean, Faculty of Education, University of Sana'a, 1977–79; Adviser to Rector, University of Sana'a, 1979–; *Publications:* five collections of poems; numerous other works on poetry and for the theatre; *Languages:* Arabic, English, French; *Address:* Sana'a University, P O Box 247, Sana'a, Yemen Arab Republic.

ABDUL AKHAR, Ahmad Mustafa, Egyptian politician; born 1925; Sohag, Egypt; *Religion:* Muslim; *Education:* BA, Agriculture, Cairo University, Egypt; *Career:* Ministry of Agriculture, 1950–57; FAO, 1957–61; Director of Nasr Food Canning Company, 1961; member of the Sohag Arab Socialist Union (ASU) Committee, 1963–67; Secretary of the Sohag ASU Committee, 1968; elected to the ASU Central Committee; elected to the People's Assembly, 1969; re-elected to ASU Central Committee, 1971; elected Secretary for Membership, Finance and Administration, 1971; Chairman of the Sohag People's Council, 1971; re-elected to People's Assembly, 1971; Assistant of ASU 1st Secretary, Sayed Marei for Upper Egypt Affairs, 1972; served on the ASU Disciplinary Committee, 1973; Deputy Minister in the Presidency, 1973; Governor of Giza, 1974–; *Address:* Governorate of Giza, Cairo, Egypt.

ABDUL ALEM, Colonel Abdullah, Yemen Arab Republic army commander; born 1946, Yemen Arab Republic; married 1972; one son, one daughter; *Religion:* Muslim; *Education:* Military College, 1966; *Career:* Commander of a battalion of Beni Hashish; in charge of political affairs in the province; Commander of Infantry, 1968–69; Commander of the province of al-Maghadir, 1970–71; Commander of Commandos and Paratroops, 1971–; member of the Presidential Council, 1971–; member of three-man Command Council, 1977–; *Decorations:* Maarib Medal, 1971; Independence Medal, Jordan, 1976; Sudanese Medal, 1st Class, 1976; *Interests and Recreations:* sports, reading, history; *Languages:* Arabic, French; *Address:* Paratroopers Camp, Sana'a, Yemen Arab Republic.

ABDUL BAKI, Abdul Razzak Muhammad, Syrian politician; born Hama, Syria; married; three sons, two daughters; *Religion:* Muslim; *Education:* Diploma in Pharmacy, 1954; *Career:* Director of Sugar and Agricultural Industries; Minister of Municipal and Rural Affairs, 1972–74; Minister of Housing, 1974–76; Founder of Socialist Unionist Party in Syria; Deputy Secretary General of the Socialist Unionist Party; *Interests and Recreations:* travel, tennis, politics; *Languages:* Arabic, French; *Address:* Al Usra Pharmacy, Homs, Syria; telephone: 29020.

ABDUL ELAH, Ahmad Abdullah, People's Democratic Republic of Yemen politician; *Career:* Minister of Education until 1974; Permanent Secretary, Ministry of Foreign Affairs, 1974–1976; member of the Central Committee and the People's Supreme Council; Study Visit to USSR, 1976; *Address:* People's Supreme Council, Aden, People's Democratic Republic of Yemen.

ABDUL ELAH BIN ABDUL AZIZ, HRH Prince, Saudi Arabian Prince/administrator; born 1938, Riyadh, Saudi Arabia; son of late King Abdul Aziz; full brother of Prince Badr Bin Abdul Aziz; *Religion:* Muslim; *Career:* Governor of al-Qasim, 1980–; *Address:* Principality of al-Qasim, Saudi Arabia.

ABDUL FATTAH, Abdul Rahim, Saudi Arabian businessman; born 1903, Jeddah, Saudi Arabia; *Religion:* Muslim; *Career:* in printing profession since 1927; Owner and Manager of Al-Fatah Press; *Address:* Al-Fatah Press, Jeddah, Saudi Arabia; telephone: Office — Jeddah 51143, 54280; Residence — Jeddah 51300.

ABDUL FATTAH ABDULLAH, Mahmud, Egyptian politician; born 1918, Minufiyah, Egypt; married; four children; *Religion:* Muslim; *Education:* BSc, Mechanical Engineering, Cairo University, Egypt 1940, Cairo Military Academy, 1940; *Career:* Assistant to the Minister of War for Technical and Financial Affairs with the rank of General, supervising the technical institutes and organizations within the armed forces; Secretary to the Higher National War Committee chaired by the late President Sadat; Minister of State for Cabinet Affairs (Secretary to the Cabinet), 1973; Minister of State for Presidential Affairs, 1974; Minister of State for Cabinet Affairs and Control, 1975; member of the newly-formed Higher Arms Procurement and Reduction Committee, 1975; attended many of the meetings in Aswan with Dr Kissinger, 1974; accompanied the late President Sadat to the ensuing inter-Arab meetings; *Interests and Recreations:* former President of the Armed Forces Club; Dean of the Engineers Syndicate, 1973–74; *Languages:* Arabic, English; *Address:* General Trade Union for Engineers, 90 Galaa Street, Cairo, Egypt.

ABDUL GADER, Major General Muhammad Abdul Aziz, Sudanese politician/army officer; born 1929, Omdurman, Sudan; married; four children; *Religion:* Muslim; *Education:* Military Academy, Khartoum; Staff courses in the UK and USA; *Career:* promoted Lieutenant Colonel, 1963; Military Attaché, Addis Ababa, Ethiopia; promoted to Colonel, 1965; Headquarters, 1966; Commander of the Sudanese Battalion to Egypt, 1967; Headquarters, 1968; Senior Staff Officer, South of Sudan, 1969; Deputy Chief of Staff, Headquarters, Sudan, 1970; Chief of Staff, 1971–72; Sudanese Ambassador to Uganda, 1972–73; Governor of Kassala Province, 1973; *Languages:* Arabic, English; *Address:* Ministry of Defence, Khartoum, Sudan.

ABDUL GADER, Zain al-Abdin Muhammad Ahmad, Sudanese politician; born 7 May 1940, Sudan; *Religion:* Muslim; *Education:* Omdurman Military Academy, 1959; course in parachuting in UK, 1962; *Career:* Commissioned 2nd Lieutenant, 1959; 1st Lieutenant, 1964; Paratroopers Training Centre course in UK, 1969; course of Company's Commander, Jebeit, 1968; Colonel, 1968; member of the Political Bureau, Assistant General Secretary of the Sudanese Socialist

Union (SSU) for Popular Organizations; Minister of Youth and Sports, 1975; *Interests and Recreations:* poetry, music, football, swimming; *Languages:* Arabic, English; *Address:* Ministry of Youth and Sports, Khartoum, Sudan; telephone: 81189.

ABDUL GANI, Rida Siraj, Saudi Arabian engineer; born 1939; *Religion:* Muslim; *Education:* MA, PhD, Bradford University, UK; *Career:* Assistant Professor of Engineering, University of Petroleum and Minerals, Dhahran; *Address:* University of Petroleum and Minerals, P O Box 144, Dhahran, Saudi Arabia; telephone: 867 3000; telex: 601060 UPM SJ.

ABDUL GHAFFAR, Hasim Hassan, Saudi Arabian dental surgeon; born 1931, Mecca, Saudi Arabia; *Religion:* Muslim; *Education:* MDS (Master of Dental Surgery); *Career:* Head of Dental Section, later Director of Hospital, Students' Hospital, Riyadh; Director, School Health Services, Ministry of Education; Fellow of International Dental College; member of American Association of Dentists; member of Executive Council, World Health Organization (WHO), Geneva; attended several medical conferences; *Decorations:* Commander of Order of Cedar of Lebanon; *Address:* P O Box 2121, Riyadh, Saudi Arabia; telephone: Office — Riyadh 26000; Residence — Riyadh 62000.

ABDUL GHAFFAR, Mahmud Shamsuddin, Egyptian diplomat; married; one son, one daughter; *Religion:* Muslim; *Career:* Consul General in Paris, worked in the textile industry; First Under Secretary, Ministry of Foreign Affairs, Ambassador to Spain, 1975; *Interests and Recreations:* motoring, golf; *Languages:* Arabic, English, French; *Address:* Ministry of Foreign Affairs, Cairo, Egypt.

ABDUL GHAFFAR, Mansur Mahmud, Saudi Arabian official; born 1936, Yanbou, Saudi Arabia; *Religion:* Muslim; *Education:* general; training course in the Institute of Public Administration, London, UK, and Ireland; *Career:* Secretary to Director General of Customs Department; Director, Mail Parcels, Customs Division; Director, Jeddah Sea Port Custom House; member of Customs Committee, Western Region Customs Secretariat *Publications:* lectures on customs organization and procedure, the Institute of Public Administration, Jeddah Branch; *Decorations:* Medal of Japanese Customs Department; *Interests and Recreations:* music, reading; *Address:* Jeddah Sea Port Customs House, Jeddah, Saudi Arabia; telephone: Office — Jeddah 31748; Residence — Jeddah 5351.

ABDUL GHAFUR, Adil Salim, Iraqi physician/academic; born 1935, Baghdad, Iraq; married; two sons, one daughter; *Religion:* Muslim; *Education:* MB, ChB, College of Medicine, Baghdad, Iraq; FRCP, Fellow of the Royal College of Physicians and Surgeons of Canada; FACC, Fellow of the American College of Cardiology; *Career:* Consultant Cardiologist and Chief of Cardio-Pulmonary Laboratory, Veterans Administration Hospital, Dayton, Ohio, USA, 1970; Secretary General, Iraqi Cardio-Thoracic Society, 1975; Chairman, Department of Cardiology, Medical City Teaching Hospital of the College of Medicine, Baghdad University, Baghdad, Iraq, 1980–; *Publications:* Editor of the Journal of the Faculty of Medicine, Baghdad, Iraq, 1973; numerous publications in scientific and medical journals in English, French and Arabic; *Interests and Recreations:* reading, travel, painting, music, jogging, swimming, tennis; member of the Hunting Club of Baghdad; *Languages:* Arabic, English; *Address:* 8/9/95 University District, Yarmuk Post Office, Baghdad, Iraq; telephone: 555 2630.

ABDUL HALIM, Ahmad, Sudanese official; born 15 April 1933, Wad Medani, Sudan; married; three sons, one daughter; *Religion:* Muslim; *Education:* BSc in Economics and Political Sciences, Alexandria University, Alexandria, Egypt; Postgraduate Diploma in Librarianship, London, UK; Associate of the Library Association; *Career:* Assistant Librarian, University of Khartoum, Sudan, 1958–64; Director, School of Extra-Mural Studies, University of Khartoum, 1964–69; Under Secretary, Ministry of Youth, Sports, Social Affairs and Religious Affairs, 1969–71; Deputy Minister of Culture and Information, 1971–72; Member of the Political Bureau, Sudanese Socialist Party, SSU 1972–79; Leader of the People's Assembly, 1973–75; Minister of Culture and Information, 1975–76; Leader of the People's Assembly, 1976–78; Assistant Secretary General, Sudan Socialist Union; Chairman of the Board of Directors, Dar al- Ayyaam for Printing and

Publishing; Assistant Director General, Arab Organization for Higher Education, Culture and Sciences; Director, Khartoum Institute of Arabic Language; Assistant Secretary General for Information and Foreign Affairs, Sudanese Socialist Union, 1972–80; *Publications:* numerous books and articles on Education, Arabic and Islamic bibliographies, literary criticism and other subjects; *Decorations:* Order of Dustour, 1972; Order of the Republic, 1st Class, 1975; Order of the Yemen Republic, 1976; Order of the Lion, Senegal, 1976; *Languages:* Arabic, English; *Address:* Khartoum International Institute for Arabic Language, P O Box 26, Khartoum, Sudan.

ABDUL HAMID, Abdul Latif, Sudanese diplomat; born 1 January 1938, Dankala, Sudan; married; three daughters; *Religion:* Muslim; *Education:* BA, Literature, University of Khartoum; PhD, Literature and Humanities, Sorbonne, Paris; Diploma, International Relations, International Institute of Management; *Career:* 3rd Secretary, Sudan Embassy in Nigeria, 1961–65; 2nd Secretary, Italy, 1965–66; 1st Secretary, 1968; 1st Secretary, Counsellor, Chad, 1971–73; Counsellor, UK, 1973–74; Minister Plenipotentiary, France, 1978–79; Sudan Ambassador to Lebanon, 1980–; *Publications:* PhD Thesis *The Mahdi Movement in Sudan,* in French; *Interests and Recreations:* reading, tennis, swimming; *Languages:* Arabic, English, French; *Address:* Sudan Embassy, P O Box 2504, Beirut, Lebanon; Mme Curie Street, Minkara Building, Ras Beirut, Lebanon; telephone: 353270, 350056.

ABDUL HAMID, Nazmi, Egyptian banker/ economist; born 1906; married; *Religion:* Muslim; *Education:* Degree in Economics, University of Leeds, UK; *Career:* economist; many years Lecturer in Economics at Alexandria University, Egypt; Economic Adviser to the new government, following the 1952 Revolution; Deputy Governor of the National Bank in Alexandria; Deputy Governor of the Egyptian Central Bank, 1960–71; Deputy Governor, 1966; Governor, 1967; appointed Egyptian Governor, IMF, 1968, Arab International Bank, 1972; member of the Economic Advisory Council, 1973; member of the National Council for Production and Economic Affairs, 1974; *Address:* Ministry of Economy, Cairo, Egypt.

ABDUL HAMID, Shafie, Egyptian diplomat; born 7 October 1927, Cairo, Egypt; married; one son, two daughters; *Religion:* Muslim; *Education:* BA, Law and Political Economics, Cairo University, Egypt, 1948; *Career:* Consul, Egyptian Embassy, Paris, 1950–55; 1st Secretary, UN Mission, 1956–60; Deputy Director, International Organisation, 1960–64; First Counsellor, New York, 1964–69; Director of International Organisation, 1969–71; Minister Plenipotentiary 1972; Director of Legal Affairs, 1973; Ambassador to the Vatican, 1974–; Rapporteur of the UN for the Law of the Sea, and later Vice President of the Conference of the UN for the Law of the Sea; *Decorations:* Order of the Egyptian Republic, 1972; Order of the Great Merit, Egypt, 1977; Order of the Magna Cruce of PIUS IX, 1977; *Interests and Recreations:* tennis; member of the Cirocolo degli Scacchi, Rome, the Gezira Sporting Club, Cairo, the Tahrir Club, Cairo; *Languages:* Arabic, English, French; *Address:* Embassy of the Republic of Egypt to the Holy See, 9 Piazza della Citta Leonina, Rome, Italy.

ABDUL JABBAR, Ahmad Khalil, Saudi Arabian diplomat; born 1927, Mecca, Saudi Arabia; *Religion:* Muslim; *Education:* BA, American University, Beirut, Lebanon, 1943; MA in Political Science, Georgetown University, Washington D.C., USA, 1943; *Career:* Secretary of Political Section, The Royal Court, Riyadh, 1943–46; member of Saudi Arabian Delegation to United Nations Conference, San Francisco, 1945; 1st Secretary, Counsellor, Saudi Legation, later Embassy to USA, also Delegate to United Nations, 1946–52, 1952–55; Assistant to Head of Prime Minister's office for political affairs with rank of Deputy Minister of State, 1955, 1960; Ambassador to Japan and Republic of China, 1960–63; Ambassador to West Germany, 1964–65; Ambassador, Foreign Ministry, Jeddah, 1965, 1966; Ambassador to Italy, 1966–80; *Address:* Ministry of Foreign Affairs, P O Box 495, Jeddah, Saudi Arabia.

ABDUL JABIR, Taysiir Muhammad, Jordanian official/economist; born 1 June 1940, Jordan; married; one son, two daughters; *Religion:* Muslim; *Education:* PhD in Economics, University of Southern California, USA, 1970; *Career:* Director, Economic Research Department, Central Bank of Jordan, 1970–72; Director, Economic Department, Ministry of Foreign Affairs, Amman, 1973–74; Economic Expert, UNECWA, Beirut, Lebanon, 1975–76; Secretary General, National Planning Council, 1977–79; Under Secretary, Ministry of Labour, 1979–; member of the Board of Directors, Vocational Training Corporation and Social Security Corporation; member of the Jordan Economists Association; member of the American Economists Association; *Publications: Studies in Arab Economical Integration,* Cairo, 1972, in Arabic; *Jordan's Experience and Policies in Reverse Transfer of Technology,* UNCTAD Report, 1980; numerous studies in various journals and magazines, in Arabic and English; column writer in daily *Jordan Times; Decorations:* Order of Jordanian Star, 1975; Knight of the Order of the Republic of China, 1973; *Interests and Recreations:* tennis, gardening; *Languages:* Arabic, English; *Address:* P O Box 429 Amman, Jordan; telephone: 661 821.

ABDUL KADIR, Yahia, Egyptian diplomat; born 1920, Alexandria, Egypt; *Religion:* Muslim; *Education:* LLB, Cairo University, Cairo, Egypt, 1943; *Career:* Ministry of Foreign Affairs, Secretary then Counsellor, Egyptian Embassies to Yugoslavia, Sudan, Italy; Ambassador to Saudi Arabia, 1964–68; Ambassador to Yugoslavia, 1968–71; Chairman, Egyptian Radio and TV, 1971; Ambassador to USSR, 1971–74; Ambassador to Greece, 1974–; *Decorations:* Egyptian Order of the Republic, 1961; Order of the Yugoslavian flag with cordon, 1968; Egyptian Order of Merits, 1970; Great Cross of Greek Order of the Phoenix, 1976; *Address:* Egyptian Embassy, 3 Leoforos Vassilissis Sofias, Athens, Greece; 1095 Cornish al Nil Street, Garden City, Cairo, Egypt.

ABDUL KARIM, Amin, Iraqi politician; born 1921, Baghdad, Iraq; *Education:* College of Law, Baghdad; *Career:* joined government service 1943; various government posts including Director General of Finance and Revenues; President, State Organization of Banks, 1943–68; Minister of Finance, 1968–74; *Address:* Ministry of Finance, Baghdad, Iraq.

ABDUL KARIM, Ibrahim, Bahraini politician/economist; born 1940; *Religion:* Muslim; *Education:* BA in Economics, Baghdad University, Baghdad, Iraq, 1965; *Career:* Personnel Relations Supervisor, Bahrain Petroleum Company; Director of Economic Affairs, Ministry of Finance and National Economy; Director of Oil and Economy, 1971; Parliamentary Secretary, Ministry of Finance and National Economy, 1972; Deputy Minister of Finance, 1973–76; Minister of Finance and National Economy, 1976–; *Address:* Ministry of Finance and National Economy, P O Box 333, Manama, Bahrain; telephone: 256114; telex: 8933 MALEYA BN.

ABDUL KARIM, Tayih, Iraqi politician; born 1933, Ana, Iraq; *Education:* Teachers Training College, 1950–51; BA, English Literature, College of Education, Baghdad University, Baghdad, Iraq, 1959; LLB, Al-Mustansiriyah University, Baghdad, Iraq, 1968–69; *Career:* Deputy Governor, Basra Governorate, Ministry of Interior, 1963; Ambassador, Iraqi Embassy, Sudan, 1969; Under Secretary, Ministry of Education, 1970; member, Regional Leadership, Arab Baath Socialist Party, 1970; Chairman, Economic Affairs Bureau, Revolutionary Command Council, 1971; Chairman, Arab Affairs Bureau, Revolutionary Command Council, 1972; re-elected member, Regional Leadership, Arab Baath Socialist party, 1973; Minister of Oil, 1974–82; President, Iraq National Oil Company, 1977; member, Revolutionary Command Council, 1977; *Address:* Ministry of Oil, Baghdad, Iraq.

ABDUL KHALIQ, Mustafa, People's Democratic Republic of Yemen politician/lawyer; born 1945; *Education:* Law Studies, Baghdad University, Iraq; *Career:* magistrate; Secretary of Aden Municipality and Prosecutor of the People's Court in the First Governorate; appointed Secretary to People's Democratic Republic of Yemen-USSR Friendship Association, 1970; Minister of Justice and Waqfs, 1971–73; Ambassador to USSR, 1973–74; member of People's Supreme Council; *Address:* People's Supreme Council, Aden, People's Democratic Republic of Yemen.

ABDUL KUDDUS, Ihsan, Egyptian writer; born 1 January 1919; son of late Rose el-Yousef, actress and journalist; *Religion:* Muslim; *Education:* Cairo University, Egypt, and in France; *Career:* lawyer, 1942; joined *Rose al-Yousef* magazine, 1942; imprisoned for attack on government, 1945; Chief Editor of *Rose el-Yousef;* imprisoned 1950–51; first novel published 1954; Editor in

Chief, *Akhbar al-Yaum*, 1974; resident writer in *Al-Ahram*, 1974; Chairman of *Al-Ahram*, 1975; *Publications:* numerous novels and short story collections; *Languages:* Arabic, English, French; *Address: Al-Ahram*, Galaa Street, Cairo, Egypt.

ABDUL LATIF, Ahmad, Saudi Arabian official/economist; born 1935, Jeddah, Saudi Arabia; *Religion:* Muslim; *Education:* BA in Economics, American University in Cairo, Egypt, 1957; extensive training with the IMF, Washington D.C., and in commercial banks in New York and London; *Career:* Director of Banking Control Department, Saudi Arabian Monetary Agency (SAMA); Director General of Foreign Department (SAMA); member of SAMA Higher Investment Committees; member of the Board of Riyadh Bank; member of the Board of The Gulf International Bank, Bahrain; contributed to the formulation of the Banking Control Law in Saudi Arabia; Bank Controller; helped establish and run The Saudi Institute for Public Education, a voluntary organization to fight illiteracy; *Publications:* articles broadcast by the Saudi English Broadcasting Station; *Interests and Recreations:* reading; *Address:* Saudi Arabian Monetary Agency, King Abdul Aziz Street, Airport Road, P O Box 2292, Riyadh, Saudi Arabia; telephone: 69418.

ABDUL LATIF, Fawzi Hussain, United Arab Emirates diplomat; born 18 April 1942, Sharjah, United Arab Emirates; married; one son, 1974; *Religion:* Muslim; *Education:* BA, Economics and Commerce, Jordanian University, 1971; Diplomatic Course, UN Institute for Training and Research in Abu Dhabi and UN; *Career:* 3rd Secretary, UAE delegation to UN, 1972; Minister Delegate in Ministry of Foreign Affairs, 1975; Ambassador to Zaire, 1975–; *Interests and Recreations:* writing, Arabic poetry, riding, hunting, swimming, travel, chess, backgammon; *Languages:* Arabic, English, some French and Lingala; *Address:* Office — UAE Embassy, Kinshasa, P O Box 1999, Congo; telephone: 69370, 69581, 59535; Residence P O Box 1219, Dubai, United Arab Emirates; telephone: 4035.

ABUL MAGD, Ahmad Kamal, Egyptian lawyer/politician; born 1930, Cairo, Egypt; five children; *Religion:* Muslim; *Education:*

Cairo University, Egypt; Law Studies, University of Paris, France; spent nine months in London in 1935 studying Constitutional Law; *Career:* Lecturer, University of Michigan, USA; various teaching posts in Cairo; Cultural Counsellor, Embassy to USA, 1966; appointed member of the Provisional Secretariat of the Arab Socialist Union (ASU), 1971; elected ASU Secretary for Youth, 1971; Minister of State for Youth, 1972; served on ASU Disciplinary Committee; Chairman of the ASU Committee, 1973; Minister of State for Cabinet Affairs during October War 1973; Minister of Information, 1974–75; ASU Secretary for Ideology, 1975–; *Languages:* Arabic, English, French; *Address:* c/o Law School, University of Kuwait, P O Box 5969, Kuwait.

ABDUL MAGID, Yahya, Sudanese politician/engineer; born 1926, Omdurman, Sudan; married; *Religion:* Muslim; *Education:* Diploma in Civil Engineering, Gordon Memorial College, 1950; Diploma in Hydrology, Imperial College, London, UK; *Career:* Part-time Lecturer, Khartoum University, Sudan; member of the British Association of Civil Engineers; practical training with British companies specialising in the construction of irrigation projects; Under Secretary, Ministry of Irrigation, 1969; Secretary of the Sudanese Engineering Society, 1963–65; Minister of Irrigation and Hydro-electric Power, 1971; Minister of State for Irrigation, Ministry of Agriculture, 1973–74; Minister of State for Irrigation and Hydro-electric Power, 1975–77; Minister for Irrigation and Hydro-electric Power, 1977; has been closely involved in the Jonglei Canal Scheme; member of International Committee for Hydraulic Law; *Address:* c/o Ministry of Energy and Power, Khartoum, Sudan.

ABDUL MAHMUD, Fatma, Sudanese official/physician; married; two children; *Religion:* Muslim; *Education:* in New Halfa, Omdurman, Sudan; Diploma in Medicine, 1967; University of Moscow, USSR, 1967; MA in Public Health, University of Moscow, USSR; *Career:* Ministry of Health, 1967–69; Deputy Minister, Social Affairs Department, 1972; Minister of State for Social Welfare, 1975; Minister of Social Affairs, 1976–; *Address:* Ministry of Social Affairs, Khartoum, Sudan.

ABDUL MAJID, Amin, Saudi Arabian official; born 1935; *Education:* Diploma in Commerce; Certificate of Public Administration; courses in Management; *Career:* Assistant Director, Zakat (Islamic alms tax) and Income Tax Department, 1968; former Chairman, Information Committee, Arab Union of Air Transport; Manager, Public Relations, Saudi Arabian Airlines (SAUDIA), 1975; former Chairman, Al-Thagr Sports Club; member, Jeddah Municipal Council, 1974–; Writer in Saudi newspapers, 1961–; Co-ordinator, SAUDIA-YEMENIA Affairs; Executive Representative, SAUDIA; *Publications:* a collection of short stories; *Interests and Recreations:* reading, music, swimming; *Address:* Saudi Arabian Airlines, P O Box 620, Jeddah, Saudi Arabia; telephone: Office— 686 2337; Residence— 642 5261.

ABDUL MAJID BIN ABDUL AZIZ, HRH Prince, Saudi Arabian Prince/administrator; born 1941, Riyadh, Saudi Arabia; son of late King Abdul Aziz; *Religion:* Muslim; *Career:* Governor of Tabuk; *Address:* Council of the Principality of Tabuk, Saudi Arabia.

ABDUL MAJID, Shaikh Adnan Abdul Rahman, Saudi Arabian businessman; born 1948, Mecca; married; two sons, one daughter; *Religion:* Muslim; *Career:* worked for Ministry of Information, Saudi Arabian Airlines, 1960–73; Partner in two advertising companies; Owner of Saudi International Corporation for marketing, market research, advertising, publicity and public relations; Owner, Saudi International Trade and Industry Fair Organization; former Vice President of Third World Fair Organization Association, Algiers, 1967; *Interests and Recreations:* bowling, chess; *Languages:* Arabic, English; *Address:* P O Box 4571, Jeddah, Saudi Arabia; telephone: 6672056, 6671691, 6671692.

ABDUL MALIK, Anwar, Egyptian academic/sociologist; born 23 October 1924, Cairo, Egypt; one daughter; *Religion:* Christian; *Education:* BA, British Institute, Cairo, 1940–44; BA in Philosophy, Faculty of Arts, Ain Shams University, Cairo, Egypt, 1954; DSoc, Sorbonne, University of Paris, 1964; Dès-L, Sorbonne, Paris, 1969; *Career:* actively involved in the development of national progressive trends in Egypt and the Arab World, through free-lance journalism, 1940–

59; Associate Editor, *Ros al-Yusuf, Al-Masa, Al-Magallah, Al-Iza'ah;* script writer, Egyptian Broadcasting System, 2nd Cultural Programme, 1956–59; Research Professor, Sociological Section, Centre Nationale de la Recherche Scientifique, Paris, 1960–; Assistant Professor, Ecole des Hautes Etudes en Sciences Sociale, Paris, 1965–; Visiting Professor, University of Chile, Santiago, 1969, University of Candido Mendes, Rio de Janeiro, Brazil, 1969, El Colegio de Mexico, 1969, University of Uppsala, 1971, Université Catholique de Louvain, Belgium, 1970, Freie Universitat Berlin, 1972–, University of Ain Shams, Cairo, 1975–76; Vice President of the International Sociological Association, 1974–81; President of International Sociological Association, Research Committee on national movements and imperialism, 1966–; participated in over 50 international meetings; frequent scientific consultant to UNESCO; Project Co-ordinator, Human and Social Development Programme, the United Nations University, Tokyo, 1978–; *Publications: Egypt, Société Militaire,* Paris, 1962; *Anthologie de la Littérature Arabe Contemporaine,* Paris, 1965; *Dirassat fi'l Thaqafah al-Wataniyah,* Beirut, 1967; *La Pensée Politique Arabe Contemporaine,* Paris, 1970; *Sociologie de l'Impérialisme,* Varna, 1970; *La Dialectique Sociale,* Paris, 1972; *Idéologie et Renaissance Nationale l'Egypte Moderne,* Paris, 1969; *L'Armée dans la Nation,* 1975; *Specificité et Théorie Sociale,* 1977; *Al Fikr al-Arabi fi Ma'rakat al Nahdah; Intellectual Creativity in Endogenous Culture,* 1982, Tokyo, co-author; *Science and Technology in the Transformation of the World,* Tokyo, 1982, co-author; several books translated into English, Japanese, Spanish, Italian, Portuguese, Serbo-Croatian; numerous articles and reports in professional journals; *Interests and Recreations:* music, opera, swimming, travel, ballet, cinema, football, cooking; member of the International Society for the Comparative Study of Civilization, of the Egyptian Philosophical Society, Association Internationale des Sociologues de Langue Française la Gesellchaft der Freunde von Beyreuth, the International Institute of Strategic Studies, the Glyndebourne Opera Festival Society; and several other associations and societies; *Languages:* Arabic, English, French, Italian, Spanish; *Address:* The United Nations University, Centre National de la Recherche Scientifique de l'Homme, 54 Boulevard

Raspail, 75006 Paris, France; telephone: Office — 544 3979; Residence — 588 8713; telex: MSH203104 F; 13 Al-Badr Street, Heliopolis, Cairo, Egypt.

ABDUL MEGUID, Adli, Egyptian official/economist; born 1929, Egypt; *Religion:* Muslim; *Education:* in Egypt; PhD, Economics, University of Wisconsin, USA, 1956; *Career:* Assistant Professor, Alexandria University, Egypt 1956–59; Lecturer, University of Khartoum, Sudan, 1959–62; UN Adviser to Sudanese Ministry of Economy, 1962–65; Chief of Investments and Export Promotion, UN Industrial Development Organization (UNIDO), 1965–75; Chief of Egyptian Economic Mission in the USA, 1975; *Address:* Egyptian Economic Mission in USA, 720 Fifth Avenue, 6th Floor, New York, NY 10019, USA.

ABDUL MEGUID, Ahmad Ismat, Egyptian diplomat; born 1923, Alexandria, Egypt; married; two sons; *Religion:* Muslim; *Education:* BA in Law, Alexandria University, Alexandria, Egypt, 1944; Diploma in Political Science, University of Paris, France; PhD in International Law, University of Paris; *Career:* Attaché and 3rd Secretary, Embassy of Egypt, London, 1950–54; Head of UK Affairs Desk, Ministry of Foreign Affairs, Cairo, 1954–56; member of Egyptian Delegation, which negotiated the British evacuation from Suez Canal, leading to the Anglo-Egyptian Agreement, 1954; Counsellor, Permanent Mission of Egypt, European Office, United Nations, Geneva, Switzerland, 1957–61; Assistant Director, Legal Department, Ministry of Foreign Affairs, 1961–63; Minister Plenipotentiary, Embassy of Egypt, Paris, France, 1963–67; Director of Cultural Affairs and Technical Assistance Department, Ministry of Foreign Affairs, Cairo, 1967–69; Secretary General of the Committee of Cultural Relations and Technical Assistance of Egypt, 1969; Official Spokesman of Egyptian Government and Head of Information Organisation, Cairo, 1969–70; Ambassador of Egypt to France, 1970; Minister of State for Cabinet Affairs, Cairo, 1970–72; Permanent Representative of Egypt to the United Nations, 1972; Chairman of the Group of 77 at the United Nations, 1972–73; Chairman of the Preparatory Committee for World Food Council, 1974; Chairman of Arab Group for the introduction of Arabic as a working language at United Nations, 1974;

Chairman of the Cairo Preparatory Conference for Geneva Peace Conference, 1977; Ambassador Extraordinary and Plenipotentiary and Permanent Representative of Egypt to the United Nations, 1977–; *Publications:* numerous articles in international law journals; *Decorations:* 1st Class Decoration, Arab Republic of Egypt, 1970, Order of Merit, 1967, and Grand Croix, 1971, France; *Languages:* Arabic, English, French; *Address:* Egyption Mission, 36 East 67th Street, New York, NY 10021, USA.

ABDUL MUHSIN BIN ABDUL AZIZ, HRH Prince, Saudi Arabian Prince/administrator; born 1927, Riyadh, Saudi Arabia; seventh surviving son of late King Abdul Aziz; *Religion:* Muslim; *Career:* Minister of Interior, 1960–61; Governor of the Holy City of Medina, 1965–; *Address:* Principality of Medina, Medina, Saudi Arabia.

ABDUL MUN'IM, Abdul Qadir Ahmad, Sudanese businessman; born 6 March 1920, Sudan; married; two sons, three daughters; *Religion:* Muslim; *Education:* BA in Commerce, American University of Cairo, Egypt; Diploma in Business Administration; *Career:* Owner and Director of two commercial companies; member of the Board, Mineral Water Co Ltd; Chairman of the Board, Sudan Batteries Co Ltd; member of Khartoum Municipal Council, of the Board of the Building Insurance Co, of the Board, Al Khartoum Bank Ltd; Chairman of the Board, Al-Jazira Commercial Co Ltd; *Interests and Recreations:* reading, social activities; *Languages:* Arabic, English; *Address:* P O Box 44, Khartoum, Sudan; telephone: Office — 70100/196; Residence — 71888.

ABDUL MUN'IM, Muhammad, Egyptian journalist; born 10 December 1937, Cairo, Egypt; married; three sons; *Religion:* Muslim; *Education:* BA in English Literature, Cairo University, Cairo, Egypt; *Career:* Officer, Armed Forces, 1957–68; Military Correspondent, *Al-Ahram* newspaper and sub-editor, 1968–; *Publications: October 6th:* First Electronic Warfare 1974–75; *Interests and Recreations:* billiards, swimming; *Languages:* Arabic, English; *Address:* 7 Ibn Marwan Street, Dokki, Cairo, Egypt; telephone: 989459.

ABDUL NABI, Hidayat, Egyptian journalist; born 10 November 1948, Heliopolis, Egypt; *Religion:* Muslim; *Education:* BA in Economics and Political Science, American University in Cairo, Egypt; MA in International Relations, Fletcher School of Law and Diplomacy, Hedford, USA, 1975; *Career:* Researcher, *Al-Ahram,* newspaper, 1971–74; Graduate Assistant, American University in Cairo, 1974–75; Script writer, TV and radio programmes, 1975–77; Diplomatic Reporter, *Al-Ahram* newspaper 1974–77; *Interests and Recreations:* tennis, swimming; *Languages:* Arabic, English, some French; *Address:* AL-*Ahram* Newspaper, Al-Galaa Street, Cairo, Egypt; telephone: 59010 ext 122, 242.

ABDUL QADIR, al-Mordhy al-Tayib, Sudanese politician; born 2 April 1927; married; five sons; *Religion:* Muslim; *Education:* Teachers' Institute, Bakht al-Redha, 1946; Sudanese Military College, 1948; Military Science, Camberley Staff College, UK; training courses in Pakistan and USA; *Career:* 2nd Lieutenant, 1950; Colonel, Sudanese Army; Director of Sudanese Military Intelligence; Military Attaché, Embassy to USA, 1966–67; Military Attaché, Embassy to UK, 1968–69; retired 1969; member of Committee for Resettlement of Refugees of Southern Sudan; member of First Constituent Assembly; Chairman of the National Defence Committee and Chairman of the 10th Constitutional Law Committee; Governor of Darfur Province, 1973–74; Secretary of the Sudanese Socialist Union (SSU) and Governor of the District of North Darfur, 1974; Chairman of the Board of Darfur General Transport Company, 1976; *Decorations:* Long Service Medal; Order of the Two Niles, 2nd Class; Order of the Constitution; *Interests and Recreations:* reading poetry, history, biographies of military commanders and politicians; *Languages:* Arabic, English; *Address:* North Darfur Province, El-Fasher, Sudan; telephone: 2001.

ABDUL QADIR, Haguig Salih, Moroccan academic; born 1948, Morocco; married; two sons; *Religion:* Muslim; *Education:* Degrees in Education and Psychology; *Career:* Teacher, 1965; Inspector of Education, 1974; Professor of Psychology, 1976; *Publications:* textbooks for primary schools, 1980; textbook in mathematics, 1982; publisher of *Al-Tarbiya wa-l Ta'liim,* since 1982; *Interests and Recreations:* reading in psychology,

literature; *Languages:* Arabic, French, English; *Address:* P O Box 35 Ya'cub Al-Mansur, Rabat, Morocco.

ABDUL QADIR, Muhammad al-Fousi, Saudi Arabian academic/Islamic scholar; born 1941, Medina, Saudi Arabia; *Religion:* Muslim; *Education:* BA in Shari'a (Islamic Law), Faculty of Shari'a; MA, Edinburgh University, UK; PhD, Principles of Islamic Jurisprudence; *Career:* Lecturer, Assistant Professor, member of Shari'a Department, Council of King Abdul Aziz University; Head of Shari'a Department, Faculty of Sharia, King Abdul Aziz University, Mecca, of Faculty of Muslim Students Association of USA and Canada, of Muslim Students Society of Britain and Ireland; delegate to Education Festival, India, 1975; *Publications: The Traditional View of Malik Bin Anas,* Life and Works, MA Dissertation; *Maliki Legal Doctrine in the West,* PhD Law Thesis; *Address:* Faculty of Shari'a, King Abdul Aziz University, Mecca, Saudi Arabia; telephone: Office — Mecca 22114/115.

ABDUL QAWI YAFAI, Muhammad, People's Democratic Republic of Yemen official; born 1946; *Career:* Director of Culture, Ministry of Information and Culture; Permanent Secretary, Ministry of Culture and Tourism; made official visits to USSR and North Korea; *Address:* Ministry of Culture and Tourism, Aden, People's Democratic Republic of Yemen.

ABDUL RAHMAN BIN ABDUL AZIZ, HRH Prince, Saudi Arabian Prince/businessman; born 1931; third son of late King Abdul Aziz and Hassa Bint Sudairi; *Religion:* Muslim: *Education:* Military Cadet, California Military High School, California, USA; Diploma of the Military Academy, California, USA; BBA in Economics and Business Administration, University of California, USA; *Career:* Founder of the National Gypsum Company; businessman; established modern farms in various provinces of the Kingdom; Founder of Printing, Publication and Press Organization, Jeddah; Founder of Al Khat Printing, Publication and Translation, Dammam; Founding member of Riyadh and Jeddah Electric Power Companies, Electric Company, of Eastern Province, Saudi Gas Co, and of a number of cement plants in Saudi Arabia; *Address:* Prince Abdul Rahman Bin Abdul Aziz Mansion, Riyadh, Saudi Arabia.

ABDUL RAHMAN BIN FAISAL, HRH Prince, Saudi Arabian Prince/army officer; born 1942; son of late King Faisal; married; *Religion:* Muslim; *Education:* Princeton University, USA; Graduate of the Royal Military Academy, UK, 1963; represented the Royal Military College in fencing; *Career:* army officer; Director of the Armed Forces Armoured Project; *Languages:* Arabic, English; Ministry of Defence and Aviation, Riyadh, Saudi Arabia.

ABDUL RAHMAN, Ibrahim Hilmi, Egyptian UN official/politician; born 5 January 1919, Sharqiyah, Egypt; married; *Religion:* Muslim; *Education:* BSc, Cairo University, Egypt, 1934–38; London University, UK, 1938–39; PhD in Astrophysics, Edinburgh University, UK, 1939–41; Cambridge University, UK, 1941–42; *Career:* Assistant Professor, Cairo University, 1942–52; Secretary General, Council of Ministers, 1953–58; Secretary General, Supreme Science Council, 1956–58; Secretary General, Atomic Energy Commission, Egypt, 1955–59; Secretary General, National Planning Commission, Egypt, 1957–60; Director, Institute of National Planning, Egypt, 1960–63; Commissioner for Industrial Development, UN, New York, 1963–66; Executive Director, United Nations Industrial Development Organisation (UNIDO), Vienna, Austria, 1967–74; returned to Egypt as Technological Adviser to the Prime Minister, 1974; Minister of Planning and Administrative Development, 1975–76; *Publications: National Planning Memoirs; Academic Studies in Astrophysics,* 1942–52; numerous reports and publications on industrial development; *Interests and Recreations:* farming, music, photography, folk art, international and industrial development, national planning, scientific and technical policies, operational research, astronomy; member of the Institut d'Egypte, Society for International Development; *Languages:* Arabic, English, French; *Address:* Office — UNIDO, P O Box 707, A-1011, Vienna 1, Austria; telephone: 0222 43500.

ABDUL RAHMAN, Mufida, Egyptian politician; born 1910; married; *Religion:* Muslim; *Edcuation:* Law, Cairo University, Egypt 1939; *Career:* Lecturer, Cairo Univerity; elected member of the National Union, 1959; later elected member of the Consultative Committee of the Women's Section of the Union; elected one of the seven women members of the National Assembly, 1960; member, Government Committee on Women's Affairs; elected to the National Congress of the Arab Socialist Union (ASU), 1968; appointed by the President to the National Assembly, 1969; member of the General Committee of the Citizens War Committee, 1970; member of the ASU Central Committee, 1971, elected to the People's Assembly, 1971; Chairman of its Social Welfare Sub-committee; Chairman of the Association of Muslim Women; *Address:* Arab Socialist Party Central Committee, Cairo, Egypt.

ABDUL RAZZAQ, Saud Abdul Aziz Muhammad, Kuwaiti businessman; born 1908; married; two sons; *Religion:* Muslim; *Education:* in Kuwait; *Career:* Public Health Administration, 1953–61; Constituent Assembly member, 1962; member of National Assembly, 1963–67; Deputy Speaker of National Assembly, 1963–65; Speaker and President of National Assembly, 1965–67; Chairman of Al-Ahli Bank, 1967; businessman in Kuwait and Bombay; *Languages:* Arabic, Urdu; *Address:* Al-Ahli Bank of Kuwait, P O Box 1387, Commercial Area No.5, Kuwait; telephone: 411101, 20; telex: 22067.

ABDUL SALAM, Othman Hashim, Sudanese economist; born 1937; *Religion:* Muslim; *Education:* Economics Degree, University of Chicago, USA; *Career:* Economic Commission for Africa (ECA), Addis Ababa, Ethiopia, 1962–67; African Institute for Economic Development and Planning, Dakar, Senegal, 1968–69; Sub-regional Office of UN Economic Commission for North Africa, 1971–74; Deputy Chairman of Sudan Development Corporation (SDC) 1974; *Address:* Sudan Development Corporation, P O Box 710, 69 Africa Road, Khartoum, Sudan.

ABDUL WAHAB, Shaikh Ahmad, Saudi Arabian official; born 1923, Mecca, Saudi Arabia; married; *Religion:* Muslim; *Education:* general, training in diplomatic ceremonials and protocol; *Career:* Chief of Protocol at the Viceroy's Cabinet, during King Faisal's appointment as Viceroy of Hijaz; Chief of Protocol at the Royal Cabinet, 1964–; accompanied the late King Faisal on his state visits to Arab, European, Asian, African and American States; has accompanied the late King Khalid on similar state visits; *Address:* The Royal Cabinet, Riyadh, Saudi Arabia.

ABDUL WASIE, Abdul Wahab Ahmad, Saudi Arabian politician; born 1929, Jeddah, Saudi Arabia; *Religion:* Muslim; *Education:* BA in Commerce and Economics, Cairo University, Egypt; Higher Diploma in Taxation, Alexandria University, Egypt; *Career:* Assistant Director, Budget Department, Ministry of Finance and National Economy, 1953; Director General of Financial Affairs, Ministry of Education, 1954; Director General of Education; Assistant Under Secretary of State for Education Affairs, 1964; Under Secretary gf State, Ministry of Education, 1965; State Minister; President of Board of Supervision and Investigation, 1971; Minister of Pilgrimage and Waqf, 1975–; Chairman, Waqf Higher Council, 1975–; Chairman, Higher International Council of Mosques, 1975–; member of Okez Press and Publishing Organization, of the Higher Committee on Education Policy, of the Higher Pilgrimage Committee, of the Supreme Council of Universities, and of the Supreme Council of Youth Welfare; attended International Conference on Education, Geneva; several UNESCO conferences, Paris; Conference on Eradication of Illiteracy, Egypt; Conferences of the Ministers of Education, Iraq, Kuwait, Libya, Iran; chaired conferences of Ministers of Waqf and Islamic Affairs, Mecca; *Publications: Madarisuna wal Tarbiya; Education in Saudi Arabia,* in English, 1970; several textbooks on mathematics and book-keeping; *Decorations:* King Abdul Aziz Order, 1st Class; Tunisian Republic Order, 1st Class; Golden Star Order, 1st Class, Republic of China; Belgian Republic Order, 1st Class; *Interests and Recreations:* reading, walking; *Languages:* Arabic, English; *Address:* P O Box 2103, Riyadh, Saudi Arabia; telephone: Office — 410 3636; Residence — 478 5222.

ABDULLAH, Abdul Malik Muhammad, Yemen Arab Republic politician/physician; born 1942, Yemen Arab Republic; married; two sons, one daughter; *Religion:* Muslim; *Education:* BSc, Medicine, Ain Shams University, Cairo, Egypt; Diploma in Public Health, Gynaecology and Obstetrics, Ain Shams University, Cairo, Egypt; *Career:* General Practitioner, Jumhuriyah Hospital, Taiz; Director, Taiz Health Centre; World Health Organization (WHO) Representative, Taiz; Director General, Medical Section, Taiz Province; Director, Nasser Hospital; Minister of Health, 1975–; *Publications: Bilharizia in Yemen thesis; Interests and Recreations:* reading; *Languages:* Arabic, English; *Address:* Southern Airport District, Al-Safiyah, Sana'a, Yemen Arab Republic; telephone: 2502.

ABDULLAH, Abdul Sami, Egyptian artist/caricaturist; born in Cairo, Egypt; married; two sons, one daughter; *Religion:* Muslim; *Education:* Teachers Training College, Cairo, Egypt; *Career:* caricaturist, worked for *Rose al-Yusuf* magazine, 1946, *Akhbar al-Yaum* newspaper, 1955, *Dar al-Shaab,* 1958, *Al-Gumhuriyah* newspaper; Head of Technical Department, *Al-Gumhuriyah,* 1964, *Al-Musawwar,* 1965–; exhibited at the Formalism Art Exhibition, 1963, 1966; *Publications: Black and White,* collection of cartoons, in Arabic; several collections of short stories, 1963, 1972; *Interests and Recreations:* walking, music, theatre; member of Zamalek Club; *Languages:* Arabic, English, French; *Address:* Dar al-Hilal, 16 Sharia Muhammad Ezz al-Arab, Cairo, Egypt; telephone: 50836.

ABDULLAH, Abdul Rahman, Sudanese politician; born 1932, Northern Province, Sudan; *Religion:* Muslim; *Education:* BA, Khartoum University, 1954; graduated from School of Public Administration, 1956; MA, Administrative Science, New York, USA, 1963; *Career:* Sub District Officer, Ministry of Interior, Sudan; Institute of Public Administration; Director of Institute of Public Administration, 1963–65; Director, African Administrative and Research Institute, Morocco, 1965; Director of the National Institute for Public Administration, Libya; Deputy Minister of Local Government, 1971; Minister of Public Service and Administrative Reform, 1971; Minister of Industry and Mines, 1977; Minister of Transport, 1977–; *Address:* Ministry of Transport, Khartoum, Sudan; telephone: 71291.

ABDULLAH BIN ABDUL AZIZ, HRH Prince, Saudi Arabian Crown Prince; born August 1921; son of late King Abdul Aziz and Shammar mother; *Religion:* Muslim; *Career:* Commander of National Guard, 1963–; Second Deputy to Prime Minister, 1975–82; Crown Prince and First Deputy Prime Minister, 1982–; visited UK as official guest of Minister of Defence, July 1973; paid State Visit to France; *Interests and Recreations:* hunting, horse racing; Chairman of Riyadh Horsemanship Club; *Address:* Royal Court, Riyadh, Saudi Arabia.

ABDULLAH BIN FAISAL, HRH Prince,
Saudi Arbian Prince/businessman; born
1921; eldest son of late King Faisal; married;
three sons; *Religion:* Muslim; *Education:*
general court education supplemented by
private tutoring and extensive reading;
Career: Assistant and Special Adviser to late
King Faisal when he was Viceroy of Hijaz
Province; Minister of Interior for Hijaz, and
Minister of Interior, 1951; resigned as
Minister of Health, 1954, and as Minister of
Interior, 1958; businessman; wide range of
business interests including Arabian Estab-
lishment for Trading and Navigation, estab-
lished 1962, to take over remaining business
of Gellatly Hankey; owner and Chairman of
Board of several companies and agencies
including General Motors Agency, Saudi
Shipment Co, Sony Electronics and others;
Founder of King Faisal International Charity
Society; *Publications:* collection of poems in
Arabic; *Interests and Recreations:* reading,
poetry, writing, football; Chairman of Jeddah
Al Ahli Football Team; *Address:* Prince
Abdullah Al Faisal Palace, Jeddah, Saudi
Arabia.

**ABDULLAH BIN MUSAED BIN ABDUL
RAHMAN, HRH Prince,** Saudi Arabian
Prince/businessman; born 1939, Riyadh,
Saudi Arabia; *Religion:* Muslim; *Education:*
MA in Economics; *Career:* member of the
Board of Directors of First Arabian Invest-
ment Co, Luxembourg, of Saudi Investment
Co, Jeddah; Chairman of Board of Saudi
Carrier Co, Riyadh; member of the Board of
Bank of America, Cairo, Egypt; member of
Constituent Committee, South Cement Plan,
Jizan; *Interests and Recreations:* reading,
swimming; *Address:* P O Box 580 Riyadh,
Saudi Arabia; telephone: Office— Riyadh 22
900, 22 974; Residence— Riyadh 51 858;
telex: 20055 Marco, Riyadh.

ABDULLAH, Ismail Sabri, Egyptian eco-
nomist; born 25 December 1924, Malawi;
married; *Religion:* Muslim; *Education:* PhD,
Economics, University of Paris, France, 1955;
Career: Lecturer in Economics, Universities
of Alexandria and Cairo, Egypt, later
Professor of Economics, University of Cairo,
Cairo, Egypt; Adviser to late President
Nasser, 1954; member of the Arab Socialist
Union, 1966–; one of the founders of the
Editorial Board of the Marxist monthly
review, *Al-Talia,* up to its suppression in
1977; Director, Al-Ahram Economic Re-

search Organisation, 1968; Director of the
Institute of National Planning, 1969; Chairman, Third World Forum, 1976–; member of
the Governing Council of the Society of
International Development; Consultant to
several UN organisations, including UNIDO,
ILO, and UNCTAD, as well as Arab League
and inter-Arab institutions; *Publications:*
Lectures in Economics, 1954; *The Organisa-
tion of the Public Sector; Confrontation with
Israel,* 1969; *Political Papers,* 1972; various
articles in French, Arabic and English;
*Towards a New International Order; Lang-
uages:* Arabic, French, English; *Address:* 39
Dokki Street, P O Box 43 Orman, Cairo,
Egypt.

ABDULLAH, Jalal Muhammad Salih, Iraqi
academic; born 1932, Kirkuk, Iraq; married;
two sons, one daughter; *Religion:* Muslim;
Education: BSc in Chem; PhD; FRSC;
Career: Demonstrator, University of
Baghdad, Baghdad, Iraq, 1962; Assistant
Professor, University of Baghdad, 1968;
Professor, University of Baghdad, 1973; Dean
of the College of Sciences, University of
Baghdad; member of the Iraqi Academy of
Sciences, 1979–; the Jordanian Academy of
Arabic Languages, 1980–; *Publications:*
numerous researches published in interna-
tional professional journals; several chemistry
textbooks published by the Ministry of Edu-
cation; Editor of the Iraqi Journal of
Sciences; *Languages:* Arabic, English, Ger-
man; *Address:* Hayy al Bunuq 4202/6/5,
Baghdad, Iraq; telephone: 8829680.

ABDULLAH KHODJA, Kamil, Algerian
official/economist; born Constantine, Algeria; *Education:* Degree in Economics;
Career: participated in Economic Study
Commission of National Liberation Front
(FLN); practical experience of economic
planning in Morocco; member of the Provisional Executive, 1962; Director, later Director General of Planning, Ministry of Finance;
Secretary of State for National Plan, 1970;
took leading role in drafting and implementation of Four-Year Plan, 1969–73; Secretary
of State for Planning, April 1977; *Address:*
Ministry of Planning, Algiers, Algeria; telephone: 780323; telex: 52516.

ABDULLAH, Rahmatalla, Sudanese diplomat; born 1922; *Religion:* Muslim; *Education:* Trinity College, Cambridge University,
UK; *Career:* Ambassador to India and Japan,

1959–60; Ambassador to Nigeria, 1960–61; Minister of National Education, 1964–65; Head of Department, Sudanese Institute of Education; Executive Secretary and Assistant General Manager, Sudan Gezira Board; Deputy Under Secretary for Foreign Affairs, 1965–67; Ambassador to France, Netherlands, Switzerland and Spain, 1968–70; Ambassador to Zaire, 1970–72; Permanent Representative to the UN, New York, 1972–74; Personal Envoy of the Government to the Organization of African Unity, OAU, Summit Meetings; Representative of Sudan at various UN, OAU, regional African, and other international conferences; *Languages:* Arabic, English, French; *Address:* P O Box 2790, Khartoum, Sudan.

ABDULLAH, Taha Ibrahim al-, Iraqi official; *Career:* Minister of Irrigation, July 1969; member of the State Planning Council, August 1969; member of the Supreme Agricultural Council, May 1972; President of Baghdad University, February 1974–80; Minister of Planning, 1980–82; *Languages:* Arabic, English; *Address:* Ministry of Planning, Baghdad, Iraq.

ABELA, Albert, Lebanese businessman; born 1921, Jezzine, Lebanon; *Education:* general; *Career:* Chairman and Managing Director, Albert Abela Company SAL; *Interests and Recreations:* member of the Beirut Yacht Club; *Address:* Office — Société Albert Abela, Starco Centre, P O Box 11– 3203, Beirut, Lebanon; telephone: 250570; Residence — Ramlet Al Baida, Beirut, Lebanon.

ABID, Ali, Tunisian artist/cariacaturist; born 15 December 1938, Tunis, Tunisia; married; six sons, three daughters; *Religion:* Muslim; *Education:* general; *Career:* cariacaturist for several Tunisian newspapers; currently exclusive cariacaturist of *Dialogue* magazine; held various exhibitions, Tunis, 1972; Cité Internationale des Arts, Paris, France, 1974; International Salon of Humour, Bordighera, Italy; annual participant International Salon of Cariacature, Montreal, Canada; 1st Prize for the Ali Riahi Festival from La Marsa Commune; *Interests and Recreations:* graphic arts, member of the National Union of Plastic and Graphic Arts; *Languages:* Arabic, French; *Address:* Dialogue Magazine, Tunis, Tunisia; telephone: 264899.

ABILLAMA, Fayik Maged, Lebanese academic; born 1936, Mtein, Lebanon; married; two sons, three daughters; *Education:* HEC, Faculty of Law and Economic Sciences, Sorbonne, Paris; Diploma and PhD, Economics; HEC, Higher Commercial Studies, Paris; Diploma of the International Monetary Fund, (IMF), Washington, 1972–73; *Career:* Bank Sabbag, 1963–65; Manager, Bank Sabbag Hamra Branch, 1964–65; Professor and member of the Board, Faculty of Business Administration, Lebanese University, 1971–76; Manager, Central Bank, 1965–76; International Consultant, 1976–1980; Dean, Faculty of Business Administration and Management of Saint Joseph University, Beirut, 1980–; former President, Lebanese Student Association in France; *Interests and Recreations:* horse riding; *Languages:* Arabic, French; *Address:* Office — USJ Campus des Sciences Humanines, Rue Huvelin, P O box 293, Beirut, Lebanon; Residence — Abillama Building, Rue du Chalet Suisse, Jdeidet al Metn, Lebanon; telephone 891033.

ABSY, Ahmad Rashid, Bahraini official; born 29 April 1931, Bahrain; *Religion:* Muslim; *Education:* American University of Beirut, Lebanon; *Career:* joined ARAMCO, Saudi Arabia, 1954–58; Script-writer for Dhahran Television, 1958–65; Producer/Director, Saudi Television, Jeddah, and later News Director 1965–69; Dirctor of Public Relations, Ministry of Defence, Bahrain, 1969–77; Lieutenant Colonel, Assistant Chief of Staff, Ministry of Defence, 1977–; *Address:* P O Box 13, Manama, Bahrain.

ABU ADAL, Georges, Lebanese businessman; born 15 September 1920, Beirut, Lebanon; married; three sons; *Religion:* Christian; *Education:* St. Joseph University, Beirut, Lebanon; *Career:* Chairman of the Board of Georges Abu Adal and Company Establishments, of Editions Orientales (publishing *Magazine),* Al-Usbu Al-Arabi, of Alimentary and Household Products Company, SOGEPA; Director of ABC, United Lebanese Timber Industries Company (OKAL), Lebanese and Near East Television, Functional Art; partner in Middle East Media; Honorary Consul General of Honduras; President of the Employers' Association; made goodwill visits to several African countries as Special Ambassador for President Franjieh, 1971; *Interests and Rec-*

reations: collecting Russian and Greek icons; *Languages:* Arabic, French; *Address:* Office — Sursock Street, Sayigh Buildings, Beirut, Lebanon; telephone: 334215; Residence — Madrassit Al-Salaam Street, Mouracade Building, Beirut, Lebanon.

ABU AL-GASIM, Major Muhammad Ibrahim, Sudanese politician; born 1937, Omdurman, Sudan; married; *Religion:* Muslim; *Education:* in Omdurman and Khartoum; Military Academy, 1961, with rank of 2nd Lieutenant; posted to Al-Obeid; parachute course at Aldershot, UK, 1962; subsequently assisted in the setting up of a paratroop unit in Khartoum; *Career:* member of the Revolutionary Command Council, 1969; Minister of Local Governments, 1969; Minister of the Interior, 1970; Assistant Prime Minister for Services; Minister of Health, 1971; played important part in the establishment of the Sudanese Socialist Union (SSU); appointed Joint Deputy Secretary General of SSU, 1973; Deputy Secretary General, SSU, 1974; Minister of Agriculture, Food and Natural Resources; *Address:* P O Box 285, Khartoum, Sudan; telephone: 70895.

ABU ASSALI, Dib, Syrian banker; born 1932, Syria; *Education:* University of Paris, France; *Career:* branch manager, Arab Unity Bank; Manager, Commercial Bank of Syria, 1967–73; Chairman and General Manager, Commercial Bank of Syria, 1973–; *Address:* Commercial Bank of Syria, Moawiya Street, P O Box 933, Damascus, Syria; telephone: 118890/1.

ABU CHAKRA, Shaikh Muhammad, Lebanese religious leader; born 1910, Amatour, Lebanon; married; *Religion:* Muslim; *Education:* general; *Career:* elected Shaikh Akl, spiritual leader of Druze community, 1948; *Publications: Loubab el-Ouloum; Address:* Rue Abou Chaara, Beirut, Lebanon; telephone: 222244, 231315.

ABU DAWUD, Ismail Ali, Saudi Arabian businessman; born 1915, Jeddah, Saudi Arabia; *Education:* general education; *Career:* employee at Sharqeh Ltd, Saudi Arabian Mining Syndicate; established own business including two factories; President of Jeddah Chamber of Commerce; Chairman of Boards of Directors of Social Insurance Organization and Riyadh Bank; member of

Franco-Arab Chamber of Commerce; *Address:* Baghdadia, Jeddah, Saudi Arabia; telephone: Office — Jeddah 27345, 25365; Residence — Jeddah 22827, 27650.

ABU ELISH, Izzat, Egyptian physician; resident in the USA; born 28 January 1931; married; two sons, one daughter; *Religion:* Muslim; *Education:* MB, ChB, Ain Shams University, Cairo, Egypt, 1947–54; Diploma in Anaesthesia, Ain Shams University, 1958; PhD in Anaesthesia, Ain Shams University; *Career:* Professor of Anaesthesia, School of Medicine, University of Pittsburgh, USA; Chief of Obstetric Anesthesia, Magee Women's Hospital; member of Alleghney County Medical Society, American Medical Association, American Society of Anaesthesiologists, International Anesthesia Research Society, Society of Middle East Anesthesiologists, Egyptian American Scholars Association; *Publications: Principles of Anaesthesia;* various articles on anaesthetics in professional journals; *Childbirth .... A Joy not a Suffering; Pain Control in Obestetrics,* Lippincott Co; *Interests and Recreations:* swimming, tennis; *Languages:* Arabic, English, French; *Address:* Office — Department of Anaesthesiology, Magee Women's Hospital, Forbes Avenue and Halket Street, Pittsburgh, PA 15213, USA; telephone: (412) 647 4145; Residence — 2361 Haymaker Road, Monroeville, PA, 15146; telephone: (412) 372 1634.

ABU FADEL, Henry, Lebanese diplomat; born 1918, Lebanon; married; two daughters; *Education:* American University of Beirut, Lebanon; Metropolitan College, London; *Career:* Professor of Arabic Language, History, Geography and Mathematics, 1938–43; Ministry of Foreign Affairs, 1945–; led several diplomatic missions abroad; currently rank of ambassador, Ministry of Foreign Affairs; *Publications: Revolt in Political Thought; Lebanon and its Treaties and Conventions,* six volumes; numerous articles and poems in newspapers; *Decorations:* Lebanese Merit, Lebanon; National Order of Cedar, Lebanon; George I, Greece; Grand Croix de L'Ordre de Saint Marc; *Interest and Recreations:* walking; president of Lions Club of Mount Lebanon; president of Alumni Club of LHS; member of several associations; *Languages:* Arabic, English, French; *Address:* Ministry of Foreign Affairs, Ashrofieh, Beirut, Lebanon.

ABU FADIL, Munir, Lebanese politician; born 1914, Ain Enoub, Lebanon; married; three children; *Religion:* Christian; *Education:* National College, Choueifat, Lebanon; Law School, Jerusalem, Palestine; *Career:* Palestine Government, 1935–45; Commander of the Force of Al-Jihad Al-Mukadass, under Arab League and Palestine Arab Higher Committee, 1948–49; elected Deputy for Aley District, 1957; re-elected 1960, 1964, 1968, 1972–; elected for 14 sessions as Vice President of Chamber of Deputies; re-elected Vice President, 1978; member of the Finance, Foreign Affairs and Defence Parliamentary Committees; member of the Board of Directors of Banque de Crédit Agricole, of Industriel et Foncier SAL, of Globe Tours Co SAL; Managing Director, Enterprises and Contracting Co, Beirut; *Languages:* Arabic, English, French; *Address:* Office— National Assembly, P O Box 11 3315, Parliament Street, Beirut, Lebanon; Residence— Jumblat Station, Beirut, Lebanon; telephone: Office— 233371; Residence— 363381/366622.

ABU FURAYWAH, Musa Ahmad, Libyan official; *Religion:* Muslim; *Career:* Director General, Ministry of Planning; Minister of Planning, 1976–77; Secretary for Planning, General People's Committee, 1977–80; Secretary of the General People's Committee for Economy and Light Industries, 1980–; *Address:* Secretariat of the General People's Committee for Economy and Light Industries, Tripoli, Libya; telephone: 37023, 34468; telex: 20351.

ABU GARBIA, Bahjat, Palestinian politician; born 1925, Hebron, Palestine; *Career:* former member of the Baath Party in Syria; member of first Palestine Liberation Organization (PLO) Executive Committee 1964; together with Dr Samir Ghusha formed Palestinian Popular Struggle Front (PPSF); appointed PPSF representative in the newly formed Central Committee of the Palestine Resistance Movement (later PLO), 1970; appointed member of the six-man General Secretariat, 1970; following PPSF affiliation to Fatah was elected member of PLO Executive Committee July 1971; in 1973 PPSF joined Arab Liberation Front (ALF) PFLP and PFLP-General Command (PFLP-GC) in the Rejection Front.

ABU GHARIB, Ali Haidar Y., Egyptian physician/WHO official; born 4 September 1923, Sohag, Egypt; married; four daughters, two sons; *Religion:* Muslim; *Education:* MB, BCh, Cairo University, Egypt, 1943–51; PhD, London School of Hygiene and Tropical Medicine, London University, UK, 1955–56; DSc, Calcutta University, India Institute of Public Health, 1958–61; *Career:* Superintendent, Provincial Government Hospitals, Ministry of Health, Cairo, 1951–55; Lecturer, High Institute of Public Health, University of Alexandria, Egypt, 1956–68; Team Leader, World Health Organisation (WHO) Cholera Control Team, Inter Regional HQ, stationed in Calcutta and Manila; Team Leader, WHO Intercountry Communicable Diseases Control Team, Western Pacific Region, Manila, Philippines, 1967–71; Regional Adviser for Communicable Diseases Control, WHO Regional Office for Africa, Brazzaville, Congo, 1971–74; Regional Adviser and Chief, Communicable Diseases Control, WHO Regional Office for Africa, Brazzaville, Congo, 1974; Director of Disease Prevention and Control, African Region of WHO, 1979–; Consultant, National Academy of Sciences, Medical Centre, Washington, D.C., USA, 1963 (temporary honorary assignment for co-authorship of a publication); winner of the National Prize on Medical Research for 1963 by the High Council of Medical Research, Ministry of Scientific Research, Cairo; Fellow of the Royal Society for Tropical Medicine, London, UK; member of the Egyptian Public Health Association; *Publications:* numerous publications on research and control of tropical diseases and health problems, in English, French, German, in medical periodicals in England, USA, Germany, India, Egypt; *Interests and Recreations:* swimming, running, riding; member of Alexandria Sporting Club and Clayman Sporting Club, Brazzaville, Congo; *Languages:* Arabic, English, French; *Address:* World Health Organisation, P O Box 6, Brazzaville, Congo; telephone: 813860/5.

ABU GHAZALA, Dawud Sulaiman, Jordanian official/diplomat; born 1 December 1913, Amman, Jordan; married; *Education:* Politics and History, American University of Beirut, Lebanon, 1935; LLB, London University, UK, 1940; Lawyers Association Permit, Lincoln's Inn, London , 1942; *Career:* Judge in Palestine, 1948–51; Judge of

Jerusalem Appeal Courts, 1951–52; Judge seconded to Khartoum High Court, 1956–59; Director General, Aqaba Port Authority, 1959–61; Governor of Jerusalem, 1961; Minister of Communications, 1962; Governor of Jerusalem, 1963–65; Ambassador in Foreign Ministry, 1966; Ambassador to Spain, 1966; Ambassador to Iran, 1967; member of Court of Cassation, 1971; *Decorations:* Star of Jordan, 2nd Class; Order of Holy Sepulchre, 1st Class; Independence Medal, 1st Class; *Address:* Shmessani, Amman, Jordan; telephone: 667468.

ABU GHAZALA, Hani Fuad F., Saudi Arabian engineer/official; born 1943, Jeddah, Saudi Arabia; *Education:* BSc, Civil Engineering; *Career:* Civil Engineer, Municipalities Agency; Head of Technical Department, Abha Municipality; Vice President of Abha Municipality; *Interests and Recreations:* reading, travel; *Address:* Town Planning Office, Abha, Saudi Arabia; telephone: Office Abha 6352.

ABU GHAZALA, Lieteuant General Muhammad Abdul Halim, Egyptian military commander/politician; born 1 January 1930, Al-Bihaira, Egypt; married; two sons, three daughters; *Religion:* Muslim; *Education:* MA, Economics, USA Army War College; MA, Military Science, War College of Egypt; *Career:* Commander of Artillery Brigade, 1968; Commander of Artillery Division, 1969; Commander of the Artillery of the 2nd Field Army, 1971; Chief of the Artillery Corps, 1972; Director of the Military Intelligence and Reconnaisance Department, 1974; Defence Attaché, Washington, USA, 1976; Chief of Staff of the Egyptian Armed Forces, 1980; Minister of Defence and Military Production, 1981; Chief of Defence Staff, 1980; Commander in Chief of the Egyptian Armed Forces, 1981–; Minister of Defence and Military Production, 1981; Field Marshal, 1981; Deputy Prime Minister, 1981; *Publications: Soviet Military Strategy; History of the Art of War,* five volumes; *The Guns Opened Fire at Noon: the October War; Mathematics and Warfare; Decorations:* Order of The Republic, 1st Class; Order of the Star of Honour, 1974; The Memorial Order of the UAR Establishment, 1958; The Liberation Order, 1952; The October 6th Medal, 1973; Medal of The 20th Anniversary of the Revolution, 1972; Medal of Long Service and Exemplariness, 1st Class, 1971;

Medal of The 10th Anniversary of the Revolution, 1962; The Army Day Medal, 1959; The Muhammad Ali Memorial Medal, 1949; The Distinguished Service Ribbon, 1978; The Training Ribbon, 1977; The Victory Ribbon, 1957; The Independence Ribbon, 1956; The Evacuation Ribbon, 1955; *Interests and Recreations:* reading, chess, tennis, basketball, soccer; *Languages:* Arabic, Russian, French, English; *Address:* Ministry of Defence, Cairo, Egypt; telephone: 600736, 829785; c/o The Defence Attaché, Egyptian Embassy, 24 South Audley Street, London W1Y 5PJ; telephone: 493 6306, 493 4279.

ABU GHAZALA, Talal, Jordanian businessman/accountant; born 22 April 1938, Jaffa, Palestine; married; four children; *Religion:* Muslim; *Education:* BA in Business Administration, American University of Beirut, 1960; *Career:* Audit Clerk, General Partner, and later Chairman Elect, Accounting Firm, 1960–67; founder of Talal Abu Ghazala and Co, Public Accountants, of Talal Abu Ghazala Associates Ltd, of Management and Industrial Consultants, of Trade Marks, of Patents and Designs Registration, of Arab International Projects Co, of Projects Co, of Project and Investment Banking Advisory Services, and of Talal Abu Ghazala International, UK, 1979; Chairman, Board of Directors, Talal Abu Ghazala International; Trustee, AUB; member of various international, professional and business associations; Sponsor of the Talal Abu Ghazala Graduate School of Business and Management, AUB, 1978; *Publications: The Abu Ghazala English/Arabic Dictionary of Accountancy,* Macmillan Press, London, 1978. *Decorations:* Order of Independence, Jordan, 1967; Old Mercury International Award for Productive Development and International Cooperation; Order of the State of Bahrain, 1978; *Interests and Recreations:* tennis, swimming; *Languages:* Arabic, English, French; *Address:* Talal Abu Ghazala International, P O Box 4628, Safat, Kuwait; telephone: 443900; telex: 2119 AUDTORS KT.

ABU HAIDAR, Jarir Amin, Lebanese academic; resident in UK; born 17 April 1932, Lebanon; married; two sons, one daughter; *Religion:* Christian *Education:* BA, American University of Beirut, Lebanon; BA, PhD, London University, UK; *Career:* Programme Assistant, BBC Arabic Service; Arabic

Literature Department, School of Oriental and African Studies, London University, 1962–; *Publications:* articles in English in *Journal of Arabic Literature;* articles in Arabic in *Huna London; Interests and Recreations:* gardening, mountaineering, music; Spanish folk literature; *Languages:* Arabic, English, Spanish, French; *Address:* School of Oriental and African Studies, University of London, London WC1, UK; telephone: 637 2388 ext 494.

ABU HAIDAR, Munir Ibrahim, Lebanese businessman; born 1927, Hammana, Lebanon; married; *Religion:* Christian; *Education:* BA in Economics, American University of Beirut, Lebanon, 1949; *Career:* worked for Arabic-American Oil Company in Saudi Arabia, 1948–53; set up private air-freight firm 1953, mainly for carriage of foodstuffs to oil companies in Saudi Arabia; Chairman of Trans Mediterranean Airways SAL, formed company into joint-stock company, 1959; Trans Mediterranean Airways, inaugurated the first regular round the world air-freight service, April 1971; *Interests and Recreations:* riding, shooting, skiing, water sports, classical music; *Languages:* Arabic, English, French; *Address:* Office — TMA, Beirut International Airport, Beirut, Lebanon; telephone: 385353; Residence — Spears Street, Greidiny Building, Beirut, Lebanon; telephone: 369844.

ABU HAIDAR, Najib, Lebanese official/ physician; born 1923, Hammana, Lebanon; married; *Religion:* Christian; *Education:* International College, Beirut; Doctor of Medicine, American University of Beirut, Lebanon, 1948; Harvard University, USA, 1951–55; *Career:* specialist in endocrinology; Mayor of Hammana; Minister of Education in Saeb Salam's non-parliamentary cabinet, January 1971; Presidential Adviser on Education, 1972–76; President of the Association of the Friends of Jerusalem; *Interests and Recreations:* sports, riding; *Languages:* Arabic, French, English; *Address:* Minkara Centre, Madame Curie Street, Beirut, Lebanon.

ABU HAJAR, Abdul Wahab A., Saudi Arabian aviation official; born 1 January, 1934; *Education:* BA, Cairo University, Egypt; *Career:* Manager of Banking and Administration, Head Office, Riyadh Bank Ltd, Jeddah, Saudi Arabia, 1958; Director General, Printing Press and Publication Corporation, Jeddah, 1963; Corporate Secretary General, Board of Directors, Saudi Arabian Airlines Corporation, Jeddah, 1964–; Managing Director, Saudi Institute for General Education, Girls Schools, Jeddah, 1957–77; member of the Saudi Arabian Airlines Sports Club; *Address:* Corporate Secretary General, Board of Directors, Saudi Arabian Airlines, P O Box 620, Jeddah, Saudi Arabia; telephone: Office — 02 631 5140, ext 2225; Residence — 02 687 7146.

ABU HAMDAN, Jamal, Jordanian writer/ administrator; born 1944, Amman, Jordan; *Religion:* Muslim; *Education:* Licence in Law; *Career:* Broadcaster and Producer in Cultural Section of Jordan Radio, 1966; Lawyer, 1969; Information and Publications Manager for ALIA (Royal Jordanian Airlines), 1969–; Writer; *Publications: The Second Exodus,* political essay, 1967, Beirut; several short story collections and plays; *Love Poems of the World,* translated with introduction, Beirut; collection of children's stories; travel, political and literary articles in Lebanese and Jordanian press; *Interests and Recreations:* travel, writing; founding member of Jordanian Writers Association; founding committee member of Arab Theatre Federation; *Languages:* Arabic, English; *Address:* ALIA, P O Box 302, Amman; telephone: Office — 22311; Residence — 71405.

ABU HASSAN, Khaldun Abdul Rahman, Jordanian businessman; born 23 December 1940, Amman, Jordan; married; one son, three daughters; *Religion:* Muslim; *Education:* BA in Business Administration, American University of Beirut, Lebanon; MA in Business Administration, University of Denver, USA, 1966; *Career:* Assistant General Manager, Jordan Insurance Co Ltd; Deputy General Manager, Jordan Insurance Co Ltd; Director, Amman Chamber of Industry, Jordan Gulf Bank, Jordan Public Mining Co Ltd, Jordan Public Administration Institute, Jordan National Committee, International Chamber of Commerce; Deputy Chairman, Jordan Paper and Cardboard Co Ltd; *Languages:* Arabic, English; *Address:* Jordan Insurance Co Ltd, P O Box 279, Amman, Jordan; telephone: 22186; telex: 21486 JICJO.

23

ABU HEILAH, Abdullah Nassir, Saudi Arabian academic; born 20 December 1943, Saudi Arabia; married; *Education:* BSc in Botany and Zoology, Riyadh University; PhD in Mycology and Plant Pathology, Glasgow University, Scotland, 1975; *Career:* Demonstrator, Botany Department, University of Riyadh, 1969–70, Lecturer, 1975–77, Assistant Professor, 1977–80, Associate Professor, 1980–; Vice Dean of the University Libraries, Riyadh University; *Publications:* numerous research papers on mycology and plant pathology, published in Arab and international professional journals; *Interests and Recreations:* reading, photography, travelling; member of the Saudi Arabian Biological Society; member of the British Mycological Society; *Address:* Botany Department, Faculty of Science, Riyadh University, Riyadh, Saudi Arabia; telephone: 0148 11000 ext 2083.

ABU HUSSAIN, Abbas Hamza al-Marzuqi, Saudi Arabian physician/administrator; born 1940, Mecca, Saudi Arabia; *Religion:* Muslim; *Education:* MB; ChB; MD; *Career:* Chief of Surgical Department, King's Hospital, Mecca; Director, Ajiad Hospital, Mecca; Director, Mecca Health Affairs; Director General of Mecca District Health Affairs, Mecca, Jeddah, Taif; member of Pilgrimage Subcommittee; member of Mina Area Development Committee; attended Arab Medical Conference, Beirut, Lebanon, conference on Disease Classification, Geneva; Conference on War Medicine, Cairo; *Interests and Recreations:* table tennis, reading; *Address:* Al-Zahra Quarter, Mecca, Saudi Arabia; telephone: Office — Mecca 24825; Residence — Mecca 25277.

ABU HUSSAIN, Hassan Hamza al-Marzuqi, Saudi Arabian official; born 1936, Mecca, Saudi Arabia; *Religion:* Muslim; *Education:* BSc, Accountancy; MBA, Public Administration; *Career:* Deputy Director of Administration, Economic Researcher, Chief Financial Analyst, Director of Planning, Bureau of Agriculture Directorate; Director of General Administration, Central Planning Organization; Director General, Private Office of Minister of Pilgrimage; Director General of Religious Affairs and Libraries Department; Director General, Mecca District, Waqfs (Islamic Endowments) Directorate; Director General of Investment for Islamic Endowments; Supervisor of *Islamic Orientation* Magazine; Deputy for President of the Central Planning Office, Board of the Industrial Research and Development Centre; attended several FAO conferences; attended conference on The Economy, Mecca, and conference on The Message of the Mosque; *Address:* Directorate of Endowments, P O Box 43, Mecca, Saudi Arabia; telephone: Office — 5434300; Residence — 5436800, 5739617.

ABU ISMAIL, Ahmad, Egyptian economist/politician; born 1915; *Religion:* Muslim; *Education:* Degree in Commerce, Cairo University, Egypt, 1937; PhD in Economics, Birmingham University, UK, 1942; *Career:* Professor and Dean of Economics, Cairo University; Director of State Railways and the Maritime Transport Organization; elected to the People's Assembly, 1971; Chairman of the Planning and Budget Committee; appointed to the National Council for Production and Economic Affairs, 1974; Minister of Finance, 1975–1976; accompanied the late President Sadat to the Salzburg meeting with President Ford, 1975; *Address:* Ministry of Finance, Cairo, Egypt.

ABU IZZIDIN, Halim Said, Lebanese diplomat; born 11 June 1918, Abadieh, Lebanon; married; one son, one daughter; *Religion:* Muslim; *Education:* BA, American University of Beirut, AUB, Lebanon; LLB, University of Paris, France; LLD, Indiana College, USA; *Career:* Foreign Service; Consul General, Lebanese Embassy, Cairo, 1944–46; Counsellor, 1946–50; Director of Political Affairs, 1950–53; Director General of Information, 1953–57; Lebanese Delegate to Bandung Afro-Asian Conference, 1955; Ambassador to India, 1957–59; Governor of North Lebanon, 1959–64; Director of Political Affairs, 1964–66; Ambassador to Egypt, 1966–71; Ambassador and Permanent Delegate of Lebanon to UNESCO, 1971–77; *Publications: Lebanon and Its Provinces,* 1963 (in English); *Foreign Policy in Lebanon,* (in Arabic); *Decorations:* Commander of the Cedar; Syrian Order of Merit; Band of the Order of the Egyptian Republic; Band of Jordan Independence Order; Band of Tunisian Republic Order; Band of the Phoenix Order; and others; *Interests and Recreations:* Arab affairs, international affairs, legal affairs, history, reading, hiking; *Languages:* Arabic, English; *Address:* Abu Alhassan Building, Makdisi Street, Beirut, Lebanon.

ABU JABIR, Kamil S., Jordanian academic; born 1932, Amman, Jordan; married; two daughters; *Religion:* Christian; *Education:* BA and PhD in Political Science, Syracuse University, Syracuse, USA, 1961 and 1965; postdoctoral studies in Oriental Department, Princeton University, USA; *Career:* Lecturer, Syracuse University, USA, 1965; Assistant Professor, University of Tennessee, 1965–67; Associate Professor, Smith College, 1967–69; Associate Professor, University of Jordan, 1969–71; Professor, University of Jordan, 1971–; Dean of Faculty of Economics and Commerce, Jordan University, 1972–73; Minister of National Economy, 1973; Dean, Faculty of Economics and Commerce, 1973–79; Professor, University of Jordan, 1979–80; Director, Queen Alia Jordan Social Welfare Fund, 1980–; President of the Council of Technical Consultation Services and Studies Centre, Jordan University; Secretary General of Jordan World Affairs Council; *Publications: The Arab Baa'th Socialist Party: History, Ideology and Organisation,* Syracuse, Syracuse University, 1966, in English; *United States of America and Israel,* Cairo, 1971, in Arabic; *Israeli Political System,* Cairo, 1973; co-author, *Government and Politics of the Contemporary Middle East,* Homewood, 1970; *Concise Encyclopaedia of the Middle East; Modern Socialism,* New York, 1968; *The Arab-Israeli Confrontation,* 1967; *Legislatures in Contemporary Societies,* 1975; *Legislatures and Development,* 1976; various articles and book reviews; *Decorations:* Order of the Jordanian Star, 1975; *Interests and Recreations:* reading, walking, politics, economics, sociology, anthropology; Secretary General of Jordan Royal Society for the Conservation of Nature; member of the Italian Academy for New Humanism; *Languages:* Arabic, English, Spanish; *Address:* The Queen Alia Jordan Social Welfare Fund, P O Box 5118 Amman, Jordan.

ABU JABIR, Rauf Saad, Jordanian businessman; born 1 December 1925, Salt, Jordan; married; two sons, one daughter; *Religion:* Christian; *Education:* Bishop's School, Amman; BBA in Economics and Commerce, American University of Beirut, Lebanon, 1946; *Career:* established Saad Abu Jaber and Sons, 1946; started general agency of Al-Sharq Insurance Company, 1946; established Jordan Brewery Company Limited, 1955; founded Jordan Dairy Company Limited, 1968; established United Insurance Company Limited, 1972; joined National Paints Company Limited, 1974; also underwriting member at Lloyds; former President of Jordan Dairy Company Limited; President, United Insurance Company Limited, Jordan Insurance Association; Honorary Consul General of the Netherlands in Jordan; *Decorations:* from HM Queen Juliana of the Netherlands; Officer of Orange Order of Nassau, 1970; *Interests and Recreations:* swimming, tennis, travel; member of many clubs and societies; President of the Bishop's School Club; Vice-President of the Friends of Jordan University Society; former President of the Royal Riding Club; President of Orthodox Philanthropic Society; former Vice President of Board of Governors of the Bishop's School; President of the Young Men's Christian Association, Amman; *Languages:* Arabic, English; *Address:* P O Box 312, Amman, Jordan; telephone: Office — 25161/2/3, 37967; Residence — 30128; telex: 21323.

ABU KHATER, Joseph, Lebanese politician/diplomat; born 1905, Zahle, Lebanon; married; *Religion:* Christian; *Education:* Licence in Law, St. Joseph University, Lebanon and in France; *Career:* Diplomatic Service; successively, Lebanese Ambassador to Italy, Austria and Mexico, 1944; Secretary General of the Ministry of Foreign Affairs; Ambassador to Egypt, 1958–66; Permanent Lebanese Delegate to the Arab League; in this capacity rejoined the Central Administration; retired 1967; elected Deputy for Zahle, March 1968; Minister of National Education in Government of Rashid Karami, 1969; Adviser to the Greek-Catholic Community Council, 1969–; Minister of Education, 1969; *Decorations:* Commander, National Order of the Cedar; various other decorations, local and foreign; *Languages:* Arabic, French; *Address:* Homsi Buidling, Roche, Beirut, Lebanon.

ABU KHATER, Tawfiq, Lebanese businessman; resident in the United Arab Emirates; born 1934, Palestine; married; *Religion:* Christian; *Career:* Manager, Shell Markets Middle East, United Arab Emirates, 1971; General Adviser, oil and development problems, to HH Ruler of Ras al-Khaimah; Director, Petroleum Affairs, 1973; Commercial and Financial Representative, Government of Ras al-Khaimah, 1973–; *Decorations:* Commander of the Cedar of Lebanon;

Languages: Arabic, English; *Address:* 43 Berkeley Square, London W1X 5FP; telephone: 408 0438.

ABU KHATER, Victor E., Lebanese businessman/management adviser; resident in the USA; born 1942, Tabaraiah, Palestine; married; three children; *Religion:* Christian; *Career:* Secretary to HH the Ruler of Ras al Khaimah, 1965–73; Director, Personnel Department and Department of Water and Electricity, 1965–73; Chargé d'Affaires, Petroleum Department; member of Board of Telecommunications; Director, Ras Al Khaimah Rock Co; Management Adviser to several European firms, 1973–75; Sole UK Representative, Redfield AG of Switzerland, 1977–78; member of Board, Al Ahlia Insurance Co, Ras Al-Khaimah, 1977–; President, Victor Investments Inc, California, USA, 1979–; Founder, Saratoga National Bank, California, USA; *Decorations:* Lebanese Order of Merit, Chevalier Grade; *Interests and Recreations:* tennis, swimming; *Languages:* Arabic, English; *Address:* 19400 Pinnacle Ct, Saragota, CA 95070, USA; P O Box 8707, Beirut, Lebanon.

ABU LUHUM, Lieutenant Colonel Ali, Yemen Arab Republic diplomat/army officer; *Religion:* Muslim; *Career:* member of the Command Council, 1974; Ambassador to Syria, 1975; *Address:* Embassy of the Yemen Arab Republic, Damascus, Syria.

ABU MAIZER, Muhammad Abdul Muhsin, Palestinian politician; born 1933, Hebron; *Religion:* Muslim; *Education:* educated as lawyer; *Career:* member of the Executive Committee and Head of Palestine Liberation Organization (PLO), Department of National, Pan-National and Returnees Affairs; sometime member of the Baath party; worked as a journalist; Editor of both a Syrian and a Lebanese newspaper in 1960s; member of the Higher Islamic Committee in Arab Jerusalem; worked as Fatah representative in Algeria, Iraq, 1969, and France, 1968; member of Fatah Central Committee, 1973; expelled by Israelis from West Bank, 1973; Head of Palestinian National Front (PNF) in Occupied Territories, 1974; elected to PLO Executive Committee as Representative of PNF, 1974; participated in PLO delegation to Moscow, 1974; PLO spokesman and head of Pan-Arab and Returnees Affairs Department; member, Occupied Homeland Affairs Department, 1977; *Publications: La Palestine Libérée,* Paris, 1968.

ABU NAMA, Al-Sharif Ali Muhammad, Saudi Arabian politician; born 1915, Mecca, Saudi Arabia; *Religion:* Muslim; *Education:* Islamic education, Mecca, Saudi Arabia; *Career:* member of Shura Council (The Advisory Body) of the Kingdom of Saudi Arabia, 1955–; member of the Council's Financial and Administration Regulations Committees; supervises own farms in Wadi Fatma area; *Interests and Recreations:* reading; *Address:* Al-Halqah al-Jiddah Square, Al-Etaibiyyah, Jarwal, Mecca, Saudi Arabia; telephone: Office — Jeddah 29078; Residence — Jeddah 23276.

ABU NAWAR, Major General Ma'an, Jordanian politician/army officer; born 26 July 1928; married; three sons, ten daughters; *Religion:* Muslim; *Education:* Diploma, London University, UK, 1963; *Career:* Jordanian Armed Forces, 1943; Colonel commanding Infantry Regiment, 1956; Commander, Infantry Brigade, 1957; Counsellor, Jordan Embassy, London, 1963; Director of Civil Defence, 1964; Director of Public Security, 1967; Assistant Chief of Staff, Jordan Army and later Major General, 1969–72; Editor, military weekly, *Al Aksa;* Minister of Culture and Information, 1972–73; Ambassador, Jordan Embassy, London, UK, 1973–76; Minister of Youth and Culture, and Minister of Tourism and Antiquities, 1980–; *Publications: The Battle of Karameh; In the Path of Jerusalem; The State of War and Peace; History of Jordan Army; The Olympic Games Old and New; Decorations:* Star of Jordan, 1st Class; *Interests and Recreations:* reading, music, theatre, sports, President of Jordan Olympic Committee and Football Federation; *Languages:* Arabic, English; *Address:* Ministry of Tourism and Antiquities, Amman, Jordan.

ABU NOSSIR, Muhammad, Egyptian politician/lawyer; born 1915; *Religion:* Muslim; *Career:* Lawyer, 1936–39; Advocate, State Legal Department, 1939–44; Advocate, State Legal Department of Cabinet, 1944–46; Assistant Counsellor and Secretary General, State Council Public Works Section, 1953; Supervisor, Administrative Contracts Section, State Council, 1954; Deputy Minister of Commerce and Industry, 1954; Head of

Trade Mission to India and Japan, 1957; member of official Egyptian Delegation to Afro-Asian Bandung Conference, 1955; Head of Trade Mission to China, 1955, to UK, 1956; Head of Economic Mission to Syria, 1956; Minister of Commerce and Industry, 1956–58; Minister of Municipal and Rural Affairs, 1958–61; Chairman, Board of Directors, General Egyptian Housing and Urbanising Organization, 1961–; Minister of Housing and Public Utilities, 1964–66; member of Secretariat General of Arab Socialist Union (ASU), 1966–; Chairman, Preparatory Committee, New Permanent Constitution, 1966; Minister of Justice, 1968–69; *Address:* 4 Al-Salih Ayyoub Street, Cairo, Egypt.

ABU ODEH, Adnan Said, Jordanian politician; born 10 November 1933, Nablus; married; three sons, two daughters; *Education:* Certificate of Teachers College, Amman, 1954; BA in English Literature, Damascus University, Syria, 1959; *Career:* Teacher in Jordan, 1954–56; Teacher in Kuwait and Trucial States, 1959–66; Officer in General Intelligence Service, 1966–70; Minister of Culture and Information, and of Tourism and Antiquities, 1970–72; Secretary General of the Arab National Union, 1972–73; Minister of Culture and Information, 1973; member of the Board of Trustees of Jordan Universities, 1973; Chief of the Royal Cabinet, 1973; Minister of Culture and Information, 1973–74; member of the Senate, 1974–76; Minister of Culture and Information, and President of the Executive Bureau for the Affairs of the Occupied Territories, 1976–79; member of the Senate, 1979; member of the National Consultative Council, 1980; Minister of Information, 1980–; member of the World Affairs Council; *Publications:* numerous articles and papers on the Middle East and Israel published in professional journals; *Decorations:* Order of Independence; Order of the Jordanian Star; *Interests and Recreations:* cycling, reading, Arabic literature, history, poetry, philology; *Address:* Ministry of Information, P O Box 1854 Amman, Jordan; telephone: 41467; Residence — P O Box 9009 Amman, Jordan; telephone: 841303.

ABU QURA, Ahmad Salih, Jordanian official/physician; born 1918, Salt, Jordan; married; five children; *Religion:* Muslim; *Education:* BA in Medicine, Syrian University,

1948; specialized in Radiology, London University, UK, 1950–51; specialized in Radiology, Harvard University, USA, 1956; *Career:* Director of Radiology Section, 1951–56; Minister of Health, 1965–66; Minister of Social Affairs and Labour, 1966; Secretary General of Jordanian National Red Crescent Society, 1962–63; *Decorations:* Independence Medal, 3rd Class; Order of the Star of Jordan, 1st Class; Order of Tunisian Republic; Grand Knight of the Order of the Italian Republic; Bernadotte Medal of International Red Cross Committee; *Address:* P O Box 147, Amman, Jordan; telephone: 73141.

ABU RABAH, Abdul Rahman, Jordanian official; born 1932, Ramallah, Jordan; married; seven children; *Education:* BA in Education and Psychology; MA in Tourism and Transport; PhD in Tourism; *Career:* Head of the Jerusalem Office, Ministry of Tourism, Amman; Secretary General, Arab Organization of Tourism, League of Arab States, 1967–; Under Secretary, Ministry of Tourism, Amman, 1973–74; *Publications:* several works on Tourism; Editor in Chief of *Arab Tourism; Interests and Recreations:* folklore; *Languages:* Arabic, English; *Address:* Arab Organization for Tourism, P O Box 2354, Amman, Jordan.

ABU RASHID, Abdul Razzak Rashid, Saudi Arabian official/mineralogist; born 1941, Mecca, Saudi Arabia; *Education:* BSc and MSc in Geology of Mining; *Career:* Deputy Governor of Petromin for Minerals; member of the Royal College of Mining, UK; *Publications:* a number of research papers; *Interests and Recreations:* football; *Languages:* Arabic, English; *Address:* P O Box 2032, Jeddah, Saudi Arabia; telephone: Office — 6533348; Residence — 6693969.

ABU RIJAL, Ali Ahmad, Yemen Arab Republic official; born 1933, Sana'a; *Religion:* Muslim; *Education:* Shari'a (Islamic Law) studies, Law, Literature, Administrative Studies, Sana'a; *Career:* Clerk, Ministry of Wqaf, 1943–58; Principal, Industrial School, 1958–61; Official Superintendent to the Minister of Public Works and Industry, 1961–62; General Manager, Ministry of Works, 1962–68; Under Secretary, Ministry of Public Works, 1968–76; Governor of Sana'a, 1976–77; Governor of Hodaidah, 1977–; founder of Yemen Studies Centre; former Chairman, Cooperative Societies,

Sana'a, 1975–78; *Interests and Recreations:* research into Yemen heritage and its preservation, politics and development, Yemeni music and classical music; *Languages:* Arabic, English; *Address:* Governorate of Hodaidah, P O Box 3397, Republic Place St, Hodaidah, Yemen Arab Republic.

ABU RISHA, Umar, Syrian poet; born 1910, near Aleppo, Syria; *Education:* in Aleppo; American University of Beirut; Chemistry, UK; *Career:* Librarian, Aleppo Public Library; various diplomatic posts including Syrian Cultural Attaché, Arab League; Ambassador to Brazil, India; *Publications:* various volumes of poetry, poetic drama and narrative poetry; *Languages:* Arabic, English; *Address:* Ministry of Foreign Affairs, Damascus, Syria.

ABU RIZK, James, Arab-American lawyer/politician; born 24 February 1931, South Dakota, USA; married; two sons, one daughter; *Religion:* Christian; *Education:* South Dakota School of Mines; BSc in Civil Engineering, 1961; Doctor of Jurisprudence, University of South Dakota Law School, 1966; *Career:* US Navy, 1948–52; Civil Engineer, 1961–63; Attorney at Law, 1966–; member of US House of Representatives, 1971–73; member of US Senate,1973–79; currently practicing Attorney in Washington D.C.; member of US Committee on Energy and Natural Resources; Chairman on the Subcommittee on Parks and Recreation; member of US Senate Committee on Judiciary; Chairman of Subcommittee on Administrative Practice and Procedure; member of US Senate Committee on the Budget; Chairman, US Senate Committee on Indian Affairs; Chairman, American Indian Policy Review Commission; *Publications:* numerous articles and papers in various journals and magazines; *Interests and Recreations:* photography; member of the National Association of Arab-Americans; founder and Chairman, American-Arab Anti-Discrimination Committee; *Languages:* English; *Address:* Aburizk, Sobol and Trister, 21 Dupont Circle, Washington D.C. 20036, USA.

ABU ROKBA, Hassan Abdullah, Saudi Arabian academic; born 1942; Jeddah, Saudi Arabia; *Religion:* Muslim; *Education:* PhD, Business Administration; *Career:* Lecturer, King Abdul Aziz University; Vice-Dean,

Faculty of Economics and Administration, King Abdul Aziz University, Jeddah, Saudi Arabia; Dean of the Faculty of Economics and Administration, King Abdul Aziz University; President, Chairman of the Board of Directors of Research and Development Centre; President of the Board of Directors, Prince Fawwaz's Project for Co-operative Housing; *Publications:* research papers in the field of administration; *Al-I'laam; Interests and Recreations:* reading, travel; *Address:* Faculty of Economics, King Abdul Aziz University, P O Box 1540, Jeddah, Saudi Arabia; telephone: Office — 687 9033; Residence — Jeddah 34160; telex: 401141 KAUNI SJ.

ABU SA'DA, Hassan Ali, Egyptian diplomat; married; one son; *Religion:* Muslim; *Education:* MA in Military Sciences, Military College, Nassir Academy; *Career:* Military Officer; Ambassador of Egypt to UK, 1979–; *Decorations:* Order of Merit, 1st Class, Egypt, 1979; Military Star of Honour, Egypt; the Medal of HM King Abdul Aziz Al-Saud, 1st Class, Saudi Arabia, 1975; fourteen military medals during 33 years of military service; *Interests and Recreations:* walking, chess, reading, painting; *Languages:* Arabic, English, French; *Address:* 75 South Audley Street, London W1Y 5DQ, UK; telephone: 4992401.

ABU SABE, Murad Ali, Egyptian academic/microbiologist, born 4 March 1937, Egypt; resident in USA; married; two sons, one daughter; *Religion:* Muslim; *Education:* BSc, Agricultural Sciences, Alexandria University, Egypt, 1958; PhD in Microbiology, University of Pittsburgh, USA, 1958; MSc in Genetics, University of California, USA, 1962–70; *Career:* Instructor, Alexandria University, 1958; Pre-doctoral Fellow, 1960–65; Lecturer, Cairo University, Egypt, 1966–68; Assistant Professor, Rutgers University, USA, 1968–74; Associate Professor, Rutgers University, 1974–; *Interests and Recreations:* member of the Genetics Society of America, American Society for Microbiology, American Association for the Advancement of Science, Egyptian Genetics Society and Society for Applied Microbiology; *Address:* Department of Microbiology, Rutgers University, New Brunswick, New Jersey 08903, USA.

ABU SALIM, Muhmmad Ibrahim, Sudanese academic/historian; born 1928, Halfa District, Sudan; married; three sons, four daughters; *Religion:* Muslim; *Education:* Diploma, Khartoum University College, 1955; PhD in History, 1966; *Career:* Assistant Archivist, 1955; Civil Service, 1957; Director of the Central Records Office with rank of Under Secretary; Visiting Professor of History, University of Khartoum, Sudan, 1976; headed various State Boards and Committees of which the most important was the Committee of the Redistribution of Sudan's Provinces; *Publications: Calendar of Mahdi's Proclamations; Cultural Movements in the Mahdist Period; History of Khartoum; Some Tuni Land Certificates; The Fur and the Land; The Mahdists and the Land; Documents from 18th Century Sennar* (in English); *Memo of Osman Digna; Collection of Poems of Tawfic Salih Gibril,* and numerous other books; *Interests and Recreations:* swimming, indoor activities, history, archives, English and Arabic literature, Sudanese culture; Chairman and member of the Sudanese Philosophical Association; Chairman of the Sudanese Historical Society; former Secretary General of Arab Branch of International Council of the University of Khartoum; member of the Board of the Faculty of Arts, Faculty of Social and Economic Studies, Institute of African and Asian Studies, University of Khartoum; *Languages:* Arabic, English, Nubian; *Address:* Office — Central Records Office, P O Box 1914, Khartoum, Sudan; telephone: Office — 71813; Residence — 79100.

ABU SAQ, Muhammad Othman, Sudanese politician; born November 1938, Sudan; married; two sons; *Religion:* Muslim; *Education:* BA, History and Arabic, University of Khartoum, Sudan; MA in History and Politics, University of Aberdeen, UK; PhD in Islamic Political Thought, University of Edinburgh, UK; *Career:* secondary school teacher, 1961–62; Teacher, Training Institute, 1965; Lecturer, Department of Political Science, University of Khartoum, 1965–74; Secretary for Thought and Propagation, Sudanese Socialist Union, SSU, 1974–80; Minister of State for Culture and Information, 1977–80; Minister of Culture and Information, 1980–; *Publications:* conference papers, pamphlets on ideology and SSU institutions; *Interests and Recreations;* swimming, indoor games, political thoughts; *Languages:* Arabic, English; *Address:* Ministry of Culture and Information, Khartoum, Sudan.

ABU SHADI, Muhamad Mahmud, Egyptian banker; born 15 August 1913, Fayum, Egypt; married; three sons, one daughter; *Religion:* Muslim; *Education:* BCom, Cairo University, Cairo, Egypt, 1934; Postgraduate course in Banking, American University, Washington D.C., 1962; PhD, Business Administration, University of Colorado, USA, 1973; *Career:* Controller General, Insurance Department, Ministry of Finance, 1949–52; Director General, Government Insurance and Provident Funds, 1952; Chairman and Managing Director, Development and Public Housing Co,1954–55; Deputy Governor, National Bank of Egypt, 1955–60; Managing Director, National Bank of Egypt, 1960–67; Chairman and Managing Director, 1967–70; Chairman, Union des Banques Arabes et Français, UBAF, Paris, 1970–; Chairman of UBAF, London, 1972; Chairman, National Bank for Development, Cairo, 1980; Deputy in Parliament, Egypt, 1980; Associate member of the Chartered Institute of Patent Agents, London,1946; Fellow of International Banking Association, Washington D.C.; member of the Overseas Bankers Association Club, London, UK, of the International Bankers Association, Washington D.C.; *Publications: The Art of Central Banking and its Application in. Egypt,* 1952; *Central Banking in Egypt,* 1952; *Will New York Attract Arab Capital,* 1974; *The Experience of Arab-French Banks* 1974; *The Role of Finance in Promoting Arab European Business Relationships,* 1976; *Decorations:* Order of the Republic of Egypt, 1955; Order of Merit, Egypt, 1971; Officier de la Légion d'Honneur, France, 1980; *Interests and Recreations:* tennis, swimming; *Languages:* Arabic, English, French; *Address:* Office — UBAF, 4 Rue Ancelle, 92521 Neuilly Cédex, France; Residence— 52 Avenue Foch, Paris 16e, France.

ABU SHAKRA, Mufid, Lebanese aviation official; born 1 June 1931, Chouf, Lebanon; married; two daughters, one son; *Religion:* Muslim; *Education:* Lebanese Baccalauréat, 1951; Degree in Mathematics and Physics, 1955; Air Navigation Licence, Beirut, 1957; Diploma in Aeronautical Technology, Paris, France, 1960; Diploma, National Institute of Administration, Beirut, 1970; *Career:* Chief of Technical Section of Civil Aviation, Directorate General of Civil Aviation, Lebanon, 1972; Representative of Lebanon on International Civil Aviation Organization (ICAO) Council; Third Vice President on ICAO Council, 1973–74; Chairman of Unlawful Interference Committee, 1975–; member of the Air Transport Committee to ICAO, 1972–; *Interests and Recreations:* swimming; member of Les Amis de l'Histoire, Paris, Académie de Sciences Techniques, Lebanon; *Languages:* Arabic, English, French; *Address:* Lebanese Delegation to ICAO, International Aviation Square, 1000 Sherbrooke St West, Montreal PQ, Canada H3A 2R2; telephone: 285 8282.

ABU SHARAF, Louis, Lebanese politician; born 1914, Zahle, Lebanon; married; seven children; *Religion:* Christian; *Education:* graduate in Arabic Literature and History, Ecole de la Sagesse; *Career:* taught Arabic literature at several colleges; long-standing member of Katayeb (Falange); Deputy for Kesrouan, 1960, 1968, 1972; Chairman, Parliamentary Education Committee, 1972; Minister of Industry and Oil in Rashid al Solh's Cabinet, 1974; *Languages:* Arabic, French; *Address:* Jounieh, Lebanon; telephone: 930913.

ABU SHERIF, Bassam, Palestinian politician; *Education:* American University of Beirut, Lebanon; *Career:* member of Popular Front for the Liberation of Palestine (PFLP); official spokesman of the PFLP and Editor of *Al-Hadaf,* in succession to Ghassan Khanafani, who was assassinated by Israeli agents, 1972; seriously wounded by letter bomb in the *Al-Hadaf* office, 1972; *Address:* Al-Hadaf Newspapers, P O Box 212, Beirut, Lebanon.

ABU SINEINA, Amin, Sudanese politician/official; born 10 October 1933; married; three sons, one daughter; *Religion:* Muslim; *Education:* BSc, Cairo University, Egypt, 1959; PhD, London University, UK, 1963; *Career:* Senior Lecturer, University of Khartoum, 1960–69; Project Manager, FAO, 1971–74; Ambassador to UN, Geneva, 1974–75; Deputy Minister of Industry, 1975–76; Minister of State for Industry, 1976–77; Minister of State for Agriculture, Food and Natural Resources, 1977–; *Publications:* numerous articles in various international journals; *Decorations:* Order of the Republic, 2nd Class, Sudan; *Interests and Recreations:* politics, music, bridge; *Address:* P O Box 285, Khartoum, Sudan; telephone: Office — 70895; Residence — 73306.

ABU SITTA, Palestinian politician; *Career:* Independent (Pro-Fatah) member of the Palestine Liberation Organization (PLO), Executive Committee and Head of PLO Occupied Homeland Department; only member of the original 1964 Executive Committee who still holds his office; former member of Ahmed Shukairy's Revolutionary Committee, 1967; re-elected to the Executive Committee chaired by Yassir Arafat, 1969; appointed member of the six-man General Secretariat, 1970; remained member of the new Executive Committee, 1971; re-elected member of PLO Executive Committee, 1973; member PLO delegation to Moscow, led by Yassir Arafat 1974; Chairman, Occupied Homeland Affairs Department.

ABU SOUAN, Camille, Lebanese lawyer/journalist; born 30 August 1919, Beirut, Lebanon; *Education:* Licence in Law, St. Joseph University, Beirut, Lebanon; *Career:* Barrister at Law; founder of the magazine *Le Cahiers De L'Est;* Secretary General, National Commission of UNESCO; Secretary General of the Pen Club; Curator, Sursock Museum; President, Cultural Committee of the newspaper *L'Orient;* Lebanese Representative to various general conferences of UNESCO, and to numerous other international conferences; travelled on journalistic and political assignments to China, Japan, West Germany, USA, USSR, the Arab World, and other countries; one of the founders of the Association for the Protection of Ancient Sites and Dwellings; *Publications:* numerous articles and studies; lectures; a translation of Khalil Gibran's *The Prophet; Decorations:* Laureate of the Institute of France, 1947; French Academy Medal, 1948; Officer, National Order of the Cedar, 1954; *Address:* L'Orient, P O Box 2488, Rue Banque du Liban, Beirut, Lebanon.

ABU SU'UD, Aziz Ali, Saudi Arabian businessman; resident in Bahrain; born 21 December, 1942, Qatif, Saudi Arabia; married; one son; *Religion:* Muslim; *Education:* BA, Business Administration, American University of Beirut, Beirut, Lebanon, 1966–71; *Career:* joined Arab Commercial Enterprises Group of Companies, Al-Khobar,

Saudi Arabia, 1962, (Insurance, Reinsurance, Surveyors and Travel Agents) and progressed to Regional Manager post; Claims Manager and Assistant Company Manager, Dammam, Saudi Arabia, 1964–66; Visiting Manager, Abu Dhabi, United Arab Emirates, 1971–72; Manager, 1972–73, Oman; Manager, 1973–78, Bahrain; Regional Manager, Bahrain and United Arab Emirates, 1979–80; Regional Manager, Arab Commercial Enterprises, Bahrain, Qatar, and United Arab Emirates, 1980–; member of the Chartered Insurance Institute, London; *Interests and Recreations:* reading; *Languages:* Arabic, English; *Address:* Arab Commercial Enterprises, P O Box 781, Awal Building, Suite 47, Manama, Bahrain; telephone: 251656.

ABU SU'UD, Khalid, Kuwaiti financial official; born 1930, Jerusalem, Palestine; *Religion:* Muslim; *Education:* BCom, Accounts, Public Finance and Business Administration, Cairo University, Cairo, Egypt, 1954; *Career:* joined Ministry of Finance as a junior economist, 1956; Director of Revenue, Income Tax and Investments 1967–; assisted in the drafting of Kuwait's commercial, financial and budget laws and regulations; Assistant Under Secretary for Investments; Financial and Investment Adviser to the HH Amir of Kuwait, 1979–; *Languages:* Arabic, English; *Address:* Office of HH Amir of Kuwait, Sief Palace, P O Box 24374, Kuwait; telephone: 430616; telex: 2796 OFFPRIM.

ABU TALIB, Muhammad Gamal, Egyptian engineer; born 3 November 1943, Egypt; resident in UK; married; *Religion:* Muslim: *Education:* BSc in Civil Engineering, Ain Shams University, Cairo, Egypt, 1965; MSc in Engineering, Sheffield University, England, 1971; PhD, Sheffield University, England, 1969–74; *Career:* Field Engineer with the Arab Contractors, Egypt and Iraq, 1966–69; full-time research student, Sheffield University, England, 1969–74; Geotechnical Engineer with McClelland Engineers, London, Grade II, 1974, Grade III, 1975, Project Engineer, 1977; Senior Engineer, Consulting Engineering Office, CEO, Soil Division, Saudi Arabia, 1978; Chief Engineer, 1979; Chartered Engineer; member of the Institution of Civil Engineers, UK, 1976, of American Society of Civil Engineers, 1979, of the Institution of Engineering Profession, Egypt; *Publications:*

numerous articles in professional journals; *Interests and Recreations:* reading, squash, bridge, photography; *Address:* c/o CEO – Soil Division, P O Box 1736, Alkhobar, Saudi Arabia; telephone: Dammam 8321676; Residence— Alkhobar 8646616 ext. 132; 8 Mossdale, Chevely Park, Belmot, Durham, UK; telephone: 0385 48773.

ABU ZAID, Hikmat, Egyptian politician/academic; born 1923, Assiut, Egypt; *Religion:* Muslim; *Education:* BA, Literature, Cairo University, Egypt, 1940; Diploma in Education, University of Edinburgh, UK; MA from University of St. Andrews, UK, 1950; Doctorate in Educational Psychology from London University, UK, 1957; *Career:* teacher in several secondary schools in Egypt; Lecturer in Psychology, College for Women, University of Ain Shams, Cairo, Egypt; Minister of Social Affairs, 1962–65 (first woman to hold Ministerial rank in modern Egypt); Professor at Cairo University; member of the Egyptian National Peace Council; alternate member of the Arab Socialist Union (ASU) Central Committee, 1968; Secretary of Art and Literature Committee; member of the ASU Secretariat General, 1970; member of the General Committee of the Citizens War Committees, 1970, National Council for Services and Social Affairs, February 1974; Professor at College for Women, Ain Shams University, Cairo; *Decorations:* Lenin Peace Prize, December 1970; *Languages:* Arabic, English; *Address:* College for Women, Ain Shams University, Cairo, Egypt.

ABU ZAID, Laila, Morrocan journalist/writer; born 1950, Al-Ksida, Morocco; *Religion:* Muslim; *Education:* Licence in English; Diploma in Journalism; *Career:* Journalist, Morocco, 1970; Correspondent for television and radio, 1973–; member of the Council for the Minister of Information, for the Council of the Prime Minister; correspondent for the BBC; member of the Higher Council for Relief and Development; *Publications: Social Problems in the USA,* 1974; *Women's Situation in Morocco,* 1975; *Communism,* 1976; *The British Life and Society,* collection of short stories, 1979; *Interests and Recreations:* journalism, reading, travel, swimming; *Languages:* Arabic, French, English; *Address:* Office of the Prime Minister, Rabat, Morocco; telephone: 33408.

ABU ZAID, Major Ma'mun Lamuhin, Sudanese politician/army commander; born 1939, Omdurman, Sudan; married; one son, one daughter; *Religion:* Muslim; *Education:* graduate of Sudanese Military Academy, 1962; military courses in UK and Egypt; *Career:* commissioned 2nd Lieutenant, 1962; promoted to Major, 1969; member of the Revolutionary Command Council; Minister for Presidential Affairs and Head of the Security Department, 1969–71; Secretary General of the Sudanese Socialist Union; resigned, 1972; returned to office as Director of the Politburo and Adviser to the President on Arab Affairs, 1975; Minister of the Interior, 1976–77; Minister of Local Popular Government, February 1977; Minister of Energy and Mining, 1977; *Decorations:* Bravery Medal; Medal of Faithful Son of the Sudan; Star of Haile Selassie; Medal of Maarib Dam, Yemen Arab Republic; *Interests and Recreations:* poetry, theatre, drama, tennis, squash, reading, cinema; *Languages:* Arabic, English; *Address:* Ministry of Energy and Mining, Khartoum, Sudan.

ABU ZAID, Muhammad Hamdi, Egyptian diplomat; born 1918; married; one son, one daughter; *Religion:* Muslim; *Education:* Egyptian Air Force Academy; *Career:* served as a pilot, 1949–60; retired at the rank of Group Captain; attended RAF Navigational Course at Hamble, UK, 1951; appointed member of the First Revolutionary Council, 1952; Director of the Office of Asian Affairs in the Presidency, 1960–62; Ambassador to Yugoslavia, 1962–68; Ambassador to Mexico, 1968–73; Head of the Western European Department, Ministry of Foreign Affairs, 1973–74; Ambassador to Syria, 1974–75; Minister of Civil Aviation, 1975–76; Ambassador to USSR, 1976; *Languages:* Arabic, English; *Address:* Ministry of Foreign Affairs, Giza, Cairo, Egypt.

ABU ZAID, Mustafa Fahmi, Egyptian politician/ lawyer; born 1928; married; three children; *Religion:* Muslim; *Education:* Law, Cairo University, Egypt, 1949; *Career:* member of Faculty of Law; Lecturer, Alexandria University, Egypt, Professor and Head of Department of Constitutional and Administrative Law; seconded as Professor and Head of Department of General Law at Arab University of Beirut, Lebanon, 1968; member of the Committee of the Arab Socialist Union (ASU); elected member of the Central Committee of the ASU Reorganization, 1971; elected member of the National Assembly; Prosecutor General with ministerial rank; Minister of Justice, 1974–75; *Languages:* Arabic, English; *Address:* Ministry of Justice, Cairo, Egypt.

ABU ZAID, Omar Mustafa, Jordanian businessman; born 1931, Jaffa, Palestine; married; three sons; *Religion:* Muslim; *Education:* general; *Career:* General Manager and Chairman of the Board of Mustafa Abu Zaid and Sons Company Ltd, Amman, Jordan; member of the Board of Construction Equipment and Machinery Company Ltd, United Arab Building Materials Company Ltd, of the Board of Directors of Amman Chamber of Commerce, 1974–78; member of the Council of Jordan Federation of Chambers of Commerce, 1974–78; major shareholder and member of the Board of Directors of Ready Mix Cement Industries Company Ltd, Alhilal Trading Company Ltd, Amman, Jordan; *Interests and Recreations:* member of several clubs; *Languages:* Arabic, English, French; *Address:* P O Box 435, Amman Jordan; telephone: 36300, 41228, 42668, 61714; telex: 1641 JO.

ABU ZAID, Othman Mahmud, Egyptian journalist; resident in Qatar; born 2 December 1933, Kafr al-Shaikh, Egypt; married; one son, one daughter; *Religion:* Muslim; *Education:* BA in Journalism, Faculty of Arts, Cairo University, 1958; *Career:* Journalist, Middle East News Agency, 1959; Directror of Gulf Area, Middle East News Agency, 1966; Director and Editor, The Qatar News Agency, 1975; Adviser to the Qatari News Agency, 1980; *Publications:* several papers and articles on the Middle East; *Decorations:* Ordre du Chevalier, Morocco; awarded The Prize of Production, Egypt; *Interests and Recreations:* jogging, swimming; *Languages:* Arabic, English; *Address:* Qatar News Agency, P O Box 3299, Al-Doha, Qatar; telephone: 320684.

ABU ZAID, Salah, Jordanian official/ diplomat; born 21 April 1923; married; *Religion:* Muslim; *Education:* one year law study, Syrian University, Damascus; Honorary Diploma in Radio and Television, Syracuse University, USA, 1957–59; *Career:* Teacher in Irbid, 1943; Government Official in Arab National Bank, 1946–50; Publicity Officer in Statistics Department, 1950–53; translator at

Jordanian Development Board, 1953–55; Chief Clerk at Department of Press and Publications, 1955–57; Director of Amman Broadcasting Service, 1958–59; Assistant to Director General of Jordanian Broadcasting Service, 1959–60; Director General of Jordanian Broadcasting Service, 1961–62, and of Press and Publications Department, 1962; Director General of National Guidance and Information Department, 1963; Minister of Information, 1964–65 and 1967; Minister of Information, Tourism and Antiquities, 1967–68; Ambassador to UK, 1969–70; Personal Adviser to HM King Hussain, 1971–72; Foreign Minister, 1972; Senator, 1973–74; Chairman, Foreign Relations Committee, 1973–74; Minister of Culture and Information, 1974–76; Ambassador to Court of St. James, London, 1976–80; Chairman and director, the Arab Information Centre For Public Relations, 1978–; *Publications: Al-Hussain Bin Talal,* 1958; *Decorations:* Arab Renaissance Medal; Star of Jordan; Cedar of Lebanon, various other medals; *Address:* P O Box 5105, Amman, Jordan; telephone: 667576.

ABU ZAKI, Rauf, Lebanese journalist; born 1941, Lebanon; married; three daughters; *Religion:* Muslim; *Career:* worked in news agencies, 1961–63; Editor and Head of Economics Department of the Lebanese *Al-Nahar* daily newspaper; founder of the *Orient Press* news agency, specialized in Lebanese economic affairs, 1972; Editor in Chief of *Al-Iktisaad al-Lubnaani wal Arabi* magazine, published by the Chamber of Commerce and Industry, Beirut, 1972–79; currently Editor in Chief and Director General of *Al-Iktisaad wal A'maal* magazine; Director General of the Arab Company for Publishing SAL, *Ibico; Languages:* Arabic, French; *Address:* Minkara Center, Mme Curie Street, P O Box 113/6194, Beirut, Lebanon; telephone: 353577/8/9; telex: 23370 LE APPICO.

ABU ZINADA, Abdul Wahab, Saudi Arabian businessman; born 1943; *Religion:* Muslim; *Education:* BA, English; *Career:* Secretary, Jeddah Chamber of Commerce and Industry; Director of Public Relations, National Advertising Agency; Director of Public Relations, International Markets Agency; Assistant Director of Jeddah Chamber of Commerce and Industry, member of Board, Saudi Agency for International Trade and Industry; *Publications:* poems, articles and short stories published in local newspapers; *Interests and Recreations:* swimming, travel; *Address:* Jeddah Chamber of Commerce and Industry, P O Box 1264, Jeddah, Saudi Arabia; telephone: Office — Jeddah 6423535; telex: 401069 GHURFA SJ.

ABUL ATTA, Abdul Azim Abdullah, Egyptian politician/engineer; born 1925; *Religion:* Muslim; *Education:* BSc and MSc in Irrigation Studies, Alexandria University, Egypt; *Career:* Deputy Director of Irrigation Works; Deputy Engineer in charge of Uganda Dam; Technical Secretary to the Minister of Works; Director of the High Dam Office in Moscow; Under Secretary for the High Dam, 1964; Deputy Chairman of the Land Reclamation Authority, 1970; Chairman of the Land Development Projects Authority; Minister of Irrigation, April 1975; Minister of Agriculture and Irrigation, 1976; Minister of Irrigation, 1977; *Address:* Ministry of Irrigation, Cairo, Egypt.

ABUL ELA, Abdul Salaam, Sudanese businessman; born 1901; *Religion:* Muslim; *Education:* Gordon College, Khartoum; *Career:* Head of Abulela Trading Corporation (export and import of food stuffs and general merchandise), one of Sudan's largest commercial firms; Chairman of the Sudan Chamber of Commerce, member of the Board of the Industrial Bank; *Languages:* Arabic, English; *Address:* Abullela Building, Abbas Square, P O Box 121, Khartoum, Sudan; telephone: 70020, 71173, 42968.

ABUL ELA, Saad, Sudanese businessman; born 1920; married; *Religion:* Muslim; *Education:* general; *Career:* Partner of his brother Abdul Salaam Abul Ela, managing the Abul Ela Trading Corporation and the Abul Ela Group of Companies; member of the Advisory Board to Radio Omdurman, 1954; composer and an authority on Sudanese music; *Languages:* Arabic, English; *Address:* Abullela Building, Abbas Square, P O Box 121, Khartoum, Sudan; telephone: 70020, 71173, 42968.

ABUL FARAJ, Ghalib Hamza, Saudi Arabian official; born 1931; *Education:* BSc, Electrical Engineering; *Career:* technical expert; technical consultant; Director General of Press and Publications Department, Ministry of Information; member of Archaeological Council; Head of Saudi Permanent Committee, Arab League; *Publications:* two collections of short stories; *The Vienna Affairs,* novel on the attack on OPEC ministers in Vienna; *Decorations:* Order of Merit, Commodore Grade, Lebanon, Order of Merit of the Republic, 2nd Grade, Egypt; *Languages:* Arabic, English; *Address:* Press and Publications Directorate, Ministry of Information, Riyadh, Saudi Arabia; telephone: Office— Riyadh 20525.

ABUL HAGGAG, Yusif Ibrahim, Egyptian academic; born 15 October 1919, Luxor, Egypt; married; one son, three daughters; *Religion:* Muslim; *Education:* BA in Geography, Cairo University, 1944; PhD in Physical Geography, London University, 1954; *Career:* junior geologist in American Oil Companies, Egypt, 1944–48; Demonstrator and Assistant Lecturer in Geography, Cairo and Ain Shams Universities, 1948–51; Research Student, London School of Economics, London, 1951–54; Lecturer, then Professor, Ain Shams University, 1955–74; Director Middle East Research Centre, Ain Shams University, 1974–77; Dean, Faculty of Arts, Ain Shams University, 1977–78; teaching positions in Wisconsin University, 1968–70, Waterloo Lutheran, 1970–72, Baghdad, Riyadh and UAE Universities; Chairman, Department of Geography, United Arab Emirates University, Al Ain, UAE; member of The Institute of British Geographers, 1951–54, the Association of American Geographers, 1968–72, the Board of Egyptian Geographers Society, 1973–78, the National Committee of Enviromental Problems in the Academy of Scientific Research and Technology, Cairo, the Lake Nassir Project, 1976–78; *Publications:* articles published in the *Bulletin of the Society of Geographers,* Egypt; various papers and books mainly on the physical, regional and economic geography of the Middle East and Africa, in Arabic; four works translated into Arabic; *Languages:* Arabic, English, French; *Address:* 9 Murad Street, Flat 9, Giza, Egypt; telephone: 897854.

ABUL HAJ, Rif'at Ali, Arab American academic; born 21 November 1933, Jerusalem, Palestine; *Religion:* Muslim; *Education:* BA, Washington and Lee University, Lexington, Virginia, USA; MA, PhD, Princeton University, USA; *Career:* Assistant Professor, St. Lawrence University, Canton, NY, USA; Associate Professor, Department of History, California State University, Long Beach, USA; Professor, Department of History, California State University, USA; Professor of History of the Near East and Modern Europe; *Publications: The Rebellion of 1703; The Structure of Ottoman Politics; Interests and Recreations:* swimming; member of the Royal Asiatic Society, the Past and Present Society, the Middle East Association of America, the American Historical Association; *Languages:* Arabic, English, Turkish, French, German; *Address:* California State University, Long Beach, 1250 Belflower Boulevard, Long Beach, CA 90840, USA.

ABUL JADAYEL, Anwar Ass'ad, Saudi Arabian businessman; *Education:* general; *Career:* Chief of Jeddah Customs Department; Director of Jeddah Customs House, Secretary General of Hejaz Customs Houses, 1954; owner of real estate, cold storage warehouse, ice-making plant, and contracting companies. *Publications:* articles published in Saudi Press on current political issues; *Interests and Recreations:* reading; *Address:* P O Box 72, Jeddah, Saudi Arabia; telephone: Jeddah 23726.

ABUL NASR, Mahmud, Egyptian diplomat/ UN official; born 23 June 1931, Cairo, Egypt; married; *Religion:* Muslim; *Education:* Licence in Law, Cairo University, Egypt; Institut des Hautes Etudes Internationales, University of Paris, France; *Career:* member of the Bar Association, Egypt, 1952–54; Egyptian Embassy to France, 1955–56; Egyptian Consulate, Genoa, Italy, 1957–59; Egyptian Embassy to Albania, 1959–61; member of the Permanent Mission of Egypt to UN, New York, 1964–68; Head, Human Rights Section, International Organization Department, Ministry of Foreign Affairs, Cairo, 1969–71; Counsellor, Deputy Permanent Representative of Egypt to UN, Geneva, Switzerland, 1971–; member of UN Committee on Elimination of All Forms of Racial Discrimination; *Languages:* Arabic, English, French, Italian; *Address:* Office — Ministry of Foreign Affairs, Cairo, Egypt.

ABUL SAMH, Abdullah A., Saudi Arabian official/journalist; born 1935, Mecca, Saudi Arabia; *Education:* BA, Journalism, Cairo University, Egypt; MA, Radio and TV, Syracuse University, USA; *Career:* Head of

Public Relations, Ministry of the Interior; Director of the Administration, Ministry of Petroleum; General Manager of Jeddah TV Station; Director of the Administration, Ministry of Information; Director General of Saudi News Agency; Deputy Chairman of Board of Directors, Industrial Services Co; *Publications:* various articles in local press; miscellaneous radio and TV talks; *Address:* P O Box 1032, Dammam, Saudi Arabia; telephone: Office— Dammam 21956; Residence— 22775.

ACCAD, Muhammad Rifat, Syrian banker; born 23 May 1922, Damascus, Syria; married; one son, two daughters; *Education:* Licence in Law, Damascus University, 1949; Specialized in Banking, Belgium, 1955; *Career:* Director of Exchange Office, 1961; Director, Vice Governor then Governor of Central Bank, 1973–77; Governor, Central Bank of Syria, 1978–; Alternate Governor (IMF), 1978; Representative of Syrian Central Bank, Board of Directors, European Arab Bank, 1978–; Alternate Governor Arab Monetary Fund, 1977; *Publications:* several articles and research papers published in different Syrian and Arab economic journals; *Interests and Recreations:* basketball; *Languages:* Arabic, French, English; *Address:* P O Box 5432, Damascus, Syria; telephone: 716468, 224800.

ACHAHBAR, Lieutenant Colonel Muhammad, Moroccan military administrator; born 1935; Morocco; married; *Religion:* Muslim; *Education:* educated at Spanish Military Academy, Avila, Spain; *Career:* Intendance Branch, 1957; promoted Lieutenant Colonel, 1971; Director of Intendance in the Morocco Army, 1971–73; Senior Intendance Officer in the Moroccan Forces; Secretary General of National Defence Administration, 1973–; *Languages:* Arabic, French, Spanish; *Address:* Ministry of Defence, Rabat, Morocco.

ACHOUR, Habib, Tunisian politician/trade unionist; born 1913, Kerkennah Islands, Tunisia; married; eleven children; *Religion:* Muslim; *Career:* Inspector of Roads; active member of the Neo-Destour; trade unionist; for many years a personal friend of President Bourguiba whom he helped escape from Sfax in 1945; led group of Sfax Unions out of the Union Générale des Travailleurs Tunisiens (UGTT) in opposition to the policies of

Ahmed Ben Salah, 1956; founded the Union des Travailleurs Tunisiens which united with UGTT, 1957; Assistant General Secretary in UGTT, with special responsibility for economic affairs and co-operatives; Secretary General in 1963; member of the Political Bureau of the Party; Deputy for Sfax in National Assembly 1969; extensive travels abroad on International Confederation of Free Trade Unions and ILO business; *Languages:* Arabic French; *Address:* Union Générale Tunisienne du Travail (UGTT), 29 place M'Hamed Ali, Tunis, Tunisia.

ADASSANI, Mahmud Khalid al- , Kuwaiti official; born 31 January 1934, Kuwait; married; one son, two daughters; *Religion:* Muslim; *Education:* BS in Petroleum Studies, 1958; *Career:* joined Kuwait Oil Company, 1958–; Assistant Petroleum Engineer, 1958–59; Petroleum Engineer, 1959–60; Director, Kuwait Oil Company, 1960–; Technical Assistant, General Oil Affairs Department, Government of Kuwait, 1960–62; Director, Technical Department, 1962–66; Assistant Under Secretary for Oil Affairs, Ministry of Finance, later Under Secretary, Ministry of Oil, 1975–; Director, Kuwait Metal Pipe Industries, 1970–; Kuwait Representative in OAPEC Executive Office, 1974–; OPEC Governor for Kuwait, 1976–; Chairman, Crude Oil and Gas, 1976–; Chairman, Joint Committee of the Saudi-Kuwaiti Neutral Zone, 1974; *Languages:* Arabic, English; *Address:* P O Box 3242, Safat, Kuwait.

ADASSANI, Muhammad Yusuf al- , Kuwaiti diplomat/politician; born 1926, Kuwait; *Religion:* Muslim; *Career:* Chief of Kuwait Municipality; Ambassador to Saudi Arabia, and non-resident Ambassador to Somalia, 1967–69; Ambassador to Lebanon, 1969–76; Minister of Planning, 1976–; *Address:* Ministry of Planning, P O Box 15, Safat, Kuwait; telephone: 420211.

ADHAM, Anwar Adam, Sudanese lawyer; born 1934, Al Obeid, Sudan; married; *Religion:* Muslim: *Education:* LLB, Cairo University, Egypt, 1958; *Career:* Sudan Bar, 1960; Advocate and Commissioner for Oaths; Partner, Adham and Abu El Reash & Co; *Languages:* Arabic, English; *Address:* P O Box 2272, Khartoum, Sudan; telephone: 79279, 81489.

ADHAM, Shaikh Kamal Ibrahim, Saudi Arabian politician/businessman; born 1929, Mecca, Saudi Arabia; married; three sons, one daughter; *Religion:* Muslim; *Education:* Victoria College, Alexandria, Egypt; Trinity College, Cambridge University, UK; *Career:* Adviser to late King Faisal when Crown Prince; Special Adviser to late King Faisal in Royal Cabinet, 1964; Adviser at the Royal Cabinet of late King Khalid and Special Envoy to Arab and foreign countries in political missions and consultations; international business interests; was involved in Saudi-Japanese oil agreement in Saudi-Kuwait Neutral Zone, 1958; *Decorations:* several orders of merit from Arab and foreign countries; *Interests and Recreations:* painting, swimming, football, poetry, Arabic music; *Languages:* Arabic, French, English, Turkish, Italian; *Address:* P O Box 478, Jeddah, Saudi Arabia; telephone: Jeddah 642 3403.

ADIB, Abdul Hayy, Egyptian artist/scenarist; born 23 November 1928, Mahallat Kubra, Egypt; married; three sons; *Religion:* Muslim; *Education:* BA, Drama and Theatre Institute; *Career:* film scenarist since 1957; one of the first film producers and cinema writers in Egypt; member of the Cinema Association at the Chamber of the Cinema Industry; *Publications:* short stories and screenplays for 120 Egyptian feature films of which the most important *Bab Al-Hadid,* 1957; *Um Al-Arusa; Interests and Recreations:* cinema and stage, reading contemporary and classical literature, swimming, walking; *Languages:* Arabic, English; *Address:* 36 Sharif Street, Cairo, Egypt; telephone: 43780.

ADIB, Albert, Lebanese journalist; born 1 July 1908, Mexico; *Career:* editor of various magazines, Cairo, Egypt, 1927–30, Beirut, Lebanon, 1930–38; President, Academy of Oriental Music, Beirut, 1933–38; Director General, Radio Levant Broaadcasting Station, Beirut, 1938–43; Editor and Proprietor, *Al-Adib Review,* Beirut, 1942–; member of various academies and foreign cultural institutes; *Publications: Liman,* poems, 1952; *Decorations:* Chevalier of the Order of the Cedar, Lebanon; *Languages:* Arabic, French; *Address:* Revue Al-Adib, P O Box 11 878, Beirut, Lebanon.

ADIB, Hoda, Lebanese artist/musician; born 26 December 1943, Beirut, Lebanon; *Religion:* Christian; *Education:* Diploma in Piano, National Conservatoire of Music, Beirut, Lebanon; *Career:* Teacher of Piano, National Conservatoire of Music, Beirut, 1970–; Teacher of Musical Initiation in government schools, 1972–75; Teacher of Solfeggio, Center of Research and Pedagogical Development, Beirut, 1977–; organizer of Experimental Poetry at French Cultural Center, and at the Goethe Institute, Beirut, 1980; *Publications: Pantheses,* collection of poems in French, 1968; *Demi-Pause,* in French, 1970; *Trois Cubes,* in Arabic, 1971; and several other collections of poetry; *Interests and Recreations:* theatre, ballet, painting, music; *Languages:* Arabic, French, English; *Address:* P O Box 11878 Beirut, Lebanon; telephone: 386 697.

ADJALI, Abdul Hamid, Algerian diplomat; born 1932, Constantine, Algeria; married; *Religion:* Muslim; *Career:* active in Algerian General Workers Union (UGTA); Chargé d'Affaires with rank of Counsellor, Leopoldville, Congo, 1964; Director of Political Affairs Office, Ministry of Foreign Affairs, and Head of Latin American Affairs and Asian Division, Ministry of Foreign Affairs; *Languages:* Arabic, French, English; *Address:* Ministry of Foreign Affairs, Rue Ibn Badran, Algiers, Algeria.

ADLI, Ibrahim, Syrian UN official; born 3 November 1921, Damascus, Syria; married; *Education:* LLB, Damascus University, Syria, 1941–44; MA in Law, American University, Washington D.C., USA, 1947–52; PhD in Economics; *Career:* Head of Income Tax Department, Ministry of Finance, 1952–54; Director of Internal Revenue, Ministry of Finance, 1954–58; Director of Personnel, Ministry of Finance, 1958–60; Director General, Pension and Insurance Fund, Syrian Government, 1960–62; Chairman of the Board and Director General, Banque de Syrie et d'Outre-Mer, Damascus, 1962–63; Resident Representative, UN Development Programme, UNDP, Kuwait, 1966–72; Resident Representative, UNDP, Libya, 1972–78; Resident Representative, UNDP, Riyadh, Saudi Arabia, 1978; Resident Co-ordinator, UN Systems Operational Activities for the Development of Saudi Arabia, 1981–; *Publications:* several articles on economics and finance in professional journals; *Decorations:* Syrian Order of Merit; *Languages:* Arabic, English, French, Turkish; *Address:* UNDP, P O Box 558, Riyadh, Saudi Arabia.

ADONIS, Ali Said, Lebanese poet, born 1930, Lattakia, Syria; married; one daughter; *Education:* Licence ès-Lettres, Damascus University, Syria; *Career:* journalist; poet; founder of the *Shi'r* magazine for poetry; founder and Director of the *Mawaqif* magazine *Publications: Premiers Poemes; Feuilles dans le Vent; Les Chants de Mihiar le Damascene; Anthologie de la Poésie Arabe des Origines à nos Jours; Le Livre des Métamorphoses et de l'Emigration dans les Régions du Jour et de la Nuit; La Scène et les Miroirs; Decorations:* special prize awarded by the Association des Amis du Livre, 1969; *Interests and Recreations:* swimming, reading, music; *Address:* P O Box 1489, Beirut, Lebanon; telephone: 284985.

ADRA, Abdul Rahman, Lebanese diplomat; born 1912, Tripoli, Lebanon; married; one daughter; *Education:* BA, Commerce and Economics; MA, PhD, History, Aix en Provence University, France; Faculty of Science, Marseille, France; American University of Beirut , Lebanon; *Career:* Lecturer, AUB, 1937–40; founder of industrial company, 1940–45; Counsellor and Chargé d'Affaries, Embassy to Saudi Arabia, 1946–47; Counsellor, Embassy to Brazil, 1947–48; in charge of UNESCO and international conferences in Lebanon, 1948–52; Ambassador to Pakistan, 1954–55; Ambassador to Iran, 1956–64; Head, UN Department, Ministry of Foreign Affairs, 1964–66; Ambassador to Morocco, 1967–68; Ambassador to Algeria, 1968–73; Ambassador to Malaysia, 1973–78; now retired; *Decorations:* Grand Officer, National Order of the Cedar; Grand Cordon, Hamayoun Order, Iran; *Interests and Recreations:* swimming, book-collecting, coin-collecting, archaeological excavation; member of the Lion's Club; *Languages:* Arabic, English, French; *Address:* Madame Curie Street, Beirut, Lebanon.

ADWAN, Maitre Georges, Lebanese lawyer; born 1947, Lebanon; *Religion:* Christian; *Education:* BA in Law and Political Science, Beirut, Lebanon; PhD in Comparative International Law, 1973; *Career:* private law practice, Beirut, Lebanon; member of

Lebanese Forces, 1976–; Assistant President, Lebanese Forces, 1976–77; *Interests and Recreations:* swimming, table tennis, skiing; *Languages:* Arabic, English, French; *Address:* Sehnaoui Building, 7th Floor, Hotel Dieu Street, Beirut, Lebanon; telephone: 215500.

ADWOK, Luigi, Sudanese politician; born 1929, Agodo, Kodak District of the Upper Nile Province, Sudan; *Education:* Degree from Bakht al-Ruda Intermediate Teacher Training College, 1954; *Career:* School Teacher, 1952–58; elected to the Constituent Assembly for the Liberal Party; retired in late 1958; Businessman; Teacher, Headmaster of Tambura Intermediate School, 1963–64; member of the Supreme Council of State, 1964; resigned June, 1965; independent member of the Constituent Assembly, 1967–69; resumed private business; Sudan Research Unit, 1969–71; member of the Preparatory Committee of the Sudan Socialist Union (SSU), 1971; Minister of Works, 1971; Commissioner of the Upper Nile Province with the rank of Minister, 1971; member of the SSU Political Bureau and of the Transitional Higher Executive Council with responsibility for the Public Services and for Administrative Reform, 1972; member of the Southern Region High Executive Council for Education, April 1972; Alternate Assistant Secretary General of the SSU, 1974; member of the People's Assembly since 1974; *Address:* Sudanese Socialist Union (SSU), P O Box 1850, Khartoum, Sudan.

AFIFI, Azmi Ahmad, Egyptian UN official; born 22 June 1921, Egypt; married; *Religion:* Muslim; *Education:* BA, Agricultural Science, Cairo University, Egypt, 1937–41; Entomological Award, 1941; University of California, Berkeley, USA, 1945–46; PhD, Food Technology and Economy, University of Massachusetts, Amherst, USA, 1946–49; *Career:* Demonstrator, Biological Sciences, Cairo University, 1941–45; Associate Professor of Agricultural Industry, Ain Shams University, 1950–57; Director, Rural Industry Department, Ministry of Labour and Social Affairs, Cairo, 1954–56; Assistant Secretary General, Scientific Council, Egypt, 1956–57; Adviser, Small Scale Industry, ILO, Switzerland and Libya, 1957–64; Chief, Industrial Institutions Secretariat, Centre for Industrial Development, UN, New York, 1964–67; Assistant Director, Industrial Institutions Division, UN, New York, 1967–68; Deputy Director, Industrial Services and Institutions Division, UN Industrial Development Organization (UNIDO), 1968–72; Deputy Director, Industrial Technical Division, UNIDO, Vienna, 1972–74; Senior Adviser to the Executive Director, UNIDO, Vienna 1974–; *Interests and Recreations:* reading, fishing, chess, planning and programming, industrial technology and administration, management; *Languages:* Arabic, English; *Address:* Office UNIDO, P O Box 707, A 1011 Vienna 1, Austria; telephone: 0222 43500; Residence — 4/1 Schreiberweg, A 1190, Vienna, Austria; telephone: 323140.

AFIFI, Major General Hilmi al-Bar, Egyptian military commander; born 1922; married; three children; *Religion:* Muslim; *Education:* graduated from Egyptian Military Academy, 1942; *Career:* commissioned in artillery; attended course at Middle East Anti-Aircraft School, Haifa, Palestine; served in Egyptian anti-aircraft units in Suez Canal Zone; course at Egyptian Staff College, 1956; attended Air Defence Course at Soviet Air Defence Academy, Odessa, USSR; Chief of Staff of Air Defence Command, October 1973 War; attended Farnborough Air Show, UK, 1974; Commander of Air Defence, 1975; *Languages:* Arabic, English; *Address:* Ministry of Defence, Cairo, Egypt.

AFLAQ, Michel, Syrian politician/writer; born 1910, Damascus, Syria; *Religion:* Christian; *Education:* Damascus and University of Paris, France, 1928–34; *Career:* taught history in a secondary school in Damascus, 1935–42; wrote articles for Damascus press on current political and social affairs; founded Baath (Renaissance) Party, 1940, together with a group of student followers, with Salah Bitar as lieutenant; founded party newspaper *Al-Baath,* 1946; imprisoned by Husni Zaim Government; Minister of Education, 1949; paid long visit to South America, 1950; returned to Syria but left for Lebanon with Akram Hourani and Salah Bitar after failure of anti-Shishlaki move in 1952; returned to Syria, October 1953; when agreed to amalgamate Baath Party with Hourani's Arab Socialist Party National (i.e. Pan Arab) Command and as such played major role in union of Syria and Egypt, 1958; withdrew to Beirut following ousting of Baath in Syria, 1959; member of National Council of Revolutionary Command following Baathist movement, March 1963, and participated in Egyptian-Syrian-Iraqi union talks, March-April 1963; accompanied Amin al-Hafiz to Baghdad, November 1963, in effort to maintain Baath Government in Iraq; returned to Beirut following February 1966 change of régime; made several visits to Iraq, 1966–70; re-elected Secretary General to Baath National Command and again in 1970; regular visitor to Iraq; *Publications:* numerous essays and articles on political ideology; *Languages:* Arabic, French; *Address:* Ministry of Information, Baghdad, Iraq.

AFRA, Saad Abdullah, Egyptian diplomat; born 1924, Alexandria, Egypt; married; *Religion:* Muslim; *Education:* BA, Law, Cairo University, Cairo, Egypt; MA, Political Sciences, Cairo University, Cairo, Egypt; *Career:* army officer by profession; Director of Egyptian Information Service, 1957–60; joined Ministry of Foreign Affairs, rank of ambassador, 1960; Ambassador to Poland, 1962–68; Director, East European Affairs, 1968–70; Under Secretary of State, Ministry of Foreign Affairs, 1970; Ambassador to Yugoslavia, 1971–74; Under Secretary of State, Ministry of Foreign Affairs, 1975–79; Ambassador to Greece, 1979–; *Languages:* Arabic, English, French; *Address:* Egyptian Embassy, 3 Leoforos Vassilissis Sofias, Athens, Greece.

AGEEL, Abdullah O., Saudi Arabian businessman; born 16 August 1934, Bombay, India; *Religion:* Muslim; *Education:* Fallah School, Jeddah; BA, Economics, Randolph Macon College, Virginia, USA, 1961; *Career:* government work with Supreme Planning Council and Ministry of Information; Business Consulting Representative, engaged in recruitment of managerial personnel for Saudi Airlines; became one of two Saudi members of New York Stock Exchange; representative of product companies and agricultural business in Saudi Arabia; owner of Abdullah Ageel Establishment, Jeddah; *Interests and Recreations:* swimming, fishing, Islamic culture; *Languages:* Arabic, English; *Address:* Abdullah Ageel Establishment, Alireza Building, King Abdul Aziz Street, c/o P O Box 8, Jeddah, Saudi Arabia; telephone: Jeddah 22233, ext 39; telex: Jeddah 40037 ZENREZA SJ.

AGGAD, Omar A., Saudi Arabian businessman; born 20 April 1927, Jaffa, Palestine; married; *Education:* BSc in Engineering, Manchester University, UK; Industrial Administration, Birmingham Faculty of Technology, UK; *Career:* Chairman, Aggad Investment Co, Riyadh, Saudi Arabia; Managing Director, Saudi Plastic Products Co, (Sappco); Chairman, Arabian Plastic Manufacturing Co, (Aplaco); Chairman, Sappco Texaco Insulation Products Co, (Saptex); Managing Director, Prefabricated Building Co Ltd, (Nabco); Chairman, Arabian Technical Contracting Co, (Artec); President, Aluminium Products Co Ltd, (Alupco), and Aluminium Manufacturing Co, (Alumaco); Managing Director, Steel Products Co Ltd, (Stepco), and Health Water Bottling Co, Nissah; Partner, Hygienic Paper Factory; Chairman, Saudi International Petroleum Carriers Co Ltd, (Sipca), Kone Lifts Saudi Ltd, and Saudi Continental Co; Founder and member of the Board of the Saudi British Bank; *Languages:* Arabic, English; *Address:* Aggad Investment Co, P O Box 2256, Riyadh, Saudi Arabia; telephone: 464 2862, 404 2862; telex: 200 276 Aggad SJ.

AGGIOURI, Rene, Lebanese journalist, born 1922, Beirut, Lebanon; married; *Education:* Licence in Law, St. Joseph University, Beirut, Lebanon; *Career:* journalist; Director and Editor of the French daily newspaper *L'Orient;* member of the National Board of Tourism; *Publications: Le Conflit de Palestine dans le Jeu des Puissances,* 1968; *Decorations:* awarded the *Pierre Mille* Prize, 1967; *Languages:* Arabic, French; *Address:* Office — l'Orient Newspaper, P O Box 688, Beirut, Lebanon; telephone: 250220.

AGOUMI, Abdul Wahab; Moroccan artist/ musician; born 10 October 1920, Fes, Morocco; married; one son, one daughter; *Religion:* Muslim; *Education:* Diploma in Music, Faud 1 University, Cairo, Egypt; Diploma of Ecole Normale, Paris, France; Diploma in Musical Composition, Internationale of Compstella; *Career:* Professor of Music; Director of the National Conservatoire of Music, Dance and Dramatic Art; Head of the Music Section of the Ministry of State for Cultural Affairs; composer, singer and producer on Radio-Télévision-Maroc; Head of Music Education Bureau in State Secretariat attached to the Prime Minister for Mutual Aid and Handicrafts; Adviser to the Minister of State for Cultural Affairs; Secretary General of the Moroccan Authors' and Writers' Society; member of the Paris Society of Composers; member of the Arab League Association for Musical Education; member of the Association of Arab Writers in Morocco; represented Morocco in several congresses of music in Egypt, Algeria, Tunisia, Morocco, Romania, Spain, France, Syria, Turkey, USSR, China, Italy, etc; *Publications:* records of Arab and symphonic music recorded by Marconi, Paris, France; *Decorations:* Order of Ouissam El-Rida, exceptional category, Morocco, 1972; *Interests and Recreations:* music, reading, riding; *Languages:* Arabic, French; *Address:* 14 Rue Ibn Toumert, Rabat, Morocco; telephone: 22089.

AHERDANE, Mahjubi, Moroccan politician; born 1921, Qulems, Morocco; married; *Religion:* Muslim; *Education:* Military College, Meknes, 1940; *Career:* Captain in the French Army; Caid (District Administrator) of Qulmes, 1949–53; Governor of Rabat Province after Independence; one of the founders of the Mouvement Populaire Parti; Minister of Defence, 1961; reappointed November 1963; elected Rabat Representative of Chamber of Counsellors, 1963; Minister of Agriculture, 1964; Minister of Defence, 1966–67; elected Deputy of Khemisset, 1970; Secretary General of the Mouvement Populaire Parti; appointed member of Government by HM King Hassan, 1977; Minister of State for Posts and Telecommunications,1977; *Publications:* various poems; *Interests and Recreations:* impressionist painting, has held exhibitions in Paris, Geneva and London, 1969; *Languages:* Arabic, French; *Address:* Prime Minister's Office, Rabat, Morocco.

AHMAD, Abdullah Awadh, Yemen Arab Republic lawyer; born 13 February 1939, Aden, Yemen Arab Republic; married; three daughters; *Religion:* Muslim; *Education:* Law College, University of Alexandria, Egypt; *Career:* Director, Legal Adviser's Office, 1968; Assistant Legal Adviser, 1970; Deputy Legal Adviser to the Revolutionary Council and to the Council of Ministers; Chairman of the Central Appeal Committee for arbitration on tax disputes, 1977; member of the People's Constitutional Council (The Parliament), 1978–; member of the Supreme Judicial Council, 1979; *Publications:* two articles in *Sharia and Law* magazine, 1973;

Interests and Recreations: reading, history, law, music, theatre; *Languages:* Arabic, English; *Address:* Legal Office for the State, P O Box 1292, Presidential Palace, Sana'a, Yemen Arab Republic; telephone: 72752/72511.

AHMAD, Abdullah Ismail, Iraqi politician; born 1927, Erbil, Iraq; *Religion:* Muslim; *Career:* joined the Kurdish Democratic Party (KDP), 1951; member of KDP Central Committee; Minister of State, 1974–; leader of the Movement of Progressive Kurds; *Languages:* Kurdish, Arabic; *Address:* c/o Kurdish Democratic Party, Aqaba Bin Nafi Square, Baghdad, Iraq.

AHMAD, Ahmad Iskandar, Syrian journalist; *Religion:* Muslim; *Career:* Editor of *Al-Thawra,* the Baath Party Newspaper; Minister of Information, 1974; owner of political daily newspaper *Tishrin,* 1979; *Address:* Ministry of Information, Autostrad Meza, Damascus, Syria.

AHMAD, Ahmad Muhammad, Egyptian official; born 28 May 1921, Cairo, Egypt; married; one son, six daughters; *Religion:* Muslim; *Education:* BSc in Military Science, 1945; Licence in Journalism, 1960; *Career:* army officer, 1945; teacher, Army Education Corps, 1949; Private Secretary to late President Nassir, 1952; Deputy Adviser and Private Secretary to late President Nasser, 1970; Minister of Local Administration, 1970; Minister of Presidential Affairs, 1971; Deputy Prime Minister, 1971; Secretary General, Federation of Arab Republics' Presidential Council, 1971; Acting Head of the Federation Council of Ministers, 1976; Head of the Egyptian Olympic Committee; Head of the Egyptian Football Union; Chairman, Al-Hurriyah School, Bab al-Louq, Cairo; *Decorations:* Flag Decoration of Yugoslavia, 3rd Class, 1960; Order of the Throne, 2nd Class, Morocco, 1960; Order of the Two Niles, 2nd Class, Sudan, 1960; Order of the Star, 2nd Class, Afghanistan, 1960; Star of Ethiopia, Commando Class, 1962; Order of Maarib, 3rd Class, Yemen Arab Republic, 1964; Order of Merit, 2nd Class, Tunisia, 1965; Alawi Medal, 1st Class, Morocco, 1965; Order of the Flag Golden Crown, Yugoslavia, 1965; Order of Stitota Commando Class, Poland, 1965; Order of Merit Grand Officer Class, Mauritania, 1976; Order of Merit Commando Class, Brazzaville, Congo, 1969; Order of the Two Niles, 1st Class, Sudan, 1969; Medal of National Merit Commando Class, Central African Republic, 1970; Order of the Flag, 1st Class, Hungary, 1970; *Languages:* Arabic, English; *Address:* 5 Ibrahim Naguib Street, Garden City, Cairo, Egypt.

AHMAD, Ahmad Sulaiman Muhammad, Sudanese diplomat; born 1923, Wad Medani, Sudan; married; *Religion:* Muslim; *Career:* Lawyer; Minister of Agriculture in the First Transitional Government formed after the October 1964 Revolution; Minister of Agriculture in Third Transitional Government, 1965; Ambassador to USSR, Minister of Economics and Foreign Trade; transferred to Ministry of Industry and Mining, 1970; Minister of Justice in the new Government, 1971; Ambassador to UK, 1973–75; *Languages:* Arabic, English, French; *Address:* Ministry of Foreign Affairs, Khartoum, Sudan.

AHMAD BIN ABDUL AZIZ, HRH Prince, Saudi Arabian Prince/administrator; born 1942; youngest of seven sons of late King Abdul Aziz and late Hassa Bint Sudairi; married; two children; *Religion:* Muslim; *Education:* BA in Political Sciences, Redlands University, Southern California, USA, 1968; *Career:* businessman; Chairman of the Board of National Gypsum Co, and several other companies and firms, 1969–70; Deputy Governor of Mecca, 1971–75; Vice Minister of the Interior, 1975–; *Languages:* Arabic, English; *Address:* Ministry of the Interior, P O Box 2833, Riyadh, Saudi Arabia; telephone: 4011944; telex: 201622 MORS SJ.

AHMAD, Ibrahim, Iraqi politician; born 1920, Sulaimaniyah, Iraq; *Religion:* Muslim; *Education:* law studies; *Career:* lawyer; member of the National Council of Peace Partisans, 1959; founder of the Kurdistan Democratic Party, 9 January 1960; later Secretary General of the Kurdistan Democratic Party for some years; *Languages:* Kurdish, Arabic; *Address:* Kurdistan Democratic Party, Aqba Bin Nafi Square, Baghdad, Iraq.

AHMAD, Ibrahim Muhammad Ahmad, Sudanese businessman; born 21 January 1920, Khartoum, Sudan; married; three sons, one daughter; *Religion:* Muslim; *Education:* Gordon Memorial College, 1956; Diploma in

Commerce and Accounting, National University, Cairo, Egypt, 1956; *Career:* government employee, 1937–48; Audit Assistant, Russell and Company, Chartered Accountants, 1948–55; Manager, I.I. Zahman Enterprise, 1955–58; Sudan Travel and Tourist Agency, 1958–67; Director, Abul Ezz Contracting Company, Tripoli, Libya, 1967–68; Sudan Employers Consultative Association, 1968–; Managing Director, Tahir Commercial Agencies (manufacturers' representatives, commission agents, imports and exports, government tenderers); Managing Director, Sudan Market and Trade; *Interests and Recreations:* gardening, motor cars, president of Port Sudan Rotary Club, 1964–65; *Languages:* Arabic, English; *Address:* P O Box 1758, Khartoum, Sudan; telephone: 71381.

AHMAD, Jamal Muhammad, Sudanese diplomat/politician; born 1913, Wadi Halfa, Sudan; *Religion:* Muslim; *Education:* Gordon College, Khartoum, Sudan; University of Exeter, UK; Oxford University, UK; *Career:* Lecturer in Modern History, University of Khartoum, 1947–57; Ambassador to Iraq, 1956–57; Ambassador to Ethiopia, 1959–64; temporary appointment as Sudan Representative at the United Nations, December 1964; Sudanese Ambassador to UK, 1965; returned to Sudan, 1966 and played important part in the Organization of African Unity Council of Ministers meeting of March 1966; Ambassdor, 1966–67; Under Secretary of Foreign Affairs; Ambassador to UK, 1969–70; General Manager of the newly established *Al-Ra'i Al-'Aam* Publishing Corporation, 1970; Ambassador, Ministry of Foreign Affairs, 1972; accompanied the Head of State on several overseas visits; member of the Board of *Al-Sahafa,* 1974; Minister of State for Foreign Affairs, 1975; Minister of Foreign Affairs, 1975–76; *Publications: The Intellectual Origins of Egyptian Nationalism,* 1960; *Languages:* Arabic, English; *Address:* Ministry of Foreign Affairs, Khartoum, Sudan.

AHMAD, Karamalla Awad, Sudanese politician; born 1926, Sudan; *Religion:* Muslim; *Education:* Diploma, Institute of Social Studies, The Hague, 1956 Netherlands; MA, Economics, University of Manchester, England; *Career:* Administration Office, Sudan, 1949–53; Assistant District Commissioner, 1954–55; Lecturer, Public Administration, University of Khartoum, 1955–57; Head of Department of Public Law and Administration, University of Khartoum, Sudan, 1958–66; Governor, Bahr al-Ghazal Province, 1966–69; Under Secretary, Ministry of Local Government, 1969–72; Deputy Minister and Governor, Red Sea Province, 1973–75; Minister of State, Secretary of Sudan Socialist Union, 1975–77; Minister of Public Service and Administrative Reform and member of the Central Committee of the Sudan Socialist Union, 1977–; *Address:* Ministry of Public Service and Administrative Reform, Khartoum, Sudan.

AHMAD, Khalid Muhammad, United Arab Emirates journalist; born 1950, Dubai, United Arab Emirates; *Religion:* Muslim; *Education:* Degree in Journalism, Cairo University, Egypt, 1973–74; *Career:* 3rd Secretary, Diplomatic Service, Ministry of Foreign Affairs; Chief Editor of *Al-Ittihad* and *Akhbar al-Imarat al-Arabiya,* published by Ministry of Information; member of the board of UAE Press and Publishing Organization; *Interests and Recreations:* travel, hunting, football; *Languages:* Arabic, English; *Address:* P O Box 791, Abu Dhabi, United Arab Emirates.

AHMAD, Laila Nadine Abdul Aziz, Egyptian academic; born 29 May 1940, Cairo, Egypt; *Education:* BA in English, Girton College, Cambridge University, UK, 1958–61; PhD in English, Girton College, Cambridge University, 1966–71; *Career:* Assistant Lecturer, Ain Shams University, Cairo, Egypt, 1962–63; Assistant Lecturer, Al-Azhar University, Women's College, Cairo, 1963–65; Inspector of English Language Teaching in the United Arab Emirates, and Adviser to Ministry of Education on English Language Teaching Development, Ministry of Education, United Arab Emirates; Associate Professor, Chairman of Department of Foreign Languages, University of the United Arab Emirates; member of the British Society for Middle Eastern Studies; *Publications: E.W. Lane and English Ideas of the Middle East in the Nineteenth Century,* 1976; *Languages:* English, Arabic, French; *Address:* University of the United Arab Emirates, P O Box 15551, Al-Ain, United Arab Emirates; 27 Marlowe Road, Cambridge, UK; telephone: 63805.

AHMAD, Muhammad al-Hassan A.S., Sudanese agriculturalist; born 1947, Sudan; married; two sons; *Religion:* Muslim; *Education:* BSc, Agriculture, University of Khartoum, 1971; MPhil, Agriculture, Nottingham, UK, 1977; currently registered for PhD at Edinburgh University, Scotland, UK; *Career:* Assistant Inspector of Agriculture, Khartoum Province, 1971–72; Plant Propagation Officer, Northern Sudan, 1972–74; Head of Hudeiba Plant Propagation Station, 1977–80; *Publications:* articles in the *Journal of the British Grassland Society,* 1978, vol 33, pp35–40; *Acta Horticulturae 83,* 1978, and others; *Interests and Recreations:* football, tennis, table tennis, travel; *Languages:* Arabic, English; *Address:* 11/5 Craigmillar Castle Avenue, Edinburgh, Scotland, UK.

AHMADI, Muhammad Bin Mussa al-, Moroccan academic/lawyer; born 24 December 1951; married; *Religion:* Muslim; *Education:* Diploma of Higher Studies in Public Law; Diploma in International Relations, Geneva, Switzerland; PhD in Law; *Career:* Lecturer, Faculty of Law, University of Casablanca, Morocco; Lecturer, National School of Public Administration; participated in conferences on the Law of the Sea, and on Refugees; *Publications:* several articles and papers on the Law of the Sea and other legal subjects published in professional journals; *Interests and Recreations:* swimming, tennis; *Languages:* Arabic, French, English; *Address:* 10 Rue du Mont Ventoux, Casablanca, Morocco; telephone: 250148.

AHMAR, Colonel Ali Abdullah Salih al-, Yemen Arab Republic army commander; born 1916; married; one son, *Religion:* Muslim; *Education:* Military College (Tank Section); Training Course at Southern Headquarters; *Career:* Lieutenant; 1st Lieutenant; Captain; Colonel; Commander of Armoured Forces; Military Commander of Taiz; *Interests and Recreations:* riding, volley-ball; *Address:* Taiz, Yemen Arab Republic.

AINI, Muhsin Ahmad al-, Yemen Arab Republic politician; born 1923, Yemen Arab Republic; *Religion:* Muslim; *Education:* Cairo University, Egypt; University of Paris, France; *Career:* teacher in Aden, 1958–61; Secretary of the Teachers' Union and Representative of Aden Trades Unions; Republican Foreign Minister following the 1962 Revolution; later appointed Permanent Representative to the UN; also accredited Ambassador to USA, 1965; Prime Minister, 1976; Ambassador of Yemen Arab Republic to USSR, 1968–70; Prime Minister, 1970; Ambassador to France, 1971; Prime Minister, 1971–72; Ambassador to UK, 1973–74; Prime Minister, 1974–75; Permanent Representative to the UN, 1979–; *Address:* Permanent Mission of Yemen Arab Republic to UN, 747 Third Avenue, New York, NY 10017.

AISHA, HRH Princess Lalla, Moroccan Royal Princess; eldest daughter of late King Mohammed V; born 1930; married; two daughters; *Religion:* Muslim; *Education:* privately in Islamic and modern subjects; *Career:* made her first public appearance 1945; first public speech at girls school inauguration in Sale, 1947; announced the Sultan's idea that Moroccan women should play a full part in national life; has promoted female emancipation; leader of Moroccan Delegation to Arab Women's Congress in Damascus, September 1957; visited Syrian front lines and was appointed Honorary Colonel of the Syrian Army; President of National Mutual Aid; played prominent part in measures for the relief of Agadir, 1960; Moroccan Ambassador to UK (Morocco's first woman ambassador), 1965–69; Ambassador to Italy, 1969–72; Honorary President of the National Union of Moroccan Women since May, 1969; *Languages:* Arabic French; *Address:* Palais Royale, Rabat, Morocco.

AISSA, Brahim, Algerian diplomat; born 19 June 1935, Algeria; married; *Education:* Diploma in Economic Science, Prague School of Economics, Czechoslovakia, 1963; *Career:* Embassy to Guinea, 1963–65; Embassy to Bulgaria, 1966–68; Department of International Organization, Ministry of Foreign Affairs, 1968–72; Delegate, International Labour Conference; Counsellor, Permanent Mission of Algeria, UN, Geneva, Switzerland, 1972; *Publications: Le Commerce Extérieur de l'Algérie et les Problèmes de sa Nationalisation,* 1963; *Languages:* Arabic, French, Czech, English; *Address:* Ministry of Foreign Affairs, 6 Rue Ibn Badran, Algiers, Algeria.

AIT-MESSAOUDENE, Said, Algerian politician/army officer; born 1933; *Career:* Major in Air Force at Officers Flying School, Salon, France, 1955; trained in various countries, and qualified as fighter pilot; member, National Liberation Army (ALN); led Algerian military missions to China, Iraq and USSR during War of Independence; course at Aeronautical Division of Moscow Military Academy; Commander of Air Force; Counsellor for Aviation Affairs in Presidency; Director General of Air Algérie, 1968; Minister of Posts and Telecommunications, 1972–77; Minister of Public Health, 1977–80; Minister of Light Industries, 1980–; *Languages:* Arabic, French; *Address:* Ministry of Light Industries, Rue Ahmed Bey de Constantine, Algiers, Algeria; telephone: 606066; telex: 52790.

AIYOUTY, Yassin al-, Eyptian UN official/academic; born 14 April 1928, Sharqiya, Egypt; married; *Education:* Diploma, Teachers Institute, Cairo, Egypt, 1948; BS, State Teachers College, Trenton, New Jersey, USA, 1953; MA, History, Rutgers University, New Brunswick, New Jersey, USA, 1954; PhD, Political Science, New York University, USA, 1966; *Career:* Teacher, Cairo, Egypt, 1948–52; Department of Public Information, UN, Geneva and New York, 1958–62; Officer in Charge, Radio and Visual Services (Arabic), UN, New York, USA, 1962–64; Special Assistant to the Executive Director, UN Institute for Training and Research, (UNITAR), 1964–70; Deputy Director of Training (UNITAR), 1970–71; Political Officer, Department of Political and Security Council Affairs, UN, New York, USA, 1971–73; Senior Political Affairs Officer, and later Principal Officer and Secretary of UN Council for Namibia, Department of Political Affairs, Trusteeship and Decolonisation , UN, 1973–; Professor of African and Middle Eastern Studies, State University of New York, Stony Brook, USA; member of the Egyptian Society of International Law, of the American Political Science Association; fellow of the African Studies Association USA, of the Middle East Studies Association for North America; *Publications: Refugees South of the Sahara, an African Dilemma,* 1970; *The UN and Decolonisation — The Role of Afro Asia,* 1971; *Africa and International Organisation,* 1974; *The Organistion of African Unity After Ten Years — A Comparative Perspective,* 1975 and 1976; numerous articles in professional journals and newspapers in Arabic and English; *Decorations:* New York University Founders Day Award, 1966; *Interests and*

Recreations: walking, cycling, gymnastics, fishing; *Languages:* Arabic, English, French, Spanish, Hebrew; *Address:* Office — Department of Political Affairs, Trusteeship and Decolonisation, UN, UN Plaza, New York, NY 10017, USA; telephone: (212) 754 1234; Residence — 2 Peter Cooper Road, New York, NY 10010, USA.

AJAJ, Safuh Galib, Jordanian businessman; born 1 December 1929; married; five sons; *Religion:* Muslim; *Education:* general; *Career:* Chairman of the Board and General Manager, Al-Zahra Manufacturing and Trading Company and Al-Nasr Company for Plastic Manufacture; owner of a factory for the production of footwear and leather goods; member of the Board of Amman Chamber of Industry, 1972–76; *Interests and Recreations:* swimming, reading, riding; *Languages:* Arabic, English; *Address:* Office— King Talal Street, Amman, Jordan; P O Box 2441, Amman, Jordan; telephone: Office — 23626, 38091; Factory — 92291; Residence — 814887.

AJMANI, Buti Bin Obaid al-, United Arab Emirates official; born 1939, Abu Dhabi; married; five sons; *Religion:* Muslim; *Education:* private education; *Career:* ADB Company; five years with the British Bank of the Middle East; Deputy Director of Ports and Customs, Abu Dhabi; Head of Personnel Department; Under Secretary, Administration and Organization Department; *Interests and Recreations:* Arabic classical poetry and literature, swimming, fishing; member of the Board of the Tourist Club; *Languages:* Arabic, English, Persian, Urdu; *Address:* P O Box 371, Abu Dhabi, United Arab Emirates; telephone: Office — 41690; Residence — 41778.

AKALWIN, Natali Olwak, Sudanese politician/academic; born Upper Nile Province, Shilluk, Sudan; *Education:* LLB, University of Khartoum; LLM, London University, UK; DPhil thesis in Shilluk Customary Law, Oxford University, UK; *Career:* Regional Minister for Regional Administration and Legal Affairs, Southern Region, 1973; Senior Lecturer in Law at the University of Khartoum; *Languages:* Arabic, English; *Address:* University of Khartoum, Khartoum, Sudan.

AKASHEH, Farid Abdullah, Jordanian politician/physician; born 14 September 1921, Karak, Jordan; married; four sons, two daughters; *Religion:* Christian; *Education:* MD, St. Joseph University, French Faculty of Medicine, Beirut, Lebanon; Wayne State University, Detroit, USA; St. Andrews University, Scotland, UK; Fellow of the American College of Surgeons, FACS; Fellow of the Royal College of Obstetricians and Gynaecologists, FRCOG; *Career:* Medical Officer for Karak District, 1950–52; Senior Medical Officer for Amman District, 1952–56; Director and Chief Surgeon, Government Maternity and Gynaecology Hospital, Amman, 1957–65; Minister of Social Welfare and Labour, 1967; Minister of Health, 1972–73; specialist in gynaecology and obstetrics; member of the Jordan Medical Association, the Royal College of Obstetricians and Gynaecologists, London, UK; *Publications:* several works on obstetrics and gynaecology in English; *Decorations:* Order of Jordanian Star, 1965, 1967; 1st Cross of the Holy Land from the Greek Orthodox Patriarch, Jerusalem, 1965; *Interests and Recreations:* reading, chess; *Languages:* Arabic, English, French; *Address:* P O Box 2173, Amman, Jordan; telephone: 41943.

AKBIK, Adnan Muhammad, Syrian banker; born 5 March 1932, Damascus, Syria; resident in Tunisia; married; one daughter, two sons; *Religion:* Muslim; *Education:* BA, Law and Economics; Doctorate of State, Paris; *Career:* joined the Syrian Bar, 1959–60; Controller, Arab Bank, Damascus, 1960–64; Assistant Manager, Arab Bank, Morocco, 1964–69; Manager of Arab Bank, Casablanca and Rabat, Morocco, 1969–72; Manager of the Arab Bank, Tunisia, 1972–79; Executive Manager, Arab Bank, Tunisia, 1979–; Lecturer, Banking School, Tunisia; *Interests and Recreations:* philately, horse riding, swimming, gardening, theatre; *Languages:* Arabic, English, French, Italian, German; *Address:* Arab Bank, P O Box 520, Tunis, Tunisia; telephone: 258840.

AKHATARZADEH, Muhammad, Bahraini businessman; born 3 July 1937, Bahrain; married; two sons, two daughters; *Religion:* Muslim; *Education:* general; *Career:* Hotel Director and partner, Moon Organisation, Moon Plaza Hotel; Managing Director, Moon Supermarket/Department Store; *Interests and Recreations:* tennis, football, swim-

ming; *Languages:* Arabic, English, Persian, Urdu; *Address:* P O Box 26218 Bahrain; telephone: 728319.

AKHRAS, Mahmud al-; Jordanian official; born 9 Janurary 1927, Jerusalem; married; one son, one daughter; *Religion:* Muslim; *Education:* ALA in Librarianship, England, 1965; FLA in Librarianship, British Library Association, 1975; *Career:* Teacher, Ministry of Education, Jordan, 1949–52; Secretary, Scholarship Committee, 1953–56; Head of Libraries Division, Ministry of Education, Jordan, 1958–61, 1964–66, 1969–79; Librarian, University of Jordan, 1962–64; Library Expert, Saudi Arabian Ministry of Education, 1966–68; Expert, Department of Documentation and Information, Arab League Educational, Scientific and Cultural Organisation, 1979–; member of the British Library Association, Jordan Library Association; Chief Editor, *Arab Magazine for Information,* Tunisia, 1980; *Publications:* Classifications in Arabic, 1965; *Manual of School Libraries,* 1972; *Palestine-Jordan Bibliography 1900–70,* 1972; *Library and Research,* 1969; *Palestine-Jordan Bibliography, 1971–75,* 1976; *Decorations:* Jordanian State Prize in Research, 1977; *Interests and Recreations:* reading; *Languages:* Arabic, English; *Address:* Arab League, Education, Scientific and Cultural Organization, P O Box 1120, Tunis, Tunisia; telephone: 892122.

AKHRAS, Shafiq Abdul Mawla, Syrian banker/economist, born 10 July 1929, Homs, Syria; married; three daughters, two sons; *Religion:* Muslim; *Education:* PhD, Financial Economics; *Career:* Inspector, then Director, Société Générale de Banques, Paris, 1952–58; Secretary General for Planning and Economic Affairs, United Arab Republic, Damascus and Cairo, 1958–61; Director General, Economic Development Organization, 1961–62; Chairman and President, Omayad Bank, Syria, 1962–65; President and Founder, Center for Economic, Financial and Social Research, Beirut, Lebanon, 1962–66; United Nations Development Organization, Vienna, Austria, 1968–71; Managing Director, Bank al Mashrik, 1971–73; Chairman, al Saudi Banque, 1973–; *Publications:* numerous studies on Arab economics, published in the *Arab Economist* and *L'Economics des Pays Arabes; Interests and Recreations:* literature, music, tennis, swimming; *Languages: Arabic, French, English; Address: Al Saudi Banque, 49–51 Avenue George V, P O Box 2708, 75008 Paris, France; 37 Avenue Foch, 75116 Paris, France; telephone: 7208608; telex: 630349.

AKIL, Fakhir Bin Hussain, Syrian academic/psychologist; born 1919, Aleppo, Syria; married; one son, two daughters; Religion: Muslim; Education: BSc, MSc, Education, American University of Beirut; PhD, Psychology, London University; Career: Professor of Psychology, Head of the Department of Psychology, College of Education, University of Damascus since 1949; member of the British Psychological Society; Adviser to UNESCO for Egypt, Jordan and Saudi Arabia; Publications: numerous books and research papers on education and psychology in Arabic and English; Interests and Recreations: walking, reading; Languages: Arabic, English, French; Address: Rushdi al Shama Jaddah, Al Najma Square, Damascus, Sryia; telephone: 228824.

AKL, Abdul Rahman, Egyptian journalist; born Qaliubiyah, Egypt; Religion: Muslim; Education: BA in Commerce, 1964; Diploma in Higher Studies in Development, 1973; Career: Editor of the Economic Section of Al-Ahram newspaper; Languages: Arabic, English; Address: Al-Ahram Newspaper, Cairo, Egypt.

AKL, Georges, Lebanese businessman/politician; born 12 February 1917, Lebanon; married; three children; Career: commerce; import-export business in wool, cereals, cotton and hides; Deputy for Zahle, 1968; Head of the Beka'a region for the Katayeb Party (Falange); Languages: Arabic, French; Address: Office — Chamber of Deputies, Place de l'Etoile, Beirut, Lebanon; telephone: 220040; Residence — Fouad 1 Street, Wattar Building, Beirut, Lebanon; telephone: 238989.

AKL, Said, Lebanese poet/academic; born 4 July 1912, Zahla, Lebanon; Education: College of Marist Brothers, Zahla, Lebanon; Career: Professor, Faculty of Letters and Lebanese Fine Arts Academy; Professor, Lebanese University; contributor to the following newspapers: Lisaan Al-Haal, Al-Sayaad and Al-Jariida; patron of the arts; founder of the Said Akl Prize, 1962; recognized for his theory of Lebanism; Publications:

The Magdalenian, Cadmus, The Book of Roses, and several other works in prose and verse; Address: Office — Furnech Chebback, Adel Chehab Street, Beirut, Lebanon; Residence — Badaro Street, Beirut, Lebanon; telephone: 380151.

AKROUF, Dawud, Algerian official, born 1934, Setfi, Algeria; married; Education: Degree in Law, University of Rennes, France; Career: Administrator, Ministry of Labour, 1963; Secretary General, Ministry of National Economy, 1963; Secretary General, Ministry of National Education, 1964; Secretary General, Ministry of Industry and Energy, 1965; Director General of National Mechanical Construction Co (SONACOME), 1968; Languages: Arabic, French; Address: SONACOME, 18 Avenue Claude Debussy, Algiers, Algeria; telephone: 669392.

AKRUSH, Anwar Atallah, Jordanian official; born 1934, Jordan; married; two sons, one daughter; Religion: Christian; Education: Licence in Literature, University of Damascus, 1968; Master of Science, Librarianship, Michigan University, USA; Career: Librarian of the State Library of Tourism and History; Librarian of the British Council Library, Amman, Jordan; President, Jordan Library Association; part-time Lecturer, University of Jordan; Publications: numerous articles in the local press on library sciences; Languages: Arabic, English, Latin, Hebrew, Turkish; Address: P O Box 634, Amman, Jordan.

AKWAA, Brigadier Muhammad Ali al-, Yemen Arab Republic army officer/politician; born 1933, Sana'a, Yemen Arab Republic; Education: Military College, Sana'a; Career: participated in movements against last three Imams of Yemen; Free Yemenis Revolution, 1948; attempted coup, 1955; revolution of 29 September 1962; leading figure in movement which ousted President al-Sallal, 1967; has held several posts in military and civil service including Assistant Military Commander, Taiz District, Head, National Security Department, Chief of Staff, Army Operations, Head, South Yemen Relief Office attached to Presidency, and Minister of the Interior, 1973–74; Address: Bir al-Azab, Sana'a, Yemen Arab Republic.

AKWAA, Ismail Ali, Yemen Arab Republic official/diplomat; born 1920; married; two sons, one daughter; *Religion:* Muslim; *Career:* 1st Secretary, Yemen Legation, Moscow, USSR; Minister Plenipotentiary and Cultural Attaché, Cairo, Egypt; Ambassador, Ministry of Foreign Affairs; second Deputy to the Minister of Foreign Affairs; Minister of Information, 1968–69; *Publications:* research papers in history, literature, criticism and genealogy, published in several scientific Arabic magazines; *Address:* P O Box 227, Sana'a, Yemen Arab Republic.

ALAMI, Driss Bin Omar al-, Moroccan official/army commander; born 1917, Morocco; married; *Religion:* Muslim; *Education:* Military Schools of Meknes, Morocco, and Saint-Cyr, France; *Career:* Officer in French army until Independence; General Staff of Royal Moroccan Army from its formation; Military Governor of Meknes, 1956; General Staff, Commander of Moroccan Forces in Tiznit region, South Morocco, 1958; Lieutenant Colonel, 1959; Director of Cadet School in Alermirimore; Officer commanding the Gendarmerie, 1960; Governor of Casablanca, Morocco, 1961; Brigadier General, 1963; Commander of Moroccan forces in the field during the Algerian border emergency, 1963; Inspector General of the Royal Forces, 1964; Major General of the Royal Moroccan Army, 1967; Minister of Posts, Telegraphs and Communications, 1970–77; currently Chairman of Royal Air Maroc; *Languages:* Arabic, French; *Address:* Royal Air Maroc, Casablanca, Morocco.

ALAMI, Musa al-, Palestinian academic/administrator; born 1895, Jerusalem; *Religion:* Muslim; *Education:* American University of Beirut, and in UK; *Career:* academic career and government services; one of the founder members of the Arab Development Society to assist underdeveloped Arab villages in Palestine, 1943; after Second World War was Palestinian Representative to the Arab League; involved in the development of Jericho area and founded a school for refugee orphan children, 1948; returned to supervise the Jericho farm, which came under the Israeli occupation, 1971.

ALAMIN, Al-Amin Abdul Latif al-, Sudanese diplomat; born 30 May 1931, Khartoum, Sudan; married; two sons; *Religion:* Muslim; *Education:* BSc in Agriculture, Cairo University, 1957; International Relations course, London School of Economics, London, 1963–64; *Career:* Assistant Inspector, Soil Department, Agricultural Research Corporation, Sudan, 1957–60; 3rd Secretary, Ministry of Foreign Affairs, Khartoum, Sudan, 1960–61; Chargé d'Affaires, Sudan Embassy, Greece, 1961–63; Consul General, Sudan Embassy, Egypt, 1964–66; 1st Secretary, India, 1966–68; Counsellor, Sudan Embassy, Uganda, 1968–71; Counsellor, Sudan Embassy, London, 1971–72; Chargé d'Affaires, Sudan Embassy, USSR, 1972–73; Director, East European Department, Ministry of Foreign Affairs, Khartoum, 1973–74; Director, Minister Office, Ministry of Foreign Affairs, 1974–75; Director General, Political Affairs Department, Ministry of Foreign Affairs, Sudan, 1975–76; Ambassador to Nigeria, 1976–78; Sudan Ambassador to Scandinavian Countries, 1978–; represented Sudan in several conferences and congresses: Non-Alignment Conference, 1964, Arab Summit, 1964, UN General Assembly, 1975; *Publications:* papers for discussion, *Ideology in Soviet Foreign Policy, Brinksmanship in Foreign Policy;* Lectures *Sudan's Role in Africa, Problems of Development in Developing Countries with Sudan as Case Study; Interests and Recreations:* swimming, mini golf, squash, folklore, music; *Languages:* Arabic, English, French, Russian; *Address:* Embassy of the Democratic Republic of Sudan, Box 16169, 10324 Stockholm, Sweden; telephone: 0824 6695.

ALAMUDDIN, Shaikh Najib, Lebanese politician/businessman; born 9 March 1909, Baakline, Lebanon; married; two sons, one daughter; *Education:* BA in Engineering and Mathematics, American University of Beirut, AUB, Beirut, Lebanon, 1929–30; postgraduate studies, University College of Exeter, UK, 1936–37; *Career:* Teacher of Mathematics, AUB, Lebanon, 1930–33; Chief Inspector of Mathematics, Department of Education, Transjordan Government, 1933–36; Inspector General of Customs, Commerce and Industry, Transjordan Government, 1939–40; Chief Secretary, Transjordan Government Secretariat, 1940–42; Founder and Chief Executive, Near East Resources Company, Beirut, 1942–52; Director General, Middle East Airlines (MEA), 1952–56; Chairman of the Board and President, MEA, 1956–77; Honorary Chairman and Board Adviser, MEA, 1977–;

Minister of Information and Tourism, Lebanon, 1965; Minister of Public Works and Transport, 1966; Minister of Public Works and Transport in Amin Al-Hafiz Cabinet, 1973; member of the Board of Chamber of Commerce and Industry; member of the Executive Committee, International Air Transport Association, IATA, of the Board of Directors of the Institut du Transport Aérien, 1974–77, of the National Tourist Board, Lebanon, of the Board of Trustees, AUB; *Decorations:* Commander, National Order of the Cedar, Lebanon; Gold Medal, Order of Merit, Lebanon; Medal, Order of the Republic, Egypt; Medal, Jordanian Order of Independence; Chevalier de la Légion d'Honneur, France, 1967; and various others; *Interests and Recreations:* farming; *Languages:* Arabic, English, French; *Address:* Alamuddin Building, Verdun Street, Beirut, Lebanon.

ALAOUI, Moulay Abdallah, Moroccan official/businessman; born 10 July 1932, Casablanca; married; two daughters, two sons; *Education:* Institute of Higher Studies, Rabat; postgraduate, National School of Administration; *Career:* Deputy, Ministry of Youth and Sports, 1955; Principal Private Secretary, 1956–58; joined Mobil Oil Group, 1958; Principal Private Secretary to the Prime Minister, 1964; Commercial Director, Mobil Oil, 1965; Adviser on East Africa, Paris; Director General, Mobil Oil, Morocco, 1974; Committee Member, International Chamber of Commerce; *Interests and Recreations:* swimming, tennis; *Languages:* Arabic, French, English; *Address:* Office — 23 Rue Allal Ben Abdallah, Casablanca, Morocco; telephone 224174; Residence — 1 Allée de Mimosas, Casblanca, Morocco; telephone: 360029.

ALAOUI, Moulay Ahmad al-, Moroccan politician/journalist; born 1919, Fes, Morocco; married; *Religion:* Muslim; *Education:* Medical Studies in France; *Career:* worked for the nationalist cause and for the Istiqlal (Independence) Party in Paris; Head of Press and Service Information on return of HM the late King Mohammed V from exile; Minister of Information and Tourism, 1960; Minister of Tourism, 1960; Minister of Tourism and Fine Arts, 1965; Director of the Royal Cabinet; founding member of the Parti Socialiste Démocratique, 1964; Minister of Industry and Mines, 1966; portfolios for Commerce and Crafts were added in March 1967; Minister of State for Tourism and Handicrafts, 1968; Minister for National Advancement and Handicrafts, 1969; elected representative for Erfoud in legislative elections of August, 1970; Director of *Maroc Soir,* 1971; Director of *Le Matin,* 1972; Minister of State, 1982–; *Languages:* Arabic, French; *Address:* Prime Minister's Office, Rabat, Morocco.

ALAOUI, Mustafa Bilarbi, Moroccan diplomat/politician; born 1923, Fes, Morocco; married; *Religion:* Muslim; *Education:* at Fes and School for Higher Studies, Rabat; Degree in Law Studies; *Career:* joined Driss M'Hammedi in nationalist activities in Atlas Mountains; Director of Cabinet of the Minister of the Interior, after Independence; Director of Political Affairs at the Ministry of the Interior, 1959–60; active in Union Nationale des Forces Populaire, UNFP, Secretariat, and helped to establish the Farmers Union; Director of Political Affairs in the Ministry of Islamic Affairs, 1965; Governor of Casablanca, 1971; Ambassador to Italy, 1977–; *Decorations:* Commander of the Order of the Throne, Morocco, 1972; Order of Massira, Morocco; Officer of the Order of Merit; *Languages:* Arabic, French; *Address:* Embassy of Morocco, Via degli Scialoia 32, Rome, Italy.

ALAQI, Muhammad Abdul Qadir, Saudi Arabian diplomat/publisher; born 15 July 1932; *Religion:* Muslim; *Education:* BSc in Political Science, Cairo University, Egypt; *Career:* Saudi missions in Jordan, Switzerland, Guinea, Japan, UN, France, Korea; Chargé d'Affaires, Embassy to Republic of Korea; former Editor in Chief of *Al-Madina* daily newspaper; co-owner and member of Board of *Al-Madina* daily newspaper; *Publications:* several articles in local press; *Interests and Recreations:* reading, travel, swimming; *Address:* Ministry of Foreign Affairs, P O Box 495, Jeddah, Saudi Arabia; telephone: 6421322; telex: 401104 KHARJI SJ.

ALAWI, Mahmud al-, Bahraini politician; born 1910; *Religion:* Muslim; *Education:* Bahrain and University of Agra, India; *Career:* Clerk in Finance Department, Bahrain Government; Accounts Officer; Head of Finance Department, 1950; appointed to State Council, 1970; Minister of Finance and National Economy, 1971–76; retired for health reasons, 1976; special adviser to Prime Minister, 1976; *Languages:* Arabic, English; *Address:* The Prime Minister's Office, Manama, Bahrain; telephone: 253361.

ALAWI, Yusuf al-, Omani diplomat; born 1945, Salalah, Oman; married; *Religion:* Muslim; *Education:* in UK; *Career:* member of the Omani Goodwill Mission to the Arab Capitals, 1971; 2nd Secretary to the Omani Embassy, Egypt 1972, and later 1st Secretary; Chargé d'Affaires, Embassy of Oman to Lebanon, 1973; Ambassador to Lebanon, 1973–74; Under Secretary, Ministry of Foreign Affairs, 1974–; *Languages:* Arabic, English; *Address:* Ministry of Foreign Affairs, P O Box 252, Muscat, Oman; telephone: 701771; telex: 3337 MFA MB.

ALGOSAIBI, Ghazi Abdul Rahman, Saudi Arabian politician; born 1940; *Education:* MA in International Relations; PhD in International Relations; *Career:* Lecturer, Riyadh University; Dean, Faculty of Commerce, Riyadh University; Director General, Railways Authority; Minister of Industry and Electricity, 1975; member of Board of: Arab Investment Co, Real Estate Development Fund, Riyadh Charity Society, Municipal Council of Dammam, Supreme Council of Youth Welfare; Adviser, Ministry of Finance and National Economy; Adviser, Ministry of Defence and Aviation; Secretary General, Supreme Council of Oil; Minister of Industry and Electricity, 1979–; *Publications:* articles in local and foreign newspapers; three collections of poems; *Interests and Recreations:* reading, swimming; *Address:* Ministry of Industry and Electricity, P O Box 5729, Riyadh, Saudi Arabia; telephone: 4775447; telex: 201154 INDEL SJ.

ALI, Abdul Aziz Muhammad, Sudanese engineer; resident in United Arab Emirates; born 10 October 1942, Medani, Sudan; married; one son, one daughter; *Education:* BS in Civil Engineering; MSc in Structures; member of Institution of Civil Engineers, UK; *Career:* worked for Sudan Government, 1966–75; Resident Engineer, Sarjah Sport Centre, 1975–78; Chief Structural Engineer, Public Works Department, Abu Dhabi, 1978–; *Interests and Recreations:* reading, painting, walking; *Languages:* Arabic, English; *Address:* P O Box 3, Public Works Department, Abu Dhabi, United Arab Emirates; telephone: 328320; telex: 22663 EM.

ALI, Abdullah M., Kuwaiti economist; born 1937, Kuwait; married; one son, one daughter; *Religion:* Muslim; *Education:* BSc in Mathematics and Statistics, 1962; MA in Economics, 1965; Diploma in National Accounts, 1965–66; *Career:* Assistant to Chief of Statistical Department, Ministry of Education, Kuwait, 1961–62; Teacher in Shuwaikh Secondary School, 1962–63; Teaching Assistant and Lecturer in Statistics, North Dakota, USA, 1964–65; Lecturer in Statistics and National Accounts, Kuwait Institute of Economic and Social Planning, 1966–69; Co-Director, Kuwait Institue of Economic and Social Planning, 1969–71; Director, Kuwait Institute of Economic and Social Planning, 1971–72; Director General, The Arab Planning Institute, 1972–; *Publications: Balance of Payments of Kuwait, 1965/66 to 1967/68; National Accounts of Kuwait, 1965/66 to 1967/68; Interests and Recreations:* theatre, reading, member of Kuwait Cine Club; *Languages:* Arabic, English; *Address:* The Arab Planning Institute, Kuwait, P O Box 5834, Safat, Kuwait; telephone: 431897.

ALI, Ahmad Muhammad, Saudi Arabian official; born 1934, Medina, Saudi Arabia; *Religion:* Muslim; *Education:* PhD in Public Administration and Fiscal Management; *Career:* Director of Islamic Institute, Aden; Deputy Rector of King Abdul Aziz University; Deputy Minister of Education for Technical Affairs; member of King Abdul Aziz University Council, of Riyadh University Council, of Petroleum and Minerals University Council, and of Imam Muhammad Bin Saud University Council, of the Administrative Board of the Saudi Credit Bank, of the Executive Board of the Arab League Educational, Cultural and Scientific Organisation (ALECSO); founding member of the Board of King Abdul Aziz University; President of the Islamic Development Bank; participated in several UNESCO conferences and conferences of ALECSO; *Publications:* PhD thesis on Pre-Audit System in the Kingdom of Saudi Arabia and the State of New York: a comparative study; *Address:* Islamic Development Bank, P O Box 5925, Jeddah, Saudi Arabia; telephone: 29129, 33995; telex: 401407, 401137 SJ

ALI, General Kamal Hassan, Egyptian politician/army officer; born 1921; married; two children; *Religion:* Muslim; *Career:* various positions in the regular army from Tank Squadron Commander to Director of Armour; Assistant Minister of War with special responsibility for training and development, 1975; Minister of Defence and Commander in Chief of Egyptian Armed Forces; Minister of Foreign Affairs; attended several military courses in USSR, Bovington, UK, 1949, and Lulworth, UK, 1950, and Nassir Academy, Egypt; *Languages:* Arabic, English; *Address:* Ministry of Foreign Affairs, Giza, Cairo, Egypt.

ALI, HRH Prince Moulay, Moroccan businessman/former diplomat; born 1924; Marrakech, Morocco; cousin of HM King Hassan II; married; one child; *Religion:* Muslim; *Education:* in Marrakesh and Lycée Lyautey, Casablanca; *Career:* arrested by Protectorate Authorities on political charges at time when HM King Mohammed V was sent into exile; joined the Royal Family in voluntary exile in Madagascar until returning to Morocco; accompanied HM the King on state visits to US, March 1963, and to France, June 1963; represented King Hassan at marriage of King Constantine of Greece, September 1964; Director of several commercial companies in Casablanca; Ambassador to France, 1964–66; on return became President of the National Sugar Company (COSUMAR); *Decorations:* decorated by General de Gaulle as Grand Officer of the Légion d'Honneur; *Languages:* Arabic, French; *Address:* Compagnie Sucrière Marocaine et de Raffinage, P O Box 3098, 8 rue Al-Mouatamid Ibnou Abbad, Casablanca, Morocco; telephone: 242345.

ALI, Muhammad Yusuf al-, Qatari businessman/engineer; born 1941; married; *Religion:* Muslim; *Education:* graduate in Electrical Engineering, University of Colorado, USA; practical training in UK; *Career:* former Chairman of Qatar National Cement Company; now Director of Qatar Electricity Department; business interests include association with Qatar Trading Company; Arab Co-chairman of Science and Technology Subcommittee in Euro-Arab Dialogue; *Address:* Qatar Trading Co, P O Box 51 and 116, Doha, Qatar.

ALI, Said Malik al-, Iraqi engineer; *Religion:* Muslim; *Education:* engineering studies; *Career:* Director General of the Agricultural Department in the Ministry of Planning; *Address:* Ministry of Planning, Baghdad, Iraq.

ALIER, Abel, Sudanese politician; born 1933, Bor District, Upper Nile, Sudan; *Religion:* Christian; *Education:* in Southern Sudan; LLB, University of Khartoum, 1959; Law Studies as Research Fellow, University of London, UK, 1961–62; MA in Law, University of Yale, USA, 1962–64; *Career:* worked as District Judge in Al-Obeid, Wad Medani and Khartoum; resigned in 1965 to take part in the Round Table Conference on the South; represented Bor District in National Assembly, 1968–69; member of the Twelve-Man Committee to make constitutional and administrative proposals for the solution of the Southern problem; leading member of the Southern Front Party; Minister of Supply and of Internal Trade, 1969; Minister of Works, 1970; Minister of State for Southern Affairs, 1971; appointed Vice President following the October 1971 Presidential Election; member of the Preparatory Committee of the Sudanese Socialist Union (SSU), 1971; has been member of the SSU Political Bureau since its inception; played leading part in the negotiations leading to the conclusion of the Addis Ababa Agreement of February 1972 on the Southern Sudan; President of the Provisional Higher Executive Council set up under the agreement; nominated by President Nimeiri and SSU for election as President of the Higher Executive Council, December 1973, and elected unopposed; member of Board of Directors, Industrial Planning Corporation; member of National Scholarship Board; Second Vice President, January 1975–; *Languages:* Arabic, English; *Address:* People's Palace, Khartoum, Sudan.

ALIREZA, Abdullah Abdul Ghaffar, Kuwaiti businessman; born 1918, Saudi Arabia; married; two sons, two daughters; *Religion:* Muslim; *Education:* St. Xavier's, Bombay, India; *Career:* President of the Alireza Group of Companies, with extensive interests in the Middle East and other countries, and many joint ventures with important European and American companies; *Languages:* Arabic, English, French, Persian, Urdu; *Address:* Office — The Alireza Group of Companies, P O Box 60, Safat, Kuwait; telephone: 816836, 840163; telex: 22030 REZAYAT FKT/22962 NALCO KT.

ALIREZA, Abdullah Ahmad, Saudi Arabian businessman; born 1944, Jeddah, Saudi Arabia; married, three children; *Religion:* Muslim; *Education:* Falah School and Hailebury College, UK; BA Political Science, Whittier College, USA; MA, Public Administration; *Languages:* Arabic, English; *Address:* P O Box 8, Jeddah, Saudi Arabia.

ALIREZA, Abdullah Muhammad, Saudi Arabian official; born 1940 in Jeddah, Saudi Arabia; *Religion:* Muslim; *Education:* in UK and University of California, Berkleley, USA; *Career:* Head of International Marketing, General Petroleum and Mineral Organization, 1971–; Ministry of Petroleum; Chairman of ARGAS, the Saudi official geological service, 1970–72; *Languages:* Arabic, English; *Address:* ARGAS, P O Box 2109, Jeddah, Saudi Arabia.

ALIREZA, Ahmad Yusuf Zainal, Saudi Arabian businessman; born 1916; married; five sons; *Religion:* Muslim; *Career:* Chief Executive of Hajji Abdullah Alireza Co, Jeddah; *Languages:* Arabic, English, Urdu; *Address:* Hajji Abdullah Alireza Co Ltd, P O Box 8, Jeddah, Saudi Arabia.

ALIREZA, Ali Ibrahim, Saudi Arabian businessman; born 14 July 1950; *Religion:* Muslim; *Education:* BA in Political Science, Roosevelt University, Chicago, USA, 1974; MA in International Relations, University of Sussex, UK, 1975; *Career:* President of Transcontinental Corporations (Trading and Transportation); *Interests and Recreations:* classical music, tennis, swimming; *Languages:* Arabic, English; *Address:* P O Box 7101, Jeddah, Saudi Arabia; telephone: 667 2958, 667 2957.

ALIREZA, Fahd Muhammad Abdullah, Saudi Arabian businessman; born 25 December 1946, Jeddah, Saudi Arabia; *Religion:* Muslim; *Education:* Seaford College, UK; BSc in Business Administration, 1967; MA in Business Administration, 1969; *Career:* Trainee with International Telephone and Telegraph (ITT), New York, 1970; professional experience of chemical factories, shipping companies and commercial enterprises; member of Jeddah Chamber of Commerce, International Business Fraternity (Delta Sigma Pi); member of Board of International Chemical Industries and Trade Marketing, Development and Investment; Chairman of

Board of Reza Investment Company; Managing Director of International Chemical Industries; *Interests and Recreations:* travel, chess, swimming; *Languages:* Arabic, English; *Address:* Alireza Compound, Kilo 5, Mecca Road, Jeddah, Saudi Arabia; telephone: Office — Jeddah 33007, 26409; Residence — Jeddah 31371.

ALIREZA, Faisal Ali Abdullah, Saudi Arabian businessman; born 1945; married; one child; *Religion:* Muslim; *Education:* in USA; *Career:* joint business ventures with western companies; *Languages:* Arabic, English; *Address:* P O Box 90, Al Khabar, Saudi Arabia.

ALIREZA, Hisham Ahmad, Saudi Arabian businessman; born Jeddah, Saudi Arabia; *Religion:* Muslim; *Education:* Wellington College, UK; University of Berkeley, USA; *Career:* worked for Charterhouse Group, Morgan Grenfell, London, Morgan Stanley Inc in Paris and New York; currently Chairman, Saudi Bulk Transport; Executive Director, Xenel Industries, Jeddah; *Languages:* Arabic, English; *Address:* P O Box 8, Jeddah, Saudi Arabia.

ALIREZA, Hussain Ali Hussain, Saudi Arabian businessman; born 1931; *Religion:* Muslim; *Education:* MA Economics, University of California, Berkeley, USA; *Career:* member of Board of Saudi Arabian Airlines; General Agent for Mazda cars; former member of Board of Jeddah Chamber of Commerce; Founder and member of the Board of Directors of the Saudi American Bank; *Address:* P O Box 40, Jeddah, Saudi Arabia; telephone: Office — Jeddah 23509; Residence — Jeddah 32230.

ALIREZA, Ibrahim Yusuf Zainal, Saudi Arabian businessman; married; *Religion:* Muslim; *Career:* former businessman in Pakistan and India, now retired; shareholder in Hajji Alireza Company; *Languages:* Arabic, English; *Address:* P O Box 8, Jeddah, Saudi Arabia.

ALIREZA, Khalid Ahmad, Saudi Arabian businessman; born 1948, Jeddah, Saudi Arabia; *Religion:* Muslim; *Education:* Wellington College, UK; BSc and ME Industrial Engineering and Operational Research, University of California, Berkeley, California, USA; *Career:* Executive Director, Xenel

Industries Ltd; Chairman, Saudi Cable Co Ltd; member of the Board, Jeddah Chamber of Commerce; *Languages:* Arabic, English; *Address:* P O Box 8, Jeddah, Saudi Arabia.

ALIREZA, Mahmud Yusuf Zainal, Saudi Arabian businessman; born 1929, Jeddah, Saudi Arabia; married; five children; *Religion:* Muslim; *Education:* BA, University of California, Berkeley, USA, 1954; Postgraduate studies in Law, Harvard University, 1955; postgraduate Diploma in Law, King's College, London University, UK, 1957; *Career:* Partner and Director, Hajji Abdullah Alireza and Co Ltd; member of the Board of Laing Wimpey Alireza Ltd, of Standard Electric Alireza, of IMECCO, of Saudi Arabian Maritime Co Ltd, of the original Board of Founders of the Red Sea Club under the Chairmanship of HRH Prince Muhammad al Faisal; Chairman of the Board of TKK Alireza Ltd; *Interests and Recreations:* underwater fishing, hunting, bridge, photography; *Address:* P O Box 8, Jeddah, Saudi Arabia; telephone: Office — Jeddah 642 2233; Residence — 636 0590.

ALIREZA, Muhammad Abdullah, Saudi Arabian businessman/diplomat; born 1911; *Religion:* Muslim; *Education:* in India; *Career:* Minister of Commerce, 1954–58; former Adviser to the Ministry of Finance and National Economy; President of the Jeddah Chamber of Commerce; Ambassador to Egypt, 1964–68; Ambassador to France, 1971–78; President, Hajji Abdullah Alireza Company, 1978–; *Languages:* Arabic, English, French; *Address:* Hajji Abdullah Alireza Company, P O Box 8, Jeddah, Saudi Arabia.

ALIREZA, Muhammad Ahmad, Saudi Arabian engineer; born 1942, Saudi Arabia; married; three children; *Religion:* Muslim; *Education:* Haileybury College, UK; MSc in Civil Engineering, Cornell University, USA; *Career:* Chairman of Xenel Industries Ltd; *Languages:* Arabic, English; *Address:* P O Box 8, Jeddah, Saudi Arabia.

ALIREZA, Shaikh Ali Abdullah, Saudi Arabian diplomat/businessman; born 1920; married; three sons; *Religion:* Muslim; *Education:* Victoria College, Alexandria, Egypt and University of Southern California, USA; *Career:* Minister of State; special aide to the then Prince Faisal at the early General Assemblies of the United Nations; accompan-

ied Prince Faisal to the Bandung Conference of Afro-Asian States, 1955; businessman and member of the Board of the Saudi Arabia Monetary Agency, 1971–; Ambassador to USA; Deputy Minister, Econcomic and Cultural Affairs Deaprtment; *Languages:* Arabic, English; *Address:* Ministry of Foreign Affairs, P O Box 495, Jeddah, Saudi Arabia; telephone: 6433721.

ALLAF, Ibrahim Khalil al-, Saudi Arabian official; born 1931, Mecca, Saudi Arabia; *Education:* BA, Arabic Language, Literature and Islamic Study, Cairo University, Cairo, Egypt, 1953; *Career:* teacher, Assistant Principal, Mecca Educational Institute, Mecca, Saudi Arabia, 1953; Inspector General, Ministry of Education, 1957; Director, News Department, Ministry of Information, Jeddah, Saudi Arabia, 1957; Press and Publication Department; Director of Public Libraries Department, Ministry of Pilgrimage and Waqfs, 1962; Cultural Adviser, Ministry of Pilgrimage and Waqfs, 1965; Supervisor, Muslim World League Library, Mecca, Saudi Arabia, 1975–77; retired from government service, 1977, devoting time to political, literary, historical and Islamic studies; *Publications:* four collections of poetry; *Decorations:* Certificate of Merit, Dictionary of International Biography, Cambridge, 1976; Certificate of Merit, Marquis Publications, 1978/79; *Interests and Recreations:* reading, writing poetry, travel; member of Mecca Cultural Club; *Address:* Shubaika Quarter, Allaf Building, Mecca, Saudi Arabia; telephone: 24288.

ALLAF, Muwaffaq, Syrian diplomat; born 1930; married; *Career:* Syrian Diplomatic Service; Permanent Representative of Syria to UN, Geneva; Head of International Organizations Department, Ministry of Foreign Affairs; Permanent Representative, UN General Assembly, New York, USA; *Languages:* Arabic, English; *Address:* UN Headquarters, New York, USA.

ALLAM, Muhanmmad Abdul Khaliq, Egyptian official/educationalist; born 21 December 1921, Cairo, Egypt; married; two sons, one daughter; *Religion:* Muslim; *Education:* Diploma, Higher Institute of Education, 1940–44; MA in Physical Education, Ohio State University, USA, 1948–49; Directors Degree in Recreation and in Health Education, Indiana University, USA, 1953–55;

ALLAM

PhD in Health and Safety Education, In-
diana University, USA, 1955; Honorary
Degree of Doctor of Law, Indiana University,
1979; *Career:* Professor, Faculty of Physical
Education, 1950–56; Assistant Secretary
General of Supreme Council for Youth
Welfare, 1956–63; Director General of Plan-
ning, Ministry of Youth, 1963–66; Dean of
Admissions and Registration, American
University of Cairo, 1966–71; Project Man-
ager, United Nations Development Pro-
gramme (UNDP), Project in Sudan, 1971–
72; Vice President for Student Development,
American University in Cairo, 1973–; Expert
in Youth Welfare for the Arab League;
member of the Council of Helwan University,
Cairo, Egypt, and of the Education Board of
Cairo University; Head of the Commission of
Faculties of Physical Education Supreme
Council of National Universities; Board
Member of the Egyptian Society for the
Dissemination of Universal Culture and
Knowledge (ESDUCK); *Publications:* a book
on youth welfare; translation into Arabic of a
work on world history of physical education;
co-author of *The World Today in Health,
Physical Education and Recreation,* a chap-
ter on physical education and recreation in
Egypt and Africa; *Interests and Recreations:*
reading, music, swimming, tennis; member of
the Gizera Sporting Club; member of the
Automobile Club; member of the Hunting
Club; member of the National Sporting Club;
Languages: Arabic, English, French; *Address:* American University of Cairo, P O
Box 1125, Cairo, Egypt; telephone: 26229,
819921.

ALOUSI, Khalil Ibrahim Akif al-, Iraqi
physician; born 23 July 1923, Baghdad, Iraq;
married; two sons; *Religion:* Muslim; *Education:* MB, ChB, PhD, Pathology; *Career:*
Pathologist, Professor of Pathology, College
of Medicine, University of Baghdad, Iraq;
Head of Department of Pathology; retired
from University in 1975; private practitioner
in pathology; founding member of Iraqi
Cancer Association; *Publications: Aids to
Pathological Histology,* 1969, in English;
numerous research papers in professional
medical journals, in English and Arabic;
Interests and Recreations: swimming, horse
riding; *Languages:* Arabic, Turkish, English;
Address: Office — Al Alousi Laboratory,
Rass Al-Qarih, Rashid Street, Baghdad,
Iraq; telephone: 888 9224, 443 7227.

ALWAN, Muhammad Hassan, Iraqi UN
official/diplomat; born 12 November 1923,
Baghdad, Iraq; married; two sons; *Regligion:*
Muslim; *Education:* BA, American Univer-
sity of Beirut, Lebanon; MA in International
Relations and Organizations; MBA in
Management and International Finance,
Graduate School of Business, Fordham
University, New York; *Career:* government
service; Chief of Bills Department, Rafidain
Bank, Baghdad, 1948–49; Attaché, Iraqi
Ministry of Foreign Affairs, 1949; 3rd Secre-
tary, Embassy to Syria, 1949–51; Vice
Consul, Khorramshahr, Iran, 1951–54; 2nd
Secretary, Embassy to Iran, 1954–55; 1st
Secretary, Embassy to USA, 1955–60; Direc-
tor, Department of UN and International
Organizations, 1960–61; Chargé d'Affaires,
Embassy to Yugoslavia, 1961–63; Chargé
d'Affaires, Embassy to Nigeria, 1963–64;
Counsellor, Embassy to Lebanon, 1964–66;
Director General, Department of UN and
International Organizations, 1967–71; Am-
bassador, Permanent Representative to the
UN European Office, Geneva, Switzerland,
1971–72; Representative at the UN General
Assembly Sessions, 1957–71; Head of Iraqi
Delegation to UNCTAD, 1971; member of
UN Advisory Committee for Administrative
and Budgetary Questions, 1971–73; partici-
pated in Colgate University Conference on
Foreign Affairs, Africa and the Middle East,
New York, 1957, in the Summer Conference
on Political, Economic and Social Conditions
of Middle Eastern Countries, Middle East
Institute, Washington D.C., 1956–60, in the
Preparatory Conference of the First Non-
Aligned Countries, Cairo, Egypt, 1961, in the
Non-Aligned First Summit Conference of
Heads of State and Governments, Belgrade,
Yugoslavia, 1961, in the UN International
Conference on Human Rights, Tehran, Iran,
1968, in the Preparatory Conference of Third
Non Aligned Countries, Dar es-Salaam,
Tanzania, 1970, in the Non Aligned Third
Summit Conference of Heads of State and
Government, Lusaka, Zambia, 1970; *Publi-
cations: Algeria before the United Nations,*
New York, 1959; *The Dynamics of Neu-
tralism in the Arab World,* San Francisco,
1964; *Decorations:* Order of St. Silvestro,
Holy See; Knight of American Redemption,
Government of Libria; *Interests and Recrea-
tions:* travel, swimming, tennis; *Languages:*
Arabic, English, French, Persian; *Address:*
Office — United Nations Rm LX 1209, P O
Box 20, Grand Central Station, New York,

NY 10017, USA; telephone: (212) 754 1234; Residence — 39 Howard Park Drive, Tenafly, New Jersey 07670, USA; telephone: (201) 569 8713.

AMAD, Muhammad Abdul Ghani al-, Jordanian journalist; born 1930, Salt, Jordan; married; *Education:* BA in Political Science and Economics, 1955; *Career:* Bank Manager, 1962–71; Director of *Al-Ra'i* newspaper, 1972–75; Chief Editor of *Jordan Times,* 1975–; *Address:* P O Box 67120, Amman, Jordan.

AMAMI, Salahiddin al-, Tunisian engineer; born 20 January 1936, Sfax, Tunisia; married; two daughters, one son; *Religion:* Muslim; *Education:* Diploma, Institut National Agronomique de Paris, 1959–62; *Career:* Researcher and Principal Engineer, Laboratory of Bioclimatology, INRAT, Tunis, 1962–64; Head of the Laboratory of Bioclimatology, 1962–74; Tunisian counterpart for FAO Projects, 1963–67; Chief Engineer, 1971; Director of the Center of Research of Rural Engineering and of Project CATID, 1974–; General Engineer, 1979; *Publications:* numerous papers and researches published in professional journals and magazines; *Interests and Recreations:* history of agriculture in the Mediterranean; *Languages:* Arabic, French, English; *Address:* Office— CRGR, P O Box 10 Ariana, Tunisia; telephone: 231 634; Residence — 74 Avenue de l'Afrique El Menzah 5, Tunis, Tunisia; telephone: 231 139.

AMERI, Abdul Qadir Braik al-, Qatari diplomat; born 25 November 1943, Doha, Qatar; married; two sons; *Religion:* Muslim; *Education:* LLB, Beirut Arab University, 1972; Diploma of Graduate Studies in General Law, Institute of Law, Political and Administrative Sciences Faculty, University of Algeria; *Career:* Employee at the Qatar Petroleum Company for 8 years; 3rd Secretary, Qatari Foreign Ministry, 1972; Ambassador, Qatari Foreign Ministry, 1974; Ambassador to Algeria, 1974; non-resident Ambassador to Mauritania, 1974; Ambassador, Qatari Foreign Ministry, 1979; Ambassador to USA, 1980; *Interests and Recreations:* music, reading; *Languages:* Arabic, English; *Address:* New Hampshire Ave, NW Flat 1180, Washington, D.C. 20037; telephone: (202) 3380111.

AMHAWI, Farid al-, Arab-American engineer; born 29 June 1941, Alexandria, Egypt; married; two sons; *Religion:* Muslim; *Education:* BSc in Electrical Engineering, Alexandria University, Cairo, Egypt; PhD, Nuclear Engineering; *Career:* Reactor Engineer, Atomic Energy Establishment, Egypt, 1963–66; Research Engineer, Institute of Atomic Engineering, Norway, 1967–68; Teaching Assistant at North Carolina University, USA, 1968–72; Nuclear Engineer at Carolina Nuclear Power Reactor, USA, 1971–72; Senior Engineer, General Electric Nuclear Energy, 1972–; Manager General Electric Nuclear Power Reactor, Core Performances Systems; *Decorations:* The Egyptian President Finest Degree Award in Sports Achievement, 1964; *Interests and Recreations:* fencing, represented the Egyptian National Team in the World Olympic Games in Rome, 1960, and Tokyo, 1964; member of the American Nuclear Society; *Languages:* Arabic, English, French; *Address:* Office — G.E. Nuclear Energy, 175 Curtner Avenue, San José, California, USA; telephone: 297 3000; Residence -- 2070 Lucretiva Avenue, 201 San José, California, USA; telephone: 279 1590.

AMIN, Abdul Fattah Muhammad, Iraqi politician; born 1932, Salahuddin Governorate, Iraq; *Education:* graduated from College of Commerce and Economics, Baghdad University, 1955; *Career:* Ambassador to Lebanon, 1969; Under Secretary, Ministry of Economy, 1973; elected member of Baath Party Regional Command, 1974; Minister of State without Portfolio, 1977; member of the Revolutionary Command Council, 1977; retired from post as Minister of State, 1977; *Address:* Ministry of Cabinet Affairs, Baghdad, Iraq.

AMIN, AL-Tigani Muhammad al-, Sudanese official/agriculturalist; born 1 January 1934, Al-Obeid, Sudan; married; two sons; *Religion:* Muslim; *Education:* BSc in Agriculture, Cairo University, Egypt, 1956; PhD, Entomology, Rostock University, Germany, 1961; Diploma, Nematology, Netherlands, 1968; *Career:* Senior Scientist and Head of Entomology Section, the Agricultural Research Corporation, Sudan, 1970–78; Assistant Professor, 1976; Professor of Entomology, 1978; National Coordinator for Entomology Research, 1978–80; Director, Jazira Agricultural Research Station, 1980–; member of FAO/UNEP Panel of Experts on Integrated

Pest Control, Plant Protection Teams of the Arab Agricultural Organization, German Agricultural Society, Egyptian Entomological Society, and others; *Publications:* numerous research papers published in professional Sudanese and foreign journals; *Interests and Recreations:* swimming, football, reading Arabic literature and poetry; *Languages:* Arabic, German, English; *Address:* P O Box 126, Wadi Medani, Sudan.

AMIN, Muhammad Jassim al-, Iraqi diplomat/politician born 1930, Baghdad, Iraq; married; one son, three daughters; *Religion:* Muslim; *Education:* BSc in Mathematics; *Career:* Teacher of Mathematics and Physics at Iraqi secondary schools, 1955–63; Cultural Attaché at the Embassy of Iraq to Egypt, 1963–64; Teacher at the Iraqi School in Morocco, 1965–68; Vice Governor of Baghdad and Mosul, 1969–70; Director General of Administrative Affairs, Ministry of Information, Iraq, 1970–77; Director of Iraqi News Agency, Beirut; Director General of Information, Ministry of Information; Editor in Chief of *Al Thawra* newpaper; Minister of Information; Ambassador, Ministry of Foreign Affairs, Baghdad, Iraq; Ambassador of Iraq to the United Arab Emirates, 1978–80; *Interests and Recreations:* poetry, literature; *Languages:* Arabic, English; *Address:* Ministry of Foreign Affairs, Baghdad, Iraq.

AMIN, Mustafa, Egyptian journalist; born 1912; *Religion:* Muslim: *Education:* MSc, School of Foreign Service, Georgetown University, Washington D.C.; *Career:* Deputy in Parliament, 1945; founder of weekly newspaper *Akhbar al-Yaum* in collaboration with his late twin brother Ali Amin; launched weekly illustrated *Akhbar al-Saa'a,* 1946, and daily *Al-Akhbar,* 1952; together with his twin brother acceded to joint editorship of *AL-Mussawwar* and affliates, 1960; returned as Chairman of the Board, 1962; arrested and imprisoned following increasing disagreements with President Nassir's politics, 1966; released by late President Sadat in January 1974 and returned to journalism as Editor in Chief of *Akhbar al-Yaum; Publications: My First Year in Prison;* and numerous other books; *Languages:* Arabic, English; *Address:* Akhbar al-Yaum, 6 Sahafa Street, Cairo, Egypt.

AMIN, Nafisa Ahmad al-, Sudanese politician; *Religion:* Muslim; *Education:* Teacher Training College, Omdurman, Sudan; course in Domestic Science at Hull, UK; *Career:* entered teaching profession; taught in Teachers Training College; elected member of the Executive Council of the Blue Nile Province; held office in the former Women's Union in the Blue Nile Province and later President of Sudan Socialist Union (SSU); active in the co-operative movement, the anti-illiteracy campaign, in adult education schemes and in the setting up of kindergartens and health centres; member of the Khartoum Cheshire Homes Committee; Deputy Minister of Youth Affairs, Sport and Social Affairs, 1971–72; Secretary for Women's Affairs and member of the Political Bureau of the Sudan Socialist Union (SSU) as well as President of the Sudan Women's Union, 1972; member of the People's Assembly, 1974; *Languages:* Arabic, English; *Address:* Sudanese Socialist Union, P O Box 1850, Khartoum, Sudan.

AMIN, Samir, Egyptian economist; born 4 September 1931, Cairo, Egypt; *Education:* PhD in Economics, University of Paris, France; *Career:* Senior Economist, Economic Development Organization, Cairo, 1957–60; Technical Adviser for Planning to Government of Mali, 1960–63; Professor of Economics, Universities of Poitiers and Paris, France and Dakar, Senegal; Director, UN African Institute of Economic Development and Planning, 1970; *Publications: Trois Expériences Africaines de Développement, Mali, Guinea, Ghana,* 1965; *L'Economie du Maghreb,* 1967; *Le Développement du Capitalisme en Côte d'Ivoire,* 1968; *Maghreb in the Modern World,* 1970; *L'Accumulation à l'Echelle Mondiale,* 1970; *L'Afrique de l'Ouest Boquée,* 1971; *Le Développement Inégal,* 1973; *Languages:* Arabic, French; *Address:* African Institute for Economic Development and Planning, P O Box 3186, Dakar, Senegal.

AMIR, Muhammad, Algerian politician/journalist; born in Algeria; *Religion:* Muslim; *Career:* Director, Movement of Algerian Muslim Scouts, 1944; Director, Students Organizations of Algerian Popular Party, PPA, and the Movement for the Triumph of Democratic Liberties, MTLD, 1950; President of the Association of North African Muslim Students, and President of the

Movement of Anti Colonial Students, 1951; President, Muslim Union of Moroccan Students, 1952; member and Director of the Federation of the National Liberation Front Party, FLN, in France, 1955; Founder of the Maghreb Etudiants journal, 1955; Founder of the review of military health services of the Army of National Liberation, 1965; President, National Committee for the Studies of Development of the Capital, COMEDOR, 1970; President, Consultative Council of National Archives, and President, Consultative Council of the National Centre of Historical Studies, 1972; President, National Committee for Appointments of Territories, 1975; Founder of the *Archives Nationales Journal,* 1972, the *Etudes Historiques journal,* 1973; member of the Central Committee of the FLN Party, 1979; member of the Political Bureau, 1979–80; President of the Commission of Social Affairs, 1979–80; currently, President of the Audit Office; *Languages:* Arabic, French, Spanish, German; *Address:* Cour des Comptes de la République Algérienne Démocratique et Populaire, 19 rue Rabah Midat, Algiers, Algeria.

AMIRI, Hassan Ali al-, Iraqi politician; born 1941, Baghdad, Iraq; *Religion:* Muslim; *Career:* Under Secretary, Ministry of Municipalities, 1973; member of the Arab Baath Socialist Party Regional Leadership, 1974; member of the Follow-up Committee, 1974; Head of the Revolutionary Command Council Public Organizations Bureau, 1974; Vice Chairman of the Higher Agricultural Council, 1974; Minister of Internal Trade, 1976; Acting Minister of Trade, 1977; *Address:* Ministry of Trade, Baghdad, Iraq.

AMIRI, Yusif Muhammad Salih al-, United Arab Emirates businessman; born 1948, Abu Dhabi, United Arab Emirates; married; one daughter; *Religion:* Muslim; *Education:* Diploma in English; courses on the British Postal System; *Career:* Assistant Marketing Director, Abu Dhabi Telephone and Telegraph Company; General Manager, Amiri Establishments; *Interests and Recreations:* reading, swimming, hunting; *Languages:* Arabic, English; *Address:* P O Box 2666, Abu Dhabi, United Arab Emirates; telephone: Residence — 42180.

AMLY, Abdul Kadir al-, Egyptian UN official/meteorologist; born 2 May 1926, Mansura, Egypt; married; *Religion:* Muslim; *Education:* BSc, Physics and Maths, Faculty of Science, Alexandria University, Egypt, 1943–47; Diploma in Meteorology, MSc in Meteorology, Imperial College of Science and Technology, London, UK, 1950–53; *Career:* Egyptian Meteorological Department, 1948–50; Aviation Forecaster, 1953; Lecturer in Aeronautical Meteorology, Meteorological Department, 1953–56; Officer, International Affairs, Meteorological Department, Egypt, 1956–64; Technical Officer for Africa, World Meteorological Organization (WMO), Geneva, Switzerland, 1964–67; Representative, Regional Officer for Africa, WMO, Geneva, Switzerland, 1968; *Publications: Meteorology for Aviation; Interests and Recreations:* meteorology; *Languages:* Arabic, English, French; *Address:* World Meteorological Organization, 41 Avenue Giuseppe Motta, CH-1211, Geneva 20, Switzerland; telephone: (022) 346400.

AMMAR, Abbas Mustafa, Egyptian official/anthropologist born 10 December 1907, Egypt; married; *Religion:* Muslim; *Education:* BA, MA, Cairo University, Egypt, 1931–36; PhD, University of Manchester, UK, 1940; Diploma in Social Anthropology, Cambridge University, UK, 1941; *Career:* Lecturer, Cairo Intermediate College of Commerce, 1931–37; Researcher in Anthropology, Manchester University and Cambridge University, UK, 1937–42; Professor, Cairo University, 1942–47; Chief, Petitions Division, Department of Political Affairs, Trusteeship and Decolonization, UN, 1948–52; Director General, Rural Welfare Department, Ministry of Social Affairs, Egypt, 1950–51; Minister of Social Affairs, 1952–54; Minister of Education, 1954; Assistant Director General, ILO, 1954–64; Deputy Director General, ILO, 1964–74; member of the Board of Trustees, International Council for Educational Development, New York; member of the Higher Committee of the Academy of Science, Egypt; Adviser to the President of the Republic of Egypt; member of the Presidential Board for Social Policy, Egypt; *Publications: Demographic Survey of an Egyptian Province,* 1942, London School of Economics; *The People of Sharquia, an Anthropo-Socio-Economic Study of the Eastern Part of the Nile Delta,* 1946; *Ibn*

Khaldoun's Prolegomena to History; Views of a Muslim Philosopher of the 15th Century on the Growth and Fall of Human Societies; An Anthropo-Geographical Study of the Sinai Peninsula; Reorganization of the Egyptian Village in a Decentralised Administration; Decorations: Silver Eagle (state prize for Study Missions), Egypt; decorations from Lebanon, Colombia, Iraq, Dahomey; *Interests and Recreations:* reading, writing, camping, anthropology, demography, rural sociology; member of the Geographical Society of Egypt, Historical Society of Egypt, Egyptian Association for Social Studies, Pioneers Group; *Address:* Office — ILO, 154 rue de Lausanne, CH-1211, Geneva 22, Switzerland; telephone: (022) 326200; Residence — 2 rue Crespin, CH 1206, Geneva, Switzerland; telephone: (022) 460308.

AMMAR, Abdul Hamid, Tunisian diplomat; born 1935, Sousse, Tunisia; married; four children; *Religion:* Muslim; *Education:* Sadiki College, Tunis; Faculty of Law, Sorbonne, University of Paris, France; *Career:* Secretary General of the Tunisian Students Union, 1962–63; Secretary General of the Destour Party Youth Organisation, 1964; Secretary General of the Destour Party Franco-Tunisian Friendship Organisation, Les Amis de la France, 1964; President of the Union Tunisian de la Jeunesse, 1965; member of the Economic and Social Council, and Director of Youth and Sports, 1965; Director of Foreign Relations for the Socialist Destour Party; Vice President of the Municipality of Sousse; Ambassador to Zaire, 1969–71; Ambassador to Senegal, Ivory Coast, Sierre Leone and Mauritania, 1972–76; Ambassador to USSR, 1976–; *Languages:* Arabic, French, English; *Address:* Embassy of Tunisia, Rue Kachalove 28, Moscow, USSR.

AMMAR, Ferdjani Ben Hadj, Tunisian politician; born 1916, Tunis, Tunisia; married; three children; *Religion:* Muslim; *Education:* in Tunis; *Career:* active member of the Neo-Destour since 1935; Minister of National Economy in the first Bourguiba Government of April 1965; member of Union Tunisienne de L'Industrie du Commerce et de L'Artisanat (UTICA) and represented Tunisia on several missions abroad; first Vice President of the National Assembly, 1964; President of the Tunisian Group of the Interparliamentary Union; President of UTICA, of the Comité Nationale de la Solidarité Sociale and of the Co-ordinating Committee for Flood Relief in the Autumn of 1969; Director of the Destour Socialist Party, 1972; *Languages:* Arabic, French; *Address:* Union Tunisienne de l'Industrie du Commerce et de l'Artisanat (UTICA), 32 Rue Charles de Gaulle, Tunis, Tunisia.

AMMAR, Mahmud, Lebanese politician; born 1924, Burj al-Barajneh, Lebanon; married; six sons; *Religion:* Muslim; *Education:* Ecole de la Sagesse; Law Studies, St. Joseph University, Beirut, Lebanon; *Career:* lawyer, 1948; member of the Scouting Federation; elected Deputy for Baabda, 1957; member of Camille Chamoun's National Liberal Party, 1958; re-elected, 1960, 1964, 1968 and 1972; Chairman of the Parliamentary Committees on Posts, Telegraphs and Information; Minister of Information, Rashid al-Solh's Cabinet, 1974; *Interests and Recreations:* football, basketball, swimming; *Languages:* Arabic, French, English; *Address:* Office — Place Riad al-Solh, Beirut, Lebanon; Residence — Immeuble Ammar, Hazmieh, Beirut, Lebanon.

AMMASH, Salih Mahdi, Iraqi diplomat/politician; born 1924, Baghdad, Iraq; married; one son, three daughters; *Religion:* Muslim; *Education:* Military College, Staff College, Baghdad, Iraq; *Career:* Army Officer, 1954; Chief of Army Intelligence, 1958; Director of Air Force Operations, 1963; Minister of Defence, 1963; General Commander of the Joint Syrian-Iraqi Army, 1963; Minister of the Interior, 1968; member of the Revolutionary Command Council, 1968; Deputy Prime Minister, Vice President of the Republic, and member of the Revolutionary Command Council, 1970; Ambassador of Iraq to USSR, 1972; Ambasador of Iraq to France, 1974; Ambassador of Iraq to Finland, 1975–; member of both the Regional and the National Leaderships of the Arab Baath Socialist Party, 1963–73; *Publications: The Military Unity; The Successful Commandership; Men Without Leadership; From Zi-Qar to Qadisia; Qutaiba Bin Muslim; The Evaluation of 5th June Defeat; The Strategic Points in The Arab Fatherland; Moscow the Capital of Ice; The Civil Popular Defence;* and several collections of poetry; *Decorations:* Military Order of Rafidain, 1st Class; numerous other Iraqi decorations; *Interests and Recreations:* reading, writing, tennis, swimming, horse riding; *Languages:* Arabic,

English, Russian; *Address:* Office — Embassy of Iraq, 46 Kulonaarentie, Helsinki, Finland; Residence — 54/29/332 Al Rabi District, Adhamia, Baghdad, Iraq; telephone: 4438187.

AMR, Muhammad Ahmad, Egyptian journalist/diplomat; born in Cairo, Egypt; married; three sons, one daughter; *Religion:* Muslim; *Education: Career:* Commentator, Egyptian Broadcasting System, 1950–62; Editor and later Editor in Chief of *Egyptian Gazette,* 1950–59; Editor in Chief, National Publication House, Cairo, 1959–62; Editor in Chief, Middle East News Agency, Cairo, 1962; Manager, Middle East News Agency, London, UK, 1962–67; Counsellor, Information Department, Cairo, 1967–69; Press Counsellor, Permanent Mission of Egypt to the UN, New York, later Minister Plenipotentiary for Press and Information, at the Permanent Mission of Egypt to the UN, 1969–79; represented Egypt at the UN General Assembly, 1978; Under Secretary of State, Department of Information, Ministry of Foreign Affairs, Cairo, 1979–; member of the Academy of Political Science, New York, of the Centre for the Study of the Presidency, New York, USA, of the Press Syndicate, Cairo, Egypt; *Publications: Nationalism not for Sale,* 1961; *Egypt's Quest for Peace,* 1973; numerous articles in Egyptian and foreign newspapers; *Languages:* Arabic, English, French; *Address:* Department of Information, Ministry of Foreign Affairs, Cairo, Egypt.

AMRI, Hussain al-, Yemen Arab Republic diplomat; born 1943, Sana'a, Yemen Arab Republic; *Religion:* Muslim; *Education:* Damascus University, Syria; PhD, Cambridge University, UK, 1976; *Career:* Ministry of Foreign Affairs, 1962; served in Yemen Arab Republic Embassy to Syria, 1970s; Permanent Under Secretary, Minister of Foreign Affairs, 1975; *Languages:* Arabic, English; *Address:* Ministry of Foreign Affairs, Sana'a, Yemen Arab Republic.

ANAM, Ali Muhammad Said, Yemen Arab Republic businessman/politician; born 1925; married; five sons, four daughters; *Religion:* Muslim; *Education:* general; *Career:* businessman; Minister of Health, 1962; member of the Presidential Council, 1963; Chairman of the Board, Yemeni Bank for Construction and Development, 1964–65;

Minister of State, 1965–66; participated in the movement of liberation from the Imam's regime; member of the Consultative Council, 1972–75; Vice Chairman and Manager, Hail Said Company, largest Yemen Arab Republic (YAR) private company; Chairman of the Board, Yemeni Company for Industry and Commerce; Chairman of the Board, Oil and Soap Company; *Publications: Industry and Commerce Magazine; Decorations:* Order of the Nile, 1st Class, Egypt; *Interests and Recreations:* reading, Arabic and Yemeni music and songs; *Address:* Presidential Palace Street, Sana'a, Yemen Arab Republic; telephone: 5302, 5303, 5304.

ANANI, Jawad Ahmad al-, Jordanian politician/economist; born 28 June 1943, Halhul, Jordan; married; two daughters, two sons; *Religion:* Muslim; *Education:* BA in Economics, American University of Cairo, AUC, Cairo, Egypt, 1967; MA and PhD in Economics, USA, 1970, 1975; *Career:* Director of Research, Central Bank of Jordan, 1975–77; Under Secretary, Ministry of Labour, 1977–79; Director General, Social Security Corporation, 1979; Minister of Supply, 1979–80; Minister of Labour, 1980–; member of the American Economists Association; President of the Board of the Cultural Organization for Children; member of the Jordanian Higher Education Council; member of the International Affairs Association, Jordan; *Publications: Pooling of Reserves among Arab Common Market Countries,* 1974, in English; numerous articles on economic subjects published in various journals and magazines; *Decorations:* Order of the Jordanian Star, 1981; member of the Olympic Committee of Jordan; *Interests and Recreations:* tennis, volley-ball, reading, music; President of the Volley-ball Union; *Languages:* Arabic, English; *Address:* Ministry of Labour, P O Box 8160 Amman, Jordan; telephone: Residence — 41 851; Office — 667 831.

ANBARI, Salih Abdul Muhsin al-, Saudi Arabian diplomat; born 1931, Damascus, Syria; *Education:* Political Science and Economics, Freiburg University, West Germany; *Career:* diplomatic posts at Saudi Embassies in Switzerland, Tunisia, Afghanistan; Director of Foreign Ministry Bureau, Dammam; represented Saudi Arabia at Arab League Seminar on Arab numerals and beginning of Lunar months (Hijra Calendar), Tunis, 1963;

57

Chargé d'Affaires, Saudi Arabian Embassy to Libya; *Interests and Recreations:* reading; *Address:* Ministry of Foreign Affairs, P O Box 6731, Jeddah, Saudi Arabia; telephone: Office — 669 0900; Residence — 665 4004.

ANBATAWI, Munzer Fayek, Jordanian UN official/lawyer; born 1929, Nablus, Jordan; married; *Education:* Licence in Law, 1953; Doctorate in International Law, 1962; *Career:* Ministry of Justice, Tripoli, Libya, 1953–56; Barrister and Civil Magistrate in Jordan, 1957–58; Deputy Director, Institute for Palestine Studies, Beirut; and part-time Lecturer in International Law at Arab University of Beirut, Lebanon, 1965–68; Professor and Head of Political Science Department, Jordan University, 1968–75; member of Centre for Human Rights, 1976–; Secretary, Human Rights Commission, United Nations, Geneva, 1977–; *Publications: Palestinian Documents,* 1965, 1966; *Palestine Yearbooks,* 1964, 1965; *Reflection on Israeli Propaganda Policy,* 1968; *Duties of Third Parties in Contemporary Wars,* 1971, in Arabic; *Address:* Palais des Nations, CH-1211, Geneva 10, Switzerland.

ANEIZI, Ali Nuriddin, Libyan politician; born 1904, Benghazi, Libya; *Religion:* Muslim; *Education:* Secondary Agricultural School of Percia, Tuscany, Italy; Agronomic Institute of Florence; University of Naples; Oriental Institute of Naples; Institut de Grenoble, Naples; *Career:* Secretary Cyrenaica Government, 1933–35; Councillor, Benghazi Province, 1937–41; escaped to Egypt to join national independence movement, 1941–44; Secretary, Arab League, Cairo, 1945–51; member of Libyan House of Representatives, 1952–55; Vice President of House of Representatives, 1952–55; Vice President of House of Representatives; Minister of Finance, 1953–55; Founder and First Governor, Central Bank of Libya, 1955–61; Ambassador to Lebanon and Jordan, 1961–62; Minister of Petroleum, 1963–64; Chairman, Sahara Bank, 1964–70, Libya Insurance Company, 1964–71, National Navigation Company, 1964; President, Intellectual Society of Libya, 1965; member of Libyan Olympic Committee, 1967–69; *Languages:* Arabic, Italian, English; *Address:* P O Box 3760, 2 Kairawan Street, Tripoli, Libya.

ANI, Abdullah Najim al-, Iraqi academic; born 14 October 1939, Iraq; married; two daughters; *Religion:* Muslim; *Education:* BSc, University of Baghdad, Iraq; MSc, University of California, USA; PhD, Soil Science and Soil Physics, University of Nebraska, USA; *Career:* Lecturer, University of Baghdad, 1970; Assistant Professor, University of Baghdad, 1976–; Chairman of the Department of Soil Science, University of Baghdad, 1978–80; *Publications: Fundamentals of Soil Science,* (translated into Arabic); *Elements of Soil Science,* 1978, in Arabic; numerous papers in Arabic and English in professional journals; *Interests and Recreations:* volleyball, swimming, painting, English and Arabic poetry; *Languages:* Arabic, English; *Address:* Office — Department of Soil Science, College of Argiculture, University of Baghdad, Abu Gharib, Iraq; telephone: 555 1647; Residence — Hayy Al Adl 645/36/15, Baghdad, Iraq.

ANI, Badri Ahmad al-, Iraqi academic; born 1933, Iraq; married; two sons, one daughter; *Religion:* Muslim; *Education:* MA, Teachers College, Baghdad, Iraq, 1956; MSc, University of Pennsylvania, USA, 1960; PhD, University of Pennsylvania, 1961; *Career:* Teacher, 1957; Research Assistant, University of Pennsylvania, 1961–62; Lecturer, University of Baghdad, 1962; Deputy Head of Botany Department, Faculty of Sciences, University of Baghdad, 1965; Deputy Dean for Students Affairs, Faculty of Sciences, 1965; Assistant Professor, University of Baghdad, 1967; Deputy Head of Biology Department, 1974; Head of Biology Department, 1975–76; Associate Professor, 1976; Professor, 1977; Head of Biology Department, Faculty of Sciences, University of the United Arab Emirates, 1978–; participated in numerous international conferences; member of the American Botanic Sciences Association; member of the Iraqi Biology Society; member of several other societies, associations and committees; *Publications:* several books, and numerous articles published in professional journals and magazines; *Interests and Recreations:* travelling, jogging, swimming, writing; *Languages:* Arabic, English; *Address:* Faculty of Sciences, Department of Biology, P O Box 15551, United Arab Emirates University, Al-Ain, Abu Dhabi, United Arab Emirates.

ANI, Tahir Tawfiq al-, Iraqi politician; *Career:* Secretary to the Revolutionary Command Council, 1968; Private Secretary to the President, 1969; Secretary General, Revolutionary Command Council, 1969; Under Secretary, Ministry of Works and Housing, 1973; Minister of State, member of Regional Leadership, 1974; member of Arab Baath Socialist Party Regional Leadership, 1974; member of the Follow-Up Committee, 1974; President of the Higher Agricultural Council, 1975; President, High Committee for Public Service, 1976; Minister of Industry and Minerals, 1979–; *Address:* Ministry of Industry and Minerals, Baghdad, Iraq.

ANNAB, Ziyad Radhi, Jordanian banker/economist; born 1927, Karak, Jordan; married; *Education:* BA, Economics, American Univerity in Beirut, AUB, Lebanon, 1950; Diploma, Economic Planning, Toledo University, USA, 1953; study mission to the International Monetary Fund on problems of monetary policies; *Career:* various posts at the Ministry of National Economy, 1951–64; Assistant Under Secretary, Ministry of Information, 1954; Under Secretary, Ministry of National Economy, 1965–66; General Manager, Industrial Development Bank, 1966–; member of the Board of Tourist Authority, of the Committee for Promotion of Investment; Vice Chairman, Board of Jordanian Phosphate Mines; member of Jordan Electricity Authority; Chairman of Jordan Hotels and Tourism Company; *Decorations:* Order of the Jordanian Star, 3rd Class; Order of Independence, 2nd Class; *Interests and Recreations:* member of the Jordanian Automobile Club; *Languages:* Arabic, English; *Address:* Industrial Development Bank, P O Box 1982, Amman, Jordan; telephone:42216; telex:1349 IBD.

ANNAZ, Nazar Ahmad Hussain al-, Iraqi aviation official; born 5 July 1943, Mosul, Iraq; one son; *Religion:* Muslim; *Education:* BA in Law; Licence in Air Traffic Control; *Career:* Assistant Controller, 1964; Air Traffic Controller, 1969; Assistant Forecaster, 1973; Manager of Iraq Airways Office, 1975; Manager of Training and Technical Co-operation, 1977; Director of Training and Technical Co-operation, 1980–; member of the Arab Civil Aviation Council (ACAC), 1977–; *Publications: Directory of Civil Aviation Training Establishments in Arab Countries,* 1980, in Arabic; several other papers and studies on aviation; *Interests and Recreations:* aviation science, law; *Languages:* Arabic, English; *Address:* Arab Civil Aviation Council, 17 Sharia al-Nasr, Rabat, Morocco; telephone: 74101, 74187, 22907.

ANQARY, Ibrahim al-, Saudi Arabian politician; born 1935; *Religion:* Muslim; *Education:* BA, Cairo University, Egypt 1952; postgraduate studies at New York University and University of Miami, USA; *Career:* Assistant Director, then Director of the Bureau of Ministry of Education, 1954–57; diplomat, Ministry of Foreign Affairs; Head of Protocol, Ministry of Foreign Affairs; member of Saudi Delegation to UN, 1962–63; Attaché, Saudi Embassy to USA, 1963; Director General of the Ministry of Interior; Deputy Minister of the Interior, 1963–70; Minister of Information, 1970–75; Minister of Labour and Social Affairs, 1975–83; represented Saudi Arabia at several regional and international conferences; Minister of Municipality and Rural Affairs, 1983–; *Interests and Recreations:* reading, travel; *Address:* Ministry of Municipality and Rural Affairs, Riyadh, Saudi Arabia; telephone: 4025309; telex: 201063 DOMA SJ.

ANSARI, Abdul Qoddus al-Qasim al-, Saudi Arabian official/writer; born 1906, Medina, Saudi Arabia; *Religion:* Muslim; *Education:* general education and later self-educated in Arabic and Islamic religion at the Prophet's Mosque, Medina; *Career:* Clerk, Al-Madina al-Munawwarah Governorate; Editor in Chief of *Umm-al-Qura* (official Government Bulletin); Director of Regulations and Projects Department, Viceroy's Cabinet, Mecca; Director of Financial Affairs Department; Adviser, Viceroy's Cabinet; member of Education Council, Mecca; Director of Statistical Department; Chairman of the Committee of the Unification of Medical Terminology, Mecca; attended First Conference of Saudi Men of Letters, Okaz Literary Festival Conference, Riyadh; Owner, Editor in Chief, *Al-Manhal* magazine; *Publications: Atharul Madinatil Munawwarah; Tarikh Madinata Jiddah); Decorations:* Gold Medal (Literary Pioneer) awarded by King Abdul Aziz University, 1974; *Interests and Recreations:* reading, walking, travel; *Address:* 144 Arafat Street, Sharefiyyah, Jeddah, Saudi Arabia; telephone: 32124.

ANSARI, Ali Ahmad al-, Qatari politician; born 1916, Qatar; son of Ahmad Ali al Ansari, descendant of the Al Ansari tribe of Saudi Arabia; married; five sons, Ahmad Ali, Qatar Ambassador to Pakistan, Muhammad Ali, Qatar Ambassador to West Germany, Riyadh Ali, BA, Political Science, USA 1980, Hamad Ali and Fahd Ali, students; *Religion:* Muslim; *Education:* General Secondary Education Certificate, Bahrain; one year at Law College, University of Cairo; Berlitz Institute for Foreign Languages, Cairo, 1953–55; *Career:* various administrative leading posts in Saudi Arabia, 1930–46; Director of Customs in Oil Area, Qatar, 1946–53; General Director, Immigration, Passports and Nationality, Qatar, 1955–70; Minister of Labour and Social Affairs, Qatar, 1970–; Head of Arab Ministerial Follow-Up Committee for Resolutions and Activities of UNFPA, 1975–; member of the Executive Board for IUCW in Geneva, 1977–; *Decorations:* United Arab Republic Medal, 1975; UN World Peace Emblem, 1976; Medal of Lebanese Islamic Welfare Association, 1976; Medal of Sultanate of Oman, 1977; Medal of Islamic Republic of Pakistan, 1978; Medal of Republic of Venezuela, 1979; Medal of Republic of Italy, 1979; Medal of PIO MANZU International Centre on Habitat, Italy, 1979; *Interests and Recreations:* hunting, versification in poetry, music, Arabic literature; *Languages:* Arabic, English, Persian, Urdu; *Address:* Ministry of Labour and Social Affairs, P O Box 201, Doha, Qatar; telephone: 325419; Residence— 25554, 23683.

ANSI, Saud Salim Hassan al-, Omani diplomat; born 1949, Salalah, Sultanate of Oman; married; two daughters; *Religion:* Muslim; *Education:* BA, Sociology, University of Beirut, 1972; *Career:* Director, Social Services Department, 1974; Head of the Press Department, Ministry of Information, 1975; Director of Electricity Board, 1975; Director in the Sultan's Diwan, 1975; First Secretary, Embassy of Oman, Tunis, 1976; Consul General of the Sultanate of Oman, Karachi, 1977; Head of the Research and Studies Department, Ministry of Foreign Affairs, Oman, 1978; Ambassador Plenipotentiary and Extraordinary of the Sultanate of Oman, Djibouti, 1980–81; *Publications: Development in Oman,* 1973, in Arabic; several articles and studies in various magazines and papers; *Interests and Recreations:* reading, writing, swimming, tennis, music; member of History Society of Oman; *Languages:* Arabic, English; *Address:* Embassy of Oman, Djibouti; P O Box 1966 Djibouti; telephone: 35381.

ANTOUN, Charly, Sudanese UN official/engineer; born 8 December 1915, Omdurman, Sudan; married; *Education:* Certificate in Civil Engineering, Gordon Memorial College, Khartoum, Sudan, 1934–37; Certificate in Surveying, Cambridge University, UK, 1948–50; *Career:* Surveyor, Survey Department, Sudan, 1938–42; Surveyor in Charge, 1942–48; Triangulation Inspector, 1951–54; Deputy Assistant and Deputy Director, Survey Department, 1954–55; Chief, Survey Office, Survey Department, Sudan, 1955–56; Assistant Director, Survey Department, Sudan, 1956–57; Director, Survey Department, Sudan, 1957–65; Chief, Cartography Unit, Economic Commission for Africa (ECA), UN, Ethiopia, 1966; Fellow of the Royal Institute of Chartered Surveyors, London, UK; *Interests and Recreations:* tennis, land surveying; member of the Rotary Club, Marikh Football Club; *Languages:* Arabic, English; *Address:* ECA, UN, P O Box 3001, Addis Ababa, Ethiopia; telephone: 47200.

ANWAR, Muhammad Samih, Egyptian diplomat; born 10 December 1924; Cairo, Egypt; married; one son, one daughter; *Religion:* Muslim; *Education:* Bachelor of Law,. Cairo University, Egypt, 1945; *Career:* Ministry of Justice, 1946–54; First Secretary, Ministry of Foreign Affairs, 1954; appointed to Egyptian Embassies to USSR, 1957, and UK, 1963; Ambassador to Kuwait, 1966; Under Secretary, Ministry of Foreign Affairs, 1968; Ambassador to Iran, 1970; Minister of State for Foreign Affairs, 1974; Ambassador at the Ministry of Foreign Affairs, 1975; Ambassador to UK, 1975; *Decorations:* Egyptian Order of The Republic, 2nd Class; Egyptian Order of Merit, 1st Class; Order of Hamayoun, 1st Class, Iran; Order of the Flag, Yugoslavia; *Interests and Recreations:* rowing, tennis; *Languages:* Arabic, English, French; *Address:* Ministry of Foreign Affairs, Cairo, Egypt.

AOUFI, Mahfud, Algerian banker/official; born 1930, Algeria; *Education:* Law and Economics, University of Grenoble, France, and Lausanne, Switzerland; *Career:* Treasurer General of Algeria, 1965; Assistant Director of the Treasury and Credit, 1967; Secretary General, Ministry of Finance; played leading role in modernization of Algerian industry; left Ministry of Finance, October 1977; Governor, Banque Central d'Algérie, 1980–; *Languages:* Arabic, French; *Address:* 8 Boulevard Zirout Youcef, Algiers, Algeria; telephone: 647400; telex: 52709.

AOUIDJ, Farid, Tunisian official; born 1934, Tunis, Tunisia; married; three children; *Religion:* Muslim; *Education:* Sadiki College, Tunis; political and economic studies, Paris, France; *Career:* Director of Ports and Deputy Director of the Ecole Nationale d'Administration in Tunis; Chef de Cabinet of the Ministry of Post, Telephones and Telegraphs; Director of the Central Administration and Chef de Cabinet at the Ministry of Planning; paid official visit to Britain, September 1973; Secretary General of Tunis Municipality; *Languages:* Arabic, English and French; *Address:* Tunis Municipality, Tunis, Tunisia.

AOUN, Andre, Lebanese official; born 1951, Beirut, Lebanon; *Religion:* Christian; *Education:* Lebanese Licence en Droit, Lebanon; French Licence en Droit; French ENSP Hospital Administrator's Degree; *Career:* Administrator, Centre National d'Ophtalmologie, Paris, France; Administrator, Paris Area Hospital Management Centre; *Interests and Recreations:* reading, theatre, cinema, swimming, skiing; *Languages:* Arabic, French, English; *Address:* 24 Rue de Charenton, Paris 12e, France; telephone: 294 4064.

AOUN, Gilbert, Lebanese diplomat; born 1940, Beirut, Lebanon; *Religion:* Christian; *Education:* Diplome d'Etudes Supérieures de Droit Public; Licence en Sciences Politiques; *Career:* Director of Public Relations Department, Ministry of Foreign Affairs, 1971–72; Deputy Director of Protocol, 1972–73; 1st Secretary and Consul, Embassy of UK, 1973–; Acting Military, Naval and Air Attaché, Embassy to UK, 1977–; *Decorations:* from Lebanon and other countries; *Interests and Recreations:* swimming, reading; *Languages:* Arabic, French, English; *Address:* Lebanese Embassy, 21 Kensington Palace Gardens, London W8, UK; telephone: 01 229 7265

AOUN, Jean Paul, Lebanese physician; born 1941; Beirut, Lebanon; *Religion:* Christian; *Education:* Doctor of Medicine, France; Fellow of the Royal College of Physicians, Montreal, Canada; *Career:* Gastroenterologist of St. George's Hospital, Beirut; Ministry of Health and Social Security Department in Lebanon; *Publications:* several papers and researches published in professional journals in France, Canada and Lebanon; *Languages:* Arabic, French, English; *Address:* Yusif Sursock Street, Beirut, Lebanon; telephone: 326165.

AQRAWI, Hashim Hassan, Iraqi politician; born 1926, Iraq; *Religion:* Muslim; *Education:* Teachers' Diploma; *Career:* Teacher; member of the Kurdish Democratic Party, KDP, 1951; member of the KDP Central Committee, 1959; member of the KDP Executive Committee, 1970; Governor of the Dohuk, 1970; Minister of Municipalities and Rural Affairs, 1974; member of the Kurdistan Legislative Assembly, 1974; first Chairman of the Kurdish Executive Council, 1974; Secretary, Kurdistan Democratic Party, 1976; Minister of State, 1977–; member of the High Committee of the National Progressive Front; member of the National Assembly; *Languages:* Arabic, English; *Address:* Kurdistan Democratic Party, The Political Office, Baghdad, Iraq.

ARABI, Mahmud Adil, Egyptian businessman; resident in United Arab Emirates; born 5 February 1936; married; *Religion:* Muslim; *Education:* BA in Commerce and Diploma in Higher Marketing Studies; *Career:* Director of Egyptian Cotton Office, Geneva, Switzerland; Deputy General Manager, United Arab Emirates (UAE) Trading Company; *Interests and Recreations:* tennis, reading; *Languages:* Arabic, English, French; *Address:* United Arab Emirates Trading Company, P O Box 4171, Abu Dhabi, United Arab Emirates; telephone: Office — 44819; Residence — 45305.

ARABI, Nizar Ahmad al-, Saudi Arabian geologist; born 1941, Mecca, Saudi Arabia; *Religion:* Muslim; *Education:* MA, Clay Mineralogy, Wichita State University, Kansas, USA; PhD, Geophysics, Al-Azhar University, Cairo, Egypt, 1976; *Career:* Assistant Lecturer, King Abdul Aziz University, Jeddah, 1966; Geophysicist, Iraq National Oil Co, Iraq; Head of Team of Seismological

Survey carried out by foreign companies working in Iraq and contracted by the Iraq National Oil Co; Director of the Tihama Co, Riyadh; member of the Iraqi Geological Society, 1971–75; attended several conferences on geology and geophysics, USA, 1966–71; *Publications:* numerous studies and articles in professional journals and magazines; *Address:* Tihama Company, Mahallat al-Mughlag, Riyadh, Saudi Arabia; Residence — Ahmad al-Arabi, Mecca, Saudi Arabia; telephone: Mecca 22271.

ARADI, Muhammad Darwish al-, Kuwaiti official; born 1930; married; *Religion:* Muslim; *Education:* BA in Commerce and Economics, Cairo University, Egypt, 1954–58; *Career:* Director of Labour Bureau in Security Department, Ahmadi, 1958–59; Director of Investigation Department, 1960–62; Secretary to HH the Amir; Grand Chamberlain to HH the Amir, 1962–65; Director of Kuwait National Industries Company and Kuwait Automotive and Trading Company, and of several other companies; *Languages:* Arabic, English; *Address:* c/o National Industries Company, P O Box 417, Safat, Kuwait.

ARAFAH, Samir A., Arab-American engineer; born 1 January 1943, Jaffa, Palestine; *Religion:* Muslim; *Education:* BSc, Electrical Engineering; MSc, Electrical Engineering Systems Analysis and Control Theory; PhD, Electrical Engineering, Modern Systems Analysis and Control; *Career:* Scheidt and Bachmann, West Germany, Assistant Engineer, Traffic Control Systems, 1964–65; District Engineer, Ministry of Electricity and Water, Kuwait, 1968–70; Design Engineer, Energy Control Systems, ITT, London, UK, 1969; teaching and research, Southern Methodist University, Dallas, USA, 1970–73; Senior Systems Scientist, Rockwell International Corporation, California, USA, 1973; Visiting Industrial Professor, University of California, Irvine, 1974; Fullerton Visiting Industrial Professor, California State University, 1976; Senior Systems Scientist, Faculty Member, Multi-Industrial Corporation; member of The Institute of Electrial and Electronics Engineers, National Management Association, Arab-American University Graduates, Association of Egyptian-American Scholars, Institute of Professional Engineers of Jordan; Eta Kappa Nu; participated in effective efforts to promote coopera-

tion of industrial and educational institutions between the USA and the Middle East; *Publications:* several technical publications in the field of engineering management science; *Interests and Recreations:* tennis, swimming, travelling, social and human sciences, music; *Languages:* Arabic, English, French, German; *Address:* P O Box 6092, Anaheim, California 92806, USA; telephone: (714) 630 4785, 632 2424.

ARAFAT, Mahmud Zaki Ibrahim, Arab-American academic/engineer; born 20 February 1935, Cairo, Egypt; married; one son; *Education:* BSc in Civil Engineering, Ain Shams University, Cairo, Egypt, 1957; PhD, Scientific Research Institute of Concrete and Reinforced Concrete, Moscow, USSR, 1965; post-graduate studies at the Urban Institute, University of Paris, France, 1970–71; *Career:* Consultant and Research Engineer with various international corporations and government agencies since 1960; member of Faculty of the School of Civil Engineering, Ain Shams University, Cairo, Egypt, 1966–69; Associate Professor of Engineering at Pratt Institute, Brooklyn, New York, 1979–80; Licensed Professional Engineer in New York, New Jersey, France and Egypt; Licensed Professional Planner, and Licensed Construction Official and Building Subcode Official in New Jersey; contributor and reviewer for a number of technical journals; member of American Society of Civil Engineers, of American Concrete Institute, of Post-licensing Institute; Chairman of Prestressed Institute Committee on Precast Prestresed Storage Tanks; member of various national technical committees; *Publications:* numerous articles in various technical journals, numerous papers for international conferences; *Decorations:* Industrial Category Award of Merit, awarded by the Concrete Industry Board Inc of New York, for the largest twin precast concrete LNG tanks, Staten Island; *Interests and Recreations:* tennis, travel, poetry, classical music; *Languages:* Arabic, English, French, Russian; *Address:* 225 Academy Street, Jersey City, New Jersey 07306, USA; telephone: (201) 792 6167.

ARAFAT, Walid Najib, Jordanian academic; born 21 May 1921, Nablus, Palestine; resident in United Kingdom; married; two sons; *Religion:* Muslim; *Education:* BA in English, Latin, Arabic, London, UK, 1947;

BA in English, 1949; BA in Arabic London, 1950; PhD in Arabic, London, 1952; *Career:* Lecturer in Arabic, School of Oriental and African Studies, University of London, 1951–61; Reader in Arabic, University of London, 1961–72; Professor and Director of the Institute of Arabic and Islamic Studies, University of Lancaster, founded by Professor Arafat with financial support from the University of Kuwait; *Publications: Diwan of Hassan Ibn Thabit,* 1971, 2 volumes, in Arabic; numerous papers and articles in English and Arabic on Islamic science, culture, Arabic literature and criticism, compartative literature, in various journals and magazines; numerous talks in the BBC Arabic Service; *Interests and Recreations:* walking, gardening, reading, writing, literature in general, Arabic literature, development of Islam, East-West relations; Fellow of RAS, member of Council of BRSMES, of the Council and Executive Committee of SRTH of Great Britain and Northern Ireland, of the Board of Religion and Theology, CNAA; *Languages:* Arabic, English, Latin, French, German; *Address:* Institute of Arabic and Islamic Studies, Landsdale College, University of Lancaster, Lancaster LA1 47N, UK.

ARAFAT, Yassir, (Abu Ammar), Palestinian politician; born 1929, Jerusalem; *Religion:* Muslim; *Education:* studied civil engineering in Cairo, Egypt; graduated from Cairo University; received military training in the Egyptian Army, 1955–56; *Career:* elected President of the Palestinian Students' Union, 1952–57; engineer in Kuwait, 1957; founded Fatah military organization Al-Asifa which began operations against Israel in 1965; Chairman of the Fatah Central Committee and of the PLO Executive Committee; elected Chairman of the PLO Executive Committee 1969; Commander in Chief of Palestinian High Command, 1971; has paid several official visits to other countries including USSR, 1974, and China; *Languages:* Arabic, English.

ARAIM, Mahmud Ahmad, Jordanian businessman; born 1922; married; two sons, one daughter; *Religion:* Muslim; *Education:* Iraqi Military College and Iraqi Staff College; *Career:* former Army Officer; Director General, Jordanian Establishment for Trading and Engineering Equipments; *Decorations:* several Jordanian and Iraqi decorations; *Interests and Recreations:* swimming, hunting, walking; poetry, literature, history, music, military strategic studies; *Address:* P O Box 6136, Amman, Jordan; telephone: 62854.

ARAKTINGI, Michel Amin, Lebanese businessman; born 1922, Beirut, Lebanon; married; three sons, one daughter; *Religion:* Christian; *Education:* general; *Career:* businessman for the last 30 years; international entrepreneur in sugar and other commodities; involved in shipping; Owner and President of Phoenicia Line, Beirut, Mimosa Real Estates Company SAL, Beirut, Comptoir Maritime (Liban) SAL, Beirut, Middle East Sugar Traders, Beirut; *Interests and Recreations:* tennis, swimming, yachting, motoring; *Languages:* Arabic, English, French; *Address:* Mimosa Building, John Kennedy Street, P O Box 6292, Beirut, Lebanon; telephone: 366490, 36649; Residence —193 Pavilion Road, London SW1X OBJ, UK; telephone: (01) 235 1498.

ARASHI, Yahya Hussain Ahmad al-, Yemen Arab Republic official; born 1947; married; one son, one daughter; *Education:* studies in social development and labour education; *Career:* teacher, 1961–62; National Guard, 1962–63; Director, Hodeida Province Office, 1964–65; Director General, Medical Department, Hodeida Province; Director, Al-Alfi Hospital, Hodeida, 1966; Director General of Organisation, Hodeida Province, 1967; Director General, Social Affairs and Labour Organization, 1968–69; Director, Taxation Department, 1970–73; Chairman, Higher Economic Committee; Director, Yemeni Bank for Construction and Development, 1973–74; Head of the Central Organization for Auditing and Accountancy, 1974–75; Minister of Culture and Information, January, 1976; *Publications: A Study of Social Development in Yemen; Decorations:* Order of the Republic, Egypt; *Interests and Recreations:* Yemeni political, social and cultural history, volley-ball, chess; *Languages:* Arabic, English; *Address:* San'aa, Yemen Arab Republic; telephone: 3076.

ARDHAOUI, Amor, Tunisian diplomat; born 24 February 1933, Jerba, Tunisia; married; one son, one daughter; *Religion:* Muslim; *Education:* Graduate Studies, University of Toulouse, France; Diploma in Political Science; Diploma of the Institute of International Studies; *Career:* member of Neo-

Destour and Socialist Destour Party, 1951–; various diplomatic posts at Stockholm, Rabat, Addis Ababa, 1960–71; Head of the African Division, Ministry of Foreign Affairs, Tunis, 1971–72; Attaché in the Office of the Presidency of the Republic, Carthage, 1972–73; Permanent Representative of Tunisia to the UN, New York, 1973–74; Minister Counsellor, Tunisian Embassy to USA, 1974–, and Deputy Permanent Representative to UN; *Publications: Développment et réforme agraire,* University of Toulouse; *Decorations:* Order of the Tunisian Republic, 1969; Order of the Polar Star, Sweden; Order of the Alaouite Medal, Morocco, 1965; Order of the Sultanate of Oman, 1973; *Languages:* Arabic, French, English; *Address:* Embassy of Tunisia, 2408 Massachusetts Avenue, NW, Washington D.C. 20008, USA.

ARIAN, Abdullah al-, Egyptian diplomat/lawyer; born 21 March 1920, Damanhur, Egypt; *Education:* LLB and PhD, Cairo University, Egypt; Harvard University, USA, and Columbia University, New York, USA; *Career:* Assistant District Attorney, Buhairah Governorate, 1942–43; Lecturer in Law, Cairo University, 1943–45; Assistant Professor of International Law and International Organisations, Institute of Public Administration, Cairo, 1959–61; Professor of International Law, Division of Legal Studies, Institute of Arab Higher Studies, Cairo, 1959–; Counsellor, Office of the President, 1955–56; Counsellor and Legal Adviser, Permanent Mission to UN, 1957–59; Director, Department of Legal Affairs and Treaties, Ministry of Common Affairs, 1959–68; Ambassador and Deputy Permanent Representative to UN, 1968–71; Ambassador to France, 1971–74; Permanent Representative to UN Office, Geneva, Switzerland, 1974–; member of International Law Committee, 1957–58, 1961–65, 1966; Delegate to various UN and Organization of African Unity (OAU) conferences and several sessions in UN General Assembly; *Publications:* several books and articles on international law and the United Nations; *Languages:* Arabic, English, French; *Address:* Permanent Mission of Egypt to the UN, 72 rue de Lausanne, Geneva, Switzerland; Ministry of Foreign Affairs, Cairo, Egypt.

ARIDA, Joseph, Lebanese businessman; born March 1931; married; three sons; *Education:* BSc, Loughborough College, UK; *Career:* Director, Arida Brothers Company; Director, Airtex (textile firm), 1953–; Director of Lebanese Television Company (CLT), 1956, Yougo Arabe, SAL, 1962, Sphinx International, 1963; *Interests and Recreations:* skiing, tennis, riding; member of the Yacht Club; and of the St. George's Club; *Languages:* Arabic, French; *Address:* Office — P O Box 38, Tripoli, Lebanon; telephone: 620185.

ARIF, Awni al-Din, Iraqi UN official/physician born 22 November 1925, Baghdad, Iraq; married; *Education:* MB, ChB, Faculty of Medicine, Baghdad University, 1944–50; MPH, School of Public Health Administration, Columbia University, New York, USA, 1958–59; Certificate in Preventive Medicine, Oklahoma Medical School, USA, 1959; Certificate in Communicable Diseases and Statistics, National Communicable Diseases Centre, Atlanta, USA, 1959; Board of Public Health and Preventive Medicine Degree, Faculty of Medicine, Baghdad University, 1967; *Career:* military service, 1950–51; medical clinician and teacher, Faculty of Medicine, Baghdad University, 1951–58; Fellow, School of Public Health, Columbia University, New York, 1958–60; Medical Officer, WHO, Geneva, 1960–66; Director General, Preventive Medicine Service, Ministry of Health, Iraq, 1966–69; Representative of Libya, Regional Office for East Mediterranean, WHO, Libya, 1969–; Fellow of American Public Health Association; member of Supreme Scientific Research Board, Iraq; member of Medical Research Board, Baghdad University; Iraqi Medical Association; Red Crescent Society, Baghdad, Iraqi Children's Protection Society; *Publications:* numerous books on preventive medicine and diseases; *Interests and Recreations:* bridge, tennis, golf, fishing, swimming, public health administration, health planning, epidemiology; member of Mansour Club, Baghdad; *Languages:* Arabic, English, French; *Address:* WHO Office, Ministry of Health, Tripoli, Libya; telephone: 31060.

ARMANAZI, Ghaith Najib, Syrian diplomat; born 10 January 1943, Damascus, Syria; married; two sons, one daughter; *Religion:* Muslim; *Education:* BA in Economics, University of Colorado, USA; MA in Area

Studies, University of London, UK; *Career:* Information Assistant, League of Arab States, London, 1967–70; Editor, Institute for Palestine Studies, Beirut, Lebanon, 1971–74; Information Counsellor, Embassy of the United Arab Emirates, London, 1974–; *Publications: Palestinian Rights, the International Definition, Journal of Palestine Studies,* volume 111, no 3, Spring 1974; several book reviews and articles in English in *Journal of Palestine Studies* and *Monday Morning Weekly,* published in Beirut, Lebanon; also articles in Arabic for *Al-Nahar* and *Al-Shu'un al-Falastiniyah; Interests and Recreations:* tennis, squash, swimming, reading; member of the London Diplomatic Association, of the Association of Economic Representatives, London; *Languages:* Arabic, English, French; *Address:* Ali Armanazi Street, Damascus, Syria; Residence — 22 Campden Hill Court, Campden Hill Road, London W8, UK.

ARMOUTI, Ismail Nazal al-, Jordanian politician/economist; born 1931, Amman, Jordan; *Education:* BSc, Political Science, Baghdad University, 1962; Diploma, Managerial Economics, London University, UK, 1965; *Career:* Chief of Trade Department, Ministry of Economy, 1969; Director of Companies and Commercial Registration, 1969–76; Minister of Interior for Municipal and Village Affairs, 1976; *Publications: Arab Common Market,* 1969; *Theory of Arab Economic Integration,* 1975; *Address:* Ministry of Municipalities and Environment, Amman, Jordan.

ARMOUTI, Muhammad Nazzal al-, Jordanian official/businessman; born 12 August 1924, Amman, Jordan; married; four sons, five daughters; *Education:* Licence in Law, Damascus University, Syria, 1946; Diploma in Public Administration, Exeter University, UK, 1959; Preliminary Certificate in French, 1956; *Career:* Chief Clerk, Chief Justice Department, 1947; Secretary General, Ministry of the Interior, 1948; Secretary General to both House of Senates and Representatives, 1950; Inspector General, Income Tax Department, 1952; Legal Adviser to the Ministry of Finance 1954, Governor of Irbid, Ma'an, Hebron, Karak, Nablus and Salt, 1955–61; Under Secretary, Ministry of the Interior, 1961; Minister of Interior, 1964–66; Ambassador to Libya, Kuwait, United Arab Emirates, 1966–71;

Head of Political Department, Ministry of Foreign Affairs, 1971; member of the Board of Trustees of the Arab College; Chairman of Jordan-Gulf Bank Co Ltd; Chairman of Armouti Trading Co; Chairman of University of Jordan; *Publications: Citizen Guide; an interpretation of the Jordanian Constitution and Law; Decorations:* Order of the Jordanian Star, 1st Class; Jordanian Order of the Independence, 1st Class; Syrian Order of Merit, 1st Class; Grand Cross, Silver Knights Organization (Papal); Grand Decoration of Holy Sepulchre (Greek Orthodox); *Interests and Recreations:* hunting, reading, history, biographies; *Address:* P O Box 9989, Amman, Jordan.

AROP, Justin Yac, Sudanese physician/politician; born in Bahr al-Ghazal, Sudan; *Education:* MB, BSc in Sudan; postgraduate training in obstetrics and gynaecology in UK; *Career:* practice as gynaecologist in Wau Civil Hospital; appointed Regional Minister of Health and Social Welfare, 1973; responsible in collaboration with WHO for implementation of Primary Health Care Programme in Sudan; currently member of Parliament of the People's Regional Assembly, Juba, 1978–; Regional Minister of Agriculture, Food and Natural Resources, 1979–; *Interests and Recreations:* music, hunting, basket-ball; *Languages:* Arabic, English; *Address:* Ministry of Agriculture and Natural Resources, P O Box 251, Juba, Sudan.

ARRAR, Sulaiman Atallah, Jordanian journalist/politician; born 8 October 1934, Ma'a, Jordan; married; *Education:* Licence in Law, Egypt, 1961; Diploma in Civil Law, Law College, Rabat, Morocco; *Career:* Attaché, Embassy to Saudi Arabia, 1961–67; Attaché to Embassy in Morocco and Algeria, 1967–72; Governor in the Ministry of the Interior, 1971–72; Director General of *Al Ittihad Al-Watani,* 1972; General Manager and Editor in Chief of *Al-Ra'i,* 1972–; Minister of the Interior, 1976; *Publications:* various articles and short stories; *Decorations:* Star of Jordan, 1st Class; Spanish Grand Cross for Civil Service; *Address:* P O Box 6710, Amman, Jordan; telephone: 64330.

ARRAYID, Jalil Ibrahim, Bahraini official/educationalist; born 26 January 1933, Bahrain; married; two sons, one daughter; *Religion:* Muslim; *Education:* BA in Chemistry,

65

American University of Beirut, AUB, Lebanon, 1954; MEd in Science Education, Leicester University, Leicester, UK, 1964; PhD in Education, University of Bath, UK, 1974; *Career:* Teacher of Science and Mathematics, Department of Education, Bahrain, 1954–59; Inspector of Science Education, 1959–66; Principal of the Teachers' Training College for Men, 1966–72; Under Secretary, Ministry of Education, 1974–82; Deputy Chairman, High Council for Vocational Training, 1975–79; Rector, Bahrain University College of Arts, Science and Education, 1982–; founding member of the Committee of the Arabian Gulf University, 1980–; Chairman of the Council for Higher Education of the Gulf States, 1982–83, and member, 1978–; Representative of Bahrain at the Arab Bureau of Education for the Gulf States, 1975; Chairman of UNESCO/ALESCO Regional Seminar on Planning and Management of Curriculum Development in Arab Countries, Cairo, Egypt, 1976; Deputy Chairman, Second Conference of Arab Educators, Baghdad, Iraq, 1978; Deputy Chairman, UNESCO Seminar on Aims of Education in Arab States, 1978; member of the Governing Board of Bahrain University College of Arts, Science and Education; member of the British Institute of Management, the Association of Arab Educators, the Indian Institute of Public Administration, the American Chemical Society, the Association for Science Education, UK; Fellow of the Chemical Society, UK; *Publications:* numerous articles and research papers published mostly in *Al-'Uluum* magazine in Lebanon; *Interests and Recreations:* chess, table tennis, photography, painting, reading; *Languages:* Arabic, English; *Address:* University College of Arts, Science and Education, P O Box 1082, Manama, Bahrain; telephone: 259268; telex: 9094 TABIA BN.

ARRAYID, Jalil Mansur, Bahraini academic; born 1944, Manama, Bahrain; married; *Religion:* Muslim; *Education:* BA in Arabic Literature, Arab University of Beirut, Lebanon; Diploma, Institute of Arab Research and Studies; MA in Arabic Literature, Cairo University, Egypt; *Career:* teacher in primary, intermediary and secondary schools; Professor at the Institute of Tutors, Bahrain; Lecturer at University College of Bahrain; Co-ordinator at the Faculty of Arabic Language and Islamic Studies, University College of Bahrain; *Publications:* several

articles on Bahraini Arabic Heritage Three Hundred Years Ago, published in the Bahraini paper *Al-Mawaqif,* 1973; *The History, Function and Cultural Influence of Bahraini Journalism,* article published as chapter of a book with the title *Studies in Bahraini Literature,* 1979; participated in editing school books for the intermediary schools in Bahrain; *Interests and Recreations:* photography, reading, collecting antiques; *Address:* The Department of Arabic Language and Islamic Studies, University College of Bahrain, P O Box 1082; telephone: Office — 682748; Residence — 682377.

ARRAYID, Jawad Salim, Bahraini politician/ lawyer; born 1940, Manama, Bahrain; married; *Religion:* Muslim; *Education:* Law, Universities of Cairo, Leeds and London; read for English Bar; *Career:* First Bahraini Public Prosecutor, 1969; member of State Council, with responsibilities for Labour and Social Affairs, 1970; Minister of Labour and Social Affairs, 1971; worked for Industry and State Council; Minister of Cabinet Affairs, 1972–; *Languages:* Arabic, English; *Address:* The Cabinet Office, P O Box 1000, Manama, Bahrain; telephone: 253939.

AS'AD, Fakhri Ayyad, Egyptian UN official/ physician; born 13 June 1924, Mansurah, Egypt; married; one son, two daughters; *Education:* MD, Cairo University, 1947; MPH, University of California, Berkeley, USA, 1956; *Career:* Medical Officer, Rural Health, Ministry of Health, Egypt, 1947–53; Director, Technical Bureau, Qalyub Training and Demonstration Centre, Egypt, 1954–59; WHO Senior Adviser, Trachoma Control Programme, Taiwan, 1960–65; Medical Technical Manager, WHO Programme on Immunization, 1975–; *Publications:* numerous articles published in various medical journals on trachoma, influenza, etc; *Interests and Recreations:* swimming, carpentry, photography, painting, tennis; *Languages:* Arabic, English, French, Chinese; *Address:* Residence — 2 Chemin de Sous-Cherre, CH-1245 Collonge-Bellerive, Geneva, Switzerland; telephone: (022) 521625.

AS'AD, Kamil, Lebanese politician/lawyer; born 1929, Beirut, Lebanon; married; one son, one daughter; *Religion:* Muslim; *Education:* French Faculty of Law, St. Joseph University, Beirut, Lebanon; Licence in Law, Faculty of Law, Sorbonne, University of

Paris, France; *Career:* Barrister at Law; elected Deputy for Marjeyoun, 1953, 1957 and 1960; member of National Front Opposition, 1958; Minister of National Education and of Fine Arts, 1961–64; re-elected Deputy for Marjeyoun, 1964; elected President of the Lebanese National Assembly, 1964; Minister of Health, 1966; re-elected Deputy for Marjeyoun-Hasbaya, 1968; President of the Lebanese National Assembly, 1968; re-elected President of National Assembly, 1970, 1973, 1979; member of National Dialogue Committee, September 1975–; *Decorations:* many foreign and Lebanese decorations; *Interests and Recreations:* reading, tennis, riding, swimming; *Languages:* Arabic, French; *Address:* Office — Chamber of Deputies, Place de l'Etoile, Beirut, Lebanon; telephone: 220040; Maurice Barres Street, Tabet Building, Beirut; telephone: 241317, 225155; Residence — Hazmiah, Haddad Building, Beirut, Lebanon; telephone: 282750.

ASAAD, As'ad Sam'an, Egyptian banker; resident in United Arab Emirates; born 22 April 1931, Cairo, Egypt; married; one daughter, two sons; *Religion:* Christian; *Education:* BA in Commerce, Cairo University, 1954; MA, Brussels University, 1958; *Career:* Office, Central Exchange Control, National Bank of Egypt (NBE), 1948; Assistant Inspector, Credit Control Department, NBE, 1956; Assistant Manager, Main Branch, NBE, 1960; Manager, National Bank of Abu Dhabi (NBAD), Abu Dhabi, 1968; General Manager, NBAD, 1975; Chief Executive, NBAD, 1979; Chief Executive, National Bank of Abu Dhabi; President and Managing Director, Abu Dhabi International Bank, Washington D.C., USA; Director, UBAF, Arab American Bank, New York; *Interests and Recreations:* swimming, tennis, chess; *Languages:* Arabic, English, French; *Address:* P O Box 4, Abu Dhabi, United Arab Emirates; telephone: 335262.

ASAD, Brigadier Rif'at al-, Syrian politician/army commander; born 1937, Qardah, Lattakia Province, Syria; younger brother of President Asad; *Religion:* Muslim; *Education:* Political Science and Economics, Damascus University, Syria; PhD in Politics, Soviet Academy of Sciences, USSR; *Career:* Commander of Siraya al-Difa', Defence Regiment; elected to Baathist Regional Command, 1975; Head of Department of Higher Educational and Scientific Studies, Damascus; Commander of Special Defence Council; *Decorations:* decorated for service in the field in 1973 war; *Languages:* Arabic, Russian, French; *Address:* Ministry of Defence, Damascus, Syria.

ASAD, Major General Hafiz al-, President of the Syrian Republic; born 1930, Qardah, Lattakia Province, Syria; married; children; *Religion:* Muslim; *Education:* Homs Military Academy, 1955; *Career:* joined Syrian Air Force; training abroad including USSR; dismissed from armed forces, 1961, following opposition to secession from Union with Egypt; Commanding Officer of Air Force Base at Dmeir, 1963; promoted Major General and Commander, Air Force, 1964; joined National Council of the Revolutionary Command (NCRC), 1965; supporter of Salah Jadid in 1966 coup; member of Regional and International Baath Command in Jadid Government; Minister of Defence and Commander of Air Force, 1966–70; ousted Salah Jadid in peaceful takeover, November, 1970; Prime Minister, Minister of Defence; resigned from former post following election as President of the Republic, March 1971; established People's Council, February 1971; and National Progressive Front, March 1972, in both of which Baath party shares power with other parties including Syrian Communist Party; re-established diplomatic relations with UK, 1973, and US, 1974; paid private visit to London, 1965; Secretary General of the Regional and International Command; Commander in Chief of Syrian Armed Forces; *Languages:* Arabic, French; *Address:* Office of the President, Damascus, Syria.

ASAD, Nassiriddin al-, Jordanian academic; born 1923, Aqaba, Jordan; *Religion:* Muslim; *Education:* BA in Arabic Literature, Cairo University, Cairo, Egypt, 1947; MA in Arabic Literature, Cairo University, 1951; PhD in Arabic Literature, Cairo University, 1955; *Career:* Deputy Director, Cultural Department, League of Arab States, 1954–59; Dean, Faculty of Arts and Education, Libyan University, Benghazi, Libya, 1959–61; Professor of Arabic Literature, Dean of the Faculty of Arts, and President of the University of Jordan, 1962–68; Assistant Director General of Arab League Educational, Cultural and Scientific Organisation, 1968–77; Ambassador of Jordan to Saudi Arabia, 1977–78; President of the University of Jordan, 1978–80; President, Royal Academy for Islamic Civilization Research (Al-Bait Foundation), 1980–; member of the Academy of Arabic Language in Cairo and Amman; member of the Academy of Arabic Language, Damascus and Baghdad; member of the Scientific Academy of Arabic Language, Aligarh, India; *Publications: The Sources of Pre-Islamic Poetry and their Historical Value,* 1956; *Modern Literary Trends in Palestine and Jordan,* 1957; *Singing Girls in Pre-Islamic Arabia,* 1960; *Modern Poetry in Palestine and Jordan,* 1961; *Khalil Beidas, The Pioneer of Modern Fiction in Palestine,* 1963; *Muhammad Ruhi Al-Khalidi: the Pioneer of Historical Research in Palestine,* 1970; *Decorations:* Order of Independence, 1st Class, Jordan; Distinctive Decoration of Education, Jordan; Golden Medal of the Arab League Educational, Cultural and Scientific Organisation; *Address:* The Royal Academy for Islamic Civilization Research (Al-Bait Foundation), P O Box 950361, Amman, Jordan; telex: 22363, Albait JO.

ASAD, Shuja' Muhammad al-, Jordanian official; born 30 December 1928, Aqaba, Jordan; married; *Education:* Wayne State University, USA; MA, Chicago University, USA; Higher Studies in Economics, 1958–59; BLitt, American University in Cairo, Egypt, 1951; *Career:* Assessor at the Income Tax Department, 1952–56; Registrar of Trade Names and Patents, Ministry of National Economy, 1958–64; Head of Industrial Department; Head of Commercial Department; Assistant Director General of Passports, 1964–65; Assistant Director General of Tourism , 1965–71; Director of General Statistics Department, 1971–79; Regional Adviser on Census, United Nations Economic Commission for Western Asia, ECWA, Beirut, Lebanon, 1979; *Address:* Residence — P O Box 5314, Jabal Amman, Amman, Jordan; telephone: 41894.

ASADULLAH, Mahmud Muhammad Ali, Saudi Arabian academic; born Mecca, Saudi Arabia; *Religion:* Muslim; *Education:* PhD Geography; *Career:* Lecturer, Faculty of Education, Mecca; Director of Student Affairs, member of King Abdul Aziz University Council; Fellow of American National Geographical Society; member of Seminar of University Presidents, Manchester, UK; Dean of Students, and Assistant Professor,

King Abdul Aziz University; *Interests and Recreations:* football, swimming; *Address:* P O Box 745, Mecca, Saudi Arabia.

ASALI, Kamil Jamil, Jordanian journalist/librarian; born 9 November 1925, Jerusalem; married; three sons, one daughter; *Religion:* Muslim; *Education:* BA, University of London, 1950; Diploma in Law, Jerusalem Law Classes, 1951; PhD in Philosophy, Humbolt University, Berlin; *Career:* teacher at schools and colleges; journalist; broadcaster; news commentator, various radio stations since 1968; Director General, University of Jordan Library; *Publications:* several books, articles and papers in Arabic, English and German; *Decorations:* Deutsche Friedensmedaille (GDR Peace Council); *Interests and Recreations:* the cultural history of Islamic Jerusalem; *Languages:* Arabic, English, German, French, Latin; *Address:* University of Jordan, Amman, Jordan; telephone: 843555; Residence — 62539.

ASFAHANI, Muhammad Hussain, Saudi Arabian businessman; born 1920, Jeddah, Saudi Arabia; *Religion:* Muslim; *Education:* General Secondary School Certificate; *Career:* member of the Board of Asfahani Printers and Co; member, Saudi Trade Delegation to the Sudan, 1963; member of Chamber of Commerce Delegation to the Far East, 1975; General Manager of Asfahani Printers and Co, Jeddah; involved in the modernization of the local printing industry; *Address:* P O Box 497, Jeddah, Saudi Arabia; telephone: Office— Jeddah 22016, 23016; Residence— Jeddah 52204, 52116.

ASFUR, Edmond Yusif, Lebanese World Bank official/economist; born 2 August 1926; married; *Education:* MA, Oxford University, UK, 1946–50; Research Fellow, Center for Middle Eastern Studies, Harvard University, USA, 1955–56; *Career:* Economist, UN New York, USA, 1956–60; UN Adviser, Development Board of Jordan, Jordan, 1962; Associate Professor, American University of Beirut, AUB, Lebanon, 1963–68; Director, Economic Research Institute, AUB, 1964–68; Chief, Industrial Development Bureau, Lebanon, 1968–69; Senior Economist and Division Chief, Europe, Middle East and North Africa Region, IBRD (World Bank), Washington D.C., USA, 1969–; *Publications: Syria: Development and Monetary Policy,* 1959; *Saudi Arabia: Long Term Projections* *of Supply and Demand for Agricultural Products,* 1965; *Prospects and Problems of Economic Development of Saudi Arabia, Kuwait and the Gulf Principalities; Economic Development and Population Growth in the Middle East,* 1972; *Turkey: Prospects and Problems of an Expanding Economy,* 1975; *Croissance et Transformations Structurelles de l'Industrie Morocaine 1968–1976,* 1977; *Interests and Recreations:* economic development, economic policies; *Languages:* Arabic, English, French; *Address:* Office — IBRD, 1818 H Street, NW, Washington D.C., USA 20433; telephone: (202) 477 2381.

ASFUR, Farid Ibrahim, Lebanese businessman/accountant; resident in USA; born 26 August 1909, Beirut, Lebanon; married; one daughter, two sons; *Religion:* Christian; *Education:* Accounting in London; member of the Association of Certified Accountants; *Career:* Staff Accountant, Iraq Petroleum Company, 1932–53; Executive Asssistant to Managing Director, Contracting and Trading Co, Beirut, Lebanon, 1953–61; General Manager, T.S. Boutagy and Sons, Beirut, 1961–63; Chairman of the Board, Semiramis Services Co SAL, Beirut, Lebanon, 1963–72; Consultant, Middle East Lutheran Ministry, 1972–73; Administrator, US Arab Chamber of Commerce, 1973–; member of the Arab Culture Centre; *Languages:* Arabic, English, French; *Address:* US Arab Chamber of Commerce (Pacific) Inc, 433 California Street, San Francisco, California 94104, USA.

ASFUR, Khalil Muhammad Ibrahim, Jordanian official; born 1924, Amman, Jordan; married; one son, one daughter; *Religion:* Muslim; *Education:* Diploma in Public Administration, Holland; *Career:* Arab Legion, 1941; Prime Minister's Office, 1958; Official in National Assembly, 1958–75; Assistant Secretary General to National Assembly, 1958–75; Secretary General to National Assembly; *Decorations:* Order of the Star of Jordan, 3rd Class, Jordan; *Interests and Recreations:* sport, music; member of King Hussain Club, and the Royal Automobile Club, Amman, Jordan; *Languages:* Arabic, English; *Address:* National Assembly, P O Box 72, Amman, Jordan; telephone: 64121.

ASFUR, Walid Mithqal, Jordanian politician/official; born 10 December 1932, Amman, Jordan; *Religion:* Muslim; *Education:* BA in Political Science and Economics; MSc in Political Science; *Career:* Businessman, 1960–80; President, Amman Chamber of Industry, 1967–80; Deputy Mayor of Amman, 1977–80; Member of the National Consultative Council, 1978–80; Minister of Industry and Trade, 1980–; member of the Governing Body of ILO; member of the World Affairs Council; *Decorations:* Order of Jordanian Star, 1981; *Interests and Recreations:* President of the Royal Automobile Club; *Languages:* Arabic, English; *Address:* Ministry of Industry and Trade, P O Box 2019 Amman, Jordan; telephone: Office — 663 774.

ASHA, Rafik al-, Syrian diplomat; born 1910, Damascus, Syria; *Education:* American University of Beirut, Lebanon; New York City University, New York, USA; *Career:* Bank Official and Financial Analyst; Professor of Banking, Economics and Accounting, Baghdad, Iraq, 1932–41; Deputy Director General, Syrian Ministry of Supplies, 1941–43; Chargé d'Affairs, Syrian Embassy to Egypt, 1944–45; Acting Consul General, New York, USA, 1945–47; member of the Syrian Delegation to the UN General Assembly, 1946–60; Acting Permanent Delegate to the UN, 1947; Consul General, New York, 1947–52; Acting Permanent Delegate to the UN, 1948–51; 1st Counsellor, Embassy to USA, 1952; Minister Plenipotentiary, Chargé d'Affaires, USA, 1952–58; Alternate Governor, IBRD, (World Bank), 1952–55; President of the Trusteeship Council, 1956–57; President of the Arab League Council, 1959; Permanent Representative of the United Arab Republic to the UN, 1959–61; Ambassador to Rumania, 1961; Ambassador to the USSR, 1961–62; Secretary General, Ministry of Foreign Affairs, 1962–64; Permanent Representative to the UN, 1964–65; Senior Financial Adviser to UN Development Programme, UNDP, 1968–; *Languages:* Arabic, English; *Address:* UNDP, P O Box 2317, Damascus, Syria.

ASHAHNU, Abdul Latif Bin, Algerian academic/economist; born 1943, Algeria; *Education:* Economic Studies; Political Economy, Paris; *Career:* Professor, Institute of Economic Studies; Director, Research Centre for Applied Economics, National Organization of Scientific Research, Ministry of Higher Education; Secretary General, Association of Third World Economists, 1976; President, Committee of Economic and Social Affairs, National Liberation Front Party, FLN; *Languages:* Arabic, French; *Address:* 20 Rue Shahid Khalif Mutafa Bin Aknoun, Algiers, Algeria; telephone: 784 292, 786 154.

ASHAIKH, Abdul Aziz Bin Muhammad Bin Ibrahim al-, Saudi Arabian official/educationalist; born 1919, Riyadh, Saudi Arabia; *Religion:* Muslim; *Education:* graduate studies in Islamic studies; *Career:* Public Notary; research worker; Library Director, 1950; Principal of Riyadh Scientific Institute, 1952–54; Deputy Grand Qadi (Judge); Vice President, Scientific Colleges and Institutes; was involved in transforming the Scientific Colleges and Institutes into the Imam Bin Saud Islamic University, and became its President; member of the Higher Committee on Education Policy; member of the Supreme Council for the Promotion of Science, Arts and Letters; permanent member of the Major Social Scientists, USA; *Publications:* several articles and lectures in the *Muslim World League Journal* and other academic and scientific periodicals; *Interests and Recreations:* reading, travel; *Languages:* Arabic, English; *Address:* Shamali al-Morabba'a, Riyadh, Saudi Arabia; telephone: Office — Riyadh 22042; Residence — Riyadh 23732.

ASHKAR, Fuad S., Arab-American physician/educator; born 13 June 1935, Lebanon; married; one daughter, one son; *Religion:* Christian; *Education:* BS, American University of Beirut, Lebanon, 1958; MD, AUB, Lebanon; 1962; *Career:* Instructor in Medicine, University of Miami, 1968–69; Assistant Professor, Radiology and Medicine, 1969–74; Associate Professor, Radiology and Medicine, 1974–80; Professor, Radiology and Medicine, 1980–; Director of Radio Assay Laboratory, MU/JMH; President, Florida Association of Nuclear Physicians, 1979–81; President, Clinical Radio Assay Society, 1980–81; Consultant to Union Carbide Co, New York; *Publications:* numerous articles in various medical journals, 1968–80; several published books on nuclear medicine and Radio Assay, 1973–79; *Decorations:* Distinguished Medal of the National Order of the Cedars, rank of Chevalier, Republic of Lebanon; *Interests and Recreations:* gardening, hunting, sailing, archeology; *Languages:*
70

Arabic, French, English; *Address:* Office — Division of Nuclear Medicine, Jackson Memorial Hospital, 1700 NW 10th Avenue, Miami, Florida 33136; Office — 6500 SW 79 Ct, Miami, Florida, USA 33143.

ASHMAWY, Said Muhammad al-, Egyptian judge; born 1 December 1932, Egypt; *Religion:* Muslim; *Education:* BA, Law, Cairo University, Egypt, 1954; Technical Program in Investment Stimulation, USA, 1978; Harvard Law School, 1978; *Career:* Assistant District Attorney, Alexandria, 1954; District Attorney, 1956; Judge, 1961; Chief Prosecutor, 1971; Chief Prosecutor, Middle Cairo District, 1974; Counsellor of State for Legislation, 1977; High Court Judge, 1978; Chief Justice of the High Court, Chief Justice of the Court of Assize, Chief Justice of the High Court of Security of State, 1981; *Publications: Mission of Existence,* 1958, 1977, in Arabic; *History of Existentialism,* 1963, in Arabic; *Conscience of the Age,* in Arabic, 1968, 1979; *Harvest of the Mind,* 1974, in Arabic; *Roots of Islamic Law – Shari'a,* 1978, in Arabic, an English translation under publication; *Spirit of Justice,* 1982; numerous articles in Egyptian daily newspapers; *Interests and Recreations:* writing, travel, tennis, classical music; member of the Syndicate of Egyptian Writers; *Languages:* Arabic, English, French; *Address:* 9 Gezira Al-Wusta Street, Apt 19, Zamalek, Cairo, Egypt; telephone: 650 522.

ASHRAF, Anwar, Bahraini businessman; born 22 October 1933; married; one son, two daughters; *Religion:* Muslim; *Career:* Managing Director, Ashraf Brothers; *Interests and Recreations:* table tennis, cricket, swimming, chess; *Languages:* Arabic, English, Urdu, Persian; *Address:* Ashraf Brothers, P O Box 62, Manama, Bahrain; telephone: 53457.

ASHRAM, Fuad Salim, Saudi Arabian official; born 1943, Jeddah, Saudi Arabia; *Education:* BA, Geography, Riyadh University, Saudi Arabia, 1972; *Career:* Chief of Foreign Transport Department, General Postal Administration; Acting Director, Planning, Training and Budgeting Department; Director, Administrative Relations Centre, Jeddah Central Postal Studies, 1974; Director, Jeddah Central Post Service; *Address:* Jeddah Central Postal Service, Jeddah, Saudi Arabia; telephone: Office — Jeddah 32764; Residence — Jeddah 32935.

ASHREY, Muhamad T. al-, Egyptian academic; resident in USA; born 21 January 1940, Cairo; married; two daughters; *Religion:* Muslim; *Education:* BSc in Geology, Cairo University, Egypt, 1959; MSc in Geology, University of Illinois, USA, 1963; PhD, University of Illinois, 1966; *Career:* Assistant Professor, Geology Department, Cairo University, 1966–69; Assistant Professor, Associate Professor, Full Professor and Chairman, Department of Enviromental Sciences, Wilkes College, 1969–75; Staff Scientist, Enviromental Defence Fund, 1975–79; Director of Enviromental Quality, Tennessee Valley Authority, 1979–; Fellow of The Geological Society of America, American Association for the Advancement of Science; member of the Board of Directors, American Shore and Beach Preservation Association, 1977–80; *Publications:* one book and numerous scientific papers in professional journals and magazines; *Interests and Recreations:* tennis, hiking, bowling, chess, bridge; *Languages:* Arabic, English, French; *Address:* 4604 Tahoe Lane, Knoxville, TN 37918; telephone: (615) 688 8462.

ASHTAL, Abdullah Salih, People's Democratic Republic of Yemen diplomat; born 5 October 1940, Addis Ababa, Ethiopia; married; *Education:* BBA, American University of Beirut, 1966; MA, Political Science, New York University, USA, 1973; Doctoral Studies, Political Science, New York University, 1974; *Career:* Assistant Director, Sana'a Branch, Yemeni Bank for Reconstruction and Development, 1966–67; member, People's Supreme Council, 1967–68; member, General Command, National Liberation Front, 1968–72; People's Democratic Republic of Yemen (PDRY), committee, IMF, 1972; Senior Counsellor, Embassy to USA, 1970–73; Ambassador, Permanent Representative of PDRY, New York, 1973–; concurrently non-resident Ambassador to Canada, 1974–; *Languages:* Arabic, English, French; *Address:* 211 E.43rd Street, New York, NY 10017, USA; telephone: (212) 972 9570.

ASSA'AD, Muhammad Qussay Walliyuddin, Saudi Arabian geologist/administrator; born 1937, Cairo, Egypt; *Religion:* Muslim; *Education:* BSc in Geology; *Career:* Geologist; Assistant Director, then Director, Geological Department; Director, Technical Affairs; Director General for Projects, Ministry of Petroleum and Mineral Resources; member of American Federal Geological Association; Deputy Minister of Petroleum and Mineral Resources; Vice-Chairman of the Arab Company for Geophysics and Survey; attended several conferences in Saudi Arabia and abroad related to geology, mining survey, nuclear power and solar energy; *Publications:* co-author of textbook on geology for secondary schools; *Interests and Recreations:* reading, swimming; *Address:* c/o Ministry of Petroleum and Mineral Resources, P O Box 247, Riyadh, Saudi Arabia.

ASSA'AD, Omar Abdul Muhsin, Saudi Arabian physician/academic; born 1920, Medina, Saudi Arabia; *Education:* MB in General Surgery; *Career:* physician for Saudi Arabian Mission in Cairo; member of Medical Syndicate, Cairo Clinical Society, Faculty of Medicine, Cairo University; Associate of American Surgical Colleges; Director General of Medical Department, King Abdul Aziz University; contributed to preliminary studies for the establishment of the Faculty of Medicine, King Abdul Aziz University; member, Arab Medical Conferences, Cairo; member of American Surgeons Conference, Miami Beach, USA; *Publications:* medical and surgical research papers; *Interests and Recreations:* religious and literary reading; *Address:* Medical Department, King Abdul Aziz University, P O Box 1540, Jeddah, Saudi Arabia; telephone: Jeddah 26206.

ASSAF, Tawfiq, Lebanese businessman/politician; born 1915, Aley, Lebanon; married; one daughter, three sons; *Religion:* Muslim; *Education:* in Lebanon and South America; *Career:* emigrated to South America, 1936; returned to Lebanon, 1951; Founder and Chairman of the Board of Société Moderne Libanaise pour le Commerce SA (Pepsi-Cola), 1951; founder and Chairman of the Board, Bank of Beirut and the Arab Countries, 1956; co-founder and member of the Board, National Insurance Society, 1961; elected member of the Board of the Beirut Bourse, 1962; President of the Druze Community Committee; elected member of the Lebanese Parliament for Aley, 1972; Minister of Oil and Industry, 1973–74; *Interests and Recreations:* history, classical music, swimming, hunting; *Languages:* Arabic, English, Spanish; *Address:* Office — Bank of Beirut and The Arab Countries, Clemenceau

Street, P O Box 111536, Beirut, Lebanon; telephone: 366920; Residence — Aitat, Lebanon; telephone: 576145.

ASSEILY, Albert, Lebanese businessman; born Beirut, Lebanon; *Career:* President, National Cotton Spinning Company, Asseily and Company; Director and Manager, Real Estate Company for Construction; Manager, National Carpet Manufacturing Company; Manager, Oriental Films and Cinemas Company (FICINOR); *Languages:* Arabic, French, English: *Address:* Office — National Cotton Spinning Company, Trablos Street, Beirut, Lebanon; telephone: 220587; Residence — Fuad 1st Street, Beirut, Lebanon; telephone: 225747.

ASSEILY, Georges, Lebanese businessman; born 1937, Beirut, Lebanon; *Education:* BSc, Textiles, International College, American University of Beirut, Lebanon; London School of Economics, UK; University of Leeds, UK; *Career:* Production Manager, National Cotton Spinning Company, 1959; Managing Director, Edouard Asseily and Sons Establishments, 1962–; President of the Industrialists Association, 1974–77; *Interests and Recreations:* cooking, skiing, riding, swimming; *Languages:* Arabic, French, English; *Address:* Residence — Hamra Street, P O Box 5562, Beirut, Lebanon; telephoe: 223114.

ASSIOUTY, Odette, Egyptian academic; born 1941, Egypt; married; one son, one daughter; *Religion:* Christian; *Education:* BA, American University of Cairo, Egypt, 1963; MSc, University of Rhode Island, USA, 1965; Postgraduate Scholarship, 1966–70; Massey Dissertation Scholarship, 1969–70; PhD, American University, Washington D.C., USA, 1970; *Career:* Assistant Manager, Egyptian Commercial Organisation, 1959–63; Lecturer, The Collier Institute, USA, 1966–69; Professor, Howard University School of Business Studies, USA, 1969–; Chairperson to the Committee of Social Problems, 1975–; Consultant to the Arab Naval Academy, 1975–76; *Publications:* papers on foreign investment in the public sector; *Interests and Recreations:* photography, the promotion of Egyptian culture, tennis, swimming; *Languages:* Arabic, English, French; *Address:* 12236 Green Leaf Avenue, Potomac, Maryland 20854, USA.

ATALLA, Anton Abdul Nur, Jordanian lawyer/politician; born 18 October 1897, Jerusalem, Palestine; married; *Religion:* Christian; *Education:* American University of Beirut, Lebanon; Law School, Jerusalem; *Career:* Crown Counsel, 1924–27; Magistrate, 1932–37; Judge of District Court, Palestine, 1937–43; Senior Partner, A.H. Atalla and Company, Advocates, Jerusalem, 1943–48; Regional General Manager, Arab Land Bank, Jordan, 1948–73; Consultant, 1974–; member of Chamber of Deputies; Chairman of House Finance Committee, 1954–56; Minister of Foreign Affairs, 1963–64; member of Bureau of Intepretation of Constitution, 1974–; member of Senate Legal Committee and Foreign Relations Committee, 1974–; *Decorations:* Renaissance Medal 1st Class; Order of the Star of Jordan 1st Class; several foreign decorations; *Address:* Arab Land Bank, P O Box 6425, Amman, Jordan.

ATALLAH, Muhammad, Lebanese official/economist; born 20 June 1929, Sidon, Lebanon; married; two sons, one daughter; *Education:* BBA in Business Administration, American University of Beirut, AUB, Beirut, Lebanon; MA in Social Sciences, The Hague, Netherlands; PhD, University of Rotterdam, Netherlands; *Career:* Professor, AUB, Beirut, Lebanon, 1959; Director General, Arab Investment Company SAL, 1961; member of the Planning and Economic Development Council and of the Planning Commission; Lebanese Government Representative on the first Board of Intra Bank, 1967; President, Council for Development and Reconstruction; *Publications: Terms of Trade Between Agricultural and Industrial Products,* 1958; studies and lectures on Lebanese and Arab economies, since 1960; *Interests and Recreations:* swimming; *Languages:* Arabic, French, English; *Address:* Mme Curie Street, Dar Al Baida, Beirut, Lebanon.

ATALLAH, Munir Hanna, Jordanian businessman; born 8 May 1933, Jerusalem, Palestine; married; three daughters, one son; *Religion:* Christian; *Education:* BA in Economics; *Career:* Ministry of Economy, Jordan, 1955–57; Jordan Development Board, 1957–59; Managing Director, Near East Engineering Company; Vice President of Board of Trustees of Royal Academy of Aeronautics, Jordan and President of Rotary Club of Amman, 1975–76; *Address:* Near East Engineering Company, P O Box 1838, Amman, Jordan; telephone: 442278, 44278; telex: 1211.

ATALLAH, Mursi, Egyptian journalist; born 5 February 1943, Gharbiyah Province, Egypt; *Religion:* Muslim; *Education:* Diploma in English and Hebrew; Higher Diploma in Information; BSc, Agricultural Science; *Career:* Secretary, Editorial Board, *Al-Ahram* weekly, July 1976–; *Publications: October War from Operations Room,* 1974, 2nd edition 1975; *Decorations:* Order of Military Duty; *Interests and Recreations:* football, tennis; *Languages:* Arabic, English, Hebrew; *Address: Al-Ahram* Newspaper, Al-Galaa Street, Cairo, Egypt; telephone: 59010.

ATALLAH, Mutwalli Yusuf, Egyptian official; born 4 February 1923, Port Said, Egypt; married; two sons; *Religion:* Muslim; *Education:* BComm, Cairo University, Egypt, 1946; Fellow of the Higher Administration Institute, Lausanne, Switzerland, 1960; *Career:* General Manager, Egyptian Insurance, Organization, 1961–64; General Manager of *Al-Wadi* Company for Agricultural Crops Export, 1964–67; General Manager of Egypt Air, 1967–69; General Manager of the Egyptian Economy Organization, 1969–71; Under Secretary, Ministry of Economy for Imports, 1971–72; First Under Secretary of the General Organization for Arab and Foreign Investments; *Interests and Recreations:* tennis, swimming, walking; *Languages:* Arabic, English, French; *Address:* Al-Hami Hussain, Awal Al-Manyal, Cairo, Egypt; telephone: 844970.

ATALLAH, Naim Ibrahim, Anglo-Arab businessman/publisher; born 1 May 1931, Haifa, Palestine; married; one son; *Religion:* Christian; *Education:* Engineering, London University, UK; *Career:* joined Intra Bank, 1960; Manager of Intra Bank, London, 1966; Chairman and Chief Executive of the Namara Group of Companies including Quartet Books UK, USA and Australia; Director of Asprey Company Ltd; Director of Holst International, co-producer of the film *The Slipper and the Rose; Publications:* editor of *Last Corner of Arabia,* 1975; *Interests and Recreations:* the arts, drama, cycling, table tennis; *Languages:* Arabic, English, French; *Address:* 18b Wellington Court, Knightsbridge, London SW1, UK; telephone: 01 581 2171/2; telex:919034.

ATALLAH, Nasri Fuad, Jordanian official; born 1934, Haifa, Palestine; married; three children; *Education:* Dover College, UK; Degree from Georgetown University, Washington D.C., USA, 1961; Research Fellow at the Centre for International Relations, Harvard University, USA; Massachusetts Institute of Technology, USA, 1972; *Career:* Jordanian Foreign Service, 1961; Attaché, Jordanian Embassy to USA, 1961–68; Assistant Chief of the Royal Protocol, 1968–71; Secretary to HM King Hussain of Jordan, 1971–72; Private Secretary to HM the King, 1972–74; Adviser to the Minister of Tourism, 1975–; *Interests and Recreations:* cricket, squash; *Languages:* Arabic, English; *Address:* Ministry of Tourism and Antiquities, P O Box 224, Amman, Jordan; telephone: 42311/6; telex: 21741.

ATEEQI, Abdul Rahman Salim al-, Kuwaiti politician; born 5 April 1928, Kuwait; married; *Religion:* Muslim; *Education:* Mubarakiyah High School, Kuwait; *Career:* Kuwait Oil Company, 1945–48; Police Department, Kuwait, 1949–59; Private Secretary to Shaikh Sabah Al-Salim Al-Sabah; Secretary General of the Kuwait Police Department; Director General of the Kuwait Health Department, 1959–61; Special Representative of Kuwait at the UN General Assembly, New York, 1961; Ambassador to the USA, 1961–63; Under Secretary of State, Ministry of Foreign Affairs, 1963–67; Minister of Finance and Oil, 1967–75; Minister of Finance, 1975–81; Adviser to HH The Amir of Kuwait, 1981; since 1982 Chairman of the Board of Directors of Bahrain and Middle East Bank, Bahrain, of the Arabian Investment Banking Corporation (INVESTCORP) EC, Bahrain, of the Islamic Banking System International, Luxembourg; *Interests and Recreations:* reading; Chairman, Society for Handicapped People, 1973–; *Languages:* Arabic, English; *Address:* P O Box 848, Safat, Kuwait; telephone: 833787, 813993.

ATIYA, Aziz Suryal, Egyptian writer/historian; born 7 July 1898; *Religion:* Christian; *Education:* MA, PhD, DLitt, Liverpool University and London University, UK; *Career:* Charles Beard Fellow and University Fellow, Liverpool University, 1930–32; History Tutor, School of Oriental Studies, London University, 1933–34; Professor of Medieval and Oriental History, Bonn University, Germany, 1935–38; Professor of Medieval History, Cairo University, 1938–42; Professor of Medieval History, Alexandria University, 1952–54; President, High Institute of Coptic Studies, Cairo; Visiting Lecturer, US Universities, Zurich University and Swiss Institute of International Affairs, 1950–51; Visiting Professor of Islamic Studies, University of Michigan, USA, 1955–56; Luss Professor of World Christianity, Union Theological Seminary and Visiting Professor of Arabic and Islamic History, Columbia University, New York, USA, 1956–57; Visiting Professor of Arabic and Islamic History, Princeton University, USA, 1957–58; member of the Institute of Advanced Studies, Princeton University; Director, Middle East Centre, Utah University, USA, 1959–67; Distinguished Professor of History, Utah University, 1967–; corresponding member, UNESCO International Committee for the Scientific and Cultural History of Mankind; corresponding member, Coptic Archaeological Society; member of the Medieval Academy of America, member of the Mediterranean Academy, Rome; Fellow of the Royal Historical Society; *Publications: The Crusade of Nicopolis,* 1934; *The Crusade in the Later Middle Ages,* 1938; *Egypt and Aragon – Embassies and Diplomatic Correspondence between 1300 and 1330,* 1938; *Kitab Qawanin al-Dawawin by Saladin's Wazir ibn Mammati,* 1943; *History of the Patriarchs of the Holy Church of Alexandria,* 1949; *Monastery of St. Catherine in Mt Sinai,* 1949; *The Mt Sinai Arabic Microfilms,* 1954; *Coptic Music,* 1960; *Crusade, Commerce and Culture,* 1962; *History of Eastern Christianity,* 1968; *Languages:* Arabic and English; *Address:* 1335 Perry Avenue, Salt Lake City, Utah, USA.

ATRASH, Mansur al-, Syrian politician; born 1925, Jabal Druze, Syria; married; *Religion:* Muslim; *Education:* BA, Political Science, American University of Beirut, AUB, Lebanon; Degree in Law, University of Paris, France; *Career:* left Syria for Jordan 1954; after fall of Shishakli Government elected to parliament for district of Salkhad in Jabal Druze, during union with Egypt 1958–61; took active interest in Baathist newspaper *Al-Jamahir;* supporter of Salah Bitar; Minister of Social Affairs and Labour, 1963; Minister of Industry ad interim after cabinet reshuffle, May 1963; member of Presidential Council, in Salah Bitar Government, 1964;

resigned, October 1964; elected Chairman of National Council for Revolutionary Command Council, NCRC, 1965; held post until February 1966; *Languages:* Arabic, English, French; *Address:* c/o Ministry of Foreign Affairs, Damascus, Syria.

ATRASH, Said Muhammad, Libyan banker; resident in France; born 24 August 1937; married; *Religion:* Muslim; *Education:* University of Gariounis, Benghazi, Libya; *Career:* joined Arab Bank Ltd, Benghazi, Libya, 1957; National Commercial Bank of Libya, Benghazi, 1958; Central Bank of Libya, 1970; Union de Banques Arabes, 1973; Banque International Arabe, 1975–; *Languages:* Arabic, English, French, Italian; *Address:* 67 Ave Franklin Roosevelt, 75008 Paris, France.

ATTAR, Abdul Wahab Abdul Salam, Saudi Arabian official; born 1940, Mecca, Saudi Arabia; married; *Religion:* Muslim; *Education:* BCom, Cairo University, Egypt, 1967; PhD Economics, University of Southern California, USA, 1969; *Career:* Assistant Director, Planning Department, Supreme Planning Board, 1969–71; Director General, Research Department, Central Planning Organization; Under Secretary of State for Social Affairs, Ministry of Labour and Social Affairs; member of Board of Higher Committee for Social Security, Saudi Credit Bank; Supreme Council for Science, Arts and Literature; Central Committee for Community Development of Rural Areas; attended third Regional Conference of Ministers of Education and Ministers in charge of Economic Planning in the Arab States, Morocco, 1974, Conference of Social Affairs Experts, Tripoli, Libya, 1971; Conference of Population Policies, Cairo, Egypt, 1975, Conference of Arab Ministers of Social Affairs, Khartoum, 1975; *Publications:* several lectures delivered at academic circles and institutions; *Address:* Ministry of Labour and Social Affairs, Riyadh, Saudi Arabia; telephone: Office — Riyadh 27100.

ATTAR, Ahmad Abdul Ghafur al-, Saudi Arabian writer/religious scholar; born 1918, Mecca, Saudi Arabia; *Religion:* Muslim; *Education:* general; *Career:* written numerous publications on language and literature; edited several ancient Arabic manuscripts; translated poems by Indian poet Rabindranath Tagore; founder of *Okaz* daily newspaper; *Decorations:* Badge of the First Conference of Saudi Men of Letters; *Interests and Recreations:* reading, writing, travelling; *Address:* Jarwal, Mecca, Saudi Arabia; telephone: Residence — Mecca 22681.

ATTAR, Muhammad Said al-, Yemen Arab Republic UN official/economist; born 26 November 1927, Djibouti; married; four children; *Religion:* Muslim; *Education:* Diploma, Institut d'Etudes du Développement Economique et Sociale, University of Paris, France, 1958–60; Doctorate in Economics, University of Paris, France; *Career:* Chairman and Director, Yemen Bank for Reconstruction, 1963–65; Minister of State, 1965–66; Minister of Economy, 1967–68; Permanent Representative of Yemen Arab Republic (YAR) to the UN, New York, USA, 1968–71; Department Director, Ministry of Foreign Affairs, 1971–73; Permanent Representative of YAR to the UN, New York, 1973–74; Executive Secretary, and Under Secretary General, UN Economic Commission for Western Asia (ECWA), Baghdad, Iraq, 1974–; *Publications: Le Marché Industriel et les Projects de l'Arabie Séoudite,* 1962; *L'Industrie du Gant en France,* 1960; *Projects Industriels en Arabie Séoudite,* 1961; *L'Epicerie,* 1961; *Annotated Bibliography on Developing Countries,* 1962; *Le Sous-Développement Economique et Sociale du Yemen,* 1964 (French), 1965 (Arabic); *Interests and Recreations:* member of the International Sociological Association; member of the University of Paris Graduates Association; Alumni of the Institute for the Study of Economic and Social Development; *Languages:* Arabic, French, English; *Address:* UN Economic Commission for Western Asia, Airport Road, P O Box 27, Baghdad, Iraq; telephone: 95068; telex: 213468.

ATTAR, Muhammad Siraj al-, Saudi Arabian businessman; born 1924, Mecca, Saudi Arabia; *Religion:* Muslim; *Education:* commercial education in Cairo, Egypt; *Career:* member of Board of Jeddah Chamber of Commerce and Industry; member of Board of Saudi National Electric Power Co, Jeddah; member of Saudi Chamber of Commerce and Industry Delegation to the Conference of Chambers of Commerce and Industry Federation, Abu Dhabi; Honorary Consul of Mexico, Jeddah; member of Saudi Trade Delegation to Korea;

Interests and Recreations: reading, travel; *Address:* Gabel Street, Sharbatli Building, 4th Floor, Flat No 49, P O Box 1765, Jeddah, Saudi Arabia; telephone: Jeddah 26241.

ATTAR, Nawzad Ahmad Amin al-, Iraqi physician/academic; born 1 April 1941, Sulaimaniya, Iraq; married; two daughters, one son; *Religion:* Muslim; *Education:* MB, ChB, DS, University of Baghdad, Iraq; FRCS, Fellow of the Royal College of Surgeons of England, UK; FRCS, Fellow of the Royal College of Surgeons of Edinburgh, UK; *Career:* Director of the General Teaching Hospital, Sulaimaniya, Iraq, 1976–78; Dean of the College of Medicine, University of Salahuddin, Iraq, 1978–; *Interests and Recreations:* tennis, gardening; *Languages:* Kurdish, Arabic, English, French; *Address:* College of Medicine, University of Salahuddin, Arbil, Iraq; telephone: 25549, 25662.

ATTAR, Omar Saddiq, Saudi Arabian businessman, born 1929; *Religion:* Muslim; *Education:* general; *Career:* President of Saddiq and Mohamad Attar Co; member of International Air Transport Association, IATA, of American Society of Travel Agents, ASTA, of Pan American, of Trans World Airlines; Honorary Consul General of Norway; *Interests and Recreations:* swimming; *Address:* P O Box 439, Jeddah, Saudi Arabia; telephone: Office — 642 3244, 22 937.

ATTAS, Amin Aqil, Saudi Arabian official/accountant; born 1936, Mecca, Saudi Arabia; *Education:* BCom in Accountancy; *Career:* Accountant at the Arab Monetary Foundation, 1959; Head of the Department of Reversions, Ministry of Alms and Incomes, 1960–64; Deputy Director General for Alms and Incomes, 1965–67; Director General, Alms and Incomes, 1967–72; member of the Board for Social Security, 1971–72; Deputy Minister for Waqfs (Religious Endowments) Affairs, Ministry of Pilgrims; participated in the Economic Conference of the Arab League, 1964; and the Arab Ministers of Waqfs Conference, 1974; *Address:* P O Box 1030, Mecca, Saudi Arabia; telephone: Office — Mecca 34260; Residence — Mecca 22983.

ATTAS, Faisal al-; People's Democratic Republic of Yemen official; born 1938; *Career:* Governor of the Fourth Governorate, 1969–70; Governor of the Fifth Governorate; former member of the People's Supreme Council; Permanent Secretary at the Ministry of Works; Permanent Secretary of the Ministry of Communications; *Address:* Ministry of Communications, Aden, People's Democratic Republic of Yeman.

ATTAS, Haidar Abu Bakar al-, People's Democratic Republic of Yemen politician; born 1939, People's Democratic Republic of Yemen; *Education:* BSc in Electronics, Cairo University, Cairo, Egypt, 1966; *Career:* Head of Public Works Department in the Fifth Province; Minister of Works, 1969–75; Minister of Communications, 1975–77; Minister of Construction, 1977–; elected member of Central Committee, 1975; *Address:* Ministry of Construction, Aden, People's Democratic Republic of Yemen.

ATTAS, Hussain Bin Hashim al-; Saudi Arabian businessman; born 1921, Jeddah, Saudi Arabia; *Religion:* Muslim; *Education:* general; *Career:* Hotel Industry for 25 years; Owner of Al-Haramain Hotels, Al-Attas Hotels, Al-Attas Holiday Beach Hotel, Obhor, Jeddah, Jeddah Oasis Hotel (under construction), Al-Attas Tourist and and Travel Agency, Al-Attas Co for Trading and Contracting and Al-Attas Maritime Agency; *Interests and Recreations:* swimming, reading; *Address:* Al-Attas Oasis Hotel, Jeddah, Saudi Arabia; telephone: Office — Jeddah 20400, 20211; Residence — Jeddah 26874.

ATTIA, Elias, Egyptian journalist/businessman; resident in Switzerland; born 1925, Cairo, Egypt; married; two daughters; *Religion:* Christian; *Education:* MA in Law, Sorbonne, France; *Career:* Editor, *Le Journal d'Egypt,* Cairo, 1945–51; Chief Editor, *Cairo Calling,* 1950–52; Owner and Chief Editor, *Radio Monde,* Cairo, 1952–60; Partner and Editor, *Radar Advertising and Public Relations,* Cairo, 1956–61; Director, *Radintor Ltd Advertising and Public Relations,* Lausanne and Geneva, 1962–74; Editor, Foreign Supplement, *La Tribune de Genève,* 1968–72; member of the Société des Arts de Genève, the Foundation Committee of Islam and West, Switzerland, the American International Club, Geneva, the Association de la Presse Etrangère, Switzerland, the Association des Arganismes Nationaux du Tourisme Etranger en Suisse; *Interests and Recreations:* tennis, swimming, photography; *Languages:* Arabic, French, English, Italian; *Address:* Office — Arab-Swiss Chamber of Commerce and Industry, Rue de Beaumont 12, 1211 Geneva 12, Switzerland; telephone: 473202; Residence — Avenue de Cavaliers 21, 1224 Chêne-Bougéries, Geneva, Switzerland.

ATTIA, George N., Arab-American academic; born in Amioun, Lebanon; married; one son, two daughters; *Religion:* Christian; *Education:* BA in Arab History, AUB, 1949; MA in Arab History, 1950; PhD, Oriental Languages and Literature, University of Chicago, 1954; *Career:* Instructor, Prep School (now International College), Beirut, 1948–49; Instructor, Tripoli College, Tripoli, Libya, 1950–51; Assistant Professor, University of Puerto Rico, 1954–57; Associate Professor, University of Puerto Rico, 1957–60; Professor and Chairman, Department of Humanities, University of Puerto Rico, 1961–67; Head, Middle East Section, Library of Congress, Washington D.C., 1967; member of the Editorial Board of the *Middle East Journal,* Washington D.C.; Visiting Lecturer, School of Advanced International Studies, Johns Hopkins University, Washington D.C., 1969–75; *Publications: Medieval Political Philosophy* (contributor), 1963, New York, (English); *Al Kindi, The Philosopher of the Arabs,* Rawalpindi, 1966; *Address:* Office — Library of Congress, Washington D.C., 2054, USA; Residence — 4301 Bushie Ct, Alexandria, VA 22312, USA; telephone: 703 2564828.

ATTIA, Mahmud Ibrahim, Egyptian geologist; born 1900; *Religion:* Muslim; *Education:* Cairo and Imperial College of Science and Technology, London, UK; *Career:* Assistant Lecturer, School of Engineering, Giza, Egypt, 1923–25; Geologist, Geological Survey of Egypt, 1929; Assistant Director, Geological Survey of Egypt, 1939; Director, Geological Survey of Egypt, 1949; Director General, Mines and Quarries Department, 1954–56; Technical Director, Mineral Wealth Company and Sinai Manganese Company, Cairo, 1956–62; Professor of Geology, Cairo University; Associate, Royal College of Science, London 1929; Fellow of the Geological Society, London, 1930; member of Institut d'Egypte, 1946; member of the

Board, Desert Institute of Egypt, 1950; member of the Egyptian Geographical Society; *Publications: Notes on the Underground Water in Egypt,* 1942; *The Barramiya Mining District,* 1948; *New Mode of Occurrence of Iron-Ore Deposits,* 1949; *Iron-Ore Deposits of Egypt,* 1950; *Ground-Water in Egypt,* 1953; *Deposits in the Nile Valley and the Delta,* 1954; *Iron-Ore Deposits of the District East of Aswan,* 1955; *Manganese Deposits of Egypt,* 1956; *Decorations:* Egyptian Order of the Republic; State Prize in Geological and Chemical Sciences; *Languages:* Arabic, English; *Address:* 10 Diwan Street, Garden City, Cairo, Egypt.

ATTIA, Shaikh Khalid Bin Abdullah, Qatari politician/businessman; born 1930; *Religion:* Muslim; *Career:* Minister of Public Works, 1970–; major business interests; partner of Ahmad Mannai; *Address:* Ministry of Public Works, P O Box 38, Doha, Qatar; telephone: 424133,424406; telex: 4438 STATENG DOHA.

ATTIGA, Ali Ahmad, Libyan official/economist; born October 1931, Misurata, Libya; married; *Religion:* Muslim; *Education:* BSc, MSc, PhD, University of Wisconsin, USA; University of California, USA; *Career:* Assistant Economic Adviser, National Bank of Libya, 1959–60; Director of Research, 1960–64; Under Secretary, Ministry of Planning and Development, 1964–66; Director of Economic Research Division, 1966–68; Minister of Planning and Development, 1968–69; Minister of Economy, 1969; General Manager, Libya Insurance Company, 1970–; Chairman of Libya Hotel and Tourism Company, 1971–; Chairman of National Investment Company, 1971–73; Secretary General of OAPEC, 1973–; member of Board of Directors of Arab Re-Organization Company, Beirut; Vice President, UN ECOSOC, 1967–68; Vice President, Oxford Energy Club, 1974–; Chairman of the Management Committee of Oxford Energy Seminar, 1979–; *Languages:* Arabic, English; *Address:* OAPEC, P*TO Box 20501, Kuwait.

AUDA, Abdul Malik Ali Ahmad, Egyptian academic; born 25 March 1927, Dakahliyah, Egypt; married 1953; two sons; *Religion:* Muslim; *Education:* BA, Political Science, Cairo University, Egypt, 1948; MA, Political Science, 1951; PhD, Political Science, 1956;

Career: Lecturer, 1957; Professor, 1962; Professor of Political Science and Economics, College of Political Science, Cairo University, 1967; Dean of the College of Information, Cairo University; Assistant Editor of *Al-Ahram* newspaper, 1971–74; member of the Journalists Association; member of the African Political Science Association; member of the International Association of Information; *Languages:* Arabic, English; *Address:* Al-Ahram, Al-Galaa Street, Cairo, Egypt.

AWAD, Ali Mustafa, Saudi Arabian diplomat; born 1915, Mecca, Saudi Arabia; *Education:* Saudi Religious Institute, Mecca, 1932; *Career:* Consul, Embassy to Lebanon; Counsellor, Embassy to Egypt; Counsellor, Embassy to France; Acting Under Secretary of State, Ministry of Foreign Affairs; Minister Plenipotentiary, Embassy to Tunisia; Ambassador, Ministry of Foreign Affairs; Ambassador to Somalia; attended UNESCO Conference, Beirut, Lebanon, 1950 and Arab League Establishment Conference, Cairo Egypt; *Decorations:* Rafidain Order, Iraq; Order of the Republic, Egypt; Star of Somalia Order 1st Class, Somalia; *Interests and Recreations:* reading; *Address:* Ministry of Foreign Affairs, P O Box 495, Jeddah, Saudi Arabia; telephone: Office — 6421322.

AWAD, Fahmi Ibrahim, Egyptian academic/veterinary surgeon; born 1924, Cairo, Egypt; *Religion:* Christian; *Education:* Bachelor of Veterinary Medicine, Cairo University, Egypt; member of the Royal College of Veterinary Surgeons; PhD, Veterinary Medicine, London University, England; *Career:* Assistant, Cairo University, 1948; scholarship to England 1949–54; Lecturer at the Veterinary College, 1955; Head of Diagnosis Department in Sudan, 1956–61; Assistant Professor at Veterinary College, 1962; Visiting Professor, Nigeria, 1968; Head of Department and Assistant Dean, 1970; Assistant Director of the FAO, 1977; Professor and Head of Veterinary Medicine Department; Consultant to the State Company for Meat and Dairy Products; Consultant to the Arab Pharmacutical Co; Assistant Director of FAO Project for the Middle and Far East; Secretary General of the Veterinary Trade Unions; *Publications:* numerous papers in veterinary medicine; *Interests and Recreations:* member of the South Cairo Rotary Club; member of Al-Maadi and Al-Yakht

Sports Clubs; *Languages:* Arabic, English, French; *Address:* 12 Street No. 14 Maadi, Cairo, Egypt.

AWAD, General Khalafalla Amir, Sudanese army commander; born 1932; *Religion:* Muslim; *Education:* studies at Military Academies; Flying course in UK, 1956–57; Royal Air Force Staff College Course, UK 1961–62; *Career:* Second in Command, Sudan Air Force, 1964; Colonel, Officer Commanding, Air Force, 1966; Brigadier, Major General; Chief of Staff, 1972; during his last year of command of the Air Force served ex-officio, as Chairman of Sudan Airways; Minister of Defence and Commander in Chief, 1973; General, 1974; Adviser on Military and Aviation Affairs to the Presidency of the Republic, 1974–; *Address:* The Presidency, Khartoum, Sudan.

AWAD, Hussain Hadi, People's Democratic Republic of Yemen official/banker; born 1928, Yemen; *Education:* Aden Protectorate College; Gordon Memorial College, Khartoum, Sudan; Trinity College Cambridge, UK; *Career:* Deputy Accountant General; Permanent Under Secretary, Ministry of Finance, 1965–68; Permanent Under Secretary, Ministry of Commerce and Industry, 1966, later Secretary to the Currency Board; Managing Director and Chairman of the Board, 1968–72; Governor, International Monetary Fund; Adviser to the Bank of Yemen(Central Bank), 1972–80; Executive Director, Arab Monetary Fund, 1980–; member of the East African Currency Board, 1965–68; *Address:* Arab Monetary Fund, P O Box 2818, Abu Dhabi, United Arab Emirates; telephone: 28500; telex:2989.

AWAD, Louis, Egyptian writer/literary critic; born 5 January 1915, Minia, Egypt; married; *Religion:* Christian; *Education:* BA, Cairo University, Cairo, Egypt; MLitt, Cambridge University, Cambridge, UK; PhD, Princeton University, USA; *Career:* Lecturer, and later Professor of English, Cairo University, 1937–54; Literary Editor, *Al-Gumhuriyah,* 1953–54; Literary Editor, *Al-Sha'b,* 1957–59; Adviser, *Al-Gumhuriyah,* 1961; Adviser, Al-Ahram Organisation, 1962–; *Publications:* numerous works of literary criticism; *Decorations:* Order of Merit First Class, 1967; *Interests and Recreations:* literary criticism; *Languages:* Arabic, English, French, Latin, German, Greek; *Address:* Flat 16, 44 Kasr al-Ainy Street, Cairo, Egypt; telephone: Residence — 33201; Office — 758366.

AWAD, Muhammad Hadi, People's Democratic Republic of Yemen diplomat; born 5 May, 1934; married; one son, three daughters; *Religion:* Muslim; *Education:* Cambridge School Certificate, Aden, 1947–52; Diploma of Education and Certificate in Social Anthropology, Murray House College of Education, University of Edinburgh, UK, 1958–59; Certificate in Educational Planning, 1963–64; UNESCO Regional Centre of the Training of Arab Educational Personnel; *Career:* Teacher in government schools, 1953–59; Education Officer, 1960–62; Chief Inspector of Schools, 1963–65; Vice Principal of Al-Ittihad College (now Al-Sha'b College), 1965–67; Ambassador Extraordinary and Plenipotentiary to the United Arab Republic (UAR); non-resident Ambassador to Sudan, Libya, Lebanon and Iraq, 1968–70; Permanent Secretary of the Ministry of Foreign Affairs, 1970–73; Ambassador Extraordinary and Plenipotentiary to the United Kingdom, November, 1973–; non-resident Ambassador to Spain, June 1974–; non-resident Ambassador to Sweden, October 1974–; non-resident Ambassador to Denmark, January 1975–; non-resident Ambassador to the Netherlands, April 1975–; *Languages:* Arabic, English; *Address:* Embassy of the People's Democratic Republic of Yemen, 57 Cromwell Road, London SW7, UK; telephone: (01) 584 6607.

AWAD, Samuel, Sudanese UN official; born 2 April 1916, Omdurman, Khartoum, Sudan; *Religion:* Christian; *Education:* Diploma, Economics, Coptic College, 1936–40; *Career:* Revenue Accountant, British Overseas Airways Corporation, Nigeria, 1941–42; Expenditure Accountant, Egypt, 1942–49; District Accountant, British Overseas Airways, Iraq, Iran and Gulf, 1949–53; Chief Accountant, Arab Airways Limited, Jordan, 1953–59; Deputy Economist, British Overseas Airways Corporation Associated Co, UK, 1960–62; Chief, Transportation, Communications and Tourism Section, Economic Commission for Africa (ECA), UN, 1962–74; Chief, Transportation, Communications and Tourism, Economic Commission for West Asia (ECWA), UN, Iraq, 1974–; *Publications: Development of Air Transport in Africa,* 1963; *Transport of Perishable Goods and*

Farm Produce, 1965; *Interests and Recreations:* tennis, swimming, economics, development of transportation; member of the Sudan Club, Skal Club; *Languages:* Arabic, English; *Address:* ECWA, UN, P O Box 27, Baghdad, Iraq.

AWADI, Abdul Karim, Syrian politician/lawyer; born 1936, Hama, Syria; married; children; *Education:* Law Faculty, Damascus University, Syria; *Career:* joined Ministry of Education; Governor of Deir al-Zor; Director General of the Public Consumption Organisation; member of Baath Regional Command, 1970–; elected member of People's Council, 1971–; Minister of Supply and Internal Trade, 1971–75; Minister of State for Foreign Affairs, 1976–80; Minister of State for Presidential Affairs, 1980–; *Address:* Ministry of Presidential Affairs, Damascus, Syria; telephone: 331112.

AWADI, Abdul Rahman al-, Kuwaiti politician/physician; born 18 December 1936, Kuwait; married; four sons; *Religion:* Muslim; *Education:* BSc, American University of Beirut, 1958; BSc, Medicine and Surgery, Aberdeen University, 1963; MA, Health Planning, Harvard University, 1965; several other courses at Harvard University, School of PH; Honorary PhD, Si-Chang ban, Republic of Korea, 1977; *Career:* President, Medical Department, Sabah Hospital, Kuwait, 1963–64; Registrar, Medical Department, Sabah Hospital, 1966–69; Assistant Head of Preventive Medicine, Ministry of Public Health, Kuwait, 1969–70; Director, Preventive Medical Services, 1971–75; Minister of Public Health, Government of Kuwait, 1975–; President of WHO, 1979; President of Executive Bureau of Council of Arab Ministers of Health; President, International Commission for Prevention of Alcoholism, Washington, 1978; Honorary Membership, Royal College of Physicians of Ireland, 1977; *Publications: Hayatuna* magazine, for health education, appeared for 10 years; *Interests and Recreations:* walking, photography, gardening; *Languages:* Arabic, English; *Address:* Ministry of Public Health, P O Box 5, Kuwait; telephone: 433285; telex: 22729 HEALTH KT.

AWADI, Abdul Salam Abdullah M. Hadi, Kuwaiti official; born 1947, Kuwait; married; two sons, one daughter; *Religion:* Muslim; *Education:* BS in Economic and Political Science, Cairo University, 1970; Graduate Studies, International Economy and Development, University of Aberdeen, UK, 1973; *Career:* Economic Researcher, Prime Minister's Office, 1970; Representative of the Prime Minister's Office, Ministry of Trade, 1972; Deputy Director, Economic Department, Prime Minister's Office, 1974; Representative of the Prime Minister's Office, Commission for Oil and Petroleum Sales, Ministry of Oil, 1976; Director General, Real Estate, Investment Co; *Languages:* Arabic, English; *Address:* Al-Sharq, Abrag Abdullah Al-Awadi, Block 3, 9th Floor, P O Box 31, Safat, Kuwait; telephone: 440218, 421803.

AWADI, Muhammad al-, Saudi Arabian official; born 1920; *Religion:* Muslim; *Career:* former President of the Jeddah Chamber of Commerce; former Director of SAUDIA, the Saudi Arabian Airlines; Manager of the Arabian Trading Company, Jeddah; Minister of Commerce and Industry, 1975; *Languages:* Arabic, English; *Address:* Arabian Trading Company, P O Box 78 Jeddah, Saudi Arabia.

AWAR, Bashir, Lebanese politician/lawyer; born 1912, Beirut, Lebanon; *Religion:* Muslim; *Education:* Licence in Law; *Career:* Police Department; Magistrate; elected Deputy for Baabda, 1951, 1960, 1968; Minister of Public Health in Abdullah Yafi Cabinet, 1951; Minister of Justice, Public Works, Posts, Telegraphs and Telecommunications and Social Affairs successively in Cabinets of Abdullah Yafi, Saeb Salam, Sami al-Solh and Rashid Karami, 1964–68; Governor of North Lebanon; Minister of Interior in Amin al-Hafez Cabinet, 1973; *Address:* Tripoli, Lebanon; telephone: 621233.

AYAK, Arop Yor, Sudanese politician; born 1935 in the Upper Nile Province, Sudan; *Education:* University of Khartoum; attended a course on African Affairs at the School of Oriental and African Studies, University of London, UK; *Career:* Arabic Department, University of Khartoum, 1963; Minister of Public Works, 1966; University of Khartoum; seconded to be Regional Director of Information and Culture, 1972–73; Regional Director of Education, 1973–74; elected to the People's Assembly as a member of the Upper Nile Constituency, 1974; elected Deputy Speaker, 1974; elected Principal of the

University of Khartoum, 1974; *Languages:* Arabic, English; *Address:* University of Khartoum, Khartoum, Sudan.

AYARI, Chedli, Tunisian banker/economist; born 24 August 1933, Tunis, Tunisia; married; three children; *Religion:* Muslim; *Education:* LLB, University of Paris, France, 1957; PhD in Social Sciences, University of Paris, France, 1961; Agrégé, Economics, University of Paris, France, 1964; *Career:* Head of Department, Société Tunisienne de Banque, 1958; Lecturer, Faculty of Law, University of Tunis, 1958–60; Counsellor for Economic Affairs, Tunisia's Permanent Mission to the UN, 1960–64; participated in several meetings of the UN General Assembly; Executive Director of the IBRD (World Bank) and the International Finance Corporation, 1964–65; Professor and Dean of the Faculty of Law, Political Sciences and Economics, University of Tunis, 1965–69; concurrently Director, Center for Socio-Economic Studies and Research; Secretary of State for Planning, 1969–70; Minister of Education, Youth and Sports, 1970–71; Amassador to Belgium, Luxembourg and Representative to the EEC, 1972; Minister of National Economy, 1972–74; Minister of Planning, 1974–75; Chairman of the Board and General Manager, Arab Bank for Economic Development in Africa, 1975–; *Publications:* numerous articles in economic journals; *Decorations:* Grand Cordon, Order of the Tunisian Republic; Grand Cordon, Order of the Tunisian Independence; Grand Officier de la Légion d'Honneur Française; *Languages:* Arabic, French, English; *Address:* The Arab Bank for Economic Development in Africa, Baladia Road, P O Box 2640, Khartoum, Sudan; Gammarth, La Marsa, Tunis, Tunisia.

AYOUN, Bishir Zarg al-, Tunisian politician; born 1912, Jerba, Tunisia; married; *Religion:* Muslim; *Education:* general; *Career:* Destour Party member since 1938; arrested for nationalist activities in 1938 and 1954; member of the National Assembly; President of the Political Commission of the Assembly; member of the Socialist Destour Party Central Committee since 1973–; *Languages:* Arabic, French; *Address:* Parti Socialist Destourien, Building 9 April 1938, Tunis, Tunisia.

AYYAD, Shukri, Egyptian academic/writer; born 1921, Minufiyah Governorate, Egypt; *Education:* BA and PhD, Arabic Literature, Cairo University, Egypt; and USA; *Career:* journalist; teacher; diplomat; Cultural Counsellor, Embassy to Brazil; Associate Professor of Modern Arabic Literature, Cairo University; Assistant Editor, *Al-Magalla* magazine, Cairo; has translated works of fiction and criticism into Arabic; *Publications:* include two short story collections; *Experiments in Literature and Criticism,* collection of essays, 1967, in Arabic; *The Short Story in Egypt,* 1968; *Address:* Faculty of Arts, Cairo University, Cairo, Egypt.

AYYAR, Hamad Mubarak al-, Kuwaiti politician; *Religion:* Muslim; *Career:* Minister of Social Affairs and Labour, 1971–75; Minister of Housing, 1975; closely involved in the Ardiah Housing Development Plan which provided for an initial building of over 3,000 houses; *Address:* c/o Ministry of Housing, P O Box 2935, Safat, Kuwait.

AYYOUB, Ibrahim T., Arab-American academic; born 11 December 1928, Al-Husn, Jordan; married 1956; one son, one daughter; *Education:* BS, Eastern Oregon College, La Grande, Oregon, USA; MA, University of Illinois, Urbana, USA; postgraduate studies, University of Illinois and others; *Career:* Mathematics Instructor, Yokina Valley College, Washington, USA, 1960–; Chairman, Mathematics Department, Yokima Valley College, 1974–76; *Interests and Recreations:* farming, soccer; *Address:* Rt 8 Box 395, Yokima, Washington 98908, USA; telephone: 966 5970.

AYYOUB, Ibrahim Taha, Sudanese diplomat; born 20 October 1940, Wadi Halfa, Sudan; married; two sons, one daughter; *Religion:* Muslim; *Education:* BA, Arts, University of Khartoum, 1964; MA, International Public Policy, Johns Hopkins University, USA, 1976; *Career:* Attaché, Ministry of Foreign Affairs, Sudan, 1965; 3rd Secretary, Sudan Embassies, Baghdad Iraq, Amman Jordan, 1966–69; 2nd Secretary, Sudan Embassy, Addis Ababa, Ethiopia, 1969–71; Consul General of Sudan in Asmara, Eritrea, 1971–73; Director of African Department, Ministry of Foreign Affairs, Sudan, 1974–75; Ambassador to Ethiopia, 1976–77; Ambassador to Malaysia, Indonesia and Sri Lanka, 1977–78; Ambassador to New Delhi, 1978–;

Decorations: Orders from Ethiopia, 1971, Iran, 1974, Oman, 1977; *Interests and Recreations:* classical Arabic poetry, swimming, travelling; *Languages:* Arabic, English; *Address:* Sudan Embassy, 6 Jarbagh, New Delhi 110003, India; telephone: Residence — 376560; Office — 619325.

AYYOUBI, Mahmud al-, Syrian politician; born 1932; married; *Religion:* Muslim; *Education:* University of Damascus, Syria; *Career:* school teacher; Director General of Administration, Department for Euphrates River Affairs; Under Secretary, Ministry of Education, 1963; Minister of Education, 1969–71; Vice President of the Republic, 1971; member of the Syrian International Command of Baath Party, 1970; visited Cairo for talks on the proposed Egyptian-Syrian-Libyan Federation, and Khartoum for Conference of Education Ministers; closely involved in the establishment of the Federation of Arab Republics, 1971; member of the committee for establishing National Progressive Front in Syria; Vice President of National Front, 1972; Prime Minister, 1972–76; *Languages:* Arabic, English; *Address:* c/o The National Progressive Front, Damascus, Syria.

AYYOUBI, Muhammad Zuhair Bin Abdul Wahab al-, Saudi Arabian broadcasting official; born 1939, Medina, Saudi Arabia; *Education:* LLB; *Career:* TV and radio announcer; Chief Announcer; Director, Department of Culture, Radio and TV; Director of Programmes, Riyadh Radio Service; Director General, Jeddah Broadcasting Service; member of Islamic Conference, Damascus, Syria 1954, Conference of Federation of Arab Broadcasting Stations, Algiers, 1973, Conference of the Organization of Islamic States Broadcasting Stations, Riyadh, 1975, Jeddah, 1975; *Publications: Tahyyatu-l Iftar* (Breakfast Greeting); several other books, television and radio programmes; *Interests and Recreations:* sport, swimming, reading; *Address:* Jeddah Broadcasting Station, Jeddah, Saudi Arabia; telephone: 6424927; telex: 401186.

AYYOUBI, Sadik, Syrian politician; born 1925; *Education:* PhD, Economics, American University, Washington D.C., USA, 1951; *Career:* Head of Budget Department, Ministry of Finance, 1952–64; Director, Accounting and Consulting Firm, Damascus; returned to government service with economic liberalization programme, 1972; Minister of Finance, 1976; *Address:* Ministry of Finance, Damascus, Syria.

AZAR, Nasib Salim, Jordanian judge; born 1920, al-Husn, Jordan; married; *Education:* Law Diploma from Syrian University, 1943; *Career:* Amman Public Prosecutor, 1948–50; Civil Magistrate, Zerqa, 1950–51; Judge of First Court, Kerak, 1951–53; Judge of First Court, Jerusalem, 1953–55; Judge of First Court, Nablus, 1955–57; Judge of First Court, Amman, 1957–59; President of Court of First Instance, Kerak, 1959–60; President of Court of First Instance, Jerusalem, 1953–55; President of Court of First Instance, Nablus, 1955–57; President of Court of First Instance, Amman, 1957–59; President of Court of First Instance, Salt, 1960–61; President of Court of First Instance, Irbid, 1961–63; Appeal Court Judge, Amman, 1963–65; Attorney General, Amman, 1965–73; Member of Court of Cassation, 1973–; *Address:* P O Box 606, Amman, Jordan; telephone: 812502.

AZAR, Roger Fawzi, Lebanese banker; born 1 July 1943, Byblos, Lebanon; married; two daughters; *Religion:* Christian; *Education:* BA, Economics, American University of Beirut, Beirut, Lebanon; Licence en Droit, Faculty of Law, Beirut; Diploma, Economic Development, Pembroke College, Oxford University, Oxford, England; MBA, INSEAD, France; *Career:* Underwriting Department, First Boston Corporation, New York, 1970–72; Manager, First Boston (Europe) Ltd, London, 1972–73; Director, Investment Banking Department, Banque Arabe et Internationale d'Investissement, 1974–78; President and Director General, Société Financière, Azar SA; Consultant, BAII; Director, Hill Samuel and Co Ltd; Director, Lowndes Lambert Group Ltd; Director and Member, Executive Committee, Montedison SPA; *Publications:* articles on African art; seminar papers on banking; *Interests and Recreations:* flying, skiing, squash, tennis, golf, sculpture, primitive and Islamic arts; member, Lion's Club; Friend of the Museum of Man; *Languages:* Arabic, English, French, German; *Address:* 6 Avenue Frédéric le Play, Paris 7e, France; telephone: 555 0631.

AZIZ, Abdeslam al-, Moroccan journalist/writer; born 1941, Tetouan, Morocco; married; *Religion:* Muslim; *Education:* attended Law College, Qarawiyin University, Fes, Morocco, 1962; attended Arts College, Fes University, 1968; training in journalism and printing, Madrid, Spain, 1968; qualified interpreter, 1975; *Career:* Teacher in Ben Mellal Secondary School, 1964; Journalist and Art Critic for *Government News,* 1972; Journalist for Royal Documents Administration, 1974; Programme Producer, Radio-Television MAROC, 1975; Press Department, Assistant Head of State Office for National Co-operation and Traditional Industry, 1975–; *Publications:* numerous articles in Moroccan newspapers; author of several novels and short story collections; *Interests and Recreations:* writing; member of the Moroccan Authors Association, the Tangiers University Club; *Address:* Ave Hassan II, Rue Al-Adarissa, Rabat, Morocco.

AZIZ, Jean, Lebanese politician/lawyer; born 24 June 1917, Jezzine, Lebanon; *Education:* Antoura College; St. Joseph University, Beirut, Lebanon; Licence in Law, Faculty of Law, Beirut; *Career:* Magistrate, 1947; Barrister at Law; elected Deputy for Jezzine, 1957; re-elected 1960, 1964 and 1968; defeated in 1972 elections; Minister of Labour and Social Affairs, 1961–64; responsible for final draft of Social Security Law, 1963; Minister of National Education, Information and Planning, 1968; Secretary General, Rashid Karami's Parliamentary Democratic Front, 1966–; *Publications:* political speeches; poetry; political and literary critique; *Interests and Recreations:* swimming and various other pastimes; *Languages:* Arabic, French; *Address:* Office — Capucins Street, Sehnaoui Building, Beirut, Lebanon; telephone: 244311; Residence — Jezzine, Lebanon and Hazmieh, Beirut, Lebanon; telephone: 280522.

AZIZ, Tariq, Iraqi politician; born 1936, Mosul, Iraq; *Religion:* Christian; *Education:* English Studies, College of Arts, Baghdad University; *Career:* member of the staff of *Al-Jumhuriyah,* 1958; Chief Editor of *Al-Jamahiir,* 1963; worked for the Baath press in Syria until the change of regime in February 1966; Chief Editor of *Al-Thawra* Publishing House; member of the Revolutionary Command Council General Affairs Bureau, April 1972; reserve member of the Arab Baath Socialist Party Leadership, 1974–77; elected member of Baath Regional Leadership, January 1977; Deputy Prime Minister, 1981–; *Languages:* Arabic, English; *Address:* Office of Deputy Prime Minister, National Assembly, Baghdad, Iraq.

AZMEH, Abdullah al-, Syrian banker/economist; born 14 July 1928, Damascus, Syria; married; two sons, three daughters; *Religion:* Muslim; *Education:* Licence in Law, Syrian University, 1951; Diploma, Economics, Lausanne University, 1958; Doctorate in Economics and Commerical Sciences, Lausanne University, 1961; *Career:* Certified Public Accountant registered in Syria; Director of Finance, General Organization of Electricity, Syria; Director, Financial Economic Affairs, Ministry of Petroleum and Electricity; Director, Bureau of Petroleum Marketing, Ministry of Petroleum and Electricity; Deputy Minister of Economy and Trade for Monetary and Banking Affairs, Damascus, Syria; General Manager, Union de Banques Arabes et Européennes, SA; member of the Board of Directors of Industrial Bank of Syria, Bank of the Arab World, Real Estate Bank, Unione di Banche Arabe ed Europe (Italia); headed and attended several meetings and conferences on International Monetary Affairs (UNCTAD), (ECWA); conducted economic negotiations with a number of countries on behalf of the Syrian Arab Republic; *Publications:* numerous books and research papers on economic and monetary subjects of the Middle East; *Languages:* Arabic, French, English, German; *Address:* UBAE Arab German Bank SA, Grosse Gallusstr. 15, 6 Fankfurt am Main 1, West Germany.

AZMEH, Issam, Jordanian banker/businessman; resident in Switzerland; born 10 July 1928, Amman, Jordan; married; two sons, one daughter; *Religion:* Muslim; *Education:* BA in Law and Economic Sciences; *Career:* Manager, Arab Bank (Overseas) Ltd, Geneva, Switzerland; President of Arab-Swiss Chamber of Commerce and Industry, Geneva, Switzerland; *Interests and Recreations:* literature, history of the Arabs, swimming, tennis, skiing; *Languages:* Arabic, English, French; *Address:* Arab Bank (Overseas) Ltd, 1 Quai du Mont Blanc, 1211 Geneva 1, Switzerland; telephone: 327 638; Residence — 18 Avenue du Bouchet, 1209 Geneva, Switzerland; telephone: 34 85 05.

AZRAK, Abdul Wahab al-; United Arab Emirates lawyer; born 1919, Aleppo, Syria; married 1941; seven sons, one daughter; *Education:* Law Degree, Damascus University, Syria; Law Degree, Paris, France; *Career:* Secretary, Syrian Chamber of Deputies; Director General of the Military Court; Director General of Syrian Customs; First Attorney in the Civil Court; Head of Administration of Syrian Government Affairs; member of the Syrian Higher Council for Science and Law; Lecturer in the Institute of Commerce and Law; Attorney General in the United Arab Emirates; *Address:* Attorney General's Office, P O Box 753 Abu Dhabi, United Arab Emirates; telephone: 43765, 43737.

AZZABI, Ayyad Muhammad, Libyan official; born 1936, Tripolitania, Libya; *Religion:* Muslim; *Career:* Director of Commercial Agencies Department; Ministry of Economic Affairs in late 1960s; Study Fellowship, Jesus College, Oxford, UK, 1968–69; Ministry of Industry, 1969; Director of National Oil Company, 1970–; Under Secretary, Secretariat of the General People's Committee for Industry; led Libyan economic team in negotiations for union with Egypt; *Languages:* Arabic, English; *Address:* Secretariat of the General People's Committee for Industry, Tripoli, Libya.

AZZABI, Ridha, Tunisian official/engineer; born 1932, Tunis, Tunisia; *Religion:* Muslim; *Education:* graduated in Mathematics and Physics, Sorbonne, University of Paris, France; postgraduate studies in Petroleum Engineering, France; *Career:* Chief Engineer of the Bizerta Oil Refinery, 1963; Chief City Engineer of Tunis, 1964–69; Governor of Nabeul, 1969–70; Director of the National Tourist Office, 1970–73; Director General of the District of Tunis, 1973; *Languages:* Arabic and French; *Address:* Tunis Municipality, Tunis, Tunisia.

AZZAM, Henry T., Lebanese ILO official/economist; born 10 April 1949, Beirut; married; *Religion:* Christian; *Education:* BSc, MSc in Economics and Statistics, American University of Beirut; PhD in Economics, University of Southern California, Los Angeles; *Career:* Assistant Professor of Economics, University of Southern California, Los Angeles, 1976; joined ILO, Geneva, Employment and Development Department, 1977; Regional Adviser on Employment and Development for the Arab States, Regional ILO Office, Beirut, 1978–; part-time Lecturer, Economics Department, AUB, 1978–81; member of the International Economics Association, Association of Arab Demographers; *Publications:* editor, *Women, Employment and Development in the Arab World,* 1981, The Haig Mouton Publishers, in English; *The Labour Market in the Gulf in Issues of Development; The Arab Gulf States,* 1980, in English; *Consequences and Probabilities of the Migration of Manpower in the Importing and Exporting Countries,* 1981; *Al-Mustaqbal al-Arabi,* in Arabic; *Manpower in the Western World,* 1980; *Al-Iqtisaad wal-Amal; Interests and Recreations:* tennis, swimming; *Languages:* Arabic, English, French; *Address:* P O Box 114–5096, ILO Regional office for the Arab States, Beirut; telephone: Office — 802780, 802980; Residence — 227537.

AZZAWI, Hikmat al-, Iraqi politician; born 1934, Iraq; *Education:* College of Commerce and Economics; *Career:* Reserve Lieutenant, 1957–58; Central Bank, 1958–63; First Superintendent, Central Bank, 1963; Auditor, Directorate of Stores and Warehouses, Directorate of Marketing, State Company for Electrical Instruments and Equipment, 1966–68; Director General and Chairman of Government Purchasing Board, 1968; Chairman, General Establishment of Trade, 1969; member of the Baghdad Chamber of Commerce, 1969; member of Board of Directors, Central Bank, 1969; Under Secretary in the Ministry of Economy, 1969; Minister of Economy, 1972–76; Minister of Foreign Trade, 1976–77; member of Iraqi Baath Party, 1977; Minister of State for Kurdish Affairs, 1977; Chief Editor, *Al-Iktisad* economic magazine, Baghdad; member of the Iraqi Economists Association; *Languages:* Arabic, English; *Address:* C/O Iraqi Economists Association, Baghdad, Republic of Iraq.

B

BA FAQIH, Fadhl Abdullah, Saudi Arabian businessman; born 1940; *Education:* BCom Business Administration; Diploma of Industrial Business Administration, UK; training courses in British factories; management training courses; *Career:* Bureau Manager, Governor of Petroleum and Minerals, General Corporation; Administrative Assistant, Iron and Steel Plant Project; Commercial Director; member of Board, Petromin Lubricating Oil Plants; Vice-Chairman of Executive Committee, Iron and Steel Plant; Director General of Iron and Steel Plant; member of Board of Directors, Arab Iron and Steel Association; attended First Arab Iron and Steel Association Conference, Tunis 1973, Second Conference, Riyadh 1974; *Address:* Petromin Iron and Steel Plant, Jeddah, Saudi Arabia; telephone: Jeddah 32699.

BA'YOUN, Adnan Adil, Jordanian official; born 18 February 1927, Amman, Jordan; married; *Education:* general; *Career:* official at the Import and Export Committees and the Currency Board, 1945–48; Arab Bank, 1948–49; Staff member of the Jordan National Assembly, 1949–60; Assistant to the General Secretary of the Houses of the Senate and Representatives; General Secretary of the National Consultative Council, 1978–; member of the Government Officials Association, 1956–59, the Cooperative Society for Government Officials, 1959–62, the Cooperative Saving Society for Government Officials, 1962–67; Chairman, the Benevolent Society in Zerqa, 1970–; *Decorations:* Order of the Star of Jordan 3rd Class; *Address:* National Consultative Council, Amman, Jordan.

BAABA, Samih Fuad al-, Lebanese diplomat; born 1923, Tripoli, Lebanon; married; two daughters; *Religion:* Muslim; *Education:* LLD, University of Paris; *Career:* Consul, Lebanese Embassy to Paris, 1953; General Consul, Tehran, 1956; General Consul, Marseille, 1958; Head of Economic Department, Lebanese Foreign Ministry, 1959; General Consul, Istanbul, 1961; Counsellor, Paris, 1964; Ambassador to Liberia, 1966; Ambassador to Kuwait, 1968; Ambassador to Bucharest, Romania, 1980–; *Publications: How to Become a Diplomat,* in Arabic; *Decorations:* Officer of the Lebanese Order of the Cedar; Order of Merit, France; and other decorations from Liberia, Turkey, Kuwait, Iran; *Languages:* Arabic, French, English; *Address:* Ambassade du Liban a Bucharest, 18 Rue Dorolaut, Romaine; telephone: 795165, 127010.

BAALBAKI, Leila, Lebanese writer; born 1936, Beirut, Lebanon; married; one daughter; *Education:* St. Joseph University, Beirut; Diploma from the Institute of Oriental Literature, Beirut; *Career:* writer; *Publications:* various novels among which, *Je Vis; Les Dieux Monstres; Un Bateau de Tendresse pour la Lune; Interests and Recreations:* swimming, music; *Languages:* Arabic, French; *Address:* Residence — Amir Amran Street, Tousbahji Building, Beirut, Lebanon.

BAALBAKI, Rohi; Lebanese academic/ publisher; born 2 September, 1947, Beirut, Lebanon; *Religion:* Muslim; *Education:* LLM, SJD, Harvard University, Lebanese University, Beirut, Lebanon; *Career:* Director, Dar Al-Ilm Lil-Malayin Publishing House, 1972–; Professor of Law, Faculty of Law, Lebanese University, Beirut, 1978–; *Publications: Human Rights and Liberties,* 1979, in English; *English Letter Writing,* 1972, in Arabic; *Yoga,* 1967, in Arabic; *Americans in North Africa in the 18th Century,* 1970 in Arabic; *Interests and Recreations:* reading, writing, chess, travelling; member of the Union of Arab Jurists, of the Union of Lebanese Authors, of the Union of Lebanese Publishers; *Languages:* Arabic, English, French; *Address:* P O Box 1085, Beirut, Lebanon; telephone: 304445, 804271.

BAAQLINI, Mershed, Lebanese business-man/banker; born 1926, Beirut, Lebanon; married; three sons, one daughter; *Education:* engineering studies; *Career:* Chairman and General Manager, Metropolitan Bank, SAL, Green Land Company, OTAC, Beirut, Lebanon; *Interests and Recreations:* reading, gardening, travel; *Languages:* Arabic, English, French; *Address:* P O Box 11–8940, Beirut, Lebanon; telephone: 415040; telex: 23505 METROB LE.

BABIKIAN, Khatchik, Lebanese lawyer/politician; born 1924, Cyprus; married; five daughters; *Religion:* Christian; *Education:* Italian College, Beirut; Licence en Droit and PhD, French Faculty of Law, Beirut, Lebanon; attended London School of Economics, UK; *Career:* Barrister at Law; elected Deputy for Beirut, 1957, 1960, 1964, 1968, 1972; currently member of Parliament; Reporter of the Parliamentary Justice Committee; Chairman of the Parliamentary Planning Committee; Minister of State for Administrative Reform, 1960–61; Minister of Health in Rashid Karami Cabinet, 1969; Minister of Tourism, 1969–70; Minister of Information in Saeb Salam Cabinet, 1972; Minister of Planning in Amin Al-Hafez Cabinet, 1973; Minister of Justice, Chafik Wazzan Cabinet, 1980–; member of the National Dialogue Committee, 1975; Chairman of the Lebanese Management Association (LMA), 1972; Chairman of Saving and Credit Cooperative for Lebanon, 1979–; member of the American Political Science Association; member of the American International Law Association; Chairman of the Armenian Central Committee for the Church of Cilicia; took a leading part in the 1963 reconciliation between Khoren I, Catholics of Cilicia and Vazken I, Catholics of Echmiadzin; Chairman of the Armenian National Assembley in Lebanon, 1972–; Chairman of the Armenian Higher Committee for Rehabilitation of Lebanon (OMARES), 1978–79; Chairman of Housing and Assistance Association (HABEAS); Vice President, World Association of French Speaking Parliamentarians, 1982–; *Decorations:* Knight of the Order of Lebanese Merit; Officer of the Order of Italian Republic; Grand Officer of the Order of the Knights of Malta, and several other orders and medals; *Languages:* Arabic, English, French, Italian, Armenian, Turkish; *Address:* Office— PO Box 939 Beirut, Lebanon; telephone: 335773; Residence — Ashrafiah, Immeuble Babikian, Beirut, Lebanon; telephone: 32201.

BACONI, Issa Nasri, Lebanese banker; resident in USA; born 2 June 1947, Haifa, Palestine; married; one son, one daughter; *Religion:* Christian; *Education:* BA and BBA, American University of Beirut, AUB, Lebanon; *Career:* First National Bank of Chicago, Beirut, Abu Dhabi, Sydney and New York, 1968–82; Vice President and Head of Middle East Division, First Chicago International, NY, and Gulf International Bank, NY, USA, 1982–; Director of Arab Bankers Association for North America; *Interests and Recreations:* squash, tennis; *Languages:* Arabic, French, English; *Address:* Gulf International Bank, 499 Park Avenue, NY 10022, New York, USA; telephone: (212) 7500660; telex: 424027 GIBANK NY.

BADAWI, Muhammad Mustafa, Egyptian academic; resident in UK; born 10 June 1925, Alexandria, Egypt; married; one son, three daughters; *Religion:* Muslim; *Education:* BA, Alexandria University, 1946; BA, London, 1950; MA, Oxford, 1964; *Career:* Research Fellow, Alexandria University, Egypt, 1947–54; Lecturer, 1954–60; Professor of English, 1960–64; Lecturer, Brasenose College, 1964–; Fellow of St. Anthony's College, 1967–; Visiting Professor, University of Kuwait, 1973; Visiting Professor, University of Alexandria, 1977; Lecturer, Oxford University; member of the Committee of Correspondents for the Annual Bibliography of *Shakespeare Quarterly*, Washington D.C., USA, 1961–80; UNESCO Expert on modern Arabic culture, 1974; member of Advisory Board, *Cambridge History of Arabic Literature,* 1970–; co-founder and Editor of the *Journal of Arabic Literature,* Leiden, 1970–; *Publications: An Anthology of Modern Arabic Verse,* 1970; *A Critical Introduction to Modern Arabic Poetry,* 1975; *Background to Shakespeare,* 1981, in Arabic; and many other books in Arabic on Literature; *Interests and Recreations:* theatre, music, comparative literature; *Languages:* Arabic, English, French; *Address:* St. Anthony's College, Oxford, UK; telephone: 0865 59651 ext 53.

BADDOU, Abdul Rahman, Moroccan politician; born 1925, Meknes, Morocco; *Religion:* Muslim; *Education:* legal and administrative studies in Rabat; *Career:* active member of nationalist movement; refused further education by French authorities, 1944; arrested and imprisoned for organising demonstrations at Ouajda, 1952; member of the Executive Committee Istiqlal Party after his release from prison; Senior Official, Ministry of Justice for several years; Deputy of Meknes, 1963; associated with reorganisation of Judiciary and in charge of criminal affairs and pardons; Ambassador to Saudi Arabia; Morocco's representative at various international conferences; Secretary of State for Foreign Affairs, 1977–; *Languages:* Arabic, French; *Address:* Ministry of Foreign Affairs, Rabat, Morocco.

BADIB, Ali Abdul Razzaq, People's Democratic Republic of Yemen politician/diplomat; *Career:* former Ambassador to German Democratic Republic; Ambassador to Romania, 1971–74; Minister of Culture and Tourism, and Acting Minister of Information, 1975; Deputy Prime Minister, 1982; member of Political Bureau; *Address:* Prime Minister's Office, Aden, People's Democratic Republic of Yemen.

BADR BIN ABDUL AZIZ, HRH Prince, Saudi Arabian Prince; born 1933; son of late King Abdul Aziz; *Religion:* Muslim; *Education:* court education; private education in religion, politics and diplomacy; *Career:* Deputy Commander of the National Guard; several posts in government, the most recent Minister of Communications; *Address:* Presidency of the National Guard, Riyadh, Saudi Arabia.

BADR BIN ABDUL MUHSIN BIN ABDUL AZIZ, HRH Prince, Saudi Arabian Prince/poet and impresario; born 1953, Riyadh, Saudi Arabia; *Religion:* Muslim; *Education:* BA; *Career:* President of the Saudi Arts Society; works for the promotion of arts, specially poetry, music, painting and folksinging; Founder of the Saudi Arts Society, an organization for the promotion of Saudi arts in Saudi Arabia and abroad; *Publications:* collections of poems and songs; *Interests and Recreations:* reading, music, poetry; *Address:* Saudi Arts Society, Commercial and Residential Centre, Jeddah, Saudi Arabia.

BADR, Fayiz Ibrahim, Saudi Arabian official/economist; born 1939, Mecca, Saudi Arabia; *Religion:* Muslim: *Education:* BA Economics, Cairo University, Egypt; MA and PhD in Economics, University of Southern California, USA; *Career:* Adviser to the President of the Central Planning Organization; Vice President, the Central Planning Organization; Deputy Minister of Planning; President of the Saudi Ports Authority since its establishment, 1976–; member of the Royal Commission for the Development of Jubail and Yanbu industrial zones; supervised the formulation of the Kingdom's First Development Plan (1970–75) and the Second Development Plan (1975–80); *Publications:* numerous articles, research papers, and specialised reports; *Interests and Recreations:* reading, swimming; *Address:* Saudi Ports Authority, P O Box 5162, Jeddah, Saudi Arabia; telephone: Office — Jeddah 643 1031. 476 0500; telex: 21783 PORTS SJ.

BADR, Hamud Abdul Aziz al-, Saudi Arabian academic; born 1939; *Religion:* Muslim; *Education:* PhD in Public Relations and Education; *Career:* journalist; Director, Foreign Relations Department, Ministry of Labour; Director of Research and Statistics Department, Ministry of Labour; Registrar and Assistant Professor of Education, Riyadh University, Saudi Arabia; Vice Rector, Riyadh University; member of the American College Registrars and Accreditation Organization (ACRAO); member of American Public Relations Organization; *Publications:* *History of Saudi Press* in Arabic; *Public Relations in Universities* in Arabic; *Interests and Recreations:* reading, travelling; *Address:* Office — P O Box 263, Riyadh, Saudi Arabia; telephone: Office — Riyadh 65560; Residence — Riyadh 67215.

BADR-KHAN, Ali Ahmad, Egyptian artist/film director; born 25 April 1946, Giza, Egypt; married; *Religion:* Muslim; *Education:* graduated from the Higher Cinema Institute, Egypt, 1967; training grant in Rome, Italy, 1968; *Career:* film director, Production Department, Egyptian Organization for Cinema, Music and Drama; awarded critics' prize for best film of 1973; State Prize for Best Director for 1975; *Interests and Recreations:* shooting, riding; *Languages:* Arabic, English; *Address:* 5 Al-Ahram Studios Street, Giza, Egypt; telephone: 852177.

BADR, Mansur Muhammad, Libyan politician; born 1931, Derna, Libya; married; *Religion:* Muslim; *Career:* joined Libyan Armed Forces, 1954; extensive training in Turkey and UK; army officer; First Commanding Officer of Libyan Navy on its foundation, 1962; Chairman of the Marine Transport Corporation; Minister of Marine Transport, 1974–77; Secretary of Marine Transport, General People's Committee, 1977; *Address:* Secretary of Marine Transport, General People's Committee, Tripoli, Libya.

BADRAH, Abdul Rashid Ahmad, Saudi Arabian businessman; born 1927 Mecca, Saudi Arabia; *Religion:* Muslim; *Career:* sweet and biscuits industry for 20 years; Chairman and General Manager of Badrah Saudi Factories, Jeddah; established housing units for factory workers; member of Jeddah Chamber of Commerce; *Decorations:* Winner of First Golden Award of the late King Khalid for Ideal Factory in Saudi Arabia; *Address:* P O Box 1678, Binzagar Building, 6th Floor, Share Jadid, Jeddah; Saudi Arabia; telex: 400178 Rashed SJ, 401024 Badrah SJ.

BADRAN, Adnan Muhammad, Jordanian academic/scientist; born 1936, Jerash, Jordan; married; *Religion:* Muslim; *Education:* BSc, Oklahoma State University, USA, 1959; MSc, Michigan State University, USA, 1960; PhD, Michigan State University, USA, 1963; *Career:* researcher in physiology, USA, 1963–66; Assistant Professor, Associate Professor and Professor, 1966–71; Dean of College of Sciences, University of Jordan, 1971–76; President of Yarmouk University, Jordan, 1976–; developed biology curriculum and books for secondary education in Jordan; Vice President, Commission of Biology Education; represented Jordan at many international conferences and UNESCO General Assembly; member of Research Grants for Sciences and Technology for International Development (BOSTID), of National Academy of Science; *Publications:* various researches and studies in the fields of physiology and biochemistry; author and editor of several books on biological sciences; Editor, *Biology Education,* Newsletter, International Union of Biological Sciences; *Decorations:* Renaissance Medal, 2nd Class, Jordan; Khalid Ibin al-Walid and Yarmouk 1st Order Medal; *Interests and Recreations:* member of the Royal Conservation Society, of the International Association of University Presidents; Presidential Fellow of Aspen Institute; *Languages:* Arabic, English; *Address:* Yarmouk University, P O Box 566, Irbid, Jordan; telephone: 71100/5; telex: 51533, 21498, YARMUK JO.

BADRAN, Mudar Muhammad, Jordanian politician/army officer, retired; born 1934, Jerash, Jordan; married; *Religion:* Muslim; *Education:* BA in Law, Damascus University, Syria, 1957; *Career:* 1st Lieutenant, Public Security, 1957; Assistant Legal Adviser to Armed Forces, 1957; Military Representative, 1962; Defence Attorney in the Military Court, 1962–65; Assistant Chief of Jordanian Intelligence, 1965–66; Assistant Chief of Jordanian Intelligence, 1968–70; Major General, retired 1970; Secretary General of Royal Court, 1970–71; National Security Adviser to His Majesty, 1971–72; Minister in the Royal Court, 1972; member of Executive Council of Arab National Union, 1972; Deputy Head of Executive Office for Occupied Territories Affairs, 1972–73; Minister of Education, 1973–74; Minister of Defence; Minister of Foreign Affairs; Prime Minister, 1976–; *Decorations:* Independence Medal, 4th Class; Renaissance Medal, 3rd Class; Independence Medal, 1st Class, 1972; *Address:* Shmaisani, Amman, Jordan; telephone: 41211.

BADRE, Albert, Lebanese academic; born 25 April 1913, Lebanon; married; *Education:* Bachelor of Business Administration (BBA), and MA American University of Beirut (AUB); PhD, University of Iowa, USA; *Career:* Lebanese Delegate to the Economic and Social Council held USA, 1948; Professor of Political Science; Director, Economic Research Institute, AUB, Lebanon; member of the Lebanese Government's Economic Planning Committee; *Publications: National Income of Lebanon; Lebanese Industrial Development,* in Arabic; *Interests and Recreations:* Vice President, AUB Alumni Association; *Languages:* Arabic, French, English; *Address:* Office — American University of Beirut, Lebanon; telephone: 292860; Residence -- Artois Street, Halim Hanna Building, Beirut, Lebanon.

BADRI, Muhammad A. al-, Egyptian UN official/statistician; born 16 November, 1920, Cairo, Egypt; *Religion:* Muslim; *Education:* BSc in Mathematics, Cairo, Egypt, 1941–45;

PhD in Statistics, University of London, UK, 1946–48; DIC (Diploma of Imperial College) in Statistics, 1948; *Career:* Statistician, Ministry of Social Affairs, Egypt, 1948–52; Professor of Statistics and Demography, Cairo University, 1952–62; UN Expert on India, 1959–62; Chief of Estimates and Projections Section, UN Secretariat, 1965–72; Assistant Director, Population Division, UN Secretariat, 1972–80; Director, Cairo Demographic Centre, 1980–; member of the International Union for the Scientific Study of Population; member of the Population Association of America; member of the International Statistical Institute; *Publications:* numerous articles on population and statistics published in several international journals and magazines, in English, Arabic, Japanese, Hungarian, Korean; several books on statistical methodology; *Interests and Recreations:* philatelic, swimming, demography statistics; *Languages:* Arabic, English, French; *Address:* Cairo Demographic Society Building, 109 Kasr al-Aini Street, Cairo, Egypt; telephone: 30571.

BAESHEN, Ahmad Muhammad Salih, Saudi Arabian businessman; born 1902, Jeddah, Saudi Arabia; *Religion:* Muslim; *Education:* general; *Career:* Supervisor, Al-Falah Secondary Schools, Mecca and Jeddah for 25 years; Inspector, Jeddah Municipality for two years; general import business; member of Board, Jeddah Municipality, 1933–69; former Chairman, Chamber of Commerce, Jeddah, Commercial Law Court; *Interests and Recreations:* reading; *Address:* P O Box 18, Jeddah, Saudi Arabia; telephone: Jeddah 32964, 31471.

BAGHDADI, Bakr Ahmad, Saudi Arabian official; born 1940; *Religion:* Muslim; *Education:* BA; *Career:* patent expert and legal adviser, Arab and Foreign Trade Agreements Committee; Manager of Ministry of Commerce, Eastern Region Branch; member of Commercial Court; Chairman of Committee on Contravention of Bills of Exchange Regulations; *Interests and Recreations:* reading, swimming; *Address:* Ministry of Commerce Branch, King's Street, Dammam, Saudi Arabia; telephone: 832 2315; telex: 601081 TEGARH SJ.

BAGHIR AHMAD, Major General Muhammad al-, Sudanese army officer/politician; born 1927, Sudan; *Religion:* Muslim; *Education:* Khartoum branch, Cairo University; Military College, 1950; Staff Courses, UK, 1954 and 1961; Staff Courses, Egypt, 1957–59; *Career:* Military Commander, Upper Nile Province, 1959; Military Attaché, Embassy to UK, 1966; Brigadier, 1967; Commander of the Military College, Omdurman, 1967; Staff Course, Cairo Military Academy, 1968; Under Secretary, Ministry of Defence, 1969; Deputy Chief of Staff, 1970; Chief of Staff, 1970; Minister of the Interior, 1971; participated in the negotiations leading to the Addis Ababa Agreement on Southern Sudan, 1972; First Vice President of the Republic following resignation of Babiker Awadalla, 1972; member of the Sudanese Socialist Union Political Bureau; *Languages:* Arabic, English. *Address:* Office of the First Vice President, Khartoum, Sudan.

BAGHLI, Ibrahim Tahir, Kuwaiti official/archaeologist; born 1942, Kuwait; married; two sons, three daughters; *Religion:* Muslim; *Education:* BA and Diploma in History; *Career:* Archaeology Researcher, 1968; Director, Department of Antiquities and Museums, 1975–; Assistant Director General and Manager of Al-Baghli, Textile Co and Textile MFG Co; *Interests and Recreations:* walking, history, archaeology; member of the Union of Arab Historians; *Languages:* Arabic, English; *Address:* Kuwait National Museum, Ministry of Information, P O Box 193, Safat, Kuwait; telephone: Office — 4320201; Residence — 616723.

BAGU, Henry, Sudanese banker; born in Eastern Equatoria, Sudan; *Religion:* Christian; *Education:* Course in social sciences in UK, 1971–72; course at the University of Perugia, Italy; *Career:* banker by profession; Commissioner of Equatorial Province, 1972; Provincial Secretary General of the Sudan Socialist Union; *Languages:* Arabic, English, Italian; *Address:* Sudan Socialist Union (SSU), P O Box 1850, Khartoum, Sudan.

BAHA'IDDIN, Ahmad, Egyptian journalist; born 1927; married; *Religion:* Muslim; *Career:* editorial staff of *Al-Akhbar;* Editor of *Akhbar al-Yaum,* 1960–61; Editor of *Akhir Sa'a,* 1961; member of Board of Directors of *Akhbar al-Yaum;* appointed Chairman of Dar al-Hilal, 1964; Editor in Chief of *Al-Musawwar,* 1965; Chairman of the Press Syndicate, 1968–69; Chairman of the *Rose el-Yousef* Publishing House 1968–69; Editor in Chief of *Al-Ahram,* 1974–75; served as Chairman of the Union of Arab Journalists; *Languages:* Arabic, English; *Address:* Al Ahram, Galaa Street, Cairo, Egypt.

BAHAR, Abdul Aziz Ahmad al-, Kuwaiti banker/businessman; born 1929, Kuwait; *Religion:* Muslim; *Education:* BA, American University of Beirut, Lebanon, 1951; *Career:* Director General of Housing Department, Ministry of Finance, 1956–61; Director General, Kuwait Fund for Arab Economic Development, 1961–62; Chairman, Kuwait National Industries, 1963–65; Director, Kuwait Metal Pipe Industries, 1965–67; Chairman, Kuwait Insurance Company, 1965–67; Director, Kuwait Chamber of Commerce and Industry, 1962–71; Chairman, Kuwait Foreign Trading, Contracting & Investment Co, 1966–73; Director, Rifbank 1967–74; Chairman, Commercial Bank of Kuwait, 1965–78; Director, United Bank of Kuwait, London, 1970–75; Deputy Chairman, Commercial Bank of Dubai, 1970–78; Director, Arab Company Trust, 1975–78; Chairman, Arab European Financial Management Company, SAK, 1978–; Director, Central Bank of Kuwait, 1980; member of International Banking Association, of Kuwait-Saudi Arabian Neutral Zone Boundary Commission, 1961, of Industrial Development Committee, 1963–65, of Kuwait Economists Society, Trustee of Kuwait University, 1966–70; *Languages:* Arabic, English; *Address:* P O Box 460, Safat, Kuwait; telephone: 410180; telex: 2810.

BAHAR, Abdul Latif al-, Kuwaiti official; born 1940, Kuwait; *Religion:* Muslim; *Education:* Victoria College, Alexandria, Egypt; BA, Economics and Politics, Keele University, UK; *Career:* Director, Office of HH Crown Prince and Prime Minister; represented Kuwait at several bilateral conferences; *Languages:* Arabic, English; *Address:* Prime Minister's Office, P O Box 4, Safat, Kuwait; telephone: 428 956.

BAHAR, Muhammad Abdul Rahman al-, Kuwaiti businessman; born 1920, Kuwait; married; *Religion:* Muslim; *Career:* Director of National Bank of Kuwait; Director of Kuwait Chamber of Commerce and Industry; Distributor in the Gulf States for several international companies, such as Caterpillar, Burroughts, General Electric, Unilever; Representative of several shipping lines, including Jugolinija, China Ocean Shipping; *Languages:* Arabic, English; *Address:* P O Box 148, Safat, Kuwait; telephone: 433881/8; telex: 2068 KT.

BAHARETH, Muhammad Salih, Saudi Arabian businessman; born 1926; *Religion:* Muslim; *Education:* general; *Career:* Director General, Ministry of Finance, 1954; Chairman of Board of Indecom, Melli Iran Bank, Jeddah; Chairman of Endowments Subsidiary Council, Jeddah; member of Board, Bin Ladin Organization; Chairman of Bahareth Organization, Jeddah; established Jeddah Clinic; member of the Board for the Settlement of Trade Disputes; *Interests and Recreations:* reading, sport; *Address:* P O Box 404, Jeddah, Saudi Arabia; telephone: Jeddah 23666.

BAHARNA, Hussain Muhammad al-, Bahraini politician/lawyer; born 5 December 1932, Manama Bahrain; married; one son, two daughters; *Religion:* Muslim; *Education:* LLB, College of Law, University of Baghdad, Iraq, 1953; Diploma in Law, University of London, 1956; PhD, Public Law, University of Cambridge, 1961; *Career:* Legal Adviser, Ministry of Foreign Affairs, Kuwait, 1962–64; Legal Adviser and Consultant on Arabian Gulf Affairs, 1965–68; Legal Adviser, Government of Bahrain, and member of the Council of State, Bahrain, 1970–71; President of the Legal Committee of the Council of State, Bahrain, 1970–71; Minister of State for Legal Affairs, Bahrain, 1971–; member of the Bahrain Bar, 1953–54; member of Lincoln's Inn, London, 1955–57; participated and contributed to a seminar on the Law of Treaties, organised by the Hague Academy of International Law, August 1960; member of the British Institute of International and Comparative Law, UK, of the American Society of International Law, Washington D.C., USA, of the Drafting Committee for the Constitution of the Federation of the United Arab Emirates, 1970–71, and Legal Adviser to the Bahrain Delegation to the UN General Assembly, 1970–71; commissioned by the Arab League as special envoy to the North American States and Japan, to represent Arab views on Palestine, and the oil crisis to the peoples and governments of North America, November 1974; *Publica-*

tions: The Legal Status of the Arabian Gulf States, Manchester University Press, 1968, UK; Legal and Constitutional Systems of the Arabian Gulf States, Beirut, Lebanon, 1974; contributed to The National Reports on the Arabian Gulf States, International Encyclopedia of Comparative Law, vol I, Hamburg, West Germany, 1973; several articles in professional journals, The Kuwait Saudi Arabian Neutral Zone Agreement of July 7, 1965, on the Partition of the Zone, in International and Comparative Law, vol 17, July 1968, UK; presented papers at several international and regional seminars on the constitutional and legal developments in the Gulf States, 1970–76; Interests and Recreations: member of the University Graduates Club, Bahrain; member of the Urubah Club, Bahrain; Languages: Arabic, English; Address: Minister of State for Legal Affairs, Government House, P O Box 790, Manama, Bahrain; telephone: 255633.

BAHNASSI, Afif Rafiq, Syrian official/art historian; born 17 April 1928, Damascus, Syria; married; three sons, one daughter; Religion: Muslim; Education: Licence in Law; BA in History of Arts; PhD in History of Arts, Sorbonne University; Career: Director General of Fine Arts, 1958–71; Director General of Museums and Antiquities; President of International Council on Monuments and Sites, Syria; President of International Council of Museums, Syria; member of the National Committee of the UNESCO; member of the German Federal Institute of Archaeology; Publications: numerous books and articles on Syrian and Arab history, Islamic art, modern art and other subjects connected with arts and archeology, in Arabic and French; Decorations: Commander of the Order of Arts and Letters, West Germany and France; Commander of the Order of Denmark; Order of Merit, Poland and other decorations; Interests and Recreations: sculpture, painting; member of the Union of Arab Writers; Founder and Chairman of the Association of Fine Arts; Languages: Arabic, French, English; Address: Office — Directorate of the Administration of Museums and Antiquities, Damascus, Syria; telephone: 14854, 14855; Residence — 5 Rawada Street, Damascus, Syria; telephone: 334554.

BAHNINI, Hadj Muhammad, Moroccan politician/lawyer; born 1914, Fes, Morocco; married; Religion: Muslim; Education: BA and PhD in Law; Diploma in Administrative Sciences, Morocco; Career: Secretary at the Royal Palace; Magistrate, Cherifien High Tribunal; Professor at the Royal College; Director of the Royal College, 1950; in exile in South Morocco, 1952; Secretary General of the Government, 1955–1972; Minister of Justice, 1958–1965; Minister of Administrative Affairs, 1965; Minister of National Defence, 1970; Minister of Justice, 1971; Deputy Prime Minister, 1972; Minister of State, 1972; Minister of State for Cultural Affairs, 1974–; Minister in charge of the Education of the Royal Princes and Princesses; Minister of State, 1982–; Languages: Arabic, French; Address: Office of the Minister of State, Ministry of Culture, Rabat, Morocco.

BAHR, Ali Abdul Rahman al-, Yemen Arab Republic official/banker; born 20 March 1929; married; Religion: Muslim; Education: MA in Economics, USA; Career: Director of Administration of Loans and Grants, 1972; Lecturer, College of Economics, Sana'a University, 1974; Deputy Minister of Economy, 1974; Deputy Governor for the Yemeni Bank in IBRD (World Bank); member of the Board of the Central Bank; member of the Board of the Yemeni Bank; member of the Board of the Electricity Corporation; Publications: MA thesis Factors Affecting the Rate of Unemployment; Interests and Recreations: reading, classical Arabic poetry, volley-ball, swimming, tennis; Languages: Arabic, English; Address: The Electricity Corporation, Sana'a, Yemen Arab Republic; telephone: 8129, 2463.

BAIDAR, Lieutenant Colonel Hamud Muhammad, Yemen Arab Republic diplomat/army commander; born 1942, near Rawdah, Yemen Arab Republic; Religion: Muslim; Education: Sana'a Military College; Career: took part in the leadership of the Free Officers Movement, which overthrew the monarchy, and led to the creation of the Yemen Arab Republic on 26 September 1962; Chief of Staff of Republican Forces, 1962–67; Officer, Commander of Military College at Rawdah, 1968–75; Assistant to the Chief of Staff, Minister of the Interior, member of the Command Council and Governor of Ibb, until 1976; Ambassador of Yemen

Arab Republic to Algeria, 1976–; *Address:* Embassy of Yemen Arab Republic, 74 Rue de Frères, Bouraba, Algiers, Algeria.

BAKALLA, Muhammad Hassan, Saudi Arabia academic; born 1 January 1946, Mecca, Saudi Arabia; married; *Religion:* Muslim; *Education:* BA, University of Riyadh, Saudi Arabia, 1964; Diploma, Linguistics, London, UK, 1968; MPhil, University of London, 1970; PhD, University of London, 1973; *Career:* successively Teaching Assistant, University of Riyadh, 1964, Lecturer, 1974–75, Assistant Professor, 1976–78, Associate Professor, 1978–; Head, Phonetics Laboratory, University of Riyadh, 1974–; Curator, Folklore Museum, University of Riyadh, 1974–; Deputy Dean, Arabic Language Institute, University of Riyadh, 1974–; member of Royal Geographical Society, London, Society of Saudi Dialects and Folklore, of the International Linguistics Association and of various other societies and associations; *Publications: Bibliography of Arabic Linguistics,* London, Mansell, 1975; editor of *Proceeding of the First International Symposium of Teaching Arabic to Non-Arabic Speakers,* 1981, volume 1; and several others works; *Interests and Recreations:* photography, philately, numismatics, table tennis, football, chess, geography; *Languages:* Arabic, English, Indonesian, Persian, Hebrew, French; *Address:* Phonetics Laboratory, College of Arts, University of Riyadh, Riyadh, Saudi Arabia; c/o Richardson, 36 Misbourne Road, Hillingdon, Middlesex, UB10 0HN, UK.

BAKDASH, Hisham Zaki, Syrian academic/physician; born 9 August 1934, Damascus, Syria; married; one son, one daughter; *Religion:* Muslim; *Education:* MD, Damascus University, 1959; Residency and Fellowship in Neuro-surgery, University of California, Los Angeles, USA (and other institutes), 1962–69: Diploma, American Board of Neurological Surgery, USA, 1969; *Career:* Associate Professor, American University of Beirut, 1971; Assistant Professor of Neuro-surgery, Damascus University, 1974–78; Professor, Damasucs University, 1979–; Chief Neuro-surgeon, Damascus University Hospital; Professor and Chairman, Department of Neuro-surgery, Damascus University; Chairman of the Examination Committee of Specialists in Neuro-surgery, Ministry of Health, Syria, 1970–; Secretary of the Scientific Committee of Damascus Medical Association, 1977–79; founding member of the Alumni Club of UCLA, University of California, USA, 1978; member of the American Association of Neurological Surgeons, 1970; Fellow, American College of Surgeons; *Publications:* numerous papers on Neuro-surgery in professional journals, USA, 1969–70; *Arab Medical Journal,* 1970–79; text book in Neuro-surgery, in Arabic; *Interests and Recreations:* history, travelling; *Address:* Jisr Abiad, Damascus, Syria.

BAKHIT, Bassam Salim, Jordanian engineer; born 27 September 1936, Salt, Jordan; married; two daughters; *Religion:* Christian; *Education:* BSc in Soil Mechanics, University of Arizona, USA, 1960; *Career:* engineer; Owner, Chairman of the Board and Managing Director of General Enterprise Co Ltd, founded 1963; involved in the construction and building of major Jordanian projects; Assistant Manager, Jordanian Cement Factory, 1960–63; member of the Planning Council, 1961–68, of Municipality of Amman, 1961–64; *Decorations:* Order of Independence, Jordan; *Interests and Recreations:* swimming; *Languages:* Arabic, English; *Address:* General Enterprises Co Ltd, P O Box 215 Amman, Jordan; telephone: Office — 64191/2; Residence — 812374.

BAKHSH, Abdul Rahman Taha, Saudi Arabian physician; born 1936, Mecca, Saudi Arabia; *Religion:* Muslim; *Education:* MBBCh, Diploma of Surgery, Diploma of Urolology, Ain Shams University, Cairo, Egypt; *Career:* Intern, al-Dimirdash Hospital, Cairo; Registrar, Department of Surgery of Urinary Tract, Cairo University; Owner and Manager, Saudi Daar al-Shifa Hospital and Bakhsh Hospital, Jeddah; member of the British Urological Associaton, London, UK, of the American International College of Surgeons; attended conference on Urinary Tract Surgery, London, UK, 1971, 1975, 1976; *Interests and Recreations:* photography, reading on Islam and Islamic culture; *Address:* Office — P O Box 365 and 6940 Jeddah, Saudi Arabia; telephone: Jeddah Daar al-Shifa Hospital: 6444333; Bakhsh Hospital: 6510666; Residence — Jeddah 6510101.

BAKIR, Anwar Abdul Hamid, Egyptian official; born 24 November 1914; married; one son, two daughters; *Religion:* Muslim; *Edu-*

cation: LLB; Diploma in Political Economy and in Public Law; Doctorate in Law; *Career:* Under Secretary of State, Egyptian Post Organization; Secretary General of Arab Postal Union; Secretary General of the African Postal Union; member of the Council of Post Administration; President of the Editorial Committee of the *International Postal Union,* 1952–74; member of the Society of Political Economies, of the Society of Public Law; *Publications: Contrôle des Changes,* 1944; articles in the Review of *International Postal Union, The Arab Postal Union* and *Society of Political Economy; Decorations:* Order of the Republic of Egypt, 1968; *Interests and Recreations:* croquet, walking, political economy; *Languages:* Arabic, English, French; *Address:* 150 Al Nil Street, Agouza, Cairo; telephone: 815855.

BAKOR, Abdallah Yusuf, Saudi Arabian academic/engineer; born 1948, Jeddah, Saudi Arabia; *Education:* BSc in Civil Engineering, 1972; Higher Training Course for Executive Management, King Abdul Aziz University, Saudi Arabia; *Career:* Civil Engineer, Municipality Office, Engineering Department, Ministry of the Interior, 1972; member of the Third Arab Engineers Conference, Tunisia; member of the Housing Co-operative Society, Jeddah; Director of Engineering Department, King Abdul Aziz University; *Interests and Recreations:* sports, football; *Address:* Engineering Department, King Abdul Aziz University, P O Box 1540, Jeddah, Saudi Arabia; telephone: Office — Jeddah 6879033; Residence — Jeddah 6876147.

BAKOR, Muhammad A., Saudi Arabian engineer/official; born 30 November 1947, Jeddah, Saudi Arabia; *Religion:* Muslim; *Education:* BSc in Civil Engineering, Massachusetts Institute of Technology, USA, 1971; MSc in Civil Engineering, Stanford University, USA, 1972; *Career:* supervised the preparation of the Second Industrial Development Plan of the Kingdom of Saudi Arabia, 1975–76, 1979–80; member of the Technical Committee, Supreme Petroleum Council; Director of Industrial Sector, Ministry of Planning 1972–; member of Saudi-US Industrial Cooperation Team; member of International Conference on Energy and Raw Materials, Paris, France, 1974; *Interests and Recreations:* swimming; *Publications: Energy and Development: A Case Study,* USA, 1973; *Address:* P O Box 3378, Riyadh, Saudi Arabia; telephone: Riyadh 21865.

BAKR AHMAD, Muhammad, Egyptian agriculturalist/academic; born 4 April 1916, Giza, Cairo, Egypt; married; two daughters, one son; *Religion:* Muslim; *Education:* BSc in Agriculture, Cairo University, Cairo, Egypt, MSc in Agriculture, Cairo University, PhD in Botany, Birmingham University, UK; *Career:* Professor, Faculty of Agriculture, Cairo Universtiy, 1956; Minister of Land Reclamation, 1968; member of the Academy of Agricultural Sciences, USSR, 1969; Professor of Agriculture, Cairo University, 1971; Head of the Department of Agricultural Botany, 1974; Emeritus Professor, Faculty of Agriculture, Cairo University, 1976; Adviser and member of the Board of the Agricultural Research Centre, Ministry of Agriculture, 1973; Head of the Plant Resources Research Council, Academy of Scientific Research and Technology, 1975; member of the National Committee for Physiological Sciences, 1975; member of the National Committee for Biological Sciences, 1977; member of the Food and Agricultural Research Council, Academy of Scientific Research and Technology, 1979; *Publications:* various research papers on plant physiology published in national and international professional journals; *Decorations:* Order of the Republic of Egypt, 4th Class, 1956; Egyptian Order of Merit, 3rd Class, 1959; Egyptian Order of Arts and Sciences, 1st Class, 1960; Egyptian Order of the Republic, 2nd Class, 1978; *Interests and Recreations:* swimming, Honorary President of the Egyptian Universities Sports Union; member of the Board of the Egyptian Football Federation, of the Executive Committee of the African Football Confederation, of Board of the Egyptian Society for Horticulture; *Languages:* Arabic, English; *Address:* Office — Faculty of Agriculture, Cairo University, Cairo Egypt; telephone: 724107; Residence — 3 Hay'i Al-Tadris Square, Dokki, Cairo, Egypt; telephone: 702711.

BAKR, Bakr Abdullah, Saudi Arabian academic/engineer; born 1 January 1938, Taif, Saudi Arabia; married; three sons, two daughters; *Religion:* Muslim; *Education:* BSc, Petroleum Engineering, University of Texas, 1959–63; MA, Business Administration, Stanford University, 1965–67; PhD, Business Administration, USA, 1968–70; *Career:* ARAMCO, 1963–64; Assistant to the Dean of College of Petroleum and

Minerals, 1964–66; Executive Assistant to the Governor of PETROMIN, 1966–70; Dean of the College of Petroleum and Minerals, 1970–74; President of the University of Petroleum and Minerals, 1974–; member of several organizations and university boards; *Interests and Recreations:* swimming; *Languages:* Arabic, English; *Address:* University of Petroleum and Minerals, P O Box 144, Dammam, Saudi Arabia; telephone: 867 3000; telex: 60160 UPMSJ.

BAKR, Ibrahim, Palestinian-Jordanian politician/lawyer; born 8 November 1924, Nazareth, Galilee, Jerusalem, Palestine; married; children; *Education:* graduated in law, Jerusalem Law College; *Career:* practiced law in Ramallah, later in Jerusalem till the June War of 1967; actively involved in political life of Jordan, before and after June War 1967 (imprisoned several times); expelled by Israelis from West Bank of the Jordan, 30 December 1967; practised law in Amman; member of the Palestine National Council, Palestine Liberation Organization, 1968–; Vice Chairman of the PLO Executive Committee, 1969; resigned, September 1969; independent member of the Central Committee of the PLO, 1970; member of the six-man General Secretariat; resigned from, PLO 1971; later practised law in Amman; President of the Jordanian Bar Association, 1977; member of the Palestine National Council and the Palestine Central Council of the PLO; re-elected President of the Jordanian Bar Association, 1979; *Languages:* Arabic, English; *Address:* P O Box 6981 Amman, Jordan; telephone: Office — 42471; Residence — 44112.

BAKR, Ibrahim Salih, Saudi Arabian diplomat; *Education:* Graduate Studies in Political Science and Psychology, University of Columbia, New York, Georgetown University, Washington D.C., USA; *Career:* Foreign Ministry, 1948–53; Consul and member of Saudi Arabian Delegation to UN, New York, 1953–57; 1st Secretary, Egypt, 1958–59; Counsellor, Chargé d'Affaires, Ghana, 1962–64; Minister Plenipotentiary, Chargé d'Affaires, UK, 1965–66; Ambassador, Head of Western Department, Foreign Ministry, 1966–68; Ambassador to Indonesia, 1968–74; Ambassador to Iran, 1975–80; Ambassador to Venezuela, 1981–; represented Kingdom of Saudi Arabia at several conferences and meetings; *Publications:* various articles in

Yawmiyat al-Bilad; Decorations: King Abdul Aziz Order of Merit; and several other decorations from Iran, Morocco, Jordon, Egypt, Indonesia; *Address:* Saudi Arabian Embassy, P O Box 62565, Avenida Principal de la Floresta, con Fco. de Miranda-Edif. Sucre, 6 Piso La Floresta Caracas 1060 A, Venezuela; telex: 23146 Saudi VE.

BAKR, Muhammad Abdul Rahman al-, United Arab Emirates politician; married; *Religion:* Muslim; *Education:* Islamic studies; *Career:* Chairman of Audit and Accounting Department; Ambassador to Syria, 1973; Minister of Justice and Islamic Affairs and Waqfs (Religious Endowments), 1977–; *Address:* Ministry of Justice, Islamic Affairs and Waqfs, P O Box 753, Airport Road, Abu Dhabi, United Arab Emirates; telephone: 323384.

BAKR, Rashid al-Tahir, Sudanese politician/lawyer; born 1930, Sudan; *Religion:* Muslim; *Education:* in Omdurman; Hantoub Secondary School; Faculty of Law, University of Khartoum; *Career:* President of the Students' Union, University of Khartoum; qualified as an advocate; active in politics; Ambassador to Libya, 1972; member of the Sudanese Socialist Union (SSU) Political Bureau and Secretary for Farmers' Affairs, 1973; Assistant Secretary General with responsibility for Sectorial Organisations, 1974; member of the People's Assembly and elected Speaker, 1974; served briefly as Minister of Animal Resources then as Minister of Justice; lawyer, 1974–; Vice President and Prime Minister, 1976; *Address:* Prime Minister's Office, Khartoum, Sudan.

BAKUR, Yahya Muhammad, Syrian agriculturalist; born 20 February 1938, Damascus, Syria; married; two sons; *Religion:* Muslim; *Education:* PhD in Agricultural Economics; *Career:* Head of Division, Administration of Agricultural Co-operation, Lattakya, Syria, 1963; Director General of Agricultural Co-operation, Lattakya, 1965; Director General of Agricultural Co-operation in Syria, 1968; Professor, Faculty of Agriculture, University of Damascus, Syria, 1973; Director of the Regional Bureau of the Arab Organization for Agricultural Development, 1977; member of the Board of the Union of Agricultural Engineers, 1969; Chairman of the Union of Agricultural Engineers, 1975–; Secretary General of the Arab Union of Agricultural

Engineers, 1979; *Publications:* numerous books, research papers, studies and translations on the development of agriculture in Syria and the Arab World; *Languages:* Arabic, German; *Address:* The Arab Organization of Agricultural Development, the Regional Bureau, P O Box 7611; Damascus, Syria; telephone: 222159; Agricultural Engineers Trade Union, P O Box 603, Damascus, Syria; telephone: 333017.

BALI, Slahiddine, Tunisian politician; born 29 July 1926, Tunis, Tunisia; three children; *Education:* Licence in Tunisian Law and French Law; holder of two diplomas for Higher Studies for the French Doctorate of Law; *Career:* Inspector of Finance, 1949; Magistrate, 1954; Prosecutor for the Permanent Military Tribunal, 1957; Acting Colonel, Director of the Central Administration, and Head of the Office of the Secretary of State for National Defence, 1966; Secretary General for the Ministry of National Defence, 1971; Permanent Secretary of the National Defence Council, 1971–73; Minister of Justice, 1973; *Decorations:* Grand Officer of the Order of the Tunisian Republic; Knight of the Order of Tunisian Independence; Commemorative Medal for the Battle for the Evacuation of Bizerta; Grand Cordon of the Order of Egypt; Grand Officer of the Order of Merit of German Federal Republic; Commander of Alaouite Medal; Commander of the Order of Iran; *Interests and Recreations:* Secretary General of the Tunisian Olympic Committee; Vice President of the Tunisian Federation of Equestrian Sports; shooting and the modern pentathlon; President of the Rugby Federation; President of the Nautical Sports Federation; Head of the Liaison Office for Africa in the International Council for Military Sports and Head of the Tunisian delegation; *Languages:* Arabic, French; *Address:* Ministry of Justice, Tunis, Tunisia; telephone: 26088.

BALLAL, Musa Awad, Sudanese diplomat/official; born 20 January 1931, Al-Fashir, Sudan; married; three daughters; *Religion:* Muslim; *Education:* Diploma of Arts, University of Khartoum, 1956; MBA, University of Pennsylvania, USA; *Career:* Director, Management Development Centre, Khartoum, 1965–70; Deputy Managing Director, Industrial Development Corporation, Khartoum, 1970–71; Secretary General, Public Sector Corporations, Khartoum; Mini-ster of Supply and Internal Trade, 1971–72; Minister of Industry and Mining, 1972–75; Ambassador of Sudan to West Germany, 1975–78; Ambassador to Kuwait, 1978–80; Ambassador to Tunis and Permanent Representative to the Arab League, 1980–; *Decorations:* Order of the Constitution, Sudan, 1974; Order of the Al-Nilayn, 1st Class, Sudan, 1979; Grosses Kreuz, West Germany, 1975; *Languages:* Arabic, English; *Address:* Sudan Embassy, P O Box 21, Belvedere, Tunis, Tunisia; telephone: 286335.

BALMA, Ahmad, Tunisian administrator; born 24 May 1923, Tunis, Tunisia; married; *Education:* BLL, MA in Politics and Economics, University of Toulouse, France; *Career:* Administrator, Civil Service of Tunisia, and Head of Social Affairs Office, 1950–57; Head, State Insurance Service, 1957–60; Principal Director General, National Security Social Fund; Head, Ministry of Health and Social Affairs Office, 1961–71; Head, Ministry of Health and Social Affairs Office, 1971–72; Director, International Labour Office (ILO) Area Office in Algiers, 1972; *Publications:* monograph on medical services in Tunisia; *Interests and Recreations:* lectures, music, sports; member, Club Sportif Football, Club Africaine Tunis; *Languages:* Arabic, English, French; *Address:* Office — BP 226, 19 Ave Claude Debussy, Algiers, Algeria; telephone: 602970; Residence -- 326 Parc Ben Omar, Algiers, Algeria; telephone: 770335.

BAMUFLEH, Salim, Saudi Arabian official; born 1924, Mecca, Saudi Arabia; *Religion:* Muslim; *Education:* BSc in Accountancy, 1950; *Career:* Chief Accountant, Mecca Health Department; Director General of Administration, Ministry of Agriculture and Water Resources; Adviser to Ministry of Agriculture; Director General, Department for Insect Control; Director General, Agricultural Research Centre, Jeddah; attended numerous international conferences on agriculture, several FAO conferences; *Interests and Recreations:* fishing, travelling; *Address:* P O Box 2579, Jeddah, Saudi Arabia; telephone: Office — 6427777, 6427840; Residence — 665 6127.

BANAWI, Ali Muhammad, Saudi Arabian businessman/industrialist; born 1930, Jeddah, Saudi Arabia; *Religion:* Muslim; *Education:* general; *Career:* manager of family business in timber and building materials, 1948–58; started his own business, 1959; Chairman of Banawi Factories, Corrugated Cartons (SFARIBAC); member of Constituent Committee, of Board of Jeddah Industrial Zone; built a residential compound for Banawi Factory personnel; printer; producer of paper products; *Interests and Recreations:* reading, hunting, photography; *Address:* Banaway Factories, Airport Street, Sharafia, Jeddah, Saudi Arabia; telephone: Jeddah 21688.

BANDAK, Mazin al-, Palestinian journalist; born 1934, Bethlehem, Palestine; married; *Religion:* Christian; *Education:* secondary education at Al-Rashidiyah College, Jerusalem; Licence in Law, Cairo University, Egypt, 1954; *Career:* writer, journalist and publisher; General Manager, *Dar al-Quds* publishing, printing and distribution house, Beirut, Lebanon; *Publications:* in Arabic: *Israel: Mujtamaa Askari,* 1969; *Al-Harb al-Thalitha,* 1972; *Qussat al-Naft,* 1974; *Al-Muqawama al-Falastiniya,* 1965–1973; 1977; various articles in Arabic in numerous newspapers and magazines; *Interests and Recreations:* music, theatre, history, fiction, walking; member of the Egyptian Journalists' Association, and Palestinian Writers' and Journalists' Union; *Languages:* Arabic, English, French.

BANDAR BIN ABDUL AZIZ, HRH Prince, Saudi Arabian Prince/businessman; born 1921, Riyadh, Saudi Arabia; son of late King Abdul Aziz; *Religion:* Muslim; *Education:* court education in Islamic studies, modern sciences and chivalry; *Career:* Chairman of Al-Bandar International Co Ltd; *Decorations:* Order of the Republic, 1st class; Order of the Nile, Egypt; Order of the Iraqi Kingdom; *Address:* Office — PO Box 1741, Al Khobar, Saudi Arabia; Residence— PO Box 5977, Al-Badi'ah, Riyadh, Saudi Arabia; telephone: Residence— Riyadh 56457, 56458.

BANDAR BIN FAISAL, HRH Prince, Saudi Arabian Prince/air force officer; born 1943; son of late King Faisal; *Religion:* Muslim; *Education:* in USA; Staff Course, RAF Bracknell, UK, 1973; *Career:* Captain, Royal Saudi Air Force; Lightning Pilot; Head, Royal Saudi Air Force negotiation teams; *Languages:* Arabic, English; *Address:* Ministry of Defence and Aviation, Riyadh, Saudi Arabia.

BANNA, Mahmud, Lebanese diplomat/lawyer; born 17 August 1917, Beirut, Lebanon; married; two sons; *Education:* Licence in Law, French Faculty of Law, Beirut, Lebanon; *Career:* Lawyer, 1941–45; 3rd Secretary, Embassy to France, 1946–48; 1st Secretary, Embassy to Italy, 1948–52; Consul General, Istanbul, Turkey, 1952–55; Head of Political Section for East and Arab League, Ministry of Foreign Affairs; Minister Plenipotentiary to Japan and Nationalist China, 1957–61; Ambassador to Czechoslovakia and Poland, 1961–64; Director General of Internal Security Forces, 1964–70; Representative of Lebanon to the European Office of the UN, Geneva, 1971; Ambassador, Permanent Representative to UN, Geneva, Switzerland; *Decorations:* various decorations from Japan, Italy, Libya, Tunisia, Senegal, Ethiopia, Jordan; Grand Officer of the Order of Honour and Merit of Haitian Republic; *Interests and Recreations:* photography, cinema, golf, tennis, swimming, table-tennis; *Languages:* Arabic, French; *Address:* Office — Lebanese Mission to the UN, 4 Avenue de Budé, CH-1202, Geneva, Switzerland; Residence — Immeuble Hamdan, Rue de Lyon, Beirut, Lebanon.

BANNA, Sabri al-, (Abu Nidal), Palestinian politician; born 1934, Gaza, Palestine; *Career:* member of Fatah and former Fatah representative in Iraq; appointed representative in Baghdad, 1971; accompanied Muhammad Daud Odeh in 1972 on a Fatah visit to China and North Korea; criticised Fatah leadership, 1973; challenged PLO Executive Committee, 1974; was disassociated by Fatah from the organization, 1974; founded Palestine Political Committee in Baghdad, publishing the newspaper *Al-Muqawama;* supported withdrawal of Popular Front for the Liberation of Palestine (PFLP) from PLO.

BAR, Abdullah Sabih al-, People's Democratic Republic of Yemen politician; *Career:* member of Organizational Committee of National Front of People's Organization; Alternate Member of Political Bureau; member of Central Committee and of People's Supreme Council; Chairman of the Supreme Organizational Watch Committee; *Address:* People's Supreme Council, Aden, People's Democratic Republic of Yemen.

BARAJAA, Abdullah Salih, Saudi Arabian businessman; born 1942, Shahar, Saudi Arabia; *Religion:* Muslim; *Education:* business administration training; *Career:* Sales Manager of Modern Supplies Corporation, Jeddah; Sales Manager of International Products Corporation, Mecca, Al Sulaiman Co, Riyadh, Hajji Abdullah Alireza and Co, Al-Khobar; Riyadh Branch Manager, Alissayee Trading Co, Proprietor and General Manager of General National Corporation, Public Relations and Representation, Riyadh; member of Riyadh Chamber of Commerce; agent for Peat Marwick Mitchell & Co; *Address:* P O Box 4226, Riyadh, Saudi Arabia; telephone: Riyadh 28183.

BARAKAT, Abdullah Hussain, Yemen Arab Republic politician; born 26 January 1936, Sana'a, Yemen Arab Republic; married; three sons, one daughter; *Religion:* Muslim; *Education:* Military College, Sana'a, 1950; Police College, Cairo, Egypt; Licence in Law, MA in Law, Cairo University, Egypt, 1958; *Career:* Army Officer, 1950; Assistant Head of Security, Taiz, 1961; Assistant Head of National Security, 1971; Minister of Agriculture, 1965–66; Head of Agricultural Projects, Tihama; Minister of the Interior, 1967; Ambassador to Sudan, 1969; Minister of the Interior, 1971; Ambassador to Algeria, 1971–74; Minister of Youth and Social Affairs; Deputy Prime Minister for Internal Affairs, 1975; Director, Head of State's Office, 1976; *Publications: Neutrality, Non-Alignment and Positive Neutrality; The Straits and their International Significance; Decorations:* Order of the Nile, 2nd Class, Egypt, 1975; *Interests and Recreations:* tennis, table-tennis, football; *Languages:* Arabic, English, French; *Address:* Airport Street, Ring Road, Sana'a, Yemen Arabic Republic; telephone: 2795.

BARAKAT, Ahmad Kaid, Yemen Arab Republic diplomat/engineer; born 1 January 1934; married; two sons, one daughter; *Religion:* Muslim; *Education:* BSc, University of Birmingham, UK; DIC, Imperial College, London, UK, 1953–59; *Career:* worked with several American and European companies in the field of petroleum and mineral exploration, 1959–63; Director General, Ministry of Public Works, 1963–64; private employment with Arab establishments , Sana'a; Director, Kuwaiti Aid, Sana'a; Technical Administrator, Kuwaiti

Aid Office, Dubai, 1964–69; Minister of Foreign Affairs, 1969–70; Personal Representative of the President; Secretary General of the Republican Council, and Head of the General Election Commission, 1970–71; Minister of Information and Culture, and Chairman of Sana'a Co-operative Union, 1971–72; Ambassador Extraordinary and Plenipotentiary to West Germany, and non-resident Ambassador to Belgium, the Netherlands, Switzerland and Austria, Head of the YAR Mission to the EEC, 1972–77; Minister of State and Chairman of Yemen Oil and Mineral Resources Corporation; member of the People's Constituent Assembley, 1978–81; Ambassador Extraordinary and Plenipotentiary to Japan, 1981–; *Interests and Recreations:* music, poetry, folklore, swimming, gardening, cross country running,; *Languages:* Arabic, English, German, French; *Address:* Yemen Oil and Mineral Resources Corporation (YOMINCO), P O Box 81, Sana'a, Yemen Arab Republic; Embassy of Yemen Arab Republic, Pastel City Higashiyama, 6–9, Higashiyama 2–chome, Meguro-ku, Tokyo, Japan; telephone: 499 7151/2.

BARAKAT, Gamaliddin, Egyptian diplomat; born 1921, Cairo, Egypt; *Education:* BLitt, LLB, Cairo University, Cairo, Egypt; Academy of International Law, The Hague, Netherlands; Oriel College, Oxford University, Oxford, England; *Career:* 3rd Secretary, Embassy of Sudan, London, 1950–52; Political Department, Ministry of Foreign Affairs, 1953–55; Consul General Aleppo, Syria, 1955–58; Counsellor, Embassy to the USA, 1958–60; Head of Service Training Department, Ministry of Foreign Affairs, 1961–63; member of the Organization of African Unity, Expert Committee, Addis Ababa, Ethiopia, 1963–64; Ambassador to Uganda, 1964–68, and to Burundi, 1967–68; Ambassador to Finland, 1968–73; Assistant to the President and Adviser on National Security, 1973–74; Director General, Department of Cultural Relations and Technical Cooperation, Ministry of Foreign Affairs, 1974–75; Ambassador to Iraq, 1976–78; Director of Institute of Diplomatic Studies, Ministry of Foreign Affairs, Cairo, Egypt, 1978–; *Publications: Status of Aliens in Egypt,* 1949; *Lectures on Diplomacy and Diplomatic Terminology,* 1962; *Lectures on Diplomatic History and Practice,* 1975; *Decorations:* Order of Merit, 4th Class, Egypt, 1958;

Order of the Republic, 2nd Class, Egypt, 1964; Order of the Lion, Finland, 1973; *Languages:* Arabic, English; *Address:* 56 Hegaz Street, Heliopolis, Cairo, Egypt.

BARAKAT, Ghalib Zaki, Jordanian diplomat/politician; born 20 September, 1927, Jaffa, Palestine; married; one son, two daughters; *Education:* BA, American University of Beirut, Lebanon, 1949; *Career:* Teacher, National College, Tripoli, Lebanon, 1949–50; Deputy Principal, National College, Tripoli, Lebanon, 1950–52; Jordan Civil Service, 1952; Chief Clerk, Press Officer, Tourist Department, Jerusalem, 1952–54; Press Attaché, Jordan Embassy, Rome, 1954–60; Director General, Jordan Tourist Authority, Amman Jordan, 1960–72; Under Secretary to the Ministry of Tourism and Antiquities, 1960–72; President of Arab Tourism Union, 1964 and 1970 sessions; Minister of Transport, Tourism and Antiquities, 1972; Chairman, Jordan Tourist Authority, 1972–79; Lecturer, Faculty of Economics and Commerrce, University of Jordan, 1967–; Minister of Tourism and Antiquities, 1973–79; member of the Board of Directors, Royal Jordanian Airlines, 1963–74; President of Jordan Hotel and Restaurants Corporation, 1973–79; Hon President, Amman Skal Club, 1975–; President, Arab Tourism Ministers Conference, Amman, Jordan, 1978; Consultant, World Tourist Organisation, Madrid; Special Envoy, World Tourist Organisation, 1980–; Ambassador and Permanent Representative of Jordan, UN, Geneva, 1980–; *Decorations:* Chevalier de la Couronne, Belgium, 1958; Istiqlal Decoration, Grade 111, Jordan, 1959; Istiqlal Decoration, Grade 11, Jordan 1961; Kawkab Decoration, Grade 11, Jordan 1964; Commander of the Holy Order of St. Silvester, Vatican, 1964; Kawkab Decoration, Grade 1, Jordan 1974; Order of T Vladimirescu, Grade 1, Romania, 1975; La Conde Coracion des Aguila Azteca, Mexico, 1976; several medals and awards; *Languages:* Arabic, English, Italian; *Address:* Jordan Permanent Mission, P O Box 463, 1211 Geneva 1, Switzerland, P O Box 9064, Amman, Jordan; telephone: 664593.

BARAKAT, Muhammad Rushdi, Egyptian diplomat/economist; born 4 August 1936, Cairo, Egypt; married; *Religion:* Muslim; *Education:* BA in Commerce, Ain Shams University, Cairo, 1958; Diploma in Market-ing, Cairo University, 1967; Diploma in Economics and Planning, Al-Azhar University, Cairo, 1974; PhD in Economic Sciences, Budapest University, Hungary, 1979; *Career:* joined Ministry of Economic, 1960; Commercial Attaché, Embassy of Egypt in India, 1961–65; 1st Secretary, Commercial Affairs, Embassy of Egypt in Budapest, Hungary, 1974–78; Commercial Adviser, Embassy of Egypt, Washington D.C., USA, 1980–; *Interests and Recreations:* squash, tennis, swimming; *Languages:* Arabic, English, French, Hungarian; *Address:* 260 S Reynolds Street, Alexndria, VA 22304, USA.

BARAKAT, Munir, Lebanese banker; born 9 August 1945, Lebanon; married; one son, one daughter; *Religion:* Christian; *Education:* BA, American University of Beirut, Lebanon; MBA, Faculty of Business Administration, New York, USA; *Career:* Branch Manager, National Bank of Abu Dhabi, 1969–75; Senior Manager, established and managed a branch, which dealt with government banking business, Abu Dhabi, 1977; Vice President, responsible for Gulf Region, UBAF Arab American Bank, New York, USA, 1980–; founder and member of the Board of Arab Bankers Association for North America, 1983–; member of Graduates Association of American University of Beirut; *Interests and Recreations:* swimming, jogging; *Languages:* Arabic, English, French; *Address:* 81 Grand Boulevard, Scarsdale, New York, 10583, USA; telephone: (212) 223 2749; Residence — (914) 472 3577.

BARAMKI, Dimitri Constantine, Jordanian academic/archaeologist; born 1906; *Education:* St. George's School, Jerusalem; BA, American University of Beirut, Lebanon; PhD, University of London, UK; *Career:* teacher in Jerusalem, 1925–26; Inspector of Antiquities, Palestine, 1927–28; Inspector of Antiquities, 1929; Senior Archaeological Officer, 1945; Archaeological Adviser and Librarian, American School of Oriental Research, Jerusalem, 1949–51; Curator of Museums, 1951; Assistant Professor of Ancient History, American University of Beirut, 1951–53; Associate Professor of Ancient History, American University of Beirut, 1953; Professor of Ancient History, 1958–75; Professor of Archaeology, Lebanese University, 1975–80; UNESCO Expert in Prehistoric Archaeology, accredited to Libya, 1964–65; excavated numerous sites in

Palestine; *Publications:* numerous articles in the quarterly journal of the Department of Antiquities in Palestine; various other publications; *Languages:* Arabic, English; *Address:* American Univesity of Beirut, P O Box 11 0236, Beirut, Lebanon.

BARDAWIL, Fuad Philip, Lebanese businessman; born 1928, Manchester, UK; married; three sons, one daughter; *Education:* BA, Political and Economic Science, American University of Beirut, Lebanon, 1948; *Career:* Chairman, Bardawil Co; Chairman and President, Specialties Co, Dubai, United Arab Emirates, Kuwait; member of the Board of Directors of Beton SAL; *Interests and Recreations:* bowling, music, reading; founding member of the Eagles Foundation (social welfare organisation); *Languages:* Arabic, French, English; *Address:* Office — Specialties Company, P O Box 3880, Dubai, United Arab Emirates; telephone: Office — 222181; Residence — 220600.

BARGASH, Hadj Ahmad, Moroccan official/banker; born 1905, Rabat, Morocco; married; *Religion:* Muslim; *Education:* Moroccan Institute of Higher Studies, Rabat; *Career:* Pasha of Azemmour, 1930–39; Delegate of the Grand Vizier for Education; Minister of Habous, (Religious Endowments), 1950–51; Governor of Casablanca, 1955–60; paid official visit to UK, 1959; Minister of Habous, 1960, and of Islamic Affairs (added to the portfolio), 1963; Leader of delegation of Moroccan Muslims to USSR, 1968; Minister of Habous, 1971–72; President of the Board of the Banque Marocaine pour le Commerce et l'Industrie (BMCI), 1973; *Languages:* Arabic, French; *Address:* Banque Marocaine pour le Commerce et l'Industrie, SA, P O Box 573, 26 Place Mohammed V, Casablanca, Morocco; telephone: 24101; telex: 21092.

BARGASH, Muhammad, Moroccan banker/official; born 1928, Rabat, Morocco; married; two children; *Religion:* Muslim; *Education:* Licencié en Droit, and Diploma of the Ecole des Sciences Politiques, Paris, France; *Career:* Chef de Cabinet of the Deputy Prime Minister in Morocco's first Government after Independence, 1956; Director of the Cabinet of the Minister of Defence; 1st Counsellor, Moroccan Embassy to France; Director of Credit in the Bank of Morocco; Deputy Governor of the Bank of Morocco, 1964;

Head of National Advancement and Planning, Royal Cabinet, 1965; Minister of Development, 1966; High Commissioner for Planning and National Advancement, 1967; official visit to UK, 1966; Minister of Agriculture, 1967; Deputy Governor of the Bank of Morocco, 1969; President of the Banque Nationale pour le Développement Economique (BNDE), 1972; Director of the Société Générale Marocaine des Banques; *Languages:* Arabic, French; *Address:* Société Générale Marocaine des Banques, 83 Boulevard Mohammed V, P O Box 90, Casablanca, Morocco.

BAROODY, Jamil Murad, Saudi Arabian diplomat; born 8 August 1905, Souk el-Gharb, Lebanon; married; *Religion:* Muslim; *Education:* BA, American University of Beirut, Lebanon, 1924–26; *Career:* Arab Political and Economic Observer, London, UK, 1929–39; Lecturer, Princeton University, USA, 1943; Adviser, *Reader's Digest*, Arabic edition, and free-lance writer, 1944–47; Adviser to Syrian Delegation to International Business Conference, 1944; Delegation of Saudi Arabia to UN, San Francisco, 1945; Alternate Permanent Representative of Saudi Arabia to UN, 1947–57; Ambassador, Deputy Permanent Representative of Saudi Arabia, UN, New York, 1957–; Permanent Head of Saudi Mission to UN, 1962–; *Publications:* poems and numerous magazine articles; *Decorations:* Honorary Citizen of New York, 1939; Order of Merit, Gold Medal, Lebanon, 1940; Distinguished Order of King Abdul Aziz, Saudi Arabia, 1973; International Law Degree, Mexican Academy of International Law, 1971; *Languages:* Arabic, English, French; *Address:* c/o Ministry of Foreign Affairs, P O Box 495, Jeddah, Saudi Arabia.

BAROOM, Abdullah Muhammad, Saudi Arabian businessman; born 1936; *Religion:* Muslim; *Education:* general education; *Career:* private enterprise; member of Board of *Okaz* daily newspaper, Saudi Metal Co, Red Sea Insurance Co; founding member of several contracting companies; participated in the establishment of several local industries; ship owner; construction materials distribution; participated in a project of credit facilities for low-income citizens for building private houses; attended several economic conferences in the Middle East and Europe; *Interests and Recreations:* travel; *Address:*

P O Box 1346, Jeddah, Saudi Arabia; telephone: 6422366; telex: 401165 BAROOM SJ.

BAROUDI, Hassan Fahmi al-, Egyptian engineer; born 27 January 1909, Egypt; married; one son, three daughters; *Religion:* Muslim; *Education:* BA in Architecture, Cairo University, Egypt; PhD in Engineering, University of London, UK; member of Institute of Structural Engineers, London, Institute of Civil Engineers, London, of American Concrete Institute, USA; *Career:* Lecturer, Higher Engineering Institute, Cairo, 1932–37, 1941–43; Lecturer, Architectural Department, Alexandria University, 1943–46; Assistant Professor, Architecture Department, Alexandria University, 1946–50; Professor Architecture Department, Alexandria University, 1951–54; Professor, Head of Architecture Department and former Dean of Faculty, Ain Shams Universtiy, Cairo, 1955–64; retired; currently, Consulting Engineer; *Languages:* Arabic, English, French. *Address:* 7 26th July Street, Cairo, Egypt; telephone: 916240.

BASALAMAH, Abdullah Hussain, Saudi Arabian physician/academic; born 27 September 1936, Mecca, Saudi Arabia; *Religion:* Muslim; *Education:* MD 1965; MRCOG 1971; FRCOG 1981; FACS 1973; *Career:* Obstetrician and Gynaecologist, Central Hospital, Riyadh, 1965–70; Assistant Professor of Obstetrics and Gynaecology, Faculty of Medicine, Riyadh University, 1970–74; Vice Dean, Faculty of Medicine, University of Riyadh, 1973–74; Dean, Faculty of Medicine and Allied Sciences, King Abdul Aziz University, Jeddah, 1974–80; Professor and Chairman, Department of Obstetrics and Gynaecology, Faculty of Medicine and Allied Sciences, King Abdul Aziz University, Jeddah 1980–; *Publications:* several books; numerous articles on childbirth and care in various medical journals in Arabic; *Interests and Recreations:* swimming, mountaineering, reading; *Address:* Faculty of Medicine, King Abdul Aziz University, P O Box 9029, Jeddah, Saudi Arabia; telephone: Office — 6879202, ext 1341, 6882057, ext 202, Residence — 6659707.

BASHA, Adnan Khalil, Saudi Arabian journalist; born 1949, Mecca, Saudi Arabia; *Religion:* Muslim; *Education:* BA in English and Education, Faculty of Education, King Abdul Aziz University, Saudi Arabia; *Career:* former editor of *Al-Nadwa* newspaper; member of Arab Air Transport Union, International Association of Travel Agents Conferences; Editor in Chief of *Al-Jinah Al-Akhdar* monthly magazine, official publication of Saudi Arabian Airlines (Saudia); responsible for the publication of the first aviation magazine in the Middle East; established a specialized department of aviation archives; *Address:* P O Box 620, Jeddah, Saudi Arabia; telephone: Jeddah 33111, 33219.

BASHIR, Ali Abdul Rahman al-, Jordanian judge/administrator; born 1930, Salt, Jordan; married; three sons, two daughters; *Religion:* Muslim; *Education:* Licence in Law; Diploma in Public Law; Honorary Professor of the Law School, University of Nebraska, USA; *Career:* Head of Income Tax Department, Ministry of Finance; Ministry of Justice; Civil Magistrate; Public Prosecutor, Assistant Attorney General; member of the Court of First Instance; President of the Income Tax Court of Appeal; Judge on Secondment to Kuwait for six years; Governor of Kerak; Governor of Irbid; Governor of Amman; *Decorations:* Independence Medal, 1st Class; King Abdul Aziz Al Saud Medal, 1st Class; Egyptian Order of Merit, 1st Class; Honorary Citizenship from Governor of Nebraska; Honorary Citizenship of Oakland, California; *Interests and Recreations:* hunting, walking; *Languages:* Arabic, English; *Address:* Jabal Amman, Amman, Jordan; telephone: 663650.

BASHIR, Lieutenant General Muhammad Ali, Sudanese army commander; born 1932, Sudan; *Religion:* Muslim; *Education:* Military Academy; *Career:* infantry officer, 1956; joined Armoured Corps and took part in Armoured Course, Egypt, 1957; Western Command, 1964–68; six-month course in USA; promoted to GHQ as Deputy to the Director of Organisation, G Branch; Brigadier and Director of Foreign Relations, 1970; Director of Armaments Division of GHQ, 1971; member of military delegation to UK; Commander of Armoured Corps as Major General, 1971; Chief of Staff, 1973; Lieutenant General, 1974; Minister of Defence and Commander in Chief of the Armed Forces, 1976; *Languages:* Arabic, English; *Address:* Ministry of Defence, Khartoum, Sudan.

BASHIR, Muhammad Omar, Sudanese diplomat/academic and writer; born 1926, Sudan; *Religion:* Muslim; *Education:* BA, School of Arts, University of Khartoum, Sudan; degrees from Queen's University, Belfast, UK and Linacre College, Oxford, UK; *Career:* Secretary General, Round Table Conference on Southern Sudan, 1964–65; Counsellor, Ministry of Foreign Affairs; Academic Secretary and Prinicipal, University of Khartoum; Professor, Institute of African and Asian Studies, Sudan; *Publications: The Southern Sudan: Background to Conflict* 1968, London; *Educational Development in the Sudan,* 1969, London; *Revolution: Nationalism in the Sudan,* 1974, London; *The Southern Sudan From Conflict to Peace,* 1975, London; *Terramedia – Themes in Afro-Arab Relations,* 1982, London; *Languages:* Arabic, English; *Address:* University of Khartoum, Institute of African and Asian Studies, P O Box 321, Khartoum, Sudan; telephone: 77044.

BASHIR, Mustafa Badawi, Sudanese official/veterinary surgeon; born 10 July 1934, Omdurman, Sudan; married; three sons, one daughter; *Religion:* Muslim; *Education:* BSc, Veterinary Science, University of Khartoum, 1961; MSc, Animal Production, Kensas State University of Agriculture and Applied Sciences, USA, 1964–66; Special Course in Animal Production, Democratic Republic of Germany, 1972; *Career:* Assistant Inspector, Animal Production, Cattle and Grassland Research Station, Western Region, Sudan, 1961–64; Head, Cattle Research Station, Blue Nile Province, 1967–70; Cattle and Grassland Research Station, Western Region, Darfur Province, Sudan, 1970–72; member of the National People's Assembly, 1972–73; Head, Animal Production Department, Ministry of Agriculture, Food and Natural Resources, 1973–75; Head of Statistics Section, Department of Animal Production Economies, 1975–77; Assistant to the Governor for Animal Production, The Blue Nile Procince, 1977–78; Chairman of Board of Directors and Managing Director, Animal Production Corporation, Khartoum, 1978–; member of Board of Halfa Agriculture Corporation, Mechanised Farming Corporation and others; *Decorations:* Order of the Constitution, 1973; *Interests and Recreations:* walking, music; *Languages:* Arabic, English; *Address:* Khartoum, P O Box 624; telephone: 74746, 77093.

BASHIR, Taha Ahmad, Sudanese UN official/psychiatrist; born 2 June 1922, Suakin, Red Sea, Sudan; married; *Religion:* Muslim; *Education:* Diploma, Kitchener School of Medicine, Khartoum, Sudan, 1942–48; Diploma in Psychological Medicine, Institute of Psychiatry, London University, UK, 1954–56; *Career:* Senior Psychiatrist, Sudan, 1957–69; Minister of Labour, Sudan, 1969–70; Minister of Health, Sudan, 1970–71; Regional Adviser in Mental Health, Regional Office for Eastern Mediterranean, WHO, Egypt, 1972; member of the World Federation for Mental Health; Association of Psychiatrists in Africa, Sudanese National Association for Mental Health; *Publications:* author of numerous books on mental health and psychiatry; *Decorations:* Fellow of Royal College of Psychiatry; *Interests and Recreations:* literature, history, swimming, tennis, behavioural sciences; member of the Arts Society, Alexandria, Egypt; *Languages:* Arabic, English; *Address:* Office — Regional Office for Eastern Mediterranean, WHO, P O Box 1517, Alexandria, Egypt; telephone: 30090; Residence — 5 rue Ahmad Zulficar, Laurens, Ramleh, Alexandria, Egypt; telephone: 30090.

BASHIR, Tahsin M., Egyptian diplomat; born 5 April 1925; *Religion:* Muslim; *Education:* BSc in Political Economy, Alexandria University, Egypt, 1950; graduate studies at Princeton and Harvard Universities, USA; MA in Political Economy, Harvard University, USA, 1955; awarded the Commercial Bank Prize for Political Economy, 1950; awarded the Ahmed Abdel Wahab Prize for Political Economy; *Career:* Spokesman and Information Officer for Egyptian Permanent Mission to UN, 1956–58; Director of Palestine Section, Department of Information, Ministry of Presidential Affairs, Cairo, 1960; Member of the UAR (United Arab Republic) Delegation to the UN General Assembly Session, 1956, 1957, 1958, 1959, 1960, 1970; Counsellor (Press Affairs) UAR Embassy to UK, 1969–71; Aide to the Secretary General of the Arab League, Cairo, 1973; Acting Presidential Counsellor for Press Affairs, 1973–74; Official spokesman and member of the Egyptian delegation to the Geneva Peace Conference, December 1973; Supervisor of Presidential Press Affairs; Ambassador at Ministry of Foreign Affairs, 1974; permanent Egyptian delegate to Arab League, 1976; *Publications:* articles on international affairs in Arabic and French; *Languages:* Arabic, English, French; *Address:* Ministry of Foreign Affairs, Giza, Cairo, Egypt.

BASHRAHEEL, Muhammad Salih, Saudi Arabian businessman; born 1928, Mecca, Saudi Arabia; *Religion:* Muslim; *Education:* general education; *Career:* Auditor, Ministry of Finance, 1949; Accountant, Ein al-Aziziah Water Co, Mecca, later Chairman, Purchasing Committee; Secretary to Director General; Treasurer, Ein Zibaidah Water Co; Owner-Manager of Alba Trading and Contracting Corporation, Mecca, dealing in foodstuffs; *Interests and Recreations:* travel; *Address:* Aziziah, Mecca, Saudi Arabia; telephone: 27742.

BASINDWAH, Muhammad Salim, Yemen Arab Republic politician; born 18 January 1935, Aden, People's Democratic Republic of Yemen; married; two sons, two daughters; *Religion:* Muslim; *Education:* general; *Career:* merchant, 1953–56; owner and Editor of *Al-Nour al-Usbuyiah* weekly newspaper, 1960–62; owner and Editor of *Al-Haqiqa al-Usbuyiah* weekly, 1962–65; member and later Vice President of the Aden Socialist Party; one of the leaders of the Liberation Front, 1962–72; spokesman on South Yemen problem in UN Decolonization Committee, and the Fourth Committee, 1963, 1964, 1965, 1966; Minister of Social Affairs and Labour, 1974; Minister of State, and Political Adviser to the President of the Republic, 1975–77; Minister of Development and Chairman of the Yemeni Planning Agency, 1977; *Publications:* pamphlet on democracy 1973; contributor to local newspapers; *Decorations:* Order of Independence from HM the King of Jordan; Order of the Republic 1st Class, Egypt, 1976; *Interests and Recreations:* Arabic literature, travelling; *Languages:* Arabic, English; *Address:* Republican Palace, Sana'a, Yemen Arab Republic; telephone: 2367.

BASRI, Driss, Moroccan official; born November, 1938; Settat, Morocco; married; *Religion:* Muslim; *Education:* Public Law; Degree in Political Science; PhD, 1975; *Career:* Principal Commissioner at the Rabat Criminal Investigation Office; Director General of Criminal Investigation; member of the Cabinet of the Director General of Police; Director of General Affairs and of Senior Staff in the Ministry of the Interior; assistant at the Law Faculties of Rabat and Casablanca; Secretary of State for the Interior, 1974; *Languages:* Arabic, French; *Address:* Ministry of the Interior, Rabat, Morocco.

BASRI, Meer S., Iraqi writer/economist; born 19 September 1911, Baghdad, Iraq; *Education:* in Baghdad and France; *Career:* joined Ministry of Foreign Affairs, Baghdad, Iraq; Head of Section and Acting Director of Protocol; Director of *The Iraq Directory,* 1935; Secretary, later Director, Baghdad Chamber of Commerce, 1935–45; Controller of Commercial Exchange, 1937–38; Assistant Iraqi Commissioner, International Paris Exhibition, 1937; Editor, *Chamber of Commerce Journal,* 1938–45; Delegate to International Business Conference, Rye, New York, 1944; Director, Eastern Commercial Corporation, 1945–49; member of the General and Administrative Council, Baghdad; Assistant Director General of Information and Organization, Dates Board, 1947; Director of various companies; *Publications: Essays on Iraqi Economy,* 1948; *Echoes of the Lyre,* poetry; *Men and Shadows,* short stories; *The Potentate of Haiti: Carnival King; Asoka the Good King of India; The Holocaust of Shendi; Role of Arab Men of Letters,* 1969; *Leaders of Thought in Modern Iraq; Procession of the Ages,* poetry; and several other works; *Interests and Recreations:* Fellow of the Royal Asiatic Society, London, UK; *Languages:* Arabic, English, French; *Address:* 244 Dover House Road, London SW15, UK.

BASRI, Taha Yassin Hassan al-, Iraqi journalist; born 1 July, 1939, Mikdadia, Iraq; married; two sons, one daughter; *Religion:* Muslim; *Education:* BA in English Literature, University of Baghdad, 1960; *Career:* Teacher, 1960–67; Deputy Editor in Chief, *Baghdad Observer,* 1968; Press Counsellor, Iraqi Embassy, Madrid, Spain, 1970; Deputy Director General, Iraqi News Agency, 1972; Director General Iraqi News Agency, 1973–; Under Secretary, Ministry of Culture and Information, 1976; member of the Iraqi Journalists Association; *Publications:* various lectures on information and news agencies, 1974–81; *Interests and Recreations:* swimming, chess, travelling, reading, journalism; *Languages:* Arabic, English, Spanish; *Ad-*

dress: Abu Nawwas Street, P O Box 3084, Baghdad, Iraq; telephone: Office — 8888520; Residence — 5555430.

BASSAM, Abdullah Al Ali al-, Saudi Arabian businessman; born 1920, Saudi Arabia; *Religion:* Muslim; *Education:* general education in Iraq; *Career:* owner of Al-Bassam Trading and Contracting Corporation; former employee, Ministry of Finance; businessman; former member of the Chamber of Commerce, 1946; *Address:* Al-Bassam Building, Bab Mecca, P O Box 193, Jeddah, Saudi Arabia; telephone: Office — 642 2260, Riyadh 402 5815, Mecca 542 9013; Residence — 6428815.

BASSAM, Muhammad Ali al-, Iraqi academic; born 1923, Baquba, Iraq; married; four sons, one daughter; *Religion:* Muslim; *Education:* Licence in Mathematics, Higher Teachers College, Baghdad, Iraq, 1944; MA and PhD in Pure Mathematics, University of Texas, Austin, USA, 1948–51; *Career:* Assistant Professor, Baghdad University, 1951–69; Professor of Mathematics, Texas Technical University, Lubbock, Texas, 1960–65; Visiting Professor, American University of Beirut, Lebanon, 1964–65; Professor and Head of Mathematics Department, College of Science, University of Baghdad, 1965–69; Professor of Pure Mathematics, Department of Mathematics, College of Science, University of Kuwait, 1969–; *Publications:* numerous research papers published in international mathematical journals; *Interests and Recreations:* swimming, sports, music, literature, poetry; member of the American Mathematical Society; member of Cambridge Philosophical Society, UK; *Languages:* Arabic, English, French, German; *Address:* Department of Mathematics, College of Science, Kuwait University, Kuwait; telephone: 542607

BASSAT, Hisham al-, Lebanese banker/ economist; born 1936, Sidon, Lebanon; married; one son, one daughter; *Education:* BA in Business Administration, Cairo University, Egypt, 1961; PhD in Economics, Lyon University, France, 1966; *Career:* Director of Research and Statistics, Arab Bank Ltd, Beirut, 1966; Director of Research, Head Office, Arab Bank, Jordan, 1975; General Manager, Arab Bank, Beirut, 1982–; member of Board of Management of Beirut Bourse; representative member of Arab Bank on Board of Housing Bank, Development and Finance Bank; member of the Board of Institute of Banking Administration; *Languages:* Arabic, French, English; *Address:* Arab Bank Ltd, P O Box 1015, Riad al Solh Street, Beirut, Lebanon; telephone: 250240; telex: 20704 ARABNK LE.

BASSIL, Francois, Lebanese banker; born 1934, Lebanon; married; two sons, one daughter; *Religion:* Christian; *Education:* LLD, University of Louvain, Belgium; *Career:* Director, Société Commerciale et Agricole, Bassil Frères et Compagnie, and Société Bancaire Agricole (now Byblos Bank), 1962–63; Director General and Member of the Board of Directors, Byblos Bank SAL, 1964–73, 1973–79; President and Director General, Byblos Bank SAL, 1979–; President and Director General, Byblos Arab Finance Bank, Belgium, SA; President and Director General, Byblos Arab Finance Holding BARAF, SA; member of the Board of Directors of the Banque du Liban, 1966–7; member of the Board of Directors of several other real estate and financial companies; *Interests and Recreations:* swimming, tennis; member of the Overseas Bankers Club; *Languages:* Arabic, French, English, Spanish; *Address:* Byblos Bank SAL, P O Box 11 5605 Beirut, Lebanon; telephone: Office — 803 575; Residence — 334 231.

BATARJI, Abdul Rauf Ibrahim, Saudi Arabian businessman; born 1920; *Education:* general; *Career:* General Manager of Batarji National Pharmacies and Drug Stores, importers and dealers in pharmaceuticals, hospital and medical equipment; *Address:* P O Box 2, Jeddah, Saudi Arabia; telephone: 642 4468; Residence — 669 0412.

BATAWI, Mustafa Amin al-, Egyptian WHO offical/physician; born 17 February 1932, Cairo, Egypt; married; *Education:* MD, Faculty of Medicine, Cairo University, Egypt; MPH, DSc, Graduate School of Public Health, University of Pittsburgh, USA; *Career:* Health Officer, University of Alexandria, Egypt; Professor, Department of Occupational Medicine, Egypt; Inter-Regional Adviser, Occupational Health, ILO, Bangkok, Thailand; Chief Medical Officer, Office of Occupational Health, WHO, Geneva, Switzerland, 1969–; *Publications: Occupational Health in Developing Countries; Monitoring of Workers' Health; Early Detection of Health Impairment; Psy-*

cho-Social Factors at Work; numerous articles in international journals; *Decorations:* honorary member, several scientific national and international societies; *Interests and Recreations:* painting and drawing, chess, sports, medicine, public health, occupational medicine, toxicology; member of the Rotary Club, member of various sports club; *Languages:* Arabic, English, French; *Address:* Office — Occupational Health Department, WHO, 20 Avenue Appia, CH1211, Geneva 27, Switzerland; telephone: (022)912694; Residence — Villa Firdouse, Chemin du Ruisseau, CH1299, Commugny, Vaud, Switzerland; telephone: (022)762697.

BAYATI, Abdul Wahab al-, Iraqi poet; born 1926, Baghdd, Iraq; *Education:* Teacher Training College, Iraq, 1950; *Career:* teacher, 1950–53; dismissed and arrested for his political stand; left Iraq for Syria and Egypt after the tripartite agression against Egypt in 1956; settled in Cairo, Egypt; member of the editorial staff of *AL Gumhuriya* daily newspaper, Cairo, Egypt; returned to Iraq 1958; Director of Translations and Publishing, Ministry of Education, Baghdad, Iraq; Cultural Adviser, Iraqi Embassy to Moscow, USSR; Lecturer, Asian People's Institute, Moscow, USSR, 1961; travelled in a number of socialist countries; settled in Egypt once more; returned to Iraq 1968; Cultural Adviser, Ministry of Information, and later Ministry of Culture and Fine Arts, Iraq; one of the pioneers in modern Arabic poetry, with a Sufi tendency; *Publications:* numerous collections of poetry including *Poetry in Exile,* 1957; *Lament for June and the Mercenaries,* 1969; *The Moon of Shiraz,* 1975; and others, many of which are translated into other languages; *Languages:* Arabic, English; *Address:* Ministry of Culture and Fine Arts, Baghdad, Iraq.

BAZ, Muhammad Bin Abdul Rahman al-, Saudi Arabian administrator; born 1933, Saudi Arabia; *Religion:* Muslim; *Education:* BA in History; *Career:* Registrar, Riyadh University; Demonstrator, Riyadh University, 1967; Director of Water Bureau, Ministry of Agriculture and Water, 1968; Director General of General Administration for Project Implementation, Ministry of Agriculture and Water, 1975–; *Interests and Recreations:* reading, travel; *Address:* General Administration for Projects Implementation, Ministry of Agriculture and Water, Riyadh, Saudi Arabia; telephone: 4012777.

BAZ, Usama Sayyid al-, Egyptian diplomat; born 1931; one son; *Education:* PhD from USA; *Career:* Egyptian Foreign Service; Counsellor and Senior Lecturer in Ministry of Foreign Affairs Training Institute; worked in Arab Socialist Union Youth Secretariat following the dismissal of left-wing supporters of Ali Sabri, 1971; Deputy Head of Private Office of Foreign Minister Ismail Fahmi, 1974; Ambassador, Head of Foreign Minister's Private Office, 1975–; *Address:* Ministry of Foreign Affairs, Cairo, Egypt.

BAZZAZ, Saad Abdul Salam al-, Iraqi diplomat/journalist; born 1950, Mosul, Iraq; married; one son, one daughter; *Religion:* Muslim; *Education:* BA, Politics and Law, Baghdad University, 1973; Certificate, Cinema Script, Institute of Broadcasting and Television, Baghdad; *Career:* Writer, Journalist and Television Producer, 1969–; Broadcaster and Editor, Mosul Television, 1969–72; Producer, Editorial Secretary, Head of Cultural Department, Director of 2nd Channel of Baghdad Television, 1972–78; Free Lance Editor, *Alif Baa* Magazine, Baghdad, 1977–78; Assistant Director, Iraqi Cultural Centre, London, 1979–80; Press Counsellor, Iraqi Embassy, London, 1980–; Editor in Chief of *UR,* magazine of Arabic culture, London, in English; *Publications: Al-Hijerat,* short stories, Beirut 1972, in Arabic; *In Search for the Sea Bird, The Story of the Boy and the Girl,* short stories, Beirut 1980, in Arabic; *The Future of Broadcasting,* 1980, research, Baghdad; *Decorations:* Prize of the Best Radio Programme, 1975; 2nd Prize of the Union of Arabic Broadcasting Company; 1st Prize from the International Festival of Palestinian Films and Programmes, 1977; *Interests and Recreations:* chess; member of the Union of Iraqi Writers and of the Union of Iraqi Journalists; *Languages:* Arabic, English; *Address:* 177/178 Tottenham Court Road, London W1, UK; telephone: 637 5831.

BAZZI, Ali al-, Lebanese politician/diplomat; born Tyre, Lebanon; *Education:* general; *Career:* Deputy for Bint-Jbeil, South Lebanon 1957; Minister of Information, and of the Interior, 1959–60; Deputy for Marjeyoun; Minister of Public Health, 1961–64; Ambassador to Kuwait, 1964–65; Ambassador to Jordan 1966–71; member of the political party Al-Nida'a Al-Qawmay; *Interests and Recreations:* hunting; *Languages:* Arabic, French; *Address:* Residence — Boustani Street, Beirut, Lebanon.

BDEIR, Muhammad Ali, Jordanian businessman; born 1909, Damascus, Syria; married; three sons, two daughters; *Religion:* Muslim; *Education:* Islamic College in Beirut, 1925; American University in Beirut, Lebanon, 1927–29; *Career:* Member of the Chamber of Deputies, 1951–54; President of Federation of Jordanian Chambers of Commerce, 1965–; Member of Board of Trustees of Jordan University; Member of Jordan National Consultative Council, 1978–; Chairman of Transjordan Building Materials Co Ltd, Jordan Construction Materials Co Ltd, Jordan Electric Power Co Ltd, Jordan Pipes Manufacturing Co Ltd; Chairman of Amman Chamber of Commerce and the Federation of Jordan Chambers of Commerce; *Address:* P O Box 48, Amman, Jordan; telephone: 24192, 36381; telex: 21876 TBMCO.

BEBBOUCHI, Rashid, Algerian academic/mathematician; born 26 October 1945; married; two daughters; *Religion:* Muslim; *Education:* BSc, University of Algiers, 1967; Diploma in Mathematics, University of Algiers, 1968; PhD in Mathematics, University of Orsay, Paris, France; *Career:* Lecturer, University of Algiers, 1968–69; Assistant Professor, Centre Universitaire de Savoie, France, 1971–73; Assistant Professor, Université d'Oran Es-Senia, Algeria, 1973–74; Assistant Professor, 1975–81; Director of the Institute of Mathematics, Université d'Oran Es-Senia, 1975–78; President of the Scientific Council of Mathematics, Université d'Oran Es-Senia, 1979–; member of the Mathematics Society of France, 1971–; *Publications:* numerous articles and papers published in international professional journals; *Interests and Recreations:* travelling, fishing, swimming, tennis, chess, reading, music; *Languages:* Arabic, French, English, Russian, German; *Address:* Cité Grande Terre B421 Oran, Algeria; telephone: 351 519.

BEHBEHANI, Ahmad Yusif, Kuwaiti businessman; born 1941, Kuwait; married; one daughter; *Religion:* Muslim; *Education:* BA, Beirut, Lebanon; Business Administration, Geneva, Switzerland; *Career:* Chairman of Dar al Yaqza for Press, Printing and Publishing, Ahmad Yusif Behbehani Establishment, Indo-Gulf Contracting Company, Nawasser Trading Company, Al-Meerooj Petroleum Company, and AYB (GENEVA) SA; Vice President, Behbehani Motors Com-

pany; Secretary General, Kuwait Journalists Association; member of the Board of Directors of Kuwait Real Estate Investment Consorium, of Kuwait International Investment Company, of Kuwait Hotels Co, of Kuwait Travel and Tourism Agencies Association; *Publications:* Editor in Chief, *Al-Yaqza* weekly magazine; *Interests and Recreations:* reading, swimming; *Languages:* Arabic, English, Persian, French; *Address:* P O Box 6000, Safat, Kuwait; telephone: 811171.

BEIDAS, Henri, Lebanese businessman; born 5 November 1921, Beirut, Lebanon; married; one daughter; *Education:* Intermediate Diploma in Arts, London, UK; private courses in public finance and general administration; LLB, LLM, London University, UK; *Career:* attached to the government of the Palestinian Mandate, 1937; Officer in Charge of a section, Personnel Department, Office of the 1st Secretary, 1940; Inspector, Government of Palestine, 1942; Assistant Intelligence and Research Officer, Department of Labour, 1945; Assistant Secretary, Finance Department, Palestinian Government, 1946; Head of the Department created in the UK to terminate the government of the Palestinian Mandate, 1948; in charge of courses dealing with Public Administration, Law, Organizations and Methods, American University of Beirut, Lebanon; Legal Adviser and later Regional Vice President, American Life Insurance Company, London, UK, 1969–; member of the Advisory Board to the Lebanese Government on insurance matters; Chairman of the Board, Middle East Insurance and Reinsurance Company; *Interests and Recreations:* tennis, swimming; *Languages:* Arabic, French, English; *Address:* Office — American Life Insurance Company, 15 Golden Square, London W1, England; telephone: (01) 439 3976.

BELAIL, Hassan, Sudanese banker/economist; born 1930; married; three children; *Religion:* Muslim; *Education:* BA, University of Khartoum; MA, Money and Banking, University of Pennsylvania, USA, 1964; *Career:* Teacher, Secondary School; Official, Sudan State Railways; Government Service, Ministry of Finance and National Economy; Assistant Under Secretary and Director of Taxation; Assistant General Manager, Sudan Commercial Bank, 1966; Managing Director, State Cotton Organisa-

105

tion, 1970; Chairman and Managing Director, Sudan Commercial Bank, 1971; member of the Board of the Union of Arab and French Banks, 1971; Deputy General Manager, UBAF Bank Ltd, London; Minister of State for Trade, 1973–75; Director, Khartoum Branch of the Arab Investment Co, 1975–80; Governor, Central Bank of Sudan, 1980–; *Languages:* Arabic, English; *Address:* Central Bank of Sudan, P O Box 313, Khartoum, Sudan; telephone: 78064; telex: 352.

BELHADJAMOR, Moncef, Tunisian politician; born 1931, Ben Khiar, Tunisia; married, two daughters; *Religion:* Muslim; *Education:* Licence in Law; *Career:* Head of the Office of the Minister of Finance, 1970; Secretary General of Finance, 1971; Secretary General of the Government, 1973; Secretary General of the Government and Minister responsible for relations with the National Assembly, 1976; Secretary of State responsible to the Prime Minister for Public Services and Administrative Reforms, 1980; Minister of Housing, 1981; representative of Tunisia in financial and economic negotiations with AID; *Decorations:* Grand Cordon of the Order of Tunisian Independence; Grand Officer of the Order of Tunisian Republic; various foreign decorations: *Address:* Ministry of Housing, Tunis, Tunisia.

BELKACEM, Nabi, Algerian politician/oil expert; *Religion:* Muslim; *Career:* Director of Energy and Oil, Ministry of Industry and Energy, 1966; President, and Director General, Société Nationale de Recherches et d'Exploitation des Pétroles en Algerie (SN Repal), 1966–70; Wali of Themcen, 1970–76; Adviser, Presidential Office, 1975–79; Minister of Energy and Petrochemical Industries, 1979–; *Address:* 80 Ahmed Gharmool Street, Algiers, Algeria; telephone: 607788; telex: 52916 SONATRACH.

BELKHODJA, Muhammad Habib, Tunisian religious leader; born 24 October 1922, Tunis, Tunisia; married; three children; *Religion:* Muslim; *Education:* Diploma in Tunisian Law, 1944; Licence (Alimya) of the University of Zitouna, 1946; Institute of Higher Studies, Sorbonne, Paris, France; PhD in Arabic Language and Literature, University of Paris, 1964; *Career:* Professor, University of Zitouna, 1946–59; Professor of Theology, University of Tunis, 1959–62 and

1964–70; Grand Mufti of the Tunisian Republic; permanent member of the Arabic Language Academy, Cairo, Egypt; *Publications: History of Tunisian Literature from the Aghalabite Period until Today; Our Contemporary Poets* and other shorter studies of literary subjects such as *Al-Jarim; Ahmed Amine; Senoussi; Ouarghi; El-Jihad; Poetry Through the Ages; Criticism of the Poetry of el-Qartagini; Languages:* Arabic, French; *Address:* P O Box 5507, Tunis, Tunisia; telephone: 260088.

BELKHOJA, Tahar, Tunisian politician/diplomat; born 9 June 1931, Mahdia, Tunisia; married; four daughters; *Religion:* Muslim; *Education:* Sadiki College, Tunis; Agricultural Engineer, Ecole d'Agriculture, Tunis, 1956; *Career:* Deputy Secretary General of Union Générale des Etudiants de Tunisie (UGET), 1955–57; President of the International Association of Agricultural Students, 1958; Delegate of the Political Bureau to Union of Tunisian Students, 1959; Chef de Cabinet to Secretary of State for Foreign Affairs, 1960; Chargé d'Affaires, Tunisian Embassy in France, 1960; Ambassador in West Africa (Senegal, Ivory Coast, Mali, Guinea and Mauritania), 1962–66; Chef de Cabinet to the Secretary of State for Planning and National Economy, 1966–67; Director General of National Security, 1967–69; Ambassador to Dakar, 1969–70; Ambassador to Madrid, 1970; Secretary for Education, Research and Vocational Training, Office of the Minister of Agriculture, 1970; Minister of Youth and Sports, 1971; Permanent Representative of Tunisia to the UN, and Ambassador to the Vatican and Geneva, 1972; Minister of the Interior, 1973–77; Ambassador to West Germany, 1980; Minister of Information, 1980; member of the Central Committee of the Destour Socialist Party, 1965–79; member of the Higher Committee of the Destour Socialist Party, 1970–71, member of the Political Bureau, 1974–77; member of the National Assembly, 1974–79, of the Political Bureau, 1981; member of numerous missions in Europe , Africa and Asia; delegate to 14th and 24th Sessions of General Assembly of the UN, New York, 1959, 1972; Head of the Tunisian Delegation at UNCTAD meeting, Santiago, Chile, 1972; *Decorations:* Grand Cordon of the Republic of Tunisia; Order of the Tunisian Independence; Grand Cross of the Order of Merit of the German Federal

Republic; Grand Cordon of the Order of the Star of Africa; Grand Cordon of the Order of the Republic of Liberia; Grand Officer of the Légion d'Honneur of France; Grand Officer of the Orders of Sudan, Belgium, Holland, Luxembourg, Senegal, Mauritania, Central African Republic, Ivory Coast, Niger; Commander of the Order of the Republic of Guinea; *Interests and Recreations:* rugby, fishing; President of the Tunisia-France Association; *Languages:* Arabic, French, English; *Address:* Ministry of Information, Tunis, Tunisia.

BEN ABBES, Yusif, Moroccan diplomat/ physician; born 15 August 1921, Marrakesh, Morocco; married; *Religion:* Muslim; *Education:* medical studies in Algiers, 1942–5; Doctor of Medicine, 1949; *Career:* Public Health Department, Morocco; Inspector of Public Health, 1958; Head Doctor of the Prefecture of Casablanca, while remaining in charge of the Casablanca hospitals; Minister of Health, 1958–61; Minister of Health and National Education, 1961–62; Ambassador to Egypt and General Delegate to the Arab League, 1965; Ambassador to Italy and Greece, resident in Rome, 1967; Ambassdor to Algeria, 1969; Minister of Foreign Affairs, 1970–71; Ambassador to Spain, 1971; Ambassador to France and Morrocan Representative to UNESCO, 1972; non-resident Ambassador to the Vatican; *Interests and Recreations:* golf; *Languages:* Arabic, French; *Address:* 3 et 5 rue Le Tasse 75016, Paris, France.

BEN ALLAL, Muhammad, Moroccan academic; born 17 Janurary, 1950, Morocco; married; one child; *Religion:* Muslim; *Education:* Diploma in Accountancy, 1968; BA in Political Sciences, 1971; Doctorat d'Etat, International Law, University of Nice, Nice, France, 1976; *Career:* Professor of International Law and International Relations, Faculty of Law, University of Hassan II, Casablanca, Morocco, 1976–; Juridical Adviser on Legal Problems related to Gibraltar, 1980; Director, National School of Administration, Rabat, 1981; member of the Moroccan Delegation, UN Conference on the Law of the Sea, New York and Geneva; *Publications: Morocco and the Law of the Sea,* 1976, Nice, Faculty of Law; several articles in university journals; *Languages:* Arabic, French, Spanish; *Address:* 7 Rue Tachfin, Tetouan, Morocco; telephone: 4240.

BEN AYED, Abdesalem, Tunisian banker/ diplomat; born 1929 Sfax, Tunisia; married; *Religion:* Muslim; *Education:* BA in Politics and Law, University of Paris, Ecole Nationale d'Administration, Paris, France; training in French Prefecture, Ministry of Finance and Société Nationale des Chemins de Fer (SNCF), Paris, 1956; *Career:* Director of Budget, Ministry of Finance, 1956–63; Ambassador to West Germany; Tunisian representative at several international conferences, at IBRD and UN, 1964–70; Director of the Office of the Prime Minister with the rank of Secretary of State, 1970–71; Ambassador to France, 1971–73; President and Director General of the Union Bancaire pour le Commerce et l'Industrie (UBCI); *Languages:* Arabic, French; *Address:* Union Bancaire pour le Commerce et l'Industrie, 7/9 Rue Gamal Abdel Nasser, Tunis, Tunisia; telephone: 245877.

BEN BASHIR, Said, Moroccan politician/ lawyer; born 1935, Fes, Morocco; *Religion:* Muslim; *Education:* Degrees in Law and Political Sciences; further Degree and Doctorate in Public Law; *Career:* Professor of Law, Morocco; President of the Administrative Council, and UN expert at the CAFRAD; Director of the National School of Public Administration; organized various conferences on legal questions and public administration and other subjects in Morocco and other African countries; General Secretary of the Association of Moroccan Jurists; Secretary of State for Higher Education and Scientific Research, 1977; Minister of Culture and Information, 1981–; *Publications:* various studies and papers published in professional journals; *Languages:* Arabic, French; *Address:* Ministry of Culture and Information, Rabat, Morocco.

BEN BELLA, Muhammad Ahmad, Algerian politician; former President of Algeria; born 1916, Algeria; *Career:* Warrant Officer in Moroccan regiment during Second World War; Chief of OAS rebel military group, Algeria, 1947; imprisoned for political activities, 1949–52; directed Algerian national movement from exile in Libya, 1952–56; arrested again, 1956, imprisoned in France, 1959–62; appointed as Vice Premier of the Algerian Provisional Government in Tunis, 1962; Prime Minister of Algeria, 1962–65; President of Algeria, 1963–65; detained, 1965–80; restricted residence in Mslia,

1979–80; returned to live in Algiers, 1981–; *Decorations:* Lenin Peace Prize, 1964; *Address:* Algiers, Algeria.

BEN BOUCHTA, Muhammad Mahdi, Moroccan politician/businessman; born 1936, Fes, Morocco; married; three daughters; *Religion:* Muslim; *Education:* Social Sciences and Law Studies, College of Law, University of Grenoble, France; Licence en Droit; *Career:* King's Counsel in the Rabat High Court of First Instance, 1960–63; Director, Cabinet of the Prime Minister, 1963–65; Chargé de Mission in the Royal Cabinet, 1965–66; Under Secretary of State for Youth and Sports, 1967; Minister of Youth and Sports, 1968; Minister of Labour and Employment and Professional Training, 1969; Deputy in Parliament, 1970; Vice President of the Chamber of Deputies, President of the Chamber, 1971; Director, Société Marocaine de Construction Automobile (SOMACA), 1972–; *Languages:* Arabic, English, French, Spanish; *Address:* Société Marocaine de Construction Automobile, Km 12, Autoroute de Rabat, Casblanca, Morocco; telephone: 350489; telex: 25825, SOMACASA.

BEN CHERIF, Ahmad, Algerian police commander; born 1927; married; *Religion:* Muslim; *Career:* served in French Armed Forces; later joined Wilaya IV of National Liberation Army (ALN), 1957; Commander of National Gendarmerie, with rank of Colonel, 1962; elected member of National Liberation Front (FLN) Committee, 1964; member of Revolutionary Command Council, 1965; Minister of Hydraulics, Land Improvement and Enviroment, 1977; member of Politburo, 1979; President of the FLN Commission of the Supreme Council of Youth; Vice President of the Commission on Higher Education; member of the Central Committee, 1979–; *Publications: L'Aurore des Mechtas Languages:* Arabic, French; *Address:* 10 Rue des Frères Belhafidh, Hydra, Algeria.

BEN JELLOUN, Ahmad Majid, Moroccan lawyer; born 27 December 1927, Fes, Morocco; married; *Religion:* Muslim; *Education:* Licencié in Law; Diploma from Institute of Political Science, Paris, France; *Career:* lawyer in Fes; member of the King's Counsel in Marrakesh, 1956, Meknes Military Tribunal, 1956; Advocate General, Rabat Appeal Court, and Rabat Supreme Court; Secretary

General of the Ministry of Justice, 1964; Minister of Information, 1965–67; Minister, Royal Cabinet, 1967; Minister of Administrative Affairs, 1971–72; Minister of Information, 1972; Attorney General of the Supreme Court, 1974–; Professor of Law at the Law Faculty and at the École Marocaine d'Administration in Rabat; member of the Committee for the Drafting of the Penal Code and Penal Procedures Code; *Decorations:* Order of the Throne; several foreign decorations; *Languages:* Arabic, French; *Address:* Court Supreme, Le Procureur General Du Roi, Rabat, Morocco.

BEN MELIH, Fuad, Moroccan banker; born 14 July 1948, Tangier, Morocco; married; *Religion:* Muslim; *Education:* BSc, Economics and Political Sciences, University of Baghdad, Baghdad, Iraq; Diplome des Etudes Economiques Financieres et Banquaire, Paris, France; Diplome d'Etude Supérieures d'Economie d'Entreprise, Paris, France; *Career:* Director, Banque Centrale Populaire, Morocco; Secretary General, Arab Bank, Morocco; President, Personnel Council of Moroccan Banks, Morocco; *Publications:* articles in newspapers and in professional journals in Arabic and French; *Languages:* Arabic, French, English, Spanish; *Address:* Arab Bank Maroc, 174 Boulevard Muhammad V, Casablanca, P O Box 810, Morocco; telephone: 223151, 272691.

BEN SALEM, Ali, Tunisian artist/painter; born 25 December 1910, Tunis, Tunisia; married; three sons; *Religion:* Muslim; *Career:* founder of Tunisian Art Museum, Dar Monastiri, Dar Ben Abdullah, Dar Othman, Tunisian Museum of Art, 1932; Tunisian Government 1st Prize for Painting, 1936; 1st Prize, North African Miniature, 1936; official Tunisian Government Decorator for the Paris International Exihibition, 1937; Collaborator of West Africa, to the Musée de l'Homme, Paris, 1937–39; Exhibitions in Stockholm, 1939–40; Professor, Sfax College, Tunisia; Founder and Director of Fine Arts School of Sfax 1940–44; 45 one-man exhibitions at Swedish cities, 1945–72; ethnographic exhibition in Helsinki, 1972; Professor of Arts and Ethnography; personal exhibitions under the patronage of the Ministry of National Education, Paris; work represented at the Musée du Luxembourg and Musée des Arts Décoratifs, Paris; *Publications:* illustrations of books on arts and ethnography in Sweden and Tunisia, the poems of Roy Campbell and O.V. de Miles; articles on the development of arts and emancipation of Tunisian women in various Tunisian journals; *Decorations:* Commander of the Tunisia Cultural Order; Officer of the Tunisian Order of Independence, 1966; Officer of the Tunisian Order of the Republic, 1975; Gold Medal of the City of Paris; Commander of the French Order of Literature and Arts, 1973; Swedish Order of the Wasa of Literature and Arts; *Interests and Recreations:* athletics, swimming; member of the Carthage Institute since its foundation, 1930, Swedish-Tunisian Friendship Association, Stockholm; Vice President of the Tunisian Society of Deaf Mutes; *Languages:* Arabic, French, Italian, English, Swedish, Latin; *Address:* Artillerigatan 24, 114 51 Stockholm, Sweden; telephone: 086 15026.

BEN SEDDIK, Mahjub, Moroccan trade union official; born 1925; *Career:* Secretary General, Union Marocaine du Travail (UMT),1955–; President, Pan African Trade Union Federation 1961, 1964, 1966, 1971; member of Secretariat General, Union Nationale des Forces Populaires (UNFP); member of Administrative Council of International Labour Organisation; *Languages:* Arabic, French; *Address:* 232 Avenue des Forces Armées Royales, Casablanca, Morocco; telephone: 308023, 304921; telex: 21956.

BEN YAHMED, Bechir, Tunisian journalist/official; born 1928; married; *Religion:* muslim; *Education:* Sadiki College,Tunis; Ecole des Hautes Etudes Commerciales, Paris, France; *Career:* Director of Cabinet of Muhammad Masmoudi, 1954; resigned to edite French Language Weekly *l'Action,* 1955; Secretary of State for Information, 1956; Secretary of State for Information, 1957; resigned to publish *Jeune Afrique,* Paris, France; *Languages:* Arabic, French, English; *Address:* c/o rue 2 Mars 1934, Tunis, Tunisia.

BENAISSA, Hanafi, Algerian academic/journalist; born 23 December 1932; married; four sons; *Religion:* Muslim; *Education:* BA in Psychology; BA in English; PhD in Philosophy; *Career:* Head of the Cultural Exchange Service, Ministry of Education, 1962–63; Professor, Higher School of Interpretation, University of Algeria, 1963–73; Professor of Psychology, Institute of Social Sciences, University of Algeria, 1973–; Editor of *Al-Thaqafa* magazine, 1975–, member of the Union of Algerian Interpreters; member of the Union of Algerian Writers; *Publications:* numerous articles published in newspapers and magazines; translation of several books into Arabic; *Interests and Recreations:* swimming, translation, writing, journalism; *Languages:* Arabic, French, English; *Address:* Cite Chevalley Bt 14B, Bouzareah, Algiers, Algeria; telephone: 785 561.

BENBARKA, Ibrahim, Moroccan Arab League official/economist; born 10 October 1939, Rabat, Morocco; married; three daughters; *Religion:* Muslim; *Education:* BA in Economics, University of Damascus, Damacus, Syria, 1963; MA in Statistics and Research, University of Cairo, Cairo, Egypt, 1966; *Career:* Chief Statistian, 1967–; Secretary, State Office for Regional Planning and Development, 1972; Director, Regional Planning and Development, 1978–; Director of Statistics, League of Arab States, Tunisia, 1981–; *Publications:* numerous studies and researches on the economy of Morocco and the Arab World in professional journals and magazines; translated *Social Economic Indicators of Morocco,* Abdul Malik Cherkaoui; *Decorations:* Order of Reda, 1971; *Interests and Recreations:* swimming, jogging, tennis; *Languages:* Arabic, French; *Address:* 17 Avenue Abda Aviation, Rabat, Morocco; telephone: 50038, 65136.

BENCHEIKH, Tayib, Moroccan politician/economist; born 1938, Zoumi, Morocco; *Religion:* Muslim; *Education:* diplomas in economics, politics and statistics, France; *Career:* Government Official in charge of statistics and responsible for population census and housing; Director of Social and Economic Development Plan, 1971; President of the Association of African Statisticians; Secretary of State for Planning and Regional Development, 1974–81; Minister of Economic Affairs, 1982; Independent Deputy at Parliament; President of Council of Meknes Province; *Languages:* Arabic, French; *Address:* Office of the Prime Minister, P O Box 760 Rabat, Morocco.

BENHABYLES, Abdul Malik, Algerian politician/lawyer; born 1921, Setif, Algeria; married; *Religion:* Muslim; *Education:* graduated in Law; *Career:* engaged in national activities, 1943–; member of Parti du Peuple Algérien, (PPA); member of Central Committee of Mouvement pour le Triomphe des Libertés Democratiques, (MTLD); Vice President of Association des Etudiants Musulmans Nord-Africaines, (AMNA); Legal Adviser to Union Generale des Etudiants Algeriens, (UGEMA), 1955; member of Commission of Information and Propaganda for Federation de France du Front de Liberation Nationale, (FLN), 1958; Representative of FLN in Damascus, Syria and in the Far East, based in Tokyo; Assistant Director of the External Services of Gouvernement Provisoire de la Republique Algérienne, (GPRA), in Cairo; represented Algeria at various international conferences; Head of Ministry of Foreign Affairs, Eastern European Division; Secretary General of the Ministry of Foreign Affairs, 1963; Ambassador to Japan, 1964–67; Ambassador to Tunisia, 1967–70; Assistant Secretary General, Ministry of Foreign Affairs, 1970–74; Secretary General of Ministry of Foreign Affairs, 1974–77; Ministry of Justice, 1977–79; member of Central Committee of FLN Party; Secretary General of the Presidency of the Republic; *Languages:* Arabic, French; *Address:* Presidency of the Algerian Democratic and Popular Republic, al-Mouradia, Algeria; telephone: 606360; telex: 52045.

BENJELLOUN, Ali, Moroccan diplomat/lawyer; born 17 August, 1927, Fes, Morocco; married; two children; *Religion:* Muslim; *Education:* LLD, Faculty of Law, Sorbonne, Paris, France; *Career:* Casablanca Bar, 1950; President, Drafting Committee of the Dahir, Supreme Court, 1955; Chairman, Moroccan Delegation for the negotiation of the Judicial Convention between France, Morocco and Spain; Vice President, Constitutional Council, 1960; President, National Accounting Office; Professor, School of Law, Moroccan School of Administration; Minister of Justice, 1967; private law practice, 1976; Head of Moroccan Permanent Mission, UN, New York, 1976–77; Ambassador Extraordinary and Plenipotentiary to USA 1977–; non-resident Ambassador to Mexico, Guatemala and the Dominican Republic; *Decorations:* Commander of the Order of the Throne, Morocco; *Interests and Recreations:* golf; *Languages:* Arabic, French, English; *Address:* Royal Moroccan Embassy, 1601 21st Street, NW, Washington D.C. 20009, USA; telephone: 462 7979.

BENMANSOUR, Nuriddin; Moroccan physician/academic; born 1935, Morocco; married; two daughters; *Religion:* Muslim; *Education:* PhD in Medicine; *Career:* Director of Avicenne Hospital, 1975–78; Director of the National Institute of Hygiene, 1978–; Professor of Medicine; *Publications:* numerous medical papers and articles published in professional journals; *Languages:* Arabic, French; *Address:* Institut National d'Hygiene, Avenue Ibn Batouta, P O Box 769, Rabat, Morocco.

BENNANI, Ahmad, Moroccan official/banker; born 1926, Fes, Morocco; married; *Religion:* Muslim; *Education:* in Paris, France; Degree in Law and Economic Sciences; *Career:* Chef de Cabinet to Muhammad Guedira, 1956–57; Minister of State; Directeur de Cabinet to Minister of National Defence; served in several senior posts in Ministry of Finance; Secretary General of Ministry of Finance and Government Repesentative on the Board of the Bank of Morocco; Under Secretary of State for Commerce and Industry, 1963; General Manager of the Caisse Nationale de Dépôt et de Gestion, 1965; Secretary of State for Economic Affairs in Prime Minister's Office, 1966; Deputy Governor of the Bank of Morocco, 1968; Vice Chairman of the UBAF, 1980; *Languages:* Arabic, French; *Address:* 277 Avenue Muhammad V, Rabat, Morocco.

BENNIS, Abdul Latif Muhammad Bin Salim, Moroccan journalist; born 1940, Fes, Morocco; married; two sons; *Religion:* Muslim; *Education:* Diploma in Classical Arabic; university studies in Paris, France; Moroccan School of Administration; *Career:* Secretary Editor, *Nation Africaine ;* Chief Editor, *L'Opinion,* daily paper; Editor in Chief, *Le Matin,* daily paper; Director, *Maroc-Soir,* daily paper; *Interests and Recreations:* tennis; *Languages:* Arabic, French, English; *Address:* 34 Rue Muhammad Smiha, Casablanca, Morocco; telephone: 301271, 309902.

BENNIS, Muhammad Abdul Wahid, Moroccan academic/journalist; born 1948, Fes, Morocco; married; two sons; *Religion:* Muslim; *Education:* PhD in Literature, France; *Career:* teacher of Arabic language, 1972; Assistant Professor, Faculty of Literature, University of Muhammad V, Rabat, 1980;

Director of *Al-Thaqafa al-Jadida* magazine, 1974–; Literary Correspondent for *Al-Nahar al-Arabi wal Duwali* magazine; *Publications:* several poetry collections, in Arabic; studies in contemporary Arabic poetry; *Interests and Recreations:* poetry, music, painting, Arabic language; *Languages:* Arabic, French; *Address:* P O Box 505 Muhammadia, Morocco; telephone: 032, 39095.

BENNOUNA, Driss, Moroccan diplomat; born 27 April 1923, Tetouan, Morocco; married; four sons, two daughters; *Religion:* Muslim; *Education:* Diploma in Electro-Mechanic Engineering, Madrid, Spain; *Career:* Director of the Professional School, Tetouan, 1949; Chief Engineer of Production and Distribution of Electrical Energy for COOPERATIVA IHMSA and for ELECTRAS MARROQUIES, Tetouan, 1949–56; member of the Executive Committee of the Reformist National Party, 1950; participated in negotiations for independence with Spain, 1956; founding member of the Ministry of Foreign Affairs, Morocco, 1956; Counsellor, Moroccan Embassy in Cairo, Egypt, 1957–58; Director of Royal Protocol, 1959; Head of Royal Protocol, 1961; Ambassador, Ministry of Foreign Affairs, Morocco, 1967; Under Secretary of State for Royal Affairs and the Chancery, 1968; Ambassador of Morocco to Damascus, Syria, 1971; Ambassador to Beirut, Lebanon, 1974; founding member of the Academy of the Kingdom of Morocco, 1978; Ambassador to Syria, 1979–; member of the Moroccan delegation to the UN on several occasions; Head of the Morocco-Mauritanian Joint Delegation on the Affairs of Sahara to Latin American countries, 1975; Envoy of King Hassan of Morocco for special missions to Saudi Arabia, Iran, Spain and Tunis; participated in various international conferences and conferences of the Arab League and of the Non-Aligned countries; *Decorations:* Officer of the Order of the Throne, Morocco, 1963; Grand Cordon of the Order of Independence, Syria, 1974; Grand Cordon of the Order of the Republic of Egypt, 1960; and several other international decorations; *Interests and Recreations:* tennis, bridge, chess, swimming, reading; *Languages:* Arabic, Spanish, French, English; *Address:* Moroccan Embassy, 2 rue Abdelmalek Ibn Marouan, Abou Roumanah, Damascus, Syria; telephone: 335 038; Residence — 8 rue Abou Faris El Marini, 4eme etage, Rabat, Morocco; telephone: 21 783.

BENNOUNA, Mehdi Ben Hadj Abdesslam, Moroccan politician/journalist; born 22 February 1919, Tetouan, Morocco; married; four children; *Religion:* Muslim; *Education:* in Nablus, Palestine; American University of Cairo, Egypt, 1938–45; London School of Economics, London, UK; *Career:* Editor of Cairo newspaper *Al Dastour;* served with British Forces in Egypt; returned to Morocco 1945 and started private business; was sent 1947 by the National Reform Party to New York to establish contact with US public opinion on the Moroccan question; returned to Tangier; was barred entry into the Spanish Zone until 1952; began organization of Moroccan trade unions, 1955; later organized Moroccan take-over of Spanish business concerns in the former Spanish Zone; Secretary of the Directorate General of the National Consultative Assembly, with rank of Honorary Attaché, 1957; Attaché at Royal Cabinet, Press and Information Affairs, 1957; founded Moroccan News Agency (Maghreb Arabe Presse– MAP), 1959, (nationalized 1974); founded Moroccan French language newspaper *La Dépêche,* 1970; elected President of the Islamic News Agency,1973; Founder and Director of Public Relations Office, and of an industrial investments company specialized in telecommunications and electronics; *Languages:* Arabic, French, Spanish, English; *Address:* Residence — Moulay Ismail Bat, C, Bd Moulay Slimane, Rabat, Morocco.

BENNOUR, Ahmad, Tunisian politician; born 1937, Tunis, Tunisia; married; three children; *Religion:* Muslim; *Education:* Sadiki College, Tunis, Tunisia; Higher Studies at the Faculty of Law, Political and Economic Sciences, Tunis; *Career:* Assistant Secretary General, Union Générale des Etudiants de Tunisie (UGET), 1958–62; member of the Executive Committee of the Neo-Destour Party, 1962–65; Ministry of the Interior, 1965; first Delegate of the Governorate of Gefsa, 1967; Director of Political Affairs at the Directorate General of National Security, 1967–68; Director General of the Tunisian Society for the Promotion of Tourist Youth, 1969; Governor of Tunis South, 1972; Governor of Souss, 1973–74; Secretary of State, Ministry of National Defence, 1974–80; Director General of National Security, Ministry of the Interior, 1980–; *Decorations:* Commander of the Order of Tunisian Republic; Officer of the Order of Tunisian

Independence; Grand Cordon of the Order of Tunisian Republic; Grand Cordon of the Order of Tunisian Independence; *Languages:* Arabic, French, English; *Address:* Ministry of the Interior, Directorate General of National Security, Tunis, Tunisia.

BENSLAMA, Abdul Rahim, Moroccan journalist/lawyer; born 1945, Rabat, Morocco; married; one son, one daughter; *Religion:* Muslim; *Education:* Diploma in Law Studies; *Career:* Administrative Officer, Ministry of Higher Education, Morocco; Judge, Court of Rabat, Morocco; Television and Radio Programme Producer; *Publications:* Editor of *Al Tadamun al Islami,* of *Al Wa'i,* and of *Al Jihad,* magazines; *Decorations:* Order of UNESCO; *Interests and Recreations:* tennis, jogging, Chairman of Moroccan Society for Islamic Solidarity; member of several other cultural societies and associations; *Languages:* Arabic, French; *Address:* P O Box 351, Rabat, Morocco; telephone: 87130.

BENSLIMANE, Abdul Qadir; Moroccan politician/economist; born 1932, Morocco; married; two children; *Religion:* Muslim; *Educaton:* BA, Law, Faculty of Law and Political Sciences, Toulouse, France; *Career:* member of Departmental Staff, Ministry of Finance, and Head of Administrative Division, 1957–59; Head of Budget Department, Ministry of Finance; Governor, Central Bank, 1959–61; Ministerial Adviser, Embassy of the Kingdom of Morocco, Paris, France, 1961–63; General Manager, Bureau d'Etudes et de Participation Industrielles, Head of Departemental Staff of Ministry of Economy and Finance, and Permanent Representative of the Kingdom of Morocco to the Comité Permanent Consultatif du Maghreb Arabe, Rabat, 1963–66; Vice President of Comité Maghrebin, Tunis, 1965–72; Ambassador to BENELUX and the EEC, Brussels, 1972; Minister of Trade, Industry, Mining and Marine, 1972–74; Minister of Finance, 1974–77; Governor of Arab Fund for Economic and Social Development, of the Arab Bank of Economic Development in Africa, of the Islamic Development Bank, of the African Development Bank and of the African Development Fund, 1974–77; Chairman and General Manager, Banque Nationale pour le Développement Economique, Rabat, 1978; Chairman of the Communal Council of Rommani; Chairman of the Provincial Council of the Khemeissat Province; Representative of Rommani at Parliament; *Decorations:* Officer of the Order of the Throne; Commander of the French Order of Merit; Commander of the Order of the Italian Republic; *Address:* Banque Nationale pour le Développement Economique, P O Box 407, Place des Alaouites, Rabat, Morocco; telephone: 26441/23, 24274, 24297.

BENSOUDA, Ahmad Ben Yahya, Moroccan politician/official; born 1920, Fes, Morocco; married; *Religion:* Muslim; *Education:* Koranic school; Qarawiyin University, Fes, Morocco; *Career:* joined the Comité d'Action Marocaine, later Movement National, 1936; imprisoned for political activities on several occasions, 1937–46; Teacher of Arabic Language and Literature at Moulay Hassan School, Casablanca, Morocco; active in Parti Democrate de l'Indépendance, politics and journalism, 1947–55; Secretary of State for Youth Affairs and Sports, 1955–56; member of Union Nationale des Forces Populaires (UNFP), 1959; resigned 1960; Governor of Rabat Province, 1962–; Director General of Radio and Television, 1964–1965; member of the Royal Cabinet, 1965; Ambassador to Lebanon, 1966; Deputy for Larache, 1970; Ambassador to Lebanon, 1972; reappointed to Royal Cabinet, 1973; Director of Royal Cabinet, 1975; First Governor to the Sahara Provinces, 1975; Counsellor to HM Hassan II, and Director of Royal Cabinet, 1976–; *Publications:* collections of Arabic poetry; *Languages:* Arabic, French, Spanish; *Address:* The Royal Cabinet, Rabat, Morocco.

BERRADA, Abdul Salam, Moroccan official/agricultural expert; born 3 October 1931, Fes, Morocco; *Education:* Ecole Nationale d'Agriculture de Grignon; Ecole Nationale des Eaux et Forêts, Nancy, France; *Career:* Waters and Forests Administration; Director of Water and Forests Administration, 1965; Secretary General, Ministry of Agriculture and Agrarian Reforms, 1971–72; Minister of Agriculture and Agrarian Reforms, 1972–74; President, Société Cellulose du Maroc, 1972; represented Morocco at many regional and international conferences; *Languages:* Arabic, French; *Address:* Cellulose du Maroc, P O Box 429, Rabat, Morocco.

BESHARA, Antoine, Lebanese politician/trade unionist; born circa 1929, Jounieh, Lebanon; *Religion:* Christian; *Education:*

general; *Career:* Chief Accountant to the Beirut Port Company; Chairman of the Port Company Union; Chairman of the Federation of Workers in Autonomous and Private Offices; Secretary General of the Lebanese Confederation of Trade Unions; member of the Constitutional Union Party; made official visit to UK 1970; *Address:* Confédération Générale des Travailleurs du Liban (CGTL), Beirut, Lebanon.

BESSAIAH, Boualem, Algerian politician/diplomat; born 1930, Algeria; *Religion:* Muslim; *Education:* general; *Career:* Teacher of Arabic Literature, 1951–56, Algeria; Officer in National Liberation Army, 1956–62; after independence 1962, joined the Ministry of Foreign Affairs; Ambassador to Belgium, Luxembourg, and European Economic Community, 1963–70; Ambassador to Egypt, 1970–71; Secretary General of Foreign Affairs, 1971–78; Ambassador to Kuwait, 1978–80; Minister of Information, 1980–; *Publications: Etendard Interdit,* 1976; *Languages:* Arabic, French; *Address:* 119 Rue Didouche Mourad, Algiers, Algeria; telephone: 611712; telex: 52989.

BEYDOUN, Bulend Wafik, Lebanese diplomat; born 1912, Istanbul, Turkey; married; two children; *Education:* Diploma in Political Science; *Career:* entered Foreign Service; Attaché, Legation to Turkey, 1947–50; Attaché, Legation to Saudi Arabia, 1950; Attaché, Legation to Brazil, 1950–53; Ministry of Foreign Affairs; Ambassador to Nigeria, 1966–71; also accredited to Cameroons, 1968–72; Ambassador to Sudan, 1972–80; *Languages:* Arabic, French; *Address:* c/o Ministry of Foreign Affairs, Beirut, Lebanon.

BEYHOUM, Issam, Lebanese diplomat; born 1921, Beirut, Lebanon; *Education:* Licence in Law, Faculty of Law, St. Joseph University, Beirut, Lebanon; *Career:* entered Foreign Service; Consul in Alexandria, Egypt, 1946; Ministry of Foreign Affairs, 1946–47; Consul in Alexandria, 1947–50; Consul in Cairo, 1950–53; Ministry of Foreign Affairs, 1953–56; 1st Secretary, Embassy to Italy, 1956–57; Ministry of Foreign Affairs, 1957–59; Counsellor, Embassy to Egypt, 1959–60; Consul General in Alexandria, 1960–65; Chargé d'Affaires and then Ambassador to Austria, 1965–71; Ambassador to Yugoslavia, 1971;

Decorations: Officer of the National Order of the Cedar; *Address:* Ministry of Foreign Affairs, Beirut, Lebanon.

BIALI, Muhamad Ahmad al-, Egyptian journalist; born 24 October 1921, Kafr al-Shaikh, Egypt; married; one daughter; *Religion:* Muslim; *Education:* BA in Journalism, American University in Cairo, Egypt; *Career:* Cairo Correspondent, Middle East Broadcasting Station, 1951; Chief Editor, *Al-Giil al-Gadiid,* Akhbar al-Yaum Publishers, 1952; London Correspondent, *Al-Qahira* newspaper, 1953; Managing Editor, *Al-Sha'b* newspaper, 1956; Director of Middle East News Agency Offices, (MENA), Morocco, Italy, West Germany, North Africa, 1959–62; Sub Editor, Managing Editor of MENA, 1962–74; Editor in Chief, member of the Board of Directors and Vice Chairman, MENA, 1974–; *Publications: Technical Study in Egyptian Press,* 1945, in English; *Odyssey of Homer,* 1947, in English; *Middle East News Agency, 25 Years of Progress,* 1979, in English; *Middle East: Case Study,* 1980, in English; *Interests and Recreations:* writing, chess, wireless mechanics, home decor, camping, travelling, painting; expert on mass media and communications; member of the Cairo Press Syndicate, of the Journalists International Club, London, of the International Journalist Union, Prague; member of Al-Gezira Sporting Club, Cairo; *Languages:* Arabic, English, French, Italian; *Address:* Office — 4 Cherifein Street, Cairo, Egypt; telephone: 741482; Residence — 188 Al-Nil Street, Cairo, Egypt; telephone: 804083.

BIDH, Ali Salim al-, People's Democratic Republic of Yemen politician; born 1940, People's Democratic Republic of Yemen; *Education:* in Aden; engineering, Cairo, Egypt; *Career:* active in National Liberation Front (NLF); Minister of Defence, 1967–68; Foreign Minister, 1968–71; Minister of State to the Presidential Council, 1971; Minister of Planning, 1973–75; Minister of Local Government Affairs, 1975; member of the NLF Political Bureau; Head of Economic Affairs, NLF Political Bureau 1975; *Languages:* Arabic, English; *Address:* Ministry of Local Government Affairs, Aden, People's Democratic Republic of Yemen.

BIDJAOUI, Muhammad, Algerian diplomat/ lawyer; born 21 September 1929, Algeria; married; *Religion:* Muslim; *Education:* Licence in Law, Grenoble University, France, 1951; Doctorate in Law, Grenoble University, 1956; Diploma, Institute of Political Studies, Grenoble University; *Career:* Attorney, Court of Appeal, Grenoble, France, 1951–53; Researcher, National Scientific Research Centre, Paris, 1956–58; Legal Counsellor, Provisional Government of Algeria, 1958–61; Legal Counsellor, Arab League, Geneva, Switzerland, 1959–62; Director, Office of the President of National Constituent Assembly, Algiers, 1962; member, Delegation of Algeria to UN General Assembly, 1962; Secretary General, Council of Ministers, 1962–64; President, Administration Council, National Society of Algerian Railways, 1964; Dean, Faculty of Law and Economics Science, Algiers University, 1964–65; Minister of Justice and Keeper of the Seals, 1964–70; Ambassador to France, 1970; Permanent Representative to UNESCO, 1971; member, International Law Commission, UN, France, 1965; member of French Society for International Law, of Senegal Group, Permanent Court of Arbitration; Honorary member, Association of Auditors and Former Auditors, Hague Academy of International Law; *Publications:* numerous books and articles on International and Algerian Laws; *Decorations:* decorations and distinctions from Morocco, Egypt, Grenoble University, and USA; *Languages:* Arabic, English, French; *Address:* International Law Commission, UN, 18 rue Hamelin, 75016, Paris, France; telephone: 553 7149.

BIHAIRI, Ma'mun Ahmad Abdul Wahab, Sudanese politician; born 1925, Darfur, Sudan; married; several children; *Religion:* Muslim; *Education:* Victoria College, Alexandria, Egypt; BA in Economics, Brasenose College, Oxford University, UK, 1949; *Career:* government service; Inspector, Ministry of Finance, 1950; Deputy Permanent Under Secretary, Ministry of Finance, 1955; Governor of the Bank of the Sudan, 1960; member of the Commission of Constitutional Development, 1961–62; Chairman of the National Technical Development Committee, 1962; Minister of Finance, 1963; accompanied President Abboud on his state visit to UK, 1964; Managing Director of the African Development Bank, resigned in 1970; President of the Board of Trustees of the Special Fund for the Repatriation, Resettlement, Relief and Rehabilitation of Sudanese Refugees of the Southern Region with rank of Minister, 1972; member of the People's Assembly, 1974; Chairman of the People's Assembly Committee on Development and Economic and Financial Affairs, 1974–75; Minister of Finance and National Economy, 1975–77; Economic Adviser to the Prime Minister, 1977–; *Decorations:* Honorary Knight Commander of St. Michael and St. George, UK, 1964; *Interests and Recreations:* tennis; *Languages:* Arabic, English; *Address:* Ministry of Finance and National Economy, P O Box 298, Khartoum, Sudan.

BIHBAHANI, Murad Yusuf, Kuwaiti businessman; born 1925; married; *Religion:* Muslim; *Education:* in Kuwait; *Career:* extensive business interests; member of Board of Al-Ahli Bank of Kuwait; Honorary Swiss Consul; *Languages:* Arabic, English, Persian; *Address:* P O Box 1387, Safat, Kuwait; telephone: 411101; telex: 22067 KT.

BIHRUZIAN, Hashim, United Arab Emirates administrator; born 1925; married; *Career:* Accountant to the Ruler of Fujairah, Shaikh Hamad Bin Muhammad al-Sharqi; *Languages:* Arabic, Persian; *Address:* Amiri Court, P O Box 1, Government House, Fujairah, United Arab Emirates; telephone: 22111.

BIKRI, Sheikh, Algerian UN Official; born 28 April 1927, Oran, Algeria; married; *Education:* Licencié-ès-Lettres, University of Algiers, 1950–53; Agrégation des Lettres, University of Paris, France, 1960; *Career:* Assistant Professor, Constantine University, Algeria, 1960–62; Regional Director of Education for West Algeria, 1962; Permanent Secretary, Ministry of Education, 1962–64; Staff Member, Planning and Finance, UNESCO, 1964–72; Chief, Policy in Education Section, UNESCO, 1972; Director, Regional Office for Education, Beirut, Lebanon, 1973; *Publications:* numerous articles on education; *Interests and Recreations:* tennis, swimming; *Languages:* Arabic, English, French; *Address:* Regional Office for Education, UNESCO, P O Box 5244, Ave Camille Chamoun, Beirut, Lebanon.

BILBAISI, Mu'atasim Ismail al-, Jordanian diplomat; born 1933, Amman, Jordan; married; *Education:* BA Economics, American University of Beirut, Lebanon 1954; *Career:* Foreign Ministry 1959, Attaché, Embassy to Spain 1959; Foreign Ministry, Amman 1959–62; Attaché, Embassy to Lebanon 1962; Assistant Head of Protocol in Royal Court 1964–69; Head of Royal Protocol 1969–70; Minister Delegate in Foreign Ministry 1970; Ambassador to Nationalist China 1971–73; non-resident Ambassador to Japan 1971–73; non-resident Ambassador to Turkey 1973–75; Head of Ceremonies Department in Foreign Ministry 1975–76; Director General of Press and Publications 1976–77; Ambassador to Switzerland, 1977–79; Ambassador of Jordan to Lebanon, 1982–; *Decorations:* Star of Jordan 3rd Class; Independence Medal 3rd Class; Order of Holy Sepulchre 3rd Class; Order of Cedars of Lebanon; Hamayouni Order, Iran; *Address:* Embassy of Jordan, Rue Verdum, Imm Belle-Rue, Beirut, Lebanon.

BILKACEM, Sharif, Algerian politician; born 1933, Ain Beida, Morocco; married; one child; *Religion:* Muslim; *Education:* law studies; *Career:* teacher, Moulay Hassan Secondary School, Morocco; member Moroccan Istiqlal (Independence) Party and Moroccan section of Algerian Students Union (UGEMA); joined National Liberation Army (ALN) in Wilaya V and became Commanding Officer; active role in Evian negotiations with France, 1962; Commander of Western Operation Forces of National Liberation Army (ALN); elected Deputy for Tlemcen, 1962; Minister of National Guidance, 1963; elected member of National Liberation Front (FLN) Central Committee, 1964; member of the Council of the Revolution; left Ministry of National Guidance to become Secretary General of FLN; visited Yemen as Representative of President Boumedienne, 1968; Minister of State for Finance and National Plan, 1968–70; Minister of State, 1970–75; *Languages:* Arabic, French, some English; *Address:* Front de Liberation Nationale (FLN), Place Emir Abdel Kader, Algiers, Algeria.

BIN ABDALLAH, Jellal, Tunisian artist/painter; born 26 May 1921; married; *Religion:* Muslim; *Education:* self educated; *Career:* artist and miniaturist, linking traditional Arab art with modern trends derived from Mediterranean classical arts; revived and created Arab theatrical stage design as set designer for the Tunis Theatre, 1957–60; received Silver Medal for the Tunisian Pavilion, Brussels, 1958; painted the mural decorations for the Maison de Tunisie, Cité Universitaire, Paris, 1953; designed ceramics for the Palais des Congrès, Bizerta, and mosaics for Lycée Iban Khaled, and for various other buildings; exhibited at Venice Biennale, Alexandria Biennale and elsewhere; *Publications:* designer for film *Roger Mauge* (prize, Cannes Festival) and *Sidi Bousaid* (Moscow prize); *Decorations:* Officer of the Order of the Tunisian Republic; Commander of the Order of Cultural Merit; *Languages:* Arabic, French, English; *Address:* 55 Avenue President Kennedy, Sidi Bousaid, Tunisia; telephone: 270705.

BIN ABDUL SALAM, Muhammad Bin Ibrahim, Saudi Arabian official/educationalist; born 1934; *Religion:* Muslim; *Education:* BA in Arabic Literature; *Career:* Head of Professional (Technical) Board, Ministry of Education; Chief of Education Mission of Saudi Arabia to Algeria; Saudi Cultural Attaché, Morocco; attended several conferences on Islamic philosophy; *Address:* P O Box 8, Riyadh, Saudi Arabia.

BIN ABDULLAH, Abdul Aziz, Moroccan academic/writer; born 28 November 1923, Rabat, Morocco; married; six daughters, one son; *Religion:* Muslim; *Education:* Degree in Law and Literature, Algiers University, Algeria, 1946; studies in Islamic sciences with a group of Moroccan Ulemas; *Career:* Director of Property Conservation and Engineering Interests, 1957; Director of Higher Education and Scientific Research, 1958–61; Director of Bureau of Coordination of Arabization in the Arab World, Arab League, 1962–; Professor at Qarawiyin University, Fes, Morocco, Mohammed V University, Rabat, and Dar al-Hadith al-Hassaniya; *Publications: The Philosophy and Morality of Ibn al-Khatib; Aspects of Maghreb Civilization,* in Arabic; *Moroccan Art in Various Ages,* in French and Arabic; *Medicine and Doctors of Morocco,* a comparative study of Arabic and foreign texts; *The Geography of the Maghreb; The Development of Thoughts and Languages in Modern Morocco,* a series of lectures delivered at the Institute of Arabic Studies in Cairo; *Human and Cultural Encyclopedia of Morocco,* ten volumes; *The Blond Country Girl,* stories of Moroccan history, Beirut; *Arabization and the Future of the Arabic Language,* lectures delivered in the Institute of Arabic Studies, Cairo; *Towards the Elimination of Illiteracy in the Arab World,* in French; author of numerous dictionaries in various fields in Arabic, French and English; *Decorations:* Honorary Medal with rank of Knight, 1969; *Interests and Recreations:* architecture, Andalusian music, philosophy, Sufism; participated in many international conferences such as UN Conference of Experts on African Affairs; represented Morocco at Islamic and Educational conferences; *Languages:* Arabic, French, English; *Address:* 47 Madagascar Street, Rabat, Morocco; telephone: 30821; Arab League Educational, Cultural and Scientific Organization (ALECSO), P O Box 290, Rabat, Morocco.

BIN ABDULLAH, Bandar, Saudi Arabian administrator; born circa 1942; *Religion:* Muslim; *Education:* USA; Organization and Methods Course, Japan; *Career:* Director of General Provisional Affairs, Ministry of Interior, 1974; Director General of Organization and Management, Ministry of Interior, 1970–71; *Languages:* Arabic, English; *Address:* Ministry of Interior, Riyadh, Saudi Arabia.

BIN ABDULLAH, Saud, Saudi Arabian diplomat; born 1944; *Religion:* Muslim; *Education:* USA; *Career:* member of Saudi Arabian Mission to UN since 1969; served in Western Department of Ministry of Foreign Affairs, 1968–69; *Languages:* Arabic, English; *Address:* Ministry of Foreign Affairs, Jeddah, Saudi Arabia.

BIN AMEIR, Ahmad Muhammad, Omani businessman; born 1933, Muscat, Sultanate of Oman; married; two sons; *Career:* Chairman of Bin Ameir Establishment for Commerce and Contractors; Chairman of Establishment of Oman Contractors; Chairman of the International Company for Insecticides; Chairman of the Chamber of Commerce and Industry, Oman; *Interests and Recreations:* Arabic Poetry; *Languages:* Arabic, English; *Address:* P O Box 5157, Ruwi, Muscat, Oman; telephone: 701973, 701495.

BIN AMIR, Taha Sharif, Libyan politician; born 1940, Benghazi, Libya; *Religion:* Muslim; *Education:* engineering trainee in Ger-

many; *Career:* Under Secretary, Ministry of Communications; Minister of Communications and Power, 1971–75; Minister of State for Revolutionary Command Council Affairs, 1975–76; *Languages:* Arabic, English, German; *Address:* c/o General Secretariat of the General People's Committee, Tripoli, Libya.

BIN AMMAR, Hassib, Tunisian politician/businessman; born 11 April 1924, Tunis, Tunisia; married; three sons, one daughter; *Religion:* Muslim; *Education:* Degree in Physical Sciences, Faculty of Sciences, University of Paris, France; *Career:* Director of Youth and Sports, 1958; Secretary General for Youth, 1960; Deputy Mayor of Tunis, 1963; Governor Mayor of Tunis, 1964; Ambassador to Italy, 1969; Director of Destour Socialist Party, 1970; Minister of National Defence, 1970; Director of S.A. El Iskane (Real Estate); Director of S.A. Mercure (bookshop and publishing); member of the Red Crescent, 1940, Socialist Destour Party Central Committee, 1940; member of the Association Sauvegarde de la Medina, 1964; Editor of *Ech-Chabab,* organ of the Higher Committee of Youth; *Interests and Recreations:* participated in the creation of the Union of Arab Cities and in preparing the project to preserve Tunis-Carthage supported by UNESCO; *Languages:* Arabic, French, English; *Address:* 9 rue Juba, Tunis, Tunisia; telephone: 282258.

BIN AMMAR, Tahar, Tunisian politician; born 25 December 1889, Tunis, Tunisia; married; four sons; *Religion:* Muslim; *Education:* Diploma, Lycée Carnot, Tunis, Tunisia; *Career:* Prime Minister, negotiated Tunisian internal autonomy with Prime Minister Mendès of France and Prime Minister Edgar Fauré, later negotiated Tunisian Independence with Prime Minister Guy Mollet; President of the Chamber of Agriculture; President of the Grand Council, Tunisian Section; *Decorations:* Grand Cordon of Tunisian Independence; foreign decorations include Commander of the Légion d'Honneur; *Interests and Recreations:* theatre; *Languages:* Arabic, French; *Address:* 18 Place aux Chevaux, Tunis, Tunisia; telephone: 260468.

BIN BAZ, Abdul Aziz Bin Abdullah, Saudi Arabian religious leader; born 1912, Riyadh, Saudi Arabia; *Religion:* Muslim; *Education:* private tuition under a group of Ulemas in

Riyadh; Arabic and Islamic science, Quranic interpretation, Jurisprudence, Islamic history; *Career:* judge, Al-Khari, 1938–52; Teacher, Religious Institute, 1953; Lecturer, Faculty of Islamic Law (Sharia), Riyadh University, Saudi Arabia, 1953–62; Chief Mufti of Saudi Arabia and Chairman of Supreme Council of Ifta (Supreme Religious Council); Rector of Islamic University, Medina; member of Supreme Council of Grand Ulema, Muslim World League, Mecca; gives regular religious lessons in the Great Mosque, Riyadh, Ka'aba, Mecca, (during pilgrimage season), and in Prophet Muhammad's Mosque, Medina; *Publications:* several books dealing with fundamental matters of religion including: *Al-Tahqiq Wal Idah Li Kathir min Masa'ilul Haj; Naqd al-Qawmiyat Ala Sa'a al-Islam al Waqi; Decorations:* Order of Merit, awarded by President of Mauritania; *Interests and Recreations:* reading, writing of Islamic literature; *Address:* Supreme Council of Ifta (Religious Council), Riyadh, Saudi Arabia.

BIN BUTTI, Shaikh Ahmad Bin Hamid, United Arab Emirates politician; born 1930, Abu Dhabi, United Arab Emirates; married; *Religion:* Muslim; *Career:* Minister of Information; member of Abu Dhabi Executive Council; *Address:* Executive Council, P O Box 10, Abu Dhabi, United Arab Emirates.

BIN GHURAIR, Hamad Bin Majid, United Arab Emirates businessman; born 1900; married; three sons; *Religion:* Muslim; *Career:* leading Dubai entrepreneur; numerous business interests in real estate and banking; former President of the Chamber of Commerce; member of the Municipal Council; *Languages:* Arabic, Urdu, English; *Address:* Abu Dhabi Chamber of Commerce and Industry, P O Box 622, Abu Dhabi, United Arab Emirates; telephone: 330880; telex: 22449 TIJARA EM.

BIN HAMIDA, Slahiddine, Tunisian journalist; born 30 June 1934, Monastir, Tunisia; married; one son, one daughter; *Religion:* Muslim; *Education:* studies in journalism and literature, Tunisia; *Career:* Editor in Chief of *Al-Amal* newspaper, organ of Neo-Destour Party, Tunis, 1960; Director of *Al-Amal,* 1964; President, Director General of Tunis-Afrique-Presse (TAP) Agency, 1972; Director General of Radio Diffusion Télévision Tunisienne (RTT), 1974; member of the

Central Committee of the Destour Socialist Party; Vice President of the Tunis Municipal Council, 1972; member of the Administrative Board of ASBU; *Publications: Between the Barada and the Nile,* 1961; *From the Happy Yemen to Revolutionary Yemen* a study of the Yemeni Revolution, 1962; *Decorations:* Commander of the Order of Tunisian Independence, 1975; Commander of the Order of Tunisian Republic, 1972; Officer of the Légion d'Honneur awarded by the President of the French Republic, 1975; Egyptian, Iranian and other decorations; *Interests and Recreations:* the novel; member of Tunisian Writers Union; sports, chess; *Languages:* Arabic, French, English; *Address:* Office — 71 Avenue de la Liberté, Tunis, Tunisia; telephone: 287300; Residence -- 60 rue des Selliers, Tunis, Tunisia.

BIN HANI, Hisham Hussein, United Arab Emirates official/auditor; born 1938, Palestine; married; four sons; *Religion:* Muslim; *Education:* BSc in Economics; *Career:* Accountant, 1968; 1st Auditor, 1969; Chief Auditor, 1975–76; Director of Administrative and Financial Affairs, 1976; *Interests and Recreations:* economics, history, swimming, football; *Languages:* Arabic, English; *Address:* Port Zaid Authority, P O Box 422, Abu Dhabi, United Arab Emirates; telephone: 823360; telex: 2273 PORTEX EM.

BIN HARIB, Thani Bin Isa, United Arab Emirates politician; born 1946, Ajman, United Arab Emirates; *Religion:* Muslim; *Education:* Administration and Social Affairs, Cairo University, Egypt; *Career:* United Arab Emirates Minister without Portfolio; UAE Minister of Islamic Affairs and Waqfs (Religious Endowments), 1973–77; Minister of Electricity and Water, Dubai, 1977; *Address:* Ministry of Electricity and Water, P O Box 1672, Dubai, United Arab Emirates.

BIN IDRIS, Abdullah Bin Abdul Aziz, Saudi Arabian writer; born 1930; *Religion:* Muslim; *Education:* BA Islamic Law and Arabic Language; *Career:* Director of Inspectorate and Examination Department, Al-Ilmi Religious Institute; Director of Technical Education, Ministry of Education; delegated as Editor in Chief, *Al-Da'wa* (Islamic Call) newspaper; member of Board, King Abdul Aziz Archives, Riyadh; member of Al-Da'wa Al-Islamiyyah (Islamic Call) Press Organization; member of New Riyadh Literary Club;

member of Supreme Council for Welfare of Science, Arts and Letters; member of Editorial Board, Darah Journal, Society of Modern Literature, Egypt; attended Saudi Men of Letters Conference, Algiers 1975; member designate of Saudi Scientific Academy; Secretary General, Supreme Council for the Welfare of Science, Arts and Letters; *Decorations:* Order of Merit; Gold Medal awarded at Saudi Men of Letters Conference (Literary Award); *Interests and Recreations:* reading, writing, travel; *Publications: Sho'ara Najd al-Ma'asiruun;* two collections of poems; co-author of Saudi secondary school textbooks; *Address:* Supreme Council for Welfare of Science, Arts and Letters, Riyadh, Saudi Arabia.

BIN JILUWI, HH PRINCE ABDUL MUHSIN BIN ABDULLAH, Saudi Arabian Prince/administrator; born 1920; *Religion:* Muslim; *Career:* Amir of Dammam for several years; Amir of Al-Hasa, Hofuf; promoted agriculture in Al-Hasa; Governor of the Eastern Province, 1967–; *Address:* Governorate of the Eastern Province, Al Hasa, Saudi Arabia.

BIN JILUWI, HH PRINCE ABDULLAH BIN ABDUL AZIZ BIN MISA'ID, Saudi Arabian Prince/administrator; born 1931, Hail, Saudi Arabia; son of late Prince Abdul Aziz Bin Musa'id Bin Jiluwi, Governor of Hail Province for 25 years during the rule of late King Abdul Aziz Ibn Saud; *Education:* general; tuition in Islamic studies and chivalry by his father; *Career:* former Governor of Al-Qasim Province; Governor of Northern Borders Province; *Interests and Recreations:* reading; *Address:* Governorate of Northern Borders Province, Arar, Saudi Arabia; telephone: Office — Arar 13.

BIN KHALIL, Nabil, Tunisian journalist; born 30 August 1930, Tunis, Tunisia; married; *Religion:* Muslim; *Education:* Licence in Law, France; Journalism Training Centre, Paris; *Career:* Head of Tunis-Afrique Press (TAP) Office in Algiers, 1962–63; Head of TAP Office in Paris, 1963–68; Assistant Editor in Chief of TAP Agency, 1968; Editor in Chief of the television review on Radio-Télévision-Tunisienne (RTT), 1968–70; Director of Information, RTT, 1970–71; Director of Foreign Relations, RTT, 1971–72; Director of Ben Express Publishing Company, 1972–75; Editor in

Chief of *Le Temps,* French daily newspaper; *Publications: Sadiki et les Sadikiens,* co-author; *La Tunisie en Marche,* co-author; *Decorations:* Knight of the Order of Merit of the FDR (West Germany), 1968; Knight of the Order of Merit of Grand Duchy of Luxembourg, 1969; Officer of the National Order of the Republic of the Ivory Coast, 1965; *Interests and Recreations:* tennis; *Languages:* Arabic, French, English; *Address:* 129 Avenue Bourguiba, Carthage, Tunis, Tunisia; telephone: 270741.

BIN LADEN, Salim Muhammad, Saudi Arabian businessman; born 1945, Mecca, Saudi Arabia; married; *Religion:* Muslim; *Education:* Millfield School, UK; *Career:* Chairman, Bin Laden Brothers for Contracting and Development, 1972–; *Interests and Recreations:* sailing, riding, motoring, flying (qualified pilot); *Languages:* Arabic, English; *Address:* P O Box 2734, Jeddah, Saudi Arabia; telephone: 29088; telex: 401044 BINLDN SJ.

BIN MAHFOUZ, Khalid Bin Salim, Saudi Arabian banker/businessman; *Religion:* Muslim; *Career:* owner and Chairman of board of several companies and agencies for foreign companies; founding member and member of Board of Saudi Bank, Paris, France; Deputy General Manager National Commercial Bank, Jeddah; *Address:* National Commercial Bank, P O Box 3555, Jeddah, Saudi Arabia; telephone: 6423122; telex: 401086 NCB.

BIN OTHMAN, Lasaad, Tunisian politician/engineer; born 16 February 1926, Tunis, Tunisia; married; one daughter; *Religion:* Muslim; *Education:* Diploma from L'Ecole Supérieure des Mines, Paris, France; studies in sub-soil resources; *Career:* Directorate of Public Works, 1949; oil exploration, 1952–59; Director of Hydraulics and Supply, Ministry of Agriculture, 1959; Chief Engineer, Hydraulics and Supply, Ministry of Agriculture, 1963; Under Secretary of State, Ministry of Agriculture, 1967; Secretary of State, Ministry of Agriculture, 1968; Minister of Public Works, 1970–71; Director General of Tunis Air, 1973; Minister of Transport and Communications, 1973–76; Minister of Supply, 1976; Minister of Agriculture, 1980–; *Decorations:* Commander of the Order of Tunisian Republic;

Languages: Arabic, French; *Address:* Ministry of Agriculture, Tunis, Tunisia; telephone: 283293.

BIN SHAKER, Lieutenant General Sharif Zaid, Jordanian army commander; born 4 September 1934, Amman, Jordan; son of Amir Shaker who came to Jordan with HM late king Abdullah; married; one son, one daughter; *Religion:* Muslim; *Education:* Victoria College, Alexandria, Egypt, 1951; Sandhurst Military Academy, UK, 1955; Long Armour Course, USA, 1962; Staff College, Leavenworth, USA, 1964; *Career:* Companion of HM King Hussain, 1955–57; Assistant Military Attaché, Embassy of Jordan to UK, 1957–58; Commander, 1st Infantry Regiment, 1963; Lieutenant Colonel, Commander of Armoured Brigade, 1964; Commander of Royal Armoured Corps; Brigadier, Commander of 3rd Armoured Division; Assistant Chief of Staff for Operations, 1970; Major General, 1970; Chief of Staff, 1972; Lieutenant General, 1974; Commander in Chief, Jordan Armed Forces, 1976; *Decorations:* Order of the Star of Jordan 1st Class; Renaissance Medal 1st Class; numerous decorations from Arab and other countries; *Languages:* Arabic, English; *Address:* Ministry of Defence and Foreign Affairs, P O Box 1577, Amman, Jordan.

BIN SMAIL, Muhammad, Tunisian broadcasting official/journalist; born 5 June 1927, Jerba, Tunisia; married; two sons; *Religion:* Muslim; *Education:* Faculty of Law, Grenoble University, France; *Career:* Editor in Chief, *L'Action* newspaper and various journals, 1955–63; Head of the Minister of Information Office, and Director General of Tourism, 1959–60; founded and directed Ceres Productions (publishing and off-set printing); Director General of Radio Télévision Tunisienne, (RTT) 1969–70; *Decorations:* Officer of the Order of Tunisian Independence; *Interests and Recreations:* sport, skiing, tennis; *Languages:* Arabic, French, English, Italian; *Address:* 6 Rue Alain Savery, Tunis, Tunisia; telephone: 280526.

BIN TAIMUR, Tariq, Omani politician; born 1923, third son of the late Sultan Said Bin Taimur; *Religion:* Muslim; married; *Education:* in Turkey and Germany; *Career:* joined the army, trained in India, 1941–45; member of the Police and Frontier Force, 1945–57;

Administrator, Muscat-Mutrah Municipalities, 1957–59; led expeditionary force against rebels tribes; Liasion Officer of Army and Civil Forces, 1962–70; exile in Turkey and Germany; representative of various German firms in the Gulf countries; Prime Minister, 1970–71; during tenure of office, organised some government departments, and created five new ministries, including Health, Justice, Economy, Information and Education; Chairman of Central Bank of Oman, 1975–; Personal Adviser to HM Sultan Qaboos; *Languages:* Arabic, English, German, Turkish; *Address:* P O Box 202, Muscat, Oman; telephone: 745 048.

BIN TOBBAL, Lakhdar, Algerian official; born 1923, Constantine District, Algeria; *Religion:* Muslim; *Career:* undertook command of Wilaya II in 1956; member of Co-ordination and Action Centre, 1951; Minister of Interior in First Provisional Government; nominated member of Triumvirate, 1960; visited China and USSR with Ferhat Abbas, 1960; Minister of State in Provisional Government inaugurated 1960; participated in negotiations leading to Evian Agreement, 1962; Chairman of Board of National Steel-Manufacturing Company (SDS); *Languages:* Arabic, French; *Address:* Société Nationale de la Sidérurgie (SNS), 5 rue Abou Moussa, Algiers, Algeria; telephone: 647560/4.

BINAISSA, Muhammad Muhammad, Moroccan UN official/journalist; born 3 January 1937, Morocco; married; *Religion:* Muslim; *Education:* Journalism, Cairo University, Egypt, 1960–61; BA in Journalism, Communications, University of Minnesota, Minneapolis, USA, 1961–63; Documentary Films and Communications, Rockefeller Foundation, New York, 1964–65; Psychology, Columbia University, New York, 1964; *Career:* Head of Programmes, Radio Africa Maghreb, Morocco, 1956–59; Director, Youth Centre, Tangiers, Morocco, 1959–60; Reporter, Moroccan Radio and Television, Cairo, 1960–61; Permanent Mission of Morocco, New York, 1964–65; Information Officer, Office of Public Information (OPI), UN New York and Addis Ababa, 1965–67; Regional Information Officer for Africa, FAO, Accra, 1967–71; Development Support Communications Officer, FAO, Rome, 1971–73; Assistant to Director, Information Office, FAO, 1973–74; Director, Information Division, FAO, Rome, 1974; *Publications: Tout est dans la Photo,* 1973; *Rural Development Support Communication Model; Grains de Peau; Interests and Recreations:* photo journalism, communication for development, design and architecture, rural development and inter-community communications; *Languages:* Arabic, Spanish, English, French, Italian; *Address:* Office — Information Division, FAO, Via delle Terme de Caracalla, 00100 Rome, Italy; telephone: 5797; Residence -- 15 Via Guerrieri, 00100 Rome, Italy; telephone: 570164.

BINHAMUDA, Bualem, Algerian politician; born 1933, Cherchel, Algeria; *Religion:* Muslim; *Education:* LLB, University of Algiers, Algeria, 1963; *Career:* joined National Liberation Army (ALN), 1956; Captain at HQ of Wilaya IV; member of Political Bureau at Tlemcen (formerly Orléansville), 1962; member of the Parliamentary Commission of War Veterans, and of the Commission for Education, 1962–65; elected member of the Central Committee of the National Liberation Front (FLN) at April 1964 Congress; re-elected, 1964; Minister of War Veterans, 1965; Minister of Justice, 1970–77; Minister of Public Works, 1977; Minister of Finance, 1978–; *Languages:* Arabic, French; *Address:* Ministry of Finance, Palais du Gouvernement, Algiers, Algeria; telephone: 632304; telex: 52062.

BINHIMA, Muhammad, Moroccan politician; born 25 June 1924, Morocco; married; two sons, two daughters; *Religion:* Muslim; *Education:* Doctor of Medicine, Nancy College, France; *Career:* Head of Medical Department, Ministry of Health, 1954; Head of Central Department of Health, 1956; Head of Ministry of Public Health Council, 1957; Secretary General, Ministry of Public Health, 1960; Governor of Agadir, 1960–61; Minister of Public Works, 1961–62, and 1963–65; Minister of Industry and Mineral Resources, 1962–63; Minister of National Education, 1965–67; Prime Minister, with overall control of economic policy, 1967–69; Minister of Agriculture and Agrarian Reforms, 1969; Minister of the Interior in Lamrani Government, 1972–73; Minister of State for Co-operation and Training, 1973–1977; Minister of State for the Interior, 1977; Minister of Interior, 1981; Private Medical Practice, 1981–; President of Safi Municipal Council; *Decorations:* Medal of Loyalty;

decorations from governments of Belgium, Sweden, Ethiopia, Tunisia, Liberia, Egypt, Niger, France, Cameroon, Italy, Libya, Ivory Coast; *Languages:* Arabic, French; *Address:* KM 5 500 Zuar Road, Rabat, Morocco.

BINIKOUS, Abdul Kadir, Algerian politician/trade unionist; born 1930, Collo, Constantine District, Algeria; *Religion:* Muslim; *Career:* teacher; elected to Secretariat of Algerian Teachers' Trade Union, 1962; Director of General Union of Algerian Workers (UGTA), 1962; Director of the Union bulletin *Révolution et Travail,* 1964; elected Secretary General of UGTA, 1969 at Third National Congress; re-elected at Fourth UGTA National Congress, 1973; *Languages:* Arabic, French; *Address:* Union Générale de Travailleurs Algériens UGTA, Maison du Peuple, Algiers, Algeria.

BINJELLOUN, Abdul Aziz, Moroccan official; born 1934, Fes, Morocco; married; *Religion:* Muslim; *Education:* Engineering, Ecole des Ponts et Chaussées; *Career:* Head of Public Works Department in city of Tetouan, 1963–66; Private Office of the Minister of Public Works, 1966; Office of Secretary General of the Ministry; Chargé de Mission, Prime Minister's Office; Director General of the Bureau des Recherches et de Participation Minières (BRPM), 1971; Under Secretary of State, Ministry of Industry, Commerce and Mines, 1971; Minister of Industry, Commerce and Mines, 1972; Director General, BRPM; *Languages:* Arabic, French; *Address:* Bureau de Recherches et de Participation Minieres (BRPM), 27 Charia Moulay Hassan, Rabat, Morocco.

BINKIRANE, Ahmad, Moroccan official/diplomat; born 1928, Marrakesh, Morocco; married; *Religion:* Muslim; *Education:* Collège Muhammad Ben Youssef, Rabat, Morocco and Ecole Supérieure de Commerce, Paris, France 1974–51; *Career:* active in nationalist movement; member of various goodwill missions to Paris following Independence; Directeur de Cabinet at the Under Secretariat for Commerce, 1956; Director General of Commerce, 1957; Under Secretary of State for Commerce, 1958; Director of the Société Anonyme Maroc-Italienne de Raffinage (SAMIR), the Moroccan-Italian Oil Refinery Company, 1958; Deputy Head and Leader of the Moroccan Delegation to the session of the Economic Commission for

Africa, Tangier, 1960; nominated Director General of the Caisse Nationale de Dépôt et de Gestion, 1966; Under Secretary of State for Commerce, Industry, Mines and Handicrafts and Director of the Marketing and Export Office, 1968–70; Director and Editor of the French language newspaper *Le Matin* 1971; Ambassador to Belgium and the EEC 1973; *Languages:* Arabic, French; *Address: Le Matin,* rue Mohammed Smiha, Casablanca, Morocco.

BINMAHMUD, Abdul Karim, Algerian politician; born 1929, Setif, Algeria; married; *Religion:* Muslim; *Education:* University of Algiers, Algeria; *Career:* entered Government Administration; Sous-Préfet of Colomb-Bechais, 1962; Préfet of Annaba (Formerly Bone); Préfet of Constantine; elected member of Central Committee of National Liberation Front (FLN) at Party Congress, 1967; Ambassador to Syria; Préfet of Algiers; Minister of Youth Affairs and Sports; Minister of Primary and Secondary Education, 1970–77; *Languages:* Arabic, French; *Address:* Ministry of Education, Algiers, Algeria.

BINNABI, Malik, Algerian writer; born 1905, Constantine, Algeria; *Education:* in Algiers and Paris, France; *Career:* writer and journalist; *Publications:* include: *Le Phénomène Coranique,* 1947; *Labbeik,* 1948; *Vocation de l'Islam,* 1957; *Al Sira al-Fikriya Fil Balad Al Moustaamara,* 1960; *Address:* Constantine, Algeria.

BINSALIM, Abdul Rahman, Algerian army commander; born Algiers, Algeria; *Religion:* Muslim; *Career:* officer, French Army; joined National Liberation Army (ALN) and spent war years in Algeria with Houari Boumedienne in Morocco; elected Deputy to National Assembly for Annaba, 1962; member of the Commission for National Defence; member of National Liberation Front (FLN) Central Committee, 1964; accompanied President Boumedienne to Moscow, 1965; member of General Staff, 1964; Assistant Chief of Staff, 1968; member of Revolutionary Council, 1965; *Address:* Front de Libération Nationale (FLN), place Emir Abdel Kader, Algiers, Algeria.

BINZAGR, Wahib Said, Saudi Arabian businessman; born 1934; *Education:* Victoria College, Alexandria, Egypt; BSc in Econo-

mics, University of Durham, UK; *Career:* family business; founder and member of Jeddah Chamber of Commerce; member of Board of Saudi Arabian Airlines, SAUDIA, 1965–70; Governor of Jeddah, 1966; member of Board of the Riyadh Bank; founding member of King Abdul Aziz University; member of Board of UBAN–Arab Japanese Finance Ltd; member of the Board of the Arab British Chamber of Commerce, London; *Address:* Binzagr Group of Companies, P O Box 54 Jeddah, Saudi Arabia; telephone: 23529, 23769.

BIRIDO, Omar Yusif, Sudanese diplomat; born 1939, Sudan; married; *Religion:* Muslim; *Education:* BA, University of Khartoum, Sudan, 1958–63; MA in Political Science, University of Delhi, India, 1964–66; *Career:* Embassy to New Delhi, India, 1964–66; Embassy of Sudan, London, UK, 1966–69; Ministry of Foreign Affairs, Sudan, 1969–71; Counsellor, Embassy to Kampala, Uganda, 1971–73; Counsellor, Permanent Mission of Sudan to UN, New York, USA, 1973–76; Director, Department of International Organizations, Ministry of Foreign Affairs, Khartoum, 1976–77; Director, Department of African Affairs, Ministry of Foreign Affairs, Khartoum,1977–78; Ambassador, Permanent Representative of the Sudan to the UN Office, Geneva, Switzerland; *Decorations:* Order of the Republic of Sudan, 1972; *Interests and .Recreations:* photography, political, social and public issues; *Languages:* Arabic, English; *Address:* 56 Rue de Moillebeau, C.P. 56, 1211 Geneva 19, Switzerland.

BISHARA, Abdullah Yacoub, Kuwaiti diplomat; born 6 November 1936, Kuwait; married; *Religion:* Muslim; *Education:* BA, Literature and Arts, University of Cairo, Egypt 1955–59; Degree in International Relations, Balliol College, Oxford University, UK 1961–62; African Studies, St.John's University, 1972–73; *Career:* Embassy to Tunis 1963–64; Director, Office of Minister of Foreign Affairs, Kuwait, 1964–71; Ambassador to Argentina and Brazil 1974; Ambassador, Permanent Representative of Kuwait to the United Nations, New York, USA, 1971–81; Secretary General of the Gulf Cooperation Council, 1981–; *Languages:* Arabic, English; *Address:* Office — Gulf Cooperation Council, P O Box 2908, Riyadh, Saudi Arabia; telephone: 4767617, 4768432; telex: 201441 TARBIA SJ.

BISHARA, Al-Fatih Muhammad Bashir, Sudanese military commander; born 1932, Madinat al-Abyadh, Sudan; married; three sons, four daughters; *Religion:* Muslim; *Education:* Military College; various military qualifications, MA in Military Science, 1954; British Staff College; *Career:* General, 1971; Deputy Chief of Staff, Sudanese Armed Forces; *Decorations:* Independence Medal; May Revolution Medal; Worthiness Medal; Excellent Long Service Medal; Unity Medal; Star of Ethiopia, rank of Commander; German Military Officers' Cross; Egyptian Medal of Merit; Victoria Medal; Yugoslav Medal of Merit; *Interests and Recreations:* swimming, walking, gymnastics; President of the Officers' Club; member of the Care for the Handicapped Association; *Languages:* Arabic, English; *Address:* P O Box 1250, Khartoum, Sudan; telephone: Office — 72801; Residence —76134.

BISHARA, Samir, Egyptian academic/ dentist; resident in the USA; born 31 October 1935, Cairo, Egypt; married; *Religion:* Christian; *Education:* graduated in dentistry, Alexandria University, Egypt 1957; Diploma in Orthodontics, Alexandria University, 1966; Certificate in Orthodontics, University of Iowa, USA, 1970; MSc, University of Iowa 1970; *Career:* Mosassat Hospital Internship, 1957–58; Staff member 1958–68; Assistant Instructor and Graduate Student in Orthodontics, University of Iowa, 1968–70; Assistant Professor of Orthodontics, University of Iowa, 1973–76; Professor of Orthodontics, University of Iowa, 1976–; member of several scientific societies; *Publications:* several scientific papers in various national and international professional journals and books; *Interests and Recreations:* orthodontics (facial growth in normal individuals with clefts palate and lip); *Lnaguages:* Arabic, English, French; *Address:* Orthodontic Department, College of Dentistry, Iowa City, Iowa 52242, USA; telephone: (319) 353 6840; Residence — 1014 Penkridge Drive, Iowa City, Iowa 52240; telephone: (319) 353 6840.

BISHI, Ali Ahmad Nasr al-, People's Democratic Republic of Yemen army commander; born 1937, Al-Khuraiba, Second Province, People's Democratic Republic of Yemen; *Education:* Koranic School, Al-Khuraiba; *Career:* Field Commander of National Liberation Front, North West Region; Deputy Minister of Defence and Commander in Chief of the Army; member of the Central Committee; member of the People's Supreme Council; former member of Presidential Council; training course in USSR, 1974; as Commander in Chief paid official visits to China, USSR and Eastern Europe; *Address:* Ministry of Defence, Aden, People's Democratic Republic of Yemen.

BITAR, Emile, Lebanese physician; born 21 October 1931, Batroun, Lebanon; married; one son; *Religion:* Christian; *Education:* Frères College, Tripoli, Lebanon; Jesuit College, Beirut; MD, University of Montpellier, France; *Career:* specialist in rheumatic and arthritic disorders; Minister of Public Health, 1970–72; founding member and former Secretary of Lebanese Anti-Rheumatism League and of Lebanese Society of the History of Medicine; prominent member of the Democratic Party; *Publications:* various papers on rheumatic and arthritic diseases in specialist journals; *Languages:* Arabic, French, English; *Address:* Office — Immeuble Laban, rue Kantar, Beirut, Lebanon; Residence -- rue Fouad I, Beirut, Lebanon.

BITAR, Georges, Lebanese journalist; born Lebanon; *Education:* general; *Career:* journalist; United Press correspondent in Lebanon; President, Association for Foreign Press Correspondents in Lebanon; *Languages:* Arabic, French, English; *Address:* Office — Place de l'Etoile, Beirut, Lebanon.

BITAR, Muhammad Yasar, Syrian banker/ economist; born 21 June, 1922, Damascus, Syria; married; two daughters, two sons; *Religion:* Muslim; *Education:* Licence in Law; Licence in Economics; PhD, Economics; *Career:* Director, Monetary Control Bureau, 1952–54; Director General, Monetary Control Bureau, 1954–56; Director of Foreign Relations and Control Department, Central Bank of Syria, Syria, 1956–61; Deputy Governor, Central Bank of Syria, 1961–63; Economic Adviser, Algeria, 1964; Financial Adviser, Saudi Arabia, 1965–71; Adviser, Technical Assistance of the International Monetary Fund, 1971–73; Deputy Director General, then Director General, Union of Arab French Banks, 1973–; *Publications:* The Monetary Union 1955, in French, Arabic; numerous articles and lectures published in French and English; *Languages:*

Arabic, French, English; *Address:* 4 Rue Ancelle Neuly/Seine, France; telephone: 7477518.

BITAT, Rabah, Algerian politician; born 1925, Constantine District, Algeria; married; *Religion:* Muslim; *Career:* active member of Algerian People's Party, Movement for Triumph of Democratic Liberties; one of the founding members of the Revolutionary Committee for Unity and Action; Commander of Wilaya II (Constantine) and Wilaya IV (Algiers); captured 1955 and spent 1955–62 in internment with Ben Bella; member of the Political Bureau of the National Liberation Front (FLN), and Vice President in the first government of Ben Bella, 1962; Minister of State in Boumedienne Government, 1965; Minister of State for Transport, 1966; President of National People's Assembly, 1977–; member of the Political Bureau of the National Liberation Front (FLN), 1979–; assumed office as President of the Republic for 45 days upon the death of President Houari Boumedienne, 1979; *Address:* National Assembly, 18 Bd Zirout Yousef, Algiers, Algeria; telephone: 638600.

BIZRI, Amin, Lebanese politician/architect; born 1925, Beirut, Lebanon; married; one son, one daughter; *Religion:* Muslim; *Education:* Diploma in Engineering, Higher Engineering School, Beirut, 1947; Diploma in Engineering Architecture and Town Planning, Institute of Town Planning, University of Paris, France, 1952; *Career:* architect and town planner in private practice; former President of the Beirut Engineers Association, and of the Federation of Arab Engineers; Minister of Tourism and of Public Works and Transport in Selim al-Hoss Cabinet, 1976; *Languages:* Arabic, French; *Address:* Office — Immeuble Union de Paris, rue Maamari, Beirut, Lebanon; Residence — Immeuble Bizri, Sporting City, Beirut, Lebanon.

BIZRI, Fuad, Lebanese politician/engineer; born 1916, Beirut, Lebanon; *Religion:* Muslim; *Education:* Diploma in Electrical Engineering, Grenoble University, France; Diploma in Mechanical Engineering, Faculty of Aix en Provence, France; *Career:* Director General, Hydroelectric Affairs, Ministry of Public Works, 1959; Chairman of the Board, Electricity Board, Beirut, 1962; member of the Higher Council for Technical and Professional Teaching, 1964; Director, Technical Section, Office of the President of the Republic, 1964–66; Minister of Hydroelectric Affairs, 1967; Technical Adviser to the Presidency of the Republic; collaborated in the establishment of the Zouk Electrical Plant, Lebanon; Minister of Economy and Trade in Takieddin al-Solh Government, 1973–74; *Decorations:* Officer, National Order of the Cedar; Gold Medal, Order of Merit, Lebanon; *Languages:* Arabic, French; *Address:* Residence — Zreik Street, Beirut, Lebanon.

BOKHARI, Abdul Hamid Muhammad, Saudi Arabian businessman; born 1932, Jeddah, Saudi Arabia; *Religion:* Muslim; *Career:* Marine Officer, Assistant Shipping Manager, International Agencies Ltd; Amsterdam Shipping Manager, Al-Attas Agencies; Manager, Middle East Lines; Managing Director, Oriental Commercial Establishment; President, Oriental Commercial Establishment, Saudi Arabian Maritime Agencies; member of Board of Maritime Services, Jeddah, International Shipping Co; owner of tanker fleet; *Interests and Recreations:* hunting; *Address:* P O Box 160, Jeddah, Saudi Arabia; telephone: Jeddah 23900, 24489.

BOKHARI, Atif Yahya Abdullah, Saudi Arabian official/agronomist; born 1938, Jeddah, Saudi Arabia; *Education:* BSc; MSc; PhD Agricultural Production; *Career:* Agronomist, 1962–63; Director of Agricultural Experimental Station at Al-Gatif, 1963–67; Assistant Lecturer, later Lecturer, Faculty of Agriculture, 1969–71; member of Arab Economic Unity Council, Livestock Development Committee; Director General, King Faisal Bedouin Settlement Project at Harad; member of the late King Faisal Project for Bedouin Settlement, American Society of Horticulture; participated in the scientific programme for irrigating Al-Gatif Oasis; participated in the construction and development of the agricultural experimental station at Al-Gatif; member of International Conference on Irrigation, Jordan, 1966; International Conference of the Function of Universities, Riyadh, 1974; *Address:* Ministry of Agriculture and Water, Riyadh, Saudi Arabia; telephone: 4012777; telex: 201693 AGRIRS SJ

BOROLOSSY, Abdul Wahab Ali al-, Egyptian academic/physician; resident in Kuwait; born 8 February 1921, Cairo, Egypt; married; *Education:* MB, BCh, Faculty of Medicine, Cairo University, Egypt, 1936–43; PhD, Medical Science and Pharmacology, School of Pharmacy, London University, UK, 1946–49; *Career:* faculty member, Faculty of Medicine, Cairo University, 1946–60; Dean of Medicine, Assiut University, Egypt, 1960–64; Director General, Medical Insurance, Egypt, 1964–65; Vice Rector, later Rector, Assiut University, 1965–68; Minister of Higher Education, 1968–71; Minister of Scientific Research, Egypt, 1971–72; Professor, Faculty of Medicine, Cairo University, 1971–74; Rector, University of Kuwait, 1974; member of the Executive Board, UNESCO, Kuwait; *Publications:* numerous research papers on pharmacology, chemotherapy, experimental therapeutics; editor: *Essentials of Pharmacology and Therapeutics,* 1974; *Decorations:* Order of the Republic, Egypt; Flag with Stars, Yugoslavia; *Interests and Recreations:* travelling, tourism, social and youth service, member of the Rotary International Club, of the Cairo South Club, member of the Egyptian Society of Pharmacology and Experimental Thereapeutics, of the Egyptian Chemical Association; *Languages:* Arabic, English, French; *Address:* UNESCO, Kuwait; telephone: 811774.

BOUABID, Maati, Moroccan politician/lawyer; born 11 November 1927, Casablanca, Morocco; *Religion:* Muslim; *Education:* primary and secondary at Rabat and Casablanca; Licence in Law and Diploma of Higher Studies, Bordeaux University, France; *Career:* called to the Bar at Casablanca until Morocco achieved its Independence; appointed Public Prosecutor in Tangier, 1956; Attorney General at the Court of Appeal Tangier 1957; appointed Minister of Labour and Social Affairs, 1958; elected first Chairman of the Municipal Council and member of Parliament of Casablanca, 1965; Chairman of the Moroccan Lawyers' Association, 1966–77; Appointed by HM King Hassan II Minister of Justice 1977; appointed Prime Minister and Minister of Justice, 1979–; *Languages:* Arabic; French; *Address:* Council of Ministers, Rabat, Morocco.

BOUAMOUD, Muhammad, Moroccan politician; born 1928, Ouajda, Morocco; *Religion:* Muslim; *Education:* Degree in Classical Arabic and in French; *Career:* various posts at Ministry of Education in General and Technical Education; worked with Ministers of PTT and Defence, and in the Office of Prime Ministers; Minister of Primary and Secondary Education, 1974–77; Minister of Labour and Professional Training, 1977–; member of Parliament; *Languages:* Arabic, French; *Address:* c/o Ministry of Labour, Rabat, Morocco.

BOUAZZA, Tayib, Moroccan diplomat; born 1 March 1923; married; five sons, one daughter; *Religion:* Muslim; *Career:* Secretary General, Moroccan Trade Unions, 1959; President, Social Commission of the National Council; Adviser, Higher Council of Planning; Judge; Ambassador of Morocco to Yugoslavia, 1959–61; Ambassador to Scandinavian Countries, 1961–65; Head of Africa and Asia Department, Ministry of Foreign Affairs, Morocco, 1965–68; Minister Plenipotentiary, 1968–71; Ambassador to Ghana, 1971–72; Head of Africa and Asia Department, 1972–74; Ambassador to Portugal, 1974; *Decorations:* Order of the Moroccan Kingdom; Order of Merit, Nigeria, Liberia, Yugoslavia, Sweden, Norway, Cameroon, Portugal; *Interests and Recreations:* horse riding, skiing, swimming; member of the Portuguese Literature Club; *Languages:* Arabic, French, English, Portuguese; *Address:* Office — Ministry of Foreign Affairs, Rabat, Morocco; Residence— 33 Hayy Al Sa'ada, Rabat, Al Tayaran, Morocco; telephone: 52878.

BOUBKER, al Kadiri, Moroccan politician; married; *Religion:* Muslim; *Career:* active in nationalist political movement; helped prepare the Proclamation of Independence, 1944; imprisoned on political charges, 1944–46; Inspector General of the Istiqlal Party; member of the Istiqlal Party Executive Committee; founded Ecole Nahda at Sale for revival of Arabic education; founded monthly review *Al-Imane* for Islamic culture and the Association de Jeunesse pour la Renaissance Islamique; Co-founder of the Moroccan Association for the Support of the Palestine Struggle; Secretary General of the Beirut based Front for Support of the Palestinian Struggle; re-elected member of the Istiqlal Party Executive Committee at its Congress, 1974; *Languages:* Arabic, French; *Address:* Al Iman, P O Box 356 rue Arkenssous, Rabat, Morocco.

BOUCETTA, Muhammad, Moroccan politician; born 1925, Marrakesh, Morocco; married; *Religion:* Muslim; *Education:* law and philosophy, Paris, France; *Career:* called to the Bar at Casablanca, 1954; member of the Istiqlal Party and Director of the French language weekly *Al-Istiqlal,* until 1957; Director of the Cabinet to the Foreign Minister, 1957; Under Secretary of State for Foreign Affairs, 1958; Minister of Public Service and Administrative Reforms, 1960; Acting Foreign Minister, 1960; represented Morocco at the session of the United Nations General Assembly; Minister of Justice, 1961; left the government, 1963; member of the Political Committee of Istiqlal Party, 1956, and member of the Executive Committee, 1963–; one of the leaders that formed the National Block with the Union National des Forces Populaires (UNFP), Al-Koutlah Al-Wataniah, 1970; Secretary General of the Istiqlal Party, 1974; Minister of State for Foreign Affairs and Cooperation, 1977; re-elected General Secretary of the Istiqlal Party at the time of the 10th Congress in 1978; elected member of Parliament for Marakesh in 1978, Minister of State for Foreign Affairs, 1980–; *Languages:* Arabic, French; *Address:* Ministry of Foreign Affairs, Rabat, Morocco.

BOUGARY, Abdul Razzak Salih, Saudi Arabian businessman; born 1942, Mecca; *Religion:* Muslim; *Education:* Secondary School Certificate; *Career:* President, Mecca Hotel and Al-Fatah Hotel in Mecca; Proprietor and President, Bougary Trading and Contracting Establishment; President and founding member of the Cape Eleuthera Development Project, Bahamas; founder and member of the Board of Hotel Al-Hamra Nova Park, Jeddah; partner and member of the Board of Al-Bougary and Sabban Tourism Company, Jeddah; member of the Board of the Arab Solidarity Bank, Bahrain; shareholder and member of the Board of the Nova-Park Hotel Co Zurich; *Interests and Recreations:* following world economic news; *Address:* P O Box 1733, Jeddah, Saudi Arabia; telephone: 6820802, 6821049; telex: 402610 RIZK SJ.

BOUHALI, Hamid, Morocan journalist; born in Morocco; married; one son, one daughter; *Religion:* Muslim; *Education:* Teaching Certificate; *Career:* Teacher since 1965; journalist; Director of *Al-Tiqshab newspaper; Interests and Recreations:* cariacature; *Languages:* Arabic, French; *Address:* Al-Tiqshab, P O Box 6699 Sidi Othman, Casablanca 04, Morocco; telephone: 371653.

BOULOS, Jawad, Lebanese lawyer/politician; born 1900, Lebanon; married; *Education:* Licence in Law, French Faculty of Law, Beirut, Lebanon, 1922; *Career:* Barrister at Law, 1923; elected twice President of the Bar of Tripoli and North Lebanon, 1932 and 1938; Deputy, 1938–39; Minister of State for Foreign Affairs, Public Works, Health; *Publications: Les Peuples et les Civilisations du Proche-Orient,* (5 Volumes) 1962–65, comparative essays from the origins of history to the present; *Decorations:* Said Akl Prize, 1964; Commander, National Order of the Cedar, Lebanon; *Interests and Recreations:* walking; correspondent member of the Venezuelan History Academy; *Languages:* Arabic, French; *Address:* Office and Residence -- Mohamed el-Hout Street, Ghorayeb Building, Beirut, Lebanon.

BOULOS, Nassib, Lebanese businessman/lawyer; born Lebanon; *Education:* St. Joseph University, Beirut, Lebanon; Licence in Law, French Faculty of Law, Beirut; *Career:* Barrister at Law; Director of Educational Finance Company, Cosley Engineering Company, Middle East, Light Metal Products, Middle East Manufacturing Company, Minnesota (3M) Middle East, Adams Products, Baalbeck Studio; *Languages:* Arabic, French, English; *Address:* Office — Patriarch Hoyek Street, Beirut, Lebanon; Residence — Verdun Street, Beirut, Lebanon.

BOURAOUI, Sadok, Tunisian official; born 1941, Sousse, Tunisia; married; *Religion:* Muslim; *Education:* engineering studies; *Career:* engineer, Ministry of Public Works; Director General, State Public Works and Construction Co, SOMATRA, 1971–73; Director General, National Tourist Office, 1973–; Chairman of Tunis Air, 1978–79, SEREPT Company (petroleum exploration and research), 1979–80, COFIT Co (financing & development of Tunisia and real estate) 1980; *Languages:* Arabic, French; *Address:* COFIT, 31 avenue de Paris, Tunis, Tunisia; telephone: 245 200.

BOURGUIBA Jr, Habib, Tunisian politician/ banker; born 9 April 1927, Paris, France; son of President Bourguiba; married; two sons, one daughter; *Religion:* Muslim; *Education:* Licence in Law, Sadiki College, Tunis; Lycée Carnot, Dijon, France; Licence in Law, Grenoble University, France; *Career:* lawyer, 1953–56; Counsellor Tunisian Embassy to USA, 1957; Ambassador to Italy, 1957–58; Ambassador to France, 1958–61; Ambassador to USA, 1961–63; concurrently to Canada, UNO and then in 1962 to Mexico; Secretary General of the Government, 1964; Minister of Foreign Affairs, 1964–70; Minister of Justice, 1970; Chairman and General Manager of the Tunisian Bank of Economic Development, and Novotel Tunisie (hotels); Chairman and Managing Director of numerous companies; President, the Export Promotion Centre; *Decorations:* Tunisian and foreign decorations; *Languages:* Arabic, French, English; *Address:* Office — Tunisian Bank for Economic Development, 48 Avenue Habib Bourguiba; telephone: 245600; Residence — Villa Dar Es Salaam, La Marsa, Tunisia.

BOURGUIBA, Maître Habib, President of the Tunisian Republic; born 1903, Monastir, Tunisia; married; one son, one daughter; *Religion:* Muslim; *Education:* Sadiki College, Lycée Carnot, Tunis; graduated wih Law Degree and Diploma in Political Science, Sorbonne, University of Paris, France; *Career:* called to Tunisian Bar, 1930; member of Destour Nationalist Party, 1921; formed Neo-Destour Party, 1934; Secretary General of the Neo-Destour; imprisoned by the French, 1934–36 and 1938–43; escaped to Middle East, 1945; travelled to promote Tunisian independence, 1945–49; prolonged political world tour in 1951; returned to Tunis,1952; was arrested on the advice of the French Resident General; released under surveillance in France, 1954; played key role in Franco-Tunisian negotiations, 1955; returned to Tunisia, 1 June 1955; Prime Minister, Minister of Foreign Affairs, Minister for National Defence in the first independent Tunisian Government of April 1956; elected President 25 July, 1957; re-elected November 1959, November 1964, November 1969; paid official visit to Britain, 1961, USA and Canada, 1968; elected unanimously President for Life by National Assembly, 18 March, 1975; *Languages:* Arabic, French; *Address:* Office of the President, Carthage, Tunisia.

BOURGUIBA, Wassila, Tunisian First Lady; born 1912, Tunis, Tunisia; married President Habib Bourguiba, 1962; one daughter; *Religion:* Muslim; *Career:* leading member of Tunisian Independence Movement; arrested and tried by French authorities for her part in a demonstration in the town of Beja, 1952; travelled widely, accompanying her husband on numerous state visits abroad; *Languages:* Arabic, French; *Address:* Office of the President, Carthage, Tunisia.

BOURJINI, Salah, Tunisian economist; born 18 January 1938, Le Kef, Tunisia; married; two daughters, one son; *Religion:* Muslim; *Education:* Diploma in Economic Studies; BA, MA and PhD in Economics; *Career:* Teacher, Cooperation School, 1964–67; Assistant Professor, University of Kansas, USA, 1969–72; Assistant Professor, Faculty of Law and Economic Studies, Tunis, 1972–79; Adviser to the Ministry of Economy, 1972–74; Adviser to the Ministry of Planning, 1974–75; Assistant Director General, International Cooperation, Ministry of Foreign Affairs, 1976–80; Assistant Resident Representative, UNDP, Algeria, 1980–; member of the Association of American Economists, of the Association of Tunisian Economists; *Publications:* articles and papers published in professional journals; *Decorations:* Knight of the Order of the Tunisian Republic,1978; Decoration Honoraire de l'Union des Aveugles de Tunisie, 1980; *Languages:* Arabic, French, English; *Address:* Deputy Resident Representative of UNDP, P O Box 823 Algiers, Gare, Algeria.

BOUSTANI, Elie J., Lebanese lawyer/ diplomat; born 20 August 1918; *Religion:* Christian; *Education:* Licence in Law, St.Joseph University, Beirut; *Career:* Head of Department, President's Office, 1942; Head of Youth Department, 1943; Secretary, Embassy to France, 1944–45; Head of Legislation, Ministry of Justice, 1947; Counsellor, Embassy to Italy, 1956–58; Counsellor, Embassy to Spain, 1958–60; Counsellor, Embassy to UK, 1960–62; Counsellor, Embassy to Italy, 1962–64; Head of Legal Department, Ministry of Foreign Affairs, 1964–66; Ambassador to Senegal, 1966–71; concurrently accredited to Mali, Guinea, The Gambia; Director of International Relations, Ministry of Foreign Affairs, 1971; Ambassador to People's Republic of China, 1972; *Publications: Les Codes Libanais Annotés et*

Traduits; Recueil des Traités; Législation Libanaise 1954–56 and contributions to various Lebanese magazines and periodicals; *Decorations:* Officer, Order of Merit of the Italian Republic 1958; Commander, Spanish Order of Civil Merit, 1960; Grand Officer of Senegalese National Order, 1971; *Languages:* Arabic, French, English; *Address:* c/o Ministry of Foreign Affairs, Beirut, Lebanon.

BOUSTANI, Emile, Lebanese former army commander; born 1909, Jounieh, Lebanon; married; three children; *Religion:* Christian; *Education:* graduate, Damascus Military Academy, 1933; *Career:* Professor, Military Academy, 1933–34; taught improvement courses, Tripoli garrison, 1st Eastern Battalion, 1934–35; Lieutenant, 1937; Commander, Heavy Artillery Company, 1940–41; in charge of training of two auxiliary battalions in the Alaouite territory, 1941; Assistant Commander of Tripoli and of the 1st Eastern Battalion, 1941–42; Commander, Infantry Company, 1st Eastern Battalion, 1942–43; Assistant Commander, 3rd Lebanese Light-Infantry Battalion, 1943; Second in Command, Homs Military Academy, 1943–45; Head of the Premier Bureau to the Lebanese Army Headquarters, 1945; in charge of the creation of the Deuxième Bureau (Military Intelligence), 1945; Director, Telephone Services, 1946; Deputy Chief of Staff of the Army, 1946; promoted Commandant, 1946; Supply Officer, 1948; in charge of the creation of the Lebanese Air Force; Commander, Lebanese Air Force, 1949; Director, Military Engineering, 1954; promoted Lieutenant Colonel, 1953; Colonel, 1959; Commanding Officer of the Northern Region, 1959–64; Inspector of Military Training, 1964; Commander in Chief of the Lebanese Armed Forces, 1965–70, participated in negotiations with Palestine Resistance leading to Cairo Agreements, 1969; promoted General, 1965; has collaborated on the re-drafting of Army statutes; led various missions to Egypt, Iraq, USA, France, UK and Italy; *Decorations:* National Order of the Cedar; Gold Medal, Lebanese Order of Merit, 1959; Croix de Guerre, 1958; Palestinian Commemorative Medal, 1949; Medal, Moroccan Order of the Throne, 1960; Medal, Syrian Order of Merit, 1948; Legion of Merit, USA, 1956; Medal, Greek Order of the Phoenix, 1958; Commander, Brazilian Order of Merit, 1966; Medal, Jordanian Order of Merit of Independence, 1967; Grand

Cordon, Greek National Order, 1969; *Languages:* Arabic, French, English; *Address:* Villa Emile Boustani, Ballouni Kisirwan, Beirut, Lebanon; telephone: 431170.

BOUSTANI, Fuad Ephrem, Lebanese academic; born 15 August 1906, Deir el-Kamar, Lebanon; married; five sons, two daughters; *Education:* St. Joseph University, Beirut, Lebanon; Docteur ès-Lettres, University of Lyon, France, 1957; St. Edward University, Austin, Texas, USA, 1958; Georgetown University, Washington D.C., USA, 1958; *Career:* Professor of Arabic Literature, Islamic Institutions and Islamic History and Civilization, Faculty of Oriental Literature, 1933–; Professor of Near Eastern History and Civilization, Political Science Institute, 1945–55; Professor of Arabic Literature and History and Muslim Philosophy, Fine Arts Academy, 1947–53; Director, Teachers' Training College, 1942–53; Secretary General, Lebanese National Commission of UNESCO, 1948–55; Secretary General, International Commission for the Translation of Literary Classics, 1949–; Dean, Lebanese University, 1953; member of the National Commission of UNESCO; *Publications: Mungid at-Tullab,* (4th edition) 1960; *Pourquoi,* (2nd edition) 1961; *Encyclopedia Arabica,* (7 volumes) 1956–67; *St. Maron,* (3rd edition) 1967; as well as other publications on Arabic literature, Muslim civilization and Lebanese history; *Decorations:* Commander, National Order of the Cedar, 1956; Medal, Lebanese Order of Merit, with Palms, 1934; Officer of the Academy, France, 1946; Commander, Order of St. Gregoire Le Grand, 1950; Commander, Order of Alfonso X the Wise, Spain, 1952; Gold Medal, Public Education, Lebanon, 1957; Commander, Hamayoun Order, Iran, 1958; Légion d'Honneur, France, 1967, as well as other foreign decorations; *Interests and Recreations:* member of the Rotary Club; *Languages:* Arabic, French; *Address:* Office — Lebanese University, Beirut, Lebanon; Residence -- Furn el-Hayek Street, Ashrafiyeh, Beirut, Lebanon.

BOUSTANI, Myrna E., Lebanese businesswoman/politician; born 20 December 1939; daughter of Emile Boustani; married; one son, one daughter; *Religion:* Christian; *Education:* French and Lebanese Baccalauréat, College Protestant Français, Beirut, 1954; Three Wise Monkeys Finishing School,

London 1955; Licence ès-Lettres, Psychology, Ecole Superiéure des Lettres, Beirut, 1958; *Career:* member of Lebanese Parliament, Chouf Constituency, (first and only woman member), 1963–64; Partner, CAT Company; Director of Banque de l'Industrie et du Travail, of Société Hôtelière du Tourisme, Societe des Grands Hotels du Levant, Al-Boustani Co, SAL; member of the Board of the Arab British Chamber of Commerce, London, the Board of Trustees of the American University of Beirut (AUB); *Interests and Recreations:* art, architecture, music, psychology, travelling, swimming, flower arranging; *Languages:* Arabic, French, English; *Address:* c/o INCOTES, 1 Great Cumberland Place, London W1H 7AL; Lebanon: P O Box 11 1036, Beirut, Lebanon.

BOUSTANI, Nabih al-, Lebanese judge; born 1907, Deir el-Kamar, Lebanon; married; two sons, one daughter; *Education:* Licence in Law, French Faculty of Law, Beirut, Lebanon; *Career:* magistrate; successively, member of the Court of First Instance, Sidon, Lebanon; Justice of the Peace, Jezzine, Lebanon; member of the Court of First Instance, Beirut, Lebanon; Deputy Public Prosecutor, Beirut; Examining Magistrate, Tripoli, Lebanon; President, Court of First Instance, Zahle, Lebanon; President, Court of First Instance, Sidon, Lebanon; President, Court of Appeal, South Lebanon; Assistant Inspector General of Justice; Counsel, Court of Cassation; Public Prosecutor, Court of Cassation; President, Council of State, 1967–; *Decorations:* Gold Medal, Lebanese Order of Merit; *Languages:* Arabic, French; *Address:* Office — Palais de Justice, Beirut, Lebanon; Residence — River Corniche, Nassar Moufaraj Building, Beirut, Lebanon.

BOUTALEB, Abdul Hadi, Moroccan politician/businessman/diplomat; businessman and diplomat; born 1923 Fes, Morocco; married; *Religion:* Muslim; *Education:* graduated in law, Qarawiyin University, Fes, Morocco; *Career:* Arabic Tutor to HM King Hassan as Crown Prince; joined Political Bureau of the Party Democrate de l'Indépendence 1951; managed the newspaper *Al-Rai Al-Am* during 1951; participated in Aix-les-Bains consultations preceding Moroccan Independence; Minister of Labour and Social Affairs in first Moroccan Government December 1955–1956; took leading part in the formation of the Union Nationale des Forces Populaires 1959; Under Secretary of State for Information, Youth Affairs and Sports 1962–1963; Minister Delegate to Prime Minister and Minister for Mauritanian and Saharan Affairs; President, Casablanca Municipal Council since June 1963; Minister of Justice 1964; Minister of Education, Youth Affairs and Sports 1967; Minister of State 1968; Minister of Foreign Affairs 1969; elected Deputy for Al-Jadida in parliamentary elections 1970; elected President of the National Assembly 1970; returned to full time business activities 1971; Ambassador to the USA 1974–77; Counsellor and Adviser, King Hassan II, 1977; Minister of State for Information 1978; Professor in Constitutional Law and Political Institutions, College of Law, Casablanca; *Publications:* author of several books including a study of Ibn Khatib, various books on constitutional law; *Decorations:* from Morocco, France, Spain, Italy, Tunisia, Egypt including Commander of the Throne from Morocco, Grand Cordon of the Egyptian Republic, Commander du Mérite Sportif, France; *Languages:* Arabic, English, French; *Address:* 9 rue des Grenadiers, Anfa, Casablanca, Morocco.

BOUTALIB, Abdul Hafid, Moroccan official/politician; born 30 June 1928, Fes, Morocco; married; *Religion:* Muslim; *Education:* Licencié en Droit; Degrees in Arts, History and Geography; *Career:* called to the Bar in Casablanca; member of the Moroccan delegations which negotiated independence agreements with France and Spain; Directeur de Cabinet, Ministry of Administrative Affairs, 1958; Director of Administrative Affairs, 1959–60; Director of Administrative Affairs, Ministry of Interior; Director of the Royal Cabinet, 1964; Under Secretary at the Ministry of the Interior, 1964; Minister of Labour and Social Affairs, 1965; Minister of Public Works and Communications, 1968; Minister of Justice, 1969; Minister of Labour, Employment and Vocational Training, 1969; *Decorations:* from West Germany, Tunisia, Egypt, Liberia; *Languages:* Arabic, French; *Address:* 8 Rue Tedders, Rabat, Morocco.

BOUTEFLIKA, Abdul Aziz, Algerian politician; born 2 March 1937, Oran, Algeria; *Religion:* Muslim; *Education:* Faculty of Letters, Algiers University; *Career:* Secretary General, General Union of Algerian Muslim

Students (UGEMA); Commandant, Algerian Resistance 1956 in Wilaya V (Oran) and at Oujda on Moroccan border; member, Central Committee and Political Bureau, National Liberation Front (FLN), 1959–60; Secretary General of National Liberation Army (ALN) General Staff, Ghardimaou, Tunisia; member of FLN delegations to Guinea and Mali; served in Sahara at time of independence; spokesman for Colonel Boumedienne with name of Commandant Abdelkader; Minister of Youth and Sports in first Ben Bella Government; Minister of Foreign Affairs, 1963; Rapporteur, Council of Ministers, Organization of African Unity (OAU), Dakar, Senegal, 1963; Chief Delegate to Second UNCTAD Conference, New Delhi, 1968; President, Council of Ministers, OAU, Algiers, 1968; Chief of Delegation, UN General Assembly, New York, USA, 1963–; Chief Delegate, Economic and Social Council (ECOSOC), UN, Geneva, 1973; Chief Delegate of Algeria to Third UNCTAD Conference, Santiago, Chile, 1972; President, Conference of Ministers on Non-Aligned countries, Algiers, 1972–73; Chief, Delegation of Algeria to Summit Conference of Heads of Arab States, 1962–73; Chief Delegate, Conference of Ministers of Islamic countries, 1972–74; President, UN General Assembly, 1974; *Decorations:* many decorations from African governments; *Languages:* Arabic, French; *Address:* Office — Ministry of Foreign Affairs, 6 rue Claude Bernard, Le Golf, Algiers, Algeria; telephone: 604734; Residence — 12 rue Ali Boumendjel, Algiers, Algeria.

BOUTROS, Fuad, Lebanese judge/politician; born 1918, Beirut, Lebanon; married; one son, two daughters; *Religion:* Christian; *Education:* Licence in Law, French Faculty of Law, Beirut, Lebanon; University of Lyon, France; *Career:* Clerk, Mixed Appeal Court, 1940; Judge, Civil Court, Mount Lebanon, 1942; Judge, Mixed Commercial and Civil Court, Beirut, 1944; Examining Magistrate, Military Court, 1944–47; Barrister at Law, 1947–; Minister of National Education and Planning, 1959–60; Deputy for Beirut, 1960; Vice President, Chamber of Deputies, 1960–61; Minister of Justice, 1961–64; re-elected Deputy for Beirut, 1964; Deputy Premier; Minister of National Education and Defence, 1966; Deputy Premier; Minister of Foreign Affairs and Tourism, 1968; Deputy Premier; Minister of Defence, 1976; and Minister of

Foreign Affairs in Selim al-Hoss Cabinet, 1976; *Decorations:* various foreign and Lebanese decorations; *Languages:* Arabic, French, English; *Address:* Office — Damascus Street, Beirut, Lebanon; Residence — Sursock Street, Beirut, Lebanon.

BOUTROSGHALI, Wassif Y., Egyptian UN official/architect; born 13 October 1924, Cairo, Egypt; married; *Religion:* Christian; *Education:* BSc in Architecture, Faculty of Engineering, Fuad University, Cairo, Egypt, 1941–46; *Career:* member of the Central Town Planning Board, Ministry of Social Affairs; Chairman and Administrator, Egyptian Mining and Prospecting Company; Administrator, Africa Insurance Company, Egypt; Senior Partner, Consulting Architecture and Engineering Firm, Egypt; Managing Director, Subconsultant Limited and PS Industrial Company Limited, Sudan, 1964–70; Senior Technical Adviser, Technical Advisory Division, UN Development Programme (UNDP), New York, 1971; *Publications: Protection et Mise en Valeur du Patrimoine Monumental Algérien,* 1970; *The Development of Cairo; Traffic Problems; Tendency of Contemporary Arab Architecture; Decorations:* 1st Prize, Architectural Competition, Maadi, Egypt, 1960; *Interests and Recreations:* hunting; member of the Automobile Club of Egypt; member of the English Union, Cairo; member of the Société d'Archéologie Copte, Cairo; *Languages:* Arabic, English, French, German, Italian; *Address:* United Nations Development Programme (UNDP), 866 UN Plaza, New York, NY 10017, USA; telephone: (212) 754 1234.

BRAHIMI, Lakhdar, Algerian diplomat; born 1 January 1934, Algeria; married; three sons; *Religion:* Muslim; *Education:* Law and Political Science; *Career:* founding member of General Union of Algerian Muslim Students (UGEMA), 1954; Vice President of UGEMA, 1956; Permanent Representative of National Liberation Front (FLN), Jakarta, Indonesia, 1956–61; Ambassador to Egypt, also accredited to Sudan and Permanent Representative to Arab League, 1963–70; Ambassador to UK, 1971–79; *Languages:* Arabic, English, French; *Address:* Ministry of Foreign Affairs, Algiers, Algeria; telephone: 608799; telex: 52838.

BREISH, Abdul Majid, Libyan banker; born 11 October 1951, Tripoli, Libya; married; one son; *Religion:* Muslim; *Education:* BA, American University of Beirut, Beirut, 1975; Financial Analysis and Policy, International Monetary Fund, Washington D.C., 1977; *Career:* Manager, Equity Participations, Libyan Arab Foreign Bank, 1975–80; Assistant to the Chairman, Libyan Arab Foreign Bank, 1977–80; Assistant Vice President, Business Development, Arab Banking Corporation, Bahrain, 1980–; member of the Board of Directors, Farah Maghreb, Morocco, 1977–80; *Interests and Recreations:* tennis, water sports, horseback riding; *Languages:* Arabic, English, Italian, French; *Address:* P O Box 5698, Alia Building, Diplomatic Area, Manama, Bahrain; telephone: 262964.

BSEISU, Adnan Nuruddin, Bahraini banker; born 1931 Nablus; married; two sons, one daughter; *Religion:* Muslim; *Education:* BA in Economics, American University of Beirut, AUB Beirut, Lebanon, 1953; MA in Money and Banking, AUB, 1958; *Career:* Assistant Economic Researcher, Economic Research Institute, AUB, 1953; Director of Economic Research Department, Saudi Arabian Monetary Agency, 1954–57; Teacher, Economic Geography, Economic and Business Management, Al Maqased College, Beirut, 1958; Assistant Manager, and later Manager, Arab Bank Ltd, Benghazi, Hebron and Manama, Bahrain, 1959–73; part time Professor, Faculty of Commerce, University of Benghazi, Libya, 1959–62; General Manager of Financial Affairs, Gulf Air, Bahrain, 1973–80, Adviser for Financial Affairs to the Chief Executive and Board of Directors, Gulf Air, 1981; Assistant General Manager, Al Bank International E.C., Bahrain, 1981–; Chairman of the Board of Directors of Gulf Helicopters Co Ltd, 1977–81; member of the Board of Directors of Bahrain Hotels Co, 1979, and of Gulf Hotels Co, Oman and Bahrain Airport Services, 1978; member of the Board of Directors of Gulf Aircraft Maintenance Co, Abu Dhabi, 1980–81; member of the Arbitration and Reconciliation Committee, Ministry of Labour and Social Affairs, Bahrain, of the Financial and Economic Research Committee, Bahrain Chamber of Commerce and Industry; *Publications: Economic Reforms of Muhammad Ali,* 1953; *Monetary Organizations in Saudi Arabia,* 1958; numerous articles published in *Bahrain Commerce Review, Arab Newsweek* and *Al Iktissaad wal Amaal; Interests and Recreations:* reading, swimming, running; Vice President and Founder Member of Rotary Club of Manama; Visiting Consultant, School of Business, AUB; member of the Financial and Economic Research Committee, Bahrain Chamber of Commerce and Industry, of the Visiting Council of Talal Abu Ghazala School of Business and Management, AUB, of the Euromarket Institute, Vienna, Austria; *Languages:* Arabic, English; *Address:* P O Box 1013, Manama, Bahrain; telephone: 245247.

BU DHALAI, Major Ahmad Salih, People's Democratic Republic of Yemen army commander; *Career:* army officer; training course, Staff Training College, Camberley, UK, 1967; Permanent Secretary, Ministry of Communications; Permanent Secretary, Ministry of Defence; Army Chief of Staff, 1967; *Address:* Ministry of Defence, Aden, People's Democratic Republic of Yemen.

BU SAIDI, Hamad Bin Humud al-, Omani politician/official; born 1926; married; *Religion:* Muslim; *Career:* served in the Household of the late Sultan Said; Secretary to HM Sultan Qabus, 1970; Acting Head of the Diwan, 1972; Head of Diwan Affairs, 1973–; Minister, in new Ministry of Diwan Affairs, 1973; *Address:* Ministry of Diwan Affairs, P O Box 117, Ruwi, Muscat, Oman; telephone: 722022; telex: 3275 DIWAN MB.

BU SAIDI, Muhammad Bin Ahmad al-, Omani politician; born 1920; *Religion:* Muslim; *Education:* Koranic School in Nizwa; *Career:* Wali of Matrah; Minister of Justice, 1970; Minister of Land Affairs, 1972–76; Minister of the Interior, 1976; *Address:* Ministry of the Interior, P O Box 3127, Ruwi, Oman.

BU SAIDI, Salim Bin Nasr al-, Omani politician; born 1933; *Religion:* Muslim; *Career:* Petroleum Development (Oman) 1970; attended a series of courses in the UK, 1971–72; Director General of Civil Aviation; Under Secretary, Ministry of Communications, 1975; Minister of Communications, 1978–; *Address:* Ministry of Communications, P O Box 684, Ministerial Complex, Ruwi, Oman; telephone: 701799; telex: 3390 MWASALAT MB.

BUABID, Maître Abdul Rahim, Moroccan lawyer/politician; born 1920, Sale, Morocco; married; *Religion:* Muslim; *Education:* Law Degree in Paris, and two years study at Ecole des Sciences Politiques; *Career:* Ecole Franco-Musulmane, Sale; arrested and imprisoned for political activities 1944–46; called to Bar in Paris; founded French language weekly newspaper *Al-Istiqlal,* 1948; member of the Executive Committee of the Istiqlal Party with special responsibilities for trade union affairs; took part in negotiations, 1956 which led to the joint declaration of Moroccan Independence 1956, and in negotiations for Franco-Moroccan diplomatic agreement of 1956; Minister of National Economy, 1956; Vice President of the Council, 1958; Administrative Secretary General of the Union Nationale des Forces Populaires (UNFP) with special responsibility for organization of the party, 1960; shared leadership of UNFP until return of Mehdi Ben Barka in 1962; took leading part in the Second National Congress of UNFP and was confirmed in leadership; later representative for Kenitra in House of Representatives; helped form National Bloc with the Istiqlal, 1970; leader of the Union Socialiste des Forces Populaires of UNFP, 1975; returned to law practice; *Languages:* Arabic, French; *Address:* Plateau de Bettana, Sale, Morocco.

BUALLAY, Qassim Muhammad, Bahraini diplomat/official; born 15 March, 1939, Muharraq, Bahrain; *Religion:* Muslim; married; one son,two daughters; *Education:* BBA, American University of Beirut, Beirut, Lebanon, 1963; *Career:* Superintendent of Bursaries and UNESCO sections, Ministry of Education, 1961–70; member of Bahrain Delegation to UNESCO General Conference, 1966 and 1968; Programme Specialist, Division of Higher Education, UNESCO, Paris, 1970–74; 1st Secretary, Ministry of Foreign Affairs, Bahrain, 1974–75; Chargé d'Affaires, Bahrain Embassy to France, 1975–76; Ambassador to France, 1976–79; Director, Economic Affairs Directorate, Ministry of Foreign Affairs, Manama, Bahrain, 1979–; *Interests and Recreations:* music, theatre, swimming, tennis; member of the Alumni Club, Bahrain; member of La Chaîne des Rotisseurs, Bahrain; *Languages:* Arabic, English, French; *Address:* Ministry of Foreign Affairs, P O Box 547, Manama, Bahrain; telephone: 255199, 258200; telex: 8228 BN.

BUALY, Abdul Aziz Abdul Rahman, Bahraini diplomat/official; born 1939, Bahrain; married; two daughters, one son; *Religion:* Muslim; *Education:* BA, University of Baghdad, Iraq; Graduate Studies, Reading University, UK; *Career:* High School Principal, Bahrain, 1969–71; Ministry of Education; Ministry of Information; Assistant Chief of Protocol, Ministry of Foreign Affairs; Ambassador to Iran; Ambassador to USA 1976–; *Interests and Recreations:* swimming, table tennis, soccer; *Languages:* Arabic, English, Persian; *Address:* Suite 715, 2600 Virginia Avenue NW, Washington D.C. 20037, USA.

BUALY, Nassir Ben Saif al-, Omani diplomat; born 9 January 1925; married; three children; *Religion:* Muslim; *Education:* Zanzibar and Mukalla; Diploma in Economics, University of Baghdad, Iraq; *Career:* entered government service in Zanzibar and appointed to the Department of Information; followed a course sponsored by the Central Office of Information, UK 1960–61; Principal Secretary, Ministry of Commerce, Zanzibar 1965; Abu Dhabi Department of Finance 1968; Director of Social Affairs in Abdulla al-Tai Ministry of Information, Social Affairs and Labour, 1971; Director of Information, 1971; Director General of Infromation 1972; Chargé d'Affaires, Embassy to UK, 1972–73; Ambassador to UK, 1973–80; Chief of Consular Affairs, Ministry of Foreign Affairs, 1980–82; Head of Asian and Australian Affairs, 1982–; *Languages:* Arabic, English, Swahili; *Address:* Ministry of Foreign Affairs, P O Box 252, Muscat, Oman; telephone: 5846782.

BUANANI, Muhammad Abdul Salam al-, journalist/television producer; born 1929, Asila, Morocco; married; two sons, one daughter; *Religion:* Muslim; *Career:* Producer and Director on Paris Radio and Television, 1955–64; Director of Programmes, Moroccan Radio, 1964–65; represented Moroccan Television in Spain, 1965–67; Producer on Moroccan Television until 1970; Director of Programmes, Moroccan Television, 1971; Head of Department and Producer on Moroccan Television; Director of Competitions; *Publications:* numerous articles, stories and poetry published in French, Spanish, Arabic magazines; *Interests and Recreations:* fishing, poetry, history of civilization; member of Moroccan Writers

Union; *Languages:* Arabic, Spanish, French, Italian; *Address:* 14 Rue Yougoslavie, Rabat, Morocco.

BUDERBA, Ahmad, Algerian diplomat/official; born 1931, St. Eugène, Algeria; *Religion:* Muslim; *Education:* medical studies; *Career:* joined National Liberation Army (ALN) as medical lieutenant; head of National Liberation Front (FLN) Social Department based in Tunisia; Chef de Cabinet to Minister of Agriculture, 1964; Secretary General, Ministry of Agriculture, 1965; transferred to Corps of Préfets and became Wali of Medea; Wali of Annaba, 1970; Ambassador to Senegal, 1971; *Languages:* Arabic, French; *Address:* Ministry of Foreign Affairs, Algiers, Algeria.

BUDJAKDJI, Rauf Mustafa, Algerian diplomat; born 4 April 1930, Blida, Algeria; married; *Religion:* Muslim; *Education:* Diploma, Ecole Supérieure de Commerce, Algiers, 1951–54; *Career:* member, Advisory Committee for Administrative and Budgetary Questions (ACABQ) UN, 1963–64; Counsellor, Permanent Mission of Algeria, UN, New York, USA, 1962–64; Head, International Organization Division, Ministry of Foreign Affairs, 1964–71; Ambassador to the Holy See; Ambassador, Permanent Mission of Algeria, UN, Geneva, Switzerland, 1971; *Languages:* Arabic, French, English; *Address:* 8 rue Voltaire, CH-1202, Geneva, Switzerland; telephone: (022) 446969.

BUDJELLAB, Omar, Algerian physician; born 1930, Belcourt, Algiers, Algeria; married; three daughters; *Religion:* Muslim; *Education:* Faculty of Medicine, Sorbonne, University of Paris, France; *Career:* active in nationalist cause as student; worked at Franco-Moslem Hospital specialising in cardiology and qualified as cardiologist, 1967; leading cardiologist in Algeria; Mustapha Hospital, Ministry of Public Health, 1970–77; *Languages:* Arabic, French; *Address:* Ministry of Public Health, Algiers, Algeria.

BUERA, Abu Bakr Mustafa, Libyan academic/businessman; born 1941, Jardina, Libya; married; five children; *Religion:* Muslim; *Education:* MA and PhD in Management, USA; *Career:* Internal Auditor, Social Security Department, Libya, 1961–66; Chairman, Department of Business Adminis-

tration, University of Garyonis, Benghazi, Libya, 1975–81; Senior Management Adviser, Arab Organization of Administrative Sciences, Amman, Jordan, 1982–83; Associate Professor of Management, Libya, 1983–; *Publications: Managers: A Complete Approach,* 1980, in Arabic; *Principles of Management,* 1983, in Arabic; several articles in professional journals; *Languages:* Arabic, English; *Address:* P O Box 6374 Benghazi, Libya.

BUFLASA, Saif Ahmad Muhammad Saif Musbah al-, United Arab Emirates businessman; born 1945, Dubai, United Arab Emirates; married; one son, three daughters; *Religion:* Muslim; *Education:* Cable and Wireless Institute, Cairo, Egypt; Language Studies, UK; *Career:* Teacher, Ministry of Education, Bahrain; Personnel Department, Shell Company; Customs Official, Abu Dhabi; Teacher, Cultural Section, Abu Dhabi Defence Department; Secretary, the United Arab Emirates (UAE) Federal Assembly, Abu Dhabi; Deputy Managing Director and Secretary of the Board of UAE Trading Company (mixed government/public company); *Interests and Recreations:* reading, swimming; *Languages:* Arabic, English; *Address:* United Arab Emirates Trading Company, Abu Dhabi, United Arab Emirates; telephone: Office -- 23289, 43830, 23322.

BUHUSSAIN, Ahmad Abdullah, United Arab Emirates administrator; born 1948, Dubai, United Arab Emirates; married; one son, one daughter; *Religion:* Muslim; *Education:* BA in History, Baghdad University, Iraq; *Career:* Head of Cultural Department, Ministry of Education; member of the Executive Committee of the Arab Educational, Scientific and Cultural Organization, 1972; Administrative Secretary, United Arab Emirates University, 1971–; *Interests and Recreations:* reading, table-tennis; Chairman of the Board of the Ahli Club; *Languages:* Arabic, English; *Address:* United Arab Emirates University, Al-Ain, P O Box 15551, Abu Dhabi, United Arab Emirates.

BUKAIR, Abdullah Ahmad, People's Democratic Republic of Yemen physician/UN official; born 13 March 1941, People's Democratic Republic of Yemen; married; *Education:* Degree in Medicine, University of Hungary, 1963–71; *Career:* Medical Officer, Ministry of Health, 1971–73; Director of

Health Service, Ministry of Health, 1971; member, Executive Board, WHO, Aden, People's Democratic Republic of Yemen; member, Yemeni Doctors Association; *Publications:* numerous articles on health service in People's Democratic Republic of Yemen; *Interests and Recreations:* reading, sports; *Languages:* Arabic, English, Hungarian; *Address:* WHO, Queen Arwa Road, Crater, Aden, First Governorate, People's Democratic Republic of Yemen; telephone: 23159.

BULOS, Nabih Yusuf, Jordanian engineer; born 4 February 1909, New York; married; three sons, one daughter; *Religion:* Christian; *Education:* Civil Engineering, University College, Loughborough, UK; Fellow, Institution of Civil Engineers UK; Fellow Institute of Arbitrators, UK; *Career:* Assistant Under Secretary, Public Works Department, Palestine, 1929–33; Engineer, H4 Station, Iraq Petroleum Co, 1933–35; Engineer, Gaza, Palestine, 1935–37; Executive Engineer, Nazareth, 1937–1940; District Engineer, Nablus, Jerusalem, Homs (Syria), 1940–51; Area Civil Engineer, Iraq Petroleum Co, 1951–53; Under Secretary, Ministry of Public Work, Jordan, 1953–59; Chief Engineer, Shakin Engineering Construction, 1959–68; Technical Adviser, Ministry of Culture & Youth, Jordan, 1968; member, Advisory Committee, Amman Municipality, 1980–; *Publications:* numerous articles on engineering problems in Jordan, in Arabic; *Decorations:* Grand Official Star of Jordan, 1955; Grand Official, Order of Merit, Italy, 1957; *Interests and Recreations:* music, drama; *Languages:* Arabic, English; *Address:* P O Box 5247, Amman, Jordan; telephone: Office — 67187, Residence — 41844.

BULTIA, Abdul Latif Miligi, Egyptian politician/trade unionist; born 1927; married; *Career:* trade unionist since 1949; elected President of the Misr Insurance Company Union, 1952; elected President of the Insurance Workers' Union, 1953; elected Secretary General of the Egyptian Federation of Labour, 1961; elected President of the Federation of Labour, 1970; Deputy Chairman of the All-Africa Trade Unions Federation; member of the International Confederation of Arab Trade Unions (ICATU) Council, and member of the Executive Council of the International Labour Organization; member of the 1964 and 1969 National Assembly for Helwan; elected Second Deputy Speaker of the National Assembly, 1970; elected Assistant Secretary for Cairo in the Arab Socialist Union (ASU), 1968 and to ASU Central Committee, 1968; member of the National Peace Council; Minister of Labour, 1970; Minister of Manpower, 1975; Minister of Manpower and Training, 1976; Secretary General of ICATU, 1972; visited UK, 1968; *Languages:* Arabic, English; *Address:* c/o Ministry of Manpower, Cairo, Egypt.

BURGAN, Salih K., Jordanian UN official/physician; born 19 July 1918, Karak, Jordan; married; *Education:* Doctorate in Medicine and Surgery, American University of Beirut, Lebanon, 1945; *Career:* physician, Transjordan Frontier Forces, 1943–46; Director of Arab Physicians, Transjordan Frontier Forces, 1946–48; private practice, Zerka, 1948–63; member of Parliament, 1961–62; member of the Senate, 1963–69; Minister of Health, 1963–64; Minister of Agriculture and of Reconstruction and Development, 1964–66; Minister of Social Affairs and Labour, 1966; Minister of Health, 1966–67; Minister of Interior for Municipal and Rural Affairs, 1967–69; Director, Beirut UN Office, 1969–75; Assistant Director General of International Labour Organisation, ILO, 1975–; member of the British Medical Association, of the Jordanian Medical Association, of the American University of Beirut Medical Alumni Association; *Decorations:* Order of the Star of Jordan, 1st Class; Commander of the Holy Sepulchre; *Interests and Recreations:* swimming, social and labour problems, world politics, member of the Delhamieh Club; member of Lions International; *Languages:* Arabic, English; *Address:* ILO, 4 Route des Morillons, CH-1211, Geneva 22, Switzerland; telephone: 326200.

BURHAN, Hamid Othman, Sudanese agriculturalist/UN official; born 23 July 1931, Sudan; married; two daughters, two sons; *Religion:* Muslim; *Education:* Diploma, Agriculture, Khartoum, 1955; MSc, Agronomy, Colorado State University, USA, 1958; PhD, Agronomy, Arizona, USA, 1963; *Career:* Assistant Inspector of Agriculture, 1955–57; Agronomist, Agricultural Research Corporation, 1958–65, Senior Agronomist, 1965–66, Acting Head, Statistics Section, 1965–67; Head, Agronomy and Crop Physiology Section, 1966–74; Research Professor of Agronomy, 1977–; Project Manager for

UNDP/FAO Wadi Jizan Agricultural Development Project, Saudi Arabia, 1975–78; Director General and Chairman of the Board of Directors, Agricultural Research Corporation, Sudan, 1978–; chairman of several scientific and technical committees, in Sudan and other countries; Director, FAO Training Centre on Statistical Techniques in Agricultural Experimentation, Sudan, 1966; member of Honour Society Phi Kappa Phi, USA, 1958 and Gamma Sigma Delta, USA, 1963; *Publications:* numerous research papers and reports on agriculture in *Sudan Agricultural Journal,* Agriculture Research Corp; *Journal of Agricultural Science,* Cambridge, and other professional journals and magazines in Sudan and abroad; *Interests and Recreations:* jogging, football, reading, films; *Languages:* Arabic, English; *Address:* Agricultural Research Corporation, P O Box 126, Medani, Sudan; telephone: Office — 226, 431, 432; Residence — 342.

BUTROS-GHALI, Butros, Egyptian politician; born 14 November 1922, Cairo, Egypt; married; *Religion:* Christian; *Education:* Licence in Law, Cairo University, Egypt, 1946; Doctorate in Law, Faculty of Law, University of Paris, France, 1949; Diploma in Higher Studies in Economics, Paris University; Diploma of L'Institut des Sciences Politiques, Paris; *Career:* Lecturer, Cairo University, 1949–59; Director of the Department of Political Science, Cairo University, 1960–; President of the Research Centre of *Al-Ahram;* Chief Editor of *Al-Siassa Dawlya* (International Affairs quarterly), 1963; Editor of *Al-Ahram al-Iktisadi* (Economic weekly); Vice President of the Egyptian Society of International Law; member of the Commission of Jurists; member of the Commission of ILO experts; member of the Committee of the Application of Conventions and Recommendations of the ILO, Geneva; Trustee of the International Legal Centre, New York; Associate Member of the Institute of International Law, Brussels; member of the Scientific Committee of the Institute Affari Internazionale, Rome; other academic posts: Fulbright Research Scholar, New York, 1954–55; member of the Hague Academy of International Law, 1965–66; visiting Professor at the Faculty of Law, Paris University, 1967–68; Lecturer on International Law, 1969; Co-director of the First Session for the Senior Diplomats of the Arab Emirates, 1973; Minister of State, 1977; Acting Minister of Foreign Affairs, 1977; *Publications: Cours de Diplomatie et de Droit Diplomatique et Consulaire,* 1951; *Le Problème du Canal de Suez,* in collaboration with Youssef Chlala 1957; *Egypt and the United Nations,* (Co-author) 1957; *Le Principe d'Egalite des Etats et les Organizations Internationales,* 1961; *Foreign Policies in a World of Change,* (in collaboration) 1963; *Contribution à une Théorie Générale des Alliances,* 1964, Paris; *L'Organization de L'Unité Africaine,* 1969, Paris; *Le Mouvement Afro-Asiatique,* 1969, Paris; *La Ligue des Etats Arabes,* 1972, Holland; *Les Conflits de Frontières en Afrique,* 1973, Paris; over 100 articles published in Arabic, French, English; *Languages:* Arabic, English, French, German; *Address:* Ministry of Foreign Affairs, Cairo, Egypt.

BUZIRI, Najib, Tunisian diplomat/politician; born 1925; married; *Religion:* Muslim; *Education:* Sorbonne, University of Paris, France; *Career:* joined Néo-Destour Party, 1941; President of the Association des Etudiants Musulmans Nord-Africains de Paris; practised law in France; member of Tunisian delegation to autonomy negotiations, 1954–55; Chargé d'Affaires, Embassy to France; Chef de Cabinet in the Ministry of Foreign Affairs, 1957–58; Ambassador to Italy, 1958; Ambassador to West Germany, 1961; while in Rome and Bonn, special assignments at UN, including leadership of Tunisian delegations at the Vienna Conferences on Diplomatic and Consular Immunities, 1961 and 1963; member of Socialist Destour Party Central Committee, 1964–; Secretary of State for Posts, Telegraphs and Telephone (PTT), 1964–65; Ambassador to USSR, 1965–70; Ambassador to Belgium and the EEC, 1970–71; Ambassador to Morocco, 1971–73; Ambassador to Algeria, 1973–75; Ambassador to Spain, 1975; President of the Party college at La Marsa; *Languages:* Arabic, French; *Address:* Ministry of Foreign Affairs, Tunis, Tunisia.

C

CAPUCCI, Archbishop Hilarion, Syrian ecclesiastic; born 1922, Syria; *Religion:* Christian; *Career:* Head of the Greek Catholic community in Jerusalem; arrested by Israelis 18 August 1974 on charge of smuggling arms and contact with Palestinian organizations; sentenced to 12 years' imprisonment by Israeli district court 9 December 1974; released from prison November 1977.

CARACALLA, Abdul Halim, Lebanese artist/choreographer; born 1938, Baalbeck, Lebanon; married; one son, one daughter; *Religion:* Muslim; *Education:* MA, Choreography; *Career:* Founder and Director, The Caracalla Dance Company, 1970; first Ballet *Today, Tomorrow, Yesterday,* 1973; second *Bizare of the Miracle,* 1975; third *The Black Tents,* 1977; fourth *Talgal an-Nur,* 1979; toured the Middle East, Europe, Asia and America with his company; *Decorations:* Patronage of HM King Hussain, Jordan; Said Akl Art Prize; *Interests and Recreations:* sports, researching Arab culture and traditions; *Languages:* Arabic, English, French; *Address:* P O Box 14–5418, Beirut, Lebanon, telephone: 243378; telex: 21660 LE; 38 Kingston Road, Teddington, London, UK; telephone: 9778674.

CATTAN, Henry, Palestinian lawyer/writer; born 1906, Jerusalem; *Religion:* Christian; *Education:* Licence en Droit, University of Paris, France; LLM, University of London, UK; Barrister at Law, Middle Temple, UK; *Career:* lecturer, Jerusalem Law School, 1932–42; member of Palestine Law Council until 1948; practising lawyer in Palestine and Syria; gave evidence to Anglo-American Committee of Inquiry on Palestine, 1946; presented Palestinian Arab case to UN General Assembly on behalf of Arab Higher Committee, 1947; represented Palestinian Arabs in UN General Assembly sessions, 1947, 1948; appointed by Arab League for discussions with Count Bernadotte, UN mediator on Palestine; *Publications: Palestine, the Arabs and Israel; Palestine: The Road to Peace; The Law of Oil, Concessions in the Middle East and North Africa; The Evolution of Oil Concessions in the Middle East and North Africa; Palestine and International Law; The Garden of Joys, The Question of Jerusalem;* and other pamphlets and articles on Palestine; *Languages:* Arabic, English, French; *Address:* 32 Avenue George V, 75008 Paris, France.

CHADER, Fuad, Lebanese official/businessman; born 28 May 1906, Beirut, Lebanon; married; *Education:* Professional School of Customs Officers, Paris, France; *Career:* Chief Controller, Customs Department, 1938–45; Head of Customs, 1945–50; Inspector and Deputy member of the Higher Customs Authority, 1950–53; Director, Civil Aviation, 1953–58; Director General of Communications and Transport, 1958–66; President, Solairmer tourist company; owner of the gallery Le Cèdre; *Decorations:* Officer, National Order of the Cedar; Gold Medal, Lebanese Order of Merit; Grand Officer, Jordanian Order of Independence; Commander, Italian Order of Merit; Commander, Order of Orange-Nassau, Netherlands; Commander, Order of St. Grégoire le Grand; as well as various other Lebanese and foreign decorations; *Interests and Recreations:* member of the Société de Droit Aérien, Paris, France, of the French-Lebanese Association; *Languages:* Arabic, French; *Address:* Office — Solairmer, Minet el-Hosn, Beirut, Lebanon; telephone: 255319; Residence — Le Cèdre, 131 Army Street, Beirut, Lebanon; Residence — Hazmieh, Lebanon.

CHADIRJI, Rifat, Iraqi official/architect; born 6 December, 1926, Baghdad, Iraq; married; *Education:* Diploma in Architecture, Hammersmith School of Arts and

Crafts, London; *Career:* founder, Senior partner and Director of Iraq Consult, 1952–; Section Head, Baghdad Building Department, Waqaf Organisation, 1954–57; Director General, Housing Department, Ministry of Planning, 1958–59; Head of Planning Committee, Ministry of Housing, 1959–63; private practice, Iraq Consult, 1963–78; member of Mayor's Council, 1958–61; member of Iraqi Tourist Board, 1970–75; Counsellor, Mayoralty of Baghdad, 1980–82; works include Cabinet Ministers' Building, United Arab Emirates, 1978, National Theatre Abu Dhabi, 1977, Al Ain Public Library, United Arab Emirates, 1978; exhibited at Gulbenkian Hall, Baghdad, 1966, University of Khartoum, 1966, Ministry of Art and Culture, Accra, Ghana, 1966, Middle East Technical University, Ankara, Turkey, 1966, Athens Technical Institute, Greece, 1966, American University of Beirut, 1966, Arab Engineers Conference, Amman Jordan, 1966, Hammersmith College of Arts, London, 1966, Ain Shams University, Cairo, 1967, Arab Engineers Conference, Kuwait, 1975, Kuwait Engineers Union, 1975, Iraqi Cultural Centre, London, 1978, Vienna Technical University, Austria, 1978; *Decorations:* several awards and prizes; First Prize for Council of Ministers' Building, Baghdad, 1975; First Prize for New Theatre, Abu Dhabi, 1977; First Prize for Council of Ministers' Building, Abu Dhabi, 1978; Honorary member of RIBA; Loeb Fellow, Harvard University; *Interests and Recreations:* photography, travelling; *Languages:* Arabic, English; *Address:* 28 Troy Court, Kensington High St, London W8; telephone: (01) 937 3715.

CHADLI, Colonel Bendjedid, Algerian politician; President of Algeria; born 14 April, 1929; *Career:* joined struggle for the independence of Algeria, 1955; Commander for Constantine Military Region, 1962; Commander for Oran Military Region, 1963–79; member of Revolutionaryn Council, 1965; Acting Chief of Staff, 1978–79; Secretary General of National Liberation Front, 1979–; President of Algeria, Commander in Chief of Armed Forces and Minister of Defence, 1979–; *Address:* Office of the President, al-Mouradia, Algiers, Algeria; telephone: 606360.

CHAFIK, Muhammad Binali, Moroccan official/educationalist; born 17 September 1926, Morocco; married; six sons, two daughters; *Religion:* Muslim; *Education:* BA in History; Diploma in Classical Arabic; Aptitude Certificate in Inspection and Teaching; Certificate in History of Arts; Diploma in Berber; *Career:* Teacher, 1944–52; Teacher at Grammar School, 1953–55; Inspector of Primary Education, 1955–61; Inspector of General Education, 1962–64; Principal Inspector for History and Geography, 1965–67; Head of Mission at the Royal Cabinet, 1968–69, 1973–77; Assistant Secretary of State, 1970–72; Secretary of State, 1972; Director of the Royal College, 1977–; *Publications: Pensées Sous Developées,* 1972, in French; *A Grammar of Berber,* in Arabic; *Ce Que Dit le Muezzin,* 1974; several articles on education in Arabic published in professional journals and magazines; *Decorations:* Wissam Reda, Morocco; Palmes Académiques, France; *Interests and Recreations:* reading, walking, gardening; *Languages:* Arabic, French, Berber; *Address:* 42 Cité Saada, Aviation, Rabat, Morocco.

CHAHINE, Rafiq Amin, Lebanese politician; born 1925 Nabatieh Lebanon; married; two daughters; *Education:* Gerard Institute in Tulsa USA; MA, PhD, Political Sciences Southern California University, USA; *Career:* Chief of Department at the Planning and Economic Development Council Ministry of Planning 1953–59; Export-Member of the Planning Council in the Ministry of Planning 1959–1960; elected deputy of Nabatiah 1960; member of the Parliamentary Committees for the Ministries of Foreign Affairs and Planning; Minister of Planning in the Ministerial Cabinet presided by Saeb Salam (1960–61); former General Director of Palestinian Refugees Administration with rank of Ambassador 1964; re-elected member of Parliament for Nabatieh (1968); Minister of Labour and Social Affairs in the Cabinet presided by Rachid Karame 1969–70; he also represented Lebanon as member of various delegations; re-elected member of Parliament for Nabatieh 1974; Rapporteur of the Administrative and Judicial Committee 1981; Chairman of the Board for Easco International SARL; *Address:* Centre Verdun, 10th Floor, Verdun Street, Beirut, Lebanon, P O Box 13–5204; telephone: 346770, 365771; telex: EASCO 21795 IE.

CHALABI, Abdul Wahab al-, Iraqi physician/academic; born 1930, Mosul, Iraq; married; two daughters; *Religion:* Muslim; *Education:* MD, University of Istanbul, Turkey; MSc, Cairo University, Egypt; *Career:* General Practitioner, 1960; Physician, Forensic Medicine, 1965; Assistant Lecturer, 1974; Demonstrater, 1976; Assistant Professor of Forensic Medicine, 1978–; Head of Section of Forensic Medicine, College of Medicine, University of Mosul; *Publications: Atlas of Forensic Medicine,* 1979 in Arabic; several research papers published in professional journals; *Interests and Recreations:* tennis, travel; *Languages:* Arabic, English, Turkish; *Address:* College of Medicine, University of Mosul, Iraq; telephone: Office — 170 2241; Residence — 73371.

CHALABI, Fadhil Ja'afar al-, Iraqi oil official: born 1929; *Education:* BA, in Law, Baghdad University 1951; Doctorat d'Etat, Oil Economics, University of Paris, France; *Career:* Director General of Oil Affairs, Baghdad, Iraq, 1968; Permanent Under Secretary of Oil, Ministry of Oil, Iraq, 1973; Assistant Secretary General, OPEC, 1976; Deputy Secretary General, OPEC, 1978–; *Publications:* OPEC and the International Oil Industry: A Changing Structure, Oxford Press; *Languages:* Arabic, French, English; *Address:* OPEC, Obere Donaust-Rasse 93, 1020 Vienna, Austria.

CHALABI, Jawad, Iraqi banker/businessman; born 2 January 1928, Iraq; *Education:* Law School, Baghdad University, Iraq, 1949; *Career:* Executive Vice President and Director, Industrial Bank of Iraq, Baghdad, Iraq, 1955–58; Director, National Textile Company, Iraq, 1955–58; Director, Iraq Cement Company, 1955–64; Director, Commercial Bank of Iraq, 1961–64; Director, Middle East Banking Company (MEBCO) Lebanon, 1961; Director, Vegetable Oil Company, Iraq, 1962–64; Managing Director, Commercial Insurance Company, Iraq; Director, National Bank of Abu Dhabi, United Arab Emirates, 1974–77; Director, Petra Bank, Amman, Jordan, 1977; Chairman and General Manager, MEBCO, Lebanon; *Interests and Recreations:* chess, tennis, modern Arabic poetry; *Address:* Middle East Banking Company (MEBCO), P O Box 3540, Beirut, Lebanon; telephone: 220105; telex: 20729 Mebcole.

CHALABI, Talal Saleem al-, Iraqi academic/physician; born 28 February 1937, Baghdad, Iraq; married; two daughters; *Religion:* Muslim; *Education:* MB, ChB, Baghdad University, Iraq, 1961; FRCS, Royal College of Edinburgh, UK, 1969; FACS, American College of Surgeons, USA, 1979; *Career:* Consultant Orthopaedic Surgeon, 1974–; Head, Department of Surgery, Medical College, Basrah, Iraq, 1978–79; Dean, College of Medicine, University of Basrah, Iraq, 1979–; *Publications:* articles in the *Medical Journal of Basrah University; Interests and Recreations:* classical music; *Languages:* Arabic, English; *Address:* College of Medicine, University of Basrah, Basrah, Iraq.

CHAMOUN, Camille, Lebanese former President; born 3 April 1900, Deir el-Kamar, Lebanon; married; two sons; *Education:* Licence in Law, French Faculty of Law, Beirut, 1923; *Career:* lawyer, 1924; contributor to the daily newspaper Le Rêveil; elected Deputy for Mount Lebanon, 1929, 1934; Minister of Finance, 1938; Deputy for Chouf, 1943; Minister of the Interior, 1943–44; Minister Plenipotentiary for Lebanon to the UK, 1944; Head, Lebanese Delegation to the Civil Aviation Conference, Chicago, USA, 1944; Head of the Lebanese Delegation to the UNESCO Conference and to the UN Preparatory Committee, 1945; Lebanese Representative to the UN General Assembly, London, UK, and New York, USA, 1946; Minister of Finance, 1947; Minister of the Interior, 1947; re-elected Deputy for Chouf, 1947, and 1951; elected President of the Lebanese Republic September, 1952–58; founder of the National Liberal Party, 1958; re-elected Deputy for Metn, 1960; Deputy for Chouf, 1968; injured in assassination attempt, 1968; re-elected, 1972; Chairman and Director of numerous Lebanese companies; President of the National Liberal Party, 1958–; Minister of the Interior and of Posts, Telegraphs and Telecommunications and Hydroelectric Resources in Rashid Karami's Government, 1975; Deputy Premier, Minister of Foreign Affairs, Interior and Defence in Rashid Karami Government, 1976; *Publications: Stages of Independence,* in Arabic; *Crise au Moyen-Orient,* 1963; *Mes Mémoires,* 1969; *Decorations:* Grand Cordon, National Order of the Cedar, Légion d'Honneur, as well as many other foreign decorations; *Interests and Recreations:* swimming, yachting, gun collecting; *Languages:* Arabic, French, English; *Address:* Ashrafiay, Beirut, Lebanon.

CHAPRA, Muhammad Omar; Saudi Arabian banker/economist; born 1st February 1933; married 1962; three daughters, one son; *Religion:* Muslim; *Education:* PhD, Economics, University of Minnesota, USA, 1961; *Career:* Assistant Professor, Wisconsin State University, Platteville, 1960–61; Senior Economist and Associate Editor, *Pakistan Development Review,* Institute of Development Economics, Karachi, 1961–62; Reader in Economics, Central Institute of Islamic Research, Karachi, 1962–63; Associate Professor, Wisconsin State University, Platteville, 1963–64; Associate Professor, University of Kentucky, Lexington, 1964–65; Economic Adviser, Saudi Arabian Monetary Agency, 1965–; *Publications:* several articles in international journals; a number of monographs, in English; *Languages:* Arabic, English, Urdu; *Address:* Saudi Arabian Monetary Agency, P O Box 2992, Riyadh, Saudi Arabia; telephone: 4887336.

CHARARA, Muhammad Hamza, Saudi Arabian diplomat, born 8 September 1924, Medina, Saudi Arabia; married; *Religion:* Muslim; *Education:* Licence in Law, King Farouk University, Egypt 1949; Studies at the Political Science Faculty, University of Rome Italy; *Career:* Attaché at the Saudi delegation to Italy, 1951; member of the Saudi delegation to the UN, 1955–57, 1961; Counsellor Embassy to Japan, 1958–60; Minister Plenipotentiary, Embassy to Japan, 1963; Ambassador to Japan, 1964; member of the Saudi delegation to the conference of the Non-Aligned states in Belgrade 1961 and Cairo, 1964; Ambassador, Permanent Representative of Saudi Arabia at the UN, Geneva, 1965–72; Ambassador to Belgium, 1972; President of the Saudi delegation to the Conference of the Economic Cooperation of the Developing Countries (Group 77), Mexico, 1976; Ambassador and Head of Saudi Mission to the EEC June, 1973; President of the Islamic Cultural Centre of Belgium; President of the Euro-Arab Club in Brussels; Ambassador to Luxembourg, 1978; *Decorations:* Decoration of King Abdul Aziz, 1972; Grand Officer of the Order of Leopold II October, 1976; *Interests and Recreations:* golf, hunting; *Languages:* English, Italian, French; *Address:* Ministry of Foreign

Affairs, P O Box 495, Baghdadiah, Jeddah; telephone: 6421322 6421423; telex: 401104 KHARJISJ.

CHATTY, Habib M., Tunisian diplomat/politician; born 9 October 1916, M'saken, Tunisia; married; *Religion:* Muslim; *Career:* started journalist career with *Ez-Zohra, La Presse de Tunisia, Le Petit Matin, Tunis-soir,* 1937; Editor in Chief of *Ez-Zohra,* official organ of Neo-Destour 1953; Editor in Chief of *As-Sabah* on its foundation in 1950; Director of *Al-Amal,* organ of Neo-Destour; Head of the Press and Documentation Department of Neo-Destour Party 1956; member of Tunisian Delegation to UN General Assembly November-December 1956; Ambassador to Syria and Iraq 1957; Tunisian Delegate to Arab League meeting September 1958; Ambassador to Turkey and Iran 1959; accompanied President Bourguiba on his visit to UK, 1961; Ambassador to UK, 1962–64; Ambassador to Morocco 1964–70; Ambassador to Algeria 1970–72; appointed Director of the President's Office August 1972; Minister of Foriegn Affairs 1974–78; Secretary General of the Organization of the Islamic Conference (OIC), 1979–; *Decorations:* Grand Cordon of the Order of Tunisian Independence; Grand Cordon of the Order of the Tunisian Republic and many other high foreign decorations; *Languages:* Arabic, French, English; *Address:* General Secretariat of the Organization of the Islamic Conference, P O Box 178, Jeddah, Saudi Arabia; telephone: 687–4858.

CHEDID, Yusuf, Lebanese diplomat; born 26 August 1914, Marjeyoun, Lebanon; married; four daughters; *Education:* BA, Political Science, American University of Beirut, Lebanon; *Career:* Professor of Oriental History, Baghdad, and Jerusalem 1940–43; 1st Secretary, Embassy to UK, 1944–50; Head of Arab Department, Ministry of Foreign Affairs, 1951–52; Chargé d'Affaires, Embassy to Liberia, 1953–55; Consul General in Sydney, Australia, 1955–59; Consul General in Johannesburg, South Africa, 1959–62; Head of UN Department, Ministry of Foreign Affairs, 1962–64; Head of Economic Department, Ministry of Foreign Affairs, 1954–66; Ambassador Extraordinary and Minister Plenipotentiary to Turkey, 1966–71; Ambassador to Austria 1971–; *Address:* Lebanese Embassy, Schwedenplatz No 2, 1010 Wien, Austria.

CHEHAB, Amir Abdul Aziz, Lebanese politician/lawyer; born 1 December 1913, Baabda, Mount Lebanon; married; five children; *Religion:* Christian; *Education:* BA, St. Joseph University, Beirut, Lebanon; Licence in Law, French Faculty of Law, Beirut; *Career:* Magistrate; Governor of North Lebanon; later Governor, South Lebanon, 1946; Director General, Ministry of the Interior, 1956; resigned 1958 to join opposition to Camille Chamoun; Deputy for Chouf, 1960 and 1964; Chairman, Parliamentary Commission for Foreign Affairs; Administrator, St. Charles City Centre SAL; *Decorations:* Commander, National Order of the Cedar, as well as various other decorations and distinctions from Greece, Iran, Mexico, etc; *Interests and Recreations:* music; *Languages:* Arabic, French; *Address:* Office — SFAH Building, Kantari Street, Beirut, Lebanon; Residence -- Tueni Street, Beirut, Lebanon.

CHEHAB, Maurice, Lebanese academic/archaeologist; born 1904, Lebanon; *Religion:* Christian; *Education:* St. Joseph University, Beirut, Lebanon; Ecole du Louvre, Paris, France; Ecole des Hautes Etudes Historiques, Paris; *Career:* Conservator, Lebanese National Museum, 1928–37; Head of Administration, Antiquities Service, 1937–44; Professor of Diplomatic and General History, Ecole des Sciences Politiques, 1940; Director of Antiquities Service, 1944; Professor of the History of Architecture, Lebanese Academy of Fine Arts, 1942; Professor of Lebanese History, Ecole Normale, 1942; Professor of Oriental Archaeology, Institute of Oriental Literature, 1946; Director of Tyre and Anjar excavations, 1950; Professor of History and Archaeology, Lebanese University, 1953–59; Curator of Lebanese General Antiquities, 1953–59; Director General of Antiquities, 1959–; *Publications: Tyr,* 1969; *Decorations:* Chevalier of National Order of the Cedar; Officer of the Order of Arts and Letters (France); *Languages:* Arabic, French; *Address:* Antiquities Department, Rue de Damas, Beirut, Lebanon.

CHEIKH AL-ARD, Faisal, Syrian UN Official/physician; born 26 July, 1919, Damascus, Syria; *Education:* MD, Friedrich Wilhelm University, West Germany, 1938–46; MD, School of Hygiene and Tropical Medicine, UK, 1947–49; MPH, Johns Hopkins School of Public Health; Diploma, American Board of Preventive Medicine; *Career:* Director, Public Health Division, UN Korean Relief Agency, Korea, 1951, 1953; Associate Professor, Public Health Administration; District Health Officer, New Mexico State Health Department, 1957–59; Director, Social Health Centre, American University of Beirut, Lebanon, 1959–61; Director, Special Health Service, Country Health Department, Maryland, USA, 1962–69; Representative of UN Fund for Population Activities in the Arab World UNFPA, 1973; *Interests and Recreations: table tennis,* travelling; member of the Rotary International; *Languages:* Arabic, French, German, Italian, English; *Address:* Office — UNFPA, P O Box 3216, Beirut, Lebanon; telephone: 804658, 807925; Residence— 1 Avenue Charles de Gaulle, Chouran, Beirut, Lebanon; telephone: 805269.

CHEIKHROUHOU, Habib, Tunisian businessman/publisher; born 20 December 1914, Sfax, Tunisia; married; three sons, four daughters; *Religion:* Muslim; *Education:* general education; *Career:* actively involved in the Socialist Destour Party; Chairman and Managing Director, Dar As-Sabah Publishing House, publish *As-Sabah* and *Le Temp* daily newspapers; Chairman and Managing Director, Nour Company (manufacture batteries), STIPCE (manufacture chemical fertilizers), Venus (travel agency), and various other companies;former Vice President, Municipality of Carthage; *Decorations:* Order of Tunisian Republic; Egyptian Order of Merit; various other decorations from Arab and other countries; *Interests and Recreations:* theatre, former Secretary General of Sfax Sporting club, former Director of Najm Theatre Group; *Address:* 4 Rue Ali Pacha Hamba, Tunis, Tunisia; telephone: 256611.

CHERKAOUI, Abdul Malik, Moroccan official/economist; born 2 December 1941; married; two daughters; *Religion:* Muslim; *Education:* BA in Economics and Statistics, INSEE, Paris, France; *Career:* Professor, Institute of Statistics, Rabat, 1971; Director of Statistics, 1972; Director General, Cooperative Office Movement, 1972; Secretary General of Planning, 1974–; Chief Engineer, 1980; *Publications: Indicateurs Socio-Economiques du Maroc,* Morocco, 1980; several articles on social economics published in professional journals; *Decorations:* Ouissame Reda; *Interests and Rec-*

reatons: tennis, chess; *Languages:* Arabic, French, Spanish, English; *Address:* Route des Zaers, Km6, Lotissement Bellevue, Rabat, Morocco; telephone: 53841.

CHIDIAC, Jean Salim, Lebanese banker; born 1929, Zahle, Lebanon; married; 1952; two daughters, one son; *Religion:* Christian; *Education:* International College; American University of Beirut; Polytechnic School of Paris; *Career:* Founder, Zahle Bank, 1956; Owner, Char Insurance Office, 1958–62; Founder and Chairman, Société Nationale d'Assurances SAL, 1963; Chairman and General Manager, Bank of the Middle East SAL, 1974; Chairman and General Manager, Middle East Commercial Bank SAL, 1979; *Publications:* several articles on insurance, first dictionary on insurance in three languages; *Pour un Management au Liban; Interests and Recreations:* swimming, bridge; *Languages:* Arabic, English, French; *Address:* SNA Building, Tabaris Square, P O Box 11–4805, Beirut, Lebanon; telephone: 250505, 335040.

COOBAR, Abdul Majid, Libyan politician; born 1909, Tripoli; *Religion:* Muslim; *Education:* general; *Career:* employed with, and later Head of Birth Registration Section, Tripoli Municipal Council; Adviser on Arab Affairs for Tripoli Municipal Council, 1943–44; resigned from Government service, 1944; member of National Constituent Assembly, 1950, and member of Assembly Committee to draft Constitution; member of Assembly for Eastern Ghavian, 1952–55; President of Parliament Assembly, 1952–55; Deputy Prime Minister and Minister of Communications, 1955–56; re-elected for Eastern Ghavian to new Chamber of Deputies, 1955; member of Viceroy's Council, 1957; Prime Minister, 1957–60; concurrently Minister of Foreign Affairs, 1958–60; *Decorations:* Independence Award, 1st Class; *Address:* Asadu al-Furat Street 29, Garden City, Tripoli, Libya.

D

DABBAGH, Abdullah Muhammad Ali al-, Saudi Arabian businessman/agriculture expert; born 1922, Jeddah, Saudi Arabia; *Religion:* Muslim; *Education:* BA Agronomy; *Career:* Secretary, Agriculture Directorate; Director, Plant Protection Division, Agricultural Affairs Directorate; Director General of Agricultural Affairs, Ministry of Agriculture; Director General, Ministry of Agriculture; Minister of Agriculture; former member of Board of Petroleum and Minerals Organization (Petromin), Chamber of Commerce and Industry, Jeddah; member of Constituent Board, King Abdul Aziz University; Director General of Al-Bilad Press and Publishing Organization; attended several FAO regional and international conferences on Locusts; now major dealer in egg-producing farms, egg-hatching plants and animal fodder plants; *Interests and Recreations:* sports; *Address:* P O Box 1035, Jeddah, Saudi Arabia; telephone: Jeddah 28277.

DABBAGH, Hashim Salih al-, Saudi Arabian official/physician; born 1925, Hadhramaut; *Education:* MD, Tropical Medicine and Public Health; *Career:* Deputy Assistant Director of Preventive Medicine, 1952; General Director for Malaria Eradication, 1962; former member of the Saudi Red Crescent Board; Director General of Preventive Medicine, Ministry of Health, 1971–; member of the Public Sanitation Board for the Eastern Region; participated in several public health and preventive medicine conferences and symposia, the latest at Guy's Hospital, London, UK; *Address:* The General Directorate for Preventive Medicine, Ministry of Health, Riyadh, Saudi Arabia; telephone: 4024878; telex: 201628 HEALTH SJ.

DABBAGH, Hassan Ali al-, Kuwaiti diplomat; born 27 April 1923, Jaffa, Palestine; married; *Religion:* Muslim; *Education:* BA, University of London, UK, 1949–52; *Career:* Ministry of Education, Kuwait, 1950–61; Inspector of Education; Minister Counsellor, Embassy to Egypt, 1961–69; Minister Counsellor, Embassy to France, 1969–73; Consul General, Switzerland, 1973; Minister, Permanent Representative of Kuwait, UN, Geneva, 1973; *Languages:* Arabic, English, French; *Address:* Ministry of Foreign Affairs, P O Box 3, Sour Street, Kuwait; telephone: 422041; telex: 22042 KHARJIA KT.

DABBAGH, Hussain Muhammad Ali al-, Anglo-Arab academic; born 19 December 1929, Jaffa, Palestine; married; one son, one daughter; *Religion:* Muslim; *Education:* BA in Classical Arabic, London University, UK; PhD, Durham University, UK; *Career:* Assistant Lecturer in Arabic, 1956–61; Lecturer in Arabic, 1961–; seconded to University of Malaya, 1964–66; University of Ibadan, Nigeria, 1969–70; Lecturer in English, University of Kuwait, 1970–71; visited University of California by invitation, 1969; Lecturer in Arabic, Durham University, UK; member of Association of University Teachers (AUT), Durham; member of the British Society of Middle Eastern Studies (BRISMES); member of Council for the Advancement of Arab-British Understanding (CAABU), London; *Publications:* a translation of Shakespeare Sonnets into Arabic verse published in *Aswat* magazine, London, 1961; several poems published in *Al-Ra'id al-Arabi* periodical; *Interests and Recreations:* gardening, badminton, tennis, watching television, Arabic and Islamic studies; *Languages:* Arabic, English, German, Latin; *Address:* University of Durham, School of Oriental Studies, Elvet Hill, Durham, UK.

DABBAGH, Riyadh Hamid al-, Iraqi academic/geologist; born 10 September 1946, Mosul, Iraq; married; one son; *Religion:* Muslim; *Education:* BSc in Geology, 1968; Diploma, London University, 1972; MSc,

University of London, 1972; PhD, University of London, 1975; International Seminar of Hydrology, UNESCO, Moscow, 1981; *Career:* Assistant Geologist, University of Mosul, 1968; Assistant Head of Geology Department, College of Sciences, University of Mosul, 1970; Demonstrator, Geology Department, 1975; Head of Geology Department, 1976–78; Vice President, University of Mosul, 1977–; member of International Hydrologists Association, the British Geology Society, the Iraqi National Council for International Hydrology Programme, UNESCO, the Iraqi Geologists Society; Head of the Iraqi Geologists Association; Deputy Chairman, Cultural Social Centre, University of Mosul; *Publications:* numerous articles and researches in professional journals and magazines; translation of two books on hydrology, 1979, 1981; *Interests and Recreations:* reading, travelling, tennis; *Languages:* Arabic, English; *Address:* The Presidency of the University of Mosul, Mosul, Iraq; telephone: 812918, 811806; telex: 8011.

DABBAGH, Zain el-Abidin al-, Saudi Arabian diplomat; born 1925; *Religion:* Muslim; *Education:* BA in Political Science, University of Washington, USA, 1950; MA in International Relations, University of Connecticut, USA, 1952; Graduate Studies in International Law; *Career:* member of Saudi Arabian Delegation to the Japanese Peace Conference, San Francisco USA, 1951; temporary assignment at Saudi Arabian Mission to the United Nations, 1952–53; joined Diplomatic Service, Ministry of Foreign Affairs, 1955; 3rd Secretary, Embassy to Japan, 1957–59; Assistant Deputy Chief, Saudi Arabian Permanent Mission to the United Nations, New York, USA; Saudi Arabian Representative in the Sixth Legal Committee of the General Assembly, 1959–64; Deputy Chief, Saudi Arabian Delegation to the UN Conference for Trade and Development (UNCTAD), Geneva, Switzerland, 1964; member of Saudi Delegation to the Non-Aligned Conference of Heads of State, Cairo, Egypt, 1964; Counsellor, Ministry of Foreign Affairs; Head of Legal and Conference Department, 1964–66; member of Saudi Preparatory Committee for the Non-Aligned Conference of Heads of State, Algeria, 1965; Minister Plenipotentiary and Chargé d'Affaires, Embassy to Nationalist China, 1966–73; Ambassador, Political Assistant to the late Foreign Minister, Omar

Saqqaf, 1973–74; Head, Saudi Delegation to the Conference of the Development of Humanitarian Law during Armed Conflict, Geneva, 1975; attended fourteen sessions of the UN General Assembly; member of the Legal and Conference Department, 1975–80; Ambassador to Japan, 1980–; *Interests and Recreations:* sport; *Address:* 6-2 Hiroo 2-chome, Shibuya-ku, Tokyo, Japan.

DABBAS, Hashim Ahmad, Jordanian official/economist; born 1929, Salt, Jordan; married; seven children; *Education:* BA, University of Cairo, Egypt, 1955; MSc, Kansas State University, 1958; PhD Economics and Political Science, University of Missouri, USA, 1964; *Career:* Economist with Jordan Development Board, 1964–66; Director General of Statistics Department, 1966–71; Under Secretary, Ministry of Industry and Trade, 1971–80; President, General Audit Office, 1980–; President of the Jordan Economics Association, 1974–; Assistant Secretary General of the Arab Economic Union, 1974–; Secretary of the Arab Economists Union, 1976–78; Alternate Governor of the World Bank representing Jordan, 1974–80; member of the Board of Directors of the World Affairs Council in Jordan, 1980–; Permanent Jordan Representative, Arab Economic Unity Council, 1970–80; part time lecturer at the University of Jordan and other academic institutions in Jordan; Government Spokesman on the boards of several public companies; *Address:* P O Box 3218, Amman, Jordan; telephone: 62759.

DABBUS, Ali Gamaliddin, Egyptian banker; born 1923, Egypt; *Religion:* Muslim; *Education:* BCom, Faculty of Commerce, Cairo University, Egypt; *Career:* Internal Division, National Bank of Egypt, 1946–62; Chairman, Chase National Bank of Egypt, Cairo; *Address:* 12 Al Birgas Street, Garden City, Cairo, Egypt; telephone: 23904, 25265, 27219; telex: 322 Cubk Ca UN.

DACCAK, Nassuh, Syrian banker/official; born 1916, Damascus, Syria; *Education:* Licencié en Droit, Damascus University, Syria; *Career:* Head of Department of Foreign Trade, Ministry of Economy, 1947–50; Director of Trade, Ministry of Economy, 1950–51; Director of Economic Affairs, 1951–59; Chairman, Board of Directors and General Manager, Industrial Bank, 1959–62; Secretary General, Ministry of Labour and

Social Affairs, 1962–63; Chairman, Board of Credit and Money, 1971; Governor, Central Bank of Syria, 1971; Alternate Governor, IMF, Arab Fund for Social and Economic Development; member of Board of Directors, European Arab Bank; *Address:* Central Bank of Syria, P O Box 2254, Damascus, Syria; telephone: 224800; telex: 11007 MAR SY.

DAFALLA, Nazir al-, Sudanese politician/veterinary scientist; born 1 Janurary 1922, Al-Obeid, Sudan; *Education:* Veterinary Science, University of Khartoum, Sudan, 1946; Diploma, Bacteriology, University of Manchester, UK, 1950–52; *Career:* Veterinary Officer, Government Research Laboratories, Khartoum, 1946–50; Senior Research Officer, 1955–56; Senior Lecturer, Bacteriology, University of Khartoum, 1956–57; Dean, Faculty of Veterinary Science, 1958–62; Deputy Vice Chancellor, University of Khartoum, 1960–62; Vice Chancellor, University of Khartoum, 1962–68; Executive Vice President, Association of African Universities, 1968–69; Provost for Agriculture and Veterinary Medicine, Ahmadu Bello University, Nigeria, 1971–72; Speaker of the People's Assembly, 1972–74; Minister of Health and Social Welfare, 1975–76; Executive Secretary, Green Project for North Africa, UN, 1978; Minister of Education and Guidance, 1981–; *Publications:* numerous papers in the field of veterinary and biological sciences and education; *Languages:* Arabic, English; *Address:* Ministry of Education and Guidance, Khartoum, Sudan.

DAFFA, Ali Abdullah al-, Saudi Arabian academic/mathematician; born 1942, Anaiza, Saudi Arabia; married; *Religion:* Muslim; *Education:* AB, Mathematics, Ohio University, 1966; BS, Mathematics, Stephen Austin State University, 1967; MA, International Relations, East Texas State University, 1968; MS, Mathematics, Vanderbilt University, 1969; PhD, Mathematics, Peabody College and Vanderbilt University, 1973; *Career:* Assistant Professor of Mathematics, University of Petroleum and Minerals, Dhahran, Saudi Arabia, 1973–74; Chairman, Mathematics Department, University of Petroleum and Minerals, 1974–77; Dean, College of Sciences, University of Petroleum and Minerals, 1977–; Associate Professor, Mathematics Department, University of Petroleum and Minerals, 1980–; member of the Committee on Degree Equivalence, Ministry of

Higher Education and the Committee on Modern Mathematics for Secondary Schools, Ministry of Education, 1974–; *Publications:* author of several books and research papers in English and Arabic on the history of Islamic and Arabic science in the Middle Ages, and on modern mathematics; *Interests and Recreations:* reading; *Languages:* English, Arabic; *Address:* University of Petroleum and Minerals, P O 144, Dhahran, Saudi Arabia; telephone: 8602600; telex: 601060 UPMSJ.

DAFFA, Khattab Omar al-, Qatari official; born 1952, Doha, Qatar; married; two daughters; *Religion:* Muslim; *Education:* BSc in Economics and Political Science, Western Michigan University, USA; *Career:* Financial Official, Ministry of Finance and Petroleum; Director of Civil Service Department, Ministry of Finance and Petroleum; *Interests and Recreations:* football, poetry and music; *Languages:* Arabic, English; *Address:* Government House, Civil Service Department, P O Box 36, Doha, Qatar; telephone: 324062, 326244; telex: 40332 CEVSER DH.

DAGHESTANI, Najib Abu al-Alla al-, Syrian engineer; born 26 June 1940, Damascus, Syria; married; two sons; *Religion:* Muslim; *Education:* Diploma in Civil Engineering, Enfield College of Technology, UK, 1968; Postgraduate Diploma, Foundation Engineering, UK, 1969; MSc in Mining and Engineering Geophysics, University of Strathclyde, UK, 1972; *Career:* Soil and Foundation Engineer, Vocation Training Centre Project, UK, 1968–70; Counterpart to UN Expert ILO, Ministry of Communications, Syria, 1972–74; Civil and Material Engineer, Roads and Bridges, Saudi Arabia, 1974; Consultant, Deputy Resident Engineer, Roads and Bridges, Saudi Arabia, 1976; Technical Adviser to the Managing Director, Oman Building and Construction Co Ltd (OBCO), Oman, 1979; General Manager, OBCO, 1980–; *Publications:* several books and other publications: *Interests and Recreations:* swimming, scuba diving, music, painting, cinema, theatre; *Languages:* Arabic, English, French, Greek; *Address:* 62 Madan Ben Baraken Abou Romanah, Damascus, Syria; telephone: 334544; P O Box 3915 Ruwi, Sultanate of Oman; telephone: 603085, 603386; P O Box 206, Paphos, Cyprus.

DAGHIR, Abdullah, Lebanese ecclesiastic/academic; born 1 June 1914, Bikfaya, Lebanon; *Religion:* Christian; *Education:* Jesuit College, Beirut; Oriental Seminary, Beirut; Licence ès-Lettres, Sorbonne, University of Paris, France 1938; *Career:* entered Jesuit Novitiate, 1932; ordained priest 1945; Head of Arabic Studies, Secondary School of St. Joseph University, Beirut; Director of Oriental Seminary of Beirut; Rector of Maronite Seminary of Ghazir, Lebanon, 1951–57; Jesuit Provincial for the Middle East, 1957–65; Rector, St. Joesph University, 1965–72; Rector, Nôtre Dame College of Jamhour, Lebanon, 1972–77; Superior, St. Joseph Residence, Beirut; *Decorations:* Officer of the Légion d'Honneur; Medal of the Lebanese Order of Merit, 1968; *Languages:* Arabic, French; *Address:* P O Box 11 293 , Beirut, Lebanon.

DAGHIR, Nuhad J., Lebanese academic; born 23 Feburary 1935, Beirut, Lebanon; married; three sons; *Religion:* Muslim; *Education:* BSc in Agriculture, American University of Beirut, 1957; MS in Animal Nutrition, Iowa State University, 1959; PhD in Animal Nutrition, Iowa State University, 1962; *Career:* Research Assistant, Iowa State University, USA, 1958–62; Assistant Professor, American Univerisity of Beirut, Lebanon, 1962–67; Associate Professor, AUB, 1967–75; Visiting Professor, University of California, Davis, California, USA, 1969–70; Visiting Professor, Iowa State University, Iowa, USA, 1979–80; Associate Dean, Faculty of Agriculture, AUB, Beirut, 1978–79; Professor of Poultry Science and Nutrition, AUB; FAO Expert to Jordan, Animal Health Institute, 1973; member of International Standing Committee of the World Poultry Science Association on Nutrient Requirements of Poultry, of International Committee of the International Union of Nutritional Sciences, Nutrition of Animals; *Publications:* co-editor and co-author of several books on nutrition and agricultural development; articles in professional journals on poultry science and nutrition, in English and Arabic; *Interests and Recreations:* swimming, reading, tennis, writing, travelling; member of eight professional and honorary organizations; participant in civic and community projects; *Languages:* Arabic, English, French; *Address:* Office – Faculty of Agriculture and Food Sciences, AUB, Beirut, Lebanon; telephone: 340740 ext 2622; Residence — Sit Nasab Street, Yeranian Building, R25 Beirut, Lebanon; telephone: 342740.

DAGHISTANI, Jafar Abdul Hamid, Saudi Arabian businessman; born 1928, Mecca, Saudi Arabia; *Religion:* Muslim; *Education:* banking courses, London, UK; *Career:* Director, Accounting and Warehouse Depot, Juffali Brothers; Director, International Agencies; Director of Chamber of Commerce and Industry, Mecca; member of Board of Chamber of Commerce, Mecca; member of Board of Arab Banks Union, Beirut, Lebanon; *Interests and Recreations:* painting, music; *Address:* Riyadh Bank, Mecca, Saudi Arabia.

DAHABI, Mahir Antoun al-, Egyptian journalist; born 1 February 1936, Alexandria, Egypt; married; two sons; *Religion:* Christian; *Education:* BA, College of Arts, Press Department, Cairo University, Cairo, Egypt; studied journalism with the Thompson Group, UK; *Career:* joined *Rose al-Yusif* 1955; Editor, *Al-Ahram* newspaper, 1958–71, Chief of the Editing Technical Department, 1971, Assistant to the Editor in Chief *Al-Ahram* newspaper, 1980; Lecturer, Layout Techniques and Journalism, Faculty of Mass Media, Cairo University; Supervisor of *Engineer's Magazine, Arab Youth* and *Islamic Banks Magazine;* Supervisor of the production of books and publications of some Egyptian publishing houses; collaborated with Al-Ahram in the Establishment of Dar al-Kitab al-Gadid publishing house; member of the Egyptian Press Syndicate, of the International Research Association for Newspaper Technology (IFRA); *Publications:* books on Arab press; articles in *Al-Ahram; Interests and Recreations:* member of Al-Gezira Club, the Hunting Club, Al-Ahli Sporting Club; *Languages:* Arabic, English, French; *Address:* 7 Abdul Hamid Said Street, Kasr al-Nil, Cairo, Egypt; telephone: 745854; telex: 92001, 92544.

DAHAMI, Muhammad, Moroccan official/economist; born 1943, Morocco; married; two sons, two daughters; *Religion:* Muslim; *Education:* Ecole Supérieure de Commerce, Bordeaux, 1966; Political Sciences; Marketing; *Career:* Commercial and Marketing Director, 1966–75; Director General, STE SEREC Office of Economical and Commercial Studies, 1975–; Director of the magazine

Bulletin Des Décideurs, 1979–; member of Parliament, 1977–; President and Director General of SODIPRESS for Information and Publications; *Publications:* articles on marketing in various journals; *Interests and Recreations:* tennis, travelling; *Languages:* Arabic, French, Spanish, English; *Address:* 69 Rue de Calais, Casablanca 01, Morocco; telephone: 273563; telex: 21062.

DAHDAH, Najib, Lebanese diplomat; born 29 November, 1915, Beirut Lebanon; married; two sons, two daughters; *Education:* Licence in Law, St. Joseph University, Beirut, Lebanon; *Career:* Ministry of Foreign Affairs; 1st Secretary, Lebanese Legation, Cairo, Egypt, 1944–45; Consul, Alexandria, Egypt, 1945; 1st Secretary, Lebanese Embassy, Paris, France, 1945–51; Counsellor, Embassy to the Holy See, 1953–56; Minister Plenipotentiary, Embassy to Colombia, concurrently accredited to Peru, Ecuador, Venezuela, Panama, 1956–57; Director, Political Affairs Department, Ministry of Foreign Affairs, 1958–59; Ambassador to Mexico, concurrently accredited to Guatemala, Honduras, Costa Rica, Nicaragua, Salvador, Panama, 1959–65; Lebanese Delegate, UN General Assembly, 1948, 1962; Lebanese Delegate to UN Security Council, 1958; Ambassador to the Holy See, concurrently accredited to Portugal, 1965–75; Permanent Secretary, Ministry of Foreign Affairs, 1975–79; journalist, *Le Reveil,* under pseudonym *Libanius,* Beirut, Lebanon, 1979–; *Publications: Evolution Historique du Liban,* in Spanish, 1964, in French, 1965, 1968; *Decorations:* Grand Officer, Order of the Nile, Egypt; Légion d'Honneur, France; Grand Croix, Piano Order, Vatican; *Languages:* Arabic, French, Spanish; *Address:* Rue Sayde Achrafieh, Beirut, Lebanon; telephone: 216206.

DAHHAN, Umaima Izzat al-, Jordanian academic; born 1942 Damascus, Syria; *Religion:* Muslim; *Education:* PhD in Business Administration, University of Texas, Austin, USA, 1975; Associate Professor, Business Department, University of Jordan; Head of Business Department, University of Jordan; member of the Board of World Women Banking; President of Working Women Club, Jordan; *Publications:* several articles in business administration in various Iraqi universities journals; co-author of many research works published by national and international

organizations; *Interests and Recreations:* travel; *Languages:* Arabic, English; *Address:* Faculty of Economics, University of Jordan, Amman, Jordan; telephone: 61916.

DAHMAN, Zuhair, Jordanian aviation official; born 20 May 1942; married; two sons; *Religion:* Muslim; *Education:* BA in Commerce and Business Management, Ain Shams University, Cairo, Egypt; special courses in Civil Aviation and Air Transport; *Career:* News Correspondent, 1962–66; worked for the Jordanian Airlines, ALIA, since 1968; Manager of ALIA in Cairo; Manager of ALIA Office in Germany; Manager of Air Freight; Executive Manager of Airport Services Office; Deputy General Manager, and Administrative Manager, ALIA; member of the Board of Al Manar Chain Hotels; *Publications:* various articles in local newspapers and magazines; *Interests and Recreations:* tennis; writing poetry; member of the Jordanian Film Club; member of ALIA Club; *Languages:* Arabic, English; *Address:* The Royal Jordanian Airlines, ALIA, P O Box 302, Amman, Jordan; telephone: 39304.

DAHMASH, Ahmad Qassim, Yemen Arab Republic politician; born in Yemen Arab Republic; married; one son; *Religion:* Muslim; *Education:* in Yemen; *Career:* Teacher, Islamic Higher Institute, Aden, 1961–62; Director of Information, Taiz, 1964; 1st Secretary, Yemen Arab Republic Embassy to Somalia, 1965; Director of the Prime Minister's Office, 1965–67; Under Secretary, Ministry of Information, 1968; Director, Printing Corporation; Minister of Information, 1971–76; Head of Commission for Administrative Re-organization; Minister of Labour, Youth and Social Affairs, 1976–; *Interests and Recreation: folk dancing, walking; Address:* Office – Al-Jania Quarter, Sana'a, Yemen Arab Republic; telephone: 2437.

DAIFALLAH, Abdul Latif, Yemen Arab Republic politician; born 1929, Harbeth, Ibb Province, Yemen Arab Republic; married; four sons, one daughter; *Religion:* Muslim; *Education:* Military Academy, Cairo, Egypt, 1955; *Career:* 1st Lieutenant in Yemeni Army, 1955; Instructor, Military Academy and Air Force, 1958; Director of Signals, 1961; Minister of the Interior; Head of Operations Office; member of the Army High Command, 1962; President of the

Executive Council; member of the Presidential Council, 1963; Deputy Prime Minister for Agriculture, Public Works, Municipalities and Communications, 1964–67; Chief of Staff and Deputy Commander in Chief, 1968; Minister of Communications, 1971–73; Minister of Public Works, 1973; Minister of Communications, 1975–76; Deputy Prime Minister for Internal Affairs, 1976; *Interests and Recreations:* reading, history, social reform, walking; *Address:* Adjacent to the Prime Minister's Office, Idha'y Quarter, Sana'a, Yemen Arab Republic.

DAIRI, Sulaiman Muhammad al-, Jordanian official/banker; born 1928, Jordan; married; *Religion:* Muslim; *Education:* BA in Economics, American University of Cairo, Egypt, 1950; Postgraduate studies, London School of Economics, 1952–53; *Career:* Jordan Foreign Currency Department, 1950–53; Director of Foreign Currencies Department, Jordan Central Bank, 1964–65; Director of Research and Statistics, Jordan Central Bank, 1965–67; Chief Auditor and Head of Internal Organisation Department of Central Bank, 1969–71; Under Secretary, Ministry of Finance, 1971–77, Deputy President, Audit Bureau, 1977–; *Address:* P O Box 37, Amman, Jordan; telephone: 23398.

DAJANI, Abdul Salim, Jordanian UN official; born 28 December 1922, Palestine; *Religion:* Muslim; *Education:* American University of Beirut, Lebanon; Law College, Jerusalem; LLB, Law School, Suffolk University, Boston, Massachusetts, USA; *Career:* UN, New York, 1950; Programme Officer, and Acting Chief of Middle East section of UN Radio and Visual Services Division, 1950–57; various UN functions in Africa, Asia and the Pacific region, Europe and the Middle East; returned to UN Headquarters in New York, 1965; Chief of Centre Services in the External Relations Division, 1972; Chief of UN Public Services, 1972; member of UN mission to Malaysia; member of UN Joint Appeal Board and UN Appointments and Promotions Committee, 1967–76; *Languages:* Arabic, English, French; *Address:* United Nations, Room GA50, New York, NY 10017, USA.

DAJANI, Abul Wafa, Jordanian businessman; born 1912, Jerusalem, Palestine; married; three sons, two daughters; *Religion:* Muslim; *Education:* BA in Business Administration, American University of Beirut, Lebanon, 1936; *Career:* Chairman and Managing Director, Wafa Dajani and Sons Company; Director Jordanian Electric Power Company, Amman, Jordan; Director, Jordan National Bank, Amman, Jordan; Director, Arabia Insurance Company, Beirut; former Director of Amman Chamber of Industry; *Interests and Recreations:* reading, sports; member of the Rotary Club; *Languages:* Arabic, English; *Address:* P O Box 33, Amman, Jordan; telephone: Office — 24170, 24179, 36026; telex: 21336.

DAJANI, Ali Tahir, Jordanian businessman; born October 1914, Jerusalem; married; two sons, three daughters; *Religion:* Muslim; *Education:* BA, American University of Beirut, Lebanon, 1932; *Career:* Institute of Economic and Financial Studies, Jerusalem, 1946; Assistant Press Officer, Palestine Government, 1936–45; Assistant Commissioner for Commerce and Industry, 1946–48; Director, Amman Chamber of Commerce, 1950–54; Controller General, Jordan Electric Power Company, 1954–62; member of Parliament, Deputy of Jerusalem, 1963–67; Minister of Transport, 1965–66; Director, Amman Chamber of Industry, 1966–; Director of Amman Bureau of *Daily Star* and *Al-Hayat* newspapers of Beirut; Honorary Consul of Japan in Amman, 1972–74; member of Royal Fiscal Commission, 1961–62; member of the Committee for Science and Technology Development; *Publications: Jordan, Land of Opportunity,* co-author, Amman, Jordan, 1975; *Industry of Jordan,* 1965, 1969, 1973 in Arabic; *Jerusalem, Faith and Struggle,* 1974; *Economy of Jordan; Decorations:* Independence Medal, 3rd Class 1962; Order of the Jordanian Star, 1st Class 1965; Order of the Commandatore, Italy, 1962; *Interests and Recreations:* gardening, member of Jerusalem Charitable Society; member of the Jordan Literacy and Adult Education Committee; lectures at Labour Education Institute; *Languages:* Arabic, English, Hebrew; *Address:* P O Box 1791, Amman Jordan; telephone: Office — 43647/8; Residence — 41099.

DAJANI, Nijmiddin, Jordanian politician/diplomat; born 7 August, 1928, Jerusalem, Palestine; married; one son, two daughters; *Religion:* Muslim; *Education:* BA, University of Wales, Aberystwyth, UK; PhD, University of Wisconsin, Madison , Wisconsin, USA,

1957; *Career:* Department of Statistics, Ministry of Economy, Damascus, Syria, 1950–52; Economic Analyst, UNRWA, Amman, Jordan, 1952–55; UNRWA Economic Analyst, 1957–58; Director of Economic Planning and Research, 1958–62; Secretary General, Jordan Development Board, 1964–68; Vice President, Jordan Development Board, 1964–68; Ambassador to West Germany, Denmark, Sweden, Norway and Luxembourg and the European Economic Community, 1968–76; Minister of Trade and Industry, 1976–; *Publications: Yarmouk, Jordan Valley Project: an Economic Appraisal; Decorations:* Jordan Independence Medal, 1st class; Grand Cross of Federal Republic of Germany, Kingdom of Denmark, Republic of Austria, Kingdom of Sweden; *Languages:* Arabic, English, German; *Address:* c/o Ministry of Trade and Industry, P O Box 2019, Amman Jordan.

DAK, Othman, Sudanese official; *Education:* University of Khartoum, Sudan; *Career:* National Council for Research; Acting Director of the Economic and Social Research Council, 1973–74; member of the People's Assembly, 1974; Minister of State for Local Government, 1975–76; *Languages:* Arabic, English; *Address:* c/o The National People's Assembly, Khartoum, Sudan.

DAKHIL, Muhammad, Libyan businessman; born 1932, Tripolitania, Libya; *Religion:* Muslim; *Career:* schoolteacher; established commercial and contracting business in 1960's; Chairman, National Development Company; *Address:* P O Box 343 Suani Road, km 2, Tripoli, Libya. telephone: 32993, 32108.

DAKHQAN, Omar Abdullah, Jordanian official; born 1927, Amman, Jordan; married; seven children; *Education:* Civil Engineering, 1950; *Career:* Assistant Under Secretary, Ministry of Public Works, 1954; Director General of Jordan Hijaz Railway, 1956; Director General of Central Water Authority, 1964; Director of Geological and Mineral Research, 1965; Director General and Deputy President of Natural Resources Authority, 1966; retired, 1969; Director General of Jordan Phosphate Company, 1969; Minister of Agriculture, 1970–72; President of the Jordan Valley Authority, 1972–1981; Member of the National Consultative Council, 1982; *Address:* Jabal Amman, Amman, Jordan; telephone: 41514, 41802.

DAKKAK, Omar Muhammad, Syrian academic; born 17 September 1927, Aleppo, Syria; married; four sons; *Religion:* Muslim; *Education:* BA in Arabic Literture, University of Damascus; Diploma in Education, University of Damascus; Diploma in Arabic Literature, Arabic High Studies Institute, Cairo, Egypt; MA in Arabic Literature, Arabic High Studies Institute, Cairo, Egypt; Arabic Literature, Ain Shams University, Cairo, Egypt, 1966; *Career:* Lecturer, Faculty of Arts, Aleppo University, Syria, 1966–72; Vice Dean, Faculty of Arts, Aleppo University, 1966–70; Dean, Faculty of Arts, Aleppo University, 1970–80; Assistant Professor, Faculty of Arts, Aleppo University, 1972–77; Professor, Faculty of Arts, Aleppo University, 1977–80; Professor, Faculty of Arts, Riyadh University, Saudi Arabia, 1980–; member of the High Council of Literature, Arts and Social Sciences, Directorate of Arab Scientific Heritage Institute, Aleppo, 1978, Central Council of Union of Arab Writers, 1977, Al-Aksa Committee; Editor in Chief of the annual archaeological journal *AL-Adiat;* Chairman of the Aleppo University Committee for Authorship, Translation and Publication, 1973; *Publications:* several books and numerous articles in different journal on Arab poetry, Syrian and Arabic literature; *Interests and Recreations:* music, archaeology; member of the Archaeological Society, Al-Adiat; *Languages:* Arabic, French, English; *Address:* P O Box 6161, Aleppo, Syria; telephone: 10298.

DAMAK, Abdel Jalil, Tunisian journalist; born 10 October 1933, Sfax, Tunisia; married; two sons, two daughters; *Religion:* Muslim; *Education:* Press Institute; *Career:* since 1958 journalist with *Dar al-Sabah* publications, *As-Sabah, Le Temps, As-Sada;* Staff Correspondent, Sub Editor, Editor in Chief, Director; made various reporting trips to the Far East, Europe, USA, Africa; *Decorations:* Order of Tunisian Independence; Order of Tunisian Republic; Tunisian Order of Cultural Merit; *Interests and Recreations:* fishing; *Languages:* Arabic, French; *Address:* 4 Rue Ali Pach-Hamba, Tunis, Tunisia; telephone: 256611, 232916.

DANA, Othman, al-, Lebanese politician/ judge; born 1921, Beirut, Lebanon; married; three children; *Religion:* Muslim; *Education:* Licence in Law, French Faculty of Law, Beirut, Lebanon; Doctor of Law, Saint Olaf

147

Academy, London, UK, 1967; *Career:* Judge, Court of Appeal, South Lebanon, 1947; Attorney General, Court of Appeal, Beirut, 1951; Attorney General, Assize Court, Beirut, 1960; Deputy for Beirut, 1960; Minister of Public Works, 1960–61; Minister of Planning, 1961–64; re-elected Deputy for Beirut, 1964; Minister of Finance, 1964–65; founded new party, National Action of November, 1966; rejoined Saeb Salam in Beirut bloc, 1967; Minister of Public Works and Transport, 1968; re-elected Deputy for Beirut, 1968; Minister of Hydroelectric Resources in Rashid Karami Cabinet, 1969; Minister of Information, 1969–70; Minister of Health, 1973–74; *Interests and Recreations:* football, volley-ball, basket-ball; *Languages:* Arabic, French; *Address:* Residence — Army Street, Beirut, Lebanon.

DARANDARY, Malik Amin, Saudi Arabian engineer; born 1922, Medina, Saudi Arabia; *Religion:* Muslim; *Education:* BSc, Aviation Engineering; *Career:* pilot of the Royal aircraft of the late King Abdul Aziz; General Manager of Saudi Arabian Airlines, Amman, Jordan; Aviation Inspector, SAUDIA; member of several IATA conferences; *Decorations:* several Orders of Merit from the late King Abdul Aziz; First Badge of Honour from the late King Abdullah, King of Jordan; *Address:* Mecca Road, Rajhi Building, Jeddah, Saudi Arabia.

DARDEER, Hassan Muhammad, Saudi Arabian businessman/actor; born 1939, Medina, Saudi Arabia; *Religion:* Muslim; *Education:* Diploma, Technical School; *Career:* TV and radio comedian; owner of the Abha Agricultural, Industrial, Tourist and Florist Town, Abha; owner of Arts Renaissance Co for Radio and TV Production; member of Board of National Corporation for Trade, Public Relations and Trade Representation; member of National Sporting and Cultural Club; *Address:* P O Box 234, Abha, Saudi Arabia.

DARKAZALLY, Ma'mun Abdul Hadi al-, Syrian banker; born 9 October 1942, Syria; married; one son; *Religion:* Muslim; *Education:* MA in International Business, New York University, New York, USA; *Career:* Assistant Treasurer, Chase Manhattan Bank, New York, 1972; Regional Officer, Chase Manhattan Bank, Beirut, Lebanon, 1974; Deputy General Manager and Manager of

Loan, Credit and Marketing, Commercial Bank of Qatar, 1975; Regional Manager, Al Saudi Banque, Paris, France, 1979; Division Manager, Africa and Middle East, Al Saudi Banque, London, UK, 1982; Branch Manager, Al Saudi Banque, London, 1983–; *Publications: The Foundation of Bayt al-Mal Islamic Institutions;* and others; *Interests and Recreations:* squash, swimming, scuba diving, flying; reading, music, coins and stamps; member of Arab Bankers Association, London; member of American Bankers Association; *Languages:* Arabic, English, French; *Address:* 7A Inverness Gardens, London W8, UK; telephone: (01) 221 1874; Offices -- (01) 493 8942.

DARMAKI, Hamad al-, United Arab Emirates official/diplomat; born 1944; married; one son, three daughters; *Religion:* Muslim; *Education:* general; *Career:* Secretary to HH the Ruler, 1961–68; Under Secretary, Director of Labour and Social Affairs Department; Ambassador of United Arab Emirates to Oman, 1972; Assistant Director, Al–Ain Municipality; *Interests and Recreations:* swimming, travelling; *Address:* Al Ain Municipality, P O Box 1003, Al–Ain, United Arab Emirates; telephone: 642366.

DARMAKI, Khalifa Muhammad Khalfan al-, United Arab Emirates administrator; born 1948, Al-Ain, United Arab Emirates; married; *Religion:* Muslim; *Education:* general; *Career:* Director of Commercial Licence Department in Al-Ain Municipality; Director of Al-Ain Municipality; *Interests and Recreations:* hunting, swimming, travelling, sporting activities at Al-Ain Sporting Club; *Address:* Al-Ain Municipality, P O Box 1003, Al-Ain, United Arab Emirates; telephone: 641675.

DARMAKI, Muhammad Salih Bin Bidwa al-, United Arab Emirates official; born 1946, Al-Ain, United Arab Emirates; married; *Religion:* Muslim; *Career:* Under Secretary in Ruler's Diwan; *Interests and Recreations:* falconry; *Languages:* Arabic, English; *Address:* P O Box 1003, Al-Ain, United Arab Emirates.

DARMAKI, Saif Bin Ali al Dhab al-, United Arab Emirates businessman/official; born 1950, Al-Ain, United Arab Emirates; married; one son, two daughters; *Religion:* Muslim; *Education:* general; *Career:* Director of

Labour and Social Affairs, 1973–76; Director of Antiquities and Tourism, Al-Ain; Chairman and Managing Director, SEDCO Dubai Ltd, Contracting and Trading Company; *Publications: Majallat al-Siyaha* (tourism magazine); *Museum Guide* in Arabic and English; *Tourism in the UAE* in Arabic, French, English; *Interests and Recreations:* table tennis, football; *Address:* P O Box 397, Abu Dhabi, United Arab Emirates, telephone: 829000; telex: 23311 Sedco EM.

DARRIJ, Muhammad al-, Moroccan academic; born 23 January 1949, Tetouan, Morocco; married; one daughter, two sons; *Religion:* Muslim; *Education:* BA in Philosophy, University of Muhammad V, Rabat, Morocco; Diploma of Higher Studies in Education and Psychology, University of Muhammad V, Rabbat; PhD in Educational Psychology, Free University of Brussels, Belgium; *Career:* Teacher of Philosophy and Islamic Thought in Moroccan schools, 1970–75; Lecturer of Psychology, Faculty of Arts, Fes, 1975–77; Professor of Education, Royal Institute for Youth and Sports, 1977–; Professor of Education, Education Centre, Rabat, 1977–; Professor of Education and Psychology, Teachers' Training College, University of Muhammad V, Rabat, 1977–; *Publications:* numerous articles and papers in education and psychology published in professional journals; Founding Director of *Psychological and Educational Studies Journal,* in Arabic; *Interests and Recreations:* Andalusian music, tennis; President of Educational Laboratory Society; member of Moroccan Philosophy Society, of the Moroccan Society for the Revival of Andalusian Music; *Languages:* Arabic, French, Spanish; *Address:* P O Box 823 Rabat, Morocco; telephone: 65639.

DARWISH, Ahmad Sani al-, Egyptian World Bank official/engineer; born 13 October 1934, Alexandria, Egypt; married; three sons, one daughter; *Religion:* Muslim; *Education:* BA and MA in Mechanical Sciences Tripos, University of Cambridge, UK, 1955; DSc (Tech), Federal Institute of Technology, Zurich, Switzerland, 1956–57; *Career:* Research Engineer, Gebruder Sulzer, Winterhur, Switzerland, 1956–57; Technical Director, Al-Chahba Spinning and Weaving, Syria, 1958; Project Analyst, General Industrialization, Cairo, Egypt, 1959; Project

Director, El-Nasr Automotive Company, Helwan Egypt, 1959–64; Project Director, Manufacturing Industry Organisation, Cairo, 1965; Project Evaluation Engineer, International Finance Corporation, Engineering Department, 1965–69; Division Chief, Industrial Projects Department, IBRD, 1969–72; Division Chief, IBRD, Country Programme, Europe, Middle East, North Africa, (EMENA) Department, 1972–74; Assistant Director, World Bank, Projects Department, 1974–80; Director, West Africa Projects, 1980–; *Publications: A Periodic Measurement of Thermal Penetration Coefficient* 1959; *Automotive Industry in Developing Countries,* 1971, in English; *Interests and Recreations:* bridge, squash, tennis; thermodynamics, manufacturing and industrial engineering, development economics, Middle East affairs; *Languages:* Arabic, English, French, German, Italian, Spanish; *Address:* Office — IBRD,1818 H Street, NW Washington DC USA 20433; telephone: (202) 477 5371; Residence — 9112 Kittery Lane, Bethesda, Maryland; telephone: (202) 469 6383.

DARWISH, Madiha Ahmad, Saudi Arabian academic; born Mecca, Saudi Arabia; *Religion:* Muslim; *Education:* MA in Modern History, USA; *Career:* Assistant Supervisor, Girls College, Jeddah, Saudi Arabia, 1969; Teaching Assistant, 1971; Assistant Professor; member of conferences on Workshop Management, Beirut American College for Women, 1970; participated in Colloquium on Access and Admission to University Education, American University of Beirut (AUB), Lebanon, 1970; contributed to the establishment of the Girls College, Department of History, Geography and Sociology, Faculty of Arts, King Abdul Aziz University, Jeddah, Saudi Arabia; Deputy Dean, Faculty of Arts, Girls College, King Abdul Aziz University, Jeddah; contributed substantially to the field of women's education in Saudi Arabia; *Publications: Modern and Contemporary History of the Royal Kingdom of Saudi Arabia,* in Arabic (under publication); *Interests and Recreations:* reading, travel, the arts; member of the Women's Charity Group, Jeddah; *Languages:* Arabic, English; *Address:* P O Box 2571 Jeddah, Saudi Arabia; telephone: Office — Jeddah 26274; Residence — Jeddah 53911.

DARWISH, Mahmud, Palestinian poet; born 1942, Al-Barwa, near Acre, Palestine; *Career:* lived in Haifa, editing bi-weekly newspaper *Al-Ittihad;* moved to Egypt, 1973; *Publications:* include *Akhir al-Layl; Ashiq min Falastin; Awraq al-Zaitun; Languages:* Arabic, French; *Address:* c/o *Al-Arabi,* P O Box 748, Kuwait.

DARWISH, Mustafa, Egyptian official/film critic; born 1 March 1928, Cairo, Egypt; *Religion:* Muslim; *Education:* Degree in Law, Faculty of Law, Cairo University, Cairo, Egypt, 1949; Diploma in Politics and Economics, Cairo University, 1950; Diploma in Public Law, Cairo University, 1951; *Career:* Adviser to the Council of State; Chief Censor of Arts, 1962, 1966–68; Administrative Judge, 1969–1982; *Interests and Recreations:* cinema, swimming, cycling; *Languages:* Arabic, English, French, Italian; *Address:* 13 Al-Boustan Street, Cairo, Egypt; telephone: 740116.

DARWISH, Samir A., Syrian businessman; born 1937, Damascus, Syria; married; one daughter, one son; *Religion:* Christian; *Education:* Law and Political Sciences, Universities of Damascus, Syria, and of St. Joseph University, Beirut, Lebanon; *Career:* writer and later editor, Bureau des Documentations Syriennes et Arabes, (BDSA), 1955–62; Director and Manager, Bureau des Documentations Syriennes et Arabes, 1962–64; Founder of the OFA Centre de Documentation, 1964, incorporating the BDSA, 1965; Director General, Office Arabe de Presse et de Documentation, and of OFA Renseignements Commerciaux (Commercial Information); President, OFA Business Consulting Centre; Associate of MECICO, France, and of MEFIS, England and Switzerland (international consultation firms) and of others; member of the Association of Arab Economists, of the Chamber of Commerce, and of several Syrian-foreign chambers of commerce; member of several other associations and federations; *Languages:* Arabic, French, English, Italian; *Address:* P O Box 451 Damascus, Syria.

DARWISH, Yahia Hassan, Egyptian UN official; born 26 June 1914, Port Said, Egypt; married; *Education:* BA, Institute of Education, Cairo, Egypt; Diploma from the Cairo School of Social Work; BA, Teachers College, American University in Cairo; MSc, Columbia University School of Social Work, New York; *Career:* Ministry of Education, Egypt, inspector and teacher; subsequently Director, Director General; Assistant Under Secretary of State; Senior Under Secretary of State, Ministry of Social Affairs; Director, East Asia and Pakistan Region, UNICEF, Bangkok, Thailand, 1972; *Publications: Social Work, its History and Philosophy,* 1947; *Social Policy,* 1965; *Social Welfare in a Socialist Community,* 1969; *Decorations:* Order of the Republic, Egypt; *Interests and Recreations:* fishing, camping; member of the Maadi Sporting Club, the Heliopolis Sports Club, the Red Crescent Association; social work, social sciences, education, psychology; member of the Egyptian Association for Social Studies; *Languages:* Arabic, English, French; *Address:* Office — UNICEF, P O Box 2154, Bangkok, Thailand; telephone: 823131; Residence -- 19 Pra Atit Road, Bangkok, Thailand.

DAU, Khalifa Ali, Libyan academic/accountant; born 12 December 1945; married; three sons, one daughter; *Religion:* Muslim; *Education:* BSc, MAS, CMA, PhD in Acounting; *Career:* Associate Dean and Head of the Business and Economics Research Centre, Faculty of Economics, Garyounis University, 1976–78; Dean, Faculty of Economics, Garyounis University, and member of the Board of Directors, Central Bank of Libya, 1978–79; Assistant Professor of Accounting and Chairman of the Accounting Department, 1979–80; *Interests and Recreations:* football, tennis; *Languages:* Arabic, English; *Address:* Faculty of Economics, Garyounis University Benghazi, Libya; telephone: 26060.

DAW, Hussain Talaat, Egyptian UN official; born 3 July 1922, Cairo, Egypt; married; *Education:* MB, ChB, Cairo Medical School, 1940–46; DB, Cairo Medical School, 1951–53; Harwell Isotope School, 1953; training in Radiation Biology and Health Physics, University of Rochester, New York, USA, 1955–56; *Career:* Deputy Director, Central Army Laboratory, 1953–59; staff member, Cairo Radioisotope Centre, 1953–59; 1st Medical Officer, International Atomic Energy Agency (IAEA), 1959–67; Director, Egyptian Atomic Energy Establishment, 1969–71; Senior Medical Officer, Radiological, Health and Safety Office, IAEA, Vienna, Austria, 1967; *Interests and Recreations:*

swimming, chess, health physics; *Languages:* Arabic, English, Italian, French; *Address:* Office — Radiological, Health and Safety Office, International Atomic Energy Agency, Kaerntnerring 11, A-1010, Vienna 1, Austria; telephone: (0222) 524511; Residence -- Haizingerstrasse 46-1180, A-1011, Vienna, Austria; telephone: (0222) 311 8103.

DAWALIBI, Maruf, Syrian lawyer/ politician; born 1907; *Religion:* Muslim; *Education:* in Aleppo, Damascus and University of Paris, France; *Career:* Lawyer in Court of Appeal, Aleppo, 1935–39; Professor, Faculty of Law, Damascus, 1947; Minister of National Economy, 1949–50; President, Chamber of Deputies, 1951; Prime Minister, and Minister of Defence, 1951; Minister of National Defence, 1954; Prime Minister, 1961–62; member of Executive Council of World Muslim Congress, 1965; living in Saudi Arabia since 1966; returned to Syria for elections to People's Council, 1977; *Publications: La Jurisprudence dans le Droit Islamique,* 1941; *Introduction au Droit Romain,* 1947; *Introduction à la science des sources du Droit Romain,* 1949; *Précis du Droit Romain,* 1961; *Histoire Générale du Droit,* 1961; *Languages:* Arabic, French; *Address:* People's Council, Damascus, Syria.

DAWANI, Abdul Hussain Khalil, Bahraini businessman; born 20 June, 1937, Bahrain; married; two daughters; *Religion:* Muslim; *Education:* Diploma in Commercial Studies, Polytechnic of Central London; *Career:* man ager of family real estate business, 1957–65; Director of Al-Jazira Cold Storage Company; founder of a marine operations company; Director, Khalil Haji Murtatha Dawani and Sons; Chairman, Coastal Marine; *Interests and Recreations:* reading, fishing, swimming, riding; member of Rotary Club, Manama, Bahrain; *Languages:* Arabic, English; *Address:* P O Box 26087, Manama, Bahrain; telephone: Office — 712978.

DE GARANG, Enok Mading, Sudanese politician; born 1 January 1934, Upper Nile Province, Sudan; married; four children; *Education:* printing course, Manchester College of Science and Technology, 1961–63; Journalism, Africa Literature Centre, Zambia, 1965–69; *Career:* Malakal Printing Press, 1959; Manager of the Spearhead Press; Editor of *Light Magazine* and published *The Voice of Southern Sudan;* teacher, African Literature Centre, Zambia; co-founder, Southern Sudan Association, London; Director and Editor of *The Grass Curtain,* London, 1970–72; External Spokesman, South Sudan Liberation Movement, 1970–72; took part in Addis Ababa negotiations on Southern Sudan, 1972; Regional Minister for Information and official spokesman of the Transitional Higher Executive Council, 1972–73; Regional Minister for Co-operatives and Rural Development, 1973–75; elected member of the Regional Assembly for the Bor District, 1973; Regional Minister of Information, Culture, Youth and Sports, 1976; member of Central Committee of Sudanese Socialist Union; *Decorations:* Medal of Two Niles for Peace, 1st Class; *Address:* Bor District, Upper Nile Province, Sudan.

DeBAKEY, Michael E., Arab-American physician/surgeon; born 7 September 1908, Louisiana, USA; married; four sons, one daughter; *Religion:* Christian; *Education:* BSc, MD, MS, Tulane University, New Orleans, Louisiana, USA; *Career:* Assistant Professor of Surgery, Tulane University, 1940–46; Associate Professor of Surgery, Tulane University, 1946–48; Chairman, Department of Surgery, Baylor College of Medicine, Houston, Texas, USA, 1948–; Director, Cardiovascular Research and Training Centre, Baylor College of Medicine, 1964–75; Director of National Heart and Blood Vessel Research and Demonstration Centre, Baylor College of Medicine, 1975–; Vice President for Medical Affairs and Chief Executive Officer, Baylor College of Medicine, 1968–69; President, Baylor College of Medicine, 1969–79; Chancellor, Baylor College of Medicine, 1979–; member of and adviser to numerous medical associations, societies and institutes; *Publications: A Surgeon's Diary of a Visit to China,* Phoenix, Arizona, Phoenix Newspapers, Incorporated, 1974; co-author *The Living Heart,* New York, David McKay Company, 1977; author and co-author of other books on medicine and articles and papers; *Decorations:* several orders, awards and honorary degrees; *Languages:* Arabic, English, French, German; *Address:* Baylor College of Medicine, 1200 Moursound Avenue, Houston, Texas 77030, USA; telephone: (713) 797 9353.

DEEB, Boutros, Lebanese academic/ diplomat; born 1922, Banias, Syria; *Religion:* Christian; *Education:* Licence and Doctorate in Law; degree in history; *Career:* Professor in History, St. Joseph University, Beirut, Lebanon; Professor, Comparative History of the Institutions of the Middle Ages and the History of the Institutions of Muslim Public Law, Faculty of the Lebanese University, Beirut, Lebanon; Director General, Ministry of Information, 1959–65; Dean of the Faculty of Law, Lebanese University, 1964–65; Head of the Permanent Lebanese Delegation to UNESCO with rank of Ambassador, 1966–68; Director General of the Presidency of the Republic, 1969–75; Ambassador to the Vatican, 1975–77; President of the Lebanese University, 1977–79; Ambassador, Lebanese Embassy, Paris, France, 1979–82; *Decorations:* Knight of the National Order of the Cedar, Lebanon, various other decorations; *Languages:* Arabic, French, English; *Address:* c/o Ministry of Foreign Affairs, Beirut, Lebanon; telephone: 386817, 386818.

DEEB, Edward, Arab-American academic/dentist; born 28 May 1927, Lebanon; married; five daughters, one son; *Religion:* Christian; *Education:* AA, BA, University of California, Los Angeles, USA, 1951; DDS, University of Southern California, USA, 1955; *Career:* private practice in periodentistry, 1955; Instructor, University of Southern California, Dental School; Los Angeles County General Hospital, University of Southern California Medical Centre, 1956–69; Chairman, Perio-Endodontic Department, 1960–69; Assistant Chairman of Dental Attending Staff, 1966–67; Chairman of Dental Attending Staff, 1968–69; Dental Research Projects, 1956–69; Fellow of the American College of Dentists, 1977; former President, Southern California Academy of Oral Pathology; former President, Southern California Academy of Endodontics; former President, Western Study of Combined Therapy; member of the Mayor's Advisory Committee, the District Attorney's Advisory Committee, the Republican State Central Committee, Los Angeles County Olympic Committee; Expert Examiner, State of California; member of the Advisory Commission on Health and Accident Insurance, State of California; *Publications:* various articles in dental journals; *Interests and Recreations:* boating, tennis, golf; member of World Affairs Council; member of Opera Associates; member of Los Angeles County Museum Association; *Languages:* English, Arabic, Spanish, French; *Address:* 10700 Burbank Boulevard, North Hollywood, California 91601, USA; telephone: (213) 766 6126, (714) 675 1820.

DEEB, Marius, Lebanese academic; resident in USA; born 15 December 1941, Jaffa, Palestine; married; one daughter; *Religion:* Christian; *Education:* BA,MA, in Political Science, American University of Beirut, Lebanon; DPhil in Politics, Middle Eastern Studies, Oxford University, UK; *Career:* Lecturer in Politics, Lebanese University, Beirut, Lebanon, 1972–73; Curriculum Consultant, Indiana, USA, 1973–74; Visiting Assistant Professor in Political Science, Indiana University, USA, 1974–; *Interests and Recreations:* travel, classical music, bridge, swimming; *Languages:* Arabic, English, French; *Address:* Department of Political Science, Indiana University, Bloomington, Indiana 47401, USA; telephone: (812) 337 7985.

DEEB, Walid Muhammad, Jordanian academic; born 17 January 1946, Haifa; married; one daughter; *Education:* BSc in Mathematics, Jordan University, 1970; PhD, State University of New York, Albany, USA, 1974; *Career:* Assistant Professor, 1974–79, Associate Professor, Faculty of Science, University of Jordan, 1979–; *Publications:* numerous publications in mathematics; *Interests and Recreations:* squash, football; *Languages:* Arabic, English; *Address:* Department of Mathematics, University of Jordan, Amman, Jordan; telephone: Office — 843555; Residence — 843179.

DEIF, Nazih Ahmad, Egyptian economist/IMF official; born 4 March 1923; *Religion:* Muslim; *Education:* BCom, MA, PhD, Cairo University, Egypt and University of Chicago, USA; *Career:* Economic Expert with Arthur D. Little Group on Industrialization of Egypt, 1953; Director of Economic Statistics, Ministry of Finance, 1954; Senior Research Officer, National Planning Committee, 1957; Director General, National Planning Committee, 1958; Under Secretary of Planning, 1961–64; Governor, IMF Egypt, 1964–66; Minister of Finance, 1964–68; Professor, Institute of Statistical Studies and Research, Cairo University, 1969–70; Executive Director for the Middle East, IMF, 1970; UN Consultant, Family Planning, Population Board, 1978–79; Managing Director, Al-Watany Bank of Egypt, 1979–81; Chairman, Muhandis Information Co, 1981; Adviser to the Ministry of Popular Development, 1981–; *Publications:* papers on national planning issues and various UN publications; *Languages:* Arabic, English; *Address:* Residence – 95 Marghani Street, Heliopolis, Cairo, Egypt.

DENG, Francis Mading, Sudanese diplomat/ academic; born 1938; married; three sons; *Religion:* Christian; *Education:* LLB, University of Khartoum, Sudan; LLM, Yale University, USA; Doctor of Juristic Science, Yale University; postgraduate research, Kings College, London University, UK; *Career:* United Nations Human Rights Officer, 1967–72; Adjunct Professor of Legal Anthropology, New York University, 1969–70; Lecturer in Law, Columbia University, USA, 1971–72; Research Fellow in Law and Modernization, Yale University, 1971–72; Ambassador to Scandinavia, 1972–74; Ambassador to USA, 1972–74; Minister of State for Foreign Affairs, 1976; has promoted development of the borders of the Northern Sudan area as model for North-South integration; member of law, anthropology and cultural associations; *Publications: Tradition and Modernization,* 1971, Yale (received Herskovitz Award); *The Dinka of the Sudan,* 1972, New York; *The Dinka and their Songs,* 1973, Oxford; *Dinka Folk Tales,* 1974; *Dynamics of Idntification,* 1974, Khartoum; *Africans of Two Worlds,* 1978; *Decorations:* Two Presidential Awards for Scientific and Literary Works; *Interests and Recreations:* collecting and translating oral literature; writing, open air recreation; *Languages:* Arabic, English, Dinka; *Address:* Ministry of Foreign Affairs, Khartoum, Sudan; telephone: 73688.

DERBAS, Adnan Muhammad, Palestinian engineer/businessman; resident in United Arab Emirates; born 5 January 1938; married; two sons, one daughter; *Religion:* Muslim; *Education: BA,* Civil Engineering, American University of Beirut, 1960; *Career:* Consulting Engineer, Lebanon and Saudi Arabia, 1960–66; established his own construction company, *Arabconsult,* Abu Dhabi, 1967–; *Interests and Recreations:* poetry, philosophy, swimming; *Languages:* Arabic, English; *Address:* P O Box 238, Abu Dhabi, United Arab Emirates; telephone: 322668; telex: 22558 CONRAB EM.

DERHALLY, Abdul Hamid Sa'id, Saudi Arabian official/economist; born 1929, Jaffa, Palestine; married; two daughters, one son; *Education:* High Diploma in Commerce, St. Marks College, Lebanon; High Diploma in Economics and Planning, University of Grenoble, France; *Career:* Interpreter at the Royal Palace, Riyadh, Saudi Arabia, 1952–54; Chief of Translation and Press Bureau at the Presidency of Council of Ministers, 1954–62; Director General, Public Relations Department, Ministry of Petroleum and Mineral Resources, 1962–69; Director General, Ministry of Planning for the Western Region Branch, Jeddah, 1969–; member of the first OPEC Conference, Riyadh, 1959; attended the International Economic Seminars at the University of Grenoble, France, 1968, University of Turin, Italy, 1974, Harvard University, USA, 1975; participated in preparing the Annual Economic Report, the First and Second Five Year Development Plan, the South West Regional Plan, and others; participated in the 8th and 9th Islamic Conferences of Foreign Ministers, 1977, 1978; member of the Pilgrimage High Committee; member of the Islamic Commission for Economic, Cultural and Social Welfare Affairs of the Organization of the Islamic Conference; *Publications: The Role of Petroleum in the Development of Saudi Arabia,* 1968, University of Grenoble, France, (a paper in French); *Saudi Arabia..the Middle East's New Power,* 1975, Harvard University, USA, (a paper in English); *Decorations:* Order of Diplomatic Service Merit, Syngrye Medal, Republic of Korea, 1977; Order of Brilliant Star with Grand Cordon, 1977; Officier de l'Ordre Nationale du Mérite, Republic of France, 1977; *Interests and Recreations:* tennis, swimming, farming, reading, music, travel; *Languages:* Arabic, English, French, Italian; *Address:* P O Box 1221 Jeddah, Saudi Arabia; telephone: Office — Jeddah 51366, 52462; Residence — Jeddah 29189.

DHAHRY, Ali Bin Khalfan al-, United Arab Emirates official/businessman; born 1942, Abu Dhabi; married; two daughters, three sons; *Religion:* Muslim; *Education:* general; *Career:* member of the Municipal Council, Abu Dhabi; Director, Abu Dhabi Office, Cairo, Egypt; Under Secretary for Housing and Purchase, Ministry of Finance; member of the Executive Council, Emirate of Abu Dhabi; Chairman of Civil Aviation; Chairman of Board of Abu Dhabi Helicopters; member of the Board of Directors of Gulf Air; Chairman of Gulf Aircraft Maintenance Co; Vice Chairman and Managing Director, Emirates Commercial Bank Ltd; Chairman, National Staff Food Company Ltd; *Decorations:* Order of the Egyptian Republic, 3rd Class; decorations from Tunisia and Morocco; *Interests and Recreations:* hunting, sailing, water skiing, farming; *Languages:* Arabic, English, Urdu; *Address:* P O Box 915 Abu Dhabi, United Arab Emirates; telephone: 325500, 344644.

DHARIF, Ahmad Jumaa al-, United Arab Emirates businessman/official; born 1942; married; four sons, one daughter; *Religion:* Muslim; *Education:* general; *Career:* Department of Housing, 1968–71; Inspector of Industrial Section, Ministry of Oil, 1971–72; Director, National Drilling Company, 1973–; *Interests and Recreations:* hunting, swimming; member of Tourism Club, technical publications on drilling; *Languages:* Arabic, English; *Address:* National Drilling Company, P O Box 4017, Abu Dhabi, United Arab Emirates; telephone: 343363; telex: 22553 Nadril EM.

DIA, Amir, Arab-American academic/physician; born December 1929, Cairo, Egypt; married; one son, one daughter; *Religion:* Muslim; *Education:* MB, BCh, Cairo Medical School, Egypt; Internship at Demardash Hospital, Abbasia, Egypt; *Career:* Instructor in Obstetrics and Gynaecology, University of California, Los Angeles (UCLA), USA, 1970; Assistant Professor of Obstetrics and Gynaecology, UCLA, 1975; Fellow of the American College of Surgeons, 1971; Fellow of the American College of Obstetricians and Gynaecologists; Fellow of the American Fertility Society; *Publications: Family Planning,* 1974; *Laparoscopic Tubal Sterilization,* 1974; *Decorations:* American Medical Association of Physicians Recognition Award, 1974; *Interests and Recreations:* skiing, tennis, fishing, travelling; President of the Egyptian Scholars Association; member of Planned Parenthood Organization; *Languages:* Arabic, English, French, Spanish; *Address:* 2800 Via Campesina, Palos Verdes Estates, California, USA; telephone: 378 5388.

DIB, Muhammad Khalil al-, Egyptian administrator; born 23 September 1919, Belbis, Egypt; married; two sons, two daughters; *Religion:* Muslim; *Education:* BSc in Military Science; *Career:* Head of the Egyptian Delegation to the International Military Sports Council, 1960–70; Secretary, later Deputy President of the Squash Union, 1962; member of the Executive Committee of the International Military Sports Union, elected twice 1964 and 1970; member of the Egyptian Olympic Committee, 1968; Secretary General, Egyptian Football Union; Secretary General, Armed Forces Sports Union; General Manager, Egyptian Football Union; *Decorations:* Sports Decoration, 1st Class; *Interests and Recreations:* squash, Swedish exercises; *Languages:* Arabic, English, French; *Address:* 3 Al Tahawi Street, Manshiyat al-Bakri, Cairo, Egypt; telephone: 962544.

DIMECHKIE, Nadim, Lebanese diplomat; born 5 December 1919, Beirut, Lebanon; married; two sons; *Religion:* Muslim; *Education:* BA, 1940; MA in Economics, American University of Beirut, Lebanon, 1951; *Career:* Teacher, Basra, Iraq, 1940–41; Managing Director, Agricultural Industries Organisation; Director General, Ministry of National Economy, 1943–44; Counsellor, Embassy of Lebanon, London, UK, 1944–49; Consul General in Ottawa, Canada, 1949–50; Director, Economic Affairs Department, Ministry of Foreign Affairs, 1951; Minister Plenipotentiary, and Chargé d'Affaires, Embassy to Egypt, 1952–55; Minister Plenipotentiary, and Chargé d'Affaires, Embassy to Switzerland, 1955–57; Ambassador to USA, 1958–62; Director, Economic Affairs Department, Ministry of Foreign Affairs, 1962–66; Ambassador to the Court of St. James, London, UK, 1966; has participated in various international conferences and organizations; Lebanese delegate to the UN, 1946, 1950, 1957–74; President of the XVIII Session of the Arab League Council, Cairo, Egypt, 1954; Lebanese delegate to the International Conference for Commerce and Development, Geneva, Switzerland, 1964; participated in the International Conference for Commerce and Labour, London, UK, 1947; participated in the Preparatory Conference of UNESCO, London, 1948, and in the International Conference for Wheat, Paris, 1948, in the International Conference for Aviation, Montreal, Canada, 1950; *Decorations:* Commander, National Order of the Cedar, Lebanon, as well as many other distinctions and decorations from Egypt, Syria, China, Tunisia, Greece; *Interests and Recreations:* swimming, tennis; *Languages:* Arabic, French, English; *Address:* Ministry of Foreign Affairs, Beirut, Lebanon.

DIREIJ, Ahmad Ibrahim, Sudanese politician; born 1933, Darfur Province, Sudan; married; *Religion:* Muslim; *Education:* University of Khartoum, and University of Leicester, UK; *Career:* Ministry of Commerce; Department of Statistics; worked in France, Sweden and Italy before returning to the Department of Statistics; contested 1965 general election as Chairman of the Darfur Front; member of the Umma Party; Minister of Co-operation and Labour, 1966–67; re-elected in 1968 elections and became Leader of the Opposition; Adviser to the Ruler of Umm al-Qawain, United Arab Emirates, 1970; *Languages:* English, German, French, Italian; *Address:* The National People's Assembly, Khartoum, Sudan.

DJAZZAR, Sabih K, Syrian physician/WHO official; born 1923, Damascus, Syria; *Education:* Diploma, Syrian University, 1942–43; MD, Faculty of Medicine, Syrian University, 1943–50; MPH, School of Public Health, Columbia University, New York, 1951–52; MSc in Hospital Administration, Northwestern University, Chicago, 1953–54; Resident in Hospital Administration, University Hospital, University of Michigan, Ann Arbor, 1954–55; WHO Senior Staff Training Course, Geneva, 1969; WHO Training Course on Family Planning, Egypt, India, Korea, 1970; *Career:* Associate Professor of Anaesthesiology, Faculty of Medicine, Syrian University, 1952–53; Director, Damascus General Hospital, Ministry of Health, Syria 1955–56; Director General of Health Department for Civil Defence, Syria, 1956–58; Director General, Public Health Assistance and Hospitals, Ministry of Health, Damascus, Syria, 1958–63; WHO Consultant for Medical Care and Health Planning, Saudi Arabia, 1962–63; Founder, Teacher, Headmaster, Najah Girls School, 1946–65; WHO Staff Member, Adviser and Team Leader of Development of Health Services Project, Congo-Brazzaville, 1965–69; Head of WHO Mission to Togo and Dahomey, Benin; Representative Lecturer, WHO Regional Training Centre of Health Person-

nel, 1969–75; Professor of Public Health and Hospital Administration, School of Medical Assistance, Lóme, Togo, 1973–75; WHO Representative, Ghana, Ivory Coast, Upper Volta, Niger, Mali, Mauritania, Gambia, Nigeria, Gabon, Central African Republic, Chad, 1969–75; Head of WHO Mission to the Central African Republic and Chad; WHO Programme Coordinator, 1975–80; Professor of Public Health, Maternal and Child Health, and Hospital Administration, Faculté des Sciences de la Santé de Bangui, 1975–80; Special Mission on behalf of WHO with the Islamic Development Bank to Southern Sudan 1979, to Somalia 1980; External Relations Officer, Cooperative Programme for Development, WHO, Geneva 1980–; Chairman of Health Planning Committee; Committee for the Evaluation and Equivalence of Foreign Medical Diplomas; member of the Planning Committee for the Creation of the Faculté des Sciences de la Santé de Bangui 1975–80; Coordination Programme Development Unit at WHO/HQ, Geneva, 1978–80; represented WHO at different international meetings and seminars, 1969–80; Acting Officer in Charge of the Emergency Relief Operations, WHO/HQ, 1979–80; member of Syrian Association of Paediatricians, Public Health Association, Alpha Delta Mu, Northwestern University Alumni, Columbia University Alumni; *Publications:* books, articles and papers; *Decorations:* Officier du l'Ordre du Mono, Republique du Togo, 1975; Men of Achievement Award, International Biographic Centre, Cambridge, UK 1978; *Languages:* Arabic, English, French, Spanish, German; *Address:* WHO, Avenue Appia, 1211 Geneva 27, Switzerland; telephone: 346061.

DJEDIDI, Captain Bishir, Tunisian naval officer; born 1934; married; one child; *Religion:* Muslim; *Education:* graduated from French Naval Academy as 2nd lieutenant 1959; *Career:* attended French Naval War College, 1965–67, US Naval War College, 1971–72; Chief-of-Staff of the Tunisian Navy, 1964–; *Languages:* Arabic, French; *Address:* Ministry of Defence, Tunis, Tunisia.

DOSS, Leila H., Egyptian UN official; born 17 June 1921, Assiut, Egypt; *Religion:* Christian; *Education:* BA, American University in Cairo, Egypt, 1941–43; *Career:* Programme Assistant, Egyptian State Broadcasting, 1943–44; Head, Spoken Word and Classical Music Department, Egyptian State Broadcasting, 1944–45; Lecturer, English Literature and Creative Writing, American University in Cairo, 1944–46; Editor, Radio Monitoring Service, Ministry of Information, Cairo, 1946; Economic Commission for Asia and Far East, UN (ECAFE) Information Service; Acting Director, UN Information Centre (UNIC), Cairo and Rangoon; Burma Radio Officer, later Press Officer, Office of Public Information (OPI), UN, Rangoon, Cairo, Bangkok, Geneva, New York; Chief, Public Information Service, UN Industrial Development Organization (UNIDO), Vienna, Austria, 1967–; *Publications:* poems published in various magazines; *Interests and Recreations:* literature, music, handiwork, travel, cooking, journalism, broadcasting, mass communication for development; member of the International Association of Women in Radio and Television; *Languages:* Arabic, English, French; *Address:* Public Information Service, UNIDO, P O Box 707, A–1011, Vienna I, Austria; telephone: (0222) 43500.

DOUAIHY, Father Semaan, Lebanese ecclesiastic; born 1921, Zghorta, Lebanon; *Education:* Congregation of the Antonins Fathers; philosophical and theological studies, St. Joseph University, Beirut, Lebanon; *Career:* joined the Order of the Antonins Fathers; Director, St. Sarkis College, Zghorta 1953–57; Director of the monthly magazine *Al-Midan;* member of the Economic Committee of the Antonins Order, 1953–57; elected Deputy for Zghorta, 1964 and 1968; *Interests and Recreations:* reading, manual work, agriculture; *Languages:* Arabic, French; *Address:* Office — Chamber of Deputies, Place de l'Etoile, Beirut, Lebanon; Residence — Zghorta, Tripoli, Lebanon.

DOUIRI, Muhammad, Moroccan politician/engineer; born 1926, Morocco; married; two sons, one daughter; *Religion:* Muslim; *Education:* Ecole Polytechnique, Ecole Nationale Supérieure des Mines de Paris, 1945–52; *Career:* active in Istiqlal Party from early age; Leader of Istiqlal Student Group in France; member and later Head of Provisional Committee of Istiqlal Party, 1952–54; member of Istiqlal Commission, 1956–59; elected member of Istiqlal Executive Committee 1960, and re-elected since then; Minister of Public Works, 1955–58; Minister of

National Economy and Finance, 1960–62; Director of Al-Risala Press, publishing *Al Alam* in Arabic, and *L'Opinion* in French, as well as other periodicals; played a prominent role in trade union affairs; elected member of Fes Town Council, 1976; elected member of Parliament, 1977; Minister of Equipment and National Promotion, 1977; Minister of Planning, Executive Development and Vocational Training, 1981–; *Languages:* Arabic, French; *Address:* Ministry of Planning, Rabat, Morocco.

DOUMIT, Michel, Lebanese politician/businessman; born 1925, Dubayya, Lebanon; *Religion:* Christian; *Education:* St. Joseph University, Beirut; *Career:* businessman; Minister of Planning, and of Labour and Social Affairs, 1976–77; Minister of Agriculture, Industry and Oil, 1977; *Address:* Ministry of Agriculture, Beirut, Lebanon.

DOURI, Izzat Ibrahim al-, Iraqi politician; born 1932, Samarra, Iraq; *Religion:* Muslim; *Career:* teacher; member of the Baghdad Committee of the Regional Leadership of the Arab Baath Socialist Party, 1968; member of the Baath Regional Leadership; member of the Revolutionary Command Council, 1969; Chairman of the Revolutionary Command Council, Public Affairs Bureau; leading advocate of agrarian reforms drive, 1969; Minister of Agrarian Reforms, 1969; member of the Arab Baath Socialist Party, Regional Leadership, 1974; Minister of the Interior, 1974; member of the Follow-up Committee on Oil Affairs and the Implementation of Agreements; Chairman of the Supreme Agricultural Council, 1974; Vice President, Revolutionary Command Council; *Address:* c/o The Revolutionary Command Council, Baghdad, Iraq.

DRISS, Guiga M., Tunisian diplomat/politician; born 21 August 1924, Tunisia; married; four children; *Religion:* Muslim; *Education:* university education in Paris and Algiers; Licence in Law, Agrégé in History and Geography; *Career:* called to the Bar, and practised Law, 1948–52; Head of the Office of the Minister of Public Health, 1952; Director of Regional and Commercial Administration; Director of National Security, 1952–63; Commissioner General of Tourism, 1963–69; Secretary of State for Public Health and Social Affairs, 1969; Minister of Public Health, 1969; Minister of National

Education, 1973–76; Ambassador to West Germany, 1976; *Decorations:* Commander of the Order of Tunisian Independence; Grand Cordon of the Order of the Tunisian Republic; *Languages:* Arabic, French; *Address:* Ministry of Foreign Affairs, Boulevard Farhat Hached, Tunis, Tunisia.

DRISS QEYTONI, Bennacer, Moroccan engineer; born 10 October 1934, Fes, Morocco; married; three children; *Education:* BSc in Mathematics, Faculty of Sciences, Rabat; BSc in Engineering, Ecole Nationale Supérieure des Telecommunications de Paris, France; *Career:* joined Radiodiffision Television Marocaine, 1962, Assistant Head of Technical Services, 1963, Head of Technical Services, 1964, Chief Engineer, 1972, Technical Director, 1974; Director General, Radiodiffision Television Marocaine, 1978; *Decorations:* Officier de l'Ordre du Trône, Morocco, 1964; *Address:* 14 Lotissement Saada, Aviation, Rabat, Morocco.

DRISS, Rashid, Tunisian diplomat/politician; born 27 January 1917, Tunis, Tunisia; married; *Religion:* Muslim; *Education:* Centre of Economic Studies, Tunis; *Career:* Representative of Neo-Destour Party in Egypt, Spain, India, Indonesia, Pakistan; Head, Tunisian Section, North African Liberation Committee, Cairo, 1946–52; returned to Tunisia, 1955; Director, Neo-Destour Party daily *Al-Amal;* Chief, African-Asian Division, Ministry of Foreign Affairs, Deputy in Constituent Assembly, 1956–57; Secretary of State for Posts, Telegraphs and Telephones, 1957–64; Member of National Assembly and Political Bureau of Neo-Destour Party, 1959; member of Central Committee of Destour Socialist Party, 1964; member of Tunisian Delegation to UN General Assembly, New York, 1965–74; member of Political Bureau of the Destour Party, and Council of Republic, 1969; member of National Assembly, 1969; Ambassador to USA, and Mexico, 1964–70; Permanent Representative to UN, 1970; President, UN Economic and Social Council (ECOSOC), 1971; *Decorations:* Grand Cordon of the Order of the Tunisian Republic, and various foreign decorations; *Interests and Recreations:* journalism, international affairs; author of many newspaper articles; *Languages:* Arabic, French, English; *Address:* c/o Ministry of Foreign Affairs, Boulevard Farhat Hached, Tunis, Tunisia.

DRISSI QEYTONI, Muhammad, Moroccan official; born 22 December 1929, Fes, Morocco; married; two sons, two daughters; *Religion:* Muslim; *Education:* Diploma, Moroccan School of Administration, 1951; *Career:* Vice President of the General Economic Confederation; President of the Federation of Industry; President of the Moroccan Association of Textile Industry; member of Parliament, President of the Economic Commision; President Delegate, STE COFITEX; Director General, STE TISBROD; *Decorations:* Chevalier de l'Ordre du Trône, Morocco, 1974; *Interests and Recreations:* member of the Rotary Club; active member of various social organizations and societies; *Languages:* Arabic, French; *Address:* 45 rue de Toulouse -CIL-, Casablanca, Morocco.

DROOBY, Ala'uddin, Syrian physician/psychiatrist; resident in Australia; born 3 December 1925, Homs, Syria; married; two sons, one daughter; *Religion:* Muslim: *Education:* BA, American University of Beirut, Lebanon, 1947; MD, University of Lausanne, Switzerland, 1952; Diploma of Psychological Medicine, London, UK, 1957; *Career:* Senior Consultant Psychiatrist, The Lebanon Hospital for Mental and Nervous Disorders, Beirut, 1957–62; Lecturer in Psychiatry, School of Medicine, American University of Beirut, 1960–72; President of the Lebanese Society of Neurology and Psychiatry; Senior Lecturer, Department of Psychiatry, Medical School, University of Western Australia; Consultant Psychiatrist, Royal Perth Hospital and Perth Medical Centre, Perth, Western Australia; member of the Royal College of Psychiatrists, UK, 1973; member of Australian and New Zealand College of Psychiatrists, Australia, 1974; member of the Lebanese Association of Physicians; former member of Editorial Board of Lebanese Medical Journal; *Publications:* various articles on psychiatry in professional journals, in English; *Interests and Recreations:* music, travelling, walking; *Languages:* Arabic, French, Turkish, English; *Address:* Residence — 53 Bruce Street, Nedlands, Perth, Western Australia (6009); telephone: 867 728; Office — Royal Perth Hospital, Perth, Western Australia; telephone: 250010, ext 2522.

DUAIJ, Ahmad Ali al-, Kuwaiti official/businessman; born 1938, Kuwait; married; two sons, two daughters; *Religion:* Muslim;

Education: in Kuwait; BA, College of North Staffordshire, UK; Oxford University, UK; *Career:* Ministry of Foreign Affairs, 1962; Secretary of Planning Board, 1962; Secretary General with rank of Permanent Under Secretary, 1964–75; Chairman and Managing Director, Kuwait Real Estate Investment Consortium, 1975–; Head of Government Scholarship Committee; member of the Mission of Kuwait at 2nd United Nations Conference for Trade and Development, (UNCTAD), Athens, 1964; *Interests and Recreations:* reading, squash, gardening, theatre; member of Graduates Association and Kuwait Economic Society; *Languages:* Arabic, English; *Address:* Kuwait Real Estate Investment Consortium KSC, P O Box 23411, Kuwait; telephone: 448260/9.

DUDIN, Marwan Akram, Jordanian politician/official; born 4 October 1936; married; three sons, two daughters; *Religion:* Muslim; *Education:* BA in English Language and Literature; Diploma in Teaching English as a Second Language; Diploma in Management-Broadcasting, UK; *Career:* Teacher of English, Teachers Training College, Jordan, 1958–63; Translation Specialist, Aramco, Saudi Arabia, 1963–64; Dean of Students, Petroleum College, Saudi Arabia, 1964–67; Director of Administration, ALIA Royal Jordanian Airlines, 1968–71; Director General, Hashemite Broadcasting Service, 1971–73; Minister of Information, 1973; Minister of State for Prime Ministerial Affairs, 1973–74; Director General, Jordan Cooperatives, 1974–78; Ambassador to Romania, 1978–80; Director General, Cities and Villages Bank, 1980; Minister of Information, 1980–; *Decorations:* Order of Independence, Jordan, 1972; Order of the Jordanian Star, 1974; *Interests and Recreations: poetry, short stories, literary criticism;* *Languages:* Arabic, English, French; *Address:* P O Box 9936 Amman, Jordan; telephone: Residence — 30489.

DURAIB, Saud Bin Saad al-, Saudi Arabian administrator/lawyer; born 1937; *Religion:* Muslim; *Education:* MA Islamic Jurisprudence; *Career:* Bureau Manager for Director General, Ministry of Justice; Bureau Manager for Under Secretary, Ministry of Justice; former member of Board for the Settlement of Commercial Disputes; member of Al-Dawa Islamic Press Organization, Riyadh, Saudi Arabia; attended the Sixth Anti-Narcotic Conference, Riyadh, Conference on the Function of the University; Legal Adviser, Ministry of Justice; *Publications: Al-Muamalatil Masrafiyyah Wa Mawaqif al-Shariatil Islamaia Minha; Al-Sharikat Fi Fiqhil Islami Wal Qanoun Al-Wadhie; Muhammad Bin Abdul Wahab, Hamil Rayatil Islam Fil Qarnil Thani Ashar;* various contributions to local press; lectures delivered at King Abdul Aziz University; *Address:* Bureau of the Minister of Justice, Riyadh, Saudi Arabia; telephone: Office -- 4351167.

DURDA, Abu Zaid Omar, Libyan politician; *Religion:* Muslim; *Career:* Governor of Misurata; Minister of Information and Culture, 1972–74; Under Secretary, Ministry of Foreign Affairs, 1974–76; Minister of Municipalities, 1976–; played leading role in General People's Congress, 1976, together with President Muammar Qadhafi, and Major Abdul Salam Jallud; Secretary for Municipalities in General People's Committee, 1977; *Languages:* Arabic, English; *Address:* Office of the Secretary for Municipalities, Tripoli, Libya; telephone: 41995; telex: 20122.

DURI, Abdul Aziz al-, Iraqi academic; resident in Jordan; born November 1919, Baghdad, Iraq; married; two sons, two daughters; *Religion:* Muslim; *Education:* BA, London University, UK, 1940; PhD, London University, 1942; PhD, Martin Luther University, Halle-Wittenburg, East Germany; *Career:* Lecturer, Professor, Higher Teachers Training College, Baghdad, 1943–48; Director of Publications and Translations, Ministry of Education, 1948–49; Dean, College of Arts and Science, Baghdad, 1949–58; Visiting Professor, School of Oriental and African Studies, London University, UK, 1955–56; Visiting Professor, American University of Beirut (AUB), 1959–60; Professor, College of Arts, Baghdad, 1961–63; President, Baghdad University, 1963–68; Visiting Professor, AUB, 1969; Visiting Professor, Jordan University, Amman, 1969–; *Publications:* in Arabic *The First Abbasid Period,* 1945; *Studies on Later Abbasid Periods,* 1945; *Islamic Institutions,* 1950; *Introduction to the History of Early Islam,* 2nd edition, Beirut 1960, *A Study on the Beginnings of Arab Histography,* Beirut, 1960; *The Historical Origins of Arab Nationalism,* Beirut, 1960; *The Shu'ubiya,* Beirut 1962; *Introduction to Arab Economic History,* Beirut 1969;

Studies on the Economic History of Iraq in the 10th Century AD, 1974; *Arabische Wirtschaftsgeschichte,* Switzerland 1979; *Die Bibliothek des Morgenlandes,* Artemis Verlag, a translation to German; *Decorations:* The Distinguished Order of Education, Jordan; *Interests and Recreations:* member of the Iraq Academy; corresponding member of the Arab Academy, Cairo, Egypt; corresponding member of the Arab Academy, Damascus, Syria; honorary member of the Jordan Academy, Amman, Jordan; *Address:* History Department, Faculty of Arts, Jordan University, Amman, Jordan.

DUVAL, Cardinal Leon-Etienne, Algerian ecclesiastic; born 1903, France; *Religion:* Christian; *Education:* Petit Séminaire et Grand Séminaire Annecy Université Gregorienne, Rome, Italy; Doctorat en Theologie; *Career:* ordained priest 1926; Professor, Grand Séminaire, Annecy, 1930–42; Vicar General and Director of Works, Diocese of Annecy, 1942–46; Consecrated Bishop of Constantine and Hippo (Annabe), 1946; Archbishop of Algiers, 1954; Cardinal 1965; *Publications: Paroles De Paix,* 1955; *Messages de Paix,* 1962; *Laics, Prêtres, Religieux Dans l'Eglise selon Vatican 11,* 1967; *Decorations:* Officier de la Légion d'Honneur, France, 1952; *Languages:* French, Italian; *Address:* 13 Rue Khelifa Boukhalfa, Algiers, Algeria.

DUWAIDAR, Muhammad Lutfi, Egyptian academic/physician; born March 1916, Alexandria, Egypt; married; two children; *Religion:* Muslim; *Education:* Faculty of Medicine, Cairo University, Egypt, 1939; Brompton Hospital and London Chest Hospital, UK, 1948–49; *Career:* Thoracic Surgery Unit, Liverpool, UK; later in Oslo and Stockholm, 1949–50; Department of Surgery at Alexandria University, Egypt as a Lecturer, 1971, and Professor of Surgery; Dean of the Faculty of Medicine and later President of Alexandria University, 1971; *Languages:* Arabic, English, French; *Address:* University of Alexandria, Alexandria, Egypt.

E

EBAID, Soliman Muhammad, Saudi Arabian broadcasting official; born 1940; *Religion:* Muslim; *Education:* BA in Geography; *Career:* Radio Announcer, 1963–71; Director of Nida al-Islam (The Call of Islam), and the Holy Koran Radio, Jeddah, Saudi Arabia, 1972; Director of Programmes, Saudi Broadcasting Service, Jeddah; member of Saudi Arabian Delegation to the Conference of the Islamic States Broadcasting Services 1975; *Address:* Jeddah Broadcasting Service, P O Box 570, Jeddah, Saudi Arabia; telephone: 4038178; telex: 201030 SJ.

EDDE, Henri Camille, Lebanese engineer/architect; born 1923, Beirut, Lebanon; married; one son, two daughters; *Religion:* Christian; *Education:* University of St. Joseph, Beirut; Higher Engineering School, Beirut, Lebanon; *Career:* practising architect 1947–; responsible for many architectural and town planning works in Lebanon; former President of Lebanese Engineering Association; member of the Planning and Development Board; Secretary General of the International Union of Architects; Minister of Public Works and Transport, 1970; Minister of Education, 1972; Director at Dar Al-Handasah Consultants (Shair and Partners); *Interests and Recreations:* skiing, flying; *Languages:* Arabic, French, English; *Address:* Dar Al-Handasah Consultants, P O Box 7159, Beirut, Lebanon; telephone: 300256, 319130; telex: DARSAH 20697 LE.

EDDE, Michel, Lebanese lawyer/politician; born 16 February 1928, Beirut, Lebanon; married; five children; *Religion:* Christian; *Education:* St. Joseph University, Beirut, Lebanon, 1935–45; Licence in Law, French Faculty of Law 1948; *Career:* Barrister at Law; Director of Continental Development Bank SAL; Minister of Posts, Telegraphs and Telephones, 1966–68; Minister of Information, 1980–; *Decorations:* Légion d'Honneur, France, 1970; *Languages:* Arabic, French; *Address:* Office — Salamoun Building, Mexico Street, Beirut, Lebanon; telephone: 346957.

EDDE, Pierre, Lebanese politcian/businessman; born 1921, Beirut, Lebanon; President under French Mandate; married; two sons, one daughter; *Religion:* Christian; *Education:* Licence in Law, French Faculty of Law; *Career:* elected Deputy for Metn, 1951; re-elected Deputy for Baabda, 1953; Minister of Finance, 1953; elected Deputy for Beirut, 1957; Minister of Finance, 1958; defeated by Pierre Gemayel, 1960 elections; President and Director General of Beirut-Riyadh Bank; Director, Middle East Business Services and Research Corporation; Managing Director, Industrial and Commercial Company of Textiles; member of the Permanent Office for the Unity of Lebanese Throughout the World (ULM); President, Banking Association of Lebanon; Minister of Finance, 1968; has often represented Lebanon at UN General Assembly; *Languages:* Arabic, French, English; *Address:* Office — Beirut Riyadh Bank, Riad al-Solh Street, Beirut, Lebanon; Residence -- Jnah, Selim Abboud Building, Beirut, Lebanon.

EDDE, Raymond, Lebanese politician/lawyer; born 15 March 1913, Alexandria, Egypt; *Religion:* Christian; *Education:* Licence in Law, French Faculty of Law, St. Joseph University, Beirut, Lebanon; *Career:* Barrister at Law; Head of the National Bloc Political Party; Deputy for Jbeil, 1953; re-elected Deputy for Jbeil, 1957; Minister of the Interior, of Labour and Social Affairs; Minister of Posts, Telegraphs and Telephones, 1958–59; defeated in 1964 elections but re-elected Deputy for Jbeil, 1965 and 1968; Minister of Public Works, Hydroelectric Resources, Agriculture and Planning, 1968–69; candidate for Presidency, 1970; has drafted and initiated various laws on banking, rents, etc; *Decorations:* Medal, Egyptian Order of Merit 1st Class, 1959; *Interests and Recreations:* shooting, swimming; member of the Beirut Club, of the Aero-Club, and of the Cercle de l'Union Française; *Languages:* Arabic, French; *Address:* Office — Riad al-Solh Street, Beirut, Lebanon; Residence — Quartier des Arts et Métiers, Lyons Street, Beirut, Lebanon.

EFFAT, Ahmad M., Egyptian official/engineer; born 1920, Egypt; *Religion:* Muslim; *Education:* in Egypt; MSc in Naval Architecture and Marine Engineering, University of Michigan, USA, 1948; *Career:* marine engineer in Cleveland, Ohio shipyard, USA; technical surveyor, American Bureau of Shipping (ABS); employed by ABS in Japan, 1961–63; Technical Director of Alexandria Shipyards, Egypt, 1963–67; returned to ABS, 1967; returned to Egypt 1969; Minister of Maritime Transport, 1972–73; Egyptian Chairman, US-Egyptian Business Council, 1975–; *Address:* Ministry of Maritime Transport, Cairo, Egypt.

EID, Aida Martha, Lebanese UN official/economist; born 7 February, 1930, Jerusalem, Palestine; *Education:* BSc in Economics, London University, London, UK, 1952–57; Diploma in Agricultural Economics and Statistics, Rome University, Rome, Italy, 1958; *Career:* Economist, Africa Region, Food and Agriculture Organisation, FAO, Rome, Italy, 1958–61; Latin America Region, FAO, Economic Analysis Division, 1972–64; Project Economist, FAO, World Bank Cooperative Programme, 1965–69; Area Co-ordinator, Near East and Europe Region, FAO, World Bank Cooperative Programme, 1969–72; Deputy Chief, Europe, Near East and Latin America, World Bank Cooperative Programme, FAO, 1973–79; Deputy Director, FAO, Investment Centre, 1979–; *Languages:* Arabic, English, French, Spanish, Italian; *Address:* United Nations Food and Agriculture Organisation, Via delle Terme di Caracalla, 00100 Rome, Italy; telephone: 57971.

EISA, Omar Salih, Sudanese official; born 1937, Omdurman, Sudan; married; two children; *Religion:* Muslim; *Education:* Faculty of Engineering, University of Khartoum, Sudan; MA in Civil Engineering, USA, 1966; *Career:* worked in Khartoum on his return from USA; Chief Engineer in Bahr al-Ghazal Province, 1969–71; member of the Resettlement Commission, 1972; appointed member of the First People's Services Committee; played an active role in several Sudanese Socialist Union (SSU) Committees from 1972; Deputy Minister of Youth Affairs and of Sport, 1973; *Languages:* Arabic, English; *Address:* Ministry of Youth Affairs and Sports, Khartoum, Sudan.

ELBAZ, Faruk, Arab-American space scientist; born 2 January 1938, Zagazig, Egypt; married; four daughters; *Religion:* Muslim; *Education:* BSc in Chemistry and Geology, 1958; MS in Geology, 1961; PhD in Geology, 1964; *Career:* Instructor, Assiut University, Egypt, 1958–60; Instructor, Heidelberg University, West Germany, 1964–66; Geologist, Pan-Am-UAR Oil Company, Egypt, 1966–67; Supervisor, Lunar Science Planning and Lunar Exploration, Bellcom and Bell Telephone Laboratories, 1967–72; Research Director, Centre for Earth and Planetary Studies, National Air and Space Museum, Smithsonian Institution, Washington D.C., USA, 1973–; Adjunct Professor of Geology and Geophysics, University of Utah, USA, 1973–1977; Adjunct Professor of Geology, Ain Shams University, Cairo 1978–81; member of US delegation of experts for joint US/USSR Lunar Cartography, 1973; member of Science Panel; Chief, Surface Processes and Properties Panel, 1974; member of the International Astronomical Union, 1973, US Board of Geographic Names-Extraterrestrial Features, 1975, Task Group of Lunar Nomenclature, which selected landing sites for Apollo Missions; Chairman of Astronaut Training in Geology for Moon Missions, 1969–72; Principal Investigator for Earth Observations and Photography of Apollo-Soyez Mission of 1975; active in twenty professional societies of geological sciences; *Publications:* 120 scientific papers and research papers; *Annotated Bibliography* Geological Society of America 1968; *The Moon Viewed by Lunar Orbiter,* NASA, Washington 1970; *Glossary of Mining Geology* 1971; *Say it in Arabic,* New York, 1968; *Astronaut Observation from the Apollo-Soyez Mission,* Smithsonian Institution, 1977; *Space Flight and Man's Destiny* in Arabic, 1977; *Egypt as Seen by Landsat* in Arabic and English, Cairo, 1979; *Catalogue of Earth's Photographs from the Apollo-Soyez Test Project,* NASA 1979; *Apollo-*

Soyez Summary Science Report, vol ll, *Earth's Observations and Photography,* 1979; *Green Egypt* in Arabic, Cairo, 1979; *Decorations:* US Bureau of Mines Certificate of Merit in Ore Reserves and Rock Formation, National Aeronautics and Space Administration, Exceptional Scientific Achievement Medal, 1971; Alumni Achievement Award for Extraordinary Scientific Accomplishments, University of Missouri, USA, 1972; Certificate of Special Commendation, Geological Society of America, 1973; Honour Citation for Contributions to World Community AAUG, 1973; Lunar Science Team Award, 1974; Certificate of Merit of World Organization of Aerospace Education, 1979; Arab Republic of Egypt Order of Merit 1st class, 1981; *Interests and Recreations:* swimming; member of American Friends of the Middle East, Wafa wal Amal Rehabilitation Society, Egypt, Association of Arab American University Graduates; *Languages:* Arabic, English, German, French, Spanish; *Address:* National Air and Space Museum, Smithsonian Institution, Washington D.C., 20560, USA.

ELEISH, Muhammad Gamaliddin, Egyptian UN official/economist; born 30 November 1928, Cairo, Egypt; married; two children; *Religion:* Muslim; *Education:* BCom, Cairo University, Egypt 1948–51; PhD in Economics, University of Edinburgh, UK 1951–56; Post Doctoral Research, Harvard University, USA 1960–61; *Career:* Head of various units in the Ministry of National Planning, including Head of Input/Output Unit and Head of Housing and Construction Unit, Cairo Egypt 1956–61; Assistant Professor and Director of Research, Institute of Management Development, Cairo, Egypt 1961–62; Economic Affairs Officer, UN Economic Commission for Africa, Addis Ababa, Ethiopia 1962–64; UN African Institute for Economic Development and Planning, Dakar, Senegal; Lecturer in Economics and Chairman of Research Committee, 1964–66; Industrial Development Officer, UN Industrial Development Organisation (UNIDO), 1966–68, Acting Chief, Survey Section, UNIDO 1968–69, Chief, Survey Section UNIDO 1969–74, Chief, Special Studies Section; Chief, Developing Economies Section; Chief of the Intersectoral Issues Branch, Department of International Economic and Social Affairs (IESA), UN, New York, USA 1974–; *Publications:*

various publications in the field of development and economics, *The Input/Output Model in a Developing Economy,* 1963; *Uses of the Input/Output Model in Development Planning in Underdeveloped Countries,* 1965; *An Introduction to the Input/Output Model* 1962; *Use of the Input/Output Model in Calculating Foreign Exchange Requirements* 1967; *Interests and Recreations:* painting, music, tennis, previously President of the Art Club, UN Economic Commission for Africa, UNIDO, Vienna; Vice Chairman of the Art Club, UN New York; *Languages:* Arabic, English, French, Spanish; *Address:* United Nations Headquarters, Room 2645A, New York, 10017, USA; telephone: 212 754 5848.

ELIAS, Ibrahim, Sudanese official; born 29 August 1923, Omdurman, Sudan; married; *Education:* Degree in Economics and Social Studies, UK; *Career:* Deputy General Manager, Ministry of Finance and Economics; General Manager of Gulf International Company, Kuwait, and Chairman of the Corporation for Hides and Plastics; General Manager of the Blue Nile Brewery; Minister of the Treasury, 1972–73; Chairman of the El-Nilein Bank and of Sudan-Kuwait Investment Company; *Publications: Studies in Sudan Economy,* 1969; *Languages:* Arabic, English; *Address:* P O Box 466, Khartoum, Sudan; telephone: 73939.

ELMANDJRA, Mahdi, Moroccan academic/ UN official; born 13 March 1933, Rabat, Morocco; married; two daughters; *Religion:* Muslim; *Education:* BA in Chemistry and in Political Science, Cornell University, USA, 1954; PhD in Economics, London School of Economics, UK, 1957; School of Oriental and African Studies, UK, 1954–55; Faculty of Law, University of Paris, France, 1960–62; *Career:* Assistant, Faculty of Law, Rabat, Morocco, 1957–58; Assistant, Moroccan School of Administration, 1957–58; Counsellor, Permanent Mission of Morocco to the UN, New York, USA, 1958–59; Director General, Radiodiffusion Television Marocaine, 1959–60; Head of African Division, UNESCO, 1961–63; Director, Executive Office of the Director General of UNESCO, 1963–66; Assistant Director General for Social Sciences and Culture, UNESCO, 1966–69; Professor and Researcher, Centre of International Studies, London, 1970; Assistant Director General for Pre-Programming, UNESCO, 1970–74; Special

Adviser to the Director General, UNESCO, 1974–76; Professor, Faculty of Juridical, Economic and Social Sciences, University of Mohammad V, 1976–; *Publications: The Arab League 1945–55*, London 1957; *Nehru and the Modern World*, New Delhi, 1967; *The Political Aspects of the North South Dialogue*, Rome, 1978; and several other works; *Decorations:* Chevalier de l'Ordre des Arts et des Lettres, France; Men of Achievement Award, Cambridge; *Interests and Recreations:* President, World Federation of Future Studies, WFSF; member of the Society for International Development, SID, and of several other societies and associations; Languages: Arabic, English, French, Spanish; *Address:* P O Box 53, Rabat, Morocco; 12 rue Dufrenoy, 75116 Paris, France.

EMAM, Hani S. Saudi Arabian businessman/economist; born 1932, Mecca, Saudi Arabia; *Religion:* Muslim; *Education:* BSc in Economics, Columbia University, USA, 1962; MA in Economics, Columbia University, USA, 1963; *Career:* Director of Railroad Affairs, Ministry of Communications, 1955; Deputy Director, Saudi Public Relations Office, New York, USA, 1964–65; Economics Editor, *AL-Madina* daily newspaper, 1965–67; Coordinator, Saudi Government Information Programme, USA, 1965; Lecturer on Petroleum Economics, King Abdul Aziz University, Jeddah, Saudi Arabia, 1971–74; Special Representative of UN Children Fund (UNICEF) accredited to Saudi Arabia, United Arab Emirates and Qatar; member of International Resources and Finance Bank SA, Luxembourg; President, Saudi Technical Services and Trading; Director, Saudi Security and Technical Services Company Ltd; Chairman of Saudi Concrete Prefab Industries Ltd, Saudi Arabian Falcon Shipping Ltd; *Publications: The Economy of Saudi Arabia and the Economic Crises of 1956–59*, Saudi Arabia; *Address:* Villa Hani Emam, Abu Tammam Street, Ruwais, P O Box 1716, Jeddah, Saudi Arabia; telephone: Office — 653–2511 (5 lines), Residence — 665 1248.

ENNABLI, Nouriddin, Tunisian agricultural engineer; born 12 October 1940 Souss, Tunisia; married; two daughters, two sons; *Religion:* Muslim; *Education:* Ecole Nationale Supérieure Agronomique, Rennes, France; Ecole Supérieure d'Hydraulique, Toulouse, France; Diploma in Engineering in Hydraulic Agronomy; *Career:* Assistant, National Institute of Agronomy of Tunisia, 1968; Lecturer, 1973; Professor, National Institute of Agronomy of Tunisia; Head of Department of Rural Engineering, 1978–; Consultant Engineer, Groupement d'Ingénieurs Conseil GIC, and SCET International, 1973–; *Publications:* numerous articles and papers in professional journals and magazines; *Interests and Recreations:* cinema, travelling, swimming; *Languages:* Arabic, French, Scandinavian languages, English; *Address:* 12 rue Hercules, Carthage-Dermech, Tunisia; telephone: 275607.

ENNACEUR, Muhammad, Tunisian politician/lawyer; born 21 March 1934, al-Jem, Tunisia; married; five children; *Religion:* Muslim; *Education:* Institute of Higher Studies, Tunis; Licence in Law, Faculté de Droit, Paris; courses in Ministries of Labour & Employment, Belgium, France, Norway, USA; *Career:* Ministry of Labour and Social Planning 1957; Director, Labour Department 1965–77; Director General of the Office for Professional Training & Employment, 1967; Governor of Sousse, 1972; Commissioner General, Office of Tunisian Workers Abroad, Employment and Professional Training, 1973; Minister of Social Affairs, 1974–77, 1977–; President, International Labour Organization Congress, Geneva, 1976; represented Tunisia in various UN coferences & meetings, member of the Board of UNICEF, 1963–64, UN Research Institute for Social Development (UNRISD) 1966–72; President of the Executive Office of Labour and Social Affairs for Arab Ministers 1980–; Assistant Secretary General, General Tunisian Students Union (UGET); member of the Political Office of the Central Committee of the Socialist Destour Party (PSD); *Decorations:* Grand Cordon de l'Ordre de l Indépendence; Grand Cordon de l'Ordre de la Republique; Médaille d'Or du Travail, for exceptional services (Tunisia); Grand Cordon de l'Ordre Nassau (Holland); Grand Cordon de l'Ordre due Mérite National Français; Grand Officier de l'Ordre du Mérite National de la Côte d'Ivoire; Commandeur de l'Ordre National du Mérite de la RFA (West Germany); *Languages:* Arabic, French, English; *Address:* 2 Rue Juba 1er, Salamo, Tunis, Tunisia; telephone: 260 670.

ESSAFI, Muhammad, Tunisian diplomat; born 26 May 1930, Tunisia; married; one son; one daughter; *Religion:* Muslim; *Education:* BA in English; Diploma in Superior Studies, Sorbonne, Paris, France; *Career:* Ministry of Foreign Affairs; Secretary, Tunisian Embassy in London, UK, 1956; 1st Secretary, Washington D.C., USA, 1957–60; Counsellor, Head of Division of America, Ministry of Foreign Affairs, 1960–62; Minister Plenipotentiary, Head of Division of America and of International Conferences, 1962–64; Ambassador of Tunisia to the Court of St. James, London, UK, 1964–69; Secretary General, Ministry of Foreign Affairs, 1969–70; Ambassador to Moscow, USSR, 1970–74; Ambassador to Bonn, West Germany, 1974–76; Secretary General of the Ministry of Foreign Affairs, 1976–78; Ambassador to Brussels, Belgium, 1978–; *Decorations:* Grand Officier de l'Ordre de la Republique Tunisienne; Chevalier de l'Ordre de l'Indépendence, Tunisia; *Languages:* Arabic, French, English; *Address:* 278 Avenue de Tervueren, 1150 Brussels, Belgium.

ESSEBSI, Begi Qaid, Tunisian politician/lawyer; born 29 November 1926; *Religion:* Muslim; *Education:* Licence in Law, University of Paris; *Career:* joined the Neo-Destour Party, 1942; one of the Leaders of the Destour Students in Paris; Vice President of the Association of Muslim North African Students; played a prominent role in the movement of the independence of Tunisia; Director of Tourism; Director of Police and Security; Minister of the Interior, 1965–69; elected member of the Central Committee at the Party Congress of Bizerta, 1964; joined the Politburo, 1965; Elected member of the National Assembly, 1969; Minister of State in Charge of Defence; Ambassador to France, 1970; excluded from Destour Socialist Party 1974, decision repealed by President Bourguiba, 1980; Minister of State, 1980; Minister of Foreign Affairs, 1981–; re-elected member of Central Committee, 1965 and of the Politburo, 1981; *Decorations:* Grand Cordon of the Republic; Order of Independence; *Languages:* Arabic, French, English; *Address:* Ministry of Foreign Affairs, Tunis, Tunisia.

ESSEBSI, Slahiddin, Tunisian lawyer; born 28 May 1933, Tunisia; married; one son; *Religion:* Muslim; *Education:* BA in Law and Economic Sciences, University of Paris, France; Certificate of Higher Commercial Studies, Ecole des Hautes Etudes Commerciales de Paris; *Career:* Lawyer; Vice President of the Municipal Council of Tunis, 1963–72; President of the Cultural Commission; member of the National Cultural Committee, 1966–72, of the American Society of International Law; *Interests and Recreations:* fishing, golf, tennis, swimming; *Languages:* Arabic, French, English; *Address:* 25 Avenue Habib Bourguiba, Tunis, Tunisia; telephone: 243930, 256012.

ESSEYLI, Cyril, Lebanese businessman; born 10 August 1908, UK; married; two daughters; *Education:* Manchester Grammar School, UK; American University of Beirut, Lebanon; *Career:* First Vice President (Commercial) of Middle East Airlines and Air-Liban; *Languages:* Arabic, French, English; *Address:* MEA, International Airport of Beirut, Beirut, Lebanon; Residence — Chouran, Beirut, Lebanon.

EZZI, Wasfi Ben Hussain, Saudi Arabian official/businessman; born 1931, Medina, Saudi Arabia; *Religion:* Muslim; *Education:* BCom in Accountancy and Business Administration; *Career:* Civil Law Courts; Customs Department; Director of Tariffs and Rating Department, Jeddah Customs Division; founder of a textile factory; owner of Ezzi Trading Establishment, Jeddah; attended various Arab League Conferences of Arab Customs Experts, Cairo; *Interests and Recreations:* music; *Address:* P O Box 3824, Jeddah, Saudi Arabia; telephone: Office — 6432222.

F

FADALLA, Awad al Karim, Sudanese diplomat; born 1 January 1938, Omdurman, Khartoum, Sudan; married; *Education:* BA, University of Khartoum, Sudan; Diploma, Institute of Public Administration; *Career:* 3rd Secretary, Embassy to Italy; 1st Secretary, Embassy to Somalia; Ambassador, Permanent Representative of Sudan, UN, Geneva, Switzerland, 1973; *Interests and Recreations:* table-tennis; *Languages:* Arabic, English, French; *Address:* Office — 15 rue au Jeu-de-l'Arc, CH-1207 Geneva, Switzerland; telephone: (022) 354649; Residence — 42 Chemin des Chatoigners, CH-1292 Geneva, Switzerland; telephone: (022) 581851.

FADL, Abdul Qader Muhammad al-, Saudi Arabian businessman; born 1932, Jeddah, Saudi Arabia; *Religion:* Muslim; *Education:* commercial training; *Career:* Chairman, Board of al-Fadl Group of Companies, including, Al-Fadl Trading and Contracting Ltd, Alpha Shipping and Trading Agencies Ltd, Economic Development Enterprises, Electronic Maintenance Services Ltd, Al-Fadl-Binladen J. and P. Ltd, Bovis (Saudia) Ltd; member of the Board of Directors of Arabian Cement Company, Al-Jazirah Bank, Jeddah Chamber of Commerce and Industry; *Interests and Recreations:* Arabic literature and history; *Address:* P O Box 82, Jeddah, Saudi Arabia; telephone: 22815, 22850.

FADL, Ali Muhammad, Sudanese academic/ physician; born 14 April 1932, Al Fashir, Sudan; *Religion:* Muslim; *Education:* Diploma, Medicine, University of Khartoum, Sudan; DPH, University of Edinburgh; DTM, Diploma in Nutrition and PhD, University of London; *Career:* Medical Inspector, Sudan Government, 1955; Medical Registrar, Ministry of Health, Sudan, 1960; successively at the University of Khartoum, Lecturer, Department of Community Medicine, 1965, Head of Department of Community Medicine, 1971, Dean of Faculty of Medicine, 1975, Deputy Vice Chancellor, 1975, Professor of Community Medicine, 1977, Vice Chancellor, 1977–; member of the National Council for Research, 1978, the National Council for Higher Education, 1977; member of Expert Committee on Nutrition, WHO, 1979, Scientific Committee of International Federation for Family Planning, 1980, International Association of Universities, Association of Arab Universities, and of African Universities; *Publications: Trials in Treatment of Bilharzia in Sudan; Susceptibility of Certain Strains of Rats to Infection with Schistosomiasis; Decorations:* Republican Decoration, 2nd Class; Golden Medal in Education; *Interests and Recreations:* swimming, tennis, music, photography, cinema; *Languages:* Arabic, English; *Address:* University of Khartoum, P O Box 321, Khartoum, Sudan.

FAHD BIN ABDUL AZIZ, HM King, King of Saudi Arabia; born 1921; eldest son of late King Abdul Aziz and late Hassa Bint Sudairi; married; five sons, Faisal, Khalid, Sultan, Saud, Muhammad; *Religion:* Muslim; *Career:* Minister of Education, 1953; member of the Council of Ministers and of its Financial and Regulations Committees; Amir of Al Jauf and Um Laj; Minister of the Interior, 1962; Second Deputy Prime Minister, 1968–75; First Deputy Prime Minister, 1975–82; Crown Prince, 1975–82; King of Saudi Arabia, 1982–; represented late King Abdul Aziz at the Coronation of HM Queen Elizabeth II, UK, 1953; leader of Saudi delegation to discuss Anglo-Saudi relations and the future of the Gulf, London, UK, November 1970; official visits to Egypt, 1974, and to Washington, for talks on Saudi-US relations and cooperation, USA, 1974; visit to President Carter, 1977; *Languages:* Arabic, English; *Address:* Royal Court, Riyadh, Saudi Arabia.

FAHD BIN SULTAN BIN ABDUL AZIZ, HRH Prince, Saudi Arabian Prince/administrator; born 1950; *Religion:* Muslim; *Education:* BA in History, University of Riyadh, Saudi Arabia; *Career:* Director of Research Department, Ministry of Labour and Social Affairs; Director General, Social Welfare Department, Ministry of Labour and Social Affairs; Deputy Minister for Social Welfare, Ministry of Labour and Social Affairs; member of the High Council of the National Committee for Child Welfare; Vice Chairman of Saudi Olympic Committee, of Saudi Arabian Federation for Football, and of Saudi Arabian Assembly for Youth Hostels; Chairman of the Arab Federation for Athletics, and of the Saudi Arabian Federation for Athletics; member of the International Executive Board for Child Welfare; *Interests and Recreations:* hunting, billiards, table tennis, football; *Languages:* Arabic, English, French; *Address:* Ministry of Labour and Social Affairs, Riyadh, Saudi Arabia; telephone: Office — 477 6167, Residence — 465 0988.

FAHHAM, Shakir, Syrian academic/politician; born 1912, Homs, Syria; *Religion:* Muslim; *Education:* Doctor of Letters, University of Cairo; *Career:* Professor, Faculty of Letters, University of Damascus; Minister of Education, 1963; Ambassador to Algeria, 1964; Rector of the University of Damascus, 1968; Minister of Higher Education 1970–73; Minister of Education, 1973–78; Minister of Higher Education, 1978–80; elected member of the Academy of Arabic Language, Damascus, 1971; Vice President of the Academy of Arabic Language, 1966–; General Director of the Board of the Arabic Encyclopedia 1981–; *Address:* Academy of Arabic Language, Damascus, Syria.

FAHMI, Ismail, Egyptian politician/diplomat; born 1920, Egypt; married; *Religion:* Muslim; *Education:* BA, Faculty of Commerce, University of Cairo, Cairo, Egypt, 1945; *Career:* joined Ministry of Foreign Affairs, 1946; Vice Consul, Egyptian Consulate, Paris, 1947–49; member of the Permanent Mission of Egypt to the UN, 1949–57; Adviser to the Egyptian delegation to the 4th-18th Session of the UN General Assembly; member of the Egyptian delegation to the Security Council, 1949–50, 1962–63; Political Adviser to the First and Second Scientific Conferences on Peaceful Use of Atomic Energy; Representative of Egypt to the Statute Conference of the International Atomic Energy Agency, New York; Representative of Egypt on the Preparatory Commission of the International Atomic Energy Agency 1956–57; Permanent Representative of Egypt on the International Atomic Energy Agency, 1957–60; Governor of the Board of the International Atomic Energy Agency, 1957–60; member of the Egyptian delegation to the 1st-4th Annual Conference of the International Atomic Energy Agency; member of the Egyptian delegation to the African Summit Conference, Cairo, 1964; member of the Egyptian delegation to the Conference of Non-Aligned Countries, Cairo, 1964; Representative of Egypt on the Disarmament Commission, New York, 1965; Director of the Department of the International Organization and Conferences, Ministry of Foreign Affairs, Cairo, 1964–68; Ambassador of Egypt to Austria, 1968–71; Chairman of the Egyptian delegation to the General Conference of the International Atomic Energy Agency, 1968, 1969, 1970, 1971; Governor of Egypt on the Board of the International Atomic Energy Agency, 1971; Representative of Egypt on the Executive Board of the UN Industrial Development Organisation (UNIDO), 1969–71; Under Secretary of State for Foreign Affairs, 1971–73; Ambassador of Egypt to the Federal Republic of Germany, 1973; Minister of Tourism, 1973; Minister of Foreign Affairs, 1973; Deputy Prime Minister and Minister of Foreign Affairs, 1975, resigned 17 November 1977, as protest to late President Sadat's visit to Israel; *Languages:* Arabic, English, German; *Address:* Ministry of Foreign Affairs, Cairo, Egypt.

FAHMY, General Muhammad Ali, Egyptian army commander; born 11 October 1920, Cairo, Egypt; married; two sons, one daughter; *Religion:* Muslim; *Education:* Engineering Faculty, Cairo University, Egypt, 1938; Cairo Military Academy, 1939; *Career:* 2nd Lieutenant, 1939; 1st Lieutenant, 1941; Captain, 1947; Major, 1950; Staff College, 1951; Lieutenant Colonel, 1954; Colonel, 1957; Brigadier, 1962; Air Defence Academy, Kalinin, USSR, 1964–65; Major General, 1965; Lieutenant General, 1973; Inspector, Senior Officers Studies Institute, 1952; Army Operations Department, 1953; Commander of the 2nd Light Anti-Aircraft Regiment, 1957; Commander of the 14th

Anti-Aircraft Regiment, 1958; Commander of the 64th Anti-Aircraft Regiment, 1959; Commander of the 6th Artillery Group, 1961; Chief of Staff of the 5th Artillery Division, 1963; Commander of the 5th Artillery Division, 1966; Air Defence Chief of Staff, 1968, Commander in Chief of Air Defence Forces, 1969; Chief of Staff of the Armed Forces, 1975; served in World War II, Palestine War, 1948, Tripartite Aggression, 1956, Arab-Israeli War, 1967; Arab-Israeli War, 1973; *Decorations:* Order of Liberation, 1952; Memorial Order of the UAR Establishment, 1958; Military Star Order, 1971; Military Honour Order, Rank of Knight, Syria, 1974; Star of Honour Order of Palestine Liberation Organization, 1974; Yugoslav Star (Golden Belt), 1974; King Abdul Aziz Order, 1st Class, 1974; Evacuation Ribbon, 1956; Independence Ribbon, 1956; Victory Ribbon, 1957; Training Ribbon, 1st Class; Distinguished Service Ribbon, 1972; Palestine Medal with Clasp, 1949; Mohammed Ali Memorial Medal, 1949; Army Day Medal, 1959; Medal of 10th Anniversary of the Revolution, 1962; Medal of Long Service and Excellence, 1962; East Germany Army Golden Medal of Merit; Medal of the 20th Anniversary of the Revolution; 6th of October Medal; *Languages:* Arabic, English, French; *Address:* Egyptian Armed Forces Staff Headquarters, Cairo, Egypt.

FAHMY, Hussain Murad, Egyptian official/agricultural expert; born 26 May 1910, Cairo, Egypt; married; one son, one daughter; *Religion:* Muslim; *Education:* BSc in Agriculture, Cairo University, Egypt; *Career:* Director General, Department of Horticulture, Ministry of Agriculture; Honorary Secretary General, National Sporting Club, 1944–54; Honorary Secretary General, Egyptian Football Association, 1954–64; Honorary Secretary General, African Football Confederation, 1963–67; Permanent Secretary General, African Football Confederation, 1968; *Publications:* numerous botanical research papers; *Decorations:* Order of the Nile 3rd Class; *Interests and Recreations:* walking; *Languages:* Arabic, English, French; *Address:* 159 26th July Street, Zamalek, Cairo, Egypt; telephone 808909.

FAHOUM, Khalid al-, Palestinian politician; *Career:* member of the Palestine Liberation Organization (PLO) Executive Committee

under Ahmed Shukairi, 1964–67; joined PLO Central Committee as independent member, 1970; became Chairman of the Palestinian National Council (PNC), July 1971; accompanied a delegation led by Yasser Arafat to Moscow, 1972; led a delegation to President Sadat, 1972 to explain certain differences between Egyptian and PLO policy; elected Head of PLO Central Committee, January 1973, a new body of about twenty members (a forum for discussion of PLO policy formulated by the Executive Committee).

FAHOUM, Munther, Jordanian banker; born 1927, Irbid, Jordan; married; two sons, one daughter; *Religion:* Muslim; *Education:* MA, Edinburgh University, Scotland, UK; *Career:* Senior Analyst, Industrial Relations, Arabian American Oil Company, 1952–57; Assistant Manager, Arab Bank Ltd, 1957–63; Lecturer (part time), Damascus University, Syria, 1961–62; Manager, Arab Bank, 1963–75; Regional Manager, Arab Bank, 1975–; member of the Board, Industrial Development Bank, Jordan; member of the Board, Housing Bank, Amman, Jordan; *Interests and Recreations:* travel, swimming, reading; *Languages:* Arabic, English, Latin; *Address:* P O Box 68, Amman Jordan.

FAISAL BIN FAHD BIN ABDUL AZIZ, HRH Prince, Saudi Arabian Prince/administrator; born 1945; eldest son of HM King Fahd; *Religion:* Muslim; *Education:* BA in Economics and Political Sciences; *Career:* Director General of Youth Welfare, 1971–74; Chairman of Saudi Olympic Committee, of Saudi Football Federation, of Arab Football Association, and of Basketball Federation; Honorary Chairman of World Swimming Federation; President of Youth Welfare Department, rank of Minister, 1974–; member of Supreme Council for Youth Welfare, established 1974; attended International Football Federation conferences, Munich, 1972–74; attended Arab Football Federation Conference, and Arab Olympic Committees Conference of the Arab Ministers of Youth; *Interests and Recreations:* reading; *Languages:* Arabic, English; *Address:* P O Box 956, Riyadh, Saudi Arabia; telephone: Office — 402 9515; Residence — 442 0100.

FAISAL, Muhammad Abdul Rahman, Sudanese politician/lawyer; born 1934, Omdurman, Sudan; married; *Religion:* Muslim; *Education:* University of Khartoum, Sudan 1958; *Career:* worked in the Judiciary, 1958–62; International Labour Organisation, 1962–74; Minister of State for Presidential Affairs, 1974–75; *Languages:* Arabic, English, French; *Address:* Ministry of Cabinet Affairs, Khartoum, Sudan.

FAITURI, Muhammad Abdul Salam al-, Libyan official; *Religion:* Muslim; *Career:* elected Chairman of the Popular Committee for the Tripoli Governorate, 1976; Minister of Social Affairs and Social Security, 1976; Secretary for Social Affairs and Social Security in the General People's Committee, 1977; *Address:* Office of the Secretary, Secretariat of Social Security, Tripoli, Libya.

FAKHREDDINE, Muhammad, Sudanese diplomat, born 1924 Dueim, Sudan; married; one daughter; *Religion:* Muslim; *Education:* BA, Psychology and Philosophy, Durham, UK; *Career:* Counsellor, Sudan Embassy, UK, 1958–60; Ambassador to Pakistan, Afghanistan and China, 1960–64; Permanent Representative of the Sudan to the UN, 1965–71; Chairman of the Decolonization, Fourth Committee of the General Assembly of the UN, 1966; Chairman of the UN Committee on the Question of Defining Aggression, 1966; Chief of Delegation of Sudan to the Special Committee on the Peaceful Uses of the Sea-bed and Ocean Floor, 1969–70; Member of the UN Committee on Contributions, 1969–71; Under Secretary, Ministry of Foreign Affairs, 1971; Deputy Minister of Foreign Affairs, 1971–72; Sudan Ambassador to the USSR, 1973–74; Sudan Ambassador to Ethiopia, 1975; currently Director of the UN North African Centre of the Economic Commission for Africa, Tangier, Morocco; *Decorations:* Order of the Republic, Sudan; Order of Al-Nilayin, Sudan; The Star of Ethiopia, Ethiopia; *Interests and Recreations:* yoga, plastic arts; member of the Arts Council; *Languages:* Arabic, English; *Address:* UN North African Centre of the Economic Commission for Africa, 18 Ave Prince Heritier, P O Box 316, Tangier, Morocco.

FAKHROO, Ali Muhammad, Bahraini physician/politician; born 1932, Bahrain; married; *Religion:* Muslim; *Education:* BSc, American University of Beirut, Beirut, Lebanon, 1954; MD, School of Medicine, American University of Beirut, 1958; *Career:* Internship,

Baylor University Hospital, Dallas, Texas, USA, 1958–59; Junior Resident, University Hospital, Birmingham, Alabama, and later Senior Resident, 1958–61; Consultant, Internal Medicine Department, Bahrain Government Hospitals, Bahrain, 1961–63; Fellow at various hospitals in the USA specialising in Cardiology and Gastro Entrology, 1963–66; Consultant Cardiologist and Assistant Director of Medical Services, Bahrain Government, 1966–70; Head of Health Department, Bahrain Government, 1970–72; Member of Constitutional Assembly, 1972–73; Member of National Assembly, 1972–75; Minister of Health, 1971–82; Minister of Education 1982–; Member of the Executive Board of World Health Organisation, 1978–81; First Adjunct Professor, Department of Medicine, Division of Cardiology, American University of Beirut, 1979; Member of the Executive Board of the Council of Arab Ministers of Health; Trustee on the Board of the Institute of Palestine Studies; Member of the High Council of Arab Board Medical Specialties, 1979–82; Member of the Editorial Board of the *American Heart Journal,* 1978–81; Member of the High Council for Youth and Sport (Bahrain), 1977; Member of the Board of Trustees of Bahrain Centre for Studies and Research, 1981–; Trustee then President of Board of University College of Bahrain, 1979–82; President of Bahrain Red Cresent Society, 1973–82; Chairman, Committee for Protection of the Enviroment, 1980–82; *Publications:* several articles on cardiac care of coronory cases, *American Journal of Cardiology and American Heart Journal,* in collaboration with B Down and T R Harrison; *Decorations:* Shousha Foundation Prize and Medal, World Health Organization, May 1982; *Interests and Recreations:* tennis, reading; *Languages:* Arabic, English; *Address:* Ministry of Education, P O Box 43, Manama, Bahrain; telephone: 52633.

FAKHROO, Qassim Darwish, Qatari businessman; born 1910; *Religion:* Muslim; *Career:* Chairman, Qassem Darwish Fakhroo & Sons, a group of companies, including Darwish Trading Co, which started 40 years ago and has developed into a large business enterprise; member of the Board of Qassim Abdulla and Sons, Darwish Fakhroo, Darwish Travel Bureau, Gulf Housing Company Ltd, Gulf Automobiles & Trading Company, Gulf Tanker and Joinery and Oasis Hotels; *Interests and Recreations:*

reading, the philosophy and analysis of Islamic traditions and teachings, Islamic literature; *Languages:* Arabic; *Address:* P O Box 350, Doha, Qatar; telephone: offfice — 22343 22781, 22789; Residence — 22811.

FALAHI, Sami D al-, Iraqi lawyer; resident in UK; born 13 December 1936, Baghdad, Iraq; *Religion:* Muslim; *Education:* MA Law, Oxford University; MSc, Economics and Industrial Management, Loughborough University of Technology; Barrister at Law, London; Fellow, Institute of Arbitration, Institute of Commerce, Institute of Petroleum; *Career:* Lecturer in Commercial Company, Contract and Arbitration Law, 1969–; Barrister and International Legal Adviser, 1972–; *Publications:* Editor of several legal and commercial publications; numerous papers and articles on commerce, contract and company law, and on legal systems; *Interests and Recreations:* tennis, travel, reading; *Languages:* Arabic, English, French; *Address:* SDF House, 77/79 Chepstow Road, Bayswater, London W2; telephone: 221 5684/5.

FAM, Aziz, Egyptian physician/academic; born 19 May, 1919, Fayoum, Egypt; married 1961; one son, one daughter; *Religion:* Christian; *Education:* MB, BCh, Faculty of Medicine, University of Cairo, Cairo, Egypt, 1946; MCh, Faculty of Medicine, Cairo University; Fellow of International College of Surgeons, 1970; Fellow of American College of Surgeons, 1973; *Career:* Demonstrator, Cairo University Hospital, 1946–55; Lecturer in Urology, Faculty of Medicine, Cairo University, 1955–62; Assistant Professor in Urology, Faculty of Medicine and Cairo University Hospitals, 1962–1968–; Professor of Urology, Faculty of Medicine, Cairo University, 1968–; corresponding member of American Urology Association, 1973–; owner-director of private clinic of urology and genito-urinary surgery; Chief of Urology Department, Coptic Hospital, Cairo; member of the Health Committee of the National Democratic Party; Chief of the Council of the Coptic Church, Garden City; Chief and Treasurer of Project of St. Mark Hospital; *Publications:* various articles and papers on genito-urinary surgery in professional and specialist journals; *Interests and Recreations:* walking, swimming; *Languages:* Arabic, English, French; *Address:* Office — Ramses Building, Ramses Square, Cairo, Egypt; telephone: 744919, 744837.

FANEK, Fahed, Jordanian banker/businessman; born 13 April, 1934, Amman Jordan; married; three sons, two daughters; *Religion:* Christian; *Education:* BA, Faculty of Commerce, Ain Shams University, Cairo, Egypt; *Career:* Head of Section, Arab Bank, Amman Jordan, 1963–66; Senior Auditor, Saba and Company, Amman, 1966–72; Director of Finance, ALIA, 1972–74; Vice President of Finance, ALIA, 1975–; *Publications:* author of several books including, *Banks and Jordanian Economy,* 1964 (in Arabic); *Jordan in the Era of Central Bank,* 1968; *Agricultural Sector in Jordan,* 1970; *Economic Thinking in Jordan,* 1972; *Cooperation and Economic Integration between Syria and Jordan in the Field of Civil Aviation,* 1976; *Tourism in Jordan,* 1978; *Profitability of Banks in Jordan,* 1981; *Jordan Development Planning,* 1982; *Interests and Recreations:* swimming, reading, writing, travel; *Languages:* Arabic, English; *Address:* Royal Jordanian Airlines (ALIA), P O Box 302, Amman Jordan; telephone: 22317.

FAQIH, Abdul Rahman al-, Saudi Arabian businessman; born 1923, Mecca, Saudi Arabia; married; five sons, two daughters; *Religion:* Muslim; *Education:* general; *Career:* member of Municipal Council, Mecca Chamber of Commerce; member of Committee for Welfare of Prisoners; member of Board of Mecca Electric Company; *Interests and Recreations:* reading, travel; *Address:* c/o Mecca Chamber of Commerce and Industry, P O Box 1086, Mecca, Saudi Arabia; telephone: 5745775; telex: 440011 CHAMEL SJ.

FAQIH, Abdullah Salih, Saudi Arabian official; born 1939, Mecca, Saudi Arabia; *Religion:* Muslim; *Education:* general; *Career:* member of Board of Arab Centre; member of Committee for the Regulation of Graphic Material, Publications and Organizations; attended First Conference of Saudi Men of Letters, King Abdul Aziz University; Director of Publications Department, Ministry of Information; *Interests and Recreations:* reading; *Address:* Publications Department, Ministry of Information, P O Box 843, Jeddah, Saudi Arabia; telephone: 4014440.

FAQIH, Omar, Saudi Arabian official; born 1930, Mecca, Saudi Arabia; married; *Religion:* Muslim; *Education:* in Cairo, Egypt, and USA; *Career:* Deputy Minister of Communications for Posts and Telegraphs, 1973–; Director General of Saudi Railways, 1972; Deputy Minister of Commerce and Industry, 1962–72; *Languages:* Arabic, English; *Address:* Ministry of Posts, Telegraphs and Telephones, Riyadh, Saudi Arabia.

FARAH, E. Caesar, Arab-American academic; born 13 March 1929, Portland, Oregon, USA; married; five sons, one daughter; *Religion:* Christian; *Education:* BA, Stanford University, USA; MA, PhD, Arabic and Islamic Studies and the Modern Middle East, Princeton University, USA; *Career:* Public Affairs Assistant, and Cultural Affairs Officer for Educational Exchanges, Foreign Service of USA, 1957–59; Assistant Professor of History and Arabic, Portland State University, Oregon, and California State University, Los Angeles, USA, 1959–64; Associate Professor of Near Eastern Studies, Indiana University, Bloomington, USA, 1964–69; Visiting Professor of Arabic, Harvard University, USA, summers 1964,1965; Professor of Islamic and Near Eastern Studies, University of Minnesota, Minneapolis, USA; Fellow of the American Oriental Society; Fellow of the Royal Asiatic Society of Great Britain; Fellow of the Middle East Studies Association of North America; Secretary of the American Institute of Yemeni Studies, and Editor of the Newsletter; Director of the Middle East Outreach Consortium for the Upper Midwest; former President of the Cedar Society, Oregon, and the American Association of University Graduates of Minnesota; President of Stanford Club of Minnesota; Weter Memorial Fellow, Stanford University, USA; Near Eastern and P.K. Hitti Fellow, Princeton University, USA; Fulbright Research Scholar, Turkey, 1967–68; American Research Centre Fellow, Cairo, 1966; American Philosophical Society Fellow; Ford Foundation (Indiana) Fellow; *Publications: The Addendum in Medieval Arabic Historiography,* 1968; *Islam: Beliefs and Observances,* 1968, 1971, second edition 1973, third edition 1983; translator and editor of the *Eternal Message of Muhammad,* 1964, 1965, 1981, London and New York; articles in leading journals; *Interests and Recreations:* swimming, tennis; *Languages:* Arabic, English, Persian, Turkish, French, German, Urdu, Latin,

Spanish; *Address:* 3847 York Avenue South, Minnesota 55410, USA; telephone: (612) 929 4008.

FARAH, Monsignor Augustin, Lebanese ecclesiastic; born 1910, Qara, Syria; *Religion:* Christian; *Education:* French and Lebanese Baccalaureates, St. Joseph University, Beirut, Lebanon; Doctorate in Theology 1942; *Career:* joined the Order of the Pères Basiliens Chouerites, 1922; ordained 1937; Director of Seminarists, 1940; Father Superior of St. John Seminary; Professor of Latin and French, St. John Seminary, 1940–46; Professor of Philosophy, Oriental College, Zahle, Lebanon, 1946; Father Superior (ad interim), St. Eli Convent, Zahle, 1947–48; Superior-General of the Order of the Pères Basiliens Chouerites, 1949; re-elected Superior-General, 1956; elected Archbishop of Tripoli, 1961–; visited France and the Holy See 1951; *Publications:* thesis *Le Saint Esprit – d'après l'Enseignement de Saint Basile; Languages:* Arabic, French, Latin; *Address:* Greek-Catholic Archdiocese, Tripoli, Lebanon.

FARAH, Naoum, Lebanese journalist/lawyer; born 20 May 1947, Beirut, Lebanon; *Religion:* Christian; *Education:* LLB, School of Law, St. Joseph University, Beirut, Lebanon; Diploma in Legal Studies, Ecole Français Superieure des Lettres; BA in Philosophy, Lyon University, Lyon, France; *Career:* journalist on *Le Jour* and *L'Orient Le Jour,* later Foreign Correspondent, 1967–71; Legal training as barrister, 1971–74; member of the Command Council and official spokesman for the Lebanese Forces, 1978; Head of the Foreign Relations Department, Lebanese Forces, 1979; member of the Central Committee, Al Kataeb Party, 1979; founder and member of the Lebanese Christian Democratic Union, 1979; member of the International Association of Young Lawyers, the Arab Organisation for Human Rights, founder and member of the Association for Solidarity of French Speaking Lawyers in Lebanon; former Secretary General of the Committee for the Safeguard of the Constitution and Liberty of Lebanon; *Publications:* articles on politics and law in *L'Orient–L'Jour,* Magazine and *Travaux et Jours,* in Arabic and French; *Interests and Recreations:* volleyball, swimming, water skiing, hunting, chess; founder and vice president of the association of the formation of the

German-Lebanese Friendship, Bonn, 1981; *Languages:* Arabic, English, Latin, some Spanish; *Address:* Hanna Haddad Building, Amin Gemayel Street, P O Box 16-5301, Beirut, Lebanon; telephone: 339318, 339319.

FARAH, Salih, United Arab Emirates lawyer; born 24 March 1930; married; one son, one daughter; *Religion:* Muslim; *Education:* Diploma in Civil Law, University of Khartoum, Sudan; LLB, London University, UK; MA, Gray's Inn, London, UK; Barrister at Law; *Career:* Judicial Assistant in Sudan; Chief Legal Adviser, Sudan; Legal Adviser, Abu Dhabi; Adviser to HH the President of the United Arab Emirates on legal affairs; member of the British Law Society, Sudanese Law Society, London and Khartoum University Graduates Association; *Decorations:* Order of Merit, 3rd Class, Egypt; *Interests and Recreations:* walking, cycling; *Languages:* Arabic, English; *Address:* P O Box 280, Abu Dhabi, United Arab Emirates; telephone: Office — 337 204; Residence — 363 978.

FARHAN, Hamad, al-, Jordanian official/businessman; born 17 February, 1921, Irbid, Jordan, 1921; married; *Religion:* Muslim; *Education:* BSc, Physics, American University of Beirut, Lebanon, 1941; Fellowship in Economics and Education, University of London, England, 1948; *Career:* Under Secretary, Ministry of Economy, 1951–55; Minister of National Economy, 1955; Under Secretary of Ministry of National Economy, 1955–57; Director of Arab Shipping Company, 1957–; founder and promoter of various projects in Jordan, including Jordan Cement Factories, Jordan Phosphate Mines Company (a mixed public and private company), Jordan Vegetable Oil Industries, Nablus, Jordan, Jordan Petroleum, Jordan Fisheries, Jordan Paper Industries Company; Chairman of Committees implementing the East Ghor Canal Irrigation Scheme and Aqaba Port, Board member of the Jordan National Shipping Lines; *Languages:* Arabic, English; *Address:* P O Box 757, Amman Jordan; telephone: 23135, 62776.

FARHAN, Ishaq Ahmad, Jordanian academic/official; born 1934, Ain Karem, Jordan; married; three sons, four daughters; *Religion:* Muslim; *Education:* BSc, American University of Beirut, AUB, Lebanon; MSc in Physical Chemistry, AUB; MA and PhD in Education, Columbia University, USA; *Career:* Head of Teachers Education Department, 1964; Head of Curriculum Department, 1964–70; Minister of Education, and of Islamic Affairs, 1970–73; Director General of Royal Scientific Society, 1975; President of Jordan University, 1976–78; member of the National Consultative Council, 1978; Professor of Education, Yarmouk University, Jordan, 1978–; member of the Islamic Association of Studies and Research, Amman; member of Boards of Trustees of universities, community colleges, scientific associations and numerous other scientific enterprises; special expertise in curriculum and textbook development; *Publications:* books, research papers and studies published in various journals and magazines; *Decorations:* Excellent Decoration of Education, Jordan, 1974; *Interests and Recreations:* gymnastics; *Languages:* Arabic, English, German; *Address:* P O Box 19095 Amman, Jordan.

FARHAT, Abbas, Lebanese administrator; born 1928, Sidon, Lebanon; married; *Religion:* Muslim; *Career:* Head of Social Services, Ministry of Labour, 1953; later Head of Social Services at the Office of Social Development; Director General, Ministry of Labour and Social Affairs, 1967–74; Director General of the Palestinian Refugees Administration, Ministry of Interior 1974–77; Inspector General of Education, 1977–; *Languages:* Arabic, French, English; *Address:* Inspector General of Education, Central Inspection, Prime Minister's Office, Beirut, Lebanon.

FARHAT, Abdallah M., Tunisian politician; born 28 August 1914, Tunisia; married; *Religion:* Muslim; *Education:* Sousse Lycée; Institute of Higher Studies, Tunis, Tunisia; *Career:* Neo-Destour militant, 1934; Head of President Bourguiba's Office, after Independence, 1956–64; Vice President, Constituent Assembly, 1956–59; Deputy, National Assembly, 1959; Chairman and Managing Director of the National Investment Company, 1964; Secretary of State for Agriculture, and Minister of Agriculture, 1969–70; Minister of Agriculture and Head of Presidential Office, 1970; Minister of National Defence, 1972–74; Minister of Supply, 1974–76; Minister of National Defence, 1976–; Acting Minister of Interior, 1977; *Decorations:* Grand Cordon of the Order of the Tunisian Republic and many foreign decorations; *Interests and Recreations:* hunting; *Languages:* Arabic, French; *Address:* Ministry of Defence, Tunis, Tunisia.

FARID, Samir Muhammad, Egyptian UN official/statistician; born 22 March 1942, Egypt; married; two daughters; *Religion:* Muslim; *Education:* BSc in Statistics, Cairo University, 1963; PhD in Demography, Leeds University, 1969; *Career:* Lecturer, Institute of Statistics, Cairo University, 1963–70; Consultant, Office of Population Censuses and Surveys, London, 1970–77; Demographic Expert, International Statistical Institute, London, 1977–; member of the International Union of the Scientific Study of Population, the International Statistical Institute, The Hague; *Publications: The Current Tempo of Fertility in England and Wales,* HMSO, London, 1974; *Population Growth in Syria,* London, 1983, (in English); *The Demographic Transition in Egypt,* (in Arabic) CAPMAS, Cairo, (English) ISIWFS, London, in press; *Interests and Recreations:* writing, swimming, chess; *Languages:* Arabic, English; *Address:* 10 Brocas Close, London NW3, UK; telephone: Residence -- 586 7180, Office -- 828 4242.

FARID, Zuhair, Egyptian physician; born 25 December 1927, Bani Suef, Egypt; married; *Religion:* Christian; *Education:* MB, ChB in Medicine, Cairo University, Egypt, 1952; SC Fellow in Medicine, University of Chicago, USA, 1959; Diploma in Tropical Medicine, London University, UK, 1961; *Career:* Hospital House Officer, Ministry of Public Health, Egypt, 1952–54; member of the staff of US Naval Medical Research Unit No 3 (NAMRU), Cairo, 1954–56; Seymor Comen Fellow of Medicine, University of Chicago, 1957–59; member of staff of NAMRU No 3, Cairo, 1959–63; member of the Expert Committee on Brucellosis, 1963–; Lecturer, London School of Hygiene and Tropical Medicine, University of London, UK, 1963–64; Director of Tropical Medicine Department, NAMRU No 3, Cairo, 1964–; Consultant, Abbassiya Fever Hospital, Ministry of Public Health, 1967–; member of the Expert Committee on Nutrition and Parasitic Diseases, 1970; Fellow of the British Royal Society of Tropical Medicine and Hygiene; member of the American Society of Tropical Medicine and Hygiene; member of the Society of Biological Sciences; visiting lecturer, London School of Hygiene and Tropi-

cal Medicine; *Publications: Textbook of Infectious Diseases,* co-author with M. Sabbur, Dar al-Ma'arif, Cairo, Egypt 1979; articles and papers on tropical and infectious diseases published in professional British and American journals; *Decorations:* Commendatore of Italian Government, 1972; *Interests and Recreations:* reading; *Languages:* Arabic, English, French; *Address:* 9 Al-Ma'had al-Suissri, Zamalek, Cairo, Egypt; telephone: 806 229.

FARIS, Mustafa, Moroccan politician/engineer; born 17 December, 1933, Casablanca, Morocco; married; *Religion:* Muslim; *Education:* Diploma in Engineering, Ecole Nationale des Ponts et Chaussées, Paris, France; *Career:* Public Works Engineer, Port of Casablanca; Chief of Public Works, Agadir Region, following earthquake, 1960; Head, Private Office, Minister of Public Works, 1961; Director of Equipement, 1962–64; Inspector General, National Irrigation Office; Secretary of State, Prime Minister's Office, in charge of Five Year Plan, 1961; Delegate for Planning and Regional Development, Prime Minister's Office, 1971; Secretary of State, Ministry of Finance; Minister of Finance, Karim-Lamrani Government, 1972; President, Director General , Banque Nationale pour le Développement Economique, 1972–77; Minister of Agriculture, 1977–80; *Languages:* Arabic, French; *Address:* C/O Ministry of Agriculture, Rabat, Morocco.

FARRADJ, Fuad Dimitri, Jordanian businessman/engineer; born 1925, Nablus, Palestine; married; *Education:* BSc, Mechanical Engineering, Fuad University, Cairo, Egypt 1948; *Career:* Engineer, Ministry of Public Works 1949–51; Board member, Jordan Cement Factories; Engineer with CAT Co, Qatar 1951–52; Assistant Under Secretary (Mechanical and Electrical), Ministry of Public Works, 1952–56; Private Consulting Office, 1956–57; General Manager, Contracting and Concrete Construction Co 1957–62; owner and partner, Farraj and Co, (Commercial), Bureau of Engineering Services (Contractors), 1962–65; President, Association of Engineers; Minister of Municipalities and Rural Affairs, 1965–66; Chairman of Board of Directors, Bureau of Engineering Services; Director, Farradj and Co; Director, Steel Mesh Industry Co, 1966–;

Address: Bureau of Engineering Services, P O Box 974, Amman Jordan; telephone: 21662, 25616; telex: 21317 FARRAJ JO.

FARRAG, Nourilddin Mahmud, Egyptian economist/lawyer; born 27 November 1932; married; two sons; *Religion:* Muslim; *Education:* LLB, Cairo University, 1952; Postgraduate Diploma, Public Law, 1954; MSc in Economics, Finance and Banking, University College, 1959; PhD in Economics, London School of Economics, 1963; *Career:* Assistant Legal Counsel, Council of State, 1952–53; Assistant Lecturer in Commercial Law, Faculty of Law, Ain Shams University, Cairo, 1953–56; Lecturer in Economics, 1964–65; Economic Adviser, Oil Affairs, Ministry of Finance and Oil, Egypt 1965–73; Economic Adviser, Ministry of Oil, Kuwait, 1974–75; Chief Executive and General Manager Arab Petroleum Investment Corporation (APICORP), Saudi Arabia, 1980–; Director, Compagnie Arabe et Internationale d'Investissement; Vice Chairman, Banque Arabe et International d'Investment; Director, Bahrain National Gas Company; member of the American Economic Association; *Interests and Recreations:* reading, music, theatre, swimming; *Languages:* Arabic, English, French; *Address:* P O Box 448, Dhahran Airport, Saudi Arabia; telephone: 8647400, 8640193, 8640196.

FARRAN, Abdul Mun'im Salih; Palestinian official/librarian; born 15 March 1938, Nablus, Palestine; *Religion:* Muslim; *Education:* Special Programme in Library Sciences, American University of Beirut, Lebanon 1962; course of instruction in Practical Librarianship, England, 1973; *Career:* Librarian since 1960; *Interests and Recreations:* travel, reading; *Languages:* Arabic, English; *Address:* Nablus Municipal Public Library, Nablus, West Bank, Jordan; telephone: 1356.

FARRASH, Abdul Malik Othman, Saudi Arabian official; born 1934; *Religion:* Muslim; *Education:* BA in Sociology, Cairo University, Egypt, 1957; *Career:* Sociology Inspector, 1958; Assistant Director General, Youth Welfare Administration, 1962; Youth Welfare Consultant, Ministry of Labour and Social affairs, 1964; Deputy Director, Social Affairs Department, Supreme Planning Council, 1964; member of Board of Industrial Development and Research Centre, Social Committe for Social Development, Applied Geology Centre, Executive Committee, Jeddah, Saudi Arabia; Director General of Technical Co-operation Administration, Council of Ministers Central Bureau; attended several UN General Assembly meetings as member of the Saudi Arabian Permanent Delegation to UN,1965, 1967, 1973, 1975; attended Arab League Social Studies Seminar, Committee for the Follow-up of Population Activities in the Arab Countries (joint UN Demographic Fund) Arab League Committee; *Publications:* articles published in local papers; *Interests and Recreations:* tennis, swimming; *Address:* Technical Co-operation Administration, Riyadh, Saudi Arabia; telephone: Office — 20054; Residence — 22247.

FARSI, Muhammad Said, Saudi Arabian official/architect/town planner; born 1934, Mecca, Saudi Arabia; married; one son; *Religion:* Muslim; *Education:* BSc, Architecture, University of Alexandria, Alexandria, Egypt, 1963; MSc, Architecture, University of Alexandria, Egypt, 1982; *Career:* Assistant to the Director of Planning, Western Region, Saudi Arabia, 1964–67; Director General of Planning, Western Region, 1967–76; Chief of the Municipality of Jeddah, 1973–82; Mayor of City of Jeddah, 1982–; *Decorations:* Medals from Jordan, Korea, China, Italy, Tunisia, Sweden; Hororary Citizen of Argentina, Equador, Indonesia; *Interests and Recreations:* reading, walking, history, architecture; member of several clubs and associations; *Languages:* Arabic, English, French; *Address:* 47 Falastin Street, Al Hamra, 88 Jeddah, Saudi Arabia.

FASSI, Abbas al-, Moroccan lawyer/politician; born 1940, Berkane, Morocco; married; *Religion:* Muslim; *Education:* Baccalaureat, Tangier; Licencie en Droit, Mohammed V University, Rabat, Morocco; *Career:* joined Istiqlal Party in 1958; President of General Union of Moroccan Students (UGEM) 1961; member of National Council of Istiqlal and later, 1965, of Central Committee; member of the Bar of City of Rabat 1964; Secretary of Bar of Rabat 1971; member of Executive Committee of Istiqlal Party 1974; Minister of Housing and National Territory, October 1977–80; Minister of Handicrafts and Social Affairs 1981–; *Languages:* Arabic, French; *Address:* Ministry of Handicrafts and Social Affairs, Rabat, Morocco.

175

FASSI FIHRI, Ahmad, Moroccan official; born 6 August 1936, Wajda, Morocco; married; two sons, two daughters; *Religion:* Muslim; *Education:* Licence in Law; Administrative Studies; *Career:* Private Secretary to the Minister of the Interior, 1956; Head of the Office, Department of Minerals and Geology, 1958; Head of the Office of the Minister of Foreign Affairs, 1959; Chargé d'Affaires, Moroccan Embassy in Berne, Switzerland, 1960; President of Meknes Municipality, 1963; Head of the Office of the Minister of the Moroccan Sahara, 1964–; Founder and Director of the National Centre of Documentation, Ministry of Planning,1967–; Founder and Director of the College of Mass Communications,1974–; member of the National Society of Journalists; Secretary General, Moroccan Society for Futuristic Studies; *Publications:* articles and papers in the field of mass communications, in Arabic and French; *Decorations:* Order of Ridha, Morocco, 1975, 1980; *Languages:* Arabic, French; *Address:* P O Box 826 Rabat, Morocco; telephone: 73131; telex: 31052.

FASSI, Muhammad al-, Moroccan academic/ man of letters; born 2 September 1906; married; three sons, three daughters; *Religion:* Muslim; *Education:* Qarawiyin University, Fes; BA and Diploma of Higher Studies, University of Paris, France; *Career:* Editor, Assifa fi-l Maghreb; member and President, North African Students Union; Founder of the Association of Arab Culture in Paris; Teacher, Lycée Lyautey, Casablanca, Morocco; Professor, Moroccan Institute of Higher Studies, 1935–40; Tutor to Royal Princes, 1941–44; Rector of Qarawiyin University, 1942–44, 1947–52; member of Istiqlal Party Executive Committee; Minister of Education and Fine Arts, 1955, and Minister of Youth Affairs and Sports, 1956; Rector of Moroccan Universities, 1958; President of Moroccan Delegations to UNESCO General Conferences, 1956, 1958, 1960, 1964; President, Centre of Coordination, Arab National Commission, UNESCO and ALESCO, 1958–; President of the Permanent Bureau Of the National Moroccan Commission for Education, Science and Culture, UNESCO-ALESCO, 1959; member of the Academy of Arabic Language, Cairo, Egypt, and of the Academy of Iraq; President of UNESCO Executive Council, 1964; Minister of State for Cultural Affairs and Traditional Education, 1968–71; President of African Universities Associations at Rabat Conference; Vice President of the Permanent Council for the International Conference of African Research Work at Dakar and Iraq; Tutor to Royal Princes and Princesses, 1973; member of the Executive Council of UNESCO, 1979; Minister of the Royal Cabinet, 1979; *Publications:* L'Evolution Politique et Culturelle au Maroc, 1958; *La Formation des Cadres au Maroc,* 1960; *Chants Ancien des Femmes de Fes,* 1967; and several other works on Berber dialects; *Interests and Recreations:* painting; *Languages:* Arabic, French; *Address:* Avenue des Muriers, Rute des Zaers, Rabat, Morocco; telephone: 52 365.

FATANI, Jamal Abdul Gader, Saudi Arabian academic/physician; born 1936, Mecca, Saudia Arabia; married; three daughters; *Religion:* Muslim; *Education:* MMBCh, Ain Shams University, Egypt, 1965; PhD, London University, Royal Free Hospital, London, 1971; *Career:* successively at the Faculty of Medicine, Riyadh University: Lecturer, Anatomy Department, 1971, Assistant Professor, Anatomy Department, 1973, Vice Dean, Faculty of Medicine, 1975, Associate Professor, Anatomy Department, 1978, Dean, Faculty of Medicine, 1978, Head of Department of Anatomy, 1980; *Interests and Recreations:* Arabic history, football, swimming; *Address:* Faculty of Medicine, University of Riyadh, P O Box 2925, Riyadh, Saudi Arabia; telephone: 481130.

FATFAT, Madhat, Lebanese diplomat; born 1915, Tyre, Lebanon; *Education:* Docteur ès-Lettres; *Career:* Foreign Service; Secretary, Arab League Council and Cultural Attaché, Arab League Secretariat, 1945–48; Chargé d'Affaires *ad interim,* Legation to Saudi Arabia, 1948–50; Cultural Attaché, Embassy to Egypt, 1950–53; Cultural Counsellor, Arab League, 1953–55; Consul General, Port Said, Egypt, 1955–57; Consul General, Cairo, 1958; Consul General, Port Said, 1959; Permanent Lebanese Delegate to Arab League, 1960; Ambassador to Libya, 1960–68; Head of Arab League Department, Ministry of Foreign Affairs, 1968–70; Ambassador to Yemen Arab Republic, 1970–73; Head of Department, Ministry of Foreign Affairs 1973–; *Address:* Ministry of Foreign Affairs, Beirut, Lebanon.

FATHALLAH, Imad; Lebanese banker; born 22 November 1950; Beirut; married; one son; *Religion:* Muslim; *Education:* BA in Economics, American University of Beirut; MBA, European Institute for Business Administration, INSEAD, France; *Career:* Assistant Director, Bankers Trust International Ltd, 1975–; founding member, Arab Bankers Association, London, 1980; *Interests and Recreations:* squash, skiing; *Languages:* Arabic, English, French, Spanish; *Address:* Office — Bankers Trust International Ltd, 56/60 New Broad Street, London EC2, England; Residence— 80 Oakwood Court, London N14, England; telephone: 6022874.

FATHALLAH, Muhammad, Lebanese diplomat; born 3 July 1909, Beirut, Lebanon; married; two sons; *Education:* Faculty of Law, Beirut, Lebanon; Faculty of Law, Aix en Provence, France; Licence in Law, Lyon University, France; *Career:* teacher and journalist 1930–37; Barrister at Law, 1937–46; entered the diplomatic service, successively posted to São Paolo, Brazil, 1946; Chargé d'Affaires, Embassy to Iran; Chargé d'Affaires, Embassy to Greece, 1949; Counsellor, Embassy to Argentine; London, UK; Consul General, Marseilles, France; Head, UN Department, Ministry of Foreign Affairs; Minister Plenipotentiary, Embassy to Czechoslovakia, 1957; Ambassador to Yugoslavia, 1963–66; Ambassador to Spain, 1966–69; Ambassador to India, 1969–73; Ambassador to Nepal, Sri Lanka, Indonesia and Thailand, 1970–73; Ambassador to India, 1973; *Publications: Rissalat al-Widah,* 1957; *Decorations:* Commander, Royal Order of the Phoenix, Greece; *Interests and Recreations:* swimming, walking, literature, doing odd jobs; *Languages:* Arabic, French; *Address:* Office — Lebanese Embassy, 23–48 Panch Scheel Marg, New Delhi, India.

FATHY, Hassan, Egyptian official/architect; born 23 March 1900, Alexandria, Egypt; *Religion:* Muslim; *Education:* Diploma, High School of Engineering, Architectural Section, Cairo, Egypt 1926; *Career:* Architect, Department of Municipal Affairs, Cairo, 1926–30; taught at Faculty of Fine Arts, Cairo, 1930–46; delegated to Antiquities Department to design and supervise the Gourna Village Project at Luxor, Upper Egypt, 1946–53; Director of School Buildings, Ministry of Education, 1949–52; Consultant to UN Relief and Works Agency (UNWRA); returned to teaching 1953; Dean, Architectural Section, Fine Arts Faculty, 1953–57; Consultant, Doxiadis Association; Lecturer, Athens Technical Institute; member of Research Project, City of the Future, 1957–62; Director, Housing Pilot Projects, Ministry of Scientific Research, 1963–65, UN Committee for Housing in South Arabia, 1965–66; Lecturer in the Philosophy of Town Planning, Al-Azhar University, Cairo, 1966–; Lecturer on Rural Housing, Faculty of Agriculture, Cairo University; *Publications: Architecture For the Poor,* Chicago, French translation, *Construire Avec le Peuple; The Arab House in the Urban Setting,* London; in Arabic, *Urban Architecture in the Middle East,* Beirut; *Constancy, Transposition and Change in the Arab City; Decorations:* Promotion Prize for Fine Arts and Letters and Gold Medal 1956; National Prize for Fine Arts and Letters, and Order of the Republic, 1967; *Interests and Recreations:* music, philosophy of science; *Languages:* Arabic, English, French; *Address:* 4 Darb el-Labbana, Citadel, Cairo, Egypt; telephone: 935211.

FATIH, Muhammad Bushara al-, Sudanese army officer; born 1932, Al-Obeid, Sudan; *Religion:* Muslim; *Education:* Military Academy, 1950–52; training course in Egypt; Staff Course at Camberley, UK; *Career:* commissioned into Artillery; Private Secretary to President Abboud, 1958–64; staff appointment at Khartoum, 1964–65; Garrison Commander, Yei, 1965; joined Instructors' Staff at the Sudanese Staff College; Commandant, Staff College, 1970; Adjutant General, 1971; appointed Deputy Chief of Staff, 1972; *Languages:* Arabic, English; *Address:* Ministry of Defence, Khartoum, Sudan.

FATTAL, Georges, Lebanese businessman; born 5 October 1941, Beirut, Lebanon; married; *Education:* London School of Economics, UK; *Career:* company manager; Assistant Director General, Khalil Fattal and Sons Company, Luxurama and other companies; member of the Board of Filteries Réunies; member of the Governing Committee of the Lebanese Red Cross; Swedish Consul to Lebanon; *Decorations:* Officer's Cross, Sovereign and Military Order, Malta, 1969; *Interests and Recreations:* member of the Rotary Club; *Languages:* Arabic, Franch, English; *Address:* Office — Fattal Building,

Rue du Port, Beirut, Lebanon; Residence -- Salamouni Building, Mexico Street, Beirut, Lebanon.

FAWWAZ BIN ABDUL AZIZ, HRH Saudi Arabian Prince/administrator; born 1934, Taif, Saudi Arabia; son of late King Abdul Aziz; *Religion:* Muslim; *Education:* private tutoring by grand ulamas; *Career:* Governor of Riyadh for several years; Governor for Holy Mecca, 1971–79; *Decorations:* Order of the Cedar of Lebanon; Decoration from Spain, and other countries; *Interests and Recreations:* swimming, riding; *Address:* Jeddah, Saudi Arabia; telephone: Office — 25055; Residence — 25555.

FAWZI, Mahmud, Egyptian diplomat/politician; born 19 September 1900; married; one son, two daughters; *Religion:* Muslim; *Education:* Cairo University, Egypt; Rome University, Italy; Liverpool University, UK; Columbia University, USA; *Career:* Egyptian Diplomatic Service, 1923; Vice-Consul, New York and New Orleans, USA, 1926–29; Consul, Kobe, Japan, 1929–36; Director, Department of Nationalities, Ministry of Foreign Affairs, 1939–41; Consul General, Jerusalem, 1941–44; Egyptian Delegate to United Nations, 1945; Egyptian Representative to Security Council, 1949; Ambassador to UK, 1952; Minister of Foreign Affairs, 1952; Deputy Prime Minister for Foreign Affairs, 1964–67; Special Assistant to the President on Foreign Affairs, 1967–70; Prime Minister, 1970–72; Vice-President and Adviser to the President for Political Affairs, 1972; retired 1974; *Languages:* Arabic, English, French; *Address:* Ministry of Foreign Affairs, Cairo, Egypt.

FAYEZ, Muhammad Ali al-, Saudi Arabian politician; born 1937 Hail, Saudi Arabia; married; one son, three daughters; *Religion:* Muslim; *Education:* BA in Law, Cairo University, Egypt, 1960; MA in Public Administration, University of Southern California, Los Angeles, USA, 1964; *Career:* Legal Adviser to the Council of Ministers, 1960–70; Director General, General Organization for Social Insurance, (GOSI), 1970–71; Deputy Minister of Labour and Social Affairs, and Chairman of the GOSI Board of Directors, 1971–80; Governor of the General Organization for Social Insurance, GOSI, 1980–83; Minister of Labour and Social Affairs, 1983–; Vice Chairman of the Board of Directors of GOSI; member of the Supreme Board of King Saud University, of the Civil Service Board; *Interests and Recreations:* reading, swimming, travel, Arabic arts; *Languages:* Arabic, English; *Address:* Ministry of Labour and Social Affairs, P O Box 2963, Riyadh, Saudi Arabia; telephone: 4785849; telex: 201043 LABOUR SJ.

FAYEZ, Zuhair Hamid, Saudi Arabian businessman/architect; born 1944, Jeddah, Saudi Arabia; *Education:* MSc, Architecture, University of Colorado, USA; *Career:* architect in American practice, Denver, Colorado, USA; introduced up to date architectural techniques to Saudi Arabia; built the Grand Sports Gymnasium, Riyadh; Director, Zuhair Fayez Practice, Jeddah; *Interests and Recreations:* football; *Address:* P O Box 5445, Jeddah, Saudi Arabia; telephone: Jeddah 54255.

FAYIZ, Akif Mathqal al-, Jordanian politician; born 1924, Amman, Jordan; married; *Education:* university studies, Lebanon; *Career:* Director, Jordan Farmers' Association, 1945–46; member of Chamber of Deputies, 1947–50, 1950–56, 1956–61, 1961–62; Minister of Agriculture, Construction and Development, 1957; Minister of Agriculture and Defence, 1957–58; Minister of Agriculture, Construction and Development, 1958; Minister of Agriculture, 1958–59; Minister of Agriculture and Social Affairs, 1959–60; Minister of Defence, 1960–62; Minister of Public Works and Communications, 1963; member of Chamber of Deputies, 1963–66, 1967–74; Minister of Communications, Tourism and Antiquities, 1967; Minister of Communications and Minister of State for Prime Ministerial Affairs, 1967–68; Deputy Premier and Minister of Interior, 1969–70; Minister of State for Prime Ministerial Affairs, 1970; Senator, 1976–; *Decorations:* Renaissance Medal 1st Class; Star of Jordan 1st Class; Iraqi Rafidain Order 1st Class; Independence Medal 2nd Class; Moroccan Military Order 1st Class; *Address:* P O Box 1240, Amman, Jordan; telephone: 44999, 663312.

FAYROUZ, (stage name of Nohad HADDAD), Lebanese artist/singer; born 1934, Beirut, Lebanon; married; three sons, one daughter; *Education:* Certificate from the National Conservatory of Music, Beirut, Lebanon; *Career:* became famous with her first song *Itab* 1950; mainly interprets songs written by her husband; has participated in the Baalbeck International Festival, 1957, 1959, 1961, 1966 and 1969; toured and performed in Brazil, UK, Syria, Jordan, Kuwait, France; has performed in various films and musicals among which *Le Vendeur de Bagues, Bint el-Hares; al-Chaks; Le Pont de la Lune;* recorded many successful songs and plays among which *Rajioun; Le Bracelet; Baalbakiya; Decorations:* Gold Medal, Lebanese Order of Merit; as well as Jordanian and Syrian decorations; a postage stamp bearing her picture was issued in her honour by the Syrian Government, 1969; *Languages:* Arabic, French; *Address:* Shams Building, Roauché, Beirut, Lebanon.

FAYYAD, Khalid Abdullah, al-, Jordanian politician/farmer; born 18 March, 1927, Deir al-Ghusoun, Tulkarm, Jordan; married; one son, four daughters; *Religion:* Muslim; *Education:* Diploma in General Agriculture, 1946; specialist course of orchards, California Polytechnic, USA, 1961; *Career:* Director of Agriculture, Nablus, 1967; seconded as Director of Agriculture, Abu Dhabi 1967–68; retired 1973; member of Tulkarm Jordan Chamber of Deputies; appointed by HM King Hussain as member of National Consultative Council, 1978–; *Decorations:* Independence Medal, Jordan, 1972; *Interests and Recreations:* agricultural sciences, political science, walking; *Languages:* Arabic, English; *Address:* P O Box 8212, Amman Jordan; telephone: 39811.

FAYYAD, Sulaiman, Egyptian writer; born 1929, Mansura Governorate, Egypt; *Religion:* Muslim; *Education:* Al-Azhar University, Egypt; *Career:* teacher of Arabic in Egypt, and Saudi Arabia; *Publications:* collection of short stories including *Atshan ya Sabaya; Address:* c/o The General Egyptian Book Organisation, Corniche el Nil, Bulaq, Cairo, Egypt.

FEGHALI, Monsignor Joseph, Lebanese ecclesiastic/academic; born 6 February 1908, Kafr Abida, Lebanon; *Religion:* Christian; *Education:* Higher Studies, Catholic Institute of Paris, and the Sorbonne, Paris, France; BA in Philosophy; PhD in Canonical Law; Diploma of Higher Studies in History; *Career:* Representative of the Maronite Patriarch in France; Director, Franco-Lebanese Foyer of Paris; Head of Oriental Law Department,

Catholic Institute of Paris; Professor of Law, of Islamic-Christian Institutions, and of Arabic Language and Literature, University of Paris, France and University of Louvain, Belgium; *Publications: L'Histoire de Droit de l'Eglise Maronite,* Paris, 1962; *Contes, Légendes, Coutumes Populaires du Liban,* Louvain 1976, 1977, 1978, three vols (Arabic texts in Lebanese dialect with transcription, translation, linguistic and ethnographic annotation); co-author and contributor to numerous other books, reviews and dictionaries; numerous studies on Islamic law and on the disciplines of the oriental churches; *Decorations:* Chevalier de la Légion d'Honneur, France; Commandeur des Palmes Académiques, France; Grand Officer, the Order of Leopold II, Belgium; *Interests and Recreations:* member of the Asian Society, of the Society of the History of Law, of the Intenational Association for the Study of Canonical Law, of the Toulouse Academy of Legislation; *Languages:* Arabic, French; *Address:* 104 Boulevard Arago, 75014 Paris, France; telephone: 633 5141.

FEKIH, Mungi, Tunisian politician; born 25 November, 1935, Kairouan, Tunisia; married; three children; *Religion:* Muslim; *Education:* Maîtrise de Langue et Littérature Arabes; *Career:* Governor of Kairouan, Tunisia; Official, Arab Bank, African Economic Development Department, Tunis, Tunisia; Chef du Cabinet and Director of the Office of the Secretary General of the Arab League, 1979–; *Languages:* Arabic, French; *Address:* League of Arab States, 37 Avenue Khereddine Pacha,Tunis, Tunisia.

FELLAGUE-ARIOUAT, Mustafa, Algerian UN official; born 31 January, 1931, Blida, Algeria; married; *Education:* Certificate, Teachers Training College, 1951–52; Diploma, National Centre for Teachers Training, Beaumount, France, 1954–55; Diploma, Faculty of Science, Institute of Human Biometrics and Vocational Guidance, Marseille University, France, 1959–61; *Career:* military service, 1956–58; Head of Training and Recruitment, Esso Standard, Algeria, 1963–64; Personnel Officer, World Meteorological Organization, Brazzaville, 1965–68; Personnel Officer, World Meteorological Organization, Geneva, Switzerland, 1968–72; Chief Personnel Division, World Meteorological Organization, 1972–; *Interests and Recreations:* bridge, chess, bowling, fishing, reading; *Languages:* Arabic, English, French; *Address:* Personnel Division, World Meteorological Organization, 41 Avenue Giuseppe Motta, CH-1211, Geneva 20, Switzerland; telephone: 022 346400.

FENJIRO, Abdul Jalil, Moroccan journalist; born 1938, Rabat, Morocco; married; *Religion:* Muslim; *Education:* in Rabat, Fes and France; *Career:* Moroccan National News Agency, Maghreb Arabe Presse (MAP), 1962–; Director of Agency after nationalisation 1974; Moroccan Delegate to several international communication conferences; *Languages:* Arabic, French; *Address:* Maghreb Arabe Presse, P O Box 1049, Rabat, Morocco.

FERDUS, Khadijah Mustafa al-, Saudi Arabian physician; born 1943, Mecca, Saudi Arabia; *Religion:* Muslim; *Education:* MD, BCh; *Career:* former physician, Jeddah Public Hospital; member of British Medical Association; Physician, King's Hospital, Jeddah, Saudi Arabia; *Interests and Recreations:* reading, walking; *Address:* P O Box 5934, Jeddah, Saudi Arabia; telephone: Office -- 6425576.

FEZZANI, Muhammad Ali Hussain, Libyan banker; born 15 January 1938, Benghazi, Libya; married; three sons, one daughter; *Religion:* Muslim; *Education:* Secondary School Certificate; *Career:* joined Barclays Bank, Benghazi, Libya, 1956–60; Head of Department, British Bank for the Middle East, Benghazi, Libya, 1960–67; Assistant Manager, Bank of North Africa, Benghazi, Libya, 1968–70; Assistant Manager, Wahda Bank, Benghazi, Libya, 1970–71; Manager, Wahda Bank, Benghazi, Libya, 1971–73; Assistant General Manager, 1973–75; Assistant General Manager UBAF Bank Ltd, 1975–; *Interests and Recreations:* reading, music; *Languages:* Arabic, English; *Address:* 55 Corringway, Ealing, London W5; telephone: 997 7886.

FILALI, Abdul Aziz, Moroccan judge/legal arbitrator; born June 1924; *Religion:* Muslim; *Education:* Lycée Gouraud, Rabat, Morocco; Lycee Lyantey, Casablanca, Morocco; Ecole Nationale d'Organisation Economique et Sociale, Paris, France; Grenoble University, France and Institut des Hautes Etudes, Rabat; Doctor of Law; *Career:* Barrister in Casablanca, Morocco 1951–55; First President, International Tribunal of Tangier, Court of Appeal Tangier, and Court of Appeal, Rabat, 1955–; Lecturer, Institut des Hautes Etudes Marocaines, Ecole Marocaine d'Administration, then Assistant Director, Ecole Marocaine; President of Centre Africain de Formation et de Recherches Administratives pour le Development (CAFRAD), Tangier 1964–; member of Commission of Arabization of Code of Commercial Law; designated Conciliator and Arbitrator, International Centre for Settlement of Investment Disputes, Washington, D.C., USA; Arbitrator, Franco-Arab Chamber of Commerce, 1976–; *Publications: Marriage in Moroccan Law,* (Arabic), *Notes Judiciaires,* (French); *Languages:* Arabic, French; *Address:* Angle Bd, Alexandre 1 er, et Bd de la Grand Ceinture, Casablanca, Morocco.

FILALI, Abdul Latif, Moroccan diplomat; born 1928, Fes, Morocco; married; *Religion:* Muslim; *Education:* Doctor of Law, University of Paris, France; *Career:* attached to the Centre National des Recherches Scientifiques, Paris, 1954–56, historical and diplomatic research on Moroccan history; Ambassador, Ministry of Foreign Affairs, 1957; Legal Adviser to Moroccan Ministry of Foreign Affairs; member of Moroccan delegation at general sessions of UN General Assembly, 1956; Moroccan Permanent Delegation to UN, 1958; Head of Moroccan delegation at 13th UN Assembly; Chief of Royal Cabinet, 1959; Chargé d'Affaires, Embassy to France, 1960–61; Director of the Royal Cabinet and Director of Protocol at the Palace, 1961; Ambassador to the Benelux countries, resident in Brussels, 1962–63; Ambassador to China, 1965; Ambassador to Algeria, 1967; Minister of Higher Education, 1968; Ambassador to Spain, 1969; Minister of Foreign Affairs, 1971–72; Ambassador to Spain, 1974–82; Minister, Royal Court, 1982–; *Languages:* Arabic, French; *Address:* Royal Court, Rabat, Morocco.

FINAISH, Muhammad, Libyan banker/IMF official; born 13 March 1936, Tripoli, Libya; married; *Religion:* Muslim; *Education:* BCom, University of Cairo, Egypt, 1955–59; MA in Economics, 1965–67; PhD in Economics, University of Southern California, Los Angeles, USA, 1968–72; *Career:* Assistant to the Public Relations Manager, Libya Shell, Tripoli, 1960–61; Foreign Relations Director,

Senussi University, Beida, Libya, 1962; Secretary General, Bank of Libya, 1963–65; Director, Research Department, Central Bank of Libya, 1972–73; Alternate Executive Director, IMF, Washington D.C., 1974; *Languages:* Arabic, English; *Address:* International Monetary Fund, 700 19th St NW, Washington D.C. 20431, USA; telephone: (202) 393 6362.

FIQ'I, Muhammad Hassan, Saudi Arabian poet; born 1924; *Religion:* Muslim; *Education:* general; *Career:* member of Jeddah Literary Society; regular contributor to major newspapers; *Publications:* several collections of poems; articles in major daily newspapers and weekly magazines; *Address:* c/o *Al-Madina* daily newspaper, P O Box 807, Jeddah, Saudi Arabia.

FISHAWY, Saad Samuel, al-, Egyptian lawyer/financial adviser; resident in the USA; born 20 February 1924, Tanta, Egypt; married; three sons; *Religion:* Christian; *Education:* BA, Law School, University of Cairo, Egypt, 1944; winner of The Shari'a (Islamic Law), Special Award, 1944; MA, Civil Law and Economics, Law School, Cairo University, Egypt, 1950; Doctor of Law, University of Chicago Law School, Chicago University, USA, 1959; *Career:* District Attorney, Luxor, 1945; Partner, Saba Habashy law firm, Cairo, 1946–53; private law practice, Cairo, 1953–57; assisted with establishment of *Peace Through the Rule of Law,* Centre, Duke University, 1959; Attorney, IBRD (World Bank), Washington D.C., USA, 1959–63; General Counsel, Kuwait Fund for Arab Economic Development, Kuwait, 1963–66; Senior Counsel for Arab Countries, Legal Department, IBRD, Washington D.C., USA, 1966–74; Adviser, Finance Department, IBRD, Washington D.C., 1974–76; Special Adviser to the President, IBRD, Washington D.C., 1976–; Professor of Shari'a (Islamic Law), Columbia Law School, Columbia University, 1978, and Georgetown University, 1979–; *Publications: Freedom of Belief,* 1953; *Interests and Recreations:* swimming, tennis, chess; *Languages:* Arabic, English, French; *Address:* The World Bank, 1818 H Street, NW, Washington D.C., 20433, USA; Residence: 4155 North 27th Street, Arlington. Virginia 22207, USA.

FITOURI, Muhammad, Tunisian lawyer/politician; born 4 April 1925, Kairouan, Tunisia; married; *Religion:* Muslim; *Education:* Licence in Law, University of Paris, France; *Career:* practised as lawyer in Tunis, 1952–; member of the Council of the National Order of Lawyers, 1960; Barrister in the Court of Cassation, 1962; Deputy, and Tunis Municipal Counsellor, 1969; Minister of Justice, 1970; Minister of Finance, 1971; *Languages:* Arabic, French; *Address:* Ministry of Finance, Tunis, Tunisia; telephone: 262088.

FRANJIEH, Sulaiman, Lebanese former President; born 14 June 1910, Zghorta, Lebanon; married; two sons, three daughters; *Religion:* Christian; *Education:* Antoura College, Lebanon; *Career:* elected Deputy for Zghorta, 1960; Minister of Posts, Telegraphs and Telephones, 1960–61; Minister of Posts, Telegraphs and Telephones, and of Agriculture, 1961; re-elected Deputy for Zghorta, 1964, and 1968; Minister of the Interior, 1968; Minister of National Economy, 1969–70; elected President of the Lebanese Republic, 1970–76; *Decorations:* Grand Cordon, National Order of the Cedar, Lebanon 1970; *Interests and Recreations:* classical music, reading history, travel, shooting, riding; *Languages:* Arabic, French; *Address:* Rue du Patriarchat, Beirut, Lebanon.

FRAYAN, Hamad Bin Muhammad al-, Saudi Arabian official; born 1937; *Religion:* Muslim; *Education:* BA and MA in Islamic Shari'a; *Career:* successively Administrative Inspector; Judicial Inspector; Director of the Chief Justice's Office for Juridical Affairs; Deputy Director General; Director General, Judicial Affairs, Ministry of Justice; Deputy Minister for Administrative and Financial Affairs, Ministry of Justice 1980–; participated in the Conference of Arab Social Defence Organization, the Arab League, Cairo; member of AL-Gazira Press Organization; member of Riyadh Literary Club; *Publications: Development of the Judicial System in Saudi Arabia, The Gezia in Islam,* and several research papers; *Interests and Recreations:* swimming, shooting, reading; *Address:* Ministry of Justice, Riyadh, Saudi Arabia; telephone: 4351149.

FREIHA, Bassam Said, Lebanese politician/publisher; born 1939 Beirut; *Religion:* Christian; *Education:* BA in Political Science, 1961,

181

American University of Beirut, Lebanon; *Career:* President and Managing Director, Dar Assayad SAL; Political Adviser to Heads of two Arab States; Lebanese Diplomatic status; *Publications: Assayad* weekly magazine, 1943; *Al Anwar* daily newspaper, 1960; *Achabaka* weekly social features magazine, 1956; *Arab Defence Journal,* 1976; *Alidari* monthly management magazine, 1974; *Samar* weekly teenage photo story magazine, 1973; *Weekly Observer,* English language marketing and advertising magazine, 1970; *Decorations:* Jordan, Morocco, Sudan, Egypt and United Arab Emirates; *Languages:* Arabic, English, French; *Address:* Dar Assayad, P O Box 1038, Beirut, Lebanon; telephone: 452700; London Office — 5 Moore Street, London, SW3, England; telephone: 01 589 6743 ,589 7706; Paris Office — 65 Avenue d'Iena, Paris 16e, France; telephone: 501 5050.

FREIHA, Issam Said, Lebanese journalist; born 1936 Beirut; married; one son, two daughters; *Religion:* Christian; *Education:* BA in Political Sciences, AUB, 1959; *Career:* Chairman of The Board of *Dar Assayad*; Editor in Chief of all Dar Assayad publications, *Al-Anwaar* (daily), *Assayad* (weekly), Ach *abaka* (weekly), *Al Tayar* (daily), *Samar* (weekly), *Weekly Observer* (English), *Alidari* (monthly), *Reports and Background* (weekly in Arabic), *Feirouz* (monthly); member of International Press Syndicate; *Address:* Dar Assayad, P O Box 1038, Beirut, Lebanon; telephone: 452700; telex: 21660.

FREIJ, Elias, Palestinian politician; born 1918, Bethlehem; married; *Religion:* Christian; *Career:* businessman and owner of factory producing souvenirs and mementos for tourists; elected to Bethlehem Municipal Council, 1972; established Bethlehem Foundation to provide funds for the economic development of the town.

FUAD, Omar Ahmad, Egyptian banker; born 1923; *Religion:* Muslim; *Career:* Economic Chef de Cabinet to Gamal Abdul Nasser; Director of the Misr Bank, 1954; First President, Misr Foreign Trade Company; member of the National Assembly, 1964 and 1969; Chairman of the Assembly's Economic Affairs Committee; Managing Director, Chairman, Misr Bank, 1969; member of the General Committee of Citizens' War Committees, 1970; elected to People's Assembly

and was Chairman of its National Plan Committee, 1971; National Council for Production and Economic Affairs, 1974; Chairman, Banque Misr; *Languages:* Arabic, English; *Address:* 151 Muhammad Farid Street, Cairo, Egypt.

FUHAID, Khalid al-Mas'ud al-, Kuwaiti official; born Kuwait; married; *Religion:* Muslim; *Education:* Mubarakiyah School; Teachers College, Kuwait; *Career:* School Superintendent; Minister of Education, 1964–70; member of National Assembly; President of Kuwait Teachers' Association; *Address:* c/o Ministry of Education, P O Box 7, Kuwait.

FULAIJ, Abdul Latif al-, Kuwaiti politician; born 1932, Kuwait; *Religion:* Muslim; *Education:* Durham University, UK; *Career:* Assistant Secretary General of the Kuwait National Assembly; Chairman of the National Assembly, 1976; *Interests and Recreations:* fishing, swimming, gardening; *Languages:* Arabic, English, French; *Address:* The National Assembly, Kuwait.

FULAIJ, Faisal Saud al-, Kuwaiti aviation official; born 1933, Kuwait; married; *Religion:* Muslim; *Education:* Cairo University, Egypt; *Career:* Kuwait Municipality; member of the Board and Chairman, Kuwait Airways; resigned from Kuwait Airways, 1983; has represented Kuwait at various international aviation conferences; *Languages:* Arabic, English; *Address:* Kuwait Airways Corporation, P O Box 394, Kuwait; telephone: 711166; telex: 23036.

FULAYFIL, Rashid Ali, Bahraini official/physician; born 15 May 1931, Muharraq, Bahrain; married; three sons, one daughter; *Religion:* Muslim; *Education:* MD, American University of Beirut, Lebanon, 1958; BSc in Medical Sciences, American University of Beirut, 1954; *Career:* Consultant, Bahrain Government Hospital, 1962–65; Chief of Services, Teues, Algeria, 1966–69; Chief of Services, Hospital Centre of University of Oran, Algeria, 1970–72; Instructor, University of Oran Hospital, Algeria, 1972–74; Assistant Professor, University Hospital of Oran, Algeria, 1974–80; Assistant Under Secretary, Hospital and Training Affairs, Ministry of Health, Bahrain, 1980–82; Under Secretary, Ministry of Health, Bahrain, 1982–; member of Bahrain Medical Society;

Publications: co-author of numerous works on medical subjects in French; *Interests and Recreations:* tennis, gymnastics, philosophy, poetry; member of Bahrain Archaeological Society; *Languages:* Arabic, French, English, German; *Address:* Ministry of Health, P O Box 12, Bahrain; telephone: Residence — 273933; Office — 252755.

FULY, Hanafi Ahmad al-; Egyptian lawyer; born 27 September, 1927, Cairo, Egypt; resident in Saudi Arabia; married; four sons, three daughters; *Religion:* Muslim; *Education:* LLB, Cairo University, Cairo Egypt, 1952; *Career:* Assistant Public Prosecutor, 1954; Public Prosecutor, 1956; Judge, 1962; Legal Adviser, High Dam Committee, 1963; Adviser, Ministry of Electricity, 1971; Legal Adviser, Ali and Fahad Shobokshi Group of Companies, The Shobokshi Maritime Company, Tuhama Advertising and Market Research Company; member of Egyptian Lawyers Union, The International Bar Association, London; *Languages:* Arabic, English, French; *Address:* Ali and Fahad Shobokshi Group of Companies, P O Box 5470, Jeddah, Saudi Arabia; telephone: 6658208/9.

FURAYH, Othman Salih al-; Saudi Arabian academic; born 1936 Onaiza, Saudi Arabia; married; one son, two daughters; *Religion:* Muslim; *Education:* BA, Arabic Language and Literature, Cairo University, 1962; MA, Arabic Literature, University of Durham, UK, 1969; PhD, Arabic Literature, University of Khartoum, 1977; *Career:* successively at the Faculty of Arts, Riyadh University, Saudi Arabia; Tutor, 1962, Lecturer, 1969, Instructor, 1977, Assistant Professor, 1978–, and Faculty member, Riyadh University; *Decorations:* Social Board Award, Student Affairs, Riyadh University, 1979; *Interests and Recreations:* tennis, volleyball, Arabic literature, the Abbasid Period; *Languages:* Arabic, English; *Address:* Arabic Department, Faculty of Arts, Riyadh University, Saudi Arabia; telephone: 4029500, 4811000.

G

GAAFAR, Muhammad Ali Bakhit, Sudanese politician; *Religion:* Muslim; *Education:* University of Khartoum, Sudan; University of Exeter, UK; University of London, UK; PhD in Political Science, Cambridge University, UK; *Career:* Deputy Under Secretary, Ministry of Local Governments, Sudan; Lecturer in Public Administration, University of Khartoum; Minister of Local Government, 1971–75; played an important role in the negotiations leading to the Addis Ababa Agreement on Southern Sudan; active in the political development and practical organisation of the Sudanese Socialist Union (SSU); Deputy Secretary General, Sudanese Socialist Union, 1974; member of the SSU Political Bureau since its establishment; Chief Editor of *Al-Sahafa* (The Press) newspaper, 1974; Leader of the People's Assembly, and Assistant Secretary General of the SSU, 1975; *Languages:* Arabic, English; *Address:* Sudanese Socialist Union, Khartoum, Sudan.

GAI, Martin Majier, Sudanese lawyer/politician; born 1 January 1938, Sudan; married; seven children; *Religion:* Christian; *Education:* LLB, University of Khartoum; *Career:* Legal Assistant in Judiciary, 1967; Judge of Second Grade, 1969; Judge of First Grade, 1972; Province Judge, 1976; Deputy Speaker, People's Regional Assembly, Southern Region, 1978; Regional Minister, Cooperation, Commerce and Supply, 1979; Regional Minister of Coordination and Legal Affairs, Juba, 1980–; *Decorations:* Medal of Neilin, 2nd Class; *Interests and Recreations:* tennis, gardening; *Languages:* Arabic, English, Dinka; *Address:* Regional Ministry of Coordination and Legal Affairs, Juba, Sudan; telephone: 2694.

GAILANI, Ahmad Zafar, Iraqi diplomat/lawyer; born 1925, Baghdad, Iraq; married; one daughter; *Religion:* Muslim; *Education:* LLB, Law College, Cairo University, Egypt, 1947; *Career:* joined Iraqi Bar Association, 1948; Ministry of Foreign Affairs, Baghdad, 1949; Attaché, Embassy of Iraq, London, 1951–54; Vice Consul, Karmanshah, Iran, 1954–58; 2nd Secretary, Embassy of Iraq, Egypt, 1958–61; Director, Afro-Asian Section, Political Department, Ministry of Foreign Affairs, Iraq, 1961–63; Consul General, New York, USA, 1963–67; Acting Chief of Protocol in Presidential Palace, 1967–69; Minister-Counsellor, Embassy of Iraq to Spain, 1969–71; Ambassador of Iraq to Saudi Arabia, 1972–76; Ambassador of Iraq to Pakistan, concurrently accredited to Thailand, 1976–; *Decorations:* Afganistan, Star Decoration, 3rd Garde, 1951; Coronation Medal, UK, 1952; France, Order of Merit Commodore, 1968; Spain Order of Merit, 1971; *Languages:* Arabic, English, French, Persian; *Address:* Embassy of the Republic of Iraq, House No 1 Street No 15, Sector F/72, Islamabad, Pakistan; telephone: 29091/20752.

GAILANI, Muhammad Rasul al-, Jordanian official/diplomat; born 30 March, 1933, Salt, Jordan; married; *Religion:* Muslim; *Education:* BA, Law, Damascus University, Damascus Syria, 1956; *Career:* Teacher, 1953–57; 1st Lieutanent, Jordan Army, 1957; Legal Adviser, General Security, 1957–60; Deputy Director, Public Investigations, 1961–62; Director of Public Investigations, 1962–63; Director of General Intelligence, 1964–68; Ambassador, Ministry of Foreign Affairs, 1968; Director, General Security, 1968–69; Minister of Interior, 1969–70; retired 1971; Adviser to HM King Hussain for National Security, 1971–72; Ambassador, Ministry of Foreign Affairs, 1972–73; Director of General Intelligence and Adviser to HM King Hussain for National Security, 1973–74; Adviser to HM King Hussain, 1974–; *Decorations:* Order of Independence, 1st Class; Order of the Star of Jordan, 1st

Class; Renaissance Medal, 1st Class; Order of the Tunisian Republic, 1st Class; Medal of the Service of the Malaysian Crown, 2nd Class; Patriarch Athanagoros Medal, 2nd Class; *Address:* P O Box 9240, Amman, Jordan; telephone: 21116.

GAILANI, Musa al-, Jordanian diplomat; born 1933, Jordan; married; three children; *Religion:* Muslim; *Education:* in Baghdad and Cairo; *Career:* joined Ministry of Foreign Affairs, Jordan; First Secretary, Jordan Embassy, London, England, 1969–71; Head of Information, Ministry of Foreign Affairs, 1972; Director General, Jordan News Agency, and Jordan Broadcasting Service, 1973–1975; Ambassador, Embassy of Jordan, Bahrain, 1975; *Languages:* Arabic, English, French, Italian; *Address:* Ministry of Foreign Affairs, Amman, Jordan.

GALAL, Muhammad Nadir, Egyptian artist/ film director; born 29 January 1941, Cairo, Egypt; married; one son, two daughters; *Religion:* Muslim; *Education:* BA in Commerce; Diploma of the Higher Institute of Cinema; *Career:* Research Assistant, Higher Institute of Cinema, 1965; Assistant Producer, 1970; Producer and Director, 1971–; *Interests and Recreations:* cinema, chess, bridge; *Languages:* Arabic, English, French; *Address:* Office — Galal Films Company, Producers and Distributors, 85 Ramses Street, Cairo, Egypt; Residence -- 4 Granada Street, Roxy, Masr al-Gedida, Cairo, Egypt; telephone: 866642.

GAMA, Abid Husni, Saudi Arabian academic; born 1944, Taif, Saudi Arabia; *Education:* BA, Political Science, 1966; MA Political Science, 1969; MA, in History, 1971; MA in Oriental Studies, 1971; PhD in History, 1972; *Career:* Manager, Purchasing Department, Modern Industries (Tide Plant), Jeddah, 1966, 1967; Chairman of Department of History, King Abdul Aziz University, Jeddah, Saudi Arabia; attended Conference on Middle East Studies, USA, 1971; *Interests and Recreations:* tennis, swimming, photography; *Address:* P O Box 2147, Jeddah, Saudi Arabia; telephone: Jeddah 26286.

GAMASY, General Muhammad al-, Egyptian army commander; born 9 September 1921, Minufiya Governorate, Egypt; married; one son, two daughters; *Religion:* Muslim; *Edu-*

cation: Military Academy, 1939; Staff College, 1951; Nassir Higher Military Academy, 1966; Colonel, 1957; Brigadier, 1962; Major General, 1965; Lieutenant General, 1973; General, 1974; Assistant Director of Mobilization Department, 1954; Commander of the 5th Regiment, 1955; Staff Officer of the Armour Corps, 1957; Commander of the 2nd Armoured Brigade, 1959; Commander of the Armour School, 1961; Chief of Army Operational Branch, 1966; Chief of Staff of the Eastern Military Zone, 1967; Deputy Director of Military Intelligence Department, 1968; Commander of the Operational Group of the Syrian Front, 1970; Chief of the Armed Forces Training Department, 1971; Chief of the Operations Department, and Deputy Chief of Staff of the Armed Forces, 1972; Chief of Staff of the Armed Forces, 1973; Minister of War and Commander in Chief of the Armed Forces, 1974; Deputy Prime Minister, Minister of War and Commander in Chief of the Armed Forces, 1976; Commander in Chief of the Unified Arab Forces, 1976; *Decorations:* Liberation Order, 1952; Memorial Order of the UAR Establishment, 1958; Order of the Star of Honour, 1973; Training Order, 1st class, Syria, 1973; Order of the Star of Honour, PLO, 1974; Order of Military Honour, Knight Rank, Syria, 1974; Order of Courage, Libya, 1974; Order of the Nielin, 1st Class, Sudan, 1974; King Abdul Aziz Order 1st Class, 1974; Member of the Order of the British Empire, MBE; and several other medals from various countries; *Languages:* Arabic, English, French; *Address:* Ministry of Defence, Cairo, Egypt.

GAMMOH, Sami Ibrahim, Jordanian official/diplomat; born 1940 Salt, Jordan; married; one son, one daughter; *Education:* MA in Economics; *Career:* Economic Counsellor, Embassy of Jordan, Cairo, Egypt, 1968–73; Permanent Representative of Jordan, Council of Arab Economic Unity and Arab Economic Council, 1970–73; Deputy Permanent Representative of Jordan to the UN, 1975–78; Director of Private Office, Ministry of Foreign Affairs, 1978–80; Director General of Budget Department, 1980–; Chairman of the Board of Directors of *Dar al-Sha'b* daily newspaper, 1982–; member of Jordan Society for International Affairs; *Languages:* Arabic, English, French; *Address:* P O Box 1860 Amman, Jordan.

GANDOUL, Said Abdul Aziz al-, Saudi Arabian official/educationalist; born 1923; *Religion:* Muslim; *Education:* College of Sharia (Islamic Law), Mecca, Saudi Arabia; BA, Islamic Law; *Career:* Director of Religious Institute, Mecca, 1957; Assistant Director General, Department of Education, 1965; Director General, High School Education, 1966; Assistant Director General of Education; Vice President of Control and Investigation Board; member of Supreme Commission for Islamic Indoctrination; member of the Board, Imam Schools; *Publications:* several books on religion and education; *Interests and Recreations:* reading; *Address:* Riyadh University Quarter, Riyadh, Saudi Arabia; telephone: Riyadh 52877.

GARABET, Samir Nouri, Iraqi engineer; born 29 July 1934; Iraq; married , 1964; one son, one daughter; *Religion:* Christian; *Education:* BSc, Civil Engineering, University of Leeds, England, 1958; MICE, member of the Institution of Civil Engineers, UK, 1965; Chartered Engineer, the Council of Engineering Institutions, UK, 1965; *Career:* Senior Civil Engineer, Iraq Petroleum Company, 1964; Technical Assistant, General Management, Iraq Petroleum Company, 1965; Senior Assistant, Iraq Petroleum Company, 1970; Chief Engineer, Northern Petroleum Organisation, 1975; Chief Engineer, Planning, Northern Petroleum Organisation, 1978; member of the Iraqi Engineers Society; *Interests and Recreations:* swimming, tennis, badminton, travel; *Languages:* Arabic, English; *Address:* Planning Department, Northern Petroleum Organisation, P O Box 1, Kirkuk, Iraq; telephone: 5539, 7916.

GARRANA, Hassan Rashid, Egyptian lawyer/IMF official; born 20 November 1918; married; *Education:* Law Degree, Faculty of Law, Cairo University, Egypt, 1936–40; Diploma in Public Law, 1940–41; Diploma in Economics, 1941–42; PhD, 1942–45; *Career:* Counsellor, Legal Department, Government of Egypt, 1941–43; Assistant Professor, Cairo University, 1943–45; Counsellor, International Monetary Fund, USA, 1947–48; Lecturer, Department of Graduate Studies, School of Commerce, University of Alexandria, Egypt, 1950–51; Senior Lawyer, Garrana and Badr Law Office, Egypt, 1948–65; Lawyer, International Finance Corporation, USA, 1965–71; Senior Coun-sellor, International Finance Corporation, Washington D.C., USA, 1971; member of the Board of Alexandria Bar Association, of the Association of International Studies, Cairo; *Publications: Extent of Egyptian Public Authorities Right to Issue Regulations,* 1945; *Introduction to the Study of Law,* 1946; *Egyptianization of Foreign Investments in Egypt,* 1947; *Legal Aspects Relating to Imposition of Arabic Language on Foreign Companies in Egypt,* 1947; *Interests and Recreations:* fishing, member of the Alexandria Sporting Club, and of the Alexandria Fishing Club; *Languages:* Arabic, French, English; *Address:* Office — International Finance Corporation, 1818 H Street NW, Washington D.C. 20433, USA; telephone: (202) 393 6360; Residence -- 1200 N Nash Street, Apt 254, Arlington, Virginia, 22209, USA; telephone: (703) 254 7324.

GASIM, Awn Sharif al- Sudanese official/academic; born 15 October 1933, Khartoum, Sudan; married; three sons, two daughters; *Religion:* Muslim; *Education:* BA, University of Khartoum, Sudan; MA, London University, UK; PhD, Edinburgh University, UK; *Career:* Lecturer, London University, 1960–61; Lecturer, College of Arts, Khartoum University, 1961–68; Senior Lecturer, Khartoum University, 1969; Head of the Translation Department, Khartoum University, 1969; Chief Editor of *Sudanese Studies* published by the Institute of African and Asian Studies, University of Khartoum; Minister of Religious Affairs and Waqfs, 1971; *Publications: Primary Readers for the Sudan,* (in Arabic), 1969; *The Diplomacy of the Prophet Muhammad* (in Arabic), 1970; *Aspects of the Cultural Renaissance,* 1971; *Dictionary of Sudanese Colloquial Arabic,* 1971; *In the Battle of the Heritage,* 1972; *Basrawi Poetry in the Omayyad Age,* 1972; *Studies in Colloquial Arabic,* 1973; *Religion in Everyday Life,* 1974; *From the Prophet's Teaching,* 1975; *Islamica: Spiritual Heritage and National Renaissance,* 1976; *Decorations:* Order of the Constitution, 1973; Order of the Two Niles, 1975; Gold Medal of Arts, Science and Letters, 1975; *Interests and Recreations:* Islamic culture and civilization, reading, walking; *Languages:* Arabic, English; *Address:* Ministry of Religious Affairs and Waqfs, Khartoum, Sudan; telephone: 79803.

GAZZAZ, Muhammad Salih al-Shaikh,
Saudi Arabian official/Islamic scholar; born
1902, Mecca, Saudi Arabia; *Religion:* Muslim; *Career:* former Secretary General of
Muslim World League, Mecca; promotes
Islam and endeavours to safeguard its true
teaching and practice throughout the world,
assisting Islamic communities, minorities,
cultural centres, societies, mosques and
schools in Asia, Africa, Europe and the
Americas; *Address:* World Muslim League,
Holy Mecca, Saudi Arabia.

GEAGEA, Joseph Tannous, Lebanese banker;
born 1921, Lebanon; Regligion: Christian;
Education: Graduated University of St.
Joseph, Beirut, 1945; *Career:* entered
banking, specialised in the field of Foreign
Exchange; Founder and Chairman of Banque
J. Geagea SAL, 1962–; Chairman of the
Lebanese Bankers Association, 1969–;
Chairman, Union of Arab Banks for several
years; *Address:* Banque J. Geagea SAL,
Immeuble Geagea, Rue El-Arz P O Box
1704 Beirut, Lebanon; telephone: 892660,
892011.

GEBARA, Georgette, Lebanese artist/
choreographer; born 3 September 1937, Jerusalem, Palestine; *Religion:* Christian; *Education:* Ballet, Yugoslavia; *Career:* Founder,
Lebanese School of Ballet, 1964; Founder,
first ballet company in Lebanon, 1966;
Director of Branch of same school, Tripoli,
1972; Choreographer and Director of plays
and musicals, 1964–; member of panel of TV
programme for discovering and encouraging
talent, 1974–; writer, weekly half hour radio
programme on dance, 1968–70; Professor of
Dance, Institute of Fine Arts, Lebanese
University, 1966–; founding member and
representative of Lebanon, The International
Centre for Traditional Music and Dance,
Tunis, 1970; *Publications:* articles in *Schaus-
Fuhrer,* vols, IX,X,XI; Columnist, *Ciné
d'Orient;* lectures on dance; *Decorations:* Said
Akl Prize, 1972; *Interests and Recreations:*
reading, music, swimming, skiing, travel;
Languages: Arabic, English, French, Italian,
Greek, Spanish; *Address:* P O Box 113–5305,
Lebanon; telephone: office 347612; telephone: Residence 350554.

GEMAYEL, Shaikh Pierre, Lebanese former
President of Lebanon; born 1 November
1905, Bikfaya, Lebanon; married; one son,
Amin Gemayel, President of Lebanon, four
daughters; *Education:* Licence in Pharmaceutical Chemistry, French Faculty of Pharmacy and Medicine, St. Joseph University,
Beirut, Lebanon; training course at Hospital
Cochin, Paris, France; *Career:* one of the five
founding members of the Katayeb (Lebanese
Falangists), 1936; elected Head of the
Katayeb Party, 1937–; supporter of Camille
Chamoun, in 1958 crisis; Minister of Education, Agriculture and Public Works, 1958–60;
elected Deputy for Beirut, 1960; Minister of
Finance, 1960–61; later also Minister of
Health, 1961; Minister of State in charge of
Financial Policy; Minister of Public Works,
1961; resigned as Minister of State and
remained Minister of Public Works, 1961–
64; re-elected Deputy for Beirut, 1964;
Minister of Communications, and Public
Works, 1964–65; Minister of the Interior,
1966; formed alliance with Camille Chamoun
and Raymond Eddé, 1967–70; re-elected
Deputy for Beirut, 1968; Minister of the
Interior, of Tourism, of Health and of Posts,
Telegraphs and Telephones, 1968; Minister
of Public Works and Transport, 1969–70;
member of the National Dialogue Committee, 1975; *Decorations:* Gold Medal,
Lebanese Order of Merit; Officer, National
Order of the Cedar; Légion d'Honneur,
France; Grand Cordon, Egyptian Order of
the Nile; as well as many other decorations
and distinctions from Poland, Jordan, Egypt
and the Holy See; *Interests and Recreations:*
hunting; *Languages:* Arabic, French; *Address:* Office — Office of the Katayeb Party,
Rue des Libérateurs, Beirut, Lebanon; Residence— St. Joseph University Street, Beirut,
Lebanon.

GEORGE, Minor, Arab-American businessman; born 20 January 1922; maried; three
sons, one daughter; *Religion:* Christian; *Education:* BA, Western Reserve University,
Cleveland, Ohio, USA; Doctor of Law,
Cleveland Marshall Law School, Ohio, USA;
Career: lieutenant in US Navy for four years
during World War II; Sewer and Water
Contractor and Land Developer; Vice President, George Bros Inc (Sewer and Water
Contractors); President, Broad-Breck Development Corporation (Land Development);
President, Sebring Development Corporation,
(Land Development), Florida; President,
Parma International Travel Service, Ohio;
three terms as city Councilman, Parma,
Ohio; President of the National Association
of Arab-Americans, 1976; two terms as

President of Mid-West Federation of American Syrian-Lebanese Clubs; appointed by President Ford to serve on the President's Advisory Committee for Refugees; member of the Board of Directors of Middle East Educational Trust, Chevy Chase, Maryland; *Interests and Recreations:* member of the St. George Orthodox Church, Cleveland, Ohio and active in many civic and charitable organizations; *Languages:* Arabic, English; *Address:* 3370 Harris Road, Cleveland, Ohio 44147, USA.

GERMOUNI, Muhammad, Moroccan academic/banker; born 11 October 1947, Morocco; married; two sons; *Religion:* Muslim; *Education:* BA in Economics; Diploma in Higher Studies in Economics; Diploma of the Institute of Political Studies; PhD , Economics, University of Grenoble, France; *Career:* General Inspector and Director, National Bank for Economic Development, Rabat, 1972–; Professor, University of Mohammed V and Hassan II, Morocco, 1976–; Expert at the UN Economic Commission for Africa, Addis Ababa, 1978, 1979; Secretary General of the Association of Moroccan Economists; member of the Moroccan Association of Future Studies; member of the International Association of Economic Sciences; *Publications:* several essays and papers published in professional journals; *Interests and Recreations:* gymnastics, tennis, swimming, music; *Languages:* Arabic, French, English; *Address:* P O Box 407 Rabat, Morocco; telephone: 20819, 24274.

GEZAIRY, Hussain Abdul Razzaq, Saudi Arabian politican/physician, born 1934, Mecca, Saudi Arabia; *Education:* MSBCH, Cairo University, 1957; Diploma in General Surgery, Cairo University, 1960; FRCS, London, 1965; *Career:* General Practitioner, Riyadh University, 1960; Registrar, Brompton and Royal Free Hospitals, London; Founding Dean, Faculty of Medicine, University of Riyadh, 1966; Lecturer, Assistant Professor then Associate Professor in General Surgery, Faculty of Medicine, Riyadh University; External Examiner, Faculty of Medicine, Riyadh University; Minister of Health, Kingdom of Saudi Arabia, 1975–; Regional Director for the Eastern Mediterranean Region, World Health Organisation (WHO), 1982–; attended the Ordinary and Special Sessions of the Council of Arab Ministers of Health, the Ordinary and Special Sessions of

the Council of the Health Ministers of Arab States in the Gulf, the WHO Regional Sub-Committee Annual meetings for the Eastern Mediterranean, the World Health Assembly Sessions, the International Conferences for Medical Education, the Saudi Medical Seminars and Conferences, the Ministerial Consultation (under the auspices of WHO), Tehran, 1978; member of Ministerial Regional Consultation Committee, WHO, EMRO; President of the Higher Board, Arab Council for Medical Specializations, Arab Board; *Decorations:* King Abdul Aziz Decoration, Grade II; Leopold II Medal (The Grand Ornament), granted by His Majesty the King of Belgium; Bright Star Decoration National Republic of China, 1981; *Interests and Recreations:* reading, sports, music; *Address:* Ministry of Health, Airport Road, Riyadh, Saudi Arabia; telephone: 4033567; telex: 201628 Health SJ, 201157 DHELTH SJ.

GHAFARI, Lieutenant Colonel Hussain Muhammad, Yemen Arab Republic army officer/diplomat; born 1930, Yemen Arab Republic; married; one son; three daughters; *Religion:* Muslim; *Career:* Manager of Taiz Airport, 1967; Military Attaché, Yemen Arab Republic (YAR) Embassy to USSR, 1972–74; Military Attaché, YAR Embassy to Iran, 1974–76; Minister of Communications, February 1976; *Interests and Recreations:* reading history, football, table-tennis; *Address:* Sana'a, Yemen Arab Republic; telephone: 5769.

GHAIDAN, General Saadoun, Iraqi politician; born 1930, Iraq; *Education:* Military College, Baghdad, Iraq; *Career:* commissioned as 2nd Lieutenant, 1963; member of the Revolutionary Command Council, 1968; Minister of the Interior, 1970–74; Minister of Communications, 1974; Deputy Prime Minister and Minister of Transport and Communications, 1979–82; *Address:* c/o Ministry of Communications, Baghdad, Iraq.

GHAITH, Said al-, United Arab Emirates politician; born Abu Dhabi, United Arab Emirates; *Career:* Minister of State for Information; Minister of State for Cabinet Affairs, 1977–; *Address:* Ministry of State for Cabinet Affairs, P O Box 899, Khalidiya Street, Abu Dhabi, United Arab Emirates; telephone: 361033; telex: 23245 AMANA EM.

189

GHALEB, Muhammad Anaam, Yemen Arab Republic official/ economist; born 1932; married; one son, one daughter; *Religion:* Muslim; *Education:* Licence in Law, Cairo University, Egypt; MA Economics, University of Texas USA; *Career:* Director of Central Planning Organization; Minister of Economy; Minister of Education and Higher Education; Minister of Information March – June 1974; Dean of the National Institute of Public Administration and Consultant to the Central Planning Organization; *Publications:* various works in economics; *Interests and Recreations:* writing poetry and short stories, walking, reading poetry, economics, music; *Languages:* Arabic, English, *Address:* P O Box 102, Sana'a, Yemen Arab Republic; telephone: 70482.

GHALIB, Murad, Egyptian diplomat/ physician; born 1 April 1922; married; *Education:* Degree in Medicine, Cairo University, Egypt, 1945; *Career:* Professor of Medical Faculty, Cairo University, 1950; Medical Adviser in Egyptian Embassy to USSR, 1953; Secretary and Counsellor, Egyptian Embassy to USSR; Director of the President's Office for Political Affairs, 1957; Ministry of Foreign Affairs, 1959; Ambassador to the Congo, 1960; Ambassador to USSR, 1961–70; appointed to Arab Socialist Union (ASU) Elections Supervisory Committee, 1971; alternate member of the Central Committee, 1971; Minister of State for Foreign Affairs, 1971; Minister of Foreign Affairs, 1972; Special Presidential Envoy to mediate in Kuwait-Iraq border dispute, 1973; Minister of Information, 1973; Resident Minister in Tripoli, Libya, 1973; accompanied late President Sadat to Arab Summit, 1973; appointed Ambassador to Libya, 1974; Ambassador to Yugoslavia, 1974; resigned 1977; *Languages:* Arabic, English, French; *Address:* Ministry of Foreign Affairs, Cairo, Egypt.

GHALLAB, Abdul Karim, Moroccan journalist/academic; married; three sons; *Religion:* Muslim; *Education:* BA, Literature, Cairo University, Cairo, Egypt; *Career:* Minister Plenipotentiary, Ministry of Foreign Affairs, Morocco, 1956–59; Professor of Literature; Editor in Chief, *Risalat al Maghrib;* Editor in Chief, *Al Alam,* 1960–; Editor in Chief *Al Bayna,* and *Afaaq;* member of Parliament; member of the Moroccan Royal Academy; Secretary General, Moroc-

can Journalists Union; member of Moroccan Writers Union; *Publications:* several novels and short story collections, 1965–77; numerous books on literary criticism, political and historical studies, 1961–79; *Decorations:* Order of the Republic, Egypt, 1956; Order of Merit, Tunisia, 1972; *Interests and Recreations:* golf, writing; *Languages:* Arabic, French, English; *Address:* Office — 11 Avenue Allal Ben Abdullah, Rabat; telephone: 32419 20; Residence — Avenue Beni Mutir, (Al Suissi), Rabat, Morocco; telephone: 51306.

GHAMMAI, Salim Humad, al-, United Arab Emirates official, born 1945, Sharjah, United Arab Emirates; married 1973; one son, two daughters; *Religion:* Muslim; *Education:* BA in Education; *Career:* Secondary School Teacher; Secondary School Headmaster; Director of Technical Department, Ministry of Education; Assistant Under Secretary, Ministry of Education 1978–; *Interests and Recreations:* travelling, reading, football, tennis, table-tennis, cinema, previously Vice Chairman of the Board of UAE Football Association, Vice Chairman of the Board of Sharjah Sports Club; *Languages:* Arabic, English; *Address:* P O Box 897, Sharjah, United Arab Emirates.

GHANDOUR, Abdul Bassit, Lebanese judge; born 1924 Beirut, Lebanon; married; two sons, one daughter; *Religion:* Muslim; *Education:* LLB, Jesuit University of Beirut, Lebanon, 1943; *Career:* Lawyer; Magistrate, Tripoli, 1953; Examining Magistrate, Beirut, 1958; Counsellor in the Court of Appeal, Beirut, 1963; Chief Justice of the Court of Bankruptcy, Beirut, 1966; Chief Justice of the Court of Inquiry, Beirut, 1978–; member of the Central Committee of the International Union of Magistrates, 1974; *Languages:* Arabic, French, English; *Address:* Fuad al-Awwal Street, Randan Building, Beirut, Lebanon; telephone: Residence — 220459; Office — 380544.

GHANDOUR, Ali Ismail, Jordanian aviation official/engineer; born 28 May 1931, Beirut, Lebanon; married; one son; three daughters; *Religion:* Muslim; *Education:* Aeronautical Engineering, New York University, USA, 1953; *Career:* Engineer and Aviation Expert, Lebanese Civil Aviation Department, 1954– 56; Chief Engineer, later Vice President for Technical Affairs, Lebanese International

Airways 1956–62; member of the Board of Trustees, American University of Beirut; Chairman of the Centre for Contemporary Arab Studies Advisory Council Georgetown University, Washington D.C., USA; member of the Board of Trustees, Royal Scientific Society, Jordan; member of the Board, World Affairs Council, Vice Chairman of the Board of Trustees, Royal Academy of Aeronautics; Director and Vice Chairman, Arab Air Services; Chairman of the Board and President, Arab Wings; Chairman of the Board, Holiday Inn, Jordan; member of the Board, Hotels and Resthouses Corporations, Jordan; founder of the Jordanian national carrier *ALIA*, The Royal Jordanian Airlines 1963; Chairman of the Board and President of *ALIA* 1974–; *Publications: Unilateralism versus Multilateralism: A Dilemma for International Civil Air Transport Today,* August 1980; *The Economic Position of Civil Aviation in the Middle East,* April 1980 (English); *Economic Regulations of Air Transport Regionalism: Salvation for Airlines of Developing Nations,* October 1980; *The Arab-Israeli Conflict: An American Dilemma,* July 1980 and several other books on aviation and politics; *Decorations:* Grand Cordon of the Order of Al-Istiqlal (Independence), Jordan; Grand Officer of the Order of Independence, Jordan; and other national and international decorations; *Interests and Recreations:* politics (reading and research); swimming; *Languages:* Arabic, English; *Address:* P O Box 302 Amman, Jordan; telephone: Office — 39305; Residence — 64566.

GHANDOUR, Munir, Lebanese diplomat; born 1914, Beirut, Lebanon; married; three children; *Education:* Licence ès-Sciences, Geneva University, Switzerland; Docteur ès-Sciences, Biology, University of Paris, France; Licence ès-Lettres, Strasbourg University, France; *Career:* successively in the Ministry of Foreign Affairs, Secretary, Legation to Belgium, 1945–49; Chargé d'Affaires, Embassy to Greece, 1949–50; Consul General in Dakar, Senegal, 1950–52; Beirut, 1953–55; Counsellor, Embassy to France, 1950–60; Ambassador to Turkey, 1960–63; Ambassador to Iraq, 1963–66; Director, UN Department, Ministry of Foreign Affairs, 1966–68; Ambassador to Morocco, 1969–; *Decorations:* Officer, National Order of the Cedar; Légion d'Honneur, France; other Belgian and foreign decora-

tions; *Languages:* Arabic, French; *Address:* Office — Lebanese Embassy, 5 Rue de Tedders, Rabat, Morocco; Residence — Bourj Abi Haidar, Beirut, Lebanon.

GHANDUR, Muzzamil Sulaiman, Sudanese diplomat; born 1928; *Religion:* Muslim; *Education:* Staff Course at Fort Leavenworth, USA, 1963; Military Course, Nasser Military Academy, Egypt, 1968; *Career:* joined regular army; Battalion Commander, 1962–63; Military Attaché, Embassy to UK, 1967; Commander of the Infantry School Gebeit, 1967; promoted to Brigadier, 1968; appointed to Ministry of Foreign Affairs with rank of Ambassador; Ambassador to West Germany, 1971; non-resident Ambassador to Austria, 1972; Adviser to the Presidency on Foreign Economic Co-operation, 1974–; *Languages:* Arabic, English, German; *Address:* President's Office, Khartoum, Sudan.

GHANIM, Abdul Latif Muhammad al-, Kuwaiti businessman; born 1910, Kuwait; *Religion:* Muslim; *Career:* extensive business interests; founder member of the first Legislative Assembly in 1938; private enterprise 1939–60; Director General of Kuwait Municipality 1960–61; President, Constituent Assembly, 1961–62; unsuccessful candidate in the National Assembly elections, 1963; Minister of Health, 1963–64; *Address:* P O Box 588, International Airport Street, Kuwait.

GHANIM, Abdullah Yusuf al-, Kuwaiti politician/businessman; born Kuwait; married; *Religion:* Muslim; *Education:* Mubarakiyah School, Kuwait; Glasgow University, UK; *Career:* private enterprise; Minister of Electricity and Water, 1974; Second Deputy President of the Kuwait Chamber of Commerce and Industry, 1970; *Interests and Recreations:* swimming, fishing; *Languages:* Arabic, English; *Address:* Ministry of Electricity and Water, P O Box 12, Kuwait.

GHANIM, Fathi, Egyptian writer/journalist; born 1924, Cairo, Egypt; *Education:* BA Law, Cairo University, 1944; *Career:* Civil Servant; journalist; Editor of *Sabah al-Khair* weekly; Editor of *Al-Gumhuriyah* daily; Chairman of State Publishing House; writer; *Publications:* novels including: *The Man Who Lost His Shadow,* translated into English by Desmond Stewart; short story collections

191

including *Experiments in Love,* 1958; *Languages:* Arabic, English; *Address:* 89 Kasr al Ain Street, Cairo, Egypt.

GHANIM, Ismail, Egyptian academic/lawyer; born 24 August 1924, Alexandria, Egypt; *Education:* Diploma in Law, Alexandria University; Faculté de Droit, Paris, France; Institute of Comparative Law, New York University, USA; *Career:* Lecturer, Faculty of Law, Alexandria University, and Ain Shams University, Cairo, Egypt, 1951–; Dean, Faculty of Law, Arab University of Beirut, Lebanon, 1962–63; Dean, Faculty of Law, Ain Shams University, 1966–68; Vice Rector, Ain Shams University, 1968–70; Rector, Ain Shams University, 1971–74; Ambassador and Permanent Delegate to UNESCO, Paris, 1970–71; Minister of Culture, 1971; Minister of Higher Education and Scientific Research, 1974–75; member, Executive Board, Cairo Governorate; member of Board of Academy for Scientific Research; Chairman, Council for the Social Sciences 1971; *Publications:* in Arabic: *The Right to Work,* 1962; *Selling,* 1963; *Subjective Law,* 1963; in French: *Les Droits réels Principaux,* 1962; *La Théorie Générale des Obligations,* 1967; *Languages:* Arabic, French, English; *Address:* Ministry of Higher Education and Scientific Research, Cairo, Egypt.

GHANIM, Kutayba Yusuf al-, Kuwaiti businessman; born 12 October 1945, Kuwait; married; two sons, one daughter; *Religion:* Muslim; *Education:* Business Administration, University of California, Berkeley, USA; *Career:* President, Al-Ghanim Industries Inc, and A.I. International Corporation, a Kuwait based multi-national corporation involved in trading, manufacturing, wholesale distribution, shipping and financial services; *Interests and Recreation;* education and its development in the Arab world; *Languages;* Arabic, English; *Address:* Al-Ghanim Industries Inc, P O Box 24172, Safat, Kuwait; telephone: 830588; A.I. International Corporation, 650 5th Avenue, 26th floor, New York, NY 10019; telephone: (212) 2456262.

GHANIM, Muhammad Hafiz, Egyptian politician; born 29 September 1925; married; *Religion:* Muslim; *Education:* Law, Cairo University, Egypt, 1945; Degree in Political Economy, University of Paris, France, 1947; Doctor of Law, 1948; *Career:* Professor of International Law and Assistant Dean of the Law Faculty at Ain Shams University, Cairo; member of Egyptian delegation to the UN, 1955; served as Director of the Legal Department of the International Atomic Energy Agency, Vienna, Austria, 1965–; Central Committee of the Arab Socialist Union (ASU), 1968; Minister of Tourism, 1968; Minister of Health, 1969; Minister of Education, 1969–72; official visit to UK as guest of the British Council, 1971; appointed member of the Follow-up Committee to implement the formation of the Federation of Arab Republics, and member of ASU Provisional Secretariat, 1971; Secretary for Economic Affairs of ASU, 1972; Egyptian Supervisor of the Egypt/Libya merger committees, 1972; First Secretary of ASU, 1973; Secretary General of the Egyptian International Law Association, and former member of the Legal Advisory Committee of the Afro-Asian States; teacher of law to postgraduate students; Deputy Prime Minister and Minister responsible for Social Development and Services, 1976; *Publications:* in Arabic, *Public International Law,* 1964; *International Organization,* 1967; *Decorations:* State Prize for best publication in field of International Law and Political Science, 1969; *Languages:* Arabic, English, French; *Address:* 3 Sharia el-Bergass, Garden City, Cairo, Egypt.

GHANIM, Yusuf Ahmad al-, Kuwaiti businessman; born 1903; married; one son; *Religion:* Muslim; *Education:* Kuwait; *Career:* Representative, Anglo-Iranian Oil Co, Kuwait, contracted to the Kuwait Oil Co during its period of expansion; *Address:* Yusuf al-Ghanim and Sons WLL, P O Box 223, Kuwait; telephone: 830588, telex: 22069 KT.

GHANNAM, Muhammad Ahmad al-, Egyptian UN official/educationalist; born 12 January 1928, Talkha, Daqahliya, Egypt; married; *Religion:* Muslim; *Education:* BA, Faculty of Arts, Cairo University, Egypt, 1944–48; Diploma in Education, Higher Institute of Education, Cairo, 1948–50; MA in Education, Faculty of Education, Ain Shams University, Cairo, 1953–55; PhD in Educational Administration, Columbia University, New York, USA, 1956–59; *Career:* social sciences teacher in secondary schools, Egypt; Consultant in Educational Planning, Ministry of Higher Education, Cairo; Researcher, Department of Educational Research, Ministry of Education, Cairo; Instructor, Ain Shams University, Cairo, 1961; Visiting Professor of Education, Baghdad University, Iraq, 1964–67; Associate Professor of Education, Ain Shams University, 1967; Professor of Educational Administration, Faculty of Education, Ain Shams University, Cairo, 1972–74; Specialist in Educational Planning and Administration, Regional Office for Education, UNESCO, Head, Planning Centre, Regional Office for Education, 1974–; *Publications: The Teacher in Egyptian School and Society,* 1953; *The Future of Higher Education in Iraq,* 1967; *Politics in Educational Planning,* 1970; *Education in thè Arab States Viewed from the Marrakesh Conference,* 1971; *Methodology of Research in Education,* 1972; *Administrative Technology,* 1972; *Decorations:* State Prize in Arts, 1972; *Interests and Recreations:* walking, gymnastics; educational planning and administration, social and philosophical foundations of education; member of the Association of Professors of Ain Shams University, Cairo; member of the Association of the Graduates of the Institute of Education, Cairo; *Languages:* Arabic, English, French; *Address:* Office — Regional Office for Education, UNESCO, P O Box 5244, Avenue Cité Sportife, Beirut, Lebanon; telephone: 311145; Residence — Al-Tani Building, Verdun Street, Beirut, Lebanon.

GHARIB, Salahuddin Muhammad, Egyptian politician/trade union official; born 1926; married; three children; *Religion:* Muslim; *Career:* began work in textile plant; Head of Personnel at Modern Textiles Company, Alexandria, Egypt; Vice President of the Union of Spinning and Weaving Workers, 1968; elected to the national Congress of the Arab Socialist Union (ASU); elected to the ASU Central Committee, 1968; elected Secretary General of the Federation of Arab Textile Workers on its foundation, 1969; Alternate member of the ASU Organising Committee, 1970; member of the provisional Secretariat of the ASU, 1971; elected President of the Egyptian Federation of Labour and President of the Union of Spinning and Weaving Workers, 1971; elected member of the ASU Central Committee and Assistant Secretary for Alexandria, 1971; ASU Secretary for Labour, 1971, and Chairman of the Manpower Committee of the People's Assembly, after election as one of the Deputies for Alexandria; Minister of Manpower, 1972,

in addition to ASU and trade union responsibilities; Secretary for Labour in ASU, 1973; Minister of Manpower and Works, 1974–75; *Address:* Ministry of Manpower & Works, Cairo, Egypt.

GHARNIT, Abdullah, Moroccan official/ politician; born June 1929, Marrakesh, Morocco; married; *Religion:* Muslim; *Education:* Faculty of Law, University of Paris, France; *Career:* magistrate; Ministry of the Interior; several posts, Ministry of the Interior, Radio and Television (RTM); Ministry of Youth Affairs and Sports; member of the Royal Cabinet; High Commissioner at National Mutual Aid, 1968; Secretary of State in Charge of National Advancement and Handicrafts, 1972–77; Minister of Handicrafts and Social Affairs, 1977; *Languages:* Arabic, French; *Address:* Ministry of Handicrafts and Social Affairs, Rabat, Morocco.

GHAZAWI, Ahmad Ibrahim al-, Saudi Arabian official/writer; born 1900; *Religion:* Muslim; *Education:* received general and religious education; *Career:* government employee; government posts; Chairman of Supreme Committee of Haj (pilgrimage); Deputy Chairman of Municipal Council, Mecca; member of several committees of State House of Councillors; founder of First Aid Department; Chairman of State House of Councillors; Saudi delegate to inauguration of Sudanese Parliament; *Publications:* numerous poems; daily column in local press entitled *Mutala'at wa Ta'likat; Shazaratal Zahab,* a collection of articles; *Decorations:* Supreme Order of King Abdul Aziz; Badge of the Conference of Saudi Men of Letters, King Abdul Aziz University; several Orders of Merit from Arab and Islamic countries; *Interests and Recreations:* reading; *Address:* Al-Nozha, Mecca, Saudi Arabia; telephone: Mecca 27942.

GHAZZI, Ghazi Said, Syrian lawyer; born 8 November, 1938, Damascus, Syria; married 1962; one son, one daughter; *Religion:* Muslim; *Education:* Licence in Law, Damascus University; specialized in Administrative and International Law; *Career:* private law pratice, Damascus, Syria, 1962–; Consultant, Iraq Petroleum Co, 1966–72; *Interests and Recreations:* music, photography, swimming, horse riding; *Languages:* Arabic, English, French; *Address:* Salhya Street, Bureau of Legal Services, P O Box 4238, Damascus, Syria; telephone: 229798; telex: 11210 SY.

193

GHEITH, Muhammad Ahmad, Arab-American academic/geologist; born 11 February 1925, Egypt; married; one daughter, one son; *Religion:* Muslim; *Education:* BSc, Cairo University, Egypt; MS Geology, University of Minnesota, USA; PhD Geochemistry, and Economic Geology, University of Minnesota; *Career:* Lecturer, Faculty of Science, Ain Shams University, Cairo, Egypt 1952–57; Consultant Geologist to the Technical Bureau of Mining and Commerce in Egypt and Sudan 1956–57; Fellow of the School for Advanced Study, Massachusetts Institute of Technology, USA 1957; Assistant, Associate, then Professor, of Geology, Boston University , USA 1958–64; Chairman and Professor of Geology, Department of Geology, Boston University 1964–75; Visiting Professor, American Unniversity in Cairo, Egypt, Kuwait University and other universities in the Middle East 1973–74; Visiting Professor, Qatar University 1981; Professor of Geology, Boston University 1975–; UNESCO delegate 1956–78; UNESCO Consultant to the Centre of Applied Geology, Saudi Arabia 1976–78; UNESCO Consultant 1975–76; Director of Special External Programmes for the Middle East, Boston University 1980–; Fellow of the Geological Society of Egypt, Sigma XI, National Association of Geology Teachers, American Association for the Advancment of Science, American Crystallographic Association, American Association of University Professors, New York Academy of Science, International Mineralogical Association, American Geophysical Union, Association of Arab-American University Graduates, Association of Egyptian-American Scholars; former Vice-president and President, Boston Geological Society; *Publications:* many articles in technical and scientific journals in various countries; *Interests and Recreations:* swimming, ping-pong, hiking, bridge; *Languages:* Arabic, English, French; *Address:* 3 Bypass Road, Lincoln, Mass 01773, USA; telephone: Office — (617) 353 2616/3315; Residence — (617) 259 8928.

GHEZAL, Ahmad, Tunisian diplomat, born 1930, M'Saken, Tunisia; married; two children; *Religion:* Muslim, *Education:* Sadiki College, Tunis, Tunisia; Institut d'Etudes Politique, Toulous, France; *Career:* Tunisian Ministry of Foreign Affairs 1958; Tunisian Embassy, Yugoslavia 1959–62;Tunisian Embassy, Belgium and EEC 1962–67; Head of European Division, Ministry of Foreign Affairs 1969–70,Tunisian Embassy, USA 1970–74; Chef de Cabinet, Ministry of Foreign Affairs 1974–77; Director of Political Affairs, Ministry of Foreign Affairs, Tunis 1974–77; Ambassador to Austria and Hungary and Permanent Representative to international organizations in Vienna, 1977–; *Languages:* Arabic, French, English; *Address:* Embassy of Tunisia, Himmelpfortgasse 20, A-1010 Vienna, Austria.

GHINIMA, Muhammad, Tunisian banker; born 1929, Sousse, Tunisia; *Religion:* Muslim; married; two children; *Education:* Doctor of Law, Bordeaux University, France; *Career:* worked in Tunisian Railways, 1957–59; National Agricultural Bank; Director General, Agricultural Bank, 1969; Governor, Central Bank, 1972; *Languages:* Arabic, French; *Address:* Banque Centrale de Tunisie, 7 Place de Monnaia, Tunis, Tunisia; telephone: 259977.

GHIRAB, Muhammad Habib, Tunisian UN official; married; *Religion:* Muslim; *Education:* Licence in Law, Faculty of Law, University of Paris, France; *Career:* Ambassador to Spain; member, Delegation of Tunisia to UN General Assembly, 1968; Special Adviser to Secretary of State for Foreign Affairs, Tunisia, 1967–69; Assistant Secretary General for Personnel Services, UN, 1969; *Decorations:* Grand Cross of Isabel the Catholic, Spain; Great Ouissam Alouite Officer, Morocco; Commander, Order of the Republic, Tunisia; *Languages:* Arabic, English, French; *Address:* Office — United Nations Plaza, New York, New York 10017, USA; telephone: (212) 754 1234.

GHISSASSI, Abdul Latif, Moroccan politician/engineer; born 16 November 1937, Morocco; married; one son, one daughter; *Religion:* Muslim; *Education:* Engineering, Ecole Nationale de Ponts et Chaussées de Paris, France, 1961; Engineering, Aerial Bases, Ecole Nationale de l'Aviation Civile, 1962; *Career:* Professor, Ecole Mohammadia des Ingeniéurs, 1962–72; Chief Engineer for Maintenance of the Air Bases of the Northern Section, 1962–65; Chief Engineer, Air Bases Maintenance, 1966–68; Secretary General, Ministry of Public Works and Communications, 1968–72; Minister of Public Works and Communications, 1972; Director General, Société Anonyme Marocaine de l'Industrie du Raffinage (SAMIR), 1973–74; Minister of Commerce, Industry, Mines, and of Merchant Shipping, 1974–77; Minister of Finance, 1977–79; Minister of Agriculture and Land Reform, 1979–81; President of the Moroccan Delegation of UNIDO, Lima, 1975; President of the Moroccan Delegation to the Regional FAO Conference for Africa, Rome, 1980; president and member of numerous other delegations to international conferencess; *Decorations:* Chevalier de l'Ordre du Trone, Morocco, 1965; Officier de l'Ordre du Trone, Morocco, 1972; Oficier de l'Ordre du Mérite Française, 1975; Order of the Islamic Republic of Mauritania, 1977; Order of Merit, Senegal, 1981; *Languages:* Arabic, French; *Address:* c/o Ministry of Agriculture and Land Reform, Rabat, Morocco.

GHODRAN, Sayid Ali, Saudi Arabian businessman; born 1930, Saudi Arabia; *Education:* general; *Career:* Ministry of Finance, 1946–56; member of Board of the Dhahran Electric Power Co, Gulf Gases Co, Saudi Arabian Fertilizer Co (SAFCO), Assir Tourist and Trading Co, Red Sea Development Co; owner of Arabian Provision and Services Co; co-founder of *Al-Sharq* magazine; attended various Chamber of Commerce Conferences; *Interests and Recreations:* swimming; *Address:* P O Box 131, Dammam, Saudi Arabia.

GHORBAL, Ashraf, Egyptian diplomat; born 22 May, 1925, Alexandria, Egypt; married; one daughter; *Education:* BA, Cairo University, Cairo, Egypt; MA, Political Science, Harvard University, 1948; PhD, Political Science, Harvard University, 1949; *Career:* joined the Egyptian diplomatic service 1945; served in United Nations, New York and Geneva; posts at the Egyptain embassies in Paris, London and Ottawa; member of the Egyptian delegation to the Franco/Egyptian negotiations following the Suez Canal invasion, November 1956; participated in several international conferences, including the non-Aligned Conference, Belgrade, 1961, and the Tri-Lateral Conference, (Egypt, India, Yugoslavia), New Delhi, 1966; Head of Egyptian Interests, Egyptian Embassy, Washington,1968–72; Assistant Adviser, President for National Security Affairs, 1972; Press Adviser to late President Sadat, 1973, and worked closely on the formulation of Egyp-

tian foreign policy with group of experts, with special reference to the period following the 1973 War; Ambassador to Washington, participated in Camp David negotiations, 1978, 1973–82; retired from diplomatic service, 1982; *Languages:* Arabic, English, French; *Address:* c/o Ministry of Foreign Affairs, Cairo, Egypt.

GHORRA, Edouard, Lebanese diplomat; born 18 June 1913, Lebanon; married; *Education:* Patriarchal College, Beirut, Lebanon; International College, American University of Beirut, Lebanon; Licence in Law, French Faculty of Law, St. Joseph University, Beirut, Lebanon; Degree in Political Science, Pittsburgh University, Pennsylvania, USA; *Career:* Barrister at Law, 1941–45; Consul General, New York, 1945–50; member, Lebanese Delegation to the UN General Assembly, 1947–49; Alternate Representative, UN Economic and Social Council (ECOSOC), 1948–49; Consul General, Sydney, Australia, 1950–55; Head, Western Affairs Department, Ministry of Foreign Affairs, 1956–57; Director, Political Affairs Department, Ministry of Foreign Affairs, Beirut, Lebanon, 1957–58; member, Lebanese Delegation to the UN General Assembly, 1958; Ambassador to the USSR, 1959–63; member, Lebanese Delegation to the UN General Assembly, 1963; Director, Overseas Department, Ministry of Foreign Affairs, Beirut, Lebanon, 1963–65; Ambassador to Czechoslovakia and Poland, 1965–68; Vice President, UN General Assembly 1968, 1974; Lebanese Representative to the Human Rights Commission, 1969–; Lebanese Representative to ECOSOC, 1971–73; Lebanese Representative, Executive Council, UN Development Programme (UNDP); Vice President, later Chairman, Co-ordination Committee, ECOSOC, 1973; Permanent Representative of Lebanon to the UN (with rank of Ambassador), New York, USA, 1968–; concurrently Ambassador to Jamaica, 1973–; *Interests and Recreations:* swimming, fishing, philately, antiques and works of art; *Languages:* Arabic, French, English; *Address:* Office — Permanent Lebanese Mission to the UN, 866 UN Plaza, New York, NY 10017, USA; telephone: (212) 355 5460.

GHORY, Emil Antoun, Jordanian politician/lawyer; born 1907, Jerusalem; married; *Education:* Diploma, Law Institute, Jerusalem, 1946; BA in Political Science, Cincinnati

University, USA, 1933; MA in Political Science, Cincinnati University, 1933; *Career:* various posts in journalism and politics, 1933–56; head of various Palestinian Arab Committees to UN, 1949–50, 1960–66; member of Chamber of Deputies, 1967–74; Minister of Social Affairs and Labour, 1969–70; Minister of State, 1971–72; Attorney, 1974–; Member of Higher Executive Committee of Arab National Union; *Publications: The Great Conspiracy; Arab Nationalism; 15th of May; Revenge or Disgrace; Palestine; Address:* P O Box 9137, Amman, Jordan; telephone: 663297.

GHOSN, Fuad, Lebanese politician; born 1912, Kosba, North Lebanon; married; two sons, two daughters; *Religion:* Christian; *Education:* St. Joseph University, Beirut, Lebanon; Licence in Law, 1935; *Career:* Barrister, 1935–42; civil servant until re-elected deputy for Koura in succession to his father, 1953; Qaimaqam (district officer) at Marjeyoun, Batroun and Jdeidat al-Metn; Minister of Justice, and Deputy Premier, 1955; Minister of Education, and Posts and Telegraphs, 1956; stood down in favour of Charles Malik at 1957 elections; re-elected, 1960, 1964, 1968 and 1972; Minister of Guidance and Information, 1960–61; Deputy President of Chamber of Deputies, 1963; Minister of Posts and Telegraphs and Deputy Prime Minister, 1969; Deputy President of Chamber of Deputies, 1972–73; Deputy Prime Minister and Minister of Defence in Amin el-Hafez Cabinet, 1973; Deputy Prime Minister and Minister of Works, Takieddin al-Solh cabinet, 1973–74; *Languages:* Arabic, French; *Address:* Rue Doman, Ashrafiyeh, Beirut, Lebanon.

GHOSTINE, Charles, Lebanese lawyer/academic; born 18 June 1949, Lebanon; *Religion:* Christian; *Education:* Licence in Law, France and Lebanon; *Career:* Barrister; Assistant Lecturer, Faculty of Business Administration, Lebanese University, 1977–80; member of the Supreme Political Council, National Liberal Party; Vice President, Lebanese Forces, 1980–82; Secretary General of Education, National Liberal Party; *Publications:* conference papers and articles on the Lebanese cause, 1982; *Interests and Recreations:* basket-ball, swimming, reading, literature and arts; *Languages:* Arabic, English, French, Italian; *Address:* Office — National Liberal Party, Rue de Liban, Beirut,

Lebanon; telephone: 338000, 327733; Residence -- Rue Albert Naceache, Beirut, Lebanon; telephone: 216495.

GHAZALI, Ahmad, Algerian politician/oil expert; born 1937, Algeria; *Religion:* Muslim; *Education:* Ecole des Ponts et Chaussées, Paris, France; *Career:* following Independence appointed Director of Fuel and Power; Adviser on Oil Affairs, Ministry of National Economy, 1964; President, Director General of national oil company SONATRACH, 1966; played leading role in negotiations for the third pipeline and in Franco-Algerian talks of 1970; Minister of Energy and Petrochemical Industries, 1977–80; Minister of Housing and Urban Planning, 1980–; *Interests and Recreations:* tennis; *Languages:* Arabic, French; *Address:* Ministry of Housing and Urban Planning, P O Box 58, Algiers, Algeria; telephone: 773067.

GHUBASH, Said al-, United Arab Emirates politician/diplomat; born Ras al-Khaimah, United Arab Emirates; *Career:* Ambassador to USA, 1977; Minister of Planning, 1977–; President of the Board, Arab Monetary Fund, Abu Dhabi, 1982–; *Address:* Ministry of Planning, P O Box 904, Abu Dhabi, United Arab Emirates; telephone: 362271; telex: 22920.

GHUNAIM, Abdul Rahman Khalid al-, Kuwaiti official/engineer; born 4 January, 1938, Kuwait; married, two sons, two daughters; *Religion:* Muslim; *Education:* BSc in Electrical Engineering, San Jose State College, California, USA, 1962; *Career:* Engineer, Ministry of Posts, Telegraphs and Telephones (formerly), 1962; Deputy Chief Engineer, 1964; Assistant Under Secretary, Ministry of Communications, 1969–; Managing Director of Kuwait Electrical Wiring Accessories Co, Kuwait and Al-Abraq Trading Company, Kuwait; Senior member, Institute Electrical and Electronic Engineers, USA; Fellow, Institution of Electrical Engineers, London, UK; Chairman, INMARSAT Council, 1979–80, 1980–81; Plenipotentiary and Head of Delegation, all Meetings of INTELSAT, 1969–; represented Kuwait in many international and Arab conferences and meetings; Chairman and Vice President of: Kuwait Reinsurance, Kuwait Financial Centre, Arab Insurance Company, Beirut; Director of Kuwait Insurance Co, Bank of Lebanon and Kuwait, Bahrain and Kuwait

Insurance Co, United Insurance Co, Ras al-Khaima; member of Arab Insurance Federation Union; Honorary Governor of Expatriate School, Kuwait; *Publications: Telecommunications in the State of Kuwait, ITU* Journal *Telecommunications,* May 1972; *Telecommunications and Development in the Third World, Practices and Prospects, Crisis on Review,* 1976, Stockholm, Sweden; *Kuwait's Development in Communications and its Significance to Friendly Countries,* lecture, 25 April 1977, Tokyo, Japan; *Arab European Cooperation in Telecommunication Industries* lecture; *Arab European Cooperation Symposium,* 20–31 May 1978, Montreux, Switzerland, *Establishment of Telecommunication Services; View from a Developing Country* 19 September 1979, lecture *Forum 79, ITU* Geneva, Switzerland; *Interests and Recreations:* football, gardening; *Languages:* Arabic, English; *Address:* Ministry of Communicatons, P O Box 16, Kuwait; telephone: 214410; telex: 22197 KT.

GHUNAIM, Khalid Salih al-, Kuwaiti politician/businessman; born 1916; married; *Religion:* Muslim; *Education:* Kuwait; *Career:* Manager, Thunayyan al-Ghanim 1938–57; Department of Public Works; Director General of Administration and Financial Affairs, 1950–61; independent business, 1961–63; Chairman of Kuwait Insurance Co, 1960–61; Director of Kuwait National Petroleum Co, 1960–62; Director of Commercial Bank, 1960–63; member of Constituent Assembly, 1962–63; member of National Assembly, 1963; Deputy Speaker of National Assembly, 1967; Speaker of National Assembly, 1971; re-elected February, 1975 and held post until dissolution of Assembly, August 1976; *Languages:* Arabic, Persian, Urdu, some English; *Address:* The Commercial Bank of Kuwait SAK, P O Box 2861, Safat, Kuwait; telephone: 41001, telex: 22004 CBK KT.

GHUNAIM, Khalifa Khalid al-, Kuwaiti businessman/politician; born 1921, Kuwait; married; two sons, one daughter; *Religion:* Muslim; *Education:* BA, American University of Beirut, Lebanon, 1942; *Career:* private enterprise; National Bank of Kuwait, 1960; member of the Kuwait Oil Tanker Company and Kuwait Currency Board, Ambassador to UK, 1963–64; Minister of Commerce, 1964–65; Chief Kuwaiti Delegate to 1st UNCTAD Conference, Geneva, 1964; *Interests and Rec-*

reations: reading, walking; *Languages:* Arabic, English; *Address:* National Bank of Kuwait, P O Box 95, Safat, Kuwait.

GHUNAIM, Sayyid Muhammad, Egyptian academic; born 10 August 1922, Egypt; married; three sons, one daughter; *Religion:* Muslim; *Education:* BA, Cairo University, Egypt, 1945; Teachers College Diploma, Ain Shams University, Cairo, 1947; Diploma of Higher Studies, 1949; Diploma in Psychology, 1953; MA in Mental Health, Ain Shams University, 1955; PhD, Geneva University, Switzerland, 1959; *Career:* Demonstrator, Faculty of Education, Ain Shams University, 1951; Assistant Professor, 1959; Associate Professor, 1967; Associate Professor, Faculty of Arts, 1967; Professor of Psychology, Kuwait University, 1968–72; Professor of Psychology, Ain Shams University, 1973–77; Vice Dean, Faculty of Arts, Ain Shams University, 1973–77; Professor of Psychology, Faculty of Education, United Arab Emirates University, 1977; Dean of Faculty of Education, UAE University, 1979–; *Publications:* several books on psychology in Arabic; *Languages:* Arabic, French, English; *Address:* Faculty of Education, United Arab Emirates University, P O Box 15551, Al-Ain, United Arab Emirates.

GHUNAIM, Yaqub Yusuf al-, Kuwaiti politician; born 1933; *Religion:* Muslim; *Education:* Dar al-Ulum in Cairo; *Career:* Ministry of Guidance and Information; Director of Television, 1962–65; Under Secretary in Ministry of Education, 1965; Minister of Education, 1978–; *Languages:* Arabic, English; *Address:* Ministry of Education, P O Box 7, Safat, Hilali Street, Kuwait; telephone: 427041, telex: 23166 EDU KT.

GHURANI, Izzat I., Palestinian academic/economist; born 23 February 1924, Jerusalem, Palestine; married 1957; one son, one daughter; *Religion:* Christian; *Education:* Diploma in Law, 1951; MBA, 1956; PhD, Economics, 1963; *Career:* Assistant Professor of Economics, University of Texas, 1963–68; Associate Professor of Economics and Department Chairman, Pahlavi University, Iran 1968–71; Professor of Economics and Department Chairman, Abadan Institute of Technology, Iran, 1971–77; Professor of Economics, Birzeit University, 1977–; Dean, Faculty of Commerce and Economics, Birzeit University, 1978; Vice President, Finance and

Administration, Birzeit University, 1979–; member of the American Economic Association, USA, and the Conference of University Administrators, UK; *Publications: Economics and Philosophy,* 1970 (Arabic); *Location Theory,* 1973 (Arabic); *Wealth,* 1974; *The International Monetary Crisis and the State,* 1974, as well as several articles published in both Arabic and English; *Interests and Recreations:* golf; *Languages:* Arabic, English; *Address:* P O Box 14, Birzeit, Birzeit University, Occupied West Bank of the Jordan.

GHUSSAIN, Talaat, Kuwaiti diplomat; born 1920, Palestine; married; *Religion:* Muslim; *Education:* American University of Beirut; *Career:* Foreign News Editor, *Al-Sha'b,* Jaffa, Palestine, 1946–47; Controller, Arab Bank, Jaffa, 1947–48; Editor, Foreign News and Director of English Section, Jordan Broadcasting, 1948–49; Director of Press and Public Information, Yemeni Ministry of Foreign Affairs, 1949–53; also represented Yemen at UN; Secretary General, Kuwait Development Board, 1953–60; Assistant State Secretary, 1961; member of Kuwait Delegation to UN General Assembly, New York, USA; Ministry of Foreign Affairs, 1961–62; Minister Counsellor, Embassy to USA, 1962; Ambassador to USA, 1962–70; Ambassador to Morocco, 1970–71; Ambassador to Japan and Malaysia, 1971; *Languages:* Arabic, English; *Address:* c/o Ministry of Foreign Affairs, P O Box 3, Sour Street, Kuwait; telephone: 422041; telex: 22042 KHARJIA KT.

GIBAILI, Abdul Ma'bud al-, Egyptian official/scientist; born 1921; married; four children; *Education:* BSc in Chemistry, Cairo University, Egypt, 1942; PhD in Nuclear Chemistry, Sorbonne, University of Paris, France, 1956; *Career:* Assistant Professor in Nuclear Energy Agency, Egypt, 1957; Chief of Nuclear Energy Agency, Egypt, 1965; member of the Consultative Scientific Committee of the International Atomic Energy Agency, Vienna, Austria; member of the Egypt-US Joint Committee established in 1974 during President Nixon's visit to Cairo; Minister of Scientific Research and Nuclear Power, 1975–76; Minister of State for Scientific Research and Atomic Energy, 1976; *Publications:* several scientific papers, especially on nuclear industrialisation, nuclear power and desalination published in professional journals; *Languages:* Arabic, French, English; *Address:* Ministry of State for Scientific Research and Atomic Energy, Cairo, Egypt.

GIEN, Abdul Aziz Abdul Aziz al-, Saudi Arabian official/engineer; *Education:* Diploma of Civil Engineering, USA; *Career:* radio maintenance engineer; air traffic controller; member, Pilgrimage Subcommittee; member of Board of International Civil Airport Association; attended several ICAO (International Civil Aviation Organisation) conferences; Director of Jeddah International Airport; *Interests and Recreations:* swimming; *Address:* Jeddah International Airport, Jeddah, Saudi Arabia; Office— telephone: 642 7211.

GINDY, Aida, Egyptian UN official; *Career:* Senior Social Affairs Officer, Social Development Division, Department of Economic and Social Affairs (ESA), UN, New York, USA; Chief, Social Welfare Service Section, Social Development Division, ESA, UN; Chief, Social Integration and Welfare Section, Social Development Division, ESA, UN; *Languages:* Arabic, English; *Address:* Office — Social Integration and Welfare Section, Social Development Division, ESA, UN, United Nations Plaza, New York, NY 10017, USA; telephone: (212) 754 1234. Residence — 7 E 86 Street, New York, NY 10028, USA; telephone: (212) 876 0889.

GLAOUI, Abdessadek, al-, Moroccan diplomat; born in Morocco; married; *Religion:* Muslim; *Education:* Doctor of Law; *Career:* President of Marrakesh Court, 1944; Minister/Cousellor, Moroccan Embassy, USA, 1962; Ambassador to Scandinavian Countries, 1965; Ambassdor, Japan 1967; Ambassador to Federal Republic of Germany, 1968; Ambassador to France, 1970; Ambassador to USA, 1971–72; Special Adviser to the Prime Minister, 1972; President of the Supreme Court of Audit of Morocco, 1974–; *Languages:* Arabic, French; *Address:* Supreme Court of Audit, Ministère des Finances, Rabat, Morocco.

GOHAR, Yusif, Egyptian writer/lawyer; born 20 July, 1912, Egypt; married; two sons, three daughters; *Religion:* Christian; *Education:* LLB, Cairo University, Egypt, 1935; *Career:* Author; Director, National Egyptian Centre for Cinema; Director, National Film

Archive; Editor in Chief, *Cinema and Theatre Magazine;* Head of Scenario Department, Higher Institute of Cinema; Legal Adviser, Syndicate of Egyptian Writers; member of National Council for Arts and Literature; writer, *Al-Ahram* daily paper; member of the Board of Directors of the Syndicate of Egyptian Writers, of the Board of Directors of Writers Association; *Publications:* more than nine short stories collections and novels, 1940–81; *Languages:* Arabic, English, French; *Address:* Residence 9 Wadi Al-Nil Maadi, Cairo; telephone: 633350; Office — Al Ahram, Galla Street, Cairo, Egypt.

GOSAIBI, Abdul Aziz Hamid al-, Saudi Arabian businessman; born 1926, Jubail, Saudi Arabia; *Education:* general; *Career:* Managing Director and member of Board of Ahmad Hamad al-Gosaibi and Brothers, Khobar; Representative for several foreign companies; member of Khobar Municipal Council; member of Board of Great Hotel Co, Cairo; authorized member of Board of United Saudi Co for Insurance; member of Board of Dammam Electric Co, Dammam Chamber of Commerce, Riyadh Hotel, Social Security Authority; member of founding Committee of Saudi-Korean Loading and Unloading Co; contributed to the establishment of several loading and unloading companies in Dammam; contributed to the establishment of several Saudi charity societies; member of Arab European World Finance and Insurance Conference; shipping agent, owner of shipping companies; Director, Gosaibi Hotel Company, Khobar; *Decorations:* Honorary Doctorate in International Economics, London University, UK; *Address:* Prince Talal Street, P O Box 106, al-Khobar, Saudi Arabia.

GOSAIBI, Khalid al-, Saudi Arabian official; born 1934; married; *Education:* BA in Economics, University of Southern California, USA; *Career:* Government Administration, 1964; worked with the Water Project Planning Staff in Ministry of Agriculture and Water; Director General of Dammam Port, and Saudi Railways 1968–72; Vice-Governor, Saudi Arabian Monetary Agency, 1980; member of the board of Riyadh Bank, Saudi International Bank; *Languages:* Arabic, English; *Address:* c/o P O Box 1047, Jeddah, Saudi Arabia.

GOULLI, Slahiddine al-, Tunisian diplomat/lawyer; born 22 June 1919, Sousse, Tunisia; *Education:* Sousse College; LLD, University of Paris, France; *Career:* Tunisian Bar; private industry, 1949–56; active in Tunisian national movement in Europe, 1947–56; Consul General, Marseille, France, 1956–57; Counsellor, Embassy to USA; Minister, Embassy to USA; Alternate Executive Director, IBRD (World Bank); Ambassador to Belgium, also accredited to Netherlands and Luxembourg, 1962; concurrently Permanent Representative to EEC; Permanent Representative to UN, 1969; Ambassador to USA, 1969–73, concurrently to Mexico, 1970–73, to Venezuela, 1972–73; *Decorations:* Grand Cordon of the Order of the Tunisian Republic; also decorations from Belgium, Netherlands, Luxembourg; *Languages:* Arabic, French, English; *Address:* Ministry of Foreign Affairs, Tunis, Tunisia.

GUAL, Peter Gatkuouth, Sudanese politican; born 3 January, 1938; married 1966; six children; *Religion:* Christian; *Education:* BSc, Economics, University of Khartoum, Sudan; *Career:* Assistant Inspector of Finance, Bank of Sudan, 1964; Technical Adviser on Economic Planning to Ministry of Southern Sudan Affairs, 1971; Minister of State and General Adviser on Southern Sudan Affairs, 1972; member of Political Bureau, Sudanese Socialist Union, 1972; Director General, Special Fund for Southern Region, 1973; Commissioner, Upper Nile Province, 1973; Regional Minister of Finance and Economy, 1975; currently, Vice President, High Executive Council for Southern Region of the Sudan; member of the Political Bureau, Sudanese Socialist Union and Regional Minister of Finance and Economic Planning; *Decorations:* Order of Al-Nilayn, 1st Class; Order of the Constitution; Order of National Unity, Order of the Republic, 1st Class; *Interests and Recreations:* tennis, hunting, fishing; *Languages:* Arabic, English, Nuer, Dinka; *Address:* High Executive Council, Regional Ministry of Finance and Economic Planning, Juba, Sudan.

GUEDIRA, Maître Ahmad Rida, Moroccan politician/lawyer; married; *Religion:* Muslim; *Education:* law studies, Paris, France; *Career:* Director of the Imperial Printing Press, 1947–51; Minister of State for Negotiations, 1955; Minister of Defence, 1956; Minister of Information and Tourism, 1956;

Editor of the French language weekly magazine *Les Phares,* on behalf of Liberal Independents, 1959; Director General of the Royal Cabinet, 1961; Minister of the Interior and of Agriculture, 1961; organized formation of the Front pour la Défense des Institutions Constitutionelles (FDIC), 1963; Minister of Foreign Affairs, 1963–64; formed the Parti Social Démocratique (PSD), 1964; Minister of Education, 1969–70; Counsellor in the Royal Cabinet, 1977; *Languages:* Arabic, French; *Address:* The Royal Cabinet, Rabat, Morocco.

GUENNEZ, Mahmud, Algerian official/ former army officer; born Tebessa, Algeria; *Religion:* Muslim; *Career:* joined the Resistance in War of Independence, 1954; Officer, National Liberation Army, ALN; Deputy Chairman and then Chairman of the Amicale des Algériens in Europe, after Independence; President of the Defence and Interior Commision, first National Assembley; Commander in Chief of the Milce Populaire; Assistent to the Head of the ALN; Minister of War Veterans, 1970; Vice President, National People's Assembly, 1977–; Member of the Central Committee of the National Liberation Front Party; *Languages:* Arabic, French; *Address:* National People's Assembly, Algiers, Algeria.

GUETTA, Serge, Tunisian banker; *Career:* IBRD (World Bank) Washington D.C., USA, 1970–74; Resident Representative of IBRD in Zaire, 1974–; *Address:* P O Box 14816, Kinshasa, Zaire; telephone: 25214.

GUILAIGAH, Abdullah Bin Muhammad al-Salih, Saudi Arabian official; born 1940, Buradah, Saudi Arabia; *Religion:* Muslim; *Education:* BA in Arabic Language, Riyadh University, Saudi Arabia; *Career:* Demonstrator; Assistant Bureau Director, Ministry of Agriculture and Water; Director, Irrigation and Dams Division; Director General, Project Execution Administration; Director General, Ministry of Agriculture and Water Affairs; Deputy Minister for Water Affairs; Governor of Saline Water Conversion Corporation; *Interests and Recreations:* Reading; *Address:* Saline Water Conversion Corporation, P O Box 5968, Riyadh, Saudi Arabia.

GUINDI, Fadwa al-, Arab-American academic/anthropologist; born 16 July 1940, Cairo, Egypt; one son, one daughter; *Religion:* Muslim; *Education:* PhD, Anthropology, University of Texas, Austin, USA, 1972; BA, Political Science, the American University in Cairo, Egypt, 1960; *Career:* Research Assistant, Social Research Centre, American University in Cairo, 1960–65; Teaching Assistant, Department of Anthropology, University of Texas, Austin, 1967–69; NIMH Fellow, 1969–72; Assistant Professor of Anthropology, University of California, Los Angeles (UCLA), 1972–79; Associate Research Anthropologist, UCLA, 1979–81; Visiting Associate Professor of Anthropology, University of Southern Califronia, Los Angeles (USC), 1981; Fulbright Senior Research Scholar, Visiting Research Professor at the Middle East Research Centre and the Social Studies Department, Faculty of Arts, Ain Shams University, Cairo, Egypt, 1981–82; Fellow of American Anthropological Association, of Royal Anthropological Institute, of Middle East Studies Association, of American Associaton for the Advancement of Science; member of Association Internationale pour l'Etude des Religions, American Research Centre in Egypt, of American Association for University Professors, Association of Arab-American University Graduates, Association of Egyptian-American Scholars, Association of Academic Women, UCLA, Association for Women in Science, Middle East Research in Anthropology; *Publications: Life Crisis Rituals Among the Kenuz,* 1972; *The Nature of Belief Systems; A Structural Analysis of Zapotec Ritual,* 1972; *Religion in Culture,* 1977; *The Angels in the Nile: A Theme in Nubian Ritual,* 1978; and several other books; *Interests and Recreations:* music, theatre; *Languages:* Arabic, English, French, Spanish; *Address:* Department of Anthropology, Haines Hall, UCLA, Los Angeles, California 90024, USA; telephone: (213) 825 3722.

GUNAID, Muhammad Ahmad, Yemen Arab Republic politician/engineer; born 1934, Hodeida, Yemen Arab Republic; married; one daughter; *Religion:* Muslim; *Education:* BSc, Engineering, University of London, London UK; *Career:* Director, Technical Section, Hodeida Public Works, 1964–65; member of the Board of Yemen Petroleum Company, 1965; Under Secretary, Ministry of Public Works, 1967; Chairman, Mocha Agricultural Development Company, 1968; Minister of Agriculture, 1968–71; Minister of Development, 1971–72; Minister of Finance,

1973–; Deputy Prime Minister for Economic and Financial Affairs, 1977–; *Interests and Recreations:* problems and history of planning and development in the Arab World, music, gardening and flower cultivation; *Languages:* Arabic, English; *Address:* Ministry of Finance, Sana'a, Yemen Arab Republic; telephone: 5178.

GWAL, Peter Gatkuoth, Sudanese politician; born 1938, Akobo, Upper Nile Province, Sudan; married, with children; *Education:* Economic and Social Studies, University of Khartoum, Sudan; *Career:* Bank of Sudan, 1964; Adviser for Economic Planning in the Ministry of Southern Affairs, 1969; Assistant Director, Projects Section, at the Ministry of Southern Affairs, 1971; member of the Popular Commission for the National Charter; attended the Organisation of African Unity (OAU) Council of Ministers meeting in Addis Ababa, 1970; Deputy Minister of Southern Affairs in the new Government of October 1971; toured the Scandinavian countries with the Minister of Foreign Affairs to seek financial help from voluntary organisations for the refugee problem in Southern Sudan, 1971; Director General of the Special Fund for the Repatriation, Resettlement, Relief and Rehabilitation of Refugees from the Southern Region, 1972; concurrently member of the Political Bureau of the Sudanese Socialist Union (SSU); contested unsuccessfully the elections for the Regional People's Assembly, 1973; Commissioner of the Upper Nile Province, 1974; *Address:* Regional People's Assembley, Juba, Sudan.

H

HABACHI, Rene Marc, Lebanese academic/ UN official; born 6 September 1915, Cairo, Egypt; *Education:* Licence in Philosophy, Grenoble University, France, 1936–39; Doctorat d'Etat in Philosophy, Sorbornne, Paris; *Career:* Professor of Philosophy at the Lebanese, French and American Universities of Beirut, 1953–59; Dean of the Institute of Social Sciences, Centre for Education in the Arab States, 1962–66; Director of the Philosophy Division of UNESCO, Paris, France, 1972–; *Publications: Penesee Méditérranée,* four volumes, 1960–70; *Pour Philosophy,* Division of UNESCO, Paris 1972; *Philosophy Notre Temps,* in Arabic and French; *Orient, quel est ton Occident?,* 1973; *Decorations:* awarded prize for best writer in the Mediterranean Area and Italy, 1964; *Interests and Recreations:* Piano, member of the Rotary Club, Beirut, Lebanon; *Languages:* Arabic, English, French; *Address:* 24 Rue des Bernardins, 75005, Paris, France.

HABASHI, Wadi, Sudanese official/ agricultural expert; born 14 August 1917, Merowe, Sudan; married; *Religion:* Christian; *Education:* Degree from Faculty of Agriculture, University of Khartoum, Sudan, 1942; Agricultural Studies, Oxford University, UK, 1951–52; *Career:* Ministry of Agriculture; worked on the Alyab, Burgeg and White Nile development schemes; Agricultural Inspector for Khartoum Province and later for Merowe, Dongola and Halfa; Technical Adviser to Ministry of Agriculture; Assistant Director and then Director for Planning and Development, Ministry of Agriculture, 1955–66; Representative of Sudan to FAO Conference 1956 and to International Tobacco Conference, Rhodesia, 1963; Chairman, Administrative Council, El-Gash Scheme Committee; Director, Production Section, Equatoria Schemes Committee; Head, Advisory Committee for Agricultural Research; member of Gezira Scheme Administrative Council; member of Studies Committee, Faculty of Agriculture, University of Khartoum; agricultural expert with FAO, 1966–71; Director, FAO–ECA (Economic Commission for Africa) Joint Agricultural Division, Addis Ababa; joined IBRD (World Bank) and Kuwait Arab Fund for Economic Development, 1971; Minister of Agriculture, 1971–73; Minister of Agriculture, Food and Natural Resources, 1973–74; President, National Council of Research, 1974; President of Organization for African Unity, Scientific Council for Africa, 1975–; *Languages:* Arabic, English; *Address:* National Council for Research, Khartoum, Sudan.

HABBAL, Adnan Muhammad Adib al-, Saudi Arabian physician; born 1936, Mecca, Saudi Arabia; *Religion:* Muslim; *Education:* BSc in Chemistry and Biology, American University of Beirut, Lebanon, 1961; MD, School of Medicine, American University of Beirut, 1965; speciality training, Department of Radiology, Medical Centre, American University of Beirut, 1967–69, Department of Radiology and Nuclear Medicine, Rush-Presbyterian St. Luke's Medical Center, Chicago, Illinois, USA, 1969–70, Staff-member, Rush-Presbyterian St. Luke's Hospital, Chicago, 1970–72, Aramco Supervisory Management Course; *Career:* Instructor, Abraham Lincoln School of Medicine, Chicago, USA, 1967–70; Adjunct, Rush-Presbyterian St. Luke's Hospital, Chicago; Assistant Professor, Rush-Presbyterian Medical Center, Chicago, 1970–72; Chief of Radiology Services, Dhahran Health Centre, Arabian American Oil Company (Aramco), Dhahran; Consultant in Radiology, Aramco's Contract Hospitals, Al-Khobar; member of Chicago Roenthen Society, 1970; member, American Board of Radiology 1970; Corresponding member of American College of Radiology; *Publications:* several scientific papers; *Interests and Recreations:* photography; *Address:* Aramco, P O Box 2657, Dhahran, Saudi Arabia.

HABBASH, George, Palestinian politician; born 1936, Lydda, Palestine; married, with children; *Religion:* Christian; *Education:* Degree in Medicine, American University of Beirut, Lebanon; *Career:* at American University of Beirut, formed with friends *Al Urwa al-Uthqa* mainly concerned with Palestine and Arab Unity; in early 1950s helped form the Arab Nationalist Movement on the basis of this group; lived in Jordan and Syria; following the 1967 war the leaders of the ANM formed a commando group later called the Popular Front for the Liberation of Palestine (PFLP) which later split into the PFLP proper, and the Popular Democratic Front for the Liberation of Palestine (PDFLP), led by Nayef Hawatmeh and the PFLP-General Command (PFLP), led by Ahmed Jibril; joined the PLO Central Committee 1970; maintained a PFLP Representative until September 1974; leads Rejection Front, which opposes current PLO policy and unites PFLP, PFLP-GC, ALF and the Palestinian People's Struggle Front (PPSF); *Languages:* Arabic, English.

HABIB, Fawzi, Egyptian economist; born 14 June 1922; married; *Education:* LLB, Cairo University, Cairo, Egypt, 1946; Diploma in Taxation, 1946; Diploma in Economics, Cairo University, 1948; Research Associate, Johns Hopkins University, USA, 1956; research and graduate studies, New York University, Federal Reserve Bank, New York, and New York Stock Exchange; MS, Agricultural Economics, North Carolina State College, USA, 1953–54; PhD, International Finance and Development, Duke University, USA, 1954–56; *Career:* Attorney and Taxation Consultant; Legal and Financial Counsel, Bank Misr, Nile Ginning Co, Ottman Bank, Barclays Bank, Egypt, 1947–53; Representative French Insurance Co, British and other European manufacturers of chemicals and agricultural machinery, 1944–53; Associate Professor, Florida State University in Panama, 1962–64; Senior Economist, World Bank, Latin American Department, 1956–61; Financial Adviser to the President of Panama, 1962–66; Senior Investment Officer, International Finance Corporation, Washington D.C., 1966–71; Chief Investment Officer, 1971–78; Senior Adviser,

International Finance Corporation, in charge of problem cases, larger investments and development banks, 1977–; member of American Bankers Association; member of American Economics Association; *Publications: The Pace and Direction of Growth of Agricultural Export Economies,* 1958; *Factors Affecting the Foreign Demand for Long Staple Egyptian Cotton,* 1956; *Interests and Recreations:* tennis, music, travel, international finance; *Languages:* Arabic, English, French, Spanish, Italian; *Address:* International Finance Corporation, 1818 H Street NW, Washington D.C., 20433 USA; telephone: Office — (202) 477 1234; Residence — (703) 3541144.

HABIB, Malalla Ali, Omani diplomat; born 10 February 1926; married; one son, four daughters; *Education:* in Oman; *Career:* Employee, Department of Treasury, 1943–44; Translator, Department of Foreign Affairs, 1945–46; Secretary, Department of Diwan Affairs, 1946–49; Senior Clerk, Department of Foreign Affairs, 1949–52; Chargé d'Affaires, Omani Embassy to New Delhi, 1973–74; Ambassador to Cairo, 1974–77; Ambassador to Iran, 1977–79; Chief of Political Affairs, Ministry of Foreign Affairs, Muscat, 1979–81; Ambassador to UK, 1981–82; Director, Minister of Foreign Affairs Office, Muscat, Oman 1982–; *Languages:* Arabic, Persian, English, Urdu; *Address:* Ministry of Foreign Affairs, P O Box 252, Muscat, Oman; telephone: 701211; telex: 3337 MFA MB.

HABRE, Elias, Lebanese politician/trade unionist; born circa 1919, Aley, Lebanon; married; several children; *Religion:* Christian; *Career:* trade unionist; member of Executive Committee of World Federation of Trade Unions and Chairman of the National Labour Federation; President of the Union of Workers and Employees of Hotels, Cafés and Restaurants; *Address:* Federation of Independent Trade Unions, Central Building, Rue Mere Galace, Beirut, Lebanon.

HABTUR, Sultan Khalifa Sultan al-, United Arab Emirates businessman/official; born 1942; married; one son, one daughter; *Religion:* Muslim; *Education:* BA in Military Sciences, 1967; *Career:* Director of Contracting Company, 1968–70; owner of Contracting Company and General Trading, 1972–74; Secretary of State, Ministry of

Public Works; Under Secretary, Ministry of Labour since the establishment of the United Arab Emirates; member of Civil Service Council, 1972–76; member of Municipality Council; member of the Board of Abu Dhabi Electricity Company; member of the Board of Emirates Commercial Bank; *Interests and Recreations:* poetry, photography, painting, literature, volleyball, swimming, hunting; *Languages:* Arabic, English; *Address:* Ministry of Labour, P O Box 809, Abu Dhabi, United Arab Emirates.

HADARI, Mahmud S. al-, Egyptian academic/dentist; born Egypt; married; two daughters; *Religion:* Muslim; *Education:* DS, Dental Medicine and Surgery, University of Alexandria, Egypt, 1951; Diploma of Dental Extraction and Aneasthesia, University of Alexandria, Egypt, 1951; Master of Dental Surgery, University of Michigan, USA, 1957; *Career:* Demonstrator, crowns and bridges, Dental School, University of Alexandria, 1951; assigned to a mission to USA, 1956–58; Lecturer on crowns and bridges, 1959; Assistant Professor of Constructive Dentistry, 1964; Professor of Constructive Dentistry, 1972; Deputy Dean for Graduate Studies and Research, 1974; Chairman, Department of Constructive Dentistry, 1978; Dean, Faculty of Dentistry, 1978–80; President, University of Alexandria, 1980–; *Publications:* numerous research papers in professional journals; *Languages:* Arabic, English, French; *Address:* University of Alexandria, 3 Al-Geish Avenue, Shatby, Alexandria, Egypt; telephone: 70207.

HADDAD, Ahmad Ali al-, Yemen Arab Republic diplomat/official; born 2 October 1939, Yemen Arab Republic; *Religion:* Muslim; *Education:* BA, Political Science, University of Vermont, USA, 1964; Post Graduate Studies, New School of Social Science Research, New York, USA 1973–74, *Career:* Assistant Director and Director, International Organisation Department, Ministry of Foreign Affairs, 1964–65; Under Secretary, Ministry of Foreign Affairs, 1966–67; Director, Foreign Office, Taez, 1968–69; Head, Department of Economy, Technical and Cooperation Section, Ministry of Foreign Affairs, 1969–70; Minister, Embassy to the Federal Republic of Germany, 1970; member of Yemen Arab Republic Delegation to the UN General Assembly, 1970; Minister, Permanent Mission to the UN, New York,

USA, 1971–73; Minister, Deputy Permanent Representative of the Yemen Arab Republic to the UN, New York, USA, 1973–74; Head of Political Department, Ministry of Foreign Affairs, 1975–76; Ambassador, Permanent Representative to the European Office of the UN, Geneva, 1977; Ambassador, Permanent Representative to the UN, New York, USA, 1978–; *Languages:* Arabic, English, French; *Address:* 747 Third Avenue, 8th Floor, New York, NY 10017, USA; telephone: 355 1730.

HADDAD, Amin Farid, Lebanese academic/pharmacist; born 20 July 1911, Batroun, Lebanon; married; one son, two daughters; *Education:* National College, Shwayfat, Lebanon; PhD, American University of Beirut, Lebanon, 1933; MSc, Philadelphia College of Pharmacy and Science, USA, 1948; *Career:* Assistant Professor of Pharmacy, American University of Beirut, Beirut, Lebanon, 1942–49; Associate Professor, School of Pharmacy, 1949–52, Associate Professor, School of Pharmacy, 1952–, Professor and Director, 1955–77, Professor Emeritus, 1977; Director, Pharmaceutical Services of University Hospital, 1949–67; member of the American Pharmaceutical Association, the American Society of Hospital Pharmacists, the International Pharmaceutical Federation, Scientific Section; member of the Expert Advisory Panel on the International Pharmacopaeia and Pharmaceutical Preparations, WHO; Secretary, High Commission on Drugs, Lebanon, 1964–68; Chairman, Scientific Committee, Lebanese Union of Pharmacists, 1952–67; Temporary Adviser to WHO (Eastern Mediterranean Region) on pharmaceutical education, 1968–70, 1971–74; Editor, *Lebanese Pharmaceutical Journal,* 1953–63; Honorary Fellow, University of Wisconsin, Madison, USA, 1958–59; *Decorations:* Officer of the Lebanese Order of the Cedar, 1958; *Languages:* Arabic, English; *Address:* American University of Beirut, Beirut, Lebanon.

HADDAD, Farid Sami, Arab-American surgeon; of Lebanese origin; born 1922, New York; married; two sons, one daughter; *Religion:* Christian; *Education:* BA, American University of Beirut, 1941; MD, American University of Beirut, 1948; FACS, Chicago, 1957; *Career:* Chief Resident, Presbyterian Hospital, Chicago, 1951–53; Special Fellow, Memorial Hospital, New York, 1953–54; Urologist, Orient Hospital, Beirut,

1954–57; Chief of Staff, Orient Hospital, Beirut, 1957–74; President, Marj'uyum Hospital, Lebanon, 1972–77; Surgeon/Urologist, Obeid Hospital, Riyadh, 1977–78; Chief of Staff, Obeid Hospital, Riyadh, 1979–81; Chief of Urology, VA Hospital, Phoenix, AZ, USA, 1981–; President, Lebanese Urology Association, 1957–67; Editor in Chief of the *Lebanese Medical Journal,* 1961–68; Vice President, International Society of the History of Medicine, 1975–80; member of the American Board of Urology, the International Society of Medicine, the New York Academy of Medicine, the Athenaeum of Argentina, the Alpha Omega Alpha; *Publications:* numerous articles on medicine and medical history in professional journals and magazines in Arabic, English and French; *Decorations:* Knight of the National Order of the Cedar, 1961; Officer of the National Order of the Cedar, 1971; Award Medal of the Egyptian Medical Association, 1966; *Interests and Recreations:* collecting manuscripts and coins; *Languages:* Arabic, English, French, German, Italian, Spanish; *Address:* 4332E Piccadilly Road, Phoenix, AZ 85018, USA; telephone: 602 2775551.

HADDAD, George Habib, Lebanese banker; born 22 May, 1941, Beirut; married; four daughters; *Religion:* Muslim; *Education:* Accountancy Diploma, Technical School, 1958; Faculty of Law, Lebanese University, 1965; Management and Finance, *TEP* Programme, University of Virginia, USA, 1975; *Career:* Branch Manager, FA Kettaneh SA, Beirut, 1956–64; successively in Citibank NA, (New York), Operations Officer, Beirut,1964–69, Senior Operations Officer, Saudi Arabia, 1969–71, Senior Assistant Manager and Head of Corporate Group, 1971–75, Beirut; Resident Vice President, Middle East and North Africa Regional Office, Athens, Greece, 1975–77; Chairman of the Board and General Manager, Universal Bank SAL, Beirut, 1978–; *Interests and Recreations:* table tennis, member of Metropolitan Lions Club; *Languages:* Arabic, English, French; *Address:* Universal Bank SAL, P O Box 113–5024, Beirut, Lebanon; telephone: 315691, 315697.

HADDAD, George M., Arab-American academic/writer; born August 1910, Homs, Syria; married; three children; *Religion:* Christian; *Education:* BA, American University of Beirut, Lebanon; Licence-ès-Lettres,

Sorbonne, University of Paris, France; PhD, Oriental Institute of Chicago, USA; *Career:* Instructor, Government Secondary Schools, Aleppo, Syria, 1934–39; Instructor, Ministry of Education, Syria, 1939–46; Professor of Middle Eastern History, Damascus University, Syria, 1949–59; Professor of Middle Eastern History, University of California, USA, 1960–; Visiting Professor at Bowdoin College, Thiel College and University of Michigan, USA, 1957–58, 1959–60; member of Syrian delegation to the conference of Palermo, Italy for Economic and Cultural Cooperation between Mediterranean countries, 1954; member of Asian Town Hall Delegation to Lecture in USA, 1955; *Publications: Revolution and Military Rule in the Middle East,* 3 volumes, New York 1965; *Fifty years of Modern Syria and Lebanon,* Beirut, 1950; *History of Arab Civilization,* Damascus 1942, in Arabic; *Aspects of Social Life in Greco-Roman Antioch,* Chicago, 1949; complete series of history textbooks for Syrian intermediate and secondary schools, 1935–46; *Decorations:* Commander of St. Peter and St. Paul, awarded by the Greek Orthodox Patriarch of Antioch and all the East for initiative in restoration of the Monestary of St. Simon Stylites, Northern Syria; *Interests and Recreations:* research and writing on the history of the Middle East; member of the Association of the American Oriental Society of the Middle East Institute; member of the Middle East Studies Association; *Languages:* Arabic, English, French, Spanish, German; *Address:* 23 East Pueblo Street, St Barbara, California 93105, USA; telephone: Office — 961 2267; Residence — 682 7653.

HADDAD, Ghassan, Syrian politician/economist; born 26 January 1926; *Education:* DSc and PhD, Economics; Military Academy, USSR; *Career:* various military posts, 1948–61; General 1961; member of the Revolutionary Command Council; Minister of Planning, 1963–65; Professor, Planning Institute for Social and Economic Development, 1969–75; Chief Adviser, Ministry of Planning, Baghdad, and Professor, University of Baghdad, 1975–; participated in several international seminars on problems of planning; member of Union of Arab Writers, Union of Arab Economists; *Publications:* numerous articles in the fields of economics and planning; *Decorations:* Medal of Merit of Honour; Medal of Loyalty, 1st Class; *Lang-*

uages: Arabic, French, German; *Address:* Ministry of Planning, P O Box 6025, Mansoor, Baghdad, Iraq.

HADDAD, Jerrier Abdu, Arab-American engineer; born 17 July 1922; married; two sons, three daughters; *Religion:* Christian; *Education:* BEE, Cornell University, USA; *Career:* joined IBM as an Electrical Engineer, Endicott, NY, USA, 1945; Head of Engineering Design of IBM 701 Computer, 1951; Manager, IBM Endicott Laboratory, 1953; General Manager, IBM Advanced System Development Division, 1956; IBM Director of Engineering, 1963; IBM Vice President, 1967; *Decorations:* Order of Cedar, Officer Grade, Republic of Lebanon 1968; *Interests and Recreations:* fishing, tennis; member of The National Academy of Engineering; Fellow of the Institute of Electronic and Electrical Engineers; Trustee of Clarkson College of Technology; *Languages:* English; *Address:* 162 Macy Road, Briacliff Manor, NY 10510, USA; telephone: (914) 941 7061.

HADDAD, Monsignor Georges, Lebanese ecclesiastic; born 14 March 1924, Beit Chabab, Lebanon; *Religion:* Christian; *Education:* Saint Anne Seminary, Jerusalem, 1935; *Career:* ordained priest at Saint Anne Seminary, 26 June 1948; Professor at Rayak Seminary, 1948–49; Director of Furn el-Chubbak School and Priest of Falougha, 1949–50; Vicar of St. Nicholas Parish, Beirut; Secretary to the Archbishop of Beirut and Priest of the Parish of St. Jean Chrysostome, 1951–60; Patriarchal Judge Vicar at Appeal Court, 1959–65; Archimandrite and Vicar General of the Eparchy of Beirut, 1960; Bishop Metropolitan of Tyre, 1965–; *Address:* Greek-Catholic Archbishopric, Tyre, Lebanon.

HADDAD, Mustafa Hassan, Syrian academic/official; born 11 July, 1930, Syria; married; two sons; *Religion:* Muslim; *Education:* BSc, Damascus University, 1953; Doctorate in Botany, University of Paris, France, 1959; *Career:* Teacher, Secondary School of Aleppo, 1954; Lecturer, Faculty of Science, University of Damascus, 1959; Assistant Professor, 1964; Full Professor, 1969; Minister of Education, 1963–65; 1966; Minister of Higher Education, 1969–70; Minister of Petroleum, Electricity and Mineral Resources, 1970–72; President of the University

of Damascus; *Publications: Contribution to the Study of Ontogenesis of Grapes,* in Arabic; *The Capparidacese of Madagascar,* in Arabic; *Plant Organization,* a textbook; *Morphogenesis* a textbook; reviewer of the *Unified Dictionary of Scientific Terms in Botany; Languages:* Arabic, French, English, German; *Address:* Damascus University, Damascus, Syria; telephone: 27268.

HADDAD, Radhia, Tunisian politician/feminist; born 17 March 1922, Tunis, Tunisia; married; two sons, two daughters; *Religion:* Muslim; *Education:* general; *Career:* Director of the Bourguiba Nursery School; President of the National Union of Tunisian Women (Union Nationale des Femmes de Tunisie (UNFT); resigned 8 March 1972 following intervention of the Socialist Destour Party in the internal affairs of the Union; Deputy in the National Assembly, elected in 1959 (first Tunisian woman Deputy) and again in 1964 and 1969; Vice President of the International Council of Women 1970–; Assistant Secretary General of the National Union of Arab Women, 1971–; Vice President of the Tunisian Holiday Camps, 1947; Associate President of the Tunisian Girl Guides, 1947; member of the Central Committee of the Socialist Destour Party, 1968–71, resigned, 1971; member of the National Planning Council 1968–; Director of *El-Marraa* review (in Arabic), 1961–72; *Interests and Recreations:* reading, walking, gardening; *Languages:* Arabic, French; *Address:* Avenue Bourguiba, Carthage Presidence, Tunisia; telephone: 276608.

HADDAD, Robert M., Arab-American academic; born 1 October 1930, New York, USA; married; one son, three daughters; *Religion:* Christian; *Education:* BSc, University of Pittsburgh, USA, 1952; MA, University of Michigan, USA, 1954; PhD, History and Middle Eastern Studies, Harvard University, USA, 1965; *Career:* Lecturer in History, Smith College, Northampton, Massacussetts, USA, 1960–65; Assistant Professor of History, Smith College, 1965–68; Associate Professor of History and Religion, Smith College, 1968–73; Professor of History and Religion, Smith College, 1973–82; Sophia Smith Professor of History and Religion, Smith College, 1982–; Chairman, Department of History, Smith College, 1973–77; President of the Orthodox Theological Society, in America, 1974–76; member of the American Historical Association; member of the Middle East Studies Association; member of the Orthodox Roman Catholic Theological Consultation; *Publications: Syrian Christians in Muslim Society: An Interpretation*, Princeton, 1970; *The Ottoman Empire in the Contemporary Middle East*, Smith College, 1975; *On Melkite Passage to the Unia: the Case of Patriarch Cyril al-Za'iim, 1672–1720; Christian Jews in the Ottoman Empire*, Holmes and Meier, 1982; *Iconoclasts and Mu'tazila: The Politics of Anthropomorphism, Byzantiun and Islam*, Hellenic College Press, 1982; *Interests and Recreations:* carpentry; *Languages:* English, Arabic, French; *Address:* Office — Department of History, Smith College, Northampton, Mass. USA; Residence— 65 Kensington Avenue, Northampton, Massachusetts 01060, USA; telephone: (413) 586 0381.

HADDAD, Sulaiman Ahmad al-; Kuwaiti businessman; born 1930; *Religion:* Muslim; *Education:* Cairo University, Egypt; *Career:* Secretary of Educational Council of Kuwait; Financial Assistant, Ministry of Education; member of National Assembly, 1961–64; Chairman of Willco Oil, Kuwait; Deputy Chairman and Managing Director, Arab European International Trading Co, Kuwait; *Languages:* Arabic, English; *Address:* Arab European International Trading Co, ARTOC, Arab Gulf Building, P O Box 23074, Safat, Kuwait; telephone: 421390/4; telex: 2366 ASCA, 2945 ASCA.

HADDAWI, Abbas Abdullah, Saudi Arabian administrator; born 1925, Mecca, Saudi Arabia; *Religion:* Muslim; *Education:* Diploma of Higher Institute of Physical Education; *Career:* International Commissioner, Saudi Arabian Boy Scouts Association; Director General of Youth Welfare, Ministry of Education; member of Arab Scouts Committee; attended International Boy Scouts Conferences in Greece, Mexico, Japan, Morocco, Libya, Algeria, Lebanon; Chairman of Saudi Delegation to Arab Sporting Tournaments held in Morocco, Kuwait, Lebanon, Egypt; *Address:* Directorate General of Youth Welfare, Ministry of Education, Riyadh, Saudi Arabia; telephone: 4043452.

HADI, Abdul Hamid Saif Manih al-, Yemen Arab Republic official; born 1946; one son, two daughters; *Religion:* Muslim; *Education:* Police College, Cairo, Egypt, 1965; College of Law, Baghdad University, Iraq, 1969; *Career:* Police College, War HQ, 1969; legal adviser to the Ministry of Local Administration; Director of Office of Minister of Interior; member of the Consultative Council; Under Secretary, Ministry of Municipalities, with rank of Minister; member of the Development Organization; member of the Board of the Water and Electricity Corporation; *Interests and Recreations:* reading literature, history; *Languages:* Arabic, English; *Address:* Al-Idha'a (Broadcasting) Quarter, Sana'a, Yemen Arab Republic.

HADI, Mahdi Mustafa al-, Sudanese politician/diplomat; born 1932, Omdurman, Sudan; *Religion:* Muslim; *Education:* Arts Degree, University of Khartoum, Sudan; *Career:* Ministry of Foreign Affairs; Chargé d'Affaires, Embassy to Chad, 1963; member of the Sudanese Mission to the UN, 1965–69; Adviser to the Sudanese Embassy to USSR, 1969; Adviser on Foreign Affairs to the President of the Revolutionary Command Council, rank of Ambassador, 1969; Secretary of the Preparatory Committee of the Sudanese Socialist Union (SSU), 1971; Secretary General of the Presidency of the Republic with the rank of Deputy Minister, 1971; promoted to General Adviser to the Presidency with rank of Minister; member of the newly-formed Political Bureau of the SSU, 1972; Secretary for External Relations of the SSU, 1972–74; Secretary of the SSU in the Khartoum Province; Commissioner of the Khartoum Province late in 1974; *Languages:* Arabic, English; *Address:* Sudan Socialist Union, P O Box 1850 Khartoum, Sudan.

HADI, Mubarak Adam al-, Sudanese diplomat; born 1 January, 1938, Hilalilya, Sudan; married; three sons, two daughters; *Religion:* Muslim; *Education:* BA in Literature, University of Khartoum, 1961; Diploma, International Institute of Management, Paris, France; Degree, Institute of Human Rights, Strassbourg, France; *Career:* 3rd Secretary, Sudan Embassy, Jeddah, Saudi Arabia, 1961; 2nd Secretary, Press Attaché, Beirut, Lebanon, 1964; 1st Secretary, Algeria, 1967; Counsellor, Paris, 1972; Minister Plenipotentiary, Director of Press and Information

Department, Ministry of Foreign Affairs, Khartoum, Sudan; Ambassador to Zaire, 1975; Ambassador to Oman, 1979–; *Interests and Recreations:* music, playing string instruments, tennis, swimming, walking, football, reading; *Address:* Embassy of Democratic Republic of Sudan, Muscat, Oman, P O Box 5205.

HADI, Muhammad Sharif, United Arab Emirates banker; born 1943 Dubai, United Arab Emirates; married; two sons, three daughters; *Religion:* Muslim; *Education:* BA; Diploma, Banking; *Career:* Manager, United Arab Emirates Central Bank, Dubai Branch, United Arab Emirates, 1974–; *Interests and Recreations:* member of the Passport Club, Dubai; *Languages:* Arabic, English, Persian; *Address:* United Arab Emirates Central Bank, P O Box 448, Dubai, United Arab Emirates; telephone: Office — 436655; Residence — 421742; telex: 45645 CURBOR.

HADID, Muhammed Hajj Hussain, Iraqi businessman/politician; born 1906; *Religion:* Muslim; *Education:* BSc in Economics, American University of Beirut, Lebanon and London School of Economics, UK; *Career:* Finance Inspector, 1931; Head of Statistics Section, Ministry of Finance, 1932; Head of Commerce Section, Ministry of Finance, 1934; Acting Director of Commerce, 1935; Acting Director General of Revenue, 1936; elected Deputy for Mosul, 1937, 1948, 1958; Vice President, National Democratic Party, 1946–54; Minister of Supply, 1946; Minister of Finance, 1958–60; founder of National Progressive Party, 1960; now Managing Director, Consolidated Modern Enterprises Company; *Languages:* Arabic, English; *Address:* Consolidated Modern Enterprises Company WLL, 4 Shahia Building, Sadoun Street, P O Box Alwiyah 2058, Baghdad, Iraq.

HADIDY, Bahaa al-, Arab-American academic; born 21 June 1931, Cairo, Egypt; married; *Religion:* Muslim; *Education:* BSc, Cairo University, Egypt, 1954; MLS, Rutgers University, New Jersey, USA, 1963; Advanced Certificate in Information Science, University of Pittsburgh, USA, 1973; *Career:* Scientific Information Officer, National Documentation and Information Centre, National Research Council of Egypt; postgraduate studies in USA, 1961–64; Library Consultant, Case Institute of Tech-

nology, Cleveland, Ohio, USA, 1967–74; postgraduate studies, University of Pittsburgh, USA, 1965–67; Professor of Information Science, Catholic University, USA, 1974–; member of Executive Committees in: American Society for Information Science, American Library Association, American Chemical Society, Association of Egyptian-American Scholars, USA, Association of Arab-Americans, USA, Association of American Library Schools; *Publications:* numerous articles in scientific journals; *Interests and Recreations:* tennis, music, swimming; *Languages:* Arabic, English, French; *Address:* 9314 Cherry Hill Road, Apartment 804, College Park, Maryland 20740, USA; telephone: (301) 474 2563.

HADITHI, Anwar Abdul Qadir al-, Iraqi politician/diplomat; born 1926, Iraq; *Religion:* Muslim; *Education:* Military College, Bagdhdad, Iraq, 1945; *Career:* several military posts; participated in the 1958 Revolution, and the Baath Revolution of 1968; Secretary General, Revolutionary Command Council, 1963; imprisoned for three years, after the coup by Abdul Salam Arif, 1963; Minister of Labour, Social Affairs, Transport and Municipalities, 1968–77; Ambassador, Ministry of Foreign Affairs, and later Ambassador to Czechoslovakia; *Address:* Embassy of Iraq, Praha 6, No Zatorce 10, Prague, Czechoslovakia; telephone: 375031.

HAFEZ, Amin al-, Lebanese politician; born 1926, Tripoli, Lebanon; married; one son; *Religion:* Muslim; *Education:* Licence ès-Sciences Politiques et Economiques, Cairo University, Egypt; American University of Beirut, Lebanon; Doctorat ès-Sciences Economiques, Lausanne University, Switzerland; Diploma in Law, International Law Academy of the Hague, Netherlands; *Career:* Economic Adviser; Director, Institute of Industrial Research, 1954–; Professor of Political Economics, Lebanese University; elected Deputy for Tripoli, 1960, 1964 and 1968; President, Parliamentary Committee on Foreign Affairs, 1965–; Prime Minister, Minister of Information and Acting Minister of Health, 1973; elected Deputy Chairman of the Foreign Affairs Committee of the Inter-Parliamentary Union, 1971; *Publications: Structure of the Political Economy in Syria and Lebanon;* several other studies published by the Institute of Industrial Research; *Interests and Recreations:* swimming, journalism;

member of the Inter-Parliamentary Union; *Languages:* Arabic, French, English; *Address:* Office — Chamber of Deputies, Place de l'Etoile, Beirut, Lebanon; Residence -- Cornich Mazraa, Ghoneim Building, Beirut, Lebanon.

HAFEZ, Mahmud al-, Lebanese diplomat; born 1915, Beirut, Lebanon; married; four children; *Religion:* Muslim; *Education:* BA in Mathematics, American University of Beirut, and Law Degree from St. Joseph University, Beirut; *Career:* taught Mathematics and Physics at International College, 1934–45; Secretary, Legation to USA, 1945–46; Secretary, Delegation to Argentina, 1946; Chargé d'Affaires, Legation to Argentina, Chile, Uruguay 1946–49; Head of Economic Department, Ministry of Foreign Affairs, 1949–50; Consul General in Jerusalem, 1950–53; Counsellor, Embassy to Egypt, 1953–57; Consul General in Marseille, France, 1957–60; Ambassador to Saudi Arabia, 1960–63; Ambassador to India, 1963–69; Director of Economic and Cultural Affairs at Ministry of Foreign Affairs, 1969–; was for a short period Director of the Internal Security Forces; Ambassador to India, 1973–80; *Languages:* Arabic, French, English; *Address:* Ministry of Foreign Affairs, Beirut, Lebanon.

HAFFAR, Bishr Lutfi, Saudi Arabian businessman; born 1936, Damascus, Syria; *Education:* BA, American University of Beirut, 1958; MA, Heidelberg University, Germany, 1961; *Career:* Businessman in Saudi Arabia, 1967–73; Director of United Establishment for Trading in Riyadh, 1973–81; member of the Board of Bri Fiber Industries, UK, Fairway Marines, UK; Chairman of the Board of Al-Bishr Trading, Riyadh; *Address:* P O Box 3497, Riyadh, Saudi Arabia; telephone: Office — 4784448, Residence — 766533; 59 Ennismore Gardens, Flat 2, London SW7.

HAFFAR, Said Muhammad al-, Syrian academic; born 1930, Damascus, Syria; married; one son, two daughters; *Religion:* Muslim; *Education:* BSc in Natural Sciences; BA in Education and Pedagogy; MSc in Environment and Radiobiology; PhD in Industrial Fermentation; *Career:* Professor and Head of Department of Fundamental Sciences, University of Damascus, 1960–; Professor of Medical Biology, Faculty of Medicine, University of Damascus, 1973–; UNESCO Expert for Environmental Sciences and Environmental Education, University of Qatar, 1978–; Member of the International Union for Conservation of Nature and Natural Resources; Professor, Universities of Damascus and Qatar; *Publications: Man and Environment Problems,* University of Qatar, 1981; *Geocancerology,* 1983; several other books, articles and lectures; *Interests and Recreations:* music; *Languages:* Arabic, French, English; *Address:* P O Box 2713, Doha, Qatar; Supreme Council of Sciences, P O Box 4762, Damascus, Syria.

HAFIZ, Hisham Ali, Saudi Arabian journalist; born 30 March 1931, Madina, Saudi Arabia; married; three daughters, two sons; *Religion:* Muslim; *Education:* BA in Political Science, Cairo University, 1955; BA, Military Science, Cairo University, 1955; *Career:* Officer in Saudi Royal Army, 1955–56; Diplomat, Saudi Arabian Embassy in Tehran, Iran and in Washington D.C., USA, 1957–62; Editor in Chief, *Madina* daily newspaper, 1962–64; Diplomat, Saudi Arabian Foreign Ministry; member of the Saudi Permanent Delegation to UN European Headquarters, Geneva, 1964–69; currently Chairman and Director General of Saudi Research and Marketing Co; Publisher of the *Arab News,* Saudi Arabia's daily English language newspaper; *Saudi Business* weekly magzine; *Al-Sharq Al-Awsat; The International* daily newspaper; *Arab News Information Service,* twice weekly publication; *Saudi Report,* weekly magazine in English; *Al-Majalla,* weekly magazine in Arabic; *Sayidaty,* weekly magazine in Arabic; *Al-Qibla,* weekly religious magazine in Arabic; *Gulf Information Service,* twice weekly in English; founding member of the Public Projects Co, Dammam, Saudi Arabia, King Abdul Aziz University, Jeddah, Arab Transport Co, Saudi Research and Investment Co, Jeddah, Saudi Research and Marketing Co, Jeddah; *Publications:* articles in the above mentioned publications; *Interests and Recreations:* reading, travel; *Languages:* Arabic, English, French; *Address:* Saudi Research and Marketing, P O Box 4556, Jeddah, Saudi Arabia; Saudi Research and Marketing, UK Ltd, 6–7 Gough Square, Fleet Street, London EC4, UK.

HAFIZ, Ibrahim, Libyan businessman; born 1932, Fezzan, Libya; married; *Career:* built up large trading and contracting firm; also has interests in printing machinery, supplies and building materials; owner of marble and carpentry factory; has interests in major Libyan travel agency; property owner; representative of Libyan Employers' Groups, ILO; *Address:* Ibrahim Hafez Establishments, 5 Tozilli Street, Garden City, P O Box 582, Tripoli, Libya; telephone: 30149, 34736, 41080.

HAFIZ, Muhammad Ali, Saudi Arabian businessman/publisher; born 1937, Medina, Saudi Arabia; *Religion:* Muslim; *Education:* BA in Journalism, Faculty of Arts, Cairo University, Egypt, 1960; *Career:* Assistant Director General of Press, Ministry of Information, 1960; Editor in Chief, *Madina* newspaper, 1961–64; General Manager and co-owner of Madina Printing and Publishing Co; Deputy General Manager of Madina Press Organization; member of Constituent Board of King Abdul Aziz University; attended Arab League Information Conferences, 1961; Manager, Madina Printing and Publishing Co; *Publications:* daily column and editorial writings in *Madina* daily newspaper; *Interests and Recreations:* reading; *Address:* P O Box 4556, Jeddah, Saudi Arabia; telephone: 34962; telex: 401570 ARANEWS SJ.

HAIARI, Adil al-, Jordanian lawyer/economist; born 1938, Salt, Jordan; married; *Education:* LLB, Baghdad University, Iraq, 1961; MA in Law, Cairo University, Egypt, 1964; PhD in Law and Finance, Cairo University, 1968; *Career:* lecturer, College of Economics and Commerce, Jordan University, 1969–; member of Jordan Economists Association; member of Jordan Civil Lawyers Union; Assistant Secretary General of Arab Economists Union; *Publications: Tax on National Income; Constitutional Law and Jordanian Constitutional System; Address:* Jordan University, P O Box 1682, Amman, Jordan; telephone: 843555.

HAIARI, General Ali Ahmad al-, Jordanian army officer/diplomat; born 1923, Salt, Jordan; married; *Religion:* Muslim; *Education:* British Cadet Training Unit, Cairo, Egypt, 1941–42; Camberley Staff College, UK, 1949; *Career:* Officer Cadet, Jordan Arab Army, 1941–42; 2nd Lieutenant, 1942–43;

1st Lieutenant, 1943–45; Captain, 1945–47; Major, 1947–48; Lieutenant Colonel, 1948–55; Colonel, 1955–56 (three years Commander of 5th Battalion, six months Commander of 1st Division); Brigadier, 1956–; General, Chief of Staff, 1956; Chief of Staff, Jordanian Armed Forces, 1969–70; Minister of Defence, 1970; Ambassador to Cairo, 1971–72; transferred to Foreign Ministry, Amman after break in diplomatic relations, 1972–73; retired 1973; *Decorations:* Independence Medal, 1st Class; Renaissance Medal, 2nd Class; Syrian Order of Merit, 2nd Class; Egyptian Order of Merit, 2nd Class; Commodore of Lebanese Order of the Cedars; *Address:* Jabal Amman, P O Box 1168, Amman, Jordan; telephone: 38195.

HAIKAL, Yusuf, Jordanian diplomat; born 15 August 1912; *Religion:* Muslim; *Education:* London University, UK; University of Paris, France; *Career:* General Inspector of Waqfs (Religious Endowments) in Palestine; District Judge, Palestine, 1943–45; Mayor of Jaffa, 1945–48; Minister, Embassy to USA, 1949–53; Chief Jordanian Delegate with Mixed Armistice Commission, Jerusalem, 1953–54; Ambassador to UK, 1954–56; Ambassador to France, 1956–57; Ambassador to USA, 1957–58; and 1959–62; Ambassador to France, 1962–64; Ambassador to Republic of China, 1964–65; *Publications: The Prime Minister and the Evolution of the Parliamentary System,* 1937; in Arabic, *The Dissolution of Parliament,* 1935; *The Palestine Problem,* 1937; *Towards Arab Unity,* 1943; *The Forefathers of the Prophet,* 1947; *Palestine Before and After,* 1971; *Decorations:* Hutchinson Silver Medal, London School of Economics; Independence Medal, 1st Class, 1953; *Languages:* Arabic, English, French; *Address:* Ministry of Foreign Affairs, P O Box 1577, Amman, Jordan.

HAJ, Awad Ahmad Hassan al-; United Arab Emirates official/diplomat; born 1949, Dubai, United Arab Emirates; married; one son, four daughters; *Religion:* Muslim; *Education:* BA in History, Faculty of Arts, Baghdad University, Iraq, 1972; *Career:* 3rd Secretary, Chargé d'Affaires, UAE Embassy to Sudan; Director of Culture and Information, Department of Economics; Deputy Director, Department of Culture and Information, Ministry of Foreign Affairs; seconded to *Al-Ittihad* daily newspaper; Director of Bureau in Dubai and Northern Emirates,

1978–79; Deputy Director General of Administration and Finance, Ministry of Foreign Affairs, 1980; Director General, Consular and Foreigners Department, November, 1980; *Interests and Recreations:* table tennis, swimming, reading; *Languages:* Arabic, English; *Address:* Ministry of Foreign Affairs, Department of Consular Affairs and Foreigners, Abu Dhabi, United Arab Emirates; telephone: Office — 362195; Residence — 369628.

HAJ, Joseph Fuad al-, Lebanese UN official/ economist; born 27 July 1918, Ismailia, Egypt; married; two daughters; *Religion:* Christian; *Education:* BS in Public Utilities Economics, New York University, USA, 1952; MA in Public Administration, New York University, USA, 1954; *Career:* Research Assistant, UN Department for Economic and Social Affairs (ESA), United Nations, 1949–52; Programme Officer, Technical Assistance Administration, Pakistan, 1952–56; Roving Recruitment Officer, Technical Assistance Recruitment Service, Europe, 1956–59; Senior Personnel Officer, ESA, United Nations, 1959–61; Deputy Chief, Secretariat Recruitment Service Office of Personnel Services, United Nations, 1961–67; Director of Division of Administration, Economic Commission for Asia and the Far East (ECAFE), United Nations, Bangkok, 1967–74; Director of Division of Administration, Economic Commission for Latin America (ECLA), UN, Santiago, Chile, 1974–79; Consultant for Administrative Matters, 1980; *Interests and Recreations:* swimming, bridge, poker; President, Intern Student Council, USA, 1947–49; Fellow of the Smithsonian Institute; *Address:* c/o UN, ECLA, P O Box 179–D, Santiago, Chile; telephone: Office — 485051; Residence — Tabalaba 1255, Santiago, Chile; telephone: 233548.

HAJJAJI, Driss al-, Moroccan businessman; born 1952, Morocco; married; *Religion:* Muslim; *Education:* Diploma in Management and Administration; LLB; *Career:* employed in SABA and Co, 1969; Director of a branch of SABA and Co, 1974–; member of the Association for the Protection of Industrial Property in the Middle East and North Africa (APPIMAF); member of the International Association for the Protection of Industrial Property (AIPP); *Interests and Recreations:* travelling, music, cinema,

weight lifting; *Languages:* Arabic, French, English; *Address:* 48 Rue Jaafar Bnou Attia, Bourgogne, Casablanca, Morocco; telephone: 70 695.

HAJJAR, Taj, Jordanian businessman; born 10 July, 1929, Damascus, Syria; married; three sons, two daughters; *Religion:* Muslim; *Education:* MA Economics and Political Science; *Career:* Managing Director of family business in Syria for six years; President, United Trading Corporation Ltd, Amman, Jordan (member of the United Trading Group); *Interests and Recreations:* swimming, tennis; *Languages:* Arabic, English, French, German, Spanish; *Address:* P O Box 1408, Amman, Jordan.

HAJJI, Yusuf Jasim al-, Kuwaiti politician; born 1921; *Religion:* Muslim; *Career:* administrator with Ministry of Health; Minister, Ministry of Waqfs (Religious Endowments) and Islamic Affairs; *Address:* c/o Ministry of Islamic Affairs, P O Box 6, Safat, Kuwait; telephone: 424011, 433849.

HAKIM, Adnan al-, Lebanese politician/ businessman; born 1914 Beirut; married; *Religion:* Muslim; *Education:* College of *Al-Makasid al-Islamiya; Career:* Founder and Chairman of al-Nigadeh Party 1936; Deputy for Beirut, and Head of the Parliamentary Committee for Defence, 1960–64, 1968–72; Owner of *Sawt al-'Uruba* newspaper; *Languages:* Arabic, French; *Address:* Office — P O Box 3537, Beirut, Lebanon; telephone: 230693, 241339; Residence — 61 UN Street, Beirut, Lebanon; telephone: 307070, 831166.

HAKIM, Georges, Lebanese diplomat/ official; born 19 April 1913, Tripoli, Lebanon; married; one son, one daughter; *Religion:* Christian; *Education:* BA, American University of Beirut (AUB), Lebanon 1932; MA, AUB, 1934; Licence in Law, St. Joseph University, Beirut, 1937; *Career:* Lecturer in Political Economics, AUB, 1934–43; Professor of Political Economics, AUB, 1943–46; Counsellor, Legation to USA, 1946–52; Lebanese Delegate to the UN Economic and Social Council, 1946–49; Lebanese Representative to the UN General Assembly, 1946, 1949, 1954, 1959–67; Head of the UN Lebanese Delegation to the Conference on Trade and Labour, Havana, Cuba, 1947–48; Lebanese Representative to the IMF and to World Bank, 1947–51;

President of the UN General Secretariat's Commission for the study of economic development in underdeveloped countries, 1951; Minister of National Economy, 1952; Minister of Finance and of Agriculture, 1952–53; Head of the Lebanese Delegation to the Arab League, 1953; Minister of Foreign Affairs and Minister of National Economy, 1953; Minister Plenipotentiary, Embassy to West Germany, 1955; Minister of National Economy, 1956; Minister Plenipotentiary, Embassy to West Germany, 1956–58; Ambassador to West Germany, 1958; Permanent Lebanese Delegate to the UN, 1959–65; President of the UN Commission on Human Rights, 1962; Chairman of the UN Conference on Trade and Labour, Geneva, 1964; Deputy Prime Minister, and Minister of Foreign Affairs, 1965–66; Permanent Lebanese Delegate to the UN, 1966–67; Minister of Foreign Affairs, 1967–68; Vice President of the American University of Beirut, Lebanon, 1968–; *Publications:* various articles and essays on the economic development of underdeveloped countries and more specifically on Syria and Palestine; *Decorations:* Grand Officer, National Order of the Cedar; as well as many other decorations and distinctions from Iraq, Egypt, Italy, West Germany, Spain and the USA; *Languages:* Arabic, French, English; *Address:* Office — American University of Beirut, Lebanon.

HAKIM, Jacques Yussif, Syrian academic/lawyer; born 1931, Damascus, Syria; *Education:* Faculty of Law, Syrian University, Damascus, Syria; Beirut Faculty of Law and Economic Science, St. Joseph University, Beirut, Lebanon; LLD, University of Lyon, Lyon, France; Institute of Economics, University of Colorado, USA; *Career:* admitted to Syrian Bar; lawyer, Damascus; Professor, Faculty of Law and Economic Science, University of Damascus, Syria; Professor, Faculty of Law and Economic Science, University of Beirut, Beirut, Lebanon; *Publications: Le donnage de source délictuelle en Droit Musulman,* 1964; *Le vol en Droit Libanais et compare,* 1960; also articles and pamphlets; *Address:* Parliament Street, Damascus, Syria.

HAKIM, Monsignor Maximos V, Lebanese ecclesiastic; born 18 May 1908, Tanta, Egypt; descendant of Maximos II Hakim, Patriarch of the Melkite Greek Catholic Church in 1761; *Religion:* Christian; *Education:* MA in Philosophy and Theology, Saint Anne Seminary, Jerusalem, 1930; *Career:* Ordained in Jerusalem, 1930; Professor, Patriarchal College, Beirut, Lebanon, 1930–31; Vice Principal, Patriarchal College, Cairo, Egypt, 1931–34; Superior, Patriarchal College, Cairo, Egypt, 1934–43; attached to the service of the late Cyril IX Maughabghab, Melkite Patriarch, 1927–47; Archbishop of St. John of Acre, Haifa, Nazareth and all Galilee, 1943–67; member of the Greek Catholic Delegation to the Vatican II Ecumenical Council, 1962–65; Greek Catholic Patriarch of Antioch and all the East, Alexandria and Jerusalem, 1967–; President of the Greek Catholic Community Council, 1969–; *Publications: Paroissien Byzantin* first edition, 1933; founder of *Le Lien,* 1936; *Pages d'Evangiles en Galilee,* first edition, 1954; *Decorations:* Légion d'Honneur, France, 1965 and 1966; *Languages:* Arabic, French, English, Italian, Hebrew, Greek, Latin; *Address:* Greek Catholic (Melkite) Patriarchate, P O Box 22249, Damascus, Syria; telephone: 433129; Al Daher Street, 161, Cairo, Egypt; telephone: 904697.

HAKIM, Murtada K. al-, Iraqi academic; born 4 April 1932, Baghdad, Iraq; married; two sons, one daughter; *Religion:* Muslim, *Education:* PhD, Animal Science; *Career:* Assistant Professor, University of Baghdad, Baghdad, Iraq, 1975–; *Publications:* numerous research papers in professional journals; *Interests and Recreations:* gymnastics, music; *Languages:* Arabic, English; *Address:* Department of Animal Production, University of Baghdad, Baghdad, Iraq.

HAKIM, Robert, Egyptian artist/film producer; born 19 December 1907, Alexandria, Egypt; married; three children; *Education:* general; *Career:* with Paramount and Joinville Studios, 1926–33; Founder, Paris Film Productions, France, 1933, President and Director General, 1960–; producer of numerous films including *Pépé le Moko: La bête humaines, L'Homme du Sud, Casque d'Or, Thérèse Raquin,* 1953, *Nòtre Dame de Paris,* 1956, *Potbouille,* 1957; *Address:* 44 Avenue de New York, Paris 18è, France.

HAKIM, Tawfiq Hussain al-, Egyptian writer; born 1902, Alexandria, Egypt; *Religion:* Muslim; *Education:* Cairo, Rome, Doc-

213

torate in Law, University of Paris, France; *Career:* wrote his first play in French, 1926; practised as a country judge near Tanta, 1930–37; later became Head of the Investigation Department at the Ministry of Education; retired from public service to devote full time to writing; Director of Egyptian National Library; member of the Higher Council of Arts, Literature and Social Sciences and Egyptian Delegate to UNESCO, Paris; member of the National Council for Services and Social Affairs, 1974; *Publications:* numerous novels, stories and plays of which best known are *Yaumiyaat Na'ib fi-l Ariyaaf* (translated into English, German and French); *Awdat al-Ruuh; Ahl al Kahf; Al Sultaan al Haa'ir;* and numerous other plays and novels, many of which are translated; *Languages:* Arabic, English; *Address:* Residence — 1095 Corniche Road, Garden City, Cairo, Egypt; Office — 26 Murad Street, Dokki, Egypt.

HAKIMI, Said Muhammad al-, Yemen Arab Republic politician; born Yemen Arab Republic; married; two sons, four daughters; *Religion:* Muslim; *Education:* general; *Career:* businessman and trade unionist, 1960–62; Commander of the National Guard, 1962–63; member of the President's Office, 1963–64; member of the Secretariat of the National Assembly, 1964–65; Director of the Prime Minister's Office, 1967–68; Director General of Hodeida Customs, 1968–69; Director of the Customs Department, 1969–70; Minister of State for Supply (Food) Affairs, 1971–72; Governor of Taiz, 1972–74; Secretary of the Political Organization of the Yemeni Union; Deputy Chairman of the Follow-Up and Rectification Committee; Minister of Supply, 1975; *Interests and Recreations:* reading history; *Languages:* Arabic, some English; *Address:* Idha'a Quarter, Sana'a, Yemen Arab Republic.

HAKKI, Muhammad I., Egyptian diplomat/journalist; born 7 April 1933; married; two daughters; *Religion:* Muslim; *Education:* Cairo University, Egypt, 1954; Georgetown University, USA, 1957–58; Fellow of the American Political Science Association, 1963–64; Fellow of the Centre for International Affairs, 1972–73; *Career:* Press Attaché, Egyptian Embassy, Washington D.C., 1957–58; Press Attaché, Egyptian Embassy, Accra, Ghana, 1958–59; Head of the American Desk, *Al-Ahram* newspaper, 1958–66,

Foreign Editor, 1966–72; Public Affairs Specialist, IBRD (World Bank), 1973–75; Minister Counsellor for Press and Information, Embassy of Egypt, Washington D.C., USA; member of the Harvard Club, New York, USA, National Press Club, Washington D.C., USA, Journalists Association, Cairo, Egypt; *Decorations:* Medal of Merit, 1956; Medal of Merit, 1st Class, 1975; *Interests and Recreations:* squash, swimming; *Languages:* Arabic, English, French; *Address:* Al-Gazira al-Wusta Street, Zamalek, Cairo, Egypt; telephone: 803572; 7321 Yates Court Maclean, Virginia, USA; telephone: 703 821 8794.

HAKKI, Yahya, Egyptian writer; born 1905; *Religion:* Muslim; *Career:* served several years in diplomatic service and travelled widely in Europe; was early pioneer of the novella and short story; his early novel *The Lamp of Umm Hashem* translated into English; also published a study of the Egyptian short story; *Address:* c/o Egyptian General Organization for Publishing & Printing, 117 Corniche el Nilst, Cairo, Egypt.

HALABI, Najib E., Arab-American businessman/lawyer; born 19 November 1915, Dallas, Texas, USA; married; one son, two daughters; *Education:* Stanford University, California, USA; Michigan Law School and Yale University Law School, USA; *Career:* served as test pilot, US Navy, Second World War; admitted to California Bar, 1940; law practice, Los Angeles, USA, 1940–42; admitted to District of Columbia Bar, 1948; Foreign Affairs Adviser to Secretary of Defence, 1948–53; Deputy Assistant Secretary of Defence, 1952–54; worked with L.S. Rockefeller and Brothers, 1953–56; Vice President, Servo Mechanisms Incorporated, 1956–58, Executive Vice President and Director, 1959–61; Secretary and Treasurer, the Aerospace Corporation, 1959–61; President, American Technology Corporation; Administrator, Federal Aviation Agency, 1961–65; Vice President, Director, Pan American World Airways, 1965–68; President, Pan American World Airways, 1968–72, Chairman, Chief Executive Affairs, 1969–72; President, Halabi International Corporation (HICO), consulting organization, servicing major US corporations, 1973–; Director, Bank of America Corporation, Menlo Financial Corporation; admitted to New York Bar, 1973; currently private practice, New York; Trustee, Stanford University, USA; *Interests and Recreations:* golf, tennis, flying, skiing; member of Aspen Institute of Humanistic Studies, Asia Society, Eisenhower Exchange Fellowships, International Executive Service Corps, Brookings Institution Commission on the Middle East; Vice Chairman, Business Council on International Understanding; *Address:* 1822 Kalarama Sq, NW Washington D.C. 20008, USA.

HALABI, Ramzi Suhail, Lebanese businessman; born 18 March 1945, Lebanon; married; three daughters; *Religion:* Christian; *Education:* Diploma in Management Studies, Kingston Polytechnic, Kingston, UK; Higher National Diploma, Business Studies, City of London Polytechnic, London; Diploma, Chartered Accountancy; *Career:* Chairman, Sarabex Group of Companies, 1974–; pioneer in the development of money markets in the Middle East; consultant in Middle Eastern currencies; *Publications:* articles on the development of Middle Eastern money markets; *Interests and Recreations:* swimming, fishing, horse riding, tennis; *Languages:* Arabic, English, French, Italian; *Address:* Monksbridge, Thames Street, Sunbury, Middlesex, England; Sarabex Arab Corporation, 14 Moor Lane, London EC2Y 9BN; telephone: (01) 628 2187; telex: 8811663/4/5/6.

HALALI, Abdullah Hussain al-, Yemen Arab Republic diplomat/official; born 1930, Anis, Yemen Arab Republic; *Religion:* Muslim; *Education:* BSc in Commerce and Accountancy, University of Cairo, Egypt; *Career:* Director General of Technical Office (later the Central Planning Organization), 1968–71; member of the Consultative Assembly, 1971; Secretary General of the Conformation of Yemen Development Organizations, 1973–75; Minister of Social Affairs, Labour and Youth, 1975; Ambassador to Czechoslovakia, 1976; *Address:* c/o Ministry of Foreign Affairs, Sana'a, Yemen Arab Republic.

HALBUBI, Ahmad Yaqub Yusuf al-, United Arab Emirates official/economist; born 1948, Abu Dhabi, United Arab Emirates; married; *Religion:* Muslim; *Education:* BA in Economics; *Career:* Secretary to the Permanent Planning Committee, 1974; Director of Administrative and Financial Affairs Section, Ministry of Planning, 1975; *Interests and Recreations:* history, poetry, chess, hunting;

Languages: Arabic, English; *Address:* Ministry of Planning, P O Box 904, Abu Dhabi, United Arab Emirates.

HALFAWY, Muhammad al-, Egyptian UN official/chemical engineer; born 7 March 1920, Mansoura, Dakahliyah, Egypt; married; *Religion:* Muslim; *Education:* BSc and MSc in Physical Chemistry, Cairo University, Egypt; DIC, Applied Chemistry; PhD, Applied Physical Chemistry, Imperial College, London, UK; Ore Dressing, Research Associate, Massachusetts Institute of Technology, USA; *Career:* Lecturer and Associate Professor, University of Alexandria, Egypt; Professor of Chemistry, University of Baghdad, Iraq; Director General, Industrial Planning Administration, Ministry of Industry; Director General, Industrialization Organization, Ministry of Industry; Managing Director, Petrochemical Complex Project, Ministry of Industry, Egypt; Project Manager and Director, Industrial Research Institute, Sudan; Senior Industrial Development Field Adviser, United Nations Industrial Development Organization (UNIDO), Lebanon; Senior Inter-Regional Adviser, UNIDO, Vienna; *Publications: Introduction to Physical Chemistry; Manual of Qualitative Analysis ;* several articles and papers on electrolytic polishing of metals, electrodeposition, mineral dressing, the fertilizer industry and petrochemical development and industrial research; *Decorations:* Award of Honour for Services to Industry, Egypt; *Interests and Recreations:* table tennis, walking, classical music, reading; member of the Hunting Club, Cairo, Egypt; *Languages:* Arabic, English, French, German; *Address:* United Nations Industrial Development Organisation, P O Box 400, Vienna, Austria; telephone: 26313889.

HAMAD, Abdul Latif Yusif Al-, Kuwaiti politician/banker; born 1937, Kuwait; married; *Religion:* Muslim; *Education:* BA, International Affairs, Claremont College, California, USA 1958–60; attended Harvard Graduate School of Arts and Science, International Affairs Programme, 1960–62; *Career:* member of the Kuwaiti Delegation, during Kuwait applicaiton for admission to the United Nations, 1962; Acting Director General, Kuwait Fund for Arab Economic Development, 1963–81, Chairman, 1981; Director General, Kuwait Investment Company, 1965–74; Director, Kuwait Investment

Company, 1974–77; Alternate Governor for Kuwait, International Bank for Reconstruction and Development, and Affiliates, Washington D.C., 1964–81; Director, the South Arabian Gulf Society (Educational and Philanthropic), 1963–81; Chairman, Kuwait Prefabricated Building Company, 1965–78; Chairman, the United Bank of Kuwait Ltd, London 1966–81; Director, the Assistance Authority for the Gulf and Southern Arabia, 1967–81; Trustee, Arab Planning Institute, 1967–; Executive Director, Arab Fund for Economic and Social Development, 1972–81; Chairman, Campagnie Arabes et Internationale Investissements, Luxembourg, 1973–81; Trustee, Jordan University, 1974; member of the Board of Trustees, Claremont College, Claremont, California, USA, 1980; member of the Board of Trustees, World Scout Foundation, Stockholm, Sweden, 1980; Minister of Finance and Planning, Kuwait, 1981–; member of the Joint Ministerial Committee of the Board of Governors of the World Bank and International Monetary Fund (Development Committee), 1974–, the Board of Trustees, Corporate Property Investors, New York, 1975–81, the Governing Body of the Institute of Development, University of Sussex, UK, 1975–, the Brandt Commission, 1976–79, the Board of International Institute for Environment and Development, London, 1976–80, Co-chairman, 1980–, the Visiting Committee of the Centre for Middle Eastern Studies, Harvard University, 1976–; Director, Scandinavian Securities Corporation, New York, 1977–; Chairman, National Investment Group, Kuwait, 1977–79; *Interests and Recreations:* walking, swimming, reading, music, theatre; *Languages:* Arabic, English; *Address:* Ministry of Finance and Planning, P O Box 9. Kuwait.

HAMAD, Isa Ahmad al-, Kuwaiti diplomat; born 1925, Kuwait; married; two sons, two daughters; *Religion:* Muslim; *Education:* Mubarakiah School, Kuwait; *Career:* Under Secretary, and Director of Administration, Ministry of Foreign Affairs; Ambassador, Embassy of Kuwait to Rome and the Vatican; represented Kuwait at several educational conferences and was member of Kuwait delegation to the United Nations; Ambassador of Kuwait, Paris, France; *Interests and Recreations:* fishing, reading, swimming; *Languages:* Arabic, English; *Address:* Embassy of Kuwait, 2 rue de Lubeck, 75016, Paris, France.

HAMAD, Yaqub, Yusuf al-, Kuwaiti businessman/banker; born 1928, Kuwait; married; one son, three daughters; *Religion:* Muslim; *Education:* BSc in Commerce, Cairo University, Egypt; *Career:* private enterprise; member of the Board of the National Bank of Kuwait; President, Board of Al-Makhazin al-Baida Company, Kuwait; member of the Board of Hamra Contracting Company; *Interests and Recreations:* reading, swimming; *Languages:* Arabic, English; *Address:* National Bank of Kuwait, Abdullah al-Salim Street, P O Box 95, Safat, Kuwait; telephone: 422011, telex: 22451.

HAMADI, Abdullah Fadel al-, United Arab Emirates lawyer/official; born 2 October 1949, Dubai, United Arab Emirates; *Religion:* Muslim; *Education:* Degree in Law and Sharia (Islamic Law); *Career:* Adviser in the Judicial and Legislative Department, Ministry of Justice; Director, Administration, and Technical Affairs, Ministry of Justice; *Interests and Recreations:* swimming, reading; *Languages:* Arabic, English; *Address:* Ministry of Justice, Islamic Affairs and Awqaf, P O Box 753, Airport Road, Abu Dhabi, United Arab Emirates; telephone: 331433.

HAMARNAH, Michael Yacub, Jordanian official; born 8 December 1935, Jerusalem; married; two daughters, one son; *Religion:* Christian; *Education:* BA, American University of Beirut, AUB, Lebanon; Diploma in Tourism Marketing; *Career:* Teacher, 1958–62; Diplomat, 1962; Director of Tourism Authority, 1962–67; Counsellor, Jordan Tourist Authority, New York City, 1967–71; Information Director for Jordan, Washington D.C., USA, 1973–77; Director of Jordan Tourist Authority, 1977–; Director General, Ministry of Tourism and Antiquities; member of the Board of Royal Jordanian Airlines ALIA, RESTCO Hotel Corporation, Jordan Spa Company for Main Hot Springs, and of International Continental Hotel; *Interests and Recreations:* swimming; *Languages:* Arabic, English; *Address:* Ministry of Tourism and Antiquities, P O Box 224, Amman, Jordan; telephone: 42315; telex: 21741.

HAMDAN, Aziz Salih al-, Kuwaiti official/town planner; born 16 March 1914, Kuwait; married; *Education:* BA in Economics, BA in Art History, MSc in Urban Planning, University of Arizona, USA, 1961–66; Cambridge University, UK, 1969–71; *Career:*

member of Master Planning Committee, 1968–, the Municipal Central Committee, Kuwait, 1966–72; Director, Master Planning Department, Kuwait, 1966–71; Director, Department of Environment, Kuwait, 1971; Secretary General, Environment Protection Society, Kuwait, 1974; member of the Government Building Committee, the Governing Council, United Nations Environment Program (UNEP); Head, Kuwait Preparatory Committee, UN Conference on Human Settlements; member of the Graduates Society; *Interests and Recreations:* reading, travel, swimming, environment, architecture, urban and regional planning; *Languages:* Arabic, English; *Address:* Office — P O Box 5988, Kuwait; telephone: 420270.

HAMDAN, Ibrahim Yusuf, Arab-American academic/scientist; born 30 September 1938, Nablus, Jordan; married; one son; *Religion:* Muslim; *Education:* MSc and PhD, Biochemistry; *Career:* Research Associate; Research Project Leader, Biotechnology Department, Kuwait Institute for Scientific Research (KISR), 1974–; participated in Research Management Development Workshop, Amman, Jordan, 1979; attended a workshop on Principles of Management organised by KISR in collaboration with Battelle, 1979; attended and participated in numerous conferences locally and abroad; *Publications:* numerous scientific papers published in Kuwait and abroad; *Interests and Recreations:* swimming; member of the Honour Society of Sigma XI, the Honour Society of Gamma Sigma Delta, the Honour Society of Phi Kappa Phi; member of the International Editorial Board of Biotechnology Letters Journal; Alternate member of UNEP/UNESCO/ICRO Panel on Microbiology; *Languages:* Arabic, English; *Address:* Kuwait Institute for Scientific Research, Biotechnology Department, P O Box 24885, Safat, Kuwait; telephone: Office — 818681; Residence — 873267.

HAMDAN, Muhammad Aqiil al-Solaiman al-, Saudi Arabian official; born 1924, Mecca, Saudi Arabia; *Religion:* Muslim; *Education:* religious education, Ilmi Institute, Mecca, Saudi Arabia; *Career:* Ministry of Finance; Secretary to the Deputy Minister of Finance; Director of the Bureau of the Deputy Minister of Communications; Director at the Ministry of Communications; Director General of the Ministry of Communications; attended Arab League conferences on Communications, Cairo, Egypt; *Interests and Recreations:* reading, history, literature; *Address:* Bureau of the Minister of Communications, Riyadh, Saudi Arabia; telephone: Office -- 4043684; telex: 201616 HI-WAY SJ.

HAMDANI, Smail, Algerian official/lawyer; born 1930, Algeria; married; *Religion:* Muslim; *Education:* Islamic and French Law, University of Algiers, Algeria, and University of Aix-en-Provence, France; *Career:* Chef de Cabinet to Farès in Provisional Executive, 1962–63; Technical Counsellor, Office of Minister of Information, 1963; Counsellor, Embassy to Belgium, examining future relations between Algeria and EEC, 1963–64; Head of Press and Information Service of Ministry of Foreign Affairs, and Technical Counsellor to Ministry of Foreign Affairs, 1964; Director of Juridical and Consular Affairs, Ministry of Foreign Affairs, 1964–68; Counsellor for Juridical and Consular Affairs at the Presidency, 1970–77; Secretary General of the Cabinet, 1977–; *Languages:* Arabic, French, English; *Address:* Cabinet Office, Algiers, Algeria.

HAMDI, Gamil Muhammad, Egyptian, UN official/auditor; born 16 November 1929, Cairo, Egypt; married; *Religion:* Muslim; *Education:* Institut des Sciences Politiques, Paris, France, 1948–52; Ecole des Hautes Etudes Commerciales, Paris, 1951–54; *Career:* Head of Department, Auditor, Textile Company, Cairo, 1954–58; Administration Manager, Textile Company, Cairo, 1958–62; Auditor, UN Operations in the Congo, Leopoldville, 1962–64; Head, Congo Desk, Bureau of Administration, Management and Budget 1964–66; Chief, Budget Section, Bureau of Administration, Management and Budget, UN, New York, USA, 1967–68; Deputy Resident Representative, United Nations Development Programme (UNDP), Manila, Philippines, 1968–70; Deputy Resident Representative, UNDP, Ankara, Turkey, 1970–73; Resident Representative, UNDP, Bangui, Central African Republic, 1973–75; Deputy Assistant Administrator, and Deputy Regional Director for Europe, the Mediterranean and the Middle East, UNDP, New York, 1975–77; Special Representative of the Administrator, UNDP, New York, 1978; Special Representative of UNDP and Resident Coordinator of United Nations Operational activities for Development in Tunisia, 1978–81; *Languages:* Arabic, French, English, Turkish; *Address:* UNDP, P O Box 863, 61 Boulevard Bab Benat, Tunis, Tunisia; telephone: 264 011.

HAMID, Abdul Mun'im, Iraqi academic/ophthalmic surgeon; born 1 July 1928, Mosul, Iraq; married; two sons, two daughters; *Religion:* Muslim; *Education:* MB, ChB, University of Baghdad; DO, RCP, RCS, University of London, UK; Degree in Ophthalmology, University of Baghdad; *Career:* Resident House Surgeon, Basra Hospital, 1956–58; Doctor, Ramad Hospital, Baghdad, 1963–65; Director and Ophthalmologist, Najaf Hospital, 1967–69; Lecturer, Mosul Medical College, University of Mosul, 1970–75; Director, Mosul Hospital, 1972–76; Professor of Ophthalmology, Mosul Medical College, University of Mosul, 1977; Head of Ophthalmology Section, College of Medicine, University of Mosul; member of the Ophthalmological Society of UK, *Publications:* numerous articles in the University professional journal; *Interests and Recreations:* Arabic and Middle Eastern history; *Address:* Ophthalmology Section, Department of Surgery, College of Medicine, University of Mosul, Mosul, Iraq; telephone: 90570.

HAMILI, Al-Shiba Said Abdul Hadi al-, United Arab Emirates oil official; born 1950, Abu Dhabi, United Arab Emirates; married; two daughters; *Religion:* Muslim; *Education:* 10 years experience in oil industry; *Career:* Deputy Manager of Abu Dhabi Marine Areas (ADMA) Company; Under Secretary, Ministry of Petroleum and Mineral Resources; United Arab Emirates representative to Organisation of Arab Petroleum Exporting Countries (OAPEC); member of the Board of Directors of the Arab Tanker Company; *Interests and Recreations:* billiards, tennis, member of the Tourism Club; *Languages:* Arabic, English; *Address:* Ministry of Petroleum and Mineral Resources, P O Box 59, Abu Dhabi, United Arab Emirates; telephone: Office — 61076.

HAMILI, Sultan Ghanum al-, United Arab Emirates politician; born Al-Ain, United Arab Emirates; married; three sons; *Religion:* Muslim; *Education:* general education; courses in finance; *Career:* Ministry of Municipalities and Agriculture, Al-Ain, 1970;

Assistant Secretary General to Council of Ministers, Abu Dhabi, 1971; Director General of Personal Accounts to HH the Head of State, 1972; member of the United Arab Emirates Federal Assembly since its formation, 1972; Secretary General, Executive Council, Abu Dhabi, UAE; *Interests and Recreations:* reading, history, poetry, hunting, swimming, water-skiing; *Languages:* Arabic, English; *Address:* Secretary General of Abu Dhabi Executive Council, P O Box 19, Abu Dhabi, United Arab Emirates; telephone: 343206.

HAMMAD, Abdul Qasim, (Abu Adnan or Abu Qays), Palestinian politician; born Upper Galilee, Palestine; *Religion:* Muslim; *Career:* early member of the Arab Nationalist Movement; member of the Popular Front for the Liberation of Palestine (PFLP); followed Nayef Hawatmeh in founding Popular Democratic Front for the Liberation of Palestine (PDFLP) 1968; later appointed Commander of the PDFLP in Lebanon; member of Political Bureau of the PDFLP.

HAMMAD, Burhan, Palestinian UN official/lawyer; born 27 April 1929, Nablus, Palestine; *Education:* LLB, Faculty of Law, Baghdad, Iraq, 1953; LLM in International Law, Yale Law School, New Haven, Connecticut, USA, 1959; JSD in International Law, Yale Law School, 1963; *Career:* Lawyer, Nablus, 1953–56; Tourist Department, Ministry of Foreign Affairs, Jerusalem, 1956–57; Assistant Director, Arab Information Centre, West Coast Branch, San Francisco, California, USA, 1961–62; Acting Director, Arab Information Center, Southern Regional Office, Dallas, Texas, USA, 1962; Acting Director, Arab Information Center, New York, USA, 1962–63; Director, UN Section, Arab States Delegation Office, New York, 1963–73; Executive Secretary of the Group of Arab Delegations to the UN, 1963–73; Senior Adviser, Mission of Jordan to the UN, 1964–73; attended sessions of the General Assembly since the 18th Session, preparation of legal briefs, especially on Arab issues, for the use of Arab Delegations; submission of recommendations, legal and political to the Arab Governments, the Council of the League of Arab States and Arab Delegations; drafting of resolutions on various items before the UN organs; representing the Arab Group in consultations and negotiations with other groups or member states; extensive lecturing at universities, colleges, civic groups and churches on matters relevant to the UN and oil concession agreements in the Middle East; member of Jordanian Bar Association, American Society of International Law; Senior Adviser for Legal and Political Affairs, United Arab Emirates Permanent Mission to the UN, 1973–; United Arab Emirates Representative, Special Political Committee, Six Committee and the Law of the Sea Conference, 1973–; *Publications: The Right of Passage in the Gulf of Aqaba,* 1959; *The Egyptian-Israeli General Armistice Agreement in Proper Perspective; The Judicial Role in Clarifying the International Status of the Mandated Territories and the National Status of its Inhabitants; Middle Eastern Oil Concessions: Some Legal and Policy Aspects of Relations Between Grantors and Grantees* (JSD Thesis); numerous legal briefs and papers on items before the various organs of the United Nations; *Address:* Mission of the United Arab Emirates to the United Nations, 747 Third Avenue, New York, NY 10017, USA.

HAMMAD, Juma, Jordanian journalist; born 1923, Palestine; married; four sons, three daughters; *Religion:* Muslim; *Education:* Gaza Secondary School, 1942; *Career:* began writing in *Al-Ghad* magazine, 1947; worked in telegraph department, Palestine Police; self-employed until 1953; Head of Bureau of Islamic Congress, Jerusalem, 1954–60; partner in founding *Al-Manar* in Jerusalem, 1961; Director of *Al-Manar* and Editor of *Al-'Ufuq Al-Jadid* cultural magazine; founded *Akhbar Al-Yaum* newspaper in Amman, 1961–62; Editor of *Al-Manar,* 1962–67; Manager and Editor of *Al-Dastour* newspaper, 1967–73; member of the Jordanian Senate, 1971–74; Secretary General of Arab National Union, 1973–74; Partner and General Manager of Jordanian Press Organisation; member of the National Consultative Council, 1978–; *Interests and Recreations:* Arabic literature, political analysis; *Languages:* Arabic, English; *Address: Al-Ra'i* newspaper, P O Box 6710, Amman Jordan; telephone: 67171; telex: 21497.

HAMMADI, Sa'duun, Iraqi politician/economist; born 22 June 1930, Iraq; *Religion:* Muslim; *Education:* American University of Beirut, Lebanon; PhD, Agriculture and Economics, Wisconsin University, USA,

1957; *Career:* edited *Al-Jumhuriyah* newspaper; Professor of Economics, Baghdad University, Iraq, 1957; Deputy Head of Economic Research, National Bank of Libya, Tripoli, Libya, 1961–62; Minister of Agrarian Reforms, 1963; Economic Adviser to Presidential Council, Government of Syria, 1964; Economic Expert, UN Planning Institute, Syria, 1965–68; President, Iraqi National Oil Company (INOC), 1968; Minister of Oil and Minerals, 1968–74; Minister of Foreign Affairs, 1974–; *Publications: Towards a Socialist Agrarian Reforms in Iraq,* 1964; *Views About Arab Revolution,* 1969; *Address:* Ministry of Foreign Affairs, Baghdad, Iraq.

HAMMOUD BIN ABDUL AZIZ, HRH Prince, Saudi Arabian Prince; born 1947; youngest son of late King Abdul Aziz; *Religion:* Muslim; *Career:* businessman; *Address:* Royal Court, Riyadh, Saudi Arabia.

HAMMOUD, Mahmud Ali, Lebanese diplomat; born 1939, Beirut, Lebanon; *Religion:* Muslim; *Education:* Licence in Law; MA in Psychology; Licence in Literature; *Career:* Consul, Lebanese Embassy, Rabat, Morocco; 1st Secretary, Lebanese Embassy, Ankara, Turkey; Counsellor, Lebanese Embassy, London, UK; Counsellor, Lebanese Embassy, Paris, France; Ambassador to France, 1978–80; Ambassador to the United Arab Emirates, 1980–; *Interests and Recreations:* skiing, tennis; *Languages:* Arabic, English, French, Turkish; *Address:* P O Box 2714, Abu Dhabi, United Arab Emirates; telephone: 727 52 09/75 36.

HAMMOUDA, M. Faruk, Syrian aviation official; born 3 June 1933; married; two daughters; *Religion:* Muslim; *Education:* BA, University of Damascus, Syria; Postgraduate Diploma, Cairo University, Egypt; Licences of Air Navigation, Syria, USA, UK; *Career:* Chief of Operation Section, Directorate General of Civil Aviation, Damascus, Syria, 1959; Chief of Licencing and Training Section, Directorate General of Civil Aviation, Damascus, 1963; Director of Civil Aviation School, Damascus, 1966; Chief of Air Traffic Services, Arab Civil Aviation Council, ACAC, Cairo, League of Arab States, 1970; Director of Air Navigation, (ACAC), Cairo, 1978; Counsellor and Director of Air Navigation, ACAC, Rabat, Morocco, 1981–; *Publi-*

cations: Chief Editor of *Civil Aviation* magazine, Syria; numerous articles and papers; *Interests and Recreations:* chess, swimming; member of the Syrian Gliding Club; member of the Hunting Club, Cairo; *Address:* Arab Civil Aviation Council, 17 Rue al-Nasr, Rabat, Morocco.

HAMMUDI, Saad Kassim, Iraqi journalist/politician; born 1937, Baghdad, Iraq; *Career:* journalist since 1955; former Editor of *Al-Jumhuriyah* and Chairman of Al-Jamahir Press House; President of the Press Union; Vice Chairman, International Organization of Journalists, 1976; Minister of Information, 1977; Editor in Chief, *al Thawra,* daily newspaper; *Address:* P O Box 2009, Baghdad, Iraq.

HAMRANI, Shaikh Muhammad Ali al-, Saudi Arabian businessman; born 1948, Mecca; *Religion:* Muslim; *Education:* university education in UK and USA; *Career:* joined Al-Hamrani Enterprises, 1973; Chairman of Board of Directors, Al-Hamrani Enterprises, 1976; member of Board, Siraj H. Zahran and Co, of Industrial Estate, Jeddah; Chairman, Sahab for Tourism and Aviation, Benevolent Association of Al-Hamrani; Honorary member of the Board of Directors, Ittahad Sports Club, Jeddah; Chairman of Board, Al-Hamrani and Dakhil Enterprises (Jeddah Bowling Centre); member of the Board, Arabian Aviation Services Co Ltd (ARABASCO); member of Industrial Committee, Chamber of Commerce; member of Board of Directors, Industrial Park; *Interests and Recreations:* flying, scuba diving, fishing, sailing, reading; *Address:* Al-Hamrani Trading and Import Est., P O Box 1229, Jeddah, Saudi Arabia; telephone: 642 1259; telex: 401230 DANYA.SJ.

HAMUD, Daifallah al-, Jordanian politician/lawyer; born 1910, Ajloun, Jordan; married; *Education:* practical and theoretical agricultural studies, Lebanon 1935; Licence in Law, Syrian University, 1946; licence to practice law from Jordanian Government, 1946; *Career:* teacher, Ministry of Education, 1934–42; merchant in Irbid, 1942–43; Assistant Attorney General, 1951; Judge, 1951–54; member of Chamber of Deputies, 1954–56; Minister of Posts and Telephone, and Civil Aviation, 1954–55; Minister of Education and Agriculture, 1956; member of Chamber of Deputies, 1956; Secretary of

Amman Municipality, 1957–58; Governor and Secretary of Amman; seconded to Head of Amman Municipality; Chamber of Deputies, 1961–62; Senator, 1962–63; Governor of Amman, 1966–68; Minister of Interior, 1968–69; lawyer and journalist, helped edit *Al-Mithaq* and *Al-Sahafy* magazines; also participated in anti-crime and open prison conference, Cairo, 1953; *Publications:* author of various articles in Jordanian and Arab journals and magazines; *Decorations:* Star of Jordan 1st Class; Iranian Hamayouni Order; Moroccan Alawite Order; *Address:* Shmaisani, Amman, Jordan; telephone: 64985.

HAMZAOUI, Abdul Aziz, Tunisian diplomat; born 1935; married; one son; *Religion:* Muslim; *Education:* Modern Languages, Sorbonne, France; International Relations, France; MA and PhD, International Relations, the Fletcher School of Law and Diplomacy, USA; International Programme of Harvard Business School, USA; *Career:* Director of Studies, National School of Administration, 1964–66; Director, Administrative and Consular Affairs, Ministry of Foreign Affairs, 1966–69; Ambassador to Canada, 1969–73; Ministry of State for Foreign Affairs, 1973–74; Ambassador to Iran and Pakistan, 1975–79; Ambassador to Belgium, Luxembourg and the EEC, 1980–; *Languages:* Arabic, French, English; *Address:* 58 Rue Hedi Zarrouk, Sidi Bou Said, Tunisia.

HANAFI, Abdul Aziz A., Saudi Arabian engineer; born 1 January 1944, Mecca; married; one son, one daughter; *Religion:* Muslim; *Education:* BSc in Civil Engineering, USA, 1969; *Career:* Consulting Engineer; Engineer in charge of Industrial Estate, Industrial Estate and Development Centre (Government Agent), Riyadh, Saudi Arabia, 1969–74; Managing Director, Hanafi Contractors and Trading Corporation; *Interests and Recreations:* chess, swimming, Arabic poetry, travelling; *Languages:* Arabic, English; *Address:* P O Box 5995, Jeddah, Saudi Arabia; telephone: 6440011, telex: 401246 HANAFI SJ.

HANANIA, Dawud Anatas, Jordanian surgeon; born 24 June 1934, Jerusalem; married; two sons, one daughter; *Religion:* Christian; *Education:* London Matriculation Certificate, 1951; MB, BS, St. Mary's Hospital

Medical School, University of London, UK, 1957; Fellow, Royal College of Surgeons, FRCS, England, 1959–61; FACS, FACC, FICA, Hon FRCSI; *Career:* Internship, Army Base Hospital, Amman, Jordan, 1957–58; House Surgeon and Surgical Registrar, General Surgery and Casualty, the Royal Northern Hospital, London, 1959–61; Resident in General and Thoracic Surgery, Army Base Hospital, Amman, 1959, 1961–64; Attending Surgeon in General and Thoracic Surgery, Army Base Hospital, Amman, 1965–68; Fellow in Thoracic and Cardiovascular Surgery, Baylor College of Medicine, Houston, Texas, USA, 1968–69; Chairman, Department of Surgery, Army Base Hospital, Amman, 1970–73; Director, King Hussain Medical Centre, 1973–76; Chief, Thoracic and Cardiovascular Surgery Section at King Hussain Medical Centre, and Director of the Royal Medical Services, Jordan Armed Forces, 1973–; *Publications:* author and co-author of books and research papers; *Decorations:* Order of Jordanian Star, 3rd, 2nd and 1st Class; *Interests and Recreations:* tennis, horse riding; *Address:* Office — Royal Medical Services, Jordan Armed Forces, Amman, Jordan; telephone: 815572; Residence — P O Box 2135, Amman, Jordan; telephone: 814173.

HANANIA, Farid S., Lebanese academic/lawyer; born 25 December 1908, Jerusalem; married; one child; *Education:* secondary studies, St. George's School, Jerusalem; BA, Business Administration, American University of Beirut (AUB), Lebanon, 1931; BA in Law, and MA, London School of Economics, UK, 1935, 1939; LLB, Queen's College, Cambridge, UK, 1941; *Career:* called to the London Bar, 1940; lawyer, London High Court, 1940–45; Assistant Professor of Political Science and Law, AUB, 1945; Associate Professor of Political Science and Law, AUB, 1947; Delegate of American University of Beirut to UNESCO sessions, Beirut, 1948; Chairman of the Department of Political Science and Law, AUB, 1948–54; Professor, 1950; Visiting Professor, University of Virginia, USA, 1952–53; Dean of the Faculty of Arts and Sciences, AUB, 1954–65; Professor of Law and Political Science, AUB, June 1965–; *Languages:* Arabic, English; *Address:* American University of Beirut, Lebanon.

HANANIA, Jack I., Lebanese engineer/academic; born Jerusalem; *Education:* Diploma, Loughborough College, UK, 1949; BSc, University of London, UK, 1950; PhD, Leeds University, UK, 1955; *Career:* Ferguson Pailin (Switchgear Manufacturers), UK, 1949; English Electric and British Electricity Authority, 1950–52; Assistant Lecturer, Leeds University, 1953–54; Kennedy and Donkin, Consulting Engineers, UK, 1962; Bechtel Corporation, USA, 1963–64; Professor of Electrical Engineering, American University of Beirut, Lebanon; member of the Institution of Electrical Engineers, UK; member of the Architects and Engineers Association of Beirut; member of American Society for Engineering Education; *Languages:* Arabic, English; *Address:* American University of Beirut, Beirut, Lebanon.

HANNUSH, Basim Abdul Masih, Syrian UN official/economist; born 24 July 1923, Syria; married; *Education:* BA in Economics, American University of Beirut, Lebanon, 1947–49; MA in Economics, American University of Beirut, 1950–52; PhD in Economics, Harvard University, USA, 1953–56; *Career:* Economic Affairs Officer, Middle East Studies Section, ESA, UN, New York, USA; Head, Economic Unit, UN Regional Social Affairs Office, Beirut, 1963; Acting Director, UN Economic and Social Affairs Office (UNESAB), Beirut, 1965–66; Chief, Economic Section, UNESAB, 1963–72; Deputy Director, UNESAB, 1972–74; Chief, Economic Research and Planning Division, Economic Commission for Western Asia, UN, 1974–; *Publications:* numerous articles and studies on UN development programmes in the Middle East; *Interests and Recreations:* development economics, gardening, walking, tennis, swimming; *Languages:* Arabic, English, Turkish, French; *Address:* ECWA, P O Box 27, Baghdad, Iraq; telephone: 95068; telex: 213468 IK.

HARAKAT, Bennacer, Moroccan official/businessman; born 25 April 1918, Casablanca, Morocco; married; three children; *Religion:* Muslim; *Education:* general; *Career:* joined the Nationalist movement (Parti National), 1936; active in the Moroccan Independence Movement, 1944–55; official at the Ministry of the Interior, acting as magistrate, Chef de Cercle, Settat, 1956–59, transferred to Khouribga, 1959; Secretary General of Casablanca Province, 1960–63;

Secretary General of Agadir Province, 1963–64; Director, Société Filatis (cotton and synthetics mill), 1964; Director, Société *Maroc Soir*, 1971–; editor of *Le Matin*, newspapers, 1977–79; Director, Somaded SA, LMS Conseils SA; Director, Sonir SA; *Interests and Recreations:* reading, jogging; *Languages:* Arabic, French, Spanish; *Address:* 20 Rue Ahmed Amine, Casablanca 01, Morocco; telephone: 362788.

HARASANI, Hamid Muhammad, Saudi Arabian physician/businessman; born 1920, Mecca, Saudi Arabia; *Religion:* Muslim; *Education:* MB, BCh, Cairo University, Egypt, 1949; *Career:* Chief of Pilgrim Guides, 1951–61; Minister of Public Health, 1961–62; Director General, Printing and Information Establishment; member of Arabian Cement Co for Electric Power, Jeddah; physician, private clinic; member of Advisory Committee, Social Security Department; *Publications: Story of Diabetes Mellitus,* a medical book in Arabic; *Interests and Recreations:* medical reading; member of Red Sea Club; *Address:* Nozha Street, Mecca, Saudi Arabia.

HARATI, Suhaam al-, Lebanese lawyer; born 9 November, 1943, Senegal; married; one son; *Religion:* Muslim; *Education:* MGP, Faculty of Sciences, Sorbonne; Law Degree, Sorbonne; Lebanese Law Degree, St. Joseph University, Beirut; member of Lebanese Bar Association; *Career:* lawyer, Beirut, 1971; Legal Counsel to Yusuf Ahmad Al-Ghanim and Sons, Kuwait, 1976–77; Senior Attorney, Al-Saleh, Graham and James, Kuwait, 1977–80; Lawyer, Partner and Manager, Gharabally and Harati Law Firm, Kuwait; *Interests and Recreations:* hunting, travelling, football, tennis, Arabic calligraphy, contemporary Arab art, Killims; *Address:* Souk Al-Wataniah 514, P O Box 22538 Safat, Kuwait; telephone: Office — 447367; Residence — 875747.

HARAZEEN, Hamad Hassan, United Arab Emirates businessman/official; born 9 June, 1940, Palestine; married; one son, one daughter; *Religion:* Muslim; *Education:* BCom in Accountancy; attended courses in fields of financial planning, management, economics in UK and USA; *Career:* auditor with UK firm, 1960–66; Assistant Director of Finance, Qatar Government, 1966–71; Assistant Director of Finance, Abu Dhabi Govern-

ment, 1971–73; Director of Budget and Financial Affairs, Abu Dhabi Govenment 1973–82; Member of Abu Dhabi Claims Committee (Arbitration Committee), Abu Dhabi Government General Projects Committee, Higher Commission for Administrative Development, Abu Dhabi Civil Service Council, and various other committees for planning, finance, and industrial projects; Vice Chairman and Managing Director, Union Cement Company, Ras al-Khaima, United Arab Emirates; Member of the Board of Directors of National College, Chouiefat School, Abu Dhabi; Managing Director, Management and Financial Consultants (MAFCO) 1982–; *Decorations:* Honorary Citizen of Houston, Texas, USA 1975; selected by Houston City Council to serve as goodwill ambassador 1975; *Languages:* Arabic, English; *Address:* P O Box 244, Abu Dhabi, United Arab Emirates; telephone: 335108, 339400; telex:23086 GETACO EM.

HARBI, Jamal, Algerian UN official/economist; born 27 May 1940, Algeria; married; one son, one daughter; *Religion:* Muslim; *Education:* Diploma in Political Sciences, Algeria, 1962; PhD in Economics, Paris, France, 1967; *Career:* Assistant Professor, Faculty of Economic Sciences, Algiers, 1969; Assistant Administrator, United Nations World Food Programme, Cairo, Egypt, 1969; Adviser, United Nations World Food Programme, Aden, People's Democratic Republic of Yemen, 1973; Regional Administrator, United Nations Development Programme UNDP, New York, USA, 1975; Resident Representative of UNDP, Djibouti, 1979–; *Publications:* articles on economic development published in *UNDP News; Interests and Recreations:* swimming, tennis, jogging, cinema, theatre, music, travelling; *Languages:* Arabic, French, English; *Address:* P O Box 2001 Djibouti; telephone: 353 412.

HARIMI, Karim Ahmad al-, Omani politician; born 1935, Muscat, Oman; married; *Religion:* Muslim; *Education:* in Oman; short course in post office administration, UK; *Career:* Cable and Wireless, Muscat; Purchases and Imports Department, Ministry of Electricity and Water, Kuwait; Director of Posts, Telegraphs and Telephones, Oman, 1970, National Development Council, 1973; occupied several ministerial posts in the departments of Development, and of Public

Works; Minister of Posts, Telegraphs and Telephones, 1980–; *Languages:* Arabic, English; *Address:* Ministry of Posts, Telegraphs and Telephones, P O Box 3338 C.P.O. Builidng, Ruwi, Muscat, Oman; telephone: 704863; telex: 3225 GUOMAN MB/3237 POSTTEL MB.

HARIRI, Ghazi al-, Syrian academic/agriculturalist; born 2 June 1937, Daraa, Syria; married; one son, one daughter; *Religion:* Muslim; *Education:* BSc, Agriculture; PhD, Entomology, University of London, 1965; *Career:* Director of Agriculture, Syria, 1961–62; Assistant Professor, College of Agriculture, Aleppo University, 1965–70; Associate Professor, Aleppo University, 1970–75, Professor, 1975–; Dean, College of Agriculture, 1968–69, 1975–79; Vice Rector, University of Aleppo, 1979–; Consultant to International Centre for Agricultural Research in Dry Areas; member of the Panel of Experts on International Poplar Commission, FAO; President of Arab Plant Protection Society, 1979–; *Publications:* many research papers on physiology and ecology of insects published in several international scientific periodicals since 1965; *Interests and Recreations:* travel; *Languages:* Arabic, English, Hungarian, French; *Address:* University of Aleppo, Aleppo, Syria; telephone: 24004.

HARIZ, Salim Sulaiman, Lebanese lawyer; born 1918, Lebanon; married; one son; *Education:* Licence in Law and Doctorate in Law; French Faculty of Law, St. Joseph University, Beirut, Lebanon; *Career:* lawyer; magistrate; Counsellor at the Exchequer and Audit Department; Counsellor, Beirut Court of Appeal; Inspector General of Education, Faculty of Law, Lebanese University; member of the Central Council of Inspection; Director General, Ministry of Education, 1977; *Publications:* in Arabic, *The Druze Reality And The Inevitability of Evolution; Le Droit Libanais,* co-author; *Le Controle préalable de la Cour des Comptes du Liban; Decorations:* American International Academy Award; French Order of National Merit; *Interests and Recreations:* music (accordion), billiards, walking; *Address:* Office — Ministry of Education, Beirut, Lebanon; Residence -- Immeuble Akkar, Place du Musée, Rue de l'Armée, Beirut, Lebanon.

HARTHI, Hussain Muhsin al-, Saudi Arabian businessman; born 1940; *Education:* BSc, Civil Engineering; *Career:* Assistant Manager, Technical Department, Ministry of Education, Riyadh, Saudi Arabia; Vice Dean, Faculty of Engineering, University of Riyadh, Saudi Arabia; General Manager and member of the Board, National Development Company, National Quarries Company, Tihama Company (Advertising, Public Relations and Marketing Studies); *Address:* P O Box 7362, Riyadh, Saudi Arabia; telephone: 4783336.

HARTHY, Muhammad Hamad Sulaiman al-, Omani diplomat; born 15 March 1928, Oman; married; one son, two daughters; *Religion:* Muslim; *Education:* religious studies; *Career:* Ambassador of Oman to Tunisia, 1973–77; Ambassador at Ministry of Foreign Affairs; *Interests and Recreations:* Swedish exercises; *Languages:* Arabic, English; *Address:* Ministry of Foreign Affairs, P O Box 252, Muscat, Oman.

HASHIM, Abdullah Hashim al-Sayyid, Saudi Arabian businessman; born 1921, Jeddah, Saudi Arabia; *Religion:* Muslim; *Education:* general education; *Career:* Chairman and President of HASHIM Group, incorporating tin can manufacturing, manufacturers of industrial and medical gases, executive distributors of Honda products, industrial and agricultural machinery; general trading; *Decorations:* Gold Medal awarded by Ministry of Commerce; *Interests and Recreations:* fishing, travel, reading; *Address:* P O Box 44, King Khalid Road, Jeddah, Saudi Arabia; telephone: Office — 643 2242/2065, Residence — 642 8924/5; telex: 401152.

HASHIM, Dhia Dawud al-, Arab-American academic; born July 1939, Baghdad, Iraq; marrid; one daughter; *Religion:* Muslim; *Education:* BA, University of Baghdad, Iraq, 1962; MBA, University of California, Los Angeles, USA, 1965; PhD, University of Missouri, Columbia, USA, 1971; *Career:* Assistant Professor, University of Baghdad, 1965–68; Assistant Profesor, California State University, Northridge, USA, 1970–72; Associate Professor, Florida International University, Miami, USA, 1972–74; Associate Professor, California State University, Northridge, USA, 1974–76; Professor, California State University, Northridge, USA, 1977–; Visiting Professor of Accounting,

University of California, Los Angeles, USA, Summer Terms 1975, 1976, 1977, 1978, 1979, 1980; Director, Centre of International Accounting Studies, California State University, Northridge, USA, 1976–; Chairman, American Accounting Association, International Accounting Section, 1979–80; *Publications:* numerous books and research papers and articles on accounting; *Decorations:* Certificate of Appreciation, US International Revenue Service, 1973; Certificate of Appreciation, US National Association of Accountants, 1974; *Interests and Recreations:* reading, travel, swimming; Middle Eastern affairs; *Languages:* Arabic, English, Persian; *Address:* School of Business Administration and Economics, California State University, Northridge, California 91330, USA; telephone: Office — (213) 8852451; Residence — (213) 360 6935.

HASHIM, Jawad Mahmud, Iraqi financial official/economist; born 1938, Iraq; married; two sons; *Education:* BA, Economics, College of Commerce and Economics, University of Baghdad, 1959; MSc, Economic Statistics, London School of Economics and Political Science, London, 1963; PhD, Economic Statistics, London School of Economics and Political Science, 1966; *Career:* Secretary General of Arab Graduates Conference in UK, 1962–63; Research Assistant, London School of Economics and Political Science, University of London; Director General, Planning Board for Educational and Social Development; Economic Adviser to the Prime Minister; Director General, Central Statistical Organization; Chief Editor, *The Economists,* quarterly journal of the Iraqi Economists Association, 1967–68; Minister of Planning and Chairman of the Steering Committee of the Planning Board, 1968–71; Assistant Professor, Department of Statistics, University of Baghdad, 1971; Economic Adviser, Office of Economic Affairs, Revolutionary Command Council, 1971–72; Minister of Planning, 1972–74; Economic Adviser, Office of Economic Affairs, Revolutionary Command Council, 1971–72; Minister of Planning, 1972–74; Economic Adviser, Office of Economic Affairs, Revolutionary Command Council, member of the Planning Board; Chairman of the Second Session of Economic Commission for West Asia (ECWA), 1974–77; President, Arab Monetary Fund, 1977–82; *Publications: The Development of Iraqi Economy,* in Arabic;

Capital Formation in Iraq, 1957–70, 1974; *Science, Technology and Industrial Development,* 1976; *Industrialization Propects of Iraq up to the Year 2000,* May 1977; *Methods of Estimating National Products, National Expenditure and National Income,* 1972, in Arabic; *Interests and Recreations:* sports, painting, driving, reading; *Languages:* Arabic, English; *Address:* c/o Arab Monetary Fund, P O Box 2818, Abu Dhabi, United Arab Emirates; telephone: 328873.

HASHIM, Major General Hashim Said, Saudi Arabian businessman/air force officer; married; three sons, one daughter; *Religion:* Muslim; *Education:* Mecca High School; Military School at Taif, 1947; Licence from British Civil Air Training Board; trained at Air Services Training, Hamble, UK, 1949, and with Royal Air Force; *Career:* Air Attaché, Embassy to USA, 1966; Commander of Royal Saudi Air Force, 1966–72; later established business interests; involved in current industrialization programme; *Languages:* Arabic, English; *Address:* c/o Ministry of Defence, Riyadh, Saudi Arabia.

HASHIM, Muhammad Abdul Latif, Egyptian academic; resident in Bahrain; born 7 October 1925, Benha, Egypt; married; two sons, one daughter; *Religion:* Muslim; *Education:* BSc, Alexandria University, Egypt; MSc, Alexandria University; PhD, Humbolt University, Berlin; *Career:* Demonstrator, Faculty of Science, Alexandria, 1948; Lecturer, Faculty of Science, Alexandria, 1961; Assistant Professor, 1968; Professor of Botany, Kuwait University, 1973; Professor of Microbiology, Alexandria, 1975; Head of Botany Department, Alexandria, 1976; UNESCO Adviser and Chairman of Biology Department, University College of Bahrain; member of Egyptian delegation to the session of the Union of Arab Biologists, Baghdad; *Publications:* papers and articles published in international journals in English and German; *Interests and Recreations:* reading, travelling, badminton; *Languages:* Arabic, English, German, French; *Address:* University College of Bahrain, P O Box 1082, Manama, Bahrain; telephone: 682885; 532 Horriya Avenue, Alexandria, Egypt; telephone: 960263.

HASHIM, Muhammad Ali, Syrian academic/politician; born 1936, Aleppo, Syria; *Religion:* Muslim; *Education:* Degree in Medicine, University of Damascus, Syria; PhD, Medicine and Endocrinology, Moscow, USSR; *Career:* Deputy Dean, Faculty of Medicine, University of Damascus, Syria; member of Parliament, 1970–72; Minister of State, 1971–72; Minister of Higher Education, 1972–78; Professor, Faculty of Medicine, University of Damascus, Syria, 1978; *Address:* Faculty of Medicine, University of Damascus, Damascus, Syria; Barada Street Al-Khuja Building, Damascus, Syria.

HASHWE, Edward Kamal, Syrian lawyer; born 1935, Hama, Syria; married; three sons, one daughter; *Religion:* Christian; *Education:* LLB, International Law; *Career:* Director, Population Census and Legislation, Ministry of Labour, Syria, 1960–61; lawyer; journalist; member of Central Committee of Syrian Arab Socialists Party, the former Syrian Lawyers Trade Union, the Union of Arab Writers; *Publications: The Interpretation of Unified Laws of Labour; Towards a Progressive Ideology of Working Class; The Handbook of Labour Laws; The Exploration of Petrol: a Study of the Use of Arab Petrol as a Weapon; Interests and Recreations:* swimming, writing; *Languages:* Arabic, English; *Address:* Al Alassi St, Damascus, Syria; telephone: 20150.

HASSAN, Abdul Hamid, Egyptian official/ physician; born October 1941, Egypt; *Religion:* Muslim; *Education:* MB, Faculty of Medicine, University of Cairo, Cairo, Egypt, 1968; General Diploma, Cairo University, 1970; MD, General Surgery, Cairo University, 1972; *Career:* President, General Union of Students, Egypt, 1968–69; Member of the General National Conference, 1968–71; Member of the Central Committee, 1971–; Cairo Youth Secretary, 1971–73; Member of the People's Assembly, 1973–; Deputy Youth Minister, 1973–79; President Supreme Council for Youth and Sport, 1973–; Member of Arab Socialist Union, 1974–; President of Youth Department, National Council for Youth and Sports; Minister of State for Youth and Sports, 1979–; Youth Secretary, National Democratic Party; *Languages:* Arabic, English; *Address:* National Council for Youth and Sports, Youth Department, 10 Mudiriyat Al-Tahrir Street, Garden City, Cairo, Egypt; telephone: 20569, 919797.

HASSAN, Abdullah, Sudanese diplomat/ politician; born 1925; *Religion:* Muslim; *Education:* Gordon College, Khartoum, and Diploma of Arts, University of Khartoum, Sudan; *Career:* District Officer and Commissioner, 1949–56; Consul General in Uganda, 1956–58; Head, Political Section, Ministry of Foreign Affairs, 1958–64; Ambassador to Ghana, 1960–64; Director General, Ministry of Information, 1965; Ambassador to France, 1965–67; Ambassador to Ethiopia, 1967–69; Under Secretary, Ministry of Foreign Affairs, 1969–70; Ambassador to USSR, 1971; Ambassador to UK, 1972; Minister of Rural Development, 1972–73; Minister of Interior, 1973–75; Secretary General to the Presidency, 1975–; member of Sudanese Political Bureau, Sudanese Socialist Union, 1972; *Decorations:* Order of the Sudanese Republic 1st Class and numerous foreign decorations; *Languages:* Arabic, English; *Address:* President's Office, Khartoum, Sudan.

HASSAN, Ahmad Muhammad al-, Sudanese physician/academic; born 1930; *Religion:* Muslim; *Education:* Medical Degrees, Universities of Khartoum, Sudan, and Edinburgh and London, UK; *Career:* doctor, 1955–57; Research Assistant, University of Khartoum, 1958–60; Lecturer in Pathology, University of Khartoum, 1962–63; Senior Lecturer and Head of Department, University of Khartoum, 1965–66; Professor of Pathology, University of Khartoum, 1966–73; Dean, Faculty of Medicine, University of Khartoum, 1969–71; Deputy Vice Chancellor, University of Khartoum, 1971; Minister of Higher Education and Scientific Reseach, 1971–72; Chairman, Medical Research Council, National Council for Research; *Interests and Recreations:* President, Sudan Philosophical Society; *Languages:* Arabic, English; *Address:* Medical Research Council, P O Box 2424, Khartoum, Sudan.

HASSAN, Ahmad Y. al-, Syrian academic/ engineer; born 25 June 1925, Palestine; *Religion:* Muslim; *Education:* DIC, Imperial College, London, UK; PhD, University of Cairo, Egypt; *Career:* Professor of Mechanical Engineering; Dean, Faculty of English, Aleppo University, 1964–67; Minister of Petroleum, Electricity and Industrial Projects, 1967–70; President, Aleppo University, 1973–79; Director of the Institute for the History of Arabic Science, 1976–; *Publica-*

tions: *Theory of Machines,* 1964; *Machine Design,* 1965; *Power Stations,* 1966; co-author, paper on Proceedings of Royal Society of London, 1964; compendium of the *Mechanical Arts,* by al-Jazari, the book of *Ingenious Mechanics,* by Banu Musa; editor *Journal for the History of Arabic Science; Decorations:* Chevalier de la Légion d'Honneur; *Address:* 13 Brendon Drive, Esher, Surrey, KT10 9EQ, UK.

HASSAN, Ben al-Mehdi Ben Moulay Ismail Moulay, Moroccan diplomat/banker; born 1912, Fes, Morocco; married; one daughter; *Religion:* Muslim; *Career:* Khalifa of the Spanish Zone before Independence; Ambassador to UK, 1965; Ambassador to Italy, 1965–67; appointed to Banque Nationale de Development Economique (BNDE), 1967; Governor of the Bank of Morocco, 1969; *Decorations:* Ouissam Alaoui, Morocco; Charles I Medal; Great Houssni Medal; and several other decorations; *Interests and Recreations:* shooting; *Languages:* Arabic, English, Spanish, French; *Address:* Banque du Maroc, 277 Avenue Mohammad V, Rabat, Morocco.

HASSAN BIN TALAL, HRH Prince, Jordanian Crown Prince; born 1947, Amman, Jordan; younger of two brothers of HM King Hussain; married Princess Tharwat, 1968; one son, three daughters; *Religion:* Muslim; *Education:* privately and at British School in Amman; Summerfields, Harrow School, UK; Christchurch, Oxford University, UK; Degree in Oriental Studies, Arabic and Hebrew; *Career:* formally appointed Heir Apparent, 1 April 1965; acts as Regent in absence of the King; played leading part in preparing 1973–75 Three-Year Development Plan and later Five-Year Plan; largely responsible for the establishment of Jordanian Royal Scientific Society (a research centre for government policy); *Languages:* Arabic, English, French; *Address:* Royal Palace, Amman, Jordan.

HASSAN, Hani al-, Palestinian politician; born 1937, Haifa, Palestine; *Education:* graduated in Construction Engineering, University of Darmstadt, West Germany, 1960–67; *Career:* helped develop Fatah organization; European Chief of Fatah, 1967; Fatah spokesman in Jordan during the 1970 crisis; Chairman of the Palestinian Political Committee in Lebanon, 1973; deputy to Yassir Arafat in Political Affairs Department of

Fatah, 1974, and to Salah Khalaf in Jihaz al-Rasd of Fatah; has directed PLO and Fatah relations with China and led PLO delegations to China; requested Chinese support for the PLO at the UN, 1974; *Languages:* Arabic, German, English.

HASSAN, Ignatius Gama, Sudanese official/ agriculturalist; born 12 December 1941; Arapi, Eastern Equatorial Province, Sudan; married; two sons; *Education:* PhD, University of Milan, Italy, *Career:* Research Division, Montectini Edisonn Co, Milan, 1967–68; Entomologist for Eastern Africa, Nairobi, 1968–71; Chief, Pesticides Promotion Division, East and Central Africa, 1971–72; returned to Sudan after the Addis Ababa Agreement in April 1972; Minister of Agriculture, Irrigation, Forestry and Animal Production; member of the Constitutional Assembly, 1972–73; Commissioner for Jonglei Canal Area Development Project, 1979–80; re-appointed Minister of Agriculture and Natural Resources for Southern Region of the Democratic Republic of Sudan, June 1980; *Decorations:* Order of the Two Niles, 2nd Class, *Languages:* Arabic, Italian, English; *Address:* Ministry of Agriculture and Natural Resources, P O Box 251, Juba, Southern Region, Sudan; telephone: Juba 3197.

HASSAN II, Moulay Hassan Bin Muhammad, HM King of Morocco; born 9 July, 1929; eldest son of King Muhammad V; married; two sons, Prince Muhammad, born August 1963, is heir to the throne; three daughters; *Religion:* Muslim; *Education:* Law Degree, 1951; Diploma of Higher Studies in Civil Law, University of Bordeaux, France, 1952; Honorary Doctorates, Universities of Cairo, Egypt, Bordeaux, France and Dakar, Senegal; *Career:* accompanied the late King to Corsica and Madagascar, 1953–55; after Independence responsible for youth affairs, and appointed Chief of Staff, Royal Moroccan Army; Deputy Prime Minister, 28 May, 1976; formally invested as Crown Prince, 9 July, 1957; in charge of several rescue operations after Agadir earthquakes, February, 1960; Deputy Prime Minister and Minister of Defence, 1960; represented Morocco at UN General Assembly, September 1960; state visits to UK, Algeria, USA, France, Spain, Senegal, Tunisia, West Germany, USSR, Turkey, Iran, Saudi Arabia; represented Morocco at

Arab Summit Meetings and Organisation of African Unity (OAU) Summit Meetings in Cairo and Algiers; succeeded to the throne, 25 February 1961; crowned, 3 March 1961; chaired Arab Summit Conference at Rabat, Morocco, October 1974; *Publications:* Le *Défi,* 1976; *Interests and Recreations:* golf, riding, hunting, tennis; *Languages:* Arabic, French, English, Spanish; *Address:* Palais Royale, Rabat, Morocco.

HASSAN, Khalid al-, Palestinian politician; born 1928, Haifa, Palestine; *Religion:* Muslim; *Career:* active in Islamic Liberation Party; Secretary of the Development Directorate, Kuwait; joined Yassir Arafat and other founding members of Fatah, and was in part responsible for Fatah relations with Arab Governments; joined Palestine Liberation Organization Committee, 1969–1973; Head of PLO Executive Committee Political Department.

HASSAN, Khalid al Haj, Jordanian politician; born 1931, Amman, Jordan; married, with children; *Education:* MA in Mechanical Engineering and Irrigation, University of Louisiana, USA, 1953; *Career:* Civil Service posts, Director General of the Jordanian Electric Power Company, 1957; Minister of Agriculture, 1957–62; Director General of the Jordan Cement Factory, 1962–64, 1965–72; Minister of Agriculture, 1964–65, 1972–73; Minister of Transport, 1974–76; *Languages:* Arabic, English; *Address:* c/o Ministry of Transport, Amman, Jordan; telephone: 41415.

HASSAN, Ma'mun Ibrahim, Sudanese financial official/diplomat; born 1 January 1939, Wad Madani, Sudan; married; three sons; *Religion:* Muslim; *Education:* BSc in Economics and History, University of Khartoum, Khartoum, Sudan; Special Studies in Diplomatic Affairs and Economic Aid, University of Khartoum; *Career:* High School Teacher, Sudan, 1963; 3rd Secretary, Ministry of Foreign Affairs, 1963; 3rd Secretary, Sudan Embassy, Pakistan, 1963–65; 2nd Secretary, Pakistan, 1966; 2nd and 1st Secretary, Counsellor, Sudan Permanent Representation to the UN, 1966–71; Chargé d'Affaires, Sudan Embassy, German Democratic Republic, 1971–72; Head of International Organizations Department, Ministry of Foreign Affairs, Khartoum, Sudan, 1972–76; Ambassador to the Benelux Countries and

the EEC, 1976–77; Ambassador to Kuwait, 1977–78; Director General, Arab Establishment for Investment, Kuwait; *Interests and Recreations:* walking, sports, poetry, literature; *Languages:* Arabic, English, French; *Address:* Arab Establishment for Investment, P O Box 23568, Safat, Kuwait.

HASSAN, Mahmud Ali, Egyptian official/engineer; born 17 July, 1915; *Religion:* Muslim; *Education:* PhD, Engineering, Cairo and Zurich Universities; *Career:* Director General, Industrial Control Department, 1956–59; Under Secretary of State for Industry, 1959–61; Chairman, Organization for Engineering Industries, 1961–66; President, Federation of Egyptian Industries, Organisation for Metallurgical Industries; Minister of Industry, 1974–75; *Publications:* various technical papers in German; *Decorations:* Order of Trade and Industry, 1st Class, Egypt; *Languages:* Arabic, English, French, German; *Address:* 45, Road 15, Maadi, Cairo, Egypt.

HASSAN, Major General Mustafa Othman, Sudanese politician/former army officer; born 1929, Omdurman, Sudan; married; six children; *Religion:* Muslim; *Education:* Military College, 1951; Staff College, India, Artillery course, Egypt; *Career:* commissioned into Artillery; Lieutenant Colonel, Military Governor of Port Sudan, 1961; Colonel and Assistant Commander of Artillery Troops, 1965; transferred to Republic Palace as ADC; Brigadier, Deputy Chief of Staff Administration, 1969; Major General, 1970; retired from Regular Army; Deputy Minister of Defence, 1971; Deputy Minister of Transport, 1973–74; Minister of State for Construction and Public Works, 1975; Minister of Construction and Public Works, 1975–77; *Languages:* Arabic, English; *Address:* Ministry of Construction and Public Works, Khartoum, Sudan.

HASSAN, Saadat al-, Palestinian politician/diplomat; born 1928 Ramallah, Palestine; married; two children; *Education:* Degree in Chemical Engineering, Illinois Institute of Technology, USA; *Career:* lived in Jordan; Head of Arab Information Centre in Chicago, USA, 1956–64; Deputy Director of PLO Office, New York, USA; Director of PLO Office, New York 1965; *Languages:* Arabic, English.

227

HASSAN, Subhi Rashid al-, Jordanian lawyer; born 1917, Jordan; married; one daughter, four sons; *Religion:* Muslim; *Education:* BA in Law, University of Damascus, Syria; *Career:* Lawyer, 1942–46; Judge, 1946–59; Chief Judge, 1959–62; Director General, Lands and Surveying Department, 1962–71; Legal and Local Adviser, Ministry of Finance, 1971–; Head of the Military and Civil Retirement Committee, 1971–; *Decorations:* Order of the Jordanian Star; *Interests and Recreations:* gymnastics, travelling; reading, law; *Languages:* Arabic, English; *Address:* P O Box 8895, Jabal al-Hussain al-Sharqyi, Amman, Jordan; telephone: 25381.

HASSANAIN, Ali Fadil, Egyptian UN official/engineer; born 20 July 1919, Egypt; married; *Education:* BSc, Cairo University, Egypt, 1938–43; MSc in Civil Engineering, Colorado University, USA, 1946–47; PhD in Civil Engineering, Ain Shams University, Cairo, 1960–64; *Career:* Engineer, Ministry of Public Works, 1943–52; Chief Engineer, Assistant Director, Ministry of Public Works, 1952–57; Director, Ministry of Public Works, 1957–58; Chief, Foreign Aid Unit, Ministry of Planning, 1958–64; Director General, Ministry of Planning, 1964–65; Director General, Ministry of Foreign Affairs, Egypt, 1965–66; Director General, Ministry of Economy, Egypt, 1966; Deputy Resident Representative, United Nations Development Programme (UNDP), Malaysia, 1966–70; Area Officer, UNDP, New York, USA, 1970–71; Senior Area Officer, UNDP, New York, 1971; member of the Egyptian Civil Engineering Society; *Decorations:* Fellowships UNDP, US Agency for International Development; *Interests and Recreations:* civil engineering, dam engineering, iron and steel works; *Languages:* Arabic, English, French, German; *Address:* Office — UNDP, 866 UN Plaza, New York, NY 10017, USA; telephone: (212) 754 1234; Residence — 305 E 40 Street, New York, NY 10016, USA; telephone: (9212) 661 2848.

HASSANAIN, Mahmud Mustafa, Egyptian UN official/economist; born 7 November 1914, Cairo, Egypt; married; *Religion:* Muslim; *Education:* BCom, Cairo University, Egypt, 1937; BSc in Economics, PhD in Demography, London School of Economics, UK, 1938–44; *Career:* Statistical Assistant, Ministry of Finance, Egypt, 1937; Lecturer,

Faculty of Economy and Commerce, Cairo University, Egypt, 1945–48; Associate Professor, Cairo University, 1948–50; Assistant Division Chief, Middle East Division, Research Department, International Monetary Fund, 1950–51; UN Economic Adviser, Ministry of Planning, Kabul, Afghanistan, 1957–61; Senior Economic Adviser, Central Bank of Afghanistan, Kabul, 1961–64; Division Chief, Middle East Division, Research Department, International Monetary Fund (IMF); Economic Adviser, Middle Eastern Department, IMF, 1954; member of the Economic, Statistical and Legislative Society, Cairo, Egypt; *Publications: Poverty in Egypt,* 1940; *Statistical Analysis,* 1946; *Statistical Research Techniques,* 1947; *Banking Institutions in Egypt,* 1957; *Financial Economic Development in Pakistan,* 1966; *Decorations:* First Prize in Statistical Aptitudes, Cairo University, Egypt, 1937; *Interests and Recreations:* photography, gardening, cattle-ranching; economic development; *Languages:* Arabic, English, French, German, Persian; *Address:* Office — Middle Eastern Department, International Monetary Fund, 700 19th Street NW, Washington D.C. 20431, USA; telephone: (202) 393 6362; Residence -- P O Box 187, Giza Farms, Waldorf, MD 20601, USA; telephone: (301) 843 6323.

HASSANI, Bakir Hussain al-, Iraqi official/diplomat; born 12 February 1915, Baghdad, Iraq; *Education:* BSc, Business Administration, Columbia University, New York, USA, 1939; LLB, Law College, Baghdad University, Iraq, 1951; *Career:* Director of Commerce and Registrar of Companies, Trademarks and Patents, Ministry of Economics, 1947–51; Director General of Contracts and Economic Research, Development Board, 1951–54; Director General and Chairman of the Board of Directors, Tabacco Monopoly Administration, 1956–59; Envoy Extraordinary and Minister Plenipotentiary, and later Ambassador to Austria, 1959–63; Special Adviser, Director General, International Atomic Energy Agency (IAEA), 1963–76; Adviser, Saudi Arabian Permanent Mission in Vienna, 1978–; member of the Board of Directors of Rafidain Bank, and of Electricity Board; member of various trade delegations; member of various government committees; Delegate to UN for many years since 1946; Head of Delegation to 3rd and 6th General Conference of International Atomic Energy

Agency, IAEA; Governor, Board of Governors, IAEA, 1960–62; Chairman of IAEA Board of Governors, 1961–62; Lecturer at the College of Pharmacy, Military Staff College; *Decorations:* Rafidain Decoration; *Interests and Recreations:* politics, economics, riding, swimming, coin and stamp collecting; *Languages:* Arabic, English, Italian; *Address:* Via Civelli Mario 9, 21100 Varese, Italy; 43 Maidenhead Court Park, Maidenhead, Berks, UK.

HASSAWI, Mubarak Abdul Aziz al-, Kuwaiti businessman/politician; born 1925, Kuwait; married; two sons, six daughters; *Religion:* Muslim; *Education:* Secondary Education in Kuwait; course in Customs Management, Alexandria, Egypt; *Career:* Head, Customs Department, Kuwait, 1963; member of National Assembly for twelve years; Chairman, Bank of Sharjah, UAE; Chairman, Al-Mal Kuwaiti Company, Kuwait, Kuwait Commercial Real Estate Centre, Kuwait; *Interests and Recreations:* hunting, riding, swimming; member of al Qadisa Club, Kuwait; *Languages:* Arabic, English; *Address:* Bank of Sharjah, P O Box 1394, Sharjah, UAE; telephone: 352111; telex: 68039 BANKSH EM; P O Box 1368, Safat, Kuwait; telephone: 416031, 423630; telex: 22082 HASSAWI KT.

HASSEB, Khair Elddine, Iraqi economist/ UN official; born 1 August, 1929, Mosul, Iraq; *Education:* BA in Economics and Commerce, University of Baghdad, Baghdad, Iraq; MSc, Economics, London School of Economics, University of London, London, UK; PhD, Cambridge University, Cambridge, England; *Career:* Civil Service, 1947–54; Head of Research and Statistics Department, Iraq Petroleum Company, 1959–60; Director General, Iraqi Federation of Industries, 1960–63; Governor, Central Bank of Iraq, 1963–65; President, General Organisation of Banks, 1964–65; Acting President, Economic Organisation, 1964–65; Governor for Iraq, International Monetary Fund, 1963–65; Alternate Governor for Iraq, International Bank for Reconstruction and Development 1963–65; Associate Professor of Economics , University of Baghdad, 1965–71; Professor of Economics, University of Baghdad, 1971–74; Chief of Natural Resources and Science and Technology Division, United Nations Economic Division for Western Asia, 1974–80; Director General, Centre

for Arab Unity Studies, 1981; Chief of Natural Resources, Science and Technology Division, United Nations Economic Commission for Western Asia, 1982–; *Publications: The National Income of Iraq 1953–61,* 1964; *Sources of Arab Economic Thought in Iraq 1900–1971,* 1973; *Workers' Participation in Management in Arab Countries,* 1971; numerous articles in Arabic and English; *Languages:* Arabic, English; *Address:* United Nations Commission for Western Asia, P O Box 27, Baghdad, Iraq; telephone: 95068; telex; 213468 IK.

HASSO, Abdul Rahman al-, Iraqi academic/ physician; born 1 July 1934, Mosul, Iraq; married; two sons, one daughter; *Religion:* Muslim; *Education:* MB; ChB; PhD; MRC, Pathology; *Career:* Reserve Army Physician (1st Lieutenant), 1963; Pathologist, 1972; President, Laboratory of Medical Research, College of Medicine, University of Mosul, 1972; Assistant Professor, 1976–; Head of Pathology Department, 1976–; *Publications:* numerous articles and papers in professional medical journals; *Interests and Recreations:* tennis, member of the Social Cultural Centre; member of the Medical Syndicate; *Languages:* Arabic, English; *Address:* Department of Pathology, College of Medicine, University of Mosul, Iraq.

HATIM, Muhammad Abdul Qadir, Egyptian politician; born 1918, Alexandria, Egypt; married; *Religion:* Muslim; *Education:* Diploma in Political Science, Cairo University, Egypt; specialised in publicity work; *Career:* commissioned into Army 1937; Major 1950; Director General of Information, Ministry of National Guidance, 1955–57; Adviser to the President on news and information, 1957–58; attended Parliamentary Union Conference in London, 1957; Deputy Minister for Presidential Affairs with special responsibilities for press and radio, 1958; Minister of State in the Central Government of the United Arab Republic, 1958–62; Minister of Culture and National Guidance, 1962–66; Deputy Prime Minister supervising National Guidance, Tourism and Culture, 1964–66; Director of Information Bureau on the Yemen, 1966–71; Deputy Prime Minister and Minister of Information, 1971; Minister of Culture, 1971; acted as Foreign Minister during the latter's absence, 1972; Senior Deputy Prime Minister, 1973; Assistant to the President for National Council Affairs, 1974–1975; Supervisor of National Councils; Chairman of the Board of *Al-Ahram,* 1974; *Interests and Recreations:* painting, held several exhibitions; member of the Arab-Spanish Friendship Association; *Languages:* Arabic, English, French; *Address:* The Presidency, Cairo, Egypt.

HATTAR, Michael Mizyad, Arab-American academic/mathematician; born 17 March 1934, Salt, Jordan; married; one daughter, one son; *Education:* BA in Mathematics, Greenville College, Illinois, USA, 1958; MSc in Mathematics, Western Washington State University, USA, 1968; Standard Teaching Credential Specialization in Junior College, State of California, 1970; Standard Teaching Credential Specialization in Secondary Mathematics, State of California, 1976; *Career:* Professor of Mathematics, Don Bosco Technical Institute, 1962–76; Chairman, Mathematics Department, Junior College, Don Bosco Technical Institute, 1968–76; Professor of Mathematics, Mount San Antonio College, 1968–; Mathematics Instructor, Secondary Learning Centre Specialist, Ontario High School, California, 1976–; Publisher of Arabic language newspaper, *Sawt Al-Mughtarib; Publications: Linear Algebra and Matrices,* National Foundation Series adaptation into Arabic, 1972; editorials and articles in *Sawt Al-Mughtarib* newspaper; *Decorations:* Teacher of the Year Award, Industrial Education Council of San Gabriel Valley, California, 1970; Don Bosco Technical Institute, Teacher of the Year Award 1969 and 1970; Institute for the Advancement of Engineering Award, 1969; *Interests and Recreations:* table tennis, soccer; member of the Association of Arab-American University Graduates, Los Angeles Chapter, President, 1970–72; member of US Omen South Bay Chapter; President, 1974; founder of United Arab Community Club, President, 1975, 1976; member of Council of Arab-American Organisations, Southern California, 1981; First Vice President, 1976–77; founding committee member, Arab Cultural Centre of Southern California; active member of the Organisation of Arab Students and Arab Community Affairs; *Languages:* Arabic, English, French; *Address:* 1247 Dore Street, West Covina, California 91792, USA; telephone: 213 333 9197.

HAWAMDAH, Mahmud al-, Jordanian politician/engineer; born 1930, Tafila, Jordan; *Religion:* Muslim; *Education:* BSc in Mining Engineering, UK, 1956; *Career:* Engineer at Jordanian Phosphate Company, 1956–66; Director of Phosphate Project, 1966–71; Vice President, National Resources Authority, 1971–74; Minister of Public Works, 1974–76; Minister of Transport, 1976; General Manager of Dar Al Handasah Consultants (Shair & Partners), Amman, Jordan, 1980–83; *Address:* P O Box 5215, Amman, Jordan; telephone: 666916.

HAWARI, Ahmad Mahmud al-, Egyptian journalist; born 12 April 1921; *Religion:* Muslim; *Education:* Polytechnic School, Cairo, Egypt; *Career:* Director, Arab Information Centre, Press Office, New York, USA, 1955–58; Managing Editor, Middle East News Agency, Cairo, 1958–65; Chairman of the Board, Middle East News Agency; Director, Magazine Department, National Publishing House, 1965–67; Chairman, National Distributing Company, 1965–67; Publishing Manager, Al-Katib al-Arabi Publishing House, 1966–69; Adviser, Editing and Publishing Organization, 1969–71; Director General, Egyptian Book Organization, 1971–72; *Decorations:* Order of King George I of Greece, 1960; *Languages:* Arabic, English; *Address:* Office— Middle East News Agency, 4 Sherifeen Street, Cairo, Egypt; Residence— Isis Building, Gardan City, Cairo, Egypt.

HAWARI, Muhammad Abdul Qadir al-, Egyptian businessman; born 4 February 1935, Cairo, Egypt; married; two sons, one daughter; *Religion:* Muslim; *Education:* Commercial Studies; *Career:* member of the Board of Directors of the Arab-Egyptian Bank, 1958–60; Chairman, Egyptian Steel and Metal Commercial Company, 1960–67; Private business, 1967–74; member of the Permanent Committee for the Distribution of Building Materials, 1977–; owner of Ezzat Al-Hawari Stores, steel wholesalers, metal and timber; President, Egyptian Co for Trade in the Free Zones, 1980; International Football Referee (elected with 18 other referees for World Cup, Tunisia, 1977); *Decorations:* FIFA Decoration (International Federation of Association Football); Certificate of Gratitude, Ministry of Public Works; *Interests and Recreations:* football, tennis, squash, literature, travel; *Languages:* Arabic, English, French; *Address:* 76 Tarik Al-Nil, Giza, Cairo, Egypt; telephone: 982291.

HAWARI, Yassir Muhammad, Lebanese journalist; born 27 December 1929, Lebanon; married; one son, one daughter; *Religion:* Muslim; *Education:* American University of Beirut, Lebanon; BA, College of Journalism, University of London, UK; *Career:* journalist; Editor in Chief, *Al-Usbua' al-Arabi* weekly; *Publications:* several novels in Arabic; *Decorations:* Medal of the Order of the Moroccan Throne; *Interests and Recreations:* aviation, classical music, reading; *Languages:* Arabic, English, French; *Address:* Office — Al-Usbua' al-Arabi, Rue Sursock, Sayegh Building, Ashrafiyeh, Beirut, Lebanon; Residence -- Moawad Building, Chiah, Lebanon.

HAWATMEH, Nayif, Palestinian politician; born 1935, Salt, Jordan; *Religion:* Christian; *Education:* at Zarqa and at Hussein College, Amman, Jordan; later at Cairo University, Egypt; Politics and Economics, Beirut Arab University, Lebanon; *Career:* member of the Arab Nationalist Movement; following Arab-Israeli War in 1967 helped to found the Popular Front for the Liberation of Palestine (PFLP), led Popular Democratic Front for the Liberation of Palestine (PDFLP); helped edit PDFLP paper *Al-Hurriyah;* General Secretary of PDFLP; headed PDFLP delegation to Moscow, 1975.

HAWIZ, Tayib Nazhat M. al-, Iraqi economist/accountant; born 1931, Iraq; *Education:* BA in Economics, Birmingham University, UK; *Career:* Chartered Accountant, British accounting firm in UK; returned to Iraq: Professor of Accounting and Administration, Baghdad University; member of the Board of Central Bank of Iraq; member of the Board of National Insurance Company of Iraq; Vice Chairman of the Iraqi Oil Board; President of Iraqi Economists Association; Director of Finance, Arab Fund for Economic and Social Development, Kuwait, 1973–; *Languages:* Arabic, English; *Address:* Arab Fund for Economic and Social Development, P O Box 21923, Safat, Kuwait; telephone: 431870.

HAYDARI, Buland al-, Iraqi poet; born 1926; *Career:* in 1950s was one of the pioneers of the *free verse* movement which revolutionized Arabic poetry; now lives and works in London; *Publications:* since 1946 has published eight collections of poems including *Khafqat al-Tin* (The Throbbing Clay); *Aghani al-Medina al-Mayyita* (Songs of the Dead City); *Khutwat fil Ghurba* (Steps in Exile); also translations of T.S. Eliot and studies of art and literature; collection of poems translated into English, *Songs of the Tired Guard*, London, UK, 1977; *Languages:* Arabic, English; *Address:* New Era Publications (Services) Ltd, Achilles House, Western Ave, London W3 ORX; telephone: (01) 993 5014, 992 2764; telex: 916398 PANHEG.

HAYEK, Ignace Antoine II, Syrian ecclesiastic; born 14 September 1910; *Education:* Patriarchal Seminary, Charfe, Lebanon; College of Propaganda and Oriental Pontifical Institute, Rome, Italy; DPhil, Docteur es Sciences Orientales; *Career:* ordained priest, 1933; successively Director of School, Curate and Vicar General, Aleppo, Syria; Archbishop of Aleppo, 1959–69; Syrian Patriarch of Antioch, 1968; *Languages:* Arabic, French, Italian; *Address:* Syrian Catholic Patriarchate of Antioch, Damascus St, P O Box 116–5087, Beirut, Lebanon.

HAZAIMAH, Rifai, Jordanian admininistrator; born 1937, Irbid, Jordan; married; one son, five daughters; *Religion:* Muslim; *Education:* BA in Law, 1966; MA in Law, 1983; Diploma in Management, Georgetown University, Washington, USA, 1968; *Career:* Public Prosecutor, Police Court, 1968; Director, Department of Foreign Affairs, 1973; Director of Public Relations, Department of Public Security, 1974; Lawyer, 1975; Director General, Department of Civil Affairs, 1977–; *Publications:* several works on civil affairs and on taxation in Arabic; *Decorations:* Order of Independence; *Languages:* Arabic, English; *Address:* P O Box 2740, Amman, Jordan; telephone: 666477.

HAZLOUL BIN ABDUL AZIZ, HRH Prince, Saudi Arabian Prince/businessman; son of late King Abdul Aziz; born 1941, Riyadh, Saudi Arabia; *Religion:* Muslim; *Career:* Vice President of Najid Corporation; *Interests and Recreations:* hunting, sports; *Address:* Al-Hajj Wal Auqag Street, Shomal Al-Muraba, Riyadh , Saudi Arabia; telephone: Office — 25 033, Residence — 25 807.

HECHAIME, Makram, Lebanese businessman; born 17 September 1944, Lebanon; married; *Religion:* Christian; *Education:* BA in Business Administration; Commercial and Instrument Flying Pilot Licence; *Career:* Production and Personnel Manager, Laminated Plastic Sheets, SAL; Industrial Marketing Manager, Laminated Plastic Sheets; *Interests and Recreations:* skiing, water skiing, tennis; *Languages:* Arabic, French, English, Italian, German, Russian, Dutch, Spanish, Portuguese; *Address:* Office — PO Box 11–7814, Beirut, Lebanon; Residence— Kaslik, Nassif Abu-Chediac Building, Beirut, Lebanon.

HEDDA, Ali, Tunisian diplomat; born 30 October, 1930, Souss, Tunisia; married; two children; *Religion:* Muslim; *Education:* BA in Political Science, Sorbonne, University of Paris, Paris, France; *Career:* Ministry of Foreign Affairs; Embassy of Tunis, Washington D.C., USA, 1956–57; Deputy Director, Banque Centrale de Tunisie 1958–66; Minister, Embassy of Tunisia, Italy, 1966; Ambassador to Senegal, and other West African States, 1970–72; Director, International Cooperation Division, Ministry of Foreign Affairs, 1972–73; Director, Prime Minister's Office, Secretary of State, 1973; Ambassador, Embassy of Tunisia, Washington D.C., USA, non-resident Ambassador, Mexico and Venezuela; *Decorations:* Grand Officer of the Order of the Tunisian Republic; Order of the Italian Republic; *Languages:* Arabic, French, English; *Address:* Embassy of Tunisia, 2408 Massachusetts Avenue, Washington D.C., USA.

HEGELAN, Shaikh Faisal al-, Saudi Arabian diplomat; born 7 October 1929, Riyadh, Saudi Arabia; married; three sons; *Religion:* Muslim; *Education:* Faculty of Law, Cairo University, Egypt; *Career:* Ministry of Foreign Affairs, Jeddah, Saudi Arabia, 1952–54; Saudi Arabian Embassy, Washington D.C., USA, 1954–58; Chief of Protocol, Jeddah, 1958–60; Political Adviser to the late King Saud, 1960–61; Ambassador to Spain, 1961–68; Ambassador to Venezuela and Argentina, 1968–75; Ambassador to Denmark, 1975–76; Ambassador to UK, 1976–79; Ambassador to USA, 1979; *Decorations:* Order of King Abdul Aziz, Saudi Arabia; Gran Cruz Isobella Catholica, Spain; Order Del Libertador-Gran Cordon, Venezuela; Order Riobranco-Grande Official, Brazil; *Languages:* Arabic, English, Spanish, French; *Address:* c/o Ministry of Foreign Affairs P O Box 495, Baghdadiah, Jeddah, Saudi Arabia; telephone: 6421322, 6421423; telex: 401104 KHARJI SJ.

HEIKAL, Muhammad Hassanain, Egyptian journalist; born 1923; married; *Religion:* Muslim; *Education:* Diploma in Economics and Journalism, Cairo University; *Career:* entered journalism, 1944; crime reporter for *Egyptian Gazette;* war correspondent in Western Desert, World War II; joined *Akher Sa'a* weekly; roving correspondent, Greek Civil War 1948, and Palestine War and Korea, 1949; editor of *Akher Sa'a;* Political Editor of *Al-Akhbar,* 1950; Editor of *Al-Ahram,* 1957; Chairman of Board, 1960; elected to the Central Committee of the Arab Socialist Union, 1968; developed in association with *Al-Ahram,* a large advertising agency, a computer service used by many Egyptian companies, and a research centre on Palestine; Minister of National Guidance, 1970; visited Libya as Presidential Envoy to explain President Nassir's May Day appeal on the Middle East, 1970; played an important part in the formation of the joint Egypt-Libya-Sudan information services and in creating Egyptian Radio and Television Federation; resigned as Minister following the death of President Nassir, 1970; *Publications: Nasser: The Cairo Documents,* 1972; *The Road to Ramadan,* 1975, and several other books; *Languages:* Arabic, English, French; *Address:* c/o Al Ahram, Al-Galaa Street, Cairo, Egypt.

HELAISSI, Abdul Rahman al-, Saudi Arabian diplomat; born 1915, Buraida, Saudi Arabia; married; two sons, two daughters; *Religion:* Muslim; *Career:* 2nd Secretary and Chargé d'Affaires, Embassy to UK, 1948–51; Deputy Minister of Agriculture, 1954; Ambassador to Sudan; Ambassador to Italy; Ambassador to the Court of St. James, London, UK, 1966–76; also accredited to Denmark; *Interests and Recreations:* horse racing, equestrian sports; *Languages:* Arabic, English; *Address:* Ministry of Foreign Affairs, P O Box 495, Jeddah, Saudi Arabia.

HELAL, Ahmad Izzuddin Hassan, Egyptian politician /oil expert; born 1942, Alexandria, Egypt; *Religion:* Muslim; *Education:* BSc, Chemical Engineering, Cairo University, Egypt, 1946; postgraduate studies in the

Netherlands and the UK; *Career:* employed by Shell, Egypt; later joined Nassir Petroleum Laboratory; Deputy Director General of Refining, Nassir Petroleum Laboratory, 1960; Director General of Egyptian General Petroleum Corporation (EGPC), 1968; Chairman of EGPC, 1971; Minister of Petroleum and Mineral Resources, 1973; made frequent missions as emissary of late President Sadat during and after October 1973 War; Minister of Petroleum, 1974–; Minister of Industry and Mineral Resources, 1977–78; Deputy Prime Minister for Production and Minister of Petroleum, 1980–; *Languages:* Arabic, English; *Address:* Ministry of Petroleum, Cairo, Egypt.

HELAL, Karim T., Egyptian banker; born 19 August 1949, Cairo, Egypt; married; two sons; *Religion:* Muslim; *Education:* BA, Business Administration, Cairo University, Egypt; *Career:* Arab International Bank, Foreign Trade Department, Cairo, 1972–73; Junior Officer, Credit Department, Investment Department; Assistant Manager of Treasury, Correspondent Banking, Arab African International Bank, Cairo, 1973–79; started Al Bahrain Arab African Bank (ALBAAB) in Bahrain and Head of the Operations as Senior Vice President, 1979–81; Director of Arab Asian International Ltd, Hong Kong; Director of C.E. Coats, London; founding member of Arab Bankers Association, London; elected fellow of International Bankers Association, Washington; *Publications: Wanted – An Arab Bank,* April 1977, published in *Euromoney; Interests and Recreations:* reading, photography, music, squash; *Languages:* Arabic, English, French; *Address:* P O Box 5619, Manama, Bahrain; telephone: 233129.

HELMI, Mustafa Kamal, Egyptian politician/academic; born 1922, Egypt; *Religion:* Muslim; *Education:* BSc, MSc and PhD in Organic Chemistry, Cairo University, Cairo, Egypt; *Career:* Professor, Faculty of Engineering, Ain Shams University, Cairo, Egypt; Secretary General, Higher Council of the Universities, 1962; Minister of Education, Higher Education and Scientific Research, 1974–78 and from 1979–82; Chairman, Scientists Syndicate; Deputy Prime Minister of State for Education and Scientific Research, 1982–; *Languages:* Arabic, English, French; *Address:* Ministry of Education, National Centre for Educational Research, Falaky Street, Cairo, Egypt.

HELOU, Charles, Lebanese politician/former President; born 25 September, 1912, Beirut, Lebanon; married; *Education:* Licence in Law, French Faculty of Law, St. Joseph University, Beirut, Lebanon; *Career:* Barrister at Law; Journalist; founder of the daily *L'Eclair du Nord,* Aleppo, 1932; Director, Political Section of Information, 1931–34; Director of the French language daily *Le Jour,* 1935–46; Envoy Extraordinary and · Minister Plenipotentiary, Embassy to the Holy See, March 1947; Lebanese Delegate to the UN Economic and Social Council, 1948; Minister of Justice and of Information, 1949; elected Deputy for Beirut, 1951; Minister of Foreign Affairs, 1951–52; Minister of Justice and Public Health, 1954–55; Minister of Information and of National Education, 1958; Chairman of the Board, Social Development Office; one of the founders and President of the National Education Council, 1964; elected President of the Lebanese Republic, August 1964– 1970; *Publications: Le Cas des Refugies Palestiniens;* and various pamphlets on the Palestinian problem; *Decorations:* Grand Cordon, National Order of the Cedar; Légion d'Honneur, France; numerous other foreign distinctions and decorations; Honorary Doctor of Cairo University, 1965; *Address:* Kaslik, Lebanon.

HELOU, Nina, Lebanese lawyer; born 1943; married 1952; *Education:* Licence in Law, French Faculty of Law, Beirut; *Career:* Barrister at Law, first woman member of Beirut Municipality; Honorary President of Lebanon Red Cross; *Languages:* Arabic, French, English.

HELOU, PIERRE, Lebanese businessman/politician; born 1929, Beirut, Lebanon; married; three children; *Religion:* Christian; *Education:* University of St. Joseph, Lebanon; *Career:* businessman; member of Lloyds, 1969; interests in several local industries; candidate in 1972 elections; elected deputy for Aley as independent attached to Aley Bloc; Minister of State for Petroleum and Industry, 1972–73; *Languages:* Arabic, French, English; *Address:* Kaslik, Lebanon.

HENABLIA, Dhaoui, Tunisian politician; born 1922, Le Kef, Tunisia; married; *Religion:* Muslim; *Education:* medicine; *Career:* active member of the National Assembly, 1959–; Vice President, National Assembly, 1969; Minister of Agriculture and member of the Political Bureau of the Socialist Destour Party, 1971–74; member of the Political Bureau of the Socialist Destour Party, 1974–81; Minister of the Interior, 1977–79; Minister of Public Health, 1979–81; member of the National Assembly, 1959–81; *Languages:* Arabic, French; *Address:* Ministry of Public Health, Tunis, Tunisia.

HERMASSI, Elbaki, Tunisian academic/sociologist; born 26 December 1937; *Education:* Degree in Philosophy, Doctorate in Sociology, Sorbonne, University of Paris, France; PhD in Sociology, University of California, Berkeley, USA; *Career:* Research Assistant at Ecole Pratique des Hautes Etudes, Paris, 1965–66; Assistant Professor, Tunis University, Tunisia, 1966–67; Assistant Professor of Sociology, University of California, Berkeley, USA; *Publications: Leadership and National Development,* California Press, 1972; *Etat et Société au Maghreb,* Paris, 1975; *Languages:* Arabic, French, English; *Address:* Sociology Department, University of California, Berkeley, California 94720, USA; telephone: 841 3543.

HESHMAOUI, Mustafa, Algerian diplomat/army commander; born 26 July, 1934, Algeria; married; three sons, two daughters; *Religion:* Muslim; *Education:* BA in History and Geography; School of Infantry, Iraq; Frunza Staff College, Moscow, USSR; *Career:* Officer, Lieutenant, Algerian Liberation Army, 1957; Captain, 1962; Major, 1972; Commander of Unit, 1968; Secretary of the Algerian National Liberation Party, 1977; member of the Central Committee of the Party, 1979; Ambassador Extraordinary to Lebanon, 1980–; *Decorations:* Order of Bravery, 1958; *Interests and Recreations:* volleyball, chess; *Languages:* Arabic, French; *Address:* Embassy of Algeria, P O Box 4794, Beirut, Lebanon; telephone: 608402.

HIBSHI, Muhammad Ali, Saudi Arabian academic/educationalist; born 1934, Mecca, Saudi Arabia; *Religion:* Muslim; *Education:* PhD, University of London, England, 1975; *Career:* various teaching posts; Cultural Relations Department, Ministry of Education; Assistant Dean, Faculty of Islamic Law (Sharia), Mecca; member of Conference on International Education, Geneva, Switzerland; Secretary General, King Abdul Aziz University, Mecca, 1971–, Arab League Economic, Cultural and Social Organisation,

(ALESCO) Conferences; *Publications: Tatawur al Ta'liim al-'Aali fil Mamlaktil Arabia al-Saudia,* in Arabic; various other books in field of teacher training and development of education; *Interests and Recreations:* reading, travel; *Address:* University of King Abdul Aziz, P O Box 1540, Mecca, Saudi Arabia.

HIDAYAT, Salahuddin, Egyptian scientist/official; born 1920; married; *Education:* BSc, Alexandria University, Egypt; *Career:* Director of the Chemical Research Section of the Armed Forces; member of Free Officers' Movement; Director General, Atomic Energy Organization, and Director of the Office of Scientific Research in the Presidency, 1960; First Minister of Scientific Research, 1961–64; Chairman, Atomic Energy Organization, 1964–67; led the Egyptian Delegation to the UN Conference on the application of Science and Technology, 1963 and was elected Vice President of the Conference; Egyptian representative on Advisory Committee for the application of Science and Technology to development; Presidential Adviser on Scientific Research, 1967–72; Chairman of the Council of Scientific Research; Council of Ministers of the Confederation of Arab Republics, 1971; Director of Scientific and Technical Affairs in Arab League, with special responsibilities for atomic energy; President of the Egyptian Scientific Professions Syndicate; President of the Development Consultants' Association; Regional Secretary of the World Federation of Scientific Workers; *Address:* Egyptian Atomic Energy Organisation, 101 Kasr Al Aini Street, Dokki, Cairo, Egypt.

HIGAZI, Abdul Aziz, Egyptian politician; born 3 January 1923; married; three sons; *Religion:* Muslim; *Education:* Degree in Accountancy, Cairo University, Egypt; PhD, Birmingham University, UK; *Career:* Dean of the Faculty of Commerce, Ain Shams University, Cairo, and member of the Cairo Governorate; Minister of Finance, 1968–73; elected to the National Assembly, January 1969; Deputy Prime Minister, 1973, with responsibility for financial and economic affairs; launched programme for promotion of Egyptian exports in world market, 1973; Deputy Prime Minister, 1974; Prime Minister, 1974–75; *Languages:* Arabic, English; *Address:* Ministry of Cabinet Affairs, Cairo, Egypt.

HIJAZI, Arafat Mahmud, Jordanian journalist; born 11 March 1927, Hebron, Jordan; married; three sons, three daughters; *Religion:* Muslim; *Education:* Diploma in Journalism from Egyptian National College; *Career:* Head of Section, Jordanian Ministry of Interior, 1952–55; Broadcaster and Producer for Jordan Radio, 1956–59; Editor of *Al-Manar* daily newspaper; Editor of *Akhbar al-Yaum* newspaper; Publisher and Editor of *Al-Sabah* newspaper; Publisher and Editor of *Amman al-Massa* weekly; Editor of *Al-Destour;* President of Jordanian Press Association, 1970–73; member of Permanent Office of Union of Arab Journalists, 1970; member of Executive of International Press Association; member of Palestine National Council, 1964–69; President of Professional and Trade Unions Assembly, 1970; lecturer; *Publications:* twenty books, mainly on Palestine, 1950–74; translated *The Bulgarian Resistance and the Palestine Liberation War* into Russian and Bulgarian; *Interests and Recreations:* travel, reading, especially military affairs; *Languages:* Arabic, English; *Address:* c/o Al-Destour newspaper, P O Box 591, Amman, Jordan; telephone: 664153, 669345.

HIJAZI, Ismail Salim, Jordanian politician; born 3 April 1915, Hebron, Jordan; married; nine sons, three daughters; *Religion:* Muslim; *Education:* Diploma in Agriculture; Certificate in Education; *Career:* teacher, and headmaster until elected member of Chamber of Deputies for Hebron, 1954; served in eight parliaments until 1975 dissolution; member of Iraq-Jordan Federal Council, 1958; Minister of Agriculture, 1965–66; resigned at end of 1966 to stand for Parliament; Minister of Construction and Development in transitional government, 1967; *Publications:* numerous political and literary articles in Jordanian press; *Decorations:* Star of Jordan, 1st Class; Order of the Holy Sepulchre from Pope Paul VI; *Interests and Recreations:* lives and works of poets; writing poetry; riding, motoring, swimming; for the last 15 years has been collecting books on the history of Hebron and has translated English books, French books and one Turkish/Persian book by 17th century traveller to Hebron; *Languages:* Arabic, English; *Address:* P O Box 9787 Amman, Jordan; telephone: Residence 811940.

HIKMAT, Yanal Omar, Jordanian diplomat/ Royal Court official; born 1934; *Education:* BA, University of California, Los Angeles (UCLA), USA, 1956; *Career:* Head of Publications Council, 1957; Foreign Ministry, 1959–68; Attaché, Embassy to Lebanon; Assistant Head of Royal Protocol, 1968–70; Head of Royal Protocol 1971; *Address:* Royal Palace, Amman, Jordan; telephone: 663292.

HIMDY, Fuad Amin, Saudi Arabian businessman; born 1930, Mecca; married; three sons, four daughters; *Religion:* Muslim; *Education:* general; *Career:* President, Al-Imtiaz Trading and Industrial Co, Mecca; Vice President of Mecca Chamber of Commerce and Industry; *Interests and Recreations:* reading, poetry; *Languages:* Arabic, English; *Address:* P O Box 412, Mecca, Saudi Arabia; Telephone: Office— 5745278; Residence— 5424828, 5732447.

HINA'I, Al- Walid Bin Zahir Bin Ghusn al-, Omani politician; former Wali of Manah; *Religion:* Muslim; *Career:* Minister of Education, 1972; Minister of Waqfs (Religious Endowments) and Islamic Affairs, 1973; *Address:* Ministry of Waqfs and Islamic Affairs, P O Box 767, Ministerial Complex, Ruwi, Oman.

HINDAN, Abdul Rahman Abdul Aziz al-, Saudi Arabian administrator/educationalist; born 1934, Mecca, Saudi Arabia; *Religion:* Muslim; *Education:* BA in Geography; *Career:* Director of Public Education Bureau; Secretary, Professional Inspectorate; Director of Bureau, Under Secretary of State, Ministry of Education; Secretary, Supreme Council of Arts and Science; Director General, Minister of Education Bureau; attended Conferences of Arab Ministers of Education, Tripoli, Libya, Cairo, Egypt, Morocco; Baghdad, Iraq; *Publications:* collection of poems; *Interests and Recreations:* football, swimming; former Chairman of Board of Al-Hilal Sporting Club, Riyadh; *Address:* Ministry of Education Bureau, Riyadh, Saudi Arabia; telephone: 4042888.

HINDAWI, Ali Muhammad al-, Jordanian lawyer/politician; born 1911, Irbid, Jordan; married; *Religion:* Muslim; *Education:* Licence in Law, Syrian University, 1942; *Career:* Judge in Ministry of Justice, 1942; various posts in judiciary, ending as Public

Prosecutor, 1942–52; Minister of Agriculture, 1955; Minister; Senator, 1959; Assistant to the Chairman, Jordan Senate, 1963; Second Jordan Senate, 1965; Permanent member of Foreign and Judicial Committees, Committee of Education and Guidance; member of Higher Committee of Legal Interpretation, 1971; *Decorations:* Order of the Star of Jordan, 1st Class; Syrian Order of Merit, 1st Class; Renaissance Medal, 1st Class; *Address:* The Senate, Amman, Jordan.

HINDAWI, Thaugan Salim, Jordanian diplomat/official; born 18 February 1927, Jordan; married; two sons, one daughter; *Religion:* Muslim; *Education:* BA in Social Studies, Cairo University, Egypt, 1954; MEd , USA, 1956; *Career:* Teacher, 1950–53; Headmaster, 1953–54; Principal, Teachers' Training College, 1956–60; Assistant Under Secretary of Education, 1961–65; Under Secretary, Ministry of Information, 1965; Minister of Education, Information, and Social Affairs, 1965–70; Ambassador to Kuwait, 1970–73; Ambassador to Cairo, Egypt, 1977–79; President of the Board of Trustees, Community Arab College; President, Arab Community College Company; *Publications: Palestinian Issue,* textbook for Jordanian schools; *Decorations:* Order of the Jordanian Star; Order of the Egyptian Republic; Order of Kingdom of Saudi Arabia; Order of the Tunisian Republic; several other decorations from various countries; *Interests and Recreations:* chess; *Languages:* Arabic, English; *Address:* PO Box 921699 Amman, Jordan; Community Arab College, PP Box 926845 Amman, Jordan.

HITTI, Said Habib; Lebanese IMF official/economist; born 16 April 1936, Souk al-Gharb, Lebanon; married; one son, three daughters; *Religion:* Christian; *Education:* BA, American University of Beirut (AUB), Lebanon, 1957; BSc, London School of Economics, UK, 1961; BLitt. Oxford University, UK, 1967; *Career:* Economist, Middle Eastern Department of IMF, 1963–73; Resident Representative, IMF, Sudan, 1968–70; Chief of Division in Middle Eastern Department, IMF, 1973–81; Senior Adviser to Middle Eastern Department, IMF, 1981–; *Publications:* articles in IMF Staff Paper and Finance and Development; *Interests and Recreations:* classical music; *Languages:* Arabic, English, French; *Address:* Office — International Monetary Fund, 700 19 Street

NW, Washington D.C. 20431, USA; telephone: (202) 477 6068; Residence — 9932 Brixton Lane, Bethesda, Maryland, 20034, USA; telephone: (301) 365 2977.

HITTI, Yusuf, Lebanese physician/academic; born Shemlan, Lebanon; *Education:* Doctor of Medicine, Faculty of Medicine, American University of Beirut, Beirut, Lebanon; Faculty of Medicine, Harvard University, USA, 1923; *Career:* Doctor in the Ottoman Army with the rank of Captain, 1917–19; Doctor in Beirut, and later Professor at the American University in Beirut; member of Parliament, 1947–51; Cabinet Minister, 1957; *Publications: Anglo-Arab Medical Dictionary,* 1967, 4th Edition, 1979; *Decorations:* Officer of the National Order of the Cedar, 1967; Commander of the British Empire, 1971; Howard Bliss Gold Medal, 1974; *Languages:* Arabic, English, French; *Address:* Clemenceau Street, Beirut, Lebanon; telephone: 364 360/1.

HOMOUD, Kamal al-, Jordanian diplomat; born 1921, Jordan; married; *Education:* Aley National College, Lebanon, 1940; Diploma in International Relations, University of London, London, UK, 1956; *Career:* Officer in the Jordanian Army, 1941–50; Military Attaché, Jordan Embassy, London, UK, 1946–50; Foreign Ministry, 1950–52; Head of Royal Protocol, 1952–54; Counsellor, Embassy of Jordan in London, 1954–56; Charge d'Affaires, Embassy to Iran, 1957; Minister Plenipotentiary, Embassy to Chile, 1957–61; Ambassador to Iran, 1962; Head of Ceremonies Department, Ministry of Foreign Affairs, 1963–64; Ambassador to India, 1964–68; Ambassador to Iraq, 1969–71; Head of Political Department, Ministry of Foreign Affairs, 1971–72; Acting Secretary General, Foreign Ministry, 1972; Ambassador to Arab League, 1972–73; Ambassador to USSR, 1973–77; Secretary General to Foreign Ministry, 1977–79; Ambassador to China, 1979–; *Decorations:* numerous decorations and medals; *Languages:* Arabic, English; *Address:* Jordan Embassy, San Li Tun Dong Liu Jie 54, Beijing, People's Republic of China.

HONEIN, Edouard, Lebanese politician; born 1913, Lebanon; *Religion:* Christian; *Education:* St. Joseph University, Beirut, Lebanon; Licence in Law, St. Joseph University, Beirut, Lebanon; *Career:* Barrister at Law,

Beirut; member and Secretary General of the National Bloc political party, 1951–; elected Deputy for Baabda, 1957; re-elected in 1960; Minister of Social Affairs and of Labour, 1961; re-elected Deputy for Baabda, 1964; Minister for Social Affairs, 1964–65; Minister of Planning and of Tourism, 1966; Minister of National Economy; Minister of Labour and Minister for Social Affairs, 1968; resigned June 1968; re-elected Deputy for Baabda, 1968; Minister of Education and Fine Arts, 1972; resigned 1972; *Publications:* numerous articles on economic and political affairs; *Address:* Office — Chamber of Deputies, Place de l'Etoile, Beirut, Lebanon.

HOSHAN, Ahmad Hamad al-, Saudi Arabian businessman; born 5 October, 1934, Medina, Saudi Arabia; married; four children; *Career:* Assistant General Manager, Yammah Cement Company, Riyadh, Saudi Arabia, 1962–63; Assistant Regional Manager, Riyadh Bank, 1963–65; General Manager, Riyadh Government Employees Cooperative Consumer Society, 1965–66; Editor in Chief, Yamamah Press Organisation, Riyadh, Saudi Arabia, 1966–71; President, HOSHANCO; *Address:* Hoshanco Building, P O Box 509, Riyadh, Saudi Arabia; telephone: 62418; telex: 201436 HOSHAN SJ.

HOSHAN, Muhamad H. al-; Saudi Arabian lawyer; born 14 April 1929, Madina, Saudi Arabia; married; two sons, four daughters; *Religion:* Muslim; *Education:* LLB, Faculty of Law, Cairo University, Egypt, 1954; Diploma d'Etudes Superieures, University of Poitiers, France, 1965; LLD, University of Paris, France, 1966; *Career:* Director General of Pensions Department, Ministry of Finance and National Economy, 1957–61; Legal Adviser, Ministry of Finance and National Economy, 1961–70; Senior Officer for Specialized Studies, Legal Department, Organization of Petroleum Exporting Countries (OPEC), 1966–68; Associate Professor of Law, University of Riyadh, 1970–73; Chairman of Law Department, University of Riyadh, 1970–73; Attorney of Law; *Publications: Introduction to the Study of Law: A comparative approach,* co-author; editor of the *Saudi Arabian Legal Encyclopaedia, a* commentary on, and a compilation of Saudi laws and regulations, in Arabic and English; *Interests and Recreations:* philosophy, sufism, biographies, swimming, photography; *Languages:* Arabic, English, French; *Ad-*

dress: P O Box 2626 Riyadh, Saudi Arabia; telephone: Office — 4648353, 4648363, Residence — 4042191; telex: 200877 DELPHISJ, 201624 JURIST SJ.

HOSS, Salim, Lebanese politician/economist; born 20 December 1929, Beirut, Lebanon; married; one daughter; *Education:* BA in Business Administration; MA in Business Administration, American University of Beirut, Lebanon, 1952 and 1957; PhD in Economics and Business, Indiana University, USA, 1961; *Career:* Accountant, Tapline Company, Beirut, 1952–54; corresponding member of the Beirut Chamber of Commerce, 1954–55; Instructor, later Professor, American University of Beirut, Lebanon, 1955; Financial Adviser, Kuwait Fund for Arab Economic Development; President, Banking Control Commission; Prime Minister, Minister of Economy and Trade; Minister of Industry and Oil; Minister of Information, December 1976; *Interests and Recreations:* member of the American Economic Society, member of the Middle East Society, member of Associated Accountants; *Languages:* Arabic, French, English; *Address:* Office — Bank of Lebanon, Beirut, Lebanon.

HOURANI, Albert Habib, academic of Lebanese descent; born 31 March 1915, Manchester, UK; married; one daughter; *Religion:* Christian; *Education:* MA, Magdalen College, Oxford University, UK; *Career:* Fellow of Magdalen College, Oxford, 1948–58; Fellow of St. Anthony's College, Oxford, 1958–; successively Lecturer, Reader in the Modern History of the Middle East, Oxford University, 1951–79; *Publications:* numerous articles and books on the modern history of the Middle East including *Syria and Lebanon,* 1946; *Minorities in the Arab World,* 1947; *A Vision of History,* 1961; *Arabic Thought in the Liberal Age, 1798–1939,* 1962, (translated into Arabic); *Europe and the Middle East,* 1980; *The Emergence of the Modern Middle East,* 1981; *Address:* 161 Woodstock Road, Oxford, UK; telephone: 0865 53244.

HOURIEH, Muhammad Ali, Syrian academic; born 19 July 1934, Lattakia, Syria; married; one son, one daughter; *Education:* BSc, PhD, Chemistry, Imperial College, University of London, 1966; Diploma, Chemical Engineering, American Institute of

Chemical Engineering, USA; Diploma in Higher Education University of Washington, USA; *Career:* Assistant Professor of Chemistry, University of Aleppo, 1966–71; Associate Professor of Chemistry, University of Aleppo, 1971–76; Professor of Chemistry, University of Aleppo, 1976–; Vice President, University of Aleppo, 1975–79; President of University of Aleppo, 1979–; member of American Chemical Society Washington, USA, American Institute of Chemical Engineers, American Nuclear Society, USA; *Publications: Chemistry,* 1967 in Arabic; *Organic Chemistry,* 1968, in Arabic; *Analytical Chemistry* 1970; *Modern Methods of Chemical Analysis; Studies on Photoionization,* 1965, in English; several papers on energy; *Interests and Recreations:* tennis; member of The National Geographic Soc'ety, (USA); *Languages:* Arabic, English; *Address:* University of Aleppo, Aleppo, Syria; telephone: 230661, 26645, Residence — 13553.

HOUT, Shafik al-, Palestinian politician; *Education:* graduated in science, American University of Beirut, Lebanon; *Career:* school master in Beirut and later in Kuwait, joined staff of the Lebanese leading weekly magazine *Al-Hawadess,* 1956; Editor of *Al-Hawadess;* appointed Director of PLO Political Office in Beirut, 1964; in 1966 helped form *Abtal Al-Auda* (Heroes of Return) a guerrilla organization later joined to the PDFLP; contributing editor of the official magazine *Al-Muharrir.*

HOUTY, Abdul Rahman, Kuwaiti engineer/official; born 1938, Kuwait; married; one son, three daughters; *Religion:* Muslim; *Education:* BSc in Engineering, University of California, Berkeley, USA; *Career:* Ministry of Electricity and Water, 1963; Ministry of Information, 1964; Chief Engineer and Assistant Under Secretary, Ministry of Information, 1965–; President of Kuwait Society of Engineers; represented Kuwait at several conferences on Radio and Television Broadcasting in Canada, Switzerland, Egypt, Iraq, Bahrain, Qatar and Kuwait; *Interests and Recreations:* touring, sea fishing; *Languages:* Arabic, English; *Address:* Ministry of Information, P O Box 193, Safat, Kuwait; telephone: 423774.

HRAYMAL, Issa Khalfan al-, United Arab Emirates diplomat; born 1 October 1946, Sharjah, United Arab Emirates; married;

three sons; *Religion:* Muslim; *Education:* BA in Geography; various diplomas; *Career:* 3rd Secretary in Foreign Ministry, Abu Dhabi, United Arab Emirates, 1970–71; UAE Consul General in Bombay, India, 1973–74; Ambassador to Algeria; *Interests and Recreations:* poetry, economics, politics, reading, swimming; *Languages:* Arabic, English, Hindi; *Address:* Ministry of Foreign Affairs, P O Box 1, Abu Dhabi, United Arab Emirates.

HUBAISHI, Hussain Ali, Yemen Arab Republic lawyer; born 4 March, 1927; Aden; married, one son, one daughter; *Religion:* Muslim; *Career:* Principal, Balais College, 1961–68; Legal Adviser to the President and Cabinet, 1968–69; Deputy Prime Minister of the Economy and Foreign Affairs, 1969–70; Legal Adviser to the President and Minister of State, 1970–; member of the Board of Sana'a University, the National Schools Association, the High Judicial Council; *Publications: Self-Determination,* 1967; other works; *Interests and Recreations:* anthropology, sociology; *Languages:* Arabic, English, French; *Address:* The Legal Office of the State, P O Box 1292, Sana'a, Yemen; telephone: 70561.

HUDAITHI, Abdullah Ibrahim al-, Saudi Arabian businessman/official; born 14 March 1944, Saudi Arabia; married; one son, one daughter; *Religion:* Muslim; *Education:* BCom in Business and Accountancy, Riyadh University, Saudi Arabia; Diploma in Public Administration, Birmingham University, UK; Diploma in Marketing and Management, International Management Institute, Cambridge, Mass, USA; *Career:* Director of Control Department, Ministry of Agriculture and Water, Riyadh, 1967–70; Director of Technical Affairs, Ministry of Agriculture and Water, Riyadh, 1970–75; Secretary General, Saudi Hotels and Resort Areas Company, Riyadh, (SHARACO), 1975–; President, Central Corporation, Riyadh, (CECORP), 1976–; member of the Board of Prefabricated Building Co (MABCO) Ltd, Riyadh, 1976–, Prescat Structure Co, Riyadh, 1976–, Al Hudaithi Establishment, Riyadh, 1976–, Arabian Lamah Co Ltd, Riyadh, 1977–; *Interests and Recreations:* member of the Board of the Arab Tennis Federation; member of the Saudi Arabian Table Tennis and Tennis Federation; member of Al-Nazer Sport, Cultural and Social Club,

Riyadh; *Languages:* Arabic, English; *Address:* P O Box 1549, Riyadh, Saudi Arabia; telephone: 4778421.

HUGAIL, Abdullah Muhammad al-; Saudi Arabian official/businessman; born 1940, Saudi Arabia; married; three sons, one daughter; *Education:* University Degree in Arabic Language; *Career:* Assistant to the Assistant Secretary of Management, Ministry of Planning; General Manager of Employee Relations, Ministry of Municipalities; General Manager of Ministry of Municipalities; Assistant Deputy Minister of Municipalities; Partner, Trading and Development Partnership, Electrical and Mechanical Supplies, Arab-German Civil Works Co Ltd, Civil Construction and Contracting, Moroweh Public Relations and Advertising Co; member of the Founding Committee of Saudi Cairo Bank; *Publications:* articles on literature, politics and social sciences; *Interests and Recreations:* swimming, table tennis; *Languages:* Arabic, English; *Address:* P O Box 1327 Riyadh, Saudi Arabia; telephone: 4039607, 4039871, 4013204, 4013520.

HUJAILAN, Jamil al-, Saudi Arabian diplomat; born 1925, Buraida, Saudi Arabia; married; three sons; *Religion:* Muslim; *Education:* in Najd and Student Mission School in Mecca; BA, Arabic Literature, University of Cairo, Egypt; *Career:* Ministry of Foreign Affairs; 3rd Secretary, Embassy to Iran, 1953; Chargé d'Affaires, Embassy to Pakistan; Director General of Broadcasting, Press and Publications, 1960; first Saudi Ambassador to Kuwait, 1961–63; first Minister of Information, 1963–70; Ambassador, West Germany, 1974–76; Ambassador to France, 1980–; *Languages:* English, French; *Address:* Embassy of Saudi Arabia, 5 Ave Hoche, 75008 Paris, France.

HUMAIDAN, Ali, United Arab Emirates diplomat; born 20 September 1931; married; *Religion:* Muslim; *Education:* Licence in Law, Baghdad University, Iraq, 1956; Diploma in Political Science, University of Paris, France, 1967; Doctorate in Political Science, University of Paris, France, 1967; *Career:* Deputy Representative of Kuwait to UNESCO, Paris, France, 1967–69; Professor, Political Science Department, University of Kuwait, 1969–70; Legal Adviser for Federal Affairs, Government of Abu Dhabi, United Arab Emirates, 1971–72; UAE Delegate, UN General Assembly, New York, USA, 1972–74; Permanent Representative, with rank of Ambassador, of the UAE to the UN, New York, USA, 1972–80; UAE Ambassador to Canada, 1976–80; *Languages:* Arabic, French, English; *Address:* Office — Ministry of Foreign Affairs, P O Box 1, Abu Dhabi, United Arab Emirates.

HUMAIDAN, Ibrahim, Bahraini politician/lawyer; born 1939; married; *Religion:* Muslim; *Education:* Cairo University, Egypt; Rabat University, Morocco; *Career:* private practice as advocate in Bahrain; Assistant Public Prosecutor; Public Prosecutor; Legal Adviser to Ministry of Labour and Social Affairs, 1972–75; Minister of Transport, 1975–; *Languages:* Arabic, English; *Address:* Ministry of Transport, P O Box 325, Manama, Bahrain; telephone: 250917; telex: 8989 MINCOM BN.

HUMAIZI, Yaqub al-, Kuwaiti businessman; born 1930, Kuwait; married; *Religion:* Muslim; *Education:* Cairo University, Egypt; Liverpool University, UK; *Career:* private enterprise; Chairman, Livestock Transport and Trading Company; member of the Constituent Assembly, 1962; *Interests and Recreations:* travel, aquatic sports; *Languages:* Arabic, English; *Address:* Livestock Transport and Trading Company, Arabian Gulf Street, P O Box 42, Kuwait; telephone: 873784, telex: 22336.

HUNSY, Muhammad Wafik, Egyptian UN official/economist; born 24 March 1934; married; *Religion:* Muslim; *Education:* BA, Ain Shams University, Cairo, Egypt, 1950–54; MSc in Economics, University of London, UK, 1964–67; *Career:* Shell Oil Company, Egypt, 1954–57; Embassy to Sweden, 1957–62; 1st Secretary, Research Department, Ministry of Foreign Affairs, 1962–64; Head of Economic Section, Department of International Organizations, 1968–69; Head of Technical Assistance Section, Department of International Organizations, Ministry of Foreign Affairs, Egypt, 1969–72; Economic Affairs Counsellor, Permanent Mission of Egypt to UN, New York, 1972; *Publications: Money, Inflation and Economic Development in Egypt 1952–66*, 1967; *Oil, Development Cooperation and the International Monetary System*, 1974; *Interests and Recreations:* swimming, economic and diplomatic matters; member of the National Sporting Club,

239

Cairo, Egypt, Young Men's Christian Association, New York; *Languages:* Arabic, English, French; *Address:* Permanent Mission of Egypt, New York, New York, 36 E 67 Street, New York, NY 10021, USA; telephone: (212) 879 6300.

HURBLI, Abdul Sami, Syrian UN official; born 20 December 1916, Aleppo, Syria; married; *Education:* Diploma, Teachers Training College, Syria, 1936–37; BA in Education, American University of Beirut, Lebanon, 1938–41; MA in Education, American University of Beirut, 1941–42; Diploma, Child Development, Institute of Education, University of London, UK, 1945–46; PhD, Education, Teachers College, Columbia University, USA, 1947–50; *Career:* Professor of Education, Teachers Training College, Syria, 1942–45; Inspector of Education, 1946–47; Director, Education Committee, Ministry of Education, 1950–51; Programme Specialist, Adult Education, UNESCO, Paris, 1951–64; Deputy Director, Teachers and School Education, United Nations Relief and Works Agency for Palestine Refugees in the Near East (UNRWA) Lebanon, 1965–67; Chief, Higher Education Division, UNRWA/ UNESCO Department of Education, 1967; *Publications: Standardised Tests on Literacy,* Beirut, 1972; *Educational Consciousness and the Future of the Arab States,* 1955, 1961, 1972; *Interests and Recreations:* school, adult and teacher education, literacy, community development; *Languages:* Arabic, English, French; *Address:* Office — Museitbeh Quarter, Beirut, Lebanon. telephone: 300090; Residence — Beirut, Lebanon; telephone: 313846.

HUSRY, Khaldun S. al-, Iraqi writer/ diplomat; born 1923, Baghdad, Iraq; married; two sons; *Religion:* Muslim; *Education:* MA, PhD in Political Science and History; *Career:* Private Secretary to Minister of Supply, Baghdad, 1946–48; Attaché at League of Arab States, 1948–51; Private Secretary to Minister of Communications, 1951–57; freelance columnist, 1957–63; Editor of *Chronology of Arab Politics* and *Arab Political Documents,* American University of Beirut, Lebanon, 1963–65; Director of Beirut Bureau of Iraqi News Agency; Counsellor, Ministry of Foreign Affairs, United Arab Emirates; *Publications:* in Arabic, *Political Essays,* 1957; *The Revolution of July 14th and the*

Truth About the Communists in Iraq, 1960, revised and enlarged edition, 1963; edited and introduced *Memoirs of Taha al-Hashimi,* 1967; in English, *A Study in Modern Arabic Political Thought,* 1966; *The Iraqi Revolution of July 14th 1958; A Middle East Reader,* New York 1962; also various articles and reviews in Arabic and English; *Languages:* Arabic, English, Turkish, French; *Address:* c/o Embassy of United Arab Emirates, Beirut, Lebanon.

HUSSAIN, Abdul Aziz, Kuwaiti politician; born 1920 Kuwait; married; two sons, one daughter; *Religion:* Muslim; *Education:* BA, College of Arabic Language, Cairo, Egypt, 1943; Diploma, Teachers College, Cairo, 1945; Diploma of Higher Education, University of London, London, UK, 1951; *Career:* Head of the Cultural Office, Cairo, Egypt, 1945–50; Director of Education, Kuwait, 1952–61; Representative of Kuwait to the UN, 1961; Ambassador of Kuwait to Egypt, and Representative of Kuwait to the Arab League, 1961–63; Minister of State for Cabinet Affairs, 1963–65; Minister of State for Cabinet Affairs, 1971–; Director of the National Council for Culture, Arts and Literature; *Publications: Arab Society in Kuwait,* a collection of articles and papers; Founder of the review of the Kuwaiti Mission in Cairo; *Decorations:* several decorations from various countries; *Interests and Recreations:* Arabic culture; Head of the Committee of Cultural Planning; Chairman of the Board of Trustees of the Institute of the History of Arabic and Islamic Sciences, University of Frankfurt, Germany; Trustee of the Kuwait Institute for Scientific Affairs; *Languages:* Arabic, English; *Address:* Council of Ministers Secretariat, Kuwait; telephone: 430133.

HUSSAIN, Abdul Razzak, Kuwaiti official/ businessman; born 1939, Kuwait; married; two sons; *Religion:* Muslim; *Education:* BSc in Petroleum Engineering, University of California, Berkeley, USA; *Career:* Kuwait Oil Company; Assistant Under Secretary, Ministry of Oil; Deputy Chairman and Managing Director Planning Administration and Finance, Kuwait Petroleum Corporation, 1980; Chairman and Managing Director, Kuwait Foreign Petroleum Exploration Co; member of the Board of Santa Fe International Corporation; member of the Kuwait Institute for Scientific Research; member of the International Energy Development Corporation; member of the Arabian Oil Company; *Languages:* Arabic, English; *Address:* Kuwait Petroleum Corporation, P O Box 26565 Safat, Kuwait; telephone: 466466, 421979.

HUSSAIN, Aziza, Egyptian politician/women's leader; born 30 May, 1919, Gharbiyah Governorate, Egypt; married; *Religion:* Muslim; *Education:* BA in Social Science, American University of Cairo, Cairo, Egypt, 1942; Certificate, Institute of Criminological Research, Cairo, 1970; Certificate, International Academy, Helsinki, Finland, 1971; *Career:* organised pilot social work projects in cooperation with other women leaders in rural areas, for child welfare and family planning; campaigned for women's rights; organised a series of lectures on social development of rural Egypt, 1949; organised and chaired Village Committee at Cairo's Women's Club; Representative of Egypt, UN Commission on the Status of Women, 1962–77; organised social welfare societies for population and family planning, 1963; member of the Ad Hoc Committee of Experts on Fertility Studies, UN, 1966; founder and Chairman of the Board of Cairo Branch of Egyptian Family Planning Association, 1967; member of UN Advisory Mission of Family Planning to Pakistan, 1968; member of the Family Law Committee of the Ministry of Social Affairs; assisted in the creation of Arab Women's Commission of the Arab League, 1971; represented the Arab League at UN International Seminar on the Status of Women and Family Planning, Istanbul, Turkey, 1972; member of the Governing Body of International Planned Parenthood Federation (IPPF), 1966–, and Vice President for the Middle East and North Africa, 1971; elected President for the International Planned Parenthood Federation (IPPE), 1977; represented the IPPF at various international conferences; attended numerous conferences on women's rights, family planning; *Decorations:* Order of Merit, Egypt, 1977; selected by FAO to represent Goddess Ceres on the FAO Medal, 1975 on the occasion of International Women's Year; elected by UN ECOSOC as member of the Board of Trustees of the UN International Institute for Training and Research for the Advancement of Women (INSTRAW), 1979; *Interests and Recreations:* classical music, general interests in the

arts, reading, walking, yoga; *Languages:* Arabic, English, French; *Address:* 10 Ahmad Nassim Street, Giza, Cairo, Egypt.

HUSSAIN BIN TALAL, HM King of Jordan; born 14 November 1935; son of late King Talal; married 1955 Princess Dina Abdel Hamid; one daughter Princess Alia 1956; married 1961, Antoinette Gardiner (assumed name of Muna al-Hussain); two sons Prince Abdullah, 1962, Prince Faisal, 1963; twin daughters Princess Zein, Princess Aisha, 1968; married 1972, Alia Toukan, (died February 1977), daughter of Bahaeddin Toukan; one daughter Princess Haya, 1974, one son Prince Ali, 1975; married 1978 Nur Halaby; one son Prince Hamzah, 1980; *Religion:* Muslim; *Education:* Bishops School, Amman, Jordan; Victoria College, Alexandria, Egypt; Harrow School, UK; Royal Military Academy, Sandhurst, UK, 1952–53; *Career:* succeeded his father King Talal, 11 August, 1952; acceded to throne 2 May, 1953; *Publications:* Uneasy Lies the Head, 1962; *My War with Israel,* 1967; *Decorations:* Order of Renaissance; Order of the Star of Jordan; Order of Independence; numerous other decorations; *Languages:* Arabic, English; *Address:* Royal Palace, Amman, Jordan.

HUSSAIN, HH Prince Naif Bin Abdullah Bin al, Jordanian Prince; born 1914, Taif, son of late King Abdullah Bin al-Hussain; married; two sons; *Religion:* Muslim; *Education:* Victoria College, Alexandria, Egypt; *Career:* Second Lieutenant, the Arab Army, 1934; Chief of the Tribes Court of Appeal, 1939; Prince Regent several times during the absence of his father King Abdullah; Prince Regent at the death of his father and before King Talal Bin Hussain became King; *Decorations:* Order of the Jordanian Star; Order of Independence, Jordan; Order of Renaissance, Jordan; Order of Rafidain, Iraq; other decorations from Turkey and Spain; *Interests and Recreations:* riding, polo, football, cricket, hunting, fishing; *Languages:* Arabic, Turkish, English; *Address:* Royal Palace, Amman, Jordan; telephone: 37 341.

HUSSAIN, HH Prince Raad Bin Zaid al-, Jordanian politician; born 18 February 1936, Berlin, Germany; son of Amir Zaid al-Hussain; married; five children; *Religion:* Muslim; *Education:* Victoria College, Alexandria, Egypt, 1947–56; BA and MA,

Christ's College, Cambridge University, UK, 1956–63; *Career:* Research Assistant, Middle East Centre, Cambridge University, 1960–62; 1st Chamberlain to the Royal Hashemite Court, Amman, 1963–65; Director General, Jordanian Youth Welfare Organization, 1965–74; President, Jordan Olympic Committee, 1965–74; Minister of the Royal Hashemite Court, 1974–75; Lord Chamberlain to the Royal Hashemite Court; *Decorations:* Jordanian Order of Renaissance, 1964; Order of Jordanian Star, 1965; KCVO, UK, 1966; *Interests and Recreations:* squash, wind surfing, tennis, skiing, Karate, Brown Belt; private pilot's licence; President of the Jordanian Radio Amateur Association; Honorary President of the Friendship Society for the Blind; President of the Friendship Society for the Jordanian Eye Bank; President of the Sports Federation for the Handicapped; *Languages:* Arabic, English, Turkish, French; *Address:* Royal Palace, Amman 37341, Jordan.

HUSSAIN, HH Princess Fakhrilnissa Zaid al-, Jordanian painter; born 1905, Istanbul, Turkey; married; one son, one daughter; *Religion:* Muslim; *Education:* Academy of Fine Arts, Istanbul; *Career:* painter; numerous international exhibitions; President, National Royal Jordanian Fakhrilnissa Institute of Fine Arts, Amman, Jordan; *Publications:* Dictionnaire de la Peinture Abstraite, Michel Seuphor, 1957; *Decorations:* Order of Jordanian Star, 1981; Order of the Rafidain, Iraq, 1956; *Interests and Recreations:* painting; *Languages:* Arabic, French, English, Turkish, Italian, Greek, German; *Address:* c/o Prince Raad al-Hussain, Royal Palace, Amman, Jordan.

HUSSAIN, HM Queen Nour al-, Queen of Jordan; born 23 August 1951; married King Hussain of Jordan 1978; one son, Prince Hamzah, born 1980; *Education:* BA in Architecture and Design, Princeton University, USA, 1974; *Career:* participated in studies for plans and designs for modern cities in Sydney, Australia, 1974–75; participated with plans for Shahistan Pahlaoi Project, Iran, 1975–76; participated in studies of Architecture and Planning in Philadelphia and New York; Director of Planning and Design, ALIA, the Royal Jordanian Airlines, 1977; participated in the special studies of establishing the Aviation Academy in Amman; *Interests and Recrea-*

tions: reading, photography, water sports, tennis; *Address:* Royal Palace, Amman, Jordan.

HUSSAIN, Hussain, Lebanese politician/trade unionist; born 1924, Beirut, Lebanon; married; nine children; *Education:* St. John University, USA; studied trade union movements in the UK, Italy and Germany; *Career:* President, Lebanese Workers and Employees' Union; President, Lebanese Bakers' Union; member of the Higher National Economy Council; member of the Board, and Secretary General of the Central Office for Social Security, Lebanon; member of the Labour Arbitration Council in South Lebanon; representative of the workers on the Board of the Trade Union Health Department; *Decorations:* Gold Medal, Lebanese Order of Merit, 1957; Labour Medal, 1965; *Interests and Recreations:* social affairs, swimming; member of Charitable Youth Organization of Abbassieh College; *Languages:* Arabic, French, English; *Address:* Office — Bourj Hammoud, Khalil Ghossoub Building, Beirut, Lebanon; Residence -- Place des Canons, Rivoli Building, Beirut, Lebanon.

HUSSAIN, Karim Muhammad, Iraqi politician/engineer; born 1942, Baghdad, Iraq; *Religion:* Muslim; *Education:* Mechanical Engineering, University of Baghdad, 1971; *Career:* joined Iraqi Baath Party, 1958; Chairman, National Union of Iraqi Students, 1969–74; elected Chairman of General Federation of Iraqi Youth, 1974; Under Secretary, Ministry of Youth, 1975–77; member of Council of Baghdad Branch of Iraqi Baath Party; Minister of Youth, 1977; *Address:* Ministry of Youth, Baghdad, Iraq.

HUSSAIN, Saddam, President of the Republic of Iraq; born 1937, Tikrit, Iraq; married; two sons, three daughters; *Education:* Law in Egypt, 1961; Degree, College of Law, Baghdad University, 1971; *Career:* joined Arab Baath Socialist Party (ABSP), 1956; participated in attempt to overthrow Abdul Karim Qassim, 1959; sentenced to death in absentia; Member of Regional Leadership, 1963; imprisoned, 1964–66; elected member of the National Leadership while in prison, 1965; escaped from prison, 1966; Vice Secretary General of ABSP, 1966; Vice Chairman of Revolutionary Command Council (RCC), de facto, 1968–, officially, 1969; re-elected member of the National

Leadership of ABSP, 1970; member of National Leadership, Assistant Secretary General, 1977–79; awarded rank of Lieutenant General (Staff) for his efforts in constructing Iraqi Armed Forces, 1976; promoted to Field Marshal (Staff), 1979; Vice Secretary General of ABSP; Secretary General, Regional Leadership of ABSP; Chairman of the Revolutionary Command Council, President of the Republic of Iraq, 1979–; *Publications:* several political and philosophical treatises; *Decorations:* Rafidain Order (Civilian), 1974; Rafidain Order 1st Class (Military), 1976; *Address:* The President's Office, Baghdad, Iraq.

HUSSAINI, Amin Yunis al-, Jordanian politician; born 17 December 1925, Jerusalem; married; one son, one daughter; *Religion:* Muslim; *Education:* BA in Economic Sciences, American University of Beirut, AUB, Lebanon; Diploma in Law, Jerusalem; Diploma in Cooperation, UK; MA in Administration, St. Louis, USA; *Career:* Cooperative Consultant in Sudan, 1951–53; Minister of Foreign Affairs and Social Welfare, 1963–65; Minister of Transport, 1967–70; Secretary General, Federation of Jordanian Chambers of Commerce and the National Committee of the International Chamber of Commerce; *Decorations:* Order of the Jordanian Star; *Interests and Recreation:* swimming; member of the Royal Automobile Club, of Al-Hussain Sport City, of several charitable societies; *Languages:* Arabic, English, French; *Address:* Federation of Jordanian Chambers of Commerce, P O Box 7029 Amman, Jordan; telephone: 665 492.

HUSSAINI, Haidar Rafiq, Jordanian UN official/bacteriologist; born 30 August 1920, Jerusalem; married; *Education:* AB, 1943; Fellowship in Botany, American University of Beirut, Lebanon, 1945–46; Graduate Studies, University of California, USA, 1946–51; *Career:* University of California, 1949–51; Director of Health Laboratory Service, Amman, Jordan, 1952–63; Regional Adviser, Health Laboratory Service, Regional Office for Eastern Mediterranean, WHO, Alexandria, Egypt, 1963–80; *Publications:* co-author *Cellular Reactions to Phthalic Acid and Related Branched Chain Acids,* 1965; *Interests and Recreations:* tennis, football, microbiology, genetics, biochemistry, immunology; *Languages:* Arabic, English; *Address:* Beirut, Lebanon; telephone: 808511.

HUSSAINI, Khairy al-; Egyptian aviation official; *Education:* BA in Law and Economics, 1957; MA in Law and Administration, Cairo University, Cairo, Egypt, 1964; MA in Law, Institute of Air and Space Law, McGill University, Montreal, Canada; PhD in Law, Cairo University, 1976; *Career:* Legal Member, Egyptian Civil Aviation Authority, 1957; part time Lecturer in Civil Aviation Law, Cairo Institute of Civil Aviation, 1967; Director General, International Air Conventions Bureau, Civil Aviation Authority, (ICAO), 1970; Vice Chairman of the ICAO Legal Committee, 1974–; Instructor, International Organization of Air Transport, Al-Azhar University, Cairo, Egypt, 1977–78; Representative of Egypt on the ICAO Council, 1978–; participated in numerous international conferences under the auspices of ICAO, AFCAC and ACAC; *Publications:* numerous articles, papers and books; *Languages:* Arabic, English, French; *Address:* Residence— 32 Dimashk Street, Madinat al-Muhandissin, Dokki, Cairo, Egypt; Office— Civil Aviation Authority, 31 26th of July Street, Cairo, Egypt.

HUSSAINI, Muhyiddin M. al-, Jordanian diplomat/economist; born 1930, Bethlehem, Palestine; married; two sons; *Religion:* Muslim; *Education:* BA in Economics, American University of Beirut, Lebanon; MA, Stanford University, California, USA; *Career:* financial and planning economist, Jordan Development Council, 1960–64; member of Chamber of Deputies, 1965–72; Minister of Communications, 1972–74; Ambassador to Kuwait, 1975–79; Ambassador to Iran, 1979; Ambassador to Morocco, 1980–; *Decorations:* Star of Jordan, 1st Class, 1974; *Interests and Recreations:* Arabic poetry, travel, riding, tennis; President of Al-Urwa al-Wuthqa Society, Amman, 1964–71; *Languages:* Arabic, English; *Address:* Ministry of Foreign Affairs, P O Box 1577, Amman, Jordan; Jordan Embassy, Morocco.

HUWAIDI, Amin, Egyptian politician/diplomat; born 21 September 1921; *Religion:* Muslim; *Education:* Military Staff College, Egypt; General Staff College, Fort Leavenworth, USA; Press College, Egypt; *Career:* Army Officer; Political Counsellor to President Gamal Abdel Nassir; Ambassador to Morocco, 1962; Ambassador to Iraq, 1963–65; Minister of State; Minister of National Guidance; Minister of War, 1965–

243

70; Director of General Intelligence, 1967–69; *Publications: How do the Zionist Leaders Think?*, 1974; *Arab Security*, 1975; *The Israeli-Arab War 1967*, 1976; *Languages:* Arabic, English; *Address:* Ministry of Foreign Affairs, Cairo, Egypt.

HUZAYIN, Sulaiman Ahmad, Egyptian academic; born 1909; *Religion:* Muslim; *Education:* Cairo University, Egypt; Liverpool and Manchester Universities, UK; *Career:* Lecturer, Cairo University, 1935; Director General, Cultural Relations, Ministry of Education, Cairo, 1950; Under Secretary of State for Education, Cairo, 1954; Rector, University of Assiut, Egypt, 1955–65; Minister of Culture, 1965–66; member, Institute d'Egypte, 1947–; President, Institut d'Egypte, 1954; member of International Council for the Study of Geography of Africa and Asia, 1956; member of Permanent Committee of Social Affairs, League of Arab States; *Publications: Some Contributions of the Arabs to Geography*, 1932; *Some New Light on the Beginnings of Egyptian Civilization*, 1937; *The Place of Egypt in Prehistory*, 1941; *Arabia and the Far East*, 1942; and numerous articles; *Languages:* Arabic, English, French; *Address:* c/o Institut d'Egypte, 13 Sharia Shaikh Rihane, Cairo, Egypt.

I

IBEIDAT, Khalid Abdullah, Jordanian diplomat; born 6 December 1937, Ajloun, Jordan; married; one son, two daughters; *Education:* BA in Political Sciences, Cairo University, 1960; MA and PhD, Sorbonne University, France; *Career:* Ministry of Foreign Affairs, 1962; 3rd Secretary, 1963; 2nd Secretary, 1967; 1st Secretary, 1971; Counsellor, 1975; Minister Plenipotentiary, 1978; Ambassador, 1980; Lecturer at Jordanian University; *Interests and Recreations:* swimming, jogging, squash; *Languages:* Arabic, English, French; *Address:* 6 Dhahyat Al-Hussain, Amman, Jordan; telephone: 66473.

IBISH, Yusuf Hussain, Lebanese academic; born 1926, Damascus, Syria; married; two sons, one daughter; *Religion:* Muslim; *Education:* BA and MA Political Studies, American University of Beirut, AUB, Lebanon; PhD, Islamic Studies, Harvard University, USA: *Career:* Assistant Professor, AUB, 1953–56; Teacher, Fellow at Harvard University, USA, 1958–60; Associate Professor, AUB, 1960–66; Professor at Dartmouth University, USA, 1966–67; Professor of Political Studies and Public Administration, AUB, 1967–; *Publications: Al-Baqillani's Doctrine of the Imamate; Islamic Political Theory,* 1965; *Traditional Modes of Contemplation and Action,* and several other works; *Interests and Recreations:* swimming, hunting; *Languages:* Arabic, French, English; *Address:* American University of Beirut, Beirut, Lebanon; telephone: 340740.

IBRAHIM, Abdul Aziz al Sayyid, Egyptian official/educationalist; born 30 April 1907; *Religion:* Muslim; *Education:* Teachers' College and Higher Institute of Education, Cairo, Egypt; PhD, Ohio State University, USA; *Career:* Lecturer in Mathematics, Military Academy, Cairo; Professor of Education and Head of Department, Ain Shams University, Cairo; Vice Rector, Cairo University; Rector, Khartoum Branch, Cairo University; Rector, Alexandria University; Minister of Higher Education; Minister of Education; Visiting Professor, Columbia University, New York, USA; Director General, Arab League Educational, Cultural and Scientific Organization (ALECSO); member of Arabic Language Academy, Egypt; member of Scientific Academy, Iraq; *Publications: The Slide Rule for Military Cadets,* 1939; *The Preparation of Teachers in Arab States,* 1954; *The University and Culture,* 1960; *Decorations:* from Egypt, Lebanon, Morocco, Tunisia, Jordan, East Germany; *Languages:* Arabic, English; *Address:* Residence — 52 Merghani Street, Heliopolis, Cairo, Egypt.

IBRAHIM, Abdul Aziz al-Tayib, Sudanese academic/agriculturalist; born 9 June 1932, Khartoum, Sudan; married; five sons; *Education:* BSc, Cairo University, Egypt; MSc, University of Khartoum; MPH, Minnesota, USA; PhD, Minnesota, USA; *Career:* Lecturer, University of Khartoum, 1967; Senior Lecturer, University of Khartoum, 1971; FAO Expert as Reader, Makarere University, Uganda, 1975–77; FAO Expert, Veterinary Investigation Officer, Hama, Syria, 1977–78; Professor, University of Khartoum, 1979; Professor and Head of Department of Preventive Medicine and Public Health, Faculty of Veterinary Science, University of Khartoum; member of WHO Expert Panel of Food Hygiene, 1968–75; *Publications:* numerous scientific articles published in journals in Sudan, Egypt, UK, USA and Kenya; *Interests and Recreations:* tennis, photography; *Languages:* Arabic, English; *Address:* Faculty of Agriculture and Veterinary Sciences, Post Office, Khartoum, Sudan; The Sudan Journal of Veterinary Science and Animal Husbandry, P O Box 32, Khartoum North, Sudan; telephone: Office — 34175, Residence — 33133.

IBRAHIM, Abdul Kadir, Egyptian ILO official; born 29 December 1923, Cairo, Egypt; *Religion:* Muslim; *Education:* BA, American University in Cairo, Egypt, 1947–51; MA, Chicago University, Chicago, Illinois, USA, 1951–52; PhD, Princeton University, Princeton, New Jersey, 1955–57; *Career:* Research in Management, Manpower and Labour Problems in Egypt, Department of Labour and National Planning Commission, 1946–55; Research Staff, Industrial Relations Section, Princeton University, Princeton, New Jersey, USA, 1955–57; Staff Member, Field Service Department and Labour Management Relations Branch, ILO, Geneva, 1957–62; Staff Member, ILO Near and Middle East Field Office, Istanbul, Turkey, 1962–65; Senior Member, Management Development Branch, ILO, Geneva, 1965–67; Deputy Director, ILO Regional Office for Africa, Addis Adaba, Ethiopia, 1967–68; Head of Research and Studies Section, Management Development Branch ILO, Geneva, 1969–73; Director, ILO Area Office, Islamabad, Pakistan, 1973; *Publications: Training Managers for Development: Methods and Techniques (et al)*, published by UN Institute for Training and Research in *The Making of the Manager,* New York, 1974; *Socio-Economic Changes in Egypt 1952–64,* in Arthur M. Ross (ed), *Industrial Relations and Economic Development,* London, 1966; *Human Resources for Egyptian Enterprise (et al)*, New York 1958; also translated into Arabic; *Some Labour Problems of Industrialization in Egypt (et al)* in *Annals of the American Academy of Political and Social Science,* Philadelphia May 1956; *Interests and Recreations:* general reading, swimming, skiing, mountain walking, philately; *Languages:* Arabic, English, French; *Address:* c/o ILO Area Office, UN Building, 18 Sixth Avenue, Ramna 5, P O Box 1047, Islamabad, Pakistan.

IBRAHIM, Hassan, Jordanian diplomat; born 1928, Jenin, Palestine; married; *Religion:* Muslim; *Education:* BA in Politics and Law, American University of Beirut, Lebanon; MA in History, American University of Beirut, Lebanon, 1952; Diploma in General Administration from UN, 1958; MA in Public Administration, New York University, USA, 1959; *Career:* teacher in Kuwait schools, 1952–53; employee in Ministry of Economy, 1953–54; Chief Clerk in Ministry of Finance, 1954–5; served in Civil Service Commission, 1956–59; 1st Secretary at Ministry of Foreign Affairs, 1959–61; Adviser at Ministry of Foreign Affairs, 1961–63; Minister Plenipotentiary, Embassy to Egypt, 1965–68; Ambassador of Jordan to the Arab Council of Economic Unity, 1968–69; Ambassador to the Soviet Union, 1969–73; Ambassador at Ministry of Foreign Affairs, 1973; Head of Political Department in Ministry of Foreign Affairs, 1973; Secretary General of Ministry of Foreign Affairs, 1973–76; Minister of State for Foreign Affairs, 1976; Minister of Reconstruction and Development, 1976; Minister of State, 1979; Minister of the Occupied Territories Affairs, 1980; *Address:* Jabal Amman, Amman, Jordan; telephone: 44564.

IBRAHIM, Hassan, Egyptian official; born 1917, Egypt; married; *Religion:* Muslim; *Education:* Egyptian Military and Air Force Academies; *Career:* member of the Free Officers Committee, which led 1952 Revolution; member of the Revolutionary Council, 1952–56; Director of the Office of the Chief of Air Staff and member of the Revolutionary Tribunal; Minister of State for Presidential Affairs, 1954; Minister of National Production and Planning, 1955–56; Chairman, National Economic Development Organisation, 1957–59; Chairman and Managing Director, Paints and Chemical Industries, 1959–; Chairman of Al-Nasr Company, National Economic Development Organisation, 1961–; member of the Presidential Council, 1962; Vice President, 1964–65; President, Middle East Finance and Consultation Company, Egyptian Granite Company, Egyptian Catering and Contracting Company, 1974–; *Decorations:* Nile Collar, 1956; *Languages:* Arabic, English; *Address:* 6 Khartoum Street, Heliopolis, Cairo, Egypt.

IBRAHIM, Izziddin, Egyptian academic/official; resident in United Arab Emirates; born 1928, Cairo, Egypt; *Religion:* Muslim; *Education:* Arabic Literature, Cairo University, Egypt; PhD, University of London, UK; *Career:* taught and held educational posts in Libya, Syria and Qatar; Professor of Arabic Literature, Riyadh University, Saudi Arabia, 1967–; active in Islamic affairs and work of the Islamic Conference, Jeddah; Cultural Adviser to the President of United Arab Emirates and Rector of UAE University; *Publications:* co-author of numerous textbooks; *Address:* President's Office, Abu Dhabi, United Arab Emirates.

IBRAHIM, Moulay Abdallah, Moroccan politician; born 1918, Marrakesh, Morocco; married; four children; *Religion:* Muslim; *Education:* Ben Youssef University, 1946–50; Sorbonne, University of Paris, France; training course, USSR, 1956; *Career:* active in nationalist movement; associated with Comité d'Action Marocaine; later member of the Council of the Mouvement Populaire (National Party); member of the Higher Executive of the Istiqlal Party, 1944; Chief Editor of *Al-Alam,* 1950; arrested for nationalist political activity on numerous occasions, 1936–52; Secretary of State for Information, attached to the Prime Minister's Office, 1955; Minister of Labour and Social Affairs, 1956; Prime Minister, 1958; Secretary of the Casablanca Chamber of Commerce and Industry, 1961–62; re-elected to the Secretariat-General and other leading bodies of the Union Nationale des Forces Populaires (UNFP), 1962; member of the joint Political Council of the UNFP and the Union Marocaine de Travail, 1967; one of the leaders who organized Istiqlal/UNFP National Bloc to boycott parliamentary elections, August 1970; *Interests and Recreations:* reading, western classical music; *Languages:* Arabic, French; *Address:* Union Nationale des Forces Populaires, P O Box 747, Casablanca, Morocco.

IBRAHIM, Muhsin, Palestinian politician; born 1923; *Education:* American University of Beirut, Lebanon; *Career:* appointed member of the Administrative Council of the Arab Nationalist Movement (ANM), 1959; member of the Lebanese delegation at the Afro-Asian Solidarity Congress in Beirut, 1960; Secretary General of the ANM and Editor of ANM Newspaper *Al-Hurriyah,* 1963; received an official invitation to visit China, 1964; *Al-Hurriyah* expressed views of the Popular Front for the Liberation of Palestine (PFLP) on the latter's formation, but in 1969 following Ibrahim's accession to the Popular Democratic Front for the Liberation of Palestine (PDFLP) *Al-Hurriyah* became the latter's official newspaper; Head of PDFLP External Affairs Department, 1970; elected member of Presidium of Arab Front for Palestine, December 1974.

IBRAHIM, Rashid Ibrahim Sultan, United Arab Emirates administrator; born 1948; married; one daughter; *Religion:* Muslim; *Education:* BA in English Literature,

Baghdad University, Iraq; *Career:* Director of Youth and Sports Office, United Arab Emirates, 1972; Head of Personnel Section, Personnel Department; Director of Personnel Affairs, Abu Dhabi, 1974–; *Interests and Recreations:* table-tennis, travel; attempts to write short stories and plays in English; *Languages:* Arabic, French, English; *Address:* Personnel Affairs Department, Abu Dhabi, United Arab Emirates.

IBRAHIM, Saad Ahmad, Sudanese academic/physician; born 10th October 1931, Khartoum; married; two daughters; three sons; *Religion:* Muslim; *Education:* Kitchener School of Medicine, 1957; PhD, Guy's Hospital Medical School, 1964; member of the Royal College of Physicians, London, 1979; *Career:* Medical Officer, Ministry of Health, 1957–59; Research Assistant, Faculty of Medicine, 1960; Lecturer in Biochemistry, Faculty of Medicine, 1964; Senior Lecturer, 1968; Professor, 1972; Director, Board for Post-Graduate Medical Studies, 1976–77; Chairman, Medical Research Council, Sudanese National Council for Research, 1977–79; Dean, Faculty of Medicine, 1977–; WHO Visiting Professor to Aleppo Medical School, Syria, 1969–70; member, Biochemical Society, England, 1962, the International Society on Toxicology, Geneva, 1970; *Publications:* numerous books, research papers, analysis on haemoglobinopathis, inborn errors of metabolism and toxicology of snake and scorpion venoms; *Interests and Recreations:* reading, fishing, hunting; *Languages:* Arabic, English; *Address:* Faculty of Medicine, P O Box 102, Khartoum, Sudan; telephone: 72224, 76430.

IBRAHIM, Sun'allah, Egyptian writer; born 1937, Cairo, Egypt; *Education:* Law studies; *Career:* journalist; in prison for political activities, 1959–64; travelled to Lebanon 1968, East Berlin, and Moscow where he studied film-making; returned to Cairo, Egypt; published various short story collections; *Languages:* Arabic, English; *Address:* The General Egyptian Book Organization, Corniche el Nil, Cairo, Egypt.

IBRAHIMI, Talib Ahmad, Algerian politician/physician; born 5 January 1932, Setif, Algeria; married; two children; *Religion:* Muslim; *Education:* MD, Haematology; *Career:* Head, Delegation of Algeria, UNESCO, 1966, 1968, 1974; Leader, General

247

Union of Algerian Muslim Students, 1955; member of the National Liberation Front Federation, France, 1956; imprisoned by French authorities for political activities, 1957–62; Minister of National Education, 1965–70; Minister of Information and Culture, 1970–77; Minister and Adviser, President of the Republic Office, 1977–82; Minister of Foreign Affairs, 1982–; member of the Executive Board of UNESCO, 1968–74; member, Arab Academy, Damscus, Syria and Cairo; *Publications: Letters de Prison,* 1966; *De la Decolonisation a la Revolution Culturelle,* 1972; *Languages:* Arabic, French; *Address:* Ministry of Foreign Affairs, 6 Rue Ibn Batram el-Mouradia, Algiers, Algeria; telephone: 600585/9.

IDILBY, Ziad H., Arab-American banker; born 1 June 1937, Damascus, Syria; married; two sons; *Religion:* Muslim; *Education:* BA, American University of Beirut AUB, Lebanon, 1960; MBA in Investment Banking and Finance, American University, Washington D.C., USA, 1960–62; PhD in Business Administration and Finance, American University, Washington D.C., 1963–65; *Career:* First National Bank of Chicago (FNBC), 1966–81, Assistant Cashier,1968; Assistant Vice President, 1969; Acting Head of Latin America and the Carribean, International Banking Department, 1971; Elected Vice President; Chairman and General Manager, FNBC SAL, Lebanon, 1972; Head of Middle East and North Africa Region, 1974; Area Head for Middle East and Africa, London, 1975; Senior Vice President, 1975; Area Head for Europe, Middle East and Africa, London, 1978; Head of the International Banking Division, Chicago, 1981; resigned from FNBC, 1981; President, Saudi Investment and Finance Corporation (Holdings) SA, London, 1981–; member of the Boards of First National Bank of Chicago, SAL, Lebanon, Misr International Bank, Cairo, International Merchant Bank of Nigeria, Lagos, First National Bank of Chicago Ltd, London, International Commercial Bank, London, UBAF Arab American Bank, New York; *Publications: Scope and Incentive in the Private Sector Afforded by Economic Community in Syria, Iraq, Jordan and Lebanon,* PhD dissertation; *Interests and Recreations:* theatre, squash, tennis, swimming; member of Annabels Club, Les Ambassadeurs Club, Marks Club, Queens Lawn Tennis Club, Hurlingham Club; *Lang-*

uages: Arabic, English; *Address:* Saudi Investment Services (UK) Limited, 7 Old Park Lane, London SW1, UK; telephone: (01) 409 3464; telex: 263763 SAUDIN.

IDRIS, Abdullah Bin Abdul Aziz Bin, Saudi Arabian official/educationalist; born 1930; *Religion:* Muslim; *Education:* BA in Arabic Language and Islamic Law; *Career:* Inspector and Director, Examination Board, Ministry of Education; General Manager, Technical Education, Ministry of Education; Secretary General, Higher Council for Promotion of Arts and Letters; Editor and General Manager, *Al-Da'wa* daily newspaper; member of several boards of local organizations; member of Society of Modern Literature, Egypt; member of the Boards of King Abdul Aziz Research Centre, Riyadh, the Higher Council for Promotion of Arts and Letters, Da'wa Islamiyah; Director of Riyadh Literary Club; member of the Editorial Board of the Periodical of King Abdul Aziz Research Centre; founder of Campaign Against Illiteracy; Saudi Representative, Literary Festival, Basra, Iraq, 1974; member, Tenth Conference of Arab Men of Letters, Algiers, 1975; General Director of Publication and Culture, Imam Muhammad Bin Saud Islamic Centre; *Publications:* contributions to local press and radio for over 20 years; several books on literary criticism, politics and social issues; two collections of poems; textbooks for high school education; *Najd Contemporary Poets; Decorations:* Badge of First Conference of Saudi Men of Letters, King Abdul Aziz University; *Address:* Imam Muhammad Bin Saud University, P O Box 5701, Riyadh, Saudi Arabia; telephone: Office — 405 4055; Residence — 476 1003.

IDRIS, Hussain, Sudanese official/agriculturalist; born 1924, Wadi Medani, Sudan; *Religion:* Muslim; *Education:* BSc in Agriculture, University of Khartoum, 1950; BSc in Botany, Imperial College, University of London, UK, 1957; PhD in Agricultural Botany, University of Nottingham, 1963; *Career:* Agricultural Officer for Mechanised Crop Production Schemes, near Gedaref, 1950–52; Inspector of Agriculture, Sudan Northern Province, 1952–53; Lecturer in Crop Husbandry, University of Khartoum, 1953–54; Agronomist and Director of Tozi Research Station in Sudan, 1957–60; Deputy Director , Agricultural Research Division, Ministry of Agriculture, Wadi Medani,

1963–64; Director General of the Sudan Agricultural Research Corporation, Wadi Medani, 1964–70; FAO Regional Consultant on Agricultural Research, Cairo, 1971; FAO Project Manager, Agricultural Research and Training, People's Democratic Republic of Yemen, 1972–73; Minister of State for Research and Services Ministry of Agriculture, Food and Natural Resources, Khartoum, 1973–77; Co-ordinator, UNDP Project to establish Cotton Development International , New York, 1977–79; Director of the Special Unit for Technical Cooperation among Developing Countries (TCDC), UNDP, New York, 1979–; *Publications:* author of several research papers on cotton, sorghum and maize, and on the organisation and administration of agricultural research in the Sudan and in the Near East; *Languages:* Arabic, English; *Address:* 1 United Nations Plaza, New York NY 10017; telephone: 754 1234

IDRIS, Lieutenant Colonel Jum'a Awadh, Libyan army commander; born circa 1938; married; three daughters; *Religion:* Muslim; *Career:* joined Libyan Army, 1958; attended platoon commanders' course in UK, 1968; attended all-arms tactics course in UK, 1968; Director of Naval Training, 1969; promoted Lieutenant Colonel, 1970; Commander of Air Defences, 1972; participated in Anglo-Libyan talks October 1975 as head of Libyan Air Defence Scheme; *Languages:* Arabic, English; *Address:* c/o Secretariat of the General People's Committee, Tripoli, Libya.

IDRIS, Muhammad Baha Iddin, Sudanese official/businessman; born 1932, Omdurman, Sudan; married; *Religion:* Muslim; *Education:* graduated from the Faculty of Science, University of Khartoum, Sudan, 1955; PhD, West Germany, 1956–59; *Career:* Lecturer in University of Khartoum, 1959; Deputy Secretary General, National Council for Research; Minister of State for Cabinet Affairs, 1972; has extensive business interests in Sudan and Saudi Arabia; *Languages:* Arabic, German; *Address:* c/o Ministry of Cabinet Affairs, Khartoum, Sudan.

IDRIS, Muhammad Khalid, Saudi Arabian physician; born 1912, Damascus, Syria; *Religion:* Muslim; *Education:* MD, American University of Beirut, Lebanon, 1936; *Career:* established Dr Khalid Idris Hospital, 1946; pioneer in the medical services in the Western Region of Saudi Arabia since 1946; Fellow of French Gynaecological Society, Royal Society of Medicine, International College of Surgeons and American College of Surgeons; Director General of Dr Khalid Idris Hospital; *Address:* Dr Khalid Idris Hospital, Jeddah, Saudi Arabia.

IDRIS, Yusuf, Egyptian writer; born 1927, Egypt; *Religion:* Muslim; *Education:* Faculty of Medicine, Cairo University, Egypt, 1945–51; *Career:* practised medicine and published stories in leading periodicals; *Publications:* ten collections of short stories, seven plays, five novels and many collections of essays; plays include *Farahat Republic,* 1955; *King of the Cotton,* 1956; *The Crucial Moment,* 1956; short story collections include *Arkhas Layali,* 1954 and *Lughat al-Ay-Ay,* 1966; *Languages:* Arabic, English; *Address:* Al-Ahram, Galaa Street, Cairo, Egypt.

IDRISS, Suhail, Lebanese writer/editor; born 1925 Beirut, Lebanon; married; one son, two daughters; *Religion:* Muslim; *Education:* two years law studies; PhD in Literature, Sorbonne, Paris, France, 1949–52; Diploma in Journalism, Paris, 1952; *Career:* Professor, Lebanese University, 1953; Professor, Arab University of Beirut, 1954–58; Editor of *Al-Adaab* magazine, 1953–; Director General of Daar al-Adaab for Publishing and Distributing; Secretary General, Lebanese Writers Union, 1968–74; Assistant Secretary General, Asian and African Writers Union, 1974; Deputy Secretary General, Union of Arab Publishers, 1981–; Director of Lebanese Branch of the Union of Arab Writers, 1982–; *Publications:* numerous novels and short story collections; Editor of *Al-Mauhal* Arabic-French Dictionary, 1970; *Decorations:* prizes for literary achievements; *Interests and Recreations:* the novel, the short story, research; member of the Union of Lebanese writers; *Languages:* Arabic, French, English; *Address:* P O Box 4123 Beirut, Lebanon; telephone: 803778.

IMADY, Muhammad, Syrian politician/economist; resident in Kuwait; born 1930, Damascus, Syria; married; two sons, one daughter; *Religion:* Muslim; *Education:* LLB, Damascus University, 1953; Degree in Economics and Financial Studies, University of Damascus, 1953; MA in Economics, University of Damascus, 1958; PhD in Economics, University of New York, 1960;

Career: Lecturer and later Professor, Faculty of Economics and Commerce, Damascus University, 1960–; Assistant Secretary General, Ministry of Economy, 1964–67; Assistant to Minister of Planning, Syria, 1968–71; Minister of Planning, Syria, 1972; Minister of Economics and Foreign Trade, Syria, 1972–79; Chairman and Director General, Arab Fund for Economic and Social Development, Kuwait, Hononary President, Syrian Economic Association; former President, Union of Arab Economists; member of High Council of Sciences, and High Council of Universities; Head of Syrian Delegation to several economic conferences and councils; President of World Bank and Chairman of International Monetary Fund Meetings, Manilla, 1976; participated in the Algerian Conference for preparation of the proprosed Arab Fund for Economic and Social Development, 1967; President, Arab Economic Council and Economic Unity Council, 1975; Chairman, Arab Fund for Economic and Social Development; member of the Syrian People's Council; *Publications: Economic Development and Planning; National Accounts; Participation in Drawing Plans for Economic and Social Development; The Prospects of Economic Growth in the 1980's; Energy as a Source of Wealth in the Middle East; Reflections on Regional Developmnt; Finance and Intercountry Projects; Approach to Integration;* and several other lectures and researches in *Econo* mics and Development; *Interests and Recreations:* reading; *Languages:* Arabic, English, French; *Address:* Arab Fund for Economic and Social Development; P O Box 21923, Kuwait; telephone: 443860; telex: 2143/2153 Kt Inmarabi.

IMAYA, Muhammad Ali al-, People's Democratic Republic of Yemen politician/trade unionist; born 1940; *Career:* Chartered Bank; active in trade union affairs since 1967; elected Head of Bank Officials Union and Treasurer of the General Federation of Workers, 1968; Assistant General Manager of National Bank of Yemen, 1970; Minister of Labour and Social Affairs, 1971–74; *Languages:* Arabic, English; *Address:* c/o National Bank of Yemen, P O Box 5, Aden, People's Democratic Republic of Yemen.

IRHAYIM, Tarik al-, Iraqi engineer; born 3 February 1937, Iraq; married; three sons, two daughters; *Religion:* Muslim; *Education:* BSc in Petroleum Production Engineering, Birmingham University, UK, 1959; PhD in Chemical Engineering, Birmingham University, UK, 1966; *Career:* Army, 1959–61; Assistant Petroleum Engineer, Ministry of Oil, 1961–63; Reservoir Engineer, KOC, Kuwait, 1966–68; Area Reservoir Engineer, IPC, Kirkuk, 1968–70; Senior Petroleum Engineer, 1970–72; Chief Petroleum Engineer, 1972–80; Project Manager, Underground Storage, Northern Petroleum Organization, 1980–; *Publications: Thermal Analogue Studies,* 1965, in *IP* and Chemical Engineering; *Bulk Volume Measurements,* 1964; *Interests and Recreations:* swimming, reading, classical music; *Languages:* Arabic, English, French; *Address:* North Petroleum Organization, P O Box 1, Kirkuk, Iraq; telephone: Kirkuk 5650, 5535; telex: 218611 IR.

IRIYANI, Abdul Karim al-, Yemen Arab Republic politician; born 20 February 1935, Iriyan, Yemen Arab Republic; married; two daughters; *Religion:* Muslim; *Education:* University of Texas, USA; University of Georgia, USA; Yale University, USA; PhD in Biochemical Genetics; *Career:* Director of Wadi Zaid Agricultural Project, 1968–69; Head of Central Planning Organization, 1972–74; Minister of Development and Head of Central Planning Organization, 1974–77; Minister of Education and President of Sana'a University, 1977–78; Agricultural Adviser, Kuwait Fund for Development, 1978–80; Prime Minister, 1980–; *Interests and Recreations:* chess; *Languages:* Arabic, English; *Address:* Prime Minister's Office, Sana'a, Yemen Arab Republic.

IRIYANI, Abdul Rahman al-, Yemen Arab Republic former President; born 1910 Iriyan, Yemen Arab Republic; *Religion:* Muslim; *Education:* Islamic Law and Arabic Studies; *Career:* held positions in judiciary during the period of monarchy; founding member of The Free Yemenes, 1944; arrested for a couple of months, 1944; First Secretary to the Cabinet of Ministers after the Revolution, 1948; arrested for seven years after the failure of the Revolution; Deputy President, High Judicial Committee; took part in the 1955 movement; was arrested thereafter, and sentenced to death; Minister of State in the government which was formed before the 1962 Revolution; Minister of Justice in the first government after the 1962 Revolution; Vice President of the Yemen Arab Republic, 1963, Chairman of the Executive Committee,

Prime Minister, 1964; Chairman of Khams Conference, and of the Republican Representation in Hurd Conference, 1966; President of the Republican Council which is formed of three members, 1967; remained President until June 1974; an authority on Arabic literature and history, and Shari'a (Islamic Law); *Address:* c/o the Presidency, Sana'a, Yemen Arab Republic.

IRSHEID, Walid Jamil, Jordanian banker; born 4 September 1936, Haifa, Palestine; married; two sons, one daughter; *Religion:* Muslim; *Education:* BA in Commerce, University of Damascus, Syria, 1965; *Career:* Banker, Arab Bank Ltd, Latakia, Amman, Nablus, and Dubai branches; Arab Bank Regional Management, Bahrain, 1956-76 Deputy Manager, Société Générale, Bahrain, 1976-; *Interests and Recreations:* reading, music; *Languages:* Arabic, English; *Address:* Société Générale, P O Box 5275, Manama, Bahrain; telephone: Office -- 253641; Residence -- 714669.

IRYANI, Muhammad Abdullah al-, Yemen Arab Republic diplomat/army commander; born 15 July 1942, Yemen; married 1963, one son, five daughters; *Religion:* Muslim; *Education:* Military Academy, 1961; *Career:* appointed to various ranks and positions in the armed forces; Commander of the Northern Province, 1963-64; infantry commander; Deputy Chief of Staff; Deputy Defence Minister; Deputy Commander in Chief of the Armed Forces; member of the Politburo; Commander in Chief of the Armed Forces until 17 June 1974; Ambassador Extraordinary and Plenipotentiary to the UK, 1974-81; *Interests and Recreations:* tennis, swimming; *Languages:* Arabic, English; *Address:* Ministry of Foreign Affairs, Sana'a, Yemen Arab Republic.

ISLAM, Saud Salih, Saudi Arabian journalist; born 1948, Dammam, Saudi Arabia; *Religion:* Muslim; *Education:* BSc in Economics and Chemistry; MSc in Petrochemical Economics and Technology; *Career:* Business and Financial Editor, *Saudi Gazette;* Editor in Chief, *Saudi Gazette,* Saudi Arabian business English language daily; *Publications:* articles in newspapers, research in petrochemicals, research on cross-cultural influence, on managemant behaviour and practice (current PhD thesis); *Address:* Saudi Gazette, P O Box 5576 Jeddah, Saudi Arabia; telephone: 667 402; telex: 400920 SGAZET SJ.

ISMAIL, Abdul Malik, People's Democratic Republic of Yemen diplomat/politician; born 26 November 1936, Aden, People's Democratic Republic of Yemen; *Education:* Maala Technical School; Faculty of Commerce, Cairo University; *Career:* leading member of Arab Nationalist Movement, 1956-63; member of United National Front; Editor, *Al-Nour wal Haqiqa,* 1961-63; Vice Chairman, General Union of Petroleum Workers, 1961-62; Chairman, Petroleum Workers Union, 1962-64; Vice President, Arab Federation of Petroleum Workers, 1962-65; leading member of National Liberation Front, 1963-65; Director, National Front Office, Cairo, 1965-66; member of General Command of National Liberation Front, 1966-68; Minister of Labour and Social Affairs, 1967-68; Minister of Economy, Commerce and Planning, 1968-70; Permanent Representative to United Nations, 1970-73; Ambassador to Egypt, 1973-75; Ambassador to Sudan, 1975; *Address:* People's Democratic Republic of Yeman Embassy, Khartoum, Sudan.

ISMAIL, Abdullah, United Arab Emirates official/oil expert; born 1927; married; children; *Career:* formerly Iraqi Under Secretary for Oil Affairs; formerly Under Secretary in the United Arab Emirates, Ministry of Minerals; Adviser to the Ministry of Petroleum and Mineral Resources, Abu Dhabi; *Languages:* Arabic, English; *Address:* P O Box 59, Abu Dhabi, United Arab Emirates.

ISMAIL, Adel, Lebanese diplomat; born 1925, Dalhoun, Lebanon; *Education:* Docteur ès-Lettres, Sorbonne, University of Paris, France; Licence in Law, Faculty of Law, Lyon, France; Diploma in Historical Studies, University of Paris, France; *Career:* Education Inspector, Ministry of National Education; Assistant Professor of Higher Education; Assistant to the Director General, Ministry of National Education, 1956-59; Counsellor, Embassy to Italy, 1963; Consul General in Milan, Italy; Ambassador to Switzerland, 1966-67; Ambassador to Sudan and Ethiopia, 1967-69; Ambassador to Saudi Arabia, 1969-75; Ambassador to Morocco, 1975-; *Publications: Histoire du Liban..17e Siecle a Nos Jours,* seven volumes, *Le Liban: Histoire d'un Peuple Decorations:* Knight of the National Order of Cedar; various other distinctions from the French Academy; *Languages:* Arabic, French; *Address:* 5 Rue de Tedders, Rabat, Morocco; telephone: 61614.

ISMAIL ALI, Abdul Fattah, People's Democratic Republic of Yemen politician; born 28 July 1939, Aden, People's Democratic Republic of Yemen; married; *Religion:* Muslim; *Career:* member of the Higher Executive Committee of the National Front, 1965; Minister of Culture and Guidance and Yemeni Unity Affairs, 1967; Secretary General of the National Front, 1969; Secretary General of the Central Committee of the National Front; member of the Presidential Council; President of the Higher People's Council; President of the Yemeni Peace and Solidarity Council; leading member of the Afro-Asian Solidarity Council; leading member of the International Peace Council; *Publications:* in Arabic: *The Dawn of Revolution; Our National Culture from Past to Present; The Vanguard Party and its Links with the Yemeni Working Class; The Present and Future of the People's Democratic Republic of Yemen; Political Resolutions of the Fifth and Sixth Conference of the Political Organization of the National Front; The Importance of the Resolutions of the Sixth Conferences to the Completion of National Democratic Revolution; The Political Decision of the Unity Conference for the Political Organization of the National Front; The Popular Democratic Union and the Popular Vanguard Party; Decorations:* Honorary Doctorate, Moscow University, 1976; *Interests and Recreations:* literature, especially poetry; *Languages:* Arabic, English; *Address:* National Front, Aden, People's Democratic Republic of Yemen.

ISMAIL, Fayiz, Syrian politician; born 1923, Antioch; married with children; *Education:* Law, University of Baghdad, Iraq; *Career:* school teacher; joined Socialist Unionist Party on its formation in 1961–62, and currently one of its leaders; Minister for Municipal and Village Affairs, 1967–70; Minister of State, 1970; resigned 1973 for health reasons; member of Afro-Asian Solidarity Committee; leading member of National Progressive Front; *Address:* The National Progressive Front, Unionist Socialist Party, Damascus, Syria.

ISMAIL, Hassan, Egytian academic/ engineering consultant, born 1917; married; one son, three daughters; *Religion:* Muslim; *Education:* BSc in Civil Engineering, Cairo University, 1938; PhD, California Institute of Technology, 1948; specialised in hydraulic engineering, UK and USA; *Career:* Demonstrator, Lecturer and later Professor at Cairo University; Dean of Faculty of Engineering, 1968; Vice Rector for Post Graduate Studies, 1970–71; Rector of Cairo University, 1971; Minister of Education, Culture and Research, 1978–79; President of Academy of Science and Technology, 1979–80; *Languages:* Arabic, English; *Address:* President of PACER Consultants, 3 Hussain Kamal al-Din Street, Dokki, Cairo, Egypt.

ISMAIL, Muhammad Hafiz, Egyptian diplomat; born 1919; married; *Religion:* Muslim; *Education:* Military Academy, Cairo, Egypt; Royal Military Academy, Woolwich, UK, 1937, passed out of Staff College in first position, 1944; *Career:* Military Attaché, Embassy to USA, 1951; Director of the Office of the Commander in Chief, Abdul Hakim Amer; General, 1953–60; Assistant Under Secretary, Ministry of Foreign Affairs, 1960–64; Egyptian Delegate, Geneva Disarmament Conference, 1964; Ambassador to UK, 1965; Ambassador to Italy, 1967; Ambassador to France, 1968; Head of the General Intelligence Service, 1970; Minister of State, 1970; Minister of State for Foreign Affairs, 1971; Adviser to the President for National Security Affairs with rank of Deputy Prime Minister, 1971; Chef de Cabinet to the President and Adviser, 1973; Ministry of Foreign Affairs with rank of Ambassador, 1974; Ambassador to USSR, 1974–77; Ambassador to France, 1977; *Languages:* Arabic, English, French; *Address:* Ministry of Foreign Affairs, Cairo, Egypt.

ISMAIL, Muhammad Othman, Egyptian politician; born 1931, Assiut, Egypt; married; *Religion:* Muslim; *Education:* Law; *Career:* practised law in Assiut; member of the National Assembly, Deputy for Assiut, 1964; elected Secretary of the Arab Socialist Union (ASU), 1968, Governorate Committee for Assiut; elected to Central Committee of ASU; member of Central Committee's Internal Affairs Committee, 1968; re-elected to National Assembly, 1969; Governor of Aswan, 1971; Presidential Adviser for People's Assembly Affairs and Secretary for

Organization, 1972; Governor of Assiut, 1973–; *Address:* Governorate of Assiut, Assiut, Egypt.

ISSA, Fawzi Sultan al-, Kuwaiti banker; born 1944; married; *Religion:* Muslim; *Education:* American University in Beirut, Beirut, Lebanon; *Career:* Managing Director of Bank of Kuwait and the Middle East; Deputy Chairman, International Financial Advisers, investment company with British merchant bank connections; Director of Research to the Kuwait Arab Fund for Economic and Social Development; Director, United Bank of Kuwait, Jordan; *Languages:* Arabic, English; *Address:* International Financial Advisers, P O Box 4694, Fisheries Building, Kuwait; telephone: 448171.

ISSA, Husam Muhammad, Egyptian academic; resident in Japan; born 23 March, 1939, Cairo, Egypt; married; one daughter; *Religion:* Muslim; *Education:* PhD in Law, University of Paris, 1969; *Career:* Head of Faculty of Law, University of Ain Shams, Cairo, Egypt, 1969–76; Visiting Professor, Catholic University of Louvain, 1972–74; Associate Professor, University of Ain Shams, 1976–; United Nations University Programme Officer; *Publications: Capitalisme et Sociétés Anonymes,* LGDJ, Paris, 1970; *The Multi-National Companies,* Arab Organization for Studies and Publications, Beirut, 1980; *Interests and Recreations:* history; *Languages:* Arabic, French, English; *Address:* University UNU, Tokjyo Seimei Building, 15–1 Shibuya, 2 Chomi, ShibuyaKu, Tokyo, Japan; telephone: 499 2811; 2 Mukarar Aljazair Street, Dokki, Cairo, Egypt.

ISSA, Raja Issa al-, Jordanian journalist; born 14 October 1922, Jaffa, Palestine; married; *Religion:* Christian; *Education:* BA in Political Sciences, American University of Beirut, AUB, Lebanon, 1942; Diploma in Journalism, University of Columbia, New York, USA, 1960; *Career:* Journalist, *Palestine* newspaper, Jaffa, 1942–48; Publisher and Editor of *Palestine* in Jerusalem, 1951; Publisher and Editor of *Jerusalem Star,* Jerusalem, 1966; Co-owner of the Jordanian Company for Press and Publishing, 1967; Editor of *Palestine News,* 1978; Deputy Director General, Jordanian Press Organization, publishers of *Al-Ra'i* and *Jordan Times,* 1978–; Founder and Director General,

Jordanian Press Distribution Company; member of the Jordanian Journalists Syndicate; Secretary General of the Arab Distributors Union; *Publications:* numerous articles in Arabic and English in the Jordanian Press; *Interests and Recreations:* reading; *Languages:* Arabic, English, French; *Address:* PO Box 375, Amman, Jordan; telephone: 30191, 30192.

ISSAC, Jacob M., Saudi Arabian journalist/writer; born 1942, Mecca, Saudi Arabia; married; one son, one daughter; *Religion:* Muslim; *Education:* BA and High Diploma in Education; *Career:* Teacher, 1969–72; Administrative Controller, 1973–; Editor in Chief, *Hasan* magazine for children, 1977–80; Editor of children's programmes for Saudi Radio, 1979–; member of the Board of Okaz, Press and Publication Organization; *Publications:* several books and short stories for children; *Interests and Recreations:* football; *Languages:* Arabic, English; *Address:* P O Box 5588, Jeddah, Saudi Arabia; telephone: 6652670, 6652875, 6439142.

ISSAWI, Charles, Arab-American academic; born 15 March 1916, Cairo, Egypt; married; *Religion:* Christian; *Education:* Oxford University, UK; Victoria College, Alexandria, Egypt; *Career:* Ministry of Finance, Cairo, 1937–38; National Bank of Egypt, Cairo, 1938–43; American University of Beirut, Lebanon, 1943–47; Middle East Unit, United Nations Secretariat, 1948–55; Columbia University, New York, USA, 1951–75; Director of Near and Middle East Institute, Columbia University, 1962–64; Bayard Dodge Professor of Near Eastern Studies, Princeton University, New Jersey, USA, 1971–; Advisory Editor of many Middle Eastern journals; John Simon Guggenheim Fellowship, 1961–62, 1968–69; Social Science Research Council Fellowhip, 1962, 1975; American Philosophical Society Fellowship, 1967; member, Council on Foreign Relations, 1959–; member of Board of Editors, Middle Eastern Studies, Columbia University, 1958–; member, Board of Society for International Development, Washington D.C., 1963–65; Consultant to United Nations, 1956, 1958 and Food and Agricultural Organization, 1955, 1965; Vice President, Middle East Studies Association, 1968; President of the Middle East Association, 1973; *Publications: Social Analysis,* 1947, London; *An Arab Philosophy of History,*

1950, London; *Egypt at Mid-Century,* 1954, London; *The Economics of Middle Eastern Oil,* 1962; *Egypt in Revolution,* 1963, London; *The Economic History of the Middle East 1800–1914,* 1966, Chicago; *The Economic History of Iran 1800–1914,* 1971, Chicago; *Issawi's Laws of Social Motion,* New York, 1973; *Oil, The Middle East and the World,* 1972, New York; *The Economic History of Turkey,* 1980, Chicago; *The Arab World's Legacy,* 1981, Princeton; *Economic History of the Middle East and North Africa,* 1982, New York; numerous articles in various publications concerned with history and foreign affairs; *Interests and Recreations:* walking, swimming; *Languages:* Arabic, English, French, German, Russian, Italian, Spanish, Persian; *Address:* Princeton University, Princeton, New Jersey, USA.

ITANI, Khalil, Lebanese diplomat; born 1923, Beirut, Lebanon; married; *Education:* MA in History and Political Science; *Career:* Professor and Journalist until 1946; Head of Press Service, Ministry of Foreign Affairs, 1946–49; Head of UN Section at Press Service, 1949–52; Press Attaché, Embassy to USA, 1952–54; Head of Arab Department, UN Secretariat, 1955–60; 1st Counsellor, Embassy to France, 1960–64; Ambassador to Ghana, also accredited to Togo, Central African Republic and Chad, 1965–67; Ambassador to Saudi Arabia, Libya and Algeria, 1967–75; Ambassador, Ministry of Foreign Affairs, Beirut; member and Head of various Lebanese delegations to the Arab League and the United Nations Sessions, to Arab countries and to the Arab-African Summit held in Cairo, 1975–78; Ambassador to United States of America, 1978–; *Publications: Histoire Diplomatique du Liban, 1840–44; Muhammad Ali Pasha.. His Advocates and His Opponents,* and various articles in journals and magazines; *Decorations:* Commander of the French National Order of Merit; Syrian National Order of Merit; *Languages:* Arabic, French, English: *Address:* Embassy of Lebanon, 2560 28th Street NW Washington, D.C. 20008, USA.

ITAYIM, Fuad Wadih, Lebanese journalist/oil consultant; born 24 June 1929, Beirut, Lebanon; married; two sons, one daughter; *Religion:* Christian; *Education:* BA in Journalism, American University of Cairo, Egypt, 1952; *Career:* Current Affairs Analyst, Arabian American Oil Company (Aramco), Dhahran, Saudi Arabia, 1952–56; began publication of weekly petroleum newsletter *Middle East Economic Survey* in Beirut, 1957; established Middle East Research and Publishing Centre, Beirut, Lebanon, 1959; began publication of bi-annual report *International Crude Oil and Product Prices,* 1972; established Middle East Petroleum and Economic Publications, Beirut, Lebanon, 1972; established Middle East Petroleum and Economic Publications (Cyprus), Nicosia, Cyprus 1976; Director of Middle East Research and Publishing Centre; Director of Middle East Petroleum and Economic Publications; lectured at various international oil conferences and symposiums on Middle East oil affairs; *Publications: Strength and Weaknesses of the Oil Weapon,* Adelphi Papers 155, International Institute for Strategic Studies 1975; *Interests and Recreations:* member of International Institute for Strategic Studies, London; member of the Royal Automobile Club; *Languages:* Arabic, English; *Address:* P O Box 4940, Nicosia, Cyprus; telephone: 74691

IZZIDDIN, Al Sayyid Muhammad, Sudanese politician/businessman; born 1934, Dongola, Sudan; *Religion:* Muslim; *Education:* Teachers Training College; Diploma in Education and Psychology, University of London, UK, 1958; Course in Rural Education, American University of Beirut, Lebanon, 1959–60; *Career:* member of the Sudanese delegations to the 20th session of the UN General Assembly and the Arab Prime Ministers' Conference; elected to the Constituent Assembly, 1965; Minister of Industry; General Manager, Sudan Insurance and Reinsurance Company; Secretary for Workers' Affairs and member of the Political Bureau of the Sudan Socialist Union (SSU) 1972–74; speaker of the People's Assembly, 1974–; *Address:* Sudan Socialist Union, P O Box 1850, Khartoum, Sudan.

IZZIDDIN, Yusuf, Iraqi academic; born in Iraq; *Education:* BA in Arabic Literature and Language, University of Alexandria, Alexandria, Egypt; MA, University of Alexandria; PhD in Philosophy, University of London, UK; *Career:* occupied several government posts for number of years; currently Professor of Literature, Faculty of Arts, University of Riyadh, Saudi Arabia; editor in chief of *Al Kitaab* ; member of the editorial staff of *Al Jumhuriyah* for several years;

editor in chief of *Al Nadwa* ; member of the Iraqi Academy of Science; member of the Academy of Arabic Language, Damascus and Amman; member of the Indian Academy of Sciences; member of the Society of Comparative Literature; member of the Royal Society of Literature, UK; *Publica-tions:* numerous works in Arabic and in English on literature and criticism and other subjects; *Decorations:* several medals and prizes; *Languages:* Arabic, English; *Address:* Faculty of Arts, University of Riyadh, Riyadh, Saudi Arabia.

J

JAAFAR, Ahmad Muhammad, Kuwaiti oil official; born 12 January 1938; married; two sons, one daughter; *Religion:* Muslim; *Education:* South Devon Technical College, England, UK, 1957–58; Hendon College of Technology, Personnel Management Course, 1963; course in Management, Henley Staff College; *Career:* Kuwait Police Force; attended Hendon College, London, England; Inspector of Police, Kuwait Police Force; Kuwait Oil Company (KOC), Public Relations Department, London Office, 1960; Personnel Officer, Kuwait Oil Company, London Office, 1960; KOC, Personnel Department, 1964–70; Superintendent, Personnel Department, Staff Superintendent, Acting Manager for Local Relations; Acting Manager for Services; British Petroleum, London; Manager, Personnel and Local Affairs, KOC, 1971; General Manager, KOC, 1974; Chairman and Managing Director, KOC, August 1975, following nationalisation of the KOC by Kuwaiti Government; *Interests and Recreations:* football; *Languages:* Arabic, English; *Address:* Kuwait Oil Company, P O Box 393, Ahmadi, 22, Kuwait; telephone: 982929, 989111; telex: 44211 KUOCO KT, 44225 KWT.

JAAFAR, Khalid Muhammad, Kuwaiti diplomat; born 12 August 1922, Kuwait; married; four sons, three daughters; *Religion:* Muslim; *Education:* Mubarakia School, Kuwait; *Career:* Teacher in Kuwait, 1940–42; Treasurer General, Kuwait Municipality, 1943–45; Superintendent of Public Relations, Kuwait Oil Company, 1945–61; Lord Chamberlain to HH Amir of Kuwait, 1961–62; Ambassador and later Head of Press and Cultural Division, Ministry of Foreign Affairs, 1962; member of Kuwait Delegation to the United Nations, prior to Kuwait admission to the United Nations, October 1962; Ambassador to London, and Chairman of Kuwait Investment Office, London, 1963–65; Ambassador to Lebanon, 1965–70; non-resident Ambassador to France, 1965–66, and Ambassador to Turkey, 1967–70; Resident Ambassador to Turkey, 1970–72; non-resident Ambassador to Bulgaria and Greece, 1971–72; Director of Protocol, Ministry of Foreign Affairs, 1972–75; Ambassador to Washington D.C., USA, 1975–80; non-resident Ambassador to Venezuela and Canada, 1975–80; Director, Political Department, Ministry of Foreign Affairs, 1982–; *Decorations:* Ordre du Mérite National, France; Grand Cordon of the National Order of the Cedar, Lebanon; Ordre de Saint Grégoire le Grand, Holy See; Order of Francisco de Miranda, 1st Class, Venezuela; *Languages:* Arabic, English; *Address:* Ministry of Foreign Affairs, P O Box 5418, Safat, Kuwait; telephone: 422041; telex: 2204 KHARJIA KT.

JAAFAR, Moncef, Tunisian diplomat; born 1936, Tunisia; married; three children; *Religion:* Muslim; *Education:* Sadiki College, Tunis; BA, Political Science and Law, University of Bordeaux, Bordeaux, France; *Career:* active in Tunisian Students Union (UGET) , and Assistant Secretary General, UGET External Affairs; Ministry of Foreign Affairs, Tunis, 1959; Embassy of Tunisia, Morocco, 1960; Embassy to Federal Republic of Germany, 1962–63; Editor in Chief, Destour Socialist Party, French language newspaper *L'Action,* 1963; active member of the Destour Socialist Party; elected member of the Central Committee of the Destour Socialist Party, 1974; Deputy of the Tunisian National Assembly, 1969–74; Director, *L'Action,* 1979; Ambassador, German Democratic Republic, Czechoslovakia, Hungary, 1973–80; Dean of Diplomatic Corps, German Democratic Republic, 1978; Director, Political Affairs for Asia, Ministry of Foreign Affairs, Tunis, 1980; Ambassador to Japan, Republic of Korea, Indonesia, 1981–; *Lang-*

257

uages: Arabic, English, French, German; *Address:* Embassy of Tunis, 29–2, Ichiban-cho, Chiyoda-ku, Tokyo 102, Japan.

JABBES, Frej, Tunisian administrator; born 1922, Kairouan, Tunisia; married; *Religion:* Muslim; *Education:* Mathematics, University of Dijon, France; *Career:* Inspector of Schools; Administrator in Ministry of Education; Governor of Medenine, South Tunisia, 1969; Secretary of State for Education, Technical Training Department, 1960–73; Head of the Office for Tunisian Workers Abroad, 1973; Director General, Office National de l'Huile, 1973; *Languages:* Arabic, French; *Address:* Office National de l'Huile, 10 Avenue Jean Jaurès, Tunis, Tunisia; telephone: 258966, 258315.

JABBOUR, George, Lebanese businessman; born 23 July 1927, Tripoli, Lebanon; *Education:* Degree in Economics: *Career:* banker; Chairman of the Board and Managing Director, Bank of Lebanon and the Middle East; Chairman of the Board, Lombard Bank, Lebanon; also of Lebanese Tourism Company; President, Lebanese White Cements Company and of Piccadilly Company; initiated various important commercial, industrial and tourist projects in Lebanon; *Interests and Recreations:* water sports, reading, classical music; *Languages:* Arabic, French, English; *Address:* Residence — Phenicia Street, Beirut, Lebanon.

JABR, Faruk, Lebanese businessman; born 15 September 1935, Beirut, Lebanon; married; two sons, one daughter; *Religion:* Muslim; *Education:* French Baccalauréat, first and second part (Experimental Sciences); BA in Economics, American University of Beirut; MBA, Graduate School of Business, Columbia University, New York, USA; *Career:* General Manager, Hussein Aoueini and Company, Saudi Arabia, 1958–64; Managing Director, The Spinning and Weaving Industrial Company, Beirut, Lebanon; member of the Board of Directors, Arab Bank Limited, Amman, Jordan, Commercial Building Company SAL, Beirut, Arabia Insurance Company SAL, Beirut, Cementation Saudi Arabia Limited, Riyadh, Saudi Arabia; Honorary Consul General of Oman in Lebanon, 1971–74; *Decorations:* Star of Jordan, 1972, Oman Medal, 1973; *Interests and Recreations:* swimming, tennis, table tennis, billiards; *Languages:* Arabic, French,

English, German, Italian, Spanish; *Address:* Beirut P O Box 384, Beirut, Lebanon; P O Box 156, Riyadh, Saudi Arabia; telephone: 20520, 28471; telex 20087 SJ.

JABR, Issamliddin Muhammad, Egyptian banker; born 10 June 1929, Egypt; married; one daughter; *Religion:* Muslim; *Education:* BA in Commerce, 1950; *Career:* Employee at Banque Belgium, 1951; Head of Commercial Sector, 1958; Assistant Manager, Port Said Bank, 1961; Manager, Port Said Bank, Muhammad Farid Branch, 1968; Manager, Foreign Relations Department, Arab African Bank, 1970; Assistant General Manager, Arab African Bank; Deputy General Manager, Arab African Bank; General Manager, Arab African International Bank; *Interests and Recreations:* horses, football; *Languages:* Arabic, French, English; *Address:* Abdel Khalik Tharwat Street, P O Box 1143, Cairo, Egypt.

JABR, Saad Salih, businessman of Iraqi descent; resident in UK; born 1929, Baghdad, Iraq; married; *Religion:* Muslim; *Education:* BA, American University of Beirut AUB, Lebanon; MA in Business Management, Southern Illinois University, USA; *Career:* Iraq Petroleum Company; Middle East Representative for Ralph M. Parsons Company, 1955–64; independent business, 1964–; Chairman of the Board of Al-Sabr Ltd, Business Consultants and Representatives for the Middle East, 1977–; Owner of the Du Quoin State Bank and the Du Quoin State Fair, USA; *Interests and Recreations:* tennis; *Languages:* Arabic, English, French; *Address:* 3 Hill Street, London W1, UK; telephone: 491 3115.

JABRA, Jabra Ibrahim, Palestinian writer/official; resident in Iraq; born 1920, Bethelehem, Palestine; married; two sons; *Education:* Arab College, Jerusalem; BA, MA, Fitzwilliam House, Cambridge University, UK; Harvard University, USA; *Career:* Lecturer, Rashidiyah College, Jerusalem, 1944; Lecturer in English Literature, College of Arts and Sciences, Baghdad, 1948–52; Research Fellow, Harvard University, USA, 1952–54; Senior Staff, Iraq Petroleum Company, IPC, 1954–72; parttime Lecturer, Baghdad University, 1956–64; Head of Department, Iraq National Oil Company, INOC, Baghdad, 1972–77; on secondment as Head of Department, Ministry of Oil,

Baghdad; Visiting Lecturer, University of California, Berkeley, USA, 1976; Adviser, Ministry of Culture and Information, Baghdad, 1977–; President of the Association of Art Critics in Iraq; *Publications: Hunters in a Narrow Street,* 1960 (in English, 1974 Arabic translation); *The Quest for Walid Mas'uud,* 1978; co-author *World Without Maps,* 1982; poetry, *Tammuz in the City,* 1959; *Closed Circuit,* 1964; and numerous other novels and short stories and poetry collections, *The Eighth Voyage,* 1967; *Fire and Essence,* 1975; *Jawad Silim and the Monument of Liberty,* 1974; *Sources of Vision,* 1979; *The Grass Roots of Iraqi Art,* 1982; and other works in literary criticism, some of which has been translated into English, French, Italian, Spanish; numerous translations, including six plays by Shakespeare; co-founder and Editor in Chief of *Funuun Arabiya,* an art quarterly; *Interests and Recreations:* literature and the arts, painting, sculpture, baroque music; worked on several major documentary films; promoted the works of many writers, poets and artists; *Languages:* Arabic, English, French; *Address:* 15/8 Al-Mansuur, Baghdad, Iraq; telephone: 5514411.

JABRE, Jamil Louis, Lebanese writer; born 1924, Lebanon; married; *Education:* Diploma in Political Sciences, Faculty of Law, Beirut; Doctor of Letters, University of Lyon, France; *Career:* Dirctor of *Al-Hikmat* revue; Cultural Adviser to *Al-Jarida* and *L'Orient* newspaper; founding-member of Lebanese PEN Club; founder of Amis du Livre, Club du Roman; *Publications: Fever; After the Storm; Agony; May Ziade; Amin Rihani; Gibran Khalil Gibran; Tagore; Jahiz and the Society of His Times; Views on Contemporary American Literature; Dream of Nimrod; Languages:* Arabic, French, English; *Address:* Nassim Audi Building, Chalhoub Section, Zalka, Beirut, Lebanon.

JACK, Muhammad Hassan al-, Sudanese academic/agricultural expert; born 22 June 1936; married; two sons; *Religion:* Muslim; *Education:* BSc in Agriculture, University of London, UK, 1963; PhD in Agriculture, University of Edinburgh, UK, 1966; *Career:* Senior Scholar, University of Khartoum, 1961; Lecturer, Department of Animal Production, UK, 1966; Senior Lecturer, Department of Animal Production, UK, 1973; Secretary for the Cooperative Committee, Sudanese Socialist Union, Khartoum, 1976; *Publications:* numerous scientific papers in British, US, German, Sudanese journals; *Interests and Recreations:* tennis; formerly Secretary of the Sudanese Philosophical Association, Secretary of Scientific Progress; member of the Sudanese Agriculture Association; *Languages:* Arabic, English, French; *Address:* Sudanese Socialist Union (SSU), P O Box 1850, Khartoum, Sudan.

JACK, Said Ahmad al-, Sudanese politician/ engineer; born 1930, Khartoum, Sudan; *Religion:* Muslim; *Education:* University of Khartoum, Sudan; MA, PhD in USA; *Career:* Ministry of Works, 1954–56; Consultative and Design Engineer; Lecturer in Civil Engineering, University of Khartoum; worked on water and electricity projects for Shendi and Berber towns; founder and member of the Board, Sudanese Trade Union; co-founder, Sudanese Teachers Association, Khartoum University; Minister of Works, 1969–70; Minister of Transport and Communications, 1970–71; member of American Engineers Society, member of Sudanese Engineers Society; *Address:* Faculty of Engineering, University of Khartoum, Khartoum, Sudan.

JAFF, Akram Hamid al-, Iraqi UN official/ agriculturalist; born 14 July 1929, Sulaimaniyah, Iraq; married; *Religion:* Muslim; *Education:* BSc, Colorado State University, USA, 1955–57; *Career:* Director General, Ministry of Economy, 1963–65; Minister of Agriculture, Iraq, 1965–66; Minister of Agriculture, Iraq,1966–69, Lecturer, Baghdad University, 1969; Senior Agricultural Adviser and Country Representive, FAO, UN Development Programme, UNDP, Somalia, 1970–73; Officer in charge, Somalia, UNDP, 1973; FAO Representative in the Arab Republic of Egypt, 1974–80; Chief of Agricultural Operations in the Middle East, North Africa and Europe, FAO, 1980–; Rome, Italy; member of the Iraqi Management Association, Iraqi Petroleum Company; Iraqi Rafidain Bank; *Publications: Soil Born Insects and Control; Tobacco Industry in Iraq; Interests and Recreations:* reading, walking, agriculture, economics, industry; *Languages:* Kurdish, Arabic, English, Persian; *Address:* Chief, AGON, FAO, Via delle Terme di Caracalla, Rome, Italy; telephone: 57971.

JAIDAH, Ali Muhammad, Qatari oil official/
economist; born 1941, Doha Qatar; *Religion:*
Muslim; *Education:* BSc in Economics, Lon-
don School of Economics, University of
London, London, UK, 1965; MSc in Petrol-
eum Economics, University of London, 1966;
Career: Head of Economics Division, Department of Petroleum Affairs, Ministry of
Finance and Petroleum, 1966–71; Director of
Petroleum Affairs, Ministry of Finance and
Petroleum, 1971–76; Secretary General of
OPEC, 1976–78; Managing Director and
member of the Board of Directors, Qatar
General Petroleum Corporation, 1979–;
Qatar Governor of OPEC, 1976; member of
the Executive Office of OAPEC, 1976;
participated in all negotiations related to the
oil industry in Qatar, including the take over
of equity in Qatar Petroleum Corporation
and Shell Company of Qatar; participated in
establishing the Qatari national organisation
for oil, the Qatar General Petroleum Corporation and Qatar Petroleum Producing
Authority; participated and headed Qatari
Delegations to OPEC and OAPEC and other
petroleum conferences and meetings on
several occasions and in various capacities;
Publications: various papers and addresses on
pricing of oil, OPEC and the future of oil
supply, the future of world energy as seen by
oil producing countries, and OPEC and the
future energy markets, OPEC policy options;
Decorations: Decoration awarded by The
Federal President of Austria; *Languages:*
Arabic, English; *Address:* Qatar General
Petroleum Corporation, P O Box 3212, Doha,
Qatar; telephone: 831000; telex:4343
PETCOR DH.

JAKKA, Abdullah Ali Issa, United Arab
Emirates official; born 1948, Ras al-
Khaimah, United Arab Emirates; married;
one son, one daughter; *Religion:* Muslim;
Education: BA, Kuwait University, 1970;
Career: Director of Department, Ministry of
Education, 1970; deputy headmaster, 1971;
school supervisor, 1971; 3rd Secretary, Mini-
stry of Foreign Affairs, 1972; 2nd Secretary,
Ministry of Foreign Affairs; Director of
Finance and Administration, Ministry of
Waqfs (Islamic Endowments) and Islamic
Affairs; *Interests and Recreations:* football,
volleyball, swimming; *Languages:* Arabic,
English, Latin; *Address:* Ministry of Waqfs
and Islamic Affairs, P O Box 753, Abu
Dhabi, United Arab Emirates.

JALAL, Mahsun, Saudi Arabian financial
official/economist; born 26 June 1936; married; two sons, one daughter; *Religion:* Muslim; *Education:* Cairo University; PhD in
Economics, Rutgers University, USA; University of California, USA; *Career:* Lecturer;
Professor; Chairman, Department of Economics, Riyadh University, 1967–75; Consultant to various government agencies, 1967–75;
established and became Director of Consulting Centre, Riyadh; Vice Chairman, Managing Director, Saudi Fund for Development,
1975–79; member of the Civil Service
Council, 1975–79; Chairman, Saudi International Bank, Nassau, 1979–81; Director,
Saudi International Bank, London, 1975–;
Director, Saudi Basic Industries Corp; Chairman, Saudi Investment Banking Corp; Chairman, OPEC Fund for International Development, 1979–; Executive Director, IMF,
1978–81; Chairman, Tunisian Saudi Development Investment Co 1981; Chairman of a
number of investment companies; *Publications: Principles of Economics;* other books
and articles on economics, development, and
economic theory; *Decorations:* Golden Star,
1st Class, Taiwan, 1978; Tanda Mahputera,
Indonesia, 1978; l'Insigne de Chevalier de
l'Ordre National, Mali, 1978; *Interests and
Recreations:* travel, sports; *Address:* P O Box
4857, Riyadh, Saudi Arabia; 1432 Ladybird
Drive, Mclean, VA 22101, USA; telephone:
(703) 356 4526.

JALAL, Muhammad Bin Yusuf, Bahraini
businessman; born 1920, Bahrain; married;
Religion: Muslim; *Education:* general education in Bahrain and India; *Career:* Civil
Servant in Bahrain for a number of years;
entered business as joint contractor for
construction in Saudi Arabia; established his
own building construction company in Bahrain; trading interests in the field of construction include construction equipment and
building materials, mechanical plants, commercial vehicles, oil field supplies and interior
design and furnishing; other trading interests
include furniture, office supplies and equipment, travel agency and a catering company;
numerous joint ventures and associated
companies; nominated for Constitutional
Assembly 1972–73; President of Bahrain
Chamber of Commerce and Industry; Chairman of Bahrain Tourism Company and
Board member of several other Bahraini
companies; *Interests and Recreations:* travel;
Languages: Arabic, English; *Address:*

Muhammad Jalal and Sons Co Ltd, P O Box 113, Manama, Bahrain; telephone: 55544; telex: 8233 MAJAL BN.

JALLAD, Abdul Khalik, Lebanese banker; born 3 May 1938, Beirut, Lebanon; married; one son; *Education:* BBA, American University of Beirut, Lebanon, 1961; *Career:* Guest Trainee, Bank of America, San Francisco, USA, 1963–64; Department Head, Union National Bank, Beirut, 1966–69; Assistant Manager, First National Bank of Chicago, 1969–; *Address:* P O Box 424, Beirut, Lebanon.

JALLOW, Raymond, Arab-American economist/academic; born 10 October 1930, Baghdad, Iraq; *Religion:* Muslim; *Education:* BA, University of Baghdad, Iraq, 1951; MA in Business Administration, University of Southern California, USA, 1956; PhD in Business Economics, University of California, Los Angeles (UCLA), 1966; *Career:* Supervisor of Revenue Department, Iraqi Railways, 1947–1952; Auditor, Robert Young, CPA, Pasadena, California, 1956–57; Economist/Manager, Research and Planning Department, United California Bank (now First Interstate Bank), Los Angeles, 1959–66, Vice President, Chief Economist, 1966–70, Senior Vice President, Chief Economist, 1979–81; Chief Economist, Western Bancorp (now First Interstate Bancorp), 1979–81; President, Jallow International Ltd, Los Angeles, 1981–; Lecturer in USA and other countries in Economics and Monetary fields; Adviser to governments and corporations in USA, Europe, the Middle East and the Far East; Presidents of the Arab Students Association, UCLA, 1958; President of the American Muslim Association, Los Angeles, 1959–61; Faculty Member, UCLA Extension, 1964–68; First President and Founder, National Association of Business Economists (Southern California), 1968–70; member of the Economist Advisory Council, American Bankers Association, Washington D.C., 1972–75; Chairman of the Board, US Organization for Medical and Educational Needs (OMEN), 1972; member of the American Statisticians Association, the American Management Association; Board Director, US OMEN, Trust Company the Financial Committee of the Seaver Institute, the Board of Regents, California Lutheran College; Advisory member of California

Polytechnic State University; *Publications: Economic and Monetary Forecast,* 1964–80; *Asset Management and Long Range Planning for Banks,* 1967; *The Energy Crisis- Its Implications for the USA; Impact of Oil Shortages on Business and Industry,* 1973; *Revolution in International Finance,* 1974; *Interests and Recreations:* travel, reading; Middle Eastern Affairs; *Languages:* Arabic, English, French; *Address:* 2530 Park Oak Court, Los Angeles, California, 90068, USA; telephone: (213) 465 7388.

JALLUD, Major Abdul Salam Ahmad, Libyan politician; born 1940, Tripolitania, Libya; married; one child; *Religion:* Muslim; *Education:* Engineering Courses, USA; *Career:* commissioned with Army, 1965; Captain at time of September 1969 Revolution; represented Revolutionary Command Council at foreign embassies following the Revolution; headed Libyan delegation in talks leading to withdrawal of US and UK forces from Libya; Deputy Prime Minister, January 1970; took prominent role in negotiations with oil companies leading to increase in posted prices, September 1970; headed Libyan delegation in further oil talks leading to revised payments, April 1971; played important part in oil policy leading to nationalisation of the oil companies, September 1973; took over responsibility for National Oil Company, September 1973; Secretary of Economy and Industry and Acting Treasury Secretary; Prime Minister, 1972–77; member of five-man General Secretariat, 1977; *Languages:* Arabic, English; *Address:* Secretariat of the General People's Committee, Tripoli, Libya.

JAMAI, Tayib, Moroccan journalist/businessman; born 3 September 1936, Fes, Morocco; *Religion:* Muslim; *Education:* Diploma, School of Journalism and Public Relations; *Career:* Representative of Morocco at the World Assembly of Youth, Brussels, Belgium, 1964–68; Representative of the Moroccan Office of Exterior Commerce, OCE, in Africa, 1969–70; Journalist; Director of *A'maal al-Maghrib; Publications:* articles in *A'Maal al-Maghrib; Interests and Recreations:* reading, tennis; *Languages:* Arabic, French, English; *Address:* 1 Rond Point Saint Exupéry, Casablanca, Morocco; telephone: 273483, 26044.

JAMAL, Adel Mahmud, Saudi Arabian banker; born 17 May, Mecca, Saudi Arabia; *Religion:* Muslim; *Education:* BA in Economics and Political Sciences, American University, Cairo, 1968; MA in International Affairs, George Washington University, 1974; *Career:* National Commercial Bank, Jeddah, 1968–69; Saudi Arabian Ministry of Foreign Affairs and Embassy in Washington, 1969–76; Banque Arabe et Internationale d'Investissement, Paris, 1977–78; Manager, Saudi International Bank, London, 1978–; member of Arab Bankers Association, London; *Interests and Recreations:* music, arts, tennis; *Languages:* Arabic, English, French; *Address:* Saudi International Bank, 99 Bishopsgate, London EC2; telephone: 6382323.

JAMAL, Ahmad Muhammad, Saudi Arabian academic/official; born 1925, Mecca, Saudi Arabia; *Religion:* Muslim; *Education:* religious education at Al-Islami Institute, Mecca, Saudi Arabia; *Career:* formerly in the Presidium of the Judiciary, Supreme Legal Court; Notary Public Office, Ministry of the Interior; member of Endowments Council (Waqfs), of Mecca Municipal Council, of Cultural Committee of Muslim World League, of International Islamic Organizations Union; attended several Islamic conferences in Pakistan, Spain; member of Shura Council (National Advisory Council); Professor of Islamic Culture, King Abdul Aziz University, Jeddah, Saudi Arabia; *Publications: Ala Ma'idatil Qoran,* four vols; *Muftarayat Alal Islam; Muhadharat fil Thaqafatil Islamiah; Isti'mar wa kifah; Address:* Al-Thaqafah Bookshop, Mecca, Saudi Arabia.

JAMAL, Jasim Yusuf, Qatari diplomat; born 1940, Doha, Qatar; married; *Religion:* Muslim; *Education:* BA History and Political Science, North east Missouri State University, USA, 1968; MA in International Relations, New York University, USA, 1974; *Career:* Director of Administrative Affairs, Ministry of Education, 1958–63; Ministry of Education Cultural Adviser, Embassy of Qatar, USA, 1963–68; Director, Department of Cultural Affairs, Ministry of Education, 1968–72; Ambassador and Permanent Representative to UN, New York; non-resident Ambassador to Canada, Brazil and Argentina, 1972–; *Languages:* Arabic, English;

Address: Permanent Mission of State of Qatar, 747 Third Avenue, New York, NY 10017, USA; telephone: (212) 486 9335.

JAMAL, Muhammad Ahmad, Sudanese diplomat; born 1917, Sudan; married; seven children; *Education:* Gordon College, Khartoum, Sudan, 1937; BA, University College, Exeter, Devon, UK, 1946; BLitt, Oxford, UK, 1954; *Career:* Ministry of Education, 1947–50; Dean of Students, Khartoum University, 1949; Ambassador to Iraq, 1956–59; Ambassador to Ethiopia, 1959–64; Permanent Representative of Sudan to the United Nations, 1964–66; Ambassador to UK, 1965–67; Under Secretary of Political Affairs, Ministry of Foreign Affairs, Khartoum, 1967–69; Secretary, Cultural Centre, Khartoum; Adviser, *Hiwar* magazine, Beirut; member, Editorial Board, *Modern Journal of African History; Publications:* author of works in Arabic and English, among others *Intellectual Origins of Egyptian Nationalism,* 1960; articles on African affairs in journals and periodicals; translated *The Federalist Papers; Africa Rediscovered* into Arabic; *Decorations:* decoration from King of Jordan, Emperor of Ethiopia, President of Syria; *Address:* Residence: — P O Box 83, Khartoum, Sudan.

JAMALI, Abdul Hussain al-, Iraqi diplomt; born 1929, Iraq; married; *Religion:* Muslim; *Education:* LLB, Baghdad College of Law, Baghdad, Iraq; MA, Political Science, University of New York, New York, USA; *Career:* Second Secretary, Embassy of Iraq, Lebanon, 1958; First Secretary, Embassy of Iraq, Ghana, Syria, Egypt; Head of Arab Affairs Department, Ministry of Foreign Affairs, 1967–69; Ambassador, 1969–71; Under Secretary, Ministry of Foreign Affairs, 1971–; *Languages:* Arabic, English; *Address:* Ministry of Foreign Affairs, Baghdad, Iraq.

JAMALI, Ahmad Muhammad al-, Omani diplomat; born 20 September 1927, Muscat, Oman; married; *Religion:* Muslim; *Education:* American University of Beirut, Lebanon, 1952–55; *Career:* Director of Education, Oman, 1971; Counsellor, Permanent Mission of Oman, New York, 1972–74; Minister, Permanent Mission of Oman, New York, 1974–75; Ambassador to France, 1975–77; Ambassador to Jordan, 1977; Ambassador to Italy, 1982–; *Interests and*

Recreations: swimming; *Languages:* Arabic, English, German; *Address:* Embassy of Oman, Via Enrico Petrella 4, Rome, Italy; Ministry of Foreign Affairs, P O Box 252, Muscat, Oman; telephone: 701211, 701614, 701515; telex: 3337 MFA MB. telephone: 701211, 701614, 701515; telex: 3337 MFAMB.

JAMALI, Assim al-, Omani politician; born in Oman; married; four children; *Religion:* Muslim; *Education:* degree in Medicine, Pakistan; further studies in UK; *Career:* Director of Public Health, Trucial States Development Council, 1960; Minister of Health, 1970–74; led Omani delegation to UN, New York to canvass support for Omani admission to UN, 1971; served briefly as acting Prime Minister following the resignation of Sayyid Tariq al-Said, 1971; Minister without Portfolio; Minister of Land Affairs and Municipalities; Minister of Public Works; Chairman of the Bank of Oman and the Gulf, Muscat; *Languages:* Arabic, English; *Address:* Ministry of Public Works, P O Box 215, Muscat, Oman; telephone: 704414; telex: 3359 ASH GHALMB.

JAMALI, Muhammad Fadil; Iraqi academic/politician; born 20 April 1903, Iraq; married; three sons; *Education:* Diploma, Teachers Training College, Baghdad, 1920; BA, American University of Beirut, 1927; MA and PhD, Columbia University, USA, 1930, 1932; Macy Fellowship, International Institute, Teachers College, Columbia University; *Career:* elementary school teacher, 1918–22; Teacher at Teachers Training College, Baghdad, 1927–29; Lecturer on Education at Higher Teachers Training College, Baghdad, 1936–47; Director General and Supervisor General of Education and Public Instruction, 1932–43; Director General of Foreign Affairs, 1944–46; Minister to Egypt, 1949; member of Iraqi Parliament, 1946–57; member of Senate, 1957–58; President of Chamber of Deputies, 1951 and 1953; Minister of Foreign Affairs, 1946, 1947, 1949, 1952, 1954, 1958; Prime Minister of Iraq, 1953–54; Headed Iraqi Delegations to several prominent Arab and International Conferences; Headed Iraqi Delegation to UN General Assembly, 1947–52 and 1954–56; signed the UN Charter at San Francisco on behalf of the Government of Iraq, 1945; was tried by the Revolutionary Military Tribunal after the Iraqi Revolution of 1958, spent three years in prison and released 14 July, 1961; Professor of Philosophy of Education, University of Tunis, 1962; *Publications:* numerous books and other publications on education, Arab and Islamic affairs and international problems; *Decorations:* decorations from Iraq, Iran, Jordan, Lebanon, Republic of China, Spain, Tunisia, Morocco; Honorary Doctor in Foreign Service, University of Southern California, 1945; Honorary Doctor in Law, Columbia University, 1945; Distinguished Service Medal, Teachers College of Columbia University, 1954; *Interests and Recreations:* hiking, listening to music; *Languages:* Arabic, English, French, Turkish, Persian; *Address:* University of Tunisia, Avenue 9 Avril, Tunis, Tunisia.

JAMIL, Abdul Latif, Saudi Arabian businessman; born 1902; *Religion:* Muslim; *Education:* general education; *Career:* owner and Chairman of Board of Abdul Latif Jamil Corporation; owner of Jamil Housing Projects in Jeddah and Riyadh; shipowner and shipping agent; *Interests and Recreations:* travel; *Address:* Abdul Latif Jamil Corporation, P O Box 248, Jeddah, Saudi Arabia; telephone: 56119; telex: 401139 YOUSEF SJ.

JAMIL, Ghalib Ali, Yemen Arab Republic diplomat; born 1930; *Religion:* Muslim; *Education:* in Egypt; Wilamette University, Salem, Oregon, USA, 1965; *Career:* Director of the Foreign Minister's Office; Director General of the Foreign Ministry, 1966; Deputy Permanent Representative to the UN, 1967; one of the two Deputy Ministers for Foreign Affairs, 1973–75; Ambassador to Iraq, 1975; *Languages:* Arabic, English; *Address:* c/o Ministry of Foreign Affairs, Sana'a, Yemen Arab Republic.

JAMIL, Talib, Iraqi lawyer; born 1919, Baghdad, Iraq; married; two sons, one daughter; *Education:* LLB, College of Law, University of Baghdad, Baghdad, Iraq, 1941; *Career:* Lawyer, 1941–53; Director of Contracts and Legal Affairs, Ministry of Economy, 1953–54; Director of Trade, 1954–58; Director of Economy, 1958–59; Lawyer, 1959–64; Deputy Minister of Economy, President of the General Organization for Insurance, 1964; Permanent Representative of Iraq to the Council of Economic Unity, with rank of Ambassador, 1965–68; Lawyer, 1968–; *Publications: Technical Terms Book-*

lets, 1961, 1962, in Arabic and English; numerous papers and articles in professional journals and magazines; *Interests and Recreations:* reading; *Languages:* Arabic, English; *Address:* Al Baab Al Sharqi, Shari Al Khulafaa, P O Box 3036, Baghdad, Iraq; telephone: 8886783; Residence — 27254.

JAMIL, Yusuf Abdul Latif, Saudi Arabian businessman; born 1943, Saudi Arabia; *Education:* BSc in Economics, American University of Cairo, Cairo, Egypt; *Career:* President of Abdul Latif Jamil Establishment, specialists in agricultural machinery and motor vehicles and shipping; member of the Board of Directors and partner of Tihama Advertising, Public Relations and Marketing Research Company; *Languages:* Arabic, English; *Address:* Palestine Road, P O Box 248, Jeddah, Saudi Arabia; telephone: 56154; telex: 401139 YOUSEF SJ.

JAMJOOM, Ahmad Salah, Saudi Arabian official/businessman; born 1925 Jeddah, Saudi Arabia; *Religion:* Muslim; *Education:* BBA, Cairo University, Egypt; Business Administration, Harvard Law School, USA; *Career:* Executive Arab Bank Ltd; Assistant Director General, Zakat (Islamic Alms) and Revenue Tax Department; Director General, General Manager of Arabian Cement Co Ltd; Minister of State, 1958–60; Minister of Commerce and Industry, 1960–62; Chairman of Saudi Arabian Airlines, SAUDIA, 1963; Chairman of Jamjoom Vehicles and Equipment; General Manager, al-Madina Press Organization, Jeddah; Vice President, Executive Committee, King Abdul Aziz National University, later King Abdul Aziz University, 1971; member of Supreme Council of King Abdul Aziz University; founder and member of the Board of Faisal Islamic Bank; Chairman, Shorouk International Centre, London; *Publications:* articles on economic and Islamic affairs in local press and magazines; *Interests and Recreations:* reading; *Address:* P O Box 1247, Jeddah, Saudi Arabia; telephone: 687 7096; 687 1708.

JAMJOOM, Asad Hassan, Saudi Arabian official; born 1923; *Religion:* Muslim; *Education:* Diploma in Engineering; *Career:* Principal of Trades School, Jeddah, 1949; Inspector General of Industrial Education, Ministry of Education, 1958; Director General of Water Affairs, Ministry of Agriculture and Water; founding member of Saudi Popular Educa-

tion Organization; member of Board of Red Sea Club; Regional Director of Agriculture and Water Affairs, Western Region, Ministry of Agriculture and Water, 1976–; attended Conference on the Utilization of Atomic Energy in Water Desalination, Medina and FAO Conference, Rome, Italy; Ministry of Agriculture and Water Delegate to World Exhibition (EXPO), Osaka, Japan, 1970; *Interests and Recreations:* swimming, fishing, travel; *Address:* P O Box 2548, Jeddah, Saudi Arabia; telephone: 6876022; telex: 401632 WESTAG SJ.

JAMJOOM, Hisham Muhammad Nour, Saudi Arabian businessman; born 1941, Saudi Arabia; *Religion:* Muslim; *Education:* BCom, Industrial Management; *Career:* Legal Department, Ministry of Petroleum and Mineral Resources; Labour Relations Department, Arabian-American Oil Company, ARAMCO; Managing Director, Jamjoom and Bros; member of the Board of Jamjoom Foremost Dairies Ltd, Chamber of Commerce and Industry, American Management Association; Manager of Raud Trading Company; *Publications: Industrial Management and Saudi Arabia* ; several articles on management and labour relations in local journals and newspapers; *Address:* P O Box 2489, Jeddah, Saudi Arabia; telephone: 29393; telex: 401365 MONEER SJ.

JAMJOOM, Muhammad Abdul Wahid, Saudi Arabian official/economist; born 1938, Cairo, Egypt; *Religion:* Muslim; *Education:* PhD in Economics; *Career:* accountant, Executive Accounting Department, Saudi Arabian Monetary Agency (SAMA); Chief, Executive Accounting Department, SAMA; Director General of Research and Statistics Division, SAMA, 1976–; Lecturer in Economics, Postgraduate Courses, SAMA Banking Institute; Director General of Economic Research Department, SAMA; attended First and Second Conference of Ministers of Finance, meeting for the approval of Arab Bank Agreement for Economic Development in Africa, Cairo, Egypt, Islamic Banks, Preparatory Committee meetings, meetings of Arab Central Bank Governors, IMF and IBRD (World Bank) meetings, Sixth Conference of Islamic Foreign Ministers, Islamic Countries Economic Delegates and Representatives Committees, OPEC meetings, OAPEC meetings; contributed to the drafting of the Arab Banks Agreement on internal procedural regulations, Arab Monetary Fund Agreement; *Publications:* PhD thesis dealing with Saudi Arabian foreign trade and balance of payments; *Interests and Recreations:* reading, chess; *Address:* Saudi Arabian Monetary Agency, P O Box 2292, Airport Road, Riyadh, Saudi Arabia; telephone: 4769594; telex: 201734 MARKAZI SJ.

JAMJOOM, Muhammad Omar, Saudi Arabian academic/engineer; born 1946, Saudi Arabia; married; two sons, two daughters; *Religion:* Muslim; *Education:* BSc, MSc and PhD in Engineering, 1969–74; *Career:* Teaching Assistant, Virginia University, 1970–71, 1972–74; Assistant Professor, College of Engineering, King Abdul Aziz University, 1975–76; Vice Dean, College of Engineering, King Abdul Aziz University, 1976–77; Dean for College of Engineering, King Abdul Aziz University, 1977–; *Interests and Recreations:* journalism, poetry, swimming, volleyball, tennis; *Languages:* Arabic, English; *Address:* Ministry of Higher Education, King Abdul Aziz University, P O Box 1540, Jeddah, Saudi Arabia; telephone: 6890068.

JAMMAL, Ali, Lebanese businessman, born 1926, Lebanon; married; seven children; *Religion:* Muslim; *Education:* National College of Aley; American University of Beirut; *Career:* worked in Industry, Trade, Construction and Development; Chairman, General Manager, Jammal Trust Bank SAL; President, Finance and Investment (Holding), Luxembourg; *Interests and Recreations:* skiing, swimming, horse riding, tennis, music; *Languages:* Arabic, English, French; *Address:* Office — Jammal Trust Bank SAL, Riyad Solh Street, P O Box 11–5640, Beirut, Lebanon; telephone: 291564; telex: 20854 LE and Jammal 20939 LE; Cable: Jamibk Beirut; Residence — telephone: 803405.

JANABI, Nawal Yusif al-, Iraqi academic; born 1 July 1937, Baghdad, Iraq; married; one daughter; *Education:* BSc, University of Baghdad, Baghdad, 1960; MSc, George Washington University, USA, 1967; PhD, Brunel University, London, UK, 1970; *Career:* Demonstrator, University of Baghdad, 1960–64; Homograft Department, National Heart Hospital and Cardiothoracic Institute, University of London, 1970–75; Assistant Professor, Department of Microbiology, College of Medicine, Al-

Mustansiriyah University, Iraq; Professor of Microbiology, College of Medicine, Al-Mustansiriyah University; *Publications:* numerous researches and articles in professional journals; *Interests and Recreations:* music; *Languages:* Arabic, English; *Address:* Department of Microbiology, School of Medicine, Al Mustansiriyah University, P O Box 14132, Baghdad, Iraq.

JARALLAH, Ahmad, Kuwaiti journalist; born 1942, Kuwait; married; *Religion:* Muslim; *Career:* joined *Al-Rai Al-'Aam* newspaper; founder of *Al-Siyasah* newspaper, 1968; owner and editor of *Al-Siyasah* newspaper, *Arab Times* newspapers and *Arab Yearbook; Address:* Dar Al-Siyasah Printing, Publishing and Distributing House, P O Box 2270, Kuwait; telephone: 813566; telex: 2332 SIYASA KT.

JARARI, Abdullah al-Abbas al-, Moroccan official/educationalist; born 1912, Rabat, Morocco; married; four sons; five daughters; *Religion:* Muslim; *Education:* BA, Quarawyin University, Fes, Morocco; Islamic Studies; Moroccan History; Diploma in Education, American University of Beirut, AUB, Lebanon, 1964; *Career:* Professor of Education in Morocco; Inspector General of Education in Morocco; *Publications:* numerous works and articles on education; *Decorations:* Order of the Throne, Morocco; Medal from Libya; *Interests and Recreations:* Arabic and Andalusian music; member of the Moroccan Scientists Federation; member of the Council of Moroccan Scientists; *Languages:* Arabic, French; *Address:* 11 Zanqit al-Qadi Ayad, Rabat, Morocco; telephone: 24107.

JAROUDI, Saeb, Lebanese economist; born 1924, Lebanon; married; *Religion:* Muslim; *Education:* American University of Beirut, Lebanon; PhD, Economics and Politics, Columbia University, USA; *Career:* Professor of Economics at American University of Beirut, (AUB) Lebanon; Financial Adviser to the Ministry of Finance under Shaikh Jabir al-Sabah and later Abdel Rahman al-Atiqi, Kuwait, Director of Rockefeller Institute, Kuwait; Kuwait Fund for Arab Economic Development; American University Beirut, 1969; Lebanese Minister of National Economy, 1971–73; returned to Kuwait, President and Director General of the Arab Fund for Economic and Social Development, Kuwait,

1973; *Languages:* Arabic, English; *Address:* Arab Fund for Economic and Social Development, P O Box 21923, Safat, Kuwait; telephone: 431870.

JARRAH, Bashir Mahmud al-, Iraqi banker; resident in Lebanon; born 1914, Mosul, Iraq; married 1945; three sons, one daughter; *Religion:* Muslim; *Education:* Military College, Baghdad, Iraq; Diploma in Bank Management; *Career:* Chairman of Board and General Manager of Rafidain Bank, Iraq, 1964–65; *Interests and Recreations:* reading, walking, economics, Islamic art; *Languages:* Arabic, English; *Address:* P O Box 113–5509, Beirut, Lebanon.

JARRAR, Abdul Rahim Ibrahim, Jordanian official; born 1919, Jordan; *Education:* Diploma, Arab College, Jerusalem, 1935–38; BA, Special Studies, Department of Education, Government of Palestine, 1940–46; *Career:* schoolmaster, Ministry of Education, 1938–50; Mayor of Jenin, Jordan, 1958–60; private business, 1952–66, 1960–61; member of Parliament, Jordan, 1961–62, 1950–58, Governor, Ministry of Interior, Jordan, 1966–72; Representative of Jordan, Advisory Commission, United Nations Relief and Works Agency for Palestine Refugees in the Near East, (UNRWA); Under Secretary, Ministry of Development and Reconstruction; member of the National Consultative Council of Jordan, 1982–83; member of the Nablus Charitable Organisation; *Decorations:* The Independence Medal, Jordan, 1982; *Interests and Recreations:* swimming; *Languages:* Arabic, English; *Address:* National Consultative Council, P O, Box 950464, Amman, Jordan; telephone: 664 977.

JARRAR, Walid, Jordanian official/engineer; born 1932, Haifa, Palestine; married; two sons, one daughter; *Religion:* Muslim; *Education:* Diploma in Civil Engineering, Baghdad University, Iraq, 1955; Diploma in Road Engineering, Ankara University, Turkey, 1957; *Career:* Engineer, District of Ma'an, 1955; Engineer in charge of Amman-Ma'an desert road, 1956; Director of Roads, Kuwait Ministry of Public Works, 1957–59; Director of Public Works, Amman Municipality, 1965; Assistant Secretary of Amman Municipality and Technical Adviser, 1966–76; Civil Engineer Consultant 1977–83; member of Kuwait Engineering Association; member of Jordan Engineering Association;

Publications: Kuwait Roads and Modern Methods of Road Planning, Ministry of Works, Kuwait, 1959, in Arabic;, *The Uses of Asphalt* 1963; *Planning and Construction of Kuwait International Airport – First Stage 1958–59; Decorations:* Independence Medal, 3rd Class, 1957; Star of Jordan, 3rd Class, 1966; *Interests and Recreations:* theatre, travel, reading, swimming; *Languages:* Arabic, English; *Address:* Amman Municipality, P O Box 5018 Amman, Jordan; telephone: Office — 43285; Residence — 41378.

JARWAN, Saif Ali al-, United Arab Emirates politician/diplomat; born 1938, Ras al-Khaimah, United Arab Emirates; married; four sons, three daughters; *Religion:* Muslim; *Education:* general education; courses in management; *Career:* Director General of Ras al-Khaimah Municipality, 1964–73; represented Ras al-Khaimah in the Rulers' Council before the creation of the United Arab Emirates; member of committee establishing the UAE; member of the UAE delegation to UN, 1975; Ambassador to Kuwait; Ambassador to Egypt, 1977; Minister of Labour and Social Affairs, Dubai, 1978–; founder of *Ras al-Khaimah* magazine (in Arabic); participated in First, Second and Third Conferences of the Organization of Arab Cities; *Interests and Recreations:* football, member of Amman Club, Ras al-Khaimah; *Address:* Ministry of Labour and Social Affairs, P O Box 4409, Shaikh Rashid Building, Port Said Road, Dubai, United Arab Emirates; telephone: 226181.

JASSIM, Ahmad Abdul Aziz al-, Kuwaiti diplomat; born 7 April, 1938, Kuwait; married; two sons, two daughters; *Religion:* Muslim; *Education:* BA in Political Science, Cairo University, 1963; *Career:* Acting Consul General, New York and member of Kuwait Delegation to UN, 1963–67; Counsellor, Kuwaiti Embassy to Baghdad, 1967–73; Ambassador to Muscat, Oman, 1974–77; Ambassador to Islamabad, Pakistan, 1978–79; Ambassador to Iran, 1979–; *Interests and Recreations;* swimming, reading, travelling; *Languages:* Arabic, English; *Address:* Embassy of the State of Kuwait, Dehkadeh Avenue, Sazeman Aab Street, No.3/38, P O Box 420, Tehran, Iran telephone: 656331, 657806.

JASSSIM, Sa'dun Muhammad al-, Kuwaiti official; born 1933, Kuwait; married; three sons; *Religion:* Muslim; *Education:* BSc, American University of Cairo, Egypt, 1956; *Career:* Assistant for Press Affairs, Kuwait Press and Publications Department; Assistant Under Secretary for Administration and Finance, Ministry of Guidance and Information, 1962; Under Secretary, Ministry of Information, 1965–; *Decorations:* Commander of the National Order of the Cedar, Lebanon, 1971; King Abdul Aziz Order, 1st Class, Saudi Arabia; *Interests and Recreations:* swimming; member of the Society of the Protection of Environment; Chief Editor of Kuwait *Red Crescent Society Magazine; Languages:* Arabic, English; *Address:* Ministry of Information, P O Box 193, Safat, Kuwait; telephone: Office — 435905, Residence — 811905.

JAWAD, Jawad Habib, Bahraini businessman/accountant, born 1942 Bahrain; married; two daughters, one son; *Religion:* Muslim; *Education:* Institute of Cost and Management Accountants Examinations, 1970; *Career:* Bahrain Petroleum Co, 1956–70; Saba and Co, 1971–72; Talal Abu Ghazalah and Co and Price Waterhouse, 1973–79; established his own company Jawad Habib and Co; Partner of Abu Ghazlah and Co, 1980–; *Languages:* Arabic, English; *Address:* P O Box 990, Manama, Bahrain.

JAWAHIRI, Muhammad Mahdi al-, Iraqi writer; resident in Prague, Czechoslovakia; born 1902, Najaf, Iraq; married; four sons, three daughters; *Religion:* Muslim; *Education:* literature; *Career:* tea cher; Head of the Editing Department, Ministry of Culture; Member of Parliament, Iraq, 1947; President of the Writers Syndicate, 1958–78; President of the Journalists Syndicate, 1958–70; *Publications:* numerous collections of poems published in Najaf and Baghdad, Iraq, in Syria and in Lebanon, 1924–82; an autobiography in press; *Decorations:* Order of Rafidain, Iraq; Order of the Golden Cedar, Lebanon; Medal of Intellect and Culture, Morocco; *Interests and Recreations:* poetry. literature, history, biographies; *Languages:* Arabic, English, French, Persian; *Address:* Cvoir-Praha-6, Petriny-Nadaleii-13, Prague, Czechoslovakia.

JAYED , Mabruk al-, Libyan official; born 1951, Tripoli, Libya, married; three sons; *Religion:* Muslim; *Education:* Philosophy in Glasgow, 1979; *Career:* Secretary of the People's Bureau in London, 1980; *Languages:* Arabic and English; *Address:* People's Bureau of the Socialist People's Libyan Arab Jamahiriya, 5 St. James's Square, London SW1.

JAZAIRI, Idriss, Algerian diplomat; born 29 May 1936; married; four children; *Education:* MA in Political Sciences, Oxford University, UK; Graduate of the Ecole Nationale d'Administration de Paris, France; MA in Public Administration, Harvard University, USA; *Career:* member of the Office of the Director General of UNESCO, 1959–62; Adviser for Economic Affairs, Algerian Permanent Mission at UN, New York, USA, 1962–63; Head of Division, and later Director of Economic, Cultural and Social Affairs, Ministry of Foreign Affairs, 1963–70; Adviser for Economic Affairs and International Cooperation at the Presidency of the Republic, 1971–77; Assistant Secretary General, Ministry of Foreign Affairs, 1977–79; Ambassador of Algeria to Belgium, Luxembourg, and the European Community, 1980–; member of the Algerian delegation at the conference on International Economic Cooperation, Paris, 1975–77, and at different summits of Non-Aligned Countries, and at OPEC conferences; Governor and President of the Board of Governors of the Banque Africaine de Développement, 1969–72; Head of the Committee of the General Assembly of the UN on the North-South Dialogue, 1978–79; *Publications: Towards a New International Economic Order- an Evaluation of Perspectives,* published under the auspices of the governments of Algeria and the Netherlands, 1976, in French; *The Concept of International Solidarity for Development,* International Institute for Social Studies, Geneva, Switzerland, 1977, in French; *Partners in Tomorrow,* Dutton, New York, 1978, in English; *Languages:* Arabic, French, English; *Address:* Ambassade d'Algérie, 209 Avenue Molière, Bruxelles 1060, Belgium.

JAZAIRI, Muhammad, Iraqi journalist; born 30 June 1939, Basra, Iraq; married; two daughters, one son; *Religion:* Muslim; *Education:* extensive training in journalism, since 1953; self educated in literature, political and economic studies, social sciences and history, while in prison, 1961–65; *Career:* journalist; journalist with *Al-Jumhuriya,* 1972; Chief Editor, *Al-Jumhuriya ;* Editor in Chief, *Al-Jumhuriya al-'Usbuu'i ;* Editor in Chief, *Funun* magazine, 1980–; Secretary, Federation of Applied Arts Critics, 1982–; Secretary and member, General Federation of Arab Writers, 1975–; member of the Iraqi Journalists Union, 1959–, and of the Arab Journalists Union, 1968–, and of the International Organization of Journalists; member of several other cultural associations, societies and committees; *Publications:* numerous books in Arabic published in Iraq; publisher of several conference magazines; *Interests and Recreations:* gymnastics, travelling, music, literary criticism; *Languages:* Arabic, English; *Address:* Hayy al-Mathna, Mahalla 718, Street 20, Building 41, Flat 8, Zayuna, Baghdad, Iraq; telephone: Residence — 774 6216; Office — 31473, 31170.

JAZI, Dali, Tunisian lawyer; born 7 December 1942, Tunisia; married, one son, one daughter; *Religion:* Muslim; *Education:* Diploma in Higher Studies in Public Law, University of Paris, France; Diploma in Higher Studies in Political Science, University of Paris; *Career:* Attaché in the Office of the Minister of National Education, 1968–69, and 1970–71; Assistant Secretary General of the Union of Tunisian Youth in charge of foreign relations, 1970–71; lawyer in Tunis, and Assistant Professor, Faculty of Law and Political and Economic Science, Tunis; Vice President of the Tunisian Union of Young Lawyers; Treasurer of the Founding Office of the Tunisian League for the Defence of the Rights of Man; contributor to the Tunisian magazine *Contact,* 1973–74; member of the Tunisian delegation to the UNESCO General Conference, Paris, 1970; member of the Tunisian delegation to the Third Conference of the Pan-African Youth Movement, 1970; made various visits to foreign countries representing the Tunisian youth movement; *Interests and Recreations:* football, tennis, music; *Languages:* Arabic, French, English; *Address:* 14 Rue de Touraine, (Cité Jardins), Tunis, Tunisia; telephone: 283512.

JAZI, Rakan Inad al-, Jordanian politician/ army commander; born 1928, Jordan; married; *Education:* Royal Military Academy, Sandhurst, UK, 1950; Military Staff College, USA, 1959; High Military College of Nassir Academy, Egypt, 1960; *Career:* Cadet Officer, Arab Legion of Jordan, 1947; Tank Regiment Commander, 1962; Armoured Brigade Commander, 1965; Second in Command of Armoured Corps, 1969; Infantry Division Commander, 1970; Military Attaché, Embassy to UK, 1970–71; Military Adviser to HM The King, 1972; Director of Officers' Affairs, 1973; Assistant Chief of Staff for Manpower with rank of Major General, 1974; Minister for Prime Minister's Affairs, 1974, 1976; *Decorations:* Independence Medal 1st Class; Star of Jordan 2nd Class; Loyal Service Medal; Chinese Medal; *Interests and Recreations:* hunting, horse riding; *Address:* Shmaisani, Amman, Jordan; telephone: 66444.

JAZRAWI, Taha Yassin Ramadan al-, Iraqi politician; born 1938, Mosul, Iraq; *Education:* Military College, Baghdad, Iraq; *Career:* member of the Revolutionary Command Council, 1969; Chairman, Trade Council Organisation; Commander in Chief, Popular Army, 1970; Chairman, Revolutionary Command Council, Arab Affairs Bureau; Minister of Industry and Minerals, 1970; Acting Minister of the Economy, 1971; Acting Minister of Planning, 1974–76; Minister of Housing and Construction, 1976–79; First Deputy to the Prime Minister, 1979–; *Address:* Ministry of Housing and Construction, Baghdad, Iraq.

JIBOURI, Hamid Alwan al-, Iraqi politician, born 1930, Hilla, Iraq; *Religion:* Muslim; *Education:* American University of Beirut, Lebanon, 1952; *Career:* Ministry of Finance; Editor of *Al-Sha'b* newspaper, 1963; Director General of Information, Ministry of Culture and Information; Minister of State for Presidential Affairs, 1968–69; Minister of Culture and Information, 1969–70; Minister of Youth, 1970–72; Minister of Culture and Information and President of the Iraqi Youth Organization, 1972–74; Minister of State, 1974–75; Liaison Minister for the Autonomous Region of Kurdistan, 1975–76; Head of the Office of the Vice Chairman of the Revolutionary Command Council with the rank of Minister, 1976–77; Minister of State for Foreign Affairs, 1977–; *Languages:* Arabic, English; *Address:* Ministry of Foreign Affairs, Baghdad, Iraq.

JIBOURI, Hazim Ahmad al-, Iraqi UN official/agriculturalist; born 15th February 1925, Mosul, Nineveh, Iraq; married; *Reli-*

gion: Muslim; *Education:* BSc, Cairo University, Egypt, 1942–47; MSc, Utah State University, Logan, USA, 1952–53; PhD, North Carolina State University, Raleigh, USA, 1954–57; *Career:* Head, Department of Field Crops, Ministry of Agriculture, Iraq, 1957–59; Professor of Plant Genetics, University of Libya, 1958–62; Senior Agronomist, FAO, Libya, 1962–65; Agronomist, FAO, Italy, 1965–67; Regional Plant Production and Protection Officer, FAO, Thailand, 1967–74; Chief, Crop Policy and Planning Unit, Plant Production and Protection Division, FAO, Italy, 1974–75; *Publications:* numerous books and articles on agricultural subjects; *Interests and Recreations:* golf, plant breeding, agronomy, agricultural planning, international agricultural development and research; *Languages:* Arabic, English, Italian; *Address:* Office — FAO, Via delle Terme di Caracalla, 00100 Rome, Itay; telephone: 57971.

JIBOURI, Nadhima Abdul Jabbar al-, Iraqi academic/biologist; born 14 July 1937, Hindiyah, Iraq; married; two sons, one daughter; *Religion:* Muslim; *Education:* BSc in Biology, University of Baghdad, Iraq, 1962; MSc in Histology and Embryology, Texas A and M University, USA, 1971; *Career:* Laboratory Assistant, Biology Section, College of Veterinary Medicine, University of Baghdad, 1963–66; Graduate Assistant, USA, 1966–71; Assistant Professor, Biology Section, College of Veterinary Medicine, University of Baghdad, 1971; *Publications:* several scientific articles in English and one paper in Arabic; *Interests and Recreations:* chess; *Languages:* Arabic, English; *Address:* Biology Section, College of Veterinary Medicine, Baghdad University, Baghdad, Iraq; telephone: Office — 555 3264; Residence — 555 5808.

JIBRIL, Ahmad, (Abu Jihad), Palestinian politician/guerrilla leader; born 1935 in Ramle; *Religion:* Muslim; *Career:* Syrian Army; Syrian Chess Champion, 1956; left Syrian Army 1958, founded the Palestinian Liberation Front (PLF) in Syria, 1961; began military operations 1965; following 1967 War PLF was briefly part of the Popular Front for the Liberation of Palestine (PFLP), later withdrew to become the PFLP–General Command, a non-political organization which did not join the Palestine Liberation Organization (PLO); member of the Rejection Front with Dr George Habbash.

JIBURY, Falih Khidir al-, Arab-American academic/irrigation engineer; born 17 December 1934; married; one son; *Religion:* Muslim; *Education:* BSc, University of Baghdad, Iraq, 1965; MSc, Oregon State University, USA, 1958; PhD, Oregon State University, 1960; Registered Professional Engineer, State of California, 1976; *Career:* Head of Land Use and Classifications, Ministry of Development, Iraq 1955–56; Assistant Professor, University of Baghdad, 1960–61; Irrigationist, University of California, 1961–80; member of the State Water Resources Control Board, 1980–; Visiting Professor, American University of Beirut, Lebanon, 1967–68; member, California Water Commission, 1978–80; Adviser to the Libyan Ministry of Land Development, to the Iraqi Ministry of Agriculture, to the Mexican Ministry of Water Resources, and to the US National Academy of Sciences Water Management Board; member of Society of Agriculture Engineers, International Committee of Irrigation and Drainage, American Society of Agronomy Soil Science, California Society of Agronomy, Western Society of Soil Science, Irrigation Society, California Irrigation Institute; *Publications:* numerous papers published in scientific and technical journals in English and Spanish; *Decorations:* Irrigation Engineer Man of the Year, 1976; *Interests and Recreations:* jogging, tennis; *Languages:* Arabic, English; *Address:* 1820 Columbia Drive East, Fresno, California 93727, USA; telephone: (209) 251 2909.

JIDDI, Muhammad Ali al-, Libyan politician; born 1933, Fezzan, Libya; *Religion:* Muslim; *Education:* Law, University of Al-Azhar, Cairo, Egypt; *Career:* lawyer, Fezzan; judge at Souq al-Jum'a Court; Minister of Justice, 1969–77; Secretary for Justice in General People's Committee, 1977; *Address:* Office of the Secretary of Justice, Secretariat of the General People's Committee for Justice, Tripoli, Libya.

JIFRY, Abdullah Abdul Rahman, Saudi Arabian journalist; born 1938; *Religion:* Muslim; *Education:* general; *Career:* journalist, *Okaz* daily newspaper; Literary Editor of *Al-Bilad* weekly magazine; Sub-Editor, *Al-Bilad* daily newspaper; Editor, *Okaz* daily newspaper; *Publications:* daily column in daily newspaper entitled *Shadows;* two collections of short stories; numerous short stories in Saudi papers; *Interests and Recrea-*

tions: reading, travel; *Address:* Al-Jazira Daily Newspaper, P O Box 354, Riyadh, Saudi Arabia.

JIGHMAN, Yahya Hamud, Yemen Arab Republic diplomat/politician; born 24 September 1943, Yemen Arab Republic; married; *Religion:* Muslim; *Education:* Law College, Ain Shams University, Cairo, Egypt; Law College, Paris University, France; Political Science, Boston University, USA, 1964; Political Science, Columbia University, New York, USA, 1966–68; *Career:* member of the Board of Directors of the Yemeni Bank; Director General of Broadcasting, Sana'a, 1963; Head of the Higher Council for Tribal Affairs, 1963; Minister Plenipotentiary to Washington, 1963; Minister of Foreign Affairs, 1968; Minister of State and Personal Representative of ex-President Iriyani, 1969; Deputy Prime Minister for Foreign Affairs and Economics, 1969–71; President of Supreme Council of Youth, Welfare and Sports, 1970; Yemen Arab Republic Delegate Governor, IBRD (World Bank) and IMF; Ambassador to the UN, New York, 1971; Ambassador to the USA, 1972; Minister of Foreign Affairs, 1974; Deputy Prime Minister for Foreign and Economic Affairs, 1974–77; *Publications:* various articles on political, economic and literary subjects in Arab journals; *Interests and Recreations:* writing poetry, reading poetry in Arabic, English and French, listening to music, playing piano, chess, swimming, riding; *Languages:* Arabic, English, French, German; *Address:* Ministry of Foreign Affairs, Sana'a, Yemen Arab Republic.

JISHI, Hassan Jawad al-, Bahraini official; born 1925; married; two children; *Religion:* Muslim; *Education:* in Bahrain; Diploma in Education; *Career:* headmaster of primary school; teacher in Kuwait; Superintendent of Student Affairs, Kuwait; Editor of monthly magazine *Saut Al-Bahrain,* 1951–55; represented Bahrain in three Arab writers' and poets' conferences; member of Committee of National Union, Bahrain, 1953–56; returned to Bahrain, 1971; Public Relations Officer, Aluminium Bahrain Ltd (ALBA); elected Speaker of Parliament, December, 1973; *Languages:* Arabic, English; *Address:* P O Box 726, Manama, Bahrain.

JISHI, Majid Jawad al-, Bahraini official/engineer; born 1930, Bahrain; married; *Religion:* Muslim; *Education:* BSc in Civil Engineering, American University in Beirut, Lebanon, 1955; *Career:* Public Works Directorate, Bahrain, 1956; Contracting Company, Qatar, 1957–61; Ministry of Public Works, Roads Division, Kuwait, 1961–64; Engineering Consultant, Bahrain, 1964–68; Assistant Director and later Director, Department of Works and Development, Abu Dhabi, 1968–70; Director of Planning, Ministry of Development and Engineering Services, Bahrain, 1970–72; Under Secretary, Ministry of Planning, 1973–75; Minister of Works, Power and Water, 1975–; Bahrain Representative and Chairman of Asry Board of Directors, 1974–78; chaired a conference held in Bahrain and organised by the Financial Times on construction opportunities in the Gulf, 1976; *Languages:* Arabic, English; *Address:* Ministry of Works, Power and Water, P O Box 6000, Manama, Bahrain; telephone: 254 341; telex: 8525 MOWPW BN.

JISR, Bassim al-, Lebanese journalist/writer; born 1930, Beirut, Lebanon; *Education:* Collège de la Sagesse, Lebanon; French Lycée; St Joseph University, Beirut; Doctorate in Public Law, Sorbonne, Paris; *Career:* Editor in Chief, *Al-Jarida* daily newspaper, 1956; Director of the National News Agency, 1962; member of Permanent Lebanese Delegation to UNESCO, 1959–; leading journalist on *Al-Anwar* newspaper, *Al-Mustakbal,* Paris, and *Al-Hawadeth,* London; founder and General Secretary of the Democratic Party, Lebanon, 1976; *Publications: Le Retour,* a novel; *Vers un Nouveau Liban,* 1959; *Le Liban Nouveau,* 1964; *Le Liban et le Défit Israelien,* 1968; *La Loi Electorale et le Citoyen,* 1969; *Le Pacte National Libanais,* 1978; *Lebanese Conflict,* 1981; *Interests and Recreations:* swimming, painting; *Languages:* Arabic, French, English; *Address:* 8 rue Commndant Schloesing, Paris 16e, France; Residence — Rue St. Elie, Mosaithe, Beirut, Lebanon; telephone: 303041.

JISR, Hussain al-, Lebanese diplomat; born 20 March 1911, Tripoli, Lebanon; married; one son; *Religion:* Muslim; *Career:* Barrister, 1931–40; Administrator of Mount Lebanon District, 1943–47; member of the Higher Council of Common Interests, Lebanon and Syria, 1947–50; Ambassador and Head of

Economic Services, Ministry of Foreign Affairs, 1950–54; Ambassador to Saudi Arabia, 1954–59; Ambassador to Belgium, 1959–60; Ambassador to UK, Sweden and Norway, 1960–62; Ambassador to Morocco, 1962–67; Ambassador to Algeria, 1962–67; Ambassador, Political Section, Ministry of Foreign Affairs, 1967–69; Ambasssador to Spain, 1969–75; now retired; *Decorations:* Grand Officer of the Order of the Cedar, Lebanon, 1955; Grand Cordon, Italy, 1954; Grand Cordon, Brazil, 1954; Grand Cordon, Morocco, 1969; Grand Cordon, Spain, 1975; *Languages:* Arabic, English, French, Spanish; *Address:* P O Box 3366, Beirut, Lebanon; Flat 7, 28 Hyde Park Gardens London, W2, UK; telephone: 402 8541.

JOMAIH, Muhammad Abdullah al-, Saudi businessman; born 1915, Riyadh, Saudi Arabia; *Religion:* Muslim; *Education:* general education; *Career:* Partner and Chairman of the Board of Directors of Saudi Company for Lime Bricks and Building Materials; owner of can manufacturing, filling and bottling plants for Pepsi Cola, Mirinda, Teem; owner of bus assembly plant; owner and partner in lubricating oil blending plant; partner in Saudi Crowncap manufacturing plant; dealer for General Motors, Shell Lubricating Oils, Yokohama Tyres, Tubes, and Fiat Allis; representative of several international firms; founder and member of Board of Directors of National Co for Agricultural Development; *Address:* P O Box 132, Riyadh; telephone: Office — 478 8811; Residence — 4782512; telex: 201023 SJ.

JORIO, Maati, Moroccan diplomat; born 1934, Rabat, Morocco; married; *Religion:* Muslim; *Education:* Faculty of Law, Rabat; Law Degree, University of Toulouse, Toulouse, France; further studies in political science; *Career:* Ministry of Public Works, 1957–64; Ministry of the Interior, 1964; Secretary General, Ministry of the Interior; Minister of Agriculture and National Advancement, 1971–72; Ambassador to Romania, 1973; Ambassador to USSR, 1977; Ambassador to Libya, 1980–82; *Languages:* Arabic, French. *Address:* Ministry of Foreign Affairs, Rabat, Morocco.

JOUMBLAT, Khalid, Lebanese politician/agriculturalist; born 1934, Bramieh, Lebanon; married; two sons; *Religion:* Muslim; *Education:* Broummana College; Agri-culture, Cirencester College, UK; *Career:* Minister of Agriculture and Health, 1967–68; Director General of Druze Waqfs, June 1969; Minister of Finance, 1974–75; *Languages:* Arabic, English, French; *Address:* Directorate General of Druz Waqfs, Verden Street, Beirut, Lebanon; Residence: Mazboudi Street, Friends Building, Lebanon; telephone: Office — 340790/1; Residence — 223141.

JOURY, Yacoub J., Jordanian UN official; born 9 July 1922, Jerusalem, Palestine; married; *Education:* general education in Administration, Radio Programming and News Production; *Career:* Programme Assistant, Palestine Broadcasting Service, Jerusalem, 1939–48; Chief News Editor and English Commentator, Hashemite Broadcasting Service, Ramallah, Jordan, 1949–53; Press and Information Officer, Tourist Department, Jerusalem, 1953–57; Consul General and member of the Permanent Mission of Jordan, New York, 1957–62; Deputy Resident Representative, UN Development Programme, Mogadishu, Somalia, 1962–64; Deputy Resident Representative, UNDP, Dacca, Bangladesh, 1964–68; Resident Representative, UNDP, and Director of UN Information Centre, Katmandu, Nepal, 1968–75; Resident Representative, Iraq, 1975–79; Resident Representative UNDP, Kingston, Jamaica, 1979–; *Languages:* Arabic, English, French; *Address:* UNDP, 1 Lady Musgrave Road, P O Box 280, Kingston 5, Jamaica; telephone: 92/65500, 92/65666.

JUFFALI, Ahmad, Saudi Arabian businessman; born 1924, Saudi Arabia; married; four children; *Education:* in Saudi Arabia and UK; *Career:* Managing Director of several companies including E.A. Juffali and Bros, Saudi Electrical Company, Saudi Cement Company Ltd, Chairman, National Insurance Company SA (Luxembourg), Arabian Metal Industries Company Ltd, Fluor Arabia Ltd, National Automobile Industry Co Ltd, Mercedes Truck Assembly Plant, Pool Arabia Ltd, Saudia Business Machines Ltd, Steel Products Co Ltd; Honorary Consul General of Denmark; founding member of Albank Alsaudi Alhollandi; member of Saudi-German Joint Economic Commission, Saudi-US Joint Economic Commission, Chase Manhattan Bank International Advisory Committee, Wells Fargo Bank International Advisory Committee; *Address:* P O Box 1049, Jeddah, Saudi Arabia; telephone: 642 22222; telex: 401130 EAJB.SJ

JUM'A, Hussain Makki al-, Kuwaiti businessman/banker; born 1929; *Religion:* Muslim; *Career:* extensive business interests in shipping and travel; Managing Director, Al Ahli Bank, Kuwait and Dubai; member of the Board of Directors of Industrial Bank of Kuwait, UBAF, Paris, UBAF, London, UBAF Arab American Bank, New York, Arab Malaysian Development ATROC Bank Ltd; member of the Board of Kuwait Chamber of Commerce, Kuwait Investment Company (Bahrain); Adviser to Arab Investment for Asia, Kuwait, Blanket Industry Company; Chairman of Arab Japanese Finance Ltd, Tokyo, Arab Japanese Finance Ltd, Hong Kong, Aluminium Extraction Company, Kuwait; Representative of Air France, Air Afrique, Union De Transport Aériens; *Languages:* Arabic, English, French; *Address:* Al-Ahli Bank, P O Box 1387, Kuwait; telephone:: 444444, 442442; telex: 22067 KT.

JUM'A, Midhat, Jordanian diplomat; born 19 August 1920, Jordan; married; *Religion:* Muslim; *Education:* BLitt, Cairo University, Egypt, 1945; Diploma of Press Institute, Cairo University, 1948; *Career:* teacher, Salt Secondary School, 1945; Attaché at Arab League, 1946–47; 1st Secretary, Jordanian Legation to Egypt, 1948–49; Counsellor, Embassy to Egypt, 1950–53; Counsellor, Embassy to London, 1953; Chargé d'Affaires, Jordan Legation to Pakistan, 1954; Minister Plenipotentiary to Pakistan, 1955; Head of Royal Protocol, 1956; Under Secretary for Publications, Broadcasting and Tourism in Foreign Ministry, 1957; Ambassador to USA 1958; Ambassador to Morocco, 1959; Ambassador to West Germany, 1962–65; Ambassador to Lebanon, 1965–67; Ambassador to UK, 1967–69; Ambassador to Tunisia, 1969–71; Ambassador to Spain, 1971–75; Ambassador to Egypt, 1975–76; Ambassador at Ministry of Foreign Affairs, Amman, Jordan, 1976–77; *Address:* Shmaisani, Amman, Jordan.

JUM'A, Sa'ad Iddin, Jordanian official; born 1924, Tafila, Jordan; married; *Religion:* Muslim; *Education:* Diploma in Administration, USA, 1955; *Career:* Prime Minister's Office, 1947–57; Secretary to the Cabinet

1957–60; Assistant Secretary General of the Cabinet, 1960–62; Secretary General of the Cabinet, 1962; Government Representative on Oil Refinery Company Board; *Address:* Shmaisani, Amman, Jordan; telephone: 666652.

JUM'A, Salah Muhammed, Jordanian UN official/agricultural expert; born 1927, Tafila, Jordan; married; *Religion:* Muslim; *Education:* BSc in Agricultural Sciences, Cairo University, Egypt 1953; MSc in Agricultural Sciences, London University, UK 1956; *Career:* Principal of Al-Jabiha Agricultural College and Supervisor of Agricultural Studies in Ministry of Agriculture and Head of Al-Jabiha Agricultural Research Station 1956–63; Director of Forestry, Ministry of Agriculture 1962–64; Director of Agricultural Studies, Ministry of Agriculture 1965–68; Jordanian Representative, Food and Agricultural Organisation, Rome, 1968–71; Deputy General Manager of Agricultural Loans Corporation, Ministry of Supply 1972; President of the Union of Agricultural Engineers 1966–68 and 1972–76; Minister of Agriculture 1976–78; Assistant Director General, Food and Agriculture Organisation, 1978–; *Decorations:* Independence Medal 3rd Class; *Address:* UN Food and Agricultural Organisation, Via delle Terme ali Caracalla, 00100 Rome, Italy; telephone: 57971.

JUMA, Abdulla Muhammad, Bahraini electrical engineer; born 1946, Bahrain; married 1972; one son, one daughter; *Religion:* Muslim; *Education:* BSc in Electrical Engineering, University of Salford, UK, 1970; *Career:* Distribution Engineer, Electricity Directorate, Bahrain, 1970–74; Project Engineer, Electricity Directorate, Bahrain, 1976–; Assistant Director, Electricity Directorate, Bahrain, 1976–78; Director of Electricity, Electricity Directorate, Ministry of Works, Power and Water, Bahrain, 1978–; *Interests and Recreations:* golf, jogging; *Languages:* Arabic, English; *Address:* Electricity Directorate, P O Box 2, Manama, Bahrain; telephone: 259926/7; telex: 8525 MOWPW BN.

JUMA, Hassan A., Bahraini banker; born 1948, Muharraq, Bahrain; *Religion:* Muslim; *Education:* Commercial Diploma; ICMA Diploma; *Career;* Manager, National Bank of Bahrain, 1972–81; Deputy General Manager, National Bank of Bahrain, 1981–; *Interests*

and Recreations: tennis, swimming; *Languages:* Arabic, English; *Address:* National Bank of Bahrain, P O Box 106, Manama, Bahrain; telephone: 230350.

JUMAH, Hassan Fahmi, Iraqi Arab League official/agriculturalist and academic; born 15 May 1937, Baghdad, Iraq; married; one son, two daughters; *Religion:* Muslim; *Education:* BSc, Baghdad University, Iraq, 1959; MSc, University of Wisconsin, USA, 1962; PhD, University of Maine, USA, 1964; *Career:* Agricultural Engineer, Ministry of Agriculture and Agrarian Reforms, Iraq, 1959; Lecturer, Faculty of Agriculture, Baghdad University, 1964–68, Dean, Faculty of Veterinary Science, Baghdad University, 1968–69; Director General, Department of Agriculture and Natural Resources and Supervisor for overall Agricultural and Veterinary Faculties in Iraq, 1963–70; Dean, Faculty of Agriculture and Forestry, Mosul University, Iraq, 1973; Professor, 1973; Minister of Agriculture and Agrarian Reforms, Iraq, 1974–77; Adviser, Ministry of Higher Education and Scientific Research, Iraq, 1977–80; Director General, Arab Organisation for Agricultural Development, Khartoum, Sudan, 1980–; *Publications:* numerous research papers on agricultural development, agricultural education, agricultural problems; *Interests and Recreations:* swimming, political sciences; *Languages:* Arabic, English, German; *Address:* Director General, Arab Organization for Agricultural Development, P O Box 474, Khartoum, Sudan.

JUMAN-AGHA, Adnan, Syrian diplomat/ lawyer; born 12 December 1928, Aleppo, Syria; married; one son, two daughters; *Religion:* Muslim; *Education:* Licence in Law, Damascus University, Syria, 1950; Diploma in Criminology, Paris, France; *Career:* private law practice, Aleppo, 1950– 52; Attaché, Ministry of Foreign Affairs, Damascus, 1952; 3rd Secretary, Syrian Embassy to Iraq, 1954; 2nd Secretary, Syrian Embassy to West Germany, 1957–59; 2nd Secretary, United Arab Republic Embassy to Saudi Arabia, 1959–60; UAR Consul in Hamburg, 1961; Syrian Consul in Istanbul, Turkey, 1962–64; 1st Secretary, Syrian Embassy to Belgium, 1964–66; Counsellor, Syrian Embassy to USSR, 1967–70; Minister Counsellor, Syrian Permanent Delegation to UN in Geneva, Switzerland, 1972; *Interests and Recreations:* economics and political science, history of peoples, travel, swimming; *Languages:* Arabic, French, English, German, Russian, Turkish; *Address:* 3A Rue de Moillebeau, 1209 — Geneva, Switzerland; telephone: 348172.

JUMAY'AN, Mikhael, Jordanian administrator; born 1915; *Education:* American University in Cairo, Egypt; *Career:* interpreter, 1940–43; teacher, 1943–45; Government Agency Secretary, 1945–47; Assistant Chief Accountant, 1947–50; Registrar of Patents, Trademarks and Companies, 1950–55; Assistant Divisional Head, Civil Service, 1955–57; Divisional Head, 1957–62; Assistant Under Secretary, 1965–68; Director of Antiquities, 1968–70; Director, Institute of Public Administration, 1970–; represented Jordan at several Arab and international conferences; President of AUC Alumni Club in Jordan, 1977–; representative of Jordan in AUC Alumni Council; *Publications: Fundamentals of Supervision,* 1964; *Fundamentals of Public Administration,* 1969, translated into Arabic; *International Laws of Chess;* and papers on public administration; *Eastern Cultural Influences on the Western Civilzation Through the Crusades; Languages:* Arabic, English; *Address:* P O Box 2077, Amman, Jordan.

K

KA'EB, Muftah Muhammad, Libyan politician; *Religion:* Muslim; *Career:* Governor of Misurata; Minister of Municipalities, November 1974–1976; Minister for Youth Affairs, 23 October 1976–77; Secretary General, People's Committee for Popular Sports; *Address:* Office of the Secretary for Popular Sports, Tripoli, Libya.

KABBAJ, Colonel Major Muhammad, Moroccan air force chief; married; *Religion:* Muslim; *Career:* Director of Royal Air Maroc Flight Operations and Technical Flight Personnel; pilot on commercial flights; Inspector of the Moroccan Air Force; *Address:* Ministry of Defence, Rabat, Morocco.

KABBANI, Fadil Khairy, Saudi Arabian official/mineralogist; born 1916, Mecca, Saudi Arabia; *Education:* ACSM, Camborne School of Mines, UK, 1938–41; DSc in Metal Mining, Colorado School of Mines, USA, 1951–54; *Career:* Chief of Production and Distribution Section, Office of the Minister of State for Development Projects, Ministry of Finance, Jeddah, 1947; Head of Mining Department, Bureau of Mines and Companies, Ministry of Finance; Deputy Director General of Petroleum and Mineral Affairs, Ministry of Finance and National Economy, 1954–61; Assistant Deputy Minister, Directorate General of Mineral Resources, Ministry of Petroleum and Mineral Resources, Jeddah, 1961–63; Deputy Minister of Mineral Resources; Associate of Camborne School of Mines; member of Board of Directors of General Organization of Petroleum and Minerals (PETROMIN), 1962–75, the Board of Trustees of College of Petroleum and Minerals (now University of Petroleum and Minerals), 1963–75, the Management Board of International Geological Cooperation Programme (IGCP), 1973–75, Board of Governors of International Atomic Energy Agency (IAEA), Vienna, Austria, 1972–74,

Saudi Arabian Permanent Representative at the Permanent Mission to IAEA, Vienna; member of the Constituent Commission of King Abdul Aziz University, 1963–70; member of the Council of King Abdul Aziz University, 1967–71; Chairman of Council of Deans of the College of Petroleum and Minerals, 1970–71; Head of Saudi Delegations to the annual 13th to 18th Conferences of the International Atomic Energy Agency, Vienna, 1969–74; Head of Saudi Delegation to the International Conference on the Conservation of the Natural Resources, Turkey, 1970, Fourth International Conference on the Peaceful Uses of Atomic Energy, Geneva, Switzerland, 1971; Round Table Conference of the Arab Heads of Geological Surveys, Cairo, Egypt, 1971; Alternative Head of the Second Arab Conference on Mineral Resources, Jeddah 1974; represented Saudi Arabia at the Solar Energy Conference, France, 1974; *Publications: Geophysical and Structural Aspects of Central Red Sea Rift Valley; Interests and Recreations:* reading, collecting mineral crystals, stamps and coins; *Address:* Al-Kandara Airport Road, P O Box 553, Jeddah, Saudi Arabia; telephone: Jeddah 33002.

KABLI, Ridha Ali, Saudi Arabian academic/official; born 1937; *Religion:* Muslim; *Education:* PhD in Organic Chemistry, 1973; *Career:* Lecturer, Faculty of Science, Riyadh University, Saudi Arabia; Assistant Professor, Riyadh University; Dean of Students, Riyadh University; Educational Attaché, Saudi Arabian Embassy, Washington, 1977–79; Assistant Professor, King Abdul Aziz University, Jeddah, 1980–; Fellow of the Chemical Society, UK; *Publications:* two papers published in the *Journal of the Chemical Society,* UK; *Address:* Faculty of Science, King Abdul Aziz University, P O Box 1540, Jeddah, Saudi Arabia.

KABLY, Ahmad Fadil, Saudi Arabian official/trade unionist; born 1918, Mecca, Saudi Arabia; *Religion:* Muslim; *Education:* Saudi Islamic Institute, Mecca, Saudi Arabia; *Career:* cashier, government repair shop, 1947–53; Accountant, Arab Company for Pilgrims' Transport; later Inspector, Financial Affairs; Director General of Public Transport Trade Union; member of the Supreme Committee of Pilgrimage, Mecca, Municipal Council, Mecca; *Interests and Recreations:* reading, travel; *Address:* Al-Masfala, Mecca, Saudi Arabia; telephone: Mecca 22231, 27511.

KABODAN, Abdul Hamid Ahmad, Egyptian banker; born 17 June 1924, Damanhur, Egypt; married; two sons; *Religion:* Muslim; *Education:* BA in Law and Economics; Diploma of Graduate Studies in Economics and Banking, 1963; *Career:* Head of Legal Department, Barclays Bank, DCO; Manager, Barclays Bank, Algeria; General Manager, Public Organization for Banks, Ministry of External Culture, Bank of Alexandria, Cairo; member of the Board of Directors, Arab African Bank, Cairo, Misr America International Bank, Cairo; Chairman of Development Industrial Bank; *Languages:* Arabic, English, French, German; *Address:* 110 Galaa Street, Cairo, Egypt; telephone: 776803, 779174.

KADDOUMI, Faruk al-, (Abu Lutf), Palestinian politician; born 1930, Nablus, Palestine; *Education:* graduated in Economics and Political Science, Cairo University, Egypt; *Career:* founding member of Fatah; later member of Palestinian Liberation Organization (PLO) Central Committee; until 1967 was responsible for PLO relations with Egypt and Iraq; member of PLO Executive Committee, 1969; during the Lebanese crisis in November 1969 negotiated on Palestinian behalf with the Saudi Ambassador; Head of the PLO Political Department, 1974–; contributed to UN debate on Palestine, November 1974.

KADDOURI, Fakhri Yasin, Iraqi official/economist; born 1932 Baghdad, Iraq; married; three children; *Education:* BA, Faculty of Commerce, University of Baghdad, 1953; MA, Faculty of Economic Science, State University of Iowa, USA, 1958; PhD Faculty of Economic and Social Science, Cologne University, Federal Republic of Germany, 1964; International Marketing Institute, Harvard University, 1966; United National European Centre, Geneva, 1968; *Career:* Tutor, Faculty of Commerce, University of Baghdad, 1953,56,58,59; Director of Internal Commerce, Ministry of Economy, Baghdad, 1965–68; Minister of Economy, Baghdad, 1968–71; Head of Economic Affairs, Revolutionary Command Council, 1971–78; Governor of Central Bank of Iraq, 1976–78; General Secretary of Council of Arab Economic Unity, 1978–; member of Follow-up Committee for Oil Affairs and Agreements Implementations, 1971–78; member of the Council of Regulating Trade, 1968–71, 1976–78; member of Planning Council, Iraq, 1971–78; President of Iraqi Economists Association, 1973–75, 1977–78; President of Liaison Committee for Professional and Popular Organisations; *Languages:* Arabic, English; *Address:* Council of Arab Economic Unity, P O Box 925100, Amman, Jordan; telephone: 64329; telex: 21900 WEHDA JO.

KADDUR, Shaikh Abdul Hafid Bin Ahmad, Tunisian businessman/farmer and stock breeder; born 28 January 1920, Le Kef, Tunisia; married; one son; *Religion:* Muslim; *Education:* Theological Studies, Al-Khadria Mosque, Le Kef, Tunisia; *Career:* Shaikh of Al-Khadria Mosque; farmer; Honorary President of the National Syndicate of the Breeders of Thoroughbred Horses in Tunisia; *Decorations:* Order of Tunisian Independence, 1960; *Languages:* Arabic, French, English, Italian; *Address:* Haras d'Abida, Le Kef, Tunisia; telephone: 275 605.

KADHIM, Nuri Muhammad al-, Iraqi diplomat; born 1928; married; three daughters; *Religion:* Muslim; *Education:* BA in Political Science, University of South California, USA; *Career:* Ministry of Foreign Affairs, 1959; 1st Secretary, Embassy to Turkey, 1961; Director of International Conferences, UN Department, Ministry of Foreign Affairs, 1964; Counsellor, Embassy to UK, 1965; Acting Director General of Conferences and of the United Nations Department, Ministry of Foreign Affairs, 1966; Counsellor, Embassy to Austria, 1966; Legal Department; Ministry of Foreign Affairs, 1968; Ambassador in the Ministry of Foreign Affairs, and Director General of the Ministry of Foreign Affairs, Public Relations Department, 1972; *Languages:* Arabic, English; *Address:* Public Relations Department, Ministry of Foreign Affairs, Baghdad, Iraq.

KADI, Trad Sud al-, Jordanian physician/ politician; born 1938, Jordan; married; four sons; *Religion:* Muslim; *Education:* Medical College, Cracow University, Poland; *Career:* Doctor at the Ministry of Health, Jordan; Director of private clinic; Minister of Health, 1974–76; *Interests and Recreations:* hunting, political history; *Languages:* Arabic, English, Polish; *Address:* Housha, Irbid, Jordan.

KADIRI, Abdul Hafid, Moroccan politician/ agriculturalist; born 1929; *Education:* Institut National d'Agronomique, France; *Career:* Director, Muhammad Douiri's cabinet; Director, Hajj Omar Ben Abdeljalil's cabinet; Under Secretary of State for Agriculture, 1958; Director of the Bureau de Recherches et de Participations Minières; left public service, 1962; member of Istiqlal Political Committee, 1956, and Executive Committee, 1969; member of the Editorial Board, *Al Istiqlal, Nation;* Director of *L'Opinion;* Minister of Youth and Sports, 1977–80; member of Parliament, 1977–; *Languages:* Arabic, French; *Address:* c/o Ministry of Youth and Sports, Rabat, Morocco.

KAHHALAH, Subhi, Syrian official/ engineer; born 1911, Damascus, Syria; *Education:* in Damascus; Engineering, Robert College, Istanbul, Turkey, 1933; MA in Engineering, University of Illinois, USA; *Career:* Ministry of Public Works and Communications, 1941–51; Head, Irrigation Section, 1941–53; Acting Director of Irrigation, 1943–46; Director of Building and Town Planning, Ministry of Public Works, 1947; Director of Technical Department of Damascus Government, 1948–53; established Consulting Engineers Firm; appointed to Board of Euphrates Dam Scheme and Major Projects Organization, 1961; Minister of Communications, 1962–63; Minister of Planning, 1962; led economic delegation to Moscow and Peking which negotiated major credit agreements, 1963; Director General of the Euphrates Dam Authority, 1969; Minister of Euphrates Dam Affairs, 1974–76; President of Syrian Engineers Association; *Languages:* Arabic, English; *Address:* Ministry of Cabinet Affairs, Damascus, Syria.

KAHTANI, Muhammad Said Abdul Rahman al-, Saudi Arabian academic/agriculturalist; born 1940, Saudi Arabia; *Education:* PhD, Horticulture, Kansas State University, Kansas, USA; *Career:* Assistant Professor, College of Agriculture, Riyadh, Saudi Arabia; Vice Dean, College of Agriculture, Riyadh University; Dean, Colleges of Agriculture and Veterinary Medicine, King Faisal University, Eastern Province, Saudi Arabia; Acting Vice Rector and Vice Rector, King Faisal University, Eastern Province; Rector, King Faisal University, Eastern Province, 1976–; member of American Society for Horticulture Science, Plant Growth Regulator Working Group, International Society for Horticultural Science, Saudi Society for Biological Sciences; participated at several national and international conferences in the field of horticulture; *Interests and Recreations:* travelling, reading; *Languages:* Arabaic, English; *Address:* King Faisal University, P O Box 1982, Dammam, Saudi Arabia.

KAID, Ahmad, Algerian politician; born 1921, Algeria; *Religion:* Muslim; *Career:* official in Municipality; member of National Liberation Front (FLN) soon after outbreak of War of Independence, 1954; member of First National Council of the Revolutionary Army, 1956; Assistant to Houari Boumedienne when latter set up Headquarters at Oujda, 1958; visited China as member of Oussedik Delegation, 1959; served on General Staff of National Liberation Army (ALN) at Ghardimaou, Tunisia, 1960; member of FLN Delegations at Evian and Lugrin negotiations; elected Deputy for Tiaret, 1962; Minister of Tourism, 1963–64; member of National Assembly, Foreign Affairs Committee; elected member of FLN Central Committee at Party Congress, 1964; member of Council of the Revolution, 1965; Minister of Finance and the National Plan, 1965; *Responsable du Parti,* 1967–72; former member of Revolutionary Council; *Languages:* Arabic, French; *Address:* Front de Libération Générale (FLN), Place Emir Abdel Kader, Algiers, Algeria.

KAIKSOW, Salman Ahmad Salman, Bahraini businessman; born 1919, Manama, Bahrain; married; six sons, one daughter; *Religion:* Muslim; *Education:* in Bahrain and India; *Career:* founder of Salman A Kaiksow, 1930; expanded into electromechanical field, 1973; diversified into hotel and catering business by the establishment of Tylos Hotel, Manama, Bahrain, 1975; Founder of Associate Company International, for commercial trading and sponsorship of international agencies, 1978; Founder of Taram Travel, 1978; Founder of MANTECH, trading in micro computers, complete OEM systems for business use, data processing in education and media supplies, 1978; *Interests and Recreations:* travel; *Languages:* Arabic, English; *Address:* P O Box 80, Manama, Bahrain; telephone: 253735, 714428.

KAIROUZ, Shaikh Habib, Lebanese politician/businessman; born 1916, Besharreh, Lebanon; married; two sons, two daughters; *Education:* BA in Political Science, French Faculty of Law and Economic Sciences of Beirut, 1952; *Career:* President of Hoteliers Association of Lebanon, 1946–; Deputy for Besharreh, 1960, 1964, 1968, 1972–; Chairman of the Parliamentary Commission on National Economy and Tourism, 1960–69; member of the Board of Banque de Crédit Populaire, 1962–; Minister of Tourism, 1969; Minister of Economy and National Defence, 1971; Chairman of the National Council of Tourism, Lebanon, 1971–; represented Lebanon at a number of international congresses in Austria, Portugal, USA, Canada, USSR, Iran, Egypt, Iraq; *Decorations:* Grand Officer of the National Order of Cedar, Lebanon; Gold Medal, Lebanese Order of Merit; Golden Star of International Tourism, awarded by the International Federation of Tourism; High Decoration from the Republic of Haiti; Grand Silver Medal awarded by the International Committee of Arts; Gold Commander Medal, awarded by the Academy of Human Sciences and Relations, Santo Domingo, Dominican Republic; *Languages:* Arabic, French; *Address:* National Council of Tourism, P O Box 5344, Beirut, Lebanon; telephone: 340940; telex: 20898.

KAISSI, Abbas al-, Moroccan politician; born 1926, Fes, Morocco; married; three children; *Religion:* Muslim; *Education:* Qarawiyin University, Fes, Morocco; French Baccalauréat and Degrees in Arts and Law; *Career:* Conservateur Foncier (Land Registrar); Deputy Secretary General of the Government, 1966; Under Secretary of State for the Interior, 1969–71; Director of Legislation at the Ministry of Administrative Affairs; Under Secretary of State for the Interior, 1972; Minister for Administrative Affairs, 1972; Director of the Royal Cabinet, 1973; Minister of Justice, 1974–77; Secretary General of the Government, 1977–; *Languages:* Arabic, French; *Address:* Office of the Secretary General of the Government, Rabat, Morocco.

KAISSOUNI, Abdul Mun'im al-, Egyptian banker/politician; born 1916; married; *Religion:* Muslim; *Education:* BCom, Cairo University, Egypt; BSc, PhD in Economics, London University, UK; *Career:* Barclays Bank, UK, 1942–43; Adviser to the Council of Ministers for Post-War Affairs, 1944–45; Lecturer, Assistant Professor of Economics, Cairo University, 1944–50; Deputy Director General of Foreign Affairs, Ministry of National Economy, 1949–50; Director, Middle East Department, International Monetary Fund (IMF), Washington D.C., and Chief Technical Representative in the Middle East, 1946–50; National Bank of Egypt, 1950–54; Deputy Minister of Finance and Economy, 1954; Minister of Finance and Economy, 1954–60; member of the National Assembly, 1957; Minister of Economy and Commerce for Egypt in the United Arab Republic (UAR), 1958; Minister of Economy, UAR Central Government, 1958–62; Chairman of the Board of the Economic Organization; Minister of Treasury and Planning, 1962–64; Deputy Prime Minister for Economic Affairs and Finance, and Minister of Economy and Foreign Trade, 1964–65; President, UN Conference on Trade and Development, Geneva, 1964; Chairman of Arab International Bank, 1971–76; Chairman, European Arab Holding, Luxembourg, 1972; member of the National Economic Council, Egypt, 1974; Deputy Prime Minister for Financial and Economic Affairs, 1976–78; Minister of Planning, 1977–78; Chairman, European Arab Bank Group; *Address:* European Arab Bank Ltd, 107 Cheapside, London EC2V 6DT; telephone: 606 6099; telex:8812047 EURAB.

KAKISH, Fuad, Jordanian engineer/politician; born 18 October 1922, Salt, Jordan; married; *Education:* BSc in Engineering, American University of Beirut, Beirut, Lebanon, 1944; Diploma in Civil and Sanitary Engineering, Imperial College, University of London, UK, 1951; *Career:* various government technical posts since 1944 in Ministry of Public Works, Municipality of Amman; Ministry of Interior, Development Board, Municipal Loans Fund; Under Secretary of Ministry of Interior for Municipal and

Rural Affairs, 1970–71; member of Chamber of Deputies, 1973; Minister of the Interior for Municipal and Rural Affairs, 1973–74; Senator, 1974–; Engineer, designing and supervising private buildings; member of Aqaba Planning Committee, the Administrative Council of the Natural Resources Authority, the Institutional Committee of Central Electricity Authority; member and later Vice President of the Scientific Research Council; member of the Anti-Illiteracy Movement, Youth Organisation, Supply Council, Council of the Arab National Union, 1972–; member of the Foreign Affairs Committee and Financial Affairs Committee in the Chamber of Deputies, 1973; *Address:* P O Box 5252, Amman, Jordan; telephone: 65553.

KALLAL, Zuhair, Tunisian academic/physician; born 26 February 1930, Tunisia; married; one daughter, one son; *Religion:* Muslim; *Education:* MD, Paris, France; PhD in Medicine, Dijon, France; Graduate in Experimental Medicine, University of Paris; Diploma in Nutrition; *Career:* Resident at Hospital, Seine Boix Paris, 1959; Assistant, Faculty of Medicine, Paris, 1960–64; Researcher at INSERM, Paris, 1960–64; Assistant, Faculty of Medicine, Tunis, 1965; Professor of Experimental Medicine, Tunis, 1969; Director, National Institute of Nutrition, Tunis, 1968–; Director, Superior School of Sciences for Nutrition, 1972; Professor and Head of Department for Experimental Medicine, Faculty of Medicine, Tunis, 1977–; Director of Projects of FAO; Co-Researcher in several universities, Harvard, Berkeley, Columbia and others; Adviser to the Ministry of Public Health; member of several international professional associations and societies; *Publications:* numerous articles in professional journals; Founding Director of the journal *Cahiers Médicaux de Tunisie,* 1970; *Decorations:* Order of Independence, Tunisia; Order of Tunisian Republic; Chevalier de la Légion d'Honneur, France; *Interests and Recreations:* travelling, music, medical ecology, protection of the environment; *Languages:* Arabic, French, English; *Address:* 14 Avenue de la Liberté, Tunis, Tunisia; telephone: 283943, 264600.

KAMAL, Burhan, Jordanian official/engineer; born 1916, Nablus, Palestine; married; *Education:* Certificate of Mechnical Engineering, Loughborough College, Loughborough, UK, 1939; *Career:* Director of Industrial School, Haifa, Palestine, 1939–48; Director, Technical Training, Syria, 1948–50; Professor of Engineering, Engineering College, Aleppo, Syria, 1950–54; Director of Technical Trainging and Edcuation, Jordan, 1954–67; Under Secretary, Ministry of Education, 1967–69; Minister of Communications, 1969–70; member of the Board of Directors of Jordan Tobacco and Cigarette Company, Ltd, Housing Bank, Steel Pipe Company Ltd, Spinning and Textile Company, Ltd, 1970–; member of the Board of Education for Vocational Training, Ministry of Labour, 1970–; *Address:* P O Box 59, Amman, Jordan; telephone: 77114.

KAMAL, Marwan Rasim, Jordanian academic; born 27 June 1933, Anabta, Palestine; married; two sons, two daughters; *Religion:* Muslim; *Education:* BS, Roosevelt University, 1955; MS, De Paul University, 1958; PhD, University of Pittsburgh, 1961; Master of Business Administration, University of Minnesota, 1968; *Career:* Researcher and Head of Department, General Mills Inc, USA, 1961–67; Professor and Dean of Sciences, Universty of Petroleum and Minerals, Saudi Arabia, 1967–77; Professor of Chemistry and Dean of Sciences, University of Jordan, 1977–80; Dean of Agriculture, University of Jordan, 1980–; *Publications:* several publications in international journals on heterocyclic and isocyanate chemistry and energy related research; *Interests and Recreations:* tennis, squash, bridge; *Languages:* Arabic, English; *Address:* Faculty of Agriculture, University of Jordan, Amman, Jordan; telephone: Office — 843555; Residence — 43334.

KAMAL, Muhammad, Jordanian broadcasting official; born 1913, Nablus, Palestine; married; *Religion:* Muslim; *Education:* BA, American University of Beirut, Beirut, Lebanon; *Career:* Superintendent, Press Bureau, British Mandate Administration, Jerusalem, Palestine; journalist and economic writer, 1948–66; Director General, Jordanian Television, 1966–; *Languages:* Arabic, English; *Address:* Jordanian Television, P O Box 1041, Amman, Jordan; telephone: 73111; telex: 1244 KAMAL JO.

KAMAL, Munir Mark, Arab-American engineer; born 13 February 1936, Beirut, Lebanon; married; one son, two daughters;

Education: BS in Mechanical Engineering, Robert College, Istanbul, Turkey, 1956; MS and PhD in Mechanical Engineering and Mechanics, University of Michigan, USA, 1958, 1965; *Career:* Project Engineer, AC Spark Plug Division, General Motors Corporation, Flint, Michigan, USA, 1956–59; Associate Senior Research Engineer, General Motors Research Laboratory, Warren, Michigan, 1965–67; President, Country Lane Home Owners Association, 1966–68; Supervisor and Research Engineer, 1968–70; Delegate, International Safety Conference, Brussels, Belgium, 1970; Programme Manager, 1970–71; Assistant Department Head, 1971–77; Department Head, 1977; member of Industry Community, University of Michigan College of Engineering, the American Society of Mechanical Engineers; the Society of Automotive Engineers, the Country Lane Home Owners Association; *Address:* Residence — 1615 Dutton Road, Rochester, Michigan 48063, USA; Office — General Motors Research Laboratory, Twelve Mile and Mound Roads, Warren, Michigan 48090, USA.

KAMALI, Shafiq al-, Iraqi poet; born 1930, Iraq; *Career:* Minister of Youth, 1970–76; Ambassador Extraordinary, Spain, 1977–79; Minister of Information, 1979–80; Chairman of the Board, Afaq Arabiya Publishing House, 1980–; Deputy Chairman, Arab Writers Union, 1975–; *Publications:* published three collections of poems, which seek new values from the Arab past, and relates Arab history to contemporary history; *Address:* Afaq Arabia, P O Box 4032, Baghdad, Iraq; telephone: 22011, 22012.

KAMEL, Hassan, Egyptian lawyer/diplomat; born 6 September 1907; resident in Qatar; *Religion:* Muslim; *Education:* Cairo University, Egypt; Montpellier and Paris Universities, France; Doctor of Law; *Career:* member of Egyptian Mixed Courts, 1930–36; Lecturer in Administrative Law, High College of Police and Administration, 1936–37; Ministry of Foreign Affairs, 1937–59, serving in France, Italy, Syria, Portugal, Switzerland, Libya, Argentina, Turkey, Hungary; Legal Adviser, Government of Qatar, 1960; Director General, Government of Qatar, 1961–67; Adviser, Government of Qatar, 1967; Permanent Representative of Qatar to UN, 1971–72; represented Qatar at various international conferences; member of Board of Directors Shell (Qatar) Limited and Qatar Petroleum Limited; *Publications:* many legal articles; *Decorations:* Officer of Légion d'Honneur, Commander of National Order of Merit; *Languages:* Arabic, English, French; *Address:* P O Box 636, Doha, Qatar.

KAMEL, Ibrahim Mustafa, Egyptian banker/architectural engineer; resident in Switzerland; born 10 July 1938, Dakahliya, Egypt; married; one son, three daughters; *Religion:* Muslim; *Education:* BSc in Architecture, Faculty of Engineering, Ain Shams University, Cairo, Egypt, 1960; DPLG in Architecture, Ecole Nationale Superieure des Beaux Arts, Paris, France, 1968; PhD in Architecture, Cairo University, Egypt, 1969; *Career:* architectural work with various firms in Paris, France, 1962–66; Executive Vice President, Consultants International, Paris, 1966–70; President, Kamel Holdings SA and Kamel Brothers SA, Switzerland, 1973–; Executive Vice President, Islamic Investment Company, 1978–82; Executive Vice Chairman, Dar Al-Maal Al-Islami Group, 1981–; member of various Islamic economic associations; *Decorations:* Officer of the National Order of the Popular Revolutionary Republic of Guinea; *Interests and Recreations:* swimming, squash, chess; Islamic heritage and arts; Islamic applications in the field of economics, finance, and management; *Languages:* Arabic, English, French; *Address:* 7 Rue des Alpes, Geneva, Switzerland; telephone: 323205.

KAMEL, Salih Abdullah, Saudi Arabian businessman; born 1940, Mecca, Saudi Arabia; *Religion:* Muslim; *Education:* BCom in Accountancy and Administration; *Career:* Financial Inspector, Ministry of Finance Representative; Financial Adviser, Ministry of Finance; member of Board of Okaz Press and Publishing Organization, of Dar Okaz Printing Organization, Tihama Company for Advertising, Public Relations and Marketing Studies, Saudi Company for Hotels and Tourist Zones, Fast Co, Saudi Prefab Co; Chairman of Board of Avco-Dallah Corporation; Director General of Dallah Corporation; *Interests and Recreations:* reading, travel; *Address:* Avco-Dallah Corporation, P O Box 430, Jeddah, Saudi Arabia; telephone: Jeddah 55490.

KAMHAWI, Walid, Palestinian-Jordanian physician; born 1923, Nablus, Palestine; *Religion:* Muslim; *Education:* MD; Diploma in Gynaecology and Obstetrics; *Career:* General Practitioner and Director, Kamhawi Hospital, Nablus, Palestine, 1951–62; Gynaecologist, 1962–73; President, Jordan Medical Council, 1963–69; Assistant General Secretary, Arab Medical Federation, 1963–73; member of the Executive Committee of Palestine Liberation Organisation, 1964–65; President, Family Planning Society of Nablus, 1965–74; President, Palestine National Fund, Palestine Liberation Organisation, 1974–81; Governor, Arab Fund for Economic and Social Development, 1975–81; *Publications: Planned Parenthood,* in Arabic 1953; *Catastrophe and Reconstruction,* in Arabic, 1955, 1962; *Interests and Recreations:* travel, swimming, reading; *Languages:* Arabic, English, Hebrew; *Address:* P O Box 950408, Amman, Jordan.

KAMIL, Hassan Ahmad, Egyptian administrator; *Religion:* Muslim; *Education:* Military Academy; *Career:* Artillery Colonel; Chef de Cabinet to General Muhammad Naguib until end of Naguib Presidency; Head of Protocol Department, 1964; Ambassador to Greece, 1968–73; Grand Chamberlain in the Presidency, 1973–74; Director of President's Private Office, 1974; *Languages:* Arabic, English; *Address:* c/o Ministry of Foreign Affairs, Cairo, Egypt.

KAMIL, Muhammad Ibrahim, Egyptian diplomat; born January 6 1927, Egypt; married; *Religion:* Muslim; *Education:* BA in Law, Faculty of Law, Cairo University, 1947; *Career:* Legal Council of State, 1948–56; Ministry of Foreign Affairs, 1956; 3rd Secretary, Embassy to UK; Counsellor, Embassy to Mexico; Consul General in Montreal, Canada; Counsellor, Embassy to Canada; Head of News Department, Ministry of Foreign Affairs; Ambassador to Zaire in early 1960s, returning after temporary closure of Egyptian Embassy; Ambassador to West Germany, 1973–77; Minister of Foreign Affairs, 1977; *Languages:* Arabic, English, French; *Address:* Ministry of Foreign Affairs, Cairo, Egypt.

KAMIL, Mustafa, Egyptian diplomat; born 27 October 1908; *Education:* Cairo University, Egypt; Sorbonne, University of Paris, France; LLB; *Career:* Professor of Constitutional and Administrative Law, Cairo University; member of Egyptian delegation to Afro-Asian Conference, Bandung, Indonesia, 1955; Ambassador to India, 1955–58; Ambassador to USA, 1958–67; Ambassador to Belgium and Luxembourg, 1967–68; retired from diplomatic service, 1968; *Publications:* textbooks on constitutional, administrative and penal law; *Languages:* Arabic, French, English; *Address:* Al-Shams Building, 94 Sarwat Street, Apartment 15, Cairo, Egypt.

KAMMAL, Muhammad Said Wasfi, Palestinian politician; born 1938, Nablus, Palestine; *Religion:* Muslim; *Education:* in Baghdad, Iraq, and Alexandria, Egypt; *Career:* joined Arab Nationalist Movement (ANM); left ANM 1966 to join Fatah; President of the General Union of Palestine Students; Assistant Director of the PLO Cairo Office, 1973; Deputy to Farouk Kaddoumi in PLO Political Department, 1974; PLO delegate to the pre-summit meeting of Arab Foreign Ministers, 1974; joined PLO delegation to the UN for General Assembly debate on Palestine.

KANA'AN, Faisal Muhammad, Saudi Arabian geologist; born 1941, Taif, Saudi Arabia; *Religion:* Muslim; *Education:* BSc, 1964; MSc, 1966; PhD in Geology and Geochemistry; *Career:* Geologist, 1966–68; Senior Economic Geologist, Directorate General of Mineral Resources, 1968–74; Deputy Chief Geologist, Directorate General of Mineral Resources; member of Geological Society of America, USA, Society of Economic Geologists, USA; *Interests and Recreations:* soccer, track and field bowling, chess; *Address:* P O Box 1970, Jeddah, Saudi Arabia; telephone: Jeddah 33331.

KANAWATY, George D, Egyptian UN official/chemist; born 17 September, 1930, Tanta, Egypt; married; *Religion:* Christian; *Education:* BSc, Chemistry and Geology, Alexandria University, Alexandria, Egypt; MS, Management, University of Illinois, USA; PhD, Management, University of Illinois, USA; *Career:* Chemist and Head of Labour Management Relations, Misr Beida Dyers, 1950–60; ILO Expert, Production Management, Cyprus and Cambodia, 1963–68; ILO Regional Adviser, Management Development, Africa 1968–69; ILO Project Manager, Tunisia, 1969–70; Associate Professor of Management, University of Ottawa, Canada; Director, Master Programme in Management Science, University of Ottawa, Canada; Chief of Management Development Branch, ILO, Geneva, Switzerland, 1973–82; Chief of Training Department, ILO, 1982–; *Publications: Cotton Bleaching, Dyeing, and Finishing,* 1954, in Arabic; co-author of *Career Planning and Development,* 1976; *Management Consulting,* Geneva 1981; co-author and editor *Introduction to Work Study,* Geneva 1979; editor and co-author *Managing and Developing New Forms of Work Organisations,* Geneva 1981; various papers published by ILO and other organisations; *Interests and Recreations:* swimming; *Languages:* Arabic, English, French, Spanish; *Address:* International Labour Organisation, 1211 Geneva 22, Switzerland.

KANOO, Abdul Latif Jasim, Bahraini official; born 22 December 1935, Bahrain; married; two sons; *Religion:* Muslim; *Education:* DIC, Imperial College, London, UK; MSc, University of Pittsburgh, USA; PhD, University of Texas, USA; *Career:* Kuwait Ministry of Public Works, 1960–63; Consultant, 1963–67; College of Petroleum and Minerals, Dhahran, 1965–67; Director of Research and Engineering Projects, Bahrain, Ministry of Development and Engineering Services, 1971–75; Under Secretary, Ministry of Housing, 1975–; member of Physical Planning Unit, Bahrain; member of Federation of Arab Engineers, Bahrain-Qatar Joint Economic Committee, the Industrial and Cultural Cooperation Committee; represented Bahrain at various regional and international conferences; Chairman of Bahrain Aluminium Extrusion Co; Vice Chairman of Bahrain Housing Bank; Chairman of Bahrain Technical Committee for Saudi-Bahrain Causeway; *Interests and Recreations:* collecting of Korans, philatelist; President, Bahrain Society of Engineers and Bahrain Historical and Archaeological Society; member of the American Society of Civil Engineers and British Institution of Structural Engineers, Chartered Structural Engineer and Federation of Arab Engineers; *Languages:* Arabic, English; *Address:* P O Box 45, Manama, Bahrain.

KANOO, Ahmad Ali, Bahraini businessman; born 22 July, 1922, Manama, Bahrain; married; two sons, one daughter; *Religion:* Muslim; *Education:* American University of Beirut, Beirut, Lebanon; *Career:* Chairman and Chief Executive, Yusuf Bin Ahmad Kanoo Group of Companies; Chairman of the Board of National Bank of Bahrain; Chairman of the Board of Bahrain Ship Repairing and Engineering Company, Bahrain Hotels Company; Director of Bahrain Fishing Company; member of Bahrain Consultative Assembly, 1973; *Interests and Recreations:* swimming, reading, travelling, member of various sports associations; *Address:* Kanoo Building, Al-Khalifa Road, P O Box 45, Manama, Bahrain; telephone: 254081; telex: 8215 KANOO BN.

KARAM, Jihad, Iraqi diplomat; born 2 December 1936, Beirut, Lebanon; *Education:* BA in Political Science, American University of Beirut, Lebanon, 1958; MA in Political Science, American University of Beirut, 1969; *Career:* private law practice, Beirut, 1969–70; Ministry of Foreign Affairs, Baghdad, 1970–71; Chief Delegate, Conference of Group of 77, Lima, Peru 1971; Vice Chairman, Delegation of Iraq to Third UNCTAD Conference, Santiago, Chile, 1972; member, Delegation of Conference of Ministers of Non-Aligned Countries, Georgetown, Guyana, 1972; member, Delegation of Iraq to Conference of Ministers of Non-Aligned Countries, Algiers, 1973; Chief Delegate, UNCTAD Working Group on Charter of Economic Rights and Duties of States, Mexico, 1974; Chairman, Economic and Finance Committee, UN General Assembly, 1974; Ambassador to Brazil; member of the Iraqi Delegation to the Conference of Foreign Ministers of the Non-Aligned Countries, Lima, Peru, 1975; member of the Iraqi Delegation to the Conference of Foreign Ministers of the Non-Aligned Countries, India, 1981; Ambassador of Iraq to India, 1978–80; Ambassador of Iraq to Guyana, Suriname and Grenada, 1980–82; *Interests and Recreations:* international law, economics; *Languages:* Arabic, English, French; *Address:* Ministry of Foreign Affairs, Baghdad, Iraq.

KARAM, Melhem, Lebanese journalist; born 1934, Rishmaya, Lebanon; married; one son, one daughter; *Religion:* Christian; *Education:* general; *Career:* President of Students Association; journalist on *Al-Assifa* review; owner-editor of Arabic daily *Al-Bayraq,* periodical, *Sabah al-Khair* and *Alf Laila Wa Laila,* and of Lebanese News Agency;

President of Lebanese Editors Association; *Languages:* Arabic, French; *Address:* Residence — Rue Abdel Wahheb, Beirut, Lebanon.

KARAMI, Rashid, Lebanese politician; born 1921, Tripoli, Lebanon; *Religion:* Muslim; *Education:* Licence in Law, Faculty of Law, Cairo University, Egypt, 1947; *Career:* Barrister at Law, 1948–51; elected Deputy for Tripoli, 1951; Minister of Justice, 1951; re-elected Deputy, 1954; Minister of Economy and Social Affairs, 1954–55; Prime Minister and Minister of the Interior, 1955–56; Prime Minister, 1958; Minister of Defence, Finance, Economy and Information, 1958–59; Prime Minister of enlarged Cabinet, October 1959–60; re-elected Deputy for Tripoli, 1960; Prime Minister and Minister of Finance, 1961–64; Prime Minister and Minister of Defence and Finance, 1965–66; Prime Minister and Minister of Finance, 1966–68; re-elected Deputy for Tripoli, 1968; Prime Minister and Minister of Finance, 1969; resigned September 1970; Prime Minister, Minister of Defence, Finance and Information, 1975; Prime Minister and Minister of Agriculture, Tourism, Housing and Co-operatives, 1976; member of National Dialogue Committee, 1975–; *Decorations:* Légion d'Honneur, and numerous other Lebanese and foreign decorations; *Interests and Recreations:* shooting; *Languages:* Arabic, French; *Address:* Office — Presidency of the Council, Grand Serail, Beirut, Lebanon; Residence -- Bachoura, Da'aboul Building, Beirut, Lebanon.

KARARA, Hussam Mahmud, Arab-American engineer/academic; born 5 September 1928, Cairo, Egypt; married; two daughters; *Education:* BSc, Cairo University, Egypt, 1949; DSc in Science Technology, Zurich, Switzerland, 1956; *Career:* Engineer, Ministry of Public Works, Egypt; Field Engineer, Idfina Dam construction, Egypt, 1949–51; Field Engineer, La Grande Dixence Dam construction, La Grande Dixence Company, Sion, Switzerland, 1952; Scientific Collaborator, Institute of Photogrammetry, Swiss Federal Institute of Technology, Zurich, 1955–56; Assistant Professor, University of Illinois, Urbana, USA, 1956–61; Associate Professor, University of Illinois, Urbana, 1961–66; Professor of Civil Engineering, University of Illinois, 1966–; Consultant of Photogrammetric Engineering to industrial and governmental mapping agencies in the USA and abroad; member of the American Society of Photogrammetry; member of the American Congress on Surveying and Mapping; member of the American Society of Civil Engineers; member of the Canadian Institute of Surveying; *Publications:* several articles in professional journals; Editor in Chief of *Handbook of Non-Topographic Photogrammetry,* 1979; Author, Chapter 16, *Manual of Photogrammetry,* 4th edition, 1981; *Decorations:* Talbert Abrams Award, 1959, 1961; Presidential Meritorious Award, 1966, 1971, 1976, 1979; Fairchild Photogrammetric Award, 1974; and others; *Address:* Office — Department of Civil Engineering, University of Illinois, Urbana, Illinois, Ill 61801, USA; Residence — 1809 Coventry Drive, Champaigne, Illinois, IL 61820, USA.

KARIM LAMRANI, Muhammad, Moroccan official/businessman; born 1 May 1919, Fes, Morocco; *Religion:* Muslim; *Career:* Office Chérifien des Phosphates (OCP), after Independence; Director, Office Cherifien des Phosphates, 1959–63; wide business and banking interests; former President of the Compagnie Africaine des Banques; Chairman, Managing Director, Crédit du Maroc, 1966; Director General, Office Cherifien des Phosphates, 1967–; Chargé de Mission, Royal Cabinet, 1967; Minister of Finance, 1971; Prime Minister, 1971–72; elected President of the World Phosphate Institute, 1973; President, Maroc Chimie; Economic Adviser to HM King Hassan; *Languages:* Arabic, French; *Address:* Office of the Cherifien des Phosphates, Angle Route d'El Jadida et Boulevard de la Gande Ceinture, Casablanca, Morocco; telephone: 206 31.

KARMI, Ghada, Palestinian physician/medical historian, resident in UK; born 19 November 1939, Jerusalem, Palestine; *Religion:* Muslim; *Education:* MB, ChB, Bristol University, UK, 1964; member of the Royal College of Physicians, London, 1967; PhD, University of London, 1978; *Career:* practiced medicine in British hospitals, 1964–72, last post Registrar in Medicine, Middlesex Hospital, London; Wellcome Research Fellow in the History of Arabic Medicine, University of Sion, Switzerland, 1952; *Languages:* Arabic, English, French; *Address:* 39 Brondesbury Villas, London, NW6, UK.

KAROURI, Muhammad Othman al-Hassan al-, Sudanese agriculturalist; born 1 January 1939, Nuri, Sudan; married; one son, one daughter; *Religion:* Muslim; *Education:* BSc, Agriculture, University of Khartoum, 1961; MSc, Soil Science, Aberdeen University, 1962–65; PhD, Soil Science, University of London, Wye College, 1970–74; *Career:* Assistant Researcher, Agricultural Research Corporation, Sudan, 1961–62; Head, Soil Science Section, Hudeiba Research Station, Sudan, 1965–70; Head, Soba Agricultural Research Station, Sudan, 1974–77; Director, Agricultural Research Council, National Council for Research, Khartoum, 1977–; Vice President, Sudanese Soil Science Society; Part-time Lecturer, The Institute of Environmental Studies, University of Khartoum; member of The Sudanese Society for Protection of the Environment; National Committee for Education, Culture and Science; *Publications:* numerous publications in scientific journals such as *Journal of Agricultural Science* and others; numerous scientific papers published in the annual *Reports of Sudan,* Agricultural Research Corporation; *Decorations:* Eisenhower Fellow, 1977; *Interests and Recreations:* conservation of natural resources and protection of the environment; gardening, swimming, chess; *Languages:* Arabic, English; *Address:* Agricultural Research Council, P O Box 6096, Khartoum; telephone: 70707, 70701, 70702.

KASHIF ALGHITA, Bakir Ahmad, Iraqi engineer; born 1922, Iraq; married; one son, two daughters; *Religion:* Muslim; *Education:* BSc in Civil Engineering, American University of Beirut, AUB, Lebanon, 1943; MSc in Irrigation, University of California, Berkeley, USA, 1947; PhD in Irrigation and Drainage Engineering, Utah State University, USA, 1951; FICE, London, 1964; *Career:* Engineer, Directorate General of Irrigation, Baghdad, 1951; Chief Engineer, Directorate General of Irrigation, 1958; Director General of Irrigation, Baghdad, 1959; Inspector General of Irrigation, Baghdad, 1970; Professor of Irrigation, Drainage and Hydrology, College of Engineering, Baghdad University, Iraq, 1971; Consulting Engineer; head of several official Iraqi delegations; *Publications: Hydrology and Its Applications,* 1982, University of Mosul; *Hydrology for Geographers,* 1982, University of Baghdad; and several others books and researches; *Decora-*

tions: Order of Salvation, 1954; *Interests and Recreations:* walking, reading, Arabic and English poetry, chess; *Languages:* Arabic, English, French, Persian; *Address:* 12/18/601 Al-Mansur, Baghdad; telephone: 5515154.

KASSAB, Adnan Ali, Iraqi engineer; born 1934; *Religion:* Muslim; *Education:* Higher Institute of Industrial Engineering, Baghdad, Iraq; *Career:* Resident Engineer, Army Canal Project, 1961–63; Director of Administration, Government Industrial Projects, 1963–64; later arrested and imprisoned; Director General of Iraqi Ports Administration, 1968–71; President, State Construction Contracting Company, 1972–80; Consultant and Researcher, 1981–; *Address:* Al Kathrah Quarter 21/17/635, Baghdad, Iraq.

KASSIM, Habib Ahmad, Bahraini politician; born 1940; *Religion:* Muslim; *Education:* BA in Economics, American University of Beirut, Lebanon, 1965; *Career:* member of Department of Finance; worked in Bahrain Development Office, 1967; Director of Commerce and Industry, Ministry of Finance and Economy, 1971; Under Secretary in Ministry of Commerce and Agriculture, 1975; Minister of Commerce and Agriculture, 1976–; *Address:* Ministry of Commerce and Agriculture, P O Box 251, Bahrain Tower, Government Road, Manama, Bahrain; telephone: 244143; telex: 9171.

KASSIM, Tarik Jamal, Saudi Arabian banker; resident in UK; born 28 August 1946, Safad, Palestine; married; one son; *Religion:* Muslim; *Education:* Business Law and Finance, City of London Polytechnic, London, UK; *Career:* Trainee, Arabian American Oil Company (ARAMCO), Dhahran, Saudi Arabia; Management Trainee, Electro-Components (Holdings) Ltd, London, 1970–73; Institutional Sales Executive, Vickers da Costa, London, 1973–74; Chief Executive, Arab Bank Investment Company Ltd (formerly The Arab and Morgan Grenfell Finance Company Ltd), 1974–; *Interests and Recreations:* reading, photography, tennis, swimming, theatre, classical music; *Address:* Office — Arab Bank Investment Company Ltd, Empire House, First Floor, 8/14 St. Martin's-le-Grand, London EC1A 4AD; telephone: 606, 7491; Residence — Flat 1, 8 Sydney Street, London SW3 6PP.

KATHARI, Said al-Samhan al-, Omani journalist/businessman; born 1942, Najd, the Southern Region of the Sultanate of Oman; married; one son, two daughters; *Religion:* Muslim; *Education:* general; *Career:* Owner and Editor of *Al-Aqida* magazine, first published in October 1972, (Arabic); *Interests and Recreations:* literature, history, politics, geography, *Languages:* Arabic, English; *Address:* PO Box 4001, Ruwi, Oman; telephone: Office — 701000, 701081; Residence — 600776.

KATKHUDA, Louay, Syrian UN official/chemical engineer; born 18 February 1929, Aleppo, Syria; married; *Education:* Diploma in Chemical Engineering, Federated Institute of Technicians, Zürich, Switzerland, 1946–51; *Career:* Chief, Tests and Research Laboratories, Syria, 1953–54; Research Chemist, Industrial Research Institute, 1954–58; Deputy Chief, Chemical Engineering Division, 1958–60; Chief, Chemical Engineering Division, Deputy Director, Department of Technology, Industrial Research Institute, Lebanon, 1960–66; Industrial Development Officer, 1966–69; Acting Chief, Industrial Institute Section, United Nations Industrial Development Organization (UNIDO), 1960–70; Chief, Industrial Institutions Section, UNIDO, Austria; *Publications: Role of Standardization in Industrial Development,* 1954; *Requirements for Industrial Research in Developing Countries,* 1969; *Interests and Recreations:* tennis, literature, music, applied research, technology, industrial and economic development; member, Association of Lebanese Engineers, Association of French Professional Engineers, American Oil Chemists Society; *Languages:* Arabic, English, French, German; *Address:* Office — P O Box 707, A-1011, Vienna 1, Austria; telephone: (0222) 43500; Residence -- 2 Phorusgasse, A-1011 Vienna, Austria; telephone: (0222) 571192.

KATLABI, Hussain Yahya al-, Syrian agriculturalist; born 1940 Hama, Syria; married; four daughters; *Religion:* Muslim; *Education:* BSc, MSc in Agriculture (Entomology), University of Alexandria, Egypt; *Career:* Researcher, 1965–71; Chief of Entomological Research Department of Plant Protection Research, Ministry of Agriculture and Agrarian Reform, Syria; *Publications: Hylesinus Olieperda F.,* 1966, in Arabic; *Dacus Olease G. Density,* 1967, in Arabic; *A*

Guide to Olive Pests, 1975; *Control of Dasyneura Oleae L.,* 1977, in French; *Life Cycle of Dasyneurs Oleae L.,* 1979, in French; *Parasites on Dasyneura Oleae L.,* 1980, in French; *Languages:* Arabic, French, English; *Address:* 72 Jaber Iben Hayan Street, No 7 Al-Sait Building, Shamal al-Koztari, Tijara, Damascus, Syria.

KAWAR, Fakhri Anis Najib, Jordanian journalist/writer; born 9 June 1945, Jordan; married; one son, one daughter; *Religion:* Christian; *Education:* Licence in Arabic Literature, Beirut, Lebanon; *Career:* published short stories in various Arabic magazines; television plays and series for children; journalist at *Al-Ra'i* newspaper, 1974–78, 1981–; journalist, *Al-Akhbar* newspaper, Jordan, 1978–79 and 1980; *Publications:* several short stories collections; children's stage play, *Watan al-Assaafer,* 1983; *Interests and Recreations:* member of, Jordanian Writers Association, Arab Writers Association, Damascus, Jordanian Journalists Union; *Languages:* Arabic, English, Persian; *Address:* Al-Ra'i newspaper, P O Box 6710, Amman, Jordan; telephone: 67171.

KAWAR, Tawfiq Amin; Jordanian businessman; born 1927, Nazareth, Jordan; married; two sons, one daughter; *Education:* LLB, Unversity College, London University, UK; Barrister at Law, Lincoln's Inn, 1952; *Career:* Office Manager, Mines Manager, Export Sales Manager, Jordan Phosphates Mines Co SA, 1952–57; Managing Director, Amin Kawar and Sons; Honorary Consul General for Denmark in Jordan; member of the Board of Amman Chamber of Commerce, 1972 – ; member of the Consultative Board, Aqaba Port; *Decorations:* Knight of the Order of Dannebrog, Denmark; *Interests and Recreations:* tennis, squash, walking, gardening; *Languages:* Arabic, English, French; *Address:* Amin Kawar and Sons, Kawar Building, Post Office Square, P O Box 222, Amman, Jordan.

KAWARI, Issa Ghanim al-, Qatari plitician; born 20 February 1942; one son, one daughter; *Religion:* Muslim; *Education:* BA in Political Studies and Public Administration, American University of Beirut (AUB), 1969; *Career:* Shell Oil Company, Qatar; Director of the Office of HH Shaikh Khalifa Bin Hamad al-Thani, then Deputy Ruler, 1970; Director of the Office of HH Shaikh

Khalifa Bin Hamad al-Thani, Amir of the State of Qatar, 1972; Minister of Information, 1972; member of the Board of Qatar General Petroleum Corporation; member of the Board of Investments; *Languages:* Arabic, English; *Address:* The Amir's Office, P O Box 923, Doha, Qatar; Ministry of Information, Doha Qatar; telephone: 426835, 324262; telex: 4297 QPRESS DH.

KAWARI, Jassim al-, Qatari administrator; born 1942; *Religion:* Muslim; *Career:* Office Manager of Minister of Foreign Affairs, Shaikh Suhaim Bin Ahmed al-Thani; *Address:* Ministry of Foreign Affairs, P O Box 250, Government House, Doha, Qatar; telephone: 325759, 325394.

KAYAL, Alawi Darwish, Saudi Arabian politician; born 1936, Jeddah, Saudi Arabia; *Religion:* Muslim; *Education:* PhD, Political Science; *Career:* Instructor, Riyadh University, Riyadh, Saudi Arabia; Director General, Social Security Organisation; Director General of Posts; Minister of Posts, Telegraphs and Telephones; member of the American Association of Political Science; Head of Saudi Delegation to Centenary Postal Conference, Lausanne, Switzerland, 1974; *Publications: Studies in American Oil Policies The Control of Oil: East–West Rivalry in the Gulf Interests and Recreations:* swimming, fishing; *Address:* Ministry of Posts, Telegraphs and Telephones, Riyadh, Saudi Arabia; telephones: 4012233; telex: 201197 TRPSIT SJ.

KAYED, Yasin Abdul Fattah al-, Jordanian official/businessman; born 1931, Zarqa, Jordan; married; three sons, one daughter; *Religion:* Muslim; *Education:* BA in Economics, Cairo University, Egypt; *Career:* Chief of Customs, Authorities of Amman, 1969; Head of the Affairs Department, Ministry of Finance, Jordan, 1970; Assistant Deputy Minister of Finance, 1972; Deputy Minister of Finance, Customs; member of the Administrative Board of the Jordanian Oil Refinery Co, the Joint Jordanian-Syrian Free Zone Co, the Jordanian Ports Organization, the Jordanian Free Zones Organisation; *Decorations:* Order of the Jordanian Star 2nd Class; *Interests and Recreations:* reading, swimming; *Languages:* Arabic, English; *Address:* Ministry of Finance, P O Box 90, Amman, Jordan; telephone 23186.

KAYID, Hassan Ali al-, Jordanian lawyer/politician; born 1918, Jordan; married; *Religion:* Muslim; *Education:* American University of Beirut, Lebanon; Egyptian Baccalaureate 1940; Licence in Law, Cairo University, Egypt, 1948; *Career:* Public Prosecutor, Ministry of Justice, Kerak, 1946; President of the Court of First Instance, Kerak, 1953; Attorney General for Amman, 1958; Under Secretary, Ministry of Education, 1961; Under Secretary, Ministry of Justice, 1962; President of the Appeals Court, 1962; Minister of Education, 1963–64; Senator, 1963–71; Minister of Interior, 1967–68; President of Employees' Council, 1971–76; Senator, 1976–; *Decorations:* Independence Medal, 2nd Class; *Interests and Recreations:* reading Arabic poetry and prose; *Address:* Jabal Hussein, Amman, Jordan; telephone: 660833.

KAYYAL, Abdullah Abdul Aziz al-, Saudi Arabian diplomat; born 1913, Riyadh, Saudi Arabia; *Religion:* Muslim; *Education:* Diploma in Arabic and Education, Cairo University, Egypt; *Career:* private office of late HM King Faisal; official of the Ministry of Education, Eastern Region; Minister Plenipotentiary to Iraq; Ambassador to USA, Mexico, Cuba and the UN; Head of Public Works Department; Ambassador to the United Arab Emirates; Ambassador to Austria, 1980–; *Decorations:* Orders of Merit from Egypt and Syria; *Interests and Recreations:* reading, swimming, gymnastics; *Address:* Embassy of Saudi Arabia, Formanegasse 38, Vienna, Austria.

KAYYALI, Fawzi al-, Syrian lawyer/politician; born 1923, Aleppo, Syria; *Career:* lawyer; civil servant, Ministry of Labour and Social Affairs; Minister of Culture, Tourism and National Guidance, 1970–76; member of Arab Socialist Union (ASU) and Secretary General, Syrian Arab Socialist Union; *Languages:* Arabic, French; *Address:* Syrian Arab Socialist Union, Damascus, Syria.

KAZ, Abdullah Ibrahim Abdullah al-, United Arab Emirates official; born 25 May 1946, Ras al-Khaimah, United Arab Emirates; married; one son, one daughter; *Religion:* Muslim; *Education:* BA in Commerce (Accounting), 1971; *Career:* Financial Director, Electricity Authority, Ras al-Khaimah; Deputy Financial Director, Ministry of Finance and Industry; *Interests and Recreations:* football, member of Amman Sports Club;

Languages: Arabic, English; *Address:* Ministry of Finance and Industry, P O Box 433, Abu Dhabi, United Arab Emirates.

KAZEM, Muhammad Ibrahim, Egyptian academic; resident in Qatar; born 26 December 1928, Cairo, Egypt; married; two daughters, one son; *Religion:* Muslim; *Education:* BSc, College of Education, Ain Shams University, Cairo, 1950; MED, Graduate School, University of Kansas, Kansas, USA, 1955; PhD, University of Kansas, 1957; *Career:* Teacher in Egyptian Schools and in Aleppo Teachers' College, Syria, 1950–54; First President, International Educators Organization, 1956; Cultural Attaché of Egypt to the Philippines, 1959–60; Assistant Professor of Education, Ain Shams University, Cairo, 1957–63; Associate Professor, Ain Shams University, Cairo, 1963–70; Founding Dean, College of Education, Al-Azhar University, Cairo, Head of Department and Professor, Department of Foundations of Education, 1970–; Chairman of the Fund Raising Committee for the Istanbul World Conference of the World Council for Curriculum and Instruction, 1976; Founding Dean, Faculty of Education, Doha, Qatar, 1973–77; First President, University of Qatar, Doha, 1977–; Chairman, Council for Higher Education, Arab Bureau of Education for the Gulf States, Saudi Arabia, 1980–81; member of the Founding Committee of the Arab Gulf University, Bahrain, 1980–81; Board Member, Institute for the History of Arab Islamic Sciences, West Germany, 1981–83; Chairman, Finance Committee, World Council for Curriculum and Instruction, USA, 1982–; member of the Philosophy of Education Society, USA; *Publications: Educational Planning in Egypt,* International Institute of Educational Planning, Paris, 1972, in English; *Educational Needs of Children in Egypt,* National Centre for Social Research, Cairo, 1973, in Arabic; and several other books on education; articles published in journals and magazines; *Decorations:* decorations from the Philippines; *Languages:* Arabic, English; *Address:* University of Qatar, P O Box 2713 Doha, Qatar; telephone: 872 151.

KAZEMI, Zaid Abdul Hussain Hassan al-, Kuwaiti businessman; born 1916 *Religion:* Muslim; *Education:* private general education; *Career:* worked in business for Abdul Muhsin Ali Kharafi and Muhamad Almatrook, 1933; established his own business in partnership with Abdul Rahman al-Bisher, 1943: elected member of Parliament, 1963–71; member of Planning Board Council, 1972–77; member of Committee for the Revision of the Constitution, 1980; *Languages:* Arabic, English, Persian; *Address:* PO Box 47, Kuwait; telephone: 411660, 515888.

KAZIMI, Abdul Latif al-, Kuwaiti businessman; born 1925; married; *Religion:* Muslim; *Career:* has extensive business interests; member of the National Assembly until its dissolution, 1975; Chairman, United Shipping Trading and Contracting Services WLL; *Languages:* Arabic, English; *Address:* United Arab Shipping, Trading and Contracting Services, WLL, P O Box 403, Safat, Kuwait; telephone: 427026; telex: 22105 UNITED KT.

KAZIMI, Abdul Muttalib al-, Kuwaiti politician; born 1936, Kuwait; married; *Religion:* Muslim; *Education:* Cairo University, Cairo, Egypt; *Career:* Director of Budgets, Ministry of Finance; member of the National Assembly; Ministry of Oil, 1975; *Languages:* Arabic, English; *Address:* c/o P O Box 403, Safat, Kuwait.

KELLOU, Muhammad Mas'ud, Algerian diplomat; born 27 March 1931, Algeria; married; three daughters; *Religion:* Muslim; *Education:* LLB and LLD, Universities of Algiers and Montpellier, France, 1955; *Career:* member of the Front of National Liberation FLN, 1956; FLN Representative in London, 1957; Chief of the Diplomatic Mission of the Algerian Provisional Government in Pakistan, 1961; Director of Department, Ministry of Foreign Affairs, 1962; Ambassador to UK, 1963–64; Ambassador to Czechoslovakia, 1964–70; Ambassador to Argentina, 1970–75; Ambassador to the People's Republic of China, 1975–77; member of Parliament and Chairman of the Committee for Foreign Affairs, People's National Assembly, Algiers, Algeria; Ambassador to the Federal Republic of Germany, 1979–82; Ambassador to Zimbabwe, 1982–; participated in UN conferences on the Law of Treaties, Vienna, Austria, 1968, 1969, and on the Law of the Sea, Geneva, Switzerland, 1980, New York, USA, 1981; *Languages:* Arabic, French, English, Spanish; *Address:* Embassy of Algeria, 8 Pascoe Avenue, Belgravia, Hararé, Zimbabwe.

KETTANEH, Aimée, Lebanese administrator; born Lebanon; married; two sons, one daughter; *Education:* Licence in Law; *Career:* President, Baalbeck Festival Committee, 1968; honorary member of the Festival Committee, 1969–; *Decorations:* various foreign decorations among which Officer, Order of Leopold II, Belgium; *Languages:* Arabic, French; *Address:* Office — Baalbeck Festival Committee, Othman Ben Affan Street, Beirut, Lebanon; Residence -- Algiers Street, Beirut, Lebanon.

KETTANEH, Desiré Edouard, Lebanese businessman; born 31 October 1909, Beirut, Lebanon; married; two sons, one daughter; *Education:* BCom, American University of Beirut, Beirut, Lebanon, 1927; BA in Political Economy, American University of Beirut, Lebanon, 1928; *Career:* Partner Director, Eastern Distributors Corporation SAL, Beirut, 1944–, Kettaneh SA Beirut, 1952–, Jal el Dib Development Company SAL, Beirut, 1966–; Partner and Manager, Kettaneh Frères Anstalt, Vaduz, Liechtenstein, 1968–; Director General, Société Foncière pour le Lotissement et le Développement SAL, Beirut, 1969–; member of the Board of MEBCO Bank of Beirut, Bank al-Mashrek, Jordan National Bank, Iraq Manufacturing and Trading Company; *Decorations:* Knight of Magisterial Grace of the Sovereign and Military Order; Order of Independence, Jordan; Order of the Cedar of Lebanon; *Interests and Recreations:* collecting antiques; member of Automobile Club de France, Paris, Club de la Chasse et de la Nature, Paris; *Languages:* Arabic, French, English; *Address:* Office — P O Box 5094, Beirut, Lebanon.

KETTANI, Hamza al-, Moroccan academic/mineralogist; born 22 November 1940, Morocco; married; one daughter, two sons; *Religion:* Muslim; *Education:* BSc in Physics and Chemistry, University of Damascus, 1962; PhD in Mineral Chemistry, University of Paris, France, 1965; PhD in Physics, 1968; *Career:* Research Engineer, BRPM Mineral Treatment Laboratories, 1962–68; Teacher of Chemistry, Lycée Mohammad V, Rabat, 1964, 1965; Teacher of Mineral and Organic Chemistry, Ecole Normale Supérieure, 1964, 1965, 1966; Lecturer, Faculty of Science, Mohammad V University, Rabat, 1968–; Director of the Office of the Minister of Higher Education, 1968; Lecturer, Mo-

hammadia Engineering School, Mohammad V University, 1969–; Chairman, Minerology Department, Mohammad V University, Rabat, 1970–; Head of Department of Mineral Engineering, Mohammadia Engineering School, 1970–75; Visiting Professor, Laval University, Quebec, Canada, 1970; Visiting Professor, University of California, Berkeley, USA, 1972; WHO Consultant for Training of Sanitary Engineering Staff, 1977–; Director of Mohammadia Engineering School, Mohammad V University, 1975–; member of the National Association of Mining Engineers; member of the French Association of Doctors of Science; member of the National Union of Moroccan Engineers, the Moroccan Geology Association, and the Technical Committees for the Preparation of the Five Year Plan; *Publications:* numerous papers published in professional journals and magazines; *Interests and Recreations:* swimming; *Languages:* Arabic, French, English; *Address:* Ecole Mohammadia d'Ingénieurs, P O Box 765 Avenue Ibn Sina, Agdal, Rabat, Morocco.

KETTANI, Idris, Moroccan academic; born 10 October 1922, Damascus, Syria; married; two sons, one daughter; *Religion:* Muslim; *Education:* BSc in Social Sciences, Université Laval, Quebec, Canada; PhD in Social Sciences, University of Mohammad V, Rabat, Morocco; *Career:* Director, Institute of Social Sciences, Rabat, Morocco; Assistant Director General, Ministry of National Education, and Director of Islamic and Private Education, 1961; Professor, Faculty of Letters, University of Mohammad V, Rabat; *Publications: Juvenile Delinquency in Morocco,* 1975, Morocco; *The Colonial Linguistic Invasion of Morocco,* in press; *Islamic Morocco vs Atheism,* 1958, Casablanca; numerous articles and researches in newspapers and journals; *Interests and Recreations:* Islamic and social studies; founding member of several cultural, social and Islamic societies; *Languages:* Arabic, French; *Address:* Faculté des Lettres, 3 Avenue Ibn Batouta, P O Box 549, Rabat, Morocco; telephone: 71873.

KHADDAM, Abdul Halim, Syrian politican; born 1932, Syria; *Religion:* Muslim; *Education:* Law, Damascus University, Syria; *Career:* Governor of Damascus, 1964; Minister of Economy and Foreign Trade, 1969; Deputy Prime Minister and Minister of

Foreign Affairs, 1970, 1974, 1976–; member of Regional Command of the Baath Party since 1969; *Address:* Ministry of Foreign Affairs, Damascus, Syria.

KHADDOURI, Majid, Iraqi academic/writer; born 27 September 1909; *Education:* BA, American University of Beirut, Lebanon; PhD, University of Chicago, USA; *Career:* Adviser to Iraqi Delegation to San Francisco Conference, 1948; Visiting Professor in Middle Eastern History, University of Indiana, USA, 1947–48; Professor of Modern Middle East History, Higher Teachers Training College, Baghdad, 1939–47; Lecturer, Baghdad Law College, 1939–44; Visiting Professor in Middle East Politics, Universities of Chicago and Harvard, USA, 1949–50; Professor in Middle East Studies, Johns Hopkins University, USA, 1950–; Distinguished Research Professor, Johns Hopkins University, 1970–; Director of Research and Education, Middle East Institute, 1950–; Visiting Middle East Professor, Columbia University, New York, USA; member of American Society of International Law, American Political Science Association; President, Shaybani Society of International Law, Washington D.C.; *Publications: The Liberation of Iraq from the Mandate,* 1935; *The System of Government in Iraq,* 1944; *Independent Iraq,* 1951; *War and Peace in Islam,* 1955; *Islamic Jurisprudence,* 1961; *Modern Libya,* 1963; *The Islamic Law of Nations; Republican Iraq,* 1969; *Political Trends in the Arab World,* 1970; *Arab Contemporaries,* 1973; *Socialist Iraq; Languages:* Arabic, English, French; *Address:* Office — School of Advanced International Studies, Johns Hopkins University, 1740 Massachusetts Ave, NW, Washington D.C., 20036, USA; Residence — 4454 Tindall Street, NW, Washington D.C., 20016, USA.

KHADDURI, Mubarak Salih al, Omani politician/physician; born 1942, Oman; *Religion:* Muslim; *Education:* scholar of the Trucial States Scholarships Programme, University of Baghdad, 1963–71; MB, ChB, University of Glasgow, UK; Diploma in Tropical Medicine and Hygiene, University of London, UK, 1972–73; *Career:* Consultant (paediatrics and internal medicine), Ruwi Hospital, Omani Ministry of Health; Minister of Health, 1974–; *Languages:* Arabic, English; *Address:* Ministry of Health, P O Box 393, Muscat, Oman; telephone: 603807; telex: 3465 SIHA MB.

KHADER, Bishara, Palestinian writer; born 13 February 1944, Zababdeh, Palestine; *Religion:* Christian; *Education:* BA in Political Sciences, University of Louvain, Belgium; Diploma in International Relations, Johns Hopkins University; Bologna Centre, Italy; PhD in Political, Social and Economic Sciences, University of Louvain, Belgium; *Career:* Director of the Arab Research Centre, University of Louvain, 1973–; *Publications: Textes de la Révolution Palestinienne,* co-author with Na'im Khader, Paris 1975, French and Italian translations; *Anatomie de Sionisme et d'Israel,* Algiers 1974, French and Spanish translations; *Histoire de la Palestine,* 3 vols., Tunis 1976; *Dialogue Euro-Arabe et Crise Energétique,* co-author with Na'im Khader, University of Louvain Arab Research Centre 1976; *La Question Agraire dans le Monde Arabe, UCLA* 1978; *Transfers Technologiques, UCLA* 1980; *Address:* CERMAC, SHI 1348 Louvain-la-Neuve, Belgium; telephone: 010 418181.

KHADIR, Abdullah al-Hassan al–, Sudanese politician/diplomat; born 1925, Sudan; married; two sons; *Religion:* Muslim; *Education:* Diploma, Faculty of Arts, Gordon College, Khartoum, 1947; School of Public Administration, 1949; *Career:* Ministry of the Interior, 1949–56; District Commissioner; 1st Secretary, Ministry of Foreign Affairs, 1956; Consul General, Uganda and Kenya; Head of Political Section, Ministry of Foreign Affairs, 1958; Ambassador to Ghana, 1960–64; Director of Ministry of Information and Labour; Ambassador to France, 1965–69; also served on Sudanese delegations to UN and the Organization of African Unity; Under Secretary, Ministry of Foreign Affairs, 1969; Ambassador to USSR, 1972; Ambassador to the Court of St. James, London, UK, 1971–72; Minister of Natural Resources, 1972–73; Minister of the Interior, 1973–75; Secretary General to the Presidency, 1975; visited Libya and USSR in 1974; *Languages:* Arabic, English; *Address:* President's Office, Khartoum, Sudan.

KHADRA, Faisal Bin, Kuwaiti banker, born 1934; married; *Religion:* Muslim; *Education:* LLB; *Career:* Head of Bills for Collection Department, Arab Bank Ltd, 1960–64; Disbursements Officer, Kuwait Fund for Arab Economic Development, 1965–66; Chief Accountant, Assistant Manager, United Bank of Kuwait, 1966–75; Manager and later Executive Manager, Industrial Bank of Kuwait, 1975; *Publications: The Role of Arab Banks in Financing Development Projects in the Arab Countries,* 1980, in Arabic; *Interests Rates, the Factors that Influence Them and Their Effect,* in Arabic; *Interests and Recreations:* reading, music, travel; *Languages:* Arabic, English; *Address:* P O Box 24511, Safat, Kuwait; telephone: 651437.

KHAFAGY, Muhammad Abdul Mun'im, Egyptian academic/writer; born 22 July 1915, Dakahliyah, Egypt; married; one son; *Religion:* Muslim; *Education:* PhD, Al-Azhar University, Cairo, Egypt; *Career:* Professor, Chairman of Literature Department, Al-Azhar University, 1969–; Dean of the College of Arabic Languages, Al-Azhar University, 1974–78; Head of the Scientific Committees for Literature and Criticism, Al-Azhar University; President of the Society of Modern Literature, Cairo; member of the Board of The Unions of Writers; Professor and Head of the Faculty of Literature, Al-Azhar University; *Publications:* numerous books and articles in literature, poetry, theatre, Islamic studies and historical research; *Interests and Recreations:* all fields of literature, travel, chess; *Languages:* Arabic, English, Persian, Hebrew; *Address:* 6 Bank of Egypt Street, Cairo P O Box 421; telephone: 850710.

KHAIRAT, Taha, Syrian diplomat/politician; born Deraa, Syria; *Education:* MA in Law; *Career:* member of the Baath Regional Command, 1971; member of the Arab Socialist Baath Party Command in Syria, 1971; Minister of Local Administration, 1976–; Ambassador to Sofia, Bulgaria, 1982–; *Address:* Embassy of Syria, Sofia, Bulgaria.

KHAIRI, Khallusi Yusuf, Jordanian economist/politician; born 1908, Jordan; married; *Education:* BA in Politics and Economics, American University of Beirut, Lebanon, 1928; Administration and Economics, University of London, 1932; *Career:* Head of Publications in Secretariat General, Jerusalem, 1932–35; District Officer under British Mandate, 1935–45; Head of Arab Office in Washington, 1945–48; member of Chamber of Deputies, 1954–56; Minister of Commerce and Agriculture, 1949–50; member of Chamber of Deputies, 1950–51;

Minister of National Economy, 1952–53; Minister of Economy, Construction and Development, 1954–55; Minister of Economy and Finance, 1955–56; Minister of Economy, 1956; Minister of Economy and Education, 1957–58; Under Secretary, Ministry of Foreign Affairs, Baghdad, Iraq, 1958; Minister of Economy, 1959; Senator, 1959–62; Minister of Economy, Construction and Development, 1959–60; member of Palestine Delegation to UN, 1963; *Decorations:* Star of Jordan, 1st Class; Independence Medal; Renaissance Medal, 1st Class, Jordan; *Address:* Jabal Amman, P O Box 35271, Amman, Jordan; telephone: 43147.

KHAIRY, Ishaq Najati al-, Jordanian dentist; born 30 March 1947, Ramla, Jordan; married; two sons; *Religion:* Muslim; *Education:* BDS in Dentistry; PhD in Orthodontics; *Career:* Dental Surgeon, 1970; Orthodontist, Ministry of Health, 1977; Orthodontist, Jordanian Medical Center, 1980; member of the Board of Jordanian Dentists Association; Head of the Social Committee, Jordanian Dentists Association; *Publications: Vacam in Orthodontic Treatment of Children; Languages:* Arabic, English, Russian; *Address:* P O Box 2314, Amman, Jordan; telephone: Clinic — 64310; Residence — 842833.

KHAL, Yusuf A. al-, Lebanese writer/publisher; born 25 December 1917; *Education:* American University of Beirut, Lebanon; *Career:* Lecturer in Arabic Literature, American University of Beirut, 1945–47, 1955–58; Editor of *Sawt al-Mar'a,* women's monthly magazine, 1946–48; Department of Information, UN Secretariat, 1948–50; Information Officer, UN Mission for Libya, 1950–52; Editor, *Al-Hoda* daily, New York, USA, 1952–55; founder and Editor of *Al-Shi'r* poetry magazine and *Adaab* literary quarterly; owner of Gallery One, Beirut; Editorial Director, Dar al-Nahar Publishing Company, Beirut, 1967–70; Editorial Director, Société Coopérative Libanaise pour l'Edition et Diffusion, Beirut; *Publications:* numerous collections of poetry, 1945–81; translation of works by T.S. Eliot, Auden, Pound, Sandberg, Frost and others; numerous essays and critical studies; *Decorations:* Pro Mundi Beneficio Medal, Brazilian Academy of Humanities, 1975; *Address:* Ghazir, Lebanon.

KHALAF, Abbas Michel, Lebanese businessman/official; born 1934, Souq al-Gharb, Lebanon; married; three children; *Religion:* Christian; *Education:* Political Science and Administration, American University of Beirut, Lebanon; *Career:* Minister of Economy in Cabinet of Rashid al-Solh, 1974; Resident Vice President of American Life Insurance Company Operations in the Middle East; *Languages:* Arabic, English, French; *Address:* ALICO, Middle East, Beirut; telephone: 802225.

KHALAF, Kahlid Yusif, Saudi Arabian academic/official; born 27 September 1947, Saudi Arabia; married; one son, one daughter; *Religion:* Muslim; *Education:* BSc, Chemistry, University of Texas, Austin, USA, 1967; MSc, PhD, Thermo-Chemistry, University of Cincinnati, Ohio, USA, 1974; *Career:* sucessively Lecturer, University of Petroleum and Minerals, Dhahran, Saudi Arabia, 1969; Assistant Professor, 1974; Head of Chemistry Department, 1975; Director of Oil Testing Centre, 1976; Director General, Saudi Arabian Standards Organization, Riyadh, Saudi Arabia, 1978; *Publications:* four scientific articles in international research journals; several presentations in international conferences; *Interests and Recreations:* swimming, table tennis, tennis, billiards; *Languages:* Arabic, English, German, French; *Address:* P O Box 3437, Riyadh, Saudi Arabia; telephone: 4013740.

KHALAF, Karim, Palestinian politician/lawyer; born 1935, Ramallah, Palestine; married; two children; *Religion:* Christian; *Education:* graduated in law, Cairo University, Cairo, Egypt; *Career:* worked with Aziz Shehadeh; District Attorney for Ramallah, 1967; Judge in Jericho; in March 1972 Municipal Elections, of the West Bank was the youngest of the mayors elected; elected Mayor in the West Bank, 1972; signed petition to the UN when Yassir Arafat addressed the General Assembly in 1974; *Languages:* Arabic, English.

KHALAF, Salah, (Abu Iyyad), Palestinian politician; born 1933, Jaffa, Palestine; *Education:* University of Cairo, Egypt; *Career:* joined Yassir Arafat in Palestinian Students' Union; schoolmaster in Kuwait, 1967; co-operated with Farouk Kaddoumi in improving Fatah's links with Arab States; took part in the fighting in Jordan (Black September), 1970; member of Palestine Central Council, 1973.

KHALEF, Yahya, Algerian IMF official/economist; born 8 December 1929, Morocco; married; *Education:* Faculty of Law, University of Paris, France, 1953; *Career:* Director, Caisse Fédérale de Crédit Agricole, Morocco, 1958–62; Secretary General, Caisse Nationale de Crédit Agricole, Morocco, 1962; Deputy Director, Caisse Algérienne de Développement pour le Financement des Enterprises, 1963; Director of Treasury and Credit, Ministry of Finance, Algeria, 1964–70; Adviser to the Minister of Finance, Algeria, 1970–72; Executive Director, IBRD (World Bank), Washington D.C., USA, 1972; member, National Council of Credit; *Interests and Recreations:* reading, swimming; *Languages:* Arabic, French, English; *Address:* IBRD, 1818 H St NW, Washington D.C. 20433, USA; telephone: (202) 393 6360.

KHALFALLAH, Khalafallah al-Rashid Muhammad Ahmad, Sudanese judge; born 15 February 1930, Merowe District, Sudan; married; four daughters, two sons; *Religion:* Muslim; *Education:* Law Diploma, University of Khartoum, Sudan; Law Degree and Diploma in International Law, University of Cambridge, UK; LLM, University of London, UK; *Career:* Legal Assistant in the Corps of Judges, 1956–57; Judge, 1960; Legal Adviser, Ministry of Justice, 1962; Attorney General, 1967; Chief Justice of Judiciary, 1972–; elected President of the Permanent Legal Committee of the Arab League; member of the Sudanese Society for International Relations and International Law; member of the Egyptian Society of Economics, Legislation and Statistics; *Publications: Law and the Citizen,* Ministry of Information, Sudan 1967; articles in local newapapers; *Decorations:* Order of the Two Niles, 1975; Order of King Abdul Aziz, 3rd class, 1971; Jumhuriya Order, 1st Class; *Interests and Recreations:* tennis, swimming; *Languages:* Arabic, English; *Address:* P O Box 763, Khartoum, Sudan.

KHALID AL-ABDULLAH AL-FAISAL, HRH Prince, Saudi Arabian Prince/official; grandson of late King Faisal; born 1942, Taif, Saudi Arabia; *Religion:* Muslim; *Education:* BSc in Political Sciences, Cambridge University, UK; *Career:* former Official, Saudi Arabian Monetary Agency; Director General, Arab Trade, Navigation and Aviation Corporation; Chairman of the Board, AMIANTIT Industries; one of the founders of cement industry in Saudi Arabia; *Interests and Recreations:* reading, travel; *Address:* AMIANTIT Industries, P O Box 589, Dammam, Saudi Arabia; telephone: Office — Jeddah 54616; Residence — Jeddah 53340.

KHALID AL-FAISAL BIN ABDUL AZIZ, HRH Prince, Saudi Arabian Prince/ administrator; born 1940, Mecca, Saudi Arabia; son of late King Faisal and full brother of HRH Saud al-Faisal; *Religion:* Muslim; *Education:* Hun School, Princeton, USA; BA in Political Economy, Oxford University, UK; *Career:* Director General, Youth Welfare Department, 1967–71; Governor of the Southern Province, 1971–; *Languages:* Arabic, English; *Address:* Abha, Asir Province, Saudi Arabia.

KHALID BIN SULTAN BIN ABDUL AZIZ, HRH Prince, Saudi Arabian Prince/air defence commander born 1949; son of HRH Prince Sultan Bin Abdul Aziz; *Religion:* Muslim; *Education:* Sandhurst Military Academy, UK, 1968; The Command and General Staff College at Fort Leavenworth, USA; Air War College, Maxwell Air Force Base, Alabama, USA; MA in Political Sciences, Auburn University, Alabama, USA; Defence Resources Management Education Centre, the Navy's Post Graduate School, Monterey, California, USA; *Career:* Captain, Army Air Defence; Colonel, Army Air Defence Command; *Languages:* Arabic, English; *Address:* Ministry of Defence and Aviation, Airport Road, Riyadh, Saudi Arabia; telephone: 667 3664, 732 2490; telex: 201188 MDA SJ.

KHALID HASSAN, Major General Abbas, Sudanese politician/retired army officer; born 1936, Sudan; married; three children; *Religion:* Muslim; *Education:* graduated from Military College, 1958; Courses in UK 1959 and 1961; *Career:* commissioned into the Armoured Corps, 1958; played a leading part in the 25 May 1969 Revolution; Deputy Commander in Chief, and Chief of Staff with rank of Brigadier, 1969; Major General 1970; First Vice President, 1969; became one of the inaugural members of the Political Bureau of the Sudan Socialist Union (SSU), 1972;

appointed to Central Committee of the SSU 1974; *Languages:* Arabic, English; *Address:* c/o Sudan Socialist Union (SSU), P O Box 1850, Khartoum, Sudan.

KHALID, Mansur, Sudanese official/lawyer; born 1931, Omdurman, Sudan; *Religion:* Muslim; *Education:* LLB, University of Khartoum, 1957; LLM, University of Pennsylvania, USA, 1960; Diplome d'Etudes Supérieures, University of Algeria, Algeria, 1963; LLD (Doctorat d'Etat in International Law), University of Paris, France, 1965; *Career:* Attorney, Khartoum, 1957–59; Legal Officer, UN Secretariat, New York, 1962–63; Assistant Resident Representative, UNDP, Algeria, 1964–65; UNESCO Paris, Bureau of Relations with Member States, 1965–69; Visiting Professor of International Law, University of Colorado, 1968; Minister of Youth and Social Affairs, 1969–71; Chairman of the Delegation of the Democratic Republic of Sudan to the XXV session of the UN General Assembly, 1970; Special Consultant and Personal Representative of the UNESCO Director General for UNRWA Fund Raising Mission, 1970; Permanent Representative of the Democratic Republic of the Sudan to the UN, 1971; Minister of Foreign Affairs, 1971–75; President of the UN Security Council, 1972; Chairman of the OAU Ministerial Committee on the impact of oil prices on Africa and Afro-Arab economic cooperation, 1973–75; Chairman of the Delegation of the Democratic Republic of the Sudan to the XXVI, XXVII, XXVIII, XXIX sessions, and the Sixth Special Session of the UN General Assembly, 1971, 1972, 1973, 1974; Minister of Education, 1975–76; Assistant to the President for Foreign Affairs and Co-ordination, 1976; Member of the Political Bureau of the Central Committee of the Sudanese Socialist Union, 1974–78; Fellow, Woodrow Wilson Center, Smithsonian Institution, Washington, D.C., 1979–80; Consultant on Finance and Investment, 1980–; Special Consultant and Personal Representative of the Executive Director of UNEP, UN, 1981; Visiting Professor on Development Studies, University of Khartoum, 1981; *Publications: Private Laws in Sudan,* 1970; *The Nile Basin, Present and Future,* 1971; *Solution of the Southern Problem and Its African Implications,* 1972; *The Decision-Making Process in Foreign Policy,* 1973; *The Sudan Experiment with Unity,* 1973; *A Dialogue* *with the Sudanese Intellectuals; Address:* PO Box 3029, Khartoum, Sudan; 9 Jubilee Place, London SW3, UK.

KHALID, Rashid O, Sudanese IMF official/ economist; born 11 October 1930, Omdurman, Sudan; married; two sons, one daughter; *Religion:* Muslim; *Education:* BA in History, University of Khartoum, Sudan; BA in Economics, University of Saskatchewan, Canada; *Career:* Inspector of Finance, Ministry of Finance, Khartoum, Sudan, 1954–56; Economist, UN Economics Affairs Department, 1956–61; UN Budget Adviser, Government of Somalia, 1961–62; UN Adviser, Institute of National Planning, Cairo, 1962–64; Economist, International Monetary Fund, 1965–69; Fiscal Adviser, Ministry of Finance, Government of Indonesia, 1969–71; Chief of Budget Division, Fiscal Affairs Department, IMF 1971–75; Adviser, at Assistant Director Level, IMF, 1976–77; Deputy Director, Fiscal Affairs Department, IMF 1977–; *Publications: Fiscal Policy, Development Planning and Annual Budgeting,* 1969; *Control and Management of Central Government Finances in the UK,* 1970; *Mu'awiya Nur: His Life and Writings,* 2 vols, University of Khartoum Press, Sudan, 1971, in Arabic; *Interests and Recreations:* tennis, literature, history; *Languages:* Arabic, English; *Address:* 3201 Kent Street, Kensington, Maryland, 20795, USA; telephone: (301) 946 5736.

KHALID, Shaikh Hassan, Lebanese religious leader/Grand Mufti; born 1921, Lebanon; *Education:* Islamic Legal College in Beirut; Al-Azhar University, Cairo, Egypt, *Career:* Legal Assistant, Beirut Islamic Court, 1947; Qadi in Akkar, 1957; co-founder of Lebanon League of the Ulema; transferred to Mount Lebanon and was elected member of the Administration Council of Waqfs, 1959; elected to Supreme Council of Waqfs, 1962; member of official Muslim delegations to Jordan and Saudi Arabia, 1964–65; member of the High Committee of Mosques, the Foundation Association for the League of Islamic World, the Islamic Research Union in Cairo, the High Islamic Shari'a Community in Lebanon; elected Grand Mufti of the Lebanese Republic, 1966; *Publications:* in Arabic, *The Personal Attitude in Islam; Unity and Logic; The Constitution in Islam; The Martyr in Islam; The Spread of the Message in Lebanon during the 14th Hijry*

Century; Decorations: Grand Cordon of the Jordanian Order of Renaissance 1st Class, 1963; Honorary Doctorate of Al-Ahzar, Cairo, 1967; *Address:* Office — Dar-Al-Eftaa, Beirut, Lebanon; telephone: 304464, 304519; Residence — Aramoun, Lebanon; telephone: 470336, 303777.

KHALID, Sulaiman al-, Kuwaiti politician; born 1934, Kuwait; married; *Religion:* Muslim; *Education:* Cairo University, Cairo, Egypt; *Career:* Minister of Customs and Ports, 1973–75; Minister of Communications, 1975–80; represented Kuwait at several international conferences in the field of customs and ports; *Languages:* Arabic, English; *Address:* c/o Ministry of Communications and Transport, Jamal Abdul Nasser Street, Kuwait.

KHALIDI, Adnan Muhammad Tahir al-, Saudi Arabian official/educationalist; born 1943, Mecca, Saudi Arabia; *Religion:* Muslim; *Education:* MA in English; *Career:* Inspector General of English; Acting Director General, Saudi Arabian International Schools; member of the Professional Board, Secondary School Education Bureau; member of Association of Teachers of English as a Second Language, USA; International Education Union; attended Conference on teaching Foreign Languages in the Arab Countries, Damascus, Syria, Conference on Translation in the Arab Countries, Kuwait, Conference on Teaching English as a Second Language, USA; *Publications: Developing Teaching Techniques of English in the Arab Countries; English Laboratory Notes for Secondary Schools,* co-author; *Address:* Ministry of Education, Airport Road, Riyadh, Saudi Arabia; telephone: 4043048; telex: 201673.

KHALIDI, Walid, Palestinian academic/ historian; born Jerusalem, Palestine; married; three children; *Religion:* Muslim; *Education:* BA, London, UK, 1945; B Litt, Oxford University, UK, 1951; *Career:* research member, Arab Office, 1946; University Lecturer, Department of Oriental Studies, Oxford, 1952–56; resigned over UK role in Tripartite Invasion of Egypt, 1956; Assistant Professor, Department of Political Studies, American University of Beirut, Lebanon, 1957–65; Professor, Department of Political Studies, American University of Beirut, 1957–65; Professor, Department of Political Studies,

American University of Beirut, 1965–; Editor of *Arab Political Documents* and *Chronology of Arab Politics*, 1963–66; Research Associate, Department of Near Eastern Studies, Princeton University, USA, 1960–61; Adviser to Iraq Delegation to UN General Assembly in special session following Middle East June War, 1967; founder and member of Board of Trustees of Institute of Palestine Studies, Beirut, 1963; *Publications:* Editor, *From Haven to Conquest; Readings on Zionism and the Palestine Problem until 1948*, Beirut 1971; articles in *Encyclopaedia of Islam, Encyclopaedia Britannica, Cassell's Encyclopaedia of World Literature; Address:* Department of Political Studies, American University of Beirut, Beirut, Lebanon. Residence -- Madame Curie Street, Beirut, Lebanon.

KHALIFA, Abdul Rahman al-Mahdi, Jordanian politician/lawyer; born 1918, Salt, Jordan; married; five sons, three daughters; *Religion:* Muslim; *Education:* BA in Law, University of Damascus, Syria; *Career:* Assistant Attorney General; Chief Judge, Court of First Instance, Jordan, Amman; Head of Income Tax Department; Secretary General of Amman Municipality; Minister of Finance for several times; Head of the Royal Cabinet; Minister of the Royal Court; Chief Auditor; Head of the Department of Civil Service; Member of the Chamber of Deputies for several times; Member of the Senate; Lawyer; *Decorations:* Order of the Renaissance, Jordan; Order of Independence, Jordan; Order of Rafidain, Iraq; decorations from Lebanon, Syria, Greece, France and Britain; *Interests and Recreations:* walking, legal and financial affairs; *Languages:* Arabic, English; *Address:* P O Box 2316 Amman, Jordan; telephone: 42461, 665086.

KHALIFA, Ahmad Muhammad, Egyptian lawyer/official; born 1 October 1923; married; *Religion:* Muslim; *Education:* BA and Diploma in Criminal Law, PhD, Faculty of Law, University of Cairo, Egypt; *Career:* Assistant District Attorney, Egypt; Lecturer, Faculty of Law, University of Baghdad, Iraq; District Attorney, Egypt; Counsellor, Council of State, Egypt; President, African Conference of Social Welfare Ministers, Cairo, 1967; Minister of Social Affairs, Egypt; Chairman, Social Sciences Council of the Academy of Science, Egypt; member, Presidential Advisory Council for Social and Criminological Research, Egypt; Chairman, UN Sub-committee on Prevention of Discrimination, and Protection of Minorities; Chairman, UN Committee for Crime Prevention and Control; Representative of Egypt, UN Commission for Social Development; member of the International Society of Criminology, Paris; member of World Peace Through Law Centre; *Publications:* articles in *Al-Ma'arif* journal; *The Society of Deviant Behaviour*, 1955; *The General Theory of Incrimination*, 1959; *Introduction to the Study of Criminal Behaviour*, 1962; *Socialism and Methods of Social Scientific Research*, 1963; *Social Planning in Egypt*, 1970; *Decorations:* member of the Academy of Science, Egypt; *Interests and Recreations:* golf, swimming; sociology of law, criminology, social planning, human rights; *Languages:* Arabic, English; *Address:* Office — Gezira Post Office, Gezira, Cairo, Egypt; telephone: 800 886; Residence — 18 Hassan Assem, Zamalek, Cairo, Egypt; telephone: 819 384.

KHALIFA, Colonel A.S. Khalifa al-, Bahraini army commander; born 20 June 1945, Muharraq, Bahrain; *Religion:* Muslim; *Education:* Diploma in Military Science, Royal Military Academy, Sandhurst, UK; various special courses; pilot training; passed Staff College Course, UK; *Career:* Platoon Commander; Training Company Commander; Infantry Company Commander; Battalion second in command; Battalion Commander; Chief of Staff, Bahrain Defence Force; *Interests and Recreations:* general sports, golf, fishing; *Languages:* Arabic, English; *Address:* Ministry of Defence, P O Box 245, West Rifaa, Bahrain; telephone: 661656; telex: 8429 BN.

KHALIFA, HH Shaikh Isa Bin Sulman al-, Amir of Bahrain; born 1932; eldest son of the late ruler HH Shaikh Sulman Bin Hamid; married to Shaikha Hassa; nine children; *Religion:* Muslim; *Education:* private; *Career:* appointed Heir Apparent, 1958; succeeded as Head of State, November 1961; paid official visit to UK, 1974; many visits to UK, USA and Europe; *Decorations:* Order of the Knight Commander of the Memorable Order of the Garter (KCMG), UK, 1974; *Interests and Recreations:* equestrian events; *Languages:* Arabic, English; *Address:* Riffa Palace, Manama, Bahrain; telephone: 661451.

KHALIFA, Muhammad Abdul Rahman, Jordanian judge; born 1926, Salt, Jordan; *Religion:* Muslim; *Education:* Diploma in Agriculture and Economics, Tulkarm Agricultural College; Diploma in Education, Tulkarm Teachers' College; Diploma in Law, Jerusalem Law Institute; *Career:* headmaster in Palestine; lawyer since 1944; judge, 1952–56; member of Chamber of Deputies, 1956–61; Inspector General of Muslim Brothers in Jordan; Deputy President of Executive Office of Muslim Brothers Conference in Arab States; member of the Office of the Islamic Conference since 1953; Head of Al-Barr Association for Martyr's Sons in Aqaba, Jordan; President of the Islamic Centre Charitable Association 1965; *Address:* Jabal Amman, Amman, Jordan; telephone: 22586.

KHALIFA, Muhammad Dawud al-, Sudanese politician/agricultural expert; born 14 November 1924, Khartoum, Sudan; married; two sons, two daughters; *Religion:* Muslim; *Education:* BSc Agriculture, Faculty of Agriculture, University of Khartoum, 1943–48; *Career:* Ministry of Agriculture, 1948–59; Manager of Habasha Pump Scheme, 1948–49; Inspector of Agriculture, Agriculture Development of Kosti District, 1949–51; Management Supervision of the Gash Delta Scheme for producing cotton and sorghum under flood irrigation, 1951–53; Senior Inspector of Agriculture, 1953–55; Chief of Agriculture Education, 1966–69; Deputy Managing Director and member of the Board of Directors for the Agriculture Bank of Sudan; member of National Assembly and Minister of Local Government 1968–69; Director of Agricultural Consultant Services Sudan Ltd, 1970–72; Senior Agriculture Adviser/Country Representative of FAO in Iraq, 1972; *Publications: Tobacco: A Possible Cash Crop in the Future Development of the Sudan; The Philosophical Society of the Sudan,* (in English); *Interests and Recreations:* reading, horse riding; founding member of the College Council, University College for Women, Sudan; *Languages:* Arabic, English; *Address:* P O Box 1500, Khartoum, Sudan.

KHALIFA, Shaikh Abdul Aziz Bin Muhammad Bin Abdullah al-, Bahraini politician; born 1930; married; *Religion:* Muslim; *Education:* in Bahrain; BA in Arabic Language and Literature, Cairo University, Egypt; studied Hebrew, Syriac, Aramaic at School of Oriental and African Studies, University of London, UK; *Career:* Assistant Director General of Education, 1960; Deputy Head of Education, 1970; Deputy Minister of Education, 1970; Chairman, Gulf Technical College Executive Committee, 1970; resigned 1971; Minister of Education, 1971–80; *Interests and Recreations:* travel, literary and cultural interests; *Languages:* Arabic, English; *Address:* c/o Ministry of Education, P O Box 43, Manama, Bahrain.

KHALIFA, Shaikh Abdul Rahman al-, Bahraini diplomat; born 24 February 1942, Bahrain; married; one son, four daughters; *Religion:* Muslim; *Education:* BSc, Commercial Studies, Cairo University, Egypt; *Career:* Director of Protocol; Director of Administrative and Consular Affairs; Ambassador of Bahrain to the UK, 1980; Ambassador of Bahrain to the Court of St. James and Republic of Ireland, 1981–; *Interests and Recreations:* golf; President of the Volleyball Union, Bahrain; Secretary General of the Bahraini Olympic Committee; *Languages:* Arabic, English; *Address:* Embassy of the State of Bahrain, 98 Gloucester Road, London SW7; telephone: 3706213, 3705132.

KHALIFA, Shaikh Abdul Rahman Muhammad al-, Bahraini official; born 1942, Jufair, Bahrain; married; two sons, one daughter; *Religion:* Muslim; *Education:* Degree in Law; *Career:* Judge of Junior Civil Court; Judge in High Civil Court; Deputy President of High Civil Court; President of High Civil Court; Under Secretary, Ministry of Justice and Islamic Affairs; Chairman of Bahrain Islamic Bank; Chairman of the Editorial Board of *Al-Hedayah* Islamic magazine, published by Ministry of Justice and Islamic Affairs; *Interests and Recreations:* literature and law, farming; member of Graduates Club; *Languages:* Arabic, English; *Address:* Ministry of Justice and Islamic Affairs, P O Box 450, Bahrain; telephone: 255675.

KHALIFA, Shaikh Abdullah Bin Khalid al-, Bahraini politician/judge; born 1922; married; one son; *Religion:* Muslim; *Career:* Judge of Junior Courts; member of Court of Appeal; President of Rifaa Municipality, 1967; President of Manama Municipality, 1967; Head of Department of Municipalities and Agriculture and member of the State Council, 1970; Minister of Commerce and

Agriculture, 1971; Minister of Justice and Islamic Affairs, 1972–; Acting Minister of Commerce and Agriculture, 1975–76; *Address:* Ministry of Justice and Islamic Affairs, P O Box 450, Government House, Government Road, Manama, Bahrain; telephone: 253089.

KHALIFA, Shaikh Abdullah Bin Khalifa Bin Salman al-, Bahraini official; born March 1931, Bahrain; married; three sons, two daughters; *Religion:* Muslim; *Education:* private education in Bahrain; *Career:* High Court Judge, 1963; selected as member and Head of Ruling Family Council, 1975–; *Interests and Recreations:* Arabic language and history, hunting, fishing; *Languages:* Arabic, English; *Address:* The Amiri Court, P O BOX 5770, Manama, Bahrain; telephone: 661663.

KHALIFA, Shaikh Daij Bin Khalifa al-, Bahraini official; born 1938; married; *Religion:* Muslim; *Education:* in Bahrain; Nautical College, UK; *Career:* Port Manager, Minaa Sulman, 1966; Director General, Customs and Ports, 1970; Assistant Under Secretary, Ministry of Finance and National Economy, Customs and Ports Affairs; Chairman of the Arab Building Repair Yard Company; *Address:* Ministry of Finance and National Economy, Customs and Ports Directorate, P O Box 15, Manama, Bahrain; telephone: 727168; telex: 8642 BN.

KHALIFA, Shaikh Hamid Bin Isa al-, Bahraini Crown Prince/Commander in Chief of Bahrain Defence Force; born 28 January 1950, Bahrain; son of HH Shaikh Isa Bin Sulman al-Khalifa, Amir of Bahrain; married; two sons; *Religion:* Muslim; *Education:* Sandhurst and Mons, UK; Fort Leavenworth, Kansas, USA; *Career:* Commander, Bahrain National Guard, 1969–71; member of State Administrative Council, 1970–71; Minister of State for Defence, 1971–; Commander in Chief of the Bahrain Defence Force; represented Bahrain at regional and international conferences, meetings of Arab League specialist committees, etc; *Interests and Recreations:* tennis, football, golf, riding, swimming; President of the Bahrain Scientific Society; *Languages:* Arabic, English; *Address:* Ministry of Defence, P O Box 245, Bahrain; telephone: 661656; telex: 8429 BN.

KHALIFA, Shaikh Isa Bin Abdullah al-, Bahraini official; born 1934; married; *Religion:* Muslim; *Education:* Bahrain, and American University of Beirut, Lebanon; University of Southern California, BSc, 1958; joined UK Civil Aviation Authority, 1969–70, in preparation for administration of Bahrain civil aviation affairs; attached to International Civil Aviation Organisation, Montreal, Canada; Director, Civil Aviation, Bahrain, 1970; Under Secretary of State for Ministry of Development and Industry and related oil affairs, 1980–; Board member of Gulf Air and Bahrain Petroleum Company; *Languages:* Arabic, English; *Address:* P O Box 235, Ministry of Development and Industry, Manama, Bahrain; telephone: 25178; telex: 8344 TANMYA BN.

KHALIFA, Shaikh Khalid Bin Muhammed Bin Abdullah al-, Bahraini politician/judge; born 1926; son of Muhammad al-Khalifa, one of Bahrain's leading shaikhs; married; *Religion:* Muslim; *Education:* in Bahrain and Cairo University, Cairo, Egypt; *Career:* Judge in Junior Civil Court, 1950; Judge in Administration, Port and Education Councils, 1950; lived for some years in Saudi Arabia; successively, Director of Immigration, Director General of Ports and Customs, and Acting President of the Courts, 1969–; member of the State Council, 1970; Minister of Justice, 1971–75; Head of Senior Court of Appeal, 1975–; *Languages:* Arabic, English; *Address:* Directorate of Courts, Ministry of Justice and Islamic Affairs, P O Box 450, Manama, Bahrain; telephone: 254290.

KHALIFA, Shaikh Khalifa Bin Sulman al-, Bahraini politician; born 1936; married; brother of HH Shaikh Isa Bin Sulman al-Khalifa; *Religion:* Muslim; *Education:* privately and in London with tutors; *Career:* first President of the Education Council, 1957; Head of Finance, 1960; Chairman of the Administrative Council, 1966–70; Co-ordinator of Foreign Aid and Technical Assistance; Chairman of the Committee for the Registry of Commerce and the Joint Committee for Economic and Financial Studies; President of State Council on its formation, 1970; Prime Minister, 1973–; *Interests and Recreations:* travel, reading, motoring; *Languages:* Arabic, English; *Address:* Office of the Prime Minister, Guidaibiya Palace, Bahrain; telephone: 253361.

KHALIFA, Shaikh Muhammad Bin Khalifa Bin Hamid Bin Isa al-, Bahraini politician; born 1937; married; two sons, two daughters; *Religion:* Muslim; *Education:* Degree from Royal Military Academy, Sandhurst, UK; *Career:* Police Inspector, Public Security Department, 1959; Director of Immigration and Passports, 1966; Deputy Director General, Public Security Department, 1970; Minister of the Interior, 1973–; *Interests and Recreations:* tennis, basket ball; *Languages:* Arabic, English; *Address:* Ministry of the Interior, P O Box 13, Manama, Bahrain; telephone: 253333; telex: 8333 ALAMN BN.

KHALIFA, Shaikh Muhammad Bin Mubarak Bin Hamad al-, Bahraini official; born 1935; married; two children; *Religion:* Muslim; *Education:* American University of Beirut, Lebanon; Modern History, Oxford University, UK; Diploma in International Law, University of London, UK; *Career:* returned to Bahrain, 1961; attended Bahrain Courts as Candidate for the Bench; Director of Information, 1962; headed in 1968 newly formed Political Bureau which became Department of Foreign Affairs, 1969; State Council, 1970; Minister of Foreign Affairs, 1971–; *Languages:* Arabic, English. *Address:* Ministry of Foreign Affairs, P O Box 547, Government House, Manama Bahrain; telephone: 25360; telex: 8228.

KHALIFA, Shaikh Muhammad Bin Sulman al-, Bahraini administrator/judge; born 1940; married; *Religion:* Muslim; *Education:* privately in Bahrain; *Career:* President of the Education Council and President of Harbour Advisory Board, 1960; Chief of Police and Public Security in succession to the late Shaikh Khalifa Bin Muhammad, 1961; Hendon Police College, UK, 1961; Judge of the Appeal Court, 1966; resigned, 1967; *Address:* Ministry of Justice, P O Box 450, Manama, Bahrain; telephone: 253339.

KHALIFA, Sirr al-Khatim al-, Sudanese politician/educationalist; born 1917, Dueim, Sudan; married; *Religion:* Muslim; *Education:* Gordon College, Khartoum; *Career:* Assistant Director of Education for five years in South Sudan; Principal, Technical Institute, Sudan, 1959; Adviser, technical education, Yemen People's Democratic Republic, 1964; accepted invitation of the National Front to form civilian Transitional Government, 1964; Prime Minister, 1964–65; as-sembled the parties concerned in the Southern problem for Round Table Conference, Khartoum, 1965; Ambassador to Italy, 1965; Ambassador to UK, following resumption of diplomatic relations, 1968–69; Special Adviser to Ministry of Higher Education and Scientific Research, 1971; Minister of Higher Education, 1971; Minister of Education, 1973–75; *Decorations:* Honorary KCMG on occasion of HM Queen Elizabeth's visit to Sudan 1965; *Languages:* Arabic, English; *Address:* Ministry of Education, Khartoum, Sudan.

KHALIL, Ahmad Tawfik, Jordanian lawyer/politician; born 1914, Haifa, Palestine; married; *Religion:* Muslim; *Education:* BSc, Political Economy, American University of Beirut, Lebanon, 1934; LLB, Queen's College, Cambridge, UK, 1938; Barrister at Law, Inner Temple, London, UK, 1939; LLM, Queen's College, Cambridge University, 1942; *Career:* Judge, Palestine, 1940–48; Chief Magistrate, Haifa, 1948; Military Governor and Head of Armistice Committee, 1952; Senator, 1971–73, 1973–74, 1974–; *Decorations:* Independence Medal, 2nd Class, 1950; *Address:* Bilbeisi Building, P O Box 6561, Amman, Jordan; telephone: Office — 24623, 37543; Residence — 41137.

KHALIL, Ali, Egyptian UN official; born 1914, Cairo, Egypt; married; *Career:* Crédit Foncier Agricole, Egypt, 1934–36; Egyptian State Broadcasting Corporation Cairo, 1936–45; Deputy Director General, Egyptian State Broadcasting Corporation, 1944–45; Chief, Middle East Service, Radio Division, Office of Public Information (OPI), UN, New York, 1954–56; Deputy Director, United Nations Information Centre (UNIC), Cairo, 1956–61; Chief, Government Information Bureau, UN, West Iran, 1962; Chief, Liaison and Special Projects, External Relations Division, OPI, New York, 1961–65; Director, UNIC, Belgrade, 1965–70; Deputy Director, Information Services, UN, Geneva, 1970–73; Acting Director, UN Information Centre, Cairo; *Publications:* numerous articles and radio scripts; *Interests and Recreations:* broadcasting, public information; *Languages:* Arabic, English, French; *Address:* Office — UN Information Centre, P O Box 262, Cairo, Egypt; telephone: 30682; Residence -- 4 Mathaf El-Zirai, Dokki, Giza, Egypt; telephone: 810138.

KHALIL, Ali al-, Lebanese politician; born 1933, Tyre, Lebanon; married; *Religion:* Muslim; *Education:* American University of Beirut, Politics and Economics, Washington University, USA; *Career:* Professor of Politics, American University of Beirut, Lebanon, the Lebanese University; Deputy for Tyre, 1972–; Minister of Tourism, 1973; Minister of State for Administrative Reform, 1973–74; Minister of Finance, 1979–82; *Languages:* Arabic, English, French; *Address:* National Assembly, Beirut, Lebanon.

KHALIL BIN FAHD, HRH Prince, Saudi Arabian Prince; born 1947; son of HM King Fahd Bin Abdul Aziz; *Religion:* Muslim; *Career:* businessman; *Address:* Royal Court, Riyadh, Saudi Arabia.

KHALIL, Brigadier Mirghani Sulaiman, Sudanese diplomat/former army officer; born 1933, Omdurman, Sudan; married; two daughters, two sons; *Religion:* Muslim; *Education:* Military College, Sudan, 1953–55; Signals Course, UK, 1957; Diploma, Military Science, Staff College, Jordan, 1969; *Career:* Officer in the Armed Forces; commissioned in the Signals Corps at Al-Obaid; served in Khartoum, 1961; Second in Command of the Signals School, 1962–65; Military Attaché, Sudanese Embassy in Kenya, 1965–68; promoted Lieutenant Colonel and assigned to the HQ of the Sudan Armed Forces, 1968; Leader of the Eastern Command, Sudan, 1970–72; Head of the Technical Committee for the Organization of the Armed Forces of the South, 1972; Sudan Armed Forces Director of Military Intelligence, 1972–75; Ambassador to Kuwait, Lebanon and Kenya, 1975–80; Ambassador to Ethiopia, 1980–; *Decorations:* Medal of Independence; Order of Long and Excellent Service; and several other decorations; *Interests and Recreations:* polo; *Languages:* Arabic, English; *Address:* P O Box 1110, Sudan Embassy, Addis Ababa, Ethiopia.

KHALIL, Fakhruddin Khalil, Syrian banker; resident in USA; born 8 April 1933, Safita, Syria; married; four sons, one daughter; *Religion:* Muslim; *Education:* BA and MA in Economics, American University of Beirut, 1956–58; *Career:* Bank Manager and Regional Manager, Banque du Caire and Banque de l'Unité Arabe, Latakia, Syria, 1959–66; Chairman and General Manager, Commercial Bank of Syria, Damascus, Syria, 1967–

71; Director, Union De Banques Arabes et Françaises, Paris, France, 1970–71; General Representative, UBAF Group, Middle East Representative Office Beirut, Lebanon, 1972–75; Senior Executive Vice President, UBAF Arab American Bank, New York, NY, 1976–; President, American University of Beirut Alumni Association of North America Inc; member of the Board of Advisers of the College of Business Administration, St. John's University New York; Honorary Member, Omicron Delta Epsilon, St. Johns University Chapter; *Interests and Recreations:* tennis, swimming; member of the Garden City Country Club and The Board Room; *Languages:* Arabic, English, French; *Address:* 345 Park Avenue, New York, NY 10154, USA; Telephone: (212) 223 1507; Residence — 115 John St., Garden City, NY 11530, USA; telephone: 516 7949269.

KHALIL, Ismail, Tunisian World Bank official/diplomat; born 11 July 1932, Gafsa, Tunisia; married; one daughter; *Religion:* Muslim; *Education:* LLB, Faculty of Law and Institute of Political Science, University of Grenoble, France, 1957; LLM, 1957; *Career:* United States Division, Secretariat of State for Foreign Affairs, Tunis, Tunisia, 1957; Secretary, Tunisian Embassy in Rome, and Representative of Tunisia with FAO, 1957–60; Counsellor and Minister Plenipotentiary, Tunisian Embassy, Washington D.C., 1960–64; Alternate Executive Director, World Bank (for Tunisia and seven other countries), 1962–64; Ambassador, Director for International Cooperation, Ministry of Foreign Affairs, Tunis, 1964–67; elected Mayor of Gafsa, 1966–68; Secretary General, Ministry of Foreign Affairs, Tunis, 1967–69; Ambassador to London, UK, 1969–72; Ambassador to Belgium, Luxembourg, and Representative of Tunisia to the EEC, 1972–78; Director General for International Cooperation, Ministry of Foreign Affairs, Tunis, 1978–79; President, Director General, Tunis Air, Tunis, 1979–80; Executive Director, World Bank (for Tunisia and seven other countries), 1980–; participated in many sessions of the UN and represented Tunisia at several meetings of the Organisation for African Unity and the Arab League; led the Arab delegation to the Euro-Arab Dialogue, 1977; *Decorations:* Commander of the Order of the Republic, Tunisia; Officer of the Order of Tunisian Independence; various decorations from Morocco, Italy, Spain, Finland, Iran, Federal Republic of Germany, Norway, Ivory Coast, Romania, Belgium and Luxembourg; *Languages:* Arabic, French, English, Italian, Spanish; *Address:* 1818 H Street, NW, Washington, D.C. 20433, USA.

KHALIL, Kasim al-, Lebanese politician/ lawyer; born 1903, Tyre, Lebanon; married; *Religion:* Muslim; *Education:* Licence in Law; *Career:* magistrate; elected deputy for Tyre 1937, 1943, 1953, 1957 and 1972; Minister of National Economy, 1957; Vice President of Camille Chamoun's National Liberation Party; Minister of Labour and Social Affairs in Saeb Salam's Cabinet, 1972; Minister of Justice successively under Amin al-Hafez and Takieddin al-Solh, 1973–74; *Languages:* Arabic, English; *Address:* Trablos Street, Beirut, Lebanon.

KHALIL, Khairy Aziz, Egyptian journalist; born 20 October 1937, Egypt; married; one son, one daughter; *Religion:* Christian; *Education:* BA, History, Cairo University, Cairo, Egypt; *Career:* political writer and expert on Third World Affairs; Consultant, Al-Ahram Centre for Political and Strategic Studies, Arab Affairs Section, and Sino-Soviet Affairs Section; translator for Agence France Presse, Middle East News Agency, Cairo; *Publications: People's War and People's Army; The Algerian Experiment in Development and Modernisation,* (in Arabic); *Revolution and Social Change,* published by Al-Ahram Centre for Political and Strategic Studies; *The Tunisian Experiment in Development,* (in Arabic); translated several works into Arabic including, *Allende: The Lessons of Failure; Guevara: is he the Trotsky of the Cuban Revolution?; Herbert Marcuse: is he the Lenin of the Sexual Revolution?; Interests and Recreations:* military history, drama, poetry; *Languages:* Arabic, English, French; *Address:* 15 Abdu al-Hamouli Street, Abbassiya, Cairo, Egypt.

KHALIL, M. Khalil al-, Lebanese diplomat; born 8 February 1941; married; two sons, one daughter; *Religion:* Muslim; *Education:* Law; *Career:* diplomat; Ambassador of Lebanon since 1971; Ambassador of Lebanon to Bonn, Federal Republic of Germany; *Publications:* essays; *Decorations:* Hamayoun, 1978; Persepolis, 1977; *Interests and Recreations:* skiing, tennis; *Languages:* Arabic, English,

French, Persian; *Address:* Embassy of Lebanon, Rheinallee 27, 5300 Bonn 2, West Germany; telephone: 0228 352 07577.

KHALIL, Muhammad Kamaliddin, Egyptian diplomat; *Religion:* Muslim; *Career:* Lecturer in International Law and Public Law, 1941–56; Director of Research Department, Ministry of Foreign Affairs, 1956–60; Minister Plenipotentiary, Embassy to UK, 1960–61; Director, North America Department, Ministry of Foreign Affairs, 1961–64; Ambassador to Jordan, 1964–66; Ambassador to Sudan, 1966–71; Ambassador to Belgium and the EEC, 1974–78; Ambassador to France, 1978–82; Ambassador to the United States, 1982–; *Publications: The Arab States and the Arab League,* 1962; *Languages:* Arabic, English, French; *Address:* Embassy of the Arab Republic of Egypt, 2310, Decatur Place,NW, Washington DC, 20008, USA.

KHALIL, Muhammad Khalil, Jordanian lawyer; born 14 December 1925, Tayibah; married; two sons, two daughters; *Religion:* Muslim; *Education:* LLB, Liverpool University, UK, 1948; Barrister at Law, Middle Temple, London, UK, 1949; LLD, Leyden University, Holland, 1952; *Career:* Legal Adviser, Government of Libya, 1952–55; Assistant Professor of International Law, American University of Beirut, 1956–59; Lawyer, Amman, Jordan, 1959–61; Legal Adviser, Shell Co of Qatar, Doha, 1961–63; Legal Adviser, Iraqi National Oil Co, Baghdad, 1964–65; Legal Adviser, SONATRACH, Algiers, 1965–71; Legal Adviser, Ministry of Electricity and Water, Kuwait, 1972; Director, Pan Arab Consultants for Petroleum, Beirut, 1973–77; Qatar General Petroleum, 1977–; *Publications: The Arab States and the Arab League,* 1962; *The General Agreement on Participation in Respect of Crude Oil Concessions in the Arabian Gulf States: Appraisal of its Legal, Economic and Financial Aspects,* 1973; *Towards an Optimal Production and Investment Strategy of the Arab Petroleum Exporting Countries in the Light of Alternative Energy Sources Through the Year 1985,* 1974; other articles and research papers; *Languages:* Arabic, English, French, Dutch; *Address:* P O Box 5149, Doha, Qatar; telephone: Office — 43214; Residence — 25639; telex: 4683 QPPABD DH, 4315 DOHMEP DH.

KHALIL, Najih Muhammad, Iraqi academic/ engineer/politician; born 1935, Iraq; *Religion:* Muslim; *Education:* Civil Engineering, University of Wales, UK, 1957; MA, Civil Engineering, USA, 1963; PhD, Civil Engineering, Oklahoma State University, USA; *Career:* Under Secretary, Ministry of Municipal and Rural Affairs; Under Secretary, Ministry of Public Works and Housing, 1974; Chairman of the Engineers' Union, 1969; Minister of Industry and Minerals, 1977–80, Professor, University of Baghdad, Baghdad, 1980–; *Languages:* Arabic, English; *Address:* College of Engineering, University of Baghdad, Baghdad, Iraq.

KHALILI, Saud Bin Ali al-, Omani businessman/diplomat; Shaikh of the Beni Ruwaha in Sumail; *Religion:* Muslim; *Education:* under his uncle, the former Imam, Muhammad Bin Abdullah al-Khalili; *Career:* Minister of Education, 1970; led the Omani goodwill mission which successfully toured the Arab world, 1971; led a further delegation to Baghdad, Amman and Damascus to seek diplomatic recognition for Oman, 1971; Ambassador to Egypt, and the Arab League, 1972; Ambassador to Kuwait 1974–77; *Address:* c/o Ministry of Foreign Affairs, Muscat, Oman.

KHALIS, Abdul Latif, Moroccan broadcasting official; born 1935, Rabat, Morocco; married; *Religion:* Muslim; *Education:* in Rabat, Morocco; *Career:* Government Administration, 1967; Education Department; Head of Service, Educational Broadcasting Division; Head of the Cultural Division of the Educational Department; Chef de Cabinet, Ministry of Higher Education; Ministry of Posts, Telegraphs and Telephones (PTT); Ministry of Youth Affairs and Sports; Chef de Cabinet, Ministry of Labour, Social Affairs, Youth Affairs and Sports; Director General of Radiodiffusion Télévision Marocaine, 1978; *Languages:* Arabic, French; *Address:* Radidiffision Télévision Marocaine, Rabat, Morocco.

KHALIS, Salah Abdul Rahman, Iraqi academic/politician; born 9 May 1925, Basrah, Iraq; married; one son, one daughter; *Religion:* Muslim; *Education:* Licence in Arabic Language, Higher Institute for Teachers, Baghdad, 1946; PhD in Literature, University of Paris, France, 1953; *Career:* Lecturer, College of Arts, Baghdad University, 1953–

58; Director General of Education, 1958–61; Professor, Moscow University, 1961–67; Chief Editor of *Al-Thaqafa al-Jadida* journal; *Languages:* Arabic, English, Russian; *Address:* Al Tahrir Square, *Al-Thaqafa* journal, Baghdad, Iraq; telephone: 8884811, 8821366.

KHALLAF, Hussain, Egyptian UN official/ politician; born 1913; *Education:* Licence in Law, Faculty of Law, Cairo University, Egypt, 1934; Doctorate in Economics and Law, University of Paris, France, 1939; *Career:* Dean, Faculty of Commerce, Baghdad University, Iraq, 1949; Professor and Head, Politics, Economics and Finance Department, Universities of Cairo and Alexandria; Assistant Secretary of State, Ministry of Industry, 1956; member of Supreme Committee of United Arab Republic — Yemen Union, 1958–61; Chairman, State Banking Institution, Egypt, 1962–64; Minister of External Cultural Relations, 1964–65; Ambassador, Permanent Representative of Egypt, UN, Geneva, 1966–73; Head of Delegation of Egypt to Conference of UNCTAD, International Labour Organization (ILO), and General Agreement on Tariffs and Trade (GATT); Vice-Chairman, Delegation of Egypt, Peace Conference, Geneva, 1973; Under Secretary General, Council for Arab Economic Unity, 1974; member, UN Commission on Human Rights, 1974; *Publications:* articles on political economy, finance and labour law; *Languages:* Arabic, English; *Address:* Office — UN Commission on Human Rights, 20 Sharia Aisha el-Tatmouria, Garden City, Cairo, Egypt.

KHAMIS, Abdul Razzaq al-, Kuwaiti official; born 1930; married; *Religion:* Muslim; *Education:* in Kuwait; *Career:* Ministry of Interior, mainly concerned with administrative and financial affairs, Kuwait, 1948; Permanent Under Secretary, Ministry of Defence, 1974–; *Address:* Ministry of Defence, P O Box 1170, Safat, Kuwait; telephone: 810268; telex: 22784 MOD KT.

KHAMIS, Muhammad Hamud, Yemen Arab Republic official; born 1940, Yemen Arab Republic; married 1964; six sons, one daughter; *Religion:* Muslim; *Education:* Police College; *Career:* Assistant Director General of Police Staff of the Police College; Deputy Director General of Public Security, 1966–

68; Director General of Emergency Security, 1968–70; Director of the Department of General Administration of National Security, 1971–84; Director of National Security, 1972; Director of the Central Office of National Security, 1975; *Interests and Recreations:* detective novels; *Address:* National Security Office, Sana'a, Yemen Arab Republic.

KHAMIS, Salim Hanna, Lebanese statistician/former FAO and UN official; born 22 November 1919, Nazareth, Palestine; married; *Education:* BA in Mathematics, American University of Beirut, Beirut, Lebanon, 1941; MA in Physics, American University of Beirut, 1942; PhD in Statistics, University of London, London, England, 1950; *Career:* Professor of Applied Mathematics, Syrian University, Aleppo, Syria, 1948–49; Statistician, United Nations, Lake Success and New York, 1949–53; Professor of Economics, Economic Research Institute, 1953–55; Professor of Mathematics and Head of Department of Mathematics, American University of Beirut, 1955–58; Regional Statistician for the Near East, Food and Agriculture Organisation (FAO), Cairo and Rome, 1958–63; Chief, Trade and Prices Branch, Statistics Division, FAO, Rome, 1961–70; Director and Project Manager, Institute of Statistics and Applied Economics, Makerere University, Uganda, 1970–72; Chief, Statistical Methodology Group, FAO, Rome, Italy, 1972–73; Chief, Statistical Development Service, FAO, Rome, 1974–81; Project Manager and Chief Adviser, Arab Institute for Training and Research in Statistics, Baghdad, Iraq, 1976–78; Officer in Charge, Statistics Division, FAO, Rome, Italy, 1980–81; elected member of the International Statistical Institute, 1955; Vice President, International Statistical Institute, 1979–81; Fellow, American Statistical Association, 1967; member of the Council of International Association of Survey Statisticians, 1974–79; *Publications: On the Reduced Moment Problem,* 1952; *Numerical Solution to the Problem of Moments,* 1947; *Tables of Incomplete Gamma Function Ratio,* 1965; *A New System of Index Numbers for National and International Purposes,* 1972; *Programme for the 1980 World Census of Agriculture ;* and various other publications; *Languages:* Arabic, English; *Address:* 23 Hillfield Road, Hemel Hempstead, Herts HP2 4AA, UK; telephone: (0442) 3869.

KHAMMASH, Amir Besim, Jordanian politician; born 1924, Salt, Jordan; married; *Education:* Arab-British College (Middle East), 1944; military and artillery courses at the British Military Institutes in the Middle East and UK, 1944–49; Royal Air Force Academy, UK, 1949; American Military Staff College in Leavenworth, USA, 1958; *Career:* Jordan Army, 1941; Commander of Artillery Corps, 1957–62; Director of Organization and Planning at Jordan Army Headquarters, 1963–64; Chief of Staff at Jordan Army Headquarters, with rank of Major General, 1965–67; Chief of the General Staff, Jordan Army, with rank of Lieutenant General, 1967–69; Minister of Defence, 1969; Minister of Defence and Transport, 1969; Minister of the Royal Court, 1972–73; Political Adviser to HM the King, 1973–74; Senator, 1974–; *Decorations:* Independence Medals, 4th Class, 2nd Class, 1st Class; Renaissance Medal, 3rd Class; Star of Jordan, 3rd Class; Medal of Loyal Service; Libyan Medal; French Medal; *Address:* Shmaisani, Amman, Jordan. telephone: 37341.

KHAMRI, Abdullah al-, People's Democratic Republic of Yemen politician; born 1930, Aden, People's Democratic Republic of Yemen; *Education:* in Aden; *Career:* joined National Liberation Front (NLF), 1964; Director of National Liberation Front, Cairo; member of NLF Executive Committee, 1968; member of Ideological and Cultural Affairs Department, NLF Executive; Minister of Information, and Minister of State for the Council of Ministers, 1973–75; Personal Representative of the Chairman of the Presidential Council; paid study visit to USSR, 1976; Minister of State for Cabinet Affairs, 1980; *Address:* c/o Ministry of State for Cabinet Affairs, Aden, People's Democratic Republic of Yemen.

KHANE, Abdul Rahman, Algerian official/ physician; born 6 March 1931, Algeria; married; *Religion:* Muslim; *Education:* MD, Algiers University, 1968; *Career:* Officer in the National Liberation Army; Chief of Finance Department; Secretary of State, Algerian Provisional Government, 1958–62; President, Electricity and Gas Company, Algeria, 1964; Member of Board of Directors, of Sahara Organization, Algeria, 1962–65, National Society, Research and Exploration for Petroleum; President, Algerian-French, Industrial Cooperation Organisation,

1966–70; Minister of Public Works, 1966–70; Physician, Department of Cardiology, University Hospital, Algiers, 1970–72; Secretary General, Organization of Petroleum Exporting Countries (OPEC), Vienna, 1973–74; Executive Director, United Nations Industrial Development Organization, (UNDIO), Vienna 1975–; *Languages:* Arabic, English, French; *Address:* UNIDO, P O Box 400–A-1400, Vienna, Austria; telephone: 0222 26310, 3001; telex:75612.

KHARAFI, Jasim al-, Kuwaiti businessman/politician; born 1938, Kuwait; married; *Religion:* Muslim; *Education:* Victoria College, Alexandria, Egypt; *Career:* private enterprise; Director, Kharafi Industries and Establishments; member of National Assembly 1975; *Interests and Recreations:* swimming, fishing; *Languages:* Arabic, English; *Address:* Kharafi Industries and Establishments, P O Box 886, Safat, Kuwait; telephone: 813622; telex: 22071 Kharafi KT.

KHARAFI, Muhammad Abdul Muhsin al-, Kuwaiti businessman/banker; born 1911; married; *Religion:* Muslim; *Education:* in Kuwait; *Career:* Chairman, Kharafi Industries and Establishment; member of Board of Chamber of Commerce, 1963; Chairman, National Bank, of Kuwait; elected to National Assembly, 1967; Honorary member, Arab Bankers Association, London; *Address:* The National Bank of Kuwait, P O Box 95, Abdullah al Salem Street, Safat, Kuwait; telephone: 422011; telex: 22451 KT.

KHARRAT, Edward al-, Egyptian writer; born 16 March 1926, Alexandria, Egypt; *Education:* LLB, Alexandria University, Alexandria, Egypt, 1946; *Career:* Assistant Secretary General, Afro-Asian People's Solidarity Organisation, Cairo, Egypt; short stories and radio script writer; literary critic; translator and broadcaster for Egyptian Broadcasting Service; Associate Senior Member, St Anthony's College, Oxford University, UK, 1979; lectured at the School of Oriental and African Studies, University of London, London, England; editor, *The Lotus,* the *Afro Asian Writings,* quarterly of the Afro-Asian Writers Association; assisted in the editing of *Gallery 68; Publications:* two collections of short stories; several novels; translations of several works into Arabic; *Languages:* Arabic, English; *Address:* The Organization

of the Solidarity of Afro-Asian People, 45 Ahmad Hishmat Street, Zamalek, Cairo, Egypt; telephone: 816367.

KHASAWNA, Hani Muhammad al-, Jordanian diplomat, born 28 November 1939, Aidun, Jordan; married; two children; *Religion:* Muslim; *Education:* Licence in Law; PhD in Politics and International Law; *Career:* Ambassador to Romania, then to Syria; Head of the Political Department, Ministry of Foreign Affairs, Jordan; Director General of the Press and Publications, Jordan; Head of the Royal Protocol; Ambassador of Jordan to USSR; *Decorations:* Order of the Renaissance, 2nd Class, Jordan; *Interests and Recreations:* tennis, jogging, poetry, music; *Languages:* English, Arabic; *Address:* Embassy of Jordan, Moscow, USSR.

KHASAWNEH, Ali Mahmud al-, Jordanian businessman; born 10 July 1929, Irbid District, Jordan; married; two sons, two daughters; *Religion:* Muslim; *Education:* BA in Economics, American University of Beirut, Lebanon; MA in Economics, George Washington University, USA; MPhil, Economics, London University, England; *Career:* Director, Industrial Department, Ministry of Economy, 1957; Deputy Manager, Arab Bank, Khartoum, 1959–60; General Manager, Kuwaiti Oil Tanker Company, 1960–75; member of the Board of Directors, Kuwait Oil Tanker Company, Arab Consultancy Company, Jordan; Chairman and Managing Director, Arab Potash Company Ltd; Chairman, Jordan National Shipping Lines Co; member of the Institute of Directors, London and Lloyd's Shipping Exchange, London; *Decorations:* Syrian Order of Independence, 1956; *Interests and Recreations:* economics, management; *Address:* Arab Potash Company Ltd, P O Box 1470, Amman, Jordan; telephone: 66166, 66167; telex: 1683 POTASH JO.

KHASH, Muhammad Najib al-, Syrian agriculturalist; born 1927, Massyaf, Syria; married; two sons, one daughter; *Religion:* Muslim; *Education:* BSc in Botany, Zoology and Chemistry, London University, 1956; MSc and PhD in Plant Pathology Laboratory, Plant Breeding University of Arizona, USA, 1965; *Career:* Researcher, Plant Pathology Laboratory, Ministry of Agriculture, 1963–64; Director of Agricultural Scientific Research, Ministry of Agriculture, 1970–71;

General Director, the Arab Centre for the Studies of Arid Zones and Dry Lands, 1971–; member of the Board of Trustees of the International Food Policy Research Institute; *Languages:* Arab, English, French; *Address:* The Arab Centre for the Studies of Arid Zones and Dry Lands, P O Box 2440, Damascus, Syria.

KHASHO, Yusif Saad, Jordanian artist/ musician; born 24 May 1927, Jerusalem; married; one daughter; *Religion:* Christian; *Education:* Law; Piano, Composition and Orchestra Conducting; Music, Academia Gentium Pro Pace; *Career:* Lands Department, Palestine, 1945–47; music teacher, Jerusalem, 1947–48; Organist, Basilica of Holy Sepulchre, Jerusalem, 1942–48; orchestra leader in Syria and Lebanon, 1949–55; choir master, orchestra conductor and music orchestrator, 1955–66; Director of Jordanian Conservatorium of Music, 1966–68; Musical Adviser, Libya, 1969–72; Director, Musical Studies Centre, CSM, 1972–; Composer, Conductor, Pianist; *Publications:* Records, *Jerusalem Symphony,* 1968; *Symphony No 2,* 1968; and several other records; *Decorations:* Order of Independence, 3rd Class, 1966; Order of the Jordanian Star, 3rd Class, 1968; *Interests and Recreations:* reading, music, the arts; *Languages:* Arabic, English, Italian, French, Spanish, German; *Address:* Via Val Trompia 64, 00141 Rome, Italy; telephone: 893046.

KHASHOGGI, Adnan Muhammad, Saudi Arabian businessman; born 25 July 1935, Mecca, Saudi Arabia; one daughter, four sons; *Religion:* Muslim; *Education:* Victoria College, Alexandria, Egypt; BA in Business Administration, Stanford University, California, USA; *Career:* President of Triad Holding Corporation (Lebanon, Switzerland, UK, Brazil, USA); *Decorations:* Officer of the Order of the Belgian Crown; *Interests and Recreations:* literature, art, football, cricket, water-skiing; *Languages:* Arabic, English, French; *Address:* 1555 Roble Drive, Santa Barbara, California, CA 93110, USA.

KHATIB, Abdul Karim al-, Moroccan physician/politician; born 1921, al-Jedida, Morocco; one son, five daughters: *Religion:* Muslim; *Education:* MD, Surgeon; *Career:* participated in the Moroccan Resistance and the Formation of Arab Maghreb Resistance Army; founding member of the Popular

Movement, 1957; after the split in the Movement he founded the Popular Constitutional Democratic Movement; Minister of Employment and Social Affairs, 1960; State Minister in charge of African Affairs, 1961; Minister of Health, 1962; presided over the first Moroccan Parliament, 1963–65; State Minister, 1977; *Interests and Recreations:* philatelist, carpet collection, horse riding; *Languages:* Arabic, French, English, Spanish; *Address:* c/o Ministry of Health, Rabat, Morocco.

KHATIB, Ahmad al-, Syrian politician; born 1920, Damascus, Syria; married; two sons, one daughter; *Religion:* Muslim; *Career:* Secretary General, Schoolteachers' Union; member of the National Council of the Revolutionary Command, 1965; elected to Amin al-Hafez's Presidential Council, 1965; held no political office 1966–70; Head of State, 1970; resigned 1971; first President of the People's Council, 1971; Prime Minister of the Federation of Arab Republics of Syria, Egypt and Libya, 1971; member of Baath Regional Command, 1971; led parliamentary delegation to Moscow, 1971; visited Libya 1972; *Address:* Baath Party, Damascus, Syria.

KHATIB, Brigadier General Sami al-, Lebanese army officer; born Al Bekaa, Lebanon; *Education:* in Lebanon; *Career:* served as second in command of Deuxième Bureau; went into self-imposed exile on accession of President Frenjieh, 1970; returned to stand trial with other Chehabits in 1974; Commander of Arab Deterrent Forces in Lebanon, 1977; *Languages:* Arabic, French, English; *Address:* Cmdt des Forces Arabe de Dissuasion, Beirut, Lebanon.

KHATIB, Ismail Muhammad al-Arabi al-, Moroccan academic; born 1942, Tetuan, Morocco; married; two daughters; *Religion:* Muslim; *Education:* BA in Islamic Studies, Tetuan, Morocco; Higher Studies, Dar al-Hadith al-Husniya, Rabat, Morocco; *Career:* teacher in Moroccan schools, 1969; Professor, Faculty of Shari'a (Islamic Law), University of Quarawyin, Fes, Morocco, 1973; Professor of Islamic Thought, College of Islamic Studies, Tetuan, 1975–; Director of *Al-Nuur* journal; Supervisor of *Rasa'il al-Nuur* journal; *Publications:* several works in Islamic studies; *Interests and Recreations:* walking, jogging, Moroccan Andalusian heritage; President of Islamic Revival Society; member of Moroccan Scientists Federation; *Languages:* Arabic, Spanish, French; *Address:* Shakib Arslan Street 8/15, P O Box 375 Tetuan, Morocco; telephone: 4450.

KHATIB, Kassim Muhammad, Lebanese businessman; born 10 December 1932, Mellaha, Lebanon; married; two sons, one daughter; *Religion;* Muslim; *Education:* BA in Management and Commercial Law, 1962; *Career:* Teaching, 1949–52; Administrative and Executive Management Positions, 1953–69; businessman; major share holder of commercial and industrial groups; consultant for international companies, 1970–; Managing Owner, General Development Establishment (GDE), Lebanon; Deputy President, Trading and Contracting Company, Tricon, United Arab Emirates; member of the Board of Directors of Tourism Development Groups Ltd (TDG), UK, Hugh MacRae (Builders) Ltd, Scotland, Engineering Building Materials Company, United Arab Emirates; *Interests and Recreations:* swimming, hunting; *Languages:* Arabic, English; *Address:* P O Box 11–9249, Beirut, Lebanon.

KHATIB, Muhammad Fathalla al-, Egyptian politician; born 1 January 1927, Egypt; *Religion:* Muslim; *Education:* BCom, Cairo University, Egypt; PhD, University of Edinburgh, UK; *Career:* Director of Research and UN Section, Arab States Delegations Office, New York, USA, 1958–61; Professor of Comparative Government, Cairo University, 1967–71; Dean of Faculty of Economics and Political Science, 1968–71; Adviser to the President on Home, Economic and Social Affairs, 1971–72; Secretary General, Arab Socialist Union, Governorate of Cairo, 1971–72; Minister of Foreign Affairs, Federation of Arab Republics, 1971–; Presidential Adviser on Home Affairs with rank of Minister, 1971; *Publications: Power Politics in the UN,* 1962; *Local Government in the United Arab Republic,* 1964; *Studies in the Government of China,* 1965; *Studies in Comparative Government,* 1967; *Introduction to Political Science,* 1969; *Languages:* Arabic, English; *Address:* 11 Sharia Ibn Zanki, Zamalek, Cairo, Egypt.

KHATIB, Omar Ismail al-, Jordanian academic/broadcasting official; born 31 May 1931, Ain Karm, Jerusalem, Palestine; married; one son, six daughters; *Religion:* Muslim; *Education:* BA in Social Sciences, 1956; MA in Television and Radio, Syracuse University, USA; PhD in Public Communications Media, Ohio State University, USA; *Career:* Head of Production Department, Jordan Broadcasting Station, 1959–61; General Supervisor of Programmes, Jordanian Broadcasting Station, 1963–64; seconded by Jordanian Government as television and radio consultant, Saudi Arabia, 1964–67; Assistant General Manager, Jordanian TV Corporation; Director of Abu Dhabi Radio and Television; Director of Arab League Offices, Dallas, Texas, USA, 1973; Professor of Information, Jordan University, 1973–75; Consultant to the United Arab Emirates (UAE), Ministry of Culture and Information for Television Affairs, and Deputy General Manager of UAE Television; Professor of Mass Communications, University of Riyadh, Saudi Arabia, 1980–; *Interests and Recreations:* swimming, squash, reading; member of Information Committee in Arab Studies Department and various academic associations in the information field; *Languages:* Arabic, English; *Address:* University of Riyadh, P O Box 2454, Riyadh, Saudi Arabia.

KHATIB, Walid Hatim al-, Jordanian businessman; born 1 March 1938, Hebron, Palestine; married; one son, three daughters; *Religion:* Muslim; *Education:* Diploma in Structure of Business and Office Services; Diploma in Financial Administration; *Career:* Head of Department, Jordan Electricity Company Limited; Secretary to Amman Chamber of Industry; Director General of Arab Advertising Agency; member of United Advertising Association; Secretary of the Jordan Textiles Association; Secretary of the Jordan-Japan Association; Economic Correspondent of *Al-Ra'i* newspaper in Jordan; member of the Council of Arab National Union; *Publications:* various studies of Jordanian industry; published *Jordan Economic Directory,* 1975; *Interests and Recreations:* swimming, reading, driving; *Languages:* Arabic, English; *Address:* P O Box 7434, Amman, Jordan; telephone: 22142; telex: 1440.

KHATIBI, Abdul Kibir, Moroccan writer/poet; born 1938, Al Jadida, Morocco; *Career:* Director, Institute of Sociology, Rabat, Morocco, 1966–70; Professor, Faculty of Arts, Mohammad V University, Rabat;

attached to the University Center of Scientific Research; Editor in Chief of the *Social and Economic Bulletin of Morocco; Publications: Le Lutteur de Classe a la Maniere Taoiste,* poetry; *La Manière Taouée,* novel, 1971; *La Blessure de Mon Propre,* 1974; *Vomito Blanco,* essays, 1974; *Interests and Recreations:* history, literature, philosophy; *Languages:* Arabic, French; *Address:* Faculty of Arts, Mohammad V University, Rabat, Morocco.

KHATTAB, Izzat Abdul Majid, Saudi Arabian academic; born 1935; *Education:* PhD in English Literature; *Career:* Assistant Lecturer, Lecturer in English, Chairman of the English Department, Riyadh University, Saudi Arabia; Dean of Faculty of Arts, Riyadh University; Head of Research Centre, Faculty of Arts, Riyadh University; *Address:* Faculty of Arts, Riyadh Universiy, P O Box 2454, Riyadh, Saudi Arabia.

KHATTABI, Larbi, Moroccan politician; born January 1929, Tetouan, Morocco; married; three children; *Religion:* Muslim; *Education:* literary studies in France and Spain; studies in International Organisations, School for International Studies, Geneva, Switzerland; *Career:* Inspector of Education in Tetouan; Senior Civil Servant, Ministry of Posts and Telecommunications and Ministry of Foreign Affairs; Permanent Moroccan Delegate to the UN in Geneva, and later in Vienna, Austria, 1968; Minister of Employment and Social Services, 1974; President, Governing Body of International Labour Organisation, ILO, 1977; Minister of Information, 1980; Keeper of the Royal Library, 1980–; *Publications:* author of various articles published in the Arab press; *Languages:* Arabic, French, Spanish, English; *Address:* Royal Library, Royal Palace, Rabat, Morocco.

KHAYAT, Abdullah Omar, Saudi Arabian journalist/businessman; born 1937, Mecca, Saudi Arabia; *Religion:* Muslim; *Education:* general; *Career:* General Manager of Mecca Bureau of *Al-Bilad* newspaper; sub-editor of *Al-Bilad* newspaper; Editor in Chief of *Okaz* newspaper; participated in press coverage of most of late King Faisal's state visits to Arab, African and Western countries; member of the First Conference of Arab Journalists, Kuwait, 1966; currently establishing a modern computer-programmed press in the

Industrial Zone, Jeddah; Owner and Director General of Sahar Printing Press and Sahar Trading Est; member of Jeddah Chamber of Commerce and Industry; *Interests and Recreations:* travel, reading, poetry; *Address:* Sahar Trading Est., P O Box 2459, Jeddah, Saudi Arabia; telephone: Office — Jeddah 631 4583; Residence — 660 1984.

KHAYAT, John Victor, Arab-American banker/businessman; born 18 December 1934, Haifa, Palestine; two sons; *Religion:* Christian; *Education:* Prior Park College, Bath, UK; Christchurch College, Oxford University, UK; Barrister at Law, Lincoln's Inn, UK; PMD, Harvard Business School, USA; *Career:* General Manager, Eckes International (Germany), 1968; Managing Director, Felli Pizzinini SRL, Italy, 1969; Middle East Representative of a banking group in Germany, 1974–; *Interests and Recreations:* skiing, yachting, riding, shooting, Egyptology, excavations, art and music; *Languages:* Arabic, English, French, German, Italian, Spanish, Portuguese; *Address:* 22 Eaton Place, London SW1, UK; telephone: 235 5587.

KHAYAT, Shakir Albert, Arab-American businessman; born 5 December 1935, Alexandria, Egypt; married; three daughters, one son; *Education:* BSc, University of Alexandria, Egypt, 1957; SM, Massachusetts Institute of Technology, USA, 1961; MBA, Harvard Graduate School of Business Administration, USA, 1963; *Career:* Senior Associate, H.N. Whitney, Goadby and Company, New York City, 1970–73; Executive Vice President, Laidlaw-Coggeshall Inc, New York City, 1973–78; Executive Vice President, Laidlaw Adams & Peck Inc, New York City, 1978–79; Principal, Khayat and Company Incorporated, New York City, 1979–; President, Equipco Khayat, Inc, Springfield, New Jersey, USA; Director, Mitchell Energy and Development Corp, American Capital Management Inc; member of the New York Society of Security Analysts, and of the Egyptian American Chamber of Commerce SA; *Interests and Recreations:* member of the Madison Square Garden Club, New York, Harvard Club, New York, City Midday Club, New York, USA; member of Pottsville Club, Pennsylvania, USA; member of Ox Ridge Hunt Club, Connecticut, USA; member of Edgartown Yacht Club, Massachusetts, USA; *Address:*

Residence — 137 Doubling Road, Greenwich, Conneticut 06830, USA; Office — 50 Broad Street, New York, New York 10004, USA.

KHAYAT, Talal M. Nuri al-, Iraqi academic; born 31 March 1935, Mosul, Iraq; married; two sons, two daughters; *Religion:* Muslim; *Education:* MB, ChB, University of Baghdad, 1957; MSc in Biochemistry, Univeristy of London, UK, 1964; *Career:* Lecturer, University of Mosul, 1964; Assistant Professor, 1972; Head of the Department of Biochemistry, 1979; Associate Professor of Biochemistry; *Publications: Serum Proteins in Diabetics,* 1971, Iraq, in English; *Amilhar and Metabolism of Metals,* 1978, 1979, 1981, West Germany; *Thyroglobulin Biosynthesis in Various Diseases,* 1979, West Germany; *Interests and Recreations:* writing, travel, swimming, music, chess; *Languages:* Arabic, English, German, Norwegian; *Address:* Medical Biochemistry Department, Mosul College of Medicine, Mosul, Iraq; telephone: 90203.

KHAYATA, Abdul Wahab, Syrian banker/economist; born 1924, Aleppo, Syria; married; one son, two daughters; *Religion:* Muslim; *Education:* LLB; BA in Economics; PhD in Financial Studies and Economics; *Career:* Government Deputy to the Banks, Central Bank of Syria, 1954; Professor, University of Damascus, 1956–69; member of Monetary and Loans Council, Central Bank of Syria, 1959–60; Chairman of the Board and Director General, Bank of Arab Unity, 1961; Chairman and Director General, The Industrial Bank of Syria, 1962; Deputy Governor, Central Bank of Syria, 1963; Secretary General, Ministry of Planning, 1963; Minister of Planning, Syria; Regional Expert for the UN, Beirut, 1969; Deputy Director for Europe and the Middle East, UN Programme for Development, New York, 1974; Director General of the French Bank, (FRAB), 1974–78; currently, President and Deputy Chairman, the Cental Bank of Oman, 1978–; *Publications: Some Phenomena of the Arab Money Surplus,* a study submitted to the Kuwaiti Chamber of Commerce and Industry, 1974, in Arabic; *The Influence of Middle East Money on the European Market,* Beirut, 1974, a study submitted to the *Financial Times* Conference on the Middle East and Finance, in English; *French Arab Cooperation and International Econo-*

mics 1974, Casablanca, Morocco, a study submitted to the French Seminar on the Relation between Countries Producing Raw Materials for Industry, in French; *The Need for New Institutions in the Frame of the Arab European Monetary Corportation,* 1976, Montreaux, Switzerland, in English; *Interests and Recreations:* swimming, tennis, chess; *Languages:* Arabic, French, English; *Address:* central Bank of Oman, P O Box 4161, Ruwi, Sultanate of Oman; telephone: 702222; telex: 3288 MARKAZI MB.

KHAYER, Yahya Muhammad al-, Syrian academic/engineer; born 1940, Dairal Zor, Syria; married; three daughters; *Religion:* Muslim; *Education:* BSc in Civil Engineering, Damascus University; PhD, Glasgow University, UK; *Career:* Demonstrator, Damacus University, 1970; Lecturer, Damascus University, 1979; Minister of Euphrates Dam; *Interests and Recreations:* poetry, Arabic literature; *Languages:* English, Arabic; *Address:* Damascus University, Civil Engineering Department, Damascus, Syria; telephone: 332963.

KHAZEN, Shaikh Fuad Jamil al-, Lebanese engineer; born 1934, Reyfoun, Lebanon; married; one son, one daughter; *Religion:* Christian; *Education:* St. Joseph University; Civil Engineering Diploma, Higher School of Engineering, Beirut; *Career:* Civil Engineer at Taylor Woodrow, Cubitt, Marples Ridgway, 1960; President of Lebanese Contractors Syndicate, 1970; Mothercat, Saudi Arabia, Dubai Hotels Ltd; member of the Board of Directors of Contracting and Trading Co, (CAT), Mothercat and subsidary companies, Banque de L'Industrie et du Travail; *Interests and Recreations:* tennis, shooting, swimming, yachting; *Languages:* Arabic, English, French; *Address:* Office — Contracting and Trading Co (CAT), Al-Arz Street, CAT Building, P O Box 11–1036, Beirut; telephone: 221564; telex 20616; Residence — Reyfoum, Lebanon, telephone: 950006, 950045.

KHAZRAJI, Majid Muhammad al-, United Arab Emirates official; born 1943, Dubai, United Arab Emirates; married; two sons, one daughter; *Religion:* Muslim; *Education:* Licence in Law, College of Islamic Sharia, Al-Azhar University, Cairo, Egypt; *Career:* Adviser, Legal Advisory and Legislation Department, Ministry of Justice; Director,

Social Planning Department, Ministry of Planning; Acting President, State Audit Institution, United Araba Emirates; *Interests and Recreations:* reading Arabic poetry, swimming, long distance walking; *Address:* State Audit Institution, P O Box 3320, Abu Dhabi, United Arab Emirates; telephone: Abu Dhabi 23900, Dubai 664040.

KHEIR, Yahya Muhammad al-; Sudanese academic/pharmacist; born 27 December 1938; Khartoum; married; two daughters, one son; *Religion:* Muslim; *Education:* Pharmacy; *Career:* pharmacist, 1962–70; Lecturer, University of Khartoum, 1970–74; Associate Professor, University of Khartoum, 1974; Dean, Faculty of Pharmacy, University of Khartoum; *Languages:* Arabic, English; *Address:* Faculty of Pharmacy, University of Khartoum, P O Box 1996, Khartoum, Sudan; telephone: 80458.

KHEREIJI, Abdullah al-Muhammad al-, Saudi Arabian academic; born 1943, Medina, Saudi Arabia; *Religion:* Muslim; *Education:* PhD in Sociology; *Career:* Adviser to Ministry of Labour and Social Affairs; member of Middle East Conference on Sociological Sciences, Alexandria, Egypt; Assistant Professor of Sociology, King Abdul Aziz University, Jeddah, Saudi Arabia; *Publications:* several books on religion and sociology; *Address:* King Abdul Aziz University, P O Box 1540, Jeddah, Saudi Arabia; telephone: 6879033; telex: 401141 KAUNI SJ.

KHIARY, Mahmud, Tunisian politician/trade unionist; born 1911; *Education:* general; *Career:* teacher, 1931–55; Secretary General, Tunisian Union of Teachers, 1941–52; President, General Federation of Tunisian Officials, 1947–58; Secretary General, General Union of Tunisian Workers (UGTT); Minister of Posts and Telegraphs; Minister of Agriculture; member of National Constituent Assembly; Chief, UN Civil Operation in Congo, 1961–62; President Director General, Société Nationale Tunisienne de Cellulose and Société Nationale Tunisienne de Papier Alfa, 1963–72; President, Director General, Société Nationale de Mise en Valeur du Sud (SONMIVAS), 1972–74; Director General, Enterprises Générale des Travaux Publics et de Promotion de l'Habitat, 1974; *Languages:* Arabic, French; *Address:* 20 rue du Koweit, Tunis, Tunisia.

KHIDR, Abdul Fattah, Saudi Arabian academic/lawyer; born 12 October 1941, Egypt; married; two sons; *Religion:* Muslim; *Education:* LLB, Ain Shams University, Egypt, 1967; LLM, Cairo University, Egypt, 1970; LLB, Cairo University, 1975; *Career:* Research Assistant, National Research Centre, Cairo, Egypt, 1974; Expert, Institute of Public Administration, Riyadh, 1972–75; Assistant Professor, Forensic Law, Institute of Public Administration, Riyadh, 1976–79; Associate Professor, Institute of Public Administration, Riyadh, 1980–; *Publications:* several publications and reseach studies on forensic science; *Interests and Recreations:* music, running; *Languages:* Arabic, English, French; *Address:* Institute of Public Administration, P O Box 205, Riyadh, Saudi Arabia; telephone: Office — 4761600; Residence — 4647058.

KHIRBASH, Muhammad Khalfan, United Arab Emirates official; born 5 March 1957, Dubai, United Arab Emirates; married; one daughter; *Religion:* Muslim; *Education:* BA in Economics, Boston University, USA; course in international investment, Japan, 1980; *Career:* Director of Investment Department, Ministry of Finance and Industy, 1980–; member of the Management Committee of Arab Development Decade Account; member of the Board of Directors of the Emirates Industrial Bank, the Emirates Tele-Communication Corporation, the Arab Authority for Agricultural Investment and Development, Sudan; *Interests and Recreations:* swimming, reading; *Address:* PO Box 433, Abu Dhabi, United Arab Emirates; telephone: 342250.

KHIYARI, Allal al-, Moroccan official/educationalist; born 1934, Meknes, Morocco; married; four sons; *Religion:* Muslim; *Education:* Institute of Education, 1958; Dar al-Hadith al-Hassaniya, 1968; MA in Islamic and Contemporary Thought, 1976; *Career:* Head of Cultural Affairs Department, Ministry of State for Cultural Affairs, 1969; Ministry of Higher Education, 1973–; member of the Union of Islamic Universities, 1969–; member of Moroccan National Committee for Legislative Reform, Meknes, 1975–; Secretary General of the Scientists Committee 1971–75; *Interests and Recreations:* theatre, poetry; member of Moroccan Writers Union; President of the Cultural Union; Head of the Office of Authors'

Rights; *Languages:* Arabic, French; *Address:* Al-Silah, Section 3, No 4, Sale, Rabat, Morocco; telephone: 8056.

KHOGHALI, Muhammad, Sudanese businessman; born 1924; married; *Religion:* Muslim; *Education:* in Khartoum; Cambridge University, UK; *Career:* Ministry of Foreign Affairs after Independence; member of Sudanese Delegation to the UN, 1956; Head of the Department of Economics and Commerce, 1959; Permanent Under Secretary, 1965; Minister of Agriculture and Forests, 1966; relinquished office to concentrate on business interests, 1967; founding member with Abdulla Ghandour and Hamza Mirghani of the business consultancy firm SICOM; Managing Director, Blue Nile Packing Company; *Languages:* Arabic, English; *Address:* Blue Nile Packing Co, P O Box 385, Khartoum, Sudan.

KHOJAH, Abdullah Sharrar, Saudi Arabian lawyer/official; born 1922; *Religion:* Muslim; *Education:* BA in Islamic Law; *Career:* former teacher; Director of Chamber of Commerce; Director, Boycott Administration; Legal Adviser; *Address:* Ministry of Commerce, P O Box 1774, Riyadh, Saudi Arabia; telephone: 4012229; telex: 201057 TIJARAH SJ.

KHOJAH, Major General Akram, Saudi Arabian airforce commander; born 1930; married; *Religion:* Muslim; *Career:* joined Military School in Taif, 1947; obtained a Licence with British Civil Air Training Mission; trained at AST Hamble and with Royal Air Force, UK; Air Attaché, Embassy to UK, 1966–69; returned to Saudi Arabia as Base Commander, Taif; appointed Base Commander, Dhahran, 1969; Vice Commander of Saudi Air Force 1973; *Languages:* Arabic, English; *Address:* Ministry of Defence, Riyadh, Saudi Arabia.

KHOLY, Hassan Sabri al-, Egyptian diplomat; born 25 February 1922; married; *Religion:* Muslim; *Education:* Cairo University, Egypt; Military and Staff Colleges; *Career:* Infantry officer; fought in Palestine War, 1948–49; Professor, Senior Officer, Students Institute; started Infantry School, Syria, 1957; seconded to the Presidency, 1952, as Deputy Director and then Director of the Palestine Office; Personal Representative of the President, 1964–76; Ambassador, Ministry of Foreign Affairs, 1974–75; Personal Representative of Director General of UNICEF 1975; *Publications: The Palestine Case; Sinai; The Policy of Imperialism and Zionism towards Palestine during the First Half of the Twentieth Century,* and various research papers on Palestine; *Languages:* Arabic, English; *Address:* c/o The Presidency, Cairo, Egypt.

KHOLY, Hussain A. al-, Arab-American academic/mathematician; born 30 October 1933, Mansura, Egypt; married; one son, two daughters; *Religion:* Muslim; *Education:* BSc, Cairo University, Egypt, 1957; Kandidat (Russian Equivalent of PhD), Hungarian Academy of Sciences, 1961; Dr of NatSc, Eotvos Lorand University, 1961; *Career:* Demonstrator, Faculty of Sciences, Cairo University, 1957–58; Lecturer, Faculty of Sciences, Cairo University, 1961–63; Lecturer, University of Khartoum, Sudan, 1963–64; Visiting Scientist, Experimental Institute of Light Metals, Italy, 1964; Assistant Professor of Mathematics and Science, 1964–65; Assistant Professor and Chairman, Department of Mathematics and Physics, 1968–72; Professor and Chairman, Department of Mathematics and Physics, 1973–; Professor and Head of the Physics Unit, American University of Cairo, Egypt, 1972–73; Consultant to the Egyptian Government, the Libyan Government; Consultant to several American national and multinational companies, schools and scientific laboratories; *Publications:* over a dozen books, papers, published in American, British, German, Dutch and Hungarian scientific magazines since 1961; *Interests and Recreations:* swimming, reading; *Languages:* Arabic, English, French, Hungarian; *Address:* 4 Pitney Drive, Mendham, New Jersey 07945, USA.

KHOMAIS, Bakr, Saudi Arabian diplomat/economist; born October 1930, Jeddah, Saudi Arabia; *Religion:* Muslim; *Education:* MA in Public Administration, Syracuse University, USA; *Career:* Ministry of Finance; Assistant Director of Economic Affairs, Ministry of Finance; Secretary General for Technical Assistance, Supreme Planning Board; Director, Agency for Technical Cooperation, Council of Ministers; Minister Plenipotentiary; Ambassador, Ministry of Foreign Affairs; Ambassador to Indonesia; member of the Board of Directors of several Saudi and foreign companies; *Publications: The Inter-*

national Bank for Reconstruction and Development and Its Role in Assisting Underdeveloped Countries; Improvement of Management, Performance Budgeting; Address: Ministry of Foreign Affairs, P O Box 495, Jeddah, Saudi Arabia; telephone: Office — 669 0900; Residence — 665 4211; Embassy of Royal Kingdom of Saudi Arabia, Jalon Imam Bonjol 3, Jakarta, Indonesia.

KHOUADJA, Brahim, Tunisian official/engineer; born 1 January 1927, Tunisia; married; three sons, one daughter; *Religion:* Muslim; *Education:* Licence in Mathematics; Diploma in Telecommunication Engineering; *Career:* Principal Engineer, 1969, General Engineer, 1955, Chief Engineer, 1969; General Engineer, 1971, Director of Telecommunications Department, 1966; Director General of Telecommunications, 1971; Secretary of State for PTT, Ministry of Transports and Communications; *Decorations:* Citations dans l'Ordre de la République, Tunis; *Languages:* Arabic, French, English; *Address:* 14 Rue Didon, Tunis, Tunisia; telephone: 891 240.

KHOUJA, Abdul Aziz, Saudi Arabian official/academic; born 1943, Saudi Arabia; *Religion:* Muslim; *Education:* PhD in Chemistry; *Career:* successively Assistant Lecturer, Lecturer and Assistant Lecturer, Assistant Professor, Faculty of Education, King Abdul Aziz University, Mecca, Saudi Arabia; Dean, Faculty of Education, King Abdul Aziz University, participated in the development and expansion of the Faculty of Education during his five year term as Dean; Deputy Minister of Information, 1976–; Head of the Executive Council for Islamic Broadcasting Corporation; Head of Islamic Press Agency; *Interests and Recreations:* lyric poetry, reading poetry; *Address:* Ministry of Information, Nasriya Street, Riyadh, Saudi Arabia; telephone: 4039650; telex: 202640 MINMOI SJ.

KHOULI, Ussama Amin, al-, Egyptian official/engineer; born 9 October, 1923, Cairo Egypt; married; one son, one daughter; *Religion:* Muslim; *Education:* BA in Engineering; Diploma of Membership of Imperial College, London England; PhD; *Career:* Lecturer, Faculty of Engineering, Alexandria University, Egypt 1951–58; Professor, Faculty of Engineering, Cairo University, Egypt, 1965–78; Vice Dean, Faculty of

Engineering, Cairo University, Egypt, 1966–68; Director General, Scientific Computation Centre, Cairo University, Egypt, 1968–70; Cultural and Scientific Counsellor, Egyptian Embassy, Moscow, USSR, 1970–75; Assistant Director General for Science and Technology, Arab Educational, Cultural and Scientific Organisation (ALESCO)1977–80; Adviser to the Minister of Education and Science, Egypt, 1981; Senior Adviser, Kuwait Institute for Scientific Research, (KISR), 1981–; member of the Editorial Board of *Contemporary Thought,* 1968–70; member of the Council of the Egyptian Society of Engineers; *Publications: Fundamentals of Thermodynamics,* 1963; *Mechanical Vibrations,* 1971; various studies on science, technology and development in the Arab Countries; *Interests and Recreations:* music, reading; *Languages:* Arabic, English, French, some Russian; *Address:* P O Box 24885, Safat, Kuwait; telephone: 835034.

KHOULY, Ahmad Lutfi Ibrahim al-, Egyptian journalist/writer; born 1928; married; one daughter; *Religion:* Muslim; *Education:* Law; *Career:* founded *Al-Tali'a,* a monthly political review published by the Al-Ahram Organization, 1964; represented Egypt at Peace and Disarmament Conference, Vienna, 1956; Peking and Moscow, 1957, Stockholm, 1958; Moscow, 1962; visited London for talks on the setting up of a Bertrand Russell Institute for Advanced Political Studies in Cairo, 1965; appointed to Central Committee of Arab Socialist Union (ASU), 1971, elected Secretary of ASU Foreign Relations Sub-Committee; led Arab Socialist Union delegations to UK, France and Lebanon; resigned as Editor of *Al-Tali'a,* 1977; *Publications:* two volumes of short stories, three plays and three film scenarios; several books on political subjects including *Conversations with Bertrand Russell and Jean-Paul Sartre; Languages:* Arabic, English, French; *Address:* Al-Watan al-Arabi, 33 Rue Marbeuf, 75008 Paris, France; telephone: 2252 027.

KHOURI, Rifik Khalil, Lebanese businessman/lawyer; born 10 January 1937; married; one son; *Religion:* Christian; *Education:* BA in Economics, American University of Beirut, 1957; Licence in Law, Faculty of Law, Lebanese University, 1962; *Career:* joined the Beirut Bar Association, 1962; Attorney at Law; Director and Legal Counsel, Bank of Credit and Commerce International, Lebanon SAL; Director and Legal Counsel, The Procter and Gamble Manufacturing Company of Lebanon SAL; Legal Counsel of the Associated Press, Beirut and several other companies and banks; *Interests and Recreations:* music, walking; *Languages:* Arabic, English, French; *Address:* 7 Arts et Métiers Street, Tabet Building, Beirut, Lebanon; telephone: Office — 354010; Residence — 341839.

KHOURI, Samir al-, Lebanese academic/engineer; born 1926, Khartoum, Sudan; married; three sons; *Religion:* Christian; *Education:* BA, American University of Beirut, Beirut, Lebanon; BSc in Civil Engineering, AUB; MSc in Civil Engineering, Lehigh University, USA; *Career:* municipal engineer, Damascus, Syria, 1948–53; Director, Contracting and Concrete Construction Company, 1955–56; Director, Design Department, Reconstruction Authority, Lebanon, 1956–58; Instructor, Civil Engineering, AUB, 1953–55; Associate Professor, Civil Engineering, AUB, Beirut, 1959–; Director and later President, Associated Consulting Engineers (ACE)SAL, Beirut, 1958–; member of the Union of Engineers and Architects, Lebanon, the Lebanese Public Health Association, the Institute of Civil Engineers, UK; Fellow of American Society of Civil Engineers, the Institution of Public Health Engineers, UK; *Publications: Solid Waste: Its Hazards and Disposals,* 1968; *Solid and Liquid Waste Disposal in Lebanon, memo* graphed lectures on industrial waste; *Enviromental Health Through Science and Technology Decorations:* Chevalier d'Honneur OSJ; Ordre des Chevaliers Hospitaliers; *Interests and Recreations:* music, reading, writing, swimming, tennis, walking, jogging; *Languages:* Arabic, English, French; *Address:* Associate Consulting Engineers (ACE), Verdun Street, Abou Shalash Building, P O Box 11–3446, Beirut, Lebanon; telephone: 353430/1/2.

KHOURI, Zuhair Salih, Jordanian banker; born 1926, Karak, Jordan, married; one son, two duaghters; *Religion:* Christian; *Education:* London School of Economics, 1951–52; American University, Washington D.C., 1955–56; IMF, Washington, Training Course, 1960–61; *Career:* Accountant, Import–Export Department, 1945–61; Head of Section, Currency Department, 1961; Secretary to the Currency Board, 1961–64; Head of Department, Central Bank, 1964–68; Operation Manager, Central Bank, 1968–74; Chairman and General Manager, The Housing Bank, 1973–; Chairman of Jordan Lime and Bricks Company and of Jordan Security Corporation; Deputy Chairman of the Amman Development Corporation; member of the Board of the Housing Corporation, 1976–, and of the Central Bank; member of the Jordanian Bankers Association; *Decorations:* Order of the Jordanian Star; Order of Independence; *Languages:* Arabic, English; *Address:* The Housing Bank, P O Box 7693 Amman, Jordan; telephone: 67126.

KHOURY, Butros, al-, Lebanese banker/businessman; born 1907, Lebanon; married; *Career:* Chairman, Agricultural, Industrial and Real Estate Bank, Industrial Company of the East, Lebanese Company for Sugar Refining; Director and Manager, Bank of Lebanon and Overseas, Assad Jabre Oil Presses, The Lebanon International Trading Corporation, The Lebanese Cement Company, Lebanese Insurance Company; President and General Manager, Banque Al-Ahli (Banque Nationale Foncière Commercial et Industrielle); Deputy Chairman, Banque du Liban et d'Outre Mer SAL, Lebanon; *Decorations:* Silver Star Medal, Jordan, 1967; various other decorations and distinctions; *Languages:* Arabic, English, French; *Address:* Hamra, Abdel Aziz Street, Daher Centre, P O Box 11-1912, Beirut, Lebanon; telephone 346 290; telex: 20740, 21273 LE.

KHOURY, Gabriel, Lebanese trade union official; born 1911, Lebanon; married; two sons, five daughters; *Education:* Diploma in Commercial Studies; Diploma in Accounting and Book-keeping, School of Accountancy, Paris, France; *Career:* joined, and later became Director of, the Bank of Syria and Lebanon and of the Bank of Lebanon; founder of the Trade Union Movement in Lebanon, 1937; President of the Lebanese Labour Federation; President of various unions in Lebanon including Bank Employees' Union, the Federation of Employees and Workers Unions; member of the Board of the Lebanese Social Security Central Office; *Decorations:* Gold Medal, Lebanese Order of Merit; Labour Medal; *Interests and Recreations:* swimming; trade union movement and social subjects; *Languages:* Arabic, French; *Address:* Office — Beirut and the United Syndicates Unions, Beshara al-Khoury Street, Beirut, Lebanon; Residence -- Chiah Boulevard, Beirut, Lebanon.

KHOURY, Khalil al-, Lebanese lawyer/official; born 1 June 1923, Beirut, Lebanon; married; one daughter; *Education:* Licence in Law, French Faculty of Law, St. Joseph University, Beirut, Lebanon; *Career:* Barrister at Law; elected Deputy for Aley, 1960; re-elected 1964 and 1968; elected President of the Constitutional Bloc political party, 1965; Minister of Social Affairs, 1969; did not stand in 1972 election; organizer, UN Seminar for the Middle East, Beirut, Lebanon, 1949; *Decorations:* many foreign decorations and distinctions from France, Poland, Belgium and other countries; *Interests and Recreations:* swimming, tennis; member of the Beirut Club, member of the Aero Club; *Languages:* Arabic, French, English; *Address:* Office — Pharaon and Chiha Building, Beirut, Lebanon; Residence -- Verdun Street, Beirut, Lebanon.

KHOURY, Michel al-, Lebanese banker/lawyer; born 1926, Beirut, Lebanon; married; three children; *Religion:* Christian; *Education:* St. Joseph University, Beirut, Lebanon; Licence in Law, Faculty of Law and Political Science, University of Paris, Paris, France; *Career:* Attaché, Political Department, Ministry of Foreign Affairs, Beirut, Lebanon, 1946; Journalist, *Le Jour* newspaper, 1947; member of Lebanese Bar and practising lawyer, 1948–53; Director General, Darwish Y Haddad Establishments, 1953–57; Editor, *Le Jour* newspaper, 1957–63; President and founding member of National Council of Tourism, 1964–72; Minister of Information and Defence, Beirut, Lebanon, 1965–66; Minister of Tourism and Planning, Beirut, Lebanon, 1967–68; Vice President, Banque Libano Française, Beirut, Lebanon, 1968–76; Special Envoy of President of Lebanon, 1976–77; Governor, Banque du Liban (Central Bank), 1978–; *Decorations:* several decorations from Brazil, Spain, Italy and others; *Interests and Recreations:* swimming, hiking; *Languages:* Arabic, English, French; *Address:* Banque du Liban, P O Box 5544, Beirut, Lebanon; telephone: 341 230; telex: 20744, LOUBAN LE.

KHOURY, Nicola Najib, Arab-American academic/physicist; born 27 May 1933, Beirut, Lebanon; married; two children; *Education:* BA with High Distinction, American University of Beirut (AUB), Lebanon, 1952; PhD, Princeton University, USA, 1957; *Career:* Assistant Professor, AUB, 1957–58, 1960–61; member, Institute of Advanced Study, Princeton University, USA, 1959–60, and 1962–63; Associate Professor, AUB, 1961–62; Visiting Associate Professor, University of Columbia, USA, 1963–64; Consultant, Brookhaven National Laboratory, 1963–73; Associate Professor, Rockefeller University, USA, 1964–68; Professor, Rockefeller University, 1968–; Trustee, American University of Beirut; Trustee, Brearley School, New York City, USA; *Publications:* contributed articles to professional journals; *Interests and Recreations:* Fellow, American Physicists' Society; *Address:* Office— Rockefeller University, New York City, New York, NY 10021, USA; Residence— 4715 Iselin Avenue, Riverdale, New York, NY 10471, USA.

KHOURY, Reverend Elia Khader, Palestinian ecclesiastic; born 1922, Jenin District, West Bank; married; *Religion:* Christian; *Education:* in Palestine, London University, and Porton College Seminary, Colorado, USA; *Career:* Anglican priest in Nablus, Bir Zeit, Jerusalem and Ramallah; expelled by Israelis from West Bank, 1969; since then has led the Arab Anglican Communion in Amman, Jordan; supporter of Fatah for many years; representative of Palestinian Christians, Palestine Liberation Organization (PLO), 1974; candidate for Bishopric of Jerusalem supported by a majority vote of the Arab Diocesan Council, April 1974.

KHOWAITAR, Hamad al-, Saudi Arabian UN official; born 26 December 1929, Saudi Arabia; married; *Religion:* Muslim; *Education:* BA in Languages and Literature, Cairo University, Egypt, 1954; *Career:* Permanent Delegate of Saudi Arabia to UNESCO, and member of Executive Board, 1964–; Representative of Saudi Arabia, World Conference of Ministers of Education on Eradication of Illiteracy, 1965; Representative of Saudi Arabia, International Conference of Education Planning, 1968; member, International Conference on Public Education and Council of International Bureau of Education, 1964–68, 1970; member, Delegation of Saudi Arabia, UNESCO General Conference, 1964, 1966, 1968, 1970, 1972; member of the International Committee of L'Olivier Symbole, France; *Interests and Recreations:* chess, table tennis; *Languages:* Arabic, English, French; *Address:* UNESCO, 7 place de Fontenoy, 75700 Paris, France; telephone: 577 1610.

KHOWEITAR, Abdul Aziz Abdullah al-, Saudi Arabian politician/educationalist; born 1927, Saudi Arabia; *Religion:* Muslim; *Education:* PhD in History; *Career:* Vice Rector of Riyadh University, Saudi Arabia, 1955–71; Head of the Directorate of Supervision and Follow-up, 1971; Minister of Health, 1974–75; Minister of Education, 1975–; member of Chivalry Club, Charity Society; President of Arab-Saudi Scouts Society, of Supreme Council of Arts and Literature; member of Supreme Council of Education, Higher Council of Universities, Committee for Administrative Reform, Council of Pensions Fund; attended Conference of International Universities, International Conference of Public Health, Conference of ALECSO; *Publications: Fi Turuk al-Bahth,* in Arabic; editor *Tarikh Shafi Ibn Ali,* in Arabic; *Decorations:* King Abdul Aziz Order of Merit, 2nd Class; Republican Order, Democratic Republic of Sudan, 1st Class; *Interests and Recreations:* reading; *Languages:* Arabic, English; *Address:* Ministry of Education, Riyadh, Saudi Arabia; telephone: 4043048; telex: 201673 MAAREF SJ.

KHOZAI, Muhammad Ali al-, Bahraini official; born 17 May 1940, Manama, Bahrain; married; one son; *Religion:* Muslim; *Education:* BA, MA, PhD; *Career:* teacher, Primary Schools, 1958–59; teacher, Secondary Schools, 1966–68; Lecturer at Teachers Training College, 1969–70; Superintendent of Culture and Arts, 1971–75; Director of Culture and Arts, Ministry of Information, 1979; Chairman of the Board of Film Censors, Ministry of Information; *Publications: The Development of Early Arabic Drama 1847–1900,* 1981, in English; essays on literature and criticisms in the local press; *Interests and Recreations:* tennis, table tennis, chess, drama, cinema, history; member of the British Society of Middle East Studies; member of Middle East Studies Association of North America; *Languages:* Arabic, English, French; *Address:* P O Box 26613, Ministry of Information, Manama, Bahrain; telephone: 683989; telex: 8399 INFORM BN.

KHRAIBET, Ibrahim Ali Yusuf, Kuwaiti businessman; born 1906, Kuwait; married; *Religion:* Muslim; *Career:* founder of retail fabrics industry and business, 1941; member of the Social Reform Society, 1963; Chairman of Warba Construction Centre; member of National Assembly, 1963; *Address:* Warba Construction Centre, P O Box 42355, Shuwaikh, Kuwait; telex: 44192, Khuraibut, Kuwait.

KHUDAIRI, Hisham al-, Iraqi diplomat; born 25 May, 1936, Baghdad, Iraq; married; *Religion:* Muslim; *Education:* BA, Social Science, Exeter University, Exeter, UK, 1955–58; MA, Government History, Exeter University, 1958–60; *Career:* Technical Assistance Department, Ministry of Foreign Affairs, 1961; Director, International Conference Division, Ministry of Foreign Affairs, 1962–63; Embassy of Iraq, Algeria, 1963–68; Embassy of Iraq, Morocco, 1968; Embassy of Iraq, London, 1968–71; Director, West European Division, Political Department, Ministry of Foreign Affairs, 1971–72; Counsellor, Permanent Mission of Iraq, UN, New York, 1972–76; Director of UN Division, Ministry of Foreign Affairs, 1976; Minister Plenipotentiary, Permanent Mission of Iraq, UN, Geneva, 1976–78; Embassy of Iraq to the Sultanate of Oman, 1979–80; Embassy of Iraq, Guinea, 1980–81; Special Assistant to President of the UN General Assembly 36th Session, 1981; member of Secretariat of 7th Non-Aligned Conference, Baghdad, 1982; Department of International Organizations, Ministry of Foreign Affairs, 1982–; *Publications: Domestic Pressures and Foreign Policy: A Study of the Palestine Controversy, 1945–48 Interests and Recreations:* tennis, rowing; *Languages:* Arabic, English, French, Spanish, Italian; *Address:* P O Box 2139, Baghdad, Iraq; telephone: 30091.

KHUDAIRI, Muwaffaq, Iraqi businessman; born 7 July 1934, Baghdad, Iraq; married; three sons; *Religion:* Muslim; *Education:* BSc in Industrial Management, University of Denver, Colorado, USA, 1955; *Career:* member, Board of Directors of the Baghdad Chamber of Commerce, 1960–65; Economic Adviser and Marketing Consultant; *Interests and Recreations:* water-skiing, tennis, swimming, antiques, poetry; *Languages:* Arabic, English; *Address:* Central Park Hotel, Queensborough Terrace, London W2 3SS, UK.

KHULAIFAWI, Major General Abdul Rahman, Syrian politician/military commander; born 1930, Damascus, Syria; *Religion:* Muslim; *Education:* Military Academy, Homs, Syria; *Career:* served as officer; trained in

USSR; Governor of Dara'a and Hama before returning to the Army; member of Baath Party Military Bureau; represented Syria on Joint Arab Command in Cairo, 1964–67; Head of Armoured Forces Administration, 1967–68; Head of the Officers Board, Ministry of Defence, 1968–70; Minister of the Interior, 1970–71; Prime Minister, 1971–72, and 1976–78; member of Baath Party Regional Command; *Address:* Baath Party, Damascus, Syria.

KHULUSI, Safa Abdul Aziz, Iraqi academic; born 17 August 1917, Baghdad, Iraqi; married; one son, one daughter; *Religion:* Muslim; *Education:* BA and PhD, University of London, University of London, 1947; *Career:* Lecturer in European History, Military Secondary School, Baghdad, 1941; Superintendent of Translation and Publication, Ministry of Education, Baghdad, 1943–45; Lecturer in Arabic, School of Oriental and African Studies, University of London, 1945–50; Professor of Arabic Literature, Linguistics and Translation, University of Baghdad, 1950–72; Professor Emeritus, University of Baghdad, 1972; External Examiner to PhD candidates of leading British Universities; Professor of Translation and Linguistics, University of Bath, 1980–; member of the Governing Body, University of Baghdad, 1963; Chairman, National Muslim Education Council of Great Britain and Europe; member of the Executive Council of the Arab Club of Britain; *Publications: Morbid Souls,* 1941, a collection of short stories (in Arabic); *The Art of Translation in the Light of Comparative Studies,* 1956 and 1958, (in Arabic); *Analytical Translation,* 1957, (in Arabic); *Studies in Comparative Literature and Literary Schools,* 1958 (in Arabic); several other works of Literature; *Interests and Recreations:* reading, travelling, walking; *Languages:* Arabic, English, Turkish, Latin, French, Hebrew; *Address:* 53 Walton Crescent, Oxford, OX1 2JQ; telephone: (0865) 52471.

KHUMAYYIS, Abdullah Bin Muhammad Bin, Saudi Arabian official/writer; born 1921, Saudi Arabia; *Religion:* Muslim; *Education:* BA in Islamic Law, Faculty of Sharia, Mecca, Saudi Arabia; BA in Arabic Language, Faculty of Arabic Language, Mecca; *Career:* Principal, Al Ilmi Religious Institute, al-Hassa, 1956; Director, Faculty of Sharia, 1958; Director General, Presidium of Judiciary, 1959; Under Secretary of State, Ministry of Communications, 1963; Director, Riyadh Water Department, 1965; member of Board of Jazirah Press Organisation, Board of Charity, Riyadh, Editorial Board of King Abdul Aziz Archives Magazine *Darah,* Board for the Rejuvenation of Dariyyah Monuments; Secretary General, Okaz Literary Festival; President of Riyadh Literary Club; attended several literary national and international conferences; *Publications:* numerous books, collections of poetry; lectures and talks for radio and television; articles in the local press; *Decorations:* Literary Vanguard Order of Merit; Medal King Abdul Aziz University; Order of Merit for Literature, Tunisia; *Interests and Recreations:* touring the Arabian Peninsula, reading; *Address:* 39 Jarir Street, P O Box 1789, Riyadh, Saudi Arabia; telephone: 63300.

KHUSHAIM, Rida Hassan, Saudi Arabian economist/businessman; born 1938, Medina, Saudi Arabia; *Religion:* Muslim; *Education:* PhD in Business Administration, 1975; *Career:* Economist, Saudi Petroleum and Mineral Organization (Petromin), 1963–65; Assistant Manager, Directorate of Zakat (Poor Tax) and Income Tax, Eastern Province; Lecturer in Economics and Business Administration, King Abdul Aziz University; member of Dammam Chamber of Commerce and Industry, Islamic Society, USA; owner and General Manager of Khushqim Stores for Industrial Equipment; established the Khushaim Factory for Hydraulic Presses, Dammam; member of several international economic conventions; attended Chartered Accountants' Conferences, Michigan, Texas, USA; *Decorations:* Merit Membership of the Accounting Society, Arizona, USA; *Interests and Recreations:* chess, table tennis; *Address:* P O Box 119, Dammam, Saudi Arabia; telephone: Dammam 25451.

KHUSHNAW, Anwar Ibrahim Salih, Iraqi official; born 1930, Arbil, Iraq; married; five children; *Religion:* Muslim; *Education:* LLB; *Career:* Assistant Director, State Organization for Food Industries, Baghdad; Director General, National Tobacco State Company, 1974–; Chairman, Arbil Chamber of Commerce; *Interests and Recreations:* walking, reading; *Languages:* Arabic, Kurdish, Turkish, English; *Address:* National Tobacco State Company, Baghdad, Iraq; telephone: Office — 21011, 21505; Residence — 23782.

KIKHIA, Mansur Rashid, Libyan diplomat; born 1931, Libya; *Religion:* Muslim; *Education:* Faculty of Law, Cairo University, Cairo, Egypt, and Paris, France; *Career:* joined diplomatic service 1957; Chargé d'Affaires, Libyan Embassy, Paris, 1962–63; Chargé d'Affaires, Libyan Embassy to Algeria, 1963–64; Consul General, Geneva, Switzerland, 1965–67; Deputy Head of Delegation to the UN, New York, 1967–69; Chairman of Libyan Delegation to the UN General Assembly, 1970, 1972, 75–76, and Vice Chairman, 1977–78; Representative of Libyan Delegation on UN Security Council 1976,1977, presiding over the Security Council 1976, 1977; Chairman, Security Council Sanctions Committee, 1977; Vice President of the UN General Assembly, 1978; Chairman, UN Advisory Committee for the International Year of the Disabled Persons, 1979; Non-resident Ambassador of Libya to Canada, 1979–; Permanent Representative of Libya to the UN, 1970–; *Languages:* Arabic, English; *Address:* The Permanent Mission of the Socialist People's Libyan Arab Jamahiriya, 866 United Nations Plaza, New York, NY 10017, USA.

KILANI, Fuad Zaid, Jordanian physician; born 10 August 1931, Nablus, Jordan; married; *Education:* MB, BCh, Cairo University, Cairo Egypt, 1956; member of the Royal College of Physicians, Glasgow, UK, 1966; Fellow of the Royal College of Physicians, 1975; MA in Hospital Administration Baylor, USA, 1965–66; Fellowship in Cardiology, Methodist Hospital, Texas, USA, 1970; *Career:* Chief of Medical Department, Army Base Hospital, Jordan, 1966–70; Commanding Officer, Army Base Hospital, Amman, Jordan, 1970–73; Minister of Health in Jordan, 1973–74; Member of the Executive Board, World Health Organisation, 1974–77; Chairman, Society of Internal Medicine, 1978–80; *Publications: Hypermetabolic Mitochondrial Disease,* 1972; *Management of Hypertension; Angiographic Study of Some Cases of Congenital Heart Disease; Decorations:* Order of Independence, Jordan, 1st Class; Order of the Jordanian Star, 1st class; Order of Tunisian Republic, 1st Class; *Interests and Recreations:* swimming, hunting, chess, reading; *Languages:* Arabic, English; *Address:* P O Box 2641, Amman, Jordan; telephone: Office — 37377; Residence — 65736.

KILANI, Haissam al-, Syrian diplomat; born 6 August 1926, Damascus, Syria; married; *Education:* Diploma, Syrian Military Academy, Damascus, 1947; Diploma, Staff Air Force Academy, Paris, France, 1953; Diploma, Air War Superior Academy, Paris, France, 1956; University of Leipzig, East Germany, 1969–72; *Career:* Officer, Syrian Air Force, 1948–61; Chief, Syrian Air Staff, 1958; Ministerial Counsellor, Ministry of Foreign Affairs, 1962; Ambassador to Algeria, 1962; Director, Economic Department, 1963–64; Ambassador to Morocco, 1965; General Inspector, Ministry of Foreign Affairs, 1966–67; Secretary General, Ministry of Foreign Affairs, 1968–69; Ambassador to East Germany, 1969–72; Ambassador to Canada and Mexico, 1972; Ambassador, Permanent Representative to UN, New York, USA, 1972–80; *Publications: The Strategic and Military Importance of the United Arab Republic,* 1958; *When Israel Attacks,* 1964; *The Strategic Position of the Arab World,* 1966; *The Arab Military Strategy: an Historic Study,* 1968; *The Military Struggle for Arab Unity,* 1973; *Interests and Recreations:* tennis, swimming, modern history; *Languages:* Arabic, English, French, German; *Address:* Ministry of Foreign Affairs, Damascus, Syria.

KINDI, Adnan Abdul Hamid al-, Iraqi official; born 1925; *Religion:* Muslim; *Education:* University of Manchester, UK; *Career:* worked in Oil Planning and Construction Administration; President of the State Organization for Industrial Design and Construction (SOIDAC), 1970; *Languages:* Arabic, English; *Address:* State Organization for Industrial Design and Construction, Khullani Street, P O Box 5614, Baghdad, Iraq.

KINDI, Muhammad Khalifa al-, United Arab Emirates politician; born 1931, Abu Dhabi, United Arab Emirates; *Religion:* Muslim; *Career:* Director of Customs and Ports; Abu Dhabi Minister of Education; member of Government Planning Council; Minister of Planning, and Head of Department of Planning in Abu Dhabi Executive Council; Minister of Public Works and Housing, 1977–; *Languages:* Arabic, English; *Address:* Ministry of Public Works and Housing, P O Box 878, Abu Dhabi, United Arab Emirates; telephone: 362774.

KITTANI, Ismat, Iraqi diplomat/UN official; born 5 April 1929, Iraq; married; *Education:* BA, Political Science and English, Knox College, Galesburg, Illinois, USA, 1951; *Career:* High School Teacher, Iraq, 1951; Ministry of Foreign Affairs, 1952–56; Permanent Mission of Iraq, UN, New York, 1957–60; Permanent Representative of Iraq, UN Geneva, 1961–64; Chief, Specialized Agency and Administrative Committee on Coordination Office, UN, 1964; Secretary, Economic and Social Council, UN, 1965–66; Director, Executive Office of the Secretary General, UN, 1967–69; Deputy Assistant Secretary General, Office of Inter-Agency Affairs and Co-ordination (IAAC), UN, 1969–70; Assistant Secretary General, IAAC, UN, 1971–73; Assistant Secretary General, Executive Assistant to the Secretary General, UN, New York, 1973–75; Head of the Department of International Organisation, Foreign Ministry, Baghdad, Iraq, 1975–80; Rapporteur General, 5th Non-Aligned Summit, Colombo, Sri Lanka, 1976; Chairman, Political Committee, 6th Non Aligned Summit, Havana, Cuba, 1979; President, 2nd Review Conference of NP Treaty, Geneva, Switzerland, 1980; President, 36th Session of UN General Assembly, NY, 1981–82; Under Secretary, Ministry of Foreign Affairs, Baghdad, Iraq, 1980–; *Languages:* Arabic, English, French; *Address:* Ministry of Foreign Affairs, Baghdad, Republic of Iraq.

KLAT, Robert, Lebanese diplomat/UN official; born 8 July 1912, Tripoli, Lebanon; married; *Education:* Licence in Law, French University, Beirut, Lebanon, 1931–34; *Career:* Barrister at Law, 1934–45; Consul General, Alexandria, Egypt; Counsellor, Embassy to Egypt, 1946–56; Director General of Administration, later Deputy Chief of Protocol, Ministry of Foreign Affairs, 1955–62; Alternate Delegate to the UN General Assembly and Ambassador to Canada, 1959–62; Chief of Protocol, Ministry of Foreign Affairs, Lebanon, 1962–65; Ambassador to Greece, 1965–71; Director General of Public Relations, Chief of Protocol, with rank of Ambassador, Presidential Palace, Beirut, 1971–; Lebanese Representative, UN Relief and Works Agency for Palestine Refugees in the Near East (UNRWA) Advisory Board, Beirut, Lebanon, 1974; Ambassador to Italy, 1972–75; now retired; *Decorations:* Commander of the National Order of the Cedar; Grand Officer of the

Egyptian Order of Merit; Commander of the Orders of Brazil, Columbia, Iran, Austria, Greece etc; *Interests and Recreations:* riding; member of Beirut Club, Aero Club and Cercle de l'Union Française, *Languages:* Arabic, French, English; *Address:* Office — UNRWA Advisory Board, Museitbeh Quarter, Beirut, Lebanon.

KLIBI, Chedli, Tunisian Arab League official/politician; born 6 September 1925, Tunis, Tunisia; married; three children; *Religion:* Muslim; *Education:* Faculty of Literature and Philosophy, Sorbonne, University of Paris, France; Doctorate in Arabic Literature and Language; *Career:* Teacher of Arabic, 1950; Teacher, Ecole Normale Supérieure, 1957; Head of Radio-Télévision-Tunisienne (RTT), 1958–61; Secretary of State for Cultural Affairs and Information, 1961–64; Secretary of State for Cultural Affairs and Guidance, 1964; Secretary of State for Cultural Affairs, 1964; Secretary of State for Cultural Affairs and Information, 1966–69; Minister of Cultural Affairs, 1966–70; Minister of Cultural Affairs and Information, 1971–73; Director of the Presidential Cabinet, 1974–76; Minister of Cultural Affairs, 1976–78; Minister of Information, 1978–79; Secretary General of the Arab League, 1979–; member of the Central Committee of the Destour Socialist Party, 1964–; member of the Political Bureau of the Destour Socialist Party, 1968–; Mayor of Carthage, 1963–; *Publications: Les Arabes Face A La Question Palastinienne; La Culture, Un Pari De Civilisation; Reflexions Sur L'Islam et Le Monde Contemporain;* and other works; contributor and later editor of *Al Nadwa* literary magazine; editor of *Sawt al Amal,* weekly newspaper of the General Union of Tunisian Workers, 1955; articles in *L'Action,* now *Jeune Afrique, Al-Sabah* and *Al Amal; Decorations:* Grand Cordon of the Order of the Tunisian Republic, 1965; Grand Cordon of the Order of Tunisian Independence, 1967; several foreign decorations; *Interests and Recreations:* literature and journalism; member of the Arab Academy, Cairo, 1971; *Languages:* Arabic, French; *Address:* Secretariat Général de la Ligue des Etats Arabes, Avenue Khereddine Pacha, Tunis, Tunisia; telephone: 890 211.

KOBEISSI, Zulfikar, Lebanese journalist; born 19 July, 1937, Beirut, Lebanon; resident in Kuwait; married; one son; *Religion:* Muslim; *Education:* LLB, Lebanese University, Beirut; studies in journalism, Thomson Institute, Wales, UK, and American University, Washington, D.C. USA; studies in banking, Institute of Bankers, London, and National Westminster Bank, London; *Career:* General Manager, *Dar al-Qabas,* Kuwait; Manager of *Dar al-Qabas* newspaper, Kuwait; Economic Editor, *Al-Nahar* newspaper, Beirut; Correspondent, *Economist* magazine, Beirut; Assistant General Manager, *Dar Assayad,* Beirut; joint owner and editor in chief, *Al-Massarif* magazine, Beirut; member of the Lebanese Press Union; *Publications:* numerous books and studies; *Decorations:* Journalist of the Year Prize, 1969; *Languages:* Arabic, English, French; *Address:* P O Box 24166, Kuwait; telephone: 81822.

KOLEILAT, Rashid A, Lebanese UN official; born 21 November 1920, Beirut, Lebanon; married; two daughters; *Education:* International College, Beirut, Lebanon, 1937–41; BA in Economics, American University of Beirut, 1941–42; Diploma in Economic Science and Finance, School of Law, Beirut, Lebanon, 1942–45; *Career:* Assistant Manager, Koleilat and Sons, Syria and Lebanon, 1945–48; Manager, 1949–53; Representative of the UN Children Fund (UNICEF), Jordan and Syria, 1953–59; Area Representative, UNICEF, Iraq, Jordan, Lebanon, Saudi Arabia and Syria, 1960–68; Deputy Regional Director, Eastern Mediterranean Region, UNICEF, Beirut, Lebanon, 1969–; *Publications:* various UNICEF studies on social development programmes in Jordan, Syria, Saudi Arabia; *Interests and Recreations:* reading, gardening, economic and social developments; *Languages:* Arabic, English, French; *Address:* Office — UNICEF, P O Box 484, Amman Jordan; Residence— Al-Manar Building, Apt 14, Tanoukhiyin Street, Beirut, Lebanon.

KOOLI, Mongi, Tunisian politician; born 15 March 1930, Tunisia; married, three children; *Religion:* Muslim; *Education:* Licence in Public Law and Political Science, Faculté de Droit, University of Paris, France: *Career:* Secretary General of Union Générale des Etudiants Tunisiens (UGET) 1959; Director of Socialist Destour Party, 1960–64; Governor of Jendouba, 1964; Governor of Bizerta, 1967–69; Director General of National Security, 1969–70; Ambassador to Spain,

1970–75; Minister of Public Health, 1976; Minister Delegate to the Prime Minister and Director of Party, 1982–; *Decorations:* Grand Cordon of the Order of Tunisian Independence; Grand Officer of the Order of the Tunisian Republic; various foreign decorations; *Languages:* Arabic, French, Spanish; *Address:* Prime Minister's Office, Tunis, Tunisia.

KORAIEM, Muhammad Samir Salim, Egyptian official/economist; born 6 October 1930, Beni Suef, Egypt; married; one son, one daughter; *Religion:* Muslim; *Education:* BA in Accounting and Public Finance, Cairo University, Egypt, 1952; Diploma in Taxation and Public Finance, Cairo University, 1954; Diploma in Planning and Finance, International Banking School, Prague, Czechoslovakia, 1963; Professional Diploma in Management, American University in Cairo; MA in Business Management, American University in Cairo, 1975; *Career:* Tax Officer, 1952; Head of Economic Cooperation with European Countries, 1965; Deputy Director General, International Finance Department, Ministry of Economy and Economic Cooperation, 1975; Under Secretary of State for International Finance; Minister of Finance 1977; part-time researcher, Economic Department, Arab League; part-time lecturer in Business Management, American University in Cairo; Fellow of Economic Development Institute, Washington D.C., USA; *Languages:* Arabic, English, French, Italian, Czechoslovakian; *Address:* Office — 8 Adly Street, Cairo, Egypt; telephone: 916214; Residence — 983027.

KORRAYEM, Badr Ahmad, Saudi Arabian broadcasting official; born 1939; *Religion:* Muslim; *Education:* Diploma of Broadcasting Training Institute, Cairo, Egypt, 1961; BA, Sociology, King Abdul Aziz University, Jeddah, Saudi Arabia; *Career:* civil servant, Immigration Department, Jeddah, 1954–57; radio announcer; radio producer; chief news release announcer; Deputy Director of Programmes, Jeddah Radio; Deputy Director General of Jeddah Radio; accompanied the late King Faisal on his state visits to Arab, African, Asian and European countries as Chief of the Information Mission covering the visits; attended as information representative, Islamic and Arab summit conferences held in Cairo, Lahore, Khartoum, Rabat; Acting Director of the Bureau of the Minister of Information, 1976; Chief Radio Announcer and Director of Programme Implementation, Jeddah Broadcasting Service, Ministry of Information; *Address:* Jeddah Broadcasting Service, Ministry of Information, Mena Road, Jeddah, Saudi Arabia; telephone: 4038178.

KOSHAK, Abdul Qadir Hamza, Saudi Arabian official/engineer; born 1 Janurary 1939; Mecca, Saudi Arabia; married; three sons, two daughters; *Religion:* Muslim; *Education:* Diploma in Radio Engineering, Cairo Institute, Egypt, 1957; BSc in Architectural Engineering, Cairo University, Egypt, 1962; MSc in Landscape Architecture and Environmental Planning, Utah State University, USA, 1968; *Career:* Engineer, Municipalities Department, 1962; Director of Technical Department, 1963; Director of Central Admission for Engineering Services, 1968; Director General for Engineering Affairs, 1972; Assistant Deputy Minister, Ministry of Municipalities, 1976; Mayor of Mecca, 1977–; Secretary General, Islamic Capitals Organization; *Interests and Recreations:* sailing, fishing, travelling, music; *Languages:* Arabic, English, French; *Address:* Mecca Municipality, Saudi Arabia, P O Box 1210, Saudi Arabia; telephone: Office— 5421576; Residence— 5435228.

KOSHAK, Yahya Hamza, Saudi Arabian engineer; born 1940, Mecca, Saudi Arabia; *Religion:* Muslim; *Education:* MA in Civil Engineering; *Career:* Civil Engineer at Municipalities Department, Ministry of the Interior; Deputy Secretary General for Engineering Affairs of Mecca Municipality; Senior Engineer at Watson Co; resigned from government service; private business, Koshak Engineering Consultative Bureau, a specialist in civil and health engineering, water supply and construction; member of the Board of several consultative companies; member of the American Water Society; Director General of Water and Sewage Department in Western Region, 1971–81; retired in 1981 to run his own office, Architecture and Engineering; *Publications:*a paper on the dual method of water networks and, a paper on Zamzam water; *Interests and Recreations:* painting, photography; *Address:* P O Box 3507, Jeddah, Saudi Arabia; telephone: Office — 6694005; Residence 6655539.

KOSHMAN, Muhammad Nassim, Kuwaiti economist/diplomat; born 25 October 1932, Lebanon; married; three sons; *Religion:* Muslim; *Education:* Degree in Law and Economics, University of Grenoble, France; *Career:* Attorney, Court of Appeals, Dakar, Senegal, 1959–61; Chargé d'Affaires of Mauritania in Washington D.C., and Head of Permanent Mission to the UN, New York, USA, 1961–64; Executive Director of the World Bank, the International Development Association, and the International Finance Corporation, Washington D.C., and Principal Resident Representative of Mauritania to the World Bank Group with rank of Ambassador, 1963–74; Special Adviser to the President of the World Bank for liaison with OPEC members, 1974–76; Ambassador of Mauritania to USA, Mexico and Brazil, 1976–78; Investment Consultant, Washington D.C., 1978–80; Adviser to the Kuwait Fund for Arab Economic Development; *Decorations:* Senegal Grand Officer of the National Order, 1969; Grand Officer of the Order of Merit, Chad, 1970; Commander of the Order of Merit, Central African Republic, 1970; Commander of the National Orders of Congo, 1970, of Ivory Coast, 1970, of Upper Volta, 1971, of Benin, 1972; Order of San Carlos, Columbia Grand Cross, 1973; Commander of the Order of National Merit, Mauritania, 1976, and several other awards; *Interests and Recreations:* reading, writing, swimming, chess, music; *Languages:* Arabic, French, English, Woloff (West Africa); *Address:* Kuwait Fund for Arab Economic Development, P O Box 2921 Kuwait; telephone: 439 075; telex: 2025 ALSUNDUK.

KOTAITE, Asaad, Lebanese UN official; born 6 November 1924, Hasbaya, Lebanon; *Education:* Licence in Law, St. Joseph University, Beirut, Lebanon, 1948; LLD, University of Paris, France, 1952; Academy of International Law, the Hague, Netherlands; *Career:* Chief, Legal Service, Ministry of Public Works and Transport, Lebanon, 1953–56; member of the UN Transportation and Communication Commission, 1957–59; Chairman, UN Air Transportation Committee, 1965–68; Representative, International Civil Aviation Organisation Council (ICAO), 1956–70; Secretary General, ICAO, Montreal, Canada, 1970–76; President, ICAO Council, 1976–; *Languages:* Arabic, English, French, Portuguese, Spanish; *Ad-*

dress: Office — ICAO, 1000, Sherbrooke Street West, Montreal H3A 2R2, Quebec, Canada; telephone: (514) 285 8219.

KUDSI, Fawwaz Nazim al-, United Arab Emirates diplomat/lawyer; born 29 September 1941, Aleppo, Syria; married; three sons; *Religion:* Muslim; *Education:* BLL, University of Aleppo, Syria; *Career:* practiced law, Syria, 1969; Acting Director, Centre of Documentation and Research, Amiri Court, Abu Dhabi, 1970; Head of Protocol Department, Ministry of Foreign Affairs, 1972–82; Ambassador, Ministry of Foreign Affairs, United Arab Emirates, 1982–; *Decorations:* Republic of Mauritania Medal; Tunisian Republic Medal; Jordanian Medal; Saudi Medal; *Interests and Recreations:* legal, political and historical thought, tennis, riding, swimming; *Languages:* Arabic, English; *Address:* P O Box 6010, Abu Dhabi, United Arab Emirates; telephone: 337889.

KUDSI, Nazim Takkiyddin al-, Syrian politician; resident in Lebanon; born February 1906, Aleppo, Syria; married; six sons, one daughter; *Religion:* Muslim; *Education:* American University of Beirut, Lebanon during World War I; Licence in Law, Damascus University; LLD, Geneva University, Switzerland; *Career:* lawyer, 1930–43; worked with National Bloc resisting the French Occupation; elected member of the Parliament for Aleppo, 1936; re-elected 1943,1947,1949,1954; first Minister Plenipotentiary representing Syria in Washington, USA; member of the Syrian Delegation demanding France's evacuation of Syria at the UN Security Council meeting in London, 1946; Representative of Syria at numerous Arab League meetings; Head of the Syrian Delegation to the New Delhi Conference for the Liberation of Indonesia, 1949; Minister of Foreign Affairs, 1949; Prime Minister, 1950 and 1951; President of the Chamber of Deputies 1951, 1954, 1955, 1956, 1957; President of the Syrian Republic, 1961–63; *Interests and Recreations:* history, walking; *Languages:* Arabic, Turkish, English, French; *Address:* c/o Capital Guidance Ltd, 18b Charles Street, London W1; Karme Building, Rue Anis Nsouei, Beirut, Lebanon; telephone: 314150.

KUHAIMY, Shaikh Ahmad al-, Saudi Arabian diplomat; born 1925, Damascus, Syria; married; four sons, one daughter; *Religion:* Muslim; *Education:* BA in Economics and Political Science; *Career:* Political Attaché, Saudi Embassy to Iraq, 1947; successively 3rd Secretary, 2nd Secretary, 1st Secretary, Counsellor, Minister Delegate, Ambassador to Jordan; Ambassador to Iraq, 1981–; *Decorations:* King Abdul Aziz Medal; Star of Jordan, 1st Class; *Interests and Recreations:* Arabic literature, swimming, riding, hunting; *Languages:* Arabic, French; *Address:* Embassy of Saudi Arabia, Waziriyah, Baghdad, Iraq.

KULAIB, Ali Ghanim, People's Democratic Republic of Yemen official/engineer; born 27 Februrary 1924, Aden; married; one son, four daughters; *Religion:* Muslim; *Education:* BSc, Engineering, St. Andrews University, Scotland, 1955; member of the Institute of Civil Engineers, 1961; *Career:* Teacher in Aden, 1949–52; Engineer, George Wimpy, UK, 1955–58; Engineer, Senior R.E. and State Engineer, Aden, 1958–62; Director of Public Works, and Permanent Secretary, Ministry of Communications, South Yemen, 1962–68; Chairman, Little Aden Township, 1968–69; Senior Resident Engineer, Mecca Project for Watson Saudi Arabia, 1969–79; Associate Partner, 1976; Manager for Saudi City Project in Jeddah, Saudi Amoudi Group, 1980–; *Interests and Recreations:* tennis, table tennis, chess, travel; *Languages:* Arabic, English; *Address:* P O Box 2779, Saudi Amoudi Group, Jeddah, Saudi Arabia; telephone: Office — 6601823, 6656376; Residence — 6530186.

KURDI, Husni Sidu, Jordanian businessman/banker; born 1906 Amman, Jordan; married; two sons, two daughters; *Religion:* Muslim; *Education:* in Jordan; *Career:* Merchant, member of the Board of Jordanian Chamber of Commerce; member of the Board of the Bank of Jordan; Chairman and General Manager, Bank of Jordan; member of the Board of the Central Bank of Jordan; member of the Amman Municipal Council; Mayor of Amman; *Decorations:* Order of Independence, 1st and 2nd Class, Jordan; *Interests and Recreations:* horse riding, hunting, football; *Languages:* Arabic, English; *Address:* Bank of Jordan, Head Office, Jabal Amman, P O Box 2140, Amman, Jordan; telephone: 44328, 44839.

KURSHUMI, Abdullah Hussain al-, Yemen Arab Republic politician; *Career:* Minister of Works, 1962–65; Minister of Communications, 1968; Prime Minister; resigned 1970; Head of Highways Authority, 1973–74; Minister of Works, 1975; Minister of Municipalities and Public Works, 1976; Minister of Public Works, 1978; *Address:* Ministry of Public Works, Sana'a, Yemen Arab Republic.

L

LABAKI, Kisruan, Lebanese diplomat/ journalist; born 1920, Ba'abda, Lebanon; married; six children; *Education:* Political Economics, American University of Beirut, AUB, Lebanon; *Career:* Journalist, 1938–39; Editor, *Revue du Liban,* 1941; Journalist, French Delegation's Radio Services, 1940– 43; Sub-editor, *L'Orient* newspaper, 1945–49; Features Editor, *Le Soir,* 1950–65; Ambassador to Belgium, the Netherlands and Luxembourg, 1965–78; Adviser to the Presidency of the Republic, Overseas Press and Information Section, 1969; Ambassador to West Germany, 1972–78; Secretary General of the Ministry of Foreign Affairs, 1979–82; Permanent Representative of Lebanon to the UN, New York, USA, 1982–; *Languages:* Arabic, French; *Address:* 866 United Nations Plaza, Suite 580, New York, NY 10017, USA.

LABBAN, Abdul Rahman al-, Lebanese physician/psychiatrist; born 1924, Beirut, Lebanon; married; three children; *Education:* BA, American Unversity of Beirut, Lebanon; MD, London University, UK; Institute of Psychiatry; *Career:* Psychiatrist, Al-Asfouria Hospital, Lebanon, 1952; Psychiatric Hospital, Kuwait, 1953; Senior Mental Health Adviser, WHO; Director, Government Hospital for Mental Illness, Jordan, 1954–59; Chief Physician, Muslim Hospital for Psychiatric Disorders, Beirut, Lebanon, 1959–62; Director, Medical Rehabilitation Centre, Beirut, Lebanon; Vice President, National Board for Scientific Research; *Decorations:* various Jordanian decorations; *Interests and Recreations:* painting; member of the Amis du Livre; *Languages:* Arabic, French, English; *Address:* Office — Ma'mari Street, Maktabi Building, Beirut, Lebanon; Residence -- Madame Curie Street, Beirut, Lebanon.

LADGHAM, Muhammad al-Bahi, Tunisian politician; born 10 January 1913; married 1947; one son, three daughters; *Religion:* Muslim; *Education:* general; *Career:* Director General of the Interior, 1933; member of Destour Party; Director, Tunisian Chamber of Commerce, 1946; Counsellor, Tunisian Delegation at Paris, 1951; representative of Tunisia at UN, 1951; Director, Tunisian Office for National Liberation, New York, 1955; Secretary General of the Socialist Destour Party, 1955–57; Vice President, Council of Ministers, 1955–56; Secretary of State, Presidency of the Republic, 1956–59; Secretary of State for National Defence, 1959–66; Prime Minister, 1969–70; Deputy in the National Assembly, 1956–72; President of the Arab Higher Committee to supervise the Cairo Agreement of September 1970 between the PLO and Jordanian Government, 1970–71; *Address:* 8 Rue Sahnoun, Hamilcar, Tunis, Tunisia; telephone: 270 323.

LADGHAM, Salah, Tunisian diplomat; born 1927, Tunisia; married; *Religion:* Muslim; *Career:* Chargé d'Affaires, Embassy to Spain, 1960–62; Ambassador to Czechoslovakia, 1962–66; Ambassador to Netherlands, 1966–70; Director of Political Affairs, Ministry of Foreign Affairs, 1970–74; Ambassador to Turkey, 1974; *Languages:* Arabic, French, English; *Address:* Ministry of Foreign Affairs, Boulevard Farhat Hached, Tunis, Tunisia.

LAGHZAOUI, Muhamad, Moroccan diplomat/politician; born 27 September 1906, Fes, Morocco; married; six children; *Religion:* Muslim; *Education:* Collège Moulay Idriss, Fes, Morocco; *Career:* founded and developed a well known transport company; founder of several scholarships to College Moulay Idriss; member of the Committee of the Istiqlal Party; represented the Istiqlal

Party on the National Moroccan delegation to the UN, December 1952; member of the Moroccan Office of Information in New York; Director General of National Security, 1956; Director, Phosphates Office, July 1960; Personal Representative of HM King Hassan to Algeria, 1961; Co-ordinator of the Phosphates Bureau des Etudes et Participation Industrielle and Bureau des Recherches et de Participations Minières; Minister of Tourism, Industry, Mines and Handicrafts, 1963–64; elected President of the Afro-Asian Organisation for Economic Cooperation at the 5th Congress in Rabat, May 1966; Ambassador to the Court of St James, 1969–71; Ambassador to France, 1971–72; now involved in private enterprise; *Languages:* Arabic, English, French; *Address:* Laghzaoui, Souissi, Rabat, Morocco.

LAGU, Major General Joseph, Sudanese army officer; born 1931, Sudan; married; three sons, three daughters; *Education:* Military College, 1960; Military Law course in UK, 1962; *Career:* Lieutenant, 1963; joined Anyanya Movement in East Africa, 1963; took over the political and military control of the Anyanya Movement, 1968; Chairman of the Southern Supreme Military Council, 1970; Head of the Southern Sudan Liberation Movement; following the Addis Ababa Agreement rejoined the army of the Sudan as Major General, 1972; Inspector General of the Sudan Armed Forces; General Officer in Command, Southern Command; President of the Higher Executive Council, Regional Government; *Languages:* Arabic, English; *Address:* President of the Higher Executive Council, Regional Government, Juba, Sudan.

LAHLOU, Abdallah, Moroccan agriculturalist; born 18 November 1943, Fes, Morocco; married; one son, two daughters; *Religion:* Muslim; *Education:* Agronomical Engineering, National Institute of Agronomy, Paris, France; Rural Engineering of Waters and Forests, Paris; *Career:* Director of the Office of Agricultural Valuation of Ouarzazte, 1969–72; Director General, National Society of Agricultural Development, SODEA, 1972–77; Director General of the Office of Commercialization and Exportation, OCE, 1977–; Vice President of the Franco Arab Chamber of Commerce; *Interests and Recreations:* walking, jogging, cycling; *Languages:* Arabic, French, English; *Address:*

Office de Commercialization et d'Exportation, P O Box 259 Casablanca, Morocco; telephone: 366249.

LAHOUD, Colonel Faris, Lebanese naval commander; born 1930; *Religion:* Christian; *Education:* graduated from Ecole Navale de Brest, France (Naval Engineer); training courses in France and Staff College in the USA; *Career:* served active career in Navy; Commander of Navy, 1967–75; Head of the Premier Bureau since 1975; *Decorations:* Officer, National Order of the Cedar, as well as other decorations; *Languages:* Arabic, French; *Address:* Office — Army High Command, Yarze, Lebanon.

LAMRHILI, Ahmad Muhammad, Moroccan academic/sociologist; born 20 March 1945, Fes, Morocco; married; *Religion:* Muslim; *Education:* Diploma, Institute of International Relations Studies, Paris, France; Diploma, Practical School for Higher Studies, Paris; BA and PhD in Sociology, Paris; *Career:* Head of Project, Ministry of Information, Rabat, 1973–75; Director, Centre of the Formation of Journalists, Rabat, 1974–75; Assistant Professor, Faculty of Arts, Fes, 1975–79; Director of the planning of the City of Fes, 1975–79; Researcher, Institute of Studies and Research for Arabisation, Rabat, 1979–; Director of *Al-Asaas* review; member of the World Federation of Twin Towns; member of the Town-planning Collective of United Cities; *Publications:* numerous articles and papers published in journals and magazines; *Interests and Recreations:* cinema; member of Hadara Association, Fes; *Languages:* Arabic, French, English; *Address:* Al-Hurriya Street, Hayy al-Salaam, P O Box 543 Tabriquat, Sale, Morocco; telephone: 87279.

LARAKI, Ahmad, Moroccan politician/ diplomat; born October 1931, Casablanca, Morocco; *Religion:* Muslim; *Education:* in Casablanca; Surgery and Medicine, University of Paris, France, 1956; *Career:* Director of the International Organizations American Division, Ministry of Foreign Affairs; Head the Moroccan Delegation to the United Nations General Assembly Session of 1957; Permanent Delegate to the UN; Directeur de Cabinet to Ahmad Balafrej, 1958; Head of Hospital Services in Casablanca, 1959; Chef de Cabinet, subsequently Secretary General, Ministry of Health; Ambassador to Spain,

1961–65; Ambassador to USA, 1965; Foreign Minister, 1967; Prime Minister, 1969–71; Head of the Ministry of Foreign Affairs with the rank of Minister of State, 1974; *Decorations:* Order of the Spanish Throne 1961; *Languages:* Arabic, French; *Address:* Ministry of Foreign Affairs, Rabat, Morocco.

LARAKI, Izzedine, Moroccan physician/politician; born 1929, Morocco; *Education:* medical studies, University of Paris, France, 1957; *Career:* Directeur de Cabinet, Minister of Education; Chef de Cabinet, Minister of Health, 1960; Professor, Faculty of Medicine, Rabat, Morocco, 1967–72; member of the National Council, and Executive Committee, 1960, 1965; member of the Istiqlal Party; member of the Moroccan Writers Union and of the editorial committee of the *Revue de la Médicine Marocaine;* Minister of Education and Executive Training, 1977–; *Publications:* several medical and literary articles; *Decorations:* Knight of the Order of King Abdul Aziz, 2nd Class, 1980; Ordre du Palme Académique, 1980; *Interests and Recreations:* walking, horse riding; *Languages:* Arabic, French; *Address:* Ministry of Education and Executive Training, 84 Rue Beni Zenassin, Rabat, Morocco; telephone: 51451.

LARI, Ridha Muhammad, Saudi Arabian journalist; born 1938, Jeddah, Saudi Arabia; *Religion:* Muslim; *Education:* BA in Political Science; *Career:* Deputy Director, Supervisor, Auditor, Diplomatic Attaché, 3rd Secretary, 2nd Secretary, Ministry of Foreign Affairs; Deputy Editor in Chief, *Okaz* daily newspaper; political commentator; *Publications:* several articles and columns; *Decorations:* Cavalier Insignia, Governments of Spain and Senegal; *Interests and Recreations:* reading; *Address:* Okaz Daily Newspaper, P O Box 1508, Jeddah, Saudi Arabia.

LASKY, Ahmad, Moroccan official/engineer; born 30 April 1932, Casablanca, Morocco; married; three children; *Religion:* Muslim; *Education:* Diploma in Public Works Engineering; *Career:* Ministry of Public Works, 1956; Engineer for Agadir District, 1959; Chief Engineer for Casablanca District, 1960–61; Director of the Port of Casablanca, 1962; Minister of Public Works and Communications, 1965; Director General of Royal Air Maroc, 1967–77; Minister of Agriculture and Agrarian Reform, 1970; Deputy of one of the Casablanca constituencies, 1970; Ministry of Secondary, Technical and Higher Education, 1971–72; Deputy for Parliament, 1977–; *Publications:* various technical articles about bridges and harbours in professional journals; *Decorations:* Moroccan, Tunisian, Egyptian, Iranian and Greek orders; *Interests and Recreations:* football, swimming; *Languages:* Arabic, French; *Address:* 4 Allée Montsouris, Casablanca, Morocco.

LASRAM, Abdul Aziz, Tunisian politician; born 25 March 1928, Tunis, Tunisia; married; three children; *Religion:* Muslim; *Education:* Licence in Law, University of Paris, France; L'Ecole Nationale d'Administration, Paris; *Career:* administrator, Tunisian Government, 1957; Ministry of Foreign Affairs, 1958, Head, Planning Department, 1959; Counsellor, Embassy to USSR, 1960–61; Under Secretary for Commerce Division with the Secretariat of State for Planning and Finance, 1965–70; Promoted to Ambassador's rank, 1970; Director of International Co-operation, Ministry of Foreign Affairs; Secretary General, Ministry of Foreign Affairs, 1971–72; President, Director General of Tunisian National Bank, 1972–74; Minister of National Economy, 1974; *Interests and Recreations:* President of the Club Africain Sporting Association; *Languages:* Arabic, French; *Address:* Ministry of National Economy, Tunis, Tunisia; telephone: 260088.

LATRECHE, Lieutenant Colonel Abdul Hamid, Algerian official/military expert; born 1931, Algeria; *Religion:* Muslim; *Education:* Military School, Saint-Maizent, France; *Career:* 2nd Lieutenant, French Army; joined National Liberation Army (ALN); member of military staff office; Commander of Oran military sector, with rank of Major, 1964; training course in USSR; Director of Ecole des Blindés, Batna, 1966; Director of Military Aviation, 1968; Secretary General, Ministry of National Defence, 1971; *Languages:* Arabic, French; *Address:* Ministry of National Defence, Algiers, Algeria.

LIASSINE, Muhammad, Algerian politician/engineer; born 1934, Algeria; *Religion:* Muslim; *Education:* Ecole Polytechnique, Paris, France; *Career:* Director of Industrialization, Ministry of Industry, 1963; Director of Industrial Production, Office Algérien de l'Action Commerciale (OFALAC); National Managing Director, National Steel Corporation, 1964; General Manager, Bureau d'Etudes et de Réalisations Industrielles (BERI); member of the Advisory Council for Hydrocarbons, Mines and Energy, 1967; Minister of Heavy Industry, 1977–80; *Address:* Ministry of Heavy Industry, Algiers, Algeria.

LOGALI, Hilary Paul, Sudanese politician; born 1931, Juba Sudan; *Education:* Khartoum College of Cairo University; courses at Baghdad University, and courses in the UK and USA; *Career:* Inspector, 1957–64; Minister of Works and Natural Resources and Communications, 1965; Secretary General, Southern Front Party, 1965–67, Vice President, 1967–69; Minister of Labour and Cooperation, 1967–69; various commercial posts in the private sector, 1970–71; Minister of Finance and Economics, Southern Regional Government, Juba, 1972–75; Speaker, People's Regional Assembly, 1975–78; member of the Executive Office of the Central Committee, Sudan Socialist Union, 1972–77, member of the Juba Territorial Consistuency, People's Regional Assembly, 1973–78; Assistant Secretary General, Sudan Socialist Union, and Head of Southern Regional Secretariat, 1976–; Chairman, University of Juba; *Decorations:* Order of Two Niles, 1st Class; Order of Constitution, 1st Class; *Languages:* Arabic, Bari, English; *Address:* P O Box 185, Juba, Sudan.

LOZI, Ahmad Abdul Karim al-, Jordanian politician; born 1925, Jordan; married; *Religion:* Muslim; *Education:* BA in Literature, Teachers Training College, Baghdad, Iraq, 1950; *Career:* teacher, 1950–53; Assistant to Chief of Royal Protocol, 1953–56; Chief of Royal Protocol, 1956–61; Head of Ceremonies at Ministry of Foreign Affairs, 1957; Member of Chamber of Deputies, 1961–62, 1962–63; Assistant to Chief of Royal Court, 1963–64; Minister of State for Prime Minister's Affairs, 1964–65; Senator, 1965; Minister of Interior for Municipal and Rural Affairs, 1967; Senator, 1967; Minister of Finance, 1970–71; member of Board of Trustees of Jordanian University; Prime Minister and Minister of Defence, 1971, 1972–73; Senator, 1973–74, 1974–78; President of the National Consultative Council, 1978–79; Chief of the Royal Hashemite Court, 1979–; *Decorations:* Star of Jordan,

1st Class; Order of Independence, 1st Class; Order of Renaissance, 2nd Class; *Address:* The Royal Palace, Amman, Jordan.

LOZI, Omaya al-, Lebanese businesswoman/ publisher, born 1945, Beirut; married; three daughters; *Religion:* Muslim; *Education:* BA in Business Administration, American University of Beirut; *Career:* Chairman and Director of *Al-Hawadess International Magazine* after the death of her husband; *Languages:* Arabic, English, French; *Address:* Office — 3 Carrington Gardens, London SW7; telephone: 3706474; Residence — 22 Sloane Avenue, London SW3, UK; telephone: 5896610.

LOZI, Salim Abdul Karim; Jordanian administrator; born 10 April 1941, Jubaiha, Jordan; married; one son, two daughers; *Religion:* Muslim; *Education:* Diploma in Agriculture, Syria, 1962; BSc in Agriculture (Forestry), Mosul, Iraq, 1970; MSc in Forestry Science and Management, USA, 1974; PhD in Development of Natural Resources and Exploitation of Soil, Colorado University, USA, 1976; *Career:* Inspector, Amman, 1962–64; Head of Department, 1965–67; Head of Department of Nurseries and Soil Preservation, 1970–73; Lecturer, University of Jordan, College of Agriculture, 1976–80; Deputy Minister of Agriculture, 1980–; member of the Jordanian Society, Royal Society for the Protection of the Environment, Amman, Jordan; *Interests and Recreations:* tennis, squash, walking; *Languages:* Arabic, English; *Address:* Office — Ministry of Agriculture, P O Box 2099, Amman, Jordan; telephone: 39391; Residence — Jubaiha, P O Box 10, Amman, Jordan; telephone: 843030, 842100.

LUAL LUAL, Akuey Lawrence, Sudanese politician/poet; born Bahr al Ghazal, Southern Sudan; *Education:* Faculty of Arts, Khartoum University, Khartoum, Sudan; *Career:* elected to Constituent Assembly, 1968; several teaching posts, 1969–71; seconded to Resettlement Commission, 1973; elected to Regional Assembly, 1973–77; Regional Minister of High Excutive Council, Minister of Education, 1975–78; elected member of Regional Assembly, 1978; Minister of High Executive Council Affairs, 1979–; *Address:* Regional Assembly, Juba, Sudan.

LUQMAN, Ali Muhammad Ali, People's Democratic Republic of Yemen journalist/ businessman; resident in Yemen Arab Republic; born 6 August 1918, Aden, People's Democratic Republic of Yemen; married; four sons, one daughter; *Religion:* Muslim; *Education:* BA, American University, Cairo, Egypt; *Career:* Managing Editor of *Fatat al-Jezirah,* Arabic daily newspaper, 1940–62; Editor in Chief *Al-Qalam al-Adani,* Arabic weekly newspaper, 1953–63, *Al-Akhbar* Arabic daily newspaper, 1963–67; Assistant Director, Rashid Trading Corporation (General Merchants), Taiz, Yemen Arab Republic (YAR); *Publications:* poetic dramas in Arabic, *Pygmalion; Al-Dhil al-Manshood; Al-Adil al-Mafqood; Qais wa Leila; Samra al-Arab;* poetry in Arabic, *Al-Watar al-Maghmoor; Ashjan fil Lail;* and several others in English; *Al-Warrad,* in Arabic; *Interests and Recreations:* literature (especially poetry) and journalism, member of poetry clubs, literary associations and press clubs; *Languages:* Arabic, English; *Address:* P O Box 4964 and P O Box 4960, Taiz, Yemen Arab Republic; telephone: 2908.

LUTFI, Sharif, Egyptian economist/financial expert; resident in Oman; born 1932, Egypt; married; two children; *Education:* BA in Economics, Alexandria University, Egypt; postgraduate work in Budapest, Hungary; PhD, Harvard University, USA; *Career:* joined Egyptian Diplomatic Service, 1950; joined the Egyptian National Bank; Head of Research, Egyptian National Bank; transferred to Ministry of Economy; Under Secretary in charge of research, 1970; Under Secretary for Economic Cooperation, 1971; 1st Under Secretary of the Ministry, 1972; IBRD (World Bank) Financial Expert, Oman National Development Council, 1974; *Languages:* Arabic, English, Hungarian; *Address:* c/o IBRD, 1818H Street, NW, Washington, D.C. 20433, USA.

M

MA'IUF, Faruk Abdullah al-, Iraqi official/ engineer; born 30 August, 1938, Umara, Iraq; married; two sons, three daughters; *Religion:* Muslim; *Education:* BSc in Mechanical Engineering, Baghdad University, 1960; BSc in Commerce and Economics, Mustansirya University, Basrah, Iraq, 1970; *Career:* Engineer, Electricity Administration for Southern Iraq, Basrah, Iraq; Director, Electricity Administration for Southern Iraq, 1969; Director General, General Company for Fertilizers, Basrah, Iraq, 1972; Secretary General, Arab Union for the Producers of Chemical Fertilizers, Kuwait, 1976; *Publications:* articles in the *Bulletin of Union* and the *Bulletin of OAPEC on Managment, Industry and Marketing; Interests and Recreations:* reading, Arabic poetry; *Languages:* Arabic, English, *Address:* Abdulla Al Salem District, Kuwait; telephone: Office — 530677; Residence — 816634.

MA'RUF, Taha Muhiyddin, Iraqi politician; born 1924; *Education:* College of Law, Baghdad, Iraq; *Career:* joined the Ministry of Foreign Affairs; Embassy to Egypt, 1960; Ministry of Foreign Affairs, 1964; Minister, Embassy to UK, 1968; Minister of State, 1968–70; Minister of Works and Housing; Ambassador at the Ministry of Foreign Affairs, 1970; Ambassador to Italy, 1970–74; non-resident Ambassador to Albania, 1971; non-resident Ambassador to Malta, 1972; Vice President of the Republic, 1974–; led the Iraqi delegation to Sudan, 1974, and to North and South Yemen and Somalia, 1977; member of Supreme Committee of Progressive Regional and National Fronts, 1975–; *Address:* Office of the Vice President, Baghdad, Iraq.

MAALOUF, Nasri, Lebanese politician/ lawyer; born 1911, Mount Lebanon; *Religion:* Christian; *Education:* Syrian School of Law, Damascus, Syria; *Career:* prominent member of former National Appeal Party; Minister of Finance, National Economy and Social Affairs in Sami al-Solh's Cabinet, 1956; defeated in 1957 elections; Minister of Defence in Takieddin al-Solh Cabinet 1973–74; *Languages:* Arabic, French, English; *Address:* c/o Ministry of Defence, Beirut, Lebanon.

MAAMDURI, Mahmud, Tunisian diplomat/ politician; born 1925, Tunisia; married; three children; *Religion:* Muslim; *Education:* Mathematics, Sorbonne, University of Paris; *Career:* taught in Paris and Tunis; elected to the Tunisian National Assembly, 1959; Ambassador to Yugoslavia, Greece, Romania, Bulgaria, Hungary 1964–69; Ambassador to Sweden, Norway, Finland, Iceland, 1969–73; Ambassador to West Germany, 1973–74; Secretary of State in the Prime Minister's Office responsible for Information, 1974; *Publications:* author of works on the theory of Destourian Socialism of which *Vent d'Est* is best known; *Languages:* Arabic, French, English; *Address:* Office of the Secretary of State for Information, Prime Minister's Office, Tunis, Tunisia.

MAAMOURI, Muhammad, Tunisian academic; born 27 December 1941, Tunisia; married; one son, one daughter; *Religion:* Muslim; *Education:* BA in English, University of Tunis, 1963; Diploma of Higher Studies, University of Paris, 1964; MA in English and American Literature, 1965; PhD in General Linguistics, Cornell University, USA, 1967; *Career: Asso* ciate Professor, English Department, University of Tunis, 1967–76; Director, Bourguiba Institute of Modern Languages, Tunis, 1974–; Mâtre de Conference in English and Linguistics, University of Tunis, 1976–; Peace Corps Language Consultant, 1966, 1969, 1970–73; Ford Foundation Language Consultant, 1973, 1974; ALESCO Language Consultant,

1980; Director, Tunis International Linguistics Institute, summers of 1976–79; *Publications:* numerous papers and studies in international professional journals; *Decorations:* Chevalier de l'Ordre des Palmes Académiques, France, 1977; Commander of the Order of the British Empire, 1980; *Interests and Recreations:* tennis, swimming, fishing, sailing, reading, Arabic language and Arab society; *Languages:* Arabic, English, French; *Address:* Institut Bourguiba des Langues Vivantes, 47 Ave de la Liberté, Tunis, Tunisia; telephone: 282418, 282923.

MAANINOU, Muhammad Saddik, Moroccan journalist; born 1944, Tangier, Morocco; married, three sons; *Religion:* Muslim; *Education:* Licence in Law; *Career:* Head of News Department, Moroccan Television, 1974; Chief Editor, Moroccan Television, 1975; Official Commentator, Moroccan Television, 1976; Director of *Le Combat* newspaper, 1963–65; covered the October War, 1973; attended Arab Development Conference in Algiers and many international conferences; *Decorations:* Green March Medal; *Languages:* Arabic, French, English; *Address:* La Pépinière, Sale, Morocco; telephone: 32010, 80285.

MABRO, Robert Emile, Anglo-Arab academic/economist; born 26 December, 1934, Alexandria, Egypt; married; two daughters; *Religion:* Christian; *Education:* BSc in Engineering, Alexandria University, Egypt, 1956; De Universa Phil, University of Paris, France, 1964; MSc in Economics, University of London, UK, 1966; MA, Oxford University, UK, 1969; *Career:* Civil Engineer, Egypt, 1956–62; Leon Fellow, University of London, 1966–67; Lecturer, School of Oriental and African Studies, University of London, London, 1967–69; Senior Research Officer, Economics of the Middle East, Oxford University, 1969–; Fellow, St. Antony's College, Oxford University, Oxford, 1971–; Director, Middle East Centre, St. Antony's College, Oxford University, 1977–80; Director of the Oxford Energy Seminar, 1979–; Consultant, Oil Problems and Economics to ILO, IBRD, OPEC, UNIDO; *Publications: The Egyptian Economy, 1952–72,* Clarendon Press, Oxford, 1974, Arabic edition, Cairo 1976; *The Industrialisation of Egypt 1939–73,* co-author with Samir Radwan, Clarendon Press, 1976; articles in academic journals; *Interests and Recreations:*

founding member, Honorary Secretary, Oxford Energy Policy Club; member of the Royal Economic Society; *Languages:* Arabic, English, French; *Address:* St. Antony's College, Oxford University, Oxford, England; telephone: 0865 59651, 56930.

MABRUK, Hadi, Tunisian official/diplomat; born 1921, Tunisia; married; *Religion:* Muslim; *Education:* University of Algiers, Algeria; *Career:* entered Public Administration, 1939; Governor of Sbeitla, 1956–58; Governor of Gafsa, 1958–60; Governor of Le Kef, 1960–62; President of the Tunisian State Shipping Company, 1962–66; President, Director General of International Harvester Company, Tunis; Commissioner General of Textiles, and concurrently President of the National Federation of Exporters, 1967; Director of Central Administration in the Ministry of National Economy, 1973; Ambassador to France, 1973; *Languages:* Arabic, French; *Address:* Tunisian Embassy, 25 rue Barbet-de-Joury 75007 Paris, France.

MABRUK, Izzidin al-, Libyan oil official/politician; born 1931, Tripoli, Libya; *Religion:* Muslim; *Education:* LLB and LLM, University College, London, UK; *Career:* Head of Appeals Court, Tripoli; represented Libya in OPEC Legal Department, 1964–66; presented OPEC paper *From Concessions to Contracts* to the 5th Arab Petroleum Congress, Cairo, Egypt, March 1965; member of Libyan Delegation to 6th Arab Petroleum Congress, Baghdad; Minister of Petroleum, January 1970; Secretary for Petroleum, General People's Committee, March 1977; Libyan representative to OPEC; *Languages:* Arabic, English, French, Italian; *Address:* Secretariat of Oil, P O Box 256, Tripoli, Socialist People's Libyan Arab Jamahiriya.

MADANAT, Nabih Ayed, Jordanian banker; born 27 April 1931, Karak, Jordan; married; one son, one daughter; *Religion:* Christian; *Education:* in Jordan; *Career:* joined The British Bank of The Middle East, 1950; transferred to Tripoli, Libya , to assist in the opening of a new branch, 1952; British Bank of the Middle East Headquaters, London, 1970; Branch Manager, British Bank of The Middle East, 1980; member of the Arab Club of Britain, the Anglo-Jordanian Society, the Arab Bankers Association, London; *Interests and Recreations:* cards, backgammon, chess; *Languages:* Arabic, English, Italian; *Address:*

195 Brompton Road, London SW3 1LZ, UK; telephone: Office — (01) 581 0321; Residence — (01) 946 1352.

MADANI, Ayad Amin, Saudi Arabian journalist; born 1945, Jeddah, Saudi Arabia; *Education:* BSc in Production Management; *Career:* Staff Manager, Saudi Arabian Airlines Coporation (SAUDIA); Manager, Management Development, Jeddah District; former Editor in Chief of *Saudi Gazette,* English language daily; Director General, OKAZ Organization for Press and Publication; member of American Management Association, Arizona State University Alumni; member of Saudi Arabian Airlines Club; *Publications:* several articles published in local newspapers; *Interests and Recreations:* photography, chess, reading; *Address:* P O Box 5576, Jeddah, Saudi Arabia.

MADANI, Izziddine, Tunisian official/writer; born 6 June 1938 Tunis, Tunisia; married; one daughter; *Religion:* Muslim; *Education:* BA, University of Tunis; Diploma in Arabic Literature and Language, Anthropology and Sociology, College de France; *Career:* Cultural Editor, *Al-Amal* Arabic journal, 1971–73; Director of the International Festival, Hammamat, Tunisia, 1978; Director of Cultural Affairs of the City of Tunis, 1980–; Cultural Editor of *Al-Amal,* 1981–; *Publications:* numerous plays and several short story collections, 1969–82; *Languages:* Arabic, French, English; *Address:* 18 Rue des Abricotiers, Le Bardo, Tunisia; telephone: 248983.

MADEY, Robert William, Arab-American nuclear scientist; born 2 May 1933, Norwalk, Connecticut, USA; married; two daughters, one son; *Religion:* Christian; *Education:* BSc, Massachusetts Institute of Technology, USA, 1955; PhD, University of Maryland, USA, 1963; *Career:* Consultant, West Coast Electronics Laboratory, Willis Motor Corporation, California, 1955; 1st Lieutenant, US Air Force, 1955–57; Instructor and Research Assistant, University of Maryland, 1957–61; Scientific Assistant to the Chief of the Reactor Division, National Bureau of Standards, Washington D.C., 1959–63; Director of Nuclear and Space Physics Group, Grumman Aerospace, 1963–69; Adjunct Professor of Physics, New York Institute of Technology, 1968; Director of Nuclear and Space Physics Programs, Grumman Aerospace,

1969–72; Manager, Research and Development Energy Programs, Grumman Aerospace, 1972–74; Deputy Director, Energy Programs, Gruman Aerospace, 1974–75; Deputy Director, Energy Systems Division, Grumman Corporation, 1976–77; Vice President, Development, Grumman Energy Systems Inc, 1977–; co-investigator with Nobel Laureate Dr Luis Alvarez on space-born High Energy Physics Experiment, 1972–73; member of Society of Sigma XI, 1963; member of American Nuclear Society, 1963, American Institute of Aeronautics and Astronautics, 1964, American Geophysical Union, 1966, American Association of the Advancement of Science, 1966, New York Academy of Sciences, 1968, the Solar Energy Industries Association, 1978, the International Solar Energy Society, 1979; *Publications:* author and co-author of numerous scientific papers and reports in professional journals and magazines; invited speaker, lecturer and panelist for numerous industry, government and community sponsored conferences and organizations; *Interests and Recreations:* skiing, tennis, golf, backgammon, music; *Languages:* Arabic, English, German; *Address:* 7 Milford Lane, Huntington Station, New York 11747, USA; telephone: (516) 421 4665.

MADKOUR, Muhammad Abdul Khalik, Egyptian official/statistician; born 8 January 1948, Cairo, Egypt; married; two daughters; *Religion:* Muslim; *Education:* BSc, Statistics, Faculty of Economics and Political Science, Cairo University, Cairo, Egypt; Doctorat ès-Sciences de l'Information, Ecole des Hautes Etudes en Sciences Sociales, Sorbonne, Paris, France; *Career:* Statistician, Industrial Development Centre for Arab States (IDCAS), 1969–71; Co-ordinator of IDCAS activities in North Africa, 1971–73; Manager, Data Processing Department, IDCAS, 1973–80; Director General, Organisation and Microfilming Information Centre (OMIC), 1978–; Project Manager, National Scientific and Technological Information Project, ASRT, Egypt/USA AID, 1980–; Senior Research Scientist, School of Information and Computer Science, Georgia Institute of Technology, Atlanta, USA, 1980–82; member of the International Committee for Social Science Information and Documentation, France, 1979–, Higher Egyptian National Committee for Information and Scientific Publications, 1975, US-

Egyptian Joint Group on Scientific and Technical Information; *Publications:* numerous studies and reports published in professional journals; *Interests and Recreations:* bridge, soccer; *Languages:* Arabic, English, French; *Address:* 8 Nile Street, Giza, Cairo, Egypt; telephone: 709627.

MADOUH, Muhammad Mahmud, Kuwaiti businessman/official; born 1938; married; three children; *Religion:* Muslim; *Career:* wide business interests; Deputy Chairman of the Kuwait Shipping Co; Deputy Chairman of the United Arab Shipping Company; Assistant Under Secretary for Industrial Affairs, Ministry of Commerce and Industry; *Languages:* Arabic, English; *Address:* Ministry of Commerce and Industry, P O Box 2944, Kuwait.

MAGDUB, General Taha al-, Egyptian army officer; born 1925; *Career:* Chief Liaison Officer of the Egyptian Army and Assistant Head of Operations during October 1973 War; took part in all negotiations with representatives of the Israeli Army at Kilometre 101 and Geneva; signed the second Israeli-Egyptian Disengagement Agreement, 1975; member of the Egyptian Delegation at the Egyptian-Israeli negotiations in Cairo, 1975; *Address:* c/o Ministry of Defence, Cairo, Egypt.

MAGHRABY, Salahilddin al-, Arab-American academic/research scientist; born 21 October 1927, Fayoum, Egypt; married; three daughters; *Religion:* Muslim; *Education:* BSc, Mechanical Engineering, Cairo University, Egypt 1948; MSc, Industrial Engineering, Ohio State University, USA, 1955; PhD, Industrial Engineering, Cornell University, USA, 1958; *Career:* Tutor, School of Enginering, Cairo, Egypt, 1949; Engineer, Foreign Inspection Office of Egyptian State Railways in London, Brussels and Budapest, 1949–54; Research Assistant, Cornell University, Ithaca, NY, USA, 1955–58; Research Leader, Western Electric Company, Research Centre, Princeton, New Jersey, USA, 1958–62; Associate Professor, Yale University, New Haven, Conn, USA, 1962–67; Director, Graduate Programme in Operational Research, North Carolina State University, 1967–76; University Professor, Operational Research and Industrial Enginering, 1967; *Publications: The Design of Production Systems,* 1966; *Theory of Activ-*

ity Networks, 1976; *Handbook of Operations Research,* 1978; several articles and chapters in lecture series; *Interests and Recreations:* history and science fiction, tennis, swimming, design and operation of integrated and distribution systems; *Languages:* Arabic, French, English; *Address:* 124 Perquimans Drive, Raleigh, North Carolina 27609, USA; telephone: (919) 7820808.

MAGHRIBI, Mahmud Sulaiman, Libyan diplomat/politician; born 1935, Haifa, Palestine; *Religion:* Muslim; *Education:* Law Studies, Damascus University, Syria; PhD, George Washington University, USA; *Career:* Legal Adviser to Esso Petroleum Company, Tripoli, 1966; appointed Prime Minister, Minister of Finance and Agriculture, 1970; took prominent role in talks with operating oil companies leading to new posted prices, 1970; Permanent Representative to UN, 1971–72; Ambassador to UK, 1973–76; *Languages:* Arabic, English; *Address:* Secretariat for Foreign Affairs, Tripoli, Libya.

MAGHUR, Kamil Hassan, Libyan diplomat/lawyer; born 1 January 1935, Tripoli, Libya; married; *Education:* LLB, Faculty of Law, University of Cairo, 1954–56; University of Paris, University of Grenoble, France; *Career:* Assistant Counsellor, Administration of Legislation, Tripoli, 1959–60; Ministry of Justice, 1960–65; Counsellor, High Court of Appeal, 1960–69; Counsellor, Supreme Court of Libya, Benghazi, 1969–71; Delegate, UN Conference on the Law of the Sea, Caracas, Venezuela, 1974; Chief Delegate of Libya to UN General Assembly, 1972–74; Ambassador, Permanent Representative of Libya, New York, 1972; *Publications:* numerous articles in *Al-Thawra; Interests and Recreations:* international law, public affairs; *Languages:* Arabic, English, Italian; *Address:* Secretariat for Foreign Affairs, Tripoli, Libya.

MAHALLAWI, Muhammad Nagui al-, Egyptian academic/physician; born 1917, Cairo, Egypt; married; *Religion:* Muslim; *Education:* MB, ChB, Cairo University, Egypt, 1940; MD, Cairo University, Cairo, 1946; *Career:* Professor of Medicine, Ain Shams University, Cairo, Egypt; President, Ain Shams University, Cairo, Egypt; President, Egyptian Society of Nephrology; Chairman, Board of Middle East Research Centre; member of American Medical Society of

Vienna, National Committee of UNESCO, Association of the Medical Schools of Africa, Supreme Council of Universitites, Egypt; *Address:* Ain Shams University, Kasr Al-Zaafran, Abbasiyah, Cairo, Egypt; telephone: 821455.

MAHAYNI, Thabit Ghalib, Syrian academic/businessman; born 1932, Damascus, Syria; married; one son, two daughters; *Education:* AB, Economics, Boston University, Boston, USA; *Career:* Assistant Director General, Damascus Chamber of Commerce, 1958; member of the Board of Directors of the Bank of Arab Unity, 1960; member of the Council of Damascus Municipality, 1960; Lecturer, College of Business Administration, Damascus University, 1961; General Director, Damascus Chamber of Commerce, 1972; member of the People's Council, 1977; *Interests and Recreations:* music, poetry, tennis, swimming; *Languages:* Arabic, English, French; *Address:* P O Box 218 Damascus, Syria; telephone: 111339.

MAHDI, Abdul Wahab Rauf, Iraqi academic; born 18 November 1938, Hindiyah, Iraq; married; two sons, one daughter; *Religion:* Muslim; *Education:* BSc, University of Baghdad, Iraq, 1962; MSc, Animal Physiology, Oklahoma State University, USA, 1968; PhD, Animal Physiology, Texas A&M University, USA, 1971; *Career:* Reserve Army Officer, 1962–64; Demonstrator, Department of Physiology, College of Veterinary Medicine, Baghdad University, 1964–66; Graduate Assistant in USA, 1966–71; Faculty Member, College of Veterinary Medicine, Baghdad University, 1971–; Head of Department of Physiology, 1974–; *Publications:* MSc and PhD thesis in English; numerous scientific articles in professional journals in English and in Arabic; *Interests and Recreations:* fishing, cycling, chess; *Languages:* Arabic, English; *Address:* Physiology, Pharmacology and Biochemistry Department, College of Veterinary Medicine, University of Baghdad, Baghdad, Iraq; telephone: Office — 5553264; Residence — 5555808.

MAHDI, Abdullah Omar, Saudi Arabian aviation official; born 1935, Mecca, Saudi Arabia; *Religion:* Muslim; *Education:* courses in air traffic service radar technique, flight safety and investigation of flight incidents, University of Southern California,

USA; *Career:* Chief, Air Traffic Control, 1958; Director, Air Traffic Services, 1964; Director General of Civil Aviation; member of International Civil Aviation Organization (ICAO), Montreal, Canada; member of Board of Saudi Arabian Airlines; attended several ICAO conferences in Montreal and some regional ICAO conferences; *Decorations:* Shining Star Medal, Republic of China; *Interests and Recreations:* reading, golf; *Languages:* Arabic, English; *Address:* Civil Aviation Department, P O Box 887, Jeddah, Saudi Arabia; telex: 401093 CIVAIR SJ English, 400171 SEF JEDDAH Arabic.

MAHDI, Muhammad R., Anglo-Arab academic/mathematician; born 1925, Iraq; married; two sons, two duaghters; *Religion:* Muslim; *Education:* BSc, 1949; MSc, 1954; PhD, 1958; *Career:* Lecturer, College of Science, Baghdad, Iraq, 1949–52; Senior Lecturer, Mathematics, Birkbeck College, University of London, 1958–; *Publications:* papers on functional analysis in various mathematical journals; *A Palestine Chronicle,* London, 1973; *Languages:* Arabic, English, Persian, French, German, Romanian; *Address:* 7 Lodge Drive, London N13, UK; telephone: 886 0044.

MAHDI, Muhammad T., Iraqi writer/journalist; resident in USA; born 6 January 1928, Iraq; married; three daughters; *Religion:* Muslim; *Education:* High School of Commerce, Baghdad, 1948; BA, MA, PhD, University of California, Berkeley, USA, 1960; *Career:* Teaching Assistant, Department of Political Science, University of California, 1959–61; Director of Arab Information Centre, San Francisco, California, 1961–63; Secretary General, Action Committee on American Arab Relations (American-Arab Relations Committee), New York, 1964; Executive Director, Federation of American-Arab Organizations, 1967–; Executive Editor, *Action* newspaper, 1969–; Executive Secretary, Arab Anti-Defamation League, 1971; Secretary General of Arab People to American People, 1980; Executive Producer of AP-AP TV, 1982; member of American Political Science Association and American Society for Legal and Political Philosophy, etc; *Publications: Nation of Lions ... Chained,* 1962, in English; *Constitutionalism: Western and Middle Eastern,* 1963, in English; *Peace in the Middle East,*

1963, in English; *Peace in the Middle East,* 1967, in English; *Kennedy and Sirhan ... Why?,* 1968, in English; *Palestine and the Bible,* 1972, in English; *Peace in Palestine,* 1976, in English; translated several works into Arabic; *Interests and Recreations:* poetry, legal philosophy, logic, sports, walking, reciting Arabic poetry, *Address:* P O Box 416, New York, NY 10017, USA.

MAHDI, Salih Abdul Rahman al-, Tunisian artist/musician; born 9 February 1925, Tunisia; married; one son, two daughters; *Religion:* Muslim; *Education:* Licence, Arabic Literature and Law; Diploma in Administration; *Career:* Judge in Court of Tunisia, 1951; Chief of the Administration of Fine Arts, Ministry of Education, 1957; Director of Music and Arts, Ministry of Culture, 1961; Head of the National Cultural Committee, 1978–; Honorary Chairman of the Arab Union of Music, League of Arab States; member of the Executive Bureau of the International Institute for Audio-Visual Cultural Development; member of the International Institute for Comparative Music Studies and Documentation, Berlin; member of the International Folk Music Council, Denmark; *Publications: The Principles of Music,* a textbook; *The Tunisian Musical Heritage; Arabic Music; Arabic Folk Music,* 1978; Composer of Tunisian National Anthem; more than 600 musical compositions; several plays; *Decorations:* Order of the Republic, Second Class, Tunisia; Order of Labour; *Languages:* Arabic, French; *Address:* 22 Rue du Brasil, Tunis, Tunisia; telephone: 286391.

MAHFUZ, Naguib, Egyptian writer/novelist; born 11 December 1911; married; two daughters; *Religion:* Muslim; *Education:* Licence in Philosophy, Faculty of Arts, Cairo University, Egypt, 1934; *Career:* Cultural Counsellor; writer, *Al-Ahram;* member of Board of Dar al-Maaref Publishing House; *Publications:* several novels, many translated into English, French, Spanish and East European languages; *Decorations:* State Prize; Order of Independence; Order of the Republic; *Interests and Recreations:* the novel, the short story, drama, music, walking; member of Nadi al-Qussa; *Languages:* Arabic, English, French; *Address:* 172 Nile Street, Agouza, Cairo, Egypt.

MAHGOUB, Rif'at, Egyptian academic/economist; born 1926, Nile Delta, Egypt; married; *Religion:* Muslim; *Education:* Faculty of Law, Cairo University, Egypt; PhD in Economics, Sorbonne, University of Paris, France, 1953; *Career:* Lecturer, and later Professor of Economics, Cairo University; Dean, Faculty of Economics and Political Science, 1971; Secretary for Ideology, Religion and Propaganda, Arab Socialist Union (ASU); Minister for Political Affairs in the Presidency, 1973; appointed to the Committee to draft revision of the National Charter, 1973; member of the High Council of Culture, 1973; member of the National Council for Production and Economic Affairs, 1974; Deputy Prime Minister for Political Affairs in the Presidency, 1975; First Secretary of ASU, 1975–76; Dean, Faculty of Economics and Political Sciences, Cairo University, 1981; *Decorations:* Award of Merit in Social Sciences; The Golden Medal, 1980; Highest Order of the Nile, 1980; *Languages:* Arabic, English, French; *Address:* Faculty of Economics and Political Sciences, Cairo University, 113 Kasr Sl Aini Street, Cairo, Egypt.

MAHGUB, Kamil, Sudanese politician; born 1930, Sudan; *Religion:* Muslim; *Career:* Headmaster of Dongola Private School, 1955–56; Ministry of Co-operation and Rural Development following the May 1969 Revolution; member of the Political Bureau of the Sudanese Socialist Union (SSU), 1972; Head of the SSU Guidance and Development Committee; SSU Secretary for Rural Development, 1974; member of People's Assembly, 1974; *Address:* Sudanese Socialist Union, P O Box 1850, Khartoum, Sudan.

MAHGUB, Makkawi Babiker, Sudanese politician/diplomat; born 1919, Khartoum, Sudan; married; *Religion:* Muslim; *Education:* Science Graduate, University of Khartoum; University of Leicester, and University of London, UK; *Career:* Foreign Service after Independence; Ambassador to Saudi Arabia and Kuwait; resigned to take a post in Qatar as Adviser on the newly-established Qatar Foreign Service, 1970; Under Secretary, Ministry of Foreign Affairs, Sudan, 1971; returned to Qatar on secondment; Secretary for External Relations in the Sudanese Socialist Union (SSU), 1974; member of the People's Assembly; Minister of Foreign Affairs, 1975–77; *Address:* Ministry of Foreign Affairs, Khartoum, Sudan.

MAHGUB, Mansur, Sudanese politician; born 1912, Sudan; *Religion:* Muslim; *Education:* Gordon Memorial College, Khartoum, Sudan; *Career:* Department of Finance, 1935; trained with various companies in UK, 1950–51; Inspector, Auditor's Department, 1951–54; Assistant Director of Accounts, Ministry of Finance, 1954–55; Under Secretary for Internal and Monetary Affairs, 1955–58; Under Secretary, Ministry of Commerce, Industry and Supply, 1958; retired 1964; Assistant Director, Sudan Commercial Bank, 1964; Minister of Finance, 1969–70; Minister of Economy, Trade and Supply, 1970–72; *Languages:* Arabic, English; *Address:* Ministry of Finance and National Economy, Khartoum, Sudan.

MAHIEDDIN, Muhammad N., Algerian academic/lawyer; born 4 December 1944, Oran, Algeria; *Religion:* Muslim; *Education:* LLB in Public Law; Diploma in Higher Studies in Public Law, University of Algiers, Algeria; *Career:* Head of Department of Law, 1972–73; Director of the Institute of Law and Administrative Sciences of Oran, 1977–; Lawyer; *Publications:* articles and papers in French published in professional journals; *Languages:* Arabic, French, English; *Address:* P O Box 1171, Oran El Menouar, Algeria; 1 rue Derbet Wahran, Oran, Algeria.

MAHIUT, Rabah, Algerian journalist; born April 1936, Algeria; *Education:* Faculty of Law, Algiers University, 1971; *Career:* journalist with National Liberation Front (FLN) in France; editor on *Al-Shaab* (later *Le Peuple* and then *El-Moudjahid),* 1962–64; Information and Guidance Department of FLN Headquarters, Algiers, 1964–66; *El-Moudjahid,* 1967–68; producer-reporter on Radio-Télévision Algiers, 1968–71; staff reporter on *Révolution Africaine,* 1971–72; Press Attaché, Central Administration, 1972; *Publications: Le Pétrole Algérien,* 1974, Algiers; *Languages:* Arabic, French; *Address:* Revolution Africaine, 7 Rue de Stade, Hydra, Algiers, Algeria.

MAHJOUBI, Mherdan, Moroccan politician; born 1924, Oulmes, Morocco; married; *Religion:* Muslim; *Education:* Military Academy, Meknes, 1940; *Career:* Captain in the French Army, 1951–53; Commander of Oulmes, 1951–53; Governor of Rabat Province, after Independence; Founder and Secretary General of the Mouvement Populaire; Member of the National Council of the Resistance and of the Liberation Army; Minister of Defence, 1961; elected Representative of Rabat at the Chamber of Counsellors, 1963; Minister of Agriculture, 1964; Minister of Defence, 1966–67; paid official visit to Great Britain, 1967; elected Deputy for Khemissat, 1970; Minister of State for Posts and Telecommunications, 1977; *Publications:* collection of poems; publisher of *Al-Massira,* magazine (journal of the Green Marsh); *Interests and Recreations:* writing, painting, held several exhibitions of his work in Morocco, Algiers, Paris, Geneva and London; *Languages:* Arabic, Berber, French; *Address:* Ministry of Posts and Telecommunications, Rabat, Morocco.

MAHMAH , Mustafa al-, Moroccan official; born 17 May 1943, Asila, Morocco; *Religion:* Muslim; *Education:* BA in Sociology, Institute of Social Sciences, Mohammed V University, Rabat; *Career:* Assistant Under Secretary, Ministry of Waqfs and Islamic Affairs; *Publications: Traditional Society and the Stage; The Moroccan Woman and Sufism,* and several other studies of Moroccan women; *Interests and Recreations:* reading; member of the Moroccan Authors Club; *Languages:* Arabic, French, Spanish; *Address:* Apartment 3, Zankat Mecca, Building 22, Rabat, Morocco.

MAHMASSANI, Subhi, Lebanese politician/ lawyer; born 1911, Beirut, Lebanon; *Religion:* Muslim; *Education:* Higher Studies in Law and Political Economy, American University of Beirut, Lebanon; LLB, University of London, UK; Doctorate in Law, Lyons University, France; *Career:* held judiciary posts, 1939–; President of Beirut Court of Appeal, 1944–46; Barrister at Law, 1946–; Legal Counsel of the Lebanese Delegation to the Arab League in Cairo, San Francisco, USA; member of the UNESCO Conferences in Beirut, Florence; participant in the Congress of Experts of the UNESCO Society for Philosophical Sciences and Humanities, Paris, 1953, the Islamic Culture Congress, Princeton USA, 1953, the Islamic-Christian Co-operation Congress held in Bhamdoun, 1954, and Tehran, Iran, 1957; former Professor of Law, Faculty of Law, Lebanese, French and Arab Universities, Beirut, Lebanon; Honorary President, Beirut Court of Appeal; elected Deputy for Beirut, 1964;

President, Parliamentary Commission for Administration and Justice 1964; former Lecturer, Faculty of Arts and Sciences, American University of Beirut, Lebanon; Minister of National Economy, 1966; *Publications: Philosophy of Legislation in Islam Constitution and Democracy,* 1952; *Pioneers of Justice in Islam,* in Arabic, Beirut, 1980; *The Legal Docrtines of Imam Al-Awazy,* in Arabic, Beirut, 1978; *Basic Concepts of Human Rights in Islamic, Lebanese and International Law,* in Arabic, Beirut, 1979; *Jurisprudence of the Legitimate Caliphs,* under publication; and numerous other legal studies and articles; *Interests and Recreations:* member of Arab and Islamic Academies in Syria, Iraq, Egypt and India; *Languages:* Arabic, French, English; *Address:* Mahmassani Buidling, Verdun Street, Beirut, Lebanon; telephone: 814106.

MAHMASSANI, Yahya, Lebanese diplomat; born Beirut, Lebanon; married; *Education:* MA, American University of Beirut, Lebanon, 1954–61; *Career:* Counsellor, Deputy Permanent Representative of Lebanon to the UN, New York, USA; Consul General, Lebanese Embassy, Milan, Italy, 1977–; *Publications: A Central Bank for Lebanon,* 1961; *Languages:* Arabic, English; *Address:* Office — 26 Via Larga, Milano, Italy.

MAHMUD, Abdul Wahab, Yemen Arab Republic politician; born 1940, near Taiz, Yemen Arab Republic; *Religion:* Muslim; *Education:* in Cairo; PhD in Economics, University of Prague, Czechoslovakia, 1960–69; *Career:* Ambassador to France; returned as Deputy Minister of Economy, 1969; Embassy to UK, 1973–74; Minister of Economy, 1974–1975; *Address:* Ministry of Economy, Sana'a, Yemen Arab Republic.

MAHMUD, Abdullah Bin Zaid al-, Qatari judge; born 1909, Bani Tamim Province, near Riyadh, Saudi Arabia; *Religion:* Muslim; *Education:* Islamic and Arabic studies; Islamic Shari'a; *Career:* Chief Judge, Qatar, 1939; Head of Shari'a Courts and Islamic Affairs; *Publications:* numerous papers and studies in Islamic jurisprudence, theology and Shari'a, a collection of articles and papers published in two volumes; *Address:* P O Box 232, Doha, Qatar; telephone: 325593; telex: 4629 AWQAF DH.

MAHMUD ALI, Abdul Halim, Egyptian academic; born May 1910, Egypt; *Religion:* Muslim; *Education:* Al-Azhar Schools and Al-Azhar University, Cairo, 1932; PhD, Sorbonne, University of Paris, France, 1939; *Career:* Professor of Philosophy, Azhar University, 1944–50; Professor of Psychology, Al-Azhar University, 1951–64; visiting Professor, University of Omdurman, Sudan; Secretary of the Islamic Research Academy; Dean of the Faculty of Theology, Al-Azhar University; member of the General Committee of Citizens War Committees, 1970; made a tour of South East Asia, 1970; Vice-Rector of Al-Azhar, 1970; Rector, 1971; Minister of Waqfs (Islamic Endowments) and Al-Azhar Affairs, 1972–73; Grand Shaikh of Al-Azhar University, 1973–; *Publications:* several books on Islamic religion and Arabic scholars; *Languages:* Arabic, French; *Address:* Al-Azhar University, Cairo, Egypt; telephone: 904051.

MAHMUD, Khalil Othman, Sudanese businessman; born 1930; *Religion:* Muslim; *Education:* studied veterinary science in Egypt; *Career:* worked in the Sudanese Ministry of Animal Resources; financial and investment adviser, Kuwait; founder of leading Gulf firm; owner of textile, glass, pharmaceutical and other factories in Sudan; *Languages:* Arabic, English; *Address:* Gulf International (Sudan), P O Box 2316, Khartoum, Sudan.

MAHMUD, Muhammad Hamid, Egyptian politician; born 1926; married; one son, one daughter; *Religion:* Muslim; *Education:* graduated from Law College, 1950; *Career:* elected to National Assembly, 1957; Secretary of the National Assembly, 1960; Legal Adviser to Shaikh Abdullah al-Sabah of Kuwait, Arab Socialist Union (ASU), Elections Supervisory Committee during reorganization of ASU; ASU Secretary for Buheira, 1971; Assistant for Lower Egypt Affairs to Sayed Ahmed Marei; Governor of Giza, 1973–74; Minister of State for Local Government and Popular Organizations, 1974; Minister of State for Local Government, Youth, Popular and Political Organizations, 1976; *Address:* Ministry of Local Government, Youth, Popular and Political Organizations, Cairo, Egypt.

MAHMUD, Muhammad Ihab Ibrahim, Egyptian economist; resident in the United Arab Emirates; born 1934, Egypt; married; two sons; *Religion:* Muslim; *Education:* BA in Commerce, Ain Shams University, Cairo, Egypt, 1962; Diploma in Economic Planning and Development, African Planning Institute, Dakar, Senegal; *Career:* Egyptian Ministry of Finance, 1962–; Director of Budget Administration, United Arab Emirates Ministry of Finance and Industry, Abu Dhabi; *Interests and Recreations:* swimming, tennis; member of Al-Shams Club, Cairo; member of Al-Ahli Club and Gezira Club; *Languages:* Arabic, English, some French; *Address:* P O Box 3126, Abu Dhabi, United Arab Emirates; telephone: Office -- 43838; Residence -- 62684.

MAHROOS, Ali Ibrahim al-, Bahraini diplomat; born 25 July 1940, Manama, Bahrain; married; two sons, one daughter; *Religion:* Muslim; *Education:* BCom, Damascus University, Syria; MA in Political Science, Lebanese University, Lebanon; *Career:* teacher, 1965–69; 3rd Secretary, Ministry of Foreign Affairs, 1969; 1st Secretary, Director of the Office of the Minister of Foreign Affairs, 1971; Director of Administrative and Financial Department, Ministry of Foreign Affairs, 1972; Minister Plenipotentiary to Lebanon, 1974; Minister Plenipotentiary to UK, 1976; Director of Political Department, Ministry of Foreign Affairs, 1980; member of the Board of Bahrain Petroleum Co; *Interests and Recreations:* reading, history, politics, swimming; *Languages:* Arabic, English; *Address:* P O Box 55 Manama, Bahrain.

MAHRUG, Smail, Algerian banker/economist; born 1926, Algeria; married; *Religion:* Christian; *Education:* University of Paris, France; *Career:* Director of the National Committee for Technical Planning, Algeria, 1962; Technical Counsellor for Economic Affairs at the Presidency; Director General of Finance under the President, 1964; member of the Board of Société Nationale de Recherche et d'Exploitation des Pétroles en Algérie (SN Repal); Minister of Finance, 1970–76; resigned through ill health, February 1976; Chairman, Group of 24, International Monetary Fund, 1974; Chairman, Union Méditerranéenne de Banques, Paris, 1977–83; *Languages:* Arabic, French, English; *Address:* Union Médi-terranéenne de Banques, 50 Rue de Lisbonne, 75008 Paris, France; telephone: 76652/84, telex: 660213.

MAHSHIE, George T., Arab-American lawyer; born 6 May 1926, Syracuse, New York, USA; *Religion:* Christian; *Education:* BA, Liberal Arts College, Syracuse University, Syracuse, New York, 1949; LLB, College of Law, Syracuse University, 1955; *Career:* admitted to practice law in New York State Courts, Federal Courts, United States Supreme Court and various other administrative courts and agencies in th USA, 1956–; Attorney and Counsellor-at-Law; President, Henderson Harbor Development Company, Inc; President, Mahshie Realty; member of American Bar Association; member of New York Trial Lawyers Association; member of American Judicature Society; and several others; *Interests and Recreations:* swimming, jogging, fishing; participant in Arab community activities; member of the Board of Directors of the National Association of Arab-Americans; former Vice President and member of the Board of Directors of the Trustees of the United Holy Land Fund; former member of the Board of Trustees of the Antiochian Orthodox Christian, Archdiocese of New York and all North America; *Address:* Residence — 313 Wedgewood Terrace, Dewitt, New York 13214, USA; telephone: (315) 446 0611; Office — 550 East Genesee Street, Syracuse, New York 13202, USA; telephone: (315) 474 4628.

MAJALI, Habis Rufaifan, Jordanian army commander; born 1914, Kerak, Jordan; married; *Religion:* Muslim; *Education:* general; *Career:* officer cadet, Arab Legion of Jordan, 1932; Commander of the Cavalry Brigade; Commander of 10th Infantry Company; Assistant Commander of 2nd Unit, 1945; Commander of Ma'an District, 1946–47; Acting Commander of 1st Unit, 1947; Commander of 2nd Unit, 1947; formed 4th Brigade, 1947; Commander of the Hashemite Brigade, 1949; King's Senior ADC, 1949; Acting Commander of 1st Brigade, 1949; Assistant to the Chief of the General Staff, 1951; Commander of Ma'an District, 1951; Commander of Nablus, 1952; Commander of Hebron District, 1955; Chief of Police in Amman, 1955; Assistant to the Chief of General Staff, 1956; Acting Chief of General Staff, 1957; Chief of General Staff, 1957; General Commander of Western Forces,

1958; Commander in Chief of the Armed Forces, 1958; Commander in Chief of the Jordanian Armed Forces with rank of Field-Marshal, 1965; member of The Royal Consultative Council, 1957; Minister of Defence, 1967–68; Senator, 1967–; Chief Master of Ceremonies to HM The King; Commander in Chief of the Jordanian Armed Forces and General Military Governor, 1970; Minister of the Royal Court, 1976–; *Decorations:* Renaissance Medal, 1st Class; Star of Jordan, 1st Class; Independence Medal; Iraq Rafidain Medal; Syrian Medal of Merit; other Arab and foreign decorations; *Address:* Residence — Shmaisani, Amman, Jordan; telephone: 67475; Office -- Ministry of the Royal Court, Amman, Jordan.

MAJALI, Major General Abdul Salam al-, Jordanian politician/physician; born 1925, Kerak, Jordan; married; *Education:* MD, College of Medicine, Syrian University, Damascus, 1949; Diploma in Ear, Nose and Throat (ENT), FRCP, London, 1952; Fellow of the American College of Surgeons, 1961; *Career:* General Physician in Jordanian Armed Forces, 1948–52; ENT Specialist, Main Hospital, Jordanian Armed Forces, 1952–56; Commanding Officer of The Main Hospital and ENT Specialist, 1956–59; Director of Royal Medical Services and ENT Specialist, 1960–69; Minister of Health, 1969–70; Minister of Health and Minister of State for Prime Ministerial Affairs, 1970–71; Minister of State for Prime Ministerial Affairs, 1971; President of the Jordanian University, 1971; member of the Jordanian University Board Trustees, 1962; member of the Royal Committee for Pedagogy and Education, 1962; President of the World Health Organisation, Geneva, 1970; President, University of Jordan, 1981–; founded and implemented Family Treatment Project in Royal Medical Services of Jordanian Armed Forces; established Health Insurance Scheme in Ministry of Health; established College of Nursing; *Decorations:* Medal of Field Medical Activities in Palestine, 1954; Independence Medal, 2nd Class, 1956; St. John's Establishment Medal, 2nd Class, 1961; Medal of Flying Banner, 1961; Star of Jordan, 1962; Independence Medal, 1st Class, 1966; Loyal Service Medal, 1968; *Address:* Shmaisani, Amman, Jordan. telephone: 812909.

MAJALI, Salih Rufaifan al-, Jordanian politician; born 1910, Kerak, Jordan; *Religion:* Muslim; *Education:* general; *Career:* District Officer of Tafila, 1945; District Officer of Ajloun, 1947; Military Governor of Hebron, 1948; Governor of Salt, 1949; Senior Official of Finance, 1950; Companies Auditor in Ministry of Finance, 1951; Governor of Ajloun, 1953; Governor of Ma'an, 1954; Governor of Salt, 1954; Governor of Nablus, 1955; member of Chamber of Deputies for Kerak, 1956; Minister of Transport, 1956–57; Deputy for Kerak, 1961; Minister of Interior, 1963; Minister of the Interior and Agriculture, 1963; Deputy for Kerak, 1963–66; Minister of the Interior, 1963–64; Senator, 1970–71; Chairman, Council of Tribal Shaikhs, 1971–73; Adviser to HM The King on Tribal Affairs, 1973; Senator, 1974; *Decorations:* Renaissance Medal, 1st Class 1972; *Address:* P O Box 1456, Amman, Jordan; telephone: 21488.

MAJDALANI, Nassim, Lebanese banker/politician; born 1912, Beirut, Lebanon; married 1940; one son, one daughter; *Education:* American University of Beirut, Lebanon; Licence in Law, Lyon University, France; *Career:* lawyer, 1937–44; elected Deputy for Beirut, 1957 and 1960; member of Revolutionary Committee opposed to President Camille Chamoun, 1958; Vice President, Council of Ministers and Minister of Justice, 1960–61; member of Kamal Joumblatt's Progressive Socialist Party; re-elected Deputy for Beirut, 1964; Minister of Justice, 1964–65; member of the Board of Directors of N. Majdalani Bank SAL, Beirut; re-elected Deputy for Beirut, 1968; Deputy Prime Minister and Minister of National Economy, 1969; Minister of Foreign Affairs, 1969–70; unsuccessfully contested 1972 elections; Chairman, Majdalani Bank SAL, Beirut, 1972–83; *Decorations:* Grand Cordon, Tunisian Order; as well as many other foreign distinctions; *Interests and Recreations:* member of the St. Georges Club; *Languages:* Arabic, French, English; *Address:* Residence — Omar Ben Khattab Street, Beirut, Lebanon.

MAJID BIN ABDUL AZIZ, HRH Prince, Saudi Arabian Prince/administrator; born 1936; son of late King Abdul Aziz; *Religion:* Muslim; *Education:* in Riyadh, court education in politics, economics and public administration; *Career:* Minister of Municipal and Rural Affairs, 1975–80; Governor of Mecca, 1980–; *Decorations:* several Orders of Merit from various countries; *Interests and Recreations:* falconry; literature; *Languages:* Arabic, English, French; *Address:* Governorate of Hijaz, Mecca, Saudi Arabia.

MAKDAMI, Hussain Abdullah al-, Yemen Arab Republic politician; born 1927, Beni al-Harith, Yemen Arab Republic; married; three sons, two daughters; *Religion:* Muslim; *Education:* Teachers' Institute, 1952; *Career:* teacher, Sana'a Secondary School; clerk in Ministry of Finance; Director of Hodeida Hospital, 1953–61; Deputy Minister of Health, 1963–65; Minister of Education, 1975–; Secretary General of the Supreme Committee for Financial and Administrative Correction, 1976; *Decorations:* Order of the Republic of Egypt; *Interests and Recreations:* hunting, farming, reading literature and Yemen poetry; *Languages:* Arabic, English; *Address:* Ministry of Education, Sana'a, Yemen Arab Republic.

MAKDISI, George, Arab-American academic; born 15 May 1920, Detroit, Michigan, USA; married; four daughters, two sons; *Religion:* Christian; *Education:* BA, University of Michigan, 1945–47; BSc, School of Foreign Service, Georgetown University, Washington D.C., 1947–48; Georgetown University Graduate School, Princeton University, USA, 1949–50; Docteur ès-Lettres, Sorbonne, University of Paris, France, 1964; MA, University of Harvard, USA, 1973; MA, University of Pennsylvania, USA, 1973; *Career:* Assistant Professor of Near Eastern Studies, University of Michigan, 1953–57; Associate Professor of Near Eastern Studies, University of Michigan, 1957–59; Lecturer in Semitic Languages, Harvard University, 1959–61; Associate Professor of Arabic, Harvard University, 1961–63; Professor of Arabic, Harvard University, 1964–73; Chaire d'Etat, Collège de France, Paris, 1969; Professor of Arabic and Islamic Studies, University of Pennsylvania, USA, 1973–; Visiting Professor, University of Paris, Sorbonne, 1978–79; Directeur d'Etudes, Ecole Pratique des Hautes Etudes, Paris, 1981–82; Director, Center for the Study of Byzantium, Islam and the Latin West, University of Pennsylvania, 1979–; Chairman of the Department of Oriental Studies, University of Pennsylvania, 1975–78; *Publications: Ibn Aquil et la Résurgence de l'Islam Tradition-*

aliste au XIe siecle (Ve siècle de l'Hegire), 1963, Institut Français, Paris-Damascus; *The Rise of Colleges: Institutions of Learning in Islam and the West,* 1981, Edinburgh University Press; numerous articles in a variety of magazines; *Interests and Recreations:* classical music, reading, museums, walking, hiking, gardening, cooking; *Languages:* Arabic, French, English, Dutch, German, Italian, Spanish, Turkish, Persian, Latin; *Address:* Office — 841 Oriental Studies Department, Williams Hall, University of Pennsylvania, USA 19104; telephone: (215) 898 7469.

MAKKAWI, Khalil, Lebanese diplomat; born 15 January 1930; Beirut, Lebanon; married; one son, one daughter; *Education:* BA in Political Science, American University of Beirut (AUB), Beirut, Lebanon; MA in Political Science, Cairo University, Cairo, Egypt; PhD, International Relations, Columbia University, USA; *Career:* UN Section, Ministry of Foreign Affairs, 1957–59; Attaché to Permanent Mission of Lebanon at the UN, New York, USA, 1959; Deputy Permanent Representative, Lebanese Mission to the UN, New York, USA, 1961–64; First Secretary, Lebanese Embassy, Washington D.C., USA, 1964–66; Chief of International Relations Department, Ministry of Foreign Affairs, Beirut, 1967–70; Counsellor, Lebanese Embassy, London, UK, 1970–71; Minister Plenipotentiary, Lebanese Embassy, London, 1971–73; Ambassador to German Democratic Republic, 1973–78; Ambassador to the Court of St. James, London, UK, 1978–83; Ambassador to Ireland, 1979–83; member of the Lebanese Delegation to the 14th and 32nd Session of the UN General Assembly; Director, Political Affairs Department, Ministry of Foreign Affairs, 1983–; UN General Assembly, 1959, 1977; *Interests and Recreations:* music, ballet, theatre, travelling, sports; *Address:* Political Affairs Department, Ministry of Foreign Affairs, Beirut, Lebanon; telephone: 2297265.

MAKKAWI, Makkawi Awad al-, Sudanese UN official/lawyer; born 21 August 1944, Omdurman, Khartoum, Sudan; *Religion:* Muslim; *Education:* LLB, Faculty of Law, University of Khartoum, Sudan; *Career:* member of the Board, Sudanese Council for Friendship, Solidarity and Peace; Secretary General, UN Association of Sudan; Solicitor and Barrister, Sudan; Programme Assistant, UNDP, Sudan; member, Executive Committee, World Federation of United Nations Association (WFUNA), Sudan, 1971; member of Advancement of Science Society, Sudan, Sudan Law Society Preparatory Committee; *Publications: The Role of Law in the Control of the Human Environment,* 1972; *Economic and Social Problems and Environmental Issues,* 1973; *Interests and Recreations:* tennis, table-tennis; law, development, international affairs; *Languages:* Arabic, English, French; *Address:* WFUNA, P O Box 913, El-Gamaa Ave, Khartoum, Sudan; telephone: 73121.

MAKKI, Ahmad Abdul Nabi, Omani official/diplomat; born 17 December 1939, Muscat, Oman; married; *Religion:* Muslim; *Education:* BCom, and Economics, Higher Institute, Cairo, Egypt, 1961–65; *Career:* worked in Abu Dhabi for several years; returned to Oman in 1970; Director of the Prime Minister's Office, 1970; member of the Omani delegation which visited Libya, Egypt and Sudan in June 1971, to canvass support for diplomatic recognition of Oman; member of the Omani Delegation which visited the United Nations to lobby for the admission of Oman to the UN, September 1971; Under Secretary, Ministry of Foreign Affairs, 1972; Ambassador to the USA, 1973, and Permanent Representative to the UN, 1975; Ambassador to Canada, 1974; non-resident Ambassador to Argentina, 1975; Ambassador to France, 1977–81; non-resident Ambassador to Belgium, and Spain, 1978; non-resident Ambassador to Portugal, 1981; Under Secretary of Commerce and Industry, 1982–; *Decorations:* Medal of Merit, First Class, Egypt; *Interests and Recreations:* reading; *Languages:* Arabic, English; *Address:* P O Box 550, Muscat, Oman; telephone: 745195; telex: 3351 WIZARA MB.

MAKKI, Hassan Muhammad, Yemen Arab Republic politician/diplomat; born 22 December 1933, Hodaida, Yemen Arab Republic; married; *Religion:* Muslim; *Education:* University of Rome, Italy, 1953–56; Doctorate in Economics, University of Bologna, Italy, 1960; *Career:* Adviser, Ministry of Economy, 1960–62; Deputy Minister of Economy; Chairman, Yemen Bank for Reconstruction and Development, Sana'a; Minister of Economy, 1963–64; Minister of Communications, 1965; Minister of Foreign

Affairs, 1964, 1966, 1967–68; Amassador to Italy, 1968–70; Ambassador to West Germany, 1970–72; Deputy Prime Minister for Economic and Financial Affairs, 1972–74; Prime Minister, 1974; Deputy Prime Minister for Economic and Financial Affairs, 1974; Permanent Representative to UN with rank of Ambassador; Ambassador to USA, 1974–75; President of Sana'a University, 1975–76; Ambassador to Rome, 1976–79; Deputy Prime Minister for Foreign Affairs and Minister of Foreign Affairs, 1979–80; Deputy Prime Minister for Economic Affairs, 1980–; *Languages:* Arabic, Italian, English; *Address:* Prime Minister's Office, Council of Ministers, Sana'a, Yemen Arab Republic.

MAKRAM, A. Rahal, Lebanese banker; resident in Bahrain; born 1937, Beirut, Lebanon; married; one son; *Religion:* Christian; *Education:* Corporate Finance, New York Institute of Finance; MA in Economics, American University of Beirut, 1967; PhD in Business Administration, AUB, 1981; *Career:* businessman; International Officer, Francis I. Dupont, New York, Wall Street firm, 1967–68; Representative, Francis I. Dupont, Beirut ,1968–70; Representative, Bache and Co, Wall Street firm, Beirut, 1970–74; Deputy Manager, Arab Finance Corporaton, 1974–75; Manager, Citicorp International Bank Ltd, 1975–78; Senior Manager, Arab Bank Ltd, 1978–; *Interests and Recreations:* reading, literature, languages, research, chess, karate (Black Belt), swimming, tennis, table tennis, soccer, marksmanship, hunting, skiing, backgammon; *Languages:* Arabic, English, French, some Italian and some German; *Address:* Arab Bank Ltd, Offshore Banking Unit, Manama Centre, Wing 3, 2nd Floor, P O Box 813 Manama, Bahrain; telephone: Office — 256398, 257981; Residence — telephone: 713346.

MAKTOUM, HH Shaikh Rashid Bin Sa'id al-, Ruler of Dubai and United Arab Emirates Vice President and Prime Minister; born 1910; married daughter of former Ruler of Abu Dhabi; four sons, one daughter; *Religion:* Muslim; *Career:* Regent, Dubai , 1938–58; succeeded his father as fourth Shaikh of Dubai, 1958; made official visit to UK, 1969; has taken a personal interest in economic and social development of Dubai using its large oil resources; closely involved in all main business decisions and commercial ventures; *Address:* Ruler's Office, Dubai, United Arab Emirates; telephone: 361975, 431110.

MAKTOUM, Shaikh Ahmad Bin Rashid Bin Sa'id al-, United Arab Emirates police chief; born 1950; fourth son of Shaikh Rashid al-Maktoum; *Religion:* Muslim; *Education:* Mons Officer Cadet Training College in UK, 1972; *Career:* Colonel in Chief, Dubai Defence Force since 1973, and of Central Military Command since 1977; *Interests and Recreations:* hunting, motoring; *Languages:* Arabic, English; *Address:* Ministry of Defence, P O Box 874, Dubai, United Arab Emirates; telephone: 432330.

MAKTOUM, Shaikh Hamdan Bin Rashid Bin Sa'id al-, United Arab Emirates politician; born 1945; second son of the Ruler of Dubai, Shaikh Rashid al-Maktoum; *Religion:* Muslim; *Education:* in Dubai and Cambridge; *Career:* Minister of United Arab Emirates (UAE), 1971–76; UAE Minister of Finance, Economy and Industry; President of Dubai Municipal Council; President of the Governing Board of Rashid Port, Dubai, 1973–; UAE Representative at IMF, OPEC and to Arab States; frequently accompanies President of UAE, Shaikh Zaid, on state visits; *Interests and Recreations:* hunting; *Languages:* Arabic, English; *Address:* Ministry of Finance, Economy and Industry, P O Box 433, Abu Dhabi, United Arab Emirates; telephone: 341936.

MAKTOUM, Shaikh Maktoum Bin Rashid Bin Sa'id al-, United Arab Emirates politician; born 1943; first son of the Ruler of Dubai, Shaikh Rashid al-Maktoum; married; *Religion:* Muslim; *Education:* in Cambridge, 1961–64; *Career:* Deputy Ruler of Dubai; Deputy Prime Minister of United Arab Emirates (UAE); has made several official visits abroad including UK; *Languages:* Arabic, English; *Address:* Prime Minister's Office, Abu Dhabi, United Arab Emirates; telephone: 451903.

MAKTOUM, Shaikh Muhammad Bin Rashid Bin Sa'id al-, United Arab Emirates politician; born 1949; third son of the Ruler of Dubai, Shaikh Rashid al-Maktoum; *Religion:* Muslim; *Education:* Mons Officer Cadet Training College, UK; Cambridge and Sandhurst; *Career:* Director of Police and Public Security, Dubai; United Arab

Emirates Minister of Defence; responsible for establishment and development of Abu Dhabi Defence Force; *Interests and Recreations:* flying helicopters and his private aircraft, hunting, shooting; *Languages:* Arabic, English; *Address:* Ministry of Defence, P O Box 874, Dubai, United Arab Emirates; telephone: 432330.

MAKTUM, Shaikh Muhammad Bin Hasher Bin, United Arab Emirates judge; born 1925; married; one son; *Religion:* Muslim; *Career:* Supervisor of the Law Courts for several years; Chairman of the Law Courts, Dubai; *Interests and Recreations:* outdoor sports; *Address:* The Law Courts, P O Box 4700, Dubai, United Arab Emirates; telephone: 224935.

MALAIKA, Nazik al-, Iraqi poet; born 1923, Baghdad, Iraq; *Education:* Arabic Literature, Teachers' Training College, Baghdad; *Career:* pioneer of modern Arabic poetry; Lecturer, Mosul University, Iraq; *Publications:* include three volumes of poetry, *Ashiqat al-Layl,* 1947; *Shazaya wa Ramad,* 1949; *Qararat al-Mawja,* 1957; also literary studies and works of criticism in which she defines the nature of the new form adopted in much contemporary poetry; *Address:* University of Mosul, Mosul, Iraq.

MALHOUQ, Abduliah Bin Abdul Rahman al-, Saudi Arabian diplomat; born 1923, Riyadh, Saudi Arabia; *Religion:* Muslim; *Education:* BA, Faculty of Dar al-Ulum, Cairo, Egypt; *Career:* Director of Administration, Eastern Province, 1947; Chief, Press and Publicity Bureau, Embassy of Lebanon, 1955; Director, Oriental Department, Foreign Ministry, 1959; Director, Arab Department, 1960; Counsellor, Embassy of Lebanon, 1961; Minister Plenipotentiary, 1966; Ambassador to Sudan, 1968; Ambassador to Algeria; former Chairman of Al-Khott Co for Printing, Publishing and Translation; former Editor in Chief of *Akhbar al-Dhahran* newspaper, 1952–54; former member of Lebanese Political Science Society; attended several Arab League meetings including those of the Committee on the Amendment of the Charter of the Arab League, 1960–61, Arab Foreign Ministers Conference, Baghdad, 1961, Arab Information Permanent Committee Meetings, Lebanon, 1962, UNESCO Meeting, Beirut, 1964, Saudi Diplomats Meeting, Jeddah, 1973, Islamic

Thought Congress Meeting, Algiers, 1974, Islamic International Convention, London, UK, 1976; *Publications: Ilmu al-Ijtima; Al-Nahdatu al-Adabiyyah Fi Najd;* several articles on development in Saudi Arabia published in some Arab and foreign newspapers and magazines; *Decorations:* Commander of Order of Cedar of Lebanon; Order of Two Niles, Sudan; King Abdul Aziz Order, Saudi Arabia; *Interests and Recreations:* reading, swimming, walking; *Address:* Embassy of Saudi Arabia, 7 Chemin des Glycines, Algiers, Algeria.

MALIK, Adil, Lebanese journalist/newscaster; resident in London; born 6 June 1941, Al-Batrun, Lebanon; married; one son, one daughter; *Religion:* Christian; *Education:* Arabic Civilization, Oriental Institute, Beirut; *Career:* journalist, *Al-Jarida* newpaper, Beirut, 1959; Television Broadcaster, Télé-Orient, Beirut, 1961; Journalist, Foreign Desk, *Al-Nahar,* 1964; Assistant Chief Editor, *Al-Jarida,* 1965; worked for the press, radio and television, 1970–76; currently working for Radio Monte-Carlo, the BBC Arabic Service and *Al-Hawadess* magazine; Managing Director, Contact Middle East SA, Press and Television Production; *Publications: Lebanese and Arab Days,* 1970, in Arabic; *From Rhodes to Geneva,* 1974, in Arabic; television documentaries, political programmes and interviews with several heads of states and international political figures; *Interests and Recreations:* theatre, art, music; *Languages:* Arabic, French, English; *Address:* Office — c/o Middle East SA, 84 Fetter Lane, London EC4A 1EQ; telephone: 8316864; Residence — 29 Wandsworth Bridge Road, London SW6 2TA, UK; telephone: 7368104.

MALIK, Ahmad Abdullah al-, Saudi Arabian economist/administrator; born 28 December, 1937, Saudi Arabia; *Religion:* Muslim; *Education:* Military Training Mission, Saudi Arabia, 1950–53 (specializing in field supply); course in supply, USA, 1953–54; Second Lieutenant, Egyptian Military Academy, Egypt, 1954–55; several military courses in Signal Corps, Egypt, 1955–58; courses at Fort Benjamin Harrison, Adjutant General School, Indianapolis, 1963; BA Economics, University of Riyadh 1964; MA 1966; PhD 1970, Indiana University, USA; *Career:* Director of Operations, Signal School, Taif, Saudi Arabia, 1958–61; in charge of the

Saudi Signal Units for the Arab league, Kuwait, 1961–62; Director of Logistics, Signal Corps, Saudi Arabia, 1962–63; Chief of Contract Department, Ordinance Corps, Ministry of Defence and Aviation, 1970–73; founder and former Director of new Centralized Procurement Department, Ministry of Defence and Aviation, 1973–80; retired from Ministry of Defence and Aviation as Brigadier General, 1980; Director General, Foreign Department, Saudi Arabian Monetary Agency, 1980–; represented Saudi Arabia in several international conferences including, International Monetary Fund (IMF), International Bank for Reconstruction and Development; represented Ministry of Finance and National Economy in oil negotiations, Vienna and Geneva, 1971–72; member of the Boards of Directors of Saudi Credit Bank since its establishment 1972–, the Arab Organization for Military Industrialization, 1975–79, now member of its liquidation committee; member of committee on Strategy for the Third Development Plan of Saudi Arabia for the period 1980–85; *Publications:* co-author, article published by Federal Reserve Bank of San Francisco, *Monetary Sources of Inflation in Saudi Arabia,* 1979; *Decorations:* Medals from the Governments of Saudi Arabia, France, Taiwan, South Korea, Egypt; *Address:* P O Box 2992, Riyadh, Saudi Arabia; telephone: 478 7449.

MALIK, Charles Habib, Lebanese academic/philosopher; born 1906, Lebanon; married; one son; *Religion:* Christian; *Education:* BA, American University of Beirut AUB, Lebanon, 1927; MA, Harvard University, USA, 1934; University of Freiburg, Federal Republic of Germany, 1935–36; honorary degrees from fifty universities in Europe, USA and Canada; *Career:* teaching and administrative positions in AUB, 1927–76; member and sometimes Chairman, Lebanese Delegation to the UN, 1945–54, 1956–58; Minister Plenipotentiary, USA, 1945–53; Cuba, 1946–55; Lebanese Representative to the UN Economic and Social Council, ECOSOC, 1946–59; member of UN Human Rights Commission, 1947–54; Chairman of UN Human Rights Commission, 1951, 1952; participated in the UN Declaration of Human Rights; Signatory for Lebanon, Japanese Peace Treaty, 1951; Ambassador Extraordinary and Plenipotentiary to USA, 1953–55; member of UN Security Council, 1953–54; Dean of Graduate Studies, AUB,

1955–60; Minister of Foreign Affairs, Lebanon, 1956–58; Minsiter of National Education and Fine Arts, 1957–60; President of the 13th Session of UN General Assembly, 1958–59; Visiting Professor, Dartmouth and Harvard Universities, 1960; Professor, American University, Washington, 1961–62; Visiting Lecturer, Exeter Academy and Harvard College, 1962; President of the World Council of Christian Education, 1967–71; Distinguished Professor of Philosophy, 1962–76; Pascal Lecturer, Waterloo University, Canada, 1981; member, chairman, president of numerous academies, associations and societies; *Publications:* author of numerous books and articles published in Europe, USA and the Middle East; *Decorations:* decorated by the governments of Lebanon and many other countries; *Interests and Recreations:* hiking, collecting old Wedgwood china; *Languages: Languages:* Arabic, French, English; *Address:* Harvard Club, 27 W 44th Street, New York, NY 10036, USA; Cosmos Club, 2121 Mass Avenue NW, Washington D.C., 20008; AUB, Beirut, Lebanon.

MALIK, Khalid Hamad al-, Saudi Arabian journalist/publisher; born 1944, Saudi Arabia; *Religion:* Muslim; *Education:* general; *Career:* Editor of *Al-Yamma* magazine; joined *Al-Jazirah* daily as News Editor; now Editor in Chief of *Al-Jazirah;* Managing Director and Board member of Al-Jazirah Press, Printing and Publishing Organization; attended Arab Conference of Information Studies on Population, Development and Reconstruction; *Publications:* editorials and other press writings ex-officio; *Address:* Al-Jazirah newspaper, P O Box 354, Riyadh, Saudi Arabia; telephone: Riyadh 30935.

MALIK, Rida, Algerian diplomat; born 21 December 1931, Batna, Algeria; married; three children; *Education:* Licence ès-Lettres; *Career:* Member of the Governing Board of the General Union of Moslem Algerian Students (UGEMA), 1956; Director and Editor in Chief *El-Moudjahid,* party newspaper of the Algerian National Liberation Front, 1957–62; member of Algerian Delegation to the Negotiations of Evian and Spokesman of the Delegation, 1961–62; member of the Drafting Committee of the Programme of Tripoli, setting out the FLN political programme, 1962; Ambassador of Algeria to Yugoslavia, 1963–65; Ambassador of Algeria to France, 1965–70; Ambassador of Algeria to USSR, 1970–77; member of the Drafting Committee of the National Charter, 1976; Minister of Information and Culture, 1977–79; Member of the Central Committee of the Algerian National Liberation Front, 1979–; Ambassador to USA, negotiated the release of the fifty two American hostages in Iran, 1979–82; Ambassador of Algeria to London, UK, 1982–; *Languages:* Arabic, French, English; *Address:* Embassy of Algeria, 54 Holland Park, London W11 3RS; telephone: 221 7400.

MALIK, Salih Abdullah, Saudi Arabian official/academic; born 1940, Saudi Arabia; married; three daughters; *Religion:* Muslim; *Education:* BSc in Jurisprudence, 1960; BSc in Geography, 1962; MBS in Sociology, 1969; MSc in Demography, 1970, PhD in Urban Sociology, 1973; *Career:* Assistant Professor, University of Riyadh, Saudi Arabia, 1973–75; Secretary General, Imam Muhammad Bin Saud University, 1975–76; Deputy Minister for Municipal Affairs, 1976–; *Interests and Recreations:* swimming, basketball, volleyball, table tennis, reading, theatre; *Languages:* Arabic, English, French; *Address:* P O Box 9103 Riyadh, Saudi Arabia; telephone: 441711.

MALKI, Abdul Hamid, Tunisian official/judge; born 1925, Tunis, Tunisia; married; four children; *Religion:* Muslim; *Education:* Law Studies; Course at Centre National d'Etudes Judiciaires, Paris, France, 1960–61; *Career:* judge in Tunis, 1961–64; Vice President of the Court of First Instance, Tunis, 1964; President of the Chamber of Commerce, 1965–75; Governor of Gabès, 1973; Governor of Tunis, 1973; *Languages:* Arabic, French; *Address:* Tunis Governorate, Tunis, Tunisia.

MALLAKH, Kamal al-, Egyptian journalist/archaeologist; born 26 October 1920, Assiut, Egypt; *Religion:* Christian; *Education:* BA in Architecture, College of Fine Arts, Cairo; MA in Egyptian Antiquities, Cairo University, Egypt; *Career:* Deputy Editor, *Al-Ahram* newspaper; member of the Higher Council for the Arts and Literature; member of Higher Council of Antiquities; Chairman of the Egyptian Association of Writers and Critics; *Publications:* twenty two books; *Decorations:* Medal of Merit for Arts and Literature; Lebanese Order of the Cedar;

Interests and Recreations: art criticism; *Languages:* Arabic, English, French; *Address:* Office — Al-Ahram newspaper, Cairo, Egypt; Residence -- 173, 26th July Street, Zamalek, Cairo, Egypt.

MAMDUH BIN ABDUL AZIZ, HRH Prince, Saudi Arabian Prince; born 1941, Riyadh, Saudi Arabia; son of late King Abdul Aziz; *Religion:* Muslim; *Career:* businessman; *Address:* Royal Court, Riyadh, Saudi Arabia.

MAMMERI, Mouloud, Algerian writer; born 28 December 1917; *Education:* in Morocco, Algiers and Paris; *Career:* Director of Anthropological, Prehistoric and Ethnological Research Centre, Algiers; *Publications:* in French *La Colline Oubliêe,* 1952 (Prix des Quatres Jurys, 1953); *Le Sommeil du Juste,* 1955; *L'Opium et le Baton,* 1965; *Le Foehn,* (play), 1967; *Le Banquet,* 1974; collection of oral poems in Berber: *Les Isefra de Si Mohand; Languages:* Arabic, French, Berber; *Address:* 82 Rue Laperlier, El-Biar, Algiers, Algeria.

MANA, Khalid al-, Qatari politician/businessman; born 1914; *Religion:* Muslim; *Career:* Minister of Public Health, 1972; has major business interests including several agencies; *Address:* Ministry of Public Health, P O Box 42, Administration Buildings, Raygan Road, Doha, Qatar; telephone: 324911, 324566.

MANDIL, Salah Hussain, Sudanese UN official/engineer; born 8 September 1941, Omdurman, Sudan; married; one son, one daughter; *Religion:* Muslim; *Education:* BSc in Electronic Engineering, 1962–65; MSc in Electronics, 1965–66; PhD, Computer Science, Queen's University, Belfast, Northern Ireland, 1971; Diploma from Management Centre, Europe, 1974; *Career:* Lecturer, Faculty of Electrial Engineering and Deputy Manager, Computer Centre, University of Khartoum, 1966–68; Leader, Information System Technology, International Business Machines (IBM), UK Scientific Centre, Peterlee, England, 1971–73; Director, Division of Information Systems Support, Geneva, Switzerland, WHO, 1974–; *Publications:* numerous publications in computer science, information systems, health information, development and technology; *Interests and Recreations:* sports, travel, photography;

Languages: Arabic, English, French; *Address:* WHO Division of Information Systems Support, 20 Avenue Appia, CH-1211, Geneva 27, Switzerland; telephone: (022) 912619.

MANGUSH, Muhammad Ahmad al-, Libyan official; born 1937, Benghazi, Libya; *Religion:* Muslim; *Career:* Chairman of Libyan Airlines; former member of the Supreme Consultation Technical Committee; Head of National Construction Corporation; Minister of Housing and Utilities, 1971–77; Secretary for Housing and Utilities, General People's Committee, 1977–; *Address:* Office of the Secretary for Housing and Utilities, Shara Jamahiriya, Tripoli, Libya; telephone: 40148, 37867; telex: 20032.

MANNA', Abdullah Sulaiman, Saudi Arabian journalist/dentist; born 1930, Jeddah, Saudi Arabia; *Education:* BDS, Dental Surgery, Alexandria University, Egypt, 1962; *Career:* Assistant Director, Jeddah Central Hospital; Director of Health Affairs, Taif, Saudi Arabia; Executive Editor, *Al-Bilad* daily newspaper; Editor in Chief, *Iqra'a* weekly magazine; member of Jeddah Literary Club; former Vice President of Union Club, Jeddah; member of Constituent Committee, Al-Bilad Press Organization; *Publications: Lamasat; Aniis Al Hayard; Interests and Recreations:* reading, music, sport; *Address:* Rowais, Bait al-Ma'adi, Al-Bilad Press Organization, King Abdul Aziz Street, Jeddah, Saudi Arabia; telephone: Jeddah 29187.

MANNAI, Ahmad, Qatari businessman; born 1931, Bahrain; married; *Religion:* Muslim; *Education:* in Qatar; *Career:* Minister of Public Works, 1976; partner of Khalid al-Attiya; developed large commercial organisation holding agencies, including General Motors, Toshiba, Massey Fergusson, JCB and other major companies; participated in several light engineering joint ventures; *Languages:* Arabic, English; *Address:* P O Box 76, Doha, Qatar; telephone: 26251; telex: 4208 DH.

MANNAI, Salim Abdullah al-, Bahraini engineer; born 15 May 1939, Qalali, Bahrain; married; one daughter,two sons; *Religion:* Muslim; *Education:* Diploma in Surveying and Geodesy, American University of Beirut, Lebanon, 1960; BSc in Engineering, AUB,

Lebanon, 1963; MSc in Engineering, University of Florida, Gainesville, USA, 1964; *Career:* Civil Engineer, 1965–70; Senior partner and Director of Mannai Engineering Co Ltd; *Publications:* numerous essays and lectures on construction and civil engineering; *Decorations:* Golden Medal by HH The Amir of Bahrain, 1969; *Interests and Recreations:* swimming, walking, table tennis; founding member of Bahrain Society of Engineers; member of American Concrete Institute; Fellow of American Society of Civil Engineers; *Languages:* Arabic, English; *Address:* P O Box 849, Manama, Bahrain; telephone: 256587, 251329.

MANSOURI, Abdul Rahman Amin, Saudi Arabian diplomat; born 1934, Mecca, Saudi Arabia; *Religion:* Muslim; *Education:* BA in Law, Cairo University, Egypt; MA in Public Law, USA; *Career:* Ministry of Foreign Affairs, Saudi Arabia, 1955; Consul, Saudi Arabian Consulate, New York, USA, 1960–63; Minister Plenipotentiary, Saudi Arabian Embassy, Paris, France, 1965; Deputy Minister, Political Affairs Department, Ministry of Foreign Affairs, 1977–; Chairman, Legal Department, OAPEC, 1982; *Interests and Recreations:* swimming, reading; *Languages:* Arabic, English, French; *Address:* Ministry of Foreign Affairs, P O Box 495, Jeddah, Saudi Arabia; telephone: 6431906; telex: 401104 KHARJI SJ.

MANSOURI, Bin Ali, Moroccan politician/official; born 3 May 1944, Nador, Morocco; married; one child; *Religion:* Muslim; *Education:* Graduate of the College for Higher Commerce and Administration of Commerce, France, 1966; Diploma of the Spanish Chamber of Commerce, Paris, France; *Career:* Cherifian Office for Phosphates; Chief of Cabinet of the State Minister in charge of Co-operation and Training of Cadres; Minister of Tourism, 1977–79; Minister of Administrative Affairs, 1979–81; Minister of Transport, 1981–; President of the Provincial Assembly of Nador; Member of Parliament, Deputy of Nador; President of the Socio-Cultural Association of the Mediterranean Area; *Languages:* Arabic, Spanish, French; *Address:* Ministry of Transport, Rabat, Morocco.

MANSUR, Abdul Hamid, Syrian UN official/agricultural expert; born 18 March 1922, Syria; married; *Religion:* Muslim; *Education:*

BSc in Agronomy, University of Toulouse, France, 1947–50; BSc in Natural Sciences, 1949–52; PhD in Agro-Ecology, 1952–55; *Career:* Technical Director, Agricultural High School, Syria, 1955–56; Chief, Ecology and Pedology Department, Ministry of Agriculture, 1956–58; Director General of Agriculture, Ministry of Agriculture, Syria, 1958–61; Adviser to President, United Arab Republic, 1961; Director, Department of Agriculture and Irrigation, Ministry of Planning, 1961; Dean, Faculty of Agriculture, University of Aleppo, Syria, 1961–63; Director of Programming, Ministry of Planning, 1964; Professor of Mediterranean and Tropical Agronomy, University of Toulouse, France, 1964–71; Senior Agricultural Adviser and Country Representative, Algeria, FAO/United Nations Development Programme, 1971; *Publications: Contribution à l'Amélioration des Conditions de Greffage; Sur l'Intérêt du Bouturage sous Brouillard dans la Génétique du Cottonier; Essai sur l'Aptitude de Bouturage de Certains Arbres Fruitiers Méditerranées; Problèmes Pastoraux et Humaines dans les Zones Arides du Moyen Orient; Contribution à l'Etude Bioclimatologique de la Syrie,* 1964; *Interests and Recreations:* soccer, swimming, horseback riding, bowling; member, Society of Natural History, France, Association of Agricultural Engineers, France, Association of Syrian Agricultural Engineers, Inter-Arab Centre for Research and Study in the Arid Zones, Syria, La Boule-Rêvée Club, Toulouse, France; *Languages:* Arabic, French, English; *Address:* Office — BP 823, 19 avenue Claude Debussy, Algiers, Algeria; telephone: 602970; Residence -- 67 chemin Mohamed Gacem, El Mouradia, Algiers, Algeria; telephone: 606551.

MANSUR, Ahmad Abdullah al-, United Arab Emirates official; born 1943, Abu Dhabi, United Arab Emirates; married; one son, two daughters; *Religion:* Muslim; *Education:* commercial studies, Cairo, Egypt, 1960–61; *Career:* Secretary of Documents and Research Office, Amiri Court, Abu Dhabi, 1969; Deputy Director of Labour and Social Affairs Department, Abu Dhabi, 1970; Director of Purchasing and Housing Department, Abu Dhabi, 1971; Under Secretary, United Arab Emirates, Ministry of Planning, 1972–; *Interests and Recreations:* poetry, swimming; *Languages:* Arabic, English; *Ad-*

dress: Ministry of Planning, P O Box 904, Abu Dhabi, United Arab Emirates; telephone: 362271; telex: 22920.

MANSUR, Al-Fatih Ahmad al-, Sudanese journalist; born 1923, Abyad, Sudan; married; two sons, four daughters; *Religion:* Muslim; *Education:* Diploma of the Institute of Science; Special Studies in Journalism, Egypt: *Career:* Owner of Kardofan Press Organization; member of the Boards of the Cooperative Bank of Sudan, Sudan Press House, Kardofan Transport Co; former Editor in Chief of *Kordofan* newspaper; *Decorations:* Order of Science, Sudan, 1974; Order of Merit, Egypt, 1964; *Languages:* Arabic, English; *Address:* The Kardofan Press and Trading House, P O Box 49 Abyad, Sudan; telephone: 2284, 2210.

MANSUR, Ibrahim Mun'im, Sudanese politician; born 1933, Sudan; *Religion:* Muslim; *Education:* Degree in Commerce, Alexandria University, Egypt; *Career:* Ministry of Commerce; Agricultural Bank; Deputy Director of the Sudan Textile Factory; General Manager of the Gulf International Company; Minister of Economy and Commerce, 1971–73; Minister of Finance and National Economy, 1973–; *Languages:* Arabic, English; *Address:* Ministry of Finance & National Economy, Khartoum, Sudan; Gulf International, P O Box 2316 and 1377, Khartoum, Sudan.

MANSUR, Jamaluldin Muhammad, Egyptian diplomat; born 22 November 1923, Cairo; married; two daughters; *Religion:* Muslim; *Education:* BA in Political Economics, Cairo University, Egypt; BA in Military Sciences, Military College, Egypt, 1944; *Career:* member of the Free Officers Group, 1952; joined Ministry of Foreign Affairs, 1953; Consul General in Marseille, 1954–56; First Secretary and Chargé d'Affaires, Brussels, 1956–57; Consul General in Trieste, Italy, 1957–61; Chargé d'Affaires, Paris, 1963–64; Ambassador to Federal Republic of Germany, 1964–65; Head of Western Europe Department, Ministry of Foreign Affairs, Egypt, 1965–69; Ambassador to Thailand, 1969–71; Ambassador to Zaïre, 1971–73; Ambassador to Cyprus, 1973–75; Deputy Minister of Foreign Affairs, 1975–77; Ambassador and Head of the Relationship Office, Syria, 1977–78; Ambassador to Yugoslavia, 1978–81; *Decorations:* Order of Merit 2nd Class, Egypt, 1971; Order of Knighthood, Italy, 1966; Order of the Cross, Sweden, 1966; Order of the White Elephant 1st Class, Thailand, 1972; *Interests and Recreations:* hunting, fishing, reading literature, poetry, politics and economy; *Languages:* Arabic, English, French, Italian; *Address:* Ministry of Foreign Affairs, Cairo, Egypt.

MANSUR, Khalid Abdullah Tariq al-, Arab-American lawyer/businessman; born 29 January 1936, USA; *Religion:* Muslim; *Education:* BA in Philosophy and Logic, Howard University, Washington D.C., USA, 1958; Doctor of Jurisprudence Degree, School of Law, University of California, Berkley, 1961; PhD in Business Administration, California Western University, 1980; *Career:* Co-founder and senior partner, Jones, Al-Talal and Al-Mansur, International Law Business Firm; Director, First African Arabian Corporation, an investment trade and construction company; Director, Islamic Bank of North America, an international investment and commercial bank, Nassau, Bahamas; Director, First Financial Insurance, San Antonio, Texas, International Transports Systems Incorporation, Arabian Health Systems, Kapital Bank, Switzerland; *Publications:* several books and numerous articles; *Decorations:* Phi Beta Kappa Key, and others; *Interests and Recreations:* music, reading, basketball; *Languages:* Arabic, English, Spanish; 601 California St, Suite 300, San Francisco, California 94108, USA; 601 California St, Suite 300, San Francisco, California 94108, USA; telephone: (415) 981 0296.

MANSUR, Sami, Egyptian journalist; born 16 September 1935, Cairo, Egypt; *Religion:* Muslim; *Education:* BA in Political Science, Cairo University, Cairo, Egypt, 1958; MA in Political Science, Cairo University, 1962; PhD in Political Science, Cairo University, 1965; *Career:* Political Commentator, *Al-Ahram* newspaper, 1958–69; Editor, *Al-Ahram* Central Desk, 1969–76; Head, International Relations Unit, Al-Ahram Centre for Political and Strategic Studies, 1976–; *Publications: Confronting Israel,* 1963; *Nigeria: the Straying Giant,* 1965; *Masks of American Imperialism,* 1968; *The Collapse of the Revolution in the Third World,* 1969; *Militarism and Industry; Hiroshima and the Atomic Bomb; Languages:* Arabic, English; *Address:* 48 Muhammad Farid Street, Cairo, Egypt; telephone: 20330.

MANSURI, Abid Rashid Salmin al-, United Arab Emirates businessman; born 1920, Abu Dhabi, United Arab Emirates; married; six sons; *Religion:* Muslim; *Career:* owner of RASCO Company; member of Al-Ain Municipal Council; *Interests and Recreations:* Islamic thought and culture, hunting, falconry; *Address:* P O Box 1229, Al-Ain, United Arab Emirates; telephone: Office — 41788, 42011; Residence — 42128.

MANSURI, Darwish Muhammad Ali al-, United Arab Emirates administrator; born 1948, Abu Dhabi, United Arab Emirates; married, three daughters; *Religion:* Muslim; *Education:* general; *Career: Edi* tor of *Al-Ittihad* newspaper; Director of General Administration, Ministry of Foreign Affairs; Director Consulate and Passports Department, Ministry of Foreign Affairs; *Interests and Recreations:* swimming, fishing, hunting; *Languages:* Arabic, some English, some French; *Address:* Ministry of Foreign Affairs, P O Box 1, Abu Dhabi, United Arab Emirates; telephone: 362195; telex: 22217 KHARJIA EM.

MANSURI, Hamad Hamid Zaiban al-, United Arab Emirates official; born 1941; married; five sons, four daughters; *Religion:* Muslim; *Education:* general; *Career:* General Supervisor of Zaid Port, 1970; Representative of Ruler of Abu Dhabi in India, 1971; United Arab Emirates Consul General in Bombay, India; Office of Complaints and Suggestions, Ministry of State for Prime Ministerial Affairs; *Interests and Recreations:* diving, hunting, fishing, reading books on industrial technology; *Languages:* Arabic, English, Hindi, Persian; *Address:* Ministry of State for Prime Ministerial Affairs, Complaints and Suggestions Department, P O Box 899, Abu Dhabi, United Arab Emirates.

MAOUI, Abdul Aziz, Algerian diplomat/official; born 10 April, 1929, Algeria; married; *Religion:* Muslim; *Education:* Licence en Droit, University of Algiers; *Career:* several posts in government following Independence 1962; Secretary General, Ministry of Foreign Affairs, 1964; Minister of Tourism, 1965–77; Ambassador to USA, 1977–80; *Languages:* Arabic, French, English; *Address:* Ministry of Foreign Affairs, 6 Rue Ibn Batram al-Mouradia, Algiers, Algeria.

MAQBUL, General Taj al-Sirr Ahmad, Sudanese official/former army commander; born 1933, Taludi, Sudan; married; three sons, three daughters; *Religion:* Muslim; *Education:* BA, Cambridge University, UK; Certificate from Sudanese Military College; Certificate of the Indian Staff College; *Career:* 1st Lieutanant, 1954; Captain, 1958; Major, 1961; Lieutenant Colonel, 1969; Brigadier, 1970; General, 1974; retired as Major General; Chairman and General Manager, State Corporation for Cinema; *Decorations:* Order of the May Revolution, 1969; *Interests and Recreations:* music, tennis; President of the Union of the Graduates of Ahfad Schools; *Languages:* Arabic, English, French; *Address:* P O Box 2705, Khartoum, Sudan; telephone: Office — 78628, Residence — 56409.

MARAKCHI, Muhammad, Moroccan businessman; born in Fes, Morocco; married; three sons, two daughters; *Religion:* Muslim; *Education:* BSc; *Career:* member of several Moroccan economic organizations; Director General, Maghreb Industries SA; Director and Partner, CAPLAM, Kleber Colombe; Director General, Industries Marocaines Modernes, Procter and Gamble; Director, SODIPI, Camping Gaz International; *Interests and Recreations:* golf; *Languages:* Arabic, French, English; *Address:* Maghreb Industries, 35 Avenue Khalid Ibnou Loualid, Casablanca, Morocco; P O Box 2516, Casablanca, Ain Sebaa; telephone: 350596, 350597.

MARAYATI, Abdid A. al-, Arab-American academic; born 14 October 1931, Baghdad, Iraq; married; one son; *Religion:* Muslim; *Education:* BA, Bradley University, Peoria, Illinois, USA, 1952; MA, Bradley University, 1954; PhD, New York University, USA, 1959; *Career:* Secretary, delegation of Iraq, 10th Session, UN General Assembly, 1954–55; Secretary, delegation of Yemen, 11th, 12th, 13th and 14th Sessions, 1956–60; Instructor, Department of Government, University of Massachusetts, USA, 1960; Technical Assistance Officer, International Atomic Energy Agency, Vienna, Austria, 1960–62; Associate Professor, State University College of New York, USA; 1962–65; Research Fellow, Harvard University, USA, 1964–65; Associate Professor, Arizona State University, USA, 1965–68; former Chairman and Professor, Department of Political Science, Toledo University, USA, 1968; Director, Center for International Studies, University of Toledo, 1968–; Technical Assistance Officer, International Atomic Energy Agency, Vienna, Austria, 1960–62; *Publications:* numerous works, papers and articles, including *A Diplomatic History of Iraq,* New York, 1961; *Psychological Factors in the Arab-Israeli Conflict,* 1980; *Interests and Recreations:* member of American Political Science Association, Middle East Institute, Middle East Studies Association of North America, Phi Kappa Phi; *Languages:* Arabic, English, French, German; *Address:* Office — Department of Political Science, University of Toledo, Toledo, Ohio 43606, USA; telephone: (419) 537 2940, 4151; Residence — 2109 Terrace View West, Toledo, Ohio 43607, USA; telephone: (419) 531 7283.

MARDI, Colonel al Tayib al-, Sudanese official; born 1927, Sudan; married; *Religion:* Muslim; *Education:* courses in Pakistan, USA and UK; Military College, 1950; *Career:* retired from army, 1957; was recalled to service, 1959; Military Attaché, Embassy to USA and Embassy to UK; retired, 1969; Presidential Secretariat, 1972; member of the Commission for Returnees; member of the First People's Assembly, Chairman of its National Defence Committee; Commissioner of Darfur, 1973, and of Northern Darfur, when province was divided in 1974; *Languages:* Arabic, English; *Address:* Northern Darfur, Sudan.

MAREI, Sayyid Ahmad, Egyptian politician; born 26 August 1913, Egypt; married; one son; *Religion:* Muslim; *Education:* BSc in Agriculture, Cairo University, Egypt; Fellowship American University, Washington D.C., USA, 1950; *Career:* farmer and horsebreeder, 1937–53; elected to the Board of the Agricultural Credit and Co-operative Bank, 1949; Director of the Agrarian Reform Executive, 1952; President, Board of Directors, Agricultural Credit and Cooperative Bank, 1955; Minister of Agrarian Reform, 1956; Minister of Agriculture, 1957; Federal Minister of Agriculture and Agrarian Reform, 1958–1961; Third Managing Director of the Misr Bank, 1963; elected to the National Assembly, 1964; Deputy Speaker of the Assembly, 1964; led delegation to UK on an International Parliamentary Union visit in 1965; Secretary for National Capital in the Secretariat General of the Arab Socialist

Union (ASU), 1964; Minister accompanying late President Sadat to Algiers Summit, 1973, and to the Arab Israeli Disengagement talks in Aswan January 1974; Secretary General of the United Nations World Food Conference, 1974; Speaker of the People's Assembly, 1974; Assistant to late President Sadat, 1978; President of the Advisory Board for the President, 1981; *Publications: Agrarian Reform in Egypt; UAR Agriculture Enters a New Age* 1960; *Food Production in Developing Countries; Address:* Office — People's Assembly, Cairo, Egypt; Residence - - 9 Sharia Shagarat el-Door, Zamalek, Cairo, Egypt.

MARIA,   Francis, Arab-American businessman/educator and civic and ecumenical leader; born 1 January 1913, Lowell, Massachusetts, USA; *Religion:* Christian; *Education:* BA, Boston University, USA, 1936; MA, Boston University, 1937; PhD, Boston University and Harvard University, 1937–40; *Career:* Head of English Department, Tewksbury High School, Tewksbury, Massachusetts, USA, 1937–40; Academic Instructor, Assistant to Headmaster, Lowell New Trade High School, 1940–41; US Marine Air Corps, 1943–46; Assistant Personnel Director, Merrimack Manufacturing Company, Lowell, Mass; Vice President for Industrial Relations, Merrimack Manufacturing Company, 1946–57; President, Frank Maria Associates, Warner, New Hampshire and Boston, Mass, 1957–; member of the US delegation to 11th General Session of UNESCO, Paris, France, 1960–61; Special Assistant to the Governor of Massacusetts, 1961–63; Consultant and Aide to Governor of Massachusetts, 1965–67; Deputy Commissioner, Department of Banking and Insurance, 1969–75; English teacher, Newton High School, Newton, Mass., 1971–73; member of President Eisenhower's Civic Committee on People to People Programme, 1956; participated in White House Conference on World Refugee Year, 1959; *Publications:* numerous articles and papers; *Decorations:* Distinguished Public Service Award, Boston University, USA, 1957; Eastern States Federation's Outstanding Achievement Award, 1960; Award of Merit, Salaam Club of New York, 1969; Action's Man of the Year Award, 1970; and several other awards; *Interests and Recreations:* reading, writing, theatre; founding member of the American Friends of the Middle East, 1951;

founder of the American-Arabic Association, 1960; active in civic and ecumenical, cultural and humanitarian activities, and founder, president and chairman of numerous committees which have helped to promote the cause of understanding between the US and Arab countries; *Languages:* English, Arabic, French; *Address:* Office— Department of Near East and Arab Refugee Affairs, P O Box 46, Warner, New Hampshire 03278, USA; telephone: (603) 456 3454; Residence — Pumpkin Hill, Warner, New Hampshire 03278, USA.

MARINI, Abu Bakr al-, Moroccan journalist; born 1939, Sale, Morocco; married; two daughters; *Religion:* Muslim; *Education:* Degree in Education, 1958; Degree in Law, 1969; MA in Higher Studies, Dar al-Hadith al-Hassaniyah; *Career:* Head of Conferences and Editor in Chamber of Deputies, 1972; Private Secretary to the Minister of Education, 1973; founder and Editor of *Al-Fanoun* arts magazine of the Ministry of State for Educational Affairs; Editor of *Al-Atfal* (The Children) magazine; *Publications:* in Arabic: *Freedom Spoke to Me,* poetry, 1970; *The Holy Struggle; Legend about the October War,* 1973; *Umm Kalthoun: 20th Century Miracle;* four anthologies, ten plays, three collections of stories, a collection of proverbs entitled *Zanabeq Wa Ashwak; Decorations:* The Green March, 1975; *Interests and Recreations:* chess, rowing, educational issues; member of the Scientists Association; *Languages:* Arabic, French; *Address:* 14 Zanqat al-Marini, Bab Ibsayen, Sale, Morocco.

MARSAGHAWI, Hassan Sadiq al-; Egyptian judge/academic; born 15 July 1923, Zaqaziq, Egypt; married; one son, one daughter; *Religion:* Muslim; *Education:* PhD in Law, Cairo University, 1954; *Career:* Deputy Prosecutor General; Judge; Lecturer, College of Law, Alexandria University, Egypt; Professor, College of Law, Alexandria University, 1965–; Lawyer at the Court of Appeal; *Publications:* numerous books on the interpretation and implementation of different aspects of law; *Interests and Recreations:* reading, walking; *Languages:* Arabic, English, French; *Address:* 13 Kamil Gailani Street, Babsharqi, Alexandria, Egypt; telephone: 33155.

MARSOT, Afaf Lutfi al-Sayyid, Egyptian academic; born 1933, Cairo, Egypt; married; two daughters; *Religion:* Muslim; *Education:* DPhil, Oriental Studies, Oxford University, Oxford, UK, 1963; MA in Political Science, Stanford University, USA; BA in Sociology, American University in Cairo, Cairo, Egypt; *Career:* Professor of Near East History, University of California, Los Angeles, California, USA; Acting Director, Near East Centre, University of California, Los Angeles, 1966–77; member of Middle East Studies Association, American Research Centre in Egypt, the American Historical Association; *Publications:* *Egypt and Cromer,* 1967; *Egypt Liberal Experiment 1922–36,* 1976; *Interests and Recreations:* swimming; *Languages:* Arabic, English, French, German, Spanish, Italian; *Address:* Department of History, University of California, Los Angeles, California 90024, USA; telephone: (213) 825 1929.

MARTO, Michael Isa, Jordanian banker/economist; born 21 August 1940, Jerusalem; married; one daughter, one son; *Religion:* Muslim; *Education:* BA in Economics, Middle East Technical University, Ankara, Turkey, 1962; MA, PhD in Economics, University of Southern California, USA, 1968–70; *Career:* Economist, Central Bank of Jordan, Amman, 1970; Director, Economic Research Department, Royal Scientific Society, Amman, 1971–74; Lecturer, Jordan University, 1970–72; Lecturer, Institute of Bankers, 1973–74; appointed by HM King Hussain as member of the Provisional Higher Executive Committee of the Jordan National Union, 1971; Economic Adviser to HRH Crown Prince Hassan, 1974–75; Economist, World Bank, Washington D.C., 1975–77; Deputy General Manager, Jordan Fertilizer Industry Co Ltd, 1977–79; Deputy General Manager, Bank of Jordan, 1979; *Publications:* *A Money Supply Model for Jordan,* 1970, in English; *Money Supply Determination, Theory and Approach,* 1971, in English; *Food and Population in the Middle East,* 1976, in English; various economic articles published in Jordan in Arabic; *Decorations:* Order of the Jordanian Star, 1975; *Interests and Recreations:* theatre, travel, reading; *Languages:* Arabic, English, French, Turkish; *Address:* P O Box 2927, Amman, Jordan; telephone: 38034.

MARWAN, Muhammad Ashraf, Egyptian businessman; born 1944, Cairo, Egypt; married; *Religion:* Muslim; *Education:* BSc, MSc and PhD in Chemistry, Cairo University, Egypt; *Career:* Presidential Staff, 1967; Assistant of Information Secretariat, 1968; Secretary for Information to the President, 1971; Presidential Secretary for Foreign Relations, 1974; Chairman of Arab Organisation for Industrialisation, 1975; *Languages:* Arabic, English; *Address:* 5 Salah Salim Street, Heliopolis, Cairo, Egypt.

MARWAN, R. Tabari, Palestinian businessman; born 1933, Jerusalem; married; one son, four daughters; *Education:* BSc in Biology, Roosevelt University, USA; *Career:* Manager, Equipment Ltd, Kuwait, 1957–66; Managing Director and Partner, Ranya Trading, Contracting and Industrial, UAE; Partner, Jordan and Ittihad Pharmacy Company, UAE; *Interests and Recreations:* soccer; *Languages:* Arabic, English; *Address:* P O Box 602 Abu Dhabi, United Arab Emirates; telephone: 822416; telex 22386 RTCC EM.

MARZUKI, Hassan Abdul Rahman al-, United Arab Emirates administrator; born 1937, Ajman, United Arab Emirates; married; five sons, three daughters; *Religion:* Muslim; *Education:* general; *Career:* private business; Administrative Section, Ministry of Education, Qatar, 1963; Director of Fahd Bin Ali al-Thani Office, Qatar, 1962; Director of Administrative and Financial Affairs, Ministry of Youth, Abu Dhabi, 1972–; *Interests and Recreations:* reading; member of Emirates Club; *Address:* Supreme Council of Youth and Sports, Director of General Secretary Office in Abu Dhabi, P O Box 539 Abu Dhabi, United Arab Emirates.

MARZUQ, Jasim Khalid al-, Kuwaiti politician; born 1933, Kuwait; married; *Religion:* Muslim; *Education:* Cairo University, Egypt; *Career:* Deputy Head of Kuwait Municipality; Head of Kuwait Municipality; Minister of Education, 1970; Chairman of the Board of Kuwait University; Director General of the Arab Union of Municipalities; Minister of Commerce and Industry, 1978–; *Languages:* Arabic, English; *Address:* Ministry of Commerce and Industry, P O Box 2944, Safat, Kuwait; telephone: 424411; telex: 22682 COMMIND KT.

MARZUQ, Salim Khalid al-, Kuwaiti engineer/politician; born 1940; married; *Religion:* Muslim; *Education:* Degree in Engineering, USA; *Career:* Ministry of Public Works, 1970; established contracting business; has joint venture with Consultants, Mott Hay and Anderson (UK) on road building projects; entered National Assembly, 1971; re-elected, 1975, for constituency of Qibla; interested in oil affairs in Assembly; *Languages:* Arabic, English; *Address:* The National Assembly, Kuwait.

MAS'UD, Ahmad Muhammad al-, United Arab Emirates politician/businessman; born 1934, Abu Dhabi, United Arab Emirates; married; two sons, three daughters; *Religion:* Muslim; *Education:* general; *Career:* First Deputy President of the Consultative Council and President of the Abu Dhabi Chamber of Commerce and Industry; *Interests and Recreations:* swimming, hunting; *Languages:* Arabic, English; *Address:* Office — Al-Mas'oud, P O Box 322, Abu Dhabi United Arab Emirates; telephone: 41370.

MASAOOD, Abdullah Muhammad al-, United Arab Emirates businessman; born 1945, Abu Dhabi, United Arab Emirates; *Religion:* Muslim; *Education:* general; *Career:* international businessman and local merchant; co-owner of Muhammad Bin Masaood and Sons Company; *Interests and Recreations:* fishing, hunting, shooting; *Address:* Muhammad Bin Masaood and Sons, P O Box 322, Abu Dhabi, United Arab Emirates; telephone: Office — Abu Dhabi 822000.

MASAOOD, Rahma Muhammad al-, United Arab Emirates businessman/politician; born 1939, Abu Dhabi, UAE; married; four sons, three daughters; *Religion:* Muslim; *Education:* general; *Career:* Chairman, Muhammad Bin Masaood and Sons and Subsidaries; member of the Federal National Council; *Interests and Recreations:* swimming, hunting; *Languages:* Arabic, English; *Address:* Office — Muhammad Bin Masaood and Sons, P O Box 322, Abu Dhabi, United Arab Emirates; telephone: 822000; telex 22249 MASTOR EM.

MASHAT, Muhammad Sadiq al-, Iraqi diplomat; born 1930, Iraq; married; *Religion:* Muslim; *Education:* in Iraq and USA; *Career:* Under Secretary of State, Ministry of Education; Ambassador, Ministry of Foreign

Affairs; Ambassador, Embassy of Iraq, Paris, France, 1969–70; President, Mosul University, 1970; Minister of Higher Education and Scientific Research, 1977–78; Ambassador, Embassy of Iraq, Vienna, Austria, 1978–81; Ministry of Foreign Affairs, Baghdad, Iraq, 1981–; *Languages:* Arabic, English, German, French; *Address:* Ministry of Foreign Affairs, Baghdad, Republic of Iraq.

MASHHUR, Mashhur Ahmad, Egyptian politician/engineer; born April 1918; married; *Religion:* Muslim; *Education:* Engineering, Fuad I University, Cairo, Egypt; Staff College, UK; Fort Belvoir, USA; *Career:* Ministry of Transport, 1941; Army Engineer, 1942; Lecturer, Egyptian Academy of War, 1948–52; Staff Officer, Egyptian Corps of Engineers; Director of Transit, Suez Canal Authority, 1956; member of Board of Directors, Timsah Shipbuilding Company, Ismailia; Deputy Chairman, Suez Canal Authority, 1964; Chairman, Suez Canal Authority, 1965–; re-elected Secretary for Ismailia, Arab Socialist Union, 1968; elected to Central Committee of the Arab Socialist Union, 1968; *Languages:* Arabic, English; *Address:* Irshad Building, Ismailia, Egypt; 6 Lazoghli Street, Garden City, Cairo, Egypt.

MASHTA, Lieutenant Colonel Tuham, Tunisian air force officer; born 1935; married; *Religion:* Muslim; *Education:* Ecole de l'Air, Salon, France, 1957; *Career:* Flying Instructor; Commander First Air Unit, 1965–68; studied in USA, 1968–69; nominated Commanding Officer of the Tunisian Air Forces, 1971; course in France, 1971–73; Acting Chief of Staff of the Tunisian Air Force, 1974; *Languages:* Arabic, French; *Address:* Ministry of National Defence, Tunis, Tunisia.

MASMUDI, Muhammad, Tunisian politician/diplomat; born 1923, Mahdia, Tunisia; married; seven children; *Religion:* Muslim; *Education:* Licence ès-Lettres, and Diploma des Sciences Politiques, Sorbonne, University of Paris, France; *Career:* Journalist; Delegate of Neo-Destour in Paris, 1949–54; member of Executive Committee of Peoples' Congress against Colonialism and of the International Committee of Moral Rearmament; Minister of State in the Tahar Ben Ammar Government, 1954; Delegate at the Franco-Tunisian Negotiations; member of the Political Bureau

of the Neo-Destour Party, and Minister of State in the first Bourguiba Government, 1957; Minister of Information, 1958; re-elected to the Political Bureau, 1959; visited USSR for Moscow International Film Festival, 1961, and UK with President Bourguiba, 1961; headed first Tunisian goodwill mission to Peking, 1961; Ambassador to France, 1964–70; Foreign Minister, 1970–74; official visit to UK, 1971; co-author of Jerba Declaration on Tunisian-Libyan unity, 1974; *Languages:* Arabic, French; *Address:* Ministry of Foreign Affairs, Tunis, Tunisia.

MASMUDI, Mustafa, Tunisian official; born 23 May 1937, Sfax, Tunisia; married; one daughter; *Religion:* Muslim; *Education:* Licence ès-Sciences Economiques; Licence in Law, Tunis University; *Career:* Administrator in Secretariat of State for Planning and Finance, 1963–64; Head of Socialist Destour Party mission to Co-ordination Committee, 1964; Attaché in the Office of the Secretariat of State for Information, 1964–66; Head of the National Press Section in the Information Department, 1966–69; Head of the Office of the Secretary of State for Information, 1969–70; Director of Information, 1970–74; Chairman and Managing Director of Tunis-Afrique-Presse (TAP) Agency, 1974; Secretary of State in charge of Information for the Prime Minister, 1974; *Publications:* in French: *L'Economie de l'Information,* 1975; *Decorations:* Grand Officer of the Tunisian Order of Independence, 1975; various foreign decorations from Belgium, Egypt, Iran, Norway, Luxembourg; *Interests and Recreations:* theatre, cinema, swimming, chess, reading; *Languages:* Arabic, French, some English; *Address:* Secretariat of State for Information, 2 Rue d'Alger, Tunis, Tunisia; telephone: 233233.

MASOUD, Muhammad Ibrahim, Saudi Arabian politician; born 1919, Jeddah, Saudi Arabia; married; *Religion:* Muslim; *Education:* BCom, National University, Beirut, Lebanon; *Career:* Department of Minerals and Public Works, Ministry of Finance, 1941; Head, Provisions Department, Ministry of Finance, 1943–48; Minister Plenipotentiary and Inspector of Diplomatic and Consular Corps, Ministry of Foreign Affairs, 1958–59; Minister Plenipotentiary, Embassy to Iraq, 1959–61; Ambassador, 1961–68; Deputy Foreign Minister 1968–75; Minister of State and member of Cabinet, 1975; founding member of Board and Deputy Director General of *Al-Bilad* daily newspaper; member of Saudi Delegation headed by HRH Prince Abdullah Al Faisal to UK and USA and North Africa, 1957; Head of Saudi Delegation to Senegal, 1961; Personal Representative of HM the King to the meeting of personal representatives of Arab Kings and Heads of State, Cairo, Egypt, 1966; Head of joint Saudi-Kuwait Delegation to the Gulf states in negotiations for establishing the United Arab Emirates, 1970; Head of Saudi Delegation to conference of Islamic Solidarity Charter, Jeddah, 1971; Saudi representative on official visits to the United Arab Emirates, Bahrain, Qatar, 1971; Head of Saudi Delegation, Conference of Arab Foreign Ministers, Cairo, 1975; Deputy Head of Saudi Delegation, Islamic Foreign Ministers Conference, Jeddah, 1975; *Publications:* articles in local press; *Decorations:* Orders of Merit from the Governments of Spain, Egypt, Lebanon, Mauritania, Senegal, Republic of China, USA, Tunisia; *Interests and Recreations:* swimming; *Languages:* Arabic, English; *Address:* Kilo 6, Mecca Road, P O Box 5666, Jeddah, Saudi Arabia; telephone: Jeddah 30518, 30111.

MASRI, Abdullah Hassan, Saudi Arabian academic/archaelogist and anthropologist; born 5 September 1947, Mecca, Saudi Arabia; married; one son; *Religion:* Muslim; *Education:* Indiana University, Bloomington, USA, 1965–66; BA in Anthropology, California State University, Sacramento, 1967–69; MA and PhD in Anthropology, University of Chicago, 1969–73; *Career:* Director, Department of Antiquities and Museums, 1973; Director General, Department of Antiquities and Museums, 1978; Deputy Assistant Manager of Education for Cultural Affairs, 1980; Lecturer in Anthropology, University of Riyadh; member of the High Council of Antiquities, the High Council of Religious Endowment (Waqfs), Saudi Arabia, the Organization of Directors General of Antiquities of Arab Countries, the General Committee of Conferences, UNESCO, ALESCO Cultural and Scientific Organization of the Arab States, Aspen Fellowship, New York, Archaeological Society of America, and others; *Publications: Prehistory in North Eastern Arabia; Field Research Projects,* Miami, 1974; *Factors of Growth in the Civilization of South-Western Arabia,* 1974, *Journal of the Faculty of Arts,* University of Riyadh; *An Introduction to the Antiquities of Saudi Arabia,* Department of Antiquities and Museums, Riyadh, 1975; *Recent Archaeological Activities in Saudi Arabia,* 1976, Proceedings of the Seminar of Arabian Studies, Cambridge; *The Ancient and Historic Legacies of Saudi Arabia and its Place in the World,* The Continents Publishers, 1979, Lausanne; *Interests and Recreations:* swimming, riding, travelling; *Languages:* Arabic, English, French; *Address:* Department of Antiquities and Museums, Ministry of Education, P O Box 3734, Riyadh, Kingdom of Saudi Arabia; telephone: 4351686, 4355821.

MASRI, Ahmad Fathi al-, Syrian diplomat; born 21 August 1932, Damascus, Syria; married; two daughters; *Religion:* Muslim; *Education:* BA in Law; Diploma in Public Law, Faculty of Law, Damascus University, 1954; *Career:* Attorney, 1954–57; Financial Inspector, 1957–58; United Arab Republic (UAR) Diplomatic Service, 1958; UAR Embassy to Iraq, 1960–62; Syrian Chargé d'Affaires, Embassy to Cyprus, 1966–67; member of the Syrian Permanent Mission to the United Nations, 1969–75; Syrian Representative to the Special Committee with regard to the Implementation of the Declaration on Granting of Independence to Colonial Countries and Peoples, 1970–; Syrian Representative to the 11th Session of the Governing Council of the UN Development Programme; Syrian Representative to the 1st Session of the Ad Hoc Committee on International Terrorism, 1973; Syrian Representative to the First Session of the Third UN Conference on the Law of the Sea; member of the UN Visiting Mission to Gilbert and Ellice Island, 1974; Chairman of the Subcommittee of the Special Committee with regard to the Implementation of the Declaration of Granting of Independence to Colonial Countries and Peoples, 1975; Syrian Representative to the First Session of the Board of Governors of the UN Special Funds; Representative in the Preparatory Committee for the Special Session of the General Assembly devoted to the Development and the International Organisation of Legal Affairs; Ministry of Foreign Affairs, 1975–78; Chargé d'Affaires, Syrian Embassy, Santiago, Chile, 1978–; *Interests and Recreations:* music, literature, photography; *Languages:* Arabic, English, French, Spanish; *Address:* Syrian Embassy, Carmencita 11, Santiago, Chile.

MASRI, Awni Fuad al-, Jordanian politician/ engineer; born 5 January 1936 Nablus; married; two daughters, two sons; *Religion:* Muslim; *Education:* BSc in Civil Engineering, American University of Beirut, AUB, Lebanon, 1959; MSc in Civil Engineering, Purdue University, USA, 1961; *Career:* Engineer, Road Sector Develpoment Board, 1961–62; Engineer, Ministry of Public Works, Jordan, 1962–63; Director of Material Section and Study and Design, Ministry of Communications, Saudi Arabia, 1963–67; Project Manager, military base, (Benladen Organization), Jordan, 1967–68; Partner and Director, Arabtech Consulting Engineers, 1968–80; President, Engineers Association, 1980; Minister of Public Works, Jordan, 1980–; member of Jordan Engineering Society; member of the American Association of Engineers; *Publications: Effects of Different Compaction Methods on Clay Characteristics,* 1961, in English; several papers in professional journals; *Decorations:* Istiqlal Order, 1963; Order of Jordanian Star, 1981; Cwanghwa Medal, South Korea, 1981; *Interests and Recreations:* swimming, bridge, reading; member of Jordan Automobile Club and Road Society; *Languages:* Arabic, English, German; *Address:* P O Box 2038 Amman, Jordan; telephone: 41466, 665556.

MASRI, Hikmat al-, Jordanian politician/ businessman; born 1905, Nablus, Palestine; *Education:* Commerce, American University of Beirut, Lebanon, 1929; *Career:* businessman and sometime Jordanian Minister; worked with Barclays Bank in Jaffa; joined family firm in Nablus; entered Jordanian Parliament as Deputy for Nablus, 1952, and subsequently held office as Minister of Agriculture, and Minister of National Economy; Speaker of the Chamber of Deputies, 1955–56; Senator, 1962–71; closely concerned in the administration of his factories in the West Bank; *Address:* c/o The Senate, P O Box 6924, Amman, Jordan.

MASRI, Muhammad Qahtan Rafiq al-, Jordanian banker; born 29 August 1938, Nablus; married; one son, two daughters; *Religion:* Muslim; *Education:* Diploma in Commercial Studies; banking courses; *Career:* Clerk, Arab Bank Ltd, Amman, Jordan, 1956; Arab Bank Ltd, Nablus, 1957, Aden, 1958–59, Amman, 1960; Head of Department, Arab Bank Ltd, Nablus, 1960–64; Assistant Accountant, Qatar National

Bank, Doha, Qatar, 1964, Accountant, 1970, Assistant Manager, 1976, Manager, 1979, Manager of the Main Office and Assistant General Manager, Qatar National Bank, Doha, 1980–; *Interests and Recreations:* swimming, tennis; *Languages:* Arabic, English; *Address:* Qatar National Bank, P O Box 1000 and 1002 Doha, Qatar; telephone: Office — 414166, 413511; Residence — 327809.

MASRI, Munib Rashid al-, Jordanian businessman; born 23 March 1936, Nablus, Palestine; married; four sons, two daughters; *Religion:* Muslim; *Education:* BA in Geology; MA in Geology; *Career:* Assistant General Manager of Phillips Petroleum Company, Jordan, 1959; General Manager, Phillips Petroleum Company, 1961; General Manager, Phillips Petroleum Company, Algeria, 1963; General Manager and Vice President, Phillips Petroleum Company (Middle East), 1965; Minister of Public Works, 1970–71; formed Engineering and Development Group, (Holding Company) dealing in engineering, consulting, contracting, industry, insurance, real estate and trade, 1971; Underwriting member of Lloyd's, 1974; member of the Board of Directors of Arab Bank Ltd, 1974; *Interests and Recreations:* basket-ball, jogging, swimming; *Languages:* Arabic, English, Russian, French; *Address:* P O Box 6147, Amman, Jordan.

MASRI, Salah Ahmad al-, Yemen Arab Republic official; born 1919, Sana'a, Yemen Arab Republic; married; three sons, two daughters; *Religion:* Muslim; *Education:* theological studies in Yemen; *Career:* Private Secretary to Imam Ahmad, 1948; Governor of Otmah, 1954; Ambassador, Yemen Embassy, Sudan, 1955–62; Shaikh of Anss Tribe, 1959; Minister of Defence, 1962–67; represented the Royalists at conferences with the Republicans held in Sudan, Saudi Arabia; Minister of State for Presidential Affairs, 1971; *Interests and Recreations:* journalism *Languages:* Arabic, English; *Address:* P O Box 1239, Sana'a, Yemen Arab Republic; telephone: 2019.

MASRI, Tahir Nash'at al-, Jordanian diplomat/administrator; born 1942, Nablus, Palestine; married; one son, one daughter; *Education:* BA in Business Administration, North Texas State University, 1965; *Career:*

Assistant General Manager, Jordan Central Bank, 1965–73; member of Parliament, 1973–75; Minister of State for Occupied Territories Affairs 1973–74; President of Executive Office for the Occupied Territories, 1973–74; Ambassador, Embassy of Jordan to Spain, 1975–78; Ambassador to France and Permanent Delegate to the UNESCO, 1978–; *Decorations:* Order of the Jordanian Star 1st Class; La Merito Civil, Isabel La Catolica, Spain; Commander of the Légion d'Honneur, France; *Languages:* Arabic, English; *Address:* Embassy of Jordan, 80 Blv Maurice Barrès, 92200 Neuilly, France; telephone: (33–1) 62423 7879.

MASSA'DEH, Salim, Jordanian politician; born 1930, Irbib, Jordan; *Education:* Law, Damascus University, Syria; *Career:* Teacher, 1949–50; Audit Department, 1955–58; Judge, 1958–70; Ministry of the Interior, 1970; Governor; Under Secretary, 1971; Minister of Justice, 1974–76; Minister of Finance and Chairman of Board of Jordan-Kuwait Bank, 1977–79; Minister of Finance, 1979; *Address:* Ministry of Finance, P O Box 85 Amman, Jordan.

MASSARI, Muhammad al Arbi al-, Moroccan journalist; born 8 July 1936, Tetuan, Morocco; married; two sons, one daughter; *Religion:* Muslim; *Education:* Diploma from the Institute of Broadcasting, Cairo, 1959; *Career:* Producer on Moroccan Radio; Secretary of the Educational Department, 1958–64; Editor of *Al-Alam* newspaper, 1964–, Chief Editor; member of the National Council and Central Committee of the Istiqlal Party, 1965–; member of the executive committee of the Istiqlal Party, 1978–; Secretary General of Moroccan Writers' Union, 1964, 1969 and 1972; Assistant Secretary of the Moroccan Association for Support of the Palestinian Struggle; Assistant Secretary General of the Arab Journalists Union; *Publications: The Arab Battle Against Zionism and Imperialism,* 1967; *With Fatah in the Ghor,* Rabat, 1969; *Discussion About the Arabs,* Rabat, 1973; *Morocco-Spain, The Last Confrontation,* Rabat, 1975; *The Land Problem in Our Political Struggle since Independence,* Rabat, 1980; *Languages:* Arabic, French, Spanish; *Address:* Al-Alam, P O Box 141, Rabat, Morocco; 27 Lumumba Street, Rabat, Morocco; telephone: 33683.

MATAR, Muhammad Hamid, Sudanese diplomat; born 1 January, 1931, Masudiya, Sudan; married; eight children; *Religion:* Muslim; *Education:* LLB, Cairo University, Egypt, 1958; International Relations and International Law, Geneva and New York, 1963; *Career:* Lawyer, 1958; Third Secretary, Ministry of Foreign Affairs, Khartoum, Sudan, 1959; Second Secretary, 1962; First Secretary, 1965; Counsellor, 1968; Minister Plenipotentiary, 1974; Ambassador, 1977; currently, Ambassador to the People's Republic of China and the Democratic People's Republic of Korea; *Interests and Recreations:* cinema, theatre, sports; *Languages:* Arabic, English; *Address:* Embassy of Sudan, 1 Dong Er Jie, San Li Tun, Beijing, People's Republic of China.

MAZBOUDI, Zaki, Lebanese politician; born 1920, Beirut, Lebanon; married; four children; *Religion:* Muslim; *Education:* Faculty of Law, Sorbonne, University of Paris, France, 1949; PhD in Economics, University of Paris, 1951; *Career:* Ministry of Finance, 1948–66; member of Lebanese Delegations to the Arab League Economic Council, 1961–65; leader of Lebanese Delegations in the Double Taxations Agreement talks with France, 1961; member of the committee to study Lebanese relations with EEC, 1963; negotiated an agreement with United Arab Republic on nationalised Lebanese property in Egypt, 1963; Secretary General of Agriculture, Industry and Real Estate Development Bank, 1966–72, and Adviser to the Bank; Deputy for Beirut, 1972; member of Parliamentary Delegation to UK, 1973; Minister of Planning 1974–75; *Languages:* Arabic, French; *Address:* c/o Banque de Crédit Agricole Industriel et Foncier SAL, Riad El-Solh Street, P O Box 3696, Beirut, Lebanon.

MAZIAD, Hamad al-, Saudi Arabian official/lawyer; born Saudi Arabia; *Religion:* Muslim; *Education:* BA, Law, Cairo University, Egypt, 1963; MA, Comparative Law, Southern Methodist University, Dallas, Texas, USA; *Career:* Secretary of Legal Affairs, Royal Cabinet, 1964; Legal Adviser, Supreme Committee of Labour Disputes, Ministry of Labour and Social Affairs, 1966–68; Legal Adviser, Ministry of the Interior, 1971–73; Director General of Border Affairs and Chairman of the Disciplinary Committee, Ministry of the Interior; member of Supreme Committee of Adult Education and Eradication of Illiteracy, member of Permanent Joint Saudi-Kuwait Committee, UN Conference on the Law of the Sea, Caracas and Geneva, Conference for the Amendment of Anti-Narcotics Convention, Geneva, Switzerland; *Publications:* articles in local press on administrative and international law; *Interests and Recreations:* reading, sport; *Address:* Ministry of the Interior, P O Bos 2833, Riyadh, Saudi Arabia; telephone: 4011944.

MAZIDI, Faisal Mansur al-, Kuwaiti businesman/oil expert; born 2 May 1933; married; *Religion:* Muslim; *Education:* Weybridge Technical College, UK, 1951; Portsmouth Municipal College, UK, 1952–53; Politics and Economics, University of Keele, UK, 1955–58; *Career:* Department of Finance and Industry 1962–65; resigned, 1965; General Manager of Kuwait Petro Chemical Company, and Managing Director of Kuwait Chemical and Fertiliser Company, 1965–71; Chairman, Government Oil Concession Committee, 1963–65; Chairman, Government Refinary Committee, 1964–66; Consultant; Adviser to BP and Gulf Oil 1972, and Kuwait Maritime Mercantile Company, 1965–70; Director, Petrochemical Industries Company, 1971–; President, Kuwait Associated Consultants (KASCON), 1971–; Chairman, Kuwait Resources Engineering and Management International (KUREMI), 1976–; member of Kuwait Economists' Society; stood unsuccessfully as Assembly candidate for Dasman Constituency, 1975; *Publications: Natural Gas and Its Utilization,* 1963; *Kuwait as a Base for Petrochemicals,* 1965; Arab League prize for paper on natural gas, 1963; *Languages:* Arabic, English; *Address:* KASCON, P O Box 5443, Kuwait.

MAZOUNI, Muhammad Halim, Algerian official/academic; born 10 March 1937, Algeria; married; two daughters, two sons; *Religion:* Muslim; *Education:* PhD in Applied Mathematics; *Career:* Associate Professor of General Mechanics and Mechanics of Vibrations, University of Paris-Sud, France, 1964–68; Head of Project of Petroleum Refinery, 1970–73; Director of the Industrial Zone of Arzew, 1971–73; Vice President of Petro-Chemistry, LNG and Refining, SONATRACH, 1972–80; Manager, SONATRACH, National Society of Petroleum and Gas; member of the Central Com-

mittee of FLN Party, 1979; *Publications: Development of Downstream Industries,* OAPEC Seminar, Oslo, 1978, in French, and other papers and researches published in professional journals and magazines; *Interests and Recreations:* music, jogging, gymnastics, walking; *Languages:* Arabic, French, English; *Address:* 1ère rue des Jardins, No 78, Arzew, Algeria; telephone: 376 637.

MAZROUI, Abdullah M, United Arab Emirates banker/journalist; born 10 April 1952, Abu Dhabi, United Arab Emirates; *Education:* BA in Political Science and Economics, American University of Beirut, Beirut, Lebanon; *Career:* Finance Department, Foreign Investment Section, Government of Abu Dhabi; Deputy Chief Executive, Chief Executive, National Bank of Abu Dhabi, 1978–79; Managing Director, National Bank of Abu Dhabi, 1979–; Director of the Board of Gulf International Bank, Bahrain, UBAN Arab Japanese Finance Ltd, Hong Kong; former Director of The Arab Investment Company, Riyadh, The Abu Dhabi Investment Company, 1978; member of Industrial Project Committee, Government of Abu Dhabi; member of Union of Arab Banks, Lebanon; Editor of *Al-Fajir* newspaper, 1975–; *Languages:* Arabic, English, French, Urdu, Persian; *Address:* National Bank of Abu Dhabi, P O Box 4, Abu Dhabi, United Arab Emirates; telephone: 323030; telex: 22907 MASDIR EM;

MAZROUI, Rashid Muhammad, United Arab Emirates businessman; born 1950, Abu Dhabi; married; two sons, one daughter; *Religion:* Muslim; *Education:* College of Economics, Sussex University, UK; *Career:* Chairman of Mazroui Construction Technology, Marzoui International Cargo Co, Al-Mazroui Drilling Co, Gulf World Trading and Services, United Arab Emirates *Daily News; Interests and Recreations:* tennis, fishing, sailing; *Languages:* Arabic, English; *Address:* Al-Mazroui and Partners, P O Box 2035, Abu Dhabi, United Arab Emirates; telephone: 820430, 826096, 827257.

MAZRUI, Abdullah Humaid Ali, United Arab Emirates official; born 1942, Ajman, United Arab Emirates; married; one son, one daughter; *Religion:* Muslim; *Education:* BA, College of Economics and Political Science, Baghdad University, Iraq, 1968; *Career:* Deputy Director, Development Office in

Trucial States Rulers' Council; Director of Development Office, Rulers' Council; Under Secretary, Ministry of Communications, 1972; Under Secretary, Ministry of Foreign Affairs, with rank of Ambassador, 1974–77; Minister of Labour and Social Affairs, 1977; *Interests and Recreations:* general reading; *Languages:* Arabic, English; *Address:* c/o Ministry of Labour and Social Affairs, Abu Dhabi, United Arab Emirates.

MAZZAWI, Musa, Anglo-Arab academic/ lawyer and broadcaster; resident in the UK; born 21 March 1925, Haifa, Palestine; married; one son, two daughters; *Religion:* Christian; *Education:* LLB, LLM, PhD, London University, UK; Barrister, Gray's Inn, London, 1950; *Career:* Courts of Justice, Haifa, Palestine, 1943; Arab Office, London, 1946; Legal Department, Prime Minister's Office, Benghazi, Libya, 1949; various teaching and journalistic appointments 1950; Holborn College of Law, subsequently the Polytechnic of Central London, UK, 1961; active on mass media in UK in promotion and defence of Arab cause, especially on Palestine; Dean, School of Law, the Polytechnic of Central London, 1973–77; Head of English Law and Professional Studies, Professor of International Law, Polytechnic of Central London, 1977–; *Publications:* various publications and radio and television broadcasts in Arabic and English on legal and political affairs; *Interests and Recreations:* photography, gardening, walking; Arab and Islamic culture and history; Arab-Western trade and other relations; *Languages:* Arabic, English; *Address:* School of Law, Polytechnic of Central London, Red Lion Square, London WC1R 4SR; telephone: (01) 405 3144; Residence — The Lane House, Mortimer, Nr Reading, Berkshire RG7 3PP, UK; telephone: (01) 2427155; telephone: 0734 332897.

MEBAZAA, Faud, Tunisian official; born 16 June 1933, Tunis, Tunisia; married; *Religion:* Muslim; *Education:* Licence in Law and Economics, Sorbonne, University of Paris, France; *Career:* active in student Neo-Destour Party; served in Secretariat of State for Health; Director of Youth and Sports, 1964; Director of National Security, 1965; Director of Youth and Sports, 1967; Governor-Mayor of Tunis, 1969; Minister of Youth and Sports, 1973; Vice President of La Marsa Municipal Council; *Decorations:*

Commander of the Tunisian Order of Independence; *Languages:* Arabic, French; *Address:* Ministry of Youth and Sports, Tunis, Tunisia; telephone: 286843.

MEDANI, Mustafa, Sudanese diplomat; born 1 August 1931, Omdurman, Sudan; married; three sons, two daughters; *Religion:* Muslim; *Education:* BA and MA in Economics, Cambridge University, UK; *Career:* Ministry of Foreign Affairs, Sudan, 1956; member of first Sudan Delegation to the UN, 1956; Consul General, Sudanese Embassy in Damascus, Syria, 1958–60; Chargé d'Affaires, Beirut; Lebanon, 1963–65; Ambassador to Lebanon, 1965–69; Ambassador to Czechoslovakia, 1969–71; Acting Under Secretary, Ministry of Foreign Affairs, Khartoum, Sudan, 1971–72; Ambassador to Ethiopia, 1972–74; Ambassador to the UN, New York, 1974–78; Ambassador to West Germany, Bonn, 1978–; *Decorations:* Order of the Republic, Egypt, 1960; Order of the Lebanese Cedar, Lebanon, 1969; Medal, Order of the Republic, West Germany, 1978; *Interests and Recreations:* Arabic, English; *Address:* 52 Beethovenallee, Bonn 2, West Germany; Embassy of the Democratic Republic of the Sudan, Habsburgerstrasse 8, 5300 Bonn 2; telephone: 363074/75, 352881/ 82.

MEGALLI, Nabila, Egyptian journalist; born 1 September 1938, Egypt; *Religion:* Christian; *Education:* Cairo University, Cairo, Egypt; *Career:* journalist, *Middle East Economist* magazine, 1958; staff of Middle East News Agency, 1963; staff of Middle East Features Service, 1964, DPA (West German news agency), 1968–; correspondent for *Daily Telegraph*, 1968–; correspondent for *Newsweek*, 1973–, *Petroleum Intelligence Weekly*, 1961–; member of the Egyptian and Arab Journalists Unions; First Secretary of Foreign Association Correspondents; *Interests and Recreations:* reading, literature, history, walking; *Languages:* Arabic, English, French; *Address:* 139 Al-Tahrir Square, Dokki, Cairo, Egypt; telephone: 744327.

MEHRI, Hassan al-, Bahraini official/ educationalist; born 12 November 1935, Bahrain; married; two daughters; *Religion:* Muslim; *Education:* Delhi University, India, 1961; TEFL Diploma, Cardiff, UK, 1964; Diploma in Educational Administration, Reading University, UK, 1965; Visiting

Fellowship, Queen Elizabeth House, Oxford University, Oxford, England, 1974; *Career:* primary school teacher, 1951–58; deputy headmaster, 1961–67; Assistant Director, Male Education; Director of General Education, 1975; Assistant Under Secretary, 1982; Chairman, Board of Directors of Bahrain Children's Home; Representative of Regional Bureau of the Middle East for Education of the Blind; member of the Board of the American Mission Hospital, Bahrain, Film Censorship, Bahrain, the Institute of the Handicapped, Bahrain; *Publications:* various articles on educational problems in local journals; *Interests and Recreations:* fishing, volley-ball; *Languages:* Arabic, English; *Address:* Ministry of Educatiom, P O Box 43, Manama Bahrain; telephone: 258406.

MEHRIK, Yusuf Ibrahim al-, Libyan academic; born 24 May 1937, Mursi Matrouh, Egypt; married; two sons, two daughters; *Religion:* Muslim; *Education:* BSc, PhD, Analytical Chemistry, Chromotography; *Career:* Dean, Faculty of Science, Tripoli, 1970–76; Director General, Petroleum Research Centre, 1976–78; Director of Environmental Programme, NASR, 1978–; *Interests and Recreations:* bridge, reading, swimming, football, water skiing; *Languages:* Arabic, English, French; *Address:* P O Box 3545, Tripoli, Libya.

MEKKI, Hatim al-, Tunisian artist/painter; born 16 May 1918, Jakarta, Indonesia; married; *Religion:* Muslim; *Education:* Lycée Carnot, Tunis; *Career:* illustrator of *Marianne;* returned to Tunis, 1940; one-man exhibition, Tunis, 1940, and 1941, Algiers 1942, lived in Paris, 1947–50; one-man exhibition, Galérie Suillerot, 1949, Galérie L.L. Rosenburg, 1950; contributed to *Combat, La Gazette des Lettres,* Editions Charlòt; 1st Poster Prize, Paris, 1953; Painting Prize, Menton Biennale 1955, and Alexandria, 1957; painted major murals, Tunis, Bizerta, Sfax; one-man exhibition at Imperial Palace, Peking, 1962; designed over two hundred Tunisian postage stamps, also for United Nations and United Arab Emirates; prizes from the UN, the Czech Press, Italian philatelists; several times 1st International Stamp Prize, Tunis; exhibitions in the USA and the main European capitals; works at museums and private collections; George Dimitrov Prize, 1973; Counsellor at the Ministry of Foreign Affairs, 1968–72;

Lecturer at Tunis University, 1968; contributor to *L'Action* (later *Jeune Afrique),* Tunis, 1955–62; Assistant Mayor of Carthage, 1959–62; Municipal Counsellor of Carthage, 1972–75; *Decorations:* Officer of the Order of the Tunisian Republic, 1965; Commander of Cultural Merit of the Tunisian Government, 1974; Officer of the Order of the Egyptian Republic, 1965; Officer of the Order of the Imperial Crown of Iran, 1974; *Interests and Recreations:* member of the Administrative Board of the International Cultural Centre, Hammamet; *Languages:* Arabic, French, English, Indonesian, Italian, Spanish, Czechoslovakian; *Address:* Municipality of Carthage, Tunisia.

MEKKI, Ismail al-Misbah, Sudanese IMF official; born 1 January 1929, Sudan; married; *Education:* BCom, Cairo University, Egypt, 1949–53; MA in Economics, Michigan State University, USA, 1962–64; *Career:* Permanent Secretary, Ministry of Finance and Economy, 1968–71; Budget Adviser, IMF, Yemen, 1971; Alternate Executive Director, IBRD, Washington D.C., 1972; *Decorations:* Yousif Nahas Prize, Cairo University, 1953; *Languages:* Arabic, English; *Address:* Office — IBRD, 1818 H Street NW, Washington D.C. 20433, USA.

MELIBARI, Salim Ahmad, Saudi Arabian businessman/chemist; born 1940, Mecca, Saudi Arabia; *Religion:* Muslim; *Education:* PhD, Inorganic Chemistry; *Career:* Lecturer, Vice Dean, Associate Professor, Dean, Faculty of Science, Riyadh University, Riyadh, Saudi Arabia; Secretary General, Riyadh University; member of the Royal Institute of Chemists; General Manager, Dallah Industries, Riyadh, Saudi Arabia, 1978–; *Publications:* several textbooks in the field of chemistry, research papers published in scientific journals; *Interests and Recreations:* reading, travel; *Address:* Dallah Industries, P O Box 1438, Riyadh Saudi Arabia; telephone: 24899, 30323, 25625; telex: 201036 DALLAH SJ.

MELLAKH, Larbi, Tunisian politician; born 1 April 1929, Governorate of Bizerta, Tunisia; married; five children; *Religion:* muslim; *Education:* Pharmacy Section, Faculté de Médecine, Marseilles, France; *Career:* Deputy for Bizerta in the National Assembly, 1969; member of the Central Committee of the Socialist Destour Party,

1973; Secretary of State to the Minister of Supply, 1973; *Decorations:* Officer of the Order of Tunisian Independence; *Languages:* Arabic, French; *Address:* Ministry of Supply, Tunis, Tunisia; telephone: 283299.

MEMMI, Albert, Tunisian academic/writer; born 15 December, 1920, Tunisia; *Education:* Lycée Carnot, Tunis; Algiers University, Algeria; University of Paris, France; *Career:* teacher, 1955; Director, Centre of Psychology, Tunis, 1956; Researcher, Centre National de la Recherche Scientifique, Paris 1959–; Assistant Professor and Professor, Ecole Pratique des Hautes Etudes, 1959–66; 1966–70; Professor, Académie des Sciences d'Outre-Mer, 1970–; *Publications: The Pillar of Sale,* 1953; *Strangers,* 1955; *The Coloniser and the Colonised,* 1957; *Portrait of a Jew,* 1966; *The Dominated Man,* 1968; *Le Scorpion,* 1969; *Le Désert; Jews and Arabs,* 1974; *La Dépendence,* 1979; *Le Racisme,* 1982; *Decorations:* Chevalier de la Légion d'Honneur; Officer des Balmes Académiques; Commander of the Order of Nichan Iftikhar; various academic awards; *Languages:* Arabic, French; *Address:* 5 rue Saint Merri, Paris 4e, 7500 4 Paris, France.

MEMMI, André, Tunisian businessman; born 13 October 1915, Tunis, Tunisia; married; *Education:* Baccalauréat; *Career:* flour manufacturer; Treasurer of Nos Petits; *Languages:* Arabic, French, English, Italian; *Address:* 7 Rue de la Banque, Tunis, Tunisia; telephone: 246138.

MENDJELI, Ali, Algerian politician; born 1922, Algeria; *Religion:* Muslim; *Career:* member of Mouvement pour le Triomphe des Libertés Démocratiques; Political Commissioner of Wilaya II; member of First Provisional Government, 1956; Assistant to Cherif Belkacem, National Liberation Army, (ALN), 1956–58; ALN General Staff at Ghardimaou, Tunisia, 1966; served with Houari Boumedienne; member of FLN delegations to Evian and Lugrin negotiations, 1961; elected Deputy for Department of Constantine in National Assembly and appointed Chairman of National Assembly Committee on Defence and the Armed Forces, 1962; First Vice-President of the National Assembly, 1963; retained post in the new National Assembly, 1963; member of FLN Central Committee and Political Bureau at Party Congress, 1964; former member

of Revolutionary Council, 1965; *Languages:* Arabic, French; *Address:* c/o FLN, Place Emir Abdel Kadir, Algiers, Algeria.

MESSADI, Mahmud, Tunisian UN official/ educationalist; born 28 January 1911, Tunisia; married; *Religion:* Muslim; *Education:* Faculty of Letters, University of Paris, France, 1936; Licence ès-Lettres, 1939; Diplome d'Etudes Supérieures, 1947; Agrégation in Arts; *Career:* Assistant Lecturer in Arabic Language and Literature, Centre of Islamic Studies, University of Paris, and Institute of Higher Studies, Tunis; Director of Secondary Education, Ministry of Education, 1955–58; Secretary of State, Ministry of National Education, 1958–68 responsible for the Educational Reform of 1958, the ten-year educational plan and establishment of the Tunisian University, 1960; Minister of Education, Youth and Sports; Chairman, Tunisian National Committee for UNESCO, 1958–68; Head, Tunisian Delegation to UNESCO General Conference; Rapporteur, Committee of Experts on Arab Culture, UNESCO: Head of Tunisian Delegation to Congresses of Arab Ministers of Education, 1958–68; Minister of State to the Prime Minister, 1969–70; Minister of Cultural Affairs, 1973; member of Council of Consultant Fellows, International Institute for Educational Planning; member of Executive Board of UNESCO, 1974; Deputy, National Assembly and member of Central Committee of Destour Socialist Party; *Publications: Education: Present and Future; The Dam,* 1955; *Hadith Abi Houraira,* 1973; *Birth of Forgetfulness,* 1974; and numerous other articles and studies; *Decorations:* Grand Cordon of the Order of Tunisian Independence; Order of the Tunisian Republic; *Languages:* Arabic, French; *Address:* Ministry of Cultural Affairs, Tunis, Tunisia; telephone: 260088; UNESCO, 1 Rue Miollis, Paris 75732, France; telephone: 566 5757.

MESTIRI, Ahmad, Tunisian politician/ lawyer; born 2 July 1925, Tunisia; married; three sons, one daughter; *Religion:* Muslim; *Education:* Licence in Law, Faculté de Droit, Paris; *Career:* Head of the Office of the Minister of Interior, 1953; Minister of Justice, first Bourguiba government, 1956; Minister of Finance and Trade, 1958; Ambassador to Egypt, 1958–62; Ambassador to Algeria, 1962–66; Minister of National

Defence, 1966–68; Minister of Interior, 1970; expelled from Neo-Destour Party, 1942–72; expelled from National Assembly, 1973; leader of group of liberal politicians, aiming to liberalise present political regime; private law practice, Tunis; *Decorations:* Grand Cordon of the Order of Tunisian Republic; various foreign decorations; *Languages:* Arabic, French, some English; *Address:* 6 rue d'Annaba, Tunis, Tunisia; telephone: 248084.

MESTIRI, Mahmud, Tunisian diplomat; born 25 December 1929; married; *Religion:* Muslim; *Education:* Institute d'Etudes Politiques, University of Lyon, France; *Career:* Ministry of Foreign Affairs; served on several delegations to UN; alternate representative to UN, 1958–59; Head of Tunisian special diplomatic mission to Congo; Ambassador to Zaire, 1961; Minister in the Permanent Tunisian Delegation to the UN, 1962–64; Secretary General, Ministry of Foreign Affairs, 1965–67; Permanent Representative to the UN, 1967–69; Chairman, UN Special Committee on the Implementation of Declaration on the Granting of Independence to Colonised Countries and Peoples, 1968; Ambassador to Belgium and the EEC, 1969–70; Ambassador to West Germany, 1970–72; Secretary General of the Ministry of Foreign Affairs, 1973; Ambassador to USSR and Poland, 1974–76; Ambassador to the United Nations, 1976; *Languages:* Arabic, French, English; *Address:* c/o Ministry of Foreign Affairs, Boulevard Farhat Hached, Tunis, Tunisia.

MESTIRI, Said Muhammad, Tunisian physician; born 22 June 1919, Tunis, Tunisia; married; four sons, one daughter; *Religion:* Muslim; *Education:* Lycée Carnot, Tunis; Baccalauréat, 1938; Medical Studies, Faculty of Medicine, Algiers, Algeria, 1939–46; intern and doctoral thesis, Algiers, 1948; various advanced courses in France and six months in USA, 1962; Agregation in Surgery, Paris, 1969; *Career:* Intern in Algerian Hospitals, 1945–48, and Tunisian Hospitals, 1948–51; Assistant Surgeon at the Sadiki Hospital, Tunis, 1951–56; Principal Surgeon at the Habib Thameur Hospital, 1957–64; Principal Surgeon of Ernest Conseil Hospital, 1967–; Professor of the Tunis Faculty of Medicine; President of the Tunisian Surgery Association; President of the Tunisian Medical Science Society, 1960–61; foreign member of the French Academy of Surgery;

member of the Lyon Society of Surgery; former Vice President of the Council of the Tunisian Order of Medicine; participated as Surgeon and Head of the Tunisian Medical Team in Suez during the Six-day War, June 1967, and the October War in Damascus, Syria, 1973; *Publications:* Medical articles and lectures to scientific conferences; *Decorations:* Commander of Nichan Iftikhar, 1961; Bizerta Commemorative Medal, 1963; Officer of the Order of the Tunisian Republic, 1964; Chevalier of the Order of Tunisian Independence, 1968; Commander of the Order of the Tunisian Republic, 1975; *Interests and Recreations:* swimming, bridge; Hispano-Moorish architecture; Tunisian ceramics; *Languages:* Arabic, French, English; *Address:* Office — Ernest Consiel Hospital, Tunis, Tunisia; telephone: 262653, 262855; Residence — Villa les Olivier, Route de Gammarth, La Marsa, Tunisia; telephone: 270346.

METAWEH, Ibrahim Esmat, Egyptian academic/educationalist, born 8 March 1923, Cairo, Egypt; married; one son, three daughters; *Religion:* Muslim; *Education:* BSc, Cairo University, 1944; Diploma in Education, 1946; MA in Education, University of Minnesota, USA, 1952; PhD in Education, University of Minnesota, 1954; *Career:* UNESCO Expert, Tripoli, Libya, 1955–57; Exchange Mission, USSR, 1961–62; Director of Educational Planning, Ministry of Higher Education, Cairo, 1962–65; Dean, College of Education, Minia, Assiut, Tanta, Shebin Al-Koum, Kafr Al-Shaikh; *Publications:* numerous books on rural education, simplified science, educational planning, audio visual aids, fundamentals of education, practice teaching, and other subjects; *Address:* Dean, College of Education, Tanta University, Tanta, Egypt; telephone: Tanta 4943, Cairo 866497.

MHAIDI, Kadhim Abdul Hamid al-, Iraqi businessman; born 12 February 1922; *Education:* Faculty of Law, Baghdad University, Iraq; in UK and USA; *Career:* Director General, Baghdad Chamber of Commerce, 1963; General Manager, Bank of Baghdad, 1964–65; Minister of Economy, 1965; Chairman of the Board, General Trade Establishment, 1966; Minister of Economy, 1966–67; Economic Adviser to the Baghdad Chamber of Commerce, 1968; Secretary General, Federation of Iraqi Chambers of Commerce,

1969; *Languages:* Arabic, English; *Address:* Federation of Iraqi Chambers of Commerce, Mustansir Street, Baghdad, Iraq.

MHEDHBI, Bashir, Tunisian diplomat; born 1912, Tunisia; married; *Religion:* Muslim; *Education:* Sadiki College, Tunis, and in France; *Career:* Neo-Destour activist; Arabic Radio Announcer on Radio Paris, 1944; later in Berlin and Athens; returned to Tunisia 1955; Assistant Private Secretary, Ministry of National Economy; Director of the Tunisian National Radio, 1956–58; President of the nationalized Tunisian Electrical and Municipal Transport Authority, 1958–62; Ministry of Foreign Affairs, 1962–66; Ambassador to Lebanon, 1966; Ambassador to Jordan, 1967–70; Secretary General, Ministry of Foreign Affairs, 1970–71; Ministry of National Defence, 1971–72; Ambassador to the Court of St. James, London, UK, 1972–74; Ambassador to Morocco, 1974–76; *Languages:* Arabic, English, French, German, Greek; *Address:* Ministry of Foreign Affairs, Boulevard Farhat Hached, Tunis, Tunisia.

MIDANI, Zuhair al-, Syrian lawyer; born 1923, Damascus, Syria; *Education:* Arab Institute of Law, Damascus, Syria, 1947; *Career:* private law practice; Deputy for Damascus, Unification Council with Egypt, 1961; Lawyer, Syria, 1968, 1975; Secretary General, Arab Lawyers Union, 1979–; *Languages:* Arabic, English; *Address:* Arab Lawyers Union, 13 Shari Ittihad al-Muhamiin al-Arab, Garden City, Cairo, Egypt; telephone: 30978.

MIDFA, Ibrahim, United Arab Emirates politician; born 1912; married; *Religion:* Muslim; *Career:* personal adviser to the Ruler of Sharjah; *Address:* c/o Amiri Court, P O Box 1, Sharjah, United Arab Emirates.

MIDHI, Muhammed Said, People's Democratic Republic of Yemen official; *Career:* Representative of Ministry of Economy, 1968; member of the First Governorate Command, 1969; Permanent Secretary to the Ministry of Commerce, Economy and Planning; former Governor of the Bank of Yemen; elected to Central Committee, 1975; Acting Minister of Commerce and Provisions, (now the Ministry of Trade and Supply), 1975; *Languages:* Arabic, English; *Address:* Ministry of Trade and Supply, Aden, People's Democratic Republic of Yemen.

MIKDASHI, Zuhair, Lebanese academic/economist; resident in Switzerland; born 1933, Beirut, Lebanon; married; two sons; *Religion:* Muslim; *Education:* Certificate of General Literary Studies, University of Lyon, France, 1953; BA in Economics, American University of Beirut (AUB), 1954; BA in Economics, (AUB), 1956; Diploma, Financial Management and Control, International Center for the Advancement of Management Education, Stanford University Graduate School of Business Administration, USA, 1963; BLitt, International Economic Affairs, University of Oxford, UK 1958; DPhil, International Economic Affairs, University of Oxford, 1971; *Career:* Economist, Planning Board, Lebanon, 1955–56; Consultant, International Bank for Reconstruction and Development (IRBD), and Assistant to IBRD Mission Chief to Libya, Washington D.C., USA, 1958–59; Technical Assistance Fellow, Europe, UN, 1962–63; Visiting Lecturer, Arab Institute of Higher Studies and Research, Cairo, Egypt, 1966; Visiting Scholar, Institut Français du Pétrole, Paris, France, 1967; Resident Adviser to the Minister of Oil and Finance, State of Kuwait, 1966–67; Associate Visiting Professor of International Business, Graduate School of Business Administration, Indiana University, Bloomington, Indiana, USA, 1970–71; Research Fellow, Center for International Affairs, and Center for Middle Eastern Studies, Harvard University, USA, 1971–72; Visiting Fellow, Institute of Developing Economies, Tokyo, Japan, 1972; Consultant, Organization of the Petroleum Exporting Countries (OPEC) at various dates between 1964 and 1975; Tenured Professor of Business Administration, American University of Beirut, Lebanon, 1976; Adviser, Center for Natural Resources, Energy and Transport and Center for Transnational Corporations, UN, New York, USA, over different periods in 1971–77; Professor of Business Administration, Ecole des Hautes Etudes Commerciales, University of Lausanne, Switzerland, 1976–; Secretary General, Arab-European Business Co-operation Committee, 1976–; *Publications: The International Politics of Natural Resources,* 1976, Cornell University Press, New York, and Ithaca, London; 1978, (Japanese Edition), Tokyo Keizai; co-author, *An Analysis of World Energy Demand and Supply 1974–85,* 1975, The Research Institute of Overseas Investment – The Export Import Bank of Japan, Tokyo, and several other books; numerous articles and papers in international journals; *Decorations:* George Webb Medley Prize, University of Oxford, 1962; Orden Francisco de Miranda, by the President of the Republic of Venezuela, 1971; Ford Foundation Travel and Study Award in the USA, 1970–73; *Interests and Recreations:* performing arts, swimming; *Languages:* Arabic, French, English; *Address:* Office — 19 Ch des Hauts-Crets, Ch-1223, Cologny, Geneva; telephone 022 351870; Residence — 12 Chemin des Abailles-Ch-1010 Lausanne; telephone: 021 324235.

MIKHAIL, Rames Sulaiman, Egyptian UN official/meteorologist; born 10 January 1920; married; *Education:* BSc in Mathematics, 1935–39; Diploma of Graduate Studies in Meteorology, Cairo University, Egypt, 1943–44; *Career:* Meteorologist, Meteorological Department of Egypt, 1938–57; Director, International Affairs Division, Meteorological Department of Egypt, 1958–68; Chief, Programme Planning and Co-ordination, World Meteorological Organization (WMO), 1968–72; Senior Programme Officer, United Nations Environment Programme (UNEP), 1973; *Languages:* Arabic, English, French, Spanish; *Address:* UNEP, P O Box 30552, Nairobi, Kenya; telephone: 33930.

MIKHBAL, Ahmad Salim, People's Democratic Republic of Yemen official; *Career:* Governor of the Sixth Governorate; member of the Central Committee; member of the People's Supreme Council; Prosecutor General for the People's Court in the Second Governorate and Commander of the Second Governorate Security Branch, 1970; Commissioner of Security for the Fifth Governorate, 1970; Governor of the Fourth Governorate, 1976; *Address:* Fourth Governorate, People's Democratic Republic of Yemen.

MILI, Ali Fredj, Tunisian official/academic; born 30 March 1943, Monastir, Tunisia; married; two daughters, one son; *Religion:* Muslim; *Education:* MA in Sociology, University of Paris, France; Diploma, School of Higher Studies of Social Sciences; Diploma, Institute of Economic and Social Development, University of Paris; PhD in Psychology, University of Paris; *Career:* Consultant of UNESCO in Syria, 1971; Researcher for the Canadian Agency of International Development, and Consultant for the Research

Centre of International Development, 1973–74; Visiting Professor, University of Constantine, Algeria, 1973–75; Senior Psychologist, Head of Services par interim, and Professor, Universities of Monkton, New Brunswick and of Quebec, Rimouski, Canada, 1976–78; Senior Psychologist and Clinical Co-ordinator of the Admission Unit, Institute Philippe Pinel de Montréal, Canada, and Doctoral Supervisor, Quebec University, Montreal, Canada, 1979–80; Head of Project, Ministry of Social Affairs, Tunis, Tunisia, and Chief Administrator, l'Office des Travailleurs Etrangers à la Formation Professionnelle et à l'Emploi, Tunis, 1981–82; Expert and Head of Sevices, Arab Organization for Social Defence, 1982–; *Publications:* numerous researches and papers; *Interests and Recreations:* travelling, skiing, golf, archaeology; member of the Canadian Society of Psychology; *Languages:* Arabic, French, English, German; *Address:* 45 Rue Mansur Al-Dahabi, Rabat, Morocco; telephone: 22218; Rue 8716, Bloc 22, Cité Olympique 1003 Tunis, Tunisia; telephone: 281491.

MILI, Muhammad Izziddine, Tunisian international official/engineer; born 4 December 1917, Djemmal, Tunisia; married; *Education:* Ecole Normale Supérieure, St. Cloud, France; Ecole Nationale Supérieure des Telecommunications, Paris, France; *Career:* Telecommunications Engineer, Tunisia, 1947–56; Director General of Telecommunications, 1957–65; Vice Chairman, Plan Committee for Africa, International Telecommunication Union (ITU), 1961–64; Chairman ITU, 1964–65; Chairman ITU Administrative Council, 1964; Deputy Secretary General, ITU, 1965–67; Secretary General ITU, 1967–; *Decorations:* Officer of the Order of Independence, Tunisia; Commander of the Order of Tunisian Republic; and various other decorations; *Languages:* Arabic, French, English; *Address:* Office— Place des Nations, CH-1221 Geneva 20, Switzerland; telephone: 412299; Residence — 5 Route de mon Idée, CH-1226 Thonex, Geneva, Switzerland.

MINKARAH, Issam A., Arab-American academic/engineer; born 5 January 1931, Beirut, Lebanon; married; one son, one daughter; *Religion:* Muslim; *Education:* BA, American University of Beirut, Lebanon, 1952; BSc, American University of Beirut, 1953; MSc,

Rensselaer Polytechnic Institute, USA, 1957; PhD, Rensselaer Polytechnic Institute, 1963; *Career:* Site Engineer, Contracting and Trading Company, Jordan and Iraq, 1953; Bridge Designer, Consulting Engineer Firm, Albany, NY, USA; Instructor, Rensselaer Polytechnic Institute, 1962–63; Projects Manager, Contracting and Trading Company, Sudan, 1963–65; part time Lecturer, University of Khartoum, Sudan; Construction, Area Works Manager, United Arab Emirates, 1965–70; Associate Professor of Civil Engineering, University of Cincinnati, USA, 1970; member of Transportation Research Board Committee, 1972–79; member of Transportation Research Board Committee, Rigid Pavement Construction, 1974; *Publications:* various technical articles and reports on road engineering; *Interests and Recreations:* swimming, hiking; member of American Society of Civil Engineers and American Society of Engineering Education; *Languages:* Arabic, English, French; *Address:* Civil and Environmental Engineering Department, University of Cincinnati, Cincinnati, Ohio 45221, USA; telephone: (513) 475 8000.

MIQDADI, Wa'el Darwish al-, Iraqi businessman/diplomat; born 30 May 1929, Haifa, Palestine; married; one son, one daughter; *Education:* Business Course, American University of Beirut, 1950; BSc in Business Administration, Boston University, USA, 1950; MA in Government Administration, Wharton School, University of Pennsylvania, 1957; *Career:* tea cher, Kuwait, 1950–52; Controller, Arab Bank, Baghdad, Iraq, 1958–61; Commercial Assistant to General Manager, Bader Al-Mulla and Bros, Kuwait, 1961–63; General Sales Manager, Deputy General Manager, Kuwait Automative Imports Co, Kuwait, 1963–75; Ambassador, Ministry of Foreign Affairs, Baghdad, Iraq, 1975; Managing Director, Kuwait Oil Tanker Company Ltd, London, UK, 1976–; *Interests and Recreations:* reading, tennis, swimming, music; *Languages:* Arabic, English, German; *Address: Office—* Kuwait Oil Tanker Co Ltd, Berkeley Square House, Berkeley Square, London W1X 5LD, UK; *Residence —* Flat A and B, Randolph Crescent, Maida Vale, London W9, UK; telephone: (01) 286 0043.

MIRGHANI, Muhammad, Sudanese diplomat; born in Southern Sudan; *Religion:* Muslim; *Career:* served in the Sudan Police; Diplomatic Service after Independence; Counsellor, Sudanese Embassy to UK; Ambassador to Kenya, 1966; Acting Under Secretary, Ministry of Foreign Affairs on return to Khartoum, before being posted to Cairo; Under Secretary, Ministry of Foreign Affairs; *Languages:* Arabic, English; *Address:* Ministry of Foreign Affairs, Khartoum, Sudan.

MIRGHANI, Muhammad, Sudanese journalist; born 1932; *Religion:* Muslim; *Education:* University of Besançon, France; London School of Journalism, UK; *Career:* Foreign News Editor, *Al-Ayam* Press House, 1949–58; Manager, Regional News Services and Reuters, Khartoum, 1958–; Sudan correspondent for Reuters and London *Daily Telegraph* and *Sunday Telegraph; Languages:* Arabic, English, French; *Address:* Regional News Services, P O Box 972, Khartoum, Sudan.

MISHAL BIN ABDUL AZIZ, HRH Prince, Saudi Arabian Prince/former administrator; born 1926; son of late King Abdul Aziz; *Religion:* Muslim; *Career:* Minister of Defence, 1951–56; Adviser to late King Saud, 1957–60; Amir of Mecca, 1963–71; *Address:* Royal Court, Riyadh, Saudi Arabia.

MISHAL, Muhammad Said Khalil al-, Qatari official/industrialist; born 1933, Palestine; *Religion:* Muslim; *Education:* BSc in Petroleum Engineering, Cairo University, Egypt, 1957; *Career:* Head of Reservoir Engineering Division, and later Petroleum Technical Department, Ministry of Petroleum and Mining, Saudi Arabia; Head of Petroleum Department, Ministry of Finance and Petroleum, Qatar, 1972; Chairman, Qatar Fertilizer Company, 1969–; Director General, Industrial Development Technical Centre, 1972–; Director, Qatar General Petroleum Corporation, 1974–; Chairman, Qatar Steel Company, 1977–; and various others; played major role in reorganizing Petroleum Industry in Qatar, establishing the Qatar General Petroleum Corporation, nationalization of Oil Industry in Qatar, organizing industrial joint ventures with foreign firms in Umm Said Industrial Estate, south of Doha; played a leading role in industrial and infra-structural activities in Qatar, and in organizing industrial planning and activities; *Address:* Industrial Development Technical Centre, P O Box 2599, Doha, Qatar; telephone: 320 565.

MISHARI, Ahmad Hamad Abdul Muhsin al-, Kuwaiti aviation official; born 1 July 1949, Kuwait; married; two sons; *Religion:* Muslim; *Education:* BSc in Economic and Political Sciences, Kuwait, 1971; *Career:* Market Research Officer, Kuwait Airways Corporation, 1971, Sales Supervisor, 1972, Assistant Marketing Director, 1974, Marketing Director, 1975, Director General, 1977; President of the Board of Trustees and member, Kuwait Airways Corporation, 1981–; *Interests and Recreations:* football; *Languages:* Arabic, English; *Address:* P O Box 394, Safat, Kuwait; telephone: 711154; telex: 23036 KT.

MISHARI BIN ABDUL AZIZ, HRH Prince, Saudi Arabian Prince/businessman; born 1930, Riyadh, Saudi Arabia; son of late King Abdul Aziz; *Religion:* Muslim; *Education:* general; *Career:* Chirman, Al-Saada Trading and Contracting Co Ltd; *Address:* P O Box 5854, Jeddah, Saudi Arabia.

MISHARI, Hassan Bin Mishari Bin Ibrahim al-, Saudi Arabian official; born 1930, Saudi Arabia; married; *Religion:* Muslim: *Education:* BCom, Cairo University, Cairo, Egypt, 1953; MA in Industrial Management, School of Business Administration, University of Southern California, USA, 1960; *Career:* Arabian American Oil Company (Aramco), 1953–60; Director General of Al-Yamama Cement Co, Riyadh, 1960–61; Deputy Minister, Ministry of Finance and National Economy, 1961–64; Minister of Agriculture and Water, 1964; Chairman of Board, King Faisal Settlement Project, Haradh, Irrigation and Drainage Project Authority, Al-Hassa, Public Organization for Saline Water Desalination; Chairman of several Saudi delegations to FAO conferences, Rome, Italy, Arab League Food Organization conferences, World Food conference, Botanical Royal Agricultural Exhibition, UK; *Decorations:* King Abdul Aziz Order for Meritorious Government Service, granted by late HM King Faisal; Order of Merit awarded by the President of the Republic of Liberia; *Interests and Recreations:* reading; *Languages:* Arabic, English; *Address:* P O Box 209, Riyadh, Saudi Arabia.

MISMARI, Muhammad Yunis Khalifa al, Libyan diplomat; born 1937, Cyrenaica, Libya; married; two sons, three daughters; *Religion:* Muslim; *Career:* Staff Colonel and Deputy Director of Army Communications, infantry course at Warminster, UK and course at Staff College, Camberley, UK, 1968–69; established import company in Benghazi, 1973; Minister Plenipotentiary; Ambassador to the Court of St. James, London, UK, 1976; *Interests and Recreations:* Arabic literature and civilization, hunting; *Languages:* Arabic, English; *Address:* Secretariat Bureau for External Relations, Tripoli, Libya.

MISTIKAWI, Muhammad Naguib al-, Egyptian journalist; born 8 April 1918, Egypt; married; three sons, two daughters; *Religion:* Muslim; *Education:* Licence in Law, Cairo University, Egypt, 1939; *Career:* Chief Editor, Sports Section, *Al-Ahram* newspaper, 1953; member of the Olympic Committee, of the Sports Committee, High Council of Youth and Sports; President of the Wrestling Federation; former Egyptian champion of 100 metres running; former 1st Division football player; *Publications:* several books on sport and art and literature; *Decorations:* Order of the Republic, 3rd Class; Order of Merit, 3rd Class; Sports Medal, 1st Class; *Interests and Recreations:* billiards, shooting, riding, travelling, reading, music, literature; *Languages:* Arabic, French, English; *Address:* No 6 Sharia 257, Maadi, Cairo, Egypt; telephone: 35586.

MITABIQANI, Muhammad Hamid al-, Saudi Arabian engineer/official; born 1930, Al-Kark, Saudi Arabia; *Religion:* Muslim; *Education:* PhD Civil Engineering; *Career:* engineer, Ministry of Communications; Assistant Secretary General for Technical Affairs, Supreme Planning Council; Director of Industrial Education; Director General of Technical Education, Ministry of Education; member of Industrial Development and Research Centre, Saudi Arabian Standardization Organization, Supreme Committee for Personnel Training; attended conferences of UNESCO General Conference, Conference on Technical Education in the Developing Countries, Berlin, Conference of Arab Ministers of Education, Rabat, Morocco, Conference of Gulf States Ministers of Education; actively participated in the drafting of co-operation agreements in the field of technical education with the Governments of Federal Republic of Germany, France and Japan; *Publications: The Role of Technical Education in Manpower Training; Philosophy of Technical and Vocational Education in the Arab Countries; Interests and Recreations:* music; *Address:* P O Box 1491, Riyadh, Saudi Arabia; telephone: Riyadh 21632.

MITWALLI, Sami, Egyptian journalist; born 30 May 1936, Sharqiyah Governorate, Egypt; married; three sons; *Religion:* Muslim; *Education:* BA in Journalism, 1958; *Career:* editor, journalist, *Al-Ahram* newspaper; editor in Investigations Department, *Al-Ahram;* Head of the Political and Popular Organizations Department, *Al-Ahram; Interests and Recreations:* social sciences, natural sciences, economics; member of Al-Shams Club; *Languages:* Arabic, English; *Address:* Al-Ahram Newspapers, Al Gala Street, Cairo, Egypt; telephone: 59010.

MOAWAD, Wajdi Antoine, Lebanese banker; born 6 June 1945, Ibadan, Nigeria; married; two daughters; *Religion:* Christian; *Education:* LLB, St Joseph University, Beirut, Lebanon; *Career:* Vice President and Middle East Representative, Fidelity Bank, Philadelphia, USA, 1974–82; Chairman and Managing Director, First Phoenician Bank, Beirut, Lebanon, 1982–; *Languages:* Arabic, English, French, German; *Address:* The First Phoenician Bank, P O Box 11–1629, Beirut, Lebanon; telephone: 250 005/6/7/8.

MOGRABI, Nabil, Lebanese journalist/ lawyer; resident in France; born 25 September 1948; Tripoli, Lebanon; *Religion:* Muslim; *Education:* Diploma in Criminology, Paris, France, 1972; Diploma in Education, Paris, 1973; PhD in Mass Communications, Paris, 1974; PhD in Law, University of Paris, 1976; *Career:* Editor of *Al-Watan al-Arabi* magazine, published in Paris, 1976–; member of the International Institute of Journalism; University Lecturer; Legal Adviser; former Honorary Consul; Chairman of the Association of Arab Writers in France; Representative of the Union of Arab Writers in France; *Publications:* several books and numerous studies, papers and articles; *Interests and Recreations:* table tennis, walking, travel, cinema, reading; *Languages:* Arabic, English, French, Italian; *Address:* 117 Bd Murat, 75016 Paris, France.

MONTASSIR, Essam Hussain, Egyptain economist; born 1 May 1935, Egypt; married; one son, one daughter; *Religion:* Muslim; *Education:* BA in Law, Ain Shams University, 1957; Diploma in Economics, Cairo University, 1957; MA, Princeton University, 1964; Diploma in Demography, Princeton University, 1965; PhD in Economics, Princeton University, 1972; *Career:* Ministry of Foreign Affairs, Cairo, 1956–62; Ministry of Foreign Affairs, Egypt, 1967–69; Egypt Price Planning Agency, 1973; Head of the Division of Analysis, Projection and Long-Term Planning, Ministry of Planning, Cairo, 1974–76; Under Secretary of State, Plan Construction Department, Ministry of Planning, 1977; United Nations Adviser to Council of Arab Economic Unity (CAEU),1978–79; Professor of Economics at the American University of Cairo, 1979–80; Director of UN African Institute of Economic Development and Planning (IDEP) in Dakar, Senegal; *Publications:* numerous books and research papers in Arabic and English; *Interests and Recreations:* tennis, photography; *Languages:* Arabic, English, French; *Address:* 22 Taha Hussain Street, Apt 29, Zamalek, Cairo, Egypt; telephone: 807333; Office — IDEP, P O Box 3186, Dakar, Senegal.

MORCOS, Claude Kamil, Syrian businessman; resident in United Arab Emirates; born in Lattakia, Syria; married; three daughters; *Religion:* Christian; *Education:* LLB; *Career:* Commercial and Insurance experience since 1954 in Syria; manager of several commercial firms; law practice in Lattakia; General Manager, Alhai al-Mohairbi Corporation for Trading, Contracting, Catering and Services; *Interests and Recreations:* sailing, swimming, tennis, bridge; *Languages:* Arabic, English, French; *Address:* P O Box 328, Abu Dhabi, United Arab Emirates; telephone: 325347, 322833; telex: 22648 EM(Alhage).

MOSLAH, Samir Abdul Rahman, Egyptian lawyer; resident in United Arab Emirates; born 6 September 1936; married; one son, one daughter; *Religion:* Muslim; *Education:* Law Degree; Higher Studies Diploma in International Law; *Career:* Director of Technical Assistance Office, Egyptian Presidential Cabinet, 1963; Director of the Office of the Egyptian Presidential Cabinet, 1963; Director of the Egyptian Vice President's Office, 1966–68; Director of Legal Affairs, Egyptian

National Defence Council, 1970; Legal Adviser to the Egyptian Minister of Local Government, 1971; Legal Adviser to the United Arab Emirates (UAE) Council of Ministers, 1972–80; Legal Adviser to Abu Dhabi Investment Authority, (ADIA); *Interests and Recreations:* tennis, swimming, winner of long-distance swimming medal world championship Capri-Naples, 1955; *Languages:* Arabic, French, German; *Address:* ADIA P O Box 3600, Abu Dhabi, United Emirates; telephone: 326100.

MOSLY, Sami Ahmad, Saudi Arabian engineer; born 1948, Taif, Saudi Arabia; *Religion:* Muslim; *Education:* BSc in Civil Engineering, 1973; MSc, Environmental Engineering, Stanford University, USA, 1972; *Career:* Head, Follow-Up Department, Ministry of Planning, Municipality, Housing and Water Sectors; Deputy Director General, Yanbu Industrial Complex, the Royal Commission for the Development of Jubail and Yanbu Industrial Zones; member of Saudi Arabian-US Joint Co-operation Committee; *Interests and Recreations:* soccer, football, tennis, classical music; *Address:* P O Box 238, Jeddah, Saudi Arabia; telephone: Riyadh 29677.

MOSLY, Sulaiman Ahmad, Saudi Arabian official/scientist; born 1946, Mecca; *Religion:* Muslim; *Education:* BSc, 1969; MSc, 1972; PhD, 1974; *Career:* research assistant, 1970; teaching assistant, 1971; Research Supervisor, 1973, Director of Research, Research and Development Corporation, Jeddah, 1974; member of Committee of Research and Environmental Protection and Desalination; Director of Research and Training, General Organization for Saline Water Desalination; *Publications: Analysis of Psychoactive Drugs; Water Pollution; Interests and Recreations:* tennis, reading; *Address:* P O Box 238, Jeddah, Saudi Arabia; telephone: Jeddah 23395.

MOSSALLAM, Ali Abdul Rahman, Saudi Arabian official; born 1935, Qassim Region, Saudi Arabia; *Religion:* Muslim; *Education:* MA in Political Science, Indiana University, Indiana, USA; *Career:* Assistant Principal, al-Ilmi Institute, al-Ahsa; Secretary, Secondary Education Department, Ministry of Education; Assistant Director, Personnel Department; Director, Organisation and Management Unit, Ministry of Agriculture;

Director General of Organisation, Planning and Budgeting Department, Ministry of Agriculture and Water Resource; Vice President, Riyadh House Establishment; attended several international conferences on agriculture, waste disposal, human nutrition, Rome, Paris, London; *Address:* P O Box 317, Riyadh, Saudi Arabia; telephone: 38332.

MOUALLIMI, Abdallah Yahia al-; Saudi Arabian businessman; born 5 May 1952, Saudi Arabia; married; two sons; *Religion:* Muslim, *Education:* BSc in Chemical Engineering, Oregon State University, USA, 1973; *Career:* Chemical Engineer, Riyadh Oil Refinery, 1973–75; Assistant General Manager of Production, Riyadh Oil Refinery, 1975–77; General Manager, Aluminuim Products Co Ltd, Dammam, Saudi Arabia, 1977–; *Languages:* Arabic, English; *Address:* Aluminium Products Co Ltd (ALUPCO), P O Box 2080, Dammam, Saudi Arabia; telephone: 8328489.

MOUASHER, Rajai S., Jordanian businessman; born 1944, Amman, Jordan; married; *Religion:* Christian; *Education:* BSc in Chemistry, American University of Beirut, Beirut, Lebanon; MSc in Marketing, Northwestern University, Illinois, USA; PhD in Marketing, University of Illinois; *Career:* Instructor in Marketing, Northern Illinois University; Assistant Professor, Marketing, Northern Illinois University, 1970–71; Assistant for special projects, Royal Scientific Society; Manager, Project Operations Status, Information System, Royal Scientific Society; member of the Board of Directors of Jordan National Bank; Minister of Industry and Trade, 1974–76; businessman, 1976–; *Decorations:* Order of the Jordanian Star, 1st class, Jordan; Order of the Sacred Treasure, First Class, Japan; Das Grosse Goldene Ehrenzeichen am Bande für Verdienste, Austria; *Languages:* Arabic, English; *Address:* Jordan General Business Company, P O Box 2851, Amman, Jordan; telephone: 41836, 42670.

MOUASHIR, Anis, Jordanian businessman/politician; born 1932, Salt, Jordan; married; *Education:* BA in Pharmacy and Chemistry, American University of Beirut, Beirut, Lebanon, 1954; *Career:* Member and Chairman, Economic Community, National Consultancy Council (NCC); Minister of Transport, 1971; Minister of Finance and Transport, 1971–72; Minister of Finance, 1972; Chairman of the Board of Directors of Aladdin Industries Limited, Scientific and Medical Supplies Ltd, Prefabricated Structures Manafacturing Company, Amman Drug and Trading Company; *Interests and Recreations:* President of the Royal Society for the Conservation of Nature; Vice President of the Royal Endowment for Culture and Education; *Languages:* Arabic, English; *Address:* P O Box 1387, Amman, Jordan; telephone: Office — 24907, 39907, 38883, 23702; telex: 21456 SABCO JO.

MOUDARRI, Nicolas Subhi, Syrian aviation official/businessman; born 25 December 1932, Damascus, Syria; married; one son, one daughter; *Religion:* Christian; *Education:* BA; member of Institute of Marketing; *Career:* Assistant Regional Manager of Gulf Area, Air India, Bahrain, 1962–64; Manager of Al-Ghanim Travel Agency, Kuwait, 1965–67; Manager of Kuwait Airways UK, Ireland, Scandinavia, 1967–70; General Manager for Omeir Bin Yousif, Abu Dhabi, United Arab Emirates, 1970–74; Regional Manager of Gulf Air for Europe and America, 1974–80; General Commercial Manager, Gulf Air, Bahrain, 1980; *Interests and Recreations:* yoga, swimming, reading, travel; *Languages:* Arabic, French, English; *Address:* Gulf Air, P O Box 138, Manama, Bahrain; telephone: 236436.

MOUKAYED, Ass'ad, Major General, Syrian administrator/businessman; *Religion:* Muslim; *Education:* RAF Technical College, Hendon, UK; Institute of Higher Air War Studies, Cairo; Flying Course at Hendon, UK; *Career:* Chairman of Syrian Arab Airlines, 1965–68 and 1972–76; Director of Armed Forces Procurement, Syrian Ministry of Defence, 1970–80; Vice President of TAG Group (Techniques d'Avant Garde), Paris, 1980–; *Languages:* Arabic, English, French, Russian; *Address:* 65 Avenue Foch, 1er Etage-Aile droite, 75116 Paris, France.

MOUNAYER, Eustache Joseph, Syrian ecclesiastic; born 6 June 1925, Syria; *Religion:* Christian; *Education:* Seminary of Benedictine Fathers, Jerusalem, Palestine; Patriarchal Seminary, Charfe Lebanon; Pontifical University of Lateran, Rome, Italy; Doctorate, Canon Law; *Career:* ordained priest, Damascus, 1949; Secretary to Archbishop of Damascus and of Apostolic Nuncio; Presi-

dent, Ecclesiastic Court, 1954–59; Secretary to Cardinal Tappouni, Beirut, 1959–71; consecrated Patriarchal Auxiliary Bishop, 1971–78; President, Ecclesiastic Appeal Court, 1960; Director of Arabic language review, *Al-Karama;* Archbishop of Damscus, 1978–; *Publications: Les Synodes Syriens Jacobites Le Shihim Languages:* Arabic, French, Italian, Syriac; *Address:* Syrian Catholic Archbishopric, Bab Sharqi, P O Box 2129, Damascus, Syria.

MOUSLY, Ahmad Muhammad Ali, Saudi Arabian businessman; born 1906; *Religion:* Muslim; *Education:* general; *Career:* Secretary to Minister of Finance and National Economy, 1950–53; attended several economic conferences; private business; *Publications:* a biographer of late King Abdul Aziz; *Address:* P O Box 238, Jeddah; telephone: Office — 23395; Residence — 51790.

MU'ALLA, Shaikh Rashid bin Ahmad al-, United Arab Emirates Ruler of Umm al-Qawain; born 1930; married; *Religion:* Muslim; *Career:* frequently represented Shaikh Ahmad al-Mu'alla at the United Arab Emirates Supreme Council meetings and at many official functions outside Umm al-Qawain; Ruler of Umm al-Qawain, 1981–; *Address:* P O Box 225, Umm al-Qawain, United Arab Emirates.

MU'ALLA, Shaikh Ahmad Bin Rashid al-, United Arab Emirates former Ruler of Umm al-Qawain; born 1904; *Religion:* Muslim; *Career:* Ruler of Umm al-Qawain 1939–81; an authority on tribal affairs; has frequently acted as a mediator on tribal disputes; at present lives mainly at Falaj al-Mu'alla where he is developing local water and agricultural resources; *Decorations:* Medal of the British Empire, MBE, 1950, for his work as a mediator; *Address:* Ruler's Office, P O Box 225, Umm al-Qawain, United Arab Emirates; telephone: 666126; telex: 69711 MUALLA EM.

MU'ALLA, Shaikh Sultan Bin Ahmad al-, United Arab Emirates official; born 1935; second son of the former Ruler of Umm al-Qawain, Shaikh Ahmad al- Mu'alla; *Religion:* Muslim; *Career:* dealt with Umm al-Qawain dispute with Sharjah over oil resources; has wide interests in trade and development; Union Minister of Health, 1971–73; United Arab Emirates Minister of

Economy and Trade, 1973–81; Chairman of Umm al-Qawain Petroleum Department; *Languages:* Arabic, English; *Address:* P O Box 9, Umm al-Qawain, United Arab Emirates.

MUALLA, Jamil Abdul Wahid, Syrian businessman/agricultural expert; born 1919, Antioch, Syria; married; *Education:* BS, Ain Shams University, Cairo, Egypt, 1946–50; postgraduate training, State Agricultural University, Wageningen, Netherlands; *Career:* Inspector of Agricultural Education, Syria, 1950–52; Director of Agriculture, Ministry of Agriculture, Syria, 1952–58; Secretary General, Ministry of Agriculture, Syria, 1958–64; Agricultural Adviser, FAO, Congo, 1964–66; Agricultural Planning Adviser, FAO, Somalia, 1966–68; Senior Agricultural Adviser and Country Representaitve, Somalia, FAO/UNDP, 1968–70; Senior Agricultural Adviser and Country Representative, Jordan, FAO/UNDP, 1970–77; retired from FAO, founded private practice for agricultural consultancy and research, Damascus, Syria, 1977–; *Publications: Principles of Horticulture Fruit Trees in Syria;* several textbooks on the agricultural sciences; *Interests and Recreations:* photography, reading, music, horticulture; *Languages:* Arabic, French, English; *Address:* P O Box 5150, Damscus, Syria; telephone: 115773, 718832; telex: 11035 SUMERT SY.

MUSA, Ismail Al-Haj, Sudanese official/journalist; born 29 March 1944, Al-Obeid, Sudan; *Religion:* Muslim; *Education:* LLB, Faculty of Law, University of Khartoum, Sudan; MA in Sociology, University of Poitiers, France; PhD in Sociology, University of Tours, France; *Career:* Dean of Students, University of Khartoum, 1975; Minister of State for Culture and Information, 1976; Secretary, Committee of Culture and Information, Sudanese Socialist Union, 1978; Editor in Chief, *Al-Ayaam* daily, 1978–; Minister of Culture and Information, 1979–; member of the Political Bureau of the Sudanese Socialist Union, 1980–; *Publications: The Intellectual and His Role,* and other works; *Decorations:* Order of the Republic, 1st Class, Democratic Republic of Sudan, 1979; *Interests and Recreations:* reading, squash; *Languages:* Arabic, English, French; *Address:* Ministry of Culture and Information, Khartoum, Sudan; telephone: 77582.

MUALLA, Mansur, Tunisian politician/economist; born 1 May 1930, Sfax, Tunisia; married; *Religion:* Muslim; *Education:* PhD, Faculty of Law, University of Paris, France; Ecole Nationale d'Administration, Paris; *Career:* Inspectorate-General of Finance, Paris; Technical Adviser to the Ministry of Finance, 1957–58; played leading role in the creation of the Tunisian Central Bank; Director General of the Central Bank, 1958–61; President, Director General of the National Investment Company, 1961; Vice President of the African Development Bank, 1964; Under Secretary of State for Commerce, 1967; Director of Central Administration in the Secretariat of State of the Presidency, 1968–69; Secretary of State then Minister for Posts, Telegraphs and Telecommunications (PTT), 1969–70; Minister of Planning, 1970–74; Minister of Planning and Finance, 1982–; member of the Central Committee, Political Bureau, Destour Socialist Party; *Decorations:* Grand Cordon of Order of Tunisian Republic; Order of Tunisian Independence; *Languages:* Arabic, French; *Address:* 32 Avenue de la République, Carthage, Tunisia.

MUALLA, Shaikh Saud Bin Rashid al-, United Arab Emirates administrator; born 1952; *Religion:* Muslim; *Education:* Oxford University Foreign Diplomatic Course, UK, 1973–74; *Career:* President of Amiri Court, Umm al Quwain; *Languages:* Arabic, English; *Address:* Amiri Court, P O Box 225, Umm al Quwain, United Arab Emirates; telephone: 666125; telex: 69711 MUALLA EM.

MUAYYID, Faruk Yusuf al-, Bahraini businessman; born 26 May, 1944, Manama, Bahrain; married; one son, one daughter; *Religion:* Muslim; *Education:* Diploma, Mechanical Engineering, Loughborough College, UK; *Career:* Vice President of Bahrain Cinema Company; Director of Bahrain Insurance Company, Gulf Publishing Company, Bahrain Hotels Company; *Interests and Recreations:* tennis; *Languages:* Arabic, English; *Address:* P O Box 143, Manama, Bahrain; telephone: 255951; telex: 8270BN.

MUAYYID, Tariq Abdul Rahman al-, Bahraini politician; born 1943; married; two children; *Religion:* Muslim; *Education:* BA in Political Economy, University of Manchester, UK, 1967; *Career:* on return from UK joined father in managing construction materials business; nominated member of Constituent Assembly, 1972; Minister of Information, 1973–; *Languages:* Arabic, English; *Address:* Ministry of Information, P O Box 253, Juffair Road, Juffair, Bahrain; telephone: 727111; telex: 8399 INFORM BN.

MUAYYID, Yusuf Khalil al-, Bahraini banker/businessman; born 1921, Manama, Bahrain; married; two sons, four daughters; *Religion:* Muslim; *Education:* general; *Career:* businessman; Chairman, Y.K. Al-Muayyid and Sons, WLL; Vice Deputy Chairman, National Bank of Bahrain; Director, French Arab Bank; *Interests and Recreations:* tennis, riding; *Languages:* Arabic, English; *Address:* P O Box 106, Manama, Bahrain; telephone: 258800; telex: 8242 NATBNK BN.

MUBARAK, Abdul Aziz Mubarak Latif al-, United Arab Emirates official; born 1933, Abu Dhabi, United Arab Emirates; married; three sons, two daughters; *Religion:* Muslim; *Education:* BA, Administration, Business and Finance; *Career:* Assistant Under Secretary of Finance and Financial Administration, Ministry of Education, UAE; *Interests and Recreations:* gardening, football, Arabic literature; *Languages:* Arabic, English; *Address:* P O Box 3072, Abu Dhabi, United Arab Emirates.

MUBARAK, Ahmad Bin Abdul Aziz al-, United Arab Emirates judge; born 1910, Saudi Arabia; married; two sons, three daughters; *Religion:* Muslim; *Education:* private studies with Ulema in Saudi Arabia and Dubai; *Career:* Qadi (Islamic Law Judge) in Saudi Arabia, 1950–1958; Chief Qadi and Adviser for Religious Affairs to HH The Head of State; member of the Islamic Union, Mecca, Saudi Arabia 1976; *Publications:* in Arabic: *Islamic Education; The Mosque; About Islam and Muslims; The Message and the Mosque; About Law and Islam; Interests and Recreations:* hunting, religious and Islamic affairs, literature and poetry; *Address:* Sharia Chief Qadi's Office, P O Box 7, Abu Dhabi, United Arab Emirates.

MUBARAK, Khalifa Ahmad al-, United Arab Emirates diplomat; born 1947, Abu Dhabi; married; two sons, one daughter; *Religion:* Muslim; *Education:* BA in Socio-logy; Diploma in Literature; *Career:* Personnel Department, Ministry of Foreign Affairs; Ambassador to Sudan, 1973–76; Ambassador to Syria, 1976–80; Ambassador to France; UAE Representative to UNESCO; *Publications:* research on the development of the bedouin in Arabic, Beirut, 1972; *Decorations:* Order of the Two Niles, Sudan; Order of Merit, Syria; *Interests and Recreations:* hunting, football, poetry, theatre; *Languages:* Arabic, English; *Address:* Embassy of UAE, 3 Rue Lota, Paris 16, France.

MUBARAK, Muhammad Husni, Egyptian politician, President of Egypt; born 4 May 1928, Kafr al-Musailha, Minufiya, Egypt; married; two children; *Religion:* Muslim; *Education:* Military Academy, 1947–49; Air Academy, 1949–50; *Career:* Air Force, 1950–52; Instructor, Air Academy, 1952–59; Commander of an L-28 Air Squadron, and later of a TU-16 Jet Fighter Brigade; training missions to the Soviet Union, 1959–64; Higher Studies Course at Frunze Military Academy in the Soviet Union, 1964–65; Commander of various air bases, 1965–67; Director General of the Air Academy, 1967–69; Chief of Staff of the Air Forces, 1969–72; Commander in Chief of the Air Force, 1972; Lieutenant General, 1973; Vice President of Egypt, 1975; Head of Egypt's delegations to the Organization of African Unity Conferences in Uganda and Mauritius, 1975, 1976; elected Vice Chairman of the National Democratic Party; elected Secretary General of the National Democratic Party, 1981; nominated by the National Democatic Party and the People's Assembly to stand as candidate for the Presidency, 7 October 1981; elected President of the Republic, 1981; elected Chairman of the National Democratic Party, 1982; *Decorations:* Order of the Star of Sinai, 1973; *Address:* The Presidency, Cairo, Egypt.

MUCHABIK, George M., Jordanian UN official; born 29 November 1922, Jerusalem; married; two sons, one daughter; *Religion:* Christian; *Education:* Degree in Book-keeping, Accounting and Commercial Correspondence; *Career:* served in United Nations Organization in Chile, 1951–56, New York, 1957–58, Ethiopia, 1959–60; UN Operation in Congo, 1960–61; Financial Officer in Chile, 1961–62; Deputy Chief, Economic Commission for Asia and the Far East, 1962–72; Acting Chief, Division of Administration, Economic Commission for Latin America (ECLA), 1972–73; Deputy Chief, Division of Administration, ECLA, Santiago, Chile, 1973–; *Interests and Recreations:* fishing, soccer; *Languages:* Arabic, English, French, Spanish; *Address:* United Nations Building, Avenida Dag Hammarskjold, Casilla 179D, Santiago, Chile; telephone: 485051.

MUDARIS, Abdul Karim Abdul Kadir al-, Iraqi official/lawyer; born 1932, Basra, Iraq; married; one son, three daughters; *Religion:* Muslim; *Education:* Faculty of Law, University of Baghdad, Iraq, 1958; MA in Economics and Social Science, Cairo University, Cairo, Egypt, 1960; *Career:* Arab League Office, 1955; Kuwait Ministry of Justice, 1961–65; Counsellor, Arab League Office, UK, 1969; Acting Director General, Arab League Office, UK, 1970–71, 1972–74; founding member, Secretary General and Chief Executive, Arab British Chamber of Commerce, UK, 1974–; First Counsellor, Iraqi Embassy, London; *Publications:* several studies and research papers; *Interests and Recreations:* music, literature, poetry, swimming; *Languages:* Arabic, English; *Address:* Arab British Chamber of Commerce, 42 Berkeley Square, London W1, UK.

MUDAWI, Al-BaKir Yusuf, Sudanese banker; born 1933, Sudan; married; *Religion:* Muslim; *Education:* BA in Economics, University of Khartoum, Sudan, 1955; Diploma in Economics, University of Oxford, Oxford, England, 1962–64; *Career:* Ministry of Finance, Khartoum, Sudan, 1955; Bank of Sudan, 1960; Assistant General Manager, Deputy General Manager, Bank of Sudan, Khartoum, Sudan, 1967–78; General Manager, Faisal Islamic Bank, Khartoum, Sudan, 1978–; *Languages:* Arabic, English; *Address:* Faisal Islamic Bank, P O Box 2415, Khartoum, Sudan; telephone: 75367, 75371, 75374; telex: 22519 FIB SD.

MUDHAFFAR, Ismail Ali, Bahraini accountant; born 9 October 1942; married; two daughters, three sons; *Religion:* Muslim; *Education:* Associate Cost and Management Accountant, UK; *Career:* Chief Accountant, Ministry of Health, 1973; Director of Finance and Personnel Affairs, Ministry of Health, 1975; member of the Board of Bahrain Aluminium Extrusion Co; *Interests and Recreations:* billiards, table tennis, cards,

chess, reading, travel; *Languages:* Arabic, English; *Address:* P O Box 12 Manama, Bahrain; telephone: Office — 252755; Residence — 325500.

MUFFARRIJ, Abdullah Ibrahim al-, Kuwaiti official/educationalist; born 1937; *Religion:* Muslim; *Education:* Degree in Islamic Affairs, Cairo University, Egypt, 1959; *Career:* Assistant Under Secretary for Social and Cultural Affairs, Ministry of Education, 1973–75; Minister of Justice, Waqfs and Islamic Affairs, 1975–76; *Address:* Ministry of Education, P O Box 7, Kuwait.

MUFLIH, Riyadh Said al-, Jordanian lawyer/businessman; born 1909, Salt, Jordan; married; *Religion:* Muslim; *Education:* Licence in Law, Damascus University, Syria, 1930; *Career:* Clerk of the Juvenile Court, 1930–32; Chief Clerk of Irbid Court, 1932; Attorney General of Karak, 1933–35; Civil Magistrate, Irbid, 1935–37; President of Irbid Court of First Instance and member of the High Court, 1942–45; Assistant Director of Lands, 1945–47; Director of the Interior, 1947; Under Secretary, Ministry of Interior, 1951–55; Minister of State for Foreign Affairs, and Prime Minister for Ministerial Affairs; Minister of Education, 1958–59; Senator, 1963–67; Chairman of the Board of Jordan Iron and Steel Industry Company and Jordan Cement Company since their foundation; Chairman of the Board of Jordan Paper Products Company Ltd, 1978–; Chairman and Director of the National Steel Industry Company Ltd, 1979–; member of the Jordanian Chamber of Deputies, 1968–74; Government Representative on Joint Education Committee, 1970; Senator, 1974–; *Decorations:* Order of the Jordanian Star 1st Class; *Address:* Office— Jordan Iron and Steel Industry Company Ltd, P O Box 1972, Jabal Amman, Al-Tamine Building, Amman, Jordan; telephone: 38227/8; telex: 1279 JISICO; Residence — Jabal Amman, Amman Jordan; telephone: 41092.

MUFTI, Fuad Sadik, Saudi Arabian diplomat; born 1937, Medina, Saudi Arabia; *Religion:* Muslim; *Education:* BCom, Economics and Political Science, Faculty of Commerce, Cairo University, Egypt, 1960; *Career:* former Attaché, Foreign Ministry; Assistant Director, Personnel Department; Counsellor, Embassy to Lebanon; Secretary, Chargé d'Affaires, Embassy to Mali; Assistant

Director, Personnel Department, Ministry of Foreign Affairs; Secretary, Embassy to Switzerland; Chargé d'Affaires, Embassy in Cameroon and Gabon; Press Counsellor, Embassy in Paris; *Publications:* radio programmes for the Saudi Arabian Broadcasting Service; edited a weekly page in *Al-Bilad* daily newspaper, under the pseudonym Abu Lamis; novel published by Tihama Organisation, Saudi Arabia; *Interests and Recreations:* reading, writing, music; *Address:* Saudi Arabian Embassy, 5 Avenue Hoche, 75008, Paris, France.

MUFTI, Said al-, Jordanian politician; born 1898, Amman, Jordan; married; *Religion:* Muslim; *Education:* general; *Career:* Deputy Administrative Governor of Amman, 1924; Administrative Governor of Amman, 1925; Mayor of Amman, 1927; District Officer of Madaba, 1928; member of Legislative Council, 1929–31, 1931–34; Mayor of Amman, 1938; Director of the Treasury, 1939; Director of Interior, 1941; Minister of Communications, 1944; Minister of Interior, 1944–45; Minister of Finance and Minister of Communications, 1945; member of Chamber of Deputies, 1947–50; Minister of Commerce, Agriculture and Supply, 1947–48; Minister of Interior, 1948–50; Prime Minister, 1950; member of Chamber of Deputies, 1950–51; Deputy Prime Minister and Minister of Interior, 1951; member of Chamber of Deputies, 1951–54; Deputy Prime Minister, and Minister of Interior, 1951–52, 1952–53; Deputy Prime Minister, and Minister of State, 1953–54; Prime Minister, and Minister of Foreign Affairs, 1955; Prime Minister, 1956; Deputy Prime Minister and Minister of Interior, and Minister of Agriculture, 1957; member of the Arab Union Council, 1958; Senator, 1959–63; member of the Jordanian University Board of Trustees, 1962; Deputy Prime Minister, 1963; Deputy Prime Minister, 1963–64; Speaker of the Senate, 1963–67; President of the Jordan University Board of Trustees, 1967–72; Speaker of the Senate, 1967–71, 1971–73, 1973–74; *Decorations:* Independence Medal, 1st Class; Star of Jordan, 1st Class; Renaissance Medal 1st Class; Renaissance Jewelled Medal; Iraqi Rafidain Medal; Syrian Medal of Merit; Order of the Holy Sepulchre; *Address:* The Senate, Amman, Jordan.

MUGSABI, Amr Ahmad al-, Libyan administrator; *Religion:* Muslim; *Career:* senior official, Ministry of Education; member of Faculty of Agriculture, Tripoli University, Libya; Minister of State for Nutrition and Marine Wealth, 1974–77; Secretary for Nutrition and Marine Wealth, General People's Committee, 1977; *Address:* Office of Secretary for Nutrition and Marine Wealth, Tripoli, Libya.

MUHAMMAD, Abdul Hafiz, Jordanian journalist; born 1928, Haifa, Palestine; married; *Religion:* Muslim; *Career:* Secretary of the Arab Merchants Association, Haifa, 1947; member of Arab Finance House, Haifa, 1947–48; member of Haifa Municipality, 1948; Secretary of the Council of Emigrants, Nablus, 1948–51; Editor, *Al-Jazira* newspaper, Amman, 1951–53; Correspondent of Arab News Agency, 1953–59; Arab League Representative, Jordan, 1959–71; Correspondent, *Al-Usbu Al-Arabi,* 1959–82; Owner and Editor, *Akhbar Al-Usbu* newspaper, 1959–75; *Publications: The Road to the Holy Land,* 1967; *The Struggle of a Great Man,* 1968; *The River that United the Arabs,* 1964; *Address:* P O Box 605, Amman, Jordan; telephone: 665330, 667330.

MUHAMMAD AL-ABDULLAH AL-FAISAL, HRH Prince, Saudi Arabian Prince/official; born 1943, Mecca, Saudi Arabia; son of HRH Prince Abdullah Bin Faisal and grandson of late King Faisal; *Religion:* Muslim; *Education:* BCom; *Career:* Accountant, Saudi Arabian Monetary Agency (SAMA), Director, Organization and Administration Unit; Director General for Administration, Ministry of Education, 1972; Assistant Under Secretary of State for Administrative Affairs, Ministry of Educationn; Chairman of Cement Co, Qassim Sugar Co, Jeddah, AMIANTIT Industries, Dammam; *Publications:* collection of poems; *Interests and Recreations:* hunting, sports; *Languages:* Arabic, English; *Address:* AMIANTIT Industries Ltd, P O Box 589 Dammam, Saudi Arabia; Ministry of Education, Riyadh, Saudi Arabia; telephone: Office— Riyadh 21 606, Residence— Riyadh 57 885.

MUHAMMAD, Al-Bushra A. Hamid, Sudanese lawyer; resident in Yemen Arab Republic; born 1952, Dongola, Sudan; married; *Religion:* Muslim; *Education:* LLB, University of Khartoum, Sudan; Bar Examination Certificate; *Career:* Assistant Labour Inspector, Labour Department, Sudan, 1976; 2nd Class Magistrate, Sudan, 1976–77; Advocate and Commissioner for Oaths, 1977–; Resident Manager, Technical Consultation Bureau, Sudanese Consultancy Company, Sana'a, Yeman Arab Republic; Partner, Adham and Abu Al-Riish and Co, Sudanese Firm of Solicitors, Khartoum, Sudan; member of the Sudanese Bar Association, 1977; *Interests and Recreations:* swimming, basket ball; *Languages:* Arabic, English; *Address:* P O Box 2272, Sudan, Khartoum; telephone: 79279, 81489, telex: 659; P O Box 2237, Sana'a, Yeman Arab Republic; telephone: 74178, telex: 2201.

MUHAMMAD, Ali Nassir, People's Democratic Republic of Yemen President; born 31 December, 1939, Eastern District, Governorate of Abyan, People's Democratic Republic of Yemen; *Religion:* Muslim; *Education:* Teachers Training College, 1959; military training at Egyptian Commando School, 1965; training course with military engineers, 1965; *Career:* teacher, before Independence; Military Commander of the Central Front, 1964; Governor of Lahej, 1968; Minister of Local Governments, 1968; Minister of Education, 1974–75; Prime Minister and Minister of Defence, 1978–; Chairman of the Presidium of the Supreme People's Council and Secretary General of the Yemen Socialist Party, elected by First General Congress of the Yemeni Party, 1978–; *Interests and Recreations:* sports, especially swimming; *Address:* Presidency House, Steamer Point, Aden, People's Democratic Republic of Yemen.

MUHAMMAD BIN ABDUL AZIZ, HRH Prince, Saudi Arabian Prince/businessman; born 1910, Riyadh, Saudi Arabia; eldest son of late King Abdul Aziz, and full brother of late King Khalid in whose favour he withdrew his claim to the Heir Apparency in 1964; *Religion:* Muslim; *Career:* entered the Holy City of Medina at the head of the forces at the end of the Hijaz war, and was given title of Governor of Medina by his father the King; participated in the historic battle of Sabla; businessman; *Address:* Royal Court, Riyadh, Saudi Arabia.

MUHAMMAD BIN FAHD, HRH Prince, Saudi Arabian Prince/businessman; born 1950; *Religion:* Muslim; *Education:* BA in Political Sciences, USA; *Career:* businessman; Chairman of Al-Bilad Corporation; Chairman of Arabian Helicopters Ltd; *Languages:* Arabic, English; *Address:* Arabian Helicopters Ltd, P O Box 2528 Dhahran, Saudi Arabia.

MUHAMMAD BIN FAISAL, HRH Prince, Saudi Arabian Prince/businessman; born 1937; second son of late King Faisal; married; *Religion:* Muslim; *Education:* The Hun School, Princeton, USA, and Laurenceville Academy; BA, California, USA; *Career:* entered administration in 1963; employed with Saudi Arabian Monetary Agency (SAMA); formerly Director of the Office of Saline Water Conversion, Ministry of Water and Agriculture; member of numerous Saudi delegations to UN General Assembly and FAO meetings in Rome, Italy; leading role in the creation of a massive programme for desalination projects; currently President of Faisal Islamic Bank; *Languages:* Arabic, English, Turkish; *Address:* Faisal Islamic Bank, Jeddah, Saudi Arabia.

MUHAMMAD BIN TALAL, HRH Prince, Jordanian Prince; brother and personal representative of HM King Hussain of Jordan; born 1941; second son of late King Talal; married; two sons; *Religion:* Muslim; *Education:* Bishops School, Amman; Islamic College, Amman; Bryanston School, UK; cadet at Iraqi Military Academy, 1957; *Career:* President of the Council of Tribal Shaikhs, 1971; resigned on health grounds, 1973; Personal Representative of HM King Hussain, 1974; *Languages:* Arabic, English; *Address:* Royal Palace, Amman, Jordan.

MUHAMMAD, Field-Marshal Anwar, Jordanian army officer; born 1926, Amman, Jordan; married; *Religion:* Muslim; *Education:* general; *Career:* soldier in Jordanian Army, 1945; Major, 1964; King's Companion and Commander of his Personal Guard, 1964–67; Chief Companion to HM King Hussain, 1967–71; Director General of Security, 1971; *Decorations:* Military Promotion Medal; Renaissance Medal; Star of Jordan; Independence Medal, Palestine Brigades; *Address:* Jabal Amman, Jordan.

MUHAMMAD, Mahdi Abdullah, People's Democratic Republic of Yemen politician/trade unionist; *Career:* worked in Bank of Yemen; Secretary General of the General Union of Workers in Banks and Insurance Organizations (Public Sector Union), 1971; President of the General Confederation of Republic Workers, 1971, member of the Central Committee; member of People's Supreme Council; *Address:* General Confederation of Republic Workers, Aden, People's Democratic Republic of Yemen.

MUHAMMAD, Muhammad Ali Bin Salih, Saudi Arabian aviation official; born 1932, Medina, Saudi Arabia; *Religion:* Muslim; *Education:* diploma in journalism; *Career:* extensive experience in aviation, administrative and technical affairs; Director of Civil Aviation Affairs, Administration Bureau of Minister of Defence and Aviation; *Interests and Recreations:* philately, travel; *Address:* Bureau of HRH Minister of Defence and Aviation, Airport Road, Riyadh, Saudi Arabia; telex: 201188 MDA SJ.

MUHAMMAD, Zahida Ibrahim, Iraqi administrator/librarian; born 1926, Baghdad, Iraq; *Religion:* Muslim; *Education:* LLB, 1948; Victoria School of Libraries, Melbourne, Australia, 1954; Library Studies, Rutgers University, New Brunswick, New York, USA, 1958–59; six months Training Programme, Princeton University Library, New York, USA, 1959; four months Librarian Training Programme, Copenhagen, Denmark, 1967; *Career:* Director, College of Education Library, University of Baghdad, 1950–58; Librarian, Central Library, University of Baghdad, 1959–63; Director, Archives Department, Central Library, University of Baghdad, 1964–75; Director General, Central Library, University of Baghdad, 1975–; *Publications:* numerous researches and studies, and several books on library science; *Languages:* Arabic, English; *Address:* Central Library, University of Baghdad, P O Box 12 Wazyria, Baghdad, Iraq.

MUHIYDDIN, Khalid, Egyptian politician; born 1922; *Religion:* Muslim; *Education:* Military Academy; BA in Commerce, Cairo University, 1951; Cavalry Officer; *Career:* member of the Nine Man Committee of Free Officers which organized 1952 Revolution; member of the National Production Council; founded evening neswpaper *AL-Masa,* 1955 ,

and Editor until March 1959; elected member of the National Assembly; Chairman of the National Assembly High Dam Committee, 1964; Chief Editor of *Al-Akhbar,* 1964; Secretary for the press in the Secretariat General of the Arab Socialist Union (ASU), 1964; member of the Presidential Council of the World Peace Council, 1958; Secretary General of the Egyptian National Peace Council, 1967, Central Committee of ASU, 1968; re-elected to the National Assembly, 1969; Chairman of the Assembly, 1969; Chairman of the Assembly Commission Public Services; elected to People's Assembly, October 1976, and leader of Progressive Unionist Party; *Decorations:* Lenin Peace Prize, 1970; *Languages:* Arabic, English; *Address:* National Progressive Unionist Party, Kasr al Nil Street, Cairo, Egypt; 6 Gezira Street, Zamalek, Cairo, Egypt.

MUHSIN, Muhammad Said Abdullah, People's Democratic Republic of Yemen politician; born North Yemen; married; two sons; *Career:* member of the General Command, 1968; Head of the Criminal Investigation Department, 1969; Head of the Revolutionary Security Department, 1970; member of the Central Committee of the National Front Political Organization, 1972; Minister of State for Security, 1974; *Interests and Recreations:* literature, mainly fiction; sports, especially watching football; President of the Executive Committee of the Higher Sports Council in the First Governorate; *Languages:* Arabic, English; *Address:* Ministry of Security, Aden, People's Democratic Republic of Yemen.

MUHYIDDIN, Ahmad Fuad, Egyptian politician/physician; born 1926; married; one son, one daughter; *Religion:* Muslim; *Education:* Degree in Medicine; *Career:* Vice-Chairman of Federation of University Students, 1946; Professor in the Faculty of Medicine, Qasr al-Aini Hospital; Director of the Office of the Minister of Health; represented Egypt at International Disarmament Conference in Japan, 1958; Doctor in Radiography, 1961; elected member of the National Congress, 1962; member of the National Assembly, 1957, 1960, 1964; in the last National Assembly was also Chairman of the Arab Affairs Committee; appointed Arab Socialist Union (ASU) Secretary for Qalubiyah, 1965; Governor of Sharqiyah, 1968; Governor of Alexandria, 1971; Governor of Giza, 1972;

Minister of State for the Local Government Secretariat, 1973, and People's Organizations; Resident Egyptian Minister in Tripoli, Libya, 1974; Minister of Health, 1974–76; Minister of State for People's Assembly Affairs, 1976; *Address:* Ministry of People's Assembly Affairs, Cairo, Egypt.

MUHYIDDIN, Zakaria, Egyptian politician/army officer; born May 1918; married; *Religion:* Muslim; *Education:* Military Academy and Staff College, Cairo; *Career:* infantry officer; member of Free Officers Executive Committee which organized 1952 Revolution; member of the Revolutionary Command Council; Minister of the Interior, 1953; Federal Minister of the Interior, United Arab Republic, 1958; Chairman of the Aswan High Dam Committee, 1960; Minister of the Interior, 1961; member of the Presidential Council, 1962; Prime Minister, 1965–66; Deputy Prime Minister, for Economic Affairs, 1967; left politics, 1968; *Languages:* Arabic, English; *Address:* 68 Khalifa al-Mamoun Street, Manshiet al-Bakri, Cairo, Egypt.

MUKADDIM, Sadik, Tunisian politician/diplomat; born 24 February 1914, Tunis, Tunisia; married; six children; *Religion:* Muslim; *Education:* Degree in Medicine, University of Paris; *Career:* President of the Association of North African Students in Paris; Minister of Justice, 1954–55; Minister of Public Health, 1955–57; member of Constituent Assembly, 1956–59; member of National Assembly, 1959–; Secretary of State, Minister of Foreign Affairs, 1957–62; attended Monrovia Conference, 1959; accompanied President Bourguiba on his state visit to UK, 1961; Ambassador to France, 1962–64; elected President of the National Assembly, 1964 and since then elected unanimously each year; *Decorations:* Grand Cordon of the Order of Tunisian Independence; Grand Cordon of the Order of the Tunisian Republic; Honorary Knight of the British Empire; *Languages:* Arabic, French; *Address:* National Assembly, Le Bardo, Tunis, Tunisia; telephone: 262800.

MUKHTAR, Ali Muhammad Abbas, Saudi Arabian official; born 1936, Jeddah, Saudi Arabia; *Religion:* Muslim; *Education:* general; *Career:* Director of Immigration Department, Jeddah; Director of Department of Tourism; Manager of the Office of the

Minister of Pilgrimage and Endowments; Deputy Minister of Pilgrimage and Waqfs (Endowments) for Pilgrimage Affairs; Secretary General, Muslim World League; member of General Secretariat of the Conference of the Prophet's Tradition; attended Conference of Public Administration, Beirut, Lebanon; established a charity organization *Sunduq Mabarrat al-Haram,* financed through his own funds; *Interests and Recreations:* swimming, reading, sports; *Address:* Al-Nuzha, Mecca, Saudi Arabia; Muslim World League, Mecca, Saudi Arabia; telephone: Office — 5743573; Residence — 5423845.

MUKHTAR, Fuad Muhammad, Saudi Arabian official; born 1936; *Religion:* Muslim; *Education:* BCom, Accountancy, University of Surrey, UK; attended Chartered Accountancy Training Course with Whinney Murray & Co, Chartered Accountants, London, UK; *Career:* Manager, Revenues Audit Administration, Saudi Arabian Airlines (SAUDIA); Chief, Individual Companies Department, Ministry of Commerce Branch, Jeddah; Chairman, Board for the Settlement of Commercial Disputes; Assistant Director for Industry; Director, Legal Department; Director, Home Trade Department, Ministry of Commerce; member of Board of Industrial Estate, Jeddah; Director of Jeddah Industrial Estate; *Interests and Recreations:* travel, reading, playing and listening to music; *Address:* Jeddah Industrial Estate, Jeddah, Saudi Arabia; telephone: Jeddah 34929.

MUKHTAR, Muhammad Gamaliddin, Egyptian academic/archaeologist; born 14 July 1918, Alexandria, Egypt; *Religion:* Muslim; *Education:* BA in Geography, Cairo University; MA in Archaeology, Cairo University; Diploma in Education, Iowa State Teachers College; PhD Archaeology, Ain Shams University, Cairo, Egypt; *Career:* Assistant Lecturer, Institute of Education, Alexandria, 1944; Lecturer, Teachers Institute, Cairo, 1950; Assistant Professor, Faculty of Education, Cairo, 1956; Head of Scientific Section Centre of Documentation, Cairo, 1957; First Archaeologist, Centre of Documentation, Cairo, 1961; General Director of Egyptian Department of Antiquities, 1967; Under Secretary of State for Antiquities, 1968; President of Egyptian Organization of Antiquities, 1972; Professor of History and Archaeology, Helwan University, 1977; Professor of Archaeology, Faculty of Arts, Riyadh University, 1978–; Vice President of International Council of Monuments and Sites, Paris, 1974–; Vice President, and member of the Scientific Commitee For Drafting the General History of Africa, UNESCO; Honorary President of the International Society of Egyptology; Honorary member of the German, Czechoslovakian and Austrian Archaelogical Societies and the American Centre of Research, Cairo; *Publications:* Director of Second Volume of *History of Africa,* UNESCO 1980, English, French and Arabic; Director of the *Encyclopedia of Egyptian Civilization,* Cairo, Volume I 1974, Volume II 1976; numerous books and articles in Arabic, English, and French; *Decorations:* Honorary Doctor, University of Montpellier, France, 1972; Officier de la Légion d'Honueur, France; Commander, Légion d'Honueur; Decoration des Universités; Décoration de Culture, and several other medals and decorations from Poland, Germany, Italy, Austria and Columbia; *Languages:* Arabic, English, French, German; *Address:* 22 Murad Street, Cairo, Egypt; telephone: 853535; Wihdat Al Sharq Hotel, Airport Street, Riyadh, Saudi Arabia; telephone: 4038800.

MUKHTAR, Ridha Muhammad Abbas, Saudi Arabian diplomat; born 1937, Jeddah, Saudi Arabia; *Religion:* Muslim; *Education:* general; *Career:* Ministry of Foreign Affairs, 1956; served in Saudi Arabian Embassies in Turkey, France and Iran; Chargé d'Affaires, Saudi Arabian Embassy, Mauritania; Vice Consul of the Saudi Arabian Embassy in Geneva; *Interests and Recreations:* music, sport; *Address:* Ministry of Foreign Affairs, P O Box 495, Jeddah, Saudi Arabia; telephone: 642 1322; telex: 401104 KHARJI SJ.

MULHIM, Muhammad Abdul Latif al-, Saudi Arabian politician; born 1936; *Religion:* Muslim; *Education:* MA, PhD, Business Administration; *Career:* former Lecturer, Faculty of Commerce, Riyadh University; Dean, Faculty of Commerce, Riyadh University; Minister of State without portfolio, 1975–; *Publications:* university textbooks on economics and business administration; *Interests and Recreations:* reading, sport; *Address:* Council of Ministers, Riyadh, Saudi Arabia; telephone: 4044200; telex: 201039 CABINET SJ.

MULLA, Muhammad Said al-, United Arab Emirates politician/businessman; born 1925; married; *Religion:* Muslim; *Career:* several business interests; Director of the National Bank of Dubai; Director of the Dubai Electricity Company; Minister of Communications, 1977–; *Address:* Ministry of Communications, P O Box 900, Abu Dhabi, United Arab Emirates; telephone: 362901; telex: 22668 CONNSAD EM.

MULLA, Najib al-Abdullah al-, Kuwaiti businessman; born 2 August 1941, Kuwait; married; four children; *Religion:* Muslim; *Education:* in Lebanon, England, Switzerland; *Career:* Head of Al-Mulla Group of Companies; Owner of Mitsubishi, NCR, GEC (UK), and other agencies; Director of several engineering and construction businesses; *Languages:* Arabic, English; *Address:* Bader Al-Mulla and Bros, P O Box 177, Safat, Kuwait; telephone: 423231.

MUMNI, Hassan Ahmad al-, Jordanian politician/official; born 11 November 1937, Jordan; married; four sons, three daughters; *Religion:* Muslim; *Education:* BA in Law, University of Baghdad, Iraq; *Career:* Claims Officer in Kuwait; Income Tax Officer, 1962–65; Director of Judicial Affairs Ministry of Interior, 1965–70; Provincial Governor, Ministry of Interior, 1970–77; Provincial Governor, Mayor of Irbid, 1978–79; member of the National Consultative Council, 1980; Minister for Municipal Rural Affairs and the Environment, 1980–; *Publications:* several works on local government and municipal affairs in Arabic; *Decorations:* Order of the Jordanian Star, 1981; *Languages:* Arabic, English; *Address:* P O Box 1799 Amman, Jordan; telephone: 845655.

MUNAIS, Sami Ahmad Abdul Aziz al-, Kuwaiti journalist; born 1933; *Religion:* Muslim; *Education:* in Kuwait and Cairo, 1952–54; *Career:* member of Department of Public Health, 1958–63; Chief Editor, *Al Talia* weekly, 1964–; member of National Assembly, 1963–65 and 1971–75; elected Secretary to Assembly, 1971 but defeated in October; elected President of Kuwait Journalists' Association, 1972; *Languages:* Arabic, English; *Address:* Al-Tali'a, P O Box 1082, Mubarak al-Kabir Street, Kuwait.

MUNJIM, Ali Abdullah al-, Saudi Arabian businessman; born 1943, Saudi Arabia; married; two daughters, three sons; *Religion:* Muslim; *Education:* general; *Career:* Deputy Director, Abdullah Ali Al Munjim Stores; Director General, Abdullah Ali Al-Munjim Fridges and Stores, Riyadh Company for Trade and Refrigeration, Barida Company for Trade and Refrigeration; member of the Board of the Chamber of Commerce and Industry, Riyadh, 1979–; *Interests and Recreations:* travel; *Languages:* Arabic, English; *Address:* Al Sittin Balmi 2, Thaleyit Al Munkim, P O Box 1544, Riyadh, Saudi Arabia; telephone: 4766126, 4767127.

MUNTASIR, Umar al-, Libyan oil official/accountant; born 1938, Tripoli, Libya; *Religion:* Muslim; *Education:* Business Administration, American University of Beirut, Lebanon, 1960; MA, American University of Beirut, Lebanon, 1967; *Career:* Accountant for Mobil Oil, 1966; played prominent part in oil workers' strike after June 1967 war; imprisoned by pre-Revolutionary régime, February 1969, for membership of Arab Nationalist Movement; released after 1969 Revolution; Director General, Economic Department, Ministry of Petroleum and Libyan representative to OPEC, 1969; Under Secretary, Ministry of Petroleum, 1971; Chairman of Oasis Oil Company, and Director General of National Oil Company, 1973; led Libyan delegation in talks with Occidental Oil Company to settle dispute over Occidental contract, 1975; *Languages:* Arabic, English; *Address:* Oasis Oil Company of Libya, P O Box 305, Tripoli, Libya; telephone: 31116.

MUQBIL, Hanna (Abu Thair), Palestinian journalist; *Career:* Secretary of the Federation of Palestinian Writers; Editor of resistance magazine *Falastin al-Thawra;* replaced by Ahmed Abdul Rahman, former Director of *Voice of Palestine,* Syria Radio January 1974,

MUQBILI, Hussain Muhammad, Yemen Arab Republic diplomat; born 1925; married; three sons; *Religion:* Muslim; *Education:* Science School, 1948; College of Sciences, Cairo, Egypt, 1957; *Career:* participated in the 1948 revolt against Imam Yahya; Commander of the National Guard; after the failure of the Revolution went to Aden, Asmara, Sudan and Egypt; 1st Secretary, Yemeni Embassy, Amman, Jordan; Counsellor and Minister Plenipotentiary in Baghdad, 1962–65; Under Secretary, Ministry of Foreign Affairs, 1966; Director of the General Civil Service Organization; Under Secretary, Ministry of Foreign Affairs with rank of Minister; *Decorations:* Ethiopian Order, 1962; *Interests and Recreations:* writing short stories, reading, walking, poultry-farming; *Languages:* Arabic, English, German; *Address:* Bir al-Shayef, Sana'a, Yemen Arab Republic; telephone: 8488.

MUQRIN BIN ABDUL AZIZ, HRH Prince, Saudi Arabian Prince/administrator; born 1942, Riyadh, Saudi Arabia; son of late King Abdul Aziz; *Religion:* Muslim; *Career:* former Saudi Air Force pilot; Governor of Hail, 1980–; *Address:* The Northern Principality, Hail, Saudi Arabia.

MURAD, Mahmud Sidki, Egyptian official/banker; born 13 December 1918, Benha, Egypt; married; *Religion:* Muslim; *Education:* BA in Commerce, Cairo University, Egypt; Higher Studies in Commerce, Alexandria University, Egypt; *Career:* Secretary General, Ministry of Municipal and Rural Affairs; Under Secretary, Ministry of Supply; Under Secretary, Ministry of Commerce and Foreign Trade; Chairman, General Organization for Foreign Trade; Chairman, Egyptian Real Estate Bank; Deputy Governor, Central Bank; Deputy Minister of Economy and Foreign Trade; Adviser to Ministry of Economy and Trade, United Arab Emirates Government; Chairman of UAE Development Bank; Adviser to UAE Commercial Trading Co; member of Eisenhower Committee, USA; Fellow of World Bank Development Institute, Washington D.C.; Lecturer in Higher Studies Department, Faculty of Commerce, Cairo University, Egypt, and other Egyptian Institutions; Chairman and Managing Director of Delta International Bank; *Publications: The Monetary Budget,* co-author with Fuad Mursi; *Economic Development in the UAE,* and a series of information booklets for Ministry of Tourism, Abu Dhabi; *Decorations:* from Somalia and Yugoslavia; *Interests and Recreations:* long distance swimming, diving; member of the Commercial Club and the Heliopolis Club, Cairo; *Address:* 162 Al-Hegaz Street, Heliopolis, Cairo, Egypt; telephone: 753994.

MURAD, Muhammad Mutaz, Arab-American banker; born 30 June 1941, Damascus, Syria; married; one son, one daughter; *Religion:* Muslim; *Education:* BA in Accounting, Cleary College, School of Banking, University of Michigan, USA; School of Bank Administration, University of Wisconsin, USA; MA, Stonier Graduate School of Banking, Rutgers University, USA; MA in Business Administration, University of Miami, USA; Executive Management Programme, Harvard University, USA; *Career:* Comptroller, National Bank and Trust Co, Michigan, USA, 1967–73; District Comptroller, Corporate Finance Officer, Sun Bank Florida, Inc, 1973–76; Executive Vice President, Sun Bank of Miami, 1976–81; Senior Vice President and Deputy General Manager, Al-Bahrain Arab African Bank, 1981–; member of Michigan Bankers Association; Committee Member of Strategic Planning; *Publications:* various articles in banking publications; frequent speaker in seminars on banking issues; *Interests and Recreations:* racquet ball, music, reading; *Languages:* Arabic, English; *Address:* P O Box 20488, Manama, Bahrain.

MURAD, Murad Ali, Bahraini banker; born 1945, Manama, Bahrain; married; two sons; *Religion:* Muslim; *Education:* General Certificate of Education; Institute of Cost and Management, UK; *Career:* Citibank, 1972–76; National Bank of Bahrain, 1977–79; Senior Manager, Saudi National Bank of Bahrain, 1979–; member of the Board of Directors of Arab Asian Bank; Council member of Bankers Society of Bahrain; member of Arab Bankers Association, London, UK; *Interests and Recreations:* soccer, jogging; *Languages:* Arabic, English; *Address:* Saudi National Commercial Bank of Bahrain, P O Box 20363, Manama, Bahrain; telephone: 231182.

MURAD, Mustafa Kamil, Egyptian politician; born 1926; married; *Religion:* Muslim; *Education:* Military Academy, Cairo, 1948; BCom, 1954; MA in Political Science, 1957; *Career:* artillery officer, Palestine War, 1948; participated in 23 July 1952 Revolution; member of several of the National Assemblies and People's Assemblies; Chairman of the Eastern Cotton Company; elected temporary Deputy Speaker, 1971 and, following the ensuing general elections, Chairman of the Assembly's Economic Committee,

National Council for Production and Economic Affairs, 1974; took over responsibility for cotton industry, 1975; leader of the Liberal Socialist Party; *Languages:* Arabic, English; *Address:* The People's Assembly, Garden City, Cairo, Egypt.

MURAYWID, Hassan, Syrian official/diplomat; born 1927, Syria; *Religion:* Muslim; *Education:* BA, American University of Beirut, Lebanon; PhD in Political Economy, University of Wisconsin, Madison, USA; *Career:* Professor, University of Damascus, Syria; member, Executive Board, UNESCO, 1974; Minister for Foreign Affairs, and Chairman of the Cultural Committee, Damascus; member, Presidential Council of Syria; member, Commissions of Education and Foreign Affairs, Syrian National Council, and Syrian Delegation to UN General Assembly; *Publications:* numerous articles and studies on comparative international relations, political economy; *Languages:* Arabic, English, French; *Address:* 1 rue Miollis, 75732, Paris, France.

MURSI, Al-Sayyid Abdul Wahab, Egyptian painter/official; born 23 February 1931, Cairo, Egypt; married; two sons; *Religion:* Muslim; *Education:* BA, Fine Arts, Cairo University, Cairo, Egypt 1957; Diploma, Arts Institute for Teachers, 1958; *Career:* painter; General Supervisor of Exhibitions, General Organisation of Arts and Literature; Minister of Education, 1977; member of Fine Arts Graduates Association; several exhibitions in European and Arab Countries, including Museum of Modern Art, Cairo, Museum of Alexandria, Museum of Barcelona, The Goethe Institute, Cairo; Exhibitions in Paris and Frankfurt, 1981; *Decorations:* various prizes including Second Prize from Biennale Exhibition at Alexandria, 1970; Biennale Exhibition at Barcelona, Spain 1971; various prizes at Biennale Exhibitions in Paris and Madrid; *Interests and Recreations:* creative art; *Languages:* Arabic, English; *Address:* 7 Sharia Dr Mustafa al-Nagdi, Al-Sirkh Quarter, Shubra, Cairo, Egypt; telephone: 640905.

MURSI, Fuad Kamil, Egyptian aviation official/lawyer; born 16 December 1924, Malawi, Minia, Egypt; married; *Education:* LLB, Cairo University, Cairo, Egypt; LLM, Air Law, McGill University, Montreal, Canada; Doctor of Jurisprudence of International Law, Yale University, USA; Pilot Officer, Military Academy College, Cairo; *Career:* military service, 1944–46; Controller, Civil Aviation Department, 1947–50; Chief, Area Control Centre, Civil Aviation Department, Egypt, 1950–53; Director, Air Transport, Civil Aviation Department, 1955–62; Assistant Director General, 1963–65; Deputy Director General, Civil Aviation Department, 1965–68; Director General of Aeronautics, Civil Aviation Authority, Egypt, 1971–73; Representative of Egypt, International Civil Aviation Organisation Council, Canada, 1974–; *Languages:* Arabic, English, French; *Address:* Ministry of Civil Aviation, Airport Road, Cairo, Egypt; telephone: 876604; Residence — Ibn Malik Street, Giza, Egypt; telephone: 848879.

MUSA, Abdul Latif Ahmad Ibrahim al-, United Arab Emirates official; born 1940; married; three sons; *Religion:* Muslim; *Education:* BA in Sociology and Philosophy, Cairo University, Egypt, 1964; *Career:* Director of Financial and Administrative Affairs, 1971; Under Secretary, Social Services Department, 1974–; *Interests and Recreations:* swimming, basketball, volleyball; member of Abu Dhabi Tourism Club; *Languages:* Arabic, English; *Address:* P O Box 644, Abu Dhabi United Arab Emirates.

MUSA'ID, Abdul Aziz Fahad al-, Kuwaiti businessman/newspaper proprietor; born 1909; married; two sons; *Religion:* Muslim; *Education:* in Kuwait; *Career:* worked in trade with Iran and India; businessman, retail business in Kuwait, 1945; established trading and contracting company; Director of *Al-Ra'i al-'Aam* newspaper, 1961; partner in ownership of Kuwaiti hotel; candidate for National Assembly (unsuccessfully), 1963 and 1965, elected in February 1966 by-election; member of Kuwait National Assembly for twelve years; publisher of the former *Daily News,* English daily newspaper; proprietor of weekly magazine *Al-Nahda,* published by Dar Al-Ra'i al-'Aam group of newspapers; *Languages:* Arabic, Urdu, Persian; *Address:* Dar al-Ra'i al-'Aam, P O Box 695 Kuwait.

MUSA'ID BIN ABDUL AZIZ, HRH Prince, Saudi Arabian Prince; born 1923, Riyadh, Saudi Arabia; son of late King Abdul Aziz; *Religion:* Muslim; *Interests and Recreations:* literature, writing poetry; *Address:* Royal Court, Riyadh, Saudi Arabia.

MUSA'ID BIN ABDUL RAHMAN, HRH Prince, Saudi Arabian Prince/administrator; born 1922, Najd, Saudi Arabia; uncle of late King Faisal; *Religion:* Muslim; *Career:* Head of Complaint Bureau of the Councils of Ministers, 1954; mediator in dispute between Pakistan and Afghanistan, 1955; Vice President of the Council of Ministers, 1959; Minister of the Interior during the absence of the Crown Prince, July-December 1960; Minister of Finance and National Economy, 1962; *Address:* Ministry of Finance and National Economy, Riyadh, Saudi Arabia.

MUSA, Muhammad Ali Hussain, Saudi Arabian official/businessman; born 1934, Mecca, Saudi Arabia; *Religion:* Muslim; *Education:* technical education in Saudi Arabia; *Career:* technical posts, Ministry of Internal Affairs, Saudi Arabia; Director General, Financial and Administrative Affairs, Ministry of Information, Western Province; Director, Cement Company Cooperative Society; Assistant Editor of *Al-Madina* daily newspaper; Director, Asir Housing Project; Manager, Department of Publications, Mecca; Deputy Director General, Ministry of Information; member of Board of Asian Announcers, Kuala Lumpur, Malaya, 1962; Manager, Rajab and Silsila Company; Director, Public Utilities, Jeddah Municipality; *Publications:* articles in local press; television and radio talks; *Interests and Recreations:* reading, literature, poetry; *Address:* P O Box 7719, Jeddah, Saudi Arabia; telephone: 670976.

MUSA, Sulaiman, Jordanian official/writer; born 1920, Irbid, Jordan; married; *Education:* Diploma in Accountancy, 1953; *Career:* Iraq Petroleum Company, 1947–50; Teacher, 1951–56; Jordan Broadcasting, 1957–58; Editor of *Risalat al-Urdun* magazine, 1958–62; Department of Culture and Fine Arts, Editor of *Afkar* magazine, 1966–67; Head of Research Section, Ministry of Information, 1968–72; Cultural Adviser, 1973–77; Cultural Adviser, Ministry of Culture and Youth, 1978–; *Publications: History of Jordan in 20th Century,* 1959; *Hussain Bin Ali,* 1957; *Lawrence and the Arabs,* 1962, translated and published in English, 1966, and French, 1973; *The Arab Revolt,* three volumes; *Portrait of Heroism,* 1968; and several other books; *Decorations:* Independence Medal, 2nd Class, Jordan; *Address:* P O Box 5348, Amman, Jordan; telephone: 662301.

MUSAWI, Ghazi Radhi al-, Bahraini banker; born 1945, Bahrain; married; one son; *Religion;* Muslim; *Education:* BA in Commerce, Baghdad University, Iraq, 1967; MA in Economics, Bangalore University, 1971; *Career;* Teacher, Commercial School, 1968–69; Bank of Bahrain and Kuwait, 1971; Manager of Branches, Bank of Bahrain and Kuwait, 1978; Deputy General Manager, Offshore Unit, Bank of Bahrain & Kuwait, 1980–; *Interests and Recreations:* chess, reading; *Languages:* Arabic, English; *Address:* Bank of Bahrain and Kuwait, P O Box 597 Manama, Bahrain. telephone: 253388; telex: 8919 BN.

MUSSA, Abdul Karim, Tunisian diplomat/official; born 1934, Tunisia; married; *Religion:* Muslim; *Education:* Sadiki College, Tunis; *Career:* Union Générale des Etudiants Tunisiens (UGET); trained as journalist; Ministry of Information, 1956; collaborator of the official Destour Socialist Party newspaper *L'Action* (French), and *Al-Amal* (Arabic); Press Attaché, Embassy to Morocco, 1962–64; Head of National Press Division, Ministry of Information, 1964–66; Embassy to Senegal, 1966–69; Embassy to Canada, 1969–71; Deputy Tunisian Permanent Representative at the UN, 1971–73; Deputy Director of Political Affairs at the Foreign Ministry, 1973–74; Director of Information, 1974; *Languages:* Arabic, French; *Address:* Director's Office, Ministry of Information, Tunis, Tunisia.

MUSTAFA, Adnan, Syrian academic/oil official; resident in Kuwait; born 1934, Al-Aba, Syria; married; one son, three daughters; *Religion:* Muslim; *Education:* PhD in Nuclear Physics, Damascus and Southampton Universities; *Career:* Assistant Lecturer in Physics, Damascus University, 1964; Lecturer, 1969; Associate Professor, 1974; Minister of Oil and Mineral Resources, Syria, 1974–76; Professor of Physics, 1978; Chairman, Physics Department, Damascus University, 1978; Visiting Professor in Sussex and Southampton Universities, UK, 1977–78; Assistant Secretary General, OAPEC, Kuwait, 1979–; member of the Institute of Physics, UK, 1966, the European Society, Switzerland, 1970, the American Physics Society, 1971; Executive Secretary, the Arab Physics Society, 1973–; Chairman, the Syrian Society for Physics and Mathematics, 1979; *Publications: The Slide Ruler,* 1968, Dar al-Ma'aarif, Cairo, Egypt; *Experiments in Modern Physics,* 1974, Damascus University; *Physics for Universities,* 1977 and several other articles and research papers published in various scientific and professional journals; *Decorations:* Award of Dinstinction, the UPPSALA Group, Sweden, 1974; *Interests and Recreations:* music, writing, poetry, walking; *Languages:* Arabic, English; *Address:* OAPEC, P O Box 20501, Kuwait; telephone: 426885.

MUSTAFA, Burhaniddin Abdul Rahman, Iraqi politician; born 1943, Salaheddin Governorate, Iraq; *Religion:* Muslim; *Education:* Teachers' College, Baghdad, 1960; College of Law, Baghdad University, 1968; *Career:* Chairman, Iraq Ports Administration, 1975; elected member of Iraqi Baath Party's Regional Command, 1977; Minister of Youth, 1977; Minister of State without Portfolio with special responsibility for coordinating relations with the Kurdish Autonomous Region, 1977–; *Address:* Council of Ministers, Baghdad, Iraq.

MUSTAFA, General Muhammad Abdul Aziz, Egyptian official/army officer; born 8 February 1913, Alexandria, Egypt; married; two sons, two daughters; *Religion:* Muslim; *Education:* BA and MA in Military Science; *Career:* General in the Armed Forces, 1956; Deputy Minister, Ministry of War, 1959; Mayor, Red Sea Governorate, 1961; Marshal in the Army, 1964; President, Institution for Marine Wealth, 1964; Deputy Minister of Youth, 1966; President, African Football Confederation, 1958; Vice-President, International Football Federation, 1962; *Decorations:* Nile Decoration; *Interests and Recreations:* fishing, sea sports; *Languages:* Arabic, English, French, Spanish; *Address:* 460 Al-Hurriya Road, Alexandria, Egypt; telephone: 48812.

MUSTAFA, Hussain Mahmud, Egyptian engineer; resident in USA; married; two sons, one daughter; *Religion:* Muslim; *Education:* BSc in Mechanical Engineering; postgraduate studies in industrial management and finance; *Career:* Plant Engineer, Helwan Portland Cement Company, Egypt, 1948–51; Plant Engineer, Sudan, 1951; Chief Plant Engineer, Iraq Portland Cement Company, Iraq, 1952; Technical Manager, Helwan Portland Cement Company, Egypt, 1953–57; General Manager and member of the Board of Directors, Alexandria Portland Cement Company, 1957–63; Engineer and cement expert, International Finance Corporation, USA, 1970–; member of Egyptian Engineering Union; expert in cement and allied industries, with long experience in promoting, implementing and operating industrial projects; *Interests and Recreations:* tennis, sailing, fishing, travelling; member of the Kenwood Country Club, Washington D.C., of the Alexandria Sporting Club, Alexandria, Egypt; *Languages:* Arabic, English, French, Spanish; *Address:* 7213 Marbury Court, Bethesda, MD 20034, USA; telephone: (301) 320 3956.

MUSTAFA, Izzidin Ibrahim, United Arab Emirates administrator; born 1928, Cairo, Egypt; *Religion:* Muslim; *Career:* Qatar Education Service; Riyadh College of Education, Saudi Arabia; Head of Abu Dhabi Cultural Centre, and Cultural Adviser to the United Arab Emirates President, 1971; *Languages:* Arabic, English, French; *Address:* Abu Dhabi Cultural Centre, P O Box 845, Abu Dhabi, United Arab Emirates.

MUSTAFA, Makkawi, Sudanese businessman; born 1919; *Religion:* Muslim; *Education:* University of Khartoum, Sudan; *Career:* Ministry of Finance; Ministry of Commerce; Director of the Sudanese Spinning and Weaving Factory, 1959; Ministry of Planning, 1969; General Manager, Spinning Company, 1969; President of the Federation of Industries; *Address:* Khartoum Spinning and Weaving Co Ltd, P O Box 193, Khartoum North, Sudan.

MUSTAFA, Muhammad Eid, Arab-American academic/accountant; born 25 November 1934, Cairo, Egypt; married; two sons; *Religion:* Muslim; *Education:* PhD; *Career:* Professor at the Department of Accountancy, School of Business Administration, California State University, Long Beach, California, USA; Expert, International Labour Organisation, United Nations Industrial Development Organisation; member of American Accounting Association, Academy of International Business, National Association of Accountants; *Publications:* several articles and research projects for periodicals in the USA, Egypt and the UN; *Interests and Recreation:* swimming, jogging; *Languages:* Arabic, English, French; *Address:* California State University, Long Beach, California 90840, USA; telephone: 213498 4586, 4653, 4573; Residence — 714 826 1991.

MUSTAFA, Zaki, Sudanese lawyer/academic; born 1935, Sudan; married; four children; *Religion:* Muslim; *Education:* Faculty of Law, University of Khartoum, 1959; PhD, London University, UK; *Career:* Lecturer in Law, University of Khartoum and Dean of Law Faculty, 1965; Dean of the Faculty of Law, Ahmado Bello University, Nigeria, 1970–72; Visiting Professor, Haile Selassie University, Addis Ababa, Ethiopia; Attorney General of the Sudan, 1973–75; Secretary General of the joint Sudanese-Saudi Authority for the Exploitation of Red Sea Resources, 1975; part-time Adviser on Legal Affairs to President Nimeiri, 1975; Adviser to the President on Legal Reform, 1977; *Publications:* numerous law books and papers in Arabic and English; *Languages:* Arabic, English; *Address:* c/o the Presidency, Khartoum, Sudan.

MUT'EB BIN ABDUL AZIZ, HRH Prince, Saudi Arabian Prince; born 1931; son of late King Abdul Aziz; *Religion:* Muslim; *Education:* court education; private tuition in various fields; extensive reading in economics, politics and culture; *Career:* Amir of Royal Palaces Guard; Vice Minister of Defence and Aviation; Governor of Holy Mecca; Minister of Housing and Public Works, 1975–; Acting Minister, Ministry of Municipal and Rural Affairs, 1978–83; *Decorations:* various orders of merit from Arab and European countries; *Interests and Recreations:* falconry, reading; *Address:* Ministry of Housing and Public Works, Washem Street, Riyadh, Saudi Arabia; telephone: 476 4979; telex: 200415, 201142 ASHGAL SJ.

MUTABAGANI, Hamid, Saudi Arabian physician; born 1935, Medina, Saudi Arabia; *Religion:* Muslim; *Education:* MD, Medicine, Cairo University, Cairo, Egypt, 1961–62; PhD in General Surgery, 1966–67; PhD in Urology, 1969; *Career:* Physician, Ministry of Education, 1962; Cultural Counsellor, Embassy to Italy, 1965; Surgeon, Ministry of Education; Professor of Pathological Surgery, Rome University, Italy; Director General, Jeddah National Hospital; founded New Jeddah Clinic; *Publications:* several research papers in medical journals; *Decorations:* Cavalier, Medal of Honour, Italy; *Interests* *and Recreations:* fishing, photography; *Address:* Jeddah New Clinic Hospital, P O Box 7692 Jeddah, Saudi Arabia; telephone: 675888; telex: 401266 SHARK SJ.

MUTAWAKKIL, Muhammad Abdul Malik Abdul Karim al-, Yemen Arab Republic administrator; born 1942; married; four daughters, one son; *Religion:* Muslim; *Education:* BA in Literature, Journalism Department, Cairo University, Egypt; *Career:* 1st Secretary, Embassy to Egypt, 1963; Director General of Press, Ministry of Information, 1967; Head of the Tourist Department, 1970; Minister of Supply, 1976; member of the Higher Committee for Rectification and member of the Board of Sana'a University; member of the National Committee for Culture and Cooperation; *Interests and Recreations:* theatre, reading, walking, gardening, special interest in administration and the development of administrative methods; *Languages:* Arabic, English; *Address:* Kuwait Hospital Block, Sana'a, Yemen Arab Republic; telephone: 70214.

MUTAWAKKIL, Yahya M. al-, Yemen Arab Republic diplomat; born 28 May 1942, Yemen Arab Republic; married; three sons; *Religion:* Muslim; *Education:* Military Academy, Paratrooper, 1960; Military Academy, Heavy Artillery, 1961; Officers Infantry Academy, Moscow, 1963; *Career:* Director of the Office of the Commander in Chief and Prime Minister, 1968; Deputy Commander in Chief of the Armed Forces, 1969; elected member of the Consultative Assembly (Parliament), 1970; Ambassador Extraordinary and Plenipotentiary to Egypt and Libya; member of the Command Council, and Minister of the Interior, 1974; Ambassador Extraordinary and Plenipotentiary to the United States, Canada and Mexico, 1976–; *Interests and Recreations:* tennis, bowling, swimming, hunting, reading, theatre, music; *Languages:* Arabic, Russian, English; *Address:* Office — Embassy of Yemen Arab Republic, Watergate Six Hundred, Suite 860, 600 New Hampshire Ave NW, Washington D.C. 20037, USA.

MUTAWWA', Faisal al-Salih, Kuwaiti diplomat; born 1927, Kuwait; married; three sons, two daughters; *Religion:* Muslim; *Education:* BA in History, University of Cairo, Egypt; *Career:* Ministry of Education, responsible for student grants; Under Secretary, Ministry of Education; Ambassador to USSR; Ambassador to Algeria; Ambassador to France; Head of Ceremonies Department, Ministry of Foreign Affairs; Official, Economic Department, Ministry of Foreign Affairs; *Interests and Recreations:* reading, swimming, sports; *Languages:* Arabic, French, English; *Address:* Ministry of Foreign Affairs, P O Box 3, Sour Street, Kuwait; telephone: 422041, 422050, telex: 22042 KHARJIA KT.

MUTI'A, Muhammad Salih Abdullah, People's Democratic Republic of Yemen politician; born 16 June 1944, Aden, People's Democratic Republic of Yemen; married; *Religion:* Muslim; *Education:* Technical Institute, Aden; *Career:* active in National Liberation Front politics and armed struggle; member of the General Command, 1968; member of the Executive Committee, 1969–70; Minister of the Interior, 1969–73; Minister of Foreign Affairs, 1973; member of the Political Bureau of the Unified Political Organization of the National Front; *Interests and Recreations:* sports, mainly watching football; *Languages:* Arabic, English; *Address:* Ministry of Foreign Affairs, Aden, People's Democratic Republic of Yemen.

MUTTAHAR, Muhammad Bin Muhammad al-, Yemen Arab Republic academic; born 19 September, 1950; Sana'a; married; one son, two daughters; *Religion:* Muslim; *Education:* BA in Philosophy and Sociology, University of Libya, 1972; MA in Educational Management, Indiana University, USA; *Career:* Director General of Planning, Ministry of Education, 1972–73; member of the Higher Committee of Educational Development Project, 1973–74; Associate Director, Educational Development Project, 1974–76; Vice Rector, Sana'a University, 1976–; *Interests and Recreations:* literature, philosophy, sociology, tennis; *Languages:* Arabic, English; *Address:* University of Sana'a, P O Box 1247, Sana'a, Yemen Arab Republic.

MZALI, Muhammad, Tunisian politician; born 1925, Monastir, Tunisia; married; six children; *Religion:* Muslim; *Education:* BA in Philosophy, and Diploma in Higher Studies in Literature, Sorbonne, University of Paris, France; *Career:* teacher, secondary schools; Teacher, Zituna University, 1950–56; Head of the Office of the Secretariat of State, Ministry of National Education, 1956–58; Head of Youth and Sports Department,

1959–64; General Director of the Tunisian Radio and Television, 1964–68; Secretary of State for National Defence, 1968–69; Minister of National Education, Youth and Sports, 1969–71; Minister of National Education, 1971–73; Minister of Health, 1973–76; Minister of National Education 1976–80; Co-ordinator of Governmental Activities at the President's Office, 1980–; Prime Minister, and General Secretary of the Destour Socialist Party, 1980–; active member of the political party, Political Bureau and National Assembly, 1964–79; active member of Capital City Hall, 1952–72; founder and Chief Editor of a cultural review *Al-Fikr,* 1955–; member of Arab Language Academy in several Arab capitals; member of Tunisian Authors Union and took part in several cultural conferences; *Publications:* in Arabic *Democracy,* 1955; an anthology of *Al-Fikr* editorials, 1969; translation of *French Settlers and Young Tunisians,* 1972; and various other publications; *Interests and Recreations:* sports; member of Tunisian and International Olympic Committee (IOC), and other sports committees, 1959–67; *Languages:* Arabic, French; *Address:* Office of the Prime Minister, Tunis, Tunisia.

N

NA'IMI, HH Shaikh Rashid Bin Humaid al-, Ruler of Ajman, United Arab Emirates; born 1900; *Religion:* Muslim; *Career:* became Ruler of Ajman in 1928; lives mainly in Manama and Masfout, has left affairs of state to his second son Humaid; *Address:* Alzaaher Palace, Ajman, United Arab Emirates.

NA'IMI, Shaikh Humaid Bin Rashid Bin Humaid al-, United Arab Emirates Crown Prince and Deputy Ruler of Ajman; born circa 1930; second son of Ruler of Ajman, Shaikh Rashid al-Na'imi; married; *Religion:* Muslim; *Education:* in Dubai; *Career:* responsible for much of the day to day government business in Ajman; *Languages:* Arabic, English; *Address:* Al-Diwan Al-Amiri, P O Box 1, Ajman, United Arab Emirates; telephone: 422122; telex: 69520 DIWAN EM.

NAA'MA, Mustafa Rajab al, Iraqi academic/physician; born 26 February 1923, Basra, Iraq; three daughters; *Religion:* Muslim; *Education:* MB, ChB, College of Medicine, University of Baghdad, 1957; Specialization Degree in Internal Medicine, University of Baghdad, 1964; MRCP, Royal College of Physicians, England, 1976; FRCP, Royal College of Physicians, England,, 1978; *Career:* Junior Physician, 1950–53; Residency Program, USA, 1953–57; Senior Physician, Cardiologist, 1964–; Lecturer, Head of Department of Medicine, University of Basra, 1968–73; Dean, College of Medicine, University of Basra, 1971–78; Assistant Professor of Medicine and Consultant, Teaching Hospital, Basra, 1974–; member of the Arab Board for Medical Specializations; *Publications:* numerous researches and papers in professional journals, in English; *Interests and Recreations:* fishing, ancient history, anthropology, medical literature; *Languages:* Arabic, English; *Address:* College of Medicine, University of Basra, P O Box 114, Basra, Iraq; telephone: Office — (040) 214105/9; Residence — (040) 214941.

NAAMA, Abdullah Hussain, Qatari journalist/businessman; *Religion:* Muslim; *Career:* publisher and owner of weekly magazine *Al-Uruba* and *Al-Arab* daily; together with his son Khalid Naama writes day-to-day reports on Qatari scene; member of Board of Directors of Qatar Insurance Company; has wide interests in textile retail industry; *Languages:* Arabic, English; *Address:* Al-Uruba, P O Box 633, Doha, Qatar.

NAAMAN, Mitri Abdallah, Lebanese poet/publisher; born 26 October 1917, Damascus, Syria; married; six children; *Education:* Baccalaureat, 1933; *Career:* Manager, the Paulist Fathers Printing Press, Harissa, later Junieh, 1933–; Manager, Saint Paul Bookshop, Beirut, 1955–57; Representative of Saint Paul at the Master Printers Association, 1944–; Proof-reader of *Nouveau Petit Larousse Arabe,* 1965–71; Founder of *Maison Naaman pour la Culture,* 1979; *Publications:* numerous books in verse and prose; translator for Arabic series published in Paris; author of several social and critical articles and poems; editor of numerous literary and school books; *Interests and Recreations:* chiromancy, interpretation of dreams, meditation, sports, gardening and rambling; member of Master Printers Association of Lebanon; *Languages:* Arabic, French, English, Italian, Latin, Greek; *Address:* Office — Paulist Institution, St. Paul Street, Junieh, Lebanon; telephone: 951699, 930051; Residence — Sarba Junieh, Lebanon; telephone: 930439.

NAAMAN, Yusif D. al-, Iraqi surgeon/academic; born 1 December 1923, Baghdad, Iraq; married; two sons; *Education:* MB, ChB, Medical School, Baghdad, Iraq, 1949;

MSc, Surgery, Baylor University Graduate School, Houston, Texas, 1953–55; DSc, Columbia University Postgraduate Medical School, New York, NY, 1958–60; Fellow of the International College of Surgeons, FICS, 1956; Fellow of the American College of Chest Physicians; FCCP, 1958; FACC, 1960; FACS, 1961; FICA, 1962; *Career:* Rotator, Royal Teaching Hospital, Baghdad, 1948–49; Captain, Iraqi Army Medical Corps, 1949–50; Assistant Instructor, Department of Surgery, Baylor University School of Medicine, Houston, Texas, 1953–55; Instructor, Department of Surgery, Baylor University, 1955–58; Senior Research Scientist, Department of Surgery, College of Physicians and Surgeons, Columbia University, New York, 1958–60; Research Associate, College of Physicians and Surgeons, Columbia University, 1960–61; Assistant Professor of Surgery, College of Medicine, University of Baghdad, Baghdad, Iraq, 1961; Founder of the Department of Thoracic and Cardiovascular Surgery, Ministry of Health, and later University of Baghdad, 1961–; Professor of Surgery, College of Medicine, University of Baghdad, 1966–; member of several associations and societies; *Publications:* Chief Editor, *Journal of the Faculty of Medicine,* Baghdad; *Surgical Physiology in Collateral Cirulation,* 1963, in English; *An Introduction to Thoracic and Cardiovascular Surgery,* 1966; several other books; numerous researches and papers in professional journals and magazines; *Interests and Recreations:* tennis, weight lifting, hunting; *Languages:* Arabic, English; *Address:* Dept of Thoracic and Cardiovascular Surgery, University Hospital, Baghdad, Iraq.

NABRI, Malik Amin, Sudanese official; born 1923, Singa, Sudan; married; four sons, five daughters; *Religion:* Muslim; *Education:* Gordon Memorial College, Khartoum, Sudan; Sudan Police College, Khartoum; *Career:* various posts in Legal Department, 1943–50; Police College, 1951–52; Police Inspector, 1953; Chief Inspector of Police, 1956; Superintendent of Police, 1960; Vice Consul, Embassy of Sudan, Kampala, Uganda, 1964–67; Consul General, Fort Lamy, Chad, 1967–68; Commandent of Police, 1969–71; Assistant Commissioner of Police, 1972–75; Under Secretary, Ministry of Interior, 1976; Governor, Northern Province, 1977–; *Decorations:* Republic of Sudan Medal; Order of Outstanding Officer, Republic of Chad; *Interests and Recreations:* classical and modern poetry, reading, national and international current affairs; *Languages:* Arabic, English; *Address:* Governor House, Northern Province, Dongola, Sudan; telephone: 2192, 2363.

NABULSI, Hamdallah Farid , Jordanian engineer/official; born 1927, Salt, Jordan; married; three sons, one daughter; *Religion:* Muslim; *Education:* BSc in Civil Engineering, Cairo University, Egypt, 1954; *Career:* District Engineer, Ministry of Public Works, 1954–63; Head of Materials Department, Ministry of Public Works, 1963–65; Director of Building Division, Ministry of Public Works, 1965–71; Director General of Housing Corporation, 1971–; Vice Chairman of the Board of Housing Corporation; member of the Board of the Housing Bank; member of the Amman City Council; member of the Board of the Cement Factory; member of the Higher Planning Council; member of Amman Regional Council; *Publications:* papers and articles in professional journals and magazines; *Decorations:* Medal of Independence, Jordan; Order of the Jordanian Star; *Interests and Recreations:* reading; member of the City Club; Fellow of the American Society of Civil Engineers; Chairman of the Board of the Jordanian Estate Establishment Company; member of the Royal Scientific Society; *Languages:* Arabic, English; *Address:* Housing Corporation, P O Box 2110 Amman, Jordan; telephone: 430585, 43889; telex: 22024 HOUSE JO.

NABULSI, Muhammad Sa'id, Jordanian banker; born 1928, Jaffa, Palestine; married; *Religion:* Muslim; *Education:* BA in Law, Damascus University, Syria, 1951; MA in Economics, Georgetown University, USA, 1956; PhD in Economics, Georgetown University, USA, 1964; postgraduate studies, Berkeley University, California, USA; *Career:* training with the IMF, USA; Lecturer, Syrian University, Damascus, Syria, and the Jordanian University, Amman, Jordan; Adviser to the Governor of the Central Bank of Jordan, 1968; Executive Director of the Central Bank of Jordan; Director of the Institute of Banking Studies; Minister of National Economy, 1972–73; Governor of the Central Bank of Jordan, 1973–; *Publications:* *Problems of Monetary Integration in Developing Countries,* 1964; research studies in banking administration; *Address:* Central

Bank of Jordan, P O Box 37, Amman, Jordan; telephone: 30301; telex: 1250 BAKAZI JO.

NABULSI, Omar N., Jordanian lawyer/politician; born 1 April 1936, Nablus, Jordan; married; two sons; *Religion:* Muslim; *Education:* Licence in Law; MA in International Law; MA in Public and Administrative Law; postgraduate studies in economics; *Career:* Political Attaché, Arab League, Cairo, Egypt, 1960; Assistant Chief of the Royal Cabinet, Jordan, 1969; Minister of National Economy, 1970; Ambassador to UK and the Netherlands, 1972–73; Minister of Agriculture, 1973; Minister of Economy, Industry and Commerce, 1973–74; Legal Adivser to the Arab Fund for Development, 1975–77; Minister of Labour, Reconstruction and Development, 1977–80; private law practice, 1980–; *Decorations:* Order of the Jordanian Star, 1st Class; *Interests and Recreations:* Arabic poetry, theatre, cinema, squash, swimming; *Languages:* Arabic, French, English; *Address:* P O Box 35116, Amman, Jordan; telephone: Office — 64724; Residence — 67001.

NACIRI, Muhammad Makki, Moroccan academic; born 1906, Rabat, Morocco; maried; two sons, three daughters; *Religion:* Muslim; *Education:* Arabic and Islamic Studies, Morocco; Philosophy and Sociology, University of Cairo, Egypt; Educational Sciences, University of Paris, France; Law, University of Geneva, Switzerland; *Career:* Ambassador Extraordinary and Plenipotentiary to Libya, 1961–63; Governor of Agadir Province, 1963–64; member of the Constitutional Chamber of the Supreme Court, 1963, 1970; Professor, Faculty of Law, University of Muhammad V, Rabat, and University of Hassan II, Casablanca, 1960–74; Minister of Islamic Affairs and Culture, 1972–74; President of the Council of Ulama of Rabat, and member of the Council of Regency of the Moroccan Kingdom, 1980–; member of the Committee of the Liberation of Arab Maghreb, 1948–55; member of the Consultative National Assembley, 1956–59; member of the Constitutional Council, 1960; member of the Royal Commission of the Classification of Law, 1970–; member of the Superior Council of Planning, 1980–; *Publications: Les Habous Islamiques au Royaume du Maroc,* Tetouan, 1935; *Position de la Nation Marocaine a l'Egard du Protectorat,* Tetouan, 1944; several other works; numerous articles and studies published in journals and magazines; founder of *Al Maghreb Al Jadid, Al Wahda Al Maghribiya, La Voix du Maroc,* and several other journals and magazines; *Decorations:* Officier de l'Ordre du Trône, Morocco, 1963; Order of Intellectual Merit, Morocco, 1969; Ordre du Grand Cordon du Nichan al-Istiqlal, Libya, 1962; Grand Cordon, Wissam al Jumhuriya, Tunisia, 1973; Ordre de la Medaille de Couronnation, Iraq, 1953; *Interests and Recreations:* walking; member of the Royal Golf Club of Dar Al Salaam; *Languages:* Arabic, French, Spanish; *Address:* 26 Rue Hamza, Agdal, Rabat, Morocco; telephone: 71953.

NADER, Laura, Arab-American academic/anthropologist; born 30 September 1930, Winsted, Connecticut, USA; married; three children; *Education:* BA in Latin American Studies, Wells College, USA, 1952; El Colegio de Mexico; Smith College, USA, 1950–51; PhD in Anthropology, Radcliffe College, USA, 1961; Linguistic Institute, University of Michigan, 1955; *Career:* Professor of Anthropology, Department of Anthropology, University of California, Berkeley, USA, 1960–; Vice Chairman, Department of Anthropology, University of California, Berkeley, USA, 1960–; Vice Chairman, Department of Anthropology, University of California, 1968–71; Visiting Professor, Yale Law School, Yale University, USA, 1971; Fellow of the Center for Advanced Study in the Behavioural Sciences, Stanford, California, USA, 1963–64; Fellow of Woodrow Wilson Center for International Scholars, D.C., 1979–80; member of the American Anthropological Association, the Society of Women Geographers, the National Research Council, Representative to the Behavioural Division, 1969–73, the Carnegie Council on Children, 1972–, The National Academy of Sciences Committees on Energy, 1975–80; Chairman, National Institute of Mental Health, Cultural Anthropology Committee, 1968–71; *Publications:* numerous anthropological books, articles and reports on social structure, law, energy; *Languages:* English, Spanish, Arabic; *Address:* Department of Anthropology, University of California 94720, Berkeley, USA.

NADER, Muhammad Jabir, Saudi Arabian lawyer/diplomat; born 4 February 1930, Medina, Saudi Arabia; married; two sons;

Religion: Muslim; *Education:* LLB, Cairo University, Egypt, 1953; *Career:* Attaché, Saudi Arabian Embassy in Kabul, 1955–59; Counsellor, Saudi Arabian Embassy in Bonn, 1960–62; Counsellor, Saudi Arabian Embassy, Kuwait, 1962–68; Counsellor, Baghdad, 1968–69; Minister Plenipotentiary, Washington D.C., 1970–71; Director, The Saudi Arabian Public Relations Programme, USA, 1970–71; Minister Plenipotentiary, Sana'a, 1972–73; established and headed the Research Department and the Legal Department, Ministry of Foreign Affairs; represented Saudi Arabia in the Legal Committee at the UN, 1967; practiced law since 1971; established M. Jabir Nader Law Firm, 1977; Chairman, Bahra Development Co Ltd, Jeddah, Saudi Arabia; *Interests and Recreations:* music, poetry, reading, photography, swimming; *Languages:* Arabic, English, French, German; *Address:* P O Box 3595, Medina Road, Al-Fateh Printing Press Street, Jeddah, Saudi Arabia; telephone: Office — 6673296, 6673356; Residence — 682726; telex 400018 Nader SJ.

NADER, Ralph, Arab-American lawyer/academic; born 27 February 1934; *Education:* Princeton and Harvard Universities, USA; admitted to Conneticut Bar, 1958; Massachusetts Bar, 1959, and USA Supreme Court; *Career:* USA Army, 1959; law practice in Hartford, Conneticut, 1959–; Lecturer in History and Government, University of Hartford, 1961–63; Lecturer, Princeton University, 1967–68; member of the American Bar Association; has advanced the cause of consumer protection, particularly in relation to car safety in the USA; *Publications: Unsafe at Any Sppead,* 1965; *Who Runs Congress,* 1972; Editor of *The Consumer and Corporate Accountability,* 1974; *Decorations:* Woodrow Wilson Award, Princeton University, USA, 1972; *Address:* 53 Hillside Avenue, Winstead, Conneticut, USA.

NADI, Muhammad Abdul Maksud al-, Egyptian academic/nuclear physicist; born 27 January 1918, Egypt; married; three sons, one daughter; *Education:* BSc in Physics, University of Cairo, Cairo, Egypt, 1940; MSc, University of Cairo, 1945; PhD, University of London, 1948; DSc, University of Cairo, 1968; *Career:* Faculty of Science, University of Cairo, 1940–, Professor of Nuclear Physics, 1961–; Dean, Faculty of Science, 1972–73; Vice President of Mansoura University, 1973–78; Head of Physics Department, Egyptian Atomic Energy Establishment, 1961–70; Research Associate, Yale University, 1959–60; Fellow, Institute of Physics, London, UK; *Publications:* numerous publications on theory of low-energy nuclear reactions; *Decorations:* Egyptian State Prize in physics research, 1950, 1955 and 1960; *Languages:* Arabic, English; *Address:* Residence — 50 Dokki Street, Giza, Cairo, Egypt.

NAFFAH, Fuad, Lebanese politician; born 1 March 1925, Kesrouan, Lebanon; married; four children; *Education:* University of St. Joseph, Beirut, Lebanon; Licence in Law, French Faculty of Law, Beirut; *Career:* legal profession; elected deputy for Kesrouan, 1960, and 1972; Minister of Agriculture, 1970–72; Minister of Finance, 1972; Foreign Minister, 1973–74; member of Centre Bloc; *Languages:* Arabic, French; *Address:* Office — Rue Becheraal-Khoury, Beirut, Lebanon; Residence — Raouché, Beirut, Lebanon.

NAFFAH, Joseph, Lebanese diplomat; born Lebanon; two sons; *Education:* BA in Law; Diploma in Administrative and International Law, St. Joseph University, Beirut, Lebanon; *Career:* Lebanese Diplomatic Service, 1944; served in various parts of the world; Consul General, Argentina, 1961–64; Ambassador to Brazil, 1968–72; Ambassador to Mexico, Cuba, Guatemala, Costa Rica, Honduras, Salvador, Nicaragua, Panama, 1972–78; Ambassador to Japan, Philippines, South Korea, 1978–; *Publications:* author of report of the *Unification of the Alphabet in International Relations,* Latin American Conference for the Advancement of Science, Sao Paulo, Brazil, 1968; *Decorations:* Order of Aguila Aztec, 1st Class, Mexico; Commander of the Order de Mayo, Argentina; Knight of the National Order of the Cedar, Lebanon; *Interests and Recreations:* reading, classical music; founder of Brazil-Lebanon Cultural Association; founder of Lebanese House, Sao Paulo, Brazil-Lebanon Chamber of Commerce, Brazil-Lebanon Cultural Association; organiser and Honorary President of the Committee for the Construction of the Monument to Fakhr el Din, Beirut, Lebanon; *Languages:* Arabic, English, French; *Address:* Lebanese Embassy, Chiyoda House, 17–8 Nagata-cho, 2 chome, Chiyoda, Tokyo, Japan.

NAFFAH, Salim, Lebanese diplomat; born 18 November 1925; married; *Religion:* Christian; *Education:* Political Sciences and Economics, American University of Beirut; Law, University of Saint Joseph, Beirut; *Career:* Ministry of Foreign Affairs; Secretary, Lebanese Embassy to Buenos Aires; Chargé d'Affaires, Lebanese Embassy to Montevideo; Consul General in Sao Paulo, Brazil; Ambassador to Colombia, Ecuador, Peru and Bolivia; Co-founder of the Lebanese Association of Political Science; *Decorations:* Order de Mayo, 1965; A Gratidao da Cidade de Sao Paulo, 1970; Order National do Cruzeiro do Sul, 1974; Medalha Ana Neri, 1977; *Languages:* Arabic, French, English, Spanish, Portugese, Italian; *Address:* Calle 74, No. 12–44 Bogota, Columbia; telephone: 2493659, 2357790.

NAFI'E, Ibrahim A., Egyptian journalist; born 11 January 1934, Suez, Egypt; married; two sons; *Religion:* Muslim; *Education:* Degree in Law, 1956; *Career:* Diplomatic Correspondent, Cairo Radio, 1956–60; Economic Editor, *Al-Gumhuriya* newspaper, 1960–62; Economic Editor of *Al-Ahram* newspaper, 1962–67; Middle East Specialist in the International Bank for Reconstruction and Development (IBRD), Information Department, 1971–73; Head of the *Al-Ahram* Economic Department, 1974–75; Chief Assistant Editor, *Al-Ahram,* 1975–; Editor in Chief, *Al-Ahram; Publications:* translation into Arabic of Lester Pearson's Report *Partners in Development,* 1971; *Interests and Recreations:* swimming, walking; member of the Hunting Club, and Cairo Rotary Club; *Languages:* Arabic, English, French; *Address:* *Al-Ahram* Newspaper, Cairo, Egypt; telephone: 971490.

NAFISI, Abdul Wahab Yusuf al-, Kuwaiti politician; born 1935, Kuwait; married; *Religion:* Muslim; *Education:* Cairo University, Egypt; *Career:* Auditor-General's Office; representative member, Kuwait Communications Company; Minister of Commerce and Industry, 1975; *Languages:* Arabic, English; *Address:* P O Box 1568, Kuwait.

NAFISI, Ghazi Fahad al-, Kuwaiti businessman; born 1 September, 1941, Kuwait; married; two sons, one daughter; *Religion:* Muslim; *Education:* Diploma in Aeronautical Engineering, London, UK, 1966; *Career:* Operations Manager, 1969, General Man-

ager, 1971, Chairman, 1973, Kuwait Aviation Fuelling, KSC; Chairman and Managing Director, Salhi Real Estate Co, 1975–; member of Kuwait National Petroleum Co, 1972–77; member of the Board of Independent Petroleum Group, 1979; member of Kuwait Hoteliers Association, 1979; *Interests and Recreations:* hunting, swimming, travel; *Languages:* Arabic, English, French; *Address:* Salhia Real Estate Co, P O Box 23413, Safat Kuwait; telephone: 421260; telex: 2789 SAREC KT.

NAGGAR, Abdel Mon'im al-, Egyptian diplomat/army officer; *Religion:* Muslim; *Education:* Cairo Military Academy; Egyptian Staff College; Cairo University; Institut des Hautes Etudes, University of Paris, France; *Career:* army officer, 1939–57; Military Attaché, Embassy to France, 1953–54; Military Attaché, Embassy to Spain, 1955–57; Head of East European Department, Ministry of Foreign Affairs, 1958; Consul General in Bombay, India, 1959–62; Consul General in Hong Kong, 1962–63; Ambassador to Greece, 1963–64; Ambassador to France, 1964–68; Ambassador, Ministry of Foreign Affairs, 1969–71; Ambassador to Iraq, 1972–77; *Languages:* Arabic, English, French; *Address:* c/o Ministry of Foreign Affairs, Cairo, Egypt.

NAGGAR, Said al-, Egyptian UN official/economist, born 21 January 1920, Egypt; married; *Education:* LLB, Cairo University, Egypt, 1942; MSc in Economics, University of London, UK, 1948; PhD in Economics, University of London, UK, 1951; *Career:* Lecturer and Associate Professor, Cairo University; Deputy Director of Research, United Nations Conference on Trade and Development (UNCTAD), Geneva, Switzerland; Director, United Nations Economic and Social Office in Beirut, 1971–74; Director, Office of the Secretary General, UNCTAD, Geneva, Switzerland, 1974; *Publications:* *Industrialization and Income,* 1953; *History of Doctrines of International Trade,* 1957; *Principles of Economics,* 1958; *Theory of International Trade,* 1961; *History of Economic Doctrines,* 1973; *Interests and Recreations:* tennis, mountain hiking; *Languages:* Arabic, English, French; *Address:* Office of the Secretary General, United Nations Conference on Trade and Development, Palais des Nations, CH-1211 Geneva 10, Switzerland; telephone: (022) 346011.

NAGUIB, Ibrahim Naguib, Egyptian politician/architect; born 24 June 1911, married; one son, two daughters; *Religion:* Christian; *Education:* Diploma in Architecture, Cairo University, Egypt, 1931; Chartered Structural Engineer, London, 1935; RIBA Certificate, London, 1938; *Career:* Architect, State Building Department, Ministry of Public Works, Egypt, 1931; Head, Technical Department, 1944–52; Inspector, North Cairo Zone, 1952–55; Lecturer, Alexandria University, 1946–52, Ain Shams University, 1954–62; Controller of Municipal and Rural Affairs, Cairo Governorate, 1955–57; Director General of Technical Research and Inspection, Ministry of Municipal and Rural Affairs, 1957–62; Deputy Minister of Housing and Public Utilities, 1962–67; member of the Central Committee of the Arab Socialist Union (ASU), 1968–71; member of People's Assembly, Vice Chairman of Services Committee, 1968–71; Minister of Tourism, 1971–72; ASU, Secretary for Services, 1972–74; Minister of Tourism and Civil Aviation, 1974–77; Chairman, International Experts in Charge of Project for Salvaging Philae Temple; President, Afro-Asian Housing Organization, 1963–67; Vice President, Board of Egyptian Society of Engineers; member of the Institute of Structural Engineers, London; President, Society of Architects; has participated in many international scientific conferences; *Publications: Architectural Drawing,* 1940; *Buildings of Nubia,* 1945; *Code of Practice for Structural Engineering,* 1946; *Foundations of Buildings in Egypt and the Sudan,* 1951; *Village Buildings and the Farmer's House,* 1953; *The Nature of Soil and Foundations in the City of Cairo,* 1959; *Housing in Developing Countries,* 1968; *Trends in Architecture in the Arab Countries,* 1969; *Languages:* Arabic, English; *Address:* The Merryland Building, Heliopolis, Cairo, Egypt.

NAGUIB, Muhammad, Egyptian politician; born 1901, Khartoum, Sudan; *Religion:* Muslim; *Education:* Gordon College, Khartoum; Military Academy, Cairo, Egypt; *Career:* Army service from 1917; served in General Staff during World War II; Sub Governor of Sinai, and Governor of Red Sea Province in Frontier Corps; Brigadier General, Second-in-Command of Egyptian troops in Palestine, 1948–49; Director General of Infantry, 1951; Chairman of Free Officers Executive Committee, which organized July 1952 Revolu-

tion; Major General of Revolution and Commander in Chief of Egyptian Army; Chairman of the Revolutionary Command Council after Revolution, 1952; Prime Minister, 1952; first President and Prime Minister on proclamation of the Republic, 19 June 1953; resigned offices on 25 February 1954 but was reinstated 8 March; Prime Minister until April 1954, then succeeded by late President Nassir; resigned from Presidency, October 1954; *Publications: Egypt's Destiny,* 1955; *Languages:* Arabic, English; *Address:* c/o Ministry of Foreign Affairs, Cairo. Egypt.

NAHAYYAN, HH Shaikh Khalifah Bin Zaid al-, United Arab Emirates Crown Prince/politician; born 1947, Al-Ain, United Arab Emirates, and eldest son of the Ruler of Abu Dhabi, HH Shaikh Zaid Bin Sultan al-Nahayyan; married; *Religion:* Muslim; *Career:* Chairman of Abu Dhabi Executive Council; Head of Departments of Defence and Finance; Supreme Commander, Abu Dhabi Defence Force; Ruler's Representative in Eastern Province, 1966; formally designated Crown Prince and Chairman of the Defence Department, April 1969; Head of the Abu Dhabi Finance Department; Chairman of the Abu Dhabi Executive Council; Deputy Supreme Commander, Abu Dhabi Defence Force; Deputy Prime Minister of United Arab Emirates, 1977; *Address:* Ministry of Defence, P O Box 874, Abu Dhabi, United Arab Emirates; telephone: 56155.

NAHAYYAN, HH Shaikh Zaid Bin Sultan al-, Head of State of United Arab Emirates and Ruler of Abu Dhabi; born 1916; youngest brother of Shaikh Shakhbout, Ruler of Abu Dhabi, 1927–66; married; *Religion:* Muslim: *Career:* until 1966 was Governor of Eastern Province of Abu Dhabi; became Ruler following deposition of Shaikh Shakhbout in August 1966; Head (President) of State of United Arab Emirates on its formation in December 1971; presided over the development of Abu Dhabi since 1966; involved in all major decisions taken by the Abu Dhabi and UAE Governments; was re-elected President for a further five years, 27 November 1976; *Decorations:* Knight Commander of the Memorable Order of the Garter, UK; *Interests and Recreations:* hunting, falconry; *Address:* Amiri Palace, Abu Dhabi, United Arab Emirates.

NAHAYYAN, Shaikh Hamdan Bin Muhammad al-, United Arab Emirates politician; born 1930; eldest son of the late Shaikh Muhammad Bin Khalifa al-Nahayyan; married; *Religion:* Muslim; *Career:* represented Ruler of Abu Dhabi on Das Island, 1957–66; Minister of Public Works, June 1971; United Arab Emirates Minister of Public Works and Head of the Department of Works in Abu Dhabi Executive Council, 1973–77; Deputy Prime Minister, 1977–; *Address:* Deputy Prime Minister's Office, Abu Dhabi, United Arab Emirates.

NAHAYYAN, Shaikh Mubarak Bin Muhammad al-, United Arab Emirates politician; born 1935; second son of the late Shaikh Muhammad Bin Khalifah al-Nahayyan; married; *Religion:* Muslim; *Career:* Deputy Chief of Police, 1961; Commandant of Police and Minister of the Interior for Abu Dhabi, 1971, and for United Arab Emirates, December 1971; member of Abu Dhabi Executive Council, 1973; UAE Minister of Interior, 1971–; *Address:* Ministry of Interior, P O Box 398, Abu Dhabi, United Arab Emirates; telephone: Abu Dhabi 367100, 341421, 367991.

NAHAYYAN, Shaikh Shakhbout Bin Sultan Bin Zaid al-; former Ruler of Abu Dhabi, United Arab Emirates; born 1905; married; two sons; *Religion:* Muslim: *Career:* succeeded as Ruler, 1928; deposed, August 1966; now lives in Abu Dhabi; *Address:* Abu Dhabi, United Arab Emirates.

NAHAYYAN, Shaikh Sultan Bin Zaid al-, United Arab Emirates army commander; second son of the President of the United Arab Emirates and Ruler of Abu Dhabi; born 1953; married; *Education:* in Abu Dhabi and Cambridge, UK; *Career:* Lieutenant, Abu Dhabi Armed Forces, 1973; Assistant Chief of Staff, 1977; Commander in Chief, United Arab Emirates Armed Forces, 1978; representative of United Arab Emirates in Military Conferences; *Address:* Ministry of Defence, P O Box 874, Abu Dhabi, United Arab Emirates.

NAHAYYAN, Tahnoun Bin Muhammad al-, United Arab Emirates official; born 1936, Al-Ain, United Arab Emirates; married; *Religion:* Muslim; *Career:* Representative of HH Ruler of Abu Dhabi in Eastern Province; Chairman of the Board of Directors of the Abu Dhabi Petroleum Company; Head of the Municipal and Agricultural Department; *Interests and Recreations:* falconry; *Address:* P O Box 1003, Al-Ain, Abu Dhabi, United Arab Emirates; telephone: 41160.

NAHAYYN, Shaikh Sarur Bin Muhammad Bin Khalifah al-, United Arab Emirates official; born 1948; *Religion:* Muslim; *Career:* President of the former Abu Dhabi Department of Justice, subsequently Minister of Justice until the merging of the Abu Dhabi and Union Ministries in 1973; Chairman, Abu Dhabi Civil Service Commission; played a major part in the reorganization of Abu Dhabi's Electricity and Water Supply Authority, 1974; Deputy Chairman, Abu Dhabi Fund for Arab Economic Development; *Address:* Abu Dhabi Fund for Arab Economic Development, P O Box 814, Abu Dhabi, United Arab Emirates; telephone: 822865; telex: 22287 FUND EM.

NAIF BIN ABDUL AZIZ, HRH Prince, Saudi Arabian Prince/politician; born 1934; son of late King Abdul Aziz; *Religion:* Muslim; *Education:* private tuition by Great Ulamas; extensive training in politics, diplomacy and security affairs; *Career:* Governor of Riyadh, 1951–55; Deputy Minister of the Interior, 1970; Minister of State for Internal Affairs; Minister of the Interior, 1975–; made several state visits to the Gulf States and Emirates to conduct talks on the security of the region; *Decorations:* Supreme Orders from various Gulf and Arab States; Honorary PhD Degree in Civil Law from China, and from Korea, 1979; *Interests and Recreations:* falconry, reading; *Address:* Ministry of the Interior, P O Box 2833, Airport Road, Riyadh, Saudi Arabia; telephone: 4011944; telex: 201622 MORS SJ, 202811 MFORM SJ.

NAIF, HH Princess Wijdan Ali Bin, Jordanian artist/painter; born 29 August, 1939, Baghdad, Iraq; married to Prince Ali Bin Naif, son of Prince Naif Bin Abdullah Bin al-Hussain; three daughters, one son; *Religion:* Muslim; *Education:* BA in History, University of Beirut, Lebanon, 1961; *Career:* diplomat, Ministry of Foreign Affairs, Amman, Jordan, 1962; first woman to enter Jordanian Diplomatic Service; first woman representative of Jordan in the Economic and Social Council of the UN, Geneva, Switzerland, 1962; first woman representative of

Jordan to the UN General Assembly, 1964; Head of Programme Department, UNDP, Amman, Jordan, 1965–66; resigned 1966; painter; Founder of the National Jordanian Museum for Fine Arts, 1980; *Publications: The Muslim Woman in Modern Society,* in Arabic, in press; *Art in the Arab World Through the Collection of the National Museum for Fine Arts,* in Arabic and English, in press; *Interests and Recreations:* swimming, riding; Islamic art and architecture; founder and President of the Royal Society for Fine Arts, Amman; member of the World Affairs Society, Amman; *Languages:* Arabic, English, French, Turkish, Spanish; *Address:* P O Box 2296 Amman, Jordan; telephone: 44822.

NAIM, Edmond Wadih, Lebanese academic/ lawyer; born 5 September 1918, Shiyah, Lebanon; *Religion:* Christian; *Education:* University of St. Joseph, Beirut, Lebanon; Licence in Law, French Faculty of Law, Beirut, 1941; Diploma of Higher Studies in Public and Private Law; LLD, 1951; *Career:* Barrister at Law, 1942–63; Professor of the Faculty of Law, Lebanese University; Dean of the Faculty of Law, Lebanese, University, 1965; President of the Lebanese University; *Publications: La Faute dans la Législation Libançaise Comparée a la Législation Française,* 1953; *L'Idéologie du Socialisme Progressive Appliqué au Liban; Précis de Droit International Privé,* in Arabic; *Interests and Recreations:* book collecting, music; *Languages:* Arabic, French; *Address:* Office — Lebanese University, UNESCO Palace, Beirut, Lebanon; telephone: 235049; Residence — Ribiya, Rue 15, Lebanon.

NAIT BELKACEM, Mouloud Kassim, Algerian politician; born in Algeria; *Religion:* Muslim; *Education:* Philosophy, Cairo University, Egypt; Sorbonne, Paris, France; Bonn University, Federal Republic of Germany; *Career:* Representative of Provisional Government in Federal Republic of Germany and Sweden; Director of Political Affairs, Ministry of Foreign Affairs; Counsellor for Political and Diplomatic Affairs at the Presidency, 1966; Minister for Comprehensive Education and Religious Affairs, 1970; Minister of State for Religious Affairs, 1979; Member of the Central Committee, National Liberation Front Party (FLN); Counsellor, Presidency Office for Cultural and Political Affairs; represented Algeria in conferences of Islamic associations in Europe; *Decorations:* Commander of Merit, Germany, 1976; Grand Chevalier of the Order of the Italian Republic; *Interests and Recreations:* western classical music, literature, theatre; *Languages:* Berber, Arabic, French, English, German, Swedish, Norwegian, Danish, Dutch, Spanish, Italian, Russian, Czech, Greek, Latin; *Address:* The Presidency, Algiers, Algeria.

NAJA, Rafik, Lebanese politician; born 1912, Tripoli, Lebanon; six children; *Education:* American University of Beirut, Lebanon; Doctorate in Economics and Finance, University of London, UK; courses, Oxford University, UK, 1947; *Career:* principal of a college, Nigeria, 1935; businessman, Lebanon, 1940–45; political and economic adviser in Lebanon, 1948–55; Director General of Waqfs (Religious Endowments) in Lebanon, 1956; Minister of Finance, 1958; elected Deputy for Beirut 1960; Minister of National Economy, 1961–64, and 1965–66; President of the political party *Al-Hayat el-Wataniya; Interests and Recreations:* swimming; *Languages:* Arabic, French, English; *Address:* Residence — Horch Street, Beirut, Lebanon.

NAJAFI, Hassan Tawfik al-, Iraqi banker/ economist; born 1926, Mosul, Iraq; three sons, three daughters; *Religion:* Muslim; *Education:* BA in Commerce and Economy, University of Baghdad, 1951; *Career:* Director General of Issue Department; Chief of Foreign Exchange Department, Central Bank of Iraq; Under Secretary for Budget Affairs, Ministry of Finance; Governor, Central Bank of Iraq; *Publications: Modern Applications of Documentary Credits; Income Terms; Documentary Credits; Dictionary of Economics; Foreign Exchange Jurisdiction and Operation; Languages:* Arabic, English; *Address:* Central Bank of Iraq, P O Box 64, Baghdad, Iraq; telephone: 8871101; telex: 2296 CNBK IK.

NAJI, Talal, (Abu Jihad Talal), Palestinian politician; *Career:* member of Military HQ and Central Committee of the Popular Front for the Liberation of Palestine General Command (PFLP-GC), and one of the principal leaders of the group; elected to Palestine Liberation Organization (PLO) Executive Committee as First PFLP-GC member, 1974; Head of PLO Education Department, 1977.

NAJJAR, Fawzi M., Arab-American academic; born 19 December 1920, Lebanon; married; two sons; *Religion:* Christian; *Education:* BA in Political Science, American University of Beirut, Lebanon, 1948; MA in Political Science, University of Chicago, USA, 1950; PhD in Political Science, University of Chicago, 1954; *Career:* Instructor, American University of Beirut, 1954–55; Instructor, University of Chicago, USA, 1955–56, 1956–58, Assistant Professor, 1958–61, Associate Professor, 1961–66; Professor at Michigan State University, East Lancing, Michigan, USA, 1956–58, 1958–61, 1961–66, 1966–; *Publications:* numerous articles in political and cultural magazines and journals; *Interests and Recreations:* walking, swimming, Middle East and Islamic studies; member of the Middle East Institute, the American Oriental Society, the Middle East Studies Association of North America, Arab-American University Graduates Association; *Languages:* Arabic, English, French; *Address:* Social Science Department, Michigan State Universtiy, East Lancing, Michigan 48824, USA; telephone: 355 0187.

NAJJAR, Fuad A., Lebanese official/ agriculturalist; born December 1909, Abadiyyah, Lebanon; married; *Religion:* Muslim; *Education:* Agricultural Engineering, Ecole Nationale Superieure Agronomique de Montpellier, France; *Career:* Founder and Managing Director of Najjar Agricultural and Trading Company, 1943; Founder with Halim Najjar of the first Agricultural Cooperative in Lebanon, 1937; landowner; Director, Board of the Agricultural and Industrial Credit Bank, 1954–; Minister of Agriculture, 1958–60; Minister of Agriculture 1964; President of Lebanese Farmers Union, 1961–; Member of Beirut Municipal Council, 1961–; District Governor of Lions International, 1971–72; President of the Lebanese Friends of the Book Association, 1965–; *Interests and Recreations:* agriculture, agricultural cooperatives, protection of Lebanese forests, improvement of rural community; *Languages:* Arabic, English, French; *Address:* Office — Najjar Agricultural and Trading Co, Place de l'Etoile, Imm Greek Orthodox, P O Box 11–576, Beirut, Lebanon; telephone: 230636, 340977; telex: 20669 LE; Residence — Rue Sidani, A Rawdah Building, Beirut, Lebanon; telephone: 343284.

NAJJAR, Ibrahim Albert, Lebanese lawyer/ academic; born 2 September 1941, Tripoli, Lebanon; married; two daughters, one son; *Religion:* Christian; *Education:* BA in French and Lebanese Law, Faculty of Law and Political Sciences, University of Saint Joseph, Beirut, Lebanon; Diploma of Higher Studies, 1964; LLD, Faculty of Law, Paris, 1966; Professor of Law, 1969; *Career:* lawyer under training, 1963–66; Instructor, and Assistant, Faculty of Law, Paris, 1966; Auditor, Conference of Aggregation, Paris, 1964; Professor of Law, University of Beirut, Lebanon, 1969; Head of Services for Kata'eb students, 1960–66; member of the Political Bureau of Kata'eb, 1973–; Regional Chief of Koura for Kata'eb, 1970–78; Lawyer at the Court of Beirut; Professor of Law, Faculty of Law and Political Sciences, University of Saint Joseph, Beirut; member of the editorial committees of several legal and political journals; Editor of *Proche Orient-Etudes Juridiques; Publications: Les Liberalités, Théorie Générale, Testaments, Donations* 1973; *Dictionnaire Juridique, Français-Arabe, Arabe-Français; Le Mariage et le Nationalité de la Femme Mariée;* and several other works and papers published in professional journals and magazines; *Interests and Recreations:* tennis, chess, poetry, research in politics and philosophy; *Languages:* Arabic, English, French, Spanish; *Address:* 355 Rue Abdel Wahab El Inglizi, Beirut, Lebanon; telephone: 339 955, 326 520; Faculty of Law, University of Saint Joseph, P O Box 293, Beirut, Lebanon.

NAJJAR, Monsignor Rauf Salim, Jordanian ecclesiastic; born 1 January 1932, Haifa; *Religion:* Christian; *Education:* PhD in International Law and Canon Law; *Career:* President of the Ecclesiastic Tribunal, 1962–; Director and Editor in Chief of *Voice of the Holy Land* monthly review, 1968–; Director General, Al-Wassifiya Vocational Centre, 1968–; Assistant of the Roman Catholic Bishop in Amman; Chancellor of the Apostelic Delegation in Jordan, 1977; *Decorations:* Order of Independence, 1973; Commander of the Ordre International de l'Étoile de la Paix; Commander of the Order of St. John of Jerusalem; *Interests and Recreations:* law; *Languages:* Arabic, English, French, Italian, Latin, German, Spanish; *Address:* P O Box 1317 Amman, Jordan; telephone: 37440, 37678.

NAJJAR, Mustafa Abdul Qadir al-, Iraqi academic/historian; born 1935, Basra, Iraq; married; one son, three daughters; *Religion:* Muslim; *Education:* BA, University of Baghdad, Iraq, 1958; MA, University of Ain Shams, Cairo, Egypt; PhD, University of Ain Shams, Cairo, 1973; *Career:* teacher, 1959–62; school director, 1962–64; teacher, 1964–66; Assistant Professor, History Department, Faculty of Literature, Basra University, 1969–78; Director, Centre of Arab Studies, 1974–; Secretary General, Center for Arab Gulf and Arab Peninsula Studies, 1979–; member of the Arab Historians Association, the Organization of Social Sciences in the Middle East, the Editorial Board of the *For eign Affairs Magazine*, Ministry of Foreign Affairs, Iraq, the Syndicate of Iraqi Journalists; *Publications:* author and co-author of numerous books, 1971–82; articles, papers and essays in professional journals and magazines; *Interests and Recreations:* reading, scientific research, travel; *Languages:* Arabic, English; *Address:* University of Basra, Basra, Iraq; telephone: Office — 214268; Residence — 315667.

NAOURI, Issa, Jordanian writer/educationalist; born 1918, Naour, Jordan; married; *Education:* Doctor Honoris Causa, Palermo University, Italy, 1976; Doctor Honoris Causa, The World Academy of Arts and Culture, Taiwan, 1981; *Career:* school teacher, eighteen years; Inspector, and Secretary of the Board of the Federation of Catholic Schools in Amman, Jordan; Ministry of Education Administration, 1954–75; Secretary, the Jordanian Arabisation, Translation and Publication Committee, 1961–76; Founder and Chief Editor *Al-Qalam al-Jadid* monthly literary review, 1952–53; represented Jordan in thirteen Arab and world conferences, 1956–79; *Publications: Mars Burns His Arms; A House Beyond the Borders; The Literary Movement in Jordan,* in English; *The Jordanian Poet Mustafa Wahbi al-Tell,* in English; and numerous other novels, short story collection, poetry collections; *Decorations:* Jordanian Order of Education, 1977; Order of the Tunisian Republic, 1966; Cavaliere Ufficiale, Order of the Italian Republic, 1964; Cultural Silver Medal, Ministry of Foreign Affairs, Italy, 1963; awarded twice the Silver Olive, Cultural Prize, Palermo, Italy,1976; San Valantino Literary Prize for Poetry, Terni,

Italy, 1979 and 1981; *Languages:* Arabic, English, Italian; *Address:* P O Box 352, Amman, Jordan; telephone: 37784.

NAQIB, Ahmad Abdul Wahab al-, Kuwaiti diplomat; born 30 July 1933, Kuwait; *Religion:* Muslim; *Education:* Adam State College, Colorado, USA; *Career:* 1st Secretary, Embassy to UK, 1962–63; Counsellor, Permanent Mission of Kuwait to UN, 1963–66; Consul General, Nairobi, Kenya, 1966–67; Ambassador to Pakistan, 1967–70; Ambassador to the Court of St. James, London, UK, 1971–75; Ambassador, Federal Republic of Germany, 1976; *Address:* Embassy of Kuwait, 5300 Bonn 2, Rheinallee 6, Federal Republic of Germany.

NASEEF, Abdullah Omar, Saudi Arabian geologist/academic; born 1939; *Religion:* Muslim; *Education:* PhD in Geology; *Career:* Lecturer, Faculty of Science, Riyadh University, Saudi Arabia; Assistant Professor, Faculty of Science, King Abdul Aziz University, Jeddah, Saudi Arabia; Secretary General, King Abdul Aziz University; Vice Rector, King Abdul Aziz University, 1976–; member of National Geological Committee, Saudi Arabian Boy Scouts Association, Association of Muslim Sociologists in America; attended Muslim Students Associations conferences in America, Canada, UK and Ireland; contributed to and participated in the Islamic Conference, European Council of Islam, London, UK, 1975; *Interests and Recreations:* reading, travel; *Address:* P O Box 3, Jeddah, Saudi Arabia; telephone: Jeddah 29033.

NASHASHIBI, Hikmat Sharif, Kuwaiti banker; born 12 September 1943, Jerusalem, Palestine; married; one son, one daughter; *Religion:* Muslim; *Education:* BA in Business Administration; *Career:* General Manager, Kuwait International Investment Co, Kuwait; member of Steering Committee, Arab Company for Trading Securities, Kuwait; Vice Chairman, Jordan Securities Corporation, Amman, Jordan; member of the Board of Convertible Capital SA, Luxembourg, Technical Subcommittee set up by the Governors of Arab Central Banks to prepare study on developing Arab capital markets, Primary Market Committee Association of International Bond Dealers, Special Advisory Group of Experts on International Financing to the President of UNIDO; Chief Executive, Al-Mal International Group, London, 1981–;

Publications: Investing Arab Financial Surpluses, 1978, in Arabic; *Arab Development through Cooperation and Financial Markets,* 1979, in English; *Investing Arab Financial Surpluses and Developing Arab Capital Markets,* 1980, in Arabic; *Interests and Recreations:* reading, writing; *Languages:* Arabic, English; *Address:* Al-Mal International Group, 3 St. James's Square, London SW1, England; telephone: (01) 930 9575; telex: 262192 ALMAL.

NASHASHIBI, Nassiriddin, Jordanian journalist; born 1924, Palestine; *Religion:* Muslim; *Education:* Arab College, Jerusalem, Palestine; American University of Beirut (AUB), Beirut, Lebanon; *Career:* Arab Office, Jerusalem, 1945–47; Chief Chamberlain, Amman, Jordan, 1951; Director General, Hashemite Broadcasting, 1952; Editor, *Akhbar al-Yaum,* Cairo, Egypt; Chief Editor, *Al-Gumhuriya'h,* Cairo, Egypt, 1959–65; Representative of the Arab League, 1965–67; Diplomatic Editor of *Al-Ahram,* Cairo, Egypt; Freelance writer and journalist in Europe and the Middle East; *Publications: Steps in Britain,* 1948; *What Happened in the Middle East,* 1958; *Political Short Stories,* 1959; *Return Ticket to Palestine,* 1960; *Some Sand,* 1962; *An Arab in China,* 1964; *Roving Ambassador,* 1970; *The Ink is very Black,* 1976; *Decorations:* Order of the Jordanian Star; *Languages:* Arabic, English; *Address:* Al-Ahram newspaper, Galaa Street, Cairo, Egypt.

NASHIR, Abdul Aziz Abdul Wali, People's Democratic Republic of Yemen politician; born 26 May 1945, North Yemen; married; *Religion:* Muslim; *Career:* Deputy Prime Minister of the Interior, 1970–71; Minister of State for Cabinet Affairs, 1971–72; member of the Executive Committee of the National Front until elected member of the Central Committee; Minister of Industry, 1975; Acting Minister of Planning, 1975; People's Democratic Republic of Yemen Representative to IBRD (World Bank); *Interests and Recreations:* sports; *Languages:* Arabic, English; *Address:* Ministry of Industry, Aden, People's Democratic Republic of Yemen.

NASIR BIN ABDUL AZIZ, HRH Prince, Saudi Arabian Prince/politician; born 1919, Riyadh, Saudi Arabia; son of late King Abdul Aziz; *Religion:* Muslim; *Career:* first Prince to assume the post of Governor of Hijaz after the annexation of Hijaz to the Kingdom, 1947; *Address:* Royal Court, Riyadh, Saudi Arabia.

NASIR, Hanna Musa, Jordanian academic; born 1936, Jaffa, Palestine; married; three sons, one daughter; *Religion:* Christian; *Education:* MSc, American University of Beirut, Lebanon, 1961; PhD in Nuclear Physics, Purdue University, USA, 1967; *Career:* established Birzeit University, the first Arab University in Palestine; President of Birzeit University; deported in November 1974 to Lebanon by Israel on charge of supporting the Palestine Liberation Organization; elected member of the Executive Committee of the Palestine Liberation Organization, 1981; *Publications:* various articles on physics in scientific journals; *Interests and Recreations:* chess, swimming; human rights of the Palestinians under occupation and higher education of the Palestinians; *Languages:* Arabic, English; *Address:* P O Box 974, Amman, Jordan; telephone: 36835.

NASIR, Muhammad, Iraqi academic/diplomat; born 1914; *Religion:* Muslim; *Education:* BSc, MA and EdD, Teachers College, Columbia University, New York, USA; *Career:* teacher, 1931–32; Professor of Education, Baghdad University, 1941–45; Dean of College of Education, Baghdad University, 1955–63; Cultural Attaché, and Permanent Representative of Iraq to the Arab League Cultural Committee, 1945–48; Cultural Attaché, Iraqi Embassy to USA, 1948–54; Alternate Delegate to UN 5th General Assembly; President of Iraq Teachers Union, 1963–64; member of the Council, Baghdad University, 1963–64; Minister of Education, 1964; Ambassador to USSR, 1964–66; Minister of Culture and National Guidance, 1966; Professor of Educational Administration, and Chairman of the Department of Education, Kuwait University, Kuwait, 1967–; *Publications:* several Arabic textbooks; co-author, *Arabic Reading,* 1940; co-author, *Civic Education,* 1940; *Guide to Higher Education in the USA,* 1957; *Readings in Educational Thoughts,* 1973; *Readings in Arabic Islamic Thoughts,* 1977; *Languages:* Arabic, English; *Address:* Kuwait University, P O Box 8063, Salmia, Kuwait.

NASIR, Sari, Jordanian academic/writer; born in Jerusalem, Palestine; married; *Education:* BA in Sociology, 1956; MA in

Communications and Sociology; PhD in Sociology, University of Illinois, USA, 1962; *Career:* Assistant Professor, State University of New York, 1962–65; Professor, Jordanian University; Head of Sociology and Philosophy Department, 1965–; *Publications: The Arab Image in American Popular Culture; The Arab Image in Britain; Working Women in Jordanian Society; A Study of Arabs in British and American Films; The Arabs and the English,* 1976, 2nd edition 1979; *Interests and Recreations:* member of the American Sociologists Association; *Languages:* Arabic, English; *Address:* University of Jordan, Amman, Jordan; telephone: 65111.

NASIRI, Rafa, Iraqi artist/painter; born 1940, Iraq; married; *Religion:* Muslim; *Education:* Fine Arts Institute, Baghdad, Iraq, 1959; Graphic Arts, Central Academy of Fine Arts, China, 1963; studied graphic arts in Lisbon with Gulbenkian Foundation Scholarship, 1967–69; *Career:* appointed to Institute of Fine Arts, 1964; exhibited at Czech Cultural Centre, Baghdad, and International Graphic Art Exhibition, Leipzig, 1965, Iraqi Art Exhibition, Berlin, 1966, Galeria Gravura, Lisbon, Autumn Salon, Estoril, First International Triennale, India, 1968, Baghdad, Beirut, Liège, 1969, Third International Biennale of Graphic Art, Cracow, Poland, Exhibition of Iraqi Posters, Baghdad, 1970, Sultan Gallery, Kuwait and National Gallery of Modern Art, Baghdad, 1971, Four Iraqi Artists Exhibition, National Gallery of Modern Art, Baghdad, Three Iraqi Artists Exhibition, Gallery One, Beirut, First International Biennale of Graphic Art, Norway, Exhibition of Arab Art, Cyprus, Fourth International Poster Biennale, Poland, 1972, Six Iraqi and Syrian Artists Exhibition, National Gallery of Modern Art, Baghdad and Arab Cultural Centre, Damascus, Fourth International Biennale of Drawing, Rijka, Yugoslavia, Fifth International Poster Biennale, Poland; with group of Iraqi artists issued manifesto *The New Vision,* 1969; *Decorations:* Honour Prize from International Summer Academy, Salzburg, Austria; *Interests and Recreations:* reading, music; *Languages:* Arabic, English Chinese; *Address:* 17/78 Qadissiya, Baghdad, Iraq; telephone: 510370.

NASR, Abdul Rahman Salman, Sudanese administrator/diplomat; born 15 September 1932, Al-Khandak, Sudan; married; five sons; *Religion:* Muslim; *Education:* University of Khartoum, Sudan, 1956; Diploma of Public Administration, Birmingham University, UK, 1963; *Career:* Administrator in several Sudanese directorates; one year with Food Industries Corporation; member of the Management Union; Governor of Southern Darfur Province; Governor of Red Sea Province, 1977–80; Ambassador to Egypt, 1981–; attended First Agricultural Conference, Governors Conference, Administration Officers Conference, Administrative Planning Conference in Darfur and the Red Sea, and other political and social care conferences; *Decorations:* Order of the Two Niles 1st Class, Sudan; Order of the Son of Sudan, Sudan; *Interests and Recreations:* reading, chess, swimming; *Address:* Ministry of Foreign Affairs, Khartoum, Sudan.

NASR, Asaad Yusuf, Lebanese businessman/aviation official; born 1927; married; four sons; *Education:* MA in Mathematics and Law, University of Cambridge, UK; *Career:* Instructor of Mathematics and Statistics, American University of Beirut, Beirut, Lebanon, 1950–55; Consultant, Ministry of National Economy, Beirut, 1950–52; Manager, General Planning and Economics, Middle East Airlines, 1955, Executive Vice President, 1963, General Manager, 1965, Managing Director, 1976, Managing Director and Deputy Chairman, 1977; Chairman of the Board and President of the Airlines, 1977–82; Chairman, ASMA (consultancy and management company), 1982–83; Middle East and North Africa Economic Consultant, McDonnell Douglas, 1983–; *Publications: The Asna Formula: A New Concept..Cost Per Passenger Mile (kilometer),* March, 1978, Flight Transportation Laboratory, Department of Aeronautics and Astronautics, Massachussets Institute of Technology, Cambridge, Mass, USA; several articles on air transport and management systems; *Decorations:* Commander of the National Order of Chad, 1973; Officer of the National Order of Lebanon, 1974; Order of the Republic of Egypt, 1974; Order of the Legion of Honour, France, 1975; *Languages:* Arabic, English; *Address:* Justinian Building, 4th Floor Justinian Centre, Beirut, Lebanon.

NASR, Marwan, Lebanese ILO official/administrator; born 9 October 1920, Monsif, Jebail, Lebanon; married; *Education:* MA in Economics and Finance, American University of Beirut, Lebanon; *Career:* Chief, Department of Industry, Beirut, Lebanon; Executive Secretary, Association of Lebanese Industrialists, Beirut, Lebanon; member of the Board of International Institute of Labour Studies, International Labour Organisation, Geneva, Switzerland; Employers member, Governing Body, ILO, Geneva, Switzerland; *Publications: Lebanese Industry,* 1967; *Arab Labour Review,* 1974; *Interests and Recreations:* chess, swimming; member of the Arab Cultural Club, International Association of Social Security; *Languages:* Arabic, English, French; *Address:* Association of Lebanese Industrialists, Chamber of Commerce and Industry Building, Justinein Street, P O Box 11–1520, Beirut, Lebanon; telephone: 350280/2.

NASSIF, Albert, Lebanese diplomat; born 5 January 1915, Lebanon; married; five children; *Education:* Licence in Law, Faculty of Law, Cairo, Egypt, 1935; Diploma in Higher Political Economics Studies, 1937; Diploma of Higher Studies in Law, Faculty of Law, Paris, France, 1938; Doctorate in Law, Faculty of Law, Paris, France, 1942; Diploma in Higher Studies of Public Law, Faculty of Law, Paris, France, 1951; *Career:* Barrister at Law, Mixed Court, Cairo, Egypt, 1935–38; Barrister at Law, Beirut, 1940–42, and 1945–47; Editor, *Gazette des Tribunaux Mixtes d'Egypte,* 1936–38; Legal Adviser, Lebanese Supply Department, 1942; Editor, Brazzaville Radio Station, Congo, 1942–44; Editor, *Le Jour* newspaper, Beirut, Lebanon, 1944–47; Lecturer, Faculty of Law, Beirut, 1945–47; Lebanese representative to the Conference on Trade and Labour, Geneva, Switzerland, 1947, to the UN Commission for Displaced Persons, 1949, to the Diplomatic Conference of the Red Cross, Geneva, 1949, to the Human Rights Commission, 1951; 2nd Secretary, Lebanese Legation to the Holy See, 1947–50; 1st Secretary, Legation to Switzerland, 1950–53; Counsellor, Embassy to France, 1953–55, to the UNESCO Conference of Heads of Cultural Relation Departments, Paris, France, 1955; Chargé d'Affaires *ad interim,* Embassy to Belgium, 1956; Head, Cultural and Social Services, Ministry of Foreign Affairs, Beirut, 1956–57; Lecturer, Faculty of Law, Beirut, 1956–57; Counsellor, Embassy to the UK, 1957–59; Minister Plenipotentiary to Liberia, 1959–61, to Guinea, 1960, to Sierra Leone, 1961; Ambassador to India, 1961; Ambassa-

dor to Turkey, 1963–65; Head, International Section, Ministry of Foreign Affairs; Lecturer, Faculty of Political Science, Social Sciences Institute, Lebanese University, 1965–69; Ambassador to Tunisia, 1969–71; Ambassador to Switzerland, 1971–78; *Publications:* various articles published in law reviews; *Decorations:* Officer, National Order of the Cedar; Légion d'Honneur, France; as well as many other foreign distinctions and decorations; *Languages:* Arabic, French; *Address:* c/o Lebanese Embassy, Alpenstrasse 24, Bern, Switzerland; Residence — 62 Maamari Street, Beirut, Lebanon.

NASSIF, Ramsis, Egyptian UN official/journalist; born 27 December 1921; married; *Education:* BA in Journalism, American University in Cairo, Egypt, 1940–44; *Career:* UN Correspondent, Egyptian newspapers, 1949–53; UN Press Liaison, Asian-African Group, 1958–61; Spokesman for the UN Secretary General, 1961–71; Chief, Information Unit, UNCTAD, Switzerland; *Decorations:* Farouk Press Prize, 1945; *Languages:* Arabic, English, French; *Address:* Office — UNCTAD, Palais des Nations, CH-1221 Geneva 10, Switzerland; telephone: (022) 346011; Residence — 12 Chemin de la Tourelle, CH-1211 Geneva, Switzerland; telephone: (022) 982465.

NASSIR, Muhammad, Moroccan engineer/politician; born March 1934, Morocco; *Religion:* Muslim; *Education:* Diploma in Engineering from School of Geographical Sciences, Paris, France; *Career:* senior civil servant for agricultural improvement and agrarian reform; President of Commission on Foreign Affairs while Deputy for Azrou and later President of their rural community; Vice President to the Provincial Council of Meknes; member of the Mouvement Populaire; Minister of Transport, 1977; President of the National Association of Geometric and Topographical Engineers; *Languages:* Arabic, French; *Address:* Ministry of Transport, Rabat, Morocco.

NATTO, Ibrahim Abbas, Saudi Arabian academic; born 15 May 1945, Mecca, Saudi Arabia; married; two sons, one daughter; *Religion:* Muslim; *Education:* BA in Political Science, USA, 1968; MA in Public Administration, University of Texas, Austin, USA, 1970; PhD, Public Educational Administration, USA, 1973: *Career:* Educational Expert, Ministry of Education, Saudi Arabia, 1973–76; Visiting Professor, Riyadh University, 1973–74; Director, Statistical Data and Educational Documentation, 1974–76; Assistant Professor and Chairman, Management Development Programme, University of Petroleum and Minerals, 1976–77; Dean, Student Affairs, University of Petroleum and Minerals, 1977–78; Professor and Director, Preparatory Progammes, College of Industrial Management, 1979–; Head of Saudi Arabian Delegation, Cultural Committee of UNESCO 18th General Conference, Paris, 1974; represented the Saudi Arabian Ministry of Education in the Symposuim of Ministries of Education in the Arabian Gulf, Bahrain, 1975; represented the Saudi Arabian Ministry of Education in the UNESCO Symposuim on Improving Education Documentation and Information Agencies in Arab States, Cairo, Egypt; representative of World Council on Curriculum and Instruction, 1981; *Publications: Management: Basic Concepts,* 1979, co-author with Henry Albers, John Wiley & Sons, in Arabic and English; *Handbook for Students on Scholarships to the US,* 1977, published by Ministry of Education; *The Growth of Elementary Education in Saudi Arabia,* in Arabic and English; *Educational Issues in Saudi Arabia,* Jeddah, under publication by Tihama; *Local Administration in Mecca,* England, under publication by Longman; *Interests and Recreation:* jogging, chess, photography, reading; Head of Philanthropic Society, University of Petroleum and Minerals, Dhahran, Saudi Arabia; member of Pi Sigma Alpha, Phi Kappa Phi, Phi Delta Kappa, the International School Association and the International Management Association; *Languages:* Arabic, English, French; *Address:* P O Box 500 UPM, Dhahran, Saudi Arabia; telephone: (03) 8602135; (03) 8602145.

NAWWAF BIN ABDUL AZIZ, HRH Prince, Saudi Arabian Prince/administrator; born 1934, Riyadh, Saudi Arabia; son of late King Abdul Aziz; *Religion:* Muslim; *Education:* private tuition; Stanford University, USA, 1954–55; *Career:* business interests in Arab Cement and National Gypsum Companies; Amir of the Palaces and the Royal Guard, and Minister of Finance, 1961–62; special adviser to late King Faisal on Gulf affairs, 1968–74; Head of the Royal Cabinet

Office in the early 1960s; *Languages:* Arabic, English; *Address:* Royal Court, Riyadh, Saudi Arabia.

NAZIR, Ali Gamal al-, Egyptian official/ economist; born 22 January 1930, Aswan, Egypt; married; one son, one daughter; *Education:* BA in Commerce, Cairo University, Egypt, 1950; MSc, University of Pittsburgh, Pennsylvania, USA, 1958; *Career:* Assistant Division Chief, Ministry of Economy, 1961; Division Chief, Ministry of Economy, 1966; Deputy Director General, Ministry of Economy, 1970; Director General, Ministry of Economy, 1974, Under Secretary 1976; *Interests and Recreations:* swimming, tennis; member of the Automobile Club; member of the Heliopolis Sporting Club; *Languages:* Arabic, English, French; *Address:* Ministry of Tourism and Civil Aviation, 110 Kasr El Aini Street, Cairo, Egypt.

NAZIR, Fuad, Saudi Arabian diplomat; born 1928; married; *Religion:* Muslim; *Career:* diplomatic service; served in Embassy to UK, 1949–55, Embassy to Spain, 1961–63; Head of Protocol, Ministry of Foreign Affairs; Ambassador to Belgium, 1963–71; Ambassador to Egypt, 1971; Ambassador to Argentina, 1977–; *Languages:* Arabic, English, French; *Address:* Saudi Arabian Embassy, Mariscal R Castilla 2951, Buenos Aires, Argentina.

NAZIR, Hisham Muhiyddin, Saudi Arabian politician; born 31 August 1932; married; three sons, two daughters; *Education:* BA and MA, UCLA, USA; Honorary Doctorate of Law, Korean University; *Career:* Governor, OPEC, 1961; Deputy Minister of Petroleum and Mineral Resources, 1962–68; President, Planning Organization, 1968–75; Minister of State, 1971–75; Minister of Planning, 1975–; Vice Chairman, Royal Commission for Jubail and Yanbu; Director and member of the Board of Supreme Council of Petroleum; member, Higher Council of Universities, including King Abdul Aziz University, University of Petroleum and Minerals, and others; Chancellor's Associate, Life Member, UCLA, USA; *Publications: The Philosophy of Peace; Patriotism and the Responsibility of the Citizen; Wealth and the Nation..Past and Future;* and others; *Decorations:* Grand Crus, Spain; Sash of Leopold, Belgium; Hamayun Medal, 1st

Grade, Iran; National Order of Merit, France; National Cedar Medal, Lebanon; *Interests and Recreations:* reading; *Address:* P O Box 358, University Street, Riyadh, Saudi Arabia; telephone: 4023800, 4023812; telex 201075 PLAN SJ.

NEKRUF, Yunis; Moroccan diplomat; born 1916; *Religion:* Muslim; *Education:* Licencié ès-Lettres, Institute des Hautes Etudes, Rabat, Morocco; University of Bordeaux, France; Algiers University, Algeria; *Career:* Director of the Cabinet of the Minister of Education, 1955–57; Cultural Counsellor, Embassy to France, and Permanent Delegate to UNESCO, Paris, 1957–59; Director of Cultural Affairs and Technical Assistant, Ministry of Foreign Affairs, 1959–61; Counsellor, Minister Plenipotentiary, Embassy to France, 1961–64; Ambassador to Senegal, Gambia, Guinea, Liberia, 1965–67; Ambassador to Yugoslavia, 1967–68; Director of Political Affairs, Ministry of Foreign Affairs, 1968–71; Ambassador to India, 1971–74; Delegate to UN General Assembly, 1965, 1968–71; represented Morocco at various international conferences; *Publications: Méthode Active d'Arabe* 1958, and various essays and articles on Portuguese colonization; *Decorations:* Officer of the Légion d'Honneur, Palmes Académiques; Commander, Arts et Lettres, France; Officer, Ouissam Alouite, Order of the Throne, Morocco; Grand Officer of the National Order of Yugoslavia; Order of Tudor Vladimirescu of Romania; Knight of the Grand Cross, Order of Merit of the Republic of Italy; Grand Officer of the Order of Merit, Senegal; *Languages:* Arabic, French; *Address:* Ministry of Foreign Affairs, Rabat, Morocco.

NIGM, Ali M., Egyptian banker; *Religion:* Muslim; *Career:* Deputy Governor, Central Bank of Egypt; *Address:* Central Bank of Egypt, 31 Kasr El Nil Street, Cairo, Egypt.

NIJIM, Bashir K., Arab-American academic; born 13 September 1936; married; two sons; *Religion:* Christian; *Education:* BA, Augustana College, Rock Island, Illinois, USA; MA, PhD, Indiana University, Bloomington Indiana, USA; graduate studies, Johns Hopkins University,and Harvard University; *Career:* Assistant Professor of Geography, 1962; Associate Professor, 1969; Professor and Head of Department of Geography,

University of Northern Iowa, USA, 1972; Roster of Consultants regarding education in developing countries, UNESCO; member of the Association of American Geographers, American Geographical Society, National Council for Geographic Education, American Association for the Advancement of Science, the Association of Arab-American University Graduates, the Middle East Studies Association of North America; *Publications:* Editor, *Handbook of the Arab World,* 1977; Editor, *Geographical Perspectives,* an academic journal, 1972–79; author of numerous geographical publications; *Decorations:* Certificate of Meritorious Teaching Achievement, from the National Council for Geographic Education; *Languages:* Arabic, English, French; *Address:* Department of Geography, University of Northern Iowa, Cedar Falls, Iowa 50614, USA; telephone: (319) 273 2772.

NIL, Zakaria Mustafa, Egyptian journalist; born 20 July 1924, Dakahliya, Egypt; married; three daughters, two sons; *Religion:* Muslim; *Education:* Diploma in Arabic Language; *Career:* journalist, 1950–; Head of Arabic Affairs Department, *Al-Ahram* daily newspaper; covered the Iraqi Revolution, 1958, the Libyan Revolution, 1969, and the Yemen Revolution, 1962; coverd most of the Arab summit conferences; *Publications: Focus of Danger in the Arab Gulf,* 1971; and other books; *Decorations:* Order of the Tunisian Republic, 1971; *Interests and Recreations:* travel, swimming, classical literature, historical novels; member of the Hunting Club; *Languages:* Arabic, English; *Address:* Journalists City, 2 Adnan al-Madany Street, Agouza, Cairo, Egypt; telephone: 811172, 977739; Al-Ahram, Galaa Street, Cairo, Egypt.

NIMATALLAH, Yusuf Abdul Wahib, Saudi Arabian economist/official; born 1940, Jeddah, Saudi Arabia; resident in Oman; *Religion:* Muslim; *Education:* abroad; *Career:* Professor, Riyadh University, Saudi Arabia; later worked in the Saudi Ministries of Oil and Finance before being seconded to Oman in 1974 as Economic Adviser to the Ministry of Development, 1975; Deputy Governor of the Central Bank; Oil Adviser to the Ministry of Agriculture, Fisheries, Petroleum and Minerals; *Address:* Ministry of Agriculture, Fisheries, Petroleum and Minerals, P O Box 467, Muscat, Oman.

NIMEIRI, Gaafar Muhammad, President of the Democratic Republic of the Sudan; born 1930; *Education:* El Hijra Elementary School, Omdurman; Wad Medani Government School, Gezira; Hantoub Secondary School, Gezira; married; *Career:* Graduated as Second Lieutenant from Military College, and transferred to Western Command; various courses in Egypt, Federal Republic of Germany and USA; joined first batch of officers to establish the Northern Command at Shendi, 1957; Southern Command, Juba, 1959; with the Free Officers Group played leading role in the October Revolution of 1964; after its setback transferred to Western Command, Al- Fasher, subsequently to Eastern Command, Gedaref; Officer in Command of Troops at Torit, Southern Command; transferred to Infantry School at Gebeit as Second Commanding Officer and Senior Lecturer, then Officer in Command until the May Revolution, 1969; Chairman of the Revolutionary Command Council; Commander in Chief of the Armed Forces and Minister of Defence; elected by plebiscite first President of the Republic, 1971; Concluded the Addis Ababa Accord with Southern Sudan Leaders ending the 17 year old civil war in the South on the basis of Southern Region Autonomy, February 1972; Unanimously elected President of the Sudanese Socialist Union by the First National General Congress, 1974; Chairman of OAU 1978–79; promoted to Rank of Field Marshal, 1979; *Decorations:* Insignia of Honour; Grand Cordan of Honour; Order of the Revolution; Order of Loyal Son of the Sudan; Order of Bravery, First Class; Long Meritorious Service Medal; Evacuation Medal; Independance Medal; Duty Medal, 1st Class; *Languages:* Arabic, English; *Address:* Office of the President, Khartoum, The Democratic Republic of the Sudan.

NIMR, Ibrahim Muhammad, Sudanese economist/banker; born 1923; *Religion:* Muslim; *Education:* Gordon College, Khartoum; BA in Economics, University of Aberystwyth, UK; *Career:* Senior Inspector, Ministry of Finance; Bank of Sudan; General Manager, Al-Nilein Bank; Chairman, Bank of Sudan, 1973–; Chairman, Savings and Investment Council, 1973; member of Ministerial Council for National Economy, 1973–74; member of Khartoum University Council, 1974–; member of Islamic University Council, 1974; member of Board of Directors, Sudanese Development Corporation, 1974–78; Alternate Governor for Sudan, IMF, 1972–; *Languages:* Arabic, English; *Address:* Bank of Sudan, Khartoum, P O Box 313, Sudan; telephone: 78064; telex: 352.

NISF, Muhammad Yusuf al-, Kuwaiti businessman/politician; born 1915; *Religion:* Muslim; *Education:* general; *Career:* Director of the Public Works Department, 1950s; member of Joint Council of Shaikhs and Merchants set up to draft electoral regulations of the Constituent Assembly, 1961; member of Constituent Assembly, 1961; Minister of Social Affairs, 1962–63; member of Board of Chamber of Commerce; Director of Kuwait Pipe Company and Kuwait Fund for Arab Economic Development (KFAED); Chairman, Al-Ahliya Insurance Company; *Address:* Ahliya Insurance Company SAK, P O Box 1602, Ali Al Salem Street, Kuwait; telephone: 435011; telex: 22213 KT.

NO'MAN, Abdul Magid, Egyptian journalist; born 18 April 1915, Egypt; *Religion:* Muslim; *Education:* Licence in Law; *Career:* Signals Staff Officer; Assistant Director, Radar and Signals Department, Egyptian Air Force, 1965; Secretary general, Aswan Governorate; Editor in Chief, Sports Section, *Akhbar al-Yaum* newspaper, Cairo, Egypt; President, Sports Journalists Association, Egypt, 1970; President, African Sports Journalists Association, Egypt, 1974; Vice President, International Sports Journalists Association, 1974; *Publications: Football: Training and Tactics,* 1968; *Decorations:* Sports Decoration 1st Class, Egypt, 1975; Nile Decoration 5th Class, Egypt, 1950; *Interests and Recreations:* football, table-tennis, athletics; member of National Sports Club, Cairo, Aviation Sports Club, Gezira Sporting Club; *Languages:* Arabic, English, French, Italian, Russian; *Address:* 111 Al-Hegaz Street, Heliopolis, Cairo, Egypt; telephone: 869727.

NOFAL, Sayyid, Egyptian Arab League official/diplomat; born 1910; married; *Religion:* Muslim; *Education:* Cairo University, Egypt; *Career:* Head of Literary Department, *Al-Siyassa,* 1935–38; Lecturer, Cairo University, 1938; Director of Technical Secretariat, Ministry of Education; Ministry of Foreign Affairs; transferred to Arab League Secretariat; Assistant Secretary General of the Arab League, 1961; retired from diplomatic service; *Publications:* many books including *The Arab-Israeli Conflict,* 1962; *Arab Unity,* 1964; *Arab Nationalism,* 1965; *Arab Socialism,* 1966; *The Record of Israel,* 1966; *Joint Arab Action,* Vol I 1968, Vol II 1971; *The Arab Gulf or The Eastern Borders of the Arab Homeland,* 1969; *An Introduction to Israeli Foreign Policy,* 1972; *Address:* Residence — 9 Khan Younis Street, Engineers City, Dokki, Cairo, Egypt.

NOUH AHMAD, Ahmad, Egyptian politician/engineer; born 4 December 1921; *Religion:* Muslim; *Education:* Alexandria University and Air Academy, Egypt; *Career:* Lieutenant General, Pilot Engineer, General HQ Armed Forces; Technical General Manager, Misrair (Egyptian Air Lines); General Secretary, later Assistant Minister, Ministry of War; Minister of State for Civil Aviation, 1971–72; Minister of Civil Aviation, 1972–74; Minister of Tourism, 1973–74; *Address:* Ministry of Tourism, Cairo, Egypt.

NOUIRA, Habib, Tunisian diplomat; born 1925, Monastir, Tunisia; married; three children; *Religion:* Muslim; *Education:* University of Zitouna, Tunis, and Cairo, Egypt; *Career:* twice imprisoned because of nationalist political activity during World War II; worked in Cairo for the Maghreb Arab Bank, 1952; after Independence joined the Tunisian Foreign Service; Embassy to Libya, 1956–57; Embassy to Morocco, 1957–59; Embassy to Iraq, 1964–65; Embassy to Libya, 1966–67; Ministry of Foreign Affairs, Tunis; Ambassador to Kuwait, 1969–73; Ambassador to Iraq, 1973; Ambassador to Syria, 1974; *Languages:* Arabic, French; *Address:* Ministry of Foreign Affairs, Boulevard Farhat Hached, Tunis, Tunisia.

NOUIRA, Hadi, Tunisian politician; born 6 April 1911, Monastir, Tunisia; married; *Religion:* Muslim; *Education:* Law, University of Paris, France; *Career:* Sorbonne Delegate of the Neo-Destour; called to Tunis Bar, 1937; elected Secretary of the Confédération Générale des Travailleurs Tunisiens; arrested and imprisoned in France for nationalist activities, 1938–42; arrested for political activities, 1952–53; Minister of Commerce in the Tahar Ben Ammar Government, 1954; Minister of Finance in the first Bourguiba Government, 1956; Secretary of State for Finance, 1957; Minister of State, 1958; Governor of the Central Bank of Tunisia, 1958–70; Minister of Finance, 1970; Prime Minister, 1970; Secretary General of the Destour Socialist Party; acting Head of State during President Bourguiba's absence from Tunisia for medical treatment, 1971; Prime Minister, 1970; *Languages:* Arabic, French; *Address:* Office of the Prime Minister, Tunis, Tunisia.

NOUR, Muhammad Abdullah, Sudanese UN official; born 2 June 1925, Omdurman, Sudan; married; *Religion:* Muslim; *Education:* BSc in Botany, Exeter University, UK, 1948–51; PhD in Plant Pathology, Rothamsted Experimental Station, London, 1954–56; *Career:* Head, Department of Crop Protection, 1957; Dean, Faculty of Agriculture, University of Khartoum, 1957–69; Deputy Vice Chancellor, Universtiy of Khartoum, 1962–64; Minister of Agriculture and Forestry, 1969–70; Assistant Director General and Regional Representative for Near East, FAO, Egypt, 1970–78; Deputy Director General, International Centre for Agricultural Research in Dry Areas (ICARDA), Lebanon, 1978–81; Director General, International Centre for Agricultural Research in the Dry Areas, Lebanon, 1981–; member of the Association of Applied Biologists, UK; member of the Philosophical Society, Khartoum; *Address:* P O Box 114/5055 Beirut, Lebanon; telephone: 303860; telex: 22509 LE.

NOURI, Anwar Abdullah al-, Kuwaiti banker/official; born 1940, Kuwait; married; four children; *Religion:* Muslim; *Education:* BSc, University College, Bangor, North Wales, UK; *Career:* Teacher, Shuwaikh Secondary School; Cultural Attache, Kuwaiti Embassy to UK; Assistant Under Secretary, Ministry of Education, 1965–66; Secretary General, University of Kuwait, 1966–78; Chairman and Managing Director, The Industrial Bank of Kuwait, 1978–; member of the Board of Trustees, University of Kuwait; *Languages:* Arabic, English; *Address:* The Industrial Bank of Kuwait, Al-Ahli Bank Building, Oman Street, P O Box 3146, Safat, Kuwait; telephone: 653000; telex: 2469, 2582.

NOURI, Mahmud Abdul Khalik al-, Kuwaiti banker; born 1 November 1949, Kuwait; married; one son, three daughters; *Religion:* Muslim; *Education:* BA in Commerce; *Career:* General Manager, Bank of Kuwait and the Middle East; Chairman of Kuwait

Insulating Material; Managing Director, United Gulf Bank; *Languages:* Arabic, English; *Address:* P O Box 26487, Safat, Kuwait.

NOWAIS, Nasir Muhammad Ali, United Arab Emirates official; born 1945, Abu Dhabi; married; two sons, one daughter; *Religion:* Muslim; *Education:* BA, School of Journalism, Cairo University, Cairo, Egypt; *Career:* Technical Director, Ministry of Information, 1969; Head of Broadcasting, 1969–70; Head of Press and Public Relations, 1970–73; Head of Broadcasting and Television, 1973–76; Under Secretary, Ministry of Information and Culture, 1976–78; General Manager, Abu Dhabi Fund for Arab Economic Development, 1978–; *Languages:* Arabic, English; *Address:* Abu Dhabi Fund for Arab Economic Development. P O Box 814, Abu Dhabi, United Arab Emirates; telephone: 22865; telex: 2287 AH.

NOWILATY, Rashad M., Saudi Arabian diplomat; born 1929, Mecca, Saudi Arabia; *Religion:* Muslim; *Education:* BA in Political Science, Faculty of Commerce, Cairo University, Egypt, 1953; *Career:* Diplomatic Attaché, Foreign Ministry, 1953; established and directed the Press Department after 2 months training at UN Secretariat, New York, USA; one of the first Saudi Arabian diplomats to establish the Saudi Arabian Embassy in West Germany, where he served as 3rd and later 2nd Secretary, 1960; 1st Secretary, Counsellor and Minister Plenipotentiary, Lebanon, 1960–67; Personal Assistant to Minister of Foreign Affairs; Aassistant Deputy Minister, directing the Political Arab Affairs Department, 1968–72; Ambassador to the Netherlands; Adviser to Saudi Arabian Delegations to the First and Second Arab Summit Conferences, Cairo and Alexandria, 1964; Alternate Delegate of Saudi Arabia to UN General Assembly, 1967; Deputy Head of Saudi Delegations to the first three annual conferences of the Islamic Foreign Ministers, Jeddah; and to the conference for the preparation of the Islamic International Agreement establishing the International Islamic News Agency, Tehran; Head of the Saudi Mission for negotiating and signing an agreement with Egypt, for the settlement of Saudi Arabian private funds previously nationalized by Egypt; Ambassador of Saudi Arabia to Senegal, Niger and Gambia, 1976–; *Decorations:* King Abdul Aziz Order, Distinguished Grade; Lebanese Order of the Cedar; Grosses Verdienstkreuz, 1st Class, West Germany; *Address:* Foreign Ministry, P O Box 495, Jeddah, Saudi Arabia; Embassy of Saudi Arabia, Rues Béranger Feraud et Masclary, BP 109, Dakar, Senegal.

NSOULI, Al-Walid, Lebanese banker; resident in UK; born 25 February 1944, Beirut, Lebanon; married; two sons, one daughter; *Religion:* Muslim; *Education:* BA, St. Joseph University, Beirut, Lebanon; *Career:* Treasurer, Bank Al Mashrek, Beirut, 1971; Vice President, Treasury Department, Middle East, Morgan Guaranty Trust Company of New York; member of International Arab Cambiste Association; member of Arab Bankers Association, London, UK; *Interests and Recreations:* squash, basketball; *Languages:* Arabic, French, English; *Address:* 92 Oakwood Court, London W14, UK; telephone: 602 0966.

NSOULI, Moustafa, Lebanese official/economist born 1909, Beirut, Lebanon; married; three children; *Education:* BA in Commerce and Economics, American University of Beirut, Lebanon; *Career:* Teacher, Mokassed College, 1931–37; teacher in Iraq, 1937–40; businessman, 1940–42; Head, General Statistics Office, 1942–52; Director General, Ministry of National Economy, 1952–59; Director General, Ministry of Planning, 1959–66; President, Board of Directors, Civil Servants' Co-operative, 1967–70; *Publications:* various articles on economics published in the local press; *Interests and Recreations:* swimming; reading; *Languages:* Arabic, French, English; *Address:* Residence — Tadmore Street, Mousseitbe, Beirut, Lebanon.

NSOULI, Zakarya, Lebanese lawyer; born 8 November 1935; *Religion:* Muslim; *Education:* Licence in French Law, Licence in Lebanese Law; Degree in General Law; Degree in Economics; LLD, University of St. Joseph, Beirut; *Career:* Lawyer, Court of Appeal and Supreme Court, 1961–; Assistant Professor, Faculty of Law, University of St. Joseph, Beirut, 1961–75; Minister of Oil and Petroleum, 1973; Professor of Law, Beirut, 1976–; Vice President, University of St. Joseph, Beirut, 1977–80; Partner, Zakarya and Marwaan Nsouli Law Firm; *Publications:* dissertation on the standards of management contracts in Lebanese Law, 1965, in French; study on valid legal order of independent interests in Lebanon and the ways of organizing them, published in *Al-Sharq al-Adna* magazine; editorial articles published in *L'Orient le Jour*, 1965–75, in French; lectures in Al-Nadwa Al-Lubnaniya; *Interests and Recreations:* music, reading, sports; Deputy President of Lebanese Pen Club; President of Rotary Club, Beirut, 1979; *Languages:* Arabic, French, English; *Address:* P O Box 7839, Beirut, Lebanon; Nsouli Building, Anis Nsouli Street, Al-Masraa, Beirut, Lebanon; telephone: 318247, 317074.

NUBAN, Said Abdul Khair al-, People's Democratic Republic of Yemen Politician; *Career:* Permanent Secretary, Ministry of Education 1973–75; Minister of Education, 1975; *Address:* Ministry of Education, Aden, People's Democratic Republic of Yemen.

NUQUL, Elia Costandi, Jordanian businessman; born 25 December 1928, Ramlih, Palestine; married; two sons, two daughters; *Religion:* Christian; *Education:* general; *Career:* accountant, 1949–51; assistant manager, 1951–52; in 1952 established own company, Nugul Brothers (paper, converting foodstuffs, army contractors), General Manager and Senior Partner; General Manager, Arab Foam Factory Company; General Manager, Naseem Trading Company; General Manager, Nuqul Engineering and Contracting Company; General Manager, Electra Company, Vice-Chairman of Middle East Insurance Company; member of the Board of Directors of Jordan Paper and Cardboard Factories Company Limited; *Interests and Recreations:* swimming, reading; member of Board of Trustees of the National Orthodox School, Amman; Eisenhower Fellow, 1964; *Languages:* Arabic, English; *Address:* 2nd Circle, Jabal Amman, Amman, Jordan; telephone: 44251, 44767.

NURALLA, Nuralla, Syrian politician/academic; born 1924; *Education:* Law Degree and Doctorate in Finance; Diploma in Higher Commercial Studies, University of Paris, Sorbonne, France; *Career:* Ministry of Finance; Governor of the Central Bank, 1963; Ministry of Finance, 1963; Professor in Faculty of Commerce, Damascus University; Minister of Finance, 1969–74; Minister of State for Planning, 1974–76; *Languages:* Arabic, French; *Address:* Ministry of State for Planning Affairs, Damascus, Syria.

NURUDDIN, Nuruddin A., Bahraini banker; born 5 November 1945, Bahrain; married; two sons, one daughter; *Religion:* Muslim; *Education:* Graduate of the Institute of Cost and Management Accountants, UK; *Career:* Manager of Operations, Chase Manhattan Bank, Bahrain, 1975; Second Vice President, Chase Manhattan Bank, Bahrain, 1976; Deputy General Manager, National Bank of Bahrain, 1976; General Manager and Chief Executive, National Bank of Bahrain, 1979–; member of the Executive Committee and Board of Directors, Arab Latin American Bank, Lima, of the Board of Directors of Bahrain Middle East Bank, and of Bahrain Telecommunications Company, Bahrain; Chairman of Bahrain Bankers Society; member of Special Council for Training in the Banking Sector, Bahrain, the Executive Committee of Arab Bankers Association, London, UK; *Interests and Recreations:* tennis, swimming, walking; *Languages:* Arabic, English, Persian; *Address:* P O Box 106, Manama, Bahrain; telephone: 258800; telex: 8242 NATBNK BN.

NUSEIBEH, Hazim, Jordanian diplomat/politician; born 1922, Jerusalem; *Education:* American University of Beirut, Beirut, Lebanon; Princeton University, USA; Jerusalem Law School; *Career:* General Director, Broadcasting and Press Department of the Government of Jordan, 1951; Representative of Jordan, Mixed Armistice Commission, 1954–56; held various senior cabinet posts including Minister of the Royal Court, Minister of Foreign Affairs and Minister of Reconstruction and Development responsible for Palestinian Refugee Affairs, 1957–68; Ambassador to Egypt, 1969; Ambassador to Turkey; Ambassador to Italy; Permanent Representative of Jordan to UN, 1976; *Address:* Ministry of Foreign Affairs, Amman, Jordan.

NUSF, Humud Yusuf al, Kuwaiti businessman/politician; born 1918; married; eight children; *Religion:* Muslim; *Career:* family business; member of the Municipal Council, 1960–62; member of Parliament, 1963–76; Minister of Public Health, 1965; manager of family business; Minister of Public Works, 1971, 1975, 1976; *Languages:* Arabic, English; *Address:* Ministry of Public Works, P O Box 8, Mubarak Al Kabir Street, Kuwait; telephone: 43700; telex: 22753 ASHGAL KT.

NUSSAIBAH, Anwar, Jordanian politician/ lawyer; born 20 January 1913, Jerusalem; married, four sons, two daughters; *Religion:* Muslim; *Education:* BSc, Cambridge University, UK; pupillage for the Bar, Grays Inn, London, UK; *Career:* Land Office, Palestine, 1936; Magistrate, 1937–42; Lecturer in Constitutional Law, Jerusalem Law College, 1938–48; Chief Arab Delegate, Israel-Jordan Mixed Armistice Commission, 1951; Minister of Construction and Development, 1952–54; Minister of Defence and Education, 1954–55; Governor of Jerusalem, 1952; Minister of Defence, 1952–53, 1954–55; Jordanian Ambassador to UK, also to Denmark and Holland, 1965; resigned, 1967; Chairman, Jerusalem District Electricity Company, 1978–; *Decorations:* Star of Jordan 1st Class; Order of Knight of St. John's Hospital, Jerusalem; Order of Knight of the Church of the Last Supper; *Languages:* Arabic, English; *Address:* P O Box 517, Jerusalem; telephone: 23333.

NUSSAIBAH, Hazem, Jordanian politician/ diplomat; born 1922, Jerusalem; married, with children; *Religion:* Muslim; *Education:* Rawda College, Jerusalem; Victoria College, Alexandria, Egypt; American University of Beirut, Lebanon; Law School, Jerusalem; Woodrow Wilson School of Public and International Affairs; PhD in Political Studies, Princeton University, USA, 1945; *Career:* Under Secretary, Ministry of National Economy, 1957–59; President, Jordan Development Board, 1959–61; Minister of Foreign Affairs, 1962–63, 1965–66; Minister of the Royal Court, 1963–65; Professor of International Affairs, Jordan University, 1966–67; Minister of Construction and Development, 1967–69; Ambassador to Egypt, 1969–71; Ambassador to Turkey, 1971–73; Ambassador to Italy, 1973–75; also accredited to Austria and Switzerland; Ambassador to United Nations, 1976; *Publications: Ideas of Arab Nationalism,* 1956; *Languages:* Arabic, English; *Address:* 866 United Nations Plaza, Room 550–552, New York 10017, USA.

NUSSEIBEH, Zaki Anwar, United Arab Emirates official; born 29 April 1946, Jerusalem; married; *Religion:* Muslim; *Education:* Rugby School, Warwickshire, UK; MA, Economics, Cambridge University, UK; *Career:* Head of Research, Ministry of Information, Abu Dhabi, 1968–70; Director of Information, Ministry of Information, Abu Dhabi, 1970–74; Press Adviser to President of United Arab Emirates; and principal interpreter during state visits, 1974–; *Publications:* various newspaper articles and translations in periodicals; *Decorations:* Jordanian Order of Independence; Officer of Order of Merit of France; Knight of the Order of Zaire; *Interests and Recreations:* reading, theatre, poetry, swimming, skiing, travel; *Languages:* Arabic, English, French, Russian; *Address:* Manhal Place, P O Box 280, Abu Dhabi, United Arab Emirates; telephone: 4332.

NUWAISER, Muhammad al-, Saudi Arabian official; born circa 1922; *Religion:* Muslim; *Education:* general; training in politics, diplomatic ceremonial and protocol; *Career:* member of the cabinet of the late King Faisal; Chief of the Private Royal Office on King Faisal's accession to the throne, 1964; Chief of the Private Office of the late King Khalid, 1975–82; *Interests and Recreations:* reading; *Address:* The Royal Cabinet, Riyadh, Saudi Arabia; telephone: 404 4200.

O

OBAID, Ibrahim Ahmad, Saudi Arabian official; born 17 January 1939, Asir, Saudi Arabia; three children; *Religion:* Muslim; *Education:* Victoria College, Alexandria, Egypt; Pennsylvania Military College, USA; MA in Government Studies; PhD in International Politics, Indiana State University, Bloomington, USA; *Career:* commissioned 2nd Lieutenant, Saudi Army; Instructor, Saudi Command and Staff College; Adviser and Chairman of Board, PETROMIN; attended all OPEC Ministerial meetings; Director General, Office of the Minister of Petroleum and Mineral Resources; Deputy Minister, Ministry of Posts, Telephones, Telegraphs, Riyadh, Saudi Arabia; Chairman, Arab Satellite Communications Organisation; member of the International Institute for Strategic Studies; *Publications:* numerous articles in Middle East journals and magazines; several articles in local newspapers, in *Okaz* daily paper, Jeddah, and *Al-Jazirah,* Riyadh; *Decorations:* Grand Cordon of the Order of Brilliant Star, Taiwan Republic; *Interests and Recreations:* reading, swimming, boxing; *Languages:* Arabic, English; *Address:* P O Box No 10878, Riyadh, Saudi Arabia; telephone: Office — 401 2310, 401 4686; Residence — 464 0006, 464 8235.

OBAIDAT, Muhammad al-Farhan, Jordanian official/educationalist; born 1914, Irbid, Jordan; *Religion:* Muslim; *Education:* Horticultural School, Jordan, 1933–34; course in Education, Egypt; *Career:* school teacher, 1932–38; school principal, 1939–53; Assistant Agricultural Education Director, 1954–56; Director, Huwwarah Teachers Training Center, 1956–57; Director of Education, 1957–62; Director of Primary Education, Ministry of Education, 1963–64; Cultural Counsellor, Embassy to Egypt, 1964–67; retired 1967; Minister of Public Works, 1971–72; member of the Consultative Council, 1978–80; *Decorations:* Order of the Jordanian Star, 1972; Medal of Education, 1973; *Languages:* Arabic, English; *Address:* Sports City Post Office, Sheimeisani, Amman, Jordan; telephone: 66966.

OBAIDI, Mahdi Muhsin al-, Iraqi official; born 14 November 1928, Baghdad, Iraq; married; four daughters; *Religion:* Muslim; *Education:* BSc and postgraduate studies in Agricultural Economics, University of California, Berkeley, USA; *Career:* Ministry of Economy, Ministry of Trade, 1954; Permanent Secretary and Deputy Minister, Ministry of Trade, Foreign Trade Relations, 1972–; member of the Economists Association of Iraq; member of the Syndicate of Agricultural Engineers; *Publications:* research papers, University of Baghdad; *Decorations:* Knight of the Order of the Italian Republic, 1964; *Interests and Recreations:* gardening, walking; *Languages:* Arabic, English, Spanish; *Address:* Ministry of Trade, Sahat al Khalani, Baghdad, Iraq; telephone: 8880772; Residence — 35/5/1 Hayy al Ma'rifa, al Saidiya, Baghdad, Iraq; telephone: 5530494;

OBAIDLI, Ahmad, United Arab Emirates official; born 1926, Bahrain; *Religion:* Muslim; *Career:* Public Relations Officer for British Petroleum, Bahrain, 1966; Secretary to Shaikh Zaid and Head of the Palace Office; Minister, United Arab Emirates Embassy, London, UK; *Languages:* Arabic, English; *Address:* Ministry of Foreign Affairs, P O Box 1, Abu Dhabi, United Arab Emirates.

ODEH, Ali Hassan, Jordanian politician; born 1917, Jordan; married; *Religion:* Muslim; *Education:* Diploma, Institute of Law, Jerusalem; Dar al-Ulum, Cairo; BA, 1935; *Career:* Lecturer at Arab College and Rashidiya School in Jerusalem; Director of Hashimiya Secondary School, Al-Birah;

Supervisor of Religious Pedagogy and Arabic Language; Educational Director; Technical Assistant to Under Secretary, Ministry of Education; Director General, Department of Passports; Under Secretary, Ministry of Information; Governor of Belga District; Under Secretary, Ministry of Development and Construction, 1967–72; Minister of Communications, 1972; Chief of Finance Office, 1973–74; Minister of Supply, 1974–75; member of Council of Arab National Union, 1972; *Publications:* numerous textbooks; *Decorations:* Star of Jordan 1st Class, 1972; *Address:* Jabal Amman, Amman, Jordan; telephone: 42834.

ODEH, Hanna, Jordanian official/economist; born 1932, Ramallah, Jordan; *Religion:* Christian; *Education:* Diploma in Economic Planning, University of the Hague, Netherlands 1957; BA in Mathematical Economics, Rotterdam University, Netherlands 1959, MA, 1961, PhD, 1963; *Career:* Statistician for United Nations Relief and Works Agency, Beirut, 1953–55; Research Assistant, University of the Hague, 1957–58; Lecturer, University of the Hague, 1961–63; employed with Jordan Development Board, renamed National Planning Council, 1963, Secretary General, 1968–74; President of National Planning Council, 1974–; participated and took important responsibilities for Jordan's Three-Year Plan, 1973–75, Five-Year Plan, 1976–80, and latest Five-Year Plan, 1981–85; *Languages:* Arabic, English; *Address:* National Planning Council, P O Box 555, Amman, Jordan.

ODEH, Muhammad Daud, (Abu Daud), Palestinian politician; born May 1937, Selwan, near Jerusalem, Palestine; *Religion:* Muslim; *Education:* Degree in Law, Jordanian University, 1968; *Career:* teacher in Jordan and Saudi Arabia; employed with Kuwait Justice Ministry; returned to Jordan, 1968; became fulltime member of Fatah, 1968, at the invitation of Ali Hassan Salameh; set up Fatah Central Observation Department in Amman, 1968; Second in Command of the Palestinian Militia in Jordan, 1970; member of the Revolutionary Council, 1970; paid official visit, with Sabri al-Banna to North Korea, 1972; arrested on sabotage charges in Amman, 1973 and sentenced to death; sentence commuted to life imprisonment and later released under general amnesty for Palestinian guerrillas, 1973.

ODUHO, Joseph, Sudanese politician; born 1927, Sudan; married; *Religion:* Christian; *Career:* member of National Assembly and member of Sudan Africa National Union and Sudan Christian Association; Regional Minister of Housing and Public Utilities, 1972–73; Regional Minister of Education, 1973; Regional Minister of Public Works and Utilities, 1973–75; member of Political Bureau of the Sudan Socialist Union (SSU), 1972; elected to the Regional Assembly for Torit North and East, 1973; *Publications:* co-author with the late William Deng, *The Problem of the Southern Sudan; Languages:* Arabic, English; *Address:* c/o Sudan Socialist Union, P O Box 1850, Khartoum, Sudan.

OJJEH, Akram Subhi, Saudi Arabian businessman; born 21 April, 1918, Damascus, Syria; married; two sons, three daughters; *Education:* College of Lazarist Fathers, Damascus, Syria; Teachers' Diploma, Faculty of Letters, Paris, France; *Career:* import-export business between France and the Middle East, 1946; founder of Les Deux Mondes in France, Saudi Arabia and Egypt, 1947; Publisher of *Le Monde Arabe,* Paris, 1950; President and General Manager, Techniques d'Avant Garde (TAG), 1974-; purchased SS France, 1977, later sold to a Norwegian corporation, 1979; *Decorations:* Commander of Legion d'Honneur; Commander of the Order of Leopold II; Officer of Nassau Orange; *Interests and Recreations:* swimming, sports; collector of antique rugs, and masterpiece paintings; *Languages:* Arabic, French, English;Address: 6rue Leo-Delibes 75116 Paris, France; telephone: 505 1480; telex: 630843 TAG FR.

OKASHA, Tharwat, Egyptian writer/official; born 1921; married; two children; *Religion:* Muslim; *Education:* Military Academy, Cairo, Egypt, 1939; Staff College, 1948; Diploma in Journalism, Cairo University, Egypt, 1948; Doctorat ès-Lettres, Sorbonne, Paris; *Career:* Military Attaché, Egyptian Embassy to Switzerland, 1953–54; Military Attaché, Egyptian Embassy to France, 1954–56; Ambassador to Italy, 1958; Minister of Culture and National Guidance, 1958–62; Chairman and Managing Director, National Bank, 1962; appointed by President Nassir to the National Assembly, 1964; Chairman of the Assembly's Foreign Relations Committee; Deputy Prime Minister, and Minister of Culture, 1966–70; Assistant for Cultural Affairs to the President, 1970–72; Lecturer, Collège de France, France, 1972; President of the Egyptian Supreme Council of Literature, Art and the Social Sciences, and member of the Executive Board of UNESCO, 1962–70; Visiting professor at the Collège de France, Paris, 1973; Elected to a corresponding professorship of the British Academy, 1975; *Publications:* several literary studies including *The History of Art,* 8 volumes, 1971; translation of some of Khalil Gibran's works and recently translated Ovid's *Metamorphoses* and *Ars Amatoria; The Muslim Painter and the Divine,* Rainbird Publications Ltd, London, 1979; *Decorations:* awarded both silver and golden medal for his contribution to the safeguarding of Nubian archeological legacy; *Languages:* Arabic, English, French; *Address:* Villa 34, Street 14, Maadi, Cairo, Egypt.

OKKEH, Awni Muhammad, Jordanian banker; born 25 November 1937, Jerusalem; married; one son, two daughters; *Religion:* Muslim; *Education:* BSc in Economics; *Career:* Manager, Arab Bank Ltd, Nigeria, 1974–77, 1976–80; Assistant Managing Director, Nigeria Arab Bank Ltd, 1980–81; former Secretary General, Nigeria-Arab Friendship Association; *Interests and Recreations:* music, reading, tennis, swimming; *Languages:* Arabic, English, French; *Address:* P O Box 1114, Lagos, Nigeria; telephone: 660144, 961228.

OMAR, Muhammad Abdul Gadir, Sudanese official/army officer; born 5 February 1929, Omdurman, Sudan; married; three sons, two daughters; *Religion:* Muslim; *Education:* Military Academy, 1952; *Career:* Military Attaché, Embassy to Ethiopia, 1963–66; Commander of the Sudanese troops in United Arab Republic, 1967–68; Commander, Southern Command, 1969–70; member of the Preparatory Committee to prepare Regional Autonomy Document, 1971–72; Chief of Staff, Sudanese Armed Forces, 1971–72; Ambassador to Uganda, 1972–73; Commissioner of Kassala Province, 1973; attended Organization of African Unity Defence Commission Conferences and Arab League Defence Ministers Conferences; *Interests and Recreations:* hunting, photography; *Languages:* Arabic, English; *Address:* Kassala Province Headquarters, Kassala, Sudan.

OMAR, Muhammad Zayyan, Saudi Arabian academic; born 1941, Medina, Saudi Arabia; *Religion:* Muslim; *Education:* PhD in Modern History, Utah State University, USA; *Career:* Lecturer, Faculty of Arts, King Abdul Aziz University; Assistant Professor, Faculty of Arts; contributed to the creation and development of King Abdul Aziz University since its early stages; Chairman of the First Conference of Saudi Men of Letters organized by the Faculty of Arts, King Abdul Aziz University; Dean of the Faculty of Arts, King Abdul Aziz University; *Publications: Manahig al-Bahth al-Ilmi; Shai minal Tarikh;* contributes regularly to scholarly journals and Saudi newspapers; *Interests and Recreations:* reading, swimming; *Address:* Faculty of Arts, King Abdul Aziz University, P O Box 1540, Jeddah, Saudi Arabia; telephone: 29033.

OMAR, Walid al-, Iraqi businessman/engineer; born 26 October, 1942, Basra Iraq; married; one son, two daughters; *Religion:* Muslim; *Education:* BSc (Hons), Imperial College of Technology and Science, London University, London, UK, 1965; MSc, Thermal Power and Process Engineering, Imperial College of Science and Technology, 1967; DIC, 1967; *Career:* joined teaching staff of University of Basra, Iraq, taught Engineering and Marketing; established Omar Engineering Company (contracting and trading company), a substantial business enterprise with more than five hundred employees; to develop his business on inter-Arab basis, he moved to Beirut, Lebanon, 1970; after the outbreak of war in Lebanon, moved his business to London, 1975–; plays a leading role in the development of inter-Arab and international business activities and commerce, developing new industries and business opportunities; *Interests and Recreations:* reading, chess, skiing, travelling; *Languages:* Arabic, English, some French; *Address:* ROSSCAPE Holdings Ltd, CP House, 97-107 Uxbridge Road, London W5 5TL, UK; telephone: (01) 567 2020; telex: 934495 ROSINT G.

OMAR, Yahia, Omani businessman; born July, 1931, Tripoli, Libya; married; three children; *Religion:* Muslim; *Career:* Libyan Police Service, 1954; Manager, Esso Oil Company, Libya, 1955; private enterprise, 1958–69; resident in Switzerland, 1969; Political and Economic Adviser to HM Sultan Qaboos, 1971–; Chairman, Arab International Bank, Cairo, Egypt; Director, Artoc Bank, Bahamas; director and shareholder of several companies; *Languages:* Arabic, English, Italian; *Address:* c/o Omani Embassy, 64 Ennismore Gardens, London SW7, England.

OMARY, Mahmud Ali al-, Jordanian official/ auditor; born 1945 Irbid, Jordan; married; two sons; *Religion:* Muslim; *Education:* BA in Economics and Commerce, Jordan, 1969; *Career:* Auditor, Ministry of Finance, Amman, Jordan, 1970; Assistant to the Head of Advance Section, 1972; Head of the Audit Section, Amman Finance Department, Jordan, 1974; Finance Department of Abu Dhabi, on secondment, 1975; Principal Finance Officer, Finance Department, Abu Dhabi, 1978; Budget Controller, Abu Dhabi, 1981–; *Interests and Recreations:* table tennis, chess, travelling; *Languages:* Arabic, English; *Address:* Finance Department, P O Box 246, Abu Dhabi, United Arab Emirates; telephone: Office — 366 800 ext 241, Residence — 829 736.

OMRAN, Abdul Rahman Bin Hassan, al-, Saudi Arabian diplomat; born 1924, Riyadh, Saudi Arabia; *Religion:* Muslim; *Education:* general education; *Career:* employee at HRH Viceroy's Cabinet in Hijaz Province 1940; Secretary at the Royal Offices of late King Abdul Aziz, 1942–50; Second Assistant to Chief of Royal Offices; Private Secretary to Governor of Riyadh, HRH Prince Sultan Bin Abdul Aziz, 1950–61; Director General of Roads Department, 1962; Counsellor at Foreign Ministry, 1961; Director, Arab League Department, 1962; Counsellor General, Embassy to Thailand, 1962; Ambassador to Tunisia, 1975–; member of the National Club, Jeddah; *Interests and Recreations:* reading, swimming, walking; *Address:* Ministry of Foreign Affairs, Jeddah,Saudi Arabia; Embassy of Royal Kingdom of Saudi Arabia, 16 rue d'Autriche, Belvedere, Tunis, Tunisia.

OMRAN, Abdullah Hamid, United Arab Emirates administrator; born 1947, Sharjah, United Arab Emirates; married; *Religion:* Muslim; *Education:* BA in Commerce, 1972; *Career:* Director of Administrative and Financial Affairs, Ministry of Justice; Director, Technical Department, Ministry of Justice, Dubai, 1977–; *Interests and Recreations:* swimming, fishing; member of Abu Dhabi Club; *Languages:* Arabic, English; *Address:* Ministry of Justice, Islamic Affairs

and Awqaf, P O Box 3907, Shaikh Rashid Building, Dubai, United Arab Emirates; telephone: 661220.

OMRAN, Abdullah Muhammad al-, Saudi Arabian lawyer/official; born 1935; *Religion:* Muslim; *Education:* PhD in Law, USA; *Career:* adviser at the Council of Ministers; private legal practice; own private bureau of legal consultations; Minister without Portfolio; *Interests and Recreations:* reading, travel; *Address:* Council of Ministers, Riyadh, Saudi Arabia; telephone: 404 4200.

OMRAN, Adnan, Syrian diplomat; born 9 August 1934, Syria; *Religion:* Muslim; *Education:* University of Damascus, Syria; University of Moscow, USSR; Diploma, Research Studies International Law, Columbia University, New York, USA; *Career:* private law practice, Damascus, Syria, 1957–61; Ministry of Foreign Affairs, 1962–63; Permanent Mission to UN, 1963–66; 1st Secretary, Syrian Embassy, Moscow, USSR, 1966–68; Head of Mission, Syrian Embassy to German Democratic Republic, 1968–70; Director, International Organisations and Conferences Department, Ministry of Foreign Affairs, Damascus, Syria, 1970–71; Director, Palestine Department, 1971–72; Director, Special Bureau Department; Representative of Syria at several of the Committees during the Annual Sessions of the UN General Assembly, 1970–73; Ambassador to Sweden and UK, 1974–80; Assistant Secretary General for Political Affairs, League of Arab States, Tunisia, 1980–; *Decorations:* Unity Medal, Syria, 1958; Victory and Bravery Medal, Syria, 1959; *Interests and Recreations:* reading, music, soccer, table-tennis, basket-ball; *Languages:* Arabic, English; *Address:* League of Arab States, Rue Fakhreldin Basha, Tunis, Tunisia; telephone: 890100, 890110.

ONSY, Mahmud Bahir, Egyptian banker; born 14 December 1916, Egypt; married; one son, one daughter; *Religion:* Muslim; *Education:* BCom in Business and Industrial Administration, Faculty of Commerce, Cairo University, 1940; *Career:* Universal Company of Maritime, Suez Canal, Ismailia, Egypt, 1941–46; Belgium and International Bank in Egypt, 1946–60; Director General of Belgium and International Bank in Egypt, 1960–62; member of the Board of Directors and General Manager of the National Bank of

Egypt, 1962–66; Secretary General, the African Development Bank, Abidjan, Ivory Coast, 1966–68; National Bank of Egypt, Cairo, 1968–69; Founder and Secretary General, the French-Arab Chamber of Commerce, Paris, France, 1969–72; Deputy Chairman and Managing Director, the Arab African International Bank, Cairo, Egypt, 1972–; Chairman, Arab African Bank, Nouakchott, Mauritania; Deputy Chairman, African Arab Company for Foreign Trade and Development (AFARCO), Nouakchott, Mauritania; membner of the Board, Compagnie Financière et Touristique (tourism and hotel development), Tunisia; member of the International Bankers Association, Washington D.C., USA; member of the International Public Relations Association, USA; member of the European Center of Public Relations, Brussels, Belguim; *Publications:* a translation into Arabic of *Economie Financière Internationale* by Raymond Bertrand, 1975; *Decorations:* Officier de l'Ordre National du Mérite, France, 1977; *Interests and Recreations:* fencing, riding, golf, music; President of the Friends of the Cairo Conservatoire Orchestra; member of the Board of Directors of International Automobile Federation, Paris, France, 1976–, and of the Egyptian Automobile and Touring Club of Egypt, Cairo, Egypt, 1968–; Vice President and Founder of the Arab Public Relations Society, Cairo, Egypt, 1965–; Founder and Honorary Treasurer of the Association of the Egyptian-French Friendship, 1965–; *Languages:* Arabic, French, English, Italian; *Address:* Office — Arab African Interarntional Bank, 44 Abdel Khalek Sarwat Street, Cairo, Egypt; telephone: 911449, 916744; telex: 92071 ARBFR UN and 363 ARBFR UN; Residence — 2 Midan Kasr al-Doubara, Garden City, Cairo, Egypt; telephone: 26712, 842267.

ORRI, Muhammad, Saudi Arabian businessman; born 1932, Saudi Arabia; *Religion:* Muslim; *Career:* owner of passanger and cargo fleet, agent for several European and Far East shipping companies; Chairman of Board of Orri Navigation Lines, Middle East Shipping Agencies, Oceantrade Shipping Agencies, Orri Stevedores; owner of Saudi European Line, trading between UK, Scandinavia and Mediterranean and Red Sea and Gulf Ports, Saudi State Line and Saudi India Line; *Address:* Orri Navigation Lines, Mina Road, Jeddah, Saudi Arabia; 2 Ave Dem Gounari, Piraeus, 32 Greece; telephone: 4179 636; telex: 212478.

ORSAN, Ali Okla, Syrian writer/official; born 1 January 1940; married; four children; *Religion:* Muslim; *Education:* Diploma, High Institute of Dramatic Arts, Cairo, Egypt, 1963; Diploma in Drama, France; *Career:* Deputy Director of the National Theatre, Damascus, 1966; Secretary of the Artists Syndicate, 1968; Director General of Theatres and Music, 1969–74; Leader of the Artists Syndicate, 1970; member of the Executive Office of the Arab Writers Union, 1973–75; Deputy Chairman, Arab Writers Union, 1975–77; Assistant to the Minister of Culture and Information, 1976; Chairman, Arab Writers Union, 1977–; Deputy Secretary General, General Union of Arab Writers, 1979–81; Secretary General, General Union of Arab Writers, 1981–; Deputy Secretary General, Union of African and Asian Writers, 1981–; Director of the following magazines, *Al-Kaatib al-Arabi, Al-Mawqif al-Adabi, Al-Turath al-Arabi* and *Al-Adaab; Publications:* numerous plays and several other works; *Decorations:* Medal of Culture, Tunisia, 1976; Silver Star, German Democratic Republic, 1983; *Interests and Recreations:* music, literature, drama and theatre; *Languages:* Arabic, French; *Address:* PO Box 3230 or 11124, Damascus, Syria; telephone: Office -- 618568; Residence -- 720271.

OSSEIRAN, Adel, Lebanese politician; born 1905, Sidon, Lebanon; married; five daughters, one son; *Religion:* Muslim; *Education:* BA, Political Science, American University of Beirut, Lebanon, 1929; MA, American University of Beirut, Lebanon, 1939; *Career:* Deputy for South Lebanon, 1943; Minister of Supply in first Cabinet after Lebanese Independence, 1943; re-elected Deputy for South Lebanon, 1947; member of the Lebanese Delegation to the UN, 1947 and 1948; re-elected Deputy for Zahrani, 1953 and 1957; elected President of the Chamber of Deputies, 1953 and 1959; re-elected President, 1958; re-elected Deputy for Zahrani, 1960 and 1968; Minister of the Interior, 1969; Minister of Justice, 1969–70; Minister of Justice, 1974–75; Minister of Economy and Trade, Justice, Public Works and Transport, 1975–76; Minister of Justice, Education, Planning, Public Works and

Transport, 1976; *Decorations:* Grand Cordon of the National Order of the Cedar; several other foreign distinctions and decorations; *Languages:* Arabic, French, English; *Address:* Office — Trablos Street, Beirut, Lebanon; telephone: 233784; Residence — Sidon, South Lebanon.

OTAIBA, Khalaf al-, United Arab Emirates official/businessman; born 1941, Abu Dhabi, United Arab Emirates; *Career:* Director, Abu Dhabi National Oil Company; Chairman, Abu Dhabi National Insurance Company; *Languages:* Arabic, English; *Address:* P O Box 839, Abu Dhabi, United Arab Emirates; telephone: 343171,; telex: 22340 EM.

OTAIBA, Mana Said al-, United Arab Emirates politician/economist; born 15 May 1946; married; one son, four daughters; *Religion:* Muslim; *Education:* BSc in Economics, Baghdad University, Iraq, 1969; MSc in Economics, Cairo University, Egypt, 1974; Phd, 1976; *Career:* Head of Petroleum Department, Abu Dhabi, 1969; Minister of Petroleum and Mineral Resources, 1971–; Chairman of Board, Abu Dhabi National Oil Company; member of Abu Dhabi Planning Board; President of Department of Petroleum, Minerals and Industry; *Publications: Abu Dhabi Planning Board; Economy of Abu Dhabi; Organization of the Petroleum-Exporting Countries and the Oil Industry; Interests and Recreations:* reading and writing poetry, swimming, hunting, horse riding; *Languages:* Arabic, English; *Address:* Ministry of Petroleum and Mineral Resources, P O Box 59, Abu Dhabi, United Arab Emirates; telephone: 362333; telex: 22544 MPMR EM.

OTAIBA, Said Bin Ahmad al-, United Arab Emirates businessman; born 1919, Abu Dhabi; married; *Religion:* Muslim; *Education:* general education in Abu Dhabi; *Career:* private business; President of Abu Dhabi Chamber of Commerce and Industry; *Interests and Recreations:* hunting during winter season; *Address:* P O Box 467, Abu Dhabi, United Arab Emirates; telephone: 41289, 41548.

OTHMAN, Abdu Ali, Yemen Arab Republic academic/politician; born Yemen Arab Republic; *Religion:* Muslim; *Education:* University of Cairo, Egypt; MA in Sociology, University of Ohio, USA; *Career:* administra-

tor in Ministry of Labour and Social Affairs; drafted trade union legislations in 1960; Lecturer in Sociology, Sana'a University, 1973; Minister of Municipal Affairs, 1974; returned to Sana'a University in 1975; *Languages:* Arabic, English; *Address:* Sana'a University, P O Box 1247 Sana'a, Yemen Arab Republic.

OTHMAN, Abdul Wahab, Sudanese official/economist; born 1 January 1936, Sudan; married; two sons, three daughters; *Religion:* Muslim; *Education:* BA, University of Khartoum, Sudan; MSc and PhD in Economics, Charles University, Czechoslavakia; *Career:* Budget Department, Ministry of Finance and National Economy, Khartoum, 1961; Director of Purchase and Supplies, Ministry of Finance and National Economy, 1972; Director of Sudan Government Purchase Office, London, 1973; Director General of the Budget, 1975; Deputy Minister of Finance, 1978; Chairman, Sudan-Kuwait Investment Company; member of Board of Cotton Public Corporation, Public Electricity and Water Corporation, Sudan Airways, and others; *Languages:* Arabic, English; *Address:* Ministry of Finance and National Economy, Khartoum, Sudan; telephone: 77173.

OTHMAN, Ahmad, Moroccan politician/diplomat; born 3 January 1930, Morocco; married; *Religion:* Muslim; *Education:* in Rabat; Licencié en Droit, 1951; Diploma of Higher Studies in Public and Civil Law, University of Bordeaux, France; *Career:* following HM King Mohammed's return from exile joined Royal Cabinet with responsibility for legal affairs; Ministry of Foreign Affairs, 1957; Head of the European Division, 1959; Head of the American Division; leading member of Moroccan delegations to UN General Assembly, Conference on Law of the Sea and Arab League meetings; Secretary General, Ministry of National Defence, 1959; Ambassador to West Germany, 1961–62; Under Secretary of State for Industry and Mines, Ministry of Commerce, 1963; led Moroccan delegation to the Khartoum meeting of African Finance Ministers, 1963; President of Compagnie Marocaine de Navigation (COMANAV), 1963; Ambassador to USA and Canada, 1967; Minister of Administrative Affairs, 1970; Prime Minister, 1972; Minister of Defence, 1973; Prime Minister, 1974 and 1977; President, Rassemblement National des Indépendents, 1980–; *Interests and Recreations:* bridge; *Languages:* Arabic, French; *Address:* 20 Avenue Prince Monlay Abdullah, Rabat, Morocco.

OTHMAN, Al-Sayyid Muhammad, Egyptian UN official/teacher; born 3 April 1926, Sharqiyah, Egypt; married; *Religion:* Muslim; *Education:* BA in English, Cairo University, Egypt, 1946–48; Diploma in English Language and Literature, University of Exeter, UK, 1950–52; *Career:* teacher of English, secondary schools, Ministry of Education, Cairo, 1948–56; Research and Documentation work, Documentation Centre for Education, Ministry of Education, Cairo, 1956–67; Programme Specialist, UNESCO, 1958–69; Senior Reviser and Chief, Arabic Translations Section, UNESCO, France, 1970–; *Publications:* translation into Arabic of *Educational Psychology,* 1955; *The Mind Alive,* 1960; *Child Development, 1963; Interests and Recreations:* teaching, research and documentation, education, translation; *Languages:* Arabic, English, French, Spanish; *Address:* Office — UNESCO, 7 Place de Fontenoy, F-75700 Paris, France; telephone: 777 1610; Residence — 78 Avenue de Suffren, 75015 Paris, France; telephone: 734 3579.

OTHMAN, Ali Issa, Jordanian UN official; born 1920, Jerusalem, Palestine; married: *Education:* BA, American University in Cairo, Egypt, 1943–47; MA, Syracuse University, New York, USA, 1947–49; Western and Islamic Social Thought, University of Chicago, 1949–54; *Career:* Deputy Director, Regional Centre for Training in Community Development, Arab States, UNESCO, 1957–64; Head, Education Research Section, Department of Education, UNRWA/ UNESCO, 1964–71; Representative, Gulf Area, UNICEF, 1971–74; Senior Regional Programme Officer, East Mediterranean Regional Office, UNICEF, Lebanon, 1974–75; Senior Adviser for Social and Educational Development, The Arab Fund for Economic and Social Development, Kuwait, 1977–79; Chief UN Technical Adviser, Ministry of Planning, Kuwait, 1979–; *Publications: The Concept of Man in Islam,* 1961; *Educational Development of the Arab Less Developed Countries,* and *Manpower Development in the Arab World,* both studies made for the Arab Fund; numerous other articles on Arab culture, development and education; *Interests and Recreations:* development, religious and cultural thought; *Languages:* Arabic, English; *Address:* UNDP, P O Box 2993, Kuwait.

OTHMAN, Othman Ahmad, Egyptian engineer; born in Ismailia, Egypt; married; four sons, one daughter; *Religion:* Muslim; *Education:* BSc in Engineering, Cairo University, Cairo, Egypt, 1940; *Career:* Engineer; Founder of Arab Contractors Company, 1949; Chairman of the Board of Arab Contractors Company; Minister of Reconstruction and Housing, 1974–76; member of the National Assembly for Ismailia Governorate, 1976–; re-elected in 1979; main projects of the Arab Contractors in Egypt include the Aswan High Dam, the widening and deepening of the Suez Canal, Port Said Shipyards, Cairo International Airport, Suez Canal Area Reconstruction and Development Programme, and other projects in Egypt, Saudi Arabia, Libya, Jordan and Iraq; Chairman of the Syndicate of Egyptian Engineers, 1979; *Publications: My Experience,* an autobiography, 1980, Cairo; *Interests and Recreations:* swimming, fishing, theatre, cinema, reading; member of the Ismailia Sporting Club; *Languages:* Arabic, English; *Address:* Office — Arab Contractors Company, 34 Adly Street, Cairo, Egypt; Residence — Alouba Street, Al Haram, Cairo, Egypt; telephone: 851616.

OUAZZANI, Maitre Thami al-, Moroccan politician/diplomat; born 27 December 1927, Fes, Morocco; married; four children; *Religion:* Muslim; *Education:* Degree in Philosphy and Law, University of Paris, Paris, France, 1951; *Career:* called to the Bar, Casablanca, 1951; active in nationalist circles; joined the Union Nationale des Forces Populaires, 1959; Ambassador to Yugoslavia and Greece, 1961; Secretary General of the Casablanca Group of African States, 1962; Director, Bureau des Recherches et Participation Minières, 1963; Minister of Labour and Social Affairs, 1963; Minister for Public Services, 1964; Ambassador to Algeria, 1965; Minister of Tourism, 1968; Minister in the Royal Cabinet, 1968; Secretary General, Parti Démocratique Constitutionnel, 1979; Ambassador to Tunisia, 1969; Ambassador to London, UK, 1971–74; President, DIAC Company, Morocco, 1974–82; Secretary General, Parti Démocratique Constitutionnel, 1982–; *Decorations:* Grand Cordon Alouite, and Yugoslav and Tunisian decorations; *Languages:* Arabic, French, English; *Address:* 32 Bd de la Résistance, Casablanca, Morocco; telephone: 309430, 220840; telex: 2262917.

OUSSEDIK, Omar, Algerian diplomat; born 1923, Algeria; *Religion:* Muslim; *Career:* member of Algerian People's Party; served as Political Counsellor in Wilayas II and III in early period of War of Independence; member of First Revolutionary Council, 1951; Minister of State, Provisional Government, 1958; diplomatic representative of Provisional Government, Conakry, Guinea, 1958; returned to Algiers, 1962, to organize Zone Autonome; prominent leader of Wilaya IV and later spokesman of Tiz-Ouzou group; Ambassador to Bulgaria, 1963; Ambassador to USSR, 1965; Ambassador, Ministry of Foreign Affairs, 1970–74; Ambassador to India, 1974–80; *Languages:* Arabic, French; *Address:* Ministry of Foreign Affairs, 6 Rue Ibin Badran al-Moradia, Algiers, Algeria; telephone: 600585.

OUSSEIMI, Khalid, Lebanese businessman; born 13 October, 1928; married; one son, one daughter; *Religion:* Muslim; *Education:* BA in Economics and Finance, Institute of Political Sciences, Faculty of Law, French University, Beirut, Lebanon; *Career:* private enterprise with various Arab countries, 1957–60; Industry and Banking, Syria, Lebanon, 1960–63; Investment Banking, 1963–; Chairman and President of Gefinour Group of Companies, Arab Investment Company, Gefinour Holding SA, Gefinour Investment Ltd; *Interests and Recreations:* golf, tennis, swimming; *Languages:* Arabic, English, French; *Address:* Gefinour, 18 Quai Gustave Ador, Geneva, Switzerland.

OWAIDA, Abdullah Shalabi, Saudi Arabian engineer; born 1944; *Education:* BSc in Chemistry, USA, 1969; *Career:* Chemist, Jeddah Oil Refinery, 1969–71; Assistant Chief Chemist, Jeddah Oil Refinery, 1972–73; Assistant Technical Manager, Petrolube, 1974; member of American Chemical Society; Technical Manager, Petromin Lubricating Oils Co (Petrolube); *Publications:* technical articles on industrial uses of petroleum and its products; *Interests and Recreations:* reading, sports; *Address:* Petrolube, P O Box 1432, Jeddah, Saudi Arabia.

OWAIS, Sultan Bin Ali al-, United Arab Emirates businessman/banker; born 1935; married; *Religion:* Muslim; *Career:* has several business interests in Dubai, including the only remaining substantial business dealing in pearls; Chairman, National Bank of Dubai; owns property in Dubai and Sharjah; lives in Sharjah; active in local politics before the formation of the United Arab Emirates; member of Abu Dhabi Planning Board, 1969; *Languages:* Arabic, English; *Address:* National Bank of Dubai Ltd, P O Box 777, Dubai, United Arab Emirates; telephone: 222241; telex: 45421 NATNAL EM.

OWEIDHA, Rashid Bin, United Arab Emirates official/businessman; born 25 October 1938, Abu Dhabi, United Arab Emirates; married; three sons; *Religion:* Muslim; *Education:* Shari'a studies (Islamic Law) with Judge Shaikh Badr, for nine years; *Career:* Assistant to Judge, 1956–57; private business, 1957; founding member of Municipal Council, 1967; founding member of Abu Dhabi Chamber of Commerce; member of Abu Dhabi National Consultative Council 1970; Editor in Chief of *Al-Wihda,* 1973; member of the Federal National Assembly, 1971, and First Deputy Speaker; member of the National Planning Council, 1975; member of the Board of the Abu Dhabi Bank; Managing Director of Rashid Bin Oweidha Organization; Chairman of First Gulf Bank; *Decorations:* from Libya, Algeria, Sudan, Morocco, Mauritania, Tunisia, Egypt, Somalia, Syria, Iraq, Saudi Arabia; *Interests and Recreations:* reading, history, classical poetry, swimming, hunting, chess; member of al-Jazira Cultural and Sporting Club; *Languages:* Arabic, English; *Address:* Rashid Bin Oweidha Organisation, P O Box 5, Abu Dhabi, United Arab Emirates; telephone: 341192; telex: 23850 JALDI EM.

OWEISS, Ibrahim Muhammad, Egyptian academic/economist; resident in the USA; born 25 September 1931, Beheira, Egypt; married; one son, one daughter; *Religion:* Muslim; *Education:* BCom in Economics, University of Alexandria, Alexandria, Egypt; MA and PhD in Economics, University of Minnesota, USA; *Career:* teacher, Ministry of Education, Egypt, 1953–55; Military Service as Lieutenant, Egyptian Armed Forces, 1955–58; Economist and Director of Project Evaluation, Egyptian Ministry of

Industry, Cairo, 1958–60; Lecturer of Economics, University of Minnesota, USA, 1962–67; Professor of Economics, Georgetown University, Washington D.C., USA, 1967–; Director of the Institute of Arab Development, Georgetown University, 1975–77; Professional Lecturer on the Economics of the Middle East, Johns Hopkins University, USA; Senior Economic Adviser to the Government of Panama, 1976–77, while on leave of absence from Georgetown University, 1977–78; First Under Secretary of State for Economic Affairs in the Egyptian Cabinet and the Chief of the Egyptian Economic Mission to the USA in New York with rank of Ambassador; member of the American Economic Association, American Statistical Association, Royal Economic Association, National Economists Club, American Association of University Professors, Association of Arab-American University Graduates, Association of Egyptian-American Scholars, Pi Gamma Mu (National Social Science Honour Society); *Publications:* numerous articles and reports in university journals and economic journals; *The Egyptian Economy, A Challenge for the Future ;* editor and contributor to *Arab-US Economic Relations; Decorations:* Order of Merit, 1st Class, Egypt, 1978; *Interests and Recreations:* tennis, swimming; member of the University Club in New York; *Languages:* Arabic, English, French; *Address:* Department of Economics, Georgetown University, Washington D.C., 20057, USA; telephone: (202) 625 4121.

P

PACHACHI, Adnan al-, United Arab Emirates official/diplomat; born 14 May 1923, Baghdad, Iraq; married; three daughters; *Religion:* Muslim; *Education:* BA Political Science, AUB, Lebanon, 1943; PhD Political Science, USA, 1949; *Career:* joined Iraqi Foreign Service, 1944; served in Washington, USA, and Alexandria, Egypt; Director General, Ministry of Foreign Affairs, 1958–59; Iraqi Ambassador and Permanent Secretary to the UN, 1959–65; Iraqi Minister of State for Foreign Affairs, 1965–66; Minister of Foreign Affairs,1966–67; Ambassador and Permanent Representative to the UN, 1967–69; Minister of State in the Government of Abu Dhabi, 1971–74; Personal Representative of the Head of State of the United Arab Emirates and member of the Executive Council of Abu Dhabi, 1974–; *Publications: Iraq 1914–1921: a study in the development of Arab nationalism, 1949; Interests and Recreations:* classical music, swimming, tennis, walking; *Languages:* Arabic, English, French; *Address:* Al-Manhal Palace, P O Box 280, Abu Dhabi, United Arab Emirates; telephone: 342133

PACHACHI, Talal Nadim al-, Iraqi diplomat; born 17 November 1937, Baghdad, Iraq; married; one son; *Religion:* Muslim; *Education:* London School of Economics, London, 1956–57; BA in Economics, and MA, Trinity College, Cambridge University, Cambridge, 1957–60; *Career:* 3rd Secretary, Economics Department, Ministry of Foreign Affairs, Baghdad, Iraq, 1963–66; 2nd Secretary, Permanent Mission of Iraq to the UN, Geneva, 1966–69; 2nd Secretary, Embassy of Iraq, Belgium, 1966–71; Director, Department of Trade Relations, Ministry of Foreign Affairs, 1971–73; Counsellor, Permanent Mission of Iraq, UN, Geneva, 1973–75; UN Permanent Mission of Iraq, 1975–81; Ministry of Foreign Affairs, 1981–; *Interests and Recreations:* tennis, swimming, economic development, international relations; *Languages:* Arabic, English, French; *Address:* Ministry of Foreign Affairs, Baghdad, Iraq.

PARTOW, Faruk Abdul Jalil, Iraqi WHO official/physician; born 17 July 1927, Basrah, Iraq; married; *Education:* MD, Lausanne University, Switzerland, 1952; Diploma in Public Health; London School of Hygiene and Tropical Medicine, 1962; Diploma in Child Health, Royal College of Physicians and Surgeons, Glasgow, UK, 1965; Diploma of Child Health, RCPS, England, 1966; *Career:* Director, International Health Department, Ministry of Health, Baghdad, 1958–60; Director, Baghdad Health Department, Ministry of Health, 1960–63; General Practitioner, Iraq, 1963–65; Paediatric Registrar, Regional Health Board, UK, 1965–68; Paediatrician, Ministry of Health, Baghdad, 1968–69; Regional Adviser, WHO Eastern Mediterranean Regional Office, Alexandria, Egypt, 1969–72; Representative to Yemen Arab Republic, WHO Regional Office for the Eastern Mediterranean, 1972–75; Public Health Administrator, WHO Regional Office for the Eastern Mediterranean, 1975–78; Director of Communicable Diseases Control, WHO Regional Office for the Eastern Mediterranean, 1978–81; Director of Disease Prevention and Control, WHO Regional Office for the Eastern Mediterranean, August 1981–; *Interests and Recreations:* public health administration, paediatrics, Arabic literature, classical music, golf; *Languages:* Arabic, English, French; *Address:* WHO Regional Office for the Eastern Mediterranean, P O Box 1517, Alexandria, Egypt.

PESHDARI, Babekr Mahmoud al-, Iraqi politician; born 1937, Sulaimaniyah, Iraq; *Education:* LLB, University of Baghdad, Iraq, 1962; *Career:* Governor of Sulaimaniyah, 1974; Chairman, Legislative

Council, Kurdish Autonomous Area, 1974–76; Minister of Labour and Social Affairs, 1976–;member of the National Progressive Party; *Publications:* paper on non-alignment, *al-estegaba al-hadaria ila tahdiat altakhalouf,* 1981; editor of *al-amel wal Tanmia; Decorations:* Order of the Republic of Mali; *Interests and Recreations:* hunting, horse riding; *Languages:* Arabic, Kurdish; *Address:* Ministry of Labour and Social Affairs, Baghdad, Iraq.

PHARAON, Ghaith Rashad, Saudi Arabian businessman/engineer; born 1940, Riyadh, Saudi Arabia; married; three children; *Education:* American International College, Beirut, Lebanon; Colorado School of Mines, USA; Stanford University and Harvard University, USA; BSc, 1962; PhD in Oil Engineering, 1963; MBA, 1965; *Career:* Chairman of Board of seventeen local and international corporations; his companies in Saudi Arabia and abroad deal extensively in international finance, engineering and professional business management; founded Saudi Research and Development Corporation (REDEC), 1967; Chairman of Board and Managing Director of REDEC, 1967–; acquired controlling interest in Bank of the Commonwealth of Detroit, USA, 1975; contributes to development of large-scale industrial ventures both in Saudi Arabia and abroad; *Decorations:* Commendatore of the Italian Republic; *Interests and Recreations:* world-wide travel; *Address:* Saudi Research and Development Corporation, P O Box 1935, Jeddah, Saudi Arabia; telephone: Jeddah 52940; telex: 401122 REDEC SJ.

PHARAON, Ghassan N., Saudi Arabian dental surgeon; born 31 July 1944, Jerusalem; *Religion:* Muslim; *Education:* BDS, University of Liverpool, 1967; *Career:* founded Jeddah Dental Clinic, 1969; Director General, Arabian Homes (property development company), 1976; Director General, Arabian Transport Co, 1977; Founder and Director General, Medical Services Co Ltd, 1980; *Interests and Recreations:* tennis, squash, skiing; *Languages:* Arabic, English, French; *Address:* P O Box 4553, Jeddah, Saudi Arabia; telephone: 665 8784, 682 2201; telex: 402476 PHARO SJ.

PHARAON, Hattan Rashad, Saudi Arabian businessman; born 1953, Paris, France; *Religion:* Muslim; *Education:* BSc, MBA, Business Administration, San Diego, California; *Career:* General Manager of National Bunkering Co Ltd, 1977, and later Managing Director of National Bunkering Co Ltd, 1979; Managing Director, Arabian Investments Co Ltd, International Trade and Development Co Ltd; *Interests and Recreations:* economics, swimming, water skiing; *Languages:* Arabic, English, French; *Address:* P O Box 6471, Jeddah, Saudi Arabia; telephone: 667 5792, 667 4628.

PHARAON, Henri, Lebanese businessman/politician; born 1900, Beirut, Lebanon; one son; *Religion:* Christian; *Education:* Licence in Law, French Faculty of Law, Beirut, Lebanon, and University of Lyon, France; *Career:* elected Deputy 1927, 1943, 1947, and 1951; Minister of Foreign Affairs, 1946–47, during which period Lebanon joined the UN and Arab League; Minister of Foreign Affairs and Minister of Justice, 1955; President, Board of Directors, Beirut Port Management Enterprise, the Pharaon and Chiha Bank of the Beirut Real Estate Company, Lebanese Finance Corporation; Managing Director, Real Estate and Modern Buildings Company and Beirut Park Company; Minister of State in charge of legislative elections, 1968; Vice President, Greek-Catholic Community Council, 1969–; *Interests and Recreations:* tennis (former Lebanese Champion), sports promotion; breeding of thoroughbred horses; owner of the largest stable of race horses in Lebanon; President of Lebanese Jockey Club; *Languages:* Arabic, French, English; *Address:* Office — Pharaon and Chiha Bank, Place Raid al Solh, Beirut, Lebanon; telephone: 240220; Residence — Palais Pharaon, P O Box 1, Beirut, Lebanon; telephone: 229099.

PHARAON, Mazin Rashad, Saudi Arabian businessman/architect; born 1939, Riyadh, Saudi Arabia; married; *Religion:* Muslim; *Education:* qualified as architect in West Germany; *Career:* shipowner, businessman, contractor; specialised in shipment of crude oil products contracts; *Languages:* Arabic, English, French, German; *Address:* P O Box 730, Jeddah, Saudi Arabia.

PHARAON, Rashad, Saudi Arabian physician; born 1912, Syria; *Religion:* Muslim; *Education:* MD, Faculty of Medicine, Damascus University; *Career:* private physician to late King Abdul Aziz, founder of the

Kingdom of Saudi Arabia, 1936–45; joined diplomatic service; Ambassador to France, Minister of Health, Ambassador to France, 1960–66; Senior Saudi Arabian Delegate to session of UN, 1963–64; Special Adviser to the late King Faisal; Adviser to the late King Khalid Bin Abdul Aziz; *Decorations:* several orders of merit from European and Arab countries; *Interests and Recreations:* reading; *Address:* The Royal Cabinet, Riyadh, Saudi Arabia.

PRINCE, Musa Najib, Lebanese lawyer; born 27 September 1925, Hamah, Syria; married; four children; *Religion:* Muslim; *Education:* Frères College, Jimiza, Beirut; Faculty of Law, Beirut; Universities of Brussels and Paris; PhDs in law from European unviersities and institutes; several Honorary PhDs (Honores Causae) from European, North and South American uni-versities; *Career:* Barrister at Law; Honorary Minister of State; Honorary Consul; University Professor and Administrator; member of several academies and academic institutions; *Publications:* several literary, poetic, political, legal publications, amongst them *Au Pays d'Adonis,* 1947; *L'Assurance-Crime,* 1962; *Introduction à l'Armenocide,* 1967; *Un Liban à Refaire,* 1967/77; *Decorations:* Lebanese Golden Order of Merit; Order of the Cedar, Lebanon; Ordre National du Mérite, France; Italian Royal Order; Order of Italian Republic, and several others; *Interests and Recreations:* parapsychology, swimming, interested in culture; *Languages:* Arabic, French, English, Italian; *Address:* Office — Sanine Building, Albert Naccache Street, Nasra, Beirut; telephone: 227504, 247334, 251408; Residence – Ferneyne Building, Ferneyne Street, Sodeco, Beirut; telephone: 236188, 334333.

Q

QA'UD, Abdul Magid Mabruk, Libyan official/engineer; born 1943, Tripolitania, Libya; married; *Religion:* Muslim; *Education:* Degree in Engineering, University of Libya, Benghazi; Diploma in Town Planning, University of Stirling, UK; *Career:* Chief Engineer, Tripoli Municipality, 1969; Mayor of Tripoli, 1971; Minister of State for Agricultural Development, 1972; leading role in Green Revolution; Secretary for Land Reclamation and Development, General People's Committee, 1977; *Languages:* Arabic, English, Italian; *Address:* Secretariat of the General People's Committee for Land Reclamation and Land Reform, Tripoli, Libya.

QABAZARD, Muhammad Hussain, Kuwaiti businessman/industrialist; born 1920; married; six children; *Religion:* Muslim; *Career:* Director General of Ports Department, 1953–61; Ministry of Finance and Industry, Oil Affairs, 1961–62; led official goodwill visit to Far East, 1961; member of Kuwait National Assembly, 1963–67; served on several parliamentary delegations; business and property interests; member of the Board of Aminoil; developed an important business dealing in marine equipment; *Interests and Recreations:* cinephotography; *Languages:* Arabic, English, Persian, Turkish, Russian; *Address:* Parts International Co, WLL, P O Box 671, Safat, Kuwait.

QABBANI, Nizar, Syrian poet; born 1923, Damascus, Syria; *Education:* graduated from Damascus University, 1945; *Career:* served as Syrian diplomat in Embassies to Egypt, Lebanon, UK, China, Spain; resigned to set up publishing house in Beirut; prolific poet, with love and women as his main themes, and in his recent work concerned with social and political issues; *Publications:* many volumes of poetry; *Address:* Al Arabi Magazine, P O Box 748, Kuwait.

QABOOS, HM Sultan Qaboos Bin Said, Sultan of Oman; born 18 November 1940; son of Sultan Said Bin Taimur and Omani mother; married 23 March 1976, to his first cousin from North Oman; *Religion:* Muslim; *Education:* seven years in UK, first with private tutors and then full course at the Royal Military Academy, Sandhurst; *Career:* Officer with the Cameronians (Scottish Rifle), a British Infantry regiment, for six months; succeeded as Sultan after his father's abdication, 23 July 1970; Prime Minister, Minister of Foreign Affairs, and Minister of Defence; *Interests and Recreations:* youth affairs for which he set up a special ministry, 1976; takes a personal interest in the welfare of disabled ex-servicemen and orphans; horse-riding, classical music, military history; *Address:* The Palace, Muscat, Oman.

QADDOUMI, Hisham, Arab engineer; resident in Qatar; born 1942, Jerusalem; *Religion:* Muslim; *Education:* business studies and economics in USA; *Career:* Brown and Root Inc, Houston, Texas; Projects in USA, Western Europe and the Middle East; Civil Engineer, Kuwait; Engineering Adviser to HH the Amir, 1974; *Languages:* Arabic, English; *Address:* P O Box 1, Doha, Qatar.

QADDURAH, Muhammad Ibrahim, Saudi Arabian businessman; born 1930, Acre, Palestine; *Education:* London Matriculation, UK; *Career:* supervisor of shipping and petroleum inspection with Arabian-American Oil Company (Aramco); member of Executive Committee of Trading and Transportation Group owned by Shaikh Sulaiman al-Olayan; founder of paper industry and paper products; *Decorations:* Honorary Doctor of Business Studies, UK; *Interests and Recreations:* table-tennis, swimming, gardening, reading; *Address:* P O Box 61, Khobar, Saudi Arabia.

QADHAFI, Colonel Muammar al-, Libyan Head of State; born 1942, Sirte, Libya; married; three sons; *Religion:* Muslim; *Education:* in Sebha and Misurata; History, University of Libya, Benghazi, 1962–63; Libyan Military Academy; *Career:* commissioned as Signals Officer, 1965; followed courses in English language, armour and signals in UK, 1966; led the 1969 Revolution; Colonel and Commander in Chief, 1969; named Chairman of Revolutionary Command Council, 13 September 1969; Prime Minister, January 1970, Minister of Defence; succeeded as Prime Minister by Major Jalloud, while remaining Minister of Defence, 1972; Chairman of People's Congress, 1976; Secretary General, General Secretariat, March 1977–; *Publications:* studies of tactics and strategy; an account of the 1969 Revolution, serialized in Libyan press; *The Green Book,* 1973; *Languages:* Arabic, English; *Address:* The General People's Secretariat, Tripoli, Libya.

QADHAT, Salman Muhammad al-, Jordanian politician; born 1919, Jordan; married; *Religion:* Muslim; *Education:* licence in Law, Syrian University, 1946; *Career:* Ministry of Interior official, 1942–43; officer in Jordanian Army, 1947; member of Chamber of Deputies, 1950–51; District Officer for Ajloun and other areas, 1951–55; Assistant Governor of Nablus, 1955–56; Governor successively of Ma'an, Jerusalem, Kerak 1956–66; member of Chamber of Deputies, 1963–66, 1967–74; currently Head of Legal Committee and member of Foreign Affairs Committee, National Consultative Council; *Decorations:* Independence Medal, Second Class; *Interests and Recreations:* reading, travels; *Address:* Jabal Hussein, P O Box 6593, Amman, Jordan; telephone: 38044.

QADI, Abdul Qadir al-, Qatari financial official; born 1934, Palestine; married; *Religion:* Muslim; *Career:* banking, Amman, Jordan; Private Secretary to HH Shaikh Khalifa, then Deputy Ruler; Director of Financial Affairs, following latter's accession, 1972; involved in work with Qatar National Bank, and the development of Qatar Monetary Agency; established Qatar Investment Office, London; Director of Middle East Airlines; Chairman, Arab-Jordan Investment Bank, Amman, Jordan; Chairman, Gulf and Occidental Investment Co, Geneva, Switzerland; *Languages:* Arabic, English; *Address:* P O Box 949, Doha, Qatar.

QADI, Abdul Rahman Ibrahim al-, Saudi Arabian diplomat; born Saudi Arabia; *Religion:* Muslim; *Education:* LLB, Cairo University, Egypt, 1955; *Career:* diplomatic service; Delegate to the UN four times; Attaché and 3rd Secretary, Saudi Embassy to Egypt; attended all Arab Summit Conferences and Non-Aligned Countries Conferences, 1960–67; Consul General, New York, USA, 1968–70; attended all Arab Foreign Ministers meetings from 1973; member of delegation accompanying the late King Khalid during his visits to Egypt, Syria, and Jordan, 1970; Ambassador, Saudi Arabian Foreign Ministry; Director of Arab Department; Ambassador to Bahrain, 1980–; *Decorations:* Orders from Lebanon and Egypt; *Interests and Recreations:* football, music, poetry; *Address:* Embassy of Saudi Arabia, P O Box 1085, Manama, Bahrain.

QADIRI, Abu Bakr al-, Moroccan journalist; born 1914, Sale, Morocco; married; five sons, four daughters; *Religion:* Muslim; *Education:* in Morocco; *Career:* journalist; Director of *Al-Iman* monthly magazine; Director of *Al-Risaala* weekly paper; member of the Moroccan Royal Academy; member of Moroccan Scientists Federation; member of the Moroccan Writers Union; member of the Executive Council of the Islamic World Conference; Assistant Secretary General of the African Islamic Conference; Secretary General of the Moroccan Society for the Support of the Palestinian Cause; *Publications:* several books; articles in Moroccan papers and magazines; *Decorations:* Order of the Throne, Morocco; Medal of the Royal Moroccan Academy; *Interests and Recreations:* walking, Andalusian music; member of the Andalusian Music Society; *Languages:* Arabic, French; *Address:* Zankit Aknassous, P O Box 356, Rabat, Morocco; telephone: 81325, 81757; Boulevard al-Massira al-Khadra, Bettana, Sale, Morocco.

QAISI, Nuri Hammudi al-, Iraqi academic; born 1932, Baghdad, Iraq; married; three sons, two daughters; *Religion:* Muslim; *Education:* BSc in Arabic Language and Literature, Baghdad University, 1955; MA and PhD in Arabic Language and Literature, Faculty of Literature, Cairo University, 1964–67; *Career:* Lecturer, Faculty of Arabic Language, Baghdad University; Head of Faculty of Arabic Language, Baghdad University, 1974–75; Dean, College of Literature, Baghdad University, 1975–78; member of Iraqi Academy of Science, 1979; President, Iraqi Academy of Science; member of Jordanian Academy of Science; representative of Iraq at the Consultative Committee of the Arab Institute of Manuscripts, Arab League; member of the Consultative Council of the Khartoum Institute for Teaching Arabic Language to non-Arabic speakers; Professor of Ancient Literature, College of Literature, Baghdad University; President of the Institute of Arabic Research and Studies, Arab Organization for Education, Literature and Science, Arab League; *Publications:* numerous books, and researches published in Iraqi and Arab scientific journals; *Interests and Recreations:* literature and criticism, travel; *Languages:* Arabic, English; *Address:* Baghdad University, P O Box 12, College of Arts, Baghdad, Iraq; telephone: Office — 25026; Residence — 5558835.

QALAMAWI, Suhair al-, Egyptian academic/writer; born 1911; *Education:* American University in Cairo, Egypt; University of Paris, France; *Career:* Lecturer in Arabic Literature; Professor of Modern Arabic Literature and Chairman, Department of Arabic, Faculty of Arts, Cairo University; Director of Egyptian General Organization for Information, Publication, Distribution and Printing; *Publications:* several short story collections; a critical study of *The Arabian Nights,* 1939, and several other works; *Languages:* Arabic, English, French; *Address:* 4 Street Wadi al-Nil, Maadi, Cairo, Egypt.

QANDIL, Ahmad Salih, Saudi Arabian journalist/publisher; born 1913; *Religion:* Muslim; *Education:* general education in Arabic language and literature; *Career:* Director of Investigations Department, Ministry of Finance; Director of Archives Department, Ministry of Finance; Director General of Pilgrimage; Editor in Chief of *Saut al-Hijaz* daily newspaper; member of Jeddah Chamber of Commerce; member of Board of *Okaz* daily newspaper; established Mecca Commercial Co, Abir Establishment (now Qandil Commercial Establishment); owner, Qandil Establishment for Art Production; well-known poet; *Publications:* several collection of poems, radio plays, TV and radio talks; *Decorations:* Badge of Pioneer of Saudi Literature, First Conference of Saudi Men of Letters, Mecca, Saudi Arabia; *Interests and Recreations:* sport, travelling, production of

radio and TV programmes; *Address:* Al-Ihsa'a Street, Sharafia, Jeddah, Saudi Arabia; telephone: Jeddah 33254.

QARAGULI, Wahbi Abdul Razzaq Fattah al-, Iraqi diplomat; born 1929, Baghdad, Iraq; married; three children; *Education:* BA in Economics, College of Commerce and Economics, University of Baghdad, Iraq, 1954; PhD in Political Economy, Switzerland, 1962; *Career:* Deputy Permanent Representative, United Nations, Geneva, Switzerland, 1964–68; Counsellor, Iraqi Embassy, Algiers, Algeria, 1968; Counsellor, Iraqi Embassy, Peking, 1970; Minister Plenipotentiary, Iraqi Embassy, Beirut, Lebanon, 1972–76; Deputy General Director, Economics Department, Ministry of Foreign Affairs, Baghdad, 1977; Ambassador to Indonesia; non-resident Ambassador to Australia, New Zealand, Singapore, Papua New Guinea, 1977; Chief of Protocol, Presidential Palace, Baghdad, 1978; Ambassador to Malaysia, non-resident Ambassador to Philippines, 1980; Ambassador to London, UK, 1982–; *Languages:* Arabic, English; *Address:* Iraqi Embassy, 21 Queen's Gate, London SW7 5JD, UK.

QARMALLI, Hassan Baha'uddin, Saudi Arabian official/physician; born 1933; *Religion:* Muslim; *Education:* MB, Diploma of Tropical Medicine and Hygiene, London University, UK; *Career:* general practitioner; Director of Airport Quarantine; Director of King's Hospital, Jeddah; Director of Health Affairs, Taif; Director of Quarantine Department; Director of Health Affairs, Jeddah; Fellow of the Royal Society of Tropical Medicine, London, UK; former member of Committee on Health Education and Training, Jeddah; attended several WHO courses, Geneva 1968, 1969, 1971, 1972; *Publications: Health Services for Mecca Pilgrims* (a thesis); *Interests and Recreations:* reading, photography; *Address:* Health Affairs Directorate, Madaries Street, Baghdadia, Jeddah, Saudi Arabia.

QASIM, Muhammad Abdul Aziz, al-, Saudi Arabian official; born 16 September 1936, Riyadh, Saudi Arabia; *Religion:* Muslim; *Education:* MA in Public Administration and Management; *Career:* teacher; Inspector, Administrative Director, Assistant Director General, Ministry of Education; Director General of Cultural Affairs, Ministry of

Education; Assistant Deputy Minister for Financial and Administration Affairs, Ministry of Petroleum; Head of the Administrative Board of the Hamadah Agricultural Co-operative Society, Washm Region; member of the Administrative Board of the Saudi Scouts Society; took part in establishing the Social Services and Development Centres in Saudi Arabia, 1960–61; participated in several educational conferences such as UNESCO Conferences in Paris, the Education Conference in Geneva, the Scouts Conference in the UK; *Publications:* articles, papers, lectures, and radio broadcasts in the local press and radio; *Interests and Recreations:* photography, reading, collecting books; *Address:* P O Box 42205, Riyadh, Saudi Arabia; telephone: Riyadh 476 7752.

QASIMI, HH Shaikh Khalid Bin Saqr al-, United Arab Emirates politician; eldest son, Heir and Deputy of the Ruler of Ras al-Khaimah, Shaikh Saqr Bin Muhammad al Qasimi; born 1940; married; two sons; *Religion:* Muslim; *Education:* in Ras al-Khaimah, Cairo, Egypt, London, UK; Public Administration in USA, 1967; *Career:* set up a number of administrations in the Emirate of Ras al Khaimah; supervised the implementation of a number of development and construction schemes; acts as official emissary of his father the Ruler; *Languages:* Arabic, English; *Address:* P O Box 200, Ras al-Khaimah, United Arab Emirates.

QASIMI, HH Shaikh Saqr Bin Muhammad al-, United Arab Emirates Ruler of Ras al-Khaimah; born 1920; married; several children; *Religion:* Muslim; *Career:* Ruler of Ras al-Khaimah, since 1948, following Sultan Bin Salim; the only Trucial States Ruler not to subscribe to the constitution of the United Arab Emirates, UAE, in July 1970, and not to join UAE on its inauguration in December 1972; helped to develop the civil and industrial infrastructure of Ras al-Khaimah; visited UK as official guest, 1962, and USA in 1966; *Address:* Amiri Court, P O Box 1, Ras al-Khaimah, United Arab Emirates; telephone: 28161.

QASIMI, HH Shaikh Sultan Bin Muhammad al-, United Arab Emirates Ruler of Sharjah; born 1939; the fourth of six sons of Muhammad Bin Khalid; married; two children; *Religion:* Muslim; *Education:* in Sharjah; Agriculture in Cairo University, 418

Egypt; *Career:* Teacher in Sharjah Technical Training School; after leaving Cairo University, cooperated closely with the then Ruler of Sharjah, late Shaikh Khalid, from 1965; Minister of Education, 1971–72; after the assassination of his brother Khalid in January 1972 was unanimously elected Ruler by the Sharjah ruling family; since the discovery of oil off Abu Musa in 1972 leading to oil production in mid-1974, he has rapidly developed plans for the industrial expansion of Sharjah with incentives to foreign firms to make their UAE bases in Sharjah; contributed much towards the new development in Sharjah; *Languages:* Arabic, English; *Address:* P O Box 1, Sharjah, United Arab Emirates; telephone: 23135; telex: 68036 EMERY EM.

QASIMI, Khalid Abdullah Bin Humaid al-, United Arab Emirates diplomat/politician; born 1940, Umm al-Qawain, United Arab Emirates; married; one daughter; *Religion:* Muslim; *Career:* served in the Trucial Oman Scouts; United Arab Emirates Minister of Electricity and Water, 1977; UAE Ambassador to Algeria, 1977–; *Languages:* Arabic, English; *Address:* Embassy of United Arab Emirates, 26 Rue Haouis Mokrane, al Mouradia, Algiers, Algeria.

QASIMI, Shaikh Abdul Aziz Bin Humaid al-, United Arab Emirates politician; born Ras al-Khaimah, United Arab Emirates; *Religion:* Muslim; *Career:* Minister of State for Supreme Council Affairs, 1977–; *Address:* Prime Minister's Office, P O Box 899, Abu Dhabi, United Arab Emirates; telephone: 361555.

QASIMI, Shaikh Abdul Aziz Bin Muhammad al-, United Arab Emirates businessman/administrator; born 1937; brother of HH the Ruler of Sharjah, Shaikh Sultan Bin Muhammad al-Qasimi; married with children; *Religion:* Muslim; *Education:* in Sharjah by private tutors and in India; *Career:* worked in Kuwait, Saudi Arabia, Qatar; joined the Trucial Oman Scouts, 1960; commissioned after attending Mons Military Academy, UK, 1963; resigned as Captain, 1967; Wali of Khor Faqqan from, 1968; private business; unofficial Adviser to the Ruler of Ras al-Khaimah; Commander of the Sharjah National Guard, 1972–; Chairman of Sharjah Chamber of Commerce; *Languages:* Arabic, English; *Address:* P O Box 1, Sharjah, United Arab Emirates.

QASIMI, Shaikh Abdul Malik Bin Qayid al-, United Arab Emirates politician/ businessman; born 1935; *Religion:* Muslim; *Career:* short period in the Trucial Oman Scouts; United Arab Emirates Minister of State for the Supreme Council and President of the Ras al-Khaimah Chamber of Commerce, Agriculture and Industry; *Languages:* Arabic, English; *Address:* Ras al-Khaimah Chamber of Commerce, Agriculture and Industry, P O Box 87, Ras al-Khaimah, United Arab Emirates; telephone: 21348; telex: 99140 TIJARA EM.

QASIMI, Shaikh Ahmad Bin Sultan al-, United Arab Emirates politician; born Sharjah, United Arab Emirates; *Religion:* Muslim; *Career:* Minister of Justice; Minister of State, 1977–; *Address:* Prime Minister's Office, P O Box 899, Abu Dhabi, United Arab Emirates; telephone: 327354.

QASIMI, Shaikh Saqr Bin Muhammad al-, United Arab Emirates Deputy Ruler of Sharjah; born circa 1937; eldest brother of HH the Ruler of Sharjah, Shaikh Sultan Bin Muhammad al-Qasimi; *Religion:* Muslim; *Career:* has exstensive business interests; Commander of the Sharjah Security Forces; refused the succession in January 1972; *Address:* P O Box 1, Sharjah, United Arab Emirates.

QASIMI, Shaikh Saqr Bin Sultan al-, former Ruler of Sharjah, United Arab Emirates; born 1924; *Religion:* Muslim; *Education:* locally by private tutors; *Career:* formerly Ruler of Sharjah, 1951–55; later lived in Cairo and Beirut; returned to Ras al-Khaimah, 1972; now lives in Abu Dhabi; well-known as poet; *Address:* Abu Dhabi, United Arab Emirates.

QASIMI, Shaikh Saud Kaid al-, United Arab Emirates official/physician; born 1939, Ras al-Khaimah, United Arab Emirates; married; *Religion:* Muslim; *Education:* Degree in Medicine and Surgery, Cairo University, Egypt; Diploma in General Surgery; *Career:* Administrative Director of Preventive Medicine; Under Secretary, Ministry of Health; *Interests and Recreations:* oil painting, poetry, tennis, hockey; member of Sporting Club, Ras al-Khaimah; *Languages:* Arabic, English; *Address:* Ministry of Health, P O Box 848, Abu Dhabi, United Arab Emirates; telephone: 41443.

QASIMI, Shaikh Sultan Bin Saqr al-, United Arab Emirates army commander; second son of the Ruler of Ras al-Khaimah, Shaikh Saqr Bin Muhammad; born 1944; married; *Religion:* Muslim; *Education:* in United Arab Emirates; Training Course at Mons Military Academy, UK; Junior Staff Course at Warminster, UK, 1974; *Career:* served in the Trucial Oman Scouts, 1970; Commander of the Ras al-Khaimah Mobile Force, 1974; Colonel, 1975; Commander of Al Yarmuk Brigade; *Languages:* Arabic, English; *Address:* Ministry of Defence, Abu Dhabi, United Arab Emirates.

QASSAB, Khalid Abdul Aziz al-, Iraqi surgeon/academic; born 8 April 1924; married; one son, two daughters; *Religion:* Muslim; *Education:* MBCh, Graduate, College of Medicine, Baghdad, Iraq, 1946; Fellow of the Royal College of Surgeons, UK, 1954; *Career:* Residency, Teaching Hospital, Baghdad, 1947–51; Postgraduate Training, London, 1952–54; Teacher, Department of Surgery, Baghdad, 1954–58; Training in Cancer Surgery, Memorial Hospital, New York, USA, 1958–59; College of Medicine, Baghdad, Assistant Professor of Surgery, 1960–70; Professor of Surgery, 1970–77; Chairman, Department of Surgery, 1977–79; retired from government service, 1980; Consultant Surgeon to Private Hospitals, 1980–; founding member of the Iraqi Cancer Society, 1962; President, Iraqi Cancer Society, *Publications:* numerous researches and papers published in medical journals; *Decorations:* Red Crescent Silver Medal for Medical Services rendered in Palestine, 1948; *Interests and Recreations:* tennis, photography, painting; founder and first General Secretary, Iraqi Society for Plastic Arts, 1956; founding member of the Society of Plastic Arts Group, 1950; exhibited his work in many local and international exhibitions and international exhibitions; founding member of the Baghdad Society for National Heritage; *Languages:* Arabic, English; *Address:* PO Box 6193, Baghdad, Iraq.

QASUSUS, Wadi Hanna al-, Jordanian journalist; born 1920, Karak, Jordan; married; one son, one daughter; *Religion:* Christian; *Education:* BSc, American University of Beirut, AUB, Lebanon; *Career:* Press Correspondent, 1942–58; Assistant Director of Publications, 1958–66; Head of Press and Research Department in the Hashemite

Royal Court, 1966–; *Languages:* Arabic, English; *Address:* Royal Court, Amman, Jordan.

QATAMI, Jasim Abdul Aziz al-, Kuwaiti official/businessman; born 1927; *Religion:* Muslim; *Education:* Kuwait and Cairo; *Career:* police training in Egypt and UK; Director, Kuwait Metropolitan Police; resigned 1956; Manager, Kuwait Cinema Company, 1956–59; Business Manager for Yusuf al-Ghanim, 1959–61; Under Secretary, Ministry of Foreign Affairs, 1961–62; member of National Assembly, 1963–65 and 1975; resigned, 1975; various business interests; *Languages:* Arabic, English; *Address:* c/o Ministry of Foreign Affairs, Kuwait.

QATTAN, Shaikh Ibrahim Yassin al-, Jordanian judge/diplomat; born 1916, Amman, Jordan; married; two sons, four daughters; *Religion:* Muslim; *Education:* MA in Shari'a Law, Al-Azhar University, Cairo, Egypt; *Career:* Chief Clerk in Shari'a Court, Amman, 1941–1942; Judge in Karak, 1942–47; Inspector of Arabic Language and Religion, and then Under Secretary, Ministry of Education, 1948–62; Chief Judge and Minister of Education, 1962–65; Lawyer in his own Law Firm, 1965; Ambassador, Ministry of Foreign Affairs, 1965; Guiding Principal to Prince Hassan in Oxford, UK, 1965–67; Ambassador to Morocco, 1967; Ambassador to Kuwait, 1973; Ambassador to Pakistan, Indonesia and Malaysia, 1975–77; Chief Judge, 1977–; President of the Board of the Organization of the Administration and Development of Orphans Affairs; member of the Arabic Language Academies of Cairo, Egypt, Iraq and Jordan, Royal Committee of Jerusalem, Royal Academy of Islamic Organization, Jordanian Red Crescent Society; *Publications:* author and co-author of numerous works; two volumes of collections of articles, lectures and poems; *Decorations:* Order of Independence; Order of the Jordanian Star; Order of Science, Ministry of Education, Jordan; decoration from Morocco; *Interests and Recreations:* walking; member of the Jordanian Writers Federation; *Languages:* Arabic, English; *Address:* P O Box 2037 Amman, Jordan; telephone: Residence — 811 925; Office — 663 163.

QAWASMI, Fahd Dawud al-, Jordanian official/agricultural engineer; born 13 April 1939, Al-Khalil, Palestine; married; one

daughter, four sons; *Religion:* Muslim; *Education:* BSc and MSc in Agricultural Engineering, Ain Shams University, Cairo, Egypt, 1962 and 1971; *Career:* Professor, College of Teachers, 1962–69; Head of the Division of Scientific Research and Agricultural Guidance, 1971; Head of Division and Deputy Head of Department of Scientific Research and Agricultural Guidance, 1974; Head of the Municipal Council of Al-Khalil, 1976–; President of the Board of Directors of Arab Cement Company; member of the Consultative Council for the Affairs of the Occupied Territories; member of the Federation of Agricultural Engineers; member of the Higher Education Council; Member of the National Guidance Committee; *Publications:* numerous articles and papers on Palestine published in the Arab World and abroad; *Decorations:* various decorations from several countries; *Interests and Recreations:* reading, music, traditional Arabic singing, travel, gymnastics; *Languages:* Arabic, English; *Address:* P O Box 39116 Amman, Jordan; Jabal al-Hussain, Nablus Street, Jordan; telephone: Residence — 667 070.

QAYS, Samarra', (Abu Leila), Palestinian politician; born in Iraq; *Career:* formerly member of Baath Party; joined Popular Front for the Liberation of Palestine (PFLP) following the 1967 War and worked with Nayef Hawatmeh with whom he left to form Popular Democratic Front for the Liberation of Palestine (PDFLP); member of PDFLP Executive Committee.

QAYSI, Riyadh al-, Iraqi diplomat/lawyer; born 20 February 1939, Baghdad, Iraq; married; *Education:* BA in Law, College of Law, Baghdad University, 1955–59; Diploma in Law, King's College, London University, UK, 1960–61; LLM in International Law, King's College, London University, 1961–63; PhD in International Law, King's College, London University, 1963–66; *Career:* Lecturer, College of Law and Politics, Baghdad University, 1966–70; 1st Secretary, Ministry of Foreign Affairs, 1970; Counsellor, Permanent Mission of Iraq, UN, New York, 1970; member, American Society of International Law, Iraqi Society of Comparative Law; *Publications:* numerous articles and books on legal topics; *Interests and Recreations:* classical music, tennis, squash; *Languages:* Arabic, English, French; *Address:* Permanent Mission of Iraq, UN, 14 E 79 Street, New York, NY 10021, USA; telephone: (212) 737 4433.

QAZAZ, Ayad Sayyid al-, Arab-American academic; born 23 August 1941, Iraq; one daughter; *Religion:* Muslim; *Education:* BA in Sociology, University of Baghdad; MA in Sociology, University of California, Berkley, USA, 1966; PhD in Sociology, University of California, Berkley, 1970; *Career:* Assistant Professor, University of California, Berkeley, 1970; Associate Professor, California State University, 1974; Full Professor, California State University, 1980–; *Publications: Women in the Middle East and North Africa; The Arab World: a Handbook for Teachers; The Arab Community in the US; Interests and Recreations:* tennis, volleyball, walking; *Address:* Department of Sociology, California State University, Sacramento, California 94819, USA.

QISARI, Samir Muhamad, Egyptian banker; born 1930, Cairo; married; two sons; *Religion:* Muslim; *Education:* BA in Commerce; *Career:* Director General of Bank Control, 1976–77; Deputy Governer, Central Bank, 1977–78; member of the Board of Alexandria and Kuwait International Bank; *Publications: The Egyptian Banking System and the Development of Banking and Financial Laws,* in Arabic; several articles in local newspapers and economic journals; *Languages:* Arabic, English; *Address:* 1 Muhamad Taimur Street, Heliopolis, Cairo, Egypt; telephone: 878672.

QODUS, Muhammad Ahmad Abdul Hamid, Saudi Arabian businessman; born 1930; *Religion:* Muslim; *Education:* general; *Career:* Auditor, Chief, Audit Division; Assistant Director, General Board of Control Bureau, Jeddah; actively participates in contracting operations; established a factory for the manufacture of furniture; proprietor of Awg Trading and Contracting Corporation, Jeddah; *Interests and Recreations:* reading, music, football; *Address:* Commercial and Residential Centre, P O Box 5112, Jeddah, Saudi Arabia.

QOSTI, Abdul Ghani Muhammad, Saudi Arabian journalist; born 1927, Mecca, Saudi Arabia; *Religion:* Muslim; *Education:* general; *Career:* accountant, Mecca Governorate Secretariat, Mecca; editor, *Al Bilad* daily; former staff member, Okaz Press Organization; Managing Editor of *Al Bilad* daily newspaper; *Interests and Recreations:* reading, poetry, music; *Address:* Al Bilad Publishing Organization, King Abdul Aziz Street, Jeddah, Saudi Arabia.

QUBBAH, Taysir, Palestinian politician; born 1938; *Education:* politics, Cairo University, Egypt; Chairman of the General Union of Palestinian Students; *Career:* arrested by the Israelis for alleged subversive activities in the Occupied Territories; after three years in prison was deported to Jordan, 1971; Popular Front for the Liberation of Palestine (PFLP) representative on the Palestinian Liberation Organization (PLO) Executive Committee, 1971–72; campaigned in Lebanese refugee camps on behalf of the Rejection Front, 1974; led PFLP Delegation to China in his capacity as Head of the PFLP Foreign Affairs Department, 1974.

QUNTAR, Ahmad S., Jordanian aviation official/trade unionist; born 1944, Amman, Jordan; *Religion:* Muslim; *Education:* BLitt, Syrian University; Diploma in Public Administration, Harvard University, USA; various specialist qualifications in civil aviation; *Career:* Vice President, Air Transport and Tourism Trade Union, 1971, President, 1972; member of Executive Committee of Trade Union Federation, 1972; Assistant Secretary General for Education and Culture in Trade Union Federation, 1973; Secretary General of Jordan Trade Union Federation, 1974; Manager of Amman Airport, ALIA Royal Jordanian Airlines, 1974–77; Station Manager, Heathrow Airport, ALIA/The Royal Jordanian Airlines, 1977–80; Area Manager, ALIA/The Royal Jordanian Airlines, Cyprus, 1980–82; Assistant Vice President, Cargo Handling, ALIA/The Royal Jordanian Airlines, Amman Airport, 1982–; represented Jordan Trade Union Federation in international conferences; member of the Higher Committee for Advanced Training, of the Workers' Education Board, of the Organisation for the Promotion of Internal Tourism; President of the Board of Workers' Clinic; *Publications: The Internal Organisation of the Jordanian Labor Movement* (in English), Harvard, USA 1973; articles in Jordanian papers; Editor of *Sawt Ummal al-Urdan; Interests and Recreations:* reading, travel, table tennis; *Languages:* Arabic, English; *Address:* P O Box 1065, Amman, Jordan; telephone: Office— 94417 (Jordan Trade Union Federation), Residence— 816 190 ext 4.

QUOTAH, Muhammad, Saudi Arabian academic/economist; born 26th July 1943; married; one son, one daughter; *Religion:* Muslim; *Education:* MSc, Mathematics; MSc, Operations Research and System Analysis; PhD, Operations Research; *Career:* Assistant Director, Research and Development Centre; Assistant Professor of Operational Research and Mathematics, King Abdul Aziz University, Jeddah, 1979–; *Languages:* Arabic, English; *Address:* Research and Development Centre, Faculty of Economics and Administration, King Abdu Aziz University, P O Box 1504, Jeddah, Saudi Arabia; telephone: 687 9033, 687 9404 ext 1251.

QURAISHI, Abdul Aziz Bin Zaid al-, Saudi Arabian banker; born 1930, Hail, Saudi Arabia; *Religion:* Muslim; *Education:* MBA, University of Southern California, USA; *Career:* General Manager, State Railways, 1961–68; President, General Personnel Bureau, 1968–74; Minister of State, 1971–74; Governor, Saudi Arabian Monetary Agency (Central Bank), 1974–83; Governor for Saudi Arabia, International Monetary Fund and Arab Monetary Fund; Alternative Governor for Saudi Arabia, Islamic Development Bank; member of the Board of Directors of General Petroleum and Mineral Orgnaisation, Public Investment Fund, Pension Fund; *Address:* c/o Saudi Arabian Monetary Agency, P O Box 2992, Riyadh, Saudi Arabia; telephone: 69042; telex: 201736 SJ.

QUTUB, Ahmad Hassan, Saudi Arabian official; born 1944, Mecca, Saudi Arabia; *Religion:* Muslim; *Education:* BSc in Dairy Science, 1967; MSc in Nutrition, 1968; PhD in Nutrition, 1970; *Career:* Director of the Standards and Metrology Department, Ministry of Commerce and Industry, 1970–72; Director General of the Saudi Arabian Standards Organization (SASO); member of Executive Bureau of the Arab Organization for Standards and Metrology (ASMO) of the Arab League; Saudi Arabia's delegate to the General Committee of ASMO; member of the Development Committee (DEVCO) of the International Organization for Standardization (ISO), the American Dairy Science Association (ADSA), the Oklahoma State Alumni Association, USA; participated in the committee concerned with the formulation of SASO administrative and financial regulations and its organizational structure; participated in some committees concerned with revising the financial and administrative regulations of ASMO; participated in the preparatory committee for the first Arab Standards Conference; *Publications: Standardization as Related to Building Materials, with an Analytical Assessment of Standardization in Saudi Arabia; A Guide for the Preparation of Saudi Standards; A Guide for the Drafting and Editing of Saudi Standards; Interests and Recreations:* reading, photography, music; *Address:* P O Box 3437, Riyadh, Saudi Arabia; telephone: 4489369.

R

RAAFAT, Hani Muhammad Nassim, Egyptian engineer; born 29 March 1945, Cairo, Egypt; resident in the United Kingdom; *Religion:* Muslim; *Education:* BSc in Production Engineering, Ain Shams University, Egypt; Postgraduate Diploma, University of Kuwait; MSc in Production Technology, Aston University, UK; PhD in Production Technology, Aston University, UK; *Career:* Lecturer, Technical College, Kuwait, 1968–72; part-time Lecturer and Demonstrator, Department of Production Engineering, University of Birmingham, UK, 1972–77; Full time Permanent Lecturer and Certificate Course Tutor, 1977–; member of the Mechanical Engineers Association, UK; *Publications:* author and co-author of several books on engineering; *Interests and Recreations:* swimming, reading, football, snooker, mechanical engineering, systems analysis, applied statistics; *Languages:* Arabic, English, French; *Address:* Department of Occupational Health and Safety, Aston University, Gosta Green, Birmingham B4 7ET; telephone: 021 3593611 ext 6290.

RABBAT, Walid B., Syrian businessman/petroleum engineer; born 31 March 1933, Damascus, Syria; married; two sons, one daughter; *Religion:* Muslim; *Education:* BSc in Petroleum Engineering; *Career:* Director, Tanks Farms and Pipelines, Syrian Petroleum Company, 1961–73; Chairman and General Director, SADCOP, 1974–75; Managing Director, Walid Rabbat and Co, 1977–; Managing Director, Syrian Branch of Petroleum and Petrochemical Inspection, Société Générale de Surveillance SA, Geneva; *Publications: Petroleum Products Losses,* 1962; *Petroleum Tanks Calibration,* 1970; *Interests and Recreations:* swimming, bridge, reading; *Languages:* Arabic, English, French; *Address:* Office — P O Box 4398, Damascus, Syria; telephone: 2285665; telex: 411495 WARACO SY; Residence — 1st floor, Ghabra and Hammami Building, AM Riad Street, Malki, Syria; telephone: 719861.

RABBATH, Edmond, Lebanese academic/lawyer; born 1906; Aleppo, Syria; married; two sons, one daughter; *Education:* Licence in Law, Doctorate in Law, St. Joseph University, Beirut, Lebanon; Licence ès-Lettres, University of Paris, France; Diploma from the School of Political Science, Paris, France; *Career:* Barrister at Law; Professor, Faculty of Law, Lebanese University; President, International Committee for the Translation of Classics; *Publications: L'Evolution Politique de la Syrie sous le Mandat Français; Unité Syrienne et Devenir Arabe; Treatise on Constitutional Law* (2 vols), in Arabic; various articles and studies published in French and Arabic language magazines; *Decorations:* Knight, National Order of the Cedar; Gold Medal, Lebanese Order of Merit; Légion d'Honneur, France; and several other decorations; *Interests and Recreations:* Governor, International Rotary Club; *Languages:* Arabic, French; *Address:* Office — Place de L'Etoile, Beirut, Lebanon; Residence — Museum Quarter, Rabbath Building, Beirut, Lebanon.

RABIE, Abdul Aziz Muhammad Ali al-, Saudi Arabian official/educationalist; born 1926; *Religion:* Muslim; *Education:* BA in Arts and Education; *Career:* Director, Education Directorate, Medina; Chairman of Board of Co-operative Society for Government Employees; Chairman of Al Ansor Sporting Club; Chairman of Medina Literary Club; Chief of Regional Scouts Bureau; General Supervisor of Boy Scout Camps in the Service of Pilgrims; member of Okaz Literary Festival Preparatory Committee; attended the First Conference of Saudi Men of Letters, King Abdul Aziz University, the Fifth Seminar Conference on Social Studies,

Amman, Jordan, Arab Teachers Conference, Alexandria, Egypt, Conference of Arab Ministers of Education and Planning, Libya, UNESCO Conference, Paris, France, 1974, Okaz Festivals Preparatory Conference, Riyadh, Saudi Arabia, 12th Arab Scout Conference, Tunis, Tunisia; *Publications: Virtuous Behaviour in the Light of Islam;* detailed commentary on collection of poetry entitled *A Man and His Destiny;* several articles; *Decorations:* Medal of a Pioneer of Letters, awarded by King Abdul Aziz University, Jeddah; *Interests and Recreations:* mountain climbing; *Address:* Bab Al-Awali, Medina, Saudi Arabia.

RADHI, Abdullah al-, United Arab Emirates businessman; born 1943, Bahrain; married; one son, one daughter; *Religion:* Muslim; *Education:* BA in Accounting, Cairo University, Egypt; *Career:* Economic Researcher in Bahrain Chamber of Commerce and Editor of its magazine, 1970–71; Deputy Director General, Abu Dhabi Chamber of Commerce and Industry, 1972; owner of Al-Radhi Trading Company; owner of Al-Khalij (Gulf) Publishing and Printing House; *Languages:* Arabic, English; *Address:* P O Box 2375, Abu Dhabi, United Arab Emirates.

RADWAN, Samir Muhammad, Egyptian ILO official/economist; resident in Geneva, Switzerland; born 20 September 1942, Egypt; married; one daughter; *Religion:* Muslim; *Education:* BSc Economics, Cairo University, Egypt, 1963; MSc in Economic Development, University of London, UK, 1976; PhD in Economics, University of London, 1973; *Career:* Assistant Lecturer, Faculty of Economics, Cairo University, 1963–65; Research Officer, Institute of National Planning Project, Cairo, and the Aswan National Planning Project, Cairo and Aswan, 1963–64; Consultant, ILO, Exploratory Employment Policy Mission to Pakistan, 1975; Consultant, ILO Mission to Iran, 1974–75; Research Officer, Oxford University, Institute of Economics and Statistics and Senior Associate Member of St. Anthony's College, Oxford, 1972–76; Senior Economist, International Labour Organisation, Geneva, 1976–; *Publications: Capital Formation in Egyptian Industry and Agriculture 1882–1967,* 1974; *The Industrialization of Egypt,* 1976 co-author with Robert Mabro; *Egypt and an Open-Door Foreign Investment Policy,* 1975; *Agrarian Systems and Rural Development,* 1979;

Agrarian Reform and Rural Poverty in Egypt, co-editor, 1977; various articles in international journals; *Interests and Recreations:* Arabic literature, history, rowing; *Languages:* Arabic, English, French; *Address:* 31A chemin des Mollies, 1293 Bellevue, Geneva, Switzerland.

RAHAL, Abdul Latif, Algerian diplomat/politician; born 14 April 1922, Algeria; married; one son, one daughter; *Religion:* Muslim; *Education:* BSc in Mathematics, Faculty of Science, Algiers University; *Career:* teacher in Algeria, 1950–62; taught mathematics at Mostaganem and Marnia, and at Berber College, Azrou, Morocco; went to Morocco for National Liberation Front (FLN), 1956, and helped establish (FLN) Federation; Chef de Cabinet to Dr Chawki Mostefai, Delegate for General Affairs in Provisional Executive, 1962; Director of Cabinet, Office of the Presidency, 1962–63; Ambassador to France, 1963–64; Delegate, UN General Assembly, New York, USA, 1966–74; Delegate to Conference of Arab League, Organization of African Unity and Non-Aligned States; Secretary General, Ministry of Foreign Affairs, 1966–71; Ambassador, Permanent Representative of Algeria, UN, New York, USA, 1971–77; Minister of Education and Scientific Research, 1977–80; *Decorations:* numerous decorations from African Governments; *Interests and Recreations:* member of the Algerian Writers Union; *Languages:* Arabic, French, English; *Address:* c/o Ministry of Education and Scientific Research, Algiers, Algeria.

RAHAL, Makram A., Lebanese banker; resident in Bahrain; born 23 March 1937, Beirut; married; one son; *Religion:* Muslim; *Education:* PhD in Business Administration; *Career:* International Officer, Francis I. Dupont, New York, 1967–68; Representative, Francis I. Dupont, Beirut (Wall Street Firm), 1968–70; Representative, Bache and Co, Beirut (Wall Street Firm), 1970–74; Deputy Manager, Arab Finance Corporation, 1974–75; Manager, Citicorp International Bank Ltd, 1975–78; Senior Manager, Arab Bank Ltd, Bahrain, 1978–; member of the Arab Bank Association, Chicago Board of Trade; *Interests and Recreations:* karate (Black Belt), chess, sports in general, reading, research; *Languages:* Arabic, English, French, Italian, German; *Address:* Arab Bank Ltd, Offshore Banking Unit, Manama

Centre, Wing 3, 2nd Floor, P O Box 813, Manama, Bahrain; telephone: Office — 256398, 257981; Residence — 713346.

RAHALI, Rahal, Moroccan politician/physician; born 29 August 1934, Morocco; *Education:* Degree in Medicine, Bordeaux University, France; *Career:* Chief Medical Officer of Health and Surgery, Provincial Hospital and Medical Centre, Meknes; President of the Provincial and Municipal Council in Meknes; member of Mouvement Populaire; Minister of Public Health, 1977–; President of the Moroccan Red Cross, Meknes; *Languages:* Arabic, French; *Address:* Ministry of Public Health, Rabat, Morocco.

RAHALI, Sidi Muhammad, Moroccan engineer; born 16 June 1924, Casablanca; three sons, three daughters; *Religion:* Muslim; *Education:* Diploma, Professional School of Casablanca, Morocco; Diploma, Technical School of Berliet, France; *Career:* constructor and builder of coach bodies since 1942; Director, General Manager and Importer, Carrosserie Rahali, Mechanical Assemblage Factory; former Vice President of the Municipality Council of the City of Casablanca; former Vice President of the Chamber of Commerce and Industry of Casablanca; *Decorations:* Chevalier de l'Ordre du Trône du Maroc, 1968; *Interests and Recreations:* boxing; President of the Moroccan Union of Professional Boxing; *Languages:* French, Arabic; *Address:* Route Cotière 111 Km11, 2000 Ain Sebaa, Casablanca, Morocco; telephone: 350438, 350915; telex: 25970.

RAHAMA, Mubarak Othman, Sudanese diplomat/army officer; born 1929, Omdurman, Sudan; married; *Religion:* Muslim; *Education:* Company Command Course, Warminster, UK, 1958; Camberley Staff College, 1962; *Career:* joined Armed Forces; Commissioned in Camel Corps, 1952; Major, 1958; Director of Military Training, 1969; Military Attaché, Embassy of Sudan to USSR, Poland, German Democratic Republic, Bulgaria and Hungary, 1968–69; Commanding Officer of Southern Command, for the Southern Region, 1970; Resident Ambassador to Nigeria, non-resident Ambassador to Ghana and Cameroon, 1971–76; Resident Ambassador to Peking, non-resident Ambassador to Democratic People's Republic of Korea, 1976–; *Languages:* Arabic, English; *Address:* Embassy of Sudan, 27 San Li Tun, Beijing, People's Republic of China.

RAHMAH, Ahmad Mirza al-, United Arab Emirates official; born 1946, Dubai, United Arab Emirates; married; one daughter; *Religion:* Muslim; *Education:* BSc in Economics and Political Science, Baghdad University, Iraq, 1969; *Career:* Deputy Director of Housing and Purchasing Department, 1971; Director of Minerals Department, Ministry of Petroleum, 1972; Director of the Minister's Office, Ministry of Petroleum, 1973; Director of Administrative and Finance Department, Ministry of Petroleum and Mineral Resources, 1974–; *Interests and Recreations:* classical poetry, swimming, football, hunting; *Languages:* Arabic, English; *Address:* Ministry of Petroleum and Mineral Resources, P O Box 59, Abu Dhabi, United Arab Emirates; telephone: 361133; telex: 22544 MPMR EM.

RAJAB, Abdul Hafidh Salim, Omani official/politician; born 1937, Dhofar, Oman; *Religion:* Muslim; *Education:* in Salalah and Kuwait; Mechanical Engineering, Kiev University, USSR; *Career:* Lecturer in Engineering, Kuwait Technical College; Director, Government Workshop and Technical Trades School, Oman, 1971; Minister of Economy, Oman, 1971; Minister of Commercial and Social Affairs and Labour, Oman, 1972; Acting Minister of Economy, 1972; Minister of Communications and Public Works, Oman, 1973; Minister of Agriculture and Fisheries, 1979–; *Languages:* Arabic, English, Russian; *Address:* Ministry of Agriculture and Fisheries, P O Box 467, Muscat, Oman; telephone: 703200; telex: 3503 AGRIFISH MB.

RAJAB, Muhammad Zaruk, Libyan politician/accountant; born 1940, Benghazi, Libya; *Religion:* Muslim; *Education:* BSc in Economics, University of Libya, Benghazi, 1962; qualified as Chartered Accountant in UK, 1967; *Career:* Lecturer in Accountancy and Dean of the Accounting Department, University of Libya; Assistant Professor of Accountancy, 1969; Head of the Audit Division; Minister of the Treasury, 1972–77; Secretary for the Treasury, General People's Committee, 1977; *Address:* Office of the Secretary of the Treasury, Tripoli, Libya.

RAJHI, Hamad Bin Naser al-, Saudi Arabian businessman/civil engineer; born 1948, Mecca, Saudi Arabia; *Education:* BSc in Civil Engineering, University of California, USA; *Career:* Managing Director, Rajhi Consulting Engineers, the firm specializes in water supply projects and architectural work; member of the American Society of Civil Engineers; attended conference on water pollution, San Francisco, USA, 1973; *Publications:* contributed to professional journals in the field of civil engineering, water pollution; *Languages:* Arabic, English; *Address:* P O Box 7669, Riyadh, Saudi Arabia; telex: 201249 NASIR SJ.

RAJHI, Sulaiman Abdul Aziz al-, Saudi Arabian businessman/financier; *Career:* Managing Director and member of the Board, al Rajhi Company for Exchange and Commerce; 1978–; *Address:* P O Box 28, Jeddah, Saudi Arabia; telex: 401058 RAJHI SJ.

RAKAN, Sharif Ghazi, Jordanian aviation official; born 1939, Cairo, Egypt; *Religion:* Muslim; *Education:* trained as a pilot in the UK; *Career:* Officer in the Jordanian Air Force; Director General of Civil Aviation, 1971–72, and 1974–; *Languages:* Arabic, English; *Address:* Department of Civil Aviation, P O Box 7547, Amman, Jordan.

RAMADAN, Abdul Azim, Egyptian academic/historian; born 18 April 1925, Giza, Egypt; married; one son, two daughters; *Religion:* Muslim; *Education:* BA in Literature, Cairo University, Egypt; MA in Modern History; Short Studies and Seminars in Management and Public Relations, Institute of Management, Cairo; *Career:* Assistant Professor of Modern History, University of Constantine, Algeria, 1973; Professor of Modern History, Minufiya University, 1978; Head of History Department, College of Education, Minufiya University, 1981; *Publications: The Development of the National Movement in Egypt,* 3 vols, 1968, 1973, Cairo; *Abdul Nasir and the Crisis of March,* 1976, Cairo; *The Egyptian Army in Politics,* 1977, Cairo; *The Struggle of Classes in Egypt,* 1978, Cairo; *The Struggle Between the Wafd (Party) and the Throne,* 1979; *The Revolutionary Thought in Egypt before the 23 July Revolution,* 1981, Cairo; *The Egyptian-Israeli Confrontation in the Red Sea,* 1981, Cairo; numerous articles in *Rose al-Yusif* publications and *Al Jumhuriya* daily newspaper, Cairo; *Al-Arab,* London; *Interests and Recreations:* classical music, walking; member of the Society of History, the Egyptian Writers Club; founding member of the National Progressive Unionist Party; *Languages:* Arabic, English, French; *Address:* 12 Nakhla Al-Muti'i Street, Apt 4, Heliopolis, Cairo, Egypt; telephone: 21351 840, 22289 840.

RAMAHI, Saif Ahmad al-Wadi, United Arab Emirates diplomat; born 28 December 1938, Muzeira, Palestine; *Education:* Diploma in Public Law, Lebanese Academy, Beirut, Lebanon, 1956; BA in Political Science and Economics, Lebanese State University, Beirut, 1960; Certificate, International Law, City of London College, London, UK, 1960; MA in Government Studies, Southern Illinois University, USA, 1966; Public Administration, University of Birmingham, UK, 1967; PhD, Southern Illinois University, Carbandale, Illinois, USA, 1970; PhD, University of Birmingham, UK, 1981; *Career:* School Teacher, Qatar, 1956–58; School Secretary, Qatar, 1958–59; School Headmaster, Qatar, 1959–60; Area Education Superintendent, Qatar, 1960–63; Deputy Director to the Emiri Court, Office of the Ruler of Abu Dhabi, 1968–70; Director, Office of the Arab League, Dallas, Texas, USA, 1970–72; Minister Plenipotentiary, Chargé d'Affaires, UAE Embassy in Tripoli, Libya, 1973–75; Minister Plenipotentiary, Chargé d'Affaires, UAE Embassy in Tokyo, Japan, 1976–80; Visiting Professor, Jochi, Sophia University, Tokyo, Japan, 1977–80; Minister Plenipotentiary, Superintendant of Diplomatic Training, Ministry of Foreign Affairs, Abu Dhabi, UAE, 1980–81; member of the Middle East Institute, Washington D.C., the Japanese Academy of Oriental Studies, the Dallas Council of World Affairs, and several others; *Publications: Economic and Political Evolution in the Gulf States,* 1973, New York, The Carlton Press; *UAE Challenges the Desert to Bloom,* 1976, Tokyo, Universal Public Relations; several other books; numerous research papers and articles in international journals and magazines; *Decorations:* Order of Independence, Jordan; *Interests and Recreations:* calligraphy, painting, writing poetry, music; *Languages:* Arabic, English; *Address:* P O Box 3631, Abu Dhabi, UAE; telephone: 343446.

RAMBA, Lubari, Sudanese politician; born 1936, Yei District, Sudan; *Education:* American University in Beirut, Lebanon, 1958–62; *Career:* Teacher, 1962–69; Sales Manager, Mitchell-Colts Co, 1969–72; Regional Director of Education, 1972–73; First Speaker, Peoples Regional Assembly, Juba, 1973–75; Minister of Public Services and Administrative Reform, Southern Sudan High Executive Council, 1975–78; General Manager, Ugandan Refugees Project and Returnees Affairs, Juba, 1980–; *Address:* The High Council of the Southern Region, Juba, Sudan.

RAMZI, Ahmad, Moroccan politician/physician; born 1939, Casablanca, Morocco; *Religion:* Muslim; *Education:* medical studies in Montpellier University, France; PhD in General Surgery, 1959; *Career:* surgeon in Marrakesh hospital, 1963–67; member of Faculty of Medicine, Rabat; Director of Health Centre, Avicennes, 1969; Senior Medical Officer in Agadir Province, 1972; Minister of Health, 1974–75; Ambassador to Iraq, 1975–77; Minister of Religious Endowments and Islamic Affairs, 1977; *Languages:* Arabic, French; *Address:* Ministry of Religious Endowments and Islamic Affairs, Rabat, Morocco.

RAPHAEL, Farid, Lebanese banker; born 1933; married; one son, two daughters; *Education:* Licence en Droit, Université de Lyon, 1954; Licence en Droit Libanais, 1955; *Career:* Compagnie Algérienne de Crédit et de Banque, 1956; Department Manager, 1965; founded Banque Libano-Française SAL, 1968, and Banque Libano-Française (France) SAL, 1976; Minister of Justice, Finance and PTT, 1976–79; Vice Chairman and General Manager, Banque Libano-Française, 1976–; Chairman and General Manager, Banque Libano-Française SAL, 1979–; *Address:* Office — P O Box 11–808, Beirut, Lebanon; telephone: 221850, 220340; Residence — Baroody Building, Hazmieh, Beirut.

RAQABANI, Said al-, United Arab Emirates politician; born Fujairah, United Arab Emirates; *Career:* former member of the United Arab Emirates Federal Council; Minister of Agriculture and Fisheries, 1977–; *Address:* Ministry of Agriculture and Fisheries, P O Box 1509, Dubai, United Arab Emirates; telephone: 362940; telex: 4259 MAF EM.

RASHDAN, Muhammad Salim, Jordanian academic; born 25 November 1921, Salt, Jordan; married; three sons, three daughters; *Religion:* Muslim; *Education:* MA in Literature and Semitic Languages; Diploma in Administration, American University of Beirut, AUB, Lebanon; *Career:* Lecturer in higher educational institutions in Iraq, 1949–50; Lecturer, Teachers College, Damascus, Syria, 1951–53; Ministry of Education, Jordan, Supervisor; Head of Department; Editor of the magazine *Risalat al-Mu'allim,* 1953–76; Lecturer, Jordanian University, 1963–; Inspector of Texts, Jordanian Television, 1975–; *Publications:* numerous books and translations published in Jordan, Syria and Lebanon in Arabic; *Decorations:* Order of Education, Jordan; Order of Garuda, Indonesia; decoration from Qatar; *Interests and Recreations:* swimming, table tennis, travelling; member of the City Sporting Club, Jordanian Writers Society; *Languages:* Arabic, English, Persian, Hebrew, and several other Semitic languages; *Address:* P O Box 1755, Amman, Jordan; telephone: Office — 30239, Residence — 36202.

RASHED, Abdul Aziz Abdul Muhsin al-, Kuwaiti businessman; born 1904, Saudi Arabia; married; one son; *Religion:* Muslim; *Career:* one of Kuwait's leading entrepreneurs; President, Al Rashed Group (shipping, contracting to government and oil companies, telecommunications, hospital equipments, import–export); *Languages:* Arabic, English; *Address:* P O Box 241, Kuwait; telephone: 422022/5, 433762; telex: 22063 ALRASHED KT.

RASHID, Abdullah Dakhil al-, Kuwaiti engineer/businessman; born 4 January 1933, Kuwait; married; one son, one daughter; *Religion:* Muslim; *Education:* BSc in Mechanical Engineering; *Career:* Mechanical Engineer, Ministry of Electricity and Water, 1964; Deputy-Director, Salt Chlorine Plant, Ministry of Electricity and Water, 1965; Assistant Under Secretary, Ministry of Electricity and Water, 1966; Director General, National Housing Authority, 1974; Vice-Chairman, Refrigeration Industry and Cold Storage Company; *Interests and Recreations:* member of Kuwait Engineers Society and Kasma Sports Club; *Languages:* Arabic, English; *Address:* P O Box 22261, Safat, Kuwait; telephone: 412111, telex: 22684 RICSCO KT.

RASHID, Lieutenant General Nadir, Jordanian official; born 1929, Salt, Jordan; *Career:* joined the Army, 1948; entered Administration in 1950s; Director, General Intelligence; Ambassador to Morocco, 1973; President of the Board of Directors, Jordan Phosphate Mines; *Address:* Lion Trading Co, P O Box 6583, Amman, Jordan; telephone: 93102.

RASHID, Muhammad Sa'ad al-, Saudi Arabian academic; born 1940, Saudi Arabia; *Religion:* Muslim; *Education:* BA in Islamic Law and Arabic Language; Diplomas in English Law, International Law, Comparative Law, London, UK; PhD in Law, Durham University, UK, 1973; *Career:* Lecturer, Faculty of Islamic Law (Shari'a); Head of Judicial Department, Faculty of Islamic Law (Shari'a), King Abdul Aziz University; permanent member, Graduate Society, Durham University, UK; attended International Conference of Youth Magistrates, and Anti-Narcotics International Conference, Bangkok, 1975; *Publications: Procedure to Bring a Criminal Action in Saudi Arabia,* a research paper submitted to the Islamic Jurisprudence Conference, Tunis, 1974; *Narcotics, Crime and Punishment in Saudi Arabia; Narcotics as Viewed by Islamic Law,* an address to International Anti-Narcotic Conference, Bangkok, Thailand, 1975; *Constitutional System of Saudi Arabia; System of Government and Administration in Saudi Arabia; System of Government and Administration in Islam; The Judiciary System in Saudi Arabia; Interests and Recreations:* reading, travel, sport; *Address:* Faculty of Shari'a, Mecca, Saudi Arabia.

RASHID, Nassir Ibrahim al-, Saudi Arabian engineer/ businessman; born 1939, Medina, Saudi Arabia; *Religion:* Muslim; *Education:* BSc in Civil Engineering, 1965; PhD in Civil Engineering, 1970; *Career:* former Dean of Technical and Administrative Affairs; Dean, Faculty of Engineering, University of Petroleum and Minerals; member of the City Council of Al-Khobar, the Contractors Classifications Committee, the American Association of Civil Engineers (AACE); attended several conferences related to highways; owner of Rashid Engineering Office, Riyadh; *Publications: Electronic Scale for Weighing Vehicles in Motion; Dynamic Loading of Highways, Planning and Scheduling by Crucial Passage Method*

(CPM); Interests and Recreations: jogging, table tennis, reading, travel; *Address:* P O Box 4354, Riyadh, Saudi Arabia; telephone: Office — 464 1188.

RASHID, Rashid Abdul Aziz al-, Kuwaiti diplomat; born 1933, Kuwait; married; *Religion:* Muslim; *Education:* American University of Beirut, Lebanon; *Career:* Assistant Technical Director, Public Works Department, 1959–61; Assistant Secretary, Government Secretariat, 1961; Director, Political Department, Ministry of Foreign Affairs, 1961–63; Permanent Representative of Kuwait at UN, 1963–67; Under Secretary, Ministry of Foreign Affairs, 1967–; Chairman of the Kuwait Cement Company; *Languages:* Arabic, English; *Address:* Ministry of Foreign Affairs, P O Box 3, Sour Street, Kuwait; telephone: 422041, 422050; telex: 22042 KHARJIA KT.

RASHIDAT, Najib Awadh al-, Jordanian politician/lawyer; born 19 April 1922, Irbid, Jordan; married; *Education:* Licence in Arabic Law, Damascus University, Syria, 1943–44; *Career:* Civil Magistrate, Amman, 1947–48; Magistrate in Juvenile Court, 1948–49; Civil Magistrate in Ajloun, 1949–50; Assistant Attorney General, 1950–51; Public Prosecutor in Amman, 1951–54; member of the Court of First Instance, 1954–56; President of the Court of First Instance, Salt, 1956–57; member of Appeals Court, Jerusalem, 1960–61; member of Appeals Court, Amman, 1961–62; Administrative Judge, 1962; member of Chamber of Deputies, 1962–64; Dean of Lawyers, 1965–67; lawyer, 1967–69; Governor of Amman, 1969–70; Minister of Interior, 1970; Minister of Communications, 1970; private law practice, 1970; private law practice, 1970–79; Minister of Justice, 1979–80; *Interests and Recreations:* reading, poetry, social studies, books about the Arab world; *Address:* P O Box 1587, Amman, Jordan; telephone: 37927.

RASHUDI, Hamad Ibrahim, Saudi Arabian administrator; born 1939; *Religion:* Muslim; *Education:* LLB, MPA; *Career:* Assistant Chief, Transfers Division; Chief of Correspondence Division; Assistant Manager of Legal Division; National Bank; Assistant Director, later Director of Registration Department, Institute of Public Administration; Director of Documentation Centre; administration and organization specialist;

Assistant Director General of Customs; Director General of Customs; member of Board of Saudi Arabian Railways Corporation; member of Conferences of General Director of Customs, Customs Co-operation Council, Brussels, Belgium, Paris, France, Buenos Aires, Argentina; *Interests and Recreations:* reading, travel, swimming; *Address:* Customs Department, P O Box 3483, Riyadh, Saudi Arabia.

RATEB, Aisha Muhammad, Egyptian diplomat/academic; born 22 February 1928, Cairo, Egypt; two sons; *Religion:* Muslim; *Education:* PhD in International Law; *Career:* Head of Department of International Law, Faculty of Law, Cairo University, Egypt; Minister of Social Affairs, 1971–77; Ambassador of Egypt to Denmark, 1980–82; Ambassador of Egypt to Federal Republic of Germany, 1982–; *Publications: International-Arab Relationship Diplomatic and Consular Organization International Organizations; Some Legal Aspects of the Arab Israeli Conflict ;* all in Arabic except one research paper published by UN concerning the establishing of Regional Committees of Human Rights; *Decorations:* Order of the Republic, 1st Class, Egypt, 1975; Highest Order of Tunisia, 1972; Order of the French Republic; *Interests and Recreations:* reading; member of International Law Society, the Society of Political Science, the Club of the Teaching Staff; *Languages:* Arabic, English, French, German; *Address:* Embassy of Egypt, 53 Bonn 2, Kronprinzenstrasse 2, Federal Republic of Germany; 6 Ibn Malek Street, Cairo, Arab Republic of Egypt.

RATIB, Gamil, Egyptian artist/actor; resident in France; born 18 August 1926, Alexandria, Egypt; married; *Career:* performed in French plays *Othello, Hamlet, Twelfth Night, Le Malentendu, Les Parachutistes, Danse de Mort, Le Roi Clos;* French films; *Les Jeunes Loups;* British films, *Lawrence of Arabia, Trapeze;* performed in various Egyptian films; acted in US, French, Egyptian television programmes; *Languages:* Arabic, French, English, Italian; *Address:* 59 Boulevard Hugo, Neuilly, France; 17 Maahad Swisry, Zamalek, Cairo, Egypt.

RAWABDAH, Abdul Rauf Salim, Jordanian official/Mayor of Amman; born 13 February 1939, Sarih, Jordan; married; eight daughters, one son; *Religion:* Muslim; *Education:* BSc in Pharmacy, American University of Beirut, AUB, Lebanon, 1962; *Career:* Inspector of Pharmacies, 1962–64; Head of Pharmacy Section, 1964–67; Director, Department of Pharmacy, 1967–75; Director of Planning and Foreign Relations, Ministry of Health, 1975–76; Director of Administrative Services, University of Yarmuk, 1976; Minister of Communications, 1976–77; Minister of Communications and Minister of Health, 1977–78; Minister of Health, 1978–79; member of the National Consultative Council, 1978–83; Vice Chairman, National Consultative Council; Chairman, Jordan Phosphate Mines Company; Chairman, Arab Industrial Group Company; Chairman of the Board of Trustees, Jordan Community College; Vice Chairman, Jordan Fertilizer Company; Mayor of Amman, 1983– *Publications: Pharmacology,* 1965, 1981, in Arabic; *Pharmacy,* 1965, 1982, in Arabic; *Decorations:* Order of the Jordanian Star, 1976; *Interests and Recreations:* swimming, photography; *Languages:* Arabic, English; *Address:* P O Box 19222, Amman, Jordan; telephone: Office — 666 033; Residence — 661 984.

RAWI, General Abdul Jabbar al-, Iraqi army officer; born 1 June, 1898, Iraq; *Religion:* Muslim; married; five sons, one daughter; *Education:* Iraqi Military Academy; *Career:* Lieutenant, Ottoman Army, 1917; 1st Lieutenant, Iraqi Army, 1921; Captain, Iraqi Police Force, 1925; Director, Baghdad Police Department, 1935; Director General, Iraqi Police Force, 1945; Dean, Iraqi Police Academy, Baghdad, Iraq, 1952; member of Parliament for Iraqi-Jordanian Federation, 1958; now retired; *Publications: Al-Badia,* in Arabic, 1954, 1972; *Decorations:* Rafidian Decoration (Military); *Interests and Recreations:* Islamic and Arabic literature; *Languages:* Arabic, Turkish; *Address:* Mansour, Baghdad, Iraq.

RAYSUNI, Muhammad al Khadir al-, Moroccan broadcasting official/writer; born 1930, Tetouan, Morocco; married; two sons, two daughters; *Religion:* Muslim; *Education:* Institute of Religion, Qarawiyin University, Fes, Morocco; Diploma in Television, Spain, 1966; *Career:* Tetouan radio station 1952; after Independence joined National Radio Station in Rabat, 1957; producer, The People's Radio Magazine, broadcast twice weekly; Head of Department, Arabic Programme Section, Moroccan Radio and Television; *Publications:* collections of short stories, 1951 and 1967; translated many novels into Spanish; published articles in *Al-Nahar* newspaper in Tetouan; *Interests and Recreations:* walking; *Languages:* Arabic, French, Spanish; *Address:* Zanqat Al-Murg, Building No 15, Rabat, Morocco.

RAYYIS, Ghazi al-, Kuwaiti diplomat; born 23 August 1935, Kuwait; married; four children; *Religion:* Muslim; *Education:* BA in Sociology, Cairo University, 1962; *Career:* 3rd Secretary, Ministry of Foreign Affairs, Kuwait; Kuwaiti Embassy to Washington, 1965; Kuwaiti Embassy to Beirut, 1965–67; Chairman, International Affairs Department, Ministry of Foreign Affairs, Kuwait, 1967–70; Counsellor, Kuwaiti Embassy to Beirut, 1970–73; Ambassador to Bahrain, 1974–80; Ambassador to London, UK, 1980–; Ambassador to Sweden; *Languages:* Arabic, English; *Address:* Embassy of Kuwait, 46 Queen's Gate, London SW7, UK; telephone: 01 589 4533.

RAYYIS, Riad Najib al-, Syrian journalist; resident in London, UK; born 28 October 1937, Damascus, Syria; married; one son, one daughter; *Religion:* Muslim; *Education:* BSc in Economics, University of London, UK; Cambridge Technical College and School of Arts, 1957–61; *Career:* Editor of the *Arab Review,* the only Arab journal published in English in Britain at the time, while still at Cambridge, 1958, Foreign Desk of *Al-Anwar* newspaper, 1961; co-founded the weekly *Al-Muharrir;* remained its Editor until its publication as a daily newspaper, 1962–63; Thomson Fellowship in Journalism and returned to UK to work for the Sunday Times, 1964; and later Western Mail; Reporter to *Al-Nahar* on the British political and literary scene; Foreign Editor and Columnist on International and Arab Affairs, *Al-Hayat,* 1964; first Arab to report on Vietnam, 1966; toured South-East Asia reporting on situation in Thailand, Laos, Cambodia, India, Pakistan, Hong Kong, Macao, Taiwan, Singapore; Foreign Correspondent of *Al-Nahar,* covering the Yemen Civil War, the War of Independence, Aden and South Arabia, 1966–68, Iraqi Coup d'Etat, 1968, Soviet Invasion of Czechoslovakia, 1968–69, Eastern Europe, 1969–70, the Greek Colonels Coup, 1967, the Somali Dispute, 1968, Ulster, 1969, attended all the meetings that

led to the creation of the United Arab Emirates and the independence of Qatar and Bahrain; Special Consultant to UNICEF on mission to the Arabian Peninsula, 1971; edited *Al-Nahar Arab Report,* 1970–76; Managing Director of Al-Nahar Press Services, a subsidiary of *Al-Nahar* newspaper; chairman of Portico Group of Companies (Publishers), 1976–; Editor in Chief of Arabic weekly *Al-Manar,* 1977–; Columnist in *Al-Mustakbal,* weekly Arab news magazine published in Paris, 1979–, writing mostly on Gulf Affairs; *Publications: Death of Others,* a collection of poems in Arabic, 1972; *The Crucial Period,* 1965; *Land of Small Dragons — a Journey to Vietnam,* 1966; *The Struggle for Oil and Oases,* 1973; *Dhofar — the Story of the Military Struggle in the Gulf,* 1978; *Interests and Recreations:* poetry, literary criticism; *Languages:* Arabic, English; *Address:* Office — 84 Fetter Lane, London EC4A 1EQ, UK; telephone: (01) 831 6861; Residence — 4a Moore Park Road, London SW6, UK; telephone: (01) 381 0486.

RAZZAZ, Ahmad Munif al-, Jordanian politician/physician; resident in Iraq; born 1921, Damascus, Syria; married; *Religion:* Muslim; *Education:* BA in Medicine and Surgery, Cairo University, Cairo, Egypt, 1946; *Career:* member of Arab Baath Party, 1949–67; member of Jordan Regional Leadership of Baath Party, 1956–66; Secretary General, Arab Baath Party, 1965–66; medical private practice, 1967–69; Arab Baath Socialist Party, 1969; Assistant Secretary General. Baath Socialist Party, responsible for Foreign Affairs Bureau, 1977–79; Founding member of Jordan Red Crescent Society, 1948; *Publications: The Development of the Meaning of Nationalism* (in Arabic), 1961; *Liberty and Its Problems in Various Countries* (in Arabic), 1965; *The Bitter Experience* (in Arabic), 1967; *The Way to Liberate Palestine* (in Arabic), 1971; *Arab Unity: Is there a Way to it?* (in Arabic), 1971; *The Philosophy of Nationalism* (in Arabic), 1977; *Baath Socialism* (in Arabic), 1978; *Address:* c/o P O Box 1834, Amman, Jordan.

REINI, Ahmad Salih al-, Yemen Arab Republic official; born 1928, Amran, Yemen Arab Republic; married; five sons, four daughters; *Religion:* Muslim. *Education:* diploma, Broadcasting Institute, Cairo, Egypt, 1960–61; Institute of Administration, Sana'a, 1968; *Career:* teacher, 1946; Principal of

Zubaid Schools, 1947; Secretary, Ministry of Communications, 1949–62; radio broadcaster; Director General of Political Affairs; Controller General of Programmes, 1949–62; Director General of Broadcasting, 1966; Director General of Communications, 1967; Director General of Broadcasting, 1968; Head of the Broadcasting Service, 1968; Under Secretary, Ministry of Communications, 1974; Under Secretary, Ministry of Information, 1974; Deputy Minister of Information, with rank of Minister, 1975; *Decorations:* Order of Merit from President Nasser of Egypt, 1963; Medal of the Republic, 4th Class; *Interests and Recreations:* classical and modern Arabic literature, volley-ball; *Address:* Ministry of Information, Sana'a, Yemen Arab Republic.

RERHAYE, Abdul Kamal, Moroccan politician/official; born 1941, Rabat, Morocco; married; *Religion:* Muslim; *Education:* LLB; *Career:* Office of Exchange Control, 1959; Assistant Director, Office of Exchange Control, 1967; Director, Office of Exchange Control, 1969; Under Secretary of State for Tourism, 1970; Director General of Deposits and Management of Public Money, 1970; Secretary of State for Finance, 1974–77; Minister of Commerce and Industry, 1977; Minister of Finance, 1979–; *Languages:* Arabic, French; *Address:* c/o Ministry of Finance, Rabat, Morocco.

RIAD, Kamal, Egyptian UN official/civil engineer; born 24 June 1922, Egypt; married; *Education:* BCE, Cairo University, Egypt, 1941–46; MCE, Hydraulics, University of Michigan, USA, 1953–54; DSc in Technical Science, Technical High School, Delft, Netherlands, 1958–61; *Career:* various positions with the Economic Commission for Africa (ECA), Ministry of Public Works and private industry since 1947; Chief, Natural Resources Section, ECA, UN, Ethiopia, 1972; member of the Egyptian Engineering Syndicate, of the International Association for Hydraulic Research; *Interests and Recreations:* golf, swimming, philately, development of natural resources; *Languages:* Arabic, English, French; *Address:* Natural Resources Section, ECA, UN, P O Box 3001, Addis Ababa, Ethiopia; telephone: 47200.

RIAD, Mahmud, Egyptian diplomat/Arab League official; born 8 January 1917, Egypt; married; three sons; *Religion:* Muslim; *Edu-*

cation: Military Academy, General Staff College; *Career:* representative of Egypt to the Mixed Armistice Commission, 1949–52; Adviser, Delegation of Egypt to the Fifth Session of the UN General Assembly, 1950; Alternate Representative of Egypt to Seventh Session of the UN General Assembly, 1952; Representative of Egypt to the Eighth Session of the UN General Assembly, 1953; Director of the Department of Arab Affairs, Ministry of Foreign Affairs, 1954–55; Ambassador to Syria, 1955–58; Counsellor to the President of the United Arab Republic on Foreign Affairs, 1958–62; Chairman of the UAR Delegation to the UN Economic Commission of Africa, Addis Ababa, 1961; Permanent Representative of the UAR to the UN, 1961–64; Minister of Foreign Affairs, 1964–71; Deputy Premier and Minister of Foreign Affairs, 1971–72; Adviser to the President of Egypt, 1972; Secretary General of the League of Arab States, 1972–79; *Publications: The Struggle for Peace in the Middle East,* Quartet Books, London, 1981; *Interests and Recreations:* reading; *Languages:* Arabic, English, French; *Address:* c/o Ministry of Foreign Affairs, Cairo, Egypt.

RIAL, Cleto Hassan, Sudanese official; born 1 September 1935, Sudan; *Education:* Xavier University, Ohio, USA; University of Notre Dame, Indiana, USA; Institute of Social Studies, The Hague, Netherlands; Royal Institute of Public Administration, UK; *Career:* Executive Officer, Ministry of Local Government, 1958–59; teacher, Comboui College, Khartoum, 1959–60; Finance Inspector, Ministry of Finance and Economy, 1962–63; Lecturer, Institute of Public Administration, 1963–72; Secretary General, Higher Executive Council for the Southern Region, 1972; *Publications: Methods and Techniques of Community Development Programmes,* 1966; *Decorations:* Order of the Two Niles; *Languages:* Arabic, English; *Address:* Secretariat General, P O Box 17, Juba, Sudan.

RIFA'I, Abdul Mun'im al-, Jordanian diplomat/politician; born 1917, Tyre, Lebanon; married; one son; *Religion:* Muslim; *Education:* Graduate, American University of Beirut, Beirut, Lebanon, 1937; *Career:* teacher in Amman, 1938; Private Secretary of HM King Abdullah; Assistant Chief of the Royal Court, 1941–42; Consul General in Egypt, Lebanon and Syria, 1943–44; Minister Plenipotentiary in Washington, and Observer at the UN, 1949; Ambassador to Iran and Pakistan, 1950; Ambassador to Washington D.C., USA, and first Permanent Representative for Jordan at the UN, 1954–57; Ambassador to Lebanon, 1957–58; Ambassador to London, UK, 1958; Minister of National Guidance, 1958–59; Jordan's Representative to the UN, 1959–65; member of the Jordanian Delegation to the Jordanian-British Treaty negotiations, 1946; Ambassador to the Arab League in Cairo, 1966; Minister of Foreign Affairs, 1967–69; Prime Minister, and Minister of Culture and Information, 1969; Senator, 1969–71; Deputy Prime Minister, and Minister of Foreign Affairs, 1969–70; Prime Minister, 1970; retired 1970–73; Special Adviser for International Affairs to HM King Hussain of Jordan, 1973–74; Ambassador to Egypt, 1973; Ambassador to the Arab League in Cairo, 1973; Personal Representative of HM the King, 1973; Head of Jordan Delegation to Kuwait and Syria to explain the United Arab Kingdom Project, 1972, and to Non-Aligned Nations Conference, Algeria, 1973, and to Middle East Peace Conference, Geneva, 1973; *Decorations:* High Order, Jordan; Order of the Jordanian Star; Order of Independence, Jordan; *Interests and Recreations:* publishing and writing poetry; *Address:* Shmeisani, Amman, Jordan; telephone: 67572.

RIFA'I, Diya'iddin Talib al-, Jordanian lawyer/official; born 13 December 1925, Safad, Jordan; married; three sons; *Religion:* Muslim; *Education:* Licence in Law; Diploma in Public Administration, Queen Elizabeth Institute of Oxford University, UK; *Career:* Secretary of Political Department, League of Arab States, 1947–50; Private Secretary to late King Abdullah, 1950–51; First Secretary, Embassy to Spain, 1951; First Secretary, Embassy to Italy, 1953–56; Counsellor, Embassy to Iran, 1956–57; Chargé d'Affaires, Embassy to Syria, 1957–58; Chargé d'Affaires, Embassy to Saudi Arabia, 1958–59; Chargé d'Affaires, Embassy to Turkey, 1959; Assistant Under Secretary, Ministry of National Economy, 1959–62; Legal Adviser to the Civil Service Commission and Audit Bureau, 1962–66; Lawyer; Editor of a local newspaper, 1966–68; General Director of Broadcasting of the Hashemite Kingdom of Jordan, 1968–70; Information Expert to the League of Arab States, 1970–71; Representative of the League of Arab States in Nigeria, Cameroon, Ivory Coast, 1971–74; Under Secretary, Ministry of Culture and Information, 1974–76; Lawyer, 1976–; Permanent Adviser to Arab Union of Broadcasting; *Publications: The Protocol,* 1960; *Bag of Memories,* 1980; *Decorations:* Order of the Jordanian Star; Order of Independence, Jordan; Order of the Holy Tomb, Vatican; Order of Merit, Morocco; Order of Merit, Egypt; *Interests and Recreations:* swimming, table tennis, chess; member of the Jordan Writers Society; *Languages:* Arabic, English, Italian; *Address:* P O Box 9663, Amman, Jordan.

RIFA'I, Hani Hussain al-, Jordanian judge; born 1927, Dair Abu Said, Jordan; married; *Education:* LLB, Law Faculty, University of Baghdad, 1951; *Career:* Lawyer, 1952; Chief of Clerks, Attorney General Department, Amman, Jordan; Magistrate, Tafila, Jordan, 1953; Public Prosecutor, Irbid, 1953; Public Prosecutor, Salt, 1954; First Public Prosecutor, Nablus, West Bank, 1955–58; Magistrate, and member of the First Instance Court, 1959–63; member of the Appeal Court, Jerusalem, 1965; Judge in Kuwait, on secondment, 1965–71; President, First Instance Court, Salt, 1971; Vice President, Appeal Court, Amman, 1973; General Inspector of Courts, Amman, 1975; Vice Minister of Justice, 1976–; Judge in the Administrative Tribunal, Arab League, 1978; Representative of Jordan in the Legal Permanent Committee of the Arab League, and in the Asian-African Legal Consultative Committee; *Address:* Jabal Hussain, Amman, Jordan; telephone: 24606.

RIFA'I, Hassan Khalid al-, Lebanese lawyer/politician; born 1923, Baalbek, Lebanon; married; *Religion:* Muslim; *Education:* in Beirut, and Cairo; *Career:* elected Deputy for Baalbek-Hermel, 1968, and re-elected in 1972; Minister of Planning in Takieddin al-Solh Cabinet, 1973–74; *Languages:* Arabic, French; *Address:* Corniche Mazraa, Beirut, Lebanon.

RIFA'I, Hisham, Syrian UN official; born 11 August 1930, Aleppo, Syria; married; *Religion:* Muslim; *Education:* Licence en Droit; *Career:* Political Affairs Officer, Trusteeship Department, Colonial Affairs, UN, 1956; Secretary, UN Subcommittee on Aden, 1964; Chief, UN Studies and Publications Section,

1969; Chief, UN Council for Namibia Section, 1970; Secretary, UN Committee on Apartheid, Department of Political and Security Council Affairs; Chief, Political Studies and Advisory Services Section, Department of Political and Security Council Affairs Secretariat; Principal Officer of Security Council Division; *Interests and Recreations:* concert music, outdoor sports; *Languages:* Arabic, English, French, Russian; *Address:* 319 East 50th Street, New York, NY 10022, USA; telephone: (212) 759 3895.

RIFA'I, Khalid Samir al-, Jordanian engineer; born 6 December 1937; married; two sons; *Religion:* Muslim; *Education:* DLC Mechanical Engineering, Loughborough University, 1961; *Career:* Managing Director, Jordan Economic Development and Trading Co; Managing Director, Construction Contracting Co; *Decorations:* Jordanian Order of Independence; *Interests and Recreations:* amateur radio; *Languages:* Arabic, English; *Address:* P O Box 2482, Amman, Jordan; telephone: 44096, 812456; telex: 21288 KHALID JO.

RIFA'I, Najmuddine al-, Syrian diplomat/ UN official; born 21 September 1925, Aleppo, Syria; *Education:* BA, MA in Political Science, American University of Beirut, Lebanon, 1944–47; PhD, International Law, Columbia University, New York, USA, 1960; *Career:* Syrian Permanent Mission to UN, 1947; Deputy Acting Director, International Organization Department, Ministry of Foreign Affairs, 1947–58; Counsellor, Permanent Mission of United Arab Republic, 1958–59; Ambassador of Syria to Committee of Seventeen, 1959–62; Director, Deputy to Under Secretary-General, Department of Political Affairs, Trusteeship and Decolonization, UN, 1965; Ambassador on secondment, Syria; *Publications: International Political Problems of Syria,* 1948; *Evolution of Libya Towards Unity and Independence,* 1960; *Languages:* Arabic, English, French; *Address:* UN Plaza, New York, NY 10017, USA; telephone: (212) 754 1234.

RIFA'I, Rashid M. S. al-, Iraqi diplomat/ official and engineer; born 1 May 1929, Mussayeb, Iraq; married; three children; *Education:* American University of Beirut, 1948–50; BSc in Electrical Engineering, University of Bristol, UK, 1954; MSE in Electrical Engineering, Purdue University, USA, 1964; PhD in Electrical Engineering, Rice University, USA, 1967; training with British Post Office, GEC, and other companies on a Federation of British Industries Scholarship, 1957–59; *Career:* Engineer, Directorate General of Posts, Telephones and Telegraphs, Iraq, 1954–62; Chief Engineer, Public Company for Electrical Equipment and Appliances, Baghdad, 1967; Minister of State for Presidential Affairs, 1968; Minister of Oil and Minerals, 1968; Minister of State, 1969; Minister of Planning, 1971; Minister of Communications, 1972; Minister of Public Works and Housing, 1974; Ambassador, 1976; Ambassador Extraordinary and Plenipotentiary accredited to Belgium 1976, and to the Grand Duchy of Luxembourg and the European Communities; member of the Institution of Electrical Engineers in the UK, the Iraqi Engineers Union, the Society of Iraqi Engineers; *Languages:* Arabic, English, French, German; *Address:* Embassy of the Republic of Iraq, 131 Avenue de la Floride, Brussels, Belgium.

RIFA'I, Yusuf Sayyid Hashim al-, Kuwaiti official; born 1932; *Religion:* Muslim; *Education:* Kuwait University, Kuwait; *Career:* Director, Travel and Residence Department, 1949–63; Minister of Posts, Telegraphs and Telephones, 1963–64; Minister of State for Cabinet Affairs, with responsibility for co-ordination of government policies and the work of different ministers 1964–70; Chairman of Municipal Council, 1966–70; *Address:* Ministry of State for Cabinet Affairs, Kuwait.

RIFA'I, Zaid Samir al-, Jordanian diplomat/ politician; born 1936, Amman, Jordan; married; *Education:* BA in Political Science, Harvard University, USA; MA in International Law, Columbia University, USA, 1958; *Career:* Attaché in the Ministry of Foreign Affairs, 1957; Secretary of the Jordanian Embassy, Cairo, Egypt, 1957; Secretary of the Jordanian Delegation to the UN, 1957–59; Head of International Organisations Department, Ministry of Foreign Affairs, 1959; Ambassador to Court of St. James, London, UK, 1970–71; Political Adviser to HM King Hussain, 1972–73; Prime Minister, Minister of Defence and Minister of Foreign Affairs, 1974–76; *Decorations:* Medal of Independence, 1st Class; Order of the Jordanian Star, 1st Class,

Jordan; Order of the Renaissance, 1st Class, Egypt; *Languages:* Arabic, English; *Address:* Jabal Amman, Amman, Jordan; telephone: 44565.

RIFAAT, Kamaliddin Mahmud, Egyptian politician; born 1921; *Religion:* Muslim; *Education:* Cairo Military Academy; *Career:* served in armed forces, 1942–45; member of National Assembly, 1957; Deputy Minister for Presidential Affairs, 1958; Minister of Labour, 1961, 1967; member of Presidential Council; Deputy Prime Minister for Scientific Affairs, 1964; member of General Secretariat of Arab Socialist Union (ASU), 1964; Ambassador at Ministry of Foreign Affairs, 1970; Ambassador to the Court of St. James, London, UK 1971–74; *Publications: Strategy; The Social Experiment; The Third World and the Socialist Solution; National Liberation; Decorations:* Order of the Republic; Military Star; decorations from Cameroon, Morocco, Tunisia, Yugoslavia; *Languages:* Arabic, English; *Address:* Ministry of Foreign Affairs, Cairo, Egypt.

RIKAISHY, Ahmad Nassir al-, Omani official/economist; born 1945, Zanzibar; married; one daughter; *Religion:* Muslim; *Education:* BA in Economics, American University in Cairo, Egypt, 1965–69; MA in Development Economics, University of Colorado, Boulder, Colorado, USA, 1971–72; Diploma in Development Economics, University of Cambridge, UK, 1973–74; *Career:* Assistant Secretary, Office of the Financial Adviser to the Government, 1971; Assistant Economic Expert, Development Council, 1974–78; Director of Planning, Development Council, 1979–80; Director General of Planning, Development Council, 1980–; member of the American Economic Association and the American Association for the Advancement of Science; *Publications: A Study of the Agricultural Sector in Oman,* 1980, in English; *A Study of Fisheries Development in Oman,* 1980, in English; *Languages:* Arabic, English, Swahili; *Address:* Development Council, P O Box 881, Muscat, Oman; telephone: 745401.

RIMAWI, Qassim Muhammad al-, Jordanian politician; born 1918, Bait Rima, Jordan; married; two sons; *Education:* BSc, MA, PhD; *Career:* Director General, Arab Palestinian Party; Commander of the Holy Jihad Forces; member of the Executive Committee of Palestine Liberation Organization; Secretary General, the All Palestine Government; Director General of Phosphate Mines; member of the Jordanian Parliament; Chairman of the House of Deputies of Jordan; Prime Minister; member of the Senate; Professor,s Lecturer, University of Jordan; Head of the Royal Committee for Jerusalem Affairs; *Publications: State and Labour,* 1952, Cairo; *Palestine Arab Refugees,* 1952; *The Challenge of Industrialization,* Beirut; *Decorations:* Order of the Jordanian Star, 1st Class; *Interests and Recreations:* tennis, horse riding, shooting, economic and educational planning, sociology, psychological and philosophical studies; *Languages:* Arabic, English; *Address:* Jabal al-Hussain, Al-Khalil Street, Amman, Jordan; telephone: 66883, 36311.

RING, Bona Malwal, Sudanese politician/journalist; born 1935, Sudan; *Education:* studied journalism in the USA, 1962–63; *Career:* Ministry of Information, 1958; Information Officer in Wau; joined editorial staff of the *Sudan Daily,* 1961; elected Secretary General of the Southern Front, 1964; elected to the Constituent Assembly, 1968; Editor of the southern newspaper *Vigilant* until 1969; Deputy Minister of Information and Culture, 1972; Minister of State, 1973; Minister of Information and Culture, 1976–; member of the Board of *Al-Sahafa* newspaper, 1974–; *Languages:* Arabic, English; *Address:* Ministry of Information and Culture, P O Box 291, Khartoum, Sudan; telephone: 75852.

RIZK, Asaad, Lebanese official/physician; born 1931, Beirut, Lebanon; married; three sons; *Religion:* Christian; *Education:* St. Joseph Hospital, Beirut, Lebanon; Doctor of Medicine, University of Paris, France; Professor Agrégé, Faculté de France; *Career:* Director of Urological Clinic, Paris; Professor of Urology, French Faculty of Medicine, Beirut; Surgeon, Dr Tawfik Rizk Hospital, Beirut; member of the American College of Surgeons, 1969; Minister of Education and Minister of Labour and Social Welfare, 1976–79; *Publications:* various studies of digestive and urinary diseases; *Languages:* Arabic, French, English; *Address:* Office — Clinique Dr Rizk, BP 11–3288, Beirut, Lebanon; telephone: 328 8800; Residence — Immeuble Naufal, Ashrafiyeh, Beirut, Lebanon; telephone: 327953.

RIZK, Charles, Lebanese official/lawyer; born 20 July 1935, Beirut, Lebanon; married; two daughters; *Education:* University of Paris and Institute of Political Studies, Paris, France; Doctorate in Law, University of Paris, France; Licence ès-Lettres; Diploma, Institute of Political Studies, Paris, France; *Career:* Director of Studies, Civil Service Council; Lecturer, Faculty of Law and Sciences, Beirut, Lebanon; Director General, Ministry of Information, 1967–70; Director General of Litani Authority, Beirut, 1970–76; Director General, Ministry of Information, 1976–78; President, Télé Liban, 1978–; *Publications: Le Régime Politique Libanais Librairie Général de Droit et de Jurisprudence,* Paris, 1966; *Languages:* Arabic, English, French; *Address:* Office — Télé Liban, P O Box 4848, Beirut, Lebanon; telephone: 300360, 450100; telex: 20110OLE.

RIZK, Edmond, Lebanese lawyer/official; born 11 March 1934, Jezzin, Lebanon; married; six children; *Education:* Licence in Law, French Faculty of Law, St. Joseph University, Beirut, Lebanon; Lebanese Academy; *Career:* Barrister at Law, 1959–; Political Commentator, Lebanese Radio; Features Editor of the newspaper *Al-Amal;* elected Deputy of Jezzin, 1968 and 1972; member of the Bureau of the Katayeb Political Party (Falangists); Minister of Education in Amin al-Hafez Cabinet, 1973; Minister of Education and Information in Takieddin al-Solh Cabinet, 1973–74; *Publications: Le Prix d'un Cerceuil,* collection of plays; and other books; various collections of radio talks and newspaper articles; *Decorations:* National Education Medal 1st Class, Iran; Romanian Order of Merit; *Interests and Recreations:* founder of La Pléiade Libanaise Association; *Languages:* Arabic, French; *Address:* Office — Furn al-Chebbak, Lazarieh Building, Beirut, Lebanon; telephone: 285666; Residence — Ashrafiyeh, Adib Ishak Street, Chidiac Building, Beirut, Lebanon; telephone: 321666, 336336.

ROSTAMANI, Abdul Rahman Hassan al-, United Arab Emirates official; born 1943, Dubai, United Arab Emirates; *Religion:* Muslim; *Education:* Degree in Social Studies, Cairo University, Egypt, 1970; *Career:* 3rd Secretary, Ministry of Foreign Affairs, 1972; Director of Information, United Arab Emirates Government, 1972; Director of Personnel Department, 1972; Under Secretary and Director of Personnel, UAE Government; Director General, Civil Service Commission, 1976–; *Interests and Recreations:* literature, poetry, music, travel, water-skiing, swimming, sports; *Languages:* Arabic, English, Hindi; *Address:* Civil Service Commission, P O Box 899, Abu Dhabi, United Arab Emirates; telephone: 36155.

ROUSHDI, Abdul Mun'im Naguib, Egyptian banker; born 23 July 1926, Cairo, Egypt; married; one son, one daughter; *Religion:* Muslim; *Education:* BA in Economics, Cairo University, 1947; graduate studies, George Washington University, 1953; *Career:* Controller of Banks, Central Bank of Egypt, 1967; International Monetary Fund Adviser to Bank of Yemen, Aden, 1970; Deputy Chairman and Managing Director, Investment Authority, Cairo, 1975; Chairman, National Bank of Egypt, 1977; *Publications:* various pamphlets and articles on economics, finance and banking; *Decorations:* Officer of the Légion d'Honneur, France, 1979; *Interests and Recreations:* music, walking; *Languages:* Arabic, English, French; *Address:* National Bank of Egypt, 24 Sherif Street, Cairo, Egypt; telephone: 744152, 744184.

ROUSHDI, Subhi Khalil, Egyptian banker/businessman; born 2 December 1929, Egypt; married; one daughter, one son; *Religion:* Christian; *Education:* Faculty of Law, Cairo University, Egypt, 1949; *Career:* Shareholder and President, Hapi Tourist Company, 1962–; Chief Executive and Shareholder of Elsara SA, Geneva, Switzerland, company with substantial investments in Egypt, especially Ismailia Transport Company, 1975–; Board Director, Misr-Immob, Swiss company with Arab interests, formed to establish and develop residential city in Egypt and owning concession for Mokattam City, Cairo, 1975–; Partner and Chairman of Giza System Engineering, Egypt, which acts as agent for digital computer equipment and similar companies and in software and hardware computer business, 1975–; Shareholder and member of the Board, Bank für Handel und Effekten, Zurich, 1977–; Shareholder and Chairman of Overseas Bank and Trust, Cayman Island; member of the Board of International Music Society; Chairman of Allied Arab Bank, London, UK, 1977; *Interests and Recreations:* tennis, swimming, reading; *Languages:* Arabic, English, French;

Address: E1 Messaha Square, Dokki, Cairo, Egypt; telephone: 987276, 987096; Allied Arab Bank Ltd, Granite House, Cannon Street, London EC4, UK.

RUMI, Khalfan Muhammad al-, United Arab Emirates politician; born 1945, Sharjah, United Arab Emirates; married; three daughters; *Religion:* Muslim; *Education:* BA in Education, College of Education, Baghdad, Iraq; University of Southampton, UK; *Career:* Deputy Director of Education, 1970–72; Secretary of State, Ministry of Education, 1972–77; Minister of Health, 1977; member of the Constituent Committee; participated in many Arab and international conferences; *Interests and Recreations:* poetry, history, sociology, reading; *Languages:* Arabic, English; *Address:* c/o Ministry of Health, P O Box 848, Abu Dhabi, United Arab Emirates.

RUSAN, Sayyah Falih al-, Jordanian official; born 1907, Irbid, Jordan; married; *Education:* BA in Arabic Literature, American University of Beirut, Lebanon, 1933; *Career:* secondary school teacher, Irbid, Kerak, Salt, 1933–37; Head of Kerak Secondary School, 1939; Schools Inspector, 1939–45; Director of Education, 1945–47; Under Secretary, Ministry of Interior, 1947–48; Under Secretary, Ministry of Education, 1948–49; Inspector of Imports and Exports, 1948–49; Governor of Salt, 1952–53; Under Secretary, Ministry of Interior for Municipal and Rural Affairs, 1953, Under Secretary, Ministry of Defence, 1953–60; retired 1960; *Address:* Jabal Webdeh, Amman, Jordan; telephone: 22534.

RUWAIDAR, Ahmad Said, Egyptian economist/official; born 1915, Egypt; married; one son, two daughters; *Religion:* Muslim; *Education:* Doctorate in Economics; *Career:* Lecturer in Economics, Ain Shams University, Cairo, Egypt, 1955; Assistant Professor, and Professor of Economics, 1958; Director General, Ministry of Economy, 1963; Under Secretary, Ministry of Economy, 1973–75; Adviser, Ministry of Economy, 1977; Fellow of the Economic Development Institute, Washington D.C., USA; member of the Egyptian Committee for Economics and Statistics; *Publications: Economic Planning,* 1958; *Economic Development,* 1964; *Financial and Monetary Policy,* 1974; *Economic Development,* 1977; *Languages:* Arabic, English, French; *Address:* 15 Mahmoud Sidqy al-Muhandis Street, Agouza, Cairo, Egypt; telephone: 814479.

S

S'HABOU, Omar, Tunisian journalist; born 9 October 1947, Tunis, Tunisia; married; *Religion:* Muslim; *Education:* Degree in Journalism, Press Institute, University of Tunis; *Career:* Editor in Chief of Socialist Destour Party organ *L'Action,* 1971; Executive Assistant to the Director of the Socialist Destour Party; Director of *Dialogue* magazine; *Decorations:* Officer of the Order of the Tunisian Republic; *Interests and Recreations:* football, chess; *Languages:* Arabic, French, German; *Address:* 102 Rue du Pacha, Tunis, Tunisia; telephone: 264985.

SA'ATY, Hassan al-, Egyptian academic/ sociologist; born 30 September 1916, Cairo, Egypt; married; one son, one daughter; *Education:* BA, Cairo University, Cairo, Egypt, 1938; Diploma of Education, Institute of Education, Cairo, Egypt, 1939; Diploma in Social Sciences; Diploma in Mental Health, London School of Economics, University of London, London, UK, 1941–42; PhD, London School of Economics, University of London, London, 1946; *Career:* Professor, Department of Sociology and Psychology, Ain Shams University, Cairo, Egypt, 1960; Dean, Faculty of Arts, Ain Shams University, Cairo, Egypt, 1964–68; Chairman, Department of Philosophy and Sociology, Faculty of Arts, Beirut Arab University, Beirut, Lebanon; Dean, Faculty of Arts, Beirut Arab University, Beirut, Lebanon, 1968–73; Chairman, Department of Sociology, Ain Shams University, Cairo, Egypt, 1973–1977; Professor Emeritus, Department of Sociology, 1977–79; Professor and Supervisor, Sociology Section, Department of Philosophy and Sociology, Faculty of Arts, Beirut, Arab University, 1979–; member of the International Sociological Association; President of the Euro-Arab Social Research Group, 1975–; *Publications: On Criminology,* 1951, Cairo; *Juridical Sociology,* 1952, 3rd edition, 1968, Cairo; *Industrialization and Urbaniza-* *tion in Alexandria,* 1958, 3d edition, 1981; *Industrial Sociology,* 4th edition, 1980; played a leading part in the development of empirical sociological research in Egypt, 1948–; *Decorations:* Medal of the Republic, Egypt, 1977; *Languages:* Arabic, English; *Address:* 59 al-Thawra Street, Heliopolis, Cairo, Egypt.

SA'EH, Abdul Hamid al-, Jordanian judge/ Islamic scholar; born 1907, Nablus, Palestine; married; *Religion:* Muslim; *Education:* Islamic Law, Islamic Juridical School, Egypt; *Career:* Teacher of Religion and Arabic Language, Nablus; Judge in Nablus; Judge in Jerusalem; arrested and exiled by the British protectorate authorities, returned 1939; General Secretary, Higher Islamic Legal Council, Palestine; member of the Court of Appeal, Palestine; President of the Court of Appeal, Jordan; President of Higher Islamic Assembly, Jerusalem; first to be exiled from Palestine by Israeli occupation forces; Chief Judge and Minister of Waqf (Islamic Affairs), Jordan; Professor, Faculty of Islamic Law, University of Jordan; Legal Adviser to Islamic Bank, Jordan; member of Palestine National Council; General Secretary of League of Popular Forces, Jordan; President of the Committee for the Rescue of Jerusalem; founding member of the Permanent Committee for the Defence of Human Rights and Basic Freedoms in the Arab World; member of the Royal Academy for Research of Islamic Civilization, Jordan, the Aal al-Bait; attended a number of Arab and international seminars and summits on Islam; *Publications: The Status of Jerusalem in Islam,* translated and published in French; *The Influence of Islam on Arab Civilizations;* and numerous other works; *Interests and Recreations:* reading, sports; *Languages:* Arabic, English; *Address:* Jerusalem Liberation Committee, P O Box 1666 Amman, Jordan; Jabal Al-Hussain, Amman, Jordan.

SA'ID, Ahmad Abdu, Yemen Arab Republic politician; born 1930, Yemen Arab Republic; married; *Religion:* Muslim; *Education:* International College, Beirut, Lebanon; Economics, Universities of Cornell and Chicago, USA; *Career:* Minister of Finance, 1967–69, and 1971–72; Minister of Development, 1973–74; Minister of Communications, 1974; Minister for Services, later Minister without Portfolio in administration of Abdul Aziz Abdul Ghani, 1975; *Interests and Recreations:* education, founded private preparatory school in Taez; *Languages:* Arabic, English, French; *Address:* Ministry of Cabinet Affairs, Sana'a, Yemen Arab Republic.

SA'ID, Brigadier Muhammad Farhi Ali, Iraqi army officer/diplomat; born 1927, Baghdad, Iraq; married; four children; *Religion:* Muslim; *Career:* commissioned 1951; Military Attaché, Embassy to Jordan, 1963–64; Commanding Officer of the 10th Armoured Brigade, 1968; member of the Military Bureau of the Arab Baath Socialist Party; Commander of the 2nd Mountain Infantry Division, 1970; Commander of the 3rd Division; *Languages:* Arabic, English; *Address:* Ministry of Defence, Baghdad, Iraq.

SAAB, Hassan, Lebanese diplomat/academic; born 15 October 1922, Beirut, Lebanon; married; two sons; *Education:* BA, Faculty of Arts, Cairo University, Egypt, 1942; one year study at University of Paris and Collège de France, Paris, France, 1945; PhD in Political Sciences, Georgetown University, Washington D.C., USA, 1956; *Career:* Attaché, Lebanese Legation in Paris, 1944–45; Vice Consul, Istanbul, Turkey, 1946–47; Head of the Department of Press and Cultural Affairs, Ministry of Foreign Affairs, Beirut, 1947–50; Secretary, and Chargé d'Affairs ad-interim, Washington D.C., 1950–56; Professor of Islamic Philosophy, Makassad College for Girls, 1956–57; Counsellor and Head of Department of Foreign Affairs, Beirut, 1956–59; Lecturer in Political Science, AUB, 1956–60; Professor, Lebanese University of Beirut, 1956–78; Professor, St. Joseph University, Beirut, 1958–68; Director of Political Affairs, Ministry of Foreign Affairs, 1959–60; Lecturer, Institute of Arabic Studies, Cairo, 1960–68; Cultural Counsellor in North America, Lebanese Embassy, Washington D.C., 1961–64; Professor, Lebanon Military College, 1965–73; Director, Training Programme for the Diplomatic Service of the United Arab Emirates, 1969–70; Lecturer, Training Courses for Arab diplomats, Lebanese Civil Service Council, 1964–76; Visiting Professor, University of Utah, USA, and University of Kuwait, 1967–77; Dean of the Faculty of Communications, Lebanese University, 1978–; guest speaker and lecturer at various international conferences and institutions; member of the Board of the Lebanese University; founder and member of various associations, amongst others the Lebanese Association of Political Science, and the Committee for National Mobilization; Secretary General of the Lebanese Development Studies Association, 1964–; represented Lebanon at various international conferences and committees; *Publications: Islam and the Challenge of Modernity; The Challenge of World Politics to the Middle East; Prospective Approach to Arab Development;* author and co-author of several other works; *Languages:* Arabic, French, English; *Address:* Ministry of Foreign Affairs, Beirut, Lebanon.

SAAD, Ahmad Zaki, Egyptian diplomat/banker; born 21 February 1900, Egypt; married; *Education:* LLB, University of Cairo, Egypt, 1922; JD, University of Paris, France, 1928; *Career:* Assistant Attorney General of Egypt, 1922–29; Egyptian Consul, Genoa, Italy, 1929–31; Egyptian Consul, Hamburg, Germany, 1931–33; Egyptian Consul, Liverpool, UK, 1933–37; Egyptian Consul, Dublin, Ireland, 1933–37; Chargé d'Affaires, Baghdad, Iraq, 1937–38; First Secretary, Egyptian Embassy, UK, 1938; Director, Eepartment for Alien Affairs, Cairo, Egypt, 1939–44; Postmaster General, 1944; Under-Secretary of State, Ministry of Finance, 1945–51; Governor, International Bank for Reconstruction and Development, 1946–52; Governor, National Bank of Egypt, 1951–52, 1955–57; Executive Director, International Monetary Fund (IMF), 1946–70; Governor, International Monetary Fund, 1946–52; principal representative with rank of Ambassador, 1964; *Address:* Office — 1818 H Street NW, Washington D.C. 20431, USA.

SAAD, Ali Rashid al-, Saudi Arabian official/statistician; born 1 September 1929, Wadi Dawsar, Saudi Arabia; married; four sons, one daughter; *Religion:* Muslim; *Education:* BSc in Agriculture, Cairo University, 1953; American University, Cairo, 1958;

postgraduate studies in the Institute of Research and Statistical Studies, 1959; UN Fellowship to study Statistics, UK, 1965; *Career:* Director of Statistics, Ministry of Agriculture, Saudi Arabia, 1959–64; Director General, Central Department of Statistics, Ministry of Finance and National Economy, Saudi Arabia, 1965–; Leader of government delegation to several international economic and statistical conferences since 1964; member of the International Statistical Institute, The Hague, the International Association of Survey Statisticians, The Hague, the American Statistical Association, Washington; *Publications: Statistical Development in Saudi Arabia,* Central Department of Statistics, 1966; *The Multi-Purpose Survey of Saudi Arabia,* 1976; *Comparison of Male Occupation Specific Labour Force with Life Tables of Saudi Arabia,* 1977; *Foreign Trade* and other statistical publications of the Department of Statistics; *Interests and Recreations:* chess, travel, swimming; *Languages:* Arabic, English; *Address:* Central Department of Statistics, P O Box 3735, Riyadh, Saudi Arabia; telephone: Office — 401 3778; Residence — 401 4127.

SAAD BIN ABDUL AZIZ, HRH Prince, Saudi Arabian Prince; born 1919, Riyadh, Saudi Arabia; son of late King Abdul Aziz; *Religion:* Muslim; *Address:* Royal Court, Riyadh, Saudi Arabia.

SAAD, Farid Ali al-, Jordanian businessman; born 1908, Umm al Fahm, Palestine; married; *Education:* BSc, American University of Beirut, Lebanon; *Career:* science teacher; Principal Inspector of Education in Transjordan and Palestine, 1928–35; District Officer, Palestine Government, 1935–43; Manager, Arab Bank, Haifa, 1943–48; Senator, 1951–55; member of Municipality Council, Royal Fiscal Committee, Committee of Education; Chairman and Managing Director, Jordan Tobacco and Cigarette Company, Jordan Bata Company; Director, Jordan Petroleum Refinery Company; Chairman of Advisory Board, Grindlay's Bank; Chairman Arab Orphans' Committee; Deputy Mayor, Amman Municipality; Trustee of Jordan University, American University of Beirut; Minister of Finance, 1972–73; *Interests and Recreations:* gardening; *Languages:* Arabic, English; *Address:* P O Box 59, Amman, Jordan.

SAADI, Muhammad Ali al-, Iraqi academic; resident in USA; born 7 April 1933, Baghdad, Iraq; *Religion:* Muslim; *Education:* BA in Political Science and Economics, University of Montana, USA, 1962; MA and PhD in Political Science, University of Massachusetts, Amherst, USA, 1969; *Career:* Associate Professor, University of Wisconsin, 1965–69; Associate Professor, California State Polytechnic University, Pomona, USA, 1969–74; Professor of Political Science, California State Polytechnic University, Assistant Chairman, then Chairman, Department of Political Science; *Publications:* Doctoral dissertation *The Jordan River Dispute: a Case Study in International Juridical Conflicts,* and various papers on the Middle East conflict delivered at US and international professional conferences; *Interests and Recreations:* Arabic, English, Russian and French literature, classical music, jazz, Arabic music; sailing, swimming, tennis, skiing; President of Southern California Chapter, Association of Arab-American University Graduates, 1975–76; *Languages:* Arabic, English, French; *Address:* California State Polytechnic University, Pomona, California 91767, USA; telephone: (714) 624 9888.

SAADI, Mussa, Moroccan politician/engineer; born December 1937, Oujda, Morocco; *Education:* Diploma in Geological Engineering, Nancy University, France; Degree in Science, Grenoble University, France; *Career:* wide experience in mining; Secretary of State for Commerce, Industry, Mines and Merchant Navy, 1974; Minister of Mines and Energy, 1977–; Vice President of the International Geological Association; member of Parliament; President of the Provincial Council of Oujda; member of the Political Bureau of the National Democratic Party; *Publications:* papers on engineering and researches on minerals in Moroccan and other journals; *Languages:* Arabic, French; *Address:* Ministry of Energy and Mines, Rabat, Morocco.

SAADIDDIN, Ibrahim Abdallah, Egyptian economist; born 25 May 1925, Sharqiyah, Egypt; married; two sons, one daughter; *Religion:* Muslim; *Education:* BCom, Cairo University, Egypt, 1945; MSc in Management, University of Illinois, USA, 1952; PhD in Business Administration, University of Illinois, USA, 1955; *Career:* Lecturer in Cairo University, 1955–59; Expert on Organization, Central Ministry of Education, 1959–60; Expert, Ministry of Planning, 1960–61; Professor and Secretary General, National Institute of Planning, Cairo, 1961–62; Professor and member of Board, National Institute of Management Development, 1962–64; Vice-Chairman of Central Auditing Authority, 1964–71; member of Arab Socialist Union Secretariat, 1965–68; Chief Technical Adviser, United Nations Development Programme, Arab Institute of Planning, Kuwait; *Publications: Principles of Marketing*, (in Arabic) 1957; *Administrative Policies in Different Social Systems* (in Arabic) 1970; also various articles in professional journals; *Interests and Recreations:* walking; *Languages:* Arabic, English, French; *Address:* Office— Planning Institute, P O Box 5834, Kuwait; telephone: 431897; Residence — 43 Giza Street, Apt 73, Giza, Egypt.

SAADIDDIN, Mursi Abdul Hamid, Egyptian official/writer; born 1921; married; one son; *Religion:* Muslim; *Career:* Ministry of Foreign Affairs; served in Egyptian Embassy in London, Head of the Students' Office, then as Assistant Cultural Attaché, Cultural Attaché; Deputy Director of Fine Arts Council, Cairo, 1956; Censor of foreign books and publications; Assistant Secretary General, and Public Relations Officer for the Afro-Asian People's Solidarity Conference (subsequently Organization), 1958; Cultural Attaché, Embassy to East Germany, 1969–72; Controller General, Egyptian Higher Council for the Arts, 1973; Director General, Ministry of Information and Culture, 1975–78; Secretary of Egyptian Poets, Essayists and Novelists (PEN) Club and Egyptian Writers Union, as well as Chief Censor of English language publications; Chairman of the State Information Service, 1977–79; *Languages:* Arabic, English, French; *Address:* Information Department, Talaat al-Harb Street, Cairo, Egypt.

SABA, Elias, Lebanese banker/politician; born 1932, Lebanon; married; five children; *Religion:* Christian; *Education:* MA, Economics, American University of Beirut, Lebanon; DPhil, Economics, Oxford University, Oxford, England, 1957–59; *Career:* Economic Adviser, Ministry of Finance, Kuwait, 1961–67; Associate Professor, American University of Beirut, Beirut, Lebanon, 1967–69; Minister of Finance and Defence, 1970–72; Chairman and General Manager, St.

Charles City Centre, SAL; Chairman and Chief Executive, ARINIF, SA; Vice Chairman, Banque du Crédit Populaire; Director, Intra Investment Company; Chairman, Allied Bank, Beirut, Lebanon, 1983–; *Publications: Post-War Developments in the Foreign Exchange Systems of Lebanon and Syria,* 1962; *Languages:* Arabic, English, French; *Address:* P O Box 5292, Ayoub Centre, Ashrafieh, Beirut, Lebanon; telephone: 334 102; telex: 22411 BANPOL LE.

SABA, Fawzi Fuad, Saudi Arabian businessman/accountant; born 1931, Jerusalem; *Education:* BBA, Business Administration, 1958; *Career:* partner, Saba and Co; Certified Public Accountant; Partner, Arthur Anderson, Saba and Co 1957–70; founder and former President, Middle Eastern Society of Associated Accountants, 1974; Senior Partner, Coopers and Lybrand Middle East; Certified Public Accountant, specialized in petroleum industry accounting and financial problems; international taxation consultant; member of American Institute of Certified Public Accountants; member of the board of Family Investments Inc, Four D Investment Co, AHA Estates Inc; attended international conferences of Certified Accountants, Beirut, 1965, New York, 1962, Paris, 1967, Sydney, 1972, Munich, 1977; *Address:* P O Box 2679, Riyadh, Saudi Arabia; P O Box 4524 Deira, Dubai, United Arab Emirates; telephone: Office — Riyadh 476 2675; Residence — Al-Khobar 857 8011.

SABA, Hanna, Egyptian official/diplomat; born 23 July 1909; *Education:* College of Jesuit Fathers, Cairo, Egypt; Doctorate in Law, Faculté de Droit, Paris, France; Diploma, Ecole Libre des Sciences Politiques, Paris; *Career:* Minister of Foreign Affairs, 1942; Counsellor, 1946; Minister, 1952; Director of Treaties Division, UN Secretariat, 1946–50; Judicial Adviser to UNESCO, 1950–67; Assistant Director General of UNESCO, 1967–71; Alternate Chairman, UNESCO Appeal Board, 1973; Vice Chairman, Association of French and Arab Jurists; Vice Chairman of Arbitration Council, Franco-Arab Chamber of Commerce, Paris Chamber of Commerce; *Publications: L'Islam et la Nationalité,* 1932; *Les Ententes et Accords Régionaux Dans la Charte des Nations Unies,* a course at Academy of International Law, The Hague, 1952; *L'Activité Quasi Législative des Institutions*

Specialisées des Nations Unies, a course at the Academy of International Law, The Hague, 1964; *Decorations:* Grand Officer of Merit, Egypt; Officer of the Nile; *Languages:* Arabic, French, English; *Address:* 3 Boulevard de la Saussaye, Neuilly, Paris, France.

SABAH, Ali Jarrah al-, Kuwaiti official/economist; born 20 January 1950, Kuwait; married; three daughters; *Religion:* Muslim; *Education:* Economic and Political Science, Kuwait University, 1972; *Career:* Second Secretary, Economic Department, Ministry of Foreign Affairs, 1972; Counsellor, Kuwait Embassy to Tehran, Iran, 1973; Investments Department, Ministry of Finance, 1975; Director of Local and Arab Investments Department, Ministry of Finance, 1975–; Director, Arab Banking Corporation, Bahrain; Deputy Chairman, Bahrain Kuwait Insurance Company, Bahrain; Deputy Managing Director, Burgan Bank, Kuwait; Chairman, Kuwait Reinsurance Co, Kuwait; Board Member, Egyptian Kuwaiti Real Estate Development Co; *Interests and Recreations:* football; *Languages:* English, Arabic; *Address:* Ministry of Finance, P O Box 9, Kuwait; telephone: 431158.

SABAH, Hamad Ibrahim al-, United Arab Emirates administrator; born 1934, Abu Dhabi, United Arab Emirates; married; two sons; *Religion:* Muslim; *Education:* Degree in Law, Cairo University, Egypt, 1958; *Career:* Director General of the Abu Dhabi Chamber of Commerce and Industry 1968–71; Director of Customs 1971–72; Director General of Customs Department, Abu Dhabi 1976–; *Interests and Recreations:* chess, swimming; *Languages:* Arabic, English; *Address:* Customs Department, P O Box 246, Finance Department Building, Abu Dhabi, United Arab Emirates; telephone: 367774; telex: 22221 EM.

SABAH, HH Shaikh Jabir al-Ahmad al-Jabir al-, Amir of Kuwait; born 29 June 1926; third son of Shaikh Ahmad al-Jabir, Ruler 1921–50; *Religion:* Muslim; *Education:* private education; *Career:* Public Security Department; special responsiblity for Kuwait Oil Company KOC, 1950–56; Representative of HH the Ruler with KOC and Aminoil, 1956–59; President of Finance Department and Housing Department, with budgetary control over all public departments; Civil Service Commission and General Oil Affairs Office, 1959–62; Ministry of Finance and Economy, 1962–63; Minister of Finance and Industry, 1963–65; has maintained a special brief on oil and financial affairs; Prime Minister, 1965, 1977; named Heir Apparent, 1966; succeeded as Amir of Kuwait, December 1977; *Languages:* Arabic, English; *Address:* Diwan Amiri, P O Box 799, Kuwait; telephone: 439 021; telex: 22700 AMDIWAN KT.

SABAH, HH Shaikh Sa'ad al Abdullah al-Salim al-, Kuwaiti Crown Prince/Prime Minister of Kuwait; born 1930; married; *Religion:* Muslim; *Education:* in Kuwait; *Career:* Police Department, 1945–53; Metropolitan Police College, Hendon, UK, 1953–54; Deputy Head of Kuwait Police, 1954–59; Deputy President of Police and Public Security Department, 1959–61; Minister of the Interior, 1962–64; Minister of the Interior and of Defence, 1964–78; Head of Ministerial Committee on Labour Problems, 1975–; leading Government spokesman in National Assembly until its dissolution in August 1976; a leading representative of the Salim branch of the al-Sabah family; Crown Prince and Prime Minister, January 1978–; *Languages:* Arabic, English; *Address:* Prime Minister's Office, Seif Palace, Safat, Kuwait; telephone: 431901.

SABAH, Husni Yahia, Syrian physician; born 3 March 1900, Damascus, Syria; *Education:* MD, Faculty of Medicine, University of Damascus, Damascus, Syria; University of Lausanne, Switzerland, and University of Paris, France; *Career:* Assistant, Faculty of Medicine, University of Damascus, 1920–24; Instructor, Assistant Professor, and Head of Internal Medicine Department, Faculty of Medicine, University of Damascus, Syria, 1924–67; Dean of Faculty of Medicine, University of Damascus, 1938–42; Rector, University of Damascus, 1942–49; retired from University of Damascus, 1967; co-founder, former Chairman, Syrian al-Muassat Association, 1943–75; co-founder, member of the Board of Directors, al-Muassat General Hospital, 1953–; President, Syrian Association of Diabetes and Endocrinology, 1972–; member, Arab Academy of Damascus, 1946–, President, 1968–; member, Arab Academy of Cairo, 1956–; Honorary member, Arab Academy of Jordan; *Publications:* numerous books in field of edocrinology, diseases of metabolism and intoxications; co-author, *English-Arabic Medical Dictionary Decorations:* Medal of Syrian Merit; Order of Distinction; Order of the Republic of Egypt; Order of Independence, 1st Class, Jordan; *Address:* 22 Baghdad Boulevard, P O Box 450, Damascus, Syria.

SABAH, Major General Shaikh Mubarak al-Abdullah al-Jabir al-, Kuwaiti army officer; born 1934; married; seven children; *Religion:* Muslim; *Education:* Kuwait; Millfield School, UK; *Career:* served for 11 months in the ranks of the 11th Hussars in Carlisle, UK; Sandhurst Military Academy, UK, 1956–57; secondment with the South Staffordshire Regiment in Minden, West Germany, 1957; Colonel, 1959; Brigadier, 1960; Deputy Commander in Chief, 1959–61; Chief of Staff of Kuwait Armed Forces, 1961; Major General, 1962; *Languages:* Arabic, English; *Address:* Ministry of Defence, P O Box 1170, Safat, Kuwait.

SABAH, Major General Shaikh Salih al-Muhammad al-, Kuwaiti army officer; born 1931; member of the Ruling Family of the State of Kuwait; married; *Career:* joined military service, 1953; trained at Carlisle and Mons, UK, 1955; attached to tanks regiment in the British Army in Britain and West Germany; led Kuwaiti Forces in Arab-Israeli War on Egyptian Front, 1967; Deputy Chief of the General Staff, 1965–; Major General, 1974; *Languages:* Arabic, English; *Address:* P O Box 998, Kuwait; telephone: 517731.

SABAH, Nasr al-, Kuwaiti businessman; born Kuwait; *Religion:* Muslim; *Career:* Chairman, Gulf Fisheries Company; member of the Board of Directors and Delegate member of Gulf International Company; Chairman of the Boards of Directors of Lonrho, UK, United Real Estate Company, Gulf International Company; *Interests and Recreations:* collecting Islamic art treasures; hunting, riding; *Languages:* Arabic, English; *Address:* Gulf International Group (Kuwait), P O Box 3389, Kuwait; telephone: 44830; telex: 22041 HAMOOU KT.

SABAH, Salim Abdul Aziz al-Saud al-; Kuwaiti banker/economist; born 1951; married; two sons; *Religion:* Muslim; *Education:* BA in Economics, American University of Beirut, Lebanon; special courses in Morgan Bank and Chemical Bank; *Career:* Central

Bank of Kuwait, Reporter of the Technical Follow-Up Committee of Interest Rates; Economic Analyst; Head of Research Department; Deputy Director of Foreign Operations; Head of Investment Department and Deputy of Research Department, Central Bank of Kuwait; *Interests and Recreations:* reading, volleyball; *Languages:* Arabic, English; *Address:* P O Box 526, Safat, Kuwait; telephone: 443299, 659999; telex: 22173 KUMBANK KT.

SABAH, Shaikh Abdullah al-Jabir al-, Kuwaiti politician; born 1902; married; two sons; *Religion:* Muslim; *Career:* President of the Municipality; Chief Magistrate and Head of Police, 1939–55; member of Supreme Council, 1961–62; presided over the work of the Departments of Justice and of Education; Minister of Education, 1962–64; Minister of Commerce and Industry, 1965–71; on relinquishing his Cabinet post in 1971, appointed Private Adviser to the Amir; *Address:* Amiri Diwan, P O Box 799, Safat, Kuwait; telephone: 430029; telex: 22700 AMDIWAN KT.

SABAH, Shaikh Abdullah al-Mubarak al-, Kuwaiti politician; born 1915; married; *Religion:* Muslim; *Career:* Head of Police and Security Forces, 1950–61; Controller of the Broadcasting Section, 1954–61; Director General of Civil Aviation, 1950–61; Deputy Ruler, 1959–61; lives abroad, mainly in Egypt; *Address:* c/o Ministry of Foreign Affairs, P O Box 3, Sour Street, Kuwait.

SABAH, Shaikh Ali Khalifa al-, Kuwaiti politician/economist; born 1945; *Religion:* Muslim; *Education:* BA in Economics, University of California, Berkeley, USA, 1968; MA in Economics, School of Oriental and African Studies, University of London, UK; *Career:* Ministry of Finance and Oil, 1968; Assistant Under Secretary for Economic Affairs, 1972; Under Secretary, Ministry of Finance, 1975; negotiator for Kuwait in 1975 negotiations with British Petroleum and Gulf Oil leading to Kuwait nationalization of Kuwait Oil Company; Minister of Oil, 1978–; Kuwait's representative on the OPEC Board of Governors, 1974–76; Chairman of OPEC Board for the year 1975; Chairman of Gulf International Bank; member of Board of the Central Bank of Kuwait, the Arabian Oil Company; *Languages:* Arabic, English; *Ad-*

dress: Ministry of Oil, P O Box 5077, Safat, Kuwait; telephone: 415634; telex: 22363 PETROL KT.

SABAH, Shaikh Jabir al-Abdullah al-Jabir al-, Kuwaiti administrator; born 1930; eldest son of Abdullah al-Jabir; married; two sons; *Religion:* Muslim; *Education:* Victoria College, Alexandria; Law Studies, UK, 1951–52; *Career:* Deputy to his father in the Courts, later Justice Department, 1952–62; Governor of Ahmadi and the Neutral Zone, January 1962–; *Interests and Recreations:* natural history, sea-fishing, gardening; *Languages:* Arabic, English; *Address:* Ministry of Interior, P O Box 4/11, Kuwait; telex: 22507 INTERPOL KT.

SABAH, Shaikh Jabir al-Ali Salem al-, Kuwaiti politician; born 1927, Kuwait; *Religion:* Muslim; *Education:* in Kuwait; *Career:* Minister of Electricity and Water, 1963–64; Minister of Guidance and Information, 1964–71; Deputy Prime Minister and Minister of Information, 1975–; *Address:* Ministry of Information, P O Box 193, Kuwait; telephone: 447128, 437660; telex: 2030 MI KT.

SABAH, Shaikh Jabir al Athbi al-, Kuwaiti aviation official; born 1935; married; six children; *Religion:* Muslim; *Education:* in Kuwait, and Oxford University, UK; *Career:* Assistant Under Secretary for Logistics and Procurement in Ministry of Defence, 1964–74; Director General, Civil Aviation, 1974–; *Languages:* Arabic, English; *Address:* Directorate of Civil Aviation, P O Box 7, Kuwait; telephone: 710981; telex: 23038 CIVAIR KT.

SABAH, Shaikh Misha'al al-Ahmad al-Jabir al-, Kuwaiti official; born 1938; *Religion:* Muslim; *Education:* in Kuwait and at Metropolitan Police College, Hendon, UK; *Career:* Head of Security Services, 1968–; extensive business interests; *Interests and Recreations:* hunting; *Address:* Ministry of Interior, P O Box 4/11, Safat, Kuwait.

SABAH, Shaikh Nasr al-Sabah al-Nasr al-, Kuwaiti official; born 1927; *Religion:* Muslim; *Career:* Governor of Kuwait City, 1967–; *Address:* Governorate of Kuwait, Kuwait; telephone: 440008.

SABAH, Shaikh Nasr Sabah al-Ahmad al-, Kuwaiti businessman; born 1947; eldest son of Minister of Foreign Affairs, Shaikh Sabah al-Ahmad; married; *Religion:* Muslim; *Education:* in Kuwait and abroad; *Career:* has played prominent part in family investment and business activities; worked in Gulf Fisheries Company, later absorbed into United Fisheries Company of Kuwait; financial interests include fisheries and seafood as well as a wide range of investment activities; member of the Boards of Kuwait Financial Centre and of International Financial Advisers; Chairman of United Real Estate Company; was until 1976 a member of the Board of Lonrho in which the family has considerable investment; *Languages:* Arabic, English; *Address:* United Fisheries of Kuwait SAK, Shuweikh, P O Box 22044, Kuwait.

SABAH, Shaikh Sabah Ahmad al-Jabir al-, Kuwaiti politician/businessman; born 1929; fourth son of late Shaikh Ahmad al-Jabir; *Religion:* Muslim; *Education:* privately in Kuwait; *Career:* member of the Higher Executive Committee, 1954–56; President of Social Affairs Department and of Printing and Publishing Department, 1956–62; Minister of Guidance and Information, 1962; Minister of Foreign Affairs, 1963–; Acting Minister of Finance and Oil, 1965–67; Acting Minister of Information, 1971–75; Deputy Prime Minister, Minister of Foreign Affairs, Acting Minister of the Interior, 1978; Owner of Gulf Fisheries Company (now merged in United Fisheries of Kuwait); extensive business interests; together with his son, Nasr al-Sabah, is a leading shareholder in Lonrho, UK; *Interests and Recreations:* boating; *Languages:* Arabic, English; *Address:* Ministry of Foreign Affairs, P O Box 3, Kuwait; telephone: 411484; telex: 22042 KHARJIA KT.

SABAH, Shaikh Salim al-Ali al-, Kuwaiti National Guard Chief; born 1924; married; *Religion:* Muslim; *Education:* in Kuwait and Beirut; *Career:* Assistant to Head of Public Works Department, 1959–62; Minister of Public Works Department (resigned), 1962–64; President of the Municipality, 1954–63; member of the Supreme Defence Council, 1965–; Head of National Guard, 1968–; extensive business interests, especially in property; *Interests and Recreations:* mainly hunting; *Address:* Ministry of Defence, P O Box 1170, Kuwait.

SABAH, Shaikh Salim Sabah al-Salim al-, Kuwaiti politician; born Kuwait; *Religion:* Muslim; *Education:* private law studies in the UK; Oxford University, UK; *Career:* Foreign Service, 1962; Head of Political Department, Ministry of Foreign Affairs, 1964; represented Kuwait at various Middle East and African conferences including Arab Summit Conference, Casablanca, 1965; Ambassador to UK, 1965–70; Ambassador to USA and Canada, 1970–75; Minister of Social Affairs and Labour, 1975–78; Minister of Defence, 1978–; *Interests and Recreations:* riding, swimming; President of Salmiyah Sports Club; *Languages:* Arabic, English; *Address:* Ministry of Defence, P O Box 1170, Safat, Kuwait; telephone: 819288; telex: 22784 MOD KT.

SABAH, Shaikh Saud Nasr al-, Kuwaiti diplomat; born 3 October 1944; married; two sons, two daughters; *Religion:* Muslim; *Education:* Law; *Career:* Barrister at Law, Gray's Inn; Legal Department, University of Foriegn Affairs, Kuwait; Ambassador to London, UK, and to Sweden and Denmark, 1975–80; Ambassador to the United States of America, 1981–; representative of Kuwait to the Conference of Law of the Sea; *Address:* Embassy of Kuwait, 2940 Tilden Street NW, Washington D.C. 20008, USA.

SABAH, Shaikha Badria al-, Kuwaiti businesswoman; born 1920; *Religion:* Muslim; *Career:* started her business after her husband's death in the late 1960s; prominent businesswoman in Kuwait; Chairman, United Trading Group (a private banking and investment organisation); *Languages:* Arabic, English; *Address:* United Trading Group, Ali al-Salem Street, P O Box 1208, Safat, Kuwait; telephone: 420115; telex: 22212 UNTROUP KT.

SABBAB, Ahmad Abdullah al-, Saudi Arabian economist/academic; born 1942, Saudi Arabia; *Religion:* Muslim; *Education:* BS (Cum Laude), 1966; MBS, New York University, USA, 1966; PhD in Management, Marketing and Economics, New York University, USA, 1973; *Career:* supervisor, Arabian American Oil Company (Aramco), Dhahran, 1966–68; Research Assistant, Management and Marketing Department, New York University, 1969–71; part-time Consultant, Urban Assistance Corporation, Graduate School of Business, New York University, 1968–73; Director of Research and Development Centre, King Abdul Aziz University; lectured on micro-economics, William Paterson College, New Jersey, USA, 1972–73; attended Seminar for Advanced Economics, Claremont College, California, USA, 1973; attended Executive Management Programme, American University of Beirut, 1974; represented King Abdul Aziz University in the International Symposium on October 1973 War, Cairo University, Egypt; participated in the first Arabic Conference in Administrative Training, Tunisia, 1967; member of Supreme Council of King Abdul Aziz University; Chairman of First Committee in charge of Planning, Training Activities in the Kingdom of Saudi Arabia; *Address:* Apt 85, Rajhi Building No 4, Mecca Road, Kilo 3, Jeddah, Saudi Arabia.

SABBAGH, Abdul Ghani Mahmud, Saudi Arabian businessman; born 1948, Mecca, Saudi Arabia; *Religion:* Muslim; *Education:* BA in Mass Communications, USA, 1974; *Career:* owner and Director, Azhar Trading Company, Projects and Development Company; Director, Shubra and al-Haram Hotels, Mecca and Taif, Saudi Arabia; *Interests and Recreations:* reading, travel; *Languages:* Arabic, English; *Address:* P O Box 4521, Jeddah, Saudi Arabia; telephone: 6532759, 6532507; telex: 400253 AZHAR SJ.

SABELLA, Emmanuel J., Jordanian businessman; born 14 June 1932, Jerusalem; married; four daughters, two sons; *Religion:* Christian; *Education:* Leeds College of Commerce, UK; Chartered and Corporate Secretary; Associate of the British Society of Commerce; *Career:* businessman; Executive Director of several companies, dealing mainly in building materials, steel insurance and contracting; underwriting member of Lloyd's; *Interests and Recreations:* member of the Amman Rotary Club, the Royal Automobile Club; *Languages:* Arabic, English, French; *Address:* P O Box 1168, Amman, Jordan; telephone: Office — 25995, 38195; Residence — 43931.

SABIR, Muhiyiddine, Sudanese official/ anthropologist and educationalist; born 1919, Dalgo, Sudan; *Religion:* Muslim; *Education:* BA in Arabic Literature, Cairo University, Egypt, 1945; BA in Social Sciences, Paris University, France, 1948; PhD in Anthropology, Cairo University, Egypt, 1946; Doctorat ès-Lettres, Bordeaux University, France, 1951; *Career:* Under Secretary, Ministry of Social Affairs, 1954; Editor in Chief, *Al-Istiqlal* and *Sawt al-Sudan* daily papers, 1955; Lecturer, Anthropology, Cairo University, Khartoum, 1956–59; Manager, *Al-Zaman* daily paper, 1957–59; UNESCO Expert and Head of Social Science Department, Arab States Training Centre for Community Development (ASFEC), Sirs Al-Layyan, Minufiya, Egypt, 1959–68; member of the Constituent Assistant Assembly of Sudan, 1968–69; member of Khartoum University Senate, 1968; Minister of Education and of Higher Education, 1969–72; Director, Arab Literacy and Adult Education Organization (ARLO), 1973–75; Director General, Arab League Educational, Cultural and Scientific Organization (ALESCO), 1975–; member of the Afro-Asian Writers Association; the Governing Board of the International Institute for Educational Planning, UNESCO; the Advisory Committee of the Arab Planning Institute in Kuwait, and others; *Publications: Cultural Change and Commumity Development,* 1962; *Researches in Community Development Programmes,* 1963; *Nomad and Nomadism, Concepts and Approaches,* 1966; *Studies on Issues related to Development and Adult Education,* 1975, translated into English; *Adult Education as Science,* co-author, 1975; *Decorations:* Order of the Republic, Egypt, 1970; Order of the Loyal Sons of the Sudan, Sudan, 1971; National Order, Chad, 1972; Order of Education, Jordan, 1978; Order of the Republic, Sudan, 1979; National Order, Mauritania, 1981; Ordre de Palme Académiques, France, 1981; *Languages:* Arabic, French, English; *Address:* Arab League Educational, Cultural and Scientific Organization, P O Box 1120 Tunis, Tunisia.

SABRA, Muhammad Qassim, Lebanese politician/diplomat; born 1914, Bourj al-Barajneh, Lebanon; *Education:* Licence in Law, Faculty of Law, University of Paris, France; *Career:* Barrister at Law; Inspector of Finance, 1944; Director of Radio-Orient; 1st Consul General, Dakar, Senegal, 1947; Counsellor, Embassy to Argentina, 1949; Minister Plenipotentiary to Iran, 1951; Ambassador to Jordan, 1955; Minister of Information, Posts, Telegraphs and Telephones and Public Works in Abdullah al-Yafi Cabinet, 1956; Minister of Public Works, Planning and Posts, Telegraphs and Tele-

phones, 1956–57; Ambassador to Spain; Director General of Economic Affairs, Ministry of Foreign Affairs, 1967–68; Director of Political Affairs, Ministry of Foreign Affairs, 1969; *Decorations:* various foreign and Middle Eastern decorations; *Interests and Recreations:* hunting; *Languages:* Arabic, French, English; *Address:* Office — Ministry of Foreign Affairs, Beirut, Lebanon.

SABRI, Adnan Ayub, Iraqi politician; born 1925, Baghdad, Iraq; *Religion:* Muslim; *Education:* graduated from Baghdad Military College, 1948; *Career:* Assistant Military Attaché, Embassy to USA, 1963; Staff Colonel, 1968; Secretary General to the Presidency of the Republic; Minister of State, 1968; Acting Minister of Communications; Minister of Communications, 1970; Minister of Youth Affairs, 1972; Minister of Transport, 1974–76; *Address:* Ministry of Transport, Baghdad, Iraq.

SABRI, Musa, Egyptian journalist; born 1924, Egypt; *Religion:* Christian; *Education:* LLB, University of Cairo, Cairo, 1943; *Career:* joined *Akhbar al-Yaum,* 1950; Editor in Chief, *Al-Gumhuriya* newspaper, 1961–63; Editor in Chief, *Akhbar al-Yaum,* 1963–68; Chairman of the Board of Directors of *Akhbar al-Yaum,* 1969–75; Editor in Chief, *Akhbar al-Yaum,* 1975–; *Publications:* documentation of the 1973 October War; numerous articles; several novels and other books; *Languages:* Arabic, English; *Address: Akhbar al-Yaum* Newspaper, 6 Sahafa Street, Cairo, Egypt.

SABTI, Zin al-Abidin al-, Moroccan diplomat/economist; born 8 September 1935, Fes, Morocco; married; two children; *Education:* Economics, Christ Church College, Oxford University, UK; Diploma of Foreign Service Studies; Postgraduate Studies in Economic Development, United Nations Institute for Training and Research, UNITAR, New York, USA; *Career:* Counsellor, Office of the Secretary of State for Foreign Affairs, 1964–67; Minister, Counsellor, Moroccan Embassy in Madrid, Spain, 1967–71; Chef de Cabinet, Ministry of Foreign Affairs, Rabat, 1971–72; Minister Plenipotentiary and Director of Economic Affairs and of Co-operation, Ministry of Foreign Affairs, 1972–77; Ambassador of Morocco to Belgium, Luxembourg and the EEC, 1977–; non-resident Ambassador of Morocco to Ireland, 1982–;

445

representative of Morocco at various international conferences; *Publications: The Effects of International Trade on the Economic Progress of Underdeveloped Countries,* an essay, and several other essays and papers published in professional journals and magazines; *Decorations:* Order Al-Ridha, Morocco; Order of the Throne, Morocco; *Interests and Recreations:* hunting, tennis, painting, photography; *Languages:* Arabic, French, English; *Address:* Embassy of Morocco, Brussels, Belgium; Ministry of Foreign Affairs, Rabat, Morocco.

SACRE, George, Lebanese trade union official/oil expert; born 1927, Beirut, Lebanon; *Religion:* Christian; *Education:* American University of Beirut; *Career:* Departmental Manager of Mobil Oil; Chairman of the Federation of Petroleum Chemical Workers (IFPCW) Board in Denver, Colorado, USA; *Languages:* Arabic, French, English; *Address:* The Federation of Petroleum Chemical Workers (IFPCW), Denver, Colorado, USA.

SADAKA, Najib, Lebanese diplomat; born January 1915, Lebanon; married; two sons, one daughter; *Education:* BA in Literature, American University of Beirut (AUB), Lebanon, 1937; Licence in Law, Doctorate in Law, AUB, Lebanon, 1940; Licence ès – Lettres, Ecole Libre des Sciences Politiques, Paris, France; Institute of Higher International Studies, Paris, France; *Career:* Professor, Faculty of Law, American University in Beirut (AUB), Lebanon, 1945–51; Counsellor, Embassy to France, 1951–52; Director General, Ministry of National Education, Beirut, 1952–56; Assistant Secretary General, Ministry of Foreign Affairs, Beirut, 1956–58; Ambassador to Switzerland 1958–59; Ambassador to Egypt, 1959–60; Ambassador to Belgium and Representative to EEC, 1960–66; Secretary General, Ministry of Foreign Affairs, Beirut, 1966–74; member of the Board of Trustees, UN Institute for Training and Research (UNITAR); Ambassador to France, 1974; *Publications: Paternal Power in Muslim Law,* (in Arabic) 1938; *La question syrienne pendant à guerre de 1914–18,* 1940; *The Palestine Question,* (in Arabic) 1946; *Decorations:* Order of the Cedar, Lebanon; other distinctions and decorations from Spain, Greece; *Languages:* Arabic, English, French; *Address:* Chehad and Sadaka Building, Al-Janah, Beirut, Lebanon.

SADAWI, A.M. Suhaid, Libyan official/oil expert; born 1928, Beirut, Lebanon; *Education:* American University of Beirut, Lebanon; *Career:* employed with Gulf Oil, Libya, 1958–61; ILO, Geneva, 1962–63; Head, General Economic Section, OPEC, 1963; participated in negotiations for amendment of Petroleum Law, 1963; member of Pricing Commission, Libya, 1967; Chairman of Pricing Commission, 1968; Deputy Director General, Libyan National Petroleum Corporation, 1968; Secretary General, Organization of Arab Petroleum Exporting Countries (OAPEC), 1970–73; *Languages:* Arabic, English; *Address:* Arab Economists and Petroleum Affairs (Consultants), P O Box 8840, Beirut, Lebanon.

SADEK, Amal Ahmad M., Egyptian academic; born 3 April 1934, Giza, Egypt; married; one son, one daughter; *Religion:* Muslim; *Education:* BA in Music Education, Egypt, 1960; PhD in Psychology, London University, UK, 1963–68; *Career:* teacher of Music, Egyptian secondary schools, 1960–63; Lecturer of Psychology, Higher Institute of Music, Egypt, 1968–74; Associate Professor, Helwan University, Egypt and King Abdul Aziz University, 1974–77; Professor and Head of Department of Psychology and Educational Technology, Helwan, University, Egypt, 1979–; *Publications: Methods of Teaching Music; Educational Psychology;* several research papers on psychology, measurement and evaluation of musical abilities, intelligence and personality; *Decorations:* Certificate of Distinction, Egypt, 1960; *Interests and Recreations:* music, travel, sewing, knitting; *Languages:* Arabic, English, French; *Address:* Residence — 6 Dr Muhammad Hegab Street, Flat 15, Al-Nuzha, Heliopolis, Cairo, Egypt; Office — 12 Ismail Muhammad Street, Zamalek, Cairo, Egypt.

SADI, Abdullah Said M, Kuwaiti economist/oil consultant; born 10 April 1925, Gaza; married; one son, one daughter; *Religion:* Muslim; *Education:* BBA, American University of Beirut, Lebanon; MBA, Harvard Business School, USA; *Career:* Senior Kuwaiti Government Official, 1956–61; Senior Economist, OPEC, 1961–69; Director of Internaft Ltd, 1969–; *Interests and Recreations:* walking, swimming, skiing, reading; member of Harvard Business School Club;

Languages: Arabic, English; *Address:* 2 Basil Street, London SW3 1AA, UK; telephone: (01) 589 0096.

SADR, Nagib Hamad al-, Egyptian diplomat; born 1915; married; *Religion:* Muslim; *Education:* Degree in Law, 1938; *Career:* transferred from Army to Ministry of Foreign Affairs, 1956; Counsellor, Embassy to Belgium, 1957; Minister, 1958; Ambassador to Guinea, 1959; Ambassador to Cameroon, 1960; Director of African Department, Ministry of Foreign Affairs, 1964; attended Organization of African Unity meetings, 1964–68; Ambassador to Algeria, 1968–74; Under-Secretary, Ministry of Foreign Affairs, 1974; responsible for African and Press Affairs; *Address:* Ministry of Foreign Affairs, Cairo, Egypt.

SADR, Zakariya Ahmad al-, United Arab Emirates official; born 1 April 1912, Minia, Egypt; married; two sons; *Religion:* Muslim; *Education:* BSc in Marine Sciences; *Career:* Officer in Egyptian Navy, 1933–44; first Arab Suez Canal pilot, 1945–52; Head of Shipping Department of Suez Canal until nationalization in 1956; after nationalization, Director of Shipping and Traffic and member of the Board, Suez Canal Authority; Director of Zaid Port, United Arab Emirates; attended International Conference Against Pollution of the Seas, London, UK, 1962 and the Conference for Estimating Cargo Tonnage, London, UK, 1969; established compensation fund for the damage of marine pollution, Brussels, Belgium, 1971; first Vice-Chairman of the International Conference on the Transport of Atomic Materials, Brussels, 1971; member of International Ports Organization, Tokyo, Japan; *Decorations:* Order of Merit, 1st Class, Egypt, 1966; *Interests and Recreations:* swimming; *Languages:* Arabic, English, French; *Address:* c/o Port Zaid Authority, P O Box 422, Abu Dhabi, United Arab Emirates.

SAED, Saif Said, United Arab Emirates diplomat; born 1 October 1945, Sharjah, United Arab Emirates; married; *Religion:* Muslim; *Education:* BA in History and Education, Kuwait University; five months diplomatic course, Abu Dhabi, UAE, 1972; *Career:* 3rd Secretary, UAE Ministry of Foreign Affairs, 1972–73; 2nd Secretary, UAE Ministry of Foreign Affairs, 1973–74; 1st Secretary, UAE Ministry of Foreign Affairs, 1974–75; Cultural Counsellor, UAE Embassy, Cairo, Egypt, 1975; UAE Ambassador to Yemen Arab Republic, 1975–; attended 35th session of UN General Assembly, 1980; *Interests and Recreations:* Arabic literature, history, poetry, cinema, television, riding; *Languages:* Arabic, English, Urdu, Persian; *Address:* UAE Embassy, P O Box 2250, Sana'a, Yemen Arab Republic; telephone: 75559, 73322; P O Box 6666, Sharjah, UAE; telephone: 351142, 351152.

SAFADI, Hisham Jamil, Jordanian banker; born 12 October 1931, Jordan; married; *Religion:* Muslim; *Education:* BA in Business Administration, American University of Beirut, AUB, Lebanon, 1953; *Career:* Accountant, Income Tax Department, Amman, Jordan, 1953–54; Administrative Assistant, Central Government Laboratories, Amman, 1954–58; Bank Officer, Intra Bank and Al-Faiha'a Bank, Damascus, Syria, 1958–63; Secretary to the Governor of Central Bank of Jordan, Amman, 1963–64; Head of Banking Operations Division, Central Bank of Jordan, 1964–65; Assistant Manager, Banking Department, Central Bank of Jordan, 1966–68; Manager, Banking Department, Central Bank of Jordan, Amman, 1969–73; Executive Manager, Foreign Relations Department, Central Bank of Jordan, 1974–79; Director, Banking Institute, Amman, 1974–80; Deputy General Manager, Jordan Fertilizers and Industry Company, Amman, 1980–82; General Manager, Syrian Jordanian Bank, Amman, 1982–; *Decorations:* Order of the Jordanian Star, 1974; *Interests and Recreations:* reading, music; *Languages:* Arabic, English, French; *Address:* Syrian Jordanian Bank, P O Box 926, 636 Amman, Jordan; telephone: 661 138.

SAFADI, Tawfiq, (Abu Usama), Palestinian politician; born 1939; *Career:* Secretary General of the Palestinian Higher Political Committee in Lebanon; closely associated with Zuhair al-Alami, former Fatah leader who died 1971.

SAFAR, Mahmud Muhammad, Saudi Arabian official; born 1939, Mecca; married; two sons, three daughters; *Religion:* Muslim; *Education:* PhD in Civil Engineering; *Career:* Faculty Member, College of Engineering, University of King Saud, 1965; Dean of Student Affairs, University of King Saud,

1974; Secretary General, High Council of Universities, 1975–; Under Secretary for Higher Education, 1977; Under Secretary for Technical Affairs, Ministry of Higher Education, 1979–; member of the Council of High Education of the Gulf States, of the Founding Committee of the Arab Gulf University, of the American Association of Civil Engineers; *Publications:* numerous books, articles, and papers; *Decorations:* Medal from China; *Interests and Recreations:* reading, swimming, travelling; *Languages:* Arabic, English; *Address:* P O Box 18370, Riyadh, Saudi Arabia; telephone: 441 2285.

SAFDAR, Yusif Muhammad, Saudi Arabian businessman/accountant; born 1940, Mecca, Saudi Arabia; *Religion:* Muslim; *Education:* BCom, Accountancy and Administration; *Career:* former Manager of Tariffs, Saudi Arabian Airlines, SAUDIA; Sales and Reservation Manager, SAUDIA; Traffic Manager, SAUDIA; former Manager of Income Tax Division in Zakat and Income Tax Directorate; Legal Accountant and former Manager of Audit Department, Zakat and Income Tax Directorate; Director of Finance in Dallah Avco Trans Arabia; Certified Public Accountant and Auditor; member of the Board of National Club; attended several Arab Air Transport Association conferences, and International Air Transport Association, IATA, conferences; *Interests and Recreations:* reading, sport; *Address:* Appartment 7, Muhammad Nazir Building, Palestine Street, West Lona Park, Jeddah, Saudi Arabia; telephone: Office — 667280; Residence — 6671339.

SAFFAR, Salman Muhammad al-, Bahraini diplomat; born 21 June 1931, Manama, Bahrain; married; *Religion:* Muslim; *Education:* BA, University of Baghdad, 1954–58; PhD, University of Paris, 1961–70; *Career:* teacher, elementary and secondary schools in Bahrain, 1954, 1959–60; Officer in charge of Political Affairs, Ministry of Foreign Affairs, Bahrain, 1970–71; Ambassador, Permanent Representative of Bahrain to the UN, New York, USA, 1971; *Interests and Recreations:* swimming, fishing, music, international affairs; *Languages:* Arabic, English, French; *Address:* Ministry of Foreign Affairs, P O Box 547, Government House, Government Road, Manama, Bahrain; telephone: 258200; telex: 8228.

SAFWAT, Mahmud Abbas, Egyptian banker/ financial adviser; born 13 February 1919, Cairo, Egypt; married; one daughter; *Religion:* Muslim; *Education:* Administration, Institute of Administration, Egypt; Degree in Law, Fuad I University, Cairo, Egypt; Diploma in Political Science and Economics, Egypt; *Career:* Secretary General, Arab Real Estate Bank, 1956; General Manager, UAE Development Bank, 1978; Legal Adviser to banks and investment companies; *Interests and Recreations:* swimming, reading; *Languages:* Arabic, English, French; *Address:* 22 Taha Hussain Street, Zamalek, Cairo, Egypt; telephone: Office — 815067, 811658; Residence — 819589.

SAFWAT, Najdat Fathi, Iraqi writer/ diplomat; born 25 April 1923, Baghdad, Iraq; married; two daughters, one son; *Religion:* Muslim; *Education:* LLB, University of Baghdad, Iraq; Postgraduate Studies, University of London, UK; *Career:* Diplomatic Service, Ministry of Foreign Affairs, Iraq; served in London, UK, 1945–49, Amman, Jordan, 1949–50, Cairo, Egypt, 1950–54, Paris, France, 1955–56, Washington D.C., USA, 1960–63, Moscow, USSR, 1963–66; Assistant Under Secretary, Ministry of Foreign Affairs, Baghdad, 1959–60; Director General, Political Department, Ministry of Foreign Affairs, with rank of Minister Plenipotentiary, 1966–67; resigned from Ministry of Foreign Affairs, 1967; free-lance writer; Trustee, Arab Research Centre, London, UK; *Publications:* in Arabic, *Schools of Western Literature,* Baghdad, 1943; *Iliya Abu Madhi and the Literary Movement in America,* Baghdad, 1945; *Zionism in the Relations of Big Powers,* Baghdad, 1967; *Iraq Through the Memoirs of Foreign Diplomats,* Beirut, 1969; *Diplomatic Stories,* Beirut, 1970; *Birobidzhan: The Soviet Experiment for a National Home for the Jews,* Baghdad, 1973; *Decorations:* Wissam al-Nahda, Jordan,1959; *Interests and Recreations:* political and literary history of the Middle East; *Languages:* Arabic, Turkish, English, French, Russian; *Address:* 20 Woodville Gardens, Ealing, London W5, UK.

SAGABI, Muhammad Ibrahim al-, Saudi Arabian businessman; born 1913, Saudi Arabia; *Religion:* Muslim; *Education:* general; *Career:* Director, Statistical Department, Eastern Province; private enterprise in real estate, electrical equipment and glass manufacturing; member of Municipal Council; established the National Glass Manufacturing Co, Dammam; *Address:* P O Box 580, Dammam, Saudi Arabia.

SAGAR, Abdul Aziz al-, Kuwaiti businessman/politician; born 1916, Kuwait; married; three daughters, one son; *Religion:* Muslim; *Education:* in Kuwait; *Career:* businessman; Minister of Public Health; Chairman of the Board of Kuwait National Bank, 1959–65; Chairman of Kuwait Oil Tankers Company, 1961–80; Chairman of the Arab-European Bank, Brussels, Belgium; Vice Chairman of Arab Bank, Paris, France; member of the first National Assembly, 1963; President of the National Assembly, 1965; President of the Board of Kuwait Chamber of Commerce and Industry; Chairman of Red Crescent Society; *Interests and Recreations:* walking, swimming, Arab navigation; *Languages:* Arabic, English; *Address:* Kuwait Chamber of Commerce and Industry, P O Box 775, Kuwait; telephone: 433864/6, 417285; telex: 22198 GURFTIGARA KT.

SAGHIR, Abdul Rahman, Lebanese academic/agriculturalist; born 10 June 1935, Beirut, Lebanon; married; two sons, one daughter; *Religion:* Muslim; *Education:* BSc in Agriculture, American University of Beirut, 1957; MSc in Agronomy, AUB, 1961; PhD in Plant Physiology, University of California (Davis), USA, 1964; *Career:* Assistant Instructor of Agronomy, AUB, 1957–59; Graduate Assistant, AUB, 1959–61; Research Assistant, University of California, Davis 1961–64; Assistant Professor of Agronomy, AUB, 1964–69; Associate Professor of Weed Science, AUB, 1976–79; Professor of Weed Science, AUB, 1976–79; Professor and Associate Dean, AUB, 1979; member of the Weed Science Society of America, the Lebanese Association for the Advancement of Science, the European Weed Research Society, the New York Academy of Science, Sigma Xi-Davis Chapter, the AUB Club, the Union of Arab Biologists; *Publications: Effects of Herbicides on Yield and Quality of Crops;* numerous publications in international scientific journals and proceedings; abstracts and articles in Arabic; *Decorations:* Asgrow Award, American Society of Horticultural Science, 1965; Award from the Institute of World Affairs, Connecticut, USA; *Interests and Recreations:* swimming, travelling, read-

ing; *Languages:* Arabic, English, French; *Address:* Faculty of Agricultural and Food Sciences, American University of Beirut, P O Box 11 6044, Beirut, Lebanon.

SAHBANI, Tayib, Tunisian diplomat; born 1925, Tunis; married; two daughters, one son; *Religion:* Muslim; *Education:* Sadiki College, Tunis; Sorbonne, Paris, France; *Career:* teacher, secondary schools, Tunis; President of the Neo-Destour Federation of Tunis, 1954–56; elected member of the National Council of the Neo-Destour, 1955; member of the Constituent Assembly, 1956; Ambassador to Morocco, 1956; Ambassador to Egypt, 1957; Secretary General, Ministry of Foreign Affairs, 1958; Personal Representative of the UN Secretary General at Brussels, dealing with Congo, 1961; Leading negotiator for the Tunisian authorities over the Bizerta Question, 1961–62; Chef de Cabinet to President Bourguiba, 1964; Ambassador to Libya, 1967–70; Head of several goodwill missions abroad including one to the Congo at the time of Katanga Crisis; Ambassador to Yugoslavia, Bulgaria and Romania, 1973–78; Secretary General, Ministry of Foreign Affairs, 1978; Permanent Representative of Tunisia at Arab League, 1980–; *Languages:* Arabic, French; *Address:* General Secretariat of the Arab League, Tunis, Tunisia.

SAHNOUN, Hadj Muhammad, Algerian diplomat; born 8 April 1931, Algeria; *Religion:* Muslim; *Education:* BA, Constantine University, Algeria, 1960; MA, New York University, New York, USA, 1963; *Career:* Director, Political Affairs Department, Ministry of Foreign Affairs, 1963–64; Assistant Secretary General, Organisation of African Unity, 1964–73; Assistant Secretary General, Arab League, 1973–74; Ambassador, Federal Republic of Germany, 1975–82; Ambassador to France, 1982–; *Publications: Economic and Social Aspects of the Algerian Revolution,* New York, 1962; *Languages:* Arabic, French, English, German; *Address:* Rue Hamelin 18, 16e, Paris, France.

SAHYOUN, Ibrahim, Lebanese dental surgeon/academic; born 6 July 1936, Haifa, Palestine; married; two daughters, one son; *Religion:* Christian; *Education:* PhD in Dental and Maxillary Surgery; *Career:* Surgeon, American Hospital in Germany; Head of Clinic, French Faculty of Medicine, Beirut, 1962; French Faculty of Medicine,

Dental School, Beirut; Assistant Lecturer, Professor, Head of Department of Dental Surgery, 1976–; Director General of the Arab Center for Accidents Research, 1977–; Dental and Facial Surgeon; member of the Administrative Council of La Banque de Beyrouth; *Publications:* several articles on facial and dental surgery in Arab and American professional journals; *Decorations:* Médaille de l'Education National Libanaise; *Interests and Recreations:* riding, sailing; *Languages:* Arabic, French, English, German; *Address:* Hamra Street, Beirut, Lebanon.

SAID, Amina al-, Egyptian journalist; born 1914, Egypt; married; three children; *Religion:* Muslim; *Education:* BA, Cairo University, 1935; *Career:* former Chairman of the Board of Directors, Dar al-Hilal Press Institution; former Editor in Chief of *Hawa* weekly women's magazine; Consultant, Dar Al-Hilal; represented Egypt at several international conferences; member of the Higher Press Council, 1975–; *Publications:* numerous books and articles; *Languages:* Arabic, English, French; *Address:* Dar al-Hilal, 16 Muhammad Izz al-Arab Street, Cairo, Egypt.

SAID, Bishir Muhammad, Sudanese journalist; born 1921, Omdurman, Sudan; *Religion:* Muslim; *Career:* teacher, 1942–45; journalist 1945; studied journalism in UK, 1949; founder and Managing Editor of newspaper publishing firm Al-Ayam Press, 1953–; member of first Sudanese delegation to UN, 1956; Press Officer to UN Office of Public Information, New York, USA, 1961–62; member of Sudan's Constitution Commission, 1958; President, Sudan Press Association, 1957–58; member of Council of University of Khartoum, 1958–60; *Languages:* Arabic, English; *Address:* Al-Ayam Press, Khartoum, Sudan.

SAID, Edward Wadie, Palestinian academic; born 1 November 1935, Jerusalem; resident in USA; married; one son, one daughter; *Education:* BA, Princeton University; MA, PhD, Harvard University; *Career:* Assistant Professor, English Department, Columbia University, 1963–70; Professor of English and Comparative Literature, Columbia University, 1970–; Visiting Professor of Comparative Literature, Harvard University, 1974; Fellow, Center for Advanced Study, Stanford University, 1975–76; Visiting Professor in the Humanities, Johns Hopkins University, 1979; member of the Palestine National Council, Council of Foreign Relations, NY, Executive Committee, New York State Council of the Humanities; Chairman, Institute of Arab Studies, Massachusetts; *Publications: Joseph Conrad and the Fiction of Autobiography,* 1965, 1966, Harvard University Press; *Beginnings, Intentions and the Method,* 1975, 1978, Basic Books; *Orientalists and Orientalism,* 1978, Pantheon, in English, with editions in French, German, Arabic, Dutch; *The Question of Palestine,* 1975, 1980, *NY Times,* in English, with editions in German, Hebrew; *Covering Islam,* 1981, Pantheon; *Literature and Society,* 1980, Johns Hopkins; *Languages:* English, Arabic, French, German, Italian, Spanish, Latin; *Address:* 419 Hamilton Hall, Columbia University, New York, NY 10027, USA.

SAID, HH Sayyid Fahr Bin Taimur al-, Omani politician; born 1928; brother of the late Sultan Said; married; *Religion:* Muslim; *Education:* course in Military Academy in Dehra Dun, 1940; *Career:* served with the Muscat Infantry, 1948–51; joined Sayyid Tariq al-Said in Beirut, 1966; worked with the former Ruler of Abu Dhabi, Shaikh Shakhbut; returned to Oman with Sayyid Tariq al-Said, 1970; Liaison Officer to the Defence Department; Deputy Minister of Defence, 1973; Minister of the Interior, 1974; led military missions to a number of Arab countries; represented the Royal Family on foreign missions; Deputy Prime Minister for Security and Defence, 1979–; *Address:* Ministry of Defence, Bait al Falaj, P O Box 113, Muscat, Oman.

SAID, HH Sayyid Hilal Bin Hamad al-Sammar al-, Omani politician; born 1927, Sur, Oman; married; six sons, three daughters; *Religion:* Muslim; *Education:* Islamic education by private tutors; *Career:* administrative posts in the government; Minister of Justice, 1973–74; Minister of Justice, 1975–82; Minister of Interior and Justice, Awqaf and Islamic Affairs, 1982–; attended Conference of Arab Ministers of Justice, Morocco, 1977; *Languages:* Arabic; *Address:* Ministry of Justice, Awqaf and Islamic Affairs, P O Box 767, Ruwi, Oman.

SAID, Kamil Muhammad, Sudanese official; born 1 January 1931; married; two sons, one daughter; *Religion:* Muslim; *Education:* graduated from Khartoum University College, Sudan, 1954; Oxford University, UK 1965–66; *Career:* Governor of the Northern Province; member of the Commission for Reorganization of Sudanese Provinces; member of the Electoral Commission for the second National Assembly; Head of the Electoral Commissions for the National Executive Councils and Local National Councils; member of the Administrative Officers' Union; attended conference on Administrative Development and its Effect on Growth in Developing Countries, Tangiers, Morocco, 1967; attended conference on Nomad Settlement in the Sub-Saharan Belt, Niamey, Niger, 1968; *Decorations:* Order of the Republic, 2nd Class, 1975; *Interests and Recreations:* reading, painting and sculpture; *Languages:* Arabic, English; *Address:* Administrative Headquarters, Northern Province, Dongola, Sudan.

SAID, Muhammad Hilmi, Egyptian diplomat; born 28 July 1925, Cairo, Egypt; married; three sons; *Religion:* Muslim; *Education:* BA in Philosophy, Cairo University, Cairo, Egypt; Diploma in Education and Psychology; Diploma in Political Sciences, Cairo University; *Career:* Third Secretary, Ministry of Foreign Affairs, 1956; Egyptian Embassy in Moscow, 1957; First Secretary, Embassy of Egypt, Amman, Jordan, 1964; Counsellor, and Minister Plenipotentiary, Egyptian Embassy, Moscow, 1971; Ambassador of Egypt to Aden, People's Democratic Republic of Yemen, 1976; Ambassador of Egypt to Dar es Salaam, Tanzania, 1979–; *Decorations:* Order of Merit 4th Class, Egypt, 1958; Order of the Republic 3rd Class, 1971; Order of the Republic 2nd Class, 1975; Order of the Jordanian Star, 1968; *Interests and Recreations:* classical music, literature, theatre; *Languages:* Arabic, English, French, Russian; *Address:* Office — Embassy of Egypt, P O Box 1668, Dar es Salaam, Tanzania; Residence— 17 Muhammad Kamil Mursi Street, Dokki, Cairo, Egypt.

SAID, Mustafa Tawfik al-, Egyptian diplomat/lawyer; born 1908; *Religion:* Muslim; *Education:* LLB, LLD, Cairo University, Egypt; *Career:* Public Prosecutor, 1929–38; Lecturer and Assistant Professor of Criminal Law, Cairo University, 1938–42; Professor of Criminal Law, Alexandria University, 1942; Dean of Faculty of Law, Alexandria University, 1946; Attorney General, Alexandria Court of Appeal, 1949; Professor of Criminal Law, Cairo University, 1950; Dean of Faculty of Law, Cairo University, 1952; Rector of Alexandria University, 1954–58; Rector of Cairo University, 1958–61; Chairman of the Supreme Council of the Universities; Ambassador to Portugal, 1962–64; Ambassador to Somalia, 1968; Ambassador to East Germany, 1972–; *Publications: On the Scope and Exercise of Marital Rights,* 1936; *The Egyptian Penal Code Annotated,* 1937; *Crimes of Forgery Under Egyptian Law,* 1953; *Principles of Criminal Law,* 1947; *The Expansion of Higher Education in the United Arab Republic,* 1960; *Languages:* Arabic, English; *Address:* Ministry of Foreign Affairs, Cairo, Egypt.

SAID, Rafik, Tunisian diplomat; born 16 March 1930, Tunis; married; one daughter, one son; *Religion:* Muslim; *Education:* BA in French Language and Literature; Diploma in History of International Relations; *Career:* teacher, 1957–58; Head of Division, Cabinet of the Ministry of National Education, Youth and of Sports, 1958–60; Director, Bourguiba Institute of Modern Languages, University of Tunis, 1960–62; Director of Cultural Animation, Ministry of Cultural Affairs and Information, 1962–68; Chargé d'Affaires, Tunisian Embassy, Paris, France, 1970; Minister Plenipotentiary, Permanent Delegation of Tunisia at UNESCO, 1969–75; Chef de Cabinet, Ministry of Public Health, 1975; Chef de Cabinet, Ministry of National Education, and Secretary General of the National Tunisian Commission for UNESCO and ALESCO, 1976–80; Ambassador of Tunisia, Ottawa, Canada, 1980–; President of the Inter-Governmental Committee for the Right of Authors, and of the Executive Committee of the International Union of the Protection of Literary and Artistic Works, 1971–73; Vice President of the Group of Permanent African Delegates at UNESCO, 1969–75; *Publications: The Political and Social Changes in Tunisia since Independence,* Georgetown University, 1964, in French; *The Cultural Politics in Tunisia,* UNESCO, 1970, 1980, in French; and several other works; *Decorations:* Knight of the Order of Independence, Tunisia, 1976; Commander of the Order of the Tunisian Republic, 1977; Médaille Vermeil du Travail, 1978; Commander of the Ordre du Lion, Finland, 1965; *Address:* 15 rue O'Connor, Ottowa, Ontario, Canada K1S 3P8.

SAID, Rushdi Farag, Egyptian geologist/ politician; born 1920; married; two children; *Religion:* Christian; *Career:* member of the Egyptian Committee on the De-Nuclearization of the Mediterranean, 1964; member of the National Assembly, 1964; member of Secretariat General of the Arab Socialist Union (ASU), 1965; Deputy Chairman of Assembly's Foreign Relations and National Defence Committee in the new People's Assembly of November 1971; elected to Inter-Parliamentary Union Executive Council, 1972; served on the People's Assembly Committee of Enquiry into the Copt-Muslim disturbances, autumn 1972; Egyptian observer at the opening of the European Security Conference in Helsinki, January 1973; Chairman of the General Egyptian Authority for Geological Surveys and Mining Projects; *Languages:* Arabic, English; *Interests and Recreations:* geology; *Address:* General Egyptian Authority for Geological Surveys and Mining Projects, Cairo, Egypt.

SAID, Sayyid Thuwain Bin Shahib al-, Omani official; born 1924; *Religion:* Muslim; *Education:* Baghdad, Iraq and Bahrain; *Career:* teacher, Saidiyyah School, Muscat; Sultan's office, 1948–55; spent six months with Oman forces in Ibri, Fahud and Nizwa; later worked for the late Sultan in Salalah; succeeded his father as Governor of Muscat on his retirement in 1970; Personal Adviser to HM the Sultan, 1970; *Languages:* Arabic, English; *Address:* Council of Ministers, Muscat, Oman.

SAID, Sayyid Fahd Bin Mahmud al-, Omani politician; born 1944; member of the Royal Family; married; *Religion:* Muslim; *Education:* degree in Commerce, University of Cairo, Egypt; Diploma in Diplomatic Studies, Paris, France; Academy of Arts in The Hague, Netherlands; *Career:* Director in the Ministry of Foreign Affairs, Oman, 1971; Minister of State, 1971; Minister of Information and Culture, 1973; *Languages:* Arabic, English, French; *Address:* c/o Ministry of Information and Youth Culture, P O Box 600, Muscat, Oman.

SAID, Sayyid Faisal Bin Ali al-, Omani politician/diplomat; born 1928; *Religion:* Muslim; *Education:* general; *Career:* teacher; Department of External Affairs, 1955; left Oman, 1964, and lived in Cairo and Beirut until 1970; Director of Education, 1970; active in founding several new schools; Minister of Economy, 1971; Chargé d'Affaires, Ministry of Foreign Affairs, 1972; Omani Permanent Representative to the UN; Ambassador to USA, 1973; Minister of Education, 1973–76; Minister of National Heritage and Culture, 1976–; *Languages:* Arabic, English; *Address:* Ministry of National Heritage and Culture, P O Box 668, Al Khuwair, Diplomatic City, Muscat, Oman; telephone: 602555, 602225, 602565; telex: 3649 OMNHCU MB.

SAID, Sayyid Shabib Bin Taimur al-, Omani diplomat; born 1944; married; *Religion:* Muslim; *Education:* in Karachi, Pakistan; accountancy studies in UK; *Career:* spent several months on attachment to the Omani Ministry of Foreign Affairs, 1971; Chargé d'Affaires, Embassy to UK, 1971; Counsellor, Omani Mission to the UN; Ambassador to Pakistan, 1974–75; Ambassador to Morocco, 1975; *Address:* c/o Ministry of Foreign Affairs, P O Box 252, Muscat, Oman; telephone: 701211, 701614, 701515; telex: 3337 MFA MB.

SAID, Shaif Muhammad, Yemen Arab Republic official; born 1924; married; five sons, five daughters; *Religion:* Muslim; *Education:* BA in Commerce, Italy; *Career:* Director of President's Office, 1963; Assistant Governor of Taiz, 1962; Chairman of the Board of the Yemen Petroleum Company; Chairman of Yemeni Airlines, Sana'a; *Decorations:* Knight Order from Italy; *Interests and Recreations:* reading, football; *Languages:* Arabic, English; *Address:* Al-Zubair Street, Sana'a, Yemen Arab Republic; telephone: 3347, 8621.

SAIDI, Kadhim al-, Iraqi economist; born 11 November 1919, Shatra, Iraq; married; four sons, one daughter; *Religion:* Muslim; *Education:* BA in Social Sciences, Baghdad, 1942; BA in Law, 1948; Higher Diploma in Political Economy, 1950; Higher Diploma in Economic Sciences, 1951; PhD in Economic Sciences, University of Paris, France, 1953; *Career:* Adviser and Assistant General Director, Ministry of Finance, 1953–60; Lecturer,

Faculty of Law, University of Baghdad, 1956–60; Dean, Faculty of Commerce, University of Baghdad, 1964; seconded to OPEC, 1964–66; Head of Economic Department, University of Baghdad, 1971–72; Chief Editor of the *Economist,* journal of the Iraqi Economists Society, 1963–64; member and Counsellor, Bureau of Economic Affairs, Revolutionary Command Council, 1972–; member of the Planning Council, 1972–78; Economic Expert, the Council of Arab Economic Unity, 1978–80; *Publications: Budget of the State,* 1969; *Income Tax in Iraq,* 1970; numerous articles and papers on economic and public finance in the *Journal of Iraqi Economists; Languages:* Arabic, French, English; *Address:* 42/1/4/ Al-Mansour, Baghdad, Iraq.

SAKET, Bassam Khalil, Jordanian economist; born 21 January 1944; married; two sons, one daughter; *Religion:* Muslim; *Education:* BSc in Economics, Baghdad University, 1966; Postgraduate Diploma in Economics, Oxford University, UK, 1970; Diploma in Financial Analysis, IMF Washington D.C., USA, 1973; PhD in Economics, Keele University, UK, 1976; *Career:* Economic Researcher and Analyst, Central Bank of Jordan, 1966–70; Senior Economist, Head of the Domestic Economy and Development, 1970–73; Director, Economics Department, Royal Scientific Society and member of the Executive Committee, 1976–; Economic Adviser to HRH the Crown Prince, Royal Court, 1978–; *Publications:* author and co-author of numerous books on economics and economic development in the Arab world and Jordan in particular; *Interests and Recreations:* music, basket ball, squash, swimming, reading; economics and economic development, particularly economics of aid; member of the Jordanian Economists Society and of the International Development Society, Washington D.C., USA; *Languages:* Arabic, English; *Address:* Office of HRH Crown Prince Hassan, Royal Court, Amman, Jordan; telephone: 37341, 4925.

SAKIJHA, Ibrahim Ali, Jordanian journalist; born 13 March 1926, Jaffa, Palestine; married; one son, two daughters; *Religion:* Muslim; *Education:* Palestine Matriculation; *Career:* Editor, *Al-Falastin* newspaper, Jaffa, Palestine, 1944–48; Editor, *Al-Masri* newspaper, Cairo, Egypt, 1948–49; Assistant Editor, *Al-Jazira* and *Al-Nasr* dailies,

Amman, 1949–50; Assistant Editor, *Al-Falastin* newspaper, Jerusalem, 1950–67; Manager and Editor of *Al-Destour,* Amman, 1967–75; General Manager and Editor of *Al-Shaab,* Amman; Vice-Chairman of the Board of Dar al-Shaab Company for Printing, Publishing and Distribution; President of Jordanian Press Association; Adviser to Jordanian Television, 1969–71; Editor, *Sawat Al Shaab,* 1983–; member of the Secretaries' Council, International Arab Information Centre, Cairo; member of the Permanent Bureau of the Arab Press Foundation; *Decorations:* Medal of His Holiness the Pope, 1964; *Interests and Recreations:* writing short stories and articles; founded Arab Cultural Association, Jaffa; *Languages:* Arabic, English; *Address: Al-Shaab* Newspaper, P O Box 925155, Amman, Jordan; telephone: 661234, 667101.

SAKRAN, Frank Salih C., Arab-American lawyer; born 1894, Nazareth, Palestine; married; one son, two daughters; *Religion:* Christian; *Education:* Juris Doctor, George Washington University; Master of Laws in Diplomacy, American University, Washington D.C., USA; *Career:* Executive Secretary, American Council of the Middle East; Attorney, US Government, Chief Legal Section; writer and lecturer on Arab-Zionist conflict; member of the Federal Bar Association, the American Society of International Law, the World Peace Through Law; *Publications: Veterans Laws,* 1936; *Palestine Dilemma,* Washington, 1948; *And So Moscow Moved In,* Washington, 1965; *America, Zionism and the Arabs,* Washington, 1966; *Whose Jerusalem?,* Washington, 1968; *Palestine, Still a Dilemma,* Philadelphia 1976; numerous newspaper articles; *Interests and Recreations:* hunting, fishing; *Languages:* Arabic, Turkish, Greek, Portuguese, Spanish, English; *Address:* Mechanicsville, Maryland, MD 20659, USA; telephone: (301) 884 3531.

SALAAM, Saeb, Lebanese politician; born 1905, Lebanon; married; five children; *Education:* American University of Beirut (AUB), Lebanon; London School of Economics, UK; *Career:* landowner, 1927–37; founder of Middle East Airlines, Air Liban, 1945; President, Middle East Airlines, 1945–56; elected Deputy for Beirut, 1943; Minister of the Interior, 1946; Prime Minister, 1952; Prime Minister during the elections of 1953;

Minister of State, 1956; re-elected Deputy of Beirut, 1960; Prime Minister, 1960–61; Head, Lebanese delegation to the XVth Session of the UN General Assembly, 1960; Prime Minister and Minister of Defence, 1961; re-elected Deputy for Beirut, 1964, 1968 and 1972; formed *Beirut Bloc* in opposition to President Chehab and Helou, 1966–68; after 1968 elections formed centre Group with Sulaiman Franjieh and Skaf and Asad; Prime Minister and Minister of Interior, 1970–73; member of the National Dialogue Committee, 1975–; *Decorations:* Grand Cordon of the National Order of the Cedar, Lebanon; many other foreign distinctions and decorations; *Interests and Recreations:* shooting, swimming; President of Al-Mokassed Association; *Languages:* Arabic, French, English; *Address:* Office — Chamber of Deputies, Place de l'Etoile, Beirut, Lebanon; telephone: 220040; Residence — Mousseitbeh Street, Beirut, Lebanon; telephone: 231716.

SALAAM, Salim Ali, Lebanese businessman; born 1922, Beirut, Lebanon; married; two daughters, two sons; *Education:* BA, American University of Beirut, Lebanon; MA in Public Administration, Harvard University, USA; *Career:* Managing Director, and member of Board of Directors, Middle East Airlines, Beirut; Secretary General, Arab Air Carriers Organization; Vice President, National Council of Tourism, Beirut, Lebanon; *Decorations:* Knight and Commander of the National Order of the Cedar, Lebanon; Order of the Jordanian Star; Egyptian Order of Merit; *Interests and Recreations:* game hunting, fishing, swimming, shooting, golf, flying, firearms collection; President of the Golf Club of Lebanon; Secretary General of the Federation of Golf Clubs; Director of Aero Club of Lebanon; member of the Scall Club, Aero Club of London, Royal Aero Club of England, Harvard Club and Propeller Club; *Languages:* Arabic, French, English; *Address:* Office — Middle East Airlines, Beirut International Airport, P O Box 206, Beirut, Lebanon; telephone: 316316; Residence — Dr. Itayem Building, Bir Hassan, Beirut, Lebanon; telephone: 832717, 318606.

SALAH, Abdullah A., Jordanian diplomat; born 31 December 1922, Tulkarm, Jordan; *Education:* BA Politics, American University of Beirut, Lebanon, 1944; Law Studies at Palestine Law Institute, Jerusalem, 1944–48;

Career: Field Education Officer, UN Relief and Works Agency (UNRWA), Jordan, 1952–62; Ambassador to Kuwait, 1962–63; Ambassador to India, 1963–64; Ambassador to France, 1964–66, 1967–70; Minister of Foreign Affairs, 1966–67, 1970–72; Ambassador to USA, 1973; also accredited to Mexico; Senator, 1971–73; *Address:* Ministry of Foreign Affairs, P O Box 1577, Amman, Jordan.

SALAH, Butrus Alfonse, Jordanian official; born 11 November 1927, Nablus, Jordan; married; one son, one daughter; *Religion:* Christian; *Education:* Law Studies, Jerusalem, 1945–48; Administration, UK, 1957; *Career:* Teacher, Terrasanta College, Jerusalem, 1945–47; Teacher, Gaza College, 1946–47; Teacher, De Lasalle College, Jerusalem, 1947–49; Employee, Arab Insurance Company, Jerusalem and Beirut, 1948–49; Employee at Aramco, Dahran, Saudi Arabia, 1950–51; Assistant Director, CAT Company, Beirut, Lebanon, 1952–54; General Commercial Director, CAT Southern Gulf Company, Bahrain, 1954–60; Director General, SINCO Company, Amman, 1960–62; Partner and Director, Jordan Traders Company, 1962–63; Administrative Director and Public Relations Director, ALIA Airline, 1963–65; Director General, Jordanian General Relations Company, 1965–67; Director of Public Relations, Ministry of Information, 1967–69; Information Attaché, Jordanian Embassy, London, UK, 1969–70; Director of Press and Public Relations Department, Ministry of Information; Acting Director of Press and Publications Department; Director General, Jordanian News Agency, 1972–73; Director of Public Relations, Ministry of Culture and Information, 1973–76; Adviser, Ministry of Culture and Information, 1976–; Under Secretary, Ministry of Information, 1978–; member of the World Affairs Council, of the National Higher Committee of the Jerash Festival; *Decorations:* Order of the Jordanian Star, 1972; *Address:* Ministry of Information, P O Box 1854, Amman, Jordan; telephone: 41467, 21875.

SALAHIDDIN, Muhammad, Saudi Arabian journalist/publisher; born 27 December 1934, Saudi Arabia; married; *Religion:* Muslim; *Education:* MA in Political Science, Michigan University, Ann Arbor, USA; *Career:* Sub-Editor, *Al-Nadwa* daily newspaper, 1959–63; Manager of Libraries Department, Ministry of Pilgrimage and Endowments, 1963–64; Executive Editor, *Al-Madina* newspaper, 1964–65; Publisher and Editor, *Saudi Review* daily bulletin in English, 1966–; Managing Director, Marwah Advertising, Marketing and Public Relations; Political Commentator, *Al-Madina* newspaper; *Languages:* Arabic, English; *Address:* Saudi Review, P O Box 4288, Jeddah, Saudi Arabia; telephone: 57908, 676100, 693500.

SALAM, Malik Salim, Lebanese official/engineer; born 18 February 1917, Safad, Palestine; married; four children; *Religion:* Muslim; *Education:* American University of Beirut (AUB); Diploma in Civil Engineering from Loughborough, UK; *Career:* Chief Engineer, Amman Municipality; Director of Public Works, Jerusalem; established business in the Lebanon; Chairman of Central Committee for Administrative Reform, 1959; Director General of Roads and Buildings, 1960; Chairman of the Executive Council of Constructional Projects, 1970; Chairman of Beirut Water Authority, 1971; Minister of Hydro-electric Resources 1974–75; *Interests and Recreations:* riding, bridge; *Languages:* Arabic, French, English; *Address:* Rue Ibn Ruchd, El Zidania, Beirut, Lebanon.

SALAM, Muhammad Abdul Jabbar, Yemen Arab Republic journalist; born 1942; married; two sons, two daughters; *Religion:* Muslim; *Education:* Diploma in Journalism, Cairo, Egypt, 1963; Diploma in Literature and Linguistic Studies, Institute of Higher Studies, Cairo, Egypt, 1969; *Career:* Director General of Public Relations, 1963–64; Editor of *Al-Hadef* monthly, 1966–69, *Al-Kalima* monthly, 1971–75, *Al-Khadra* weekly, 1974–75; Director General of Sabaa Organization for Press and News; *Interests and Recreations:* reading and writing short stories criticism in Arabic, football; *Languages:* Arabic, English; *Address:* Southern Airport Street, Al-Safia, Sana'a, Yemen Arab Republic.

SALAMA, Albert Barsum, Egyptian lawyer/politician; born 1905, Alexandria, Egypt; *Religion:* Christian, *Education:* law, 1926; *Career:* lawyer; appointed to the newly-constituted People's Assembly, 1971, where later represented Coptic interests; served as member of Assembly's Standing Committee and on the fact-finding Commissions of 1972 and 1973; Minister of State for People's

Assembly Affairs, 1973–75; Minister of State, Cabinet Affairs, Follow-up and Control, 1976; *Languages:* Arabic, English; *Address:* Ministry of Cabinet Affairs, Cairo, Egypt.

SALAMAH, Wadi Sulaiman, Jordanian businessman/lawyer; born 4 January 1905, Jerusalem, Palestine; married; two sons, one daughter; *Education:* Diploma, American University of Beirut, 1926–28; Diploma of the Council of Legal Studies, Jerusalem, Palestine, 1933; *Career:* various posts in teaching; Secretary, Chief Justice of Palestine, 1937–42; Magistrate and Registrar, District Court of Jaffa, 1943–46; Judge, District and Land Court, Jaffa, member of the Criminal Assize Court, 1947–48; lived in Jordan, 1948–; Deputy Manager, Arab Airways Company Ltd, Amman, Jordan, 1949–52; Manager, Arab Airways Jerusalem, associated company of BOAC, 1952–58; Manager, Arabia Insurance Company, Jordan, 1961–78; member of the Tourist Advisory Board, Jerusalem; retired 1978; *Publications:* assisted in the compilation and the editing of *Law Reports of Palestine; Interests and Recreations:* Secretary of the Baden Powell Boy Scout Association of Palestine, 1922–26; member of the YMCA, Jerusalem, Goethe Institute, Amman, Orthodox Club, Amman; *Languages:* Arabic, English, German; *Address:* P O Box 5068, Amman, Jordan; telephone: 43016.

SALAMEH, Shukri S., Jordanian UN official; born 25 June 1915, Jerusalem; married; two daughters; *Religion:* Christian; *Education:* Political Science, American University of Beirut, Lebanon; Certificate and Diploma, Jerusalem Law College; Diploma in American Law, La Salle Extension University, USA; *Career:* Assistant Government Advocate, Palestine Government, 1939–41; Attorney at Law, Jaffa, Palestine, 1941–48; Arabic and English translator/interpreter, UN Mission in Libya, 1950–56; Human Rights Officer, UN Secretariat, 1956–62; Personnel Officer, UN Office of Personnel (OPS), 1962–66; Deputy Chief, Staff Services, UN OPS, 1964–66; Chief of Rules and Procedures Section, UN OPS, 1966–70; Chief of Staff Services, UN OPS, 1970–75; Director, Division of Personnel Administration, UN Secretariat, 1975; has served on a number of community associations and as Secretary of

UN School Board of Trustees; *Interests and Recreations:* tennis, fishing; member of Arab-American University Graduates Association; former President of UN Arab Club; former member of Palestine Bar Association and Jordan Bar Association; *Languages:* Arabic, English; *Address:* Office — Staff Services, OPS, UN, United Nations Plaza, New York, NY 10017, USA; telephone: 754 1234.

SALAMI, Ali Ahmad Nasir, People's Democratic Republic of Yemen diplomat/official; born 1933, People's Democratic Republic of Yemen; *Career:* entered teaching profession; active in politics and former member of the National Liberation Front (NLF) with Qahtan al-Shaabi; fostered union between Front for the Liberation of South Yemen (FLOSY) and NLF 1966; following Independence 1967 worked in Ministry of Education; Ambassador to Libya; *Address:* Ministry of Foreign Affairs, Aden, People's Democratic Republic of Yemen.

SALAWI, Gabriel Emile, Lebanese banker; resident in France; born 8 October 1929, Haifa; married; one son, one daughter; *Religion:* Christian; *Education:* BA in Economics, Cairo University, Cairo, Egypt; New York Institute of Finance, USA; *Career:* Assistant Manager, National Bank of Kuwait, 1953–62; Manager, Merrill Lynch, Beirut, Lebanon, 1962–64; Senior Vice President, Union Bank of Switzerland, Beirut, 1964–81, and Adviser to the Union Bank of Switzerland, Paris and Zurich, 1981–; Director, Banque Arabe et Internationale d'Investissement (BAII) Middle East, Bahrain; *Interests and Recreations:* tennis, swimming, skiing; *Languages:* English, French, German, Italian, Arabic; *Address:* 14 Rue Des Sablons, 75016, Paris, France; telephone: Office — 260 3401; Residence — 553 1122; 45 Bahnhofstr 8021, Zurich, Switzerland; 1001, Starco South, Beirut, Lebanon.

SALEEM, Salim A.K., Iraqi UN official; born 29 August 1925, Mosul, Iraq; married; *Education:* BA in Political Science, American University of Beirut, Lebanon, 1945–48; University of Cincinnati, Ohio, USA, 1949–51; PhD in Political Science, University of Southern California, Los Angeles, USA, 1952–58; *Career:* Diplomat, Ministry of Foreign Affairs; Director, Ministry of In-

formation; Director, Office of Public Information, UN, Lebanon; Director, United Nations Information Centre (UNIC), Beirut; *Interests and Recreations:* political affairs; *Languages:* Arabic, English; *Address:* UNIC, Ardati Street, Ras Beirut, Lebanon; telephone: 34610.

SALEH, Abdul Jawad, Palestinian politician; born 1932 in Al-Bireh, Ramallah; married; four children; *Education:* graduated in Economics, American University in Cairo, 1955; *Career:* teacher in Libya; returned to West Bank and established his own contracting business, 1965; elected mayor of Al-Bireh, 1967, and returned with large majority in 1972 municipal elections; deported to Jordan by the Israelis, 1973; member of the Palestine National Front (PNF); member of Palestinian Liberation Organisation (PLO), Occupied Homeland Affairs Department; member of Palestine Liberation Organization (PLO) Executive Committee, 1974; Deputy Head of the Occupied Homeland Department, 1974–; in charge of the Executive Office for Home Affairs.

SALEH, Anis Elie, Lebanese lawyer; born 12 August 1904, Mount Lebanon, Lebanon; married; three children; *Education:* BA, St. Joseph University, Beirut, Lebanon, 1925; Licentiate in Law, French Faculty of Law, 1928; *Career:* provincial magistrate with Government, 1928; magistrate, French Courts, Beirut, Lebanon, 1929–37; Assistant Inspector General of all courts in Beirut and Province, 1937–45; Director General, Ministry of Justice, 1946–50; Director General, Ministry of Interior and Juridical Counsellor to President of the Republic, 1951; lawyer at Court, Anis Saleh office, 1952–; Consulting Attorney, Kidder Peabody Limited, Lebanon and North America; Consulting Attorney, Van Lines Inc; Consulting Attorney, Chase Manhattan Bank; Consulting Attorney, Continental Bank of Chicago; Director of Courses, Faculty of Law, Beirut; Director of Courses for Forensic Medicine, Faculty of Medicine, 1951–55; *Decorations:* Officer, Order of Cedar of Lebanon; Medal of Lebanese Merit; Medal of Syrian Merit, 1st Class; Commander, Order of Cedar, Lebanon; Officer, Légion d'Honneur, France; *Address:* Residence — Immeuble Saleh, Rue du Liban, Beirut, Lebanon.

SALEH, Muhammad Musaad al-, Kuwaiti journalist/lawyer; born 1933, Kuwait; married; *Religion:* Muslim; *Education:* Cairo University, Egypt; *Career:* lawyer; Chairman, *Al-Hadaf* weekly magazine; journalist, *Al-Watan* daily newspaper; formerly President of the Kuwait Journalists Association and of the Kuwait Lawyers Association; *Interests and Recreations:* reading, press and parliamentary affairs; *Languages:* Arabic, English; *Address:* Dar al-Watan, P O Box 1142, Safat, Kuwait; telephone: 448211/4.

SALEM, A. Philip, Lebanese physician/academic and researcher; born 1941, Bterrem al-Koura, Lebanon; married; *Religion:* Christian; *Education:* BSc, American University of Beirut, 1961; MD, AUB, 1965; *Career:* Intern, American University Hospital, Beirut, 1964–65; Junior Assistant Resident, Department of Internal Medicine, American University Hospital, Beirut, 1965–66; Senior Assistant Resident, Department of Medicine, American University Hospital, Beirut, 1966–67; Resident, Department of Internal Medicine, American University Hospital, Beirut, 1967–68; Research Fellow, Medical Oncology, Memorial Sloan-Kettering Cancer Center, New York, 1968–70; Research Fellow, Medical Oncology, M.D. Anderson Hospital and Tumor Institute, Houston, Texas, 1970; Assistant Professor, American University Medical Center, Beirut, 1971; Director, Cancer Programme, American University Medical Center, 1972; Assistant Professor, M.D. Anderson Hospital and Tumor Institute, Department of Developmental Therapeutics, Houston, Texas, 1976; Assistant Professor, Director, Cancer Programme, American University Medical Center, Beirut, 1977; Associate Professor, American University Medical Center, Beirut, 1978; President, Lebanese Cancer Society; Secretary General, Middle East Union Against Cancer; member of the Lebanese Association of Public Health, Development Studies Association, American Association for Cancer Research, American Society of Clinical Oncology, World Health Organization Expert Committee on Cancer, WHO Committee on Mediterranean Abdominal Lymphoma International Research Project, International Scientific Advisory Committee of the Fourth International Symposium on the Prevention and Detection of Cancer, UICC International Faculty for Postgraduate Courses on Clinical Cancer Chemotherapy, Eastern Cooperative Oncology Group (ECOG), the European Organisation for Research and Treatment of Cancer (EORTC), Development Studies Association, Beirut; *Publications:* author and co-author of numerous research papers and conference abstracts in *Journal of the American Geriatrics Society, Cancer Bulletin, American Association for Cancer Research, Lebanese Medical Journal, American Review of Respiratory Diseases,* and other journals; *Interests and Recreations:* reading, travelling; *Languages:* Arabic, English; *Address:* American University Hospital of Beirut, P O Box 113–6044, Beirut, Lebanon; telephone: 340460 ext 38741, 345400.

SALIBA, Jacob Said, Arab-American businessman; born 10 June 1913, East Broughton, Quebec, Canada; married; one daughter, two sons; *Education:* BSc, Boston University, USA, 1941; *Career:* Senior Supervising Engineer, Thompson and Lichtner Co, Boston, 1944–49; President, Kingston Dress Co, Boston, 1949–51; President, Industrial and Management Associates Inc, Boston, 1951–54; President, Director Maine Dress Co, Cornish Maine, 1948–61; Executive Vice President, and member of the Executive Committee, Cortland Corp Inc, (former Brockway Motor Co Inc), New York City, 1954–59; Director and Executive Vice President, Sawyer Tower Inc, Boston, 1955–56; President, Sawyer Tower Inc, 1956–59, Director, 1955–60; Vice President, Farrington Manufacturing Co, Executive Vice President, Farrington Packing Corp, Farrington Instruments Corp, 1959–61; President, North East Industries Inc 1961; President, Fanny Farmer Candy Shops, 1963–68; President, Frozen Foods Division, W.R. Grace and Co 1966–68; President, Katy Industries Inc, 1969–, R.E. Bush Universal Inc, Midland Insurance Co; Special Consultant, Air Material Command, USAF, Drayton, Ohio, 1942–43; consignment to Chief Air Staff, USAF, 1952–54; Company Chairman, Air Force Spare Study Group, 1953; Trustee, Boston University; member, Corporation Massachusetts General Hospital, Naval Architects and Marine Engineers Methodist Clubs, Union League, New York City, Algonquin, Boston, Bridgton Highlands Country Club, Bridgton, Maine; *Address:* Office — 4368 Prudential Center, Boston, Massachusetts 02199, USA; 151 Rutledge Road, Belmont, Massachusetts 02178, USA.

SALIBA, Most Reverend Metropolitan Philip,
Arab-American ecclesiastic; born 10 June
1931, Abou-Mizan, Lebanon; *Religion:*
Christian; *Education:* Patriarchal Theological Seminary, Balamand, Lebanon; Orthodox
Secondary School, Homs, Syria; scholarships
to Kelham Theological School and University
of London, UK, 1953, Holy Cross Greek
Orthodox Theological School, Brookline,
Massachusetts; BA, Wayne State University,
Detroit, Michigan, USA, 1959; MDiv degree,
St. Vladimir's Orthodox Theological Seminary, Yonkers, New York, 1965; *Career:*
ordained to the Diaconate, 1949; Secretary to
Alexander III of Antioch; teacher of Arabic
Language and Literature and Student Adviser at Balamand Theological School, 1952;
ordained to the Holy Priesthood, 1 March
1959; Pastor of St. George Parish, Cleveland,
Ohio, USA, 1966; nominated to succeed the
late Metropolitan Antony; elevated to the
rank of Archimandrite, 1966, and consecrated to the Episcopate by Patriarch Theodosios
VI to serve as Metropolitan of the Archdiocese of New York and all North America,
1966; *Publications:* articles in Arabic and
English; *Decorations:* Commander's Badge of
the Lebanese Order of the Cedar, 1968;
Order of the Civil Merit of the Syrian Arab
Republic 1st Class, 1970; Medal of the
Highest Merit from the Syrian Government,
1974, The Order of the Bush Unburned from
the Church of Mount Sinai, 1966; *Languages:* English, Arabic, Greek, French; *Address:* 358 Mountain Road, Englewood, New
Jersey, NJ 07631, USA; telephone: (201)
871 1355.

SALIBI, George, Lebanese official/
educationalist; born 1925, Souk el-Gharb,
Lebanon; *Education:* St. Joseph University,
Beirut; American University of Beirut; PhD
in Philosophy, University of Chicago, USA;
Career: Inspector of Primary Education, then
of Secondary Education; Head, Secondary
Education Department; Director of Primary
Education, 1959–; Director of Compensation
Fund for Teachers in Private Schools;
Rapporteur of the Commission on Degree
Equivalents; Director General of the Disciplinary Council, 1967–; Co-chairman of the
Civil Service Commission; *Interests and
Recreations:* reading, education and psychology, tennis; *Languages:* Arabic, French,
English; *Address:* Latif Khoury Building,
Talaat al-Akkawi, Beirut, Lebanon.

SALIBI, Kamal, Lebanese academic/
historian; born 1929; *Education:* BA, American University of Beirut; PhD in History,
London University, London, UK, 1953;
Career: Professor of Lebanese History and
Medieval Near East, Department of History,
American University of Beirut, 1953–; *Publications: The Maronite Historians of
Medieval Lebanon* (revised PhD thesis in
collaboration with Bernard Lewis), 1959; *The
Modern History of Lebanon; Crossroads to
Civil Wars: Lebanon 1958–76; Syria Under
Islam; A History of Arabia* ; numerous
articles and research papers published in
various journals and magazines; *Languages:*
Arabic, English, French; *Address:* Department of History, American University of
Beirut, P O Box 11–0236, Beirut, Lebanon;
telephone: 804487.

SALIH, Abu Bakr Osman Muhammad,
Sudanese diplomat; born 1930, Wadi Halfa,
Sudan; married; three sons; *Religion:* Muslim; *Education:* Faculty of Arts, Khartoum
University, Sudan, 1955; *Career:* secondary
schoolmaster, 1955; 3rd Secretary, Ministry
of Foreign Affairs, 1956; 2nd Secretary,
Political Section, 1958; Secretary, 1963;
Counsellor, 1964; Minister Plenipotentiary,
1965; Ambassador, 1966; Secretary General
of the Presidency (Ministerial Rank), 1972;
Ambassador, 1973; Ambassador to France,
Switzerland and Holy See; *Publications:*
several articles in Arab and Sudanese Press;
Co-editor of *Socialist Magazine* 1972–73;
Decorations: Star Decoration, Romania; *Interests and Recreations:* chess, reading
novels, music; *Languages:* Arabic, English;
Address: 83 avenue Henri Martin, 75016
Paris, France; telephone: 514 5832.

SALIH, Awadallah S. Muhammad, Sudanese
judge/religious leader; born 1912, Omdurman, Sudan; married; seven sons; *Religion:*
Muslim; *Education:* Shari'a Law, Gordon
Memorial College, Khartoum, 1931; *Career:*
Legal Assistant, 1931; Judge, Second Grade,
1940; Judge, First Grade, 1953; Judge in the
Court of Appeal, 1959; Mufti of Sudan,
1963; retired in 1979; Head of the Islamic
Activities Revival Committee; member of the
League of Islamic World, Legal Control
Committee of Faisal Islamic Bank; *Decorations:* Order of Al-Nilayn, Sudan; *Languages:* Arabic, English; *Address:* Islamic
Activities Revival Committee, P O Box 320,
Omdurman, Sudan.

SALIH, Galobawi Muhammad, Sudanese UN official/public administration expert; born 1 January 1932, Northern Province, Sudan; married; *Religion:* Muslim; *Education:* BA in Economics; Diploma in Public Law and Administration, University of Khartoum, Sudan, 1952–57; MPA, New York University, USA, 1961–62; UN Fellowship for studies in USA, UK, Egypt, 1961–62; UN Fellowship, for studies in Africa and Europe, 1964–66; *Career:* various posts with municipal councils in Sudan, 1956–60; Executive Officer, Abu Hagar Rural Council, Blue Nile Province, Sudan, 1960–61; Head, Local Government Section, Institute of Public Administration, Sudan, 1960–65; Director, Institute of Public Administration, Khartoum, Sudan, 1965–70; Chief, Local Government Section, UN Public Administration Division, 1970–73; Chief, Section for Personnel Administration and Training, UN Division of Public Administration and Finance, 1973–77; Dean, Sudanese Public Service, Under Secretary, Ministry of Public Service and Administrative Reforms, Khartoum, Sudan, 1977–78; Director General, African Training and Research Centre in Administration for Development, Tangiers, Morocco, 1978–80, Institute of Public Administration, Riyadh, Saudi Arabia, 1981–; member of Middle East Institute, Washington D.C., USA, African Association of Public Administration and Management, Dar es Salaam, Tanzania; *Publications:* numerous books in fields of administration, development, organisational studies; *Interests and Recreations:* photography, African tribal folklore; *Languages:* Arabic, English, French; *Address:* Institute of Public Administration , P O Box 205, Riyadh, Saudi Arabia; telephone: 464 5991; telex: 201160.

SALIH, Hani Abdul Rahman, Jordanian academic; born 14 April 1937, Al-Lid; married; four sons; *Religion:* Muslim; *Education:* BA in Literature, Cairo University, Egypt; MA and PhD in Education Sciences, Tennessee University, USA, 1964–66; *Career:* Lecturer, Jordan University, Amman, 1966; Associate Professor, 1970; Professor, 1975; Dean of the College of Education, Jordan University, 1980; *Publications: The Philosophy of Education,* in Arabic, 1967; *Towards an Islamic Formulation of Curriculum Development; Curriculum Management,* 1980 and 1981, and other works; *Interests and Recreations:* swimming,

walking, reading; member of the Jordanian Society of Al-Kitab; *Languages:* Arabic, English; *Address:* College of Education, Jordanian University, Amman, Jordan; telephone: Office — 843555; Residence — 843048.

SALIH, Salih Muhammad, Sudanese banker/agricultural engineer; born Sudan; *Religion:* Muslim; *Career:* Municipal Engineer, Government service, 1942; Agricultural Engineer, 1943–45; Chief Surveyor, 1945–51; Field Inspector, Sudan Gezira Board, 1951–55; Group Inspector, 1955–56; Assistant General Manager, 1956–62; General Manager, 1962–64; Managing Director, Sudan Agricultural Bank, 1965; *Address:* Office — Sudan Agricultural Bank, P O Box 1363, Khartoum, Sudan.

SALIH, Tayib al-, Sudanese writer; born 1929, Sudan; *Education:* Khartoum University; Exeter University, UK; *Career:* twelve years in charge of Drama Department, BBC Arabic Section; Technical Adviser to Sudan Broadcasting Service, Khartoum; Director of Information, Qatar; *Publications:* include volumes of short stories and novel *The Season of Migration to the North* (translated into English); *Address:* Ministry of Information, P O Box 1836, Doha, Qatar.

SALIM, Ahmad, Egyptian Arab League official; born 24 October 1920, Alexandria, Egypt; *Religion:* Muslim; *Education:* Degree in French Literature, University of Alexandria, Egypt, 1945; Diploma in Civilization and Philology, 1952–54; Diploma in Tourist Studies, Cairo, 1963; *Career:* Professor of French, University of Alexandria; Cultural Attaché, Egyptian Embassy to Switzerland, 1960; Co-Chairman, Misr Travel and Shipping, Cairo; Tourist Counsellor, Egyptian Embassy to France, 1967–72; Director of the Arab League Office in Paris, 1975–; member of the Board of Association Mondiale pour la Formation Professionelle Touristique (AMFORT); *Interests and Recreations:* music, painting, reading, tennis; *Languages:* Arabic, French, English, some Italian; *Address:* 138 Boulevard Haussmann, Paris 8è, France.

SALIM, Air Commodore Hassan, Egyptian aviation official; born 23 June 1928, Alexandria, Egypt; married; *Education:* Flying Academy, Cairo, 1952; Management Course,

Ireland, 1972; *Career:* Egyptian Air Force and Civil Service, 1958–74; General Manager of Aeronautics for Operations and Air Transport, Civil Aviation Organization, Cairo, 1972–73; General Manager of Operations, member of the Board of Executives, Egyptair, 1973–74; Adviser to the Chairman of Egyptair; Representative of Egypt, International Civil Aviation Organization (ICAO) Council, Canada, 1974–; *Languages:* Arabic, English; *Address:* Office — ICAO Council, 1080 University Street, Montreal H3B 3A5, PQ, Canada; telephone: (514) 866 2551; Residence -- 431 Gezira Wosta, Zamalek, Cairo, Egypt.

SALIM, Hussain, Egyptian businessman; resident in United Arab Emirates; born 11 November 1933, Cairo, Egypt; married; one son, one daughter; *Religion:* Muslim; *Education:* BSc in Commerce, Cairo University, Egypt; *Career:* Director of Economic Research in the Spinning Support Fund, Cairo, Egypt; Director of General Administration of Spinning and Textiles, Arab Foreign Trading Company, Cairo, Egypt; Director General of the Egyptian Products Commercial Centre, Casablanca, Morocco; Director General of the Egyptian Products Commercial Centre, Baghdad, Iraq; Director General and member of the Board of Directors of the Arab Foreign Trading Company; Director General of the United Arab Emirates (UAE) Trading Company; *Interests and Recreations:* swimming, squash, cycling; member of the Tourism Club; member of the Sporting Club and Automobile Club, Cairo, Egypt; *Languages:* Arabic, English, French; *Address:* United Arab Emirates Trading Company, P O Box 4171, Abu Dhabi, United Arab Emirates; telephone 43830.

SALIM, Khalid, Jordanian banker/official; born 1921, Al-Husn, Jordan; married; two sons, four daughters; *Religion:* Christian; *Education:* BA in Mathematics, American University of Beirut, Beirut, Lebanon, 1941; Diploma of Education, Institute of Education, University of London, UK, 1950; PhD in Educational Administration, Columbia University, USA, 1960; *Career:* teacher, secondary school, 1941–49; Inspector of Education, 1950–56; Assistant Under Secretary of Education, 1956–62; Minister of Social Welfare and Minister of State for Prime Ministerial Affairs, 1962; Minister of National Economy and Minister of State for

Prime Ministerial Affairs, 1962–63; Governor of the Central Bank of Jordan, 1963–73; President of the National Planning Council, 1973–74; Ambassador to France and Permanent Delegate to the UNESCO, 1975–78; non-resident Ambassador to Belgium and EEC, 1975–78; Member of Executive Board of UNESCO, 1976–80; Member of the National Consultative Council; Chairman of the Board of Arab Finance Corporation, Jordan, 1979; Secretary General and member of the Arab Thought Forum, 1980–; member of the Jordanian National Commission for UNESCO, 1951–62; member of the Jordanian Scientific Association, 1956–60; member of the Board of the Arab Scientific Union, 1957–59; President of the Authority of Tourism and Antiquity, 1962–63; Governor of IMF,IBRD, 1963–74; member of the Board of Trustees of the Jordan University, 1963–76; Deputy Chairman of the Royal Scientific Society, 1970–73; Chairman of the Public Insurance Corporation, 1971–73; Chairman of the Institute of Banking Studies, 1971–73; Deputy Chairman of ALIA, 1971–74; Associate Member of the Committee of Twenty, 1972–74; member of the National Committee for Population, 1973–74; Associate member of the Development Committee (IBRD), 1974; member of the Higher Education Council, 1979–; member of the Royal Commission for Mu'ta University, 1980–; *Publications: Reorganisation of Educational Administration in Jordan,* 1960; author of several textbooks in mathematics; numerous articles on mathematics, popular science, education, economics and banking; *Decorations:* Order of Renaissance (al-Nahdah), 1956; Order of Independence, Jordan, 1958; Order of the Jordanian Star, 1962; Order of Renaissance, 1974; Grand Officier de l'Ordre de la Couronne, Belgium, 1978; Grand Officier de l'Ordre National du Mérite, France 1981; and several other foreign decorations; *Interests and Recreations:* reading, writing, bridge; *Languages:* Arabic, English, French; *Address:* Arab Finance Corporation, P O Box 35104, Amman, Jordan; telephone: Residence — 43921; Office — 66148, 66149; telex: 21875.

SALIM, Mamduh Muhammad, Egyptian politician; born 1918; *Religion:* Muslim; *Education:* Egypt and at the Metropolitan Police College, UK; *Career:* police work; promoted to Chief of the Investigation Branch at Alexandria with the rank of General; for a time was responsible for the personal security of President Nassir; Police Commander, Alexandria, 1964–67; Governor of Assiut, 1967; Governor of Gharbiyah, 1970; Governor of Alexandria, 1970–71; Minister of the Interior, 1971; member of the Arab Socialist Union Central Committee, 1971; Deputy Prime Minister, and Minister of the Interior, 1972–75; Deputy Military Governor General, 1973; Prime Minister, 1975–77; Prime Minister and Minister of the Interior, 1977; *Address:* Office of the Prime Minister, Cairo, Egypt.

SALIM, Sami Ali, Egyptian businessman; born 30 August 1937, Cairo, Egypt; married; three daughters; *Religion:* Muslim: *Education:* BA in Commerce; Management and Industrial Studies; *Career:* Manager, Chemical Industries Company, 1960–69; Commercial and Technical Consultant, T. Maneklal Company, India, 1960–69; Swastic Textile Trading and Manufacturing Company, Bombay, India, 1960–69; owner, Middle East Chemical Manufacturing Company; Area Manager, ARTOS Company, West Germany; Local Area Agent, Crossroll Company, Halifax, UK; *Interests and Recreations:* hunting, water-skiing, music; *Languages:* Arabic, English, French, German; *Address:* P O Box 510, Cairo, Egypt; Telex: 2502 UN.

SALLAM, Muhammad Abdul Aziz, Yemen Arab Republic official/diplomat; born 1933 , Taiz, Yemen Arab Republic; married; three sons; *Religion:* Muslim; *Education:* in Egypt; BSc in Biology, Temple University, Philadelphia, USA, 1954–58; Graduate School, Temple University, 1958–59; MA in Political Science, Graduate School, University of California, 1959–60; *Career:* Director of the German Trade Office, Sana'a, 1960–61; Teacher, Balquis College, Aden, 1961–62; Director, Ministry of Public Health, 1962–63; Minister and Chargé d'Affaires, Yemen Embassy, Baghdad, 1963–64; Deputy Foreign Minister, 1964–65; Chairman of the Board of Directors, Yemen Drug Company, 1965–66; Minister of Foreign Affairs, 1966–67; Director of the Office of the Prime Minister, 1970–71; Ambassador, Head of the International Department, and UN Affairs, Ministry of Foreign Affairs, 1971–72; Minister, Embassy to UK with the rank of Ambassador, 1972–74; Deputy Permanent Representative to UN, New York, 1975–76;

Permanent Representative to UN, 1976–77; Chief of Cabinet for Technical Affairs, Prime Minister's Office, 1978–; member of the Development Committee, Council of Ministers; *Languages:* Arabic, English; *Address:* 78 Hadda Road, P O Box 2661 Sana'a, Yemen Arab Republic; telephone: Residence — 74509, Office — 74509, 73091/3.

SALLOUM, Hamad Ibrahim al-, Saudi Arabian official/educationalist; born 1937, Saudi Arabia; *Religion:* Muslim; *Education:* BA, 1960; MS, 1970; PhD, 1974; *Career:* various teaching posts; Director, Teachers Training Institute, 1961–64; Principal, Secondary School, 1965–69; Director of Education, Riyadh Zone; Assistant Deputy Minister, Students Affairs, Ministry of Education, 1981; Visiting Professor, Faculty of Education, University of Riyadh, Riyadh, Saudi Arabia; member of Preliminary Committee of Higher Saudi Arabian Council for Educational Policy; President of the Executive Council of the Arab League Educational, Scientific and Cultural Organisation; member of the Board of Education Research Centre, College of Education, Riyadh University; attended several conferences in field of education and role of university; *Interests and Recreations:* reading, travel, sports; *Languages:* Arabic, English; *Address:* P O Box 1922, Riyadh, Saudi Arabia; telephone: 4024197.

SALLOUM, Nassir Muhammad, Saudi Arabian official/engineer; born 4 November, 1936, Medina, Saudi Arabia; *Religion:* Muslim; *Education:* BSc, MSc, PhD in Civil Engineering; *Career:* resident engineer, Ministry of Communications, 1965; Head of Study Department, Ministry of Communications, 1965–68; various other posts in the Ministry of Communications, Deputy Minister, 1976–; member of the American Society of Civil Engineers; member of the Board of Saudi Arabian Railways Authority; *Interests and Recreations:* reading, travel; *Languages:* Arabic, English; *Address:* Ministry of Communications, Airport Road, Riyadh, Saudi Arabia; telephone: 404 2928 ext 113/165; telex: 201616 HI-WAY SJ.

SALMAN BIN ABDUL AZIZ, HRH Prince, Saudi Arabian Prince/politician; born 1926; son of late King Abdul Aziz and Hassa Bint Sudairi; *Religion:* Muslim; *Education:* Court education at the hands of great Ulamas;

private tuition in different fields of education; *Career:* Governor of Riyadh, 1962–; Chairman of several charity projects and societies; Chairman of the Supreme Committee for the Planning of the City of Riyadh; *Interests and Recreations:* falconry, reading; *Address:* Riyadh Governorate, Riyadh, Saudi Arabia.

SALMAN, Said Abdullah, United Arab Emirates politician/diplomat; born 1945, Ras al-Khaimah, United Arab Emirates; *Religion:* Muslim; *Education:* BA, Al-Azhar University, Cairo; DEA, Faculty of Law, Sorbonne, Paris; preparing for Doctorat d'Etat, Sorbonne, Paris; *Career:* Minister of Housing, later Minister of Housing and Public works, 1973–77; Ambassador of UAE to Paris, 1977–79; Minister of Education and Youth, Abu Dhabi 1979–; member of Executive Board of UNESCO; *Address:* Ministry of Education and Youth, P O Box 295, Abu Dhabi, United Arab Emirates; telephone: 342408; telex: 22581 TARBIA EM.

SALMAN, Salah, Lebanese politician/physician; born 1936, Beirut, Lebanon; *Education:* graduated from Medical School, American University of Beirut, Lebanon, 1961; *Career:* specialist in ear, nose and throat diseases, Johns Hopkins University, USA; Professor of American University of Beirut Medical School; Minister of Health, 1972–73; Founder-President of League of Young Druze Intellectuals for Social Action; Minister of Interior and of Housing and Co-operatives in Selim al-Hoss Cabinet, 1976; *Publications:* papers in international and local medical journals on ear, nose and throat diseases; *Decorations:* Penrose Award, Faculty of Medical Sciences, 1961; *Languages:* Arabic, English; *Address:* Ministry of Interior, Beirut, Lebanon; Residence — Najjar Building, Lyon Street, Beirut, Lebanon.

SALMAN, Shaikh Salman al-Duaij al-, Kuwaiti politician; born 1939; *Religion:* Muslim; *Education:* in Cairo, Egypt and USA; *Career:* Minister of State for Legal and Administrative Affairs, 1976; Minister of Justice, 1978–; *Address:* P O Box 6, Safat, Kuwait; telephone: 432510.

SALMAWY, Muhammad, Egyptian journalist; born 26 May 1945, Cairo Egypt; married; one son, one daughter; *Religion:* Muslim;

Education: BA in English Literature, Cairo University, Cairo, Egypt; MA in Mass Communications, American University in Cairo, Cairo, Egypt; Diplomas in Drama and Modern English Literature, Oxford and Birmingham Universities; *Career:* Lecturer, Cairo University, 1966–70; Freelance editor and radio announcer, radio Cairo, 1963–75; Editor, Foreign Desk, *Al-Ahram* newspaper, Cairo, 1970–77; Expert, Board of Al-Ahram Centre for Political and Strategic Studies, 1977–79; Foreign Editor, *Al-Ahram* newspaper, Cairo, 1979–; imprisoned for political activity, 1977; member of Egyptian Press Syndicate, Cairo, the Union of Arab Journalists, Alumni of Salzburg Seminar in American Studies, Salzburg; *Publications: The Foreign Editor,* 1976; *Origins of British Socialism,* 1978; short stories and plays published in various periodicals and dailies in Egypt; numerous articles on political and social affairs, literary criticism in the local press; *Interests and Recreations:* music, plastic arts, cinema, riding, swimming, photography; member of Gezira Sporting Club, Maadi Sporting and Yacht Club, the Old Victorian Association, London; *Languages:* Arabic, English, French; *Address:* 9 Road 216, Maadi, Cairo, Egypt; telephone: 635146.

SALTI, Amir O. al-, Jordanian banker; born 22 December 1939, Amman, Jordan; married; two daughters; *Religion:* Muslim; *Education:* BA, MBA, PhD; *Career:* Assistant General Manager, Arab Development Society, 1973; Assistant Manager for Finance, Citibank, 1976–; Chairman of Department, Jordan Livestock and Poultry Company; member of the Board of Arab International Insurance Company, of Intermediate Petrochemical Industry; *Interests and Recreations:* tennis; member of the Rotary Club; *Languages:* Arabic, English, French; *Address:* Arab Jordan Investment Bank, P O Box 8797, Amman, Jordan; telephone: 668 629.

SALTI, Sami, Jordanian businessman; born 1926, Jerusalem; married; two sons, one daughter; *Religion:* Christian; *Education:* BA in Business Administration; *Career:* Managing Director of J. Salti & Sons Company (steel suppliers), 1950–; Honorary Consul General for Austria in Jordan, 1965; *Decorations:* Croix d'Officier (Grosses Ehrenzeichen) from the President of the Austrian Republic, 1972; *Interests and Rec-*

reations: tennis, swimming; *Languages:* Arabic, English, Hebrew; *Address:* P O Box 832, Amman, Jordan; telephone: 25495.

SAMI, Abdul Aziz Mahmud, Egyptian physician/academic; born 3 September 1910 Cairo, Egypt; married; one daughter; *Education:* MB, ChB, University of Cairo, Cairo, Egypt, 1936; MD, Cairo University, 1937; *Career:* Lecturer, Cairo Medical School, Cairo University, Egypt, 1937–45; Assistant Professor of Medicine, Cairo University, 1945–51; Professor, Pulmonary Diseases Department, 1951–; member, Permanent Council for National Services, 1953–55; Vice President, National Anti-Tuberculosis Association, 1956–; Dean, Medical School, University of Cairo, Egypt, 1963–67; Consultant, World Health Organisation, Expert Committee on Tuberculosis, 1964; Secretary, National Committee on Medical Education, 1965–67, 1969–; Fellow of the Royal College of Physicians, UK; member of the American College of Chest Physicians, USA; *Publications:* numerous articles and papers on chest diseases, in professional journals in Egypt; *Decorations:* Order of the Republic, 1954; State Prize for Science, 1975; Order of Merit, 1977; *Languages:* Arabic, English; *Address:* 25 Bustan Street, Falaki Square, Cairo, Egypt; telephone: 24430.

SAMI, Amin, Egyptian diplomat; born Egypt; *Education:* Licence in Law; *Career:* Egyptian Ministry of Foreign Affairs; Ambassador to Morocco; Ambassador to Mali, 1963–64; Ambassador to Poland; Ambassador to Netherlands, 1976–80; *Address:* Ministry of Foreign Affairs, Cairo, Egypt.

SAMMAN, Ahmad Abdul Aziz al-, Syrian lawyer/academic; born 1904, Damascus, Syria; *Education:* Licentiate, Doctor of Law; PhD in Political Science; Diploma in Criminology, Arabic Institute of Law, University of Paris, France; *Career:* lawyer; Professor, University of Damascus, Syria; Rector, University of Damascus, 1952–58; Minister of National Education, 1961; Dean, Faculty of Law, University of Damascus; *Publications: Precis De Droit; Les Droits Constitutionnels; Précis De La Législation Du Travail; Les Faits Et Les Points De Vues Economiques Dans Les Temps Modernes; Précis D'Economie Politique; L'Economie De La Syrie; Le Régime Monétaire De La Syrie;* La Nation Arabe; L'Economie Des; Pays Arabes; *Languages:* Arabic, French; *Address:* Nejmeh Square, Damascus, Syria.

SAMMAN, Ghada al-, Syrian writer; born 1942, Syria; *Education:* medical studies; later graduated in English Literature, 1961; *Career:* civil servant, journalist and university lecturer; member of group of young women writers, Beirut; *Publications:* three collections of short stories including *La Bahra fi Bairut,* 1963; *As-Suqut ila al Qimma; Languages:* Arabic, English; *Address:* c/o Al Arabi, P O Box 748, Kuwait.

SAMMAN, Qadi Ali al-, Yemen Arab Republic politician; born 1920, Sana'a, Yemen; married; one daughter; *Education:* Islamic Studies, Faculty of Sciences, Sana'a; *Career:* Minister of Justice, 1974; Minister of Justice, 1975; Minister of Waqfs, 1978; Minister of Waqfs, 1981–; *Address:* The Minister's Office, Ministry of Waqfs, Sana'a, Yemen Arab Republic.

SAMRA, Mahmud Dawud, Jordanian academic; born 1924, Palestine; married; one son, two daughters; *Religion:* Muslim; *Education:* BA in Arabic Studies, Faculty of Arts, Cairo University, Egypt, 1950; PhD in Arabic Studies, School of Oriental and African Studies, University of London, UK, 1958; *Career:* Deputy Editor in Chief, *Al-Arabi* magazine, 1958–62; Associate Professor of Literary Criticism, Arabic Department, University of Jordan, Jordan; Professor of Literary Criticism, 1966–; Dean, Faculty of Arts, University of Jordan, 1968–73; Vice President, University of Jordan, 1973–; Vice President of Jordan Academy of Arabic; member of Iraqi Academy of Science; Vice President of the Royal Society of Fine Arts, Jordan; President of the Association of Jordanian Writers; *Publications: Essays in Literary Criticism,* Beirut, 1959; *Contemporary Writers,* 1961, Beirut; *Western Travellers in the Levant,* 1967, Beirut; *The Angry Young Writers,* 1973, Beirut; *The Young Writers,* 1970, Amman; *On Literary Criticism,* 1974, Beirut; *Palestine,* 1974, Beirut, in Arabic; translated several books from English into Arabic; several articles and papers in English and Arabic, published mainly in *Al-Arabi, Middle East Forum; Decorations:* Order of Independence, 1st Class, Jordan, 1973; Reuvon Prize, University of London, 1958; *Interests and Recreations:* comparative literary criticism; contemporary Arabic, European and American literature; *Languages:* Arabic, English, Greek, French, Latin; *Address:* The University of Jordan, P O Box 1682, Amman, Jordan.

SANBAR, Ramzi H., Lebanese engineer/ businessman; born 1938, Haifa, Palestine; *Education:* BA and MA in Civil Engineering; Doctorate in Environmental Studies, Paris, France; *Career:* joined US Bechtel Company, constructing pipeline terminals in Libya; established R.H. Sanbar Consultants, 1970, an engineering consultant company, with branches in Kuwait, Saudi Arabia, Qatar, Sudan, UK, France, Spain, USA, Brazil; *Languages:* Arabic, French, English; *Address:* R.H. Sanbar Consultants (UK) Ltd, 18 Upper Brook Street, London W1Y 1PD, UK; R.H. Sanbar Projects Inc, 540 Madison Avenue, New York, 10022, USA; telephone: 408 2414.

SANOUSSI, Muhammad Nasir al-, Kuwaiti official; born 1938, Kuwait; married; two sons, one daughter; *Religion:* Muslim; *Education:* BA in Mass Communications, USA; Diploma in Broadcasting, USA; Institute of Drama, Cairo, Egypt; Training Courses with ITN and BBC, London, UK, 1962; *Career:* Director General of Television Programmes, Kuwait, 1964; Director General of Kuwait Television, 1972; Assistant Under Secretary for Television Affairs and Cinema, 1973–; Chairman of the Board of Directors of Modern Networks Company; member of the Board of Baalbek Studios, Lebanon; Chairman of the Board of Arab Company for International Production; member of the Board of the Gulf States Organisation for Programme Production; Chairman of Gulf Festival for Television Production and Kuwait Cine Club; *Interests and Recreations:* television and cinema productions; *Languages:* Arabic, English, French; *Address:* P O Box 25795, Kuwait TV, Kuwait City, Kuwait; telephone: 431712, 419584.

SAOUMA, Edouard, Lebanese UN official/ agriculturalist; born 6 November 1926, Beirut, Lebanon; married; one son, two daughters; *Education:* Ingénieur Agronome, School of Engineering, French University, Beirut, Lebanon, 1946–49; *Career:* Director General of Agricultural Research Institute, Beirut, Lebanon; Minister of Agriculture, Fisheries and Forestry, 1970; Director Gener-

al, Food and Agriculture Organisation, FAO, Asia and Far East Regional Office, New Delhi, 1962–65; Director, Land and Water Development Division, Agricultural Department, FAO, Rome, Italy, 1969–75; elected Director General of FAO, 1976–; *Publications:* various articles and reports on world agricultural problems; *Decorations:* Grand Croix of the National Order of the Cedar, Lebanon; Said Akl Prize, Lebanon; Mérite Agricole, France; Grand Croix de l'Ordre National du Tchad; Grand Croix de l'Ordre National du Ghana; Grand Croix de l'Ordre National de la Haute Volta; awards from Accademico Corrispondente dell' Accademia Nazionale di Agricoltura, Italy; Honorary Doctorates from Universities of Peru, Korea, Uruguay, Indonesia, Warsaw, Philippines; *Languages:* Arabic, English, French, Spanish, Italian; *Address:* Food and Agriculture Organisation of the United Nations, Via delle Terme di Caracalla, 00100 Rome, Italy; telephone: 5797; telex: 61181.

SAQUET, Labeebe Hanna, Arab-American writer/musician and teacher; born Boston, USA; married; four sons, one daughter; *Religion:* Christian; *Education:* Voice and Piano, New England Conservatory of Music, Boston, USA; Sorbonne, University of Paris, France; Boston State University, Boston; Pre-engineering Certificate, Northeastern University, Boston; Theater and Music, George Washington University, USA; University of New Mexico, Albuquerque, USA; Dance at Senia Russakof; BEd; MEd; *Career:* teacher of English, Art, Music and French for twenty six years in Boston; Chairman of Grievance Committee of Boston's Teachers Union for seven years; Director of Yankee Players Little Theater for four years; Editor of *The Messenger* and *News Letter* of the American Arab Benevolent Association; member of the Board, and New England Chairman of Maloufs International; Vice President, City of Boston Federation of Organizations; President, City of Boston Federation of Organizations; Financial Director, Massachusetts Society of Poets; *Publications: Evolution of the Theater,* 1967; *I Loved In Lebanon,* translated into Arabic 1979; *Songs of a Maid of Lebanon,* collection of poems; *Decorations:* Boston Terecentenary Decoration for best ethnic production; City of Boston Saquet Day, 6 June 1975; *Interests and Recreations:* dancing, song, piano, soft baseball, basketball, fishing, travelling; *Lang-*

uages: English, Arabic, French; *Address:* 12 Lynn Avenue, Kenberma, Hull, MA 02045, USA; telephone: 925 3755; Residence — 28 Peak Hill Road, West Roxbury, Boston, MA 02131, USA; telephone: 327 7209.

SARKIS, Elias, Lebanese politician/former President; born 18 July, 1924, Chbanieh, Lebanon; *Education:* Law School, University of St. Joseph, Beirut, Lebanon; *Career:* Judge, Auditor's Court, 1953; Legal Adviser, President of the Republic, 1959; Director General, Presidency of the Republic, 1962; Governor, Central Bank of Lebanon, 1968–76; elected President of the Republic of Lebanon, 1976–82; *Decorations:* 1st Class Medal, Jordanian Independence, 1967; *Languages:* Arabic, French, English; *Address:* Our Lady of Lourdes Street, Beirut, Lebanon.

SARKIS, Nicolas, Lebanese economist; born 1935; *Education:* in Germany and France; Doctorat en Sciences Economiques, Sorbonne, University of Paris, France; *Career:* founded Centre for Petroleum Studies, Beirut, 1965; Oil Adviser to oil exporting countries; *Publications:* various articles on oil industry; *Le Pétrole à l'Heure Arabe,* Paris, 1975; *Languages:* Arabic, French; *Address:* The Petroleum Research Centre, 7 Avenue Ingres, 75781 Paris Cédex 16, France.

SARRUF, Fuad, Lebanese academic/writer; born 1900, Hadeth, Lebanon; married; one daughter; *Education:* BA, American University of Beirut, Lebanon 1918; Honorary Doctorate in Law, University of Pacific, California, USA, 1958; *Career:* Lecturer, American University of Beirut, 1918–19; Director, Lebanon Boys School, Souk Al-Gharb, 1919–22; Editor, *Al-Muqtataf,* a monthly magazine, Cairo, Egypt, 1922–44; Public Relations Adviser and Features Editor, *Al-Ahram* newspaper, Cairo, Egypt; Vice President, American University of Beirut, 1952–68; President, American University of Beirut, 1966–74; Editor, American University of Beirut Centennial Publications (24 vols), 1966–69; member of the Baalbek Festival Committee; member of the National Commission to UNESCO, Paris, France; member of the Lebanese National Council for Research; *Publications: Conquest of Modern Science,* 1934; *Pillars of Modern Science,* 1935; *Horizon of Modern Science,* 1939; *Altar of Mars,* 1943; *The Conquest Continues,* 1944; *Eternal Fire,* 1947;

Rendevouz with History, 1951; *En Route,* 1954; *Man's Unconquerable Mind,* 1956; *At the Door,* 1957; *Horizon without Limits,* 1958; *Yacoub Sarruf: a Study,* 1960; *Man and the Universe,* 1961; *In the Frame of the UNESCO,* 1969; and numerous other books and papers; Editor of the Arabic quarterly bulletin of the American University of Beirut, Lebanon; *Decorations:* Gold Medal, Lebanese Order of Merit, 1944; Commander, National Order of the Cedar, 1956; Grand Officer, National Order of the Cedar, 1967; Extraordinary Medal , Syrian Order of Merit, 1956; Order of Independence, First Class, Jordan 1973; Grand Cordon, Order of the Cedar, Lebanon, 1975; Gold Medal of UNESCO, 1974; *Interests and Recreations:* member of the American University of Beirut Alumni Club; Regional Governor, Lion's Club of Lebanon and Jordan; correspondent member of the Cairo and Baghdad Arabic Language Academies; *Languages:* Arabic, English, French; *Address:* Cairo Street, Hamra, Ras Beirut, Lebanon; telephone: 343919.

SARTAWI, Sufyan Ibrahim, Jordanian banker/businessman; born 25 October 1930, Nablus, Jordan; married; two sons, three daughters; *Religion:* Muslim; *Education:* BA in Commerce, University of Cairo, Egypt; *Career:* Accountant, Ministry of Finance, Kuwait; Insurance Supervisor, Ministry of Trade, Kuwait; Director of Companies, Insurance and Financial Documents, Kuwait; member and Director General, Jordanian Kuwaiti Bank, Amman, Jordan; Vice Chairman of the Board and General Manager, Jordanian Kuwaiti Bank; Chairman of the Board, the Arab Company for the Manufacture and Trading of Paper; Vice Chairman of the Board of Orient Industrial Co, dry batteries manufacturers; member of the Board of the Arab International Hotels Co, the Press Co, Eva Bank, the Financial Operations Co, Kuwait, the Board of Development of the Intermediary University College; *Languages:* Arabic, English; *Address:* The Jordanian Kuwaiti Bank, P O Box 9776, Amman, Jordan; telephone: Office — 61165, 62126–9; Residence — 62922.

SASSI, M. Abdul Hamid, Tunisian official/engineer; born August 1934, Gabès, Tunisia; *Religion:* Muslim; *Education:* Civil Engineer of L'Ecole des Ponts et Chaussées, Paris, France; *Career:* Chief Engineer of Le Kef,

1961–62; Chief Engineer of Sousse, 1963–65; Chief Engineer, Ministry of Public Works in charge of Major Projects; Chairman and Managing Director of the Major Projects Organization, 1965–71; Secretary of State at the Ministry of Public Works and Housing, 1971–73; Secretary of State to the Minister of Supply; Minister of Transport and Communications, 1976; *Decorations:* Grand Officer of the Tunisian Order of Independence; *Languages:* Arabic, French; *Address:* Ministry of Transport and Communications, Tunis, Tunisia; telephone: 242400.

SASSINE, Michel, Lebanese politician; born 1928, Beirut, Lebanon; *Religion:* Christian; *Career:* candidate for Parliament, 1960; Deputy in 1968 and 1972; Vice President of the Chamber of Deputies, 1969–70; supporter of Camille Chamoun; Minister of Tourism in Cabinet of Saeb Salam; Minister of Housing in Cabinets of Amin el-Hafez, 1973, and Rashid al-Solh, 1974–75; *Interests and Recreations:* hunting; *Languages:* Arabic, French; *Address:* Immeuble Sassine, Rue Sassine, Beirut, Lebanon.

SATI, Iklil, Jordanian businessman/former diplomat; born 1926, Damascus, Syria; married; *Education:* University of Damascus, Syria; *Career:* Private Secretary to King Abdullah, 1949; Ministry of Foreign Affairs, 1950–61; Deputy Head of Royal Protocol, 1961–63; Head of Royal Protocol, 1964–66; Ambassador to Spain, 1967–70; Secretary General of Ministry of Foreign Affairs, 1970–72; businessman since retirement from Ministry of Foreign Affairs; *Interests and Recreations:* shooting; *Languages:* Arabic, English, French, Italian, Spanish, Turkish; *Address:* P O Box 5139, Amman, Jordan.

SAUD, Abdul Karim, Syrian diplomat; born 1930, Lattakia, Syria; married; two sons, one daughter; *Religion:* Muslim; *Education:* Licence in Law; Diploma in Law, Damascus, Syria; PhD in French Literature, France; *Career:* First Counsellor, Ministry of Planning, 1971–76; Lecturer of French Literature, Damascus University, 1972–75; Economic Counsellor and Lecturer of Political Economy, Damascus University; Minister Counsellor, Embassy of Syria, Cairo, Egypt, 1977; Ambassador of Syria to China, 1978–; *Interests and Recreations:* music, literature, theatre, poetry; *Languages:* Arabic, English, French; *Address:* Embassy of Syria, 6 San Li Tun, Peking, People's Republic of China.
466

SAUD AL-FAISAL, HRH Prince, Saudi Arabian Prince/politician; born 1941; son of late King Faisal; *Religion:* Muslim; *Education:* BA in Economics, Princeton University, USA; *Career:* Deputy Minister of Petroleum and Mineral Wealth, 1971–74; Minister of Foreign Affairs, 1975–; founding member of King Faisal Charity Society; Head of Saudi Arabian delegation to the UN General Assembly, 1976 session; Special Envoy of late King Khalid on several diplomatic and political missions; participated in pan-Arab efforts to end the civil war in Lebanon; member of the Saudi Arabian delegation to Arab summits since 1975; member of the seven-man follow-up committee to the Fes Summit, chaired by HM King Hassan of Morocco, 1980; member of the Saudi delegation accompanying late King Khalid on his state visits to Cairo, Pakistan, Syria and Sudan; accompanied Zaki Yamani, Minister of Petroleum to OPEC talks, 1971; played prominent role in OPEC Participation Conference, Riyadh, 1972; *Interests and Recreations:* reading; *Languages:* Arabic, English; *Address:* Ministry of Foreign Affairs, P O Box 495, Jeddah, Saudi Arabia; telephone: 6423460.

SAUD BIN ABDUL MUHSIN BIN ABDUL AZIZ, HRH Prince, Saudi Arabian Prince/administrator; born 1947; son of HRH Abdul Muhsin Bin Abdul Aziz; *Religion:* Muslim; *Education:* BA in Business Administration; *Career:* Director, Health, Housing and Environment Sectors Department, Central Planning Organization; Director of Co-ordination and Follow-up, Ministry of Health; Deputy Governor of the Holy City of Mecca Province; participated in the establishment of the first company for electric cables; attended the Conference on Health and Environment, Harvard and Johns Hopkins Universities, USA; *Interests and Recreations:* falconry, riding; *Address:* Mecca Province Emirate, Mecca, Saudi Arabia; telephone: Residence — Riyadh 54545.

SAUD BIN ABDULLAH, HRH Prince, Saudi Arabian Prince/army commander; born 1949; son of HRH Prince Abdullah Bin Faisal; married; *Religion:* Muslim; *Education:* Graduate of Sandhurst Military College, UK, 1968; *Career:* Captain of Army Air Defence; *Languages:* Arabic, English; *Address:* Ministry of Defence and Aviation, Riyadh, Saudi Arabia.

SAUD BIN FAHD, HRH Prince, Saudi Arabian Prince/businessman; born 1948; son of HM King Fahd Bin Abdul Aziz; *Religion:* Muslim; *Education:* Degree in Public Administration, USA; *Career:* businessman; *Languages:* Arabic, English; *Address:* Royal Court, Riyadh, Saudi Arabia.

SAUDI, Abdullah Ammar al-, Libyan banker; born 20 March 1937, Tripoli, Libya; married; two sons, three daughters; *Religion:* Muslim; *Education:* Commercial and Accountancy Diploma, 1955; Teachers High Certificate in Commerce, 1957; *Career:* Teacher, Technical and Commercial College, Tripoli, Libya, 1957–58; Central Bank of Libya, Head of Department, Manager, and General Manager, 1958–72; Chairman and General Manager, Libyan Arab Foreign Bank, 1972; Chairman of Libyan Arab Foreign Bank, Banco Arabe Espanol, Madrid, Spain, the Arab Financial Services Company, Abu Dhabi, United Arab Emirates; President and Chief Executive, Arab Banking Corporation, Manama, Bahrain; Vice Chairman of Arab Latin American Bank, Lima, Peru, Arab International Bank, Cairo; Director of Iveco Nederland BV, Amsterdam; *Decorations:* Great Cross of Civil Merit, HM King of Spain, 1977; President's Gold Medal, President of Italy, 1977; Award of The Most Innovative Banker of the Year from *International Herald Tribune,* 1980; Banker of the Year 1981, by Board of Editors of *Institutional Investor; Languages:* Arabic, English, Italian; *Address:* P O Box 5698, Manama, Bahrain; telephone: 232235; telex: 9432, 9433 ABC BH.

SAWAYA, Asaad F., Lebanese businessman; born 8 March 1926; married; one son, two daughters; *Religion:* Christian; *Education:* LLD; *Career:* Managing Director, Banque de l'Industrie et du Travail SAL; Chairman, Association of Banks in Lebanon; member of the Board of Al-Jihaad al-Watani Insurance Co, Société Financière et Immobilière du Port de Beyrouth, Société Immobilière pour l'Agriculture et la Construction; Vice Chairman, International Committee, International Chamber of Commerce; *Interests and Recreations:* tennis, skiing; *Languages:* Arabic, French, English; *Address:* Riad Solh Street, P O Box 11–3948, Beirut, Lebanon; telephone: 259873; telex: 20698 LE.

SAWI, Abdul Munim Mahmud al-, Egyptian writer/official; born 1918; married; four sons; *Religion:* Muslim; *Education:* BA, Faculty of Arts, Cairo University, Egypt, 1942; *Career:* war correspondent, North African, 1942–43, and Palestine War, 1948; correspondent, London, 1948–52; Press Attaché, Egyptian Embassy, London; Managing Editor, Middle East News Agency, 1958; Under-Secretary, Ministry of Culture, 1967; Chairman of the Press Syndicate, 1973; Chairman of the Board, National Council for Services and Social Affairs, 1974; Chairman of the Board, al-Tahrir Publishing House (publishers of *Al-Gumhuriyah* and *Le Progrès Egyptien*); resigned, 1977; Minister of Information and Culture, 1977; writes in *Al-Gumhuriyah; Publications:* several novels and other books; *Languages:* Arabic, English; *Address:* Ministry of Information, Television Building, Cairo, Egypt.

SAWI, Amir al-, Sudanese diplomat/official; born 1921; *Education:* Public Administration, University of Bristol, UK, 1948–49; *Career:* entered government service, 1944; Assistant Representative of Sudan in Cairo, Egypt, 1953; District Commissioner in Korti, 1956; Assistant Under Secretary, Ministry of Foreign Affairs, 1956–57; Deputy Under Secretary, Ministry of the Interior, 1960; Permanent Under Secretary, 1965–70; Under Secretary, Ministry of Public Services and Administrative Reform, 1971; Doyenne of the Sudan Civil Service; Ambassador to UK, 1976–; *Languages:* Arabic, English; *Address:* Embassy of the Democratic Republic of Sudan, 3 Cleveland Row, St. James's, London SW1, UK; telephone: 839 8080.

SAWWAF, Muhammad Mahmud al-, Saudi Arabian writer/Islamic scholar; born 1915; *Religion:* Muslim; *Education:* LLM Islamic Law, Al-Azhar University, Cairo; *Career:* teacher of Arabic Literature and Islamic Thoughts; Lecturer, Faculty of Shari'a, Baghdad, Iraq; Inspector of Mosques, Endowments General Directorate; Professor, Faculty of Shari'a, Mecca; Adviser to the Ministry of Education; member of Constituent Congress of Muslim World League, Executive Bureau of Muslim World Congress, Karachi, Permanent Bureau, General Congress on the Palestine Question, Amman, Jordan, Supreme Advisory Council, Islamic University, Medina; Special Envoy of late HM King Faisal for a number of years;

Publications: Sawt al-Islam; Al-Muslimuun Wa Islam al-Falak; Al-Mukhataat al-Isti'mariyyah Li Mukafahat al-Islam; Al-Siyam Fi'l Islam; Rihlati Ila al-Diyari Islamiyyah; Afriqia al-Muslimah; Decorations: Knight of the Most Excellent Order of Merit, awarded by the Head of Government of the Comoro Islands; *Address:* P O Box 894, Mecca, Saudi Arabia.

SAYAH, Muhammad, Tunisian politician; born 31 December 1933, Sousse, Tunisia; *Religion:* Muslim; *Education:* Training School for Higher Education, Tunis; Licence ès Lettres; *Career:* joined Neo-Destour Party, 1949; member of Union Générale des Etudiants Tunisiens, UGET, 1952–62; member of UGET Executive Bureau, 1957–62; Secretary General of UGET, 1960–62; Assistant Director of the Socialist Destour Party, and Director of *L'Action,* French language organ of the Party, 1962; Secretary General of the Destour Youth Association, 1964; Secretary General of State for Information, 1969–70; Permanent Representative of Tunisia to the United Nations Specialised Agencies, Geneva, Switzerland, 1970–71; Minister of Public Works and Housing, 1971–73; Director of Socialist Destour Party, and Minister of Youth and Sports, 1973; Minister Delegate to the Prime Minister, and Director of Socialist Destour Party, 1973; Deputy Prime Minister for Planning, 1976–80; Minister of Public Works and Housing, 1980–81; Minister of Equipment, 1981–; *Languages:* Arabic, French; *Address:* Ministry of Equipment, Cité Jardin, Tunis, Tunisia; telephone: 892299.

SAYAR, Ali Abdullah, Bahraini journalist; born 1926, Bahrain; married; *Religion:* Muslim; *Education:* Bahrain Technical School and Cairo Technical School; *Career:* worked in Saudi Arabia and Kuwait; returned to Bahrain in 1952 and co-operated with Mahmud al-Mardi in publishing *Al-Qafilah* newspaper, and later *Al-Watan;* member of the Higher Executive Committee, 1956; worked in Kuwait Ministry of Social Affairs and Labour, 1956; worked for commercial firms in Bahrain, 1957–69; founder and Editor in Chief, *Sada Al-Usbu* weekly newspaper, 1969; member of the Constituent Council, 1973; *Languages:* Arabic, English; *Address:* P O Box 549, Manama, Bahrain.

SAYARI, Hamad Saud al-, Saudi Arabian banker/economist; born 1941, Saudi Arabia; *Religion:* Muslim; *Education:* MA in Economics, University of Maryland, USA, 1971; *Career:* Director, Foreign Relations Department, Ministry of Labour and Social Affairs; Instructor of Economics, Institute of Public Administration; Chief Analyst, Central Budget Department, Ministry of Finance; Secretary General, Public Investment Fund; Director General, Saudi Industrial Development Fund; Deputy Governor, Saudi Arabian Monetary Agency, 1978–83; Acting Governor, Saudi Arabian Monetary Agency, 1983–; Chairman, Saudi Industrial Development Fund; member of Board, Arab Bank, Amman, Jordan; *Address:* P O Box 2060, Riyadh, Saudi Arabia; telephone: 477 2295.

SAYEGH, Anis, Palestinian writer; born 1931, Tiberias, Palestine; married; *Religion:* Christian; *Education:* American University of Beirut, Lebanon; PhD in History, University of Cambridge, UK, 1964; *Career:* Director of the Palestine Research Centre (researches and publishes material on the Palestine question in all its aspects), 1966; injured in letter-bomb attack, 1972; Director of the Palestine Programme at the Arab Centre for Higher Studies in Cairo, 1973.

SAYEGH, S. Samaan, Arab-American businessman/pharmacist; born 25 December 1927, Jerusalem, Palestine; married; one son, three daughters; *Religion:* Christian; *Education:* Doctorate in Pharmacy, University of Tucson, Arizona, USA; *Career:* pharmacist; President, Group Physicians Service; Chairman, American Arab Congress; President, Palestinian War Victims Society and President, American-Arab Society; *Decorations:* Man of the Year Award, City of Los Angeles, 1975; *Interests and Recreations:* all aspects of art; member of Arabic Lodge 763, Los Angeles; member of Scottish Rite 32 Degree; member of Sons of the Desert Shrine Club, of Mystic Shrine Club; *Languages:* Arabic, English; *Address:* 2035 Vista Sierra Madre, California, USA; telephone: (213) 446 8980.

SAYER, Musa'id Badir Muhammad Nasir al-, Kuwaiti businessman; born 25 September 1947, Kuwait; married; three sons, one daughter; *Religion:* Muslim; *Education:* BA in Business Administration, Kuwait University; *Career:* Owner and Director, Muhammad Nasir al-Sayer and Sons Est;

President, Musa'id Badir al-Sayer Est; member of the boards of several major companies; *Interests and Recreations:* sports; member of the Hunting and Equestrian Club, Kuwait, and the Tourist and Entertainment Club, Kuwait; *Languages:* Arabic, English; *Address:* Musa'id Badir al-Sayer Est, P O Box 21666, Safat, Kuwait; telephone: 410697, 418721, 418682.

SAYER, Sayer Badir al-, Kuwaiti businessman; born 17 September 1951, Kuwait; *Religion:* Muslim; *Education:* Aeronautical Engineering; *Career:* Managing Director, Muhammad Nasir Al-Sayer and Sons Est; Board member of Kuwait Tire Co, Toyota, Egypt; *Interests and Recreations:* chess, backgammon, hunting, scuba diving; *Languages:* Arabic, English, French; *Address:* P O Box 485, Safat, Kuwait; telephone: 434139, 427326.

SAYIGH, Bishop Salim Wahban, Jordanian ecclesiastic; born 15 April 1935, Jordan; *Religion:* Christian; *Education:* BA in Philosophy and Theology; PhD in Law; *Career:* President of the Latin Patriarchal Court in Jerusalem, 1967–79; Rector of the Latin Patriarchal Seminary, 1976–81; Bishop and Vicar General of the Latin Patriarchate in Jordan, 1982–; *Publications: Le Statu Quo des Lieux-Saints,* 1971, in French; *Decorations:* Commander of the Equestrian Order of the Holy Sepulchre of Jerusalem, 1982; *Interests and Recreations:* table tennis, volley ball, chess, history, ecclesiastical law; *Languages:* Arabic, French, English, Italian, Latin; *Address:* Latin Vicariate, P O Box 1317 Amman, Jordan.

SAYIGH, Khalil, Lebanese businessman/publisher and distributor; born 1919, Damascus, Syria; married; one son, three daughters; *Education:* Business Studies, International College, American University of Beirut; *Career:* Founder and Owner of the Librairie du Liban, Beirut, 1944–; Sayigh Bookshop, Damascus, the Sphinx Bookshop and Publishing House, Cairo, Egypt, York Press, Beirut, 1979, the Dictionaries Division, 1965, Arabic Ladybird Division, 1975; Butterfly Division, 1979, Text Books Division, Chairman, Longman Penguin Arab World Centre, Beirut, Amman, Khartoum; Representative of Longman Group Ltd, and Churchill-Livingston Medical Division, Penguin Books Ltd and Ladybird Books Ltd, in the Arab world; *Interests and Recreations:* swimming, collector of art works; *Languages:* Arabic, English, French; *Address:* Office — Librairie du Liban, P O Box 11–945, Beirut, Lebanon; telephone: 258259; telex: 21037.

SAYIGH, Yusif Abdullah, Syrian academic/economist; born 26 March 1916, Palestine; married; two sons, one daughter; *Religion:* Christian; *Education:* BA in Business Administration and Economics, American University of Beirut, Lebanon; PhD in Economics, Johns Hopkins University, Baltimore, USA; *Career:* Instructor, Assistant Professor, Associate Professor, Full Professor of Economics, AUB, 1953–74; Director of Economic Reseach Institute, AUB, 1957–59 and 1962–64; Economic Adviser, Planning Board, Kuwait, 1964–65; Research Associate, Centre for International Affairs, Harvard University, USA, 1959–60; Visiting Associate Professor, Princeton University, USA, 1960–61; Adviser to Organization of Petroleum Exporting Countries, 1974–77; Adviser to Arab Fund for Economic and Social Development, 1976–79; Adviser to Arab League, Department of Economic Affairs, 1979–80; member of the National Assembly, Palestine Liberation Organization, PLO, Central Committee of PLO, the Executive Committee and President of National Fund of PLO, 1971–74; *Publications:* in English, *The Economic Impact of the Influx of Palestinian Refugees on Lebanon, Syria and Jordan,* Karachi; *Entrepreneurs of Lebanon: the role of the business leader in a developing economy,* Cambridge, USA; *Economies and Economists in the Arab World,* Beirut; *Jordan: a country survey,* co-author; *The Mediterranean Development Project,* Rome; *The Economies of the Arab World,* London, 1977; in Arabic, *The Socio-Economic Content of the Concept of Arab Nationalism,* Beirut; *The Israeli Economy,* first edition Cairo, 1963, second edition Beirut, 1966; *The Strategy of Action for the Liberation of Palestine;* and other books; *Interests and Recreations:* tennis, swimming; member of Society for International Development, and the Federation of Arab Economists; *Languages:* Arabic, English, French; *Address:* P O Box 155-445, Beirut, Lebanon; telephone: 300407.

SAYIH, Hamid Abdul Latif al-, Egyptian banker/economist; born 1921; married; *Education:* BA in Commerce, Cairo University,

Egypt; MA in Commerce, University of Denver, USA; PhD in Finance and Economics, University of Kentucky, USA; *Career:* Director of the National Bank of Egypt, Cairo; Lecturer, Cairo University; various senior government posts since 1954; Assistant Under Secretary and later Under Secretary, Ministry of Economy, 1960; took part in talks with International Bank for Reconstruction and Development (IBRD) for the Aswan High Dam and later in financial negotiations with France and UK; Egyptian Deputy Director of IBRD; Under Secretary of International Economy, Ministry of Economy and Foreign Trade; Chairman and Governor of the National Bank, 1971; Minister of Economy and Economic Co-operation, 1976–1980; member of the Suez-Mediterranean Pipeline Finance Committee; Director of the Arab International Bank; Economic and Financial Adviser, and member of the National Production Council; *Languages:* Arabic, English; *Address:* No1 Road 255, New Maadi, Cairo, Egypt.

SAYYID AHMAD, Muhammad al-, Egyptian journalist/writer, born 29 November 1928, Cairo, Egypt; married; two sons; *Religion:* Muslim; *Education:* Electronic Engineering Diploma, Cairo University, Egypt, 1956; Licence in law, Ain Shams University, Cairo, 1957; *Career:* imprisoned for leftist activities at university, 1950–52; imprisoned for political activities, 1959–64; Director, left-wing Publishing House Al-Dimukratiya Al-Gadida; Editorial Writer for *Al-Akhbar,* 1965–68; *Al-Ahram,* 1968; writer, *Al-Ahram;* writer of political studies; member of the Legislation and Economic Society, Cairo; *Publications: On the Eisenhower Doctrine,* 1957; *Economic World Crisis,* 1958; *Study on Egyptian Socialism,* 1964; *After the Guns Fall Silent,* 1975; *Interests and Recreations:* member of Cairo Sporting Club; *Languages:* Arabic, English, French; *Address:* 22 Ibn Zanki Street, Zamalek, Cairo, Egypt; telephone: Office — 755500; Residence — 803949.

SAYYID HASSAN, Muwaffaq al-, Syrian academic/economist; born 1929, Damascus, Syria; married; two daughters, one son; *Religion:* Muslim; *Education:* BA in Law, University of Damascus; Diploma of Higher Studies in Economic Sciences, University of Paris, Sorbonne, France; PhD in Economic Sciences, University of Paris, Sorbonne,

Paris; *Career:* Lecturer, University of Damascus, 1978–83; Assistant Professor, 1983–; Dean of the Faculty of Economics and Commerce for Scientific Affairs; Head of the Division of Economic Consultations and Studies, University of Damascus; Member of the University Council for Scientific Affairs; President of the Teachers' Union Branch in the University of Damascus; *Publications: Economic Analysis,* a university textbook, Ibn Hayyan, Damascus 1981, in Arabic; *Contemporary Economic Problems,* a university textbook, *Al-Matba'a al-Jadida,* Damascus, 1982, in Arabic; PhD thesis in French; *Interests and Recreations:* swimming, economic studies, literature; *Languages:* Arabic, French; *Address:* Faculty of Economics and Commerce, University of Damascus, Damascus, Syria.

SAYYID, Hussain Muhammad al, Saudi Arabian lawyer; born 22 January 1919; married; three sons, one daughter; *Religion:* Muslim; *Education:* LLB, Alexandria University, Egypt; postgraduate Diploma, Economics and Public Law, Alexandria University; MA and PhD in Taxation, Alexandria University; *Career:* Inspector of Income Tax, 1961; University Teacher, Riyadh University, 1961–63; Dean of Faculty of Commerce, Riyadh University, 1963–70, Legal Adviser for the Rector, 1970–73, Deputy Dean of Admission and Registration, 1973–76; Legal Consultant for Saudi Basic Industries Corporation, SABIC, 1976–78; Partner, Shawwaf and Al-Sayyid Law Office; *Publications: Taxation Accounting in the Kingdom,* textbook, 1970; several articles in Saudi newspapers, magazines, Riyadh University publications and foreign professional journals in Arabic and English; *Interests and Recreations:* reading; *Languages:* Arabic, English, French; *Address:* Shawwaf and Al-Sayyid Law Office, P O Box 2700, Riyadh, Saudi Arabia; telephone: 478 5145, 478 2510.

SAYYID, Muhammad Lutfi al-, Egyptian academic/engineer; born 7 February 1932, Alexandria, Egypt; married; one son, three daughters; *Religion:* Muslim; *Education:* BSc in Electrical Engineering, University of Alexandria, 1953; MSc, PhD, University of Michigan, Ann Arbor, 1963–67; *Career:* Electrical Engineer, 1953–61; Associate, Clarkson College, Potsdam, NY, 1967–68; Professor, Cairo Institute of Technology, Helwan, 1972; Dean, Faculty of Engineering and Technology, Helwan, 1977–79; Vice President, University of Helwan, Cairo, 1979–; *Publications:* numerous publications in the field of electrical machines; *Interests and Recreations:* swimming; *Languages:* Arabic, English, French; *Address:* Residence — 10 Street No 256, Maadi, Cairo, Egypt; Office — 7 Mudiriyet Al-Tahrir Street, Garden City, Cairo, Egypt.

SAYYID, Mustafa Amr al-, Arab-American academic/chemist; born 8 May 1933, Egypt; married; seven children; *Education:* BSc, Ain Shams University, Cairo, Egypt, 1953; PhD, Florida State University, Florida, USA, 1959; *Career:* went to USA, 1954; naturalized, 1965; Research Fellow, Yale University, USA, 1957; Research Fellow, Harvard University, USA, 1959–60; Research Fellow, California Institute of Technology, USA, 1960–61; Assistant Professor, University of California, Los Angeles, USA, 1961–64; Associate Professor of Chemistry, 1964–67; Professor of Chemistry, 1967; Consultant, North American Aviation Minute Man Program, 1965–66; Editor, *Journal of Physical Electro-Optics,* 1962–65; US Navy, 1968–71; *Publications:* articles and papers in professional journals; *Decorations:* Distinguished Teaching Award, University of California, USA, 1964; Fresenius National Award, 1967; Gold Medal Award, American Chemical Society, California, 1971; elected to the US National Academy of Sciences, April 1980; Alfred P. Sloane Guggenheim Fellowship, 1965; *Interests and Recreations:* member, American Physicists Association, American Chemists Association, American Association of University Professors, Western Spectroscopy Association; *Address:* 3325 Colbert Avenue, Los Angeles, California, CA 90066, USA.

SBIH, Missoum, Algerian diplomat; born 21 December 1931, Arzew, Algeria; married; four children; *Education:* PhD in Law, University of Paris, France; *Career:* Director of Cabinet Affairs; Director General of Public Services; Director General of the National School of Administration; Secretary to the Ministry of Foreign Affairs; Professor of Law; President of the Adminsitrative Council of the Moroccan Center for Administrative Studies and Researches; Ambassador Extraordinary and Plenipotentiary to Ottowa, Canada; member of the National Council of Scientific Research; member of the National Legislative Commission; member of the National Economic and Social Council, President of the Planning section, and of the Enterprise and Social Section; *Publications: The Public Function,* Paris, 1968; *The Algerian Public Administration,* Paris, 1973; *The Administrative Institutions of the Maghreb,* Paris, 1977; and several other studies on public administration; *Interests and Recreations:* tennis, sailing; *Languages:* Arabic, French; *Address:* Ambassade d'Algérie, 435 Daly Ave, Ottowa, Canada KIN 6H3; 101 Maripos Ave, Ottowa, Canada; telephone: 232 5823.

SBIHI, Abdul Hadi, Moroccan diplomat/ agronomist; born 1925, Sale, Morocco; married; *Religion:* Muslim; *Career:* Head of the Private Office of the Minister of National Economy; Inspector, Ministry of Agriculture; Governor of the Province of Casablanca, 1961; Minister Plenipotentiary and Permanent Delegate of Morocco to FAO, 1961; Ambassador to the Ivory Coast, 1965–67; Ambassador to USSR, 1967–70; Head of the Office de Commercialisation et d'Exportation (OCE), 1970; Minister of Agriculture and Agrarian Reform, 1971; Ambassador to Norway, Sweden and Denmark, 1973; *Languages:* Arabic, French; *Address:* Ministry of Foreign Affairs, Rabat, Morocco.

SEDNAOUI, Rafik, Lebanese businessman; born 15 March 1923, Cairo, Egypt; married; two sons; *Education:* Licence in Law, French Faculty of Law, Cairo, Egypt; BSc, Harvard Business School, Harvard University, USA; *Career:* company director; director of various companies dealing with interior design and other establishments bearing the name Sednaoui; *Interests and Recreations:* riding; *Languages:* Arabic, French, English; *Address:* Office — Lyon Street, Arts et Métiers, Beirut, Lebanon; Residence — Verdun Street, Tabet Building, Beirut, Lebanon.

SEFROUI, General Abdeslam Ameur Ben Lahcen, Moroccan army commander/ diplomat; born 1923, Sefrou, Morocco; married; three children; *Religion:* Muslim; *Education:* Meknes Military Academy, 1943; *Career:* served in Morocco and Indochina; Captain, 1955; Governor of Agadir Province, after Independence; Staff Officer in African High Command, 1956; accompanied Crown Prince to Cairo, 1959; Major, 1965; Commander of 11th Battalion at Casabianca;

Governor of Ouajda Province, 1961–1965; Governor of Casablanca City, 1965–1967; Colonel, 1965; Commander of the Light Security Brigade, 1968; Commander of Meknes Military Academy, 1968; Commander of Royal Guard, 1971; General, 1971; Commander of the Moroccan Expeditionary Contingent in Syria, 1973; Commander of the Moroccan Infantry Forces and the Royal Guard, 1975–78; Ambassador of Morocco to Holland, 1978–80; *Languages:* Arabic, French, English; *Address:* Ministry of Defence, Rabat, Morocco.

SEHAIMI, Mansur Abdul Rahman, Saudi Arabian engineer/oil expert; born 1942, Mecca, Saudi Arabia; married; three sons, one daughter; *Religion:* Muslim; *Education:* BSc in Petroleum Engineering, University of Texas, USA; *Career:* Petroleum Engineer, Ministry of Oil and Mineral Resources, 1964; Development and Production Engineer, Aramco, 1965–67; Construction Engineer, Jeddah Oil Refinery, 1967–68, Shift Supervisor, Operations, 1968–70, Technical Services Supervisor, 1970–73, Technical Services Manager, 1973–75, General Manager, Productions, 1975–78, Managing Director and Assistant Chairman for Production, 1978–; *Interests and Recreations:* table tennis, swimming; *Languages:* Arabic, English; *Address:* Jeddah Oil Refinery Company, P O Box 1604, Jeddah, Saudi Arabia; telephone: 6426311.

SEHILI, Mahmud, Tunisian artist; born 27 July 1931, Tunisia; married; one son, two daughters; *Religion:* Muslim; *Education:* Sadiki College, Tunis; Fine Arts School, Tunis; Ecole des Beaux Arts, Paris, France; *Career:* exhibited with the Maghreb Group, Galerie Peinture du Monde, Paris, France; modern art shows England, USA, Sweden 1967; one man exhibitions, Tunis; Vice President, Tunisian Painters Association; Director, The Irtissem Gallery; Professor, Painting and Traditional Arts, Fine Arts School, Tunis, Tunisia; participated in exhibitions and discussions on Tunisian art, The Irtissem Gallery with group of young Tunisian painters; *Decorations:* Gold Medal, Tunisian Modern Art Exibition, Milan, 1969; *Interests and Recreations:* theatre, music; *Languages:* Arabic, French; *Address:* 4 rue Victor Hugo, Carthage Presidency, Tunis, Tunisia; telephone: 278 085.

SEHNAOUI, Antoine Elie, Lebanese businessman; born 1902, Damascus, Syria; married; *Education:* Diploma in Philosophy; *Career:* founder and General Manager, National Tube Company; founder and President, Elie Sehnaoui and Sons Establishments; *Decorations:* Knight, National Order of the Cedar, Lebanon; as well as many other distinctions and decorations from the Holy See, Belgium; *Interests and Recreations:* collecting paintings and works of art; member of the Rotary Club, Beirut, of the Beirut Aero Club, and the Beirut Club; member of the Cercle de l'Union Française; *Languages:* Arabic, French; *Address:* Office — Rue de la Marseillaise, Beirut, Lebanon; Residence -- Perthuis Street, Beirut, Lebanon.

SEHNAOUI, Antoine Michel, Lebanese businessman/banker; born 1903, Damascus, Syria; *Education:* studies in finance and commerce; *Career:* President, Euro-Lebanese Bank Corporation; Director of Eternit Company, Lebanese Cement Company, National Tube Company, Chemical Union Company; elected Deputy for Beirut 1960 and 1964; Minister of Posts, Telegraphs and Telephones, 1964–65; founder of the Belgium-Lebanese Bank; one of the founders of Al-Ahli Bank; founder of Building Construction SAL; *Decorations:* many distinctions and decorations from the Holy See, Tunisia and Belgium; *Interests and Recreations:* member of the Beirut Aero Club and the Beirut Club; *Languages:* Arabic, French; *Address:* Youssef Hani Street, P O Box 110-122, Beirut, Lebanon; telephone: 221710/13; telex: 20977 LE.

SELMI, Saida Bin Abid, Tunisian geologist; born 10 November 1946, Tunis; married; one son, one daughter; *Religion:* Muslim; *Education:* BSc, MSc in Geography; PhD in Geomorphology, University of Strasbourg, France; *Career:* Head of Laboratory, 1971; Assistant, 1973; Head of Geomorphological Laboratory, 1976; Head of the Department of Geomorphology, Ministry of Agriculture, 1979–; *Publications:* numerous papers published in professional journals; *Interests and Recreations:* reading, travelling; *Languages:* Arabic, French, English; *Address:* 11 Rue 12 Mai 64, Cité 25 Juillet, Ariana, Tunis, Tunisia; telephone: 235 052.

SENOUSSI, Ahmad, Moroccan diplomat; born 22 April 1929, Meknes, Morocco; married; three sons; *Religion:* Muslim; *Education:* Institute of Higher Political Studies, Paris, France; *Career:* member of the Cabinet of Driss M'hammedi; member of the delegation led by Mr M'hammedi to the Franco-Moroccan talks, 1955–56; Director of the Press Division, Ministry of Foreign Affairs, 1956–58; Director of Information, 1958–60; member of numerous delegations to international conferences; represented Morocco in the Congo and the Leopoldville Conference, 1960; member of Moroccan delegation to UN General Assembly, November–December 1960; Secretary General of Ministry of Information, Handicrafts and Tourism, 1961; Ambassador to Nigeria and Ivory Coast, 1965–67; Minister of Information, 1967; Moroccan High Commissioner for EXPO '67 in Montreal, Canada; Ambassador to Tunisia, 1971; Ambassador to Algeria, 1973–76; Editor of various magazines including *Maroc* (Ministry of Foreign Affairs), and *Maroc Documents* (Ministry of Information); *Decorations:* Officer of Moroccan Order of the Throne; Cross of Courage and Endurance (Mission to Congo); also decorations from Jordan and Yugoslavia; *Languages:* Arabic, French, English; *Address:* Ministry of Foreign Affairs, Rabat, Morocco.

SENOUSSI, Badriddine, Moroccan diplomat/official; born 30 March 1933, Fes, Morocco; married with children; *Religion:* Muslim; *Education:* Licence en Droit, University of Bordeaux, France; Licence ès-Lettres, Mohammed V University, Rabat, Morocco; Diploma of the Centre of Business Preparation, Paris, France; *Career:* Counsellor of the High Cherifian Tribunal, 1956–57; Chargé de Mission, Ministry of State and of Public Function, 1957; Chargé de Mission, Ministry of National Defence, 1957; General Secretary, Tobacco Management, 1958–63; Director of the Royal Cabinet, 1963–64; Under Secretary of State for Commerce, Industry, Mines, and Merchant Marine, 1964–65; Under Secretary for Administrative Affairs, 1965–66; Minister of Posts and Telecommunications, 1966–70; Deputy for Benslimane, House of Representatives, 1970; Minister of Youth, Sports and Social Affairs, 1970–71; Ambassador to USA, 1971–74; Ambassador to Iran; Ambassador to UK, 1977–80; *Decorations:* Officer of Ouissame Alouite, and various foreign decorations; *Languages:* Arabic, French, English; *Address:* The Royal Cabinet, Rabat, Morocco.

SERAFI, Ahmad Mustafa al-, Egyptian academic; resident in Canada; born 3 March 1929, Cairo, Egypt; *Religion:* Muslim; *Education:* BSc, Cairo University, Egypt; PhD, University of Manchester, UK; PhD in Engineering, Technical University of Darmstadt, West Germany; *Career:* Instructor, Cairo University, Egypt, 1950–53; part-time Instructor, Manchester College of Science and Technology (MCST), UK, 1954–56; Assistant Lecturer, MCST, UK, 1956–57; Consultant, Egyptian Electrical Commission, 1957–61; part-time Lecturer, Assuit University, Egypt, 1957–61; part-time Lecturer, Ain Shams University, Egypt, 1957–61; Lecturer, Cairo University, Egypt, 1957–61; Fellow, Alexander von Humbolt Foundation, Technical University of Darmstadt, West Germany, 1961–64; Assistant Professor, University of Libya, 1965–67; Consultant, Government of Libya, 1967–68; Head, Electrical Engineering, University of Libya, 1967–68; Visiting Professor, ETH Zurich, Switzerland, 1967–77; *Publications:* numerous publications in English, German and Arabic; *Interests and Recreations:* swimming, tennis, travelling, camping; *Languages:* Arabic, English, German, French; *Address:* Electrical Engineering Department, University of Saskatchewan, Saskatoon, Saskatchewan, S7N OWO Canada.

SERAPHIM, Juliana, Lebanese artist/painter; born 13 April 1934, Jaffa, Palestine; *Education:* commercial studies; Art Academies of Florence, Italy, and of Madrid, Spain; *Career:* secretary with the UN Relief and Works Agency for Palestine Refugees in the Near East, 1953–58; painter, 1957–; has contributed to the Baalbek Festival, to the Jeunesses Musicales du Liban, to the Congress for the Freedom of Culture; has held exhibitions of her work in Florence and Rome, Italy, Paris, France, Buenos Aires, Argentina, Alexandria, Egypt; has illustrated books and designed jewellery using oriental themes; *Decorations:* worldwide distinctions among which the Florence Prize from the Italian Cultural Centre and several others; prize from Ministry of National Education; Silver Medal, from the town of Viareggio, Italy; *Interests and Recreations:* swimming; member of the Painters Association; *Lang-*

uages: Arabic, French; Address: Khawaga
Building, Apartment No 9, Parc Tabet, Sin
el-Fil, Beirut, Lebanon.

SHAAR, Muhammad Sayid al-, Sudanese
administrator; born 22 April 1924, Omdur-
man, Sudan; married; two sons, one daughter;
Religion: Muslim; Education: BSc in Politi-
cal Science, University of Khartoum, Sudan;
Master of Public Administration, Institute of
Social Studies, The Hague, Holland; Career:
Commissioner, White Nile Province; Decora-
tions: Order of the Republic 2nd Class;
Interests and Recreations: reading, tennis;
Languages: Arabic, English; Address:
Dweim, Sudan.

SHAATH, Nabil, Palestinian politician; born
1938, Safad, Galilee, Palestine; Education:
Doctorate from the Wharton School, USA;
Career: taught economics at American
University of Beirut, Lebanon; member of
Advisory Council, Fatah Central Committee,
1971; Head of Fatah Advisory Council;
Director of Palestine Liberation Organization
(PLO) Planning Centre.

SHACKAL, John G., Egyptian UN official;
Career: Administrative Officer, Office of the
Controller, UN, New York, USA; Senior
Budget Officer, Budget Division, Office of
the Controller, UN, New York; Administra-
tive Officer, Administrative and Financial
Service, UN, Geneva, Switzerland; Chief,
Personnel Division, UN, Geneva, 1972–;
Address: UN, Palais des Nations, Ch-1211,
Geneva 10, Switzerland; telephone: (022)
346011.

SHAFEI, Muhammad Zaki, Egyptian politi-
cian/economist; born 1922; Religion: Mus-
lim; Education: Law Faculty, Cairo Univer-
sity, 1942; MA in Economics, 1947; PhD in
Political Economics, Princeton University,
USA, 1950; Career: called to the Bar, 1942;
subsequently worked for three years with UN
in New York, Cairo University branch in
Khartoum, Sudan; Dean of the Faculty of
Economics and Political Science, Cairo
University, 1960; member of the Supervising
Committee for Arab Socialist Union (ASU)
Elections, 1968; alternate member of the
ASU Central Committee and member of its
Economic Subcommittee; member of Nation-
al Council for Production and Economic
Affairs, 1974; Assistant Secretary General
for Economic Affairs, in the Arab League;

Minister of Economy and Economic Co-
operation, 1975–77; Address: Ministry of
Economy, Cairo, Egypt.

SHAFIQ, Muhammad Nuri, Jordanian offi-
cial/educationalist; born 1927, Tafilah, Jor-
dan; married; five children; Education: BA,
Cairo University, Egypt, 1950; MA, Teachers
College, Columbia University, New York,
USA, 1954; Teachers College, Columbia
University, New York, 1963; Career:
Teacher, 1950–53; Instructor, Amman
Teachers College, Jordan, 1954–59; Editor of
Risalat al-Mu'allim, 1956–59; Administra-
tor, Ministry of Education, 1959–61; Under
Secretary, Ministry of Education, 1963–67;
Administrative Adviser to the Prime Mini-
ster, 1967–68; Civil Service Commissioner
and Chairman of the Board of Directors of
Jordan Institute of Public Administration,
1968–70; Vice Chairman of Jordan Develop-
ment Board, 1970–71; President of the National Planning Council, 1971–73; Minister
of Finance, 1973; General Manager, General
Construction Co Ltd, 1973–74; Director
General, Royal Scientific Society, 1974–75;
Management Consultant to the Prime Minister, 1975–78; President and Director General, Arab Consulting Association, 1976–78;
Civil Service Commissioner, 1978–79; Mini-
ster of Education, 1979–80; Education Consultant, Arab College, 1981–82; Secretary
General, Council of Higher Education,
1982–; member of the Board of Trustees of
Jordan University, 1977–; Founder and
member of the Board of Trustees of the Arab
College, 1975–; Deputy Mayor of the City of
Amman, 1980–; member of the Arab
Thought Forum, 1981–; Publications: numer-
ous articles and research papers published in
Jordan and the Arab world; Address: P O
Box 2003, Amman, Jordan; telephone: 21033.

SHAHAT, Mahmud Abdul Hamid al-, Egyptian academic/agriculturalist; born 19 May
1930, Egypt; married; one daughter; Religion: Muslim; Education: BSc in Agricultural Sciences, Cairo University, Egypt; MSc
in Agricultural Economics, USA; PhD in
Agricultural Economics, USA; Career: Assistant Professor, 1965; Associate Professor,
1969; Head of Agricultural Economic Department, 1970; Vice Dean, 1977; Chairman
of the Permanent Promotional Committee for
Associate Professors of the Egyptian Universities; member of the Permanent Promotional Professors Committee of Egyptian

Universities; Visiting Professor, Warsaw University, Poland, 1978; External Examiner, Ife University, Nigeria, 1978–79; *Publications:* numerous research papers on agricultural reform and development in Egypt; *Interests and Recreations:* music, travelling, swimming, croquet; member of the Political Economy, Statistics and Legislation Society; member of the Heliopolis Sporting Club; *Languages:* Arabic, English, French; *Address:* Office — Faculty of Agriculture, Minya University, Egypt; telephone: 2333; Residence — 14 Alseil Street, Roxy, Heliopolis, Egypt; telephone: 879735.

SHAHBANDAR, Salah Abdul Rahman, Egyptian surgeon/academic; born 22 July 1924, Egypt; married; one son, one daughter; *Religion:* Muslim; *Education:* MB, BCh, Cairo University, 1948; MD in Surgery, Cairo University, 1953; Cancer Surgery, Memorial Sloan-Kettering Institute, NY, 1958; *Career:* Surgery Resident, Cairo University, Egypt, 1951–52; Demonstrator, Cairo University, 1952–53; Lecturer, 1954–61; Assistant Professor, Cairo University, 1961–70; Professor of Surgery, Cairo University, 1971; Vice Dean, National Cancer Institute, Egypt, 1974–77; Dean, National Cancer Institute, 1978–; member of the Board of the Massachusetts Institute of Technology, Cairo University Programme, 1977; Researcher for National Cancer Institute at the South-West Oncology Group, USA, 1978; *Publications:* medical papers in medical journals in Egypt and abroad; *Decorations:* Order of the Republic, Egypt, 1960; *Languages:* Arabic, English, French, Portuguese, Spanish, Italian; *Address:* 73 Abdel Aziz Second Street, Al Manial, Egypt.

SHAHEEN, Riad, Arab-American engineer/ businessman; born 8 October 1936, Lebanon; married; one son, one daughter; *Religion:* Muslim; *Education:* BSc in Electrical Engineering, Ohio State University, USA, 1960; *Career:* Project Engineer, Atlas Missile Site, Plattsbourgh, NY, 1961–62; Project Engineer, Minuteman Missile Site, Rapid City, South Dakota, 1962–63; Project Engineer, Shippingport Atomic Power Plant, Shippingport, Pennsylvania, 1963–64; Executive Vice-President, Electrical Contractor, 1966– 72; President, majority stock-holder and Chief Executive Officer, Long Electric Company Inc; member of Board of Directors, National Association of Arab-Americans; *Interests and Recreations:* swimming, cycling; *Languages:* English, Arabic; *Address:* Office — 1310 South Franklin Road, Indianapolis, IN 46239, USA; telephone: (317) 356 2455; Residence — 11808 Rolling Springs Drive, Carmel, Indiana 46032, USA; telephone: (317) 844 0374.

SHAHI Ahmad S. al-, Anglo-Arab academic/ anthropologist; born July 1938, Iraq; married; one daughter; *Education:* BA, University of Baghdad, Baghdad, Iraq; post graduate Diploma in Social Anthropology, Oxford University, UK; BLitt, DPhil, Oxford University; *Career:* Lecturer in Social Anthropology, Department of Anthropology and Sociology, University of Khartoum, Sudan, 1965– 70; Lecturer in Social Anthropology, Department of Social Studies, University of Newcastle Upon Tyne, UK; Fellow of the Royal Anthropological Institute, UK; member of the Association of Social Anthropologists; Fellow of the British Society for Middle Eastern Studies; *Publications:* Editor of Vol 17 *The Arab World,* of *Peoples of the Earth,* 1973; *Wisdom from the Nile,* in collaboration with Dr F.C.T. Moore, 1978; *Le Soudan,* 1979; various anthropological articles in international and African journals; *Interests and Recreations:* spent two years carrying out fieldwork on the Shaiqiyya tribe of Northern Sudan; *Languages:* Arabic, English; *Address:* Department of Social Studies, University of Newcastle Upon Tyne, NE1 7RU; telephone: 0632 28511.

SHAHID, Irfan Arif, Arab-American academic; born 1926, Nazareth, Palestine; *Education:* BA in History and Literature, Oxford University, UK, 1951; Elizabeth Procter Fellow, Princeton University, USA, 1953–54; PhD, Near Eastern Studies, Princeton University, 1954; Junior Fellow, Arab Byzantine Relations; Byzantine Studies, Dumbarton Oaks, USA, 1954–55; *Career:* Instructor of Arabic, University of California, Los Angeles, USA, 1955–56; Associate Professor, Indiana University, 1960–62; Associate Professor, Georgetown University, 1962–66, Professor, 1966–; Fulbright-Hays Fellow; *Publications: The Martyrs of Najran; Pre-Islamic Arabia; Rome and the Arabs* (in print), Dumbarton Oaks, Washington D.C.; *Byzantium and the Arabs in the Fourth Century* (in print), Dumbarton Oaks, Washington D.C.; numerous papers and articles on Arab history and literature and Arab-

Byzantine relations; *Interests and Recreations:* Arab history and literature and Arab-Byzantine relations; *Languages:* Arabic, English; *Address:* Department of Arabic, School of Languages and Linguistics, Georgetown University, Washington D.C. 20057, USA.

SHAHIDI, Brahim al-Ouazzani al-, Moroccan broadcasting official/producer; born 1929, Fes, Morocco; married; two sons, two daughters; *Religion:* Muslim; *Education:* Moroccan Institute of Higher Studies; Paris Drama School; Sarah Bernhardt Theatre; Simon Institute of Drama; National Conservatoire of Dramatic Art, 1949–55; *Career:* Teacher of Arabic, 1948–49; Head of Amateur Theatrical Department, Youth and Sports, 1958; Producer on Moroccan Radio, 1959–62; Head of Drama Department, Moroccan Radio, 1963; Deputy Head of Education and Social Affairs; Head of Drama Department, Moroccan Radio, 1963–72; Head of Programmes and Production Department, Radio and Televison, 1972–; *Publications:* articles and studies on theatre in various newspapers and magazines; *Decorations:* Wissam al-Ridha, 1st Class, 1974; *Interests and Recreations:* theatre and radio production; President of Moroccan Authors' Association; swimming, riding, chess; *Languages:* Arabic, French; *Address:* 12 Ave de France, Rabat-Agdal, Morocco; telephone: Office — 62009, Residence — 72938.

SHAHIN, Ibrahim al-, Kuwaiti official/architect; born 1948, Kuwait; *Education:* BA, Washington State University, USA; MA in Architecture, University of Pennsylvania, USA (studied under Louis Khan); *Career:* architect; member of the Board, Kuwait National Housing Authority; Head of Urban Design Section, Kuwait Municipality, 1973–76; Assistant Director, National Housing Authority, 1976, Director General, 1976–; *Languages:* Arabic, English; *Address:* National Housing Authority, P O Box 23385, Safat, Kuwait; telephone: 717804; telex: 46489 LANDUSE KT.

SHAHIN, Sulaiman Majid, Kuwaiti diplomat; born 1937, Kuwait; married; *Religion:* Muslim; *Education:* Cairo University, Egypt; *Career:* Ministry of Foreign Affairs; member of the Kuwaiti Delegation to the UN, New York, USA; Head of Department, Office of the Under Secretary, Ministry of Foreign Affairs; Ambassador to Bahrain, 1971–73; Ambassador to the United Arab Emirates (UAE), 1973–75; Ambassador to Egypt, 1975; *Interests and Recreations:* sports, reading; *Languages:* Arabic, English; *Address:* c/o Ministry of Foreign Affairs, P O Box 3, Sour Street, Kuwait; telephone: 422041, 422050; telex: 22042 KHARJIA KT.

SHAHINE, Rafic, Lebanese politician; born 1925, Nabatieh, South Lebanon; married; two daughters; *Education:* Gerard Institute, Sidon, Lebanon; American University of Beirut, Lebanon (AUB); PhD in Political Science and Economics, Southern California University, USA; *Career:* Department Head, Planning and Economic Development Council, 1953–59; member, Planning Council, Ministry of Planning, 1959–60; Deputy for Nabatieh, 1960; member of the Parliamentary Committee for Foreign Affairs and Planning; Minister of Planning, 1960–61; Director General with rank of Ambassador, Palestinian Refugees Administration, 1964; member of the Lebanese Delegation to the Conference of Arab Heads of Government, Cairo, 1965; member of the Lebanese Delegation to the summit meeting of Arab Heads of Government, Casablanca, 1965; member of the Lebanese Delegation to the United Nations, 1965; member of the Special Political Commission dealing with Palestinian Refugees, 1965–67; Deputy for Nabatieh, 1968; Minister of Social Affairs, 1969–71; *Languages:* Arabic, French, English; *Address:* Office — Chamber of Deputies, Place de l'Etoile, Beirut, Lebanon; Residence -- Osman Ben Affan Street, Beirut, Lebanon.

SHAIBANI, Muhammad Bin Abdul Rahman al-, Saudi Arabian official; born 1920, Medina, Saudi Arabia; *Religion:* Muslim; *Education:* Shari'a School, Medina; *Career:* Ministry of Finance in Dammam; Head of the Office of the Governor of the Eastern Province; Ministry of Information in Jeddah; Deputy Minister of Information, Broadcasting and Television, 1968; *Address:* c/o Ministry of Information, P O Box 570, Riyadh, Saudi Arabia.

SHAIKH AL-ARD, Medhat, Saudi Arabian diplomat/physician; born 20 April 1920; married; *Religion:* Muslim; *Education:* University of Beirut, Lebanon; MD, University of Baghdad, Iraq; *Career:* Lecturer, Jeddah Health Institute; Court Physician; Embassy to Lebanon, Beirut; Ministry of Foreign Affairs, Riyadh, 1964–66; Delegate, UNESCO General Conference, Paris, France; Ambassador to France, 1966–72; Observer, Economic and Social Council UN (ECOSOC), Geneva; Delegate, World Health Assembly, Geneva, 1972–74; Ambassador, Permanent Representative of Saudi Arabia, UN, Geneva, 1972; *Languages:* Arabic, English, French; *Address:* Ministry of Foreign Affairs, P O Box 495, Jeddah, Saudi Arabia; telephone: 642 1322.

SHAIKH, Hassan Ali al-, United Arab Emirates official; born 1940, Ras al-Khaimah, United Arab Emirates; married; five sons, two daughters; *Religion:* Muslim; *Education:* general; *Career:* Deputy Director of Labour, United Arab Emirates Ministry of Labour; Head of Visa Section, Ministry of Labour and Social Affairs; *Interests and Recreations:* literature, swimming; member of Abu Dhabi Club; *Address:* Ministry of Labour and Social Affairs, P O Box 809, Abu Dhabi, United Arab Emirates; telephone: 362042.

SHAIKH, Lieutenant General Abdullah al-, Saudi Arabian army officer; born 1932; *Religion:* Muslim; *Education:* Officer Cadet Course, Taif, 1950; *Career:* Director General of Frontier Force and Coast Guard; Ministry of the Interior; Commander of the Internal Security Force College, 1968; *Languages:* Arabic, English; *Address:* c/o Ministry of the Interior, P O Box 2833, Riyadh, Saudi Arabia.

SHAIKHLY, Abdul Qadir Jassim al, Iraqi academic/veterinary scientist; born 1 July 1940, Baghdad, Iraq; married; three sons; *Religion:* Muslim; *Education:* BVMS, College of Veterinary Medicine, University of Baghdad, 1965; PhD, University of Bristol, UK, 1972; *Career:* Veterinary Inspector, Veterinary Services of the Iraqi Army, 1965–67; Instructor in Veterinary Anatomy, University of Baghdad, 1964–68; Lecturer in Anatomy, College of Veterinary Medicine, University of Baghdad, 1972–77; Assistant Professor of Anatomy; Professor of Veterinary Anatomy; Head of the Department of Veterinary Anatomy and Histology; member of the Iraqi Veterinary Medical Society; member of the World Association of Veterinary Anatomists; *Publications:* numerous papers and researches in professional jour-

nals; *Interests and Recreations:* swimming, walking; *Languages:* Arabic, English; *Address:* Office — College of Veterinary Medicine, Al-Ameria, Baghdad, Iraq; Residence — Al-Ameria, Baghdad, House No 28/4/630, Iraq.

SHAIKHLY, Salah al-, Iraqi economist/UN official; born 13 October 1939, Baghdad, Iraq; married; two daughters; *Religion:* Muslim; *Education:* BSc in Science and Technology, University of Manchester, UK, 1963; MSc in Managment Science, University of Manchester, 1965; PhD in Econometrics and Resource Forecasting, University of Manchester, 1967; *Career:* Senior Research Officer, London School of Economics, 1966–67; Senior Lecturer, Baghdad University, and Adviser to the Planning Board for Social and Educational Planning, 1967–68; Dean of the College of Business Administration, Baghdad University, 1968–69; member of the Board of Directors, Management Development Centre, Baghdad, 1968–71; Chairman of Iraq National Computer Committee, 1969–71; member of the Board of Directors, Central Bank of Iraq; acting Director, Management Development Centre, 1968–76; President, Central Statistical Organisation, Baghdad, Iraq, 1968–76; Acting Governor, Central Bank of Iraq, 1976; President and Chairman of the Board of Directors, Iraqi Fund for External Development, 1976–77; Assistant Administrator and Regional Director for Arab States, United Nations Development Programme, New York, 1978–; *Publications: Manpower Planning: A Five Year Forecast,* Baghdad, 1969; *Textbook on Production Management,* Baghdad, 1974; *Econometric Model for Industrial Location in Arab Countries,* Cairo, 1976; *The Debt Problem of Less Developed Countries, Cause, Effects and Solutions,* Mexico, 1977; *Interests and Recreations:* tennis; *Languages:* Arabic; English; *Address:* United Nations Development Programme, 1 United Nations Plaza, New York, NY 10017, USA; telephone: 212 754 4841.

SHAIN, Hisham Mustafa al-, Egyptian banker; born 29 October 1929; married; one daughter; *Religion:* Muslim; *Education:* BA in Commerce; Diploma, Egyptian Institute of Taxation; *Career:* Assistant Manager, Bank of Cairo, Egypt; Manager, Bank of Cairo, Dubai, United Arab Emirates (UAE); Manager, Bank of Cairo, Abu Dhabi, United Arab Emirates; *Interests and Recreations:*

classical literature, tennis, chess; member of Cairo Hunting Club; *Languages:* Arabic, English, French; Address: P O Box 533, Abu Dhabi, United Arab Emirates; telephone: Office — 43036; Residence — 61406.

SHAIR, Jamal Abdu al-, Jordanian physician; born 21 June 1928, Salt, Jordan; married; three sons, one daughter; *Religion:* Christian; *Education:* BA, American University of Beirut, AUB, Lebanon, 1947; MD, Medicine and Surgery, AUB, Beirut, 1951; Diploma in Obstetrics, Dublin, Ireland, 1952; Fellow of the Royal College of Surgeons, UK, 1958; *Career:* Assistant Surgeon, UK, 1957–58; gynaecologist and obstetrician, Amman, 1960–; member of the National Consultative Council of Jordan, 1978–; Minister of Municipalities and Environment, 1979–80; Consultant Gynaecologist and Obstetrician, National Hospital, Amman; President of the Board of the National Hospital; *Publications:* weekly column in *Al-Ra'i;* numerous articles and papers in journals and magazines in Jordan and abroad; *Interests and Recreations:* political studies; *Languages:* Arabic, English; *Address:* National Hospital, P O Box 1596, Amman, Jordan; telephone: 665 760, 664 164.

SHAIR, Wahib Abdo, Jordanian businessman/accountant; born 1939, Salt, Jordan; married 1965; one son; *Religion:* Christian; *Education:* BSc in Economics, University of London, 1960; Fellow of the Institute of Chartered Accountants; *Career:* Lecturer at the American University of Beirut, 1964–66; Senior Partner of Shair and Co, 1965–; *Languages:* Arabic, English; *Address:* P O Box 351, Amman, Jordan; telephone: 43439, 61280.

SHAKER, Shaikh Ghassan I., Saudi Arabian businessman/political adviser; born 1937, Jeddah, Saudi Arabia; three sons; *Religion:* Muslim; *Education:* Victoria College, Alexandria, Egypt; St. John's College, Cambridge University, UK; *Career:* owner and President of Ghassan Shaker Est, Saudi Arabia; Vice President, Ibrahim Shaker Co, Saudi Arabia; Vice President, Ghazi Shaker and Bros, Saudi Arabia; President, Cementation Saudi Arabia Ltd; Director, Banque du Liban et d'Outre-Mer, Lebanon; Personal Adviser to HM Sultan Qaboos Bin Said, Sultan of Oman, 1972–; *Decorations:* Medal of the Egyptian Republic, 1st Class; Medal of the

Tunisian Republic, 1st Class; Order of the Jordanian Star, 1st Class; Order of Jordanian Independence 1st Class; Omani Renaissance Medal 1st Class; Omani Medal 1st Class; Iranian Hamyoun Medal; Grand Officer of the Légion d'Honneur, France; Cavalieri di Gran Croce, Italy; Merito Civil, Spain; *Interests and Recreations:* swimming, tennis, hunting; *Languages:* Arabic, English, Turkish, French; *Address:* PO Box 156, Riyadh, Saudi Arabia; 17 Grosvenor Square, Flat 11, London W1; telephone: Riyadh 20520, 28470, 28471.

SHAKIR, Abdul Magid, Tunisian diplomat; born Sfax, Tunisia; married; three children; *Religion:* Muslim; *Education:* in Tunisia and France; *Career:* President of the General Union of Tunisian Students in France; lawyer; Counsel for the defence of the Algerian Leader, Mohammed Ben Bella; Administrative Director of the Neo-Destour Political Bureau; Secretary of State for Agriculture, 1962; Secretary of State for Information; Ambassador to Algeria, 1966–70; Ambassador to Yugoslavia, 1970–72; Ambassador to Sweden, Norway, Finland and Iceland, 1973; Ambassador to Spain, 1982–; *Languages:* Arabic, French; *Address:* Embassy of Tunisia, Plaza de Alonso, Martinez 3, Madrid, Spain.

SHAKKUR, Lieutenant General Yussif, Syrian army officer; born 1926, Homs, Syria; *Religion:* Christian; *Education:* Syrian Military School; Syrian Staff College; Soviet Voroshilov Academy; *Career:* Commander, South-Western Front and South Western Region, 1963; Chief Commander, Army Artillery, 1963; Commander, Security Forces, 1964–67; Chief of Operations Branch, General Headquarters, 1967; Deputy Chief of Staff, 1968–72; Chief of Staff, 1972–74; Deputy Minister of Defence, 1974; *Decorations:* Knight of Syrian, Egyptian and Palestinian Legions of Honour; Moroccan and Syrian Orders of Merit; Commander, Order of the Cedar of Lebanon; *Languages:* Arabic, French; *Address:* Ministry of Defence, Damascus, Syria.

SHALHOUB, Ghazi Salih Bin, Saudi Arabian businessman; born 1941, Jeddah, Saudi Arabia; *Education:* Diploma of Commerce; *Career:* former officer, Saudi Arabian Airlines; member of Chamber of Commerce, Jeddah; owner and Manager, Shalhoob

Aluminium Factory; *Interests and Recreations:* reading, football; *Address:* Khalid Bin al-Wahid Street, Sharafiyya, Jeddah, Saudi Arabia.

SHALHOUB, Salih Bin Muhammad Bin, Saudi Arabian official; born Riyadh, Saudi Arabia; *Religion:* Muslim; *Career:* Assistant at late King Abdul Aziz's Court; Private Secretary to late King Abdul Aziz; Director, Ministry of Finance, Riyadh; *Interests and Recreations:* reading; *Address:* Bin Shalhoub House, Airport Street, Kandara, Jeddah, Saudi Arabia; telephone: Office — Jeddah 631 1215; Residence — Jeddah 631 1547.

SHALI, Khusruw Ghani, Iraqi academic/agriculturalist; born 1 July 1938, Sulaimaniya, Iraq; married; one son, one daughter; *Religion:* Muslim; *Education:* BSc in Agriculture, University of Baghdad, 1960; MSc in Forestry, University of Edinburgh, UK, 1967; PhD in Agriculture, University of Edinburgh, 1974; *Career:* Research Assistant, 1960; Lecturer, 1970; Dean of Students, University of Sulaimaniyah (Salahuddin University), 1974–76; Head of Soil Department, College of Agriculture, University of Sulaimaniyah, 1976–77; General Registrar, University of Sulaimaniyah, 1977; Dean of College of Agriculture, University of Sulaimaniyah, 1977–81; Assistant Professor, 1981; President of the University of Sulaimaniyah, 1981–; member of the British Society of Soil Science; member of the International Society of Soil Science; *Publications:* several articles in the University journal *ZANCO; Interests and Recreations:* travel; *Languages:* Arabic, Kurdish, English; *Address:* President of the University of Salahuddin, Arbil, Iraq; telephone: 23441; telex: 8912.

SHALLAH, Badriddine, Syrian businessman; born 1909, Damascus, Syria; *Career:* Businessman, exporter/importer of food and agricultural products; President of the Union of Syrian Chambers of Commerce and of Damascus Chamber of Commerce; *Languages:* Arabic; *Address:* Faysal Street, P O Box 150, Damascus, Syria; telephone: 110005, 111339, 118339.

SHAMAIMARI, General Hamad al-, Saudi Arabian army officer; born 1920; *Religion:* Muslim; *Education:* Military School, Taif; *Career:* commissioned, 1943; former Com-

mander of the 11th Brigade in Jordan; Deputy Chief of Staff, 1965–71; Chief of Staff, 1971; First Chief of General Staff, 1973–; *Address:* Ministry of Defence, Airport Road, Riyadh, Saudi Arabia.

SHAMI, Ahmad al-, Yemen Arab Republic diplomat/politician; *Religion:* Muslim; *Career:* royalist Foreign Minister, 1964–70; member of Republican Council, 1970–71; Ambassador to UK, 1971–73; Ambassador to France, 1973–75; *Address:* c/o Ministry of Foreign Affairs, Sana'a, Yemen Arab Republic.

SHAMI, Faruk Yahia, Saudi Arabian businessman; born 1941, Jeddah, Saudi Arabia; *Education:* MA in Marketing Psychology; *Career:* Administrative Assistant, Saudi Embassy to Austria, 1968–69; Representative of Swiss Watches Factories in Saudi Arabia, Gulf States; member of International Centre for Watches and Jewellery Factories, Lausanne, Gemmological Association of Great Britain, London, Jewellery Organisation, West Germany, Dixi Group, Buhre Group, Furrer Jacot, Switzerland, Saint Maurice Enterprises, France, Alexander Marketing Institute, USA; member of the Board of Louis Roselle Company, Orfina Company, Candino Company; Proprietor of International Markets Agency, Jeddah; President, Saudi International Food Company, Jeddah; attended several international conferences on watch trade; *Publications: Watch Trade in Saudi Arabia and Gulf States,* published under the auspices of the Union of Swiss Watch Factories; *Address:* FY Shami Building, Medina Road, Al-Fatah Street, P O Box 2391, Jeddah, Saudi Arabia; telephone: 6656309, 6655782; telex: 401500 SHAMI SJ.

SHAMI, Hassan, Moroccan official/engineer; born 1938, Fes, Morocco; *Religion:* Muslim; *Education:* Engineering, Ecole Nationale des Ponts et Chaussées, Paris, France; *Career:* Director of Public Works in Meknes; Director of the development of Casablanca Port; Director of the Port of Casablanca, 1965; Director of Hydraulics, 1969; Minister of Public Works and Communications, 1970; Director General of the Office de Commercialisation et d'Exportation (OCE), 1971; *Languages:* Arabic, French; *Address:* Office de Commercialisation et d'Exportation (OCE), 45 Avenue des F.A.R., Casablanca, Morocco.

SHAMISSI, Shaikh Hadif Bin Hamid al-, United Arab Emirates businessman; born 1931, Al-Hamawiya, United Arab Emirates; married; four sons; *Religion:* Muslim; *Career:* Deputy President of Al-Ain Municipal Council; Head of Purchasing Committee, Zaid Port, Abu Dhabi; Personal Companion to HH President of the United Arab Emirates; *Interests and Recreations:* classical poetry, falconry, hunting; member of the Falconry Club; *Languages:* Arabic, English, Urdu; *Address:* HH The Ruler's Office, P O Box 124, Abu Dhabi, United Arab Emirates.

SHAMMA, Samir, Saudi Arabian lawyer; born 1912, Safad, Palestine; *Education:* Law Studies, Palestine; *Career:* called to the Palestine Bar, 1943; Syrian Bar, 1948; Legal Adviser, Saudi Arabian Ministry of Foreign Affairs, 1950–54; Legal Adviser to the Saudi Arabian Directorate of Petroleum and Mineral Affairs, 1954–59; played a large part in negotiating and drafting the neutral Zone Offshore Concession Agreement between the Saudi Arabian Government and a Japanese firm; closely connected with the world of oil; private law practice, Jeddah; *Address:* King Abdul Aziz Street, Amir Abdullah al Faisal Building, Jeddah, Saudi Arabia; telephone: Jeddah 27286.

SHAMMAS, Elias Wahid, Lebanese businessman/publisher; born 1945, Beirut, Lebanon; married; *Education:* St. Joseph University, Beirut, Lebanon; *Career:* Managing Director, Arab Press Service, Nicosia, Cyprus, 1978–; Vice Chairman, P.H. and E. Chammas Investment Ltd, Nicosia, Cyprus; *Languages:* Arabic, English, French; *Address:* 1B Naxos Street, Nicosia, Cyprus; telephone: 55280; telex: 3712 APS CY.

SHAMMAS, Habib Abdul Nour, Lebanese businessman/insurance specialist; born 1936, Beirut, Lebanon; married; three sons; *Education:* MA, American University of Beirut, Lebanon; *Career:* Representative, American Life Insurance Company, (ALICO), Gulf Area; Senior Agency Manager, ALICO; Director, Furjaira National Insurance Company; Founder and Partner in several of the Chammas Group of Companies; Vice-Chairman, P.H. and E. Chammas Investments Ltd, Nicosia, Cyprus, 1980–; *Languages:* Arabic, English; *Address:* Fujairah National Insurance Company, P O Box 277, Fujairah, United Arab Emirates; telephone: 22527/8; telex: 89012 FINSCO EM.

SHAMMAS, Pierre Wahid, Lebanese economist/publisher; born 1941, Beirut, Lebanon; married one son, two daughters; *Education:* BA, History, University of Munich, Germany, 1958; Postgraduate Studies in Economics and Political Science, University of York, England, 1969; *Career:* Editor and later Consultant, Economic and Political Affairs, Kuwait, 1962–68; Consultant, Petroleum Economics and Political Affairs, Beirut, Lebanon, 1966–68, 1970–73; Founder and Chief Editor, Arab Press Services (APS) , and APS Consultants, Nicosia, Cyprus, 1973–; Founder and President, P.H. and E. Chammas Investments Ltd, Nicosia, Cyprus, P. Chammas for Construction and Development, Beirut, Lebanon, APS, (Media and Marketing) Ltd, Nicosia; member of the Arab British Chamber of Commerce, London, England; *Publications:* several studies and reports on petroleum and financial affairs in the Middle East and elsewhere, and Arab international affairs; *Languages:* Arabic, English, German, French, Turkish; *Address:* 1B Naxos Street, Nicosia, Cyprus; telephone: 57773, 66778; telex: 3712 APS CY.

SHAMMAS, Said Ya'qub, Kuwaiti diplomat; born 1927; married; four children; *Religion:* Christian; *Education:* Bristol College of Commerce, UK; Economics and Political Science at London School of Economics, UK; *Career:* Deputy Director General of Civil Service Commission, 1954–61; joined foreign service, 1961; attended general course for Foreign Service trainees, Oxford University, UK, 1961–62; new entrants course at Foreign Office, London; seconded to British Consulate in Antwerp, 1962; Consul General in New York and Kuwait Permanent Observer, and Representative, UN, 1962–63; Ambassador to the USSR, 1963–66; Ambassador to France, 1966–69; Head of Protocol Department, Ministry of Foreign Affairs, 1969–71; Ambassador to Kenya, 1971–73; business interests; *Languages:* Arabic, English; *Address:* P O Box 547, Kuwait.

SHAMMAS, Shukri H., Lebanese businessman/engineer; born 1909; married; three sons, two daughters; *Religion:* Christian; *Education:* BA, American University of Beirut; BSc in Civil Engineering, London University; *Career:* Teacher, Secondary School, Shweir, Lebanon, 1925–26; Gordon College, Khartoum, 1927–32; Engineering and Building Construction Dept, IPC Ltd, 1932–36; Teachers College, Baghdad, Iraq, 1937–39; Partner and Managing Director, the Contracting and Trading Co, Lebanon; President, MOTHERCAT, Scotland; Chairman and President, Tourism and Hotel Development Corporation SAL; Chairman, Rabiya Co SAL; Vice Chairman, Banque de l'Industrie et du Travail SAL; Managing Director, CAT Co and Partners, WLL, Libya; Director, Société des Grands Hôtels du Liban, SAL; Director, National Steel Construction Co, Libya; Mayor of Rabiya, 1960–; member of Board of Trustees, AUB, 1963–; Chairman, Advisory Council of the Lebanese Management Association, 1964–; Fellow, American University of Washington D.C., 1966–; *Publications: Some Problems of Science and Engineering Education in the Middle East,* 1961; *Al-Rabiya, A Residential Project in Lebanon,* 1962; *Pipelines in the Service of Petroleum Industry,* 1963; *Oil Storage,* 1965; *Lebanan's Business Outlook,* 1971; *Oil Control,* 1973; *Oil Cutbacks,* 1974; *Decorations:* Holy Cross Medal, 1956; St. Mark's Greater Cordon, 1957; Cedar's National Medal, 1972; *Interests and Recreations:* reading, tennis, swimming, bridge; member of Alumni Association of AUB; Chairman of Lebanese Management Association; member of Alumni Lions, Automobile and Rabiy and other clubs; *Languages:* Arabic, English and French; *Address:* The Contracting and Trading Co, CAT, P O Box 11–1036, Beirut, Lebanon; telephone: 221564, 221569.

SHAMS, Ibrahim Muhammad Said, Saudi Arabian banker; born 1931, Jeddah; married; three sons, one daughter; *Religion:* Muslim; *Education:* general education; *Career:* Bank of Indochina, Jeddah, 1951–62; Head of Accounts, Riyadh Bank, 1961–65; Inspector, Riyadh Bank, 1965–67, Controller, 1967–69, Manager, 1969–71, Assistant General Manager, 1971–73, Deputy General Manager, 1973–80; General Manager, Riyadh Bank, 1980–; Chairman of Gulf Riyadh Bank, Bahrain; Chairman, Saudi Travellers Cheques Company, Riyadh; member of the Board of Directors of Saudi Arabian Agricultural Bank, General Social Insurance Organization, Jeddah Oil Refinery, UBAF, Paris, and UBAF Bank Ltd, London, UK; member of the Union of Arab Banks, Beirut, Lebanon, Arab Bankers Association, London, UK, Islamic Bank International Association;

Interests and Recreations: reading; swimming; *Languages:* Arabic, English; *Address:* Riyadh Bank, P O Box 1047, Jeddah, Saudi Arabia; telephone: 647 4777.

SHAMSA, Muhammad Sadiq Bakir, Iraqi academic; born 1943, Najaf, Iraq; married; three children; *Education:* BSc in Commerce and Economics; MA in Social and Economic Sciences; PhD in Accounting; *Career:* Head of Management Development, University of Baghdad, 1977; Deputy Dean of Faculty of Management and Economics, University of Baghdad, 1977–78; Dean of Faculty of Management, Salahuddin University, 1978–; member of the Board of the Syndicate of Accountants, 1978; Deputy Chairman of the Iraqi Economists Association, Sulaimaniya, 1981; *Publications:* co-author of *Specialised Accounting,* 1979; *Tax Accounting* 1980, and other works; *Languages:* Arabic, English; *Address:* Salahuddin University, Arbil, Iraq; telephone: Office — 25514, 25413; Residence — 27824.

SHANDIRLI, Abdul Kadir, Algerian official/diplomat; born 1915, Algiers, Algeria; married; two children; *Religion:* Muslim; *Education:* School of Political Science, Algiers and University of Paris, France; *Career:* served in French Army in Algeria, 1943–45, later in France and Germany; edited newspaper for French troops in France and Germany; Editor of French newspaper in Shanghai, China, 1946–48; Head of Public Relations at UNESCO, Paris; Representative, National Liberation Front (FLN), UN, USA, during War of Independence; first Permanent Representative of Algeria at the UN, 1962; Director General of Political, Economic and Cultural Affairs, Ministry of Foreign Affairs; Director of National Oil Company SONATRACH, and Head of Special Organization set up by UN Special Fund on the planning of the Algerian chemical industry; Chairman of the National Liquid Methane Corporation (CAMEL), 1969–75; Director, Arab Fund for Economic and Social Development, 1975; *Languages:* Arabic, English, French; *Address:* Arab Fund for Economic and Social Development, P O Box 21923, Safat, Kuwait; telephone: 431870.

SHANFARI, Said Ahmad al-, Omani politician/businessman; born 1939, Salalah, Oman; *Religion:* Muslim; *Education:* Oman and abroad; *Career:* Director and Owner of several businesses in Salalah and Muscat; Minister of Agriculture and Fisheries, Petroleum and Minerals, 1974–79; Minister of Petroleum and Mineral Resources, 1979–; *Address:* Ministry of Petroleum and Mineral Resources, P O Box 551, Muscat, Oman; telephone: 603785; telex: 3280.

SHANSHAL, Lieutenant General Abdul Jibbar Khalil, Iraqi army officer; born 1920, Mosul, Iraq; married; *Career:* Chief of Staff of 3rd Division, 1963; Chief of Staff, 1963; Commander of Staff College, 1964; Commander of 4th Division, Mosul, and Commander of Mosul Garrison, 1966; Deputy Chief of General Staff (Operations), 1968; promoted Lieutenant General, 1969; Chief of General Staff, 1970; *Languages:* Arabic, English; *Address:* Ministry of Defence, Baghdad, Iraq.

SHANTY, Ahmad Mahmud al-, Saudi Arabian geologist; born 1932, Jaffa, Palestine; *Religion:* Muslim; *Education:* PhD in Geology; *Career:* geologist; Director of the Mining Administration; Director of the Geological Administration in the General Directorate of Mineral Resources; Director of the Geological Centre; Director of the Applied Geology Institute, Riyadh; member of the Association of Geological International Development (IGCP), National Committee for Geological Co-ordination, Board of the Association of Geological International Development (AGID); participated at the Atomic Energy Conference, Vienna, 1965, and the Arab Conference for Mineral Resources, Saudi Arabia; *Publications:* several papers published by the General Directorate for Mineral Resources, Saudi Arabia; *Interests and Recreations:* sport, swimming; *Address:* Applied Geology Institute, P O Box 1744, Riyadh, Saudi Arabia.

SHAQWARA, Yahya Ali, Jordanian businessman/economist; born 8 August 1938, Nablus, Jordan; married; two sons; *Religion:* Muslim; *Education:* Diploma and PhD in Economics and Social Sciences, University of Nuremburg, West Germany, 1969–72; *Career:* Head of Research Section, Ministry of Culture and Information, Jordan, 1973; Head of Economic Research Section in Royal Scientific Society, Jordan, 1975; Manager for Consultancy, Talal Abu Ghazalah International, Jordan, 1978; General Manager, Shaqwara Consultancy Bureau, Jordan,

1980–; Lecturer, Jordan University, Amman; *Publications: The Role of Mass Communication System in National Development of Jordan,* 1973 (German); *The Impact of Investment Law on Industry and Tourism in Jordan,* 1976, in Arabic; *The Role of Journalism in National Development in Jordan,* 1977, in Arabic and German; *Interests and Recreations:* Arabic and German poetry, swimming, tennis; *Languages:* Arabic, German, English; *Address:* P O Box 7214, Jordan; telephone: 65026.

SHARABI, Hisham, Arab-American academic; born 4 April 1927, Palestine; married; two daughters; *Religion:* Muslim; *Education:* BA, AUB, Lebanon; MA, PhD, University of Chicago, USA; *Career:* News Analyst, UN Press Section, 1952–53; Georgetown University, Washington D.C., 1953–; Editor, *Journal of Palestine Studies,* 1971–; Professor of History and Government, Georgetown University; member of Executive Committee, Centre for Contemporary Arabic Studies, Georgetown University the Middle East Institute, the American Historical Association, the Middle East Studies Association; *Publications: A Handbook of the Contemporary Middle East,* 1957; *Government and Politics of the Middle East in the 20th Century,* 1962, 1963, 1968; *Nationalism and Revolution in the Arab World,* 1966; *Strategy and Diplomacy in the Arab-Israeli Conflict,* in Arabic, Beirut, 1975; *Languages:* Arabic, English, French; *Address:* 5105 Worthington Drive, Washington D.C. 20016, USA; telephone: (301) 229 6716.

SHARABI, Nazim Bishara, Jordanian banker/official; born 1 March 1916, Nablus, Palestine; married; four daughters; *Religion:* Muslim; *Education:* BA in Political Science, American University of Beirut, AUB, Lebanon, 1937; MA in Political Science, AUB, 1941; Diploma in Social Studies, Birmingham University, UK; *Career:* Lecturer, AUB, 1938–41; Probation Officer, Palestine, 1942–48; Assistant Field Director, League of Red Cross Societies, East Jordan, 1948–49; Controller of Imports and Exports, Jordan, 1949–51; Under Secretary, Ministry of Social Welfare, Jordan, 1951–54; Senior Manager, Arab Bank Ltd, Head Office, Amman, Jordan, 1954–63; Minister of Finance and Minister of National Economy, 1963–64; Assistant General Manager, Arab Bank Ltd, Head Office, Amman, 1965–68;

Minister of National Economy, 1968–69; Assistant General Manager, Arab Bank Ltd, Amman, 1969; *Decorations:* Order of the Jordanian Star,1st Class; *Interests and Recreations:* tennis, reading; *Languages:* Arabic, English; *Address:* Arab Bank Ltd, Head Office, Amman, Jordan; telephone: Office — 38161, Residence — 41567.

SHARAF, Abdul Aziz Muhammad, Egyptian journalist; born 5 November 1940, Dakahliyah, Egypt; married; *Religion:* Muslim; *Education:* College of Arts, Cairo University, Egypt, 1968; MA in Journalism, 1971; PhD in Mass Communications, Cairo University, 1975; *Career:* Journalist, 1968; Teacher, Cairo University, 1972–75; Professor of Information and Mass Communications, Al-Azhar University, 1976; Literary Editor, *Al-Ahram* newspaper; member of the Egyptian Writers Association; member of the Egyptian Journalists Association; *Publications: Lutfi al-Sayyid: Philosopher of the Nation,* 1963, in Arabic; *Resistance in Contemporary Algerian Literature,* in Arabic, 1971; *Creative Vision,* 1971; *Mass Media and The Language of Civilization,* 1979; *The Art of Editing for Mass Media,* 1980, and several other publications; *Decorations:* 1st Prize, Egyptian Journalists Association, 1966; 1st Prize, Arabic Language Academy, 1970; 2nd Prize, Arab League Economic, Cultural and Social Organization, ALECSO, 1973; *Languages:* Arabic, English; *Address:* Office — Al-Ahram Newspaper, Al-Galaa Street, Cairo, Egypt; telephone: 7550; Residence — 17 Digla Street, Madinat al-Muhandisiin, Cairo, Egypt.

SHARAF, Sharif Fawwaz, Jordanian official; born 1938, Amman, Jordan; *Religion:* Muslim; *Education:* BA, American University of Beirut, Beirut, Lebanon; *Career:* Ministry of Foreign Affairs, 1961–62; Prime Minister's Office, 1962–63; member of Jordan Mission to the UN, New York, 1963–65; Ministry of Foreign Affairs, 1965–66; Secretary General, Youth Care Organisation, 1966–74; Director General, Jordan Youth and Sports Organisation, 1974–76; founder of the Royal Jordanian Theatre, and the Physical Education College, Amman, Jordan; Minister, Culture and Youth, 1976–; assisted in the creation of the Jordan National Library, and National Museum, Amman, Jordan; *Languages:* Arabic, English; *Address:* Ministry of Culture and Youth, Amman, Jordan.

SHARAF, Taysir Ahmad, Jordanian banker; resident in UK; born 2 October 1933, Haifa, Palestine; married; three sons; *Religion:* Muslim; *Education:* BA in English Literature, Damascus University, Syria, 1958; *Career:* Financial Controller, Arab Bank Ltd, Damascus, 1959; Secretary General and Manager of Foreign Relations Department, Arab Orient Bank, 1963–67; Manager, Foreign Relations Department, Commercial Bank of Syria, Damascus, 1967–68; Assistant Manager, Arab Bank Ltd, Benghazi Branch, Libya, 1969–70; Manager, Arab Bank, Tripoli, Libya, 1970–71; Manager of Arab Bank Nigeria Ltd, Kano Branch, 1972–74; Managing Director, Arab Bank Nigeria Ltd, Lagos, Nigeria, 1974–77; Manager, Arab Bank Ltd, London, UK, 1978; Representative, Al Saudi Banque, 1979–80; Manager, Al Saudi Banque, West End Branch, London, 1981–82; Manager, Bank Relations Division, Al Saudi Banque, London, 1983–; *Publications:* articles in Arabic magazines published in London; *Interests and Recreations:* reading, swimming, tennis, bridge; *Languages:* Arabic, English, French; *Address:* Office — 52/60 Cannon Street, London EC4, UK; telephone: 236 6533; Residence -- 10 Park West, London W2, UK; telephone: (01) 258 0358.

SHARAFA, Ali, United Arab Emirates official; born 1941, Sharjah, United Arab Emirates; *Religion:* Muslim; *Education:* Cairo Military Academy, Egypt; *Career:* officer in Abu Dhabi Defence Force; Director of Civil Service Commission; United Arab Emirates Ambassador to the Sudan, 1972–73; Head of Economic Department, Ministry of Foreign Affairs; Director of the Presidential Diwan; *Languages:* Arabic, English; *Address:* Amiri Palace, Abu Dhabi, United Arab Emirates.

SHARAIHA, Wadi J., Jordanian academic/economist; born 15 August 1936, Jordan; married; two children; *Education:* BA in Law Baghdad University, 1961; MSc in Economic Development, Charles University, 1963; PhD in Economic Planning and Development, Charles University, 1965; Course in Marketing and Managment, Harvard University, USA, 1969; course in Planning, Madison University, USA; *Career:* Senior Economist, Jordan Development Planning Council, 1965–67; Associate Professor, Department of Economics, University of Jordan, 1969; Professor, Department of Economic Development and Planning, University of Jordan, 1971; Head of Economics and Statistics, 1971–75; Director of Planning and Development, University of Jordan, 1974–76; Assistant Professor, Department of Economics and Statistics, University of Jordan, 1976; University Planning Adviser, University of Kuwait, 1976–78; Dean, Faculty of Economics and Commerce, Professor of Economic Development and Planning, University of Jordan, 1979–; member of the Academic Advisory Board, Georgetown University, Washington D.C., USA, 1981, the Jordan Economic Society, the Board of Directors of King Hussain Fund for Research, the Steering Committee for Industrial Development of Jordan, the Board of Trustees of National College, Amman, Jordan; Distinguished Member of the International Advisory Board of the Association for Anthropological Diplomacy, Williamsburg, USA; *Publications: Economic Development in Jordan,* published by the Higher Institute for Arab Studies, 1976; *Economic Growth and Population Policy in Jordan,* AKWA, 1971; *Arab Common Market: Economic Analysis,* 1972; *Gulf Economic Integration,* Kuwait Chamber of Commerce, 1977; *The Role of Budget in Economic Planning,* Rabat, Morocco, 1980; and several others; *Address:* University of Jordan, Amman, Jordan; telephone: 845 3555.

SHARBATLI, Abdul Rahman Hassan Abbas, Saudi Arabian businessman; born 1943; *Religion:* Muslim; *Education:* Victoria College, Alexandria, Egypt; *Career:* private enterprise; member of Board of Red Sea Insurance Co, Dhahran Electric Co, Saudi Refineries Co; *Interests and Recreations:* swimming: *Address:* P O Box 5627, Attar Building, King Abdul Aziz Street, Jeddah, Saudi Arabia; telephone: 6442631; telex: 401228 SJ.

SHARBATLI, Al-Sayyid Ibrahim Hassan Abbas, Saudi Arabian businessman; born 1952, Jeddah; *Religion:* Muslim; *Education:* Higher Diploma in Commerce and Economics; *Career:* Honorary Consul General of Panama in Jeddah; President of Saudi Arabia Marketing Corporation; Chairman of Saudi Spanish Construction Co; President of Samaco-Binladin Co; shareholder in several Saudi and Arab firms; *Interests and Recreations:* reading, swimming; *Address:* P O Box 5968, Jeddah, Saudi Arabia; telephone: Office — Jeddah 6655568, 6672951.

SHAREKH, Muhammad al-, Kuwaiti banker/businessman; born 20 September 1942, Kuwait; married; *Religion:* Muslim; *Education:* BSc in Economics, Cairo University, Egypt, 1965; MA in Development Economics, Williams College, Williamstown, Massachusetts, USA, 1968; *Career:* Kuwait Customs, 1958; Department of Posts, Telegraphs and Telephones, 1959–65; Deputy Director General, Kuwait Fund for Arab Economic Development, 1965–73; member of the Committee on Industrial Projects, Prime Minister's Office, Kuwait, 1972; Founder and main Partner, Electronics International Ltd, Kuwait, 1970–73; Alternate Executive Director, IBRD, World Bank, Washington D.C., USA, 1973–74; Chairman and Managing Director, Industrial Bank of Kuwait, 1974–77; Chairman, Al Alamiah Co, 1977– (established 1970); member of the Kuwait Economics Society; member of the Federation of Arab Economists; *Interests and Recreations:* chess, reading, history, poetry; *Languages:* Arabic, English; *Address:* Al Alamiah, P O Box 23781, Safat, Kuwait; telephone: 414141; telex: 2694 EIL.

SHARI'E, Abdullah al-Nafi'e al-, Saudi Arabian academic; born 1937, Medina, Saudi Arabia; *Religion:* Muslim; *Education:* PhD in Educational Psychology; *Career:* various posts in Ministry of Education, including inspector of schools; Lecturer, Assistant, Associate and Professor, Faculty of Education , King Abdul Aziz University, Mecca, Saudi Arabia; Professor, Faculty of Education, Riyadh University, Saudi Arabia; Vice Dean and Dean, Faculty of Education, Riyadh University; member of Supreme Council of Riyadh University; member of the Board of King Abdul Aziz Historical Archives, Institute of Public Administration, International Society of Psychology, International Society of Applied Psychology, Society of Higher Education; currently Vice Chancellor, University of Riyadh, Riyadh, Saudi Arabia; attended national and international conferences in the fields of psychology and education; *Publications:* several papers in field of psychology; *Languages:* Arabic, English; *Address:* University of Riyadh, P O Box 2454, Riyadh Saudi Arabia; telephone: 29500.

SHARI, Saduk al-, Jordanian politician/army officer; born 1923, Huwara, Irbid, Jordan; married; *Education:* various military certificates; Senior Commanders' Certificate; British Staff College Certificate, 1949; *Career:* officer cadet, 1942; 2nd Lieutenant, 1943; platoon commander and training officer; Adjutant of Army Training Centre at Sarafand, 1944; Staff Captain, Mechanised Brigade, 1945; Staff Captain, 1st Infantry Division, 1948; Brigade Major, 3rd Infantry Brigade, 1952; Commanding Officer, 8th Infantry Regiment, 1953; Commander, National Guards, 1954; Chief of Staff, Arab Jordanian Army, 1957; Deputy Commander in Chief of the Arab Hashemite Union Army, 1958; Chief of Staff, Arab Jordanian Army, 1958; retired in 1959; Director General of the Passports Department, 1971; District Governor, Irbid District, 1972; Minister of Supply, 1974; Minister of State for Foreign Affairs 1974–76; member of the Arab National Union Council, 1972; *Decorations:* Independence Medal, 4th Class; Renaissance Medal, 3rd Class; Star of Jordan, 2nd Class; Independence Medal, 1st Class; Operational Medal for World War II; Operational Medal for Palestine; Egyptian Military Medal of Merit, 1st Class; Syrian Military Medal of Merit, 1st Class; British War Star Medal; Chinese High Star Medal, 1st Class; *Address:* Tha'a Al-Ali, Amman, Jordan; telephone: 845462.

SHARIF, Abdul Sattar Tahir, Iraqi politician; born 1933, Kirkuk, Iraq; *Career:* member of the Kurdish Democratic Party (KDP); Secretary Third Branch of KDP, Secretary General, 1973; Minister of Housing, April, 1974; Minister of Municipalities, 1974–76; Minister of Transport, 1976–; Committee's Secretary General, Kurdish Revolutionary Party; *Languages:* Arabic, Kurdish; *Address:* Ministry of Transport, Baghdad, Iraq.

SHARIF, Abu Bakr Ali al-, Libyan banker/politician; born 1940, Benghazi, Libya; *Religion:* Muslim; *Education:* economic studies in Cairo, 1964–66; *Career:* businessman in Misurata; Director of the General Organization for Industrialization and Head of the General Planning Authority; Minister of Economy, 1972–77; Secretary for Trade, General People's Committee, 1977; Chairman and General Manager, Libyan Arab Foreign Bank, 1980–; *Languages:* Arabic, English; *Address:* Libyan Arab Foreign Bank, P O Box 2542, Tripoli, Libya; telephone: 41428.

SHARIF, Aziz, Iraqi politician; born 1902, Ana, Iraq; *Education:* Teachers College, Baghdad, Iraq, 1925; Law College, Baghdad, 1931; *Career:* Lawyer, Basra, 1931–34; Judge, Basra Law Courts, 1934; Lawyer, Basra and Baghdad, 1935–42; Judge, Baghdad Law Courts, member of the High Criminal Court, 1942–44; founded the People's Party, 1943, banned, 1947; founding member, Afro-Asian People's Solidarity Movement, Cairo, 1958, later in Baghdad; led Peace Movement, Baghdad, 1958–; Secretary General, Joint National Council for Peace and Solidarity, Baghdad, Iraq, 1969–; actively participated in mediation for peaceful settlement of Kurdish Question, and Declaration of March 11, 1970; Minister of Justice, 1969; Minister of State, 1976; member of the Presidential Committee, Bureau of the World Peace Council and Vice President of the Council; *Decorations:* Lenin International Peace Prize, 1960; *Address:* Secretary General, National Council for Peace and Solidarity, Baghdad, Iraq.

SHARIF, Fuad, Egyptian official; born 1926, Egypt; married; four children; *Education:* PhD in Business Administration, University of Chicago, USA; one year post-doctoral research, Harvard Business School, USA; *Career:* founder, National Institute of Management Development, Cairo, 1961; UN office, New York, wrote about management problems, 1967; assisted in the reorganization of UN internal administration; one of 23 inter-regional advisers; Minister of State for Cabinet Affairs and Administrative Development, 1976; *Address:* c/o Ministry of Cabinet Affairs, Cairo, Egypt.

SHARIF, Kamil Ismail al-, Jordanian diplomat; born 1936, Al-Arish, Jordan; married; *Education:* general; *Career:* officer in Palestine Liberation Army, 1947; Commander of Fedayeen Brigade in Palestine War with rank of Major; Commander of Fedayeen operations in the Suez Canal Zone, 1951; Ambassador to Nigeria, Germany, Taiwan and Pakistan, 1961–72; Senator, 1973–75; Minister of Waqfs, Islamic Affairs and Holy Places, 1976–; Chairman of Islamic Congress for Jerusalem; executive member of World Muslim League; executive member of World Council of Mosques; founder and editor of *Al Oustour* newspapers; *Publications: Secret Resistance at the Suez Canal,* 1957; *Decorations:* Egyptian Golden Order for Bravery; Star of Palestine Medal; *Address:* P O Box 2429, Amman, Jordan; telephone: 61957.

SHARIF, Muhammad Ahmad, Libyan official/educationalist; *Religion:* Muslim; *Education:* in USA; *Career:* Dean of the Faculty of Education, University of Libya, Tripoli; Minister of Education, 1972; led Islamic side at Islamic-Christian Dialogue, Tripoli, 1976, and Chairman of the Conference; *Address:* c/o Secretariat of General People's Committee for Education, Tripoli, Libya.

SHARIF, Muhammad al-, Syrian official/lawyer; born 1930, Syria; *Religion:* Muslim; *Education:* LLB, Faculty of Law, Damascus University, Damascus, Syria; *Career:* Assistant Director, Customs Department, 1965–66; Director General, Customs Department, 1966–74; Minister of Finance, 1974–76; Assistant Secretary General of the Council of Arab Economic Unity, Amman, Jordan, 1977–; *Address:* General Secretariat, Council of Arab Economic Unity, P O Box 925100, Amman, Jordan; West Abou Rummaneh Street, Damascus, Syria.

SHARIF, Omar (Michel Shalhoub), Egyptian artist/actor; *Education:* Victoria College, Alexandria, Egypt; *Career:* made first film *The Blazing Sun,* 1953; starred in 24 Egyptian films and two French co-production films during following five years; began international film career with *Lawrence of Arabia;* starred in *The Fall of the Roman Empire, Behold a Pale Horse, Ghengis Khan, The Yellow Rolls-Royce, Doctor Zhivago, The Night of the Generals, Mackenna's Gold, Funny Girl, Cinderella-Italian Style;* *Languages:* Arabic, English, French; *Address:* c/o Carolyn Pfeiffer Ltd, Flat 2, 10 Connaught Place, London W2, UK.

SHARIF, Rashid Bin Rajih Muhammad al-, Saudi Arabian academic/Islamic scholar; born 1944, Taif; *Religion:* Muslim; *Education:* BA in Islamic Law, Mecca, 1965; PhD in Philology and Arabic, Cambridge, 1972; *Career:* Dean of Faculty of Shari'a and Islamic Studies, Mecca; Superintendent, University of Mecca; Deputy President, University of Mecca; Vice Chancellor, Umm al-Qura University; participated in the 10th Conference on Islamic Thought, Algiers, Algeria, Conference on the Objectives of the University, Teachers Training Conference,

Mecca, the Conference of Islamic Teaching, Conference of Islamic Economy, Conference of Islamic Societies, Canada, Conference of Islamic Students Union, USA, Conference of the Islamic Research Academy, Cairo, Seminar of Shaikh Muhammad Bin Abdul Wahab, Riyadh, annual conference of the Society of Muslim Arab Students, USA, Conference on Crime Prevention; member of the Mecca Literary Club; *Publications:* *Islamic and Linguistic Studies,* under publication; *Interests and recreations:* reading, sports; *Address:* Faculty of Law, Umm al-Qura University, P O Box 715, Mecca, Saudi Arabia; telephone: 5565321; telex: 440026 JAMMKA SJ.

SHAROUNY, Yusif al-; Egyptian writer; born 14 October 1924, Munufia, Egypt; married; one son, one daughter; *Education:* BA in philosophy, Cairo University, Egypt, 1945; *Career:* Teacher, Egypt; Teacher, Sudan, 1949–57; worked for the Supreme Council for Arts, Literature and Social Sciences, 1956–; Under Secretary of State, Ministry of Culture and Information; writer and author; member of the Arab Writers Conference, Cairo 1957, 1968, Kuwait 1958, Baghdad 1965, 1970, Algeria 1975; paricipated in Al-Ghazali Festival of the Supreme Council of Arts, Literature and Social Sciences, Damascus, Syria, 1961; member of the Writers Association, of the Writers Union, and of several other literary associations; *Publications:* numerous short story collections and literary studies, 1954–79; several of his works have been translated into English, German, French and Spanish; *Decorations:* Order of the Republic, 1979; the Government Promotion Prize for Literary Criticism, 1978; the Government Promotion Prize for Short Stories, 1970; Order of Sciences and Arts, 1970; *Languages:* Arabic, English, French; *Address:* High Council of Arts, Literature and Social Sciences, 9 Hassan Sabri Street, Zamalek, Cairo, Egypt.

SHARQAWI, Abdul Rahman al-, Egyptian writer; born 1920, Egypt; *Religion:* Muslim; *Education:* graduated in Law, 1943; *Career:* worked as lawyer, civil servant, journalist; Chairman of the Board of *Rose el-Yousef,* 1977; Chairman of the Higher Council of Literature and the Arts, 1977; *Publications:* include *Al-Ard* (The Earth), translated into English; *Al-shawar'a al-Khalfiyya* (Back Streets); two verse-plays *Ma'sat Jamila* (The Tragedy of Jamila) and *Al-Fata Mahran;*

short story collection *Ahlam Saghira* (Small Dreams); *Address:* c/o Dar Akhbar al-Yom, Sharia al-Sahaafa, Cairo, Egypt.

SHARQI, Hamad Bin Saif al-, United Arab Emirates politician; born 1936, Fujairah, United Arab Emirates; *Religion:* Muslim; *Career:* Governor of Fujairah; United Arab Emirates Minister of State, 1971–73; Deputy Ruler and Chairman of Municipal Council, Fujairah, 1973–; *Address:* Amiri Court, P O Box 1, Government House, Fujairah, United Arab Emirates; telephone: 22313; telex: 89000 SHARQI EM.

SHARQI, HH Shaikh Hamad Bin Muhammad al-; Ruler of Fujairah, United Arab Emirates; born 1949; *Religion:* Muslim; *Education:* in Fujairah; Police Administration in UK, 1967–69; Mons Military Academy, UK, 1970; *Career:* member of the Supreme Council of the United Arab Emirates (UAE); first ruler of a member state in the United Arab Emirates to be appointed by a decree of the Supreme Council of the Union; United Arab Emirates Minister of Agriculture and Fisheries, 1971–74; Ruler of Fujairah, 1974–; *Address:* PO Box 1, Fujairah, United Arab Emirates; telephone: 22443; telex: 8900 SHARQI EM.

SHATA, Bakri Salih, Saudi Arabian official; born 1936, Mecca, Saudi Arabia; *Religion:* Muslim; *Education:* MA Public Administration; *Career:* General Commissioner of Saudi Arabian Pavilion, Expo, Osaka, Japan; Administrative Assistant to Under Secretary of State, Ministry of Commerce; member of various Government Committees on Government Schools Nutrition, Government Purchases and Warehouses; attended several Conferences of General Agreement on Tariffs and Trade (GATT) and UNIDO; Director General of Central Administration for Government Purchases, Ministry of Finance and National Economy; *Interests and Recreations:* swimming, bowling; *Address:* Government Purchasing Department, Ministry of Finance and National Economy, P O Box 3483, Riyadh, Saudi Arabia; telephone: 401 3334; telex: 201626.

SHATTI, Ibrahim al-, Kuwaiti official; born 1930; married; *Religion:* Muslim; *Education:* in Kuwait and Cairo; MA in Geography, Durham University, UK, 1958; *Career:* Director of Research, Ministry of Social Affairs

and Labour, 1961–62; Assistant Under Secretary, Ministry of Information, 1962–64; Assistant Under Secretary, Ministry of Foreign Affairs, 1965–67; Chairman of Kuwait Petrochemical Industries Company; Director of HH The Amir's Office, 1967–; *Publications:* editor of a history textbook; *Languages:* Arabic, English; *Address:* Amiri Diwan, P O Box 799, Safat, Kuwait; telephone: 430001; telex: 22700 AMDIWAN KT.

SHAUBAKI, Ahmad Kayid al-, Jordanian politician/engineer; born 1930, Shaubak; *Religion:* Muslim; *Education:* Civil Engineering, University of Baghdad, Iraq, Turkey and USA; *Career:* Administrator, Ministries of Communication and Public Works; Director of Roads Department, Ministry of Public Works, 1965; Minister of Public Works, 1972–74; Minister of Communications, 1974–76; Minister of Public Works, 1976; member of the National Consultative Council, 1978–; *Languages:* Arabic, English; *Address:* P O Box 9301, Amman, Jordan.

SHAWAF, Abdul Mu'in, Saudi Arabian businessman; born 24 November 1939, Hama; married; three sons; *Religion:* Muslim; *Education:* MA in Political History; *Career:* Administrative Manager; Civil Engineering Consultant, Riyadh, Saudi Arabia; Director General, Al-Rajhi Development Co Ltd, Contracting and Trading; member of Riyadh University Society; *Interests and Recreations:* swimming, table tennis; *Languages:* Arabic, English; *Address:* Al-Rajhi Development Co Ltd, P O Box 4301, Riyadh, Saudi Arabia; telephone: 476 5116, 476 0576.

SHAWAF, Bassim Adbullah al-, Iraqi engineer; born 24 December 1935; resident in USA; married; two sons, one daughter; *Religion:* Muslim; *Education:* BSc in Engineering, University of London, 1960; MSc and PhD in Engineering, University of California, Los Angeles; *Career:* Instrumentation Engineer, Iraq Petroleum Company, 1960–62; Associate Professor, California State University, Los Angeles, 1964–69; Technical Adviser, System Development Corporation, Santa Monica, California, 1969–70; Principal Engineer, Philco Ford Corporation, Aeronautics Division, California, 1970–72; Project Manager, TRW Systems and Energy Group, Redondo Beach, Calfornia, 1973–79; President, Operations Control Corp, Los Angeles,

California, 1979–80; President, Strategics Group Incorporation, Santa Monica, California; member of American Management Association; member of Institute of Electrical and Electronics Engineers; *Interests and Recreations:* tennis, reading; history of Islamic and modern politics; *Languages:* Arabic, English, French; *Address:* 546 Moreno Ave, Los Angeles, California, 90049, USA; telephone: (213) 451 9411.

SHAWAF, Tarik M.A., Saudi Arabian businessman; born 1933, Saudi Arabia; *Religion:* Muslim; *Education:* BS in Civil Engineering, Worcester Polytechnic Institute, Massachusetts, USA, 1955; *Career:* joined Bin Laden Contractors (responsible for Hofuf irrigation and drainage scheme, Wadi Jizan dam and first Riyadh water supply and treatment project); established his own firm, Saudi Consult, part of British Arabian Design Group, designing hospitals for Ministry of Health, 1967–; *Languages:* Arabic, English; *Address:* Saudi Consult, P O Box 2341, Riyadh, Saudi Arabia; telephone: 8328936; telex: 201231 SHAWAF SJ.

SHAWAN, Aziz al-, Egyptian artist/ musician; born 6 May 1916, Cairo, Egypt; married; one son, one daughter; *Religion:* Christian; *Education:* Diploma of High Commercial Studies, Cairo; *Career:* Manager, Soviet Cultural Centre, Cairo, 1956–68; Musical Adviser, Opera and Music Department, Ministry of Culture, 1973–76; Composer; *Publications: Music for Everybody,* in Arabic, General Organisation for Books; *The Evolution of Egyptian Music,* in English; *Decorations:* Decoration of Arts and Sciences, first category; *Interests and Recreations:* literature, history of Ancient Egypt; *Languages:* Arabic, English, French, Russian, Italian; *Address:* 11a Qubba Street, Roxy, Heliopolis, Cairo, Egypt; telephone: 869314.

SHAWI, Hisham Ibrahim al-, Iraqi diplomat; born 16 March 1931, Baghdad, Iraq; married; two children; *Religion:* Muslim; *Education:* BA in Political Science, American University of Beirut, Beirut, Lebanon, 1952; MLitt in International Relations, St. Anthony's College, Oxford University, Oxford, UK, 1956; *Career:* Assistant Professor and Head of Department of Politics, Universities of Baghdad, Al-Mustansyria, 1958–70; Dean, College of Law and Politics, Al-Mustansyria

University, 1970–72; Ambassador, Ministry of Foreign Affairs, 1972; Permanent Representative of Iraq, UN Office, Geneva, 1972; Minister of Higher Education and Scientific Research, 1972–74; Minister of State, 1974–75; Minister of State for Foreign Affairs, 1975–76; Ambassador, Ministry of Foreign Affairs, 1976–77; Permanent Representative of Iraq, UN, New York, USA, 1977; Head of the Diwan of the Presidency of the Republic of Iraq, 1977–78; Ambassador, Ministry of Foreign Affairs, 1978; Ambassador to the Court of St. James, London, 1978–82; Ambassador to Austria, 1982–; President of Iraqi Political Science Association, Iraqi UN Association; Representative of Iraq, Commission on Human Rights; member of the UN Subcommission on Prevention of Racial Discrimination and Protection of Minorities, 1972–74; listed in *Who's Who of the World, International Dictionary of Biography, Men and Women of Distinction; Publications: The Art of Negotiation; An Introduction in Political Science,* 1967, 1978; *From the Essence of the Matter,* 1966; *The Wilsonian Conception of International Life; Languages:* Arabic, English; *Address:* Embassy of the Republic of Iraq, Johannesgasse 26, A-1010, Vienna, Austria.

SHAWI, Khalid al-; Iraqi economist/oil official; born 30 April 1930, Baghdad, Iraq; married; two sons, one daughter; *Religion:* Muslim; *Education:* LLB, Baghdad University, 1952; Diploma, English Language, Bard College, USA, 1953; LLM, University of Michigan, USA, 1955; SJD, University of Michigan, USA, 1957; Diploma, French Language, Institut de Cape d'Aie, France; *Career:* Registrar, Ministry of Economy, Iraq, 1957; Commercial Attaché (First Secretary), Embassy of Iraq to London, 1959; General Manager, Commercial Bank of Iraq, 1963; Deputy Director, Iraqi National Oil Company, 1964; Director, State Organisation for Insurance, 1964–65; Deputy Minister of Economy, 1965; Deputy Minister of Industry and Finance, 1966; Dean, Faculty of Law and of Political Science, Mustansiriya University, 1968; Professor and Head of Department of Law, Garyunis University, Libya, 1970; Counsellor and Director of Legal Affairs, Organisation of Arab Petroleum Exporting Countries (OAPEC), 1978–; *Publications: The Role of the Corporate Entity in International Law,* 1957; *Commercial Companies (Iraqi Law),* 1968; *The*

Commercial Documents, 1971; *Theory of Taxation and the Libyan Tax Legislation,* 1974; *The Campaign of Jewish Settlement in Barqa,* 1976 (partly translated into English); *The Businessman and the Commercial Documents,* 1977; and numerous other papers; *Interests and Recreations:* music, swimming, walking, reading biographies, contemporary history and political thought; member of the Iraqi and the International Law Syndicate, the Society of Comparative Insurance; member of Mansur Club, Baghdad; *Languages:* Arabic, English, French; *Address:* OAPEC, P O Box 20501, Kuwait; telephone: Office — 426873, 448200; Residence — 512995.

SHAWI, Mundhir al-, Iraq politician/lawyer; born 21 December, 1928, Baghdad, Iraq; *Education:* LLB, College of Law, Baghdad, 1951; Doctorat d'Université, Political Science, Toulouse, France, 1956; Doctorat d'Etat in Law, France, 1961; *Career:* Professor of Constitutional Law and Jurisprudence, College of Law, Baghdad University, Baghdad, Iraq 1961–74; Head of Law Department, College of Law and Politics, Baghdad University, Baghdad, Iraq, 1969–73; Minister of Justice, 1974–; member of Iraqi Scientific Academy, 1980–; member of the National Assembly, 1980–; *Publications:* several books and articles on constitutional law and jurisprudence; papers on legal reforms; *Languages:* Arabic, French, English; *Address:* Ministry of Justice, Baghdad, Iraq.

SHAWI, Nazar Nadhif al-, Iraqi academic; born 1928, Baghdad, Iraq; one son, three daughters; *Religion:* Muslim; *Education:* BSc, University of Michigan, USA, 1952; PhD, Bacteriology, George Washington University, USA, 1956; *Career:* Lecturer, Institute of Medical Research, College of Medicine, University of Baghdad, 1956, Assistant Professor, 1960, Professor, 1965; Deputy Dean, College of Medicine, University of Baghdad, 1963, Head of Microbiology Department, 1965; Director, Central Institute for Microbiology, 1966; Technical and Administrative Superintendent of Iraqi Institutes, 1969; President of University of Mosul, 1969; President of University of Basra, 1970; Consultant, Ministry of Higher Education and Scientific Research 1975; President of Scientific Research Organization, 1977; Secretary General, Federation of Arab Scientific Research Councils, 1977–; member of

the Council of Medical and Social Research, 1967, Permanent Consultative Committee, Ministry of Health, 1968, Water Pollution Committee, 1969, Oceanic Committee, 1971, Higher Education Planning Committee, 1972, Council of Higher Education and Scientific Research in Iraq, 1976, General Health Committee, WHO, 1970, and several other committees; *Languages:* Arabic, English; *Address:* Office — Federation of Arab Scientific Research Councils, P O Box 13027, Baghdad, Iraq; telephone: 441 7344.

SHAWKI, Muhammad Tawfik, Egyptian oil official; born 22 June 1931, Alexandria; married; three daughters; *Religion:* Muslim; *Education:* Petroleum Engineering, Cairo University, Egypt, 1947; *Career:* joined the Oil Wells Co, 1947; Director of Fields, 1958; Director of Operations, General Oil Co, 1958–66; Chairman of the Board of Suez Gulf Petroleum Co, 1966–77; Expert, General Petroleum Organization, 1977; Chairman of the Board of Balaum Petroleum Co, 1977–; *Decorations:* Order of the Republic 3rd Class; *Interests and Recreations:* swimming, tennis; member of the Automobile Club, and Al-Gezira Club; *Languages:* Arabic, English, French; *Address:* 155 Muhammad Farid Street, Cairo, Egypt; telephone: 910202, 913233

SHAZLI, Lieutenant General Saad Muhammad al-Hussainy al-, Egyptian politician/soldier; born 1 April 1922; married; three daughters; *Religion:* Muslim; *Education:* Faculty of Agriculture, Cairo University, Egypt, 1938–39; Lieutenant, Military College, 1940; Weapons Course, Transportation Course, Ammunition Course, War Cases Course, Physical Training Course, 1940–43; Administration Course, 1947; Junior Officers Command Course, 1950; MA in Military Science, 1952; Paratroopers Course, Jumpmasters Course, Infantry School, Fort Benning, USA; Air Transport-Ability Course, Fort Eustis, USA, 1953; MA in Political Science, Cairo University, 1954; Command and Leadership Course in USSR, 1958–59; *Career:* 2nd Lieutenant, 1940; Officer of the Guards, 1943–48; Company Commander, 1949; Commander of Parachute School, 1954–56; Commander of Parachute Battalion, 1956–58; Commander of United Arab Republic Contingent, UN, Congo, 1960–61; Defence Attaché, London, 1961–63; General Training Department GHQ,

1964; Brigade Commander, 1965–66; Head of General Training Department GHQ, 1966; Commander of the Shazli Group, Egyptian-Israeli War, 1967; Commander of Special Forces, 1967–69; Commander of the Red Sea Distict, 1970–71; Chief of Staff of Egyptian Armed Forces, and Assistant Secretary General of the Arab League for Defence, 1971–73; Ambassador to UK, 1974–75; Ambassador to Portugal, 1975–78; Secretary General, the Egyptian National Front Party (an opposition political organization), Algeria; *Publications: How an Infantry Division Can Cross a Water Barrier,* 1973; *The Crossing of the Suez,* 1980; and several other books; Editor and Publisher of *AL Gabha,* a political magazine published in Algiers since 1980; *Decorations:* Medal of Palestine, 1948; Medal of Military Courage, 1949; Medal of Liberation, 1952; Medal of Long Service, 1961; Military Medal of Yemen, 1966; Medal of Distinguished Service, 1972; Honour Star, 1974; Order of the Republic, 1974; and numerous other foreign decorations; *Interests and Recreations:* air gliding, fencing, golf, camping, chess; *Languages:* Arabic, English, French, German, Russian, Portuguese; *Address:* P O Box 778, Alger-Garc, Algeria.

SHEBANI, Omar, Libyan academic/educationalist; born 1930; *Religion:* Muslim; *Education:* Ain Shams University, Cairo, Egypt; Boston University and George Washington University, USA; *Career:* Assistant Director, Teachers College, University of Libya, Benghazi, 1965; Director of Youth Department, 1968; Professor, University of Libya, 1970; *Languages:* Arabic, English; *Address:* University of Libya, Benghazi, Libya.

SHEHAB, Ibrahim Khalil, Egyptian academic/educationalist; born 27 December 1923, Sohag, Egypt; married; three daughters; *Religion:* Muslim; *Education:* BA in English Literature, Faculty of Arts, Cairo University, 1944; Diploma in Education, Higher Institute of Education, Cairo, 1946; MA and PhD, Teachers College, Columbia University, NY, USA, 1949–53; *Career:* Teacher of English, Orman Model Secondary School, Egypt, 1946–49; Lecturer, Higher Institute of Education, Alexandria, 1953–58; Assistant Professor of Curriculum, Teachers College, Cairo, 1958–63; Professor of Curriculum, Faculty of Education, Ain Shams University, 1963–68; Professor of Curriculum, Faculty of Education, Tripoli, Libya, 1968–70; Professor and Head of Department of Curriculum, Faculty of Education, Ain Shams University, 1972–75; UNESCO Expert, Educational Research Centre, Baghdad, Iraq, 1975–76; Professor of Curriculum, Faculty of Arts, Education and Psychology, Mustansiriyah University, Baghdad, Iraq, 1976–78; UNESCO Expert in Curriculum and Evaluation and Head of the Department of Curriculum, University College of Arts, Science and Education, Bahrain, 1978–; *Publications:* numerous research papers, articles and translations on education and teaching since 1960; *Interests and Recreations:* music, drama, travel, swimming, backgammon, cards, reading, walking; *Languages:* Arabic, English, French; *Address:* Office — University College of Arts, Science and Education, P O Box 1082, Manama, Bahrain; telephone 682748; Residence — 68 Al-Zahraa Street, Apt 4, Dokki, Giza, Egypt; telephone: 713635.

SHEHADEH, Aziz, Palestinian lawyer; born 1912, Bethlehem, Palestine; *Religion:* Christian; *Education:* graduated from Government Law School, 1936; *Career:* practised law in Jaffa until 1948; law practise partnership in Ramallah; active in refugee affairs following 1948 War; served as Secretary to the Palestine Refugee Congress delegation at the meetings of the UN Conciliation Commission, Lausanne, Switzerland, 1949; unsuccessfully contested Jordanian elections as deputy for Ramallah, 1951; now one of the West Bank's leading lawyers and was defence counsel at the trial of Archbishop Capucci, 1974; *Languages:* Arabic, English.

SHEIBAN, Abdullah Bin Ali Bin, United Arab Emirates official/businessman; born 1932, Abu Dhabi, United Arab Emirates; married; five sons; *Religion:* Muslim; *Career:* 20 years' employment in Abu Dhabi Government and later United Arab Emirates Government; Under Secretary, Ministry of Social Affairs; member of the Board of Directors of UAE Trading Company; President of the Board of Administration of the International School of Shoueifat, Abu Dhabi; *Interests and Recreations:* swimming, skiing; *Address:* P O Box 462, Abu Dhabi, United Arab Emirates; telephone: Residence — 361 462.

SHELAL, Ait, Algerian diplomat; born 1929, Messaoud, Algeria; married; three children; *Education:* qualified as doctor, University of Paris, France; *Career:* President of General Union of Muslim Algerian Students (UGEMA); Ambassador to Italy, 1967–71; Ambassador to Belgium, 1971; also accredited to Netherlands and Luxembourg; Secretary General, Non-Aligned Conference, Algiers, 1973; Delegate, North-South Dialogue, Paris, 1975–76; *Languages:* Arabic, French; *Address:* Ministry of Foreign Affairs, Algiers, Algeria.

SHELLI, Tijani M., Tunisian official; born 23 March 1931, Tunisia; married; two children; *Religion:* Muslim; *Education:* Engineering, L'Ecole Polytechnique, Paris, France, 1959; *Career:* Engineer of Public Works, le Kef, 1959–60; Assistant Chief Engineer for Roads and Bridges, then Director of Transport, 1961; Director of Maritime and Air Transport, 1962; Chairman and Managing Director of the National Tunisian Railway Company, 1965–67; Director of Industry in the Department of Planning and National Economy, 1967–69; Chairman and Managing Director of Maghreb Chemical Industries (Industries Chimiques Maghrebines, ICM), and of Gabès-Chimie-Transports, 1969; Minister of Public Transport, 1969–70; Minister of National Economy, 1970–72; Chairman and Managing Director of the Agency for the Promotion of Investments, 1973; President, Economic and Social Council 1976; *Decorations:* Grand Cordon of the Order of the Tunisian Republic; *Languages:* Arabic, French; *Address:* Agency for the Promotion of Investments, 18 Avenue Mohammed V, Tunis, Tunisia; telephone: 241047.

SHENUDA III, Egyptian ecclesiastic; born 3 August 1923; *Religion:* Christian; *Education:* BA, English, Cairo University, Egypt, 1947; graduated from Theological College, 1949; *Career:* became a monk at Wadi al-Natrun Monastery, 1954 (adopting ecclesiastical name of Antonius al-Sariani); ordained priest, 1955; Bishop for Religious and Clerical Education, 1962, taking ecclesiastical name of Bishop Shenuda; ordained Head of Coptic Orthodox Church, 1971; Pope of Alexandria and Patriarch of the See of St. Mark in All Africa and the Near East; visited Greek and Russian Orthodox Patriarchs in Istanbul, 1972; visited the Pope in the Vatican, 1973; *Languages:* Arabic, English; *Address:* St. Mark's Patriarchate, Anba Rueiss Building, Ramses Street, Abbasiyah, Cairo, Egypt.

SHERBINI, Muhammad Gharib Dusuki al-, Egyptian academic/engineer; born 8 October 1946, Sharqiyah; married; *Education:* BSc in Mechanical Engineering, Cairo University, Egypt, 1968; MSc in Mechanical Engineering, Cairo University, 1972; PhD in Mechanical Engineering, University of Salford, UK, 1975; *Career:* Demonstrator, Faculty of Engineering, Cairo University, 1968; Research Assistant, Technical University of Denmark, 1972; Teaching Assistant, Faculty of Engineering, Cairo University, 1972; Research Associate, University of Salford, UK, 1973; Research Fellow, Loughborough University of Technology, UK, 1975; Assistant Professor, Faculty of Engineering, Cairo University, 1976; Associate Professor, Faculty of Engineering, Cairo University, 1980; Consultant for a number of private firms and engineering offices in Cairo; *Publications:* numerous papers and articles in English; *Interests and Recreations:* table tennis, chess, travelling; *Languages:* Arabic, English; *Address:* Department of Mechanical Design and Production, Faculty of Engineering, Cairo University, Giza, Cairo, Egypt; telephone: 840655.

SHERZAD, Ihsan, Iraqi engineer; born 1925, Arbil, Iraq; married; one son, five daughters; *Religion:* Muslim; *Education:* BSc in Civil Engineering, Baghdad University, Iraq, 1946; MSc in Civil Engineering, University of Michigan, USA, 1950; LLB, Baghdad University, Iraq, 1962; *Career:* Engineer, Public Works Department, 1946–49; Lecturer, Engineering College, Baghdad University, 1950–67; Professor, Engineering College, 1963; Minister of Public Works and Municipalities, 1967 and 1968; Minister of Housing, 1968; Minister of Municipalities, 1970–74; Director, Iraq Consult (Engineering Consultants), Baghdad; Fellow of American Society of Civil Engineering; member of American Concrete Institute (MACI); President, Kurdish Academy, Baghdad, 1972–75; *Publications:* various articles in engineering technical journals and co-author of *Strength of Material,* 1960; *Address:* Iraq Consult, P O Box 1162, Alwiyah, Baghdad, Iraq.

SHIBAILI, Abdul Rahman Abdul Aziz al-, Saudi Arabian diplomat; born 1930, Saudi Arabia; *Religion:* Muslim; *Education:* general *Career:* Ministry of Foreign Affairs; Consul General, Jerusalem, 1967; Chargé d'Affaires, Embassy to Lebanon, 1972; Ambassador, Foreign Ministry; attended several Arab League and UN cnferences; worked at the Royal Cabinet for five years before joining Diplomatic Corps; *Decorations:* Commander of National Order of Cedar of Lebanon; *Interests and Recreations:* swimming; *Address:* Foreign Ministry, P O Box 495, Jeddah, Saudi Arabia; telephone: 642132; telex: 401104 KHARJI SJ.

SHIBAILI, Abdul Rahman, al-, Saudi Arabian broadcasting official; born Unaiza, Saudi Arabia; *Religion:* Muslim; *Education:* PhD Radio, TV and Cinema Studies, 1941; *Career:* Assistant Director of Programmes, Riyadh Broadcasting Service, 1965–66; Director of Programmes, Riyadh TV Service, 1966–68; Director General, TV Department; attended several Arab and international information conferences; *Publications:* PhD thesis on Saudi information; *Address:* Ministry of Information, P O Box 843, Riyadh, Saudi Arabia; telephone: 4038178.

SHIBL, Yusuf A., Lebanese economist; born 23 November 1934, Acre, Palestine; married; one son, one daughter; *Religion:* Muslim; *Education:* BA in Economics, American University of Beirut; MA in Economics, AUB; PhD in Economics, University of California, Los Angeles; *Career:* Economic Adviser, Ministry of Finance, Saudi Arabia, 1965–7; Assistant Professor of Business Administration, AUB; Senior Economist, Dar Al-Handasa, Beirut; Lecturer, AUB School of Business; Chairman and Partner, Dar Al-Handasa Consultants; *Publications:* The Aswan High Dam; Foreign Trade of Israel; Fiscal Policy in Israel; Economics of Defence; Inflation: Economic Analysis vs Political Set Up; *Interests and Recreations:* football, swimming, travel, oriental music; *Languages:* Arabic, English, French; *Address:* Dar Al-Handasa Consultants, Serdan Street, P O Box 7159, Beirut, Lebanon.

SHIBLEY, George Edward, Arab-American lawyer; born 6 May 1910, New York, USA; married; two sons; *Religion:* Christian; *Education:* AB in Political Science, Stanford University, USA, 1927–31; LLB, Stanford University Law School, USA, 1931–34; LLD, Stanford University Law School, 1965; *Career:* admitted to California Bar, State of California, 1935, US District Court, Southern District of California, USA, 1942; senior partner, George E. Shibley Law Offices, 1935–43, and 1950–77; senior partner of Shibley, Warner and Litwin, 1943–50; Legal Counsel of Cedars Investment Co Inc, 1961–; Counsel, US Court of Appeal, Ninth Circuit, 1963, US District Court, Northern District of California, 1971, US Supreme Court, 1977; Delegate to Third Conference of the Inter-American Bar Association; member of Board of Directors (intermittently President and Secretary) and Legal Counsel of US Omen Inc, 1963–77; Legal Counsel, Palestine Arab Fund, 1970–77; Legal Counsel, Palestine War Victims Society, 1970–77; Member of Board of Directors, American Arab Educational Foundation, 1970–77; Attorney and Counsellor, Solicitor and Advocate and Proctor in Admiralty; *Publications:* numerous magazine and newspaper articles on the Arab world, Arab culture, history and international relations, on Syrian and Lebanese independence, Arab-Israeli conflict and the Palestinian Revolution, mostly in US and English publications from 1928 to the present time; *Decorations:* Distinguished Service Award, MGM, 1933; Medal of Valour, Lichtenberg, 1945; Superior Achievement Award, Alsace, 1964; Distinguished Service Award, US Omen, 1966; Citation, Defensor de Mexicanos, Semanal Hoy, Mexico City, 1944; Award of Merit, Palestinian Voice, 1972; *Interests and Recreations:* member of the Los Angeles County Museum of Art, Natural History Museum Alliance, Little Theatre Alliance; participated since 1927 in acting, directing, writing and production of dramatic works; *Languages:* English, Spanish, Arabic, Italian, French; *Address:* Law Offices, George E. Shibley, 505 Heartwell Building, 19 Pine Avenue, Long Beach, California 90802, USA; telephone: (203) 437 2295.

SHIDID, Sayyid Abbas, Egyptian UN official; born 1 August 1913, Cairo, Egypt; married; *Education:* Diploma in Political Science, Institut des Hautes Etudes Politiques, Paris, France, 1929–32; Licence in Law, Faculty of Law, University of Montpellier, France, 1933–36; *Career:* Chief Editor, European Department, Egyptian State Broadcasting, 1943–45; Director, European Department, Egyptian State Broadcasting, 1945–54; Controller General, European and Overseas Programmes, Egypt, 1954–61; Deputy Director, UN Operation in the Congo, Zaire, 1962–63; Deputy Chief, Radio Service, UN, New York, 1964–65; Acting Director, UN Information Centre (UNIC), Egypt, Saudi Arabia, Yemen, 1965–66; Adviser, African Development Bank, Ivory Coast, 1967; Director, UNIC, Senegal, 1967–70; Director, UNIC, Bucharest, 1970–; *Publications: The UN Information System*, 1971; *Interests and Recreations:* member of the Gezira Sporting Club; member of the Baneasa Diplomatic Club; member of the International Association for Mass Communication Research; *Languages:* Arabic, French, English, Italian; *Address:* Office — UN Information Centre, 16 Rue Aurel Vlaicu, Bucharest 2, Ilfov, Romania; telephone: 125639; Residence -- 13–19 Alecu Russo, Bucharest 2, Romania; telephone: 121420.

SHIHABI, Imad Hikmat, Syrian army officer; born 1931, Syria; married; *Religion:* Muslim; *Education:* in Syria, USA, USSR; *Career:* armed forces; General Chief of Staff, Syria, 1976–; *Languages:* Arabic, Russian, English; *Address:* GHQ, Chief of Staff Office, The Armed Forces, Damascus, Syria.

SHIHABI, Samir al-, Saudi Arabian diplomat; born 1925, Jerusalem, Palestine; *Religion:* Muslim; *Education:* BA in Economics, American University of Beirut, Lebanon, 1945; American University, Cairo, Egypt, 1947; *Career:* successively 2nd Secretary, 1st Secretary, Counsellor, Minister Plenipotentiary, Ministry of Foreign Affairs; Saudi Ambassador to Turkey and Somalia; Ambassador, Ministry of Foreign Affairs; Saudi Ambassador, Pakistan, 1979–; *Decorations:* King Abdul Aziz High Order of Merit; *Interests and Recreations:* sport; *Address:* Embassy of Saudi Arabia, Plot 436-F, Rama 614, Islamabad, Pakistan.

SHIHABIDDIN, Adnan, Kuwaiti academic/nuclear scientist; born 1 November 1943, Jaffa; married; two daughters; *Religion:* Muslim; *Education:* BSc in Electrical Engineering; MSc in Nuclear Engineering; PhD in Nuclear Engineering, University of California, Berkeley, USA; *Career:* Assistant Professor, Kuwait University, 1970–76; Adviser to the Prime Minister's Office on nuclear energy, 1970–76; Consultant, Kuwait Institute for Scientific Research, Energy Division, 1973–74, Lawrence Berkeley Laboratory, Berkeley, California, 1971–75; member of the Nuclear Energy Committee of Kuwait, 1975–; Associate Professor, Physical Department, Kuwait University, 1976; visiting Associate Professor, Nuclear Engineering Department, University of California, Berkeley, USA, 1978; Project Manager, Feasibility Study for establishing Arab Fund for Scientific and Technological Development, 1977–79; Vice Rector, Kuwait University, 1976–80; Vice Chairman of Kuwait National Technology Committee, 1976–; Director General, Kuwait Institute for Scientific Research, 1976–; member of Board of Governors International Atomic Energy Agency, 1979–; *Publications:* co-author of *Tables of Isotopes,* September 1980, 7th Edition, John Wiley and Sons, Inc; numerous articles and researches in journals and magazines; *Interests and Recreations:* sports, chess; *Languages:* Arabic, English; *Address:* Kuwait Institute for Scientific Research, P O Box 24885, Safat, Kuwait; telephone: 818631, 835183.

SHIHADEH, Musa Mustafa, Arab-American businessman/chemical engineer; born 18 January 1931, Ramallah, Palestine; married; three children; *Religion:* Muslim; *Education:* BA in Polymer Chemistry, Brooklyn Polytechnic Institute, Brooklyn, USA; MA in Chemical Engineering, Brooklyn Polytechnic Institute, USA; *Career:* Production Chemist for Manhattan Adhesives, 1954–55; Production Chemist, Montrose Chemical, 1956; Consultant for US Coatings, Goodyear and other plastics and resin manufacturing industries, 1957–59; President, Advanced Polymer Inc, 1959–60 (corporation acquired by Helene Curtis, 1961); Vice-President, Toch Brothers, 1962–67; formed Guard Polymer Inc which manufactures coating resins and building material chemicals, 1967–74; merged with Con Chem, Inc, Vice-President, Technical Director, 1974–77; Consultant and President of Atlantic Development Corporation and Clover Chemical Corporation, licencing and engineering of chemical products; President and owner of several corporations including Atlantic Development Corporation, Clover Chemical Corporation; member of the Chemical and Engineering Society, of Arab-American University Graduates Association, of Resin and Coatings Society; *Interests and Recreations:* tennis, boating, swimming; *Languages:* Arabic, English, German, Russian; *Address:* 11 Cerrito Place, Rolling Hills Estates, California 90274, USA; telephone: (213) 530 7008.

SHIHAIL, Faisal Muhammad al-, Saudi Arabian official; born 1953; *Religion:* Muslim; *Education:* MA in Public Administration; *Career:* Director General of Posts and Lighthouses, 1961–69; Director General and member of Board, Al-Jazirah Press Organisation, 1966–69; Assistant Deputy Minister for Communications; member of Saudi Olympic Committee; Vice-Chairman of the Saudi Football Federation, Al Hilal Sporting Club; Constituent member of Riyadh Private Schools; member of Board of Arab League, Arab Maritime Transport Academy; Vice-Chairman of the Inter Governmental Maritime Consultant Organisation, 1971–73; Saudi Chief Delegate to Conference on the Law of the Sea, Caracas, Venezuela, 1973; member of Maritime Safety Conference, Conference on Freight Line, London, UK; Lecturer, Riyadh University; *Publications:* books on public administration, planning and control; *Interests and Recreations:* swimming, chess, reading; *Address:* Ministry of Communications, Airport Road, Riyadh, Saudi Arabia; telephone: 4042928; telex: 201616 HI-WAY SJ.

SHIHATA, Ibrahim Fahmi, Egyptian official/legal adviser; resident in Austria; born 1937, Egypt; married; one son, two daughters; *Education:* BA in Law, Cairo, 1957; Diploma in Public Law and Finance, Cairo, 1958; Doctor of Juridical Science, Harvard University, USA, 1964; *Career:* member of the Council of State, Cairo, 1957–59; member of the Technical Bureau of the President of Arab United Republic, Damascus, 1959–60; Lecturer in International Law, Ain Shams University, 1964–66; Legal Counsel, Kuwait Fund, 1966–70; Associate Professor, International Law and International Economic Law, Ain-Shams University, 1970–72; Senior Legal Adviser, Kuwait Fund, 1972–76; Director General, Organization Petroleum Exporting Countries Fund, 1976–; member of the Executive Board of the International Fund for Agricultural Development, Rome; member of the Executive Board of the International Fertilizer Development Centre, USA; *Publications:*

numerous books and papers published in Arabic and English; *Interests and Recreations:* poetry and music; *Languages:* Arabic, English, French; *Address:* P O Box 995, Vienna 7, Austria.

SHINAIBAR, Abdul Aziz Abdullah al-, Saudi Arabian official/petroleum engineer; born 1936; *Education:* BSc in Petroleum Engineering; *Career:* Technical Adviser, Minister's Bureau, Ministry of Petroleum, 1967; Director, Development Division, 1968; Director, Minister's Bureau, 1971; Director General, Ministry of Petroleum, 1975; Under Secretary of State for Administrative Affairs, Ministry of Petroleum and Mineral Resources; member of Board of Trustees, University of Petroleum and Minerals; member of Board, Public Organization for Sea Water Desalination; Vice President, World Petroleum Conference, Arab Petroleum Conference, Atomic Energy Conference; *Address:* Ministry of Petroleum and Mineral Resources, P O Box 247, Riyadh, Saudi Arabia; telephone: 4780552; telex: 200997 PETROL SJ.

SHINAISHIN, Osman Abdul Magid, Arab-American engineer; born 18 March 1933, Egypt; married; three children; *Education:* BSc, Cairo University, 1952; MSc, Michigan University, 1960; PhD, University of California, Berkeley, 1965; *Career:* Instructor, high school, Egypt, 1952–57; Research Assistant, University of California, Berkeley, 1962–64; Research Engineer, Boeing Co, Seattle, 1965–68; General Electric Co, Schenectady, 1968–73; Manager, Accoustics Centre, Mechanical and Technical Incorporation, Latham, NY, 1974–76; Senior Programme Manager, MSF, 1976–; Graduate Examiner, Rensselaer Polytechnic Institute, Troy, NY, 1972–74; External Doctoral Examiner, 1972–74; Consultant, Environmental Protection Agency, 1974; Trustee, Islamic Community Center NY, Albany, 1973–74; *Address:* 9916 Meadow Lark Rd, Vienna, VA 22180; Office— NSF, Washington D.C. 20550, USA.

SHINDY, Wagih M., Egyptian economist/academic; born 1 February 1936, Cairo, Egypt; married; one son, one daughter; *Religion:* Muslim; *Education:* LLB, University of Ain Shams, Cairo, Egypt; MA in International Trade and International Trade Law, Georgetown University, Washington

D.C., USA; PhD in International Finance, Georgetown University, Washington D.C., USA; *Career:* Commercial Attaché, Egyptian Embassy to Washington D.C., USA; Egyptian Representative, Trade Committee, FAO; Assistant Professor, Howard University, Washington D.C.; Permanent Representative, International Economy Organization, Washington D.C.; Vice Chairman, International Cotton Advisory Committee; Chairman, Finance Committee, International Cotton Advisory Committee; Chairman, Information Committee, International Cotton Advisory Committee; Acting Commercial Counsellor, Washington D.C.; Associate Professor, American University of Cairo, Egypt; Visiting Professor, King Abdul Aziz University, Jeddah, Saudi Arabia; Professor and Chairman, Economics Department, Mansura University, Egypt; Under Secretary of State, Ministry of Economy and Economic Co-operation; Chairman of the Arab Investment Bank, Cairo, Egypt; *Publications: International Trade Between Theory and Practice,* 1972; *International Trade Organizations ,* 1979, Cairo; *International Payments and International Currency Crisis,* 1974, Cairo; articles on international finance, international trade, international payments, and petroleum economics; *Interests and Recreations:* reading, music, sports; member of the International Rotary Club; *Languages:* Arabic, English; *Address:* Office — 8 Adly Street, Cairo, Egypt; Arab Investment Bank, 1113 Cornich al Nil, Cairo, Egypt; telephone 809800; Residence — 4 Granada Street, Roxy, Heliopolis, Cairo, Egypt.

SHIQUER, Haddou, Moroccan politician; born 1932, Morocco; married; *Religion:* Muslim; *Education:* Licencié ès-Lettres, Faculté des Lettres, Rabat, Morocco; *Career:* teacher, secondary schools in Rabat for twelve years; Deputy for Khemisset in the first Moroccan Parliament; Under Secretary of State for the Interior, 1963; Minister of Posts, Telegraphs and Telephones, 1964; Minister of Agriculture, 1966; Minister in the Royal Cabinet, 1967; Minister of National Defence, 1967; Minister of Primary Education, 1968–72; Minister of National Education, 1972–73; elected Deputy for Khouribga in parliamentary elections, 1970; Minister of the Interior, 1973–77; Minister for Relations with Parliament, 1977; *Languages:* Arabic, French; *Address:* Ministry for Relations with Parliament, Rabat, Morocco.

SHIRAWI, Yusuf Bin Ahmad al-, Bahraini official; born 1927; married; six daughters; *Religion:* Muslim; *Education:* in Bahrain; BA in Chemistry, American University of Beirut, AUB, 1950; Diploma in Chemistry, Glasgow University, UK, 1953–55; *Career:* Official, Bahrain Education Department, 1956; Assistant Secretary to Head of Oil Affairs Department, 1956; Ministry of Finance, 1963; Head of Development Bureau, 1967; Bahrain Representative to the Provisional Council of the United Arab Emirates, 1968; Chairman of Gulf Technical College Executive Committee; Government Director at Aluminium Bahrain Company; Director of Gulf Aviation, later Gulf Air, 1970; member of the State Council with responsibilites for development, 1970; Minister of Development and Industry, 1975–; *Languages:* Arabic, English; *Address:* Ministry of Development and Industry, P O Box 235, Manama, Bahrain; telephone: 253361; telex: 8344 TANMYA BN.

SHISHTAWY, Saied A. al-, Egyptian UN official/agriculturalist; born 12 March 1929, Tanta, Egypt; married; *Education:* BSc in Agriculture, Cairo University, Egypt, 1955; MSc in Rural Sociology, Columbus, The Ohio State University, USA, 1961; PhD in Agricultural Economics, Columbus, The Ohio State University, USA, 1963; *Career:* Scientific Officer, National Research Center, Cairo, Egypt, 1955–60; Researcher, Columbus, The Ohio State University, USA, 1963–64; Assistant Professor, Bluefield State College, West Virginia, USA, 1963–64; Planning Adviser, Institute of National Planning, Egypt, and Visiting Professor of Agricultural Economics, Cairo University, Egypt, 1964–65; Human Resources Expert, FAO, Iraq and Tanzania, 1965–69; Agricultural Production Economist, FAO, 1969–70; Deputy Chief, Near East and North Africa Regional Bureau, FAO, 1970–73; Chief, Regional Bureau for the Near East and North Africa, Development Department, FAO, Italy, 1974–; member of the Society for International Development; *Publications: Effect of Membership Relations on Patronage in a Farmer Co-operative,* 1961; *Statistical Analysis of the Inter-relationships of Major Factors Affecting Management of Fifty One Ohio Agricultural Co-operatives,* 1963; *Survey and Plan of Irrigation Investment and Development in the Pangami and Wami River Basins in Tanzania,* 1968; *Study* *of Selected Agrarian Reform Programmes in Iraq,* 1970; *Decorations:* Alpha Kappa Delta; Gamma Sigma Delta; Honorary Scientific Societies; *Interests and Recreations:* golf, swimming, reading, music; *Languages:* Arabic, English, French, Italian; *Address:* Office — Regional Bureau for the Near East and North Africa Development Department, FAO, Via delle Terme di Caracalla, 001000 Rome, Italy; Residence — Via Alessandro Magno, 193 Casal Palocco, Rome, Italy; telephone: 06 6091155.

SHOBOKSHI, Abdul Majid, Saudi Arabian journalist; born 1927, Jeddah, Saudi Arabia; *Religion:* Muslim; *Education:* general; *Career:* Director, Passports Department; Director, Jeddah Police Department; Director, Pilgrimage Department, Jeddah; Assistant Director General, Pilgrimage Affairs; member of Board, Al-Bilad Press Organization; founder member of charity fund, Jeddah; member of Constituent Board, King Abdul Aziz University; Editor in Chief, *Al-Bilad* daily newspaper; attended Arab Journalists Conferences; *Interests and Recreations:* reading; *Address: Al-Bilad* daily Newspaper, King Abdul Aziz Street, Jeddah, Saudi Arabia.

SHOBOKSHI, Ali Hussain, Saudi Arabian businessman; born 1940, Mecca, Saudi Arabia; *Religion:* Muslim; *Education:* BSc in Business Administration, Cairo University, Cairo, Egypt; *Career:* President and owner of Ali Fahd Shobokshi Group; Chairman of Shobokshi Maritime, Okaz Organisation for Press and Publication, Dar Okaz Printing and Publishing, Saudi Development Company, Shobokshi Preusse Teerbau Engineering Ltd, Arab International Airlines; Vice President of Arab Greek Chamber of Commerce, Vice Chairman of Tihama Advertisement, Public Relations and Marketing Studies Company; Founder and member of the Board of Directors of Saudi Cairo Bank, Faisal Islamic Bank; member of the Board of Directors of Saudi National Shipping Company, International Maritime Services Company Ltd, Red Sea Insurance Company, Arab Investment Company, Information Production Company; *Address:* Shobokshi Building, Shobokshi Street, P O Box 5470, Jeddah, Saudi Arabia; telephone: 33318, 26868; telex; 40008 GAC SJ.

SHOBOKSHI, Fahd Hussain, Saudi Arabian businessman; born 1939, Saudi Arabia; married; three children; *Religion:* Muslim; *Education:* BA Business Administration, USA, 1963; *Career:* Vice President and Owner, Ali and Fahd Shobokshi Group; President, General Agencies Corporation; Chairman of Saudi Paper Converting Company, IPCO Marine Saudi Arabia, Shobel Real Estate Investment Company; member of the Board of Directors, International Maritime Services Company Ltd, Saudi Hotels and Resorts Areas Company, Shark Housing and Development Company, Shams Pyramids Company, Cairo, Misr-Abu Dhabi Company, Arab Investment Company, Cairo; founder and partner of Faisal Islamic Bank, Cairo and Sudan; member of the Board of Directors of Okaz Company for Distribution, Saudi Advertising International; *Address:* Shobokshi Building, Shobokshi Street, P O Box 5470, Jeddah, Saudi Arabia; telephone: 33318, 26868; telex: 40008 GAC SJ.

SHOCAIR, Amin Khalil, Jordanian businessman/pharmacist; born 1925, Amman, Jordan; married; *Education:* Certificate of Services, College of Medicine, Syrian University, Damascus, 1944; Degree in Pharmacy, School of Pharmacy, College of Medicine, Damascus University, Damascus, 1948; *Career:* elected President, first Council of the Jordanian Pharmaceutical Association upon establishment, 1957–59; President of same association, 1977–81; member of the Executive Council of Arab Pharmacists Union, APU, 1979–81; Chairman of the Board of Directors of the Arab Pharmaceutical Manufacturing Co Ltd, Salt, Jerusalem Insurance Co Ltd, Amman, Afro-Arab Techni Chemicals Ltd, Lagos, Nigeria; Owner and Manager of al-Hayat Pharmacy, Amman, the Arab Drug Store, Amman; organiser of the first professional seminar *Pharmacy Profession on the Verge of the 21st Century,* February 1980; member of the National Executive Council; *Publications:* numerous articles, lectures, and speeches on cultural, political and scientific subjects; *Decorations:* Gold Medal of APU, 1st Class; *Languages:* Arabic, English; *Address:* Office — King Hussain St, Abdali, Amman, Jordan; telephone: 64139/94.

SHOIB, Muhammad Othman, Egyptian physician/UN official; born 22 August 1921; married; *Religion:* Muslim; *Education:* MB,

BCh, Medicine Faculty, Cairo University, Egypt, 1938–46; MPH, Harvard University, USA, 1947–48; DPH, Columbia University, USA, 1949–50; Johns Hopkins University, USA, 1966; *Career:* Senior Lecturer, Preventive Medicine, Faculty of Medicine, Cairo University, 1950–54; Head, Department of Preventive Medicine, Cairo University, 1956–58; Head, Department of Occupational Health, Higher Institute of Public Health, Alexandria University, Egypt, 1956–59; Director, International Health Division, Ministry of Health, Cairo, 1954–59; Director General, Ministry of Health, 1959–60; Chief Medical Officer, Social and Occupational Health, World Health Organization (WHO), Geneva, 1960–64; Director of Health Service, Regional Office for Eastern Mediterranean, WHO, Alexandria, Egypt 1964–; member of the Egyptian Medical Association, Egyptian Public Health Association, American Public Health Association, American Academy of Occupational Medicine, Argentine Association for Industrial Medicine, Finnish Association for Industrial Medicine; *Publications:* co-author: *Principles of Public Health,* 1945; contributor: *Epidemiology of Communicable Diseases,* 1958; *Decorations:* Order of the Republic, Egypt; *Interests and Recreations:* photography, swimming, golf, public health, occupational health; member of the Egyptian Automobile Club, Smouha Sporting Club, Syrian Arab Club, Alexandria Sporting Club; *Languages:* Arabic, English, French; *Address:* Office — Regional Office for Eastern Mediterranean, WHO, Abdel Hamid Badawi Street, Alexandria, Egypt; telephone: 30090.

SHOMALI, Ahmad Abdul Aziz, United Arab Emirates official/educationalist; born 1945, Bahrain; married; three sons, two daughters; *Religion:* Muslim; *Education:* BA in Social Sciences, Baghdad University, Iraq; *Career:* Administrative Affairs Supervisor, Ministry of Education; Head of Educational Planning Section, Ministry of Education; *Interests and Recreations:* travel, fishing; *Languages:* Arabic, English; *Address:* Ministry of Education, P O Box 295, Abu Dhabi, United Arab Emirates.

SHOMAN, Abdul Majid Abdul Hamid, Jordanian banker; born 1912, Beit Haneena, Jordan; married; two sons; *Religion:* Muslim; *Education:* BSc, MA, New York University, New York, USA; *Career:* Chairman and Manager, Arab Bank Ltd; Vice Chairman, Board of Directors, Morocco; member of the Board of Directors of Union de Banques Arabes et Françaises UBAF, Arab-American Bank, New York; Chairman, Jordan Petrol Refinery Company Ltd; member of the Board of Directors, Central Bank of Jordan; Vice President, Arab Bank Overseas Ltd, Zurich, Switzerland; Chairman, Union de Banques Arabes et Européennes, Luxembourg and Frankfurt; Chairman, Commercial Building Company, Beirut; member of the Board of Directors, Arab Japanese Finance Ltd; *Decorations:* Independence Medal, 2nd and 3rd Class, Jordan; Renaissance Medal; *Interests and Recreations:* walking; *Languages:* Arabic, English; *Address:* Arab Bank Ltd, P O Box 68, Amman, Jordan; telephone: 38161/9; telex 1230, BANKARABI JO.

SHOMAN, Ahmad R, Arab-American academic/engineer; born 8 August 1929, Sharqiyah, Egypt; married; three sons, two daughters; *Religion:* Muslim; *Education:* BSc, MSc, PhD in Mechanical Engineering; *Career:* Instructor of Mechanical Engineering, Cairo University, 1950–53; Assistant Professor of Mechanical Engineering, University of Washington, Seattle, USA, 1956–60; Associate Professor of Mechanical Engineering, New Mexico State University, Las Cruces, New Mexico, 1960–65; Professor of Mechanical Engineering, New Mexico State University, 1965–; Visiting Professor, New Laval University, Quebec, Canada, 1966–67; Consultant on Supersonic Research Project, ARO Inc; Consultant on Gas Turbine Turbo Machinery, Industrial Products Division of Boeing Company, 1959–63; Consultant to Service Technology Corp; Consultant on Rankine Cycle Power Plants, the DuPont Company; Consultant to the US Army Research Office, North Carolina; member of the American Society of Engineers; Chairman of the Southern New Mexico West Texas Subsection, 1963–64, Director, 1964–65; member of Sigma XI; Honorary member of Pi Tau Sigma; Fellow of the American Association for the Advancement of Science; Researcher in Energy and Energy Systems, and on Enhanced Oil Recovery Systems; *Publications:* articles in technical journals and reviews; *Languages:* Arabic, English, French, German; *Address:* Office — New Mexico State University, Department of Mechanical Engineering, P O Box 3450, Las Cruces, New Mexico; Residence — 1006 Bloomdale Street, Las Cruces, New Mexico 88001, USA; telephone: (505) 523 5358.

SHOMAN, Khalid, Jordanian banker; born 13 October, 1931, Brooklyn, USA; married; *Religion:* Muslim; *Education:* Victoria College, Alexandria, Egypt; BA, MA, Economics, Jesus College, Cambridge University, England; *Career:* Assistant General Manager, member of the Board of Directors, Arab Bank Ltd, 1958; Deputy General Manager, Deputy Chairman, Arab Bank Ltd, 1974–; Deputy Chairman, Deputy General Manager, Arab Computing Co, Amman; member of the Board of Directors of Arab Bank Investment Co, London, Arab Bank Switzerland Ltd, Arab German Bank, Arab National Bank, Saudi Arabia, Arab Bank, Morocco, Arab Bankers Association, London, Royal Jordanian Airlines, Jordan, Jordanian Air Academy, Jordan; *Interests and Recreations:* swimming, squash, fishing, scuba diving; *Languages:* Arabic, English, French, German; *Address:* Arab Bank Ltd, P O Box 68, Amman, Jordan; telephone: 37080.

SHORFI, Abdullah, Moroccan diplomat/politician; born 1927, Fes, Morocco; married; *Religion:* Muslim; *Career:* Royal Cabinet on Declaration of Independence, 1956; Counsellor, Embassy to Spain; Chargé d'Affaires, Embassy to France; Consul General, New York, USA; member of the Permanent Delegation to the United Nations; Director of the European Department, Ministry of Foreign Affairs; Ambassador to West Germany; returned to the Ministry of Foreign Affairs, Secretary General, 1961; Under Secretary of State, 1964; Ambassador to Spain, 1967–69; Ambassador to USSR, 1970–73; Ambassador to the Court of St. James, London, UK, 1973–76; *Languages:* Arabic, French, English, German; *Address:* Ministry of Foreign Affairs, Rabat, Morocco.

SHRAIBI, Larbi, Moroccan official/physician; born 1921, Casablanca, Morocco; *Education:* in Casablanca; Medical Degrees from the Universities of Casablanca, and Paris, France; *Career:* Ministry of Public Health, 1956; Head of the Department of Skin Diseases, Casablanca, 1960–63; Minister of Public Health, 1963; Director General of the Société Chérifienne des Pétroles (SCP), 1969; *Languages:* Arabic, French; *Address:* Société Chérifienne des Pétroles (SCP), P O Box 79, 27 Cheria Moulay Hassan, Rabat, Morocco; telephone: 21995/97.

SHRYDEH, Burhan Najib, Jordanian businessman/official; born 17 September 1939, Jordan; two sons, two daughters; *Religion:* Muslim; *Education:* BSc in Mathematics and Physics; MA in Business Administration; PhD in Management Science; *Career:* Research Mathematician, Allen Bradley Co, Milwaukee, USA, 1960–61; Operation Research Analyst, US Steel South Works, Chicago, USA, 1961–64; Project Manager, Computer Systems, Interlake Steel Corporation, Chicago, USA, 1965–68; Co-operative Manager, Computer Systems and Programing, Admiral Corporation, Chicago, USA, 1968–70; Manager, Store Merchandising Systems, Montgomery Ward, USA, 1970–74; Manager, Economic Data Bank, Royal Scientific Society, Amman, Jordan, 1975–76; Director General, Jordan Department of Statistics, 1979–; *Publications: Economic Data Bank Development in a Developing Nation; Interests and Recreations:* theatre, music, painting, bridge, chess, golf, tennis; *Languages:* Arabic, English; *Address:* Department of Statistics, P O Box 2015, Amman, Jordan.

SHU'ABI, Major Salih Muslih Qasim Majdul, People's Democratic Republic of Yemen politician; born 1940; *Career:* from 1965 participated in armed struggle in Shaibi and Dathina areas in association with Ali Ahmed Nasr al-Bishi; Commander of the 22nd Brigade since its formation in June 1970; member of the Political Bureau; member of the People's Supreme Council; Minister of the Interior; *Address:* Ministry of the Interior, Aden, People's Democratic Republic of Yemen.

SHUAIB, Faisal Abdul Salam, Kuwaiti businessman; born 1934, Kuwait; married; *Religion:* Muslim; *Education:* Mubarakiyah School, Kuwait; BA in Politics, University of Nottingham, UK; *Career:* Ministry of Foreign Affairs, Kuwait; 2nd Secretary, Kuwaiti Embassy to UK, 1963–65; Ministry of Commerce, 1965–66; business entrepreneur, 1966–; Director, Muhammad A. Shuaib and Sons, Abdul Salam Shuaib and Sons, Faisal A. Shuaib, Public Relations and Advertising; Kuwaiti Delegate to GATT in Geneva, 1964–66; represented Kuwait at the first UNCTAD, Geneva, 1964; *Interests and Recreations:* theatre, music, cinema, swimming, fishing, antiques, cooking; *Languages:* Arabic, English; *Address:* P O Box 115, Safat, Kuwait.

SHUAIB, Hamid Abdul Salam, Kuwaiti official/architect/town planner; born Kuwait; married; two sons, two daughters; *Religion:* Muslim; *Education:* Diploma in Architecture, Oxford Polytechnic, England; Diploma, Civic Design, University of Liverpool, Liverpool, UK; University of Liverpool, 1962–64; *Career:* various architectural firms, London 1958–60; Assistant Architect, Ministry of Public Works, Kuwait, 1960–62; Assistant Director, Technical Affairs, Kuwait Municipality, 1965–72; Chief Architect, Kuwait Municipality, 1972–; founding member and former President, Kuwait Society of Engineers, Kuwait Environmental Protection Society; Partner, Pan-Arab, Consultant Engineers, Planners and Architects; *Publications:* articles on planning; *Interests and Recreations:* music, theatre, tennis, swimming; *Languages:* Arabic, English, French; *Address:* P O Box 10, Safat, Kuwait; telephone: 419728; telex: 22570 BALDIA KT.

SHUAIB, Muhammad Abdul Salam al-, Kuwaiti businessman; born 1924, Kuwait; married; three sons, two daughters; *Religion:* Muslim; *Education:* in Kuwait; *Career:* teacher; businessman; Managing Director, Muhammad A. Shuaib and Brothers Trading Company Ltd; Director, Abdul Salam Shuaib's Sons Trading Company Ltd; member of the Board of Directors of the Kuwait Chamber of Commerce and Industry; member of the Board of Directors, The Port Authority, 1979–; *Interests and Recreations:* sports, swimming, fishing; *Languages:* Arabic, English; *Address:* P O Box 115, Safat, Kuwait.

SHUKAIR, Mahmud Abd Alayyan, Jordanian journalist/writer; born 15 March 1941, Jerusalem; married; three sons, two daughters; *Religion:* Muslim; *Career:* worked for *Al-Jihad,* Jerusalem and *Al-Quds;* contributed to *Al-Fajr* and *Al-Sha'ab; Publications:* short story collection *Khubz Al-Akharin;* short story collection *Al-Turab;* children's novel *Al-Arous Al-Makhtoufd;* published numerous short stories and articles on cultural affairs in various Arabic magazines, several television series; *Interests and Recreations:* table tennis, listening to classical music; member of Jordanian Short Story Writers' Association; *Languages:* Arabic, English, some Hebrew; *Address:* P O Box 2793, Jordanian Writers' Association, Amman, Jordan.

SHUKRALLAH, Ibrahim, Egyptian official; born 1 February, 1921, Egypt; married; two sons, one daughter; *Religion:* Christian; *Education:* BA, English Literature, Cairo University, Cairo, Egypt; BA, Psychology, American University in Cairo; Diploma, Institute of Higher Arab Studies, Cairo; *Career:* News Editor, *Egyptian Mail,* Cairo, 1941–42; founder and Editor in Chief, *Trablus al-Gharb,* daily newspaper, Libya, 1943; Editor, *Corriere di Tripoli,* Libya, 1944; Foreign News Editor, *Sawt al-Umma,* daily newspaper, 1948; Assistant Directory of Information, Press Office, Arab League, 1946–57, Deputy Director of Information, 1961; joint editor, *Arab Observer,* 1964–65; Arab League Representative, Ottawa, Canada, 1965–70; Acting Chief of Mission to UN, 1970; Director of Information, Arab League, 1971–74; Chief Representative of Arab League Mission, India and South East Asia, 1974–79; Assistant Secretary General, Arab British Chamber of Commerce, London, 1982–; *Publications: Images from the Arab World,* London 1943; *Non-Ali gnment: Hope and Fulfilment,* Cairo, 1961; *The Show Trial of Adolf Eichmann,* Cairo, 1962; collection of poems (in Arabic), 1982; *Languages:* Arabic, English, French; *Address:* Arab British Chamber of Commerce, 42 Berkeley Square, London W1, England; telephone: 01 491 4245; telex: 22171 ARABRI G.

SHUKRI, Adel Muhammad, Egyptian economist; resident in the United Arab Emirates; born 1931, Cairo, Egypt; married; three daughters; *Religion:* Muslim; *Education:* PhD in Economics, Cairo University, Egypt; PhD in Political Science, Berlin University; *Career:* Attaché in Egyptian Embassy to Germany; Secretary in Egyptian Embassy, Czechoslovakia; Director of Research Department, Maritime Transport; Assistant Lecturer in Economics and Political Science, University of Khartoum, Sudan; Expert in UN Technical Aid Programme; Economic Adviser to United Arab Emirates Government; Founder and President of Euro-Arab Consultant and Implementation Group (ECOJECT); *Publications:* articles on economics and politics; *South East Asia Treaty Organization,* Cairo, 1958; *Nazism Between Ideology And Practice,* Cairo, 1964; *Interests and Recreations:* poetry, music, tennis, billiards, chess; *Languages:* Arabic, English, French, German; *Address:* P O Box 1, Abu Dhabi, United Arab Emirates; telephone:

Office — 62635; Residence — 61373; 18 Aly Ibn Aby Taleb St, Muhandisiin, Cairo; P O Box 55, Orman, Giza, Cairo, Egypt.

SHUKRI, Ahmad al-Siba'i, Moroccan academic/lawyer; born 1938, Sidi Qassim, Morocco; married; two sons, one daughter; *Religion:* Muslim; *Education:* Licence in Law; Diploma in Higher Studies in Law; PhD in Law; *Career:* Assistant Professor, Faculty of Law, 1962; Lecturing Professor, 1969; Professor, 1971–; Head of Mission at the Royal Cabinet; Professor of Law at Hassan II University, Casablanca, at Muhammad V University, Rabat, and Dar al-Hadith al-Husniya, Rabat; member of the Moroccan Lawyers Federation, of the Academic Council of the Faculty of Law, of the Editorial Board of the Moroccan magazine, *Law, Politics and Economics,* published by the Faculty of Law; *Publications:* several books on Moroccan law, in Arabic; numerous articles in Moroccan magazines and papers; *Interests and Recreations:* reading literature and history; tennis, football; member of the Tennis Club; *Languages:* Arabic, French; *Address:* Rue Zarhun, Zankit Barq al-Lail, Villa Shukri Suisse, Rabat, Morocco.

SHUKRI, Fahmi Mahmud, Iraqi Arab League official/financial expert; born 1927, Baghdad, Iraq; married; one daughter; *Religion:* Muslim; *Education:* LLB, University of Baghdad, 1957; MA in Finance, Copenhagen University, Denmark, 1961; MA in Economics, University of Stockholm, Sweden, 1963; *Career:* Director of Planning and Research, Ministry of Finance, Iraq, 1964–73; Director of the Research Centre, Arab Organization of Administrative Sciences, Arab League, Amman, Jordan; Lecturer in Financial Administration; Administrative and Financial Adviser; *Publications:* numerous research papers for international seminars and conferences; *Supreme Financial Audit: Its Scope and Its Organisation,* Amman, Jordan, 1983; *Languages:* Arabic, English; *Address:* Arab Organization of Administrative Sciences, P O Box 17159, Amman, Jordan.

SHUKRI, Muhammad Aziz, Syrian academic/lawyer; born Damascus, Syria; married; *Religion:* Muslim; *Education:* Licence in Law, Damascus University, Damascus, Syria, 1959; LLM, University of Virginia, USA, 1961; Doctor of Juridical Science, Columbia University, USA, 1965; *Career:* Associate Judge at the Council of State, 1959–60; Lecturer, International Law, Damascus University, 1964–70; Assistant Professor of International Law and Organizations, Assistant Dean for Academic Affairs, University of Kuwait, 1974–77; *Publications: The Concept of Self Determination in the United Nations,* 1965; *The Acquisition of Nationality in the Laws of the Arab States,* 1961; numerous books and articles in the field of international law and organisations; *Interests and Recreations:* music, table tennis; *Languages:* Arabic, English; *Address:* 15 Al-Mughira Ben Shuba Street, Damascus, Syria; telephone: 338420.

SHUKRI, Sabih Mahmud, Iraqi banker; born 18 December 1928, Baghdad, Iraq; married; *Religion:* Muslim; *Education:* BA in Economics and Commerce, Baghdad University, Baghdad, Iraq; PhD candidate, International Business Law; *Career:* thirty-six years in banking; trained with leading European banks; acting General Manager, Rafidain Bank, Baghdad, Iraq, 1958; Manager, Rafidain Bank, London; Chief Manager, Arab Bank, London, 1977; Director, Arab Morgan Grenfell Finance Company Ltd; Managing Director and Chief Executive, Allied Arab Bank, London, 1977–; member of the Board of Arab-British Chamber of Commerce and Chairman of Finance Committee; Deputy Chairman, Arab Bankers Association, London, 1981, resigned April 1983; member of the Board of Institute of Bankers, and senior lecturer in banking, Jordan; Chairman of World of Islam Encyclopaedia; Treasurer of World of Islam Festival and member of its Management Committee; Chairman and Chief Executive, The International Who's Who of Arab World Ltd; *Interests and Recreations:* riding, classical music; Chairman and founder of International Music Society, 1980; life member of London Philharmonic Society; art collector; Chairman of the Board of Trustees of Islamic Museum, London 1983–; *Languages:* Arabic, English; *Address:* Allied Arab Bank, Granite House, Cannon Street, London EC4; International Who's Who of the Arab World Ltd, 37 Park Street, London W1; telephone: 493 8885; telex: 268663 IWWAW.

SHUMMO, Ali Muhammad, Sudanese official; born 25 September 1932, Khartoum, Sudan; married; one son, four daughters; *Religion:* Muslim; *Education:* BA in Islamic

Law and Jurisprudence; MA in Psychology and Pedagogy; Postgraduate Studies in Co-operative Law; MSc; *Career:* Director General, Sudan Television, 1965–71; Deputy Under Secretary, Ministry of Information and Culture, Sudan, 1971; Under Secretary, Ministry of Information and Culture, Sudan, 1971–73; Adviser to the Minister of Information and Culture, Abu Dhabi, United Arab Emirates (UAE), 1973–77; Minister of State for Youth and Sports, 1977–78; member of the Board of Trustees of International Broadcasting Institute; member of International Advisory Committee for Libraries, Documentation and Archives; former President of Arab States Broadcasting Union, also Chairman of Programme Committee; member of the NAB, USA; former member of the Administrative Council of the International Radio and Television Organization and President of the Jury for Developing World; *Publications:* contributor to *Broadcasting System,* published 1975 by Dr. Sydney Head; has contributed to different organizations with articles and designs for projects; *Decorations:* medals from Emperor Haile Selassie of Ethiopia; President Lubke of the FDR (West Germany); *Interests and Recreations:* walking; Prize, International Television Festival 1966; *Languages:* Arabic, English; *Address:* c/o Ministry of Culture and Information, Khartoum, Sudan.

SIBAI, Omar al-, Syrian politician/engineer; born 1924, Aleppo, Syria; married; *Education:* Aleppo; Diploma in Electrical Engineering, Sorbonne, University of Paris, France; *Career:* member of Aleppo Electricity Workers' Union; Manager, tractor and motor assembly factory, Aleppo; Minister of Communications, 1970, reappointed in 1974 and 1976; member of Syrian Communist Party Politburo; visited Prague, 1966; *Address:* Ministry of Communications, Damascus, Syria.

SIBAIE, Ahmad Muhammad al-, Saudi Arabian journalist; born 1905; *Religion:* Muslim; *Education:* general; *Career: Sawtal Hijaz* press editor, editor in chief, one of the earliest newspapers in the country; secretary to several charity societies; Inspector, Ministry of Finance; Founder and Editor of *Al-Nadwah* daily newspaper; Founder and Editor of *Quraysh* magazine; Secretary of Society for the Defence of Palestine, 1939; attended Second Arab Men of Letters Conference, Kuwait, 1971; *Publications:* six books for schools; *Yawmityat Majnoun Ba'is; Daouna Namshi; Qala Wa Qultu; Tarikhu Makka; Address:* Jarwal al- Biban, Mecca, Saudi Arabia; Al-Shohada, Taif, Saudi Arabia.

SIDAROUS, HE Cardinal Stephanos I, Egyptian ecclesiastic; born 1904; *Education:* Jesuits College, Cairo, Egypt; Faculté de Droit, and Ecole Libre des Sciences Politiques, Paris, France; *Career:* Barrister in Egypt, 1926–32; Vincentian Priest, 1939; Professor, Seminaries of Evreux, Dax, Beauvais, France, 1939–46; Rector of the Coptic Catholic Seminary, 1946–53; Rector of the Coptic Catholic Seminary, Tahta and Tanta, and Maadi, 1953–58; Auxiliary Bishop of the Patriarch of Alexandria, 1947; Patriarch of Alexandria, 1958; Created Cardinal, 1965; *Languages:* Arabic, English, French, Italian, Latin; *Address:* 34 Ibn Sandar Street, Kubbah Bridge, Cairo, Egypt; telephone: 821740, 827816.

SIDDIQNI, Georges, Syrian official/writer; born 1934, Lattakia, Syria; *Religion:* Christian; *Education:* in Lattakia and Damascus University; *Career:* teacher; Minister of Information, 1973–74; member of Baath Regional Command and International Command; Head of Cultural Research Bureau, 1975; *Publications:* author of several novels and various articles; *Interests and Recreations:* President of the Union of Arab Writers in Syria; *Address:* Culture and Research Bureau, Damascus, Syria.

SIDI BABA, Dey Ould, Moroccan diplomat/official; born 1921; married; *Religion:* Muslim; *Career:* elected to Mauritanian Territorial Council as delegate for Ardrar, 1946; former Mauritanian Minister of Commerce, Industry and Mines; former member of the Grand Council of French West Africa, and Counsellor for the territory of Mauritania; declared allegiance and became resident of Morocco, 1958; Adviser to Moroccan Ministry of Foreign Affairs; member of the Moroccan delegation to the UN General Assembly, 1958, 1959; Chairman of the Afro-Asian Group in the 4th Decolonization Committee, UN General Assembly, 1959; Ambassador to Guinea, 1961; Moroccan Representative at the UN Committee on Ruanda Burundi; Director of the African Division, Ministry of Foreign Affairs; Deputy in the Moroccan Permanent Delegation to the UN, New York, Head of the Delegation, 1964; member of the Royal Cabinet, with rank of Minister, 1967; Ambassador to Saudi Arabia, 1971; Director of the Royal Cabinet, 1972; Minister of Education, 1973; Minister of Habous (Religious Endowments) and Islamic Affairs, 1974–77; Speaker of Parliament, 1977; *Decorations:* Commander of the Alaouite Throne; Niger Grand Order of Merit; Officer of the Libyan Order of Independence; Commander of the Syrian Order of Merit; *Languages:* Arabic, French; *Address:* Parliament Building, Rabat, Morocco.

SIDKY, Izziddin, Egyptian dental surgeon/academic; born 20 May 1914, Alexandria, Egypt; married; five children; *Education:* BDS, University of Cairo, Egypt; Higher Dental Diploma in Oral Surgery, 1950; *Career:* Professor of Operative Dentistry and Endodontics, Dental School, University of Cairo; Chairman, Operative, Endodontics, Crown and Bridge Department; Dean, Faculty of Dentistry; President, Supreme Board of Dental Education; President, Board of Dental Examiners; President, Egyptian Dental Syndicate; member, Egyptian Dental Association; Editor in Chief, *Egyptian Dental Journal; Publications:* author of three books on dentistry; contributed articles to professional journals; *Address:* Residence — 5 Midan Falaky, Cairo, Egypt.

SIDQI, Aziz, Egyptian politician; born 1 July 1920; *Religion:* Muslim; *Education:* Cairo University, Egypt; PhD in Engineering, Harvard University, USA; *Career:* Technical Adviser in the Prime Minister's Office after the 1952 Revolution; Director General of the Productivity Centre of the International Labour Office, 1955; Director General of al-Tahrir Province Authority; Minister of Industry, 1956; Federal Minister of Industry in the United Arab Republic of Egypt and Syria, 1958; Deputy Prime Minister for Industry and Mineral Wealth, 1964; Minister of Mining, Petroleum and Light Industries; Adviser on Industrial Affairs to the President, 1967; Minister of Industry, 1968; Petroleum and Mining added to the Portfolio, 1968; Military Production added in 1969–70; Deputy Prime Minister for Production and Trade, 1970; Chairman of the Provisional Secretariat of the Arab Socialist Union (ASU), 1971 and supervised the elections to the ASU; First Deputy Prime Minister, 1971; Prime Minister, 1972–73; Personal Assistant to the late President Sadat, 1973–75; *Address:* c/o Ministry of Industry, Cairo, Egypt.

SIGINI, Omar Abdullah, Saudi Arabian financial official/banker; born 1924, Mecca, Saudi Arabia; *Religion:* Muslim; *Education:* MA in Public Administration; *Career:* Director General of Banks Control Department, Saudi Arabian Monetary Agency (SAMA); Controller of Arab Banks Union; member of Board of Saudi Credit Bank, United Bank, Dammam; member of Board of Bank Melli Iran, Jeddah; member of Founding Committee, International Gulf Bank, Bahrain; Executive Director, Islamic Bank of Development and representative of Saudi Arabia at the Bank; contributed in the implementation of Saudi banking policy; contributed in developing banking services, Saudi Arabia; attended Arab-European Seminar, Switzerland, and Arab Banking Seminar, Beirut; *Address:* Islamic Development Bank, P O Box 5925, Jeddah, Saudi Arabia; telephone: 33994; telex: 401137 BANKISLAMI SJ.

SIJELMASSI, Muhammad, Moroccan diplomat; born 1932, Fes, Morocco; married; *Religion:* Muslim: *Education:* in Morocco; Law studies at Universities of Bordeaux, France, and Rabat, Morocco; *Career:* Chef de Cabinet, Ministry of Labour, 1956; admitted to the Magistrature, 1957; Chargé de Mission in Cabinet of Prime Minister, 1965; Chargé de Mission, Royal Cabinet, 1966; Under Secretary of State, Royal Cabinet, 1967; Under Secretary of State in Ministry of Foreign Affairs, 1967; represented Morocco at Organization of African Unity, Foreign Ministers Conference, Addis Ababa, 1970; Minister in the Royal Cabinet, 1970; Ambassador to Algeria, 1971; Ambassador to USSR, 1973–77; Ambassador to Norway, Denmark and Sweden, 1977–; *Languages:* Arabic, French; *Address:* Moroccan Embassy, Oregards Alle 19, 2900 Hellerup, Denmark.

SIKSIK, Dawud Sulaiman, United Arab Emirates official; born 25 December 1944, Jaffa, Palestine; married; one son, one daughter; *Religion:* Muslim; *Education:* Al-Hussein College, Amman, Jordan; UN Vocational Centre, Jerusalem; *Career:* Private Secretary to HH Ruler of Abu Dhabi, 1967–72; Private Secretary to HH the President of the United Arab Emirates,

1972–74; Minister Plenipotentiary attached to Presidential Palace as Director of Administration and Finance; *Decorations:* Order of Independence, Jordan; Rafidain Order, Iraq; *Interests and Recreations:* reading, theatre, swimming, water-skiing, tennis; *Languages:* Arabic, English; *Address:* Manhal Palace, Abu Dhabi, United Arab Emirates.

SIMBAWA, Amin Muhammad Ibrahim, Saudi Arabian businessman; born 1946, Mecca, Saudi Arabia; *Religion:* Muslim; *Education:* MA in Industrial Management, 1970; *Career:* Lecturer in Industrial Management at the Royal Technical Institute, Riyadh, 1971; Lecturer in Industrial Management at the Higher Technical Institute, Riyadh, 1972; Director of Commercial Education, 1973–75; member of the Saudi Arabian Delegation to West Germany, 1974; General Director of Mecca Textile Mill; *Interests and Recreations:* reading, sport; *Address:* P O Box 608, Gararah, Mecca, Saudi Arabia.

SINDI, Abdul Aziz Muhammad, Saudi Arabian engineer; born 1946; *Religion:* Muslim; *Education:* BSc in Civil Engineering; *Career:* Project Engineer, Governorate Building, Qassim, 1971; Engineer in charge of asphalt laying, Mecca Governorate Secretariat, 1971; Chief, Engineering Department, 1973; Director, Technical Department, 1973; Director of Engineering Department, Mecca Municipality, 1973–; member of Higher Pilgrimage Technical Sub-Committee, Technical Board of Real Estate Development Fund, Arab Town Planning Organization, Board of Governorate Secretariat; attended Arab Cities Organization Conference, Baghdad; *Interests and Recreations:* music; *Address:* Mecca Municipality Secretariat, Mecca, Saudi Arabia; telephone: Office — 5423075.

SINDI, Ali Abdul Rasuul, Saudi Arabian businessman; born 1933, Mecca, Saudi Arabia; married; four sons; *Religion:* Muslim; *Education:* in Saudi Arabia; *Career:* Administrative Section of Civil Aviation Department; Assistant Director General of Civil Aviation, 1953–68; Chairman, Express Contracting and Trading, 1968–; *Interests and Recreations:* tennis; *Languages:* Arabic, English; *Address:* P O Box 2951, Jeddah, Saudi Arabia; telephone: 6654585; telex: 401082 SINDICO SJ.

SINDI, Kamil, Saudi Arabian aviation official; born 1930, Mecca, Saudi Arabia; married; *Religion:* Muslim; *Education:* training courses in USA; *Career:* Administrator, Director, Jeddah Airport; Inspector General of Civil Aviation, 1965; Director General of Civil Aviation; Assistant Chairman of the Board, Saudi Arabian Airlines, and Deputy to the Minister of Defence and Aviation (Civil Aviation); *Languages:* Arabic, English; *Address:* Saudi Arabian Airlines, P O Box 167, Saudia Main Building, Jeddah, Saudi Arabia; telephone: 686 0000; telex: 401007 SAUDIA SJ.

SIRRY, Muhsin Hussain al-, Yemen Arab Republic banker; born 22 December 1934; married; four sons; *Religion:* Muslim; *Education:* BA in Commerce, Dublin University, Irish Republic; *Career:* Minister of Economy, 1966; President of Yemeni Bank, 1973; *Interests and Recreations:* the science of banking, football, chess, reading; *Languages:* Arabic, English; *Address:* The Bank of Yemen, Sana'a, Yemen Arab Republic; telephone: 5561.

SKAFF, Georges, Lebanese journalist/politician; born 28 January 1928, Zahle, Lebanon; *Education:* Oriental College, Zahle, Lebanon; French Lycée, Beirut, Lebanon; BA in Political Science, Faculty of Law; *Career:* journalist, Editor and later Editor in Chief, *Al-Jarida* newspaper; Director General, UNIPRESS (Press and Public Relations Company), 1965–; Publisher and Editor, *Rijal al-Aamal,* an economic magazine/journal published in Arabic and in French; Editor in Chief, *Al-Dyar* a political magazine; Minister of Economy and Trade, Finance and Posts, Telegraphs and Telecommunications, 1976; *Publications: Réalités Libanaises,* 1960; *Vers un Liban meilleur,* 1961; *Notre Vigne à Allyne,* (poetry in prose), 1961; *Le Liban Nouveau,* 1963; *Monsieur Dix Heures* (short stories); *Decorations:* Gold Medal, Lebanese Order of Merit; *Interests and Recreations:* swimming, tennis, gardening, reading; *Languages:* Arabic, French; *Address:* Office — *Al-Jarida* newspaper, Trablos Street, Beirut, Lebanon.

SKAFF, Jean, Lebanese banker/businessman; born 4 April 1908, Zahle, Lebanon; *Education:* Diploma from the School of Civil Engineering, St. Louis, Missouri, USA; *Career:* banker; businessman; elected Deputy for Zahle, 1951; Minister of Agriculture; President, Board of Directors, Modern Hotels Company; Director Agricultural Credit Bank; *Interests and Recreations:* walking, tennis, swimming; member of the Beirut Aero Club; founder of the Bekaa Sports Club; the Baalbek Festival; *Languages:* Arabic, French; *Address:* Office — Rue du Port, P O Box 1787, Beirut, Lebanon.

SKAFF, Joseph Elias, Lebanese politician; born 1922, Lebanon; married; one son, one daughter; *Religion:* Christian; *Education:* BA in Political Sciences, St. Joseph University, Beirut; *Career:* Deputy of South Lebanon, 1947; Deputy of Zahle, 1953, 1957, 1960, 1964 and 1972; Minister of Agriculture; Minister of Labour and Social Affairs; Minister of Public Health; Minister of Hydraulic Resources and Electricity; Minister of National Defence, 1980–; represented Lebanon as member and then president of several Parliamentary Delegations to different countries, since 1948; *Decorations:* Order of National Cedar for High Officers; various other distinctions and decorations; *Interests and Recreations:* swimming and reading; *Languages:* Arabic, French, English; *Address:* Al-Midan, Zahle, Lebanon; telephone: 823515, 823022.

SKALLI, Ali, Moroccan diplomat; born 1927, Fes, Morocco; married; four children; *Religion:* Muslim; *Education:* BA in Law and Political Sciences, University of Paris, France; *Career:* Société Métallurgique, Luxembourg, 1954–56; Counsellor, Moroccan Embassy to France, 1956; Ministry of Foreign Affairs, Morocco, Head of Consular Affairs, Head of Social Affairs, Head of International Organizations, Head of European Affairs; Minister Plenipotentiary and Chargé d'Affaires, Moroccan Embassy in Paris, France; Ambassador to Federal Republic of Germany, 1970; Secretary General, Ministry of Foreign Affairs, 1971–74; Ambassador, Permanent Representative to the UN, and the international organizations in Geneva and Austria, 1974; *Languages:* Arabic, French; *Address:* c/o Ministry of Foreign Affairs, Rabat, Morocco.

SLAOUI, Maître Driss, Moroccan diplomat/politician; born 1926, Fes, Morocco; married; *Religion:* Muslim; *Education:* in France; *Career:* Governor of Casablanca, 1955; Sous-Directeur, Chef de Sûetré Régionale,

Casablanca, 1956; Under Secretary of State for the Interior, 1958; Minister of Industry, Commerce and Mines, 1960–61; Secretary General of the Casablanca Group of African states in charge of the Group Liaison Office, Bamako, Mali, 1961–62; Director of the Royal Cabinet, 1962; Minister of Finance, 1963; leading member of the Front pour la Défense des Institutions Constitutionelles (FDIC); Founding member of the Parti Social-Democrate (PSD) set up by Maître Ahmed Guedira; Minister of National Economy, Finance and Agriculture, 1963; Governor of the Bank of Morocco, 1964; Minister of Justice, 1968; responsible for the development of the Casablanca Region under the Five-Year Plan; Director General of the Royal Cabinet, 1969–71; Permanent Representative at UN, Geneva, 1974; Representative to International Court of Justice in Western Sahara dispute, 1975; *Languages:* Arabic, French; *Address:* c/o Ministry of Foreign Affairs, Rabat, Morocco.

SLIM, Muhsin, Lebanese politician/lawyer; born 17 October 1918; married; three sons; *Education:* Collège des Frères; Licence in Law, St. Joseph University, Beirut, Lebanon; *Career:* Barrister at Law; elected Deputy for Beirut, 1960; President of the Committee for upholding the Constitution and Liberties; Secretary General, Arab Institute for Legislation and Legal Research; *Decorations:* many foreign and local distinctions and decorations; *Interests and Recreations:* member of the Cercle de l'Union Française; member of many literary and scientific associations; *Languages:* Arabic, French; *Address:* Office — Place de l'Etoile, Arida Building, Beirut, Lebanon; Residence — El-Ghobeyri, Beirut, Lebanon.

SLIM, Tayib, Tunisian diplomat; born 1914, Tunis, Tunisia; *Religion:* Muslim; *Education:* in Tunis and Paris; *Career:* active in the Neo-Destour movement, Paris, 1939; sentenced to 20 years' hard labour for political activities, 1941; released 1943; spent several years in Italy, Germany, Spain; later in Cairo, India and South-East Asia, fundraising and supporting the nationalist movement; returned to Tunis 1955; Ambassador to the Court of St. James, London, UK, 1956, also accredited to Denmark, Norway, Sweden; elected to the Political Bureau of the Neo-Destour Party, 1959; Permanent Representative of Tunisia at the UN in New York;

Minister of State and Personal Representative of the President, 1967–70; represented the President at the Rabat Summit Conference, 1969; Ambassador to Morocco, 1970–72; Secretary of State responsible for the Environment, 1972–73; Permanent Representative to the UN, Geneva, Switzerland; Ambassador to Austria, 1973; Ambassador to Canada, 1973; Permanent Representative to UN, 1982–; *Interests and Recreations:* sailing; *Languages:* Arabic, English, French; *Address:* Permanent Mission of Tunisia to UN, 40 East Street, New York, NY 10021, USA.

SLIMANI, Othman, Moroccan economist; born 13 October 1941, Fes, Morocco; married; one child; *Religion:* Muslim; *Education:* Degrees in Law and Economic Sciences; *Career:* Inspecteur des Finances; Secretary General, Ministry of Finance Department; several assignments abroad, particularly with the IMF in Washington; Secretary of State for Economic Affairs in Prime Minister's Office, 1977; Director General, Crédit Immobilier Hotelier, 1980–; *Languages:* Arabic, French; *Address:* 68 rue de Reins, Casablanca, Morocco.

SMAILA, Milad Abdul Salam, Libyan politician; *Religion:* Muslim; *Career:* Under Secretary, Ministry of Planning; Minister of State for Cabinet Affairs, 1976–77; Secretary for General People's Committee Affairs, General People's Committee, 1977; *Address:* General People's Committee, Tripoli, Libya.

SOGHAIER, Adnan Abdul Khalik, Lebanese UN official/agronomist; born 22 July 1928, Palestine; married; two sons, one daughter; *Religion:* Muslim; *Education:* Matriculation and Diploma in Agriculture, Khadoori Agricultural College, Tul Karm, Palestine, 1948; BSc in Agriculture, Kansas State University, Manhattan, Kansas, USA, 1951; MSc in Agronomy, Kansas State University, Manhattan, Kansas, USA, 1952; *Career:* Marketing Assistant, Bunge Grain Corporation, 1952; Agronomist, Food and Agriculture Organisation, Cyrenaica, Libya, 1952–54; Agronomist and Team Leader, FAO, Cyrenaica, Libya, 1955–57; Senior Agronomist, FAO, Tripolitania, Libya, 1958–60; Seed Improvement Adviser and Project Supervisor, FAO, Pakistan, 1961–65; Project Leader, Seed Improvement and Certification, FAO, Iraq, 1966–70; Senior Agricultural Adviser

and Country Representative, FAO, UNDP, Syria, 1971–77; FAO Representative, Sudan, 1978–80; Resident Representative of the United Nations Development Programme, UNDP, and UN Co-ordinator in Iraq, 1980–82; UNDP Resident Representative and UN Co-ordinator in Saudi Arabia, 1982–; *Publications: Crop Agronomy and Improvement in Tripolitania* , 1961; *Seed Improvement in West Pakistan,* 1966; *Cereal Seed Status: Ethiopia,* 1968; *Wheat and Barley Improvement through Seed Production and Certification,* 1971; *Interests and Recreations:* music, reading, swimming; member of Gamma Sigma Delta Club, the Society of Agronomy; *Languages:* Arabic, English, and some Italian; *Address:* UNDP Resident Representative Office, United Nations Development Programme, P O Box 558, Riyadh, Saudia Arabia.

SOLAIM, Sulaiman Abdul Aziz al-, Saudi Arabian politician/academic; born 1941; *Education:* BCom, Cairo University, Egypt; MA in International Relations, University of Southern California, USA; PhD in International Relations, Johns Hopkins University, USA, 1970; *Career:* Director, Department of Foreign Relations and Conferences, Ministry of Labour; Assistant Director General of General Organization of Social Insurance; Professor of Political Science, Riyadh University, 1972–74; Deputy Minister of Commerce and Industry for Trade and Provisions, 1974–75; Minister of Commerce, 1975–; Chairman of Board, Saudi Arabian Specifications and Standardization Organization, Wheat Silos and Flour Mills Organization; *Address:* Ministry of Commerce, P O Box 1774, Airport Road, Riyadh, Saudi Arabia; telephone: 4039567; telex: 201057 TIJARAH SJ.

SOLH, Rashid al-, Lebanese politician; born 1924, Beirut, Lebanon; married; one daughter; *Religion:* Muslim; *Education:* Collège des Frères and Mokassed College; Law Degree from University of St. Joseph, Beirut; *Career:* in the judiciary, 1948–60; successively Judge, President, Labour Arbitration Court, Examining Magistrate, Attorney General in the Shari'a (Personal Status) Court of Beirut; stood unsuccessfully for Parliament, 1960; elected deputy for Beirut, 1964; was in the Beirut Bloc of deputies opposed to Presidents Chehab and Helou; defeated in 1968 elections; re-elected 1972; committee member, Lebanese-Soviet and Lebanese-German Democratic Republic Friendship Societies; Prime Minister and Minister of the Interior, 1974–75; *Languages:* Arabic, French; *Address:* Bourj Abu-Haidar, Beirut, Lebanon.

SOLH, Takiddin al-, Lebanese politician; born 1909, Beirut, Lebanon; married; *Religion:* Muslim; *Education:* studies in Law and History, American University of Beirut (AUB), Lebanon; *Career:* journalist; contributed to *Al-Nida'a* and *Al-Dyar* newspapers, 1931–35; teacher of literature, Lycée, 1935–43; Director, Ministry of Information, 1943–44; Counsellor, Lebanese Embassy, Egypt, 1944–47; President, Press Syndicate, 1947; Adviser, Arab League, 1942–50; elected Deputy for Zahle, 1957; re-elected Deputy for Baalbek-Hermel, 1964; President, Parliamentary Committee for Foreign Affairs; Minister of the Interior, 1964–65; member of the National Commission to UNESCO; Vice President, National Tourist Board, 1966–; joined Saeb Salam in Beirut Bloc, 1967; defeated in 1968 elections; Prime Minister and Minister of Finance, 1973; resigned in September 1974 following loss of support from People's Socialist Party; *Interests and Recreations:* football; *Languages:* Arabic, French, English; *Address:* Office — Riad el Solh Street, Beirut, Lebanon; Residence — May Ziade Street, Quartier des Arts et Métiers, Beirut, Lebanon.

SOROUR, Ihab Zaki, Egyptian diplomat; born 1 January 1935, Cairo, Egypt; married; one son, two daughters; *Religion:* Muslim; *Education:* BA in Military Science, 1953; BA in Commerce, 1956; MA in Arts and Political Science, 1960; PhD in Political Science, 1970; Diploma in Foreign Trade Planning, UN Geneva, 1971; *Career:* President of African Affairs Bureau, 1953–67; Director, Economic Research Department, Ministry of Economy and Foreign Trade, 1968–71; Commercial Counsellor, Tokyo, Japan, 1972–74; Political Counsellor for Ministry of Foreign Affairs, Cairo, Egypt, 1974; member of Egyptian Delegation to United Nations, New York, 1975; Chargé d'Affaires of Egypt to New Zealand, 1975; Ambassador of Egypt to New Zealand, 1976–; paricipated in various official Egyptian delegations since 1970; *Publications:* several articles on political economy in local and foreign press; *Decorations:* Order of the Revolution, 1953; Order

of the Republic, 1975; *Interests and Recreations:* tennis, squash, hunting, swimming, travel, chess, backgammon; member of the Economic and Legislative Association, Cairo, Egypt, International Law Association, Cairo, Egypt, African Assembly, Cairo, Egypt, International Trade Centre, Geneva, Switzerland; World Trade Centre, NY, USA, and the Foreign Correspondents Club, Tokyo, Japan; *Address:* Embassy of Egypt, P O Box 10386, Wellington, New Zealand.

SOUDAH, Claude Anton, Arab-American banker/international financial manager; born 8 June 1937, Jerusalem, Palestine; married; three daughters; *Religion:* Christian; *Education:* BA, College of Business Administration, Seattle, University of Washington, 1966; American Institute of Banking, Seattle Chapter; School for International Banking, University of Colorado, 1972; Pacific Coast Graduate School, University of Washington, 1977; *Career:* Management Trainee, International Division, Seattle-First National Bank, Seattle, Washington, 1966–67, Assistant Vice President, International Division, 1967–71, Vice President and Manager, Seattle Office, International Division, 1972–74, Vice President and Manager, Americas Region, International Division, Washington, 1974–79, Vice President and General Manager, Europe Region, International Division, London, 1979–; member of Overseas Bankers Club; member of Arab Bankers Association, London; member of Woolnoth Society; *Interests and Recreations:* reading, writing, stamp collecting, travel, backgammon, soccer, basket-ball; *Languages:* Arabic, English; *Address:* 28 Hanover House, St. John's Wood High Street, London NW8 7DY; telephone: (01) 722 0725.

SOUELEM, Nadir Muhammad, Egyptian academic/plastic surgeon; born 1926, Cairo, Egypt; *Religion:* Muslim; *Education:* MB, BCh, Cairo, Egypt; FRCS, London, UK; *Career:* Registrar, Senior Registrar, Cairo; Lecturer in General Surgery, Ain Shams University, Cairo, Egypt; plastic surgeon, East Grinstead, UK; Assistant Professor of Plastic Surgery, Ain Shams University; Professor of Plastic Surgery, Ain Shams University; Head of the Burns and Facio-Maxillary Department, and of the Plastic Surgery Department, Ain Shams University; *Publications:* more than 20 research papers on plastic surgery, published in local and foreign journals; *Decorations:* Order of the Republic, 1958; *Interests and Recreations:* tennis, swimming, diving, music; member of the International Association for Sports Medicine, member of the Medical Committee of the African Football Confederation, President of the Egyptian Association for Plastic Surgery; *Languages:* Arabic, English, French; *Address:* Office — 26 Adly Street, Cairo, Egypt; telephone: 977834; Residence - - la Shafik Mansour Street, Zamalek, Cairo, Egypt; telephone: 810473.

SOURANI, Jamil al-, Palestinian politician/ diplomat; born 1923, Jerusalem; *Education:* American University of Beirut, Lebanon; *Career:* lawyer in Gaza, 1947; and Chairman of the Palestinian Lawyers' Association, 1959; member of the Legal Committee of the Palestine National Union; member of Palestine Liberation Organization (PLO) Executive Committee, 1966; member of the PLO Revolutionary Committee, 1967; led a PLO delegation to North and South Yemen, 1968; Palestinian visiting representative to North Korea and East Berlin, 1969, PLO Delegation to the Arab Foreign Ministers' Conference in Cairo, Egypt, 1973; visited London, 1974, with request to British Government to support the Palestinian cause at the UN General Assembly.

SOUSS, Ibrahim, Palestinian UN official; born 3 August 1943, Jerusalem, Palestine; *Education:* Institut d'Etudes Politiques, Paris; Fondation Nationale des Sciences Politiques, Paris; Ecole Normal de Musique; Royal College of Music, London; Hochschüle für Musik, München; *Career:* President of the General Union of Palestine Students, Paris, 1971–72; PLO Permanent Observer to UNESCO, Paris, France, 1975–80; Director of PLO Liaison and Information Bureau in France, 1978–; *Languages:* Arabic, English, French, Italian, German, Russian; *Address:* Palestine Liberation Organisation Bureau, 3 rue Merimée, 75016 Paris, France.

SOUSSA, Antoine Michel, Lebanese businessman; resident in Jordan; born 1928, Haifa, Palestine; married; four daughters; *Religion:* Christian; *Education:* University of Haifa, preparatory year in medicine, 1947; *Career:* Eastern Tobacco Co, Cairo, Egypt, 1948–52; later Assistant Manufacturing Superintendent, Eastern Tobacco Co; Founder and Managing Director, Jordan Printing

and Packaging Co Ltd; member of the Board of Directors of Jordan Tobacco and Cigarette Co Ltd; member of the Board of Directors of Chamber of Industry, 1961–; member of the Board of the Directors of Jordan Social Security; Vice President of Jordan Craft Centre Co; member of the Advisory Board of the Greek Catholic Community, Amman; Assistant General Manager, Jordan Tobacco and Cigarette Co, 1961–81; Founder and Partner of Rainbow Supermarket; represented Jordanian employers at the seminar of the International Labour Organisation, Beirut, 1961; Delegate of the Chamber of Industry to the Tripartite Committee for Amendment of the Jordan Labour Law, 1960, 1967, 1970, 1980/81; Employers Representative, ILO 67th Conference, Geneva; Treasurer of Cerebral Palsy Foundation, Jordan; *Interests and Recreations:* tennis, swimming; winner of several sports awards; Head of the Frères College Scout Movement in Haifa; member of the Royal Automobile Club of Jordan, and several social and sporting clubs in Amman; *Address:* P O Box 6868, Amman, Jordan.

SOUSSI, Major General Habib, Tunisian army officer; born 1914, Tunisia; married; seven children; *Religion:* Muslim; *Education:* two-year course at the Ecole Supérieure de la Guerre, Paris, France, 1963; *Career:* after Independence, Tunisian Armed Forces; Chief of Staff of the Tunisian Brigade in the Congo, 1960–61; Commandant of Aviation and trained as a pilot, 1962; Chief of Staff of the Tunisian Army, 1967; *Decorations:* won several decorations while serving in the French Army; Honorary CBE (Commander of the British Empire) on the occasion of President Bourguiba's visit to the UK; *Languages:* Arabic, French, English; *Address:* Ministry of Defence, Tunis, Tunisia.

STETIE, Salah, Lebanese diplomat/writer; born 28 September 1928, Beirut, Lebanon; married; *Education:* Licence ès-Lettres; Diploma in Modern and Contemporary Literature; Law Studies, University of Paris, Sorbonne, France; Ecole du Louvre, Paris, France; *Career:* Professor, Academy of Literature, Beirut; Professor, Faculty of Literature, Lebanese University, Beirut; Editor in Chief, *L'Orient Littéraire;* Lebanese Cultural Counsellor, Permanent Delegation to UNESCO; Assistant Permanent Lebanese Delegate to UNESCO; *Publications:* numerous articles and research papers published in

Mercure de France; Le Figaro Littéraire; Al-Adab, and other literary reviews and journals; co-author with painter R.E. Gillet of *La Nymphe des Rats; Les Porteurs de Feu; Froide Gardée; La Mort-abeille; Uz En Poésie, La Unième Nuit, Invasion de l'Arbre et du Silence,* Gallimard; *Decorations:* Knight of the National Order of Cedar, Lebanon; Commander, French Order of Merit; Knight, French Order of Arts and Letters; *Interests and Recreations:* swimming, antiquary of paintings and rare books; member of the Automobile Club of Lebanon, of the French Pen Club and the French Writers Society; *Languages:* Arabic, French; *Address:* Office — Permanent Delegation of Lebanon to the UNESCO, Place de Fontenoy, Paris 75007, France; telephone: 577 1610; Residence — Louis David Street, Paris 75016, France; telephone: 870 0192; Solaiman Bustani Street, Stetie Building, Beirut, Lebanon; telephone: 308779.

STINO, Kamal Ramzi, Egyptian official; *Religion:* Christian; *Career:* Minister of Supplies, 1959 and 1962–63; Deputy Prime Minister for Supply and Internal Trade, 1964–66; member, General Secretariat of Arab Socialist Union, 1966; Director General, Arab Organization for Agricultural Development; *Address:* Arab Organization for Agricultural Development, 4 el-Gamaa Street, P O Box 474, Khartoum, Sudan.

SUBHI, Abdullah al-Salim al-, Saudi Arabian official; born 1943, Medina, Saudi Arabia; *Religion:* Muslim; *Education:* BCom Business Administration, University of Riyadh, Saudi Arabia; *Career:* Director of Public Relations, 1970; Deputy Director of the Customs Department, Medina, 1972; Director of Customs Department; *Publications:* articles on public commerce; *Interests and Recreations:* swimming, reading, riding; *Address:* The Bank Building, Flat 17, Medina, Saudi Arabia.

SUBHI, Muhammad Ibrahim, Egyptian official/engineer; resident in Switzerland; born 28 March 1925, Alexandria, Egypt; married; two sons, one daughter; *Religion:* Muslim; *Education:* BA in Engineering, Cairo University, Cairo, Egypt, 1949; one year fellowship studying transport and communications services, Vanderbilt University, Nashville, Tennessee, USA, 1955–56; *Career:* Engineer, construction of roads and airports in the Engineer Corps, 1950; Technical Secretary of Communications Commission, Permanent Council for Development and National Production, 1954; Technical Director, Office of the Minister of Communications for Posts, Railways and Co-ordination, 1956–61; attended the Universal Postal Union Congress, Ottawa, Canada, 1957; Director General, Sea Transport Authority; member of the Technical Committees of the Postal Organisation, Egypt, 1961–64; Under Secretary of State for Communications and member of the Board of the Postal Organisation, 1964–68; Chairman of the Postal Organisation, Egypt, and Secretary General of the African Postal Union, 1968–74; Head of the Egyptian Delegation to the Universal Postal Union, Tokyo and Lausanne Congress, 1969–74; Director of the Executive Bureau in charge of Egyptian projects in Africa, 1964–74; Director General of the International Bureau of the Universal Postal Union, Berne, Switzerland, 1975–; *Decorations:* Order of Merit, 1st Class, Egypt, 1974; Heinrich von Stephan Medal, Federal Republic of Germany, 1979; Order of Postal Merit, Gran Placa, Spain, 1979; *Interests and Recreations:* croquet, philately, music; *Languages:* Arabic, English, French, German, Spanish; *Address:* Office — Woltpoststrasse 4, 3000 Berne 15, Switzerland; telephone: 432211.

SUBHI, Shaikh Mahmud Muhammad Abdul Salam, Libyan academic/Islamic scholar; born 1924, Tripoli, Libya; *Religion:* Muslim; *Education:* graduated from University of Al-Azhar, Cairo, 1950; *Career:* elected to Chamber of Deputies, 1956; Dean of Faculty of Islamic Studies, University of Libya, 1969; named member of Benghazi Constitution Committee of Arab Socialist Union, 1971; member of Libyan delegation to Islamic Conference, Tripoli, December 1970; Head of Islamic Call Society; has travelled frequently and accompanied Colonel Qadhafi on his first visit to Europe. *Address:* Al Fateh University, Faculty of Islamic Studies, P O Box 13040, Tripoli, Libya.

SUCCAR, Abdul Latif, Syrian diplomat; born 27 December 1924, Damascus, Syria; married; *Education:* BA in History and Political Science, American University of Beirut, Lebanon, 1943–47; MA in Government, New York University, USA, 1949–53; *Career:* Secretary, Syrian Permanent Mission to UN, New York, 1948; Political Affairs Officer,

1979; *Interests and Recreations:* croquet, philately, music; *Languages:* Arabic, English, French, German, Spanish; *Address:* Office — Woltpoststrasse 4, 3000 Berne 15, Switzerland; telephone: 432211.

SUBHI, Shaikh Mahmud Muhammad Abdul Salam, Libyan academic/Islamic scholar; born 1924, Tripoli, Libya; *Religion:* Muslim; *Education:* graduated from University of Al-Azhar, Cairo, 1950; *Career:* elected to Chamber of Deputies, 1956; Dean of Faculty of Islamic Studies, University of Libya, 1969; named member of Benghazi Constitution Committee of Arab Socialist Union, 1971; member of Libyan delegation to Islamic Conference, Tripoli, December 1970; Head of Islamic Call Society; has travelled frequently and accompanied Colonel Qadhafi on his first visit to Europe. *Address:* Al Fateh University, Faculty of Islamic Studies, P O Box 13040, Tripoli, Libya.

SUCCAR, Abdul Latif, Syrian diplomat; born 27 December 1924, Damascus, Syria; married; *Education:* BA in History and Political Science, American University of Beirut, Lebanon, 1943–47; MA in Government, New York University, USA, 1949–53; *Career:* Secretary, Syrian Permanent Mission to UN, New York, 1948; Political Affairs Officer, UN, New York, 1951–61; Consultant, Syrian Foreign Ministry, 1956–61; Deputy Civilian Officer, UN Operation in the Congo, 1961–63; Chief, Foreign Aid Section, UN Operation in the Congo, 1962–63; Acting Director, Bureau of Economic Coordination, Zaire, 1963; Deputy Resident Representative, Somalia, 1965–68; Resident Representative, United Nations Development Program, Yemen, 1968–71; Regional Representative for Saudi Arabia and the Gulf Area, 1971; *Interests and Recreations:* reading, swimming, travel; international economic development; international relations; international trade and business finance; *Languages:* Arabic, English, French; *Address:* Office — UNDP, P O Box 558, Al-Washem Street, Riyadh, Saudi Arabia; telephone: 22564, 63153.

SUCCARI, Owais R., Arab-American academic; born 30 May 1939, Damascus, Syria; *Religion:* Muslim; *Education:* BA in Business Administration, Damascus University, Damascus, Syria, 1961; PhD in International Business, Louvain University, Belgium, 1968;

Career: Ministry of Planning, Damascus, Syria, 1961–64; Professor of Management, Louvanium University, Kinshasa, Zäre, 1968–71; Associate Professor, Management Department, DePaul University, Chicago, USA, 1972–; Executive Director, MidAmerica-Arab Chamber of Commerce, Chicago, USA, 1974–; member of the Academy of Management, the Academy of International Business, Chicago Association of Commerce and Industry, Chicago Council on Foreign Relations, European International Business Association; *Publications: International Petroleum Market: Policy Confrontation Between the Common Market and the Arab Countries,* Louvain, Belgium, 1968; *Interests and Recreations:* reading, music, tennis, swimming, sailing; *Languages:* Arabic, English, French; *Address:* MidAmerica-Arab Chamber of Commerce, 135 S. LaSalle Street, Suite 2050, Chicago, Illinois 60603, USA; telephone: 312 782 4654.

SUDAIRI, Abdul Muhsin Muhammad al-, Saudi Arabian UN official/agriculturalist; born 1936, Riyadh; married; three children; *Religion:* Muslim; *Education:* BSc in Agriculture, Colorado University; MSc in Agriculture, Arizona University, USA; *Career:* several posts at the Ministry of Agriculture and Water, Riyadh, Saudi Arabia; Permanent Representative of Saudi Arabia to the FAO with rank of Ambassador, 1972; Head of the Middle East Group of FAO; Head of the Group of Oil Exporting Countries during the UN Conference for the establishment of the International Fund for Agricultural Development, 1975; elected Head of Committee of the International Food Programme, 1976; elected Head of the Preparatory Committee of the International Agricultural Fund; Head of International Agricultural Fund, 1977; *Publications:* numerous articles published in various international journals and magazines; *Interests and Recreations:* swimming, walking; *Languages:* Arabic, English; *Address:* The International Fund for Agricultural Development, Via del Sevafico 107, Rome 00142, Italy; telephone: 54591.

SUDAIRI, Abdullah al-, Saudi Arabian official; born 1930; *Religion:* Muslim; *Education:* in USA; *Career:* Amir of Wadi Sirhan region of the north, responsible for agricultural development and Bedouin resettlement; organised the establishment of Municipal

Affairs Division of the Ministry of the Interior; Deputy Minister of Municipal Affairs, Ministry of the Interior, 1964–; *Interests and Recreations:* bridge; *Languages:* Arabic, English; *Address:* Ministry of the Interior, P O Box 2833, Riyadh, Saudi Arabia; telephone: 4011944; telex: 201622 MORS SJ.

SUDAIRI, Khalid Bin Ahmad al-, Saudi Arabian politician; born 1914; married; *Religion:* Muslim; *Career:* Governor of various provinces including Jizan; appointed Governor of the Northern Territories and Tabuk, 1943; Amir of the Eastern Province, 1946, played important part in negotiations with Arabian-American Oil Company (ARAMCO); Amir of Badana on Tapline; Minister of Agriculture, 1956–60; Governor of Najran, 1962–78; succeeded by his son Fahd as Governor of Najran, and son Sultan as Deputy Governor; *Address:* Governorate of Najran, Saudi Arabia.

SUDAIRI, Saad al-Nasser al-, Saudi Arabian official; born 1935, Saudi Arabia; *Education:* BA in Law; *Career:* Governor of Al Ghat, 1962–67; Deputy Governor Medina, 1967–; Chairman, Uhud Sporting Club; member of Supreme Committee of Pilgrimage; *Interests and Recreations:* sports, swimming, reading; *Address:* Governorate of Medina, Medina, Saudi Arabia.

SUDAIRI, Turki Bin Ahmad Bin Muhammad al-, Saudi Arabian politician; born 1899; *Religion:* Muslim; *Career:* Governor of Jawf, 1930; Governor of Assir, 1932; Governor of Jizan, 1957; *Address:* Jizan, Saudi Arabia.

SUDAIRI, Turki Bin Khalid, al-, Saudi Arabian official; born 1936, Abha, Saudi Arabia; *Education:* BA in Political Science; *Career:* Head, International Commercial Relations, Ministry of Commerce, 1962; Assistant Director, Department of Statistics, Ministry of Finance, 1964; General Secretary, Central Organisation for Management, 1966; Vice President, Civil Service Commission, 1971; President, Civil Service Commission, 1971–; *Languages:* Arabic, English; *Address:* Civil Service Commission, P O Box 9194, Riyadh, Saudi Arabia; telephone: 4020880; telex: 201445 CIVIL SJ.

SUGAIR, Salih Abdullah al-, Saudi Arabian diplomat; born 1930, Buraidah, Saudi Arabia; *Religion:* Muslim; *Education:* BA in Law; MA in Political Science; *Career:* 3rd, 2nd and later 1st Secretary to Royal Cabinet; Minister Plenipotentiary, Ministry of Foreign Affairs, Director of UN Department of International Conferences, Press and Public Relations Department, Department of Islamic Affairs, Ministry of Foreign Affairs; Ambassador to Oman; Ambassador to India, 1976; participated in several Arab Foreign Ministers Conferences, UN General Assembly Sessions, Arab League Committees; member of Saudi Arabian Mission to UN, 1960–65; former Chairman, Islamic Solidarity Fund, Organisation of Islamic Conference; *Decorations:* King Abdul Aziz Order of Merit, 1st Grade; King Abdul Aziz Excellent Grade Decoration; The Sultanate of Oman Decoration; Order of the Cedar, Lebanon; the Ordre National du Lion, Senegal; *Interests and Recreations:* reading, swimming; *Address:* Ministry of Foreign Affairs, P O Box 495, Jeddah, Saudi Arabia; telephone: 642 1322, 642 1423; telex: 401104 KHARJI SJ.

SUHAIMAT, Ali Muhammad, Jordanian politician/engineer; born 1936, Karak, Jordan; married; two sons, two daughters; *Religion:* Muslim; *Education:* BSc in Civil Engineering, 1960; *Career:* Engineer, Government of Jordan, 1960–64; Engineer with private contractors, 1964–68; member of Jordan Development Board, 1968–71; Under Secretary, Ministry of Transport, 1971–73; private business, 1973–76; Minister of Transport, 1976–79, 1979–; Minister of State for Prime Ministerial Affairs, 1979–; *Decorations:* Order of the Jordanian Star; Award from Austria, 1981; *Address:* P O Box 7403, Amman, Jordan; telephone: Residence — 661 955.

SUIDAN, Jad Anis, Lebanese banker; resident in Saudi Arabia; born 17 November 1947, Haifa; married; *Religion:* Christian; *Education:* BA in Business Administration, American University of Beirut, AUB, Lebanon, 1969; *Career:* Whinney Murray and Co, UK and the Middle East; member of the Institute of Chartered Accountants of England and Wales, 1975–79; Controller, Arab Investment Company SAA, 1979; Deputy Director General and Chief Executive, Arab Investment Co SAA, 1981–83; Director General, Arab Investment Co SAA,

1983–; *Interests and Recreations:* tennis, swimming; reading; *Languages:* Arabic, French, English; *Address:* The Arab Investment Company SAA, P O Box 4009, Riyadh 11491, Saudi Arabia; telephone: 482 3444.

SUKI, Wadi Najib, Arab-American physician/academic; born 26 October 1934, Khartoum, Sudan; married; *Education:* BSc, American University of Beirut, Lebanon, 1955; MD, 1959; *Career:* Fellow in Experimental Medicine, Southwestern Medical School, University of Texas, Dallas, USA, 1959–61; Resident in Internal Medicine, Parkland Memorial Hospital, Dallas, 1963–65, Instructor, 1965–66; Assistant Professor of Internal Medicine, 1966–68, Associate Professor of Medicine, Baylor College of Medicine, Houston, Texas, 1968–71, Professor, 1971–; Chief of Renal Section, Methodist Hospital, Houston; Attending Physician, Ben Taub General Hospital, Houston; Consultant VA Hospital, Houston; Consultant in Nephrology, Wilford Hall, USAF Medical Center, Lackland AFB, Texas; recipient of research and training grants, National Institute of Health, USPHS, 1968; Fellow of the American College of Physicians; member of the International Society of Nephrology, American Soceity of Nephrology, American Federation of Clinical Research, American Physiological Society, American Society of Clinical Investigation, Association of American Physicians; Secretary Treasurer, Southern Society for Clinical Investigation, 1974–77; President, Southern Society for Clinical Investigation, 1978–79; Associate of the European Dialysis and Transplantation Association; member of Alpha Omega Alpha; member of the Editorial Board of *The Kidney,* 1970–76, *Kidney International,* 1976–, *Journal of Clinical Investigation,* 1976–80, *Mineral and Electrolyte Metab,* 1977–, *Renal Physiol,* 1978–, *Nephron,* 1979–, *Seminars in Nephrology,* 1980–; Associate Editor, *American Journal of Nephrology,* 1980–; Chairman of the Medical Advisory Council, Kidney Foundation, Houston and Greater Gulf Coast, 1969–71; Chairman, National Medical Advisory Council, National Kidney Foundation, 1971–73; member of the Executive Committee, Council on Kidney in Cardiovascular Disease, American Heart Association, 1971–75; member of the Scientific Advisory Board, 1972–80; Secretary of the Scientific Advisory Board, 1977–78; President of the Scientific Advisory Board, National Kidney Foundation, 1979–80; *Publications:* regular contributor to several professional journals; *Address:* Residence — 2330 N. Braeswood, Houston, TX 77030, USA; Office — 6565 Fannin St, Houston, TX 77030, USA.

SUKKER, Yusif Yacoub, Jordanian businessman; born 15 May 1944, Salt, Jordan; married; one daughter, one son; *Religion:* Christian; *Education:* BA in Economics, American University of Beirut, Lebanon, 1967; MSc in Program National Development, ISS, Holland, 1971; *Career:* Head of External Trade and Statistics Department, Central Bank of Jordan, 1968–72; General Manager, Philips Division, Amman, Jordan, 1975–77; General Manager, Transmed Jordan Trading Shareholding Co Ltd, 1977–; *Interests and Recreations:* swimming, riding; *Languages:* Arabic, English; *Address:* P O Box 2431, Amman, Jordan; telephone: Office — 41968; Residence — 42494; telex: 21631.

SULAIMAN, Abdul Aziz Abdullah al-, Saudi Arabian businessman; born 1934, Mecca, Saudi Arabia; *Religion:* Muslim: *Education:* in Egypt; Lafayette University, USA; Technical Financial Training, Chase Manhattan Bank, New York; *Career:* Deputy Minister of Petroleum and Monetary Affairs, 1951–53; Vice Chairman, Saudi Arabian Monetary Agency SAMA, 1953–55; Chairman of the Board of Saudi Hotel Co, Arabian Cement Co Ltd, Jeddah, Rolaco Trading and Contracting, Siraj Zahran Co, Sulaimaniyah Real, Saudi Light Industry, Saudi Capital Corporation, Zahran Contracting Co, Cement Product Industry Co, Al-Jezira Bank; founder of Saudi Maritime Navigation Co; member of the Board of Société Financière pour le Moyen-Orient, Beirut, FRAB Bank, Paris, France, FRAB Holding, Luxembourg, Boonton Molding Co, New Jersey, USA, Saudi National Electric Co, Jeddah, Saudi Refinery Co, Jeddah; founder and Chairman of the Board of Al-Hamadany Society for Chivalry and Preservation of Arab Legacy; *Publications:* political and economic articles published in local press; *Decorations:* Lebanese Order of Merit; *Interests and Recreations:* reading, riding, music; *Address:* P O Box 222, Jeddah, Saudi Arabia; telephone: Office — 665 8148; telex: 401029 ROLACO SJ.

SULAIMAN, Abdul Muhsin Abdul Rahman al-, Saudi Arabian businessman/engineer; born 1946, Jeddah, Saudi Arabia; *Education:* BSc in Electrical and Industrial Engineering, 1971; MA in Audio Visual Media, Western Michigan University, USA; *Career:* member of Industrial Managment Society; owner and Director, Best Trading Corporation, Jeddah, Saudi Arabia; shareholder and member of the Board of Directors of IPCO Marine SA, Al-Sulaiman Travels, Avis Saudi Arabia, Saudi Cars and Trade Company; *Interests and Recreations:* photography, deep sea fishing; *Languages:* Arabic, English; *Address:* P O Box 1271, Jeddah, Saudi Arabia; telephone: 52930.

SULAIMAN, Ahamd al-Abdullah al-, Saudi Arabian businessman; born 1938, Mecca, Saudi Arabia; *Religion:* Muslim; *Education:* BCom, International Commerce; *Career:* Director of the Office of Shaikh Abdullah al-Sulaiman, 1960–68; Deputy Head, Siraj Zahran and Partners, 1961–63; owner of al-Sawary Trading and Contracting Company, Sawary USA, Sawary Investment Corporation, Ahmad Abdullah al-Sulaiman General Trading Company; President, Siraj Zahran and Company, Technical Services Contracting and Trading Company; Director of Tihama Advertising Organisation, *Al-Bilad* daily newspaper; *Address:* Abdullah Sulaiman and Sons, P O Box 2337, Jeddah, Saudi Arabia; telephone: 29044.

SULAIMAN, Ahmad, Sudanese official/diplomat; born 1924, Sudan; *Education:* Faculty of Law, University of Cairo, Egypt; *Career:* Minister of Agriculture, 1964; Ambassador to USSR; Minister of Economy and Foreign Trade, 1969–70; Minister of Industry and Mining, 1970-71; Minister of Justice, 1971–73; Chairman, Sudan Peace Committee; delegate, World Peace Council Conference; delegate, Afro-Asian People's Solidarity Organization; *Address:* Office — Ministry of Justice, Khartoum, Sudan.

SULAIMAN, Badr al-Din, Sudanese politician; born 23 March 1933, White Nile Province, Sudan; married; one son, three daughters; *Religion:* Muslim; *Education:* Degree in Law, University of Khartoum, Sudan; *Career:* Administrative Officer in Local Government, 1960; practising lawyer, 1960–68; director in private industrial sector, 1968–72; member of the Political Bureau of the Sudanese Socialist Union (SSU) and of the First National Assembly, 1972; member of the second National Assembly, 1975; Assistant Secretary General of the SSU, 1976–; Minister of Industry, 1975–77; Chairman of the Al-Ayyam Printing and Publishing Company, 1974; *Decorations:* Order of the Republic 1st Class; Order of Kuwait 1st Class; *Interests and Recreations:* football, tennis; President of the Omdurman Graduates Club; *Languages:* Arabic, English; *Address:* Al-Ayyam, P O Box 363, Khartoum, Sudan.

SULAIMAN, Hikmat, Iraqi diplomat; born 17 August 1917, Iraq; *Education:* American University of Beirut, Lebanon; University of Georgetown, USA; *Career:* Ministry of Foreign Affairs, 1933; Attaché, Embassy to Turkey, 1936–39; Acting Consul, Istanbul, Turkey, 1939; Secretary in Charge of Foreign Exchange Control, National Bank of Iraq, 1946–49; Attaché, Embassy to Lebanon, 1949–50; Attaché, Embassy to USA, 1950–54; Attaché, Embassy to Pakistan, 1954–55; Consul General, Jerusalem, 1955–58; Consul General, Damascus, Syria, 1958–60; Deputy Under Secretary, Ministry of Foreign Affairs, 1960–61; Minister, Embassy to West Germany, 1961–63; Ambassador to France, 1963–66; Ambassador to Morocco, 1966; now retired; *Publications: Oil Iraq: Rules of Diplomacy and Protocol,* 1961; *Decorations:* Grosses Bundesverdienstkreuz; *Address:* c/o Ministry of Foreign Affairs, Baghdad, Iraq.

SULAIMAN, Izzat Ibrahim, Egyptian diplomat; born 1919; married; *Career:* entered Ministry of Foreign Affairs, 1973; Head of the Department of Arab Affairs; Ambassador to Iran, 1974–77; *Languages:* Arabic, English, Turkish; *Address:* Ministry of Foreign Affairs, Cairo, Egypt.

SULAIMAN, Michael Wadie, Arab-American academic; born 26 February 1934, Tiberias, Palestine; married; one son, one daughter; *Religion:* Christian; *Education:* BA, Bradley University, USA, 1960; PhD, University of Wisconsin, USA, 1965; *Career:* Assistant Professor of Political Science, Kansas State University, USA, 1968–72; Associate Professor of Political Science, Kansas State University, USA, 1968–72; Professor of Political Science, Kansas State University, Kansas, 1972–; Head of Department, Political Science, Kansas State University, 1975–; *Publications: Political Parties in Lebanon- The Challenge of a Fragmented Political Culture,* New York, 1967; *American Images of Middle East Peoples: Impact of the High School,* 1977; numerous articles in journals of political science and Middle East affairs; *Interests and Recreations:* table-tennis, chess; member of Middle East Studies Association, the Arab-American University Graduates, the Middle East Institute, the American Research Centre in Egypt, the American Political Science Association; *Languages:* Arabic, English, French; *Address:* Kansas State University, Department of Political Science, Kedzie Hall, Room 204, Manhattan, KS 66506; telephone: (913) 532 6842; Residence — 427 Wickham, Manhattan, KS 66502; telephone: (913) 539 2127.

SULAIMAN, Muhammad Sidki, Egyptian politician/engineer; born 1919; *Religion:* Muslim; *Education:* Fuad I University, Cairo, Egypt; *Career:* Colonel in Egyptian Army, 1962; Minister for the High Dam, 1962–66; Prime Minister, 1966–67; Deputy Prime Minister, Minister of Industry and Power, 1967–70; President, Soviet-Egyptian Friendship Society; *Decorations:* Order of Lenin; *Languages:* Arabic, English; *Address:* Ministry of Industry and Power, Cairo, Egypt.

SULAIMAN, Mustafa Dawud, Egyptian financial official/accountant; born 17 March 1929, Cairo; married; three sons, two daughters; *Religion:* Muslim; *Education:* BSc in Commerce and Finance, 1955; Diploma in Cost Accountancy, 1960; *Career:* Finance Manager, 1974; General Manager, Egyptian Real Property Co for Land Reclamation; contracting and commercial business; part-time Chartered Accountant; member of the Commerce Club, the Egyptian Accountants Association; *Interests and Recreations:* interested in international trade concerning building and construction equipment; *Languages:* Arabic, English; *Address:* 2 Dr Abdul Hamid Said Street, Cairo, Egypt.

SULAYTI, Hamad Ali, Bahraini official/educationalist; born 3 January 1942, Bahrain; married; two sons, *Religion:* Muslim; *Education:* BA Education and Psychology; Diploma of Education; MA in Educational Planning and Administration; PhD in Curriculum Development and Library Sciences; *Career:*

Teacher, Elementary Schools, 1958–60; Teacher of Education and Psychology, Bahrain Teachers Training College, 1967–69; Superintendent of Educational Planning and Cultural Affairs, 1970–71; Director of Educational Planning, 1972–75; Assistant Under Secretary for Planning, Curricula and Cultural Affairs, Ministry of Education, 1975–; Acting Secretary General, Bahrain Centre for Studies and Research; member of the Manpower Planning Council; Chairman of the Committee for Curriculum Development; member of the Trustees, Arab Institute for Economic and Social Planning; member of the Educational Board; *Publications:* numerous articles on education in national and Arab journals; *Interests and Recreations:* fishing, sailing, table-tennis; member of Alumni Club; *Languages:* Arabic, English; *Address:* Ministry of Education, P O Box 43, Manama, Bahrain; telephone: Office — 259265; Residence — 671526; telex: 9094 TARBIA BN.

SULTAN, Ahmad Ismail, Egyptian engineer/politician; born 14 April 1923, Port Said, Egypt; married; *Religion:* Muslim; *Education:* Faculty of Engineering, Cairo University, Egypt, 1945; management of electricity generating station, UK and France; National Defence College, 1967; *Career:* Shift Engineer, Maintenance and Project Engineer, various power stations, 1945–64; Director and member of the Executive Board, Electrical Projects Corporation, 1964–68; Governor of Minufiya, 1968–71; Minister of Power, 1971–76; Deputy Prime Minister for Production and Minister of Power and Energy, 1976–78; Consultant Engineer since October 1981; *Decorations:* Order of the Republic 1st Class; *Languages:* Arabic, English; *Address:* Office — 2 Okasha street, Dokki, Cairo, Egypt.

SULTAN, Amin Kassim Muhammad, Yemen Arab Republic businessman; born 4 March 1928; married; three sons, three daughters; *Religion:* Muslim; *Education:* Diploma in Commerce, London Chamber of Commerce, 1949; *Career:* commerce, 1948; established Al-Kawthar factory, textile and tyre factories; co-founder of the first National Bank; merchant and commercial adviser; President of the Yemen Chamber of Commerce for 6 years; member of the Board of Directors of the Central Bank; owner of Amin Kassim Sultan and Partners; representative of several companies; *Interests and Recreations:* reading economics, religious and political books, hockey, football, swimming; *Languages:* Arabic, English; *Address:* P O Box 4888, Taiz, Yemen Arab Republic.

SULTAN BIN ABDUL AZIZ, HRH Prince, Saudi Arabian Prince/politician; born 1922; son of late King Abdul Aziz and Hassa Bint Sudairi; *Religion:* Muslim; *Education:* Court education in religion, culture and diplomacy; tuition at the hands of great Ulamas; extensive reading in various fields; *Career:* President of the Royal Guard in Riyadh; Minister of Communications; Minister of Defence and Aviation, and Inspector General, 1962–; paid official visits to Egypt, Syria, France, Jordan, USA; member of most Saudi delegations headed by late King Faisal to Arab and Islamic Summit Conferences, state visits and UN General Assembly sessions; Chairman of the Supreme Committee for Administrative Reform; Vice President of the Supreme Council of Higher Education; *Decorations:* Order of Merit 1st Class from various Western and Arab countries; *Address:* Ministry of Defence and Aviation, Airport Road, Riyadh, Saudi Arabia; telephone: 667 3664, 732 2490; telex: 201188 MDA SJ.

SULTAN BIN FAHD, HRH Prince, Saudi Arabian Prince/army officer; born 1951; son of HM King Fahd Bin Abdul Aziz; *Religion:* Muslim; *Education:* in USA; Graduate of the Royal Military Academy, Sandhurst, UK; *Career:* in the Armed Forces; Army Lieutenant in Infantry; *Languages:* Arabic, English; *Address:* Ministry of Defence and Aviation, Airport Road, Riyadh, Saudi Arabia; telephone: 6673664, 7322490; telex: 201188 MDA SJ.

SULTAN, Brigadier Shaikh Faisal Bin, United Arab Emirates businessman/official; born 1940; third son of Shaikh Sultan Bin Salim, former Ruler of Ras al-Khaimah; married; *Religion:* Muslim; *Career:* joined Trucial Oman Scouts, 1954; Mons Officer Cadet School, UK; Jordanian Forces; member of the staff of the Crown Prince of Abu Dhabi, 1970; Under Secretary, Ministry of Defence, 1971; Chief of Staff, Abu Dhabi Defence Forces, 1973; Chairman of GIBCA Group of Companies, and other companies and banks; *Languages:* Arabic, English; *Address:* GIBCA, P O Box 2570, Abu Dhabi, United Arab Emirates.

SULTAN, Faisal, Lebanese diplomat; born 1919, Tripoli, Libya; married; five children; *Education:* Licence in Law, Faculty of Law, Damascus University, Syria; *Career:* Attaché, Protocol Department, Ministry of Foreign Affairs, 1947–52; UN Department, Ministry of Foreign Affairs, 1952–53; Consul in Jerusalem, 1953–56; Secretary, Embassy to Egypt, 1956–60; Ministry of Foreign Affairs, 1960–63; Consul General in Alexandria, Egypt, 1963–70; Ambassador to Turkey, 1971–78; Ambassador to Kuwait, 1978–; *Decorations:* Officer of the Spanish Civil Order of Merit; *Languages:* Arabic, French, English; *Address:* Embassy of Lebanon, Kuwait.

SULTAN, Ibrahim Muhammad al-, Saudi Arabian diplomat; born 1930, Saudi Arabia; *Religion:* Muslim; *Career:* Director General, Royal Office; Attaché, Embassy to Morocco; Office Director, Ministry of Foreign Affairs; Counsellor, Ministry of Foreign Affairs, Minister Plenipotentiary; Under Secretary of State for Administrative and Financial Affairs, Foreign Ministry; Ambassador to Jordan, 1977–; *Decorations:* Officer, Order of the Cedar, Lebanon; Key to the City of Seoul, awarded on an official visit; Sultan Qadarat, Philippines; Shining Star, National Republic of China; decoration from Iran; *Interests and Recreations:* reading, swimming; *Address:* Embassy of Saudi Arabia, Amman, Jordan; telephone: 814154, 814155.

SULTAN, Mahmud Abdullah, Saudi Arabian businessman; born 15 December 1933, Medina, Saudi Arabia; married; four sons, one daughter; *Religion:* Muslim; *Education:* Diploma in Business Administration, American University of Beirut, AUB, Lebanon; Diploma in Management, Boston, Massachusetts; *Career:* Saudi Arabian Mining Syndicate, various posts, 1945–51; Arabian American Oil Company, Assistant Superintendent, Superintendent, Manager, 1952–64; Jeddah Oil Refinery Company, Manager, General Manager and Director of the Board, 1964–79; Chairman and Managing Director, Petromin Lubricating Oil Company; *Interests and Recreations:* reading, table tennis; *Languages:* Arabic, English; *Address:* Petromin Lubricating Oil Company, P O Box 1432, Jeddah, Saudi Arabia; telephone: 49626.

SUNBUL, Salim Saudi Arabian diplomat; born 1928; *Religion:* Muslim; *Education:* BA in Political Science, Faculty of Commerce, Cairo University, Egypt, 1953; *Career:* Attaché, Foreign Ministry 1953; 3rd Secretary, Saudi Embassy, UK, 1955, Assistant Director of Protocol, 1956; Acting Chargé d'Affaires, Saudi Embassy, France; Chargé d'Affaires, Saudi Legation, Cyprus, 1960; Head of Department of Protocol, Foreign Ministry; *Decorations:* several Orders of Merit from Arab countries; *Address:* Foreign Ministry, P O Box 495, Jeddah, Saudi Arabia; telephone: Office — Jeddah 6421322; telex: 401104 KHARJI SJ.

SUNNA, Sami Jadalla, Jordanian UN official/agricultural engineer; born 31 January 1931, Jordan; married; *Education:* Agricultural Engineering, Ecole Nationale d'Agriculture de Grignon, France, 1949–53; Iowa State University, USA, 1957–58; PhD in Plant Ecology, University of Montpellier, France, 1960–63; *Career:* Principal, Rabba Agricultural School, Jordan, 1953–55; Assistant Director, Agronomy Division, Ministry of Agriculture, 1955–63; Chief, Agricultural Planning Section, Jordan Development Board, 1963–66; Director, Agricultural Marketing Department, Jordan, 1966–68; Assistant Director, Agricultural Research and Extension Department, Ministry of Agriculture, Jordan; Adviser, World Food Programme (WFP), Egypt, 1968–72; Senior Adviser, WFP/UNDP, Algeria, 1972–75; Director General, Jordan Valley Authority, 1975–76; Deputy Director General, Agricultural Credit Corporation, 1976–80, and later Director General 1980–; Secretary of the Jordan Agricultural Engineering Association; *Interests and Recreations:* agricultural development; *Languages:* Arabic, English, French; *Address:* P O Box 77, Amman, Jordan; telephone: 664266.

SURSOCK, Yvonne, Lebanese businesswoman/conservationist; born Lebanon; married; three sons, one daughter; *Education:* Ecole Supérieure des Lettres, Beirut, Lebanon; Town Planning Institute, London, England; *Career:* Founder and President of the Association for the Protection of Sites and Old Buildings; President of the Committee and Director General of Nicolas Sursock Museum, 1960–66; President, Jeunesses Musicales du Liban; member of the Baalbek Festival Association; Vice President of Royal Bank of Canada (Middle East) SAL, 1960–69; member of the Board of Bank Trad-Credit Lyonnais, Beirut; member of the Board of Port of Beirut Financial and Real Estate Company; Vice President, Société du Parc de Beyrouth; member of the Committee of Protection Maternelle and Infantile (Ecole Sociale); Vice President, Committee of Dar al-Fan; *Interests and Recreations:* sports, swimming, skiing, horse riding; *Address:* APSAD, P O Box 154, Beirut, Lebanon; telephone: 334267.

SUWEIDI, Abdullah Bin Nassir al-, Qatari politician/businessman; *Religion:* Muslim; *Career:* private enterprise; Minister of Communications and Transport, 1970–; *Address:* Ministry of Communications and Transport, P O Box 3416, Doha, Qatar; telephone: 324098, 426262; telex: 4800 MINCOM DH.

SUWEIDI, Ahmad Khalifa al-, United Arab Emirates politician; born 1937, Abu Dhabi, United Arab Emirates; married; three sons, three daughters; *Religion:* Muslim; *Education:* BA in Economics and Political Science, Cairo University, Egypt; *Career:* Assistant to Minister of Finance, Abu Dhabi, 1957; Director of the Amiri Court, Abu Dhabi, 1958; Head of the Amiri Court, Abu Dhabi, 1970; Minister of State for Ruler's Affairs, Abu Dhabi, 1971; United Arab Emirates Minister of Foreign Affairs, 1972–; member of Abu Dhabi Executive Council; Chairman of the Board, Abu Dhabi National Bank; *Interests and Recreations:* Arabic literature, poetry, history, golf, water-skiing, billiards, tennis, swimming, fishing; *Languages:* Arabic, English, French; *Address:* Ministry of Foreign Affairs, P O Box 1, Abu Dhabi, United Arab Emirates; telephone: 367012; telex: 22217 KARJIA EM.

SUWEIDI, Muhammad Habrush, United Arab Emirates official; born 1946; *Religion:* Muslim: *Education:* in Qatar and two years in UK; Baghdad University, Iraq; *Career:* Deputy Director of the Amiri Court, 1969; United Arab Emirates Minister of State for Financial and Industrial Affairs; member of Abu Dhabi Executive Council, 1971; *Languages:* Arabic, English; *Address:* c/o Abu Dhabi Executive Council, Abu Dhabi, United Arab Emirates.

SUWEIDI, Musbah Muhammad al-, United Arab Emirates official; born 1950, Sharjah, United Arab Emirates; married; one son; *Religion:* Muslim; *Education:* Diploma in Commerce, Kuwait, 1970; Diploma, International Institute of General Commerce, Cairo, Egypt, 1972; *Career:* Chief Accountant, Sharjah Electricity Company, 1970; Accountant, Ministry of Finance; Head of Salaries Department, Ministry of Finance; Deputy Director of Financial and Administrative Affairs, Ministry of Islamic Affairs and Waqfs, 1975; Deputy Chairman of Wahda Company for General Contracting and Trading, Sharjah, United Arab Emirates; *Interests and Recreations:* short-story writing, swimming, football, travel; *Languages:* Arabic, English; *Address:* Al-Wahda General Contracting and Trading Company, Sharjah, United Arab Emirates; telephone: Sharjah Office — 24286; Residence — Abu Dhabi 44354.

SWAIDI, Luay Tawfik al-, Iraqi businessman/lawyer; born 1935, Baghdad, Iraq; married; one son; *Religion:* Muslim; *Education:* Degree in International Law, Law College, Baghdad University; *Career:* Chairman and Director of several Iraqi companies; Director of Spinconsult; member of Iraqi Bar Association, Iraqi Chamber of Commerce; *Interests and Recreations:* tennis, riding, swimming, painting; *Languages:* Arabic, English, French; *Address:* Flat 3 Chesham House, 30–31 Chesham Place, London SW1, UK.

T

TA'I, Muhibiddin al-, Iraqi engineer/official; *Education:* trained as civil engineer; *Career:* four years Head of Society of Civil Engineers in Iraq; Under Secretary of Ministry of Works and Housing, 1968; Head of the Central Follow-up and Inspection Committee, Ministry of Planning, 1972; Under Secretary, Ministry of Industry, 1972; Under Secretary, Ministry of Interior, 1980–; *Languages:* Arabic, English; *Address:* Ministry of Interior, Baghdad, Iraq.

TABBAH, Ezzat Fuad, Jordanian businessman; born 24 September 1915, Damascus, Syria; married; two sons, one daughter; *Religion:* Muslim; *Education:* Degree in Law; *Career:* Chairman and General Manager, Ezzat F. Tabbah and Sons Company; Honorary Consul General of Chad Republic, Jordan; *Decorations:* Order of the Jordanian Star, 3rd Class; *Languages:* Arabic, English, French; *Address:* P O Box 229, Amman, Jordan; telephone: 22161/2, 41509; telex: 1703 FOUAD JO.

TABBAH, Tawfik, Jordanian businessman; born 18 August 1921; married; four daughters; *Religion:* Muslim; *Career:* founder and President of Royal Jordanian Airlines (ALIA), 1964; founder and member of the Board of Directors, Central Bank of Jordan, Amman; Vice Chairman, Amman Chamber of Commerce; Chairman, United Trading Group; *Decorations:* Independence Medals, 2nd and 3rd Class, Jordan; *Interests and Recreations:* flying, swimming, riding; *Address:* United Trading Company Ltd, P O Box 1408, Amman, Jordan; telephone: 36385.

TABBARAH, Riad Bahige, Lebanese UN official/economist; born 21 July, 1933, Baghdad, Iraq; married; *Education:* BA in Economics, American University of Beirut, Beirut, Lebanon, 1953–56; MA in Economics, Northwestern University, Evanston,

Illinois, USA, 1956–58; PhD in Economics, Vanderbilt University, Nashville, Tenn, USA, 1964; *Career:* Senior Statistician, Tennessee Department of Employment Security, USA, 1960–62; Senior Consultant, US Department of Labour, USA, 1960–61; Demographer, United Nations Economic Commission for Africa, Ethiopia, 1962–64; Social Affairs Officer, UN Department of Economic and Social Affairs, UN, New York, USA, 1965–70; Associate Research Demographer, University of California at Berkeley, USA, 1970–71; Chief, Population Policy Section, Population Division, UN, New York, USA, 1971–75; Chief, Population Division, United Nations Economic Commission for Western Asia, Beirut, Lebanon, 1975–, currently based in Baghdad, Iraq; *Publications: Demographic Techniques for Manpower Planning in Developing Countries,* 1962; *Population Policy and Birth Control,* 1964; *Toward a Theory of Demographic Development,* 1971; *The Adequacy of Income: A Social Dimension in Economic Development,* 1972; *Population and Development in Lebanon,* 1977; *International Migration and National Population Policies,* 1978; *Background to the Lebanese Conflict,* 1979; *Interests and Recreations:* tennis, photography; member of the American Economic Association, the International Union for Scientific Study of Population, the Population Association of America; *Languages:* Arabic, English, French; *Address:* Office — Population Division, Economic Commission for Western Asia, P O Box 27, Baghdad, Iraq; telephone: 96031/9.

TADLAOUI, Muhammad al-, Moroccan engineer; born 18 October 1939, Meknes, Morocco; married; one son; *Religion:* Muslim; *Education:* BSc, Civil Engineering, University of London, London, UK; DIC, Imperial College, England, UK; MICE, Institution of Civil Engineers; *Career:* Research Engineer, England, UK, 1962; Project Engineer, England, UK, 1966; Consulting Engineer, Morocco, 1972; Founder and General Director of Consulting Engineering Firm SOCOPLAN, 1975–; co-founder of the Association of Consulting Engineers of Morocco (AMCI), Morocco, 1976; member of the Bureau of the Association of Consulting Engineers (AMCI), External Relations, Morocco, 1977–; member of the National Commission of Engineering, Morocco, 1980–; *Interests and Recreations:* tennis, swimming, Arabic literature, history of war; *Languages:* Arabic, English, French; *Address:* Residence — Al-Mansour, Zankat Moulay Slimane, Rabat, Morocco; telephone: 21020, 23280.

TAHA HUSSAIN, Mu'nis, Egyptian UN official; born 8 September 1921; married; one daughter; *Religion:* Muslim; *Education:* Degree in Literature, Cairo University; Agrégation de Lettres, University of Paris, France; Doctoratès-Lettres, University of Paris; *Career:* Professor of French Language and Literature, Cairo University, 1951–61; senior UNESCO Official, 1962; Head of International Diffusion of Culture, UNESCO, Paris; *Publications: L'Islam dans la littérature romantique en France,* Cairo, 1962, and numerous articles in Egyptian journals; *Interests and Recreations:* comparative literature, the plastic arts, theatre, music, swimming; *Languages:* Arabic, French, English, Italian, Spanish; *Address:* 27 rue Leconte de Lisle, Paris 75016, France; telephone 2246054.

TAHA, Muhammad Fathi, Egyptian official/meteorologist; born 15 January 1914, Cairo, Egypt; *Religion:* Muslim; *Education:* BA, Physics, Cairo University, Cairo, Egypt, 1930–34; DIC, Imperial College, London University, London, England, 1937–38; *Career:* Lecturer, Faculty of Science, Cairo University, Cairo, Egypt, 1942–44; Vice President and member, World Meteorological Organisation Regional Commission for Africa, 1947, 1955–59, 1959–63; member of the Outer Space Exploration Committee, Academy of Science, 1967; Chairman, National Committee, Geodesy and Geographies, Academy of Science, 1967–75; President, Permanent Meteorological Committee, Arab League, 1971–; Chairman, Board of Directors, Egyptian Meteorological Authority, 1971–76; President, World Meteorological

Organisation, 1971–79, member of the Executive Committee, 1955–; Under Secretary of State, Egypt, 1964–76; member of the Union of Scientific Workers, Egypt; Meteorological Adviser, Ministry of Aviation, 1976–; *Publications: Climates of the Near East; Climates and Meteorology North of the Tropic of Cancer,* 1960; *Decorations:* Order of Merit, 3rd Class, 1954, 1st Class, 1976, Egypt; *Interests and Recreations:* sports, aeronautical meterology; member of several sports clubs; *Languages:* Arabic, English; *Address:* Koubry al-Qubba Post Office, Cairo, Egypt; telephone: 86202.

TAHER, Abdul Hadi Hassan, Saudi Arabian official/oil expert; born 1931, Medina, Saudi Arabia; married; two sons, one daughter; *Education:* University of Cairo, Egypt; University of Ain Shams, Cairo, Egypt; University of California, Berkeley, USA; *Career:* joined Saudi Arabian government service, 1955; Director General, Ministry of Petroleum and Mineral Resources, 1961; Governor General, Petroleum and Mineral Organisation (PETROMIN), 1962; Minister of State for PETROMIN, 1978; Chairman and Managing Director, Jeddah Oil Refinery Co; Head of Saudi Delegation, Conference on International Economic Cooperation CIEC, Paris, 1976–77, and co-Chairman of the Conference's Energy Commission; member of Board of Directors, Arabian American Oil Co ARAMCO and its Executive Committee; Honorary Member, American Society of Petroleum Engineers and American Management Association CEO Club; part-time Lecturer, University of Riyadh, Petroleum Economics, 1960s; *Publications: Income Determination in the International Petroleum Industry,* Pergamon Press, Oxford, 1966; *Development and Petroleum Strategies in Saudi Arabia,* in Arabic, 1970; *Energy: A Global Outlook,* Pergamon Press, 1981; lectures and papers on economics and petroleum affairs; *Languages:* Arabic, English; *Address:* Ministry of Petroleum and Mineral Resources, P O Box 345, Riyadh, Saudi Arabia.

TAHER, Thabet Abdul Rauf al-, Jordanian businessman; born 1928, Nablus, Palestine; married; one son; *Religion:* Muslim; *Education:* MA in Public Administration, Netherlands; Diploma in Marketing, Harvard University, USA; Diploma in Industrial Management, Netherlands; *Career:* Head of

Division, Civil Service Commission; Administrative Assistant, Secretary of the Board of Directors, General Manager, Jordan Phosphate Mines Company Ltd; Director General, Arab Mining Company; member of the Board of Directors of Jordan Phosphate Company, Jordan Fertilizer Company; Vice Chairman, Arab Potash Company, Jordan; member of the Amman Chamber of Industry, Amman, Jordan; Vice President, World Phosphate Institute, 1974; *Languages:* Arabic, English; *Address:* P O Box 20198, Amman, Jordan; telephone: 42637; telex: 1489 ARMICO JO.

TAIBA, Mahmud, Saudi Arabian official/engineer; born 1936; married; *Religion:* Muslim; *Career:* entered Arabian American Oil Company (Aramco); later studied electrical engineering in USA under Aramco auspices; on return, appointed to Ministry of Commerce; Director General of Industrial Research and Development Centre, 1967; *Languages:* Arabic, English; *Address:* The Saudi National Oil Company, P O Box 1458, Dhahran, Saudi Arabia.

TAIE, Muhammad Adil, Saudi Arabian official/accountant; born 1931, Qoos, Egypt; *Religion:* Muslim; *Education:* BCom, Cairo University, 1953; Graduate Studies in Taxation, Cairo, 1957; *Career:* Chief Accountant Drug Co, Egypt, 1958; Chief Accountant, Saudi Contracting Co, 1960; Chief Accountant, Ministry of Communications, 1963; Financial Expert, General Board of Control, 1964; Director, Financial Affairs, Ministry of Petroleum and Mineral Resources, Jeddah; Financial Controller, Ministry of Petroleum and Mineral Resources, Jeddah; *Interests and Recreations:* swimming; *Address:* Ministry of Petroleum and Mineral Resources, P O Box 345, Jeddah, Saudi Arabia; telephone: Jeddah 643 3133, ext 28.

TAIMA, Fuad Khazal, Arab-American businessman; born 1935, Baghdad, Iraq; married; one son, four daughters; *Religion:* Muslim; *Education:* Baghdad College, 1953; BSc in Business, Wharton School, University of Pennsylvania, 1957; MA in Business Administration, Wharton School, University of Pennsylvania, 1960; *Career:* Economic Consultant to Arab World UN Mission, 1960–68; President, Averroes Incorporation, 1971–; co-founder, National Association of Arab Americans, 1972; co-founder, Mid-Atlantic US Arab Chambers of Commerce, 1975; co-founder, Northern Virginia Export Import Association, 1974; Vice President, AAUG, Washington D.C., 1970–72; Regional Vice President, US Arab Chamber of Commerce, 1976–; President, Taima and Associates Incorporation, 1971–; *Interests and Recreations:* tennis, swiming, cycling; socio-economic philosophies, literature; member of Les Ambassadeurs Club, London, and of the Middle East Institute; *Address:* Averroes Incorporation, 6825 Redmond Drive, Drawer T. McLean, Virginia, USA; telephone: (703) 3564077.

TAJIR, Sayyid Muhammad Mahdi al-, United Arab Emirates diplomat/businessman; born 26 December 1931, Bahrain; married; six children; *Religion:* Muslim; *Education:* Preston Grammar School, Lancashire, UK; *Career:* Director, Port and Customs, Dubai, 1955–63; Director of HH the Ruler of Dubai's Affairs, and Director of Petroleum Affairs Department, Dubai, 1963–; Director, National Bank of Dubai Ltd,1963; Director, Dubai Petroleum Company, 1963; Chairman, Dubai National Air Travel Company, 1966; Director, Qatar-Dubai Currency Board, 1965–73; Chairman, South Eastern Dubai Drilling Company, 1968–; Director, United Arab Emirates Currency Board, 1973–; Director, Dubai Dry Dock Company, 1973–; United Arab Emirates Ambassador Extraordinary and Plenipotentiary to Court of St. James, London, 1972–82; Ambassador of United Arab Emirates to the Court of St. James, 1983–; Vice Chairman of the World of Islam Festival, 1976; Chairman of the Board of the Arab-British Chamber of Commerce, London, UK; Adviser to the Ruler of Dubai; Director, Allied Arab Bank Ltd, London, 1977–; *Decorations:* Honorary Citizen of the State of Texas, USA, 1963; *Interests and Recreations:* patron of arts and culture; *Languages:* Arabic, English, Persian; *Address:* United Arab Emirates Embassy, 30 Prince's Gate, London SW7 1PT; telephone: 581 1281.

TAKAWI, Abdullah Mahmud al-, United Arab Emirates diplomat; born 1 August 1948, Ras al-Khaimah; married; three sons, one daughter; *Religion:* Muslim; *Education:* OND, Business Managment, Exeter, UK, 1970; *Career:* Secretary of the Department of Education, 1970; Arab Planning Institute, Kuwait, 1974; Officer, British Bank of the

Middle East; Manager of Finance and Administration to the Higher Supreme Council Affairs, Ministry of Foreign Affairs; 3rd Secretary, 1976; member of UAE Delegation to 31st Session of UN General Assembly, 2nd Secretary, 1977, 1st Secretary, 1978; Head of the Mission, Embassy of UAE, Decca, Bangladesh; *Interests and Recreations:* horse riding, travel, reading; *Languages:* Arabic, English, Bengali; *Address:* Embassy of the United Arab Emirates, House No. SWB(1), Road No. 7, Gulsan Model Town, Decca, Bangladesh.

TAKIEDDIN, Khalil, Lebanese diplomat; born 1906, Baaklin, Lebanon; married; two children; *Education:* Licence in Law, French Faculty of Law, St. Joseph University, Beirut, Lebanon; *Career:* Secretary General, Lebanese Parliament, 1943; Ministry of Foreign Affairs; Minister Plenipotentiary to the USSR, 1946–50; Minister Plenipotentiary to Sweden, 1950–52; Minister Plenipotentiary to Mexico, 1952–55; Ambassador to Egypt, 1955–57; Ambassador to Turkey, 1957–60; Ambassador to the Court of St. James, London, UK, 1960–65; *Publications: Memoirs of an Ambassador,* as well as numerous articles in local and foreign press; *Decorations:* Grand Cordon, Egyptian Order of the Nile; Holder of the Northern Star, Sweden; *Languages:* Arabic, French; *Address:* Residence — Abdel Aziz Street, Beirut, Lebanon.

TAKKIEDDINE, Diana, Lebanese musician/pianist/educator; born Davao, Philippines; *Education:* Lobregat Music Academy, Manila, Philippines; Diploma, The National Music Conservatory, Beirut, Lebanon; further studies in Paris, Rome, Vienna and Salzburg; BA in Philosophy, American University of Beirut (AUB), Lebanon; *Career:* international concert pianist; soloist; performed with internationally famous orchestras; performed on numerous radio programmes in France, UK, Lebanon and others; Piano Chairman, Beirut National Music Conservatory; Lecturer, Fine Arts Department, AUB; Music Consultant, International College; member of the Board of National Conservatory; member of the Board of the Organizing Committee for the International Festival, Jibran, Lebanon, 1970; Founder and Managing Director of the Arab Institute for the Development of Arts (AIDA); interpreted and recorded Lebanese music overseas; member of the Chopin Society, Warsaw, Poland; *Decorations:* Gold Medal, Lebanese Order of Merit; *Interests and Recreations:* walking, swimming; *Address:* Residence— 91 Bishop's Road, London SW6, UK; telephone: (01) 736 8967, (01) 731 3351; Fayez Makarem Building, Madame Curie Street, Beirut, Lebanon; Office — Department of Fine Arts, American University of Beirut, Lebanon; telephone: 292860 ext 2527, 2290.

TAKLA, Laila I., Egyptian politician; married; two sons; *Religion:* Christian; *Education:* LLB, Faculty of Law, Cairo University, Egypt; Diploma, Social Studies, University of Southern California, USA; MA, University of Southern California, California; PhD, New York University, USA; *Career:* Lecturer in Administration, New York University, USA; Lecturer, Higher Institute of Administration, Cairo University, Cairo, Egypt; Chairman, Foreign Affairs Committee, People's Assembly; member of the Central Committee of the Arab Socialist Union, 1971; member of the National Specialised Councils, 1972, the History of the Revolution Committee; Public Administration Expert, Arab League, 1969; Representative of Egypt, UN General Assembly, 1973–; Vice President, International Parliamentary Union, 1977; Chairman of the Committee on Education; President of the Finnish-Egyptian Society, 1976; Chairman, National Committee on Environmental Law; Chairman, UN Experts Group on the Advancement of Women, 1976; *Publications: Public Administration: Principles and Dynamics,* 2 Volumes, 1968, 1971, 1976; *The Six Hour War: An Analysis of the Arab-Israeli October War,* 1973; *The Ombudsman: A Comparative Study,* 1971; *Interests and Recreations:* swimming, tennis, sculpture, folk arts; *Languages:* Arabic, English, French; *Address:* People's Assembly, Cairo, Egypt.

TAKLA, Philippe Habib, Lebanese politician/banker; born February 1915, Zouk, Lebanon; married; two sons; *Education:* Licence in Law, French Faculty of Law, St. Joseph University, Beirut, Lebanon, 1935; *Career:* Barrister at Law; Editor in Chief, *Gazette des Tribunaux Libano-Syriens;* elected Deputy, 1945; Minister of National Economy, and of Posts, Telegraphs and Telephones, 1946; Minister of Foreign Affairs, and National Education, 1947; re-elected Deputy 1945,

1947 and 1957; Minister of Foreign Affairs, 1958; Minister of Justice and National Economy, 1959–60; Minister of Foreign Affairs; Minister of National Economy and of Tourism, 1960; Minister of Foreign Affairs, 1960–64; Governor, Bank of Lebanon, 1964; Minister of Foreign Affairs, 1964–65; Governor, Bank of Lebanon, 1965–67; Lebanese Representative and Governor, IMF, 1965; Minister of Foreign Affairs, and Minister of Justice, 1966; Head, Permanent Delegation of Lebanon to the UN, 1967; Ambassador to France, 1968–71; Minister of Foreign Affairs in Rashid al-Solh Government, 1974; Minister of Foreign Affairs, Education and Planning in Rashid Karami's Government, 1975–76; *Decorations:* Légion d'Honneur, France; many other foreign decorations and distinctions; *Languages:* Arabic, French; *Address:* Residence — 42 rue Copernic, Paris 75016, France; telephone: 727 5209.

TAKY, Ziad al-, Lebanese banker/economist; resident in Kuwait; born 10 February 1941; married; two sons; *Religion:* Muslim; *Education:* BSc in Finance, 1963; MSc in Economics, 1965; MBA, 1966; PhD in Economics, 1970; *Career:* Assistant Professor, American University of Beirut, AUB, Lebanon, 1971–72; Associate Professor, Haigazian College, 1973–76; Senior Economist, Industrial Bank of Kuwait, 1976–79; Chief Economist, The National Bank of Kuwait, 1979–; *Publications: Monetary Policy in an Open Developing Economy,* Lebanon, 1971; several articles in economic and financial magazines; *Decorations:* Omicron Delta Epsilon, Economic Honorary Medal; *Interests and Recreations:* tennis, bowling, swimming; member of the Hunting and Equestrian Club of Kuwait; *Languages:* Arabic, French, English; *Address:* The National Bank of Kuwait, P O Box 95, Safat, Kuwait; telephone: 463803 telex: 44836 NATBANK KT.

TAKYIDDIN, Fawzi Abdul Razzak, Syrian physician; born 1915, Damascus, Syria; *Education:* University of Berlin, Germany; University of Zurich, Switzerland; *Career:* MD Assistant, University of Berlin, 1942–44; Zurich University, 1945–47; founder of the National Hospital, Damascus, 1947; practised medicine, specialising in cardiology, Damascus, 1947; member of the Pediatry Association and the Cardiologues Association; *Address:* The National Hospital, Damascus, Syria.

TAL, Hajim Khalaf al-, Jordanian official; born 1920, Irbid, Jordan; married: *Education:* BA in History and Politics, American University of Beirut, Lebanon 1945; MA, Karachi University, Pakistan, 1960; *Career:* Minister Plenipotentiary, Foreign Ministry 1947–62; Under Secretary, Ministry of Interior, 1962–67; private business, 1967–71; Assistant Secretary General of Tribal Shaikhs Council 1971–72; Inspector General, Ministry of Finance, 1972; Director General, Municipal and Village Loan Fund, 1972–80; Director General, Orphans Institute, 1980–83; *Decorations:* Renaissance Medal, 2nd Class; Star of Jordan, 2nd Class; *Address:* Sweilih, Amman, Jordan; telephone: Office — 23591; Residence — 842344.

TAL, Mraiwid al-, Jordanian diplomat; born 1928, Irbid, Jordan; married; two children; *Religion:* Muslim; *Education:* London School of Economics, UK, 1955–57, and University of Pittsburgh, USA, 1961; *Career:* joined UN and worked as Economic Consultant in Saudi Arabia, Lebanon and Morocco, and at UN Headquarters in New York; Counsellor at Ministry of Foreign Affairs, 1962–67; Counsellor, Embassies to West Germany and Tunisia, 1967–69; Head of UN Department at the Ministry of Foreign Affairs, 1969–70; Chief of Royal Protocol, 1970; Secretary General to the Royal Diwan and Private Secretary to the King, 1970–72; Economic Adviser to HRH Prince Hassan, 1972–74; *Languages:* Arabic, English; *Address:* The Royal Court, Amman, Jordan.

TAL, Naim Abdul Qadir al-, Jordanian official; born 1918, Irbid, Jordan; married; two sons, two daughters; *Education:* in Lebanon; *Career:* Teacher, Ministry of Education, 1940–44; Administrator, 1944–45; Director of Department, 1953–58; District Officer, 1958–62; Mayor of Irbid, 1963–67; member of the Chamber of Deputies, 1967–; *Decorations:* Medal of Independence 4th Class; Knight of the Order of the Holy Sepulchre; *Address:* Ma'mun Street, Irbid, Jordan; telephone: 2160.

TALAL BIN ABDUL AZIZ, HRH Prince, Saudi Arabian Prince/UN official and former diplomat; born 10 August 1931, Taif, Saudi Arabia; son of late King Abdul Aziz; married; eight children; *Religion:* Muslim; *Career:* Comptroller of the Royal Household, 1947; Minister of Communications, 1951;

Ambassador to France, 1955; Minister of Finance and National Economy, 1961; Vice Chairman of the Supreme Council, 1961; Vice Chairman of the Supreme Commission, in charge of Mecca Holy Shrines and facilities, 1961; Special Envoy for UNICEF, 1980–; President of AGFUND (Arab Gulf Programme for UN Development Organization), 1981–; *Languages:* Arabic, English; *Address:* UNICEF, P O Box 18009 Riyadh, Saudi Arabia; telephone: 401 1320, 402 1358, 401 3504; telex: 202989 SJ.

TALFAH, Khairallah, Iraqi official; born 1919, Iraq; married; *Career:* Governor of Baghdad, 1969; member of Higher Education and Scientific Research Council 1970; Head of the Civil Service Board, 1973–82; *Address:* Civil Service Board, Baghdad, Iraq.

TALHI, Jad'allah Azzuz al-, Libyan official; *Religion:* Muslim; *Education:* Degree in Geology, University of Louvain, Belgium; *Career:* joined Mines Department of Ministry of Industry and Minerals, responsible for mineral resources, especially phosphates, iron and radioactive materials; Minister of Industry and Minerals, 1972–77; Secretary for Industry and Minerals, General People's Committee, 1977; *Languages:* Arabic, English; *Address:* Office of the Secretary for Industry and Minerals, Tripoli, Libya.

TALHUNI, Bahjat, Jordanian politician; born 1913, Jordan; married; two sons, one daughter; *Religion:* Muslim; *Education:* Licence in Law, Syrian University, 1936; *Career:* lawyer, 1936–38; Judge, 1938–52; President of the Court of Appeal in Amman, 1952–53; Minister of the Interior, 1953; Minister of Justice, and Acting Chief Justice, 1953–54; Chief of the Royal Cabinet, 1954–60; Prime Minister, 1960–62; Senator, 1962–63; Chief of the Royal Cabinet, 1963–64; Prime Minister, 1964–65; Senator, 1964–67; Personal Representative of HM the King, 1967–69; member of the Royal Consultative Council, 1967; Prime Minister and Minister of Foreign Affairs, 1967–68; Senator, 1968–71; Prime Minister and Minister of the Interior and Defence, 1968; Chief of the Royal Court, 1969; Prime Minister, 1969–70; Senator, 1973–74; Chief of the Royal Cabinet, 1973–74; President of the Committee for the Preparation of the Civil Law, 1971–77; President of the Senate, 1974–83; Private Counsellor for His Majesty King

Hussain, 1983; member of the Board of Trustees to the Jordan University, 1962–76; elected Honorary Member for Life, Arab Parliamentary Union, 1983; *Decorations:* Star of Jordan; Renaissance Medal, 1st Class; other Arab and foreign decorations; *Address:* P O Box 119, Amman, Jordan. telephone: 22058.

TALIB, Bassam, Syrian journalist; born 1945, Damascus; resident in Qatar; married; one son; *Religion:* Muslim; *Education:* BA in Philosophy and Sociology; *Career:* Editor of *Diyaruna Wal Aalam,* a magazine financed by the Ministry of Finance and Petroleum since 1976; *Publications:* a novel in Arabic; *Interests and Recreations:* reading; *Languages:* Arabic, English, French; *Address:* P O Box 3534, Doha, Qatar.

TAMIMI, Adnan Amin, Iraqi UN official; born 5 October 1919, Nablus, Jordan; married; *Education:* BA, American University of Beirut, Lebanon; Diploma, Birmingham University, UK; MS, Columbia University, New York, USA; *Career:* Deputy Resident Representative, UN Development Programme (UNDP), Egypt; Senior Programme Officer, United Nations Industrial Development Organization (UNIDO), Vienna, Austria; Assistant Chief, Technical Assistant Unit, Economic Commission for Asia and the Far East (ECAFE), UN, Bangkok, Thailand; Programme Officer, Technical Assistant, Administration, UN, New York; Social Affairs Officer, Department of Economic and Social Affairs (ESA), UN; Social Affairs Officer, United Nations Economic and Social Office in Beirut (UNESOB), Beirut; Senior Programme Management Officer, Section for Africa, UNIDO, Vienna; *Interests and Recreations:* sports, tennis, swimming, reading; *Languages:* Arabic, English; *Address:* UNIDO, P O Box 707, A-1011 Vienna 1, Austria; telephone: (0222) 4350.

TAMIMI, Hamdi A., Arab-American academic; born 20 August 1924, Hebron, Palestine; married; five children; *Education:* BSc, Sterling College, USA, 1950; MSc, University of Colorado, School of Medicine, Denver, Colorado, USA, 1954; PhD, 1957; *Career:* Fellow in Microbiology, Colorado School of Medicine; Instructor at School of Nursing, Colorado General Hospital, 1955–57; Research Associate and acting Chairman,

Department of Microbiology, School of Dentistry, Washington University, St. Louis, USA, 1957–59; Professor and Department Chairman, Department of Microbiology, School of Dentistry, University of the Pacific, San Francisco, USA, 1960–; Lecturer, University of California, Berkeley, USA, 1961–76; Consultant, Mary's Help Hospital, Daly City, California, USA, 1968–73; Lecturer on Human Diseases, College of Marin, Kentfield, California, USA, 1968–79, Merck Chemical Company, San Francisco, USA, 1969, Veteran Administration Hospital, San Francisco, USA, 1975–78; Chairman, Faculty Appointments and Promotions Committee, University of the Pacific, 1964–66; member of the Committee on Pre-Professional Education and Admission, American Dental Association, Chicago, Illinois, USA, 1970–73; member of the National Board of Dental Examiners; the American Association of Dental Schools, Chicago, Illinois, 1972–77; President, Islamic Center of San Francisco, Inc, San Francisco, California, USA, 1968–73; member of the New York Academy of Sciences, American Society for Microbiology, American Association of University Professors, International Association of Dental Research; and several others; *Publications:* numerous articles in professional journals; *Address:* Residence — 113 Yolo Street, Corte Madera, CA 94925, USA; Office — 2155 Webster Street, San Francisco, CA 94115, USA.

TARAMAN, Khalil Shawki, Arab-American academic/engineer; born 10 July 1939, Cairo, Egypt; married; two sons; *Religion:* Muslim; *Education:* BSc in Mechanical Engineering, Ain Shams University, Egypt, 1964; MSc in Mechanical Engineering, Ain Shams University, 1967; MSc, University of Wisconsin, USA, 1969; PhD, Texas Technical University, USA, 1971; *Career:* Instructor, Ain Shams University, Cairo, Egypt, 1964–67; Instructor, University of Wisconsin, 1967–69; Research Fellow, Texas Technical University, 1969–70; Assistant Professor, University of Detroit, 1970–73; Associate Professor, University of Detroit, 1973–76; Director, Manufacturing Engineering, University of Detroit; Professor and Chairman, Mechanical Engineering Department, University of Detroit, 1977–; Consultant to Ford Motors, General Electric, US Arabian Development and Bendix; supervised research at Chrysler and Carboloy Systems of General Electric;

member of the American Institute of Industrial Engineers, Westinghouse and General Motors, Numerical Control Society, American Society of Engineering Education, of the American Society of Mechanical Engineers; International Director of the Society of Manufacturing Engineers; member of the Egyptian American Scholars' Association; Chairman of the Founder Chapter, Society of Manufacturing Engineers; member of the International Education Committee; Vice Chairman, the International Machining Technology Division; member of the International Honor Awards Committee; Chairman of the Material Removal Council; member of Alpha Pi Mu Honor Society of Industrial Engineers, the Pi Tau Sigma Honor Society of Mechanical Engineers; *Publications: Computer Aided Design/Computer Aided Manufacturing,* 1980, SME Books; numerous articles and reviews in engineering and technical journals; *Decorations:* Medal of Science, the Best Instructor and Outstanding Educator of America; *Interests and Recreations:* travelling, classical music, tennis; *Languages:* Arabic, English; *Address:* Office — Department of Mechanical Engineering, University of Detroit, Detroit, Michigan 48221, USA; telephone: (313) 927 1242.

TARAWNAH, Ahmad Mahmud al-, Jordanian politician; born 1920, Karak, Jordan; married; two sons, one daughter; *Religion:* Muslim; *Education:* BA in Law, University of Damascus, Syria; *Career:* Judge, 1942–50; member of the Chamber of Deputies, 1950–60; President of the Chamber of Deputies; member of the Regency Council; Minister of Agriculture and Commerce, 1950; Minister of Communications and Public Works, 1954; Minister of Education, 1957; Minister of Finance, 1958; Minister of Defence, 1959; Minister of Justice, 1960; Chief of the Royal Court; President of the East Ghor Canal Authority, 1963; Chief of the Civil Service Commission, 1965; Deputy Prime Minister and Minister of the Interior, 1972–73; President of the National Consultative Council; Senator; *Publications:* numerous articles published in journals and magazines; *Decorations:* Order of Independence, Jordan; Order of the Jordanian Star, Jordan; Order of Renaissance, Jordan; Higher Order of Renaissance, Jordan; Order of Education, Jordan; Order of the Tunisian Republic; Order of Al-Alawi, Morocco; several other decorations from various countries; *Interests and Recreations:* riding, chess, backgammon, walking, gymnastics, reading, Arabic and English poetry, history and religion, law; *Languages:* Arabic, English; *Address:* P O Box 2453, Jabal, Amman, Jordan; telephone: 21512, 41719.

TARAWNEH, Naji Hussain, Jordanian judge; born 15 November 1930; married; *Religion:* Muslim; *Education:* BA in Law, Damascus University, Syria, 1954; *Career:* Judge at the Ministry of Justice, 1955–72; President of the Income Tax Board of Appeal, 1972–74; Minister of Justice 1974–76; *Address:* Jabal Amman, Amman, Jordan; telephone: 44744.

TARCICI, Adnan, Yemen Arab Republic diplomat; born 14 July 1918, Halba, Akkar, Lebanon; married; *Religion:* Muslim; *Education:* Diploma from the National School of Oriental Languages (Ecole Nationale des Langues Orientales), Paris, France; Doctoratès-Lettres, *Career:* member of a Lebanese Mission to Yemen, 1946; member of the Yemen Delegation to the UN General Assembly, 1947–74; Minister, Yemen Embassy, Lebanon, 1953; Adviser, First Republican Council, Sana'a, Yemen Arab Republic (YAR), 1962; Permanent Representative with the rank of Ambassador of Yemen to the UN, Geneva, Switzerland, 1963; Ambassador to France, 1977; *Publications: Yemen,* 1948; *Yemen and the Civilisation of the Arabs,* 1963; *The Queen of Sheba's Land,* 1973; *Interests and Recreations:* solar energy, development of solar cookers; *Languages:* Arabic, French, English; *Address:* c/o Ministry of Foreign Affairs, Sana'a, Yemen Arab Republic.

TARYAM, Abdullah Omran, United Arab Emirates journalist/politician; born 1945, Sharjah, United Arab Emirates; married; two sons, one daughter; *Religion:* Muslim; *Education:* BA in Literature and History, Cairo University, Egypt, 1966; *Career:* Director of Education, Sharjah Government, 1968–71; Editor, *Al-Khalij* newspaper; Minister of Justice in first United Arab Emirates Government, 1971–72; Minister of Education, 1972–77; Minister of Education, 1977; *Decorations:* Order from Tunisia and Morocco; *Interests and Recreations:* literature, poetry, volley-ball, basket-ball, tennis; *Languages:* Arabic, English; *Address:* P O Box 30, Al Wahda Street, Sharjah, United Arab Emirates; telephone: 353777; telex: 68055.

TARZI, Zahdi Labib, Palestinian diplomat/journalist; born 1924, Jerusalem, Palestine; married; two children; *Education:* Law Degree; *Career:* Civilian Service, British Army, World War II; active journalist in Palestinian nationalist movement; Representative of Palestine Liberation Organisation (PLO), Brazil, 1964; Representative of PLO, Office of the League of Arab States, Argentina; Head of the League of Arab States Office, Spain; PLO Delegation, UN, New York, 1974–75; Permanent Observer, PLO, UN, 1975–; *Decorations:* Knight of the Order of the Holy Sepulchre, Patriarch of Jerusalem, 1966; *Address:* Mission of the Palestine Liberation Organisation to the United Nations, 115 East 65th Street, New York, NY 10021; telephone: (212) 288 8500; telex: 621082 PLO NY.

TASHKANDI, Abdul Aziz Muhammad Issa, Saudi Arabian surgeon/ophthalmic specialist; born 1926, Mecca, Saudi Arabia; *Religion:* Muslim; *Education:* Cairo, MB, ChB, 1958; Alexandria, DOMS, 1964; UK Postgraduate studies for MS; DOMS Barraquer Institute, Spain; *Career:* Ophthalmic Surgeon and Director of the Eye Hospital in Jeddah, 1960; Medical Officer, Cairo University Hospital, Moorfields Eye Hospital, UK, and others in the UK; Eye Surgeon and Director of the Nasseriya Eye Hospital; external examiner, the Riyadh Faculty of Medicine; member of Egyptian Medical Association, 1958, Egyptian Ophthalmic Committee, 1958, Oxford Ophthalmic Congress, 1966, the Barraquer Institute, 1975; appointed by the Ministry of Health to supervise and improve ophthalmic services in Saudi hospitals, undertaking inquiry into operations for cataract by non-professionals in some rural districts; *Publications:* several scientific articles and lectures; radio and television interviews; *Interests and Recreations:* swimming, reading, gardening; *Address:* Nasseriya Eye Hospital, P O Box 118, Riyadh, Saudi Arabia; telephone: 4025600.

TAWASHI, Rashad Kamel, Egyptian academic/pharmaceutical researcher; resident in Canada; born 26 September 1933, Giza, Egypt; married; four children; *Education:* PhD in Philosophy, University of Basel,

Switzerland, 1960; *Career:* Research Pharmacist, Ciba A.G., Basel, 1960–61; Lecturer in Pharmaceutical Technology, University of Alexandria, Egypt, 1961–65; Research Associate, University of Michigan, Ann Arbor, USA, 1965–67; recipient of grants from the Medical Research Council of Canada, 1968–80; Assistant Professor of Industrial Pharmacy, University of Montreal, Canada, 1967–70; Associate Professor, University of Montreal, 1970–75; Professor, University of Montreal, 1975–; participated in the establishment of the first School of Pharmacy, University of Tripoli, Libya, 1976; Consultant to various pharmaceutical companies in Quebec, Canada; Visiting Professor of European Institute of Industrial Pharmacy, Montpellier, France, 1973; member of the Medical Research Council of Canada Grant Committee, 1972, of the American Association for the Advancement of Science, American Pharmaceutical Association, Canadian Association for Research Toxicology, Academy of Pharmaceutical Sciences; member of the Association of Egyptian-American Scholars, the Montreal Pharmacists Discussion Group and Vice Chairman for the year 1974; *Publications:* numerous articles published in pharmaceutical and professional journals; *Decorations:* MRC Visiting Scientist Award, the Federal Institute of Technology, Zurich, Switzerland, 1971; *Address:* Residence — 66 Hyde Park, Beaconsfield, Quebec, Canada; Office — Faculty of Pharmacy, Casa Postale 6128, University of Montreal PQ, Canada H3C 3J7.

TAWFIK, Tawfik Ibrahim, Saudi Arabian official; born 1937, Riyadh, Saudi Arabia; *Religion:* Muslim; *Education:* MBA, Business Administration; courses in marketing and administration; *Career:* Director, Exhibitions Department, Ministry of Commerce; Director, Industrial Estates Department; acting Director General of Industry; Director of Industrial Information, Industrial Development and Research Centre; Director General of Supply, Ministry of Commerce; Deputy Minister of Commerce for Supply, Ministry of Commerce; attended several UNIDO Conferences, UN Industrial Development Organization; *Interests and Recreations:* travel, football; *Address:* Ministry of Commerce, Riyadh, Saudi Arabia; telephone: Office — Riyadh 402 1116.

TAWFIQ, Shaikh Muhammad Omar, Saudi Arabian official/man of letters; born 1922; *Religion:* Muslim; *Education:* Dar Ulum al-Shari'a (School of Islamic Sciences), Medina, Saudi Arabia; *Career:* teacher at Dar al-Aytam, Medina; Directorate of Telegrams and Posts; Director, *Umm al-Qura* Official Bulletin; Office of Attorney General; retired from civil service; businessman; appointed by the late King Faisal as Minister of Communications, 1962; reappointed for the same portfolio in late King Khalid's First Cabinet, 1972–76; Chairman of the Hijaz Railways Company; Acting Minister of the Pilgrimage, 1963–70; contributed, through extensive writings, to the development of Saudi cultural life; *Publications:* articles, radio talks, active participation in literary and cultural papers and magazines; *Interests and Recreations:* reading, writing; *Address:* c/o the Ministry of Communications, Airport Road, Riyadh, Saudi Arabia; telephone: 4042928.

TAWFIQ, Zakaria Muhammad Abdul Fattah, Egyptian politician; born 1920; married; *Religion:* Muslim; *Career:* Bank Misr; Commercial Counsellor, Embassy to Spain, 1954–57; worked for some years in Ministry of Economy with special responsibility for the cotton trade; Under Secretary, Ministry of Economy, 1962; Chairman of the Egyptian General Cotton Organization, 1968–75; Minister of Foreign Trade, 1975–76; Minister of Trade and Supply, 1976; Chairman, General Union of Chambers of Commerce, 1976–; President, Afro-Asian Organization for Economic Co-operation (AFRASEC), 1972; *Languages:* Arabic, Spanish, English; *Address:* Ministry of Trade and Supply, Cairo, Egypt.

TAWIL, Bahgat Ahmad al-, Egyptian UN official; born 23 November 1917, Alexandria, Egypt; married; *Religion:* Muslim; *Education:* BCom, Cairo University, Egypt, 1935–39; MA in Statistics, Columbia University, New York, USA, 1942–44; Doctoral Studies, Economics and Statistics, 1946–49; Research, National Income Estimation, 1950–52; *Career:* Instructor, 1940–46; Visiting Lecturer, School of Social Work, Cairo, Egypt, 1952–57; Special Assistant and Counsellor, Embassy to USA, 1953–55; Director General, Department of Statistics and Census, Cairo, 1957–61; Director, Regional Statistical Training Centre, 1961–62; Head of Statistics and Demography Division, Economic Commission for Africa, UN, Addis Ababa, 1962–65; Deputy Director, Office of Technical Co-operation, Department of Economic and Social Affairs, New York, 1965–72; Representative of the Secretary General, Pakistan, 1971; Acting Director, Office of Technical Co-operation, Department of Economic and Social Affairs, UN, 1972–73; Director, Office of the Assistant Secretary General for Special Political Questions, UN, 1973; member of Al-Ruwaad, Social Welfare Group, Cairo; member of the Egyptian Statistical Society; member of the National Club of Commerce, Cairo; *Interests and Recreations:* economic analysis, management; member of the Maadi Sporting Club, Cairo, Egypt; *Languages:* Arabic, French, English; *Address:* Office — Office of the Assistant Secretary General for Special Political Affairs, UN, United Nations Plaza, New York, NY 10017, USA; telephone: (212) 754 1234; Residence — 209 Highbrook Avenue, Pelham, NY 10803, USA; telephone: (914) 738 5534.

TAWIL, Ibrahim Abdul Fattah al-, Egyptian banker/lawyer; born 6 March 1925, Alexandria, Egypt; married; two sons; *Education:* BA, Law, Alexandria University, 1946; *Career:* Lawyer, 1946; Arab African International Bank (AAIB), Legal Department, 1965; Manager, Arab African International Bank, Legal Department, 1970; Assistant General Manager, Arab African International Bank, 1975; Legal Adviser and Secretary General of the Board, AAIB, 1979–; *Interests and Recreations:* reading, tourism; member of Egyptian Bar Association, Egyptian Automobile Club, Algezira Sport Club; *Address:* 44 Abdul Khalek Tharwat Street, Cairo, Egypt; telephone: 916710, 920390; telex: ARBFR 92071, ARBFRO 363.

TAWIL, Joseph Elias, Arab-American ecclesiastic; born 25 December 1913, Damascus, Syria; *Religion:* Christian; *Education:* Philosophy and Theology, St. Anne's Seminary, Jerusalem, Palestine; LLD, St. Bonaventure University, USA, 1974; *Career:* ordination as a priest, Jerusalem, 20 July 1936; Professor, Patriarchal College, Cairo, Egypt, 1936–39; Dean of Studies, Patriarchal College, Cairo, 1943–54; Publisher of *Le Lein* review of the Greek Catholic Patriarchate, 1943–54; Greek Catholic Patriarchal Vicar in Alexandria, Egypt, 1954–60; elected Archbishop by

Greek Catholic Synod, 1959; Greek Catholic Patriarchal Vicar of Damascus, Syria, 1969–70; Melkite Greek Catholic Apostolic Exarch for the USA, 1970; Melkite Greek Catholic Eparch of Newton, 1976; *Languages:* Arabic, French, Greek, Latin, English; *Address:* 19 Dartmouth Street, West Newton, Massachusetts, 02165, USA; telephone: (617) 969 8957.

TAYAR, Adnan Muhammad al-, Iraqi banker; born 30 June 1930, Baghdad, Iraq; married; five daughters; *Religion:* Muslim; *Education:* BA in Law, 1953; *Career:* Central Bank of Iraq, 1948; Director of Investment, Central Bank of Iraq, 1962; Director General, Iraqi Bank of Credit, 1969; Director General, Bank of Commerce, 1970; Chairman of the Board of Directors of Bank Al-Rafidain, 1974; Director of Bank Al-Rafidain, 1971–82; Deputy Chairman, Iraq-Brazil Bank, 1982–; *Interests and Recreations:* swimming, walking; *Languages:* Arabic, English; *Address:* Rua Carlos Gois 64/202 Levlon, 22440 Rio de Janeiro, Brazil; telephone: 2394418.

TAYARA, Muhammad Ghassan, Syrian engineer/politician; born 30 September 1938, Syria; married; one son; *Religion:* Muslim; *Education:* Diploma in Engineering, Moscow, USSR; PhD in Technology; *Career:* Director of Center of Technical Training, and Center of Development and Production, Damascus, Syria, 1974–80; President of the Syndicate of Syrian Enginers, 1980–; member of Parliament, 1980–; *Publications:* articles and papers on production and development published in professional journals and magazines; *Interests and Recreations:* swimming; *Languages:* Arabic, English, Russian; *Address:* P O Box 2336 Damascus, Sahat Yusif al-Azma, Bina Dar, Syria; telephone: 113540, 114916; telex: 411962.

TAYEBI, Muhammad Bel Hadj, Algerian politician; born 1918, Sidi Bel Abbes, Algeria; *Religion:* Muslim; *Career:* Regional Commander of Wilaya V (Oran), 1956–59; Commander of North-West Operational Zone (Moroccan-Algerian border area), 1962; military member of National Liberation Front (FLN) mission in Rabat, Morocco; Director General of Sûreté Générale, 1963–64; elected member of FLN Central Committee at April 1964 Congress; Ambassador to Brazil, 1965; Préfet of Oran, 1965;

member of Council of Revolution, 1965–; one of five members of National Liberation Front (FLN) Executive Secretariat, 1965–67; Minister of Agriculture, 1968; *Languages:* Arabic, French, Spanish; *Address:* c/o Ministry of Agriculture, 12 Boulevard Colonel Amirouche, Algiers, Algeria; telephone: 668950/4.

TAYER, Ahmad Hamid al-, United Arab Emirates official/financial administrator; born 1950, United Arab Emirates; married; *Religion:* Muslim; *Education:* BA in Economics, Faculty of Economics and Political Science, Cairo University, Cairo, Egypt, 1973; *Career:* Director, Economic Department, Ministry of Finance, Industry, 1973–74; Director General, Ministry of Finance and Industry, 1974–78; member of the Board of Arab Investment and Foreign Trade Bank, Board of Amman Insurance Company; Alternate Governor of United Arab Emirates at International Monetary Fund and World Bank, Islamic Development Bank; Assistant Under Secretary, Ministry of Finance and Industry, 1978–; *Interests and Recreations:* literature, football, science, economics; *Languages:* Arabic, English; *Address:* Ministry of Finance and Industry, P O Box 433, Abu Dhabi, United Arab Emirates; telephone: 44330; telex: DB 5722.

TAYIB, Abdul Malik al-, Yemen Arab Republic diplomat; born 1935, al-Nadra, Yemen Arab Republic; *Religion:* Muslim; *Education:* in Sana'a; *Career:* Minister of Education, 1968–69; candidate for the three members Republican Council, May 1972; Head of Council of Ministers, Action Committee, 1972–73; Ambassador to Libya, 1973–74; Minister for Local Government in the administration of Muhsin Al-Aini, 1974–75, and of Abdul Aziz Abdul Ghani; Ambassador to Libya, 1976; Ambassador to Morocco; member of the Command Council; *Address:* P O Box 400, Sana'a, Yemen Arab Republic.

TAYIB, Abdullah al-, Sudanese academic; born 1921, Al-Damer, Sudan; married; *Education:* Gordon College, Khartoum, 1936–42; PhD, London University, UK, 1950; *Career:* Lecturer in Arabic, School of Oriental and African Studies, University of London, UK; Head of Arabic Department, Bakht al-Redha Teachers Training Institute, Department of Arabic, Khartoum University,

Dean, Faculty of Arts, 1961–64, 1964–66; Head of Faculty of Arabic, Provost, Faculty of Arabic, Abdullahi Bayero College, Kano, Nigeria, 1964; Professor of Arabic, Dean of Faculty of Arts, University of Khartoum, 1966; member of the Committee for reviewing the structure of Khartoum University; Vice Chancellor, University of Juba, 1975–76; Professor Emeritus, University of Khartoum; Maître de Conférence, Arabic Department, University of Mohammed Ben Abdullah, Fes, Morocco; *Interests and Recreations:* Arabic language and literature; member of the Academy of Arabic Language, Cairo, Egypt; *Languages:* Arabic, English, French; *Address:* PO Box 1996, Khartoum, Sudan.

TAYIB, Muhammad Said, Saudi Arabian official/businessman; born 1937; *Religion:* Muslim; *Education:* BA in Economics and Political Science; *Career:* Assistant Director of the Department of Immigration and Passports, Mecca; Head of the Department of Practical Studies, Al-Thaghr Model Schools, Jeddah; General Manager of the Office of the Minister of Pilgrimage and Endowments; contributed regularly to local newspapers; Director General of Tihama for Advertising, Public Relations and Market Research; participated actively in the establishment of King Abdul Aziz University, Jeddah; *Interests and Recreations:* reading, writing, swimming; *Address:* Tihama, P O Box 5455, Jeddah, Saudi Arabia; telephone: Office — 644 4444, Residence — 660 4077.

TAYYARA, Abdul Rahman al-, Lebanese economist/accountant; born 1911; married; *Religion:* Muslim; *Education:* Higher Studies of Commerce; *Career:* Head of Income Tax, 1945; Head of Department of Commerce, Islamic Regar College of Beirut (Makaasid School), 1950–59; Head of Lebanese Treasury, 1952; Director, Monetary Department, Ministry of Finance, 1953; Professor of Accounting, Centre of Financial Studies, Lebanese University, 1954–62; Director General, Posts and Telegrams, 1956; Director General, National Economy, 1959; Professor of Accounting, National Institute for General Management, Civil Service Council, 1962; Head of Central Inspection and Control Committee, 1962; Head of Civil Service Council, 1974; Chairman and Director General, National Bank for Industrial and Touristic Development; *Publications: Gener-*

al Finance in the Republic of Lebanon, 1956, Institute of Higher Arabic Studies, Arab League; *Accounting of Private Companies; Accounting of Financial Companies,* Centre of Financial Studies, Lebanese University; *Accounting Simplified,* 1962, National Institute for General Management, Civil Service Council; *Decorations:* Lebanese Golden Order of Merit, 1954; Knight, Officer and Commander of the National Order of the Cedar, 1949, 1957, 1958; Officer of the National Order of Merit, France, 1968; *Interests and Recreations:* photography, chess, hunting; *Languages:* Arabic, French, Italian, English; *Address:* National Bank for Industrial and Touristic Development, Rue Riad al-Solh, Building Arab Bank, P O Box 8412; telephone: 254850, 252601.

TAZI, Abdul Haq al-, Moroccan politician; born 20 September 1932; *Education:* Degree in Agronomic Engineering, Paris Institute of Agronomy, 1954–56; Degree in Rural Engineering; *Career:* President of Istiqlal Party Students Body, Paris, 1956–58; Engineer for Meknes and Tafilalt Provinces, 1959; Chief of Department Staff, Ministry of Agriculture, 1960; Member of Istiqlal Party National Council, 1961; Director, National Land Development Agency, 1962; Engineer in private sector, 1963; Member of the Executive Committee of Istiqlal Party, 1964–; Secretary General of Istiqlal Youth, 1968–76; Municipal Seat at Fes City Council, 1976; Secretary of State for Vocational Training, 1977; Secretary of State for Co-operation, 1980; Secretary of State for Foreign Affairs, 1981; *Languages:* Arabic, French; *Address:* c/o Ministry of Foreign Affairs, Rabat, Morocco.

TELL, Safwan Khalaf al-, Jordanian academic; born 12 December 1938, Irbid, Jordan; married; two sons, one daughter; *Religion:* Muslim; *Education:* BA in Archaeology; MA in Archaeology and Byzantine and Islamic Arts; PhD in Islamic Art and Architecture; *Career:* Inspector of Antiquities, Department of Antiquities, Jordan, 1968–74; Instructor, Jordan University, 1974–80; Head of Department of Antiquities, Jordan University, 1975–79; Assistant Director of Jordan University and Director of Cultural and Public Affairs, 1976–81, Associate Professor, 1981; Head of Department of Antiquities, Jordan University, 1975–79; Assistant Director of Jordan University and

Director of Cultural and Public Affairs, 1976–81; Assistant Secretary General, Federation of Arab Universities, Riyadh, Saudi Arabia, 1982–; *Publications: Development of Arabic Script in the First Hijri Century,* in Arabic; *Development of Coins in Jordan,* in Arabic; *Interests and Recreations:* sports; *Languages:* Arabic, English, Turkish; *Address:* P O Box 2873, Riyadh, Saudi Arabia.

TELL, Said M. al-, Jordanian politician/academic; born 1934, Irbid, Jordan; married; *Education:* BA in Mathematics and Education, American University of Beirut, Beirut, Lebanon, 1957; MA in Education, American University of Beirut, 1960; PhD, 1963; *Career:* several teaching posts, Irbid, 1953–58; Instructor, Hawara Teachers College, 1958–65; Cultural Counsellor, Jordan Embassy, Lebanon, 1965–69; Assistant Professor, University of Jordan, 1969–72; Professor of Education and Dean of the College of Education, University of Jordan, 1972–78; Minister of Communications, 1978; *Publications:* several articles on teaching methods and educational subjects published in various professional journals in Arab countries; translated several textbooks in the field of education; *Languages:* Arabic, English; *Address:* P O Box 921234, Amman, Jordan; telephone: 62322.

THABIT, Rashid Muhammad, People's Democratic Republic of Yemen diplomat/politician; *Career:* Minister of Information; Minister of Broadcasting; Minister of State for Cabinet Affairs; Ambassador, Ministry of Foreign Affairs, 1975; Ambassador to Egypt, 1975; member of Central Committee; *Address:* c/o Ministry of Foreign Affairs, Aden, People's Democratic Republic of Yemen.

THANI, Brigadier Shaikh Hamad Bin Jassim al-, Qatari Chief of Police; born 1949; brother of HH the Ruler; married; four sons, one daughter; *Religion:* Muslim; *Education:* Qatar and UK; Police training, Hendon Police College, UK; LLB, Beirut Arab University; *Career:* Chief of Police, 1972; responsible for development of Qatar Police into a modern force; *Languages:* Arabic, English; *Address:* P O Box 920, Doha, Qatar.

THANI, HH Shaikh Khalifa Bin Hamad al-, Amir of Qatar; born 1934, Rayyan, Qatar; *Religion:* Muslim; *Career:* Head of Security in first oil project in Qatar; Head of Civil

Courts; Minister of Education; Deputy Amir, 1960; Chairman, Qatar and Dubai Monetary Agency, 1966; Minister of Foreign Affairs and President of the Council of Ministers, 1971; Minister of Finance and Chairman of Council for State Investment, 1972; succeeded his cousin Shaikh Ahmad Al-Thani as ruler, 1972; played an important role in the economic and social development of Qatar; *Address:* Diwan al-Amiri, P O Box 1, Doha, Qatar; telephone: 415888; telex: 4297 DH.

THANI, Major General Shaikh Hamad Bin Khalifa al-, Qatari Heir Apparent/army commander; born 1949; eldest son of HH the Ruler, Shaikh Khalifa Bin Hamad al-Thani; married; two sons, one daughter. *Religion:* Muslim; *Education:* in Qatar and UK; passed out of Royal Military College, Sandhurst, UK, 1971; *Career:* Commander in Chief of Qatar Security Forces, 1972; played leading part in the re-equipment and modernization of Qatar Armed Forces; concerned with officer training; designated Heir Apparent, 1977; Minister of Defence 1977–; *Address:* Ministry of Defence, Doha, Qatar; telephone: 328523.

THANI, Shaikh Abdul Aziz Bin Khalifa al-, Qatari politician; born 12 December 1948, Doha, Qatar; *Religion:* Muslim; *Education:* BA in Political Science and Economics, 1972; MA, 1974, Northern Indiana University, USA; *Career:* Deputy Minister of Finance and Petroleum, 1972; Minister of Finance and Petroleum, 1972–; President of the Qatar Monetary Agency, 1972–; Chairman, Qatar National Petroleum Company, 1973–; senior member of Qatar Investment Board; as Minister of Petroleum was closely associated with the two operating companies, Qatar Petroleum Company and Shell Qatar, during the take-over of their equity by the Government of Qatar; Chairman of OPEC, December 1976; *Languages:* Arabic, English; *Address:* Ministry of Finance and Petroleum, P O Box 36, Government House, Doha, Qatar; telephone: 324281, 320558; telex: 4315 DOHMFP DH.

THANI, Shaikh Ahmad Bin Saif al-, Qatari diplomat; born 1946; married; *Religion:* Muslim; *Education:* in Bahrain; Diploma in Public Administration, London, UK, 1971; *Career:* Ambassador to the Court of St. James, London, UK, 1971–77; *Languages:* Arabic, English; *Address:* Ministry of Foreign Affairs, P O Box 250, Government House, Doha, Qatar.

THANI, Shaikh Faisal Bin Thani al-, Qatari politician; born 1900; *Religion:* Muslim; *Career:* Minister of Industry and Agriculture, 1970–; *Address:* Ministry of Industry and Agriculture, P O Box 1966, Doha, Qatar; telephone: 324948; telex: 4096 SINZRA DH.

THANI, Shaikh Khalid Bin Hamad al-, Qatari politician; born 1937; elder brother of HH the Amir, Shaikh Khalifa Bin Hamad al-Thani; married; one son; *Religion:* Muslim; *Education:* Royal Military College, Sandhurst, UK; *Career:* Minister of Interior, 1972–; involved in development of Police Service in collaboration with Commander of Police, Shaikh Hamad Bin Jassim al-Thani; *Address:* Ministry of Interior, P O Box 2433, Doha, Qatar; telephone: 421044, 426214.

THANI, Shaikh Muhammad Bin Jabir al-, Qatari politician/businessman; born 1916; married; one son; *Religion:* Muslim; *Career:* private enterprise in freight firms, Qatar Flour Mills, and Al-Darbi Building Contractors; Minister for Municipal Affairs, 1972–; *Address:* Ministry for Municipal Affairs, P O Box 2727, Doha, Qatar; telephone: 326107.

THANI, Shaikh Nasir Bin Khalid al-, Qatari politician/businessman; born 1915; married; *Religion:* Muslim; *Career:* leading businessman in Doha; interests in National Qatar Cinema Corporation; President of Qatar Israel Boycott Committee; Minister of Economic and Commercial Affairs, 1970–; *Address:* Ministry of Economic and Commercial Affairs, P O Box 1968, Doha, Qatar; telephone: 325828, 325885; telex: 4488 ECOM DH.

THANI, Shaikh Suhaim Bin Hamad al-, Qatari politician; born 1940; brother of HH the Ruler, Shaikh Khalifa Bin Hamad al-Thani; *Religion:* Muslim; *Career:* Minister of Foreign Affairs, 1972–; *Address:* Ministry of Foreign Affairs, P O Box 250, Doha, Qatar; telephone: 427767, 325079.

THOUR, Ali Lutf al-, Yemen Arab Republic politician; born 18 September 1940; married; one son, three daughters; *Religion:* Muslim; *Education:* College of Commerce, Cairo

University, 1964; training course on Development, USA, 1965; BSc, 1968; *Career:* member of the Higher Economic Committee, 1964–65; Government Representative and member of the Board in the Yemeni Company, 1965–66; member of the Board of the Yemeni Bank for Reconstruction and Development (YBRD) and Manager of the Sana'a Branch, 1966–67; Deputy Chairman, Yemeni Bank for Reconstruction and Development, 1967–68; Chairman of the Yemeni Bank, 1968; Deputy President of the Yemen National Assembly; Chairman of the Assembly's Economic Committee, 1968–69; Minister of Finance, 1969–70; Chairman of YBRD, 1970–73; Minister of Economy, 1973–74 and 1974–76; Executive member of the Board of the Yemeni Bank, 1966–76; *Interests and Recreations:* poetry, fiction, swimming; *Languages:* Arabic, English; *Address:* Ministry of Economy, Sana'a, Yemen Arab Republic.

THUWAINI, Abdul Muhsin, Kuwaiti businessman; born 1930; married; *Religion:* Muslim; *Education:* in Kuwait; *Career:* contractor; member of the Board of Directors of Kuwait Chamber of Commerce and Industry; Chairman of Kuwait Contractor Unions; member of the board of several shareholding companies; *Languages:* Arabic, English; *Address:* P O Box 446, Safat, Kuwait.

THUWAINI, Major General Abdul Latif Faisal al-, Kuwaiti official; born 1927, Kuwait; married; nine children; *Religion:* Muslim; *Education:* in Kuwait; courses in London on security and police affairs; *Career:* attended Interpol conferences on Crime Prevention and Offenders Treatment, local conferences for police commanders; *Interests and Recreations:* hunting, fishing, riding; founding member of Al-Ahly Sports Club (The Kuwait Club now), and of Teachers Club; founding member of the Hunting and Riding Club; member of the Administrative Board and Manager of Hunting and Riding Club; Manager of a horse racing club; *Languages:* Arabic, English; *Address:* Ministry of the Interior, P O Box 4, Safat, Kuwait; telephone: 816111.

TIBAH, Mustafa Abdullah, Saudi Arabian official/physician; born 1926; *Education:* BM,B Ch; *Career:* Surgeon, Arab American Oil Company (Aramco), 1957–60; Director

and Surgeon, King's Hospital, Jeddah, 1960–62; Director and Surgeon, Tobruk Military Hospital, 1962–63; Assistant Director of Medical Service, Ministry of Defence, 1963–64; Director, Jeddah Quarantine; Director General of Curative Medicine, Ministry of Health, 1978–; *Interests and Recreations:* reading, contemplation; *Address:* Ministry of Health, Airport Road, Riyadh, Saudi Arabia; telephone: 4044792; telex: 20 1628 HEALTH SJ.

TIBBU, Muhammad Ali, Libyan politician; born 1930, Fezzan, Libya; *Religion:* Muslim; *Career:* Lecturer, Faculty of Agriculture, University of Libya; Assistant Director General, Agricultural Bank, Sebha; Minister of Agriculture and Agrarian Reform, 1970–77; Secretary for Agriculture and Agrarian Reform, General People's Committee, 1977; *Languages:* Arabic, French; *Address:* Office of the Secretary for Agriculture and Agrarian Reform, Tripoli, Libya.

TIGANI, Muhammad al-Tom al-, Sudanese official/educationalist; born Sudan; *Religion:* Muslim; *Career:* Ministry of Education; Dean, Higher Teachers Training Institute; Under Secretary; Chairman of the Board of the Management Development and Productivity Centre, 1973; Secretary for Youth Affairs and Sport of the Sudanese Socialist Union (SSU), 1974–75; Minister of State for General Education, 1975–76; *Address:* Ministry of Education, Khartoum, Sudan.

TLASS, Lieutenant General Mustafa Abdul Qadir, Syrian army commander; born 11 May 1932, Homs, Syria; married; two daughters, two sons; *Religion:* Muslim; *Education:* Diploma in Military Sciences; PhD in Military Sciences, Vorshelov Command and General Staff Academy, USSR; *Career:* Tank Battalion Commander of the 5th Armoured Brigade, 1963; participated in the Liberal Officers Movement in Homs, 1962; Chief of National Security Court, Central Region; elected member of the Regional Leadership of the Baath Arab Socialist Party, 1965; Major General, 1968; Vice Commander in Chief of the Army and Armed Forces, Minister of Defence, 1972–; *Publications:* numerous books and other publications; *Decorations:* awarded 28 Syrian, Arab and foreign Medals and Orders; *Interests and Recreations:* military and historical studies, reading, writing, horse riding, tennis, swimming; *Languages:* Arabic, French, English; *Address:* Al-Ammawiyun Square, Headquarters of the Army and Armed Forces, Damascus, Syria.

TOBIA, Maguid, Egyptian writer; born 25 March 1938, Egypt; *Religion:* Christian; *Education:* BSc in Mathematics, 1960; Diploma, Institute of Script Writing, 1968; MA in Film Production, 1971; *Career:* Official, Higher Council of Arts and Literature, 1969–78; author of several film scripts and scenarios; Official of Ministry of Culture, and freelance writer; member of the Egyptian Writers Union, Chamber of Cinema Industry, Society of Egyptian Film Critics, Story Committee, Supreme Council of Culture; *Publications:* several novels and short story collections; including *The Music Kiosk, Hanan; Decorations:* winner of Short Story Club Award, 1964; First Prize from Egyptian Cinema Institute for film scenarios; State Encouragement Prize for the Best Novel; *Interests and Recreations:* reading, literature, cinema, travel; *Languages:* Arabic, English; *Address:* 15 al-Lewaa Abdul al-Aziz Ali, Heliopolis, Cairo, Egypt.

TOLBA, Mustafa Kamal, Egyptian UN official/educationalist; born 8 December 1922, Egypt; married; *Religion:* Muslim; *Education:* BSc in Botany, Faculty of Science, Cairo University, Cairo, Egypt, 1939–43; DIC, Imperial College, University of London, London, UK, 1946–49; PhD in Microbiology, Imperial College, University of London, 1946–49; *Career:* Assistant Lecturer, Lecturer, Assistant Professor and Professor of Microbiology, Cairo University, Egyptian National Research Centre and Baghdad University, Iraq, 1943–; Secretary General, National Science Council, Egypt, 1959–63; Cultural Counsellor and Director, Egyptian Education Bureau, Washington D.C., USA, 1963–65; Under Secretary of State, Higher Education, 1965–70; Minister of Youth, Egypt, 1971; President, Academy of Scientific Research and Technology, Egypt, 1971–73; Deputy Executive Director, UN Environment Programme, 1973–75; Executive Director, UN Environment Programme, Nairobi, Kenya, 1975–; *Publications:* numerous scientific papers in professional journals in India, Iraq, Federal Republic of Germany, Sweden, USA, UK; *Decorations:* decorations from Egypt, Jordan, Spain, Czechoslovakia; *Interests and Recrea-*

tions: table tennis, music, travelling; *Languages:* Arabic, English; *Address:* United Nations Environment Programme, P O Box 30552, Nairobi, Kenya; telephone: 333930.

TOM, Ali al-, Sudanese UN official; born 30 June 1931, Khartoum, Sudan; married; *Religion:* Muslim; *Education:* Diploma in Agricultural Science, University of Khartoum, Sudan, 1951–56; Diploma in Agricultural Economics, Oxford University, UK, 1958–59; Certificate in Agricultural Planning, National Planning Institute, Egypt, 1962; *Career:* Inspector of Provincial Agriculture, Sudan, 1956–58; Senior Agricultural Planning Economist, Ministry of Agricultural Planning, Sudan, 1959–63; Agricultural Planning Economist, FAO, 1963–65; Regional Land Tenure and Settlement Officer for Africa, FAO, Addis Ababa, Ethiopia, 1965–68; Investment Economist, FAO, Rome, Italy, 1968–69; Minister of Agrarian Reform and Production, Sudan, 1969–70; Minister of Agriculture, Sudan, 1970–71; Director, FAO Agricultural Division, Economic Commission for Africa (ECA), UN, Addis Ababa, 1971; member, International Association of Agricultural Economists, International Development Association, African Association for Advancement of Agricultural Science, Arab Association of Agricultural Engineering, Sudan Agricultural Society, Sudan Philosophical Society; *Publications:* numerous books on agricultural development and reform; *Interests and Recreations:* basketball, table tennis, swimming, photography, music, numismatics; member, Ethiopian Creative Arts Centre; *Languages:* Arabic, French, English, Italian; *Address:* ECA, UN, P O Box 3001, Addis Ababa, Ethiopia; telephone: 47200.

TOMEH, George J., Syrian academic/diplomat; born 15 April 1922, Damascus, Syria; married; two sons, one daughter; *Religion:* Christian; *Education:* BA, MA and PhD, American University of Beirut AUB, Lebanon and Georgetown University, Washington D.C., USA, 1947–52; *Career:* Alternate Governor, IMF, 1950; Director, UN and Treaties Department, Ministry of Foreign Affairs, 1953–54; Assistant Professor of Philosophy, and Assistant Dean of Arts and Sciences, AUB, 1954–56; Director, Research Department, Ministry of Foreign Affairs, 1956–57; Consul General for United Arab Republic, New York, 1958; Minister Plenipotentiary, New York, 1961; Consul General and Deputy Permanent Representative of Syria to UN, 1961–63; Minister of Economy, 1963–64; Professor of Philosophy, Damascus University, 1964–65; Ambassador and Permanent Representative to the UN, 1965–72; Adviser to the Organization of Arab Petroleum Exporting Countries, OAPEC; Professor of Philosophy, School of Arts, University of Kuwait, 1980–; *Publications:* in Arabic, *The Idea of Nationalism,* 1954; *The Philosophy of Leibniz,* 1954, 1956, 1965; *The Making of the Modern Mind,* 1957, 1966; in English, *Islam, Yearbook of Education and Philosophy,* 1957; *Neutralism in Syria,* 1964; *Challenge and Response.. a Judgment of History,* 1969; *Decorations:* Syrian Order of Merit, 2nd Class, 1957; Syrian Order of Merit, Excellence Class, 1968; Commander of the Order of St. Peter and St. Paul, 1957; *Interests and Recreations:* swimming, walking, political and economic thought; *Languages:* Arabic, English, French; *Address:* P O Box 23558, Kuwait.

TOUQAN, Muhammad Abdul Rahman, Jordanian banker; born 1918, Salt, Jordan; *Religion:* Muslim; *Education:* Law degree, Damascus University, Syria; *Career:* Manager, Jordan National Bank; occupied several ministerial posts, including Tourism and Communications; Deputy Governor of Central Bank of Jordan; Chairman, Petra Bank; *Address:* Arab Shipping Co Ltd, P O Box 757, Amman, Jordan.

TOUQAN, Salah Ala'iddin, Jordanian lawyer/politician; born 1914, Salt, Jordan; married; *Religion:* Muslim; *Education:* Licence in Law, University of Damascus, Syria, 1938; *Career:* Attorney General and various judicial appointments; Minister of Finance, 1956–57; Senator, 1961–62; member and President of the Chamber of Deputies, 1962–63; Head, Audit Bureau, 1967–73; Senator 1973–; *Decorations:* Order of the Jordanian Star, 1st Class; Renaissance Medal, 1st Class; *Address:* Jabal Webdeh, Amman, Jordan; telephone: 25254.

TOURI, Rashid, Algerian academic; born 1928; *Religion:* Muslim; *Education:* Degree in Mathematics, Science Faculty, Algiers University, Algeria; Agrégation in Mathematics, Sorbonne, University of Paris, France; *Career:* teacher in Algiers; taught in secondary schools; Lecturer in Mathematics,

Science Faculty, Algiers University; Dean of the Faculty of Science, Algiers University 1964; Rector of Algiers University, 1970; *Languages:* Arabic, French; *Address:* University of Algiers, Faculty of Science, 2 Rue Didouche Mourad, Algiers, Algeria.

TRIKI, Mahmud, Tunisian politician/journalist; born 26 April 1936; married; one son, one daughter; *Religion:* Muslim; *Education:* Licence de Droit et Sciences Economiques, Paris, France; *Career:* Head of Department, Tunisian Agricultural Bank, 1965; Editor in Chief, Socialist Destour Party organ *L'Action,* 1967; Director of the Tunisian Party Company, 1969; Prime Minister's Office, 1970; Director of Political Affairs in the Prime Minister's Office, 1972; Chairman and Managing Director of Tunis-Afrique-Presse (TAP); President of the Union of Arab Press Agencies; Coordinator of the Press Agencies of the Non-Aligned Countries; *Decorations:* Officer of the Order of the Tunisian Republic, 1972; Chevalier of the Order of Tunisian Independence, 1976; Grand Officer of the Egyptian Order of Merit, 1972; *Interests and Recreations:* sociology, theatre, poetry, football, hunting, archaeology; *Languages:* Arabic, French; *Address:* 25 Avenue Habib Bourguiba, Tunis, Tunisia; telephone: 249000.

TUENI, Ghassan Gibran, Lebanese journalist/diplomat; born 5 January 1926, Beirut, Lebanon; married; two children; *Religion:* Christian; *Education:* BA in Philosophy, American University of Beirut, Lebanon, 1945; MA in Political Science, Harvard University, Boston, Massachusetts, USA, 1947; *Career:* Professor, Political Science Department, American University of Beirut, Lebanon; Editor in Chief, *Al-Nahar* newspaper, 1948–; founder and Professor, School of Law and Political Science, Lebanon 1951–54; elected Deputy for Mount Lebanon, 1951; elected Deputy for Beirut, 1953; Chairman of the Foreign Affairs Committee; Vice President, Chamber of Deputies, 1951–53; member of the Lebanese Delegation to the UN, 1957; Roving Ambassador, attached to the UN and to South America, 1967; Deputy Prime Minister and Minister of Education and Information, 1970–71; Head of UNICEF Mission to Saudi Arabia and the Gulf States, May 1971; Minister of Oil, Industry, Tourism, Labour and Social Affairs, 1975; Minister of Information, 1976;

Lebanese Permanent Representative to UN, 1976–82; Publisher, *Al-Nahar* newspaper, 1982–; founder and President, Business Services and Research Corporation Ltd; founder and President and Managing Director, Press Co-operative; founded French language daily *L'Orient-Le Jour*, 1965; owner and publisher of merged *L'Orient-Le Jour*, 1971; *Address:* P O Box 11–226, Beirut, Lebanon.

TUHAMI, Abdul Rahman, Moroccan official/physician; married; *Religion:* Muslim; *Education:* Faculty of Medicine, Toulouse, France; specialist training in Neurology, France; *Career:* Averroes Hospital, Casablanca, Morocco; in charge of hospitals at Youssefiyya, Essaouira and Demi-Mellal; Chief Physician, Averroes Hospital, Casablanca, 1971; Minister of Public Health in Lamrani Government, 1972; Private Physician to HM the King since 1974; Minister of Public Health, 1975–77; *Languages:* Arabic, French; *Address:* Ministry of Public Health, Rabat, Morocco.

TUHAMI, Hassan, Egyptian politician; born 1924; married; *Religion:* Muslim; *Career:* Vice President of the Islamic Conference, 1959; Ambassador to Austria, 1961; Chief Observer on the Egyptian Delegation to the International Atomic Energy Agency; member of the Cabinet, 1968; Secretary General of the Cabinet, 1969; Director General of the Arab Socialist Union (ASU), 1969; Minister of State, 1970; Presidential Adviser, 1970; Secretary General, Islamic Conference, 1971; *Address:* c/o The Presidency, Cairo, Egypt.

TUHAMI, Muhammad Sharif al-, Sudanese politician/geologist; born 7 December 1934; married; two daughters, two sons; *Religion:* Muslim; *Education:* BSc in Geology, Panjab University, India, 1958; MSc in Geology, University of Arizona, USA, 1962; PhD in Geology, University of London, 1976; *Career:* Geologist, Sudanese Geology and Mining Corporation, 1958–66; Director, Water Corporation, 1966–69; Adviser to a number of foreign companies, 1969–78; Minister of Energy and Mining, 1978–; member of the Central Committee of the Sudanese Socialist Union; *Decorations:* Order of the Two Niles (Al-Nilayn), 1st Class, Sudan; *Interests and Recreations:* tennis; *Languages:* Arabic, English; *Address:* Ministry of Energy and Mining, P O Box 2087, Khartoum, Sudan; telephone: 75599.

TULFAH, Major General Adnan Khairallah, Iraqi politician/army commander; born 1940, Iraq; married; one son, two daughters; *Education:* Military Academy, Staff College, Baghdad, Iraq; BA, College of Arts, Mustansiriyah University, Baghdad, Iraq; *Career:* joined Armed Forces as Second Lieutenant; National Guard Commander; joined Baath Socialist Party, 1957; occupied several posts in the Party; took active part in 14th Ramadan, 1963 Revolution; elected member of the Military Office of the Party; member of the Regional Command, Baath Socialist Party, Revolutionary Command Council, 1977–; Minister of Defence, 1977–; Deputy Prime Minister, Minister of Defence, 1979–; Deputy Commander of the Armed Forces, 1979–; *Address:* Ministry of Defence, Baghdad, Iraq.

TUMA, Elias H., Arab-American academic/economist; born 12 November 1928, Palestine; married; one son, two daughters; *Education:* BA in Sociology, University of Redlands, California, USA, 1958; PhD in Economics, University of California, Berkeley, USA, 1962; *Career:* Postgraduate Fellow, Near Eastern Centre, University of California, Los Angeles, USA, 1962–63; Assistant Professor of Economics, San Fernando Valley State College, California, USA, 1962–63; Assistant Professor of Economics, University of Saskatchewan, Canada, 1963–65; Assistant Professor of Economics, University of California, Davis, 1965–67; Associate Professor of Economics, University of California, 1967–71; Associate Dean, College of Letters and Science, University of California, Davis, 1968–71; Professor of Economics, University of California, Davis, 1971–; Director of University of California Education Abroad Program, American University of Cairo, Egypt, 1981–83; Consultant for FAO, 1975–76; Inter-Regional Consultant, United Nations, 1965; Special Consultant, United Nations, 1964; *Publications: Twenty-Six Centuries of Agrarian Reform,* 1965; *Economic History and Social Sciences.. Problems of Methodology,* 1971; *European Economic History, Tenth Century to the Present,* 1971; *Peace Making and the Immoral War.. Arabs and Jews in the Middle East,* 1972; *Food and Population in the Middle East: The Economic Case for Palestine,* 1978; numerous articles for newspapers and journals; *Interests and Recreations:* woodwork, photography, gardening, international affairs; *Languages:* Arabic, English, Hebrew; *Address:* 604 Barbera Place, Davis, California 95616, USA; telephone: (916) 756 3822; Department of Economics, Politics and Mass Communication, American University in Cairo, Cairo, Egypt; 113 Sharia Kasr el-Aini, Cairo, Egypt.

TUNI, Sayyid Muhammad, Egyptian academic; born 27 April 1926, Bani Swaif, Eygpt; married; *Education:* PhD in Animal Husbandry, Animal and Poultry Nutrition; *Career:* Teacher, Al-Azhar University, 1950; Teacher, Minia Agricultural Secondary School, 1951; Deputy Principal, Aswan Agricultural School; Associate Professor, High Institute of Agriculture, Minia, 1956; Associate Professor, College of Agriculture, Minia, 1967; Professor, Minia Agriculture College, 1973; Professor and Head of Department of Animal Husbandry, Minia Agricultural College, 1973–; *Publications:* numerous essays published in various academic journals; *Languages:* Arabic, French, English, German; *Address:* College of Agriculture, University of Minia, Egypt.

TUNISI, General Muhammad Tayib al-, Saudi Arabian official; born 1920; *Religion:* Muslim; *Career:* Ministry of Defence; received combat commission; ordnance training course in USA; Director of Supply, Ministry of Defence; Director General of Public Security (Police), 1967; *Languages:* Arabic, English; *Address:* c/o Office of the Director General of Public Security, Riyadh, Saudi Arabia; telephone: 403 6510.

TUQAN, Abir Dajani; Lebanese lawyer; resident in Kuwait; born 14 March 1945, Jaffa, Palestine; married; *Religion:* Muslim; *Education:* Chatelard School and Brillantmont, Lausanne, Switzerland; Barrister at Law, Middle Temple; Islamic Law, London University, UK; *Career:* practised law at both the criminal and civil Bar in UK; was first (and only) Arab woman to be called to the English Bar (Honourable Society of Middle Temple); Lawyer, Graham and James, lawyers and legal advisers, Kuwait; *Interests and Recreations:* opera, reading, film production, skiing, swimming, charity work; committee member of Red Crescent Society; *Languages:* Arabic, English, French, Italian; *Address:* P O Box 1245, Safat, Kuwait.

TUQAN, Baha'iddin, Jordanian diplomat; born 1910; married; *Religion:* Muslim; *Education:* BA, American University of Beirut, Lebanon; *Career:* Arab Legion; Secretary to Officer Commanding, 1932–37; on staff member of BBC, London, 1942; Income Tax Assessor, Transjordan Government, 1945–46; Governor of Belqa District, 1946–47; Secretary to Transjordan Delegation to negotiate Independence Treaty, London, 1946; Transjordan Consul General in Jerusalem, 1947–48; Minister to Egypt 1948–51; Minister to Turkey, 1951–54; Under Secretary, Ministry of Foreign Affairs, 1954–56; Ambassador to UK, 1956–58; Permanent Representative to UN, 1958, 1971–72; Under Secretary, Minister of Foreign Affairs, 1962; Head of Arab League Office in Rome, Italy, 1966–70; Ambassador to UN; Senator 1973; *Publications: Short History of Transjordan,* 1945; *Languages:* Arabic, English; *Address:* P O Box 5192, Amman, Jordan.

TUQAN, Fadwa, Palestinian poet; born Nablus, Palestine; *Publications:* her volumes of poetry include *Wahdi ma a al-Ayyam,* 1955; *Wajadtuha; Atina Hubban; Languages:* Arabic, English; *Address:* c/o *Al-Arabi,* P O Box 748, Kuwait.

TURABI, Hassan Abdullah al-, Sudanese politician/lawyer; born 1930, Sudan; married; three sons, three daughters; *Religion:* Muslim; *Education:* LLB, Faculty of Law, University of Khartoum, Sudan, 1955; LLM, London University, London, England, 1957; Doctorat en Droit, Paris University, Paris, France, 1964; *Career:* Lecturer, Law Faculty, University of Khartoum, Sudan, 1957; Dean, Law Faculty, University of Khartoum, Sudan, 1964; Secretary General, Islamic Charter Front; member of the Constituent Assembly, 1965–68; Constitutional Expert in Sudan, 1967 and Gulf States, 1969; leading member of the the political opposition to President Nimeiri, 1969, terms of detention exceeding six years; elected member of Politbureau, Ruling Party, following national reconciliation; Attorney General, member of the Cabinet, 1978–; *Languages:* Arabic, English, French; *Address:* Attorney General's Office, P O Box 302, Khartoum, Sudan; Residence — P O Box 1515, Khartoum, Sudan.

TURKI, Abdul Aziz Abdullah al-, Saudi Arabian oil official; born 12 August 1936, Jeddah, Saudi Arabia; married; two children; *Religion:* Muslim; *Education;* BA in Business Administration, Cairo University, Egypt, 1964; *Career:* Banque de l'Indochine, 1949–52; American Embassy in Jeddah, 1953–54; ARAMCO, 1954–66; Director, Office of the Minister of Petroleum and Mineral Resources, 1966–68; Director of General Affairs, Directorate of Mineral Resources, 1968–70; Assistant Secretary General, OAPEC, 1970–75. Deputy Minister of Petroleum and Mineral Resources, 1975–; Secretary General, Supreme Advisory Council for Petroleum and Mineral Affairs; Saudi Arabia's Governor to OPEC; member of the Petromin Board of Directors; Vice President of the Executive Committee for the East-West Pipeline, Petroline; member of the Board of Directors of ARAMCO; Director of Arabian Oil Company Ltd; Chairman of the Board of Directors of Arab Maritime Petroleum Transport Co, AMPTC; *Interests and Recreations:* tennis, swimming; *Languages:* Arabic, English; *Address:* Ministry of Petroleum and Mineral Resources, P O Box 247, Riyadh 11191, Saudi Arabia.

TURKI, Abdul Rahman Ali al-, Saudi Arabian businessman; born 1930; *Religion:* Muslim; *Education:* BBA, USA; *Career:* Government Official, Ministry of Communications, Railroads and King Abdul Aziz Port; chairman of private businesses, a group of companies founded with foreign capital in Saudi Arabia, including industrial projects, engineering, pipe laying, dredging, industrial camp catering and adminstration, import of electronic, electrical, and construction materials, manufacturing of industrial goods related to oil and gas industries, and marine goods, shipping and transport; *Address:* P O Box 718, Dammam, Saudi Arabia; telephone: Office — 832 2579; Turki Trading and Shipping Co Ltd, 17a Curzon Street, London W1Y 7FE; telephone: (01) 491 3664; ATCO Development Incorporation, Memorial Towers, 5400, Memorial Drive, Suit 606, Houston, Texas 77007; telephone: (713) 880 1100; telex: 601067 TURKI SJ.

TURKI, Abdullah Bin Abdul Muhsin Bin Abdul Rahman al-, Saudi Arabian academic/ Islamic scholar; born 1940, Saudi Arabia; *Religion:* Muslim; *Education:* PhD, Islamic Jurisprudence; *Career:* several teaching posts; Inspector, Religious Colleges' and Institutes' Presidium; Lecturer, Faculty of Islamic Law (Shari'a), Riyadh University, Riyadh, Saudi Arabia; Dean, Faculty of Arabic Language and Social Sciences, Riyadh University; Vice Rector, The Islamic University of Imam Muhammad Ibn Saud, 1978–; *Publications:* various books in field of jurisprudence; several radio and television programmes; *Interests and Recreations:* reading; *Address:* The Islamic University of Imam Muhammad Ibn Saud, P O Box 5701, Riyadh, Saudi Arabia; telephone: 4042472; telex: 201166 UNIVER SJ.

TURKI BIN FAISAL, HRH Prince, Saudi Arabian Prince/businessman; born 1947; son of late King Faisal; married; *Religion:* Muslim; *Education:* Hun School, Princeton, USA; Laurenceville Academy, Georgetown, USA; postgraduate studies, London University, UK, 1973; *Career:* Counsellor to Royal Diocese, 1973–; Assistant to Kamal Adham, 1973–; *Address:* Royal Court, Riyadh, Saudi Arabia.

TURKI, Brahim, Tunisian diplomat; born 13 November 1930; married; three children; *Religion:* Muslim; *Education:* Licence in Law, France; *Career:* Ministry of Foreign Affairs, 1956; economic training with UN General Secretariat, 1959–60; Personal Private Secretary to the Prime Minister, 1961; rank of Minister, 1962; Consul General in Paris, 1962–63, Minister Counsellor, Embassy to Algeria, 1965–67; Director of Political Affairs, Ministry of Foreign Affairs, 1967–70; Ambassador to the Netherlands, 1970–74; Ambassador to UK, 1974–76; Secretary of State, Minister of Foreign Affairs, 1976; twice Tunisian delegate to the UN; has taken part in many Maghreb, Arab and African summit meetings; *Decorations:* Commander of the Order of the Tunisian Republic; Grand Cordon of the Dutch Order of Nassau; various other foreign decorations; *Languages:* Arabic, French, English; *Address:* Ministry of Foreign Affairs, Tunis, Tunisia; telephone: 260088.

TURKI, Fawaz, Palestinian writer; born 10 June 1940, near Haifa, Palestine; *Education:* Bournmouth College, Hampshire, UK; *Career:* teacher in Australia and Europe; employed with Victoria Education Department, Australia; travelled widely in India; now lives in Paris as teacher and writer;

Publications: The Disinherited: Journal of a Palestinian Exile, New York and London, 1972; *Languages:* Arabic, English, French.

TURKI, Kamaluddin Zaki al-, Egyptian diplomat; born 1920, Cairo, Egypt; married; *Religion:* Muslim; *Career:* served in Egyptian Air Force, 1958; Ministry of Foreign Affairs; Counsellor, Embassy to Libya, 1964; Consul General, Marseilles, 1964–66; Ambassador to Congo-Brazzaville, 1966–70; Ambassador to Denmark, 1970–73; Head of East European Department, Ministry of Foreign Affairs, 1973–74; Head of West European Department, 1974; *Languages:* Arabic, English; *Address:* Ministry of Foreign Affairs, Cairo, Egypt.

TURKI, Mansur Ibrahim al-, Saudi Arabian official/economist; born 1942; *Religion:* Muslim; *Education:* BSc in Economics and Political Science, University of Riyadh, Saudi Arabia, 1963; MSc in Economics, Colorado State University, Fort Collins, Colorado, USA, 1967; PhD in Economics, Colorado State University, Fort Collins, Colorado, 1971; course in Administration, University of Wisconsin, Madison; course in Marketing Management, International Marketing Institute, Cambridge, Mass, 1974; Honorary Doctor of Law, Wayne State University, Detroit, Michigan, USA, 1977; *Career:* Assistant Instructor, Department of Economics, University of Riyadh, 1963; Assistant Professor, Department of Economics, University of Riyadh, 1971; Vice Dean, College of Commerce, University of Riyadh, 1972–74; Economic Adviser, Ministry of Finance and National Economy, 1973–74; Co-ordinator, Saudi Arabian-USA Joint Commission on Economic Co-operation, 1974–; Deputy Minister of Finance and National Economy for Economic Affairs, 1974–70; President, University of Riyadh, Chairman, University Board, 1979–; member of the Technical Committee of the Supreme Council of Petroleum, 1974–79, Arab Experts on Economic Cooperation, the Arab League, Tunis, 1976–; Alternate Governor, International Monetary Fund, Washington D.C., 1977–79, Arab Fund for Economic Development in Africa, Khartoum, Sudan; Chairman of Sudan-Egyptian Construction Co, Cairo, Egypt, 1976–, National Shipping Co, 1978–80; Vice Chairman, the Saudi Company for Hotels and Resort Areas, Riyadh, 1975–78; member of the Board of the Arab Fund for Economic Development in Africa, Khartoum, Sudan, 1975–79, Saudi Company for Basic Industries, Riyadh, 1977–79, the Saudi Fund for Development, 1974–, General Petroleum and Minerals Organization, 1976–79, University of Petroleum and Minerals, Dharan, 1979–, Joint Saudi Arabian-USA Board of Solar Energy Project, 1977–, Saudi Arabian Joint Commissions on Economic Affairs with Bahrain, Kuwait, Taiwan, Riyadh, 1975–80, Supreme Coucil of Universities, Riyadh, 1979–; *Publications: Economic Theory and Islamic Economy; Removing Disbalance as Means of Increasing Agricultural Production; Decorations:* Grand Officier de l'Ordre de Léopold, Belgium; Order of Diplomatic Service, Republic of Korea; El Merito, Spain; Grand Officer of the First Order of Mauritania; Grand Cordon of the Order of the Brilliant Star Taiwan; Grand Cordon of the Brilliant Cloud Taiwan; *Interests and Recreations:* swimming, table tennis; *Address:* University of Riyadh, P O Box 2454, Riyadh, Saudi Arabia; telex: 201019 RUNIV SJ.

TUWAIJIRI, Ahmad Salih al-, Saudi Arabian official/economist; born 1942, Riyadh, Saudi Arabia; *Religion:* Muslim; *Education:* MA in Industrial Economics; Higher Diploma in Industrialization; *Career:* economic research staff member, Petroleum and Minerals Organisation (PETROMIN); Director, Industrial Research Department, Industrial Development and Research Centre; Director General of Industry, Ministry of Industry; Deputy Minister of Industry and Power, 1976–79; Chairman, Foreign Investment Committee; Vice Chairman, Managing Director, Saudi Consulting House, 1979–; Chairman of the Board of Directors of Saudi Kuwait Cement Co; member of the Board, Arab League Industrial Development Centre, Saudi Standardisation Organisation, Iron and Steel Plant, Jeddah; member of the Constituent Committee, the Foreign Investment Committee, the Technical Industrial Bureau; member of American Saudi Committee of Joint Co-operation and other committees; attended three UN (UNIDO) Conferences, Vienna, Austria, Conference on the Industrial Development of the Arab Countries, Libya, Wood Industries Development Conference, Vienna, Conference on the Message of the University, Riyadh; *Publications: Notes on Economics,* Institute of Public Administration; Study on the Influence of Customs Protection on National Industries; co-author of *Industrial Investment Directory of Saudi Arabia; Interests and Recreations:* riding, football, table tennis, reading; *Address:* P O Box 1267, Riyadh, Saudi Arabia; telephone: 448 4533, 448 4588.

U

UBAIDAT, Ahmad Abdul Majid, Jordanian politician; born 1938, Jordan; married; three sons, two daughters; *Religion:* Muslim; *Education:* BA in Law, Baghdad University, Iraq, 1960–61; *Career:* 1st Lieutenant in Public Security, 1961–64; Assistant Director of Intelligence Services, 1964–74; Director of Intelligence Services with rank of General, 1974–82; Minister of the Interior, 1982–; *Decorations:* Independence Medal, 4th Class, 1965; Renaissance Medal, 3rd Class, 1971 and 2nd Class, 1973; *Address:* Shmaisani, Amman, Jordan; telephone: 38949.

UBAIDI, Abdul Ati al-, Libyan politician; born 1943, Cyrenaica, Libya; married; *Religion:* Muslim; *Education:* University of Libya, Benghazi; University of Manchester, UK; *Career:* Lecturer in Economics and Social Studies, University of Libya, 1967; Minister of Labour and Social Affairs, 1970–74; Acting Minister of Foreign Affairs, 1970; Minister of Labour, and the Civil Service, 1974–77; Chairman of the General People's Committee, 1977; *Languages:* Arabic, English; *Address:* General People's Committee, Tripoli, Libya.

UJAILI, Abdul Salam al-, Syrian writer/politician; born 1918, Rakka, Syria; *Education:* medical degree, Damascus University, Damascus, Syria; *Career:* private medical practice, Rakka, Syria; Minister of Education, Foreign Affairs, Culture and Information, 1962; Deputy for Rakka, Syrian Parliament, 1947; leading exponent of short stories; *Publications:* large number of short stories published in Arabic; *Address:* P O Box 25, Rakka, Syria.

UMRAN, Ahmad al-, Bahraini politician/adviser to HH the Amir; born 1909, Bahrain; married; three children; *Religion:* Muslim; *Education:* American University of Beirut, Beirut, Lebanon, 1933; *Career:* Bahrain Electricity Department, 1936; Secretary of Muharraq Municipality, 1940; Director of Education, 1945; Director General of Education, 1960; appointed to State Council on its establishment in January, 1970; Minister of Education, 1971–73; Adviser to HH the Amir, 1973–; *Interests and Recreations:* fishing; *Languages:* Arabic, English; *Address:* Amiri Palace, P O Box 1, Manama, Bahrain; telephone: 661451, 661545.

URAISH, Mahmud Abdullah, People's Democratic Republic of Yemen diplomat/politician; born 1943, Rada, North Yemen; *Career:* entered oil industry with British Petroleum; active in trade union politics and was Secretary of the Caltex Branch of the General Union of Petroleum Workers; Acting General Secretary of Petroleum Workers' Union 1965; Finance Minister, 1967; Adviser to the President on Planning Affairs with rank of Minister, 1969; Acting Finance Minister, 1969; Deputy Prime Minister for Financial and Economic Affairs, 1969; Minister of Finance, 1971–74; Ambassador to German Democratic Republic, and non-resident Ambassador to Czechoslovakia, Poland and Hungary; member of the Central Committee; member of the People's Supreme Council; *Languages:* Arabic, English, German; *Address:* Ministry of Foreign Affairs, Aden, People's Democratic Republic of Yemen.

'USH, Muhammad Abul Faraj al-, Syrian academic; born 1916, Damascus, Syria; married; two sons, five daughters; *Religion:* Muslim; *Education:* Licence in History, University of Damascus, 1950; Diploma in Education, University of Damascus, 1950; Doctorate in History (Arabic Literature), University of Saint Joseph, Beirut, 1974; Seminar Training on Sasanian, Arab Sasanian and Islamic Coins, American Numismatic Society, New York, 1964–65;

Career: Director of Education, Deir al-Zor, Syria, 1950–51; Professor of History, Damascus, 1951–53; Curator of Islamic Art Section, National Museum of Damascus, 1953–55; Chief Curator, National Museum of Damascus, 1955–65; Director of the Historical Documents (Archives), Damascus, 1965–67; Director General of Antiquities and Museums, 1967; Chief Curator of the National Museum, Damascus, 1968–74; Professor of History and Archaeology, University of Qatar, 1974–; reporter for *Numismatic Literature,* Islamic Art Publications, SPA, New York; *Publications:* several books and researches on Islamic art, numismatics, archaeology and epigraphy, published in Arabic, French and English; *Interests and Recreations:* numismatics, Islamic art, Islamic history, epigraphy, travel, swimming; *Languages:* Arabic, French, English; *Address:* Muhajireen, Shamsiyyah, 5th Jeddah, 73 Damascus, Syria; telephone 333805, 669524.

UWAIDH, Ahmad Abdullah, Yemen Arab Republic official/businessman; born 1947, Hadramaut; married; one son; *Religion:* Muslim; *Education:* BA, Commerce, University of Damascus, Damascus, Syria; *Career:* Accountant, Internal Trading Co, Mukalla, 1971–72; Director of Finance and Administration, Directorate of Trade; Deputy Director General for Finance and Administration, Internal Trading Co 1974–79, Acting Director General, 1979–; *Interests and Recreations:* arts, swimming, table-tennis, Arabic literature; *Languages:* Arabic, English; *Address:* Internal Trading Co, Sana'a, Yemen Arab Republic.

W

WADUD, Muhammad al-, Yemen Arab Republic politician/physician; born 1930, near Taiz, Yemen Arab Republic; *Religion:* Muslim; *Education:* MD, University of Prague, Czechoslovakia; *Career:* practised at Taiz Hospital, 1965–66; Minister of Health, 1968–69, and 1974–75; Director of Health for Taiz, 1969–74; *Languages:* Arabic, English; *Address:* Ministry of Health, Sana'a, Yemen Arab Republic.

WAHAIBI, Khalfan Bin Nasr al-, Omani politician/administrator; born 1940; *Religion:* Muslim; *Education:* secondary education in Qatar; *Career:* Qatari Department of Health, 1964; Petroleum Development, Oman; Trade Relations Manager, Petroleum Development, Oman; Acting Minister of Education, 1973; Minister of Social Affairs and Labour, 1973–80; *Languages:* Arabic, English; *Address:* Ministry of Social Affairs and Labour, P O Box 560, Muscat, Oman; telephone: 702233.

WAHBY, Muhammad, Egyptian diplomat/writer; born 7 March 1934, Cairo, Egypt; married; *Religion:* Muslim; *Education:* BA, English Literature, Cairo University, Cairo, Egypt, 1955; MA, Political Science, New Delhi University, India, 1964; *Career:* Arab League, Cairo; Press Attaché, Arab League Office, New Delhi, India, 1961–65; Deputy Chief Representative, Arab League Office, New Delhi, 1965–70; Acting Chief Representative, Arab League Office, New Delhi, 1970–72; Director, Information and Planning, Arab League Office, Cairo, 1972–74; Acting Director, Arab League Office, London, 1974–76; Deputy Director, Arab League Office, London, 1976–79; Elizabeth Collard Grant (for research and publications), for the improvement of Arab-European relations, 1979; Consulting Editor, *Middle East Economic Digest,* 1979–80; Press Attaché, Egypt, Embassy to Federal Republic of Germany,

1980–; talks and lectures on Arab affairs in Britain, India, and other European countries; Editor of *Al-Arab,* New Delhi (English monthly magazine), 1965–72; member of the Strategic Studies Institute, London; *Publications:* articles published in *Rose al Yousef, National Herald, Patriot Arab Socialism,* New Delhi, 1966; *Arab Quest for Peace,* New Delhi, 1971; co-author *West Asian Crisis,* 1967; *Meerut,* 1968; *Interests and Recreations:* violin, squash, swimming, literature, theatre; *Languages:* Arabic, English, French; *Address:* Embassy of Egypt, Kronprinzenstrasse 2, 53 Bonn 2, Federal Republic of Germany.

WAHID, Rida, Lebanese politician/physician; born 1920, Tyre, Lebanon; married; *Religion:* Muslim; *Education:* Medical Education in Lebanon; *Career:* practiced as a physician, 1950–60; Head of Lebanese Delegation to the BIT, 1960–67; elected Deputy for Tyre, left Parliament in 1960; Minister of Labour and Social Affairs, February 1964, and September of the same year, during the Presidency of Charles Helou, and remaining as Director General at the Ministry of Health; Minister of Health, the last two months of Rashid Karami's Cabinet, 1966; Consultant Delegate to the BIT, Tehran, Iran, for Medical Care Branch, 1975; Director General of Social Security Scheme, 1967; *Decorations:* Chevalier of the Légion d'Honneur and various other decorations; *Languages:* Arabic, French; *Address:* Caisse Nationale de Sécurité Sociale, Beirut, Lebanon; Residence — Rue Karm Ghazzaoni, Beirut, Lebanon; telephone: 243660.

WAJIH, Muhammad Abdul Khadim al-, Yemen Arab Republic official; born 1940, Zabid, Yemen Arab Republic; *Religion:* Muslim; *Education:* UK, 1960–62; BSc Economics, University of London, UK,

1962–65; *Career:* on return to Yemen entered National Assembly; Director General, Yemen Petroleum Company, 1971; Director General of the Bajil Cement Factory, 1971–75; Minister of Agriculture in Administration of Abdul Aziz Abdul Ghani, 1975; *Languages:* Arabic, English; *Address:* Ministry of Agriculture, Sana'a, Yemen Arab Republic.

WAKIL, Abdul Wahid al-, Egyptian businessman/architect; born 7 August 1943, Giza, Egypt; *Religion:* Muslim; *Education:* BSc, Faculty of Engineering, Ain Shams University, Cairo, Egypt; *Career:* Lecturer, Department of Architecture, Ain Shams University, 1965; worked with Professor Hassan Fathy for Ministry of Culture and Ministry of Tourism on various projects and research, 1970; began to work privately designing palaces and private residences in indigenous style, developing traditional style in building industry; *Publications:* article on *Modern Concepts of Arab Architecture, Arab News,* Jeddah, June 1976; *Construire Comme Nos Aieux,* Safa, Beirut 1972; *Interests and Recreations:* music, sailing; *Languages:* Arabic, English, French; *Address:* 27 Mohammed Kamel Morsi, Dokki, Cairo, Egypt; telephone: 705564.

WAKIL, Muhammad al-, Arab-American academic/nuclear engineer; born 9 March 1921, Alexandria, Egypt; divorced; one son, one daughter; *Education:* BS, University of Cairo, Cairo, Egypt, 1943; MS, University of Wisconsin, Madison, USA, 1947; PhD, University of Wisconsin, Wisconsin, 1949; *Career:* Lecturer, University of Alexandria, Alexandria, Egypt, 1950–52; Research Associate, University of Wisconsin, Wisconsin, USA, 1954–55; Assistant Professor, University of Minnesota, USA, 1954–55; Associate Professor, University of Wisconsin, 1957–61; Professor of Mechanical and Nuclear Engineering, 1961; member of American Society for Mechanical Engineers, American Nuclear Society, American Society for Engineering Education, Combustion Institute; *Publications: Nuclear Power Engineering,* 1962; *Nuclear Heat Transport,* 1971 (Japanese translation 1972); *Nuclear Energy Conversion,* 1971 (Japanese translation 1975); also contributed articles to professional journals; *Decorations:* award of Meritorious Paper, American Society of Mechanical Engineering, 1952; award for Excellence in Instruction of Engineers, American Society of Mechani-

cal Engineers, 1969; Benjamin Smith Reynolds Award, University of Wisconsin, USA, 1970; Distinguished Teaching Award, Nuclear Engineering Division, American Society of Engineers, 1971; American Nuclear Society, Arthur Holly Compton Award 1979; Fulbright Scholar, 1966, 1978; *Interests and Recreations:* member Sigma Xi, Pi Tau Sigma, Tau Beta Pi; *Languages:* Arabic, English; *Address:* 1010 Edgehill Drive, Madison, Wisconsin, W1 53705, USA.

WAKIL, Rahim al-, Iraqi artist/sculptor; born 30 June 1936, Iraq; married; *Religion:* Muslim; *Education:* Diploma, Fine Arts Institute, Baghdad, Iraq, 1954–59; National Diploma of Design and Sculpture, Chelsea College of Arts, London, England, 1960–65; *Career:* Head, Department of Sculpture and Art Adviser, National Museum, Baghdad, Iraq, 1965–71; Lecturer, Institute of Fine Arts, Baghdad, 1971–; member of Iraqi Artists Union, International Association of Arts, Baghdad Group; actively involved in the organisation of the National Museum prior to its opening, 1966; *Interests and Recreations:* display, illumination, preservation of antiquities display, interior design; *Languages:* Arabic, English; *Address:* Institute of Fine Arts, Mansour, Baghdad, Iraq.

WAL, Michael, Sudanese politician; born in Upper Nile Province, Sudan; *Education:* BA, MSc, New York State, USA; *Career:* member of the Sudan African National Union, in 1960s; participated in the Addis Ababa negotiations, 1972; Regional Minister for Cabinet Affairs, 1972–73; stood unsuccessfully for the Regional Assembly Elections in the Intellectuals Constituency, 1973; Chairman of the Regional Development Corporation, 1973; *Languages:* Arabic, English; *Address:* c/o Regional People's Assembly, Juba, Sudan.

WALI, Ibrahim al-, Iraqi diplomat; born 1930, Baghdad, Iraq; married; three children; *Career:* entered Ministry of Foreign Affairs; 2nd Secretary, Geneva, Switzerland, 1959; Embassy to Yugoslavia, 1962; Embassy to Yemen Arab Republic, 1964; Embassy to Stockholm; Chief of Protocol at Republican Palace, 1966; Embassy to Yugoslavia, 1966; Embassy to Kuwait, 1970; Minister, Embassy to France, 1972; Director General of Ministry of Foreign Affairs Political Department,

1974; *Languages:* Arabic, English, French, Swedish; *Address:* Ministry of Foreign Affairs, Baghdad, Iraq.

WANNOUS, Mounir, Syrian Arab League official/engineer; born 1934, Tripoli, Lebanon; *Education:* civil engineering studies, Damascus and France; *Career:* Deputy Minister for Technical Affairs, Ministry of Municipal and Rural Affairs, 1964–70; Minister of Euphrates Dam, 1970–74; consultancy and contracting office (private practice), 1974–80; Director General, The Standing Conference on Housing and Town Planning, League of Arab States, Tunis, 1980–83; *Languages:* Arabic, French; *Address:* League of Arab States, Avenue Khereddine Pacha, Tunis, Tunisia; telephone: 890211; PO Box 4731, Damascus, Syria.

WARRAD, Faik, Palestinian politician; born 1920, Tilfit, near Nablus, Jordan; *Career:* member of Communist Party, late 1930s; active after 1948 in West Bank politics; manager, the National Bloc newspaper *Al-Jabha* in the election campaign of September 1954; elected to Jordanian Parliament as member for Ramallah, 1956; leader of the Ansar, newly formed commando group (Partisans), 1970; member of the Palestine National Council, 1971; accompanied Yassir Arafat on visit to Moscow, 1974.

WARZAZI, Halima Embarek, Moroccan diplomat; born 1933, Casablanca, Morocco; married; *Religion:* Muslim; *Education:* Licence in Literature, Cairo University, Cairo, Egypt; *Career:* joined Ministry of Foreign Afffairs, 1957; Cultural Attaché, Embassy of Morocco to the USA, 1959; member of the Moroccan Delegation to the UN General Assembly, 1959–81; joined Ministry of Health, 1962; returned to Ministry of Foreign Affairs, member of the Minister's Office, 1964; President of the Social Affairs Committee, of UN General Assembly, 1966; member of the International Institute of Human Rights; member of the International Civil Service Commission of the UN; former member of the Committee of Experts on Elimination of Racial Discriminations; former member of the Commission on the Status of Women; member of the Subcommission Against Discriminatory Measures and of the Protection of Minorities; *Languages:* Arabic, French, Spanish, English; *Address:* c/o Ministry of Foreign Affairs, Rabat, Morocco.

WAZEN, Anwar E., Lebanese banker; born 31 July 1947; married; one daughter; *Religion:* Christian; *Education:* Licence in Economics, University of St. Joseph, Beirut, Lebanon; *Career:* Banking, 1973–; currently with CITICORP International Group; voting member of the Association of International Bond Dealers, 1978; *Interests and Recreations:* tennis; *Languages:* Arabic, English, French, German; *Address:* CITIBANK, P O Box 545, Manama, Bahrain; telephone: 257184, 257193.

WAZIR, Khalil al-, (Abu Jihad), Palestinian politician; born 1936, Acre, Palestine; *Career:* colleague of Yassir Arafat, 1950s; joined the group which later became nucleus of Al-Fatah; worked in the Gulf, 1960s; moved to Algiers to supervise Fatah training camp, 1964; accompanied Arafat on first Fatah mission to China, 1964; since 1964 has been responsible for the organization and training of Fatah forces.

WAZIR, Muhammad Abdul Kaddus al-, Yemen Arab Republic diplomat; born 1932, Yemen Arab Republic; *Religion:* Muslim; *Education:* American University of Beirut, Lebanon; *Career:* Ministry of Foreign Affairs, 1959; Yemeni Legation, Italy, 1959; attended Haradh Conference as royalist delegation, 1966; Ambassador to Lebanon, accredited to Jordan, Pakistan, Turkey, 1975–78; Ambassador to Jordan, 1978–79; Ambassador to Bonn, accredited to Berne, Vienna, The Hague, EEC, Brussels, 1979–; *Languages:* Arabic, English, Italian; *Address:* Embassy of Yemen Arab Republic, Kraterstrasse 7, 5300 Bonn 2, West Germany.

WAZZAN, Chafiq al-, Lebanese politician/lawyer; born 1925, Beirut, Lebanon; married; two sons; *Religion:* Muslim; *Education:* Law Degree, University of St. Joseph, Beirut, Lebanon; *Career:* lawyer since 1947; candidate in 1964 elections; elected Deputy for Beirut, 1968; defeated 1972; former leader with Amin al-Uraissi of the National Organization Party; Minister of Justice, 1969; Prime Minister, 1980–; *Interests and Recreations:* social affairs, discus-throwing; Vice President of the Law and Political Science Faculty Alumni Association; *Languages:* Arabic, French; *Address:* Office — Rue du Parlement, Immeuble Asseyli, Beirut,

Lebanon; telephone: 254345; Residence — Rue Haroun el-Rashid, Immeuble Wazzan, Beirut, Lebanon.

WIEU, Andrew W. Riang, Sudanese politician/administrator; born 1928, Malakal District, Sudan; *Education:* School of Public Administration, Khartoum University College, Khartoum, Sudan, 1954; graduate studies, Wheaton College, Illinois, USA, 1976–77; Honorary LLD, Wheaton College, USA, 1977; MA, International Development and Human Needs, The American University, School of International Service, Washington D.C., USA; *Career:* various administrative and judicial posts: Local Government Inspector, 1956–64; Minister of Agriculture, 1965; member of the Constituent Assembly, 1968–69; Land Inspector, Southern Region, 1970–72; member of National People's Assembly, Deputy Speaker, 1972–73; Minister, Department of Inter-departmental Coordination, 1973–75; Minister, Presidential Administrative and Financial Affairs, 1975–76; various committees and commissions, Ministry of Southern Affairs Advisory Committee, Public Service Administrative Reform Committee, Southern Sudan Relief and Resettlement Commission, Sudan Socialist Union Central Committee; *Decorations:* The Order of the Two Niles, 2nd Class, Sudan, 1972; Order of the Republic, 2nd Class, Sudan, 1975; Order of Merit, Great Officer, Senegal, 1975; Order of Marib,

Yemen Arab Republic, 1976; *Address:* Development Extension and Consultancy Services, P O Box 533, Khartoum, Sudan.

WISHAHI, Hussain Ali, businessman/electrical engineer; born 1934; *Education:* BSc, Electrical Engineering, Illinois University, Urbana, USA; *Career:* Head, Planning Department, Riyadh Electrical Company; Manager, Electrical Construction Department, Dammam Electric Company; Owner and Manager, the Electrical Engineering Office, Riyadh; *Interests and Recreations:* swimming, shooting, reading, travel; *Address:* P O Box 1599, Riyadh, Saudi Arabia; telephone: Office — Riyadh 448 6400; Residence — 402 5299.

WOL WOL, Lawrence, Sudanese politician; born 1936, Sudan; *Education:* University of Khartoum, Sudan; subsequently in East Africa; Fribourg University, Switzerland; Bordeaux University, France; *Career:* Secretary of the Anyanya Movement delegation at the Addis Ababa negotiations, 1971–72; Minister of State for Planning, 1972; Minister of Planning, 1973; member of the Political Bureau of the Sudanese Socialist Union (SSU), 1972; elected to the Regional Assembly for Gogrial East, 1973; Head of the Regional Ministry of Commerce, Industry and Supply, 1973; *Languages:* Arab, English, French; *Address:* Regional Ministry of Commerce, Industry and Supply, Juba, Sudan.

Y

YACOUB, George, Iraqi UN official/lawyer; born 9 February 1923, Iraq; married; three sons, one daughter; *Religion:* Christian; *Education:* LLB, Baghdad Law College, Baghdad, Iraq, 1948; Postgraduate studies, Yale University and University of Michigan, USA, 1953–55; *Career:* private law practice and freelance journalism, 1948–53; editor and broadcaster, Baghdad, Beirut, London, 1955–59; Public Information Division, UNICEF, New York, 1959–62; Press and Publications Division, New York, 1962–65; Director, UN Information Centre, Karachi, Islamabad, 1968–72; Press and Publications Division, Office of Public Information, New York, 1972–73; Chief of Policy and Programmes Section, Information Centre Service, New York, 1974; UN Spokesman, UN Forces, Cyprus, 1974–81; Principal Officer, UN Radio and Visual Services, New York, 1981–; *Publications:* numerous articles and editorials in Baghdad, Beirut newspapers, 1948–59; *Interests and Recreations:* jogging, tennis, reading, writing essays and political articles, music; *Languages:* Arabic, English, some Turkish and Kurdish; *Address:* Room 827B, United Nations Plaza, New York, NY 10017, USA; telephone: (212) 754 1234.

YACOUB, Magdi, Egyptian surgeon/pioneer in heart transplant; born 1936, Egypt; married; three children; *Education:* Cairo Medical School, Cairo University, Cairo, Egypt; *Career:* Cairo University Medical School Hospital, Cairo, Egypt; Brompton Hospital, London, England; National Heart Hospital (where he worked under Mr Donald Ross, pioneer heart transplant surgeon), London, England; Assistant professor, Chicago Medical School (where he studied the techniques of Professor Norman Shumway of California), Chicago, USA; Harefield Hospital (where he formed a team for heart transplant surgery), Middlesex, England, 1969–; *Publications:* numerous papers and articles in the field of heart transplant surgery and cardiovascular diseases; *Languages:* Arabic, English; *Address:* 24 Upper Wimpole Street, London W1M 7TA, England; telephone: 01 935 6223.

YAFI, Abdul Karim Tawfik, Syrian academic; born 1919, Homs, Syria; married; one son, one daughter; *Religion:* Muslim; *Education:* Bachelor of Arts; Bachelor of Science; PhD, Arts and Science; *Career:* Professor of Sociology and Demography, University of Damascus, Syria; member of Arab Academy of Syria; member of the International Union for the Scientific Study of Population; *Languages:* Arabic, French, English; *Address:* 77 Abdel Munim Street, Malky, Damascus, Syria; telephone: 712606.

YAFI, Abdullah al-, Lebanese politician; born 1901, Beirut, Lebanon; married; four children; *Education:* Doctorate in Law, Faculty of Law, University of Paris, France; *Career:* Barrister at Law, Beirut, 1926; elected Deputy for Beirut, 1932; Prime Minister and Minister of Justice, 1938–39; member of the Lebanese Delegation to the Arab League Preparatory Conference, 1944; member of the Lebanese Delegation to the UN Charter Conference, San Francisco, USA, 1945; Minister of Justice, 1946–47; Prime Minister and Minister of the Interior, Defence and Information, 1953–54; Prime Minister and Minister of the Interior, 1956 and Minister of Planning, 1956; Prime Minister and Minister of Information, 1966; Prime Minister and Minister of Defence, 1968; re-elected Deputy for Beirut, 1968; Prime Minister, Minister of Finance, Education, Social Affairs and Information, 1968–69; member of National Dialogue Committee, 1975–; *Decorations:* Grand Cordon, Lebanese Order of Merit; as well as many other foreign and local distinctions and decorations; *Languages:*

Arabic, French; *Address:* Office — Riad al-Solh Street, Beirut, Lebanon; Residence -- Fouad I Street, Beirut, Lebanon.

YAFI, Muhammad Salim al-, Syrian Arab League official/diplomat; born 21 December 1920; *Religion:* Muslim; *Education:* LLB, Damascus University, Syria; *Career:* Ministry of Supply, 1943–45; Ministry of Foreign Affairs, 1945; Attaché, Embassy to Egypt, 1945; Attaché, Embassy to Turkey, 1946; Consul in Mersin, Turkey, 1949; Chargé d'Affaires, Embassy to Saudi Arabia, 1952; Ministry of Foreign Affairs, 1954; Director General, Arab Palestinian Organization; Delegate to Consultative Committee UN Relief and Works Agency (UNRWA), 1954; Chargé d'Affaires, Embassy to Switzerland, 1956; Assistant Secretary General, Ministry of Social and Labour Affairs, 1958–62; Director General, Palestinian Refugees Organization, 1958–62; member of United Arab Republic Higher Council of Radio and Television, 1959–62; Counsellor for Palestinian Affairs, Ministry of Foreign Affairs, 1962; Director of Arab Affairs, Ministry of Foreign Affairs; Director of Administrative and Cultural Affairs, Ministry of Foreign Affairs, 1962; Lecturer, Faculty of Commerce, Damascus University, 1962–64; Minister, Embassy to France, 1964–65; Minister, Chargé d'Affaires, Ambassador to Belgium, 1966–68; Director of European Affairs, Ministry of Foreign Affairs, 1968; Assistant Secretary General for Political Affairs, 1969; Assistant Minister of Foreign Affairs, 1970; Assistant Secretary General of the Arab League, 1970; President of Conciliation Committees of Jordan, 1970, Oman, 1971, Yemen, 1972–73; *Publications: A Study of the Palestinian Question and its Evolution,* 1961; *Languages:* Arabic, French; *Address:* c/o Arab League, Avenue Khereddine Pacha, Tunis, Tunisia; telephone: 890 211.

YAGHI, Abdul Rahman Abdul Wahaab, Jordanian academic/linguistic expert; born 1924, Palestine; married; four children; *Religion:* Muslim; *Education:* BA, MA, PhD in Arabic Literature, 1950–60; *Career:* International Expert with UNESCO for Arabic Language, 1962–64; Full Professor of Modern Arabic Literature, Faculty of Arts, University of Jordan, Amman, 1964–; President of Jordanian Society of Writers, 1979–; member of the Jordanian Committee of the World Peace Council; *Publications:* thirty books published in Beirut, Cairo, Amman (Arabic); *The Soldier who Dreamt of White Lilies* (translated into English); articles on Arabic literature published in the *Year Book of Encyclopaedia Britannica,* 1975–76; seven books translated from English into Arabic; *Interests and Recreations:* modern Arabic literature, swimming, tennis; *Languages:* Arabic, English; *Address:* Faculty of Arts, University of Jordan, Amman, Jordan.

YAGHI, Hashim Abdul Wahab, Jordanian academic; born 1921, Palestine; married; two sons, one daughter; *Religion:* Muslim; *Education:* Bachelor, MA and PhD in Arabic Literature, Cairo University, 1951–60; *Career:* Lecturer, University of Libya, 1960–61; Lecturer, King Abdul Aziz University, Saudi Arabia, 1961–62; Lecturer, Associate Professor, Full Professor, Jordan University, 1962–; taught at Kuwait University, 1975–77; Dean of Scientific Research and Higher Studies, Jordan University, 1978–80; *Publications: The Outlook of the Modern Lebanese Society,* 1964 (Arabic); *Our Culture in Fifty Years; Criticism in Modern Literature; Schools of Modern Criticism;* and other books on literature; *Interests and Recreations:* music, walking, poetry; *Languages:* Arabic, English; *Address:* Faculty of Arts, Jordan University, Amman, Jordan; telephone: Office — 843555; Residence — 37025.

YAHIA, Anis Hassan, People's Democratic Republic of Yemen politician; born 1935, Aden; *Career:* various teaching posts; actively involved in the Independence Movement; elected to Political Bureau of National Front Party, 1975; Minister of Economy and Industry, 1971–73; Minister of Communications, 1973–75; member of the People's Supreme Council; Vice Chairman of Presidium of Yemen's Council for Peace and Solidarity, 1976; Secretary, Central Committee, Department of Economic Affairs, 1976–79; Minister of Fishery Resources, 1979–; *Address:* Ministry of Fishery Resources, Aden, People's Democratic Republic of Yemen.

YALA, Muhammad Hadj, Algerian politician/diplomat; *Religion:* Muslim; *Career:* diplomat for Provisional Government before Independence; Assistant Representative, Belgrade, Yugoslavia; Representative in Prague, Czechoslovakia; travelled widely in

USSR and Eastern Europe; Head of Eastern Europe Division, Ministry of Foreign Affairs after Independence; Ambassador to Guinea, 1963; Ambassador to People's Republic of China, 1964; Préfet of Algiers, 1965; Préfet of Constantine, 1970; Wali of Constantine; Minister of Commerce, 1977–80, Minister of Interior, 1980–; President of Franco-Algerian Society; *Languages:* Arabic, French; *Address:* Ministry of Interior, Palais du Gouvernement, Algiers, Algeria; telephone: 630465/7.

YAMANI, Ahmad, (Abu Mahir), Palestinian politician; born 1925; *Career:* one of the original supporters of George Habbash in the Arab Nationalist Movement; led the Palestinian section which formed Abtal al-Auda (Heroes of the Return), 1966; was one of the founders of the Popular Front for the Liberation of Palestine (PFLP), 1967; Secretary General of the Palestine Workers' Federation in mid-1960s; Head of the Tripoli, Libya Office of the PFLP, 1969; commanded PFLP with Wadia Haddad, 1970, in Jordan during the temporary absence of George Habbash; elected to the Executive Committee of the Palestinian Liberation Organization (PLO) as representative of the PFLP, 1973; led delegation from PLO to Peking to request Chinese support, 1973; Head of PFLP during illness of George Habbash, 1973; left PLO Executive Committee when the PFLP withdrew from the PLO, 1973; accompanied Yassir Arafat on visit to Moscow, 1973; Head of PLO Popular Organization, 1974.

YAMANI, Muhammad Abdullah Abdu, Saudi Arabian politician/academic; born 1939, Mecca, Saudi Arabia; married; three sons, one daughter; *Religion:* Muslim; *Education:* BSc, Geology, University of Riyadh, 1963; MSc and PhD, Geology, Cornell University, USA, 1968; Diploma and special course in University Administration, Wisconsin University, USA; *Career:* Professor, University of Riyadh; Deputy Dean, College of Science, Riyadh University; Deputy Minister of Education for Technical Affairs; Vice Rector, King Abdul Aziz University, Jeddah; Rector, King Adul Aziz University; Minister of Information, 1975–83; *Publications: The Difficult Equation,* (Arabic); *Economic Geology in Saudi Arabia,* (Arabic); *Unidentified Flying Object (UFO),* (Arabic); and other publications; *Interests and Recreations:* reading, football, writing short stories

and novels; UFO research; *Languages:* Arabic, English; *Address:* c/o Ministry of Information, Riyadh, Saudi Arabia; telephone: 4024343.

YAMANI, Shaikh Ahmad Zaki, Saudi Arabian politician; born 30 June 1930, Mecca, Saudi Arabia; *Religion:* Muslim; *Education:* LLB, Cairo University, 1951; MA, Comparative Law, New York University, USA; PhD, Harvard University, USA, 1955–56; Honorary PhD, Nihon University, Japan 1969; Honorary PhD, Osmania University, India, 1975; *Career:* Legal Adviser, established one of the first private legal practices in Saudi Arabia, 1956; Legal Adviser to Oil Department, Tax Department, Ministry of Finance, 1956–58; Legal Adviser to Council of Ministers, 1958–60; Minister of State, 1962; member, Council of Ministers, 1960; Minister of Petroleum and Mineral Resources, 1962–; Director, Arabian American Oil Company (Aramco), 1962; Chairman of Board of Directors, General Petroleum and Minerals Organization, 1963–; Chairman of Board of Directors, Saudi Arabian Fertiliser Co, 1966–; Secretary General, Organization of Arab Petroleum Exporting Countries, 1968–69; Chairman, Saudi Arabian-Sudanese Joint Commission for Exploitation of the Red Sea Resources, 1974; President, the Supreme Consultative Council for Petroleum and Mineral Affairs, 1975; member of several international law associations; *Publications: Islamic Law and Contemporary Issues,* in English and Arabic; *Interests and Recreations:* music, astrology; *Languages:* Arabic, English; *Address:* Ministry of Petroleum and Mineral Resources, P O Box 247, Riyadh, Saudi Arabia; telephone: 4762552; telex: 200997 PETROL SJ.

YAQUB, Adil Muhammad, Arab-American academic/mathematician; born 19 January 1928, Nablus, Jordan; married; two children; *Education:* AB, University of California, Berkeley, USA, 1950; MA, 1951; PhD, 1955; *Career:* Instructor, Purdue University, West Lafayette, Indiana, USA, 1955–57; Assistant Professor, 1957–60; Associate Professor of Mathematics, University of California, Santa Barbara, USA, 1960–67, Professor, 1967–; member of the American Mathematics Society, Mathematics Association of America, and of Sigma Xi, Pi Mu Epsilon; *Publications: Introduction to Linear and Abstract Algebra,* 1971; contributor to research articles in professional and mathematical journals; *Address:* 602 Litchfield Lane, Santa Barbara, CA 93109, USA.

YASSIN, Al-Sayyid, Egyptian academic/writer; born 9 March 1933, Alexandria, Egypt; married; two sons, one daughter; *Religion:* Muslim; *Education:* Licence in Law, Alexandria University, Egypt, 1957; MSc in Criminology, Institute of Criminology; *Career:* Research Assistant, National Institute of Criminology, 1957; Researcher, National Institute of Criminology, 1960; Expert, National Institute for Social and Criminal Research (Head of Criminal Behaviour Unit), 1967; Director of the Political and Strategic Studies Centre, Cairo, 1975–; part-time Lecturer, College of Information, Cairo University; Lecturer, Institute of Research and Arabic Studies, Cairo; Professor of Sociology (seconded), American University in Cairo; *Publications: Foundations of Social Research,* Cairo; *Studies in Criminal Behaviour and Treatment of Criminals,* Cairo; *Social Analysis of Literature,* Cairo; *Contemporary Criminal Policy,* Cairo; *The Arabic Personality between Israeli and the Arabic Understanding,* Cairo; *Interests and Recreations:* tennis; *Languages:* Arabic, English, French; *Address:* American University of Cairo, 113 Kasr al-Aini Street, Cairo, Egypt.

YASSIN, Anas Yussuf, Saudi Arabian diplomat; born 1 May 1934, Taif, Saudi Arabia; married; two children; *Education:* Victoria College, Alexandria, Egypt, 1944–52; University of California, California, USA, 1954–56; Honorary Doctorate, University of Osmania, Hyderabad, India; *Career:* Director, National Gibson Company, Riyadh, Saudi Arabia, 1958–59; Chairman, Arab Trading Company, 1959–61; founder, Al-Nasr Trading Office, Jeddah, 1962; Foreign Ministry, 1963; member, Saudi Arabian Delegation to 19th General Assembly of United Nations with rank of Ambassador, 1964; Foreign Ministry, Jeddah, Saudi Arabia; Delegate, 21st General Assembly of United Nations; Ambassador to India, 1968; *Address:* Ministry of Foreign Affairs, P O Box 495, Jeddah, Saudi Arabia; telephone: 6421917; telex: 401104 KHARJI SJ.

YASSIN, Badr al-, Kuwaiti financial official; born 1938, Kuwait; married; *Religion:* Muslim, *Education:* Mubarakiyah School, Kuwait; Cairo University, Egypt; accountancy studies; *Career:* Assistant Under Secretary, Ministry of Finance, Ministry of Commerce; Head of the Kuwait Investment Office, London, 1965; Founder and Head of Kuwait Auditing Office; *Languages:* Arabic, English; *Address:* Kuwait Auditing Office, P O Box 2115, Safat, Kuwait.

YASSIN, Muhammad Othman, Sudanese UN official; born 1915; *Religion:* Muslim; *Education:* BSc in Economics, London School of Economics, UK; *Career:* joined Sudanese Political Service, 1945; Liaison Officer, Ethiopia, 1952–53; Governor of Upper Nile Province, 1954–55; Permanent Under Secretary of Foreign Affairs, 1956–65; member of Sudanese delegation to UN, 1956; Delegate to Independent African States Conference, Monrovia, Liberia, 1969; delegate to Conference on Positive Action for Peace and Security in Africa, Accra, Ghana, 1960; delegate to Independent African States Conference, Leopoldville, Congo, 1960; Special Adviser to UN on training of diplomats, 1961–62; Special Envoy to Ethiopia and Somalia on border dispute; member of Organization of African Unity (OAU), Committee for Conciliation between Algeria and Morocco; organizer of first African Finance Ministers Conference, Khartoum, 1963; joined UN Office of Technical Co-operation, 1966; Resident Representative, UN Development Programme (UNDP), Jordan, 1970–75; Chairman, Board of Directors, Sudan Commercial Bank, 1975; *Publications: The Sudan Civil Service,* 1954; *Analysis of the Economic Situation in the Sudan,* 1958; *Problems of the Transfer of Power: the Administration Aspect,* 1961; *Germany and Africa,* 1962; in Arabic; *The Poet's Ballads, Tewfiq the Poet; Decorations:* Knight of Great Rank of Humane Order of African Redemption of Liberia; Grand Officer of Order of African Redemption of Liberia; Grand Officer of Order of Menelik II, Ethiopia; Order of Egyptian Republic; Star of Yugoslavia; First Order of Jordanian Independence; *Languages:* Arabic, English; *Address:* Sudan Commercial Bank, P O Box 1116, Khartoum, Jordan; Residence — P O Box 2201, Khartoum, Sudan.

YASSIN, Salim Said, Syrian politician/academic; born 10 October 1937, Lattakia, Syria; married; three daughters, two sons; *Education:* BA, University of Damascus,

Syria, 1960; MA, Economics, University of Colorado, USA, 1963; PhD, 1965; *Career:* Director, Lattakia Petroleum Installation, 1960–61; Civil Service, 1961–65; Assistant Professor of Economics, University of Aleppo, Syria, 1966–70; Vice Dean, Faculty of Commerce, University of Aleppo, 1967–69; Vice President, then Acting President, 1969–71; Associate Professor of Economics; President of University of Lattakia, Syria, 1971–78; Minister of Transport, 1978–80; Minister of Planning, 1980–82; Minister of Economy and Foreign Trade, 1982; member of the Supreme Board of Syrian Universities, 1969–78, National Planning Institution, 1971–, Technical Commission Union of Arab Universities, 1970–78; Syrian People's Council, 1971–73; *Publications: The Theory of Correlation,* 1968; *International Trade,* 1970; *Address:* Baghdad Street, Lattakia, Syria; Ministry of Economy and Foreign Trade, Damascus, Syria.

YATA, Ali, Moroccan politician/journalist; born 1920, Tangier, Morocco; married; *Religion:* Muslim; *Career:* Secretary General of Communist Party of Morocco, 1945; Editor of *Al Mukafih,* later of *Al Kifah Al Watani;* founder of the Party of Liberation and Socialism; founder of newspaper *Al Bayaan,* November 1972; founder of Party of Progress and Socialism, 1974; *Languages:* Arabic, French; *Address:* P O Box 152, Casablanca, Morocco; telephone: 222 238.

YATEEM, Hussain Ali, Bahraini businessman; born 1914; married; two sons, three daughters; *Religion:* Muslim; *Education:* Bahrain, and Brighton Grammar School, England; *Career:* involved in first oil concession in Bahrain, 1932; established first water distillation and ice plant, 1938; opened plants for industrial gas; general agencies (Carrier Brown Boveri); Chairman of A.M. Yateem Brothers; former President, Bahrain Chamber of Commerce and Bahrain Red Crescent Society; Director of Bank of Bahrain, Bahrain Slipway Company Ltd and Gulf Hotels; founding member of Gulf Aviation Company Limited; *Interests and Recreations:* swimming, walking, yachting, gardening; *Languages:* Arabic, English; *Address:* P O Box 60, Manama, Bahrain; telephone: 253444, 253450.

YATEEM, Shahrazad Hussain, Bahraini businesswoman/art expert; born 1 October 1951, Manama, Bahrain; *Religion:* Muslim; *Education:* studied Fine Arts, Beirut College for Women, Beirut, Lebanon, Paris University and Sorbonne, Paris, France; *Career:* opened art gallery, Bahrain, 1973, second gallery, 1979; *Interests and Recreations:* archaeology; vice president, Bahrain Historical and Archaeological Society, 1974–, tennis, swimming, yoga; *Languages:* Arabic, English, French; *Address:* P O Box 60, Manama, Bahrain.

YAZGHI, Muhammad Driss al-, Moroccan journalist; born 28 September 1935, Fes, Morocco; married; two sons; *Religion:* Muslim; *Education:* BA in Law; *Career:* Head of Services, Equipment Budget, Ministry of Finance, 1960; Lawyer, 1964; member of the Central Committee of the National Union of Popular Forces, UNFP, 1962; member of the Political Bureau of the Socialist Union of Popular Forces, USFP, 1975; Director of *Al-Muharrir* daily paper, 1975–; Director of *Liberation* weekly paper in French; member of Parliament; member of the Central Committee of the Moroccan Society for the Support of the Palestinian Cause; member of the National Syndicate of the Press; member of the Arab Writers Union; *Publications:* articles in newspapers and magazines; *Interests and Recreations:* jogging, swimming, poetry, painting; *Languages:* Arabic, French; *Address:* 5 Ibn Tufail Street, Les Oranges, Rabat, Morocco.

YAZID, Muhammed, Algerian diplomat/politician; born 1923, Blida, Algeria; married, one son, two daughters; *Religion:* Muslim; *Career:* active member of Algerian People's Party; President of North African Students' Association in France, in charge of Federation in France for Movement for the Triumph of Democratic Liberties (MTDL); imprisoned by French for political activities, 1948–50; member, Revolutionary Committee for Unity and Action, and National Liberation Front (FLN), Cairo, 1954; represented FLN at Afro-Asian Bandung Conference with Ait Ahmad, 1955; represented FLN at UN, 1956–; Minister of Information in Provisional Government, 1958–62; played leading role in Provisional Government's acceptance of Evian Agreements; has led many missions abroad; President of Afro-Asian People's Solidarity Organization, Algiers, 1964; re-elected to National Assembly, 1964; President of National Assembly Foreign Affairs Commission; Ambassador to Lebanon, 1971; *Languages:* Arabic, French, English; *Address:* Ministry of Foreign Affairs, Algiers, Algeria.

YUNES, Manuel, Lebanese businessman; born 21 June 1920; married; two sons, two daughters; *Religion:* Christian; *Education:* Licence in Philosophy and Letters, University of Venezuela; Doctor of Philosophy, Central University of Venezuela; *Career:* Professor of Oriental Studies, Central University of Venezuela, 1952–55; member of Lebanese Chamber of Deputies, 1964–68; member of Founding Committee of the International Centre for the Sciences of Man of UNESCO, Byblos, Lebanon, 1968; President of the Real Estate Improvement Company; Vice President, Rifbank Beirut, Lebanon; President of the Founding Committee of the Lebanon National Refinery; founder and President of the International Centre for the Study of Tolerance; candidate for the Presidency of the Lebanese Republic, 1976; *Publications:* in Spanish: *Una Concepcion Filosofica de la Cultura,* 1953 (translated into Arabic, 1954); in Arabic, *The Reform of Lebanon,* 1959; *The Regional Neutrality of Lebanon,* 1963; *Lebanon and the New Generations,* 1969; *Draft Laws Presented to the Lebanese Parliament,* 1964–68; *Decorations:* Grand Officer of Order of the Cedar; *Interests and Recreations:* philosophy, politics, poetry, swimming, Alpine climbing; *Languages:* Arabic, Spanish, English, French, Latin, German; *Address:* P O Box 7040, Beirut, Lebanon.

YUNIS, Adil Assad, Arab-American physician/academic; born 17 March 1930; married; one son, two daughters; *Education:* BA and MD, American University of Beirut, Lebanon, 1950 and 1954; *Career:* Intern and Assistant Resident, American University Hospital, Beirut, 1954–56; Resident, Barnes Hospital, St. Louis, USA, 1956–57; practised medicine, specialising in haematology, Miami, Florida, USA, 1964–; Chief of Haematology Department, Jackson Memorial Hospital, Miami, 1965–; Assistant Professor of Medicine, Washington University, USA, 1963–64; Assistant Professor of Medicine and Director of Haematology Research, University of Miami, 1964–65; Director, Division of Haematology, 1965–; Assistant Professor of Medicine, 1965–68; Professor of Medicine and Biochemistry and Director of the Howard Hughes Laboratories for Haematology Research, 1968; Leukemia Scholar, 1961–66; member of the American Society of Clinical Investigation, of the American Society of Hematology; also member of the American Society of Biological Chemists and of the Association of American Physicians; *Decorations:* Research Career Development Award, USPHS; *Languages:* Arabic, English; *Address:* Residence — 11415 Nogales St, Coral Gables, FL 33156, USA; Office — 1550 NW 10th Avenue, Miami, FL 33136, USA.

YUNIS, Mahmud, Egyptian engineer/politician; born 3 April 1912; *Religion:* Muslim; *Education:* Royal College of Engineers; MSc Cairo University, Egypt; Staff College; *Career:* Engineer, 1937; Military Operations Directorate, 1943; Lecturer, Staff College, 1944, and 1947; Director, Technical Affairs Office, Military General HQ, 1952; Managing Director and Chairman, General Petroleum Authority, 1954; Counsellor, Ministry of Commerce and Mining; Managing Director, Suez Canal Authority following nationalization of Suez Canal Company, 1956; Chairman of Suez Canal Authority, 1957–65; President, Engineers Syndicate, 1954–65; Director and Chairman, Compagnie Orientale des Pétroles d'Egypte (COPE), 1958–65; member of National Assembly, 1964; Deputy Prime Minister for Transport and Communications, 1965–66; Deputy Prime Minister for Electric Power, Oil and Mining, 1966–67; Deputy Prime Minister for Petroleum and Transport, 1967–68; Consultant to Italian State Oil Company ENI; currently, private consulting firm, Beirut, Lebanon; *Decorations:* Order of Merit, 1st Class; Order of the Nile, 3rd Class; Military Star; Liberation Medal; Order of the Republic, 1st Class; Palestine Medal; Grand Cordon of the Order of Yugoslav Standard; Grand Officer of the Panamanian Order of Vasco Nuñez de Balbao; Republican Medal, 3rd Class; Military Service Medal, 1st Class; *Languages:* Arabic, English; *Address:* P O Box 7272, Beirut, Lebanon; 26 July Street No 21, Cairo, Egypt.

YUSIF, Muhammad Musa Abdullah al-, Omani official; born 1948, Muttrah, Oman; married; two sons, one daughter; *Religion:* Muslim; *Education:* Oman; Aberdeen College of Commerce; City of London College; *Career:* Petroleum Development, Oman, 1966–67; Auditor, Whinney Murrey & Co. 1967–71; Petroleum Development, Oman, 1971–72; Director of Accounts and Treasury, 1972–74; Director General of Finance, 1974–75; Permanent Under Secretary for Finance and Director General of Finance, 1975–; member of Development Council and Financial Affairs Council; Governor, Central Bank of Oman and Arab Monetary Fund; Chairman of Oman Development Bank; Chairman of Holiday Inn, Salalah; Chairman of Oman National Insurance Co; Fellow of the Association of Certified Accountants; *Languages:* Arabic, English; *Address:* P O Box 506, Muscat, Oman; telephone: 745 240; telex: 3333 MALIYA MB.

YUSUF, Abdullah Yaqub, United Arab Emirates official; born 1949, Umm al-Qaiwain, United Arab Emirates; *Religion:* Muslim; *Education:* BA in Arabic, History Department, Al-Azhar University, Cairo, Egypt; *Career:* Director of Internal Trade, Ministry of Economy and Commerce, 1974; *Interests and Recreations:* history of civilizations, hunting, swimming, travelling; *Languages:* Arabic, English; *Address:* P O Box 3397, Abu Dhabi, United Arab Emirates.

YUSUF, Ibrahim M., Egyptian physician/academic; born 20 November 1940, Egypt; married; one daughter; *Religion:* Muslim; *Education:* BS, Ain Shams University, Cairo, Egypt, 1961; MSc, University College of Wales, England, 1965; PhD, University of Edinburgh, Scotland; *Career:* Research Associate, Michigan State Universtiy, Michigan, USA, 1967–69; Research Associate, Banting and Best, Department of Medical Research, University of Toronto, Canada, 1969–70; Research Associate, Department of Pathology, University of Toronto, Canada, 1970–72; Assistant Professor, Department of Pathology, University of Toronto, 1972–78; Assistant Professor, Department of Pathology, University of Toronto, 1974–78; Associate Professor, Department of Paediatrics, University of Montreal, Montreal, Canada, 1978–; member of Canadian Biochemical Society, American Association for the Study of Liver Diseases, Society for Experimental Biology and Medicine; Scholar of Canadian Hepatic Foundation, 1977–78; *Publications:* several papers in scientific journals on chloestasis bile acids; *Interests and Recreations:* travelling, driving; member of the American-Egyptian Scholars Association; *Languages:* Arabic, English, French; *Address:* Centre de Recherche, Hôspital Ste-Justine, 3175 Côte Ste-Catherine, Montreal, Quebec, Canada; telephone: (514) 731 4931 ext 247.

YUSUFI, Muhsin Muhammad Abdullah al-, Yemen Arab Republic administrator/politician; born 1939, Marib, Yemen Arab Republic; married; two sons, one daughter; *Religion:* Muslim; *Education:* Police College, 1965; *Career:* Lieutenant, Police Force; Chief, Sana'a Security Department, 1968; Chief, Taiz Security Department, 1971; Minister of the Interior, 1975–78; member of the Republican Group, People's Legislative Council of the Yemen Arab Republic; Governor of Taiz, 1978–; *Interests and Recreations:* reading; *Address:* Governor House, Taiz, Yemen Arab Republic.

Z

ZAANOUNI, Mustafa, Tunisian UN official/politician; born 19 December 1928, Sousse, Tunisia; married; four children; *Education:* Licence en Droit, Paris, France; Diplôme de Doctorat d'Etat en Economie, Politique et Sciences Economiques, Paris; Diplôme de l'Ecole Nationale d'Administration, Paris; *Career:* Head of Department, Secretariat of State for Planning, 1956–58; Head of Economic Affairs Department, Secretariat of State for Agriculture, 1959–64; Lecturer, Higher Law School, Higher Agricultural School and Co-operative School, Tunis, 1957–64; Supervisor of FAO Special Fund Projects, 1964–66; Expert in Agricultural Economics for FAO-IBRD, World Bank Co-operation Programme, 1966–69; Chairman of the National Centre for Industrial Studies, 1970; Secretary of State for Agriculture, 1971; Secretary of State for Planning, 1972–74; Minister of Planning, 1975–80; Assistant Administrator and Regional Director for Arab States of the United Nations Development Programme, 1982–; *Decorations:* Grand Officer of the Order of the Tunisian Republic; *Languages:* Arabic, French; *Address:* League of Arab States, Tunis, Tunisia; telephone: 296855.

ZACCOUR, Makram Michele, Lebanese banker/stockbroker; born 19 August 1935, Cheyah, Lebanon; *Religion:* Christian; *Education:* Degree in Business Administration, University of California, Berkeley, USA; Phi Beta Kappa; *Career:* Manager, Ultratex Textile Mills, Cali, Colombia, South America, 1958–66; Account Executive, Merrill Lynch, 1966–; Manager, Beirut Office, Merrill Lynch, 1973; Senior Vice President, Merrill Lynch, 1978; Managing Director, Merrill Lynch London Retail Office, 1979; Chairman of the Board, Merrill Lynch, Middle East, SAL, 1980; Managing Director, Merrill Lynch Pierce Fenner & Smith Ltd; *Languages:* Arabic, English, Spanish, French; *Address:* Merrill Lynch Pierce Fenner & Smith Ltd, 153 New Bond Street, London W1Y 9PA, UK; telephone: (01) 493 7242.

ZAHAR, Abdul Rahman, Egyptian WHO official/entomologist; born 22 August 1916, Cairo, Egypt; married; *Religion:* Muslim; *Education:* BS, Faculty of Agriculture, Cairo University, Egypt, 1935–38; PhD, University of Edinburgh, Scotland, UK, 1945–48; London School of Hygiene and Tropical Medicine, University of London, England, 1965–66; *Career:* Instructor, School of Agriculture, Egypt, 1938–42; Demonstrator in Entomology, Faculty of Agriculture, Cairo University, 1942–44; Entomologist, Insect Control Section, Ministry of Health, Cairo, Egypt, 1949–52; Entomologist, Malaria Control Project, World Health Organisation, Saudi Arabia, 1952–55; Team Leader, Malaria Control Project, Saudi Arabia, 1956–58; Senior Adviser, Regional Eradication Training Centre, Cairo, 1959–62; Regional Entomologist, Regional Office, Africa, World Health Organisation, Brazzaville, 1962–65; Regional Entomologist, Regional Office, Eastern Mediterranean, World Health Organisaton, Alexandria, Egypt, 1966–70; Entomologist, Division of Malaria and Vector Biology and Control, World Health Organisation, Geneva, Switzerland; retired, 1977; member of the Royal Entomologists Society, London, England, Royal Society of Tropical Medicine and Hygiene, London, Entomological Society of Switzerland; *Publications: The Ecological Distribution of Black Flies in South-East Scotland,* 1951; *Review of the Ecology of the Malaria Vector in the Eastern Mediterranean Region,* 1974; series of studies on *Leishmaniasis Vecators/ Resnoirs and their Control in the Old World 1979–81;* scientific papers and articles in professional journals; *Interests and Recreations:* tennis, fishing; member of the Alexandria Sporting Club; *Languages:* Arabic, English, French; *Address:* 48 Chemin des Coudriers, 1209 Genève, Switzerland.

ZAHID, Abdul Majid, Saudi Arabian businessman; born 1927, Jeddah, Saudi Arabia; married; four children; *Education:* Mechanical Engineering, GMI, USA; graduate studies, Stamford Business School, USA; *Career:* President and Chief Executive Officer, Arabian Motors and Engineering Company Ltd; member of the Board of Trans Arabian Technical Services, Saudi Bulkhandling, National Pipe Company, J. A. Jones Construction, Saudi Arabia; Consultant to several leading US and European corporations; *Interests and Recreations:* tennis, swimming, shooting, camping; *Languages:* Arabic, English; *Address:* P O Box 166, Dammam, Saudi Arabia; Flat 3, 17 Ennismore Gardens, London SW7 1AA; telephone: 832 2626; telex: 601033 AMAECO SJ.

ZAHID, Yusuf, Saudi Arabian businessman; born 1920; *Education:* general; *Career:* owner of the Zahid Tractor and Heavy Machinery Company; former head of the family firm, M.M. Zahid and Brothers (firm was divided in 1972 between Yusuf Zahid and his brothers Ibrahim Zahid and Abdul Zahid); *Languages:* Arabic, English; *Address:* P O Box 1588, Kilo 5, Mecca Road, Jeddah, Saudi Arabia; telex: 401042 ZAHTRAC SJ.

ZAHRAN, Muhsin Muharram, Egyptian academic/architect; born 1935, Cairo; married; one son, one daughter; *Religion:* Muslim; *Education:* BSc in Architecture, Ain Shams University, Cairo; MSc in Architecture, Urban Design, MIT, USA; Master of Fine Arts in Architecture, Princeton University, USA; PhD in Architecture, Princeton University; TAU Beta, Polytechnical Institute, USA; *Career:* Architect, Government Design Bureau, Cairo, 1965–66; Assistant Professor of Architecture, Alexandria University, 1966; Associate Professor of Architecture, Alexandria University, 1972; Professor of Architecture, Alexandria University, 1977; Dean, Faculty of Architecture, Beirut Arab University, Lebanon, 1978–; United Nations Consultant and Expert, ECWA, Beirut, 1975–80; UNESCO, Paris, 1976–77; UNEP, Nairobi, 1976–77; UNCHS, Nairobi, 1976–77; UNCHBP, New York, 1975–78; *Publications:* articles on housing, urban housing,

architecture and design, in English and Arabic; *Decorations:* Educational Medal, Egypt, 1959; Alexandria University Medal, Egypt, 1977; TAU Beta Polytechnical Institute Medal, 1962; *Interests and Recreations:* tennis, hiking, swimming, soccer; *Languages:* Arabic, English, French; *Address:* 23 Roushdy Street, Roushdy, Alexandria, Egypt; telephone: 75550; Arab University of Beirut, P O Box 115020, Beirut, Lebanon; telephone: 3001100.

ZAID, Abdul Muhsin Bin Sulaiman al-, Saudi Arabian diplomat; born 1916, Saudi Arabia; *Religion:* Muslim; *Education:* general; *Career:* Diplomatic Attaché, Consulate General, Syria and Lebanon; various diplomatic posts up to the rank of Ambassador; Ambassador to Syria, 1976–; *Decorations:* Orders from Saudi Arabia, Syria, Senegal and Tunisia; *Address:* Embassy of Saudi Arabia, Avenue al Jala'a, Damascus, Syria.

ZAIDAN, Ahamd Muhammad, Saudi Arabian official; born 1915, Mecca, Saudi Arabia; married; four sons, five daughters; *Religion:* Muslim; *Education:* Radio Technical Centre, 1932; Diploma of Meteorology from RAF, Iraq 1944; Diploma of Telecommunication, GPO, England, 1951; *Career:* Director of Royal Mobile Radio Station, 1933; Director, Jeddah Radio Station, 1936; Director, Technical Institute of Telecommunication, 1937; Regional Director, Posts Telegraphs Telephones (PTT), Khobar, Dhahran, 1939; Director, Meteorological Service, 1944; Director, Radio Monitoring Service, 1951; Technical Director, HRH The Viceroy's Office, 1954; Inspector General, PTT, 1955; Director General of PTT, 1957; Deputy Minister, PTT; 1963–72; President, BETA Co Ltd, Jeddah, 1973–; Chairman of the Arab Postal Union Conference, 1957, Arab Telecommunication Union Conference, 1966, Plan Committee for Asia and Oceania, 1968–80; member of the Administrative Council of the International Telecommunication Union, ITU, 1966–77, and others; represented Saudi Arabia in several International Telecommunications conferences and conventions; *Decorations:* Diploma of Honour from ITU; *Interests and Recreations:* fishing; member of Radio Society of Great Britain, American Radio Relay League; *Languages:* Arabic, English, French; *Address:* BETA Company Ltd, P O Box 2011, Jeddah, Saudi Arabia; telephone: 643 7300.

ZAIDAN, George C., Egyptian economist/ UN official; born 11 February 1939, Cairo, Egypt; married; *Education:* BLL, Cairo University, 1955–59; BSc in Economics, London School of Economics, UK, 1959–63; PhD in Economics, Harvard University, USA, 1963–67; *Career:* various posts in International Bank for Reconstruction and Development (IBRD), Washington D.C., USA, 1969–74; Chief, Operations Division, Population and Nutrition Project Department, IBRD, Washington D.C., USA 1975–78; Chief, Country Programme Review Division, Programming and Budgeting Department; Chief, Industrial Development and Finance Division, Europe, Middle East and North Africa Region, IBRD, Washington D.C., USA, 1978–; in charge of Division responsible for preparing, appraising and supervising all World Bank Group Loans to development banks and for industrial sector work in countries of Europe, Middle East and North Africa; *Publications: Costs and Benefits of Family Planning Programmes,* 1971; *Population Growth and Economic Development,* 1969; *Costs and Benefits of a Prevented Birth: Conceptual Problem and an Application,* Egypt, 1968; co-author, *The Population Work of the World Bank,* 1968; *Interests and Recreations:* tennis, bridge, table tennis, squash, demography, economic development; *Languages:* Arabic, English, French, Italian; *Address:* Office — IDF Division, Projects Department, Europe, Middle East and North Africa Region, 1818 H Street, NW, Washington, D.C. 20433, USA; telephone: (202) 477 2784; Residence — 7007 Longwood Drive, Bethesda, Maryland 20817, USA; telephone: (301) 469 7081.

ZAIDAN, Ziyad, Saudi Arabian official/ architect; born 1946, Mecca, Saudi Arabia; *Religion:* Muslim; *Education:* BA, University of Detroit, USA, 1972; MA, University of Detroit, USA; *Career:* Designer and Architect, Wakelq-Kushner Architects and Engineers, 1968–70; Architect and Planner, City of Troy Planning Department; President, IDEA Centre; member of Jeddah Chamber of Commerce, Board of Prince Fawwaz Project for Cooperative Housing; attended UN Habitat Conference, Tehran, 1975; *Decorations:* Magna Cum Laude; IDEA Centre won two design competitions from the Ministry of Municipal and Rural Affairs; *Interests and Recreations:* riding; *Address:* P O Box 1999, Jeddah, Saudi Arabia; telephone: 40015, 46026; telex: 400220 IDEAMC SJ.

ZAIWAR, Ali, Egyptian journalist/army officer; born 2 March 1922, Cairo, Egypt; married; two sons; *Religion:* Muslim; *Career:* General in the Armed Forces, retired 1974; held various posts in the Army dealing with sports; Secretary General, Army Sports' Union for eight consecutive years; Secretary of Football Studies, Egyptian Football Union, 1960–62; Editor, Sports Section of various Egyptian newspapers, 1958–; Editor, sports section of the *Akhbar al-Yaum* Organization, Cairo; Manager, Al-Ahly Football Team; Radio Sports Commentator, 1958; Television Sports Commentator, 1960; *Decorations:* various military decorations and orders; *Interests and Recreations:* walking, swimming, table-tennis; honorary member of the Gezira Sporting Club, of the Aviation Club, of Al-Ahly Club, 1939–; *Languages:* Arabic, English; *Address:* 57 Al-Hejaz Street, Masr al-Gedida, Cairo, Egypt; telephone: Office -- 930643; Residence -- 867449.

ZAKI, Abdul Rahman Muhammad, Sudanese lawyer; born 1939, Delgo, Sudan; married; three daughters; *Religion:* Muslim; *Education:* LLB, LLM, London, UK; *Career:* Legal Assistant, Attorney General's Chambers, 1962–64; Assistant Legal Council, Attorney General's Chambers, 1964–67; Legal Council, Attorney General's Chambers, 1967–71; Advocate, 1972; Provincial Judge, 1972–73; Deputy Advocate General, 1973–74; Legal Counsel to the People's Assembly, 1974–75; Under Secretary, Attorney General's Chambers, 1975–76; Attorney General, 1976; *Interests and Recreations:* picnics, table-tennis, psychology; *Languages:* Arabic, English; *Address:* Attorney General's Chambers, P O Box 302, Khartoum, Sudan.

ZAKI, Hassan Abbas, Egyptian financial official/economist; resident in United Arab Emirates; born 2 January 1917, Port Said, Egypt; married; three daughters; *Religion:* Muslim; *Education:* BA in Economics, Cairo University, Cairo, Egypt; graduate studies, American University, Washington, USA; *Career:* Government Representative, Alexandria Stock Exchange; Commercial Secretary, Egyptian Embassy, 1953; Director General of Currency Control Administration, 1955; Minister of Treasury, 1958; Minister of

Economy and Supply, 1961; Minister of Economy and Trade, 1966–71; Adviser to HH the President of the United Arab Emirates; member of the Board of Abu Dhabi Fund, Abu Dhabi National Oil Company, Abu Dhabi Investment Organisation, Abu Dhabi Currency Board; Governor of the International Monetary Fund for the UAE, Washington, USA; Vice Chairman of the Board of the Arab International Bank, Cairo, Egypt; Chairman of the Board of the Arab International Company for Hotels and Tourism, Cairo, Egypt; Chairman of the Board of the Société Arabe Internationale de Banque (SAIB), Cairo, Egypt; *Publications:* various articles on monetary affairs, international trade and cotton policies; *Decorations:* from Egypt, Yugoslavia, Greece, Romania, Somalia, Italy; *Interests and Recreations:* economics, Sufism, social studies; member of the Banking Club; *Languages:* Arabic, English, French; *Address:* Amiri Court, P O Box 849, Abu Dhabi, United Arab Emirates; telephone: 36548, 36381.

ZALZALA, Abdul Hassan, Iraqi Arab League official/diplomat; born 14 January 1928, Amara, Iraq; married; four children; *Religion:* Muslim; *Education:* Law College, Baghdad, 1948; PhD in Economics, Indiana University, USA, 1957; *Career:* Director, Loans and Investments Department, Central Bank of Iraq, 1957; Director, Foreign Exchange Department, 1957; Acting Director, Statistics and Economic Research Department, 1959–62; Deputy Governor of The Central Bank, 1962–63; Chairman, Board of Administration, Central Bank, 1962–63; Ambassador to Iran, 1963–64; Minister of Industry, 1964; Minister of Planning, 1964; Acting Minister of Finance, 1965; Ambassador to Austria, 1965–66; Ambassador to Egypt and Somalia, 1966; Ministry of Foreign Affairs, 1968; Governor of the Central Bank, 1969–73; Ambassador to Canada, 1974–76; Under Secretary General of the Arab League for Economic Affairs, 1976–; *Publications:* economic, political, literary articles in Arabic and English in local and foreign newspapers and magazines; *Address:* Under Secretary General for Economic Affairs, Arab League Office, P O Box 1120, Tunisia, Tunis.

ZALZALAH, Hadi, Arab-American engineer; born 5 August 1936, Baghdad, Iraq; married; one son, one daughter; *Education:*

BS, Purdue University, Indiana, USA, 1961; postgraduate studies at Indiana University, USA, 1955–57, Institute of Technology, 1960; studies at Roosevelt University, 1960; *Career:* Project Engineer, Ingersol Milling Machine Company, Rockford, Illinois, USA, 1961–65; Vice President, Electro Corporation, design and manufacturing company for machine tools, 1965–66; Chief Electronics Engineer, Pratt and Whitney Machine Tool Division, Cudahy, California, USA, 1967–; *Address:* Residence — 31281 Ganado Drive, Palos Verdes Peninsula, CA 902704, USA; Office -- 8420 Atlantic Avenue, Cudahy, CA 90201, USA.

ZAMAKHSHARI, Tahier Abdul Rahman, Saudi Arabian writer; born 1914, Mecca, Saudi Arabia; *Religion:* Muslim; *Education:* general; *Career:* Secretary, Secretariat of the Holy Capital; Secretary, Customs Secretariat; Riyadh Municipality; Radio and TV service; member of Al-Tawfir Co; attended several literary symposia in Lebanon, Syria, Egypt and Tunisia; *Publications:* 14 collections of poetry; *Ahlam al-Rabie Hamasat,* and others; some novels and short stories; *Decorations:* Tunisian Republic Medal of Honour, 3rd Class; Tunisian Republic Medal of Honour for Culture, 2nd Class; *Address:* Waqf al-Zakaria, Flat 2, Sharafiyya, Jeddah, Saudi Arabia.

ZAMIL, Khalik Abullah al-, Saudi Arabian engineer/businessman; born 1948, Alkhobar, Saudi Arabia; married; two daughters; *Religion:* Muslim; *Education:* BSc in Civil Engineering; *Career:* Engineer; Industrial Studies and Development Center ISDC, 1972–74; Zamil Air Conditioning Factory, 1974–76; President, Zamil Soule Steel Buildings Company Ltd, 1977–; member of the Board of AH Al-Zamil Group of Companies, Saudi American Bank; Vice President, Chamber of Commerce in the Eastern Province; *Interests and Recreations:* basketball, running; *Languages:* Arabic, English; *Address:* P O Box 9, Alkhobar, Saudi Arabia; telephone: 864 2567, 833 1479.

ZANDO, Ahmad, Egyptian economist/official; born 1917; *Religion:* Muslim; *Education:* BCom, Cairo University, Egypt, 1938; *Career:* taught for some time at Commercial Institute in Alexandria; formed State Audit Department, 1942; later Controller General of this Department; Director General of

Exchange Control, 1958; Director General of the Budget Department, Ministry of Economy; Under Secretary at the Treasury; member of the Board of Directors of the Economic Development Organization; Director of the Office of the Minister of Treasury, 1961; Deputy Minister, 1962; Minister of Economy and member of the Egyptian Executive Council, 1962; Governor of the Central Bank, 1964–67; Planning Adviser to the President, 1967, with responsibility for the National Planning Institute; Governor of the Central Bank, 1971; *Address:* c/o Central Bank of Egypt, 31 Kasr Al Nil Street, Cairo, Egypt.

ZARIFA, Salim Shukri, Egyptian engineer; born 3 December 1923, Cairo, Egypt; married; two children; *Education:* BSc in Engineering, University of Cairo, Egypt; *Career:* partner, International Engineering and Trading Bureau, Cairo; Technical Director, Egyptian Diesel and Components Industries, Cairo; *Interests and Recreations:* member, Gezira Sporting Club, Cairo; *Address:* Residence— 32 Shagaret Al Dorr Street, Zamalek, Cairo, Egypt.

ZAWAWI, Omar Abdul Mun'im al-, Omani businessman/physician; born 1930, Muscat, Oman; married; *Religion:* Muslim; *Education:* Medicine, Cairo University Medical School, Cairo, Egypt; Master of Public Health, Harvard University, USA; *Career:* practiced as doctor; established Waled Associates Agency; Counsellor to HM Sultan of Oman, Sultan Qaboos; businessman; *Languages:* Arabic, English; *Address:* Zawawi Trading Company, P O Box 58, Muscat, Oman; telephone: 600102, 600407; telex: 3232 ZAWAWI.

ZAWAWI, Qais Abdul Mun'im al-, Omani politician; born 1935, married; three sons; *Religion:* Muslim; *Education:* general; *Career:* businessman in Dubai; returned to Oman following the death of his father, 1966, to run the family business; appointed Minister of State for Foreign Affairs, 1973; Vice-Chairman of the National Development Council, 1974; Minister of State for Foreign Affairs; *Address:* Ministry of Foreign Affairs, P O Box 252, Muscat, Oman.

ZAWI, Tahir Ahmad al-, Libyan religious leader; born 1890, Tripoli, Libya; *Religion:* Muslim; *Education:* Islamic Studies, Al-

Azhar University, Cairo, Egypt, 1912–18, 1924–37; *Career:* actively participated in the political life of Libya and Egypt; joined Ministry of Waqf, Egypt, 1940–53; Editor, *Al-Siyasa* newspaper, organ of the al-Dastour Party, Egypt; Secretary and Chief Correspondent for the Tripolitania Committee for Independence of Libya, 1943–52; Mufti of Libya, 1969; *Publications: Omar al-Mukhtar; Encyclopedia of Libyan Cities; Struggle of Libyan Exiles; Tripolitania Rulers; Languages:* Arabic; *Address:* Mufti of the Arab Socialist Jamahiriyah of the People of Libya, P O Box 385, Tripoli, Libya.

ZAYANI, Rashid al-, Bahraini businessman/banker; born 1915; married; *Religion:* Muslim; *Career:* private enterprise; Chairman of Bank of Bahrain and Kuwait; member of Constituent Assembly, 1972–73; *Languages:* Arabic, English; *Address:* Bank of Bahrain and Kuwait, P O Box 597 Manama, Bahrain; telephone: 253388; telex: 8919 BAHKUBANK BN.

ZAYAT, Latifa al-, Egyptian writer/academic; born 1926, Egypt; *Career:* Assistant Professor, English Department, Ain Shams University, Cairo, Egypt; *Publications:* several collections of short stories and novels, including *The Open Door;* literary studies of T.S. Eliot and Ford Madox Ford; *Address:* University of Cairo, Faculty of Arts, English Department, Cairo, Egypt.

ZAYYAT, Fuad, Syrian businessman; born 24 August 1941, Damascus, Syria; married; three daughters; *Religion:* Christian; *Education:* Law, University of Damascus, Syria; *Career:* Chairman, GENVICO Group of Companies with branches in Damascus, Geneva, London, Nicosia, Beirut, Washington; *Interests and Recreations:* music; *Languages:* Arabic, English, French, Spanish; *Address:* King Faisal Street, P O Box 692, Damascus, Syria; telex: 411381.

ZAYYAT, Muhammad Abdul Salaam al-, Egyptian politician; born 1917; *Religion:* Muslim; *Career:* elected to Chamber of Deputies in the last elections before the July 1952 Revolution and subsequently a member of the 1957, 1964 and 1969 National Assemblies; Secretary to the Provisional Committee to supervise elections to the Arab Socialist Union (ASU), 1968; elected Secretary General of the National Congress, 1968;

elected Secretary General of the Fourth ASU National Congress, 1970; member of the Provisional Secretariat of the newly formed ASU Central Committee, 1971; Adviser for Political Affairs to the President, with rank of Deputy Prime Minister, 1971; Deputy Prime Minister without Portfolio, 1972; member of the Foreign Relations Committee of the People's Assembly; *Address:* The People's Assembly, Cairo, Egypt.

ZAYYAT, Muhammad Hassan al-, Egyptian diplomat; born 14 February 1915, Egypt; married; three children; *Religion:* Muslim; *Education:* BA and MA and Diploma in Oriental Studies, Cairo University, Cairo Egypt; DPhil, Oxford University, England; *Career:* Lecturer, Associate Professor, Alexandria University, Alexandria, Egypt, 1942; Cultural Attaché, Embassy of Egypt, Washington, USA, 1950–54; Chargé d'Affaires, Tehran, Iran, 1955–57; member, UN Advisory Council for Somalia, 1957–60; Egyptian Alternate Representative, UN New York, 1962–64; Ambassador, Embassy of Egypt, New Delhi, India and Nepal, 1964–65; Under Secretary of State, Ministry of Foreign Affairs, Cairo, 1965; represented Egypt, Organisation of African Unity, Summit Conference, 1974; made several tours of East and West Africa; Head of the State Information Service, 1967; Head of the Permanent Information Committee, Arab League, 1968; Egypt Permanent Representative, UN, New York, 1969; Minister of State for Information, 1972; Foreign Minister, 1972–74; Adviser to the President of Egypt, 1974–75; member of the Board of the Middle East Research Centre, Ain Shams University, Cairo, Egypt, 1976–; member of the Institut d'Egypte, Cairo, Egypt, 1980–; *Decorations:* Grand Cordon of the Order of the Nile, Egypt; decorations from Lebanon, Tunisia, Mauritania, Somalia, Italy, Belgium, Poland, Iran, Thailand, Chad, Senegal; *Languages:* Arabic, English, French, Persian; *Address:* 7 Hassan Sabri Street, Zamalek, Cairo, Egypt; telephone: 807096.

ZEBAN, Akash al-, Jordanian army officer/politician; born 1927, Jordan; married; *Education:* military studies at Cadets' College, 1943; Staff College, UK, 1953; *Career:* training officer; section and battalion Commander; infantry battalion staff officer; Talal Divisional Staff Officer, 1952–54; commander of infantry and armoured battalion;

three times Head of Royal Bodyguard; Founder and Commander of Royal Armoured Force; Assistant Commander of War Operations, 1964; Jordanian Ambassador to Kuwait, 1964; retired, 1968; Deputy Director of Public Security for Irbid, 1969; retired with rank of Governor in Ministry of Interior, 1970; Governor of Salt, 1970; Minister of Defence, 1970; retired; *Publications:* various books on military and historical subjects; *Decorations:* Renaissance Medal 1st Class; Independence Medal 1st Class; Star of Jordan 1st Class; Military Bravery Medal; various foreign orders; *Interests and Recreations:* hunting, swimming, riding, reading; *Languages:* Arabic, English; *Address:* Jabal Hussein, Amman, Jordan; telephone: 63662.

ZEBDI, Kamil, Moroccan official/ethnographer; born 17 July 1927, Rabat, Morocco; *Education:* Diploma, L'Ecole du Louvre, Paris, France; *Career:* curator of museums; Cultural Attaché, Embassy to France; Cultural Attaché, Embassy to Denmark; now ethnographer, Ministry of Cultural Affairs of Morocco; *Publications:* Le Cri du Royaume, 1960; Kyrielle, 1967; Échelle pour le Futur du Maroc, 1974; Seve, 1981; *Decorations:* Award from L'Académie Française, 1960; *Address:* P O Box 99, Rabat, Morocco.

ZEERA, Said, Bahraini administrator; born 1920, Bahrain; married; *Religion:* Muslim; *Education:* general education in Bahrain; *Career:* Secretary to the Council of Ministers, State of Bahrain; *Languages:* Arabic, English, Persian, Urdu; *Address:* Secretariat, Council of Ministers, P O Box 78, Manama, Bahrain.

ZEID, Abdul Razzak al-Khalid al-, Kuwaiti businessman; married; *Religion:* Muslim; *Education:* Cairo University, Egypt; *Career:* private enterprise; represented Kuwait, labour conferences in Geneva; founding member of the Kuwait Chamber of Commerce and Industry, 1952; Honorary Treasurer of the Chamber; *Interests and Recreations:* walking, swimming; *Languages:* Arabic, English, French; *Address:* Kuwait Chamber of Commerce and Industry, P O Box 775, Safat, Kuwait; telephone: 433854; telex: 22198 GURFTIGARA KT.

ZEIN, Abdul Latif, Lebanese lawyer/politician; born 1931, South Lebanon; married; one daughter; *Religion:* Muslim; *Educa-*

tion: American University of Beirut, Lebanon; Law Degree, University of St. Joseph, Beirut, Lebanon; *Career:* lawyer since 1953; Deputy for Nabatiyeh, 1960; re-elected 1964, 1968 and 1972; Minister of Agriculture, 1969; *Interests and Recreations:* swimming, skiing, tennis; *Languages:* Arabic, English, French; *Address:* Office — Immeuble Salam, Rue Bechara el-Khoury, Beirut, Lebanon; Residence — Immeuble Shonhaibar, Rue Verdun, Beirut, Lebanon.

ZEIN, HM Queen, Queen Mother of Jordan; born 1918, Egypt; daughter of Sharif Jamil Bin Nassir and sister of Sharif Nassir; married late King Talal; three sons HM King Hussain, HRH Prince Muhammad, HRH Prince Hassan; *Religion:* Muslim; *Languages:* Arabic, French, English; *Address:* Royal Palace, Amman, Jordan.

ZEINE, N. Zeine, Lebanese academic/historian; born 5 April 1908, Haifa, Palestine; married; one son, two daughters; *Education:* BA, Collège des Frères, Lebanon, 1929; MA, American University of Beirut, Lebanon, 1945; PhD, School of Oriental and African Studies, University of London, London, UK; *Career:* Professor of Modern History of the Near East, American University of Beirut, Lebanon; *Publications: Arab Turkish Relations and the Emergence of Arab Nationalism; The Struggle for Arab Independence; Western Diplomacy and the Rise and Fall of Faisal's Kingdom in Syria; Interests and Recreations:* stamp collecting, tennis, photography, gardening; *Languages:* Arabic, English, Persian, French; *Address:* Department of History, American University of Beirut, Beirut, Lebanon; telephone: 317768.

ZENINED, Abdelslam, Moroccan politician; born 1934, Ouezzane, Morocco; married; two daughters, one son; *Religion:* Muslim; *Education:* Bordeaux and Sorbonne Universities, France; Institut des Hautes Etudes Internationales, Geneva, Switzerland, 1961–62; *Career:* several posts in the Ministry of Foreign Affairs, Head of Personnel, Economic Division, 1959–60, Economic Division, 1960–61, African Division, 1963; Prime Minister's Cabinet, 1964; Chef de Cabinet, 1964; Director of the Cabinet, Minister of Agriculture and Agrarian Reform; Secretary General of the Ministry of Information, 1967–72; Director of General Affairs, Prime Minister's Cabinet, 1972; Secretary of State in Prime Minister's Cabinet for General Affairs, and Saharan Affairs, 1974; Secretary of State for General Affairs in Prime Minister's Cabinet, 1977–79; Minister of Tourism, 1979–; *Languages:* Arabic, French; *Address:* Ministère du Tourisme, Rabat, Morocco.

ZENTAR, Mahdi Mrani, Moroccan diplomat; born 6 December 1929, Meknes, Morocco; married; one daughter; *Religion:* Muslim; *Education:* Baccalauréat, University of Bordeaux, France; LLB, Faculty of Law, Rabat University, Morocco; Licence en Droit, University of Paris, France; *Career:* lawyer in Casablanca, 1955; Head of the Office of the Minister charged with negotiating independence, 1956; Director General of Information, Ministry of Foreign Affairs, 1957; Director of the National Tourism Office, 1958; Consul General in Paris, 1959; Legal Adviser, Ministry of Foreign Affairs, 1960; Director of Political Affairs, Ministry of Foreign Affairs, 1961; Ambassador to Algeria, 1963; Ambassador to Yugoslavia, 1966; Ambassador to Egypt, 1967; Ambassador to the UN, New York, 1971; Ambassador to Italy, 1974; member of the Commission of Arbitration, Mediation and Conciliation in the Organization of African Unity (OAU), 1969; Ambassador to France, 1982–; *Decorations:* Officer of the Order of the Throne, Morocco, 1963; Grand Officer of the Order of the Yugoslav Flag, 1967; Greek decoration; *Interests and Recreations:* political and economic writing; travel, photography, swimming, gastronomy, music; *Languages:* Arabic, French, English, Spanish, Italian; *Address:* Embassy of Morocco, Rue le Lasse 3 et 5, 16e, Paris, France.

ZERDANI, Abdul Aziz, Algerian lawyer/politician; born 1934, Canrobert, Algeria; married; *Career:* Political Commissioner of Wilaya I, Aurès; later Private Secretary to Krim Belkacem; entered Ministry of Foreign Affairs of Provisional Government, 1961; Deputy for Batna in National Assembly, 1962; re-elected 1964; President of National Assembly Economic Commission; Director of *Le Peuple* newspaper and former regular contributor to *Révolution Africaine;* elected member of National Liberation Front (FLN) Central Committee April 1964 Congress, and helped draft the Algerian Charter; Minister of Labour, 1965–67; now a practising lawyer; *Address:* Al Chaab, 1 Place Maurice Audin, Algiers, Algeria.

ZGHAL, Muhammad, Tunisian official; born 1929, Sfax, Tunisia; married; *Religion:* Muslim; *Education:* graduated in Science, Sorbonne, University of Paris, France; *Career:* after Independence became first Director of Information; Head of Tunisian Press Agency (TAP); Head of State Phosphate Company; Director of Information, 1969; Chef de Cabinet, Ministry of Information, 1970–71; Chef de Cabinet, Ministry of the Interior, 1971; Secretary of State for Education, 1971; *Languages:* Arabic, French; *Address:* Ministry of Education, Tunis, Tunisia.

ZHIRI, Kassim, Moroccan diplomat; born 25 March 1920; *Religion:* Muslim; *Education:* Institute of Higher Studies, Rabat, Morocco; *Career:* Manager, *Al-Maghreb* and *Al-Alam* daily newspapers; Director General Moroccan Broadcasting Station, 1956–59; Ambassador to Senegal, 1960–61; Ambassador to Yugoslavia, 1962–64; Director of Information, Ministry of Foreign Affairs, 1966; Permanent Delegate of League of Arab States to UN, Geneva, 1966–68; Minister of Secondary and Technical Education, 1968–69; Ambassador to Mauritania, 1970–72; Ambassador to People's Republic of China, 1972–73; founder of Free School, El-Jedida; *Publications: Biography of Mohammed V,* 1962; *The Gold of Sons,* novel; political commentaries and social and historical studies; *Decorations:* Moroccan and Yugoslav decorations; *Languages:* Arabic, French; *Address:* 61 rue de la Marne, Rabat, Morocco.

ZIADEH, Farhat J., Arab-American academic; born 8 April 1917, Ramallah, Palestine; married; five daughters; *Religion:* Christian; *Education:* BA, American University of Beirut, Beirut, Lebanon, 1937; LLB, University of London, England, 1940; Barrister at Law, Lincoln's Inn, London 1946; *Career:* Instructor, Princeton University, USA, 1943–45; Magistrate, Government of Palestine, 1946–48; Lecturer, Assistant Professor, Associate Professor, Princeton University, 1948–66; Professor, University of Washington, Seattle, USA, 1966–; Chairman, Near East Department, University of Washington, 1970–; former member of the Board

of Directors, American Research Centre, Egypt; former President, Middle East Studies Association; *Publications: An Introduction to Modern Arabic,* 1957; *Reader in Modern Literary Arabic,* Princeton, 1964; *Philosophy of Jurisprudence in Islam of Mahmassani,* Brill, 1964; *Lawyers, The Rule of Law and Liberalism in Modern Egypt,* Stanford, 1968; *Property Law in the Arab World,* London, 1979; editor, *Adab al Qadi,* American University Press, Cairo, 1979; *Interests and Recreations:* swimming, Islamic institutions and Islamic law; *Languages:* Arabic, English, French, Turkish, Hebrew; *Address:* Department of Near Eastern Studies, University of Washington, Seattle, Washington 98195, USA; telephone: (206) 543 6033.

ZIDI, Mekki, Tunisian engineer; born 1929, Thala, Tunis; married; four children; *Religion:* Muslim; *Education:* Metallurgical and Mining Engineer, Ecole Polytechnique, Paris, France; Ecole des Mines; *Career:* Steel Work, al-Fouladh, Bizerta, Tunisia; President, Steel Works and Director of Mines, 1967–70; Secretary of State, Ministry of National Economy, 1970–75; President, Office National des Mines, Tunis, 1975–; *Languages:* Arabic, French; *Address:* Office National des Mines, 26 rue d'Angleterre, Tunis, Tunisia.

ZIMAITY, Muhamad Abdul Maguid, Egyptian aviation official; born 7 December 1922; married; one son; *Religion:* Muslim; *Education:* BSc in Aero-Engineering, 1944; Associate Fellow, Royal Aeronautical Society, London, 1955; Chartered Engineer, Council of Engineering Institutions, London, 1969; *Career:* Egyptian Airforce, 1948–56; General Manager, Société Aéronavale Mediterranéenne SAM, Cairo Airport, 1956–57; Adviser, Vocational Training Centre, 1958–60; United Arab Airlines, General Manager, Procurement and Supply, 1961–69; United Arab Airlines, Technical Director General, 1970; Director General, General Organization for International Exhibitions and Fairs, 1973–75; Vice President, Egypt Air, Corporate Planning, 1975–80; Adviser to Chairman, Egypt Air; member of the Scientific Research Academy and the Transport Research Council; Reporter for different scientific and technical seminars, workshops, symposia; External Examiner, Faculty of Commerce, Cairo and Ain Shams Universities, for MSc in Business Administration and Air Transport Economics; *Publications:* compiler and editor, *Dictionary of Technical Terms*, 1962, in English and Arabic, reprinted several times; compiler and editor, *Technical Directory, Aeronautical Engineering*, 1976, published by Leipzig; articles in the *Engineering Magazine* on aviation science and technology; *Decorations:* Order of Liberation; Order of Merit 1st Class, 1980; *Interests and Recreations:* music, reading, writing, translation, editing, organising seminars, technoeconomics and feasibility studies, science and technology, literature; *Languages:* Arabic, English, French, Italian; *Address:* 41 Nakhla Metei Street, Heliopolis, Egypt; telephone: 864712.

ZINE, Abdallah Yahia al-, Yemen Arab Republic official; born 28 June 1943, Sana'a, Yemen; married; two children; *Religion:* Muslim; *Education:* Licence en Sciences de l'Information, Université d'Alger, 1968; Diplôme et Doctorat en Sciences de l'Information, Sorbonne, Université de Paris, 1975; *Career:* Director General, Yemen News Agency; Assistant to the General Secretary of the National Assembly; Director General, Yemen Radio and Television Office; Director of Information and Culture at the Presidency; *Publications: Le Yemen et ses Moyens d'Information, Etude Historique, Politique, Juridique, Sociale et Critique, 1872-1974*, published by the SNED, 1978; *Interests and Recreations:* swimming, tennis, table tennis; *Languages:* Arabic, French, English; *Address:* P O Box 278, Sana'a, Yemen.

ZINTANI, Abdul Wahab Muhamad al-, Libyan diplomat/engineer; born 13 October 1936, Zintan, Libya; married; four sons, three daughters, *Religion:* Muslim; *Education:* BSc in Electrical Sciences; Diploma in Engineering; Diploma in Wireless Engineering; *Career:* Officer and Teacher of Wireless Engineering and Electricity, 1959–69; Chief of Benghazi Municipality, 1971; Mayor of Benghazi, 1973; Ambassador to Cyprus, Lebanon, USSR, Finland, Sweden; *Publications:* articles in *Al-Hagiga* and *Al-Amal* newspapers, 1970; *Radio and Television Engineering; The Slide Rule; The Revolution of Jungles; Documents of the Unity; The Middle East War; The Fairytale of the Iron Curtain; Interests and Recreations:* football, tennis, swimming, horse riding, scientific writing; *Languages:* Arabic, English, Russian; *Address:* c/o Ministry of Foreign Affairs, Tripoli, Libya.

ZOGHBI, Elie, Egyptian ecclesiastic; born 11 January 1912, Cairo, Egypt; *Religion:* Christian; *Education:* graduated in theological studies, St. Anne Seminary, Jerusalem 1935; *Career:* ordained to ministry of Greek Catholic Melkite Order, 1936; Professor in secondary seminary, St. Anne Seminary, Jerusalem, 1937–41; parish priest, Cairo, 1941–49; parish priest, Alexandria, Egypt, 1949–51; Archimandrite, 1951; Bishop and Vicar General, Egypt and Sudan, 1954–68; Archbishop of Baalbek, Lebanon, 1968; *Address:* Residence — Archevêché Grec Catholique Melkite de Baalbek, Baalbek, Lebanon.

ZOUHEIRI, Bashir Ali, Syrian banker/chartered accountant; resident in UK; born 1927, Damascus, Syria; married; four sons, one daughter; *Education:* MA in Commerce and Finance, Cairo University, 1953; Certified Chartered Accountant, Syria, 1958; *Career:* Controller, the Rafidain Bank, Damascus, 1950–52; Manager, General Controller of Foreign Exchange, Ministry of Finance, Syria, 1952–56; Manager of Accountancy and General Inspector, Central Bank of Syria, Damascus, 1956–60; General Manager, Arab World Bank, Damascus, 1960–68; Technical Adviser to the Governor of Central Bank of Jordan, 1968–69; Technical Adviser, Banking Sector, Ministry of Finance, Algeria, 1969–71; Chairman and General Manager, Commercial Bank of Syria, Damascus, 1971–73; joint General Manager, European Arab Bank, Brussels, Belguim, 1973–78; Group General Manager, European Arab Bank, UK, 1979–; member of the Association of Chartered Accountants, Syria; Chairman, Arab Bankers Association, London; *Publications:* several books and articles on banking, economy, insurance and economic development; *Interests and Recreations:* tennis; *Languages:* Arabic, French, English; *Address:* European Arab Bank Ltd, 107 Cheapside, London EC2; telephone: 01 606 6099.

ZOUHIR, Latifa, Tunisian broadcasting official; born 9 August 1933; married; one son, one daughter; *Religion:* Muslim; *Education:* Degree in Modern Literature; MA in literature; *Career:* two years of journalism; broadcaster on Tunisian Radio; Director of International Programmes on Radio-Télévision-Tunisienne (RTT), 1970; member of the Higher Information Council; *Publica-*

tions: essay in French *La Littérature maghrébine d'expression française;* broadcast literary criticism; *Decorations:* Order of the Tunisian Republic, 1974; *Interests and Recreations:* tennis, swimming, reading, music; *Languages:* Arabic, French, English, Italian; *Address:* 53 Rue du 1er Juin, Tunis, Tunisia; telephone: 280099.

ZU'BI, Hatim Sharif, Jordanian lawyer/politician/banker; resident in Bahrain; born 17 June 1927, Nazareth, Palestine; married; four sons; *Religion:* Muslim; *Education:* LLB, University College, University of London, London, UK, 1949; Barrister at Law, Lincoln's Inn, 1950; *Career:* Legal Adviser, Ministry of Finance, Saudi Arabia, 1950–54; Lecturer, American University of Beirut, Beirut, Lebanon, 1954; Manager, Banque du Caire, Amman, Jordan, 1956–60; Director and Secretary, Jordan Hotels and Tourism Company, 1956–65; Vice Chairman, Jordan Phosphate Mines Company, 1962–65; Director and Deputy General Manager, Cairo Amman Bank, 1960–65; Minister of National Economy, 1965–69; Acting Minister of Foreign Affairs; Minister of Communications; Acting Minister of Finance, 1969–70; Chairman of Jordan Electricity Authority; Chairman of Agricultural Marketing Board; Governor for Jordan at the World Bank; Chairman of Arab Economic Council, Arab League; Director and Deputy Manager of Cairo Amman Bank, Amman, 1970–71; Legal Consultant and Attorney, International Legal Practice, Amman, Abu Dhabi, Dubai, Sharjah, Manama; Fellow of the Institute of Arbitrators, UK; member of the Bar Association; *Decorations:* Order of the Jordanian Star, 1st Class; Order of the Tunisian Republic, 1st Class; Order of the National Order of the Cedar, 1st Class, Lebanon; GBE Knight Grand Cross of the Most Excellent Order of the British Empire; Grand' Ufficiale nell Ordinario al Merito della Republica Italiana; *Interests and Recreations:* horse riding, swimming, tennis, shooting, fishing; member of Jordan Archaeological Society; *Languages:* Arabic, English, some French; *Address:* Hatim S. Zu'bi, P O Box 502, Manama, Bahrain; telephone: 251911, 251695, 258207.

ZUAYTER, Akram, Jordanian diplomat/politician; born 1909, Jordan; *Education:* American University of Beirut, Lebanon; College of Law, Jerusalem; *Career:* teacher, secondary schools, Nablus Acre, Palestine, 1927–30; Chief Editor, *Mira'at al-Shark* and *Al-Hayat,* Jerusalem, 1930–31; Professor of History, Baghdad, Iraq, 1934–35; Secretary, Palestine National Committee, 1936; exiled, 1937–50; member, Palestine Permanent Committee, 1950; Inspector of Education, Iraq, 1940–41; President, Arab Delegation to Latin America for Palestine Cause, 1947–48; Counsellor, Syrian Delegation, Arab League, 1950; Ambassador to Syria, 1962–63; Ambassador to Iran, 1963–65; Minister of Foreign Affairs, Jordan, 1966; Senator, 1967–; Minister, Royal Hashemite Court, 1967–; member of Consultative Council, 1967–; Ambassador to Lebanon, 1971; member of the Jordan Academy of Arabic, the Royal Academy of Islamic Civilization; President of the Islamic Cultural Centre, Beirut, Lebanon; *Publications: Recent History,* 1941; *Mission to a Continent,* 1950; *The Palestine Cause,* 1954, and other books, essays and articles; *Decorations:* Grand Cordon of the Order of the Jordanian Star; Order of Independence, Jordan; Knight Grand Cross Order of St. Michael and St. George, UK; and other decorations from Lebanon, Libya, and Iran; *Address:* Dar al-Handasah Consultants, P O Box 7159, Beirut, Lebanon.

ZUBAIR, Muhammad Omar, Saudi Arabian academic/economist; born 1 September 1936; *Religion:* Muslim; *Education:* MA, PhD, Economics, 1971; *Career:* Dean, Faculty of Economics and Public Administration, King Abdul Aziz University, Mecca; Head of the Economics Department; Vice Rector, King Abdul Aziz University; Head of the Economics Department, Ministry of Finance; Chairman of King Abdul Aziz University Council; Rector of King Abdul Aziz University, 1976–; member of Supreme Council of Saudi Universities; attended UN Conference of Trade and Development, Islamic Conference London, UK, 1975, International Conference of Islamic Economics, Mecca, 1976; *Publications:* several research papers on Islamic economics; *Interests and Recreations:* travel, reading; *Address:* King Abdul Aziz University, P O Box 1540, Jeddah, Saudi Arabia; telephone: 687 9033; telex: 401141 KAUNI SJ.

ZUBAIR, Shaikh Muhammad, Omani businessman; born 1940, Husn, Oman; married; six children; *Religion:* Muslim;

Education: Studies in Public Administration; *Career:* worked with Petroleum Development, Oman; established Muscat Trading Company, 1966, Zubair Enterprises with a number of subsidiary companies, 1973, partnership with Balfour Kirkpatrick; *Languages:* Arabic, English; *Address:* Office — Zubair Enterprises, P O Box 127, Muscat, Oman; telephone: 722821; telex: 3258 MUSTRD MB.

ZUBI, Yusif Muhammad al-, Jordanian aviation official; born 25 July 1946, Salt, Jordan; married; *Religion:* Muslim; *Education:* LLB, Damascus University, Syria, 1970; Diploma in Air Space Laws, McGill University, Montreal, Canada, 1976; LLM, McGill University, 1977; *Career:* Chief of International Affairs, Jordan Civil Aviation, 1971–73; Chief of Bilateral Agreements, Jordan Civil Aviation, 1973–75; Chief of Air Transport, Jordan Civil Aviation, 1975–78; Deputy Director of Air Transport, Jordan Civil Aviation, 1978–81; Director of Air Transport, Arab Civil Aviation Council (ACAC), Rabat, Morocco, 1981–; member of Air and Space Association, McGill University, Montreal; *Interests and Recreations:* reading, travelling, backgammon; *Languages:* Arabic, English; *Address:* Arab Civil Aviation Council, 17 Al-Nasr Street, P O Box 4410, Rabat, Morocco; telephone: Office — 74187; Residence — 70021.

ZUHAIR, Harb Salih al-, Saudi Arabian engineer/businessman; born 4 July 1938, Zubair, Iraq; married; one son, two daughters; *Religion:* Muslim; *Education:* Civil Engineering, Portsmouth College of Technology, Portsmouth, UK, 1961; Diploma of Technology; *Career:* Civil Engineer, Ministry of Communications, Saudi Arabia, 1961–68; Chief of Maintenance and Rural Road Department; Deputy Chief Engineer of the Roads Department; Director of Planning, Ministry of Communications for Posts Telephones Telegraphs, Roads and Ports; resigned from Ministry of Communications, 1968; Managing Director of family company SADCO, 1968; Chairman, Electronic Equipment Marketing Co, Modern Arab Contractors, Saudi Arabia, Trust Investment and Development Est Holding Co, Riyadh, Saudi Arabia; Partner and Director, Société Bancaire Arabe, Paris, France; *Interests and Recreations:* reading, music, swimming, tennis, sailing, hunting; *Address:* P O Box 3750, Riyadh, Saudi Arabia.

ZUHAIR, Lieutenant General Asaad al-, Saudi Arabian diplomat/army commander; born circa 1930; *Religion:* Muslim; *Education:* joined Military School at Taif in 1947; A Licence with the British Civil Air Training Mission; trained at AST Hamble, 1949; followed by RAF training, UK; *Career:* Air Attaché, Embassy to USA and later to Pakistan, 1966–71; Director of the Royal Saudi Air Force; Commander of the Royal Saudi Air Force, 1972; Lieutenant General, 1974; Ambassador to Taiwan, 1979–; *Languages:* Arabic, English; *Address:* Embassy of Saudi Arabia, 321 Shih Pai Road, See 2, Pei Tou, Taiwan.

ZURAYK, Constantine, Lebanese academic/diplomat; born 1909, Damascus, Syria; married; four children; *Education:* BA, American University of Beirut, Lebanon, 1928; MA, University of Chicago, 1929; PhD, Princeton University, 1930; Doctorate in Literature (h.c.), University of Michigan, 1967; *Career:* Assistant Professor of History, American University of Beirut (AUB), 1930–42; Associate Professor of History, AUB, 1942–45; 1st Counsellor, Syrian Legation to the USA, 1945–46; Minister Plenipotentiary for Syria to USA, 1945–47; Delegate to the UN Security Council and to the UN General Assembly, 1946–47; Vice President and Professor of History, American University of Beirut, 1947–49; Rector, Syrian University, 1949–52; Vice President, AUB, 1952–54; Acting President, AUB, 1945–57; Distinguished Professor of History, AUB, 1956–; President of the International Association of Universities, 1955–70; *Publications:* numerous books and other publications; *Decorations:* Commander, National Order of the Cedar, Lebanon; Medal of the Syrian Order of Merit, 1st Class; Syrian Order of Merit; Public Instruction Medal 1st Class, Lebanon; *Interests and Recreations:* corresponding member of the Arab Academies in Syria and Iraq; Chairman, Institute for Palestinian Studies; member of the AUB Alumni Club; *Languages:* Arabic, French, English; *Address:* Office — American University of Beirut, P O Box 11-7164, Beirut, Lebanon; Residence — Artois Street, Beirut, Lebanon; telephone: 343174.

ZUWAI, Muhammed Abdul Kassim, Libyan politician; *Religion:* Muslim; *Career:* Under Secretary, Ministry of Information and

Culture; Minister of State without Portfolio, 1947–77; Secretary for Information and Culture; General People's Committee, 1977;

Address: Office of the Secretary for Information, Tripoli, Libya.

LIST OF
PROFESSIONAL
CATEGORIES

ACADEMICS
ARTISTS/MUSICIANS/PAINTERS
ARMED FORCES/POLICE CHIEFS
BANKERS/ECONOMISTS/AUDITORS/ACCOUNTANTS
BUSINESSMEN/BUSINESSWOMEN
DIPLOMATS
ENGINEERS/AGRICULTURAL ENGINEERS/ELECTRONIC
ENGINEERS/INDUSTRIAL/ENGINEERS
INTERNATIONAL OFFICIALS
JOURNALISTS/WRITERS/POETS
LAWYERS/JUDGES
OFFICIALS/ADMINISTRATORS
OIL OFFICIALS/FINANCIAL OFFICIALS/AVIATIONS OFFICIALS/
ADMINISTRATORS/BROADCASTING OFFICIALS
TRADE UNION OFFICIALS
PHYSICIANS/DENTAL SURGEONS/DENTISTS/SURGEONS
POLITICIANS
RELIGIOUS LEADERS/ECCLESIASTICS
SCIENTISTS/VETERINARY SURGEONS/SPACE SCIENTISTS/
AGRICULTURALISTS/GEOLOGISTS/NUCLEAR SCIENTISTS

LIST OF COUNTRIES

Democratic and Popular Republic of Algeria
State of Bahrain
Arab Republic of Egypt
Republic of Iraq
Hashemite Kingdom of Jordan
State of Kuwait
Republic of Lebanon
Socialist People's Libyan Arab Jamahiriya
Kingdom of Morocco
Sultanate of Oman
PLO/Palestine
State of Qatar
Kingdom of Saudi Arabia
Democratic Republic of Sudan
Syrian Arab Republic
Republic of Tunisia
United Arab Emirates
Yemen Arab Republic
People's Democratic Republic of Yemen
United Kingdom
United States of America

INDEX

ALGERIA

The Democratic and Popular Republic of Algeria lies in North Africa. The country is bounded to the east by Tunisia and Libya, to the south by Niger and Mali and to the north by the Mediterranean Sea.

Area: 2,381,441 square kilometres.

Population: (1981 estimation) 19,300,000.

National Flag: The flag has equal vertical stripes of green and white, with a red crescent moon and five pointed red stars superimposed in the centre.

Administrative Organisation: The country is divided into thirty one wilayas (departments).

Main Cities: Algiers (capital), Constantine, Annaba, Oran.

Languages: Official Language: Arabic; Others: French.

Currency: Algerian Dinar (DA).

Measures: The metric system is in force.

RELIGIOUS LEADERS/ECCLESIASTICS

BAHRAIN

The State of Bahrain is situated in the Arabian Gulf. The country's closest neighbours are Saudi Arabia to the west and Qatar to the east.
Area: The total land area is 662 square kilometres.
Population: (1981 estimation) 360,000.
National Flag: The flag is scarlet with a vertical white stripe at the hoist and the two colours are separated by a serrated line.
Administrative Organisation: There are six principal islands in the Bahrain group of which Bahrain is the largest.
Main Cities: Manama (capital), Muharraq, Isa, Awali.
Languages: Official Language: Arabic; Others: English.
Currency: Bahraini Dinar (BD).
Measures: The metric system is in force.

EGYPT

The Arab Republic of Egypt occupies the northeastern tip of Africa. The country is bordered by Libya to the west, Sudan to the south and Gaza strip in the north east. To the north its coastline runs along the Mediterranean and to the east along the Red Sea and the Gulf of Aqaba.

Area: 1,000,253 square kilometres.

Population: (1981 estimation) 43,200,000.

National Flag: The flag is a horizontal tricolour of red, white and black. The white stripe is charged with an eagle emblem in gold.

Administrative Organisation: The country is divided into twenty one governorates.

Main Cities: Cairo (capital), Alexandria, Port Said, Port Suez, Aswan, Tanta, Mahalla al-Kubra.

Languages: Official Language: Arabic; Others: English, French.

Currency: Egyptian Pound (£E).

Measures: The metric system is in force, but some local measures are still in use.

575

IRAQ

The Republic of Iraq closest neighbours are Turkey to the north, Iran to the east, Kuwait and Saudi Arabia to the south, and Syria and Jordan to the west.
Area: 437,522 square kilometres.
Population: (1981 estimation) 13,800,000.
National Flag: The flag is horizontal tricolour, red, white and black. The white band is charged with three five pointed green stars.
Administrative Organisation: The country is divided into eighteen governorates.
Main Cities: Baghdad (capital), Mousal, Basra (main port), Kirkuk.
Languages: Official Language: Arabic; Others: English.
Currency: Iraqi Dinar (ID).
Measures: The metric system is in force. Also some local measures are in use.

JORDAN

The Hashemite Kingdom of Jordan is situated on both banks of the Jordan River. The country's closest neighbours are Syria to the north, Iraq to the east, Saudi Arabia to the south and occupied territories to the west.
Area: 97,739 square kilometres.
Population: (1981 estimation) 3,500,000.
National Flag: The flag is a horizontal tricolour of black, white and green with a red triangle, containing a seven pointed star at the hoist.
Administrative Organisation: The country is divided into eight administrative provinces, three of which are occupied by Israel.
Main Cities: Amman (capital), Aqaba (main port), Irbid.
Languages: Official Language: Arabic; Others: English.
Currency: Jordanian Dinar (JD).
Measures: The metric system is in force.

ACADEMICS

ABU JABIR, Kamil S.	25
ARAFAT, Walid Najib	62
ASAD, Nassiriddin al-	67
BADRAN, Adnan Muhammad /scientist	88
BARAMKI, Dimitri Constantine /archaeologist	98
DAHHAN, Umaima Izzat al-	145
DEEB, Walid Muhammad	152
FARHAN, Ishaq Ahmad /official	173
KAMAL, Marwan Rasim	279
KHATIB, Omar Ismail al- /broadcasting official	304
NASIR, Hanna Musa	391
NASIR, Sari /writer	391
RASHDAN, Muhammad Salim	427
SALIH, Hani Abdul Rahman	459
SAMRA, Mahmud Dawud	463
SHARAIHA, Wadi J. /economist	483
TELL, Safwan Khalaf al-	528
YAGHI, Abdul Rahman Abdul Wahaab /linguistic expert	546
YAGHI, Hashim Abdul Wahab	546

ARMED FORCES/POLICE CHIEFS

BIN SHAKER, Lieutenant General Sharif Zaid	119
HAIARI, General Ali Ahmad al- /diplomat	211
MAJALI, Habis Rufaifan	335
MUHAMMAD, Field-Marshal Anwar	369
ZEBAN, Akash al- /politician	558

ARTISTS/MUSICIANS/PAINTERS

HUSSAIN, HH Princess Fakhrilnissa Zaid al-	242
KHASHO, Yusif Saad /musician	303
NAIF, HH Princess Wijdan Ali Bin /painter	387

BANKERS/ECONOMISTS/AUDITORS/ACCOUNTANTS

ANNAB, Ziyad Radhi /economist	59
AZMEH, Issam /businessman	82
FAHOUM, Munther	169
FANEK, Fahed /businessman	171
IRSHEID, Walid Jamil	251
KHAIRI, Khallusi Yusuf /politician	290
KHOURI, Zuhair Salih	310
MADANAT, Nabih Ayed	328
MARTO, Michael Isa /economist	347
MASRI, Muhammad Qahtan Rafiq al-	351
NABULSI, Muhammad Sa'id	382
OKKEH, Awni Muhammad	403
SAFADI, Hisham Jamil	447
SAKET, Bassam Khalil	453
SALIM, Khalid /official	460
SALTI, Amir O. al-	462
SARTAWI, Sufyan Ibrahim /businessman	465
SHARABI, Nazim Bishara /official	482
SHARAF, Taysir Ahmad	483
SHOMAN, Abdul Majid Abdul Hamid	497
SHOMAN, Khalid	498
TOUQAN, Muhammad Abdul Rahman	532

BUSINESSMEN/BUSINESSWOMEN

ABU GHAZALA, Talal /accountant	22
ABU HASSAN, Khaldun Abdul Rahman	23
ABU JABIR, Rauf Saad	25
ABU ZAID, Omar Mustafa	32
AJAJ, Safuh Galib	43
ARAIM, Mahmud Ahmad	63
ATALLAH, Munir Hanna	72
BDEIR, Muhammad Ali	105
DAJANI, Abul Wafa	146
DAJANI, Ali Tahir	146
FARRADJ, Fuad Dimitri /engineer	174
HAJJAR, Taj	212
KAWAR, Tawfiq Amin;	285
KHASAWNEH, Ali Mahmud al-	302
KHATIB, Walid Hatim al-	304
KURDI, Husni Sidu /banker	318
MASRI, Munib Rashid al-	351
MOUASHER, Rajai S.	363
MOUASHIR, Anis /politician	363

579

OIL OFFICIALS/FINANCIAL OFFICIALS/ AVIATION OFFICIALS/ADMINISTRATORS/ BROADCASTING OFFICIALS/ TRADE UNION OFFICIALS

PHYSICIANS/DENTAL SURGEONS/ DENTISTS/SURGEONS

POLITICIANS

RELIGIOUS LEADERS/ECCLESIASTICS

KUWAIT

The State of Kuwait is situated in the northwest extreme of the Arabian Gulf. The country's closest neighbours are Iraq to the northwest and Saudi Arabia to the south.
Area: 20,150 square kilometres.
Population: (1978 estimation) 1,199,000.
National Flag: The flag has horizontal green, white and red stripes, with a black trapezoid next to the staff.
Administrative Oraganisation: The country consists of four districts.
Main Cities: Kuwait (capital), Al Ahmadi (main port).
Languages: Official Language: Arabic; Others: English.
Currency: Kuwaiti Dinar (KD).
Measures: The metric system is in force.

LEBANON

The Republic of Lebanon is situated on the eastern shore of the Mediterranean Sea. The country's closest neighbours are Syria to the north and east.
Area: 10,400 square kilometres.
Population: (1981 estimation) 3,000,000.
National Flag: The flag has horizontal stripes of red, white and red. In the centre of the white strip is a cedar tree.
Main Cities: Beirut (capital), Tripoli, Siada.
Languages: Official Language: Arabic; Others: French, English.
Currency: Lebanese Pound (£Leb).
Measures: The metric system is in force.

ACADEMICS

ABILLAMA, Fayik Maged	19
ABU HAIDAR, Jarir Amin	22
BAALBAKI, Rohi; /publisher	85
BADRE, Albert	88
BOUSTANI, Fuad Ephrem	127
CHEHAB, Maurice /archaeologist	139
DAGHIR, Nuhad J.	144
DEEB, Boutros /diplomat	151
DEEB, Marius	152
HABACHI, Rene Marc /UN official	203
HADDAD, Amin Farid /pharmacist	205
HANANIA, Farid S. /lawyer	221
IBISH, Yusuf Hussain	245
KHOURI, Samir al- /engineer	310
MALIK, Charles Habib /philosopher	340
MIKDASHI, Zuhair /economist	358
NAIM, Edmond Wadih /lawyer	388
RABBATH, Edmond /lawyer	423
SAGHIR, Abdul Rahman /agriculturalist	449
SALIBI, Kamal /historian	458
SARRUF, Fuad /writer	465
ZEINE, N. Zeine /historian	559
ZURAYK, Constantine /diplomat	563

ARMED FORCES/POLICE CHIEFS

BOUSTANI, Emile	127
KHATIB, Brigadier General Sami al-	303
LAHOUD, Colonel Faris	322

ARTISTS/MUSICIANS/PAINTERS

ADIB, Hoda /musician	36
CARACALLA, Abdul Halim /choreographer	135
FAYROUZ (stage name of Nohad HADDAD) /singer	178
GEBARA, Georgette /choreographer	188
SERAPHIM, Juliana /painter	473
TAKKIEDDINE, Diana /pianist	520

BANKERS/ECONOMISTS/AUDITORS/ACCOUNTANTS

AZAR, Roger Fawzi	81
BACONI, Issa Nasri	86
BARAKAT, Munir	98
BASSAT, Hisham al- /economist	103
BASSIL, Francois	103
CHIDIAC, Jean Salim	140
FATHALLAH, Imad;	177
GEAGEA, Joseph Tannous	188
HADDAD, George Habib	206
JALLAD, Abdul Khalik	261
JAROUDI, Saeb	265
KHOURY, Butros, al- /businessman	310
KHOURY, Michel al- /lawyer	311
MAJDALANI, Nassim /politician	336
MAKRAM, A. Rahal	338
MOAWAD, Wajdi Antoine	362
NSOULI, Al-Walid	398
R'AHAL, Makram A.	424
RAPHAEL, Farid	427
SABA, Elias /politician	440
SALAWI, Gabriel Emile	456
SARKIS, Nicolas	465
SHAMMAS, Pierre Wahid /publisher	480
SHIBL, Yusuf A.	492
SKAFF, Jean /businessman	504
SUIDAN, Jad Anis	510
TAKY, Ziad al- /economist	521
TAYYARA, Abdul Rahman al- /accountant	527
WAZEN, Anwar E.	543
ZACCOUR, Makram Michele /stockbroker	553

BUSINESSMEN/BUSINESSWOMEN

ABELA, Albert	19
ABU ADAL, Georges	19
ABU HAIDAR, Munir Ibrahim	23
ABU KHATER, Tawfiq	25
ABU KHATER, Victor E. /management adviser	26
AKL, Georges /politician	45
ARAKTINGI, Michel Amin	63
ARIDA, Joseph	64
ASFUR, Farid Ibrahim /accountant	69
ASSAF, Tawfiq /politician	71
ASSEILY, Albert	72
ASSEILY, Georges	72
BAAQLINI, Mershed /banker	86
BARDAWIL, Fuad Philip	99
BEIDAS, Henri	105
BOULOS, Nassib /lawyer	125

DIPLOMATS

ENGINEERS/INDUSTRIAL ENGINEERS/ AGRICULTURAL ENGINEERS/ ELECTRONIC ENGINEERS

INTERNATIONAL OFFICIALS

JOURNALISTS/WRITERS/POETS

LAWYERS/JUDGES

LIBYA

The Socialist People's Libyan Arab Jamahiriya extends along the Mediterranean coast of north Africa. The country's closest neighbours are Egypt to the east, Sudan to the southeast, Niger and Chad to the south and Tunisia and Algeria to the west.

Area: 1,759,537 square kilometres.

Population: (1981 estimation) 3,100,000.

National Flag: The flag is plain green. A new design is presently underway.

Administrative Organisatin: The country is divided into ten governorates.

Main Cities: Tripoli (capital), Benghazi, Zawia.

Languages: Official Language: Arabic.

Currency: Libyan Dinar (LD).

Measures: The metric system is in force.

MOROCCO

The Kingdom of Morocco is situated in the extreme northwest of Africa. The country's closest neighbours are Algeria to the east and Muritania to the south. To the northeast its coastline runs along the Mediterranean Sea and to the west the Atlantic Ocean.

Area: 622,014 square kilometres.
Population: (1981 estimation) 21,600,000.
National Flag: The flag is red with a five pointed green star in the centre.
Administrative Organisation: The country is divided into thirty five administrative districts.
Main Cities: Rabat (capital), Casablanca, Fes, Marrakech, Tangier.
Languages: Official Language: Arabic; Others: French.
Currency: Moroccan Dirham (DH).
Measures: The metric system is in force.

OMAN

The Sultanate of Oman lies in the extreme southeast of the Arabian Peninsula. The country is bordered to the southwest by South Yemen, to the south and east by the Arabian Sea, to the north by the Gulf of Oman and to the northwest by the United Arab Emirates and Saudi Arabia.

Area: 300,000 square kilometres.

Population: (1981 estimation) 910,000.

National Flag: The flag has horizontal stripes of white, red and green, with a vertical red stripe at the hoist.

Administrative Organisation: The country is divided into forty wilayats (governorates).

Main Cities: Muscat (capital), Matrah, Salalah.

Languages: Official Language: Arabic; Others: English.

Currency: Riyal Omani (RO).

Measures: The imperial, metric and local systems are all in use, although the metric system was officially adopted in 1974.

BUSINESSMEN/BUSINESSWOMEN

BIN AMEIR, Ahmad Muhammad	116
KHALILI, Saud Bin Ali al- /diplomat	300
OMAR, Yahia	403
ZAWAWI, Omar Abdul Mun'im al- /physician	557
ZUBAIR, Shaikh Muhammad	562

DIPLOMATS

ALAWI, Yusuf al-	48
ANSI, Saud Salim Hassan al-	60
BUALY, Nassir Ben Saif al-	131
HABIB, Malalla Ali	204
HARTHY, Muhammad Hamad Sulaiman al-	223
JAMALI, Ahmad Muhammad al-	262
SAID, Sayyid Shabib Bin Taimur al-	452

JOURNALISTS/WRITERS/POETS

KATHARI, Said al-Samhan al- /businessman	285

OFFICIALS/ADMINISTRATORS

MAKKI, Ahmad Abdul Nabi /diplomat	338
RAJAB, Abdul Hafidh Salim /politician	425
RIKAISHY, Ahmad Nassir al- /economist	434
SAID, Sayyid Thuwain Bin Shahib al-	452
YUSIF, Muhammad Musa Abdullah al-	550

POLITICIANS

BIN TAIMUR, Tariq	119
BU SAIDI, Hamad Bin Humud al- /official	130
BU SAIDI, Muhammad Bin Ahmad al-	130
BU SAIDI, Salim Bin Nasr al-	130
HARIMI, Karim Ahmad al-	222
HINA'I, Al- Walid Bin Zahir Bin Ghusn al-	235
JAMALI, Assim al-	263
KHADDURI, Mubarak Salih al /physician	289
QABOOS, HM Sultan Qaboos Bin Said	415
SAID, HH Sayyid Fahr Bin Taimur al-	450
SAID, HH Sayyid Hilal Bin Hamad al-Sammar al-	450
SAID, Sayyid Fahd Bin Mahmud al-	452
SAID, Sayyid Faisal Bin Ali al- /diplomat	452
SHANFARI, Said Ahmad al- /businessman	482
WAHAIBI, Khalfan Bin Nasr al- /administrator	541
ZAWAWI, Qais Abdul Mun'im al-	557

PLO/PALESTINE

QATAR

The State of Qatar is situated on the west coast of the Arabian Gulf. The country's closest neighbours are Saudi Arabia to the west and the United Arab Emirates to the south.
Area: 11,400 square kilometres.
Population: (1981 estimation) 220,000.
National Flag: The flag is maroon and white with a nine point zigzag interlock.
Main Cities: Doha (capital), Umm Said.
Languages: Official Language: Arabic; Others: English.
Currency: Qatari Riyal (QR).
Measures: The metric system has been adopted, but imperial measures are still used.

SAUDI ARABIA

The Kingdom of Saudi Arabia occupies four fifths of the Arabian Penisula. It is bordered by Kuwait, Iraq and Jordan to the north, South Yemen and Oman to the south, the United Arab Emirates and Qatar to the east and North Yemen and the Red Sea to the west.
Area: 2,263,587 square kilometres.
Population: (1981 estimation) 10,400,000.
National Flag: The flag is green and bears white inscription 'There is no God but God and Muhammad is the prophet of God', above a white sword.
Main Cities: Riyadh (capital), Jeddah (main port), Mecca, Medina.
Languages: Official Language: Arabic; Others: English.
Currency: Saudi Riyal (SR).
Measures: The metric system is in force.

ACADEMICS

ABA HUSSAIN, Mansur Muhammad /official	1
ABBAD, Abdul Muhsin Bin Hamad al-	2
ABDUL QADIR, Muhammad al-Fousi /Islamic scholar	15
ABU HEILAH, Abdullah Nassir	24
ABU ROKBA, Hassan Abdullah	28
ASADULLAH, Mahmud Muhammad Ali	68
BADR, Hamud Abdul Aziz al-	87
BAKALLA, Muhammad Hassan	92
BAKR, Bakr Abdullah /engineer	93
DAFFA, Ali Abdullah al- /mathematician	143
DARWISH, Madiha Ahmad	149
FATANI, Jamal Abdul Gader /physician	176
FURAYH, Othman Salih al-;	183
GAMA, Abid Husni	186
HIBSHI, Muhammad Ali /educationalist	234
JAMAL, Ahmad Muhammad /official	262
JAMJOOM, Muhammad Omar /engineer	265
KABLI, Ridha Ali /official	275
KAHTANI, Muhammad Said Abdul Rahman al- /agriculturalist	277
KHALAF, Kahlid Yusif /official	291
KHATTAB, Izzat Abdul Majid	305
KHEREIJI, Abdullah al-Muhammad al-	307
KHIDR, Abdul Fattah /lawyer	307
MASRI, Abdullah Hassan /archaelogist and anthropologist	350
NATTO, Ibrahim Abbas	393
OMAR, Muhammad Zayyan	403
QUOTAH, Muhammad /economist	422
RASHID, Muhammad Sa'ad al-	428
SHARI'E, Abdullah al-Nafi'e al-	484
SHARIF, Rashid Bin Rajih Muhammad al- /Islamic scholar	486
TURKI, Abdullah Bin Abdul Muhsin Bin Abdul Rahman al- /Islamic scholar	535
ZUBAIR, Muhammad Omar /economist	562

ARMED FORCES/POLICE CHIEFS

KHOJAH, Major General Akram	308
SHAIKH, Lieutenant General Abdullah al-	477
SHAMAIMARI, General Hamad al-	479

BANKERS/ECONOMISTS/AUDITORS/ACCOUNTANTS

BIN MAHFOUZ, Khalid Bin Salim /businessman	118
CHAPRA, Muhammad Omar; /economist	138
JAMAL, Adel Mahmud	262
KASSIM, Tarik Jamal	284
KHUSHAIM, Rida Hassan /businessman	313
MALIK, Ahmad Abdullah al- /administrator	340
NIMATALLAH, Yusuf Abdul Wahib /official	395
QURAISHI, Abdul Aziz Bin Zaid al-	422
SABBAB, Ahmad Abdullah al- /academic	444
SAYARI, Hamad Saud al- /economist	468
SHAMS, Ibrahim Muhammad Said	481

BUSINESSMEN/BUSINESSWOMEN

ABDUL FATTAH, Abdul Rahim	8
ABDUL MAJID, Shaikh Adnan Abdul Rahman	13
ABDULLAH BIN FAISAL, HRH Prince /businessman	18
ABU DAWUD, Ismail Ali	20
ABU SU'UD, Aziz Ali	30
ABU ZINADA, Abdul Wahab	33
ABUL JADAYEL, Anwar Ass'ad	34
AGEEL, Abdullah O.	38
AGGAD, Omar A.	39
ALIREZA, Abdullah Ahmad	50
ALIREZA, Ahmad Yusuf Zainal	50
ALIREZA, Ali Ibrahim	50
ALIREZA, Fahd Muhammad Abdullah	50
ALIREZA, Faisal Ali Abdullah	50
ALIREZA, Hisham Ahmad	50
ALIREZA, Hussain Ali Hussain	50
ALIREZA, Ibrahim Yusuf Zainal	50
ALIREZA, Khalid Ahmad	50
ALIREZA, Mahmud Yusuf Zainal	51
ALIREZA, Muhammad Abdullah /diplomat	51
ASFAHANI, Muhammad Hussain	68
ATTAR, Muhammad Siraj al-	75
ATTAR, Omar Saddiq	75
ATTAS, Hussain Bin Hashim al-;	76
BA FAQIH, Fadhl Abdullah	85
BADRAH, Abdul Rashid Ahmad	88

DIPLOMATS

ENGINEERS/INDUSTRIAL ENGINEERS/ AGRICULTURAL ENGINEERS/ ELECTRONIC ENGINEERS

RELIGIOUS LEADERS/ECCLESIASTICS

SCIENTISTS/VETERINARY SURGEONS/ SPACE SCIENTISTS/AGRICULTURALISTS/ GEOLOGISTS/NUCLEAR SCIENTISTS

SUDAN

The Democratic Republic of Sudan is situated in northeast Africa. The country's closest neighbours are Egypt to the north and Ethiopia and the Red Sea to the east, the Central African Republic, Chad and Libya to the west and Kenya to the south.
Area: 2,505,813 square kilometres.
Population: (1981 estimation) 19,600,000.
National Flag: The flag has three horizontal stripes of red, white and black with a green triangle at the hoist.
Administrative Organisation: The country is divided into six regions, each with its own regional assembly.
Main Cities: Khartoum (capital), Omdurman, Port Sudan, Juba.
Languages: Official Language: Arabic; Others: English.
Currency: Sudanese Pound (S£).
Measures: The metric system is gradually replacing traditional weights and measures.

ACADEMICS

ABU SALIM, Muhmmad Ibrahim /historian	29
FADL, Ali Muhammad /physician	167
IBRAHIM, Abdul Aziz al-Tayib /agriculturalist	245
IBRAHIM, Saad Ahmad /physician	247
JACK, Muhammad Hassan al- /agricultural expert	259
KHEIR, Yahya Muhammad al-; /pharmacist	307
TAYIB, Abdullah al-	527

ARMED FORCES/POLICE CHIEFS

ABBOUD, General Ibrahim /politician	5
AWAD, General Khalafalla Amir	78
BAGHIR AHMAD, Major General Muhammad al- /politician	89
BASHIR, Lieutenant General Muhammad Ali	100
BISHARA, Al-Fatih Muhammad Bashir	122
FATIH, Muhammad Bushara al-	177
LAGU, Major General Joseph	322

BANKERS/ECONOMISTS/AUDITORS/ACCOUNTANTS

ABDUL SALAM, Othman Hashim	16
BAGU, Henry	89
BELAIL, Hassan /economist	105
MUDAWI, Al-BaKir Yusuf	367
NIMR, Ibrahim Muhammad /banker	396
SALIH, Salih Muhammad /agricultural engineer	459

BUSINESSMEN/BUSINESSWOMEN

ABDUL MUN'IM, Abdul Qadir Ahmad	14
ABUL ELA, Abdul Salaam	33
ABUL ELA, Saad	33
AHMAD, Ibrahim Muhammad Ahmad	40
KHOGHALI, Muhammad	308

MAHMUD, Khalil Othman	334
MUSTAFA, Makkawi	377

DIPLOMATS

ABBAS, Al-Obeid Khalifa	4
ABDUL HAMID, Abdul Latif	10
ABDULLAH, Rahmatalla	18
AHMAD, Ahmad Sulaiman Muhammad	40
AHMAD, Jamal Muhammad /politician	41
ALAMIN, Al-Amin Abdul Latif al-	46
AYYOUB, Ibrahim Taha	80
BALLAL, Musa Awad /official	95
BASHIR, Muhammad Omar /academic and writer	101
BIRIDO, Omar Yusif	121
DENG, Francis Mading /academic	153
FADALLA, Awad al Karim	167
FAKHREDDINE, Muhammad	170
GHANDUR, Muzzamil Sulaiman	191
HADI, Mubarak Adam al-	208
HASSAN, Abdullah /politician	225
JAMAL, Muhammad Ahmad	262
KHALIL, Brigadier Mirghani Sulaiman /former army officer	298
MATAR, Muhammad Hamid	352
MEDANI, Mustafa	354
MIRGHANI, Muhammad	360
RAHAMA, Mubarak Othman /army officer	425
SALIH, Abu Bakr Osman Muhammad	458
SAWI, Amir al- /official	467

ENGINEERS/INDUSTRIAL ENGINEERS/AGRICULTURAL ENGINEERS/ELECTRONIC ENGINEERS

ALI, Abdul Aziz Muhammad	48

INTERNATIONAL OFFICIALS

ABBAS, Makki	4
ANTOUN, Charly /engineer	60
AWAD, Samuel	78
BASHIR, Taha Ahmad /psychiatrist	101

SYRIA

The Syrian Arab Republic is situated on the eastern shore of the Mediterranean Sea. The country is bordered by Turkey to the north, Iraq to the east and Jordan to the south and Lebanon to the west.
Area: 185,180 square kilometres.
Population: (1981 estimation) 9,100,000.
National Flag: The flag is horizontal tricolour of red, white and black. The central stripe bearing a falcon emblem in gold.
Administrative Organisation: The country is divided into thirteen administrative districts.
Main Cities: Damascus (capital), Aleppo, Homs, Hama.
Languages: Official Language: Arabic; Others: French.
Currency: Syrian pound (£Syr).
Measures: The metric system is in force.

ACADEMICS

AKIL, Fakhir Bin Hussain /psychologist	45
BAKDASH, Hisham Zaki /physician	92
DAKKAK, Omar Muhammad	147
FAHHAM, Shakir /politician	168
HADDAD, Mustafa Hassan /official	207
HAFFAR, Said Muhammad al-	210
HAKIM, Jacques Yussif /lawyer	213
HARIRI, Ghazi al- /agriculturalist	223
HASHIM, Muhammad Ali /politician	224
HASSAN, Ahmad Y. al- /engineer	225
HOURIEH, Muhammad Ali	237
KHAYER, Yahya Muhammad al- /engineer	306
MAHAYNI, Thabit Ghalib /businessman	331
MUSTAFA, Adnan /oil official	376
SAYIGH, Yusif Abdullah /economist	469
SAYYID HASSAN, Muwaffaq al- /economist	470
SHUKRI, Muhammad Aziz /lawyer	500
TOMEH, George J. /diplomat	531
'USH, Muhammad Abul Faraj al-	539
YAFI, Abdul Karim Tawfik	545

ARMED FORCES/POLICE CHIEFS

SHAKKUR, Lieutenant General Yussif	478
SHIHABI, Imad Hikmat	493
TLASS, Lieutenant General Mustafa Abdul Qadir	530

BANKERS/ECONOMISTS/AUDITORS/ACCOUNTANTS

ABU ASSALI, Dib	20
ACCAD, Muhammad Rifat	35
AKBIK, Adnan Muhammad	44
AKHRAS, Shafiq Abdul Mawla	44
AZMEH, Abdullah al- /economist	82
BITAR, Muhammad Yasar /economist	122
DACCAK, Nassuh /official	142
DARKAZALLY, Ma'mun Abdul Hadi al-	148
KHALIL, Fakhruddin Khalil	298
KHAYATA, Abdul Wahab /economist	306
ZOUHEIRI, Bashir Ali /chartered accountant	561

BUSINESSMEN/BUSINESSWOMEN

DARWISH, Samir A.	150
MORCOS, Claude Kamil	362
MUALLA, Jamil Abdul Wahid /agricultural expert	365
RABBAT, Walid B. /petroleum engineer	423
SHALLAH, Badriddine	479
ZAYYAT, Fuad	557

DIPLOMATS

ALLAF, Muwaffaq	51
ARMANAZI, Ghaith Najib	64
ASHA, Rafik al-	69
JUMAN-AGHA, Adnan /lawyer	273
KHAIRAT, Taha /politician	290
KILANI, Haissam al-	314
MASRI, Ahmad Fathi al-	350
OMRAN, Adnan	404
RIFA'I, Najmuddine al- /UN official	433
SAUD, Abdul Karim	466
SUCCAR, Abdul Latif	509

ENGINEERS/INDUSTRIAL ENGINEERS/AGRICULTURAL ENGINEERS/ELECTRONIC ENGINEERS

DAGHESTANI, Najib Abu al-Alla al-	143
TAYARA, Muhammad Ghassan /politician	526

INTERNATIONAL OFFICIALS

ADLI, Ibrahim	36
CHEIKH AL-ARD, Faisal /physician	139
HANNUSH, Basim Abdul Masih /economist	221
HURBLI, Abdul Sami	240
KATKHUDA, Louay /chemical engineer	285
MANSUR, Abdul Hamid /agricultural expert	343
RIFA'I, Hisham	432
WANNOUS, Mounir /engineer	543
YAFI, Muhammad Salim al- /diplomat	546

TUNISIA

The Republic of Tunisia lies on the Mediterranean coast of Africa. The country is bordered by Algeria to the west and Libya to the east.
Area: 163,610 square kilometres.
Population: (1981 estimation) 6,600,000.
National Flag: The flag is red charged with white disc containing a red crescent moon and a five pointed red star.
Administrative Organisation: The country is divided into eighteen governorates.
Main Cities: Tunis (capital), Sfax, Djerba, Sousse, Bizete, Kairaoun.
Languages: Official Language: Arabic; Others: French.
Currency: Tunisian Dinar (TD).
Measures: The metric system is in force.

603

UNITED ARAB EMIRATES

The United Arab Emirates lies along the eastern Gulf coast of the Arabian Peninsula. The country is bordered by Qatar to the northwest, Saudi Arabia to the south and west, and Oman to the east and northeast.
Area: 86,449 square kilometres.
Population: 980,000.
National Flag: The flag has horizontal stripes of green, white and black, with a vertical red stripe at the hoist.
Administrative Organisation: The country consists of seven emirates, they are: Abu Dhabi, Ajman, Dubai, Fujairah, Ras Al Khaimah, Sharijah, Umm Al Qaiwain.
Main Cities: Abu Dhabi (capital), Dubai.
Languages: Official Language: Arabic; Others: English.
Currency: United Arab Emirates Dirham (UD).
Measures: The imperial and metric systems are in use, as well as local weights and measures.

OIL OFFICIALS/FINANCIAL OFFICIALS/ AVIATION OFFICIALS/ADMINISTRATORS/ BROADCASTING OFFICIALS/ TRADE UNION OFFICIALS

POLITICIANS

NORTH YEMEN

The Yemen Arab Republic is situated in the southwestern corner of the Arabian Peninsula. It is bordered on the north and east by Saudi Arabia, to the south by South Yemen, and to the west by the Red Sea.

Area: 195,000 square kilometres.

Population: (1981 estimation) 5,300,000.

National Flag: The flag has three horizontal stripes of red, white and black, with a five pointed green star in the centre.

Administrative Organisation: The country is divided into six governorates.

Main Cities: Sana'a (capital), Hodaida (main port), Taiz.

Languages: Official Language: Arabic; Others: English.

Currency: Yemeni Riyal (YD).

Measures: imperial system in Sana'a. Local weights and measures used in the rest of the country.

SOUTH YEMEN

The People's Democratic Republic of Yemen is situated in the south eastern part of the Arabian Peninsula. To the west and northwest it is bounded by the Yemen Arab Republic, to the north by Saudi Arabia, to the east by Oman, and to the south by the Gulf of Aden and the Arabian Sea.

Area: 290,274 square kilometres.

Population: (1981 estimation) 2,000,000.

National Flag: The flag has horizontal stripes of red, white and black with light blue triangle, containing a five pointed red star at the hoist.

Administrative Organisation: The country is divided into six governorates.

Main cities: Aden (capital), Lahaj.

Languages: Official Language: Arabic; Others: English.

Currency: South Yemeni Dinar (YD).

Measurements: imperial system used in Aden. Local weights and measures used in the rest of the country.

ARMED FORCES/POLICE CHIEFS

BISHI, Ali Ahmad Nasr al-	122
BU DHALAI, Major Ahmad Salih	130

DIPLOMATS

ASHTAL, Abdullah Salih	71
AWAD, Muhammad Hadi	78
ISMAIL, Abdul Malik /politician	251
SALAMI, Ali Ahmad Nasir /official	456
THABIT, Rashid Muhammad /politician	528
URAISH, Mahmud Abdullah /politician	539

JOURNALISTS/WRITERS/POETS

LUQMAN, Ali Muhammad Ali /businessman	325

OFFICIALS/ADMINISTRATORS

ABDUL QAWI YAFAI, Muhammad	15
ATTAS, Faisal al-;	76
AWAD, Hussain Hadi /banker	78
KULAIB, Ali Ghanim /engineer	318
MIDHI, Muhammed Said	358
MIKHBAL, Ahmad Salim	359

PHYSICIANS/DENTAL SURGEONS/DENTISTS/SURGEONS

BUKAIR, Abdullah Ahmad /UN official	132

POLITICIANS

ABDUL ELAH, Ahmad Abdullah	8
ABDUL KHALIQ, Mustafa /lawyer	11
ATTAS, Haidar Abu Bakar al-	76
BADIB, Ali Abdul Razzaq /diplomat	87
BAR, Abdullah Sabih al-	96
BIDH, Ali Salim al-	113
IMAYA, Muhammad Ali al- /trade unionist	250
ISMAIL ALI, Abdul Fattah	252
KHAMRI, Abdullah al-	301
MUHAMMAD, Ali Nassir	369
MUHAMMAD, Mahdi Abdullah /trade unionist	370
MUHSIN, Muhammad Said Abdullah	370
MUTI'A, Muhammad Salih Abdullah	378
NASHIR, Abdul Aziz Abdul Wali	391
NUBAN, Said Abdul Khair al-	399
SHU'ABI, Major Salih Muslih Qasim Majdul	498
YAHIA, Anis Hassan	546

UK

(Anglo-Arab)

ACADEMICS

BUSINESSMEN/BUSINESSWOMEN

USA

(Arab-American)

SCIENTISTS/VETERINARY SURGEONS/
SPACE SCIENTISTS/AGRICULTURALISTS/
GEOLOGISTS/NUCLEAR SCIENTISTS

MEDITERRANEAN S

MOROCCO

ALGERIA

MAURITANIA